AN INTRODUCTION TO POSITIVE ECONOMICS

WITHDRAWN

AN INTRODUCTION TO

POSITIVE ECONOMICS

EIGHTH EDITION

RICHARD G. LIPSEY
K. ALEC CHRYSTAL

OXFORD UNIVERSITY PRESS

Oxford University Press, Walton Street, Oxford OX2 6DP

Oxford New York
Athens Auckland Bangkok Bogota Bombay
Buenos Aires Calcutta Cape Town Dar es Salaam
Delhi Florence Hong Kong Istanbul Karachi
Kuala Lumpur Madras Madrid Melbourne
Mexico City Nairobi Paris Singapore
Taipei Tokyo Toronto

and associated companies in
Berlin Ibadan

Oxford is a trade mark of Oxford University Press

© 1995 Richard G Lipsey and K Alec Chrystal

Eighth edition published 1995

British Library Cataloguing in Publication Data
Data available

Library of Congress Cataloging in Publication Data
Data available
ISBN 0–19–877424–9
ISBN 0–19–877425–7 (Pbk.)

International student edition
ISBN 0–19–259020–0

10 9 8 7 6 5 4 3 2

Printed on acid-free paper by
Mateu Cromo, Spain

To Diana

Contents

∾ Foreword

We live in exciting, momentous, often hopeful, but sometimes frightening, times.

At centre stage in current history is the end of communism — the event itself and its aftermath. The century-old battle between free markets and government planning as alternatives for organizing economic activity has been settled within the last decade — and settled with a degree of decisiveness that is rare for great social issues. The failure of central planning in the former USSR and its Eastern European satellites, and the failure of old-fashioned socialism and agricultural collectivism in African and Asian countries, has been recognized (with a very few exceptions) by the very governments that were most committed to these systems. At the end of a century of experimentation, the much criticized, free-market, capitalist system has proved itself superior to centrally planned, or highly government-regulated, systems.

We who are living through one of history's most decisive moments need to understand why it is that market-oriented economies perform so much better than fully planned or highly government-controlled economies. This is a core issue in economics since economic theories are expressly designed to understand the successes (and, where they occur, the failures) of free-market, capitalist societies.

Accepting the triumph of market-oriented economies does not imply the belief that governments have no place in the economy and that the best government is the smallest government (a philosophy known as *laissez faire*). What it does entail is a reconsideration of the place of government in the economy along two main lines, both of which economists are actively studying.

First, creating income and wealth through economic activity is usually best accomplished through the activities of private citizens buying and selling in largely unregulated markets. But this is not the end of the story. Although market economies certainly work better than planned economies, they do not work perfectly. One of today's great social issues is to reallocate the responsibilities of government, leaving it to do what it can best do and leaving the private sector to do what it can best do. We ask: 'What is the desirable role of government in improving the functioning of a basically market-oriented economy?'

Second, although it is desirable to create income and wealth, we also care about how that income and wealth are distributed among all citizens. Poverty for a minority in the midst of plenty for the majority has always been a problem in wealthy societies — just as poverty for the majority has always been a problem for the world's poorer countries which group includes most countries, with the exception of the advanced industrial nations during the last couple of hundred years. We ask: 'What is the place of government in pursuing social policies that alleviate the poverty and suffering of those who do not share in the income and employment that market economies create for the majority?'

Many other problems are pressing. The world's population continues to grow by leaps and bounds; environmental problems are everywhere: pollution is a continuing worry in many places, the world's stock of fish is being depleted rapidly, and deforestation is widespread in such varied areas as Madagascar and the southern slopes of the Himalaya Mountains; in many of the countries of South East Asia, people's incomes are doubling every 12–15 years, while in many African countries, incomes are stagnant and, in some, they are even falling; at least 20 million employable Europeans are without work; the United Kingdom has gone in the space of less than a lifetime from the richest country in Western Europe to one of the poorest; many economists feel that the world is going through a technological revolution based on new, computer-based, information and communication technologies that is at least as profound as the First Industrial Revolution in the eighteenth century.

In all these issues (and many more), economists have been in the forefront of analysing, explaining, and, where appropriate, offering solutions. Economists have succeeded in these tasks mainly because their subject has a core of useful theory that explains how markets work and evaluates their outcomes in terms of successes and failures. Although some economic analysis is extremely abstract and sometimes even economists wonder about its value, the basic core of economic theory is the secret of the subject's success. As a result of this theory, economics has an excellent record of illuminating important issues in a way that leads to deeper understanding and useful policy recommendations.

Those who read this book are setting out on the study of a subject which, as the above discussion suggests, is highly relevant to understanding and improving the world in which we live. Approached in the right way, your study will be an adventure. Theory will have to be learned, and some will find the theory fun in itself. Those who do not, will find that, surprisingly early in their studies, theories can be used to add to one's understanding of real issues. Of course, the world is complex, and fully understanding its economic aspects requires much more economics than can be packed into any elementary textbook. But mastery of the subject to the level of this one book will contribute greatly to your understanding of many important issues and many of the policies directed at them.

Good luck and good studying!

RICHARD LIPSEY
ALEC CHRYSTAL

Vancouver, BC,
  and
London, England
January 1995

∾ Preface

The eighth edition of *Positive Economics* incorporates the most radical revisions since the first edition. The new edition builds upon some of the tried and tested material from earlier editions but, at almost every point, it incorporates new theoretical developments and extensive new applications, all of which are intended to illustrate and enliven the exposition of the theory. Every chapter has been extensively rewritten and many chapters are entirely new.

This preface is in two main parts. The first is intended to help teachers identify some of the themes and key innovations in this edition while the second tells students a bit about how to approach the study of economics, especially as it is presented in this book.

....

Primarily to the instructor

Of course there is no reason why interested students should not read this section. After all, you may be interested in what we have to say to instructors. Those students who are not should skip to page xxi where we direct a few important remarks to students.

Our General Approach

First, we outline a few aspects of our general approach to the subject.

Our Intended Audience   *Positive Economics* is an introductory textbook, starting at an elementary stage and progressing, in some places, to an intermediate level. Although it is designed to be read as a first book in economics, we hope it will not be without interest for someone who has already studied one of the many existing textbooks written at a pre-university standard such as Lipsey and Harbury's *First Principles of Economics* (Oxford: Oxford University Press, 2nd edn. 1990). Our present book is intended for students who wish to understand economics in some depth. Hence, economic theories are built up in a logically coherent and consistent way and we do not skip over difficult concepts that will be needed later on. Nor do we teach things that make matters easy at an early stage but which will have to be 'unlearned' later on. We have always given first priority to making the theoretical analysis readable and fully understandable. Nowhere is a theoretical concept introduced merely to be bowed to. Instead, everything that is introduced is fully explained. This requires much space, which is obtained at the cost of leaving out masses of descriptive data which is available elsewhere. In all our writing in this book we take our theme from Albert Einstein:

Everything should be made as simple as possible, but not simpler

Encourage critical Assessment Often when students feel that there is something wrong with what they have been taught, they do not know how to go about being critical of it in an effective way. We have made a point of telling readers what is going on, to say now we are doing comparative-static equilibrium analysis or whatever it might be, and we have devoted considerable space to an analysis of both sensible and silly criticisms of the theories described—much more space than can be found in any other textbook written at a comparable level.

We do not accept the view that the possibility of criticizing what has been learned should go unmentioned because, if it is raised, students will only make hasty and confused criticisms. Good students will always attempt criticisms and evaluations. It seems to us that their criticisms are more likely to be informed and relevant if they are given instruction in how to set about effectively assessing and even challenging what they have been taught than if they meet a conspiracy of silence on this topic.

Emphasize empirical applications Economic theory is meant to be about the real world. Economists seek, by the use of theory, to explain, understand, and predict real-world phenomena, and theory must therefore be related to, and tested by, empirical observations. The student of economic theory needs to ask at every stage what are the relevant empirical magnitudes and quantities. This is the theme that we have stressed by ending all the Parts in microeconomics with a chapter devoted to issues of one or more of the following: applying, measuring, and testing the theories and relationships studied in that Part.

Separate positive from normative analysis The distinction between positive and normative statements is well known to professional economists. Economic theory cannot, of course, ever show us what we ought to do, but only what will happen if we do certain things. The uses and limitations of economic theory in dealing with matters of public policy is a theme which recurs throughout the book. Policy issues are raised for purposes of illustration in many chapters; a whole Part—Part 6—is devoted to microeconomic policy, while six chapters—39–44—deal with macroeconomic policy issues.

Some General Themes

Next we turn to a few of the general themes we have tried to weave into the book as a whole.

THE POWER OF THE MARKET

Since the last edition of this book was published, the century-long conflict between capitalism and communism has ended. What a decade ago was the most powerful communist economy in the world, the USSR, has disappeared, both as a nation and as a planned economy. Mixed capitalism, the system of economic organization that has long prevailed in much of the industrialized world, now prevails in virtually all of it. (Although the transformation of formerly planned economies into market economies is proving more difficult than many thought.) Many less developed economies are also moving in this direction. The reasons for the failure of the planned economies of Eastern Europe are discussed in Chapter 1 as a contrast to the reasons for the relative success of market-oriented economies. This goes along with a discussion of alternative economic systems all of which is intended to set the stage for a theme that recurs throughout the book: the understanding of how market economies work and why, with all their imperfections, they work better than any known alternative.

GLOBALIZATION

The last twenty-five years have seen enormous world-wide economic changes. Flows of trade and investment between countries have risen so dramatically that it is now common to speak of the 'globalization' of the world economy. Today, it is no longer possible to study any economy without taking into account developments in the rest of the world.

Here are a few examples of our treatment of the international aspect in the micro half of the book. The discussion of agricultural policy in Chapter 7 has a major international dimension. Foreign direct investment and transnational corporations are introduced in the first chapter on the theory of the firm (Chapter 10) and then receive detailed attention in several subsequent chapters, including Chapter 17 on the organization of firms, and Chapter 26 on trade policy. The newer methods of 'lean production' or 'flexible manufacturing', first developed in Japan and now displacing the older mass production techniques, are discussed in connection with the firm (Chapters 10, 14, and 17), and with economic growth (Chapter 33) and economic development (Chapter 34). Chapter 26 provides detailed discussions of commercial policies that seek to regulate or limit the free flow of international trade and investment. It also outlines the basic theory of customs unions and describes trade-liberalizing arrangements such as the General Agreement on Tariffs and Trade (GATT), the European Union, and the North American Free Trade Agreement (NAFTA).

Our basic framework for macroeconomic theory and policy is also organized around globalization. We develop the theory of national income determination in an *open* economy from the outset—rather than starting, as is so often done, with a closed economy which is opened to international trade and investment many chapters later.

Change in the terms of trade is one of the factors used to explain the existence of a negatively sloped aggregate demand curve (Chapter 31). Hence, international relative prices are placed right at the heart of the functioning of the macro-model.

Monetary policy and institutions are developed from an international perspective. Various exchange rate regimes and the evolution of globalization in finance provide the context for the incorporation of monetary factors into macroeconomics. A whole chapter (39) is devoted to the analysis of monetary and fiscal policy in an open economy model with perfect capital mobility, and the differences between fixed and floating exchange regimes are analysed.

The EU dimension affects macroeconomics in several places. Most notably, the potential implications of a single currency are discussed (Chapter 38), as are the implications for fiscal policy of the Maastricht convergence criteria (Chapter 42). A high level of equilibrium unemployment seems to be a bigger problem in the EU than in North America, so international comparisons are used to give new insights into this central topic in macroeconomics (Chapter 41).

ECONOMIC GROWTH

For a long time economic growth has been the poor sister of economic theory. It is hardly mentioned in microeconomics and it usually gets a single chapter in the macroeconomics section of most introductory textbooks—a chapter that is often skipped due to the time taken to teach the model relevant to the study of short-term fluctuations.

Yet, as we say in Chapter 33:

Economic growth is the single most powerful engine for generating long-term increases in living standards. What happens to our material living standards over time depends primarily on the growth in national income (as measured, for example, by the GDP) in relation to the growth in population. The removal of a serious recessionary gap, or the elimination of all structural unemployment, might cause a once-and-for-all increase in national income by, at the very most, 5–10 per cent. However, a growth rate of 3 per cent per year raises potential income by 10 per cent in 3 years, *doubles* it in about 24 years, and quadruples it in 48 years. Even a 1 per cent growth rate doubles potential income over one normal lifetime of about 70 years.

Economic growth has been attracting more and more attention from both theorists and empirical economists. At the macro level, there has been a renewed interest in growth as theorists have investigated the implication of accepting the well-documented fact that innovation is largely endogenous to the economic system. At the micro level, the tradition of detailed study of endogenous innovation goes back for at least three decades. Economists have established, by masses of detailed studies, many characteristics of the endogenous innovative process. These studies have given rise to many generalizations which are the stylized facts on which empirically relevant theories are being built. On the policy level, economists and policy-makers are rediscovering what the classical economists knew: microeconomic policies, instituted for reason of static efficiency or equity, can have major effects on growth so that there may be a trade-off between equity and static efficiency on the one hand and growth (or dynamic efficiency) on the other hand.

The importance of growth as a means of influencing living standards in the long term and the renewed interest in growth among economists is reflected at many places in the new edition. In our basic theory of the firm we deal with three runs: the short run in which only some factor inputs can be varied; the long run in which all inputs can be varied, but within the confines of static technology; and the very long run when technology can change in response to the economic signals of altered prices and profits—as it constantly does. Later, in the micro half of the book, we show that considerations of economic growth have strongly influenced many public policies in many countries over the last two decades. Policies that used to be thought of as being exclusively concerned with static efficiency and equity have been influenced by consideration of their effect on long-term growth.

The growing interest in the microeconomics of growth and technical change is also reflected in the main growth chapter (33) which covers microeconomic issues related to innovation as well as the more traditional macroeconomic treatment. This chapter is placed as part of the core of macro theory, rather than as an afterthought as so often happens in first-year textbooks. We also treat development economics in the same place. We feel that once growth is admitted into the core of macro theory and its microeconomic aspects are recognized, the issues traditionally treated in development economics become relevant to our understanding of growth economics. After all, with the rise of Japan, the four Asian tigers, and the many other newly industrializing nations of Asia and South America, the old dichotomy between advanced nations to whom one kind of economics applied, and developing nations to whom another kind of economics applied, is no longer tenable. We have, however, made this chapter easy to skip for those who do not want to follow us all this way.

THE IMPORTANCE OF ECONOMIC POLICY

Most chapters of the book contain some discussion of economic policy. We have two main goals in mind in these discussions. First, we aim to give students practice in using economic theory, because applying theory is both a wonderfully effective teaching method and a reliable test of students' grasp of theory. Second, we want to introduce students to the major policy issues of today.

Both goals reflect our view that students should see that economics is useful in helping us to understand and deal with the world around us.

Microeconomic policy   We first mention policy issues in Chapter 1 and give several detailed illustrations of the use of economic theory to study policy issues in Chapter 6 on Demand and Supply in Action. Chapter 15 studies tax issues (among other things) as examples of 'the theory of the firm and industry in action'. Chapter 16 deals with regulation and anti-monopoly policy, while Chapter 17 considers some of the many policy issues that arise from takeovers, mergers, and foreign investment. Many other issues, such as minimum wages (Chapter 19), the economics of non-renewable resources (Chapter 20), and privatization (Chapters 16 and 23), all relate to public policy. Part 6 is wholly directed to the theory and practice of microeconomic policy. In line with what was said earlier, we consider growth as well as static efficiency and equity as goals in the chapter on the aims and objectives of public policy (Chapter 24). The micro half of the book ends with a long chapter devoted to issues of commercial policy—policies related to international trade and investment. As well as covering the traditional issues of tariff policy, it deals with non-tariff barriers, trade in services, investment, and regional agreements with respect to trade and investment liberalization.

Macroeconomic policy   Perceptions of macroeconomic policy have changed radically in the last few years. We explain the old views (Chapter 36 appendix) but we also incorporate the new (Chapters 40–4).

Macroeconomic debates for the last three decades have been dichotomized as between monetarists and Keynesians. The original classification applied to an argument about whether monetary or fiscal policies were better for controlling aggregate demand. The natural rate hypothesis added an equilibrium concept to the model, which, if it were accepted, implied that the best that policy could do was return the economy to the natural or potential level of output. Under that analysis, distinctions between monetarists and Keynesians melted into minor issues of timing.

New classical (and later real business cycle) economics sought to change the conception of policy by assuming that the economy was always in equilibrium. This meant that unemployment and the business cycle were always an optimal response to whatever shocks appeared. Policy-makers could create shocks but they could not systematically offset them, or so it seemed. Wherever this view was accepted, macroeconomics lost its *raison d'etre*.

New Keynesian economics took on the challenge of explaining involuntary unemployment in a world in which agents are optimizing (or close to optimizing). New Keynesians have directed much attention to the issue of why wages do not tend to adjust to clear labour markets. Efficiency wages and insider–outsider models produce new Keynesian explanations of what used to be called 'classical' unemployment, and new Keynesian policy prescriptions include a wide range of microeconomic 'supply side polices' which used to be associated with monetarist approaches.

Even more importantly, theoretical work on hysteresis and endogenous growth makes it clear that the level of potential national income at any point in time may not be independent of where the economy has just been and what policy-makers have just done. Policy mistakes can lead to permanent losses and change the course of the economy in the long run.

As a result of the debates between the new classical and the new Keynesian economists, macroeconomics has been revitalized. A central aim of this book is to communicate the importance of the new ideas to a new generation of students.

Guidance on using this textbook for short or modular courses

Many first courses in economics are only one semester (or equivalent) in length. We have aimed for comprehensive coverage in this text, which necessarily means the inclusion of a large amount of optional material. We have also aimed for flexibility in the use of the text, and so suggested coverage in chapters for various types of courses are listed below.

[A note of chapters with a concentration on policy issues: 6, 16, 17, 22–26, 38, 40–44]

A short Introduction to Economics course (twenty weeks)

Chapters 1, 4–6, 7 or 8, 10–16, 18–19, 27–32, 35–36, 38, 40–41

A short course for Business students (twenty weeks)

Chapters 1, 4–6, 7 or 8, 10–17, 18–19, 26–32, 35–38, 40–41, 43

An Introduction to Microeconomics course (one semester)

Chapters 1, 4–6, 7 or 8, 9–15, 18–20, 22–24

An Introduction to Macroeconomics course (one semester)

Chapters 27–32, 35–44 [Alternatively, for a course with a growth emphasis include chapters 33 and 34; for a course with an international emphasis the key chapters are 37 and 39]

Changes from the Seventh Edition

In this section we lay out some of the most important changes that we have made in going from the Seventh to the Eighth edition.

CHANGES IN MICROECONOMICS

Chapter 1 gives an introduction to both the importance of growth as a major long-run determinant of living standards and of the globalization of markets, thus introducing themes that are carried throughout the whole book. It also discusses the reasons for the failure of planned economies as a preliminary to understanding the strengths of the market as a co-ordinating system. We have added a new box on comparative advantage that introduces students to the idea of gains from specialization at the outset.

Chapter 2 contains a new discussion of the nature and uses of economic models. (All too often in other books, the word model just appears more or less unexplained.) It also has a new box on the issue of the possibility of value-free enquiry.

Chapter 6 contains new examples of the Channel tunnel and newspaper circulation wars as well as a new box on road pricing to give a modern look to this important chapter that allows students to exercise their newly acquired skills in demand and supply theory. The older examples of rent control and agriculture have been rewritten to focus them on illustrating 'price theory in action'. The chapter draws four extremely important lessons about the price system, the sort of messages we hope students will remember long after they have forgotten the intricacies of indifference curves and isoquants.

Part 3 on demand has been reworked to give two chapters, one on marginal utility and one on indifference analysis. There are new boxes on the Slutzky decomposition that is used in empirical work and on empirical applications of the income and substitution effect. The part concludes with a revised and enlarged chapter on choice under risk which covers many items of current interest, including moral hazard, adverse selection, and portfolio diversification.

Two new boxes, one on transnational corporations and one on Coase's theory of the firm, have been added to Chapter 9.

A new box on what is variously called lean production or flexible manufacturing has been added to Chapter 11. This is the system that is eliminating the old Fordist mass production system that served the economy well for more than fifty years. We have focused the last part of the chapter more on the microeconomics of the firm by stressing the new interest of economists in endogenous technological changes that are induced at the micro level by changes in economic signals.

We have rewritten Chapter 14 to include more material on, and examples of, strategic behaviour, contestable markets, game theory, and prisoner's dilemma, as well as new boxes on 'Globalization of Production and Competition' and 'Brand Proliferation in Alcoholic Drinks'.

Chapter 15, 'The Theory of the Firm and Industry in Action', gives the comparative statics of changes in demand and costs including those induced by taxes. It concludes with an extended study of OPEC as an example of 'the theory in action'.

The analysis of optimality has been brought forward to Chapter 16 which gives the theoretical case for anti-monopoly policy and then goes on to consider actual policy in the United Kingdom.

Chapter 17 considers takeovers and mergers and then goes on to their international aspect when foreign companies are involved and, more generally, to discuss foreign direct investment. This leads naturally to a discussion of whether or not firms maximize profits and to alternative theories of firm behaviour. Instead of 'coming out of the blue' as it did in previous editions, this treatment of alternative theories is now motivated by the earlier discussion, since one reason for takeovers is that the target firm is thought not to be maximizing its profits.

Part 5 on distribution is now organized to give the basic theory in Chapter 17, an expanded and updated discussion of labour markets in Chapter 18, and discussions of the currently popular topic of non-renewable resources (an aspect of land) and capital in Chapter 19. Several new boxes have been added to the distribution chapters including one discussing the electricity and the coal industries. The part concludes with a chapter on distribution theory in action in which the response of wage differentials and the movement of labour to economic signals is discussed, followed by a wholly new discussion of the effects on factor markets and wage differentials of the opening of trade in manufactured products between the newly industrializing countries and the developed countries.

Part 6 on microeconomic policy has been reworked and extensively updated. There is a new discussion of the Coase theorem and a new box on the relation between efficiency and redistribution. The section on market failure and environmental protection policies has been greatly extended to cover many current issues in policy. Boxes give applications to such issues as the problem of fish as an example of a common property resource.

The final micro part covers real trade theory. There is a much extended chapter on the gains from trade covering not only static comparative advantage but modern work on dynamic comparative advantage, resource creation (human capital), and strategic trade theory. The final chapter gives a long discussion of commercial policy starting with the usual arguments for and against free trade but extending to include the modern issues of non-tariff barriers. Systems frictions that arise because what used to be purely domestic policies with respect to labour standards, investment practices, and environmental protection now have impacts on trade and become involved in trade policy disputes. The chapter concludes with an analysis of the theory and practice of regional trade liberalizing agreements with applications to the EU and the NAFTA.

CHANGES IN MACROECONOMICS

It is easy to summarize what has changed in the macroeconomics chapters—almost everything. This is not to say that all the macro chapters are untried, rather these chapters incorporate much material that has proved successful in the US and Canadian book entitled *Economics* (US edition by Lipsey, Courant, Purvis, and Steiner and Canadian edition by Lipsey, Purvis, and Courant). There is, however, also a significant amount of material original to this edition of *Positive Economics* which has been developed to reflect the specific needs of European students, especially those based in the United Kingdom, and some material, such as the careful development of the Phillips curve in Chapter 40, which has been retained from the seventh edition of *Introduction to Positive Economics*, because we could not improve on it.

The algebra used in the text of the seventh edition has been dropped. This makes the text more readable and enables us to go much further in developing concepts that are difficult to handle algebraically. A key innovation in the development of the macro model is that we move very rapidly from the Keynesian cross to the AS/AD framework. An open economy with flexible prices thus becomes the standard early on, rather than being introduced much later in the treatment, as in the seventh edition. We discuss fiscal policy in this context and then move on to consider growth and development before we discuss money.

The coverage of growth in the core of macroeconomics is symptomatic of our perceptions of the key developments in economics. Macro texts used to say that macroeconomics was about the cycle but not about the trend. This is no longer true. Hysteresis, endogenous growth, and real business cycle literatures all make it clear that the trend and cycle are interrelated.

The normal and logical development is to introduce the monetary sector before the aggregate demand curve—since the transmission mechanism is by far the most important reason for the AD curve's negative slope. By postponing the full explanation of the AD curve's slope, and relying on some sufficient conditions for its negative slope in terms of wealth and international terms of trade effects, we are able to use the AD curve effectively before discussing the monetary sector. This has the huge didactic advantage that we can close the model before having to take a major detour to discuss monetary institutions and the monetary sector. Once the monetary sector is added (Chapter 36), we show how the AD curve can be derived from IS/LM and then use a two quadrant diagram with IS/LM and AS/AD as the standard format for applying the model to a variety of policy scenarios. It is a great help that the AS/AD environment is already familiar before students see the formal derivation of AD from IS/LM.

The following are some specific features of the macroeconomics half of the book that are worthy of mention. Some survive from the seventh edition, although usually in amended form; others are largely, or wholly, new.

An introductory chapter (27) talks about the main issues of macroeconomics and shows long historical data series before any theory is introduced.

A simple bar chart shows the relationship between income, expenditure, and output-based measures of national income using 1993 UK national accounts data, in a new chapter (28) that explains all the important concepts used in national income accounting.

Attention is given to the assumptions used in building macro models (Chapter 29) before we start on theory. Many of these are temporary but the importance of the single homogeneous product assumption, often neglected in other texts, is highlighted.

As in earlier editions, the macro model is built around the equilibrium concepts of potential national income and the NAIRU. New IMF estimates of potential GDP for the United Kingdom are used to illustrate its historical level.

As in earlier editions, the short-run aggregate supply curve (Chapter 31) is derived assuming fixed input prices, but it is also related to the short-run optimization of firms and their underlying cost structures.

Unlike many other treatments, we do not end our core macroeconomic theory with a given long-run aggregate supply curve, putting the causes of its shifts beyond the scope of our treatment. Rather, we end our core macro theory part with two chapters that discuss growth, both in developed and developing countries.

The discussion of money and monetary policy has been substantially updated to reflect the financial innovations of the last decade or so. There is a new exposition of the money multiplier and there is an analysis of competitive banking (Chapter 35). The latter is central to the explanation of modern monetary policy which operates through interest rates rather than via the monetary base or reserve ratios (Chapter 38). We think this is a major improvement on textbooks which go through the fixed ratios story and then say that monetary policy doesn't actually operate that way. Our exposition makes it clear that policy operates via the influence of interest rates on the demand for bank loans.

The exchange rate and exchange rate regimes are discussed (Chapter 37), and the significance of perfect capital mobility is analysed in detail (Chapter 39). There are also boxes explaining key financial terms and discussing key institutional developments such as the euro-currency markets and globalization of finance. The appendix to Chapter 37 gives a historical review of the evolution of exchange rate regimes, including the ERM.

Monetary policy is viewed from the perspective of targets and indicators. The demise of explicit monetary targets is explained, as is the experience with exchange rate targeting. The post-1992 policy of inflation targeting is set out, as are the difficulties of targeting a lagging indicator. Alternative monetary indicators are discussed, including Divisia index numbers (Chapter 38). There is also a discussion of the costs and benefits of adoption of a single currency for the EU.

Chapter 40 offers a detailed discussion of the relationship between inflation and unemployment. It is distinctive in that it presents a step-by-step account of the relationship between the Phillips curve and the SRAS curve. There is also a taxonomy of various inflationary shocks combined with an analysis of the effects of policy accommodation or validation.

Chapter 41, on employment and unemployment, is one of the most important chapters in the macro section of the book. It reflects the large amount of research in this area which has taken place over the last decade or so and associated especially with New Keynesians. Traditional macroeconomics focused only on cyclical unemployment. Recent work has focused more on equilibrium unemployment. Key concepts, such as efficiency wages, insider–outsider models and menu costs, are explained and some of the policy implications of the new approaches are outlined.

Fiscal policy has always been central to macroeconomics, but introductory texts have paid little attention to the longer-term issues associated with deficits and debt. Chapter 42 is devoted to these issues entirely. Data are presented showing national debt over the last century and there are tables illustrating the changing composition of public expenditure, both in the UK and EU. A box analyses the sustainability of deficits and the notion of Ricardian equivalence is critically assessed. There is also a discussion of the functions of the public sector as a producer, indicating some of the likely long-term demands on the public purse.

Business cycle research has been very active in recent years and a new chapter (43) reflects some of the more important developments. Characteristics of cycles are illustrated using UK data, and the older macro approaches (Keynesians and monetarists) are explained, along with newer views (new classical and real business cycles). The method of dynamic modelling applied to business cycle is an important complement to the traditional comparative static methodology of mainstream macroeconomics.

The final macro chapter (44) tries to give some perspective to the evolution of macroeconomics as well as re-emphasizing the importance of evidence in the evolution of positive economics as a whole.

Primarily to the Student

Here we give a bit of advice to beginners on how to approach a book in economics. Of course, there is no reason why instructors should not read on as well. After all, they may be interested in what we have to say to students.

Format

Before we pass to consider substance, a few words about the format of the book may be of assistance.

Figures, tags, and captions   The formal analysis related to each figure is given in a caption attached to that figure. This has the advantage of keeping the reasoning physically attached to its associated figure and in allowing that reasoning to be studied at the point that seems best to the reader. The text is made self-sufficient by providing an intuitive explanation of the formal reasoning given in each figure caption. This means that the text can be read on its own, without the figure captions—say, on first reading or for revision. The basic analytical reasoning that is the core of economics is, however, given in the captions *all of which must be carefully studied by all students.*

Captioning also permits both a fast reading of the text for the general intuitive drift of the argument without captions, and an easy revision of specific points by reading some captions on their own.

Each figure caption begins with a tag line in bold type that states its main message.

Summaries   Every chapter ends with a set of summary points. They provide a useful review as well as a warning that some of the chapter needs to be reread when the reasoning behind one or more of the summary points cannot be reconstructed.

Topics for review   Every chapter also ends with a series of topics for review. These can be treated in the same way as the summaries: as checks on what has just been learned, and as signals during revision.

Boxes   Frequent use is made of boxes which are set off from the body of the chapter by a different type and use of a colour surround. The main unifying point about all the boxes is that they contain material that can be omitted without loss of continuity. They include empirical illustrations, more detailed elaborations of various points made in the text, points of historical interest, and occasional formal proofs, all of which may be of interest to some, but not all, readers.

Glossary   The first time a technical term is used extensively in the text it is printed in **bold** type so that it can be easily recognized as such. The definitions of all such terms are gathered together in a Glossary printed at the end of the book.

Approaches to the Study of Economics

You need to study a book on economics in a different way from how you would study a book on, say, history or English literature. Economic theory has a logical structure that builds on itself from stage to stage. Thus if you only imperfectly understand some concept or theory, you will run into increasing difficulty when, in subsequent chapters, this concept or theory is taken for granted and built upon. Because of its logical structure, quite long chains of reasoning are encountered; if A then B, if B then C, if C then D, and if D then E. Each step in the argument may seem simple enough, but the cumulative effect of several steps, one on top of the other, may be bewildering on first encounter. Thus when, having followed the argument step by step, you encounter the statement 'it is now obvious that if A then E', it may not seem at all obvious to you. This is a problem which everyone encounters with chains of reasoning. The only way to deal with it is to follow the argument through several times. Eventually, as the reasoning becomes familiar, it will become obvious that, *if A then E*.

Economics has its own technical language or jargon. At first you may feel that you are merely being asked to put complicated names to common-sense ideas. To some extent this is true. It is a necessary step, however, because loose thinking about vaguely formed ideas is a quick route to error in economics. Furthermore, when you begin to put several ideas together to see what follows from them, jargon—the single clearly defined term to refer to these ideas—becomes a necessary part of your equipment. To help you recognize them as such, technical terms are printed in **bold type** the first time they are used. As a further aid, their definitions are gathered together into a Glossary printed at the end of the book.

A book on economics is to be worked at, and understood step by step. It is usually good to read a chapter quickly in order to see the general run of the argument, and at this stage you might omit the captions to the figures. You must then reread the chapter carefully, making sure that the argument is understood step by step. On this reading, you *must* study the captions to all the figures carefully. They contain the reasoning on which the intuitive discussion of the text is based. If you do not understand the captions, you have not understood economics. You should not be discouraged if, occasionally at this stage, you find yourself spending an hour on only two or three pages.

A pencil and paper are necessary pieces of equipment in your reading. Difficult arguments should be followed by building up one's own diagram while the argument unfolds, rather than relying on the printed diagram which is, perforce, complete from the beginning. Numerical examples should be invented to illustrate general propositions.

The Summaries and Topics for Review are there to help you. After your reading of each chapter, and when revising for exams, you should read them and check that you understand the meaning of the topics and the reasoning behind the summary points. Difficulties in doing so provide a signal that you need to reread some or all of the chapter.

After the book has been read in this detailed manner, it should be reread fairly quickly from cover to cover; it is often difficult to understand why certain things are done until one knows the end-product, and, on a second reading, much that seems strange and incomprehensible will be seen to have an obvious place in the analysis.

In short, the technical vocabulary aside, one must seek to understand economics, not to memorize it. Theories, principles, and concepts are always turning up in slightly unfamiliar guises. If you have understood your economics, this poses no problem; if you have merely memorized it, this spells disaster.

Write to us

Economics is a subject in which one never stops learning. We are grateful to many users—students and teachers—who have taken the trouble to write to us pointing out errors, making comments, and offering suggestions. We hope that readers will continue to teach us with as many further comments and criticisms as they have in the past. We try to acknowledge every such letter. If you write and do not hear from us, write again—the post (or our filing systems) have let us down!

Acknowledgements

Finally we wish to say a word of thanks to those people who have made this book possible. In so far as the ideas and viewpoints expressed in the first edition were novel, they were the common property of all of Lipsey's colleagues who in the late 1950s and early 1960s were members of the LSE *Staff Seminar on Methodology, Measurement and Testing in Economics*. All that Lipsey did in the first edition was to give a slightly personal expression to this general viewpoint.

Valuable research assistance on the eighth edition has been provided by Cliff Bekar, Ken Carlow, and Selby MacLeod. Saira Abbasi and Robyn Wills have shown unlimited patience in providing the many and varied secretarial duties associated with the production of the book. Many anonymous advisers read the manuscript and contributed greatly towards improvements. Sue Appleton Hughes provided creative editing for which, now that it is over, the authors are grateful. The usual disclaimer of course holds here: for all remaining shortcomings and mistakes, the authors may blame each other, but the reader should blame us both.

R.G.L
K.A.C

Simon Fraser University
Vancouver, B.C.
   and
City University Business School
London, England

January 1995

PART ONE

Scope and method

∾ CHAPTER 1

Economic issues

WHY has the history of most industrial nations been one of several years of boom and plenty, followed by several years of recession and unemployment bringing poverty to many? Why, during the 1930s in most countries, was up to one person in four unemployed while factories lay idle and raw materials went unused—why, in short, was everything available to produce urgently needed goods that were not produced? Why, in the 1990s, did unemployment in most countries reach the highest levels ever attained since the Great Depression of the 1930s?

What determines the level of wages, and what influences do unions have on the share of national income received by labour? Is it possible that, having fully achieved the purpose of putting labour on an equal footing with management, unions have outlived their usefulness?

How do ordinary commercial banks create money within broad limits? How can governments create money without limits? If money is valuable, why do economists insist that countries with large supplies of it are no richer than countries with small supplies?

Are full employment and stable prices compatible, or must governments make agonizing choices between them?

Is government intervention needed to keep markets working effectively, or would we be better off with a policy of *laissez-faire* that minimized government intervention? What are the effects of a government's taxing and spending policies?

These are a few of the questions with which economists concern themselves, and on which the theories of economics are designed to shed some light.

This chapter is a general introduction to the subject matter of economics. It is divided into four main parts. The first deals with the general nature of the issues that concern economists. The second deals with the alternative ways in which a nation's economic activities can be structured, emphasizing the two contrasting extremes of decentralized market economies and centrally planned economies. The third looks briefly at the origins of market economies and the evolution of some of their key characteristics such as specialization and the division of labour. The fourth and final section discusses how people's living standards are affected by the availability of jobs, the productivity of labour in those jobs, and the distribution of the income produced by those jobs. It reveals an economy characterized by ongoing change in the structure of jobs, in the production techniques used by the workers, and in the kinds of goods and services produced.

The issues discussed in this chapter will arise again at many places throughout the book. Because most of them are interrelated, it helps to know the basic outlines of all of them before studying any one of them in more depth.

The source of economic problems

ALL of the above issues, as well as many others that we will meet in our study, have common features—features that make them economic rather than something else, such as political or biological. Our first task in this chapter is to look for some of the similarities that suggest an underlying unity to these apparently diverse issues.

Most of the problems of economics arise out of a basic fact of life:

The production that can be obtained by fully utilizing all of a nation's resources is insufficient to satisfy all the wants of the nation's inhabitants; because resources are scarce, it is necessary to choose among the alternative uses to which they could be put.

Resources and scarcity

Kinds of resources   The resources of a society consist not only of the free gifts of nature, such as land, forests, and minerals, but also of human capacity, both mental and physical, and of all sorts of man-made aids to further production, such as tools, machinery, and buildings. It is sometimes useful to divide these resources into three main groups: (1) all those free gifts of nature, such as land, forests, minerals, etc., commonly called *natural resources* and known to economists as **land**; (2) all human resources, mental and physical, both inherited and acquired, which economists call **labour**; and (3) all those man-made aids to further production, such as tools, machinery, and factories, which are used up in the process of making other goods and services rather than being consumed for their own sake, which economists call **capital**.

Often a fourth resource is distinguished. This is **entrepreneurship** from the French word *entrepreneur*, meaning one who undertakes tasks. Entrepreneurs take risks by introducing both new products and new ways of making old products. They organize the other factors of production and direct them along new lines. (When it is not distinguished as a fourth factor, entrepreneurship is included under labour.) Collectively, these resources are called **factors of production**, and sometimes just 'factors' for short.

Kinds of production   The factors of production are used to make products which are divided into goods and services: **goods** are tangible, such as cars or shoes; **services** are intangible, such as haircuts and education. Economists often refer to 'goods' when they mean goods and services. They also use the terms *products* and *commodities* to mean goods and services.

Goods are themselves valued for the services they provide. A car, for example, provides transportation (and possibly also satisfaction from displaying it as a status symbol). The total output of all goods and services in one country over some period, usually taken as a year, is called its **national product**.

The act of making goods and services is called **production**, and the act of using these goods and services to satisfy wants is called **consumption**. Anyone who makes goods or provides services is called a **producer**, and anyone who consumes them to satisfy his or her wants is called a **consumer**.

Judging definitions   The division of resources into land, labour, capital, and entrepreneurship, and the division of output into goods and services, are matters of definition. Definitions cannot be judged as we would matters of fact; they are to be judged instead on the grounds of usefulness and convenience. The question 'Is this fourfold division of factors likely to be a useful one?' can be discussed fruitfully. The question 'Is this fourfold division of factors the correct one?' is unlikely to give rise to fruitful discussion, and it certainly has no definite answer.

Useless arguments about which of many competing definitions of some concept is the correct one are so common that they have been given a name: *essentialist arguments*. An essentialist argument concerns purely semantic issues; they occur whenever we agree about the facts of the case, but argue about what name to use to indicate the agreed facts. For example, we may agree about what happened in the Soviet Union between 1921 and 1989, but argue about whether that can be called true communism. We are then having an essentialist argument about definitions.

Scarcity   In most societies goods and services are not regarded as desirable in themselves; few people are interested in piling them up endlessly in warehouses, never to be consumed. Usually the purpose of producing goods and services is to satisfy the wants of the individuals who consume them. Goods and services are thus regarded as *means to an end*, the satisfaction of wants.

In relation to the known desires of individuals for such products as better food, clothing, housing, schooling, holidays, hospital care, and entertainment, the existing supplies of resources are woefully inadequate.[1] They are sufficient to produce only a small fraction of the goods and services that people desire. This gives rise to the basic economic problem of *scarcity*.

CHOICE AND OPPORTUNITY COST

Choices are necessary because resources are scarce. Because a country cannot produce everything its citizens would like to consume, there must exist some mechanism to decide what will be done and what left undone; which goods will be produced and which left unproduced; what quantity of each will be produced; and whose wants will be satisfied and whose left unsatisfied. In most societies these choices are influenced by many different people and organizations, from individual consumers to business organizations, labour unions, and government officials. One of the differences among economies such as those of the United States, the United Kingdom, India, and Taiwan is the amount of influence that various groups have on these choices.

If you choose to have more of one thing, then, where there is an effective choice, you must have less of something else. Think of a man with a certain income who considers buying bread. We could say that the cost of this extra bread is so many pence per loaf. A more revealing way of looking at the cost, however, is in terms of what other consumption he must forgo in order to obtain his bread. Say that he decides to give up some cinema attendances. If the price of a loaf is one-fifth the price of a cinema seat, then the cost of five more loaves of bread is one cinema attendance; or, put the other way around, the cost of one more cinema attendance is five loaves of bread.

Now consider the same problem at the level of a whole society. If the government elects to build more roads, and finds the required money by building fewer schools, then the cost of the new roads can be expressed as so many schools per mile of road.

The economist's term for costs expressed in terms of forgone alternatives is **opportunity cost**. If some course of action is adopted, there are typically many alternatives that might be forgone. For example, when the government decides to build the road, it might cut expenditure on schools, on research laboratories, or on a proposed modernization of the postal service. To get a precise measure of opportunity cost, economists count the sacrifice as that of the *best available alternative*. Thus, in the above example we ask: If the government had not built the roads, what was the best alternative use of its funds? That alternative is what is given up to get the roads.

---

[1] We do not need to decide if it would ever be possible to produce enough goods and services to satisfy all human wants. We only need to observe that it would take a vast increase in production to raise the living standard of all the citizens of any country to that currently enjoyed by its richer citizens. Even if this could be done, it is doubtful that all citizens would find their wants fully satisfied.

The concept of opportunity cost emphasizes the need for choice by measuring the cost of anything that is chosen in terms of the best alternative that could have been chosen instead. The sacrificed alternative measures the cost of obtaining what is chosen.

Our discussion may now be summarized briefly. Most of the issues studied in economics are related to the use of scarce resources to satisfy human wants. Resources are employed to produce goods and services, which are used by consumers to satisfy their wants. Choices are necessary because there are insufficient resources to satisfy all human wants.

BASIC ECONOMIC PROBLEMS

Most of the specific questions posed at the beginning of this chapter (and many other questions as well) may be regarded as aspects of seven more general questions that arise in *all* economies.

1. *What products are being produced and in what quantities?* The answer to this question determines the allocation of the economy's scarce resources among alternative uses, called its **resource allocation**. Choosing to produce a particular combination of goods means choosing a particular allocation of resources among the industries producing these goods. For example, producing a large output of food requires that a large amount of resources be allocated to food production.

2. *By what methods are these products produced?* This question arises because output can almost always be produced in more than one technically possible way. Agricultural goods, for example, can be produced by farming a small quantity of land very intensively, using large quantities of fertilizer and machinery, or by farming a large quantity of land extensively, using only small quantities of fertilizer and machinery. Similarly, any particular manufactured good can usually be produced by several different techniques. One technique may use a large quantity of labour and only a few simple machines; another, a large quantity of automated machines and only a few workers.

3. *How is society's output of goods and services divided among its members?* Why are some individuals and groups able to consume a large share of the national output, while other individuals and groups are able to consume only a small share? The superficial answer is that the former earn large incomes while the latter earn small incomes. But this only pushes the question one stage back. Why do some individuals and groups earn large incomes while others earn only small incomes? The basic question concerns the division of the national product among individuals and groups. Economists wish to know why any particular division occurs in a free-market society and what forces, including government intervention, can cause it to change. When they speak of the division of the national product

among any set of groups in the society, economists speak of the **distribution of income**.

4. *How efficient is the society's production and distribution?* These questions quite naturally arise out of questions 1, 2, and 3. Having asked what quantities of goods are produced, how they are produced, and to whom they are distributed, it is natural to go on to ask whether the production and distribution decisions are efficient.

The concept of *efficiency* is quite distinct from the concept of *justice*. The latter is what we will learn in Chapter 2 to call a 'normative concept'. A just distribution of the national product would be one that our value judgements told us was a *good* or a *desirable* distribution. Efficiency and inefficiency are what we will learn in Chapter 2 to call 'positive concepts'. Current production methods are inefficient if it is possible to produce more of at least one product *without* simultaneously producing less of any other merely by adopting alternative production methods. The economy's output is said to be inefficiently distributed if a redistribution of that output among individuals could make at least one person better off *without* simultaneously making anyone worse off.

Questions 1–4 are related to the allocation of resources and the distribution of income and are intimately connected, in a market economy, to the way in which the price system works. They are grouped under the general heading of **microeconomics**.

5. *Are the country's resources being fully utilized, or are some of them lying idle?* We have already noted that there are not enough resources to produce all of the products that people desire. Yet during periods of recession unemployed workers want jobs, the factories in which they could work are available, the owners want to operate their factories profitably, raw materials are available in abundance, and the goods that could be produced by these resources are wanted. Yet, for some reason, nothing happens: the workers stay unemployed, the factories lie idle, and the raw materials remain unused. The cost of such unemployment is felt both in terms of the goods and services that could have been produced by the idle resources, and in terms of the effects on people who are unable to find work for prolonged periods.

Economists study why market economies experience such periods of unemployment *which are unwanted by virtually everyone in the society*, and ask if such unemployment can be prevented by government action.

6. *Is the purchasing power of money constant, or is it being eroded because of inflation?* The world's economies have often experienced periods of prolonged and rapid changes in price levels. Over the long swing of history, price levels have sometimes risen and sometimes fallen. In recent decades, however, the course of prices has almost always been upward. Economists ask many questions about the causes and consequences of changes in the price level.

7. *Is the economy's capacity to produce goods and services growing from year to year, or is it remaining static?* The misery and poverty described in the England of a century and a half ago by Charles Dickens are no longer with us as a mass phenomenon. This is largely due to **economic growth**, increases in the total output of goods and services that the economy is capable of producing . The nation's capacity to produce goods and services has grown about 2 per cent per year faster than its population since Dickens's time. Why the capacity to produce grows rapidly in some economies, slowly in others, and not at all in yet others is a critical problem which has exercised the minds of some of the best economists over the centuries.

Questions 5, 6, and 7 are usually studied in a branch of economics called **macroeconomics**.

There are, of course, other questions that arise, but these seven are the major ones common to all types of economies. Most of the rest of this book is devoted to their detailed study. We shall study how decisions on these questions are made in free-market societies, the (often unexpected) consequences of settling these questions through the price system, and why governments sometimes intervene in an attempt to alter the decisions.

THE PRODUCTION-POSSIBILITY BOUNDARY

Four of the above questions that are most easily confused can be distinguished by introducing a simple diagram.

Consider one choice that faces all economies today: how many resources to devote to producing 'guns for defence' and how many to devote to producing goods for all other purposes. This is a problem in the allocation of resources, which is illustrated in Figure 1.1.[2] The United States, Israel, and (perhaps surprisingly) many of the world's poorer, less developed countries devote quite large proportions of their total resources to defence expenditures, as also did the former Soviet Union. These countries have correspondingly less resources available to produce goods for civilian uses. Some European countries, such as France, devote quite large amounts to military purposes, while others, such as Germany, devote only a little. The United Kingdom is located towards the lower end of this list, devoting only 3.7 per cent of its total resources to military purposes.

The horizontal axis measures the quantity of military goods produced, while the vertical axis measures the quantity of all other goods, which we call 'civilian goods'. The red line on the figure shows all those combinations of military and civilian goods that can be produced if all resources are fully employed. It is called a **production-possibility boundary**. Points outside the boundary show combinations that cannot be obtained because there are not enough resources to produce them. Points on the boundary are just obtainable: they are the combinations that can just be produced using all the available supplies of resources.

[2] If you are not sure about the use of graphs, you might wish to study pp. 53–5 now.

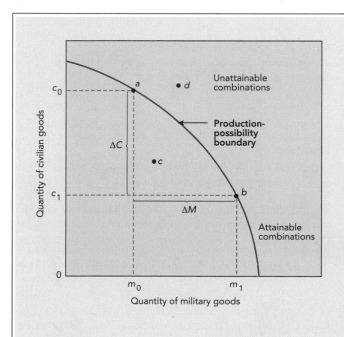

Figure 1.1 A production-possibility boundary

The negatively sloped boundary shows the combinations that are just attainable when all of the society's resources are efficiently employed. The quantity of military goods produced is measured along the horizontal axis, the quantity of civilian goods along the vertical axis. Thus, any point on the diagram indicates some amount of each kind of good produced. The production-possibility boundary separates the attainable combinations, such as a, b, and c, from unattainable combinations, such as d. It is negatively sloped because in a fully employed economy more of one good can be produced only if resources are freed by producing less of other goods. For example, moving from point a (whose coordinates are c_0 and m_0) to point b (whose coordinates are c_1 and m_1) implies producing an additional amount of military goods, indicated by ΔM in the figure, at an opportunity cost of a reduction in civilian goods by the amount indicated by ΔC. Points a and b represent efficient uses of society's resources. Point c represents either an inefficient use of resources or a failure to use all the resources that are available.

A single production-possibility boundary illustrates three concepts: scarcity, choice, and opportunity cost. Scarcity is implied by the unattainable combinations beyond the boundary; choice, by the need to choose among the attainable points on the boundary; opportunity cost, by the negative slope of the boundary which shows that obtaining more of one type of output requires having less of the other.

Increasing opportunity cost   The production possibility curve of Figure 1.1 is drawn with a slope that gets steeper as one moves along it from left to right. The increasing slope indicates increasing opportunity cost as more and more of either product is produced. Consider, for example, starting at the vertical axis where all production is of civilian goods with nothing for the military. A small increase in military production moves the economy slightly along the curve, indicating a reduction in the production of civilian goods. However, the flatness of the curve indicates that the loss of civilian goods is small. Now consider being at point *b*, where most production is of military goods (a situation not found except in the midst of a major war). At *b* the curve is very steep. This indicates that, if even more military goods are to be produced, the sacrifice in civilian goods is very large.

The increasing steepness of the production possibility curve as one moves along it from left to right indicates that, the higher the production of either goods, the greater is the opportunity cost of obtaining a further increase in its production.

The boundary can also be used to illustrate four of the questions discussed earlier.

Question 1.   The question of where to produce on the production-possibility boundary is a question about the allocation of resources. In this example, each point on the boundary implies a different allocation of resources between the production of military and civilian goods. The United States, Israel, France, Germany, and the United Kingdom will each be at different points along their own production possibility curves.

Questions 4 and 5.   An economy can always be located inside its boundary. This is wasteful because production of all goods and services is then less than it could be if points on the boundary were attained. An economy can be producing inside its production-possibility boundary either because some of its resources are lying idle (question 5), or because its resources are being used inefficiently in production (question 4).

Question 7.   If the economy's capacity to produce goods is increasing through time, the production-possibility boundary will be moving outwards over time, as illustrated in Figure 1.2. More of *all* goods can then be produced.

Notice that, if an economy is at some point on an

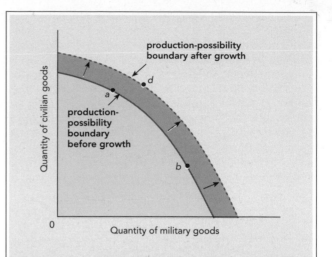

Figure 1.2 The effect of economic growth on the production-possibility boundary

Economic growth shifts the production-possibility boundary outward, allowing more of all commodities to be produced. Before growth in productive capacity, points *a* and *b* were on the production-possibility boundary and point *d* was an unattainable combination. After growth, point *d* becomes attainable, as do all points within the dark blue band.

unchanging production-possibility boundary, having more of one thing necessarily implies having less of something else. It is, however, possible to have more of everything if: (1) resources previously unemployed are now employed; (2) resources previously used inefficiently are now used efficiently; or (3) economic growth shifts the production-possibility boundary outwards.

A note on terminology   We have used the term 'production-possibility boundary'. 'Boundary' emphasizes that the points on the line are maximum points. It is always possible to produce at points *inside* the line by not employing some factors of production, or by using them inefficiently. Two other terms, 'frontier' and 'curve', are often used instead of boundary.

The words 'production possibility' emphasize the alternative possibilities available to the society. However, the term 'transformation' is often used instead. The idea behind the term 'transformation' is that society can, in effect, 'transform' one product into another by moving resources from the production of one product into the production of the other. Speaking of transforming one product into another stresses the idea of opportunity cost. Of course, one good is not literally transformed into another as ancient alchemists sought to transform base metals into gold; but, by moving resources from producing one type of good to producing another, quantities of the first type of good are sacrificed to gain quantities of the second type.

You can make up six terms by combining the following words:

$$
\left.\begin{array}{l}
\text{Production possibility} \\
\text{or} \\
\text{Transformation}
\end{array}\right\} \text{with} \left\{\begin{array}{l}
\text{Curve} \\
\text{or} \\
\text{Boundary} \\
\text{or} \\
\text{Frontier}
\end{array}\right.
$$

All six terms mean the same thing; all six are commonly used.

Economics: a working definition

Listing the problem areas of economics outlines its scope more fully than can be done with short definitions. Economics today is regarded much more broadly than it was even half a century ago. Earlier definitions stressed only the alternative and competing uses of resources, and focused on choices among alternative points on a stationary production-possibility boundary. Other important problems concern failure to reach the boundary (problems of inefficiency or underemployment of resources) and the outward movement of the boundary over time (problems of growth and development).

Broadly defined, modern economics concerns:

1. the allocation of a society's resources among alternative uses and the distribution of the society's output among individuals and groups at a point in time;
2. the ways in which allocation, distribution, and total output change over time;
3. the efficiencies and inefficiencies of economic systems.

Alternative economic systems

AN economic system is a distinctive method of providing answers to the basic economic questions just discussed. All such systems are complex. They include producers of every sort—publicly and privately owned, as well as domestically owned and foreign owned. They include consumers of every sort—young and old, rich and poor, working and non-working. They include laws (such as those relating to property rights), rules, regulations, taxes, subsidies, and everything else that governments use to influence what is produced, how it is produced, and who gets it. They are also influenced by customs of every conceivable kind, and the entire range of contemporary mores and values.

Types of economic system

Although each nation's economic system is in some ways distinct from all others, it is helpful to distinguish three pure types, called *market, traditional,* and *command* economies. These economies differ in the way in which economic decisions are *co-ordinated.* All real economies contain some elements of each method.

MARKET SYSTEMS

In a **market economy**, millions of consumers decide what products to buy and in what quantities; a vast number of firms produce those products and buy the factor services that are needed to make them; and millions of owners of factors of production decide to whom and on what terms they will sell these services. These individual decisions collectively determine the economy's allocation of resources among competing uses.

In a market economy, the allocation of resources is the outcome of millions of independent decisions made by consumers and producers, all acting through the medium of markets.

Early economists observed that, although most products were made by a large number of independent producers, they were made in approximately the quantities that people wanted to purchase. Natural disasters aside, there were neither vast surpluses nor severe and persistent shortages in relation to the demand for these products. These economists also saw that most labourers were able to sell their services to employers most of the time, in spite of the fact that the kinds of products made, the techniques used to make them, and the places in which they were made changed over time.

How does the market produce this order without conscious direction by some central co-ordinating body? It is one thing to have the same products produced year in and year out when people's wants and incomes do not change; it is quite another to have production adjusting continually to changing wants, incomes, and techniques of production. Yet the market does produce this relatively smooth adjustment—although with occasional, and sometimes serious, interruptions. Because of the importance of prices in market economies, we say that they employ a **price system**. This term refers to the role that prices play in determining the allocation of resources and the distribution of national product. Economists' great insight is that:

Markets function without conscious control because individuals take their private decisions in response to publicly available signals such as prices, while these signals in turn respond to the collective actions entailed by the sum of all individual decisions; in short, the price system is an automatically functioning social-control mechanism.

A *social-control mechanism* is a technical term for anything that influences social behaviour. Prices, which provide an incentive for people to adopt certain patterns of behaviour voluntarily, are one example; laws, which force behaviour into certain patterns, are another.

In 1776 the great Scottish economist Adam Smith (1723–90) published *The Wealth of Nations*. This great book was the culmination of early attempts to understand the workings of market economies. Smith spoke of the price system as 'the invisible hand' because it co-ordinated decision-taking that was decentralized among millions of individual producers and consumers.

An example   Suppose that, under prevailing conditions, farmers find it equally profitable to produce either beef or potatoes. As a result, they are willing to produce some of both products, thereby satisfying the demands of individuals to consume both. Now suppose that consumers develop a greatly increased desire for potatoes and a diminished desire for beef. This change occurs because of the discovery that too much red meat is harmful to one's health.

When consumers buy more potatoes and less beef, a shortage of potatoes and a surplus of beef develops. To unload their surplus stocks of beef, merchants reduce the price of beef because it is better to sell it at a reduced price than not to sell it at all. Merchants find, however, that they are unable to satisfy all their customers' demands for potatoes. These have become scarce, so merchants charge more for them. As their price rises, fewer potatoes are demanded. Thus, the rise in its price limits the quantity demanded to the available supply.

Farmers see that potato production has become more profitable than in the past because the costs of producing potatoes remain unchanged while their market price has risen. Similarly, they see that beef production has become less profitable than in the past because costs are unchanged while the price has fallen. Attracted by high profits in pota-

toes and deterred by low profits or potential losses in beef, farmers expand the production of potatoes and curtail the production of beef. Thus, the change in consumers' tastes, working through the price system, causes a reallocation of resources—land and labour—out of beef production and into potato production.

The reaction of the market to a change in demand leads to a reallocation of resources. Beef producers reduce their production; they will therefore be laying off workers and generally demanding fewer factors of production. Producers of potatoes expand production; they will therefore be hiring workers and generally increasing their demand for factors of production.

Labour will have to switch from beef to potato production. Certain types of land, however, are better suited for producing one product than the other. When farmers increase their potato production, their demands for the factors especially suited to growing potatoes also increase—and this creates a shortage of these resources and a consequent rise in their prices. Meanwhile, with beef production falling, the demand for land and other factors of production especially suited to growing cattle is reduced. A surplus results, and the prices of these factors are forced down.

Thus, factors particularly suited to potato production will earn more, and will obtain a higher share of total national income than before. Factors particularly suited to beef production, however, will earn less and will obtain a smaller share of the total national income than before.

All of the changes illustrated in this example will be studied more fully in subsequent parts of this book; the important thing to notice now is how changes in demand cause reallocations of resources in the directions required to cater to the new levels of demand.

This example illustrates the point made earlier: *The price system is a mechanism that co-ordinates individual, decentralized decisions.*

TRADITIONAL SYSTEMS

A *traditional economic system* is one in which behaviour is based primarily on tradition, custom, and habit. Young men follow their fathers' occupations—typically, hunting, fishing, and tool making. Women do what their mothers did—typically, cooking and fieldwork.[3] There is little change in the pattern of goods produced from year to year, other than those imposed by the vagaries of nature. The techniques of production also follow traditional patterns, except when the effects of an occasional new invention are felt. The concept of private property is often not well defined and property is frequently held in common. Finally, production is allocated among the members according to long-established traditions. In short, the answers to the eco-

[3] To a modern reader it may sound sexist to divide the occupations in this way. But through most of history, this was the male–female division of labour in most rural societies.

nomic questions of what to produce, how to produce, and how to distribute are determined by traditions.

Such a system works best in an unchanging environment. Under static conditions, a system that does not continually require people to make choices can prove effective in meeting economic and social needs.

Traditional systems were common in earlier times. The feudal system, under which most people lived in medieval Europe, was a largely traditional society. Peasants, artisans, and most others living in villages inherited their general positions in that society, as well as their specific jobs, which they handled in traditional ways. For example, the blacksmith made customary charges for dealing with horses brought to him, and it would have been unthinkable for him to decline his services to any villager who requested them.

Today only a few small, isolated, self-sufficient communities still retain mainly traditional systems; examples can be found in the Canadian Arctic and the Himalayas. Also, in many of the world's poorer countries, significant aspects of economic behaviour are still governed by traditional patterns.

COMMAND SYSTEMS

In command systems, economic behaviour is determined by some central authority, which makes most of the necessary decisions on what to produce, how to produce it, and who gets it. Such economies are characterized by the *centralization* of decision-making. Because centralized decision-makers usually lay down elaborate and complex plans for the behaviour that they wish to impose, the terms **command economy** and **centrally planned economy** are usually used synonymously.

The sheer quantity of data required for the central planning of an entire economy is enormous, and the task of analysing it to produce a fully integrated plan can hardly be exaggerated, even in the age of computers. Moreover, the plan must be a rolling process, continually changing to take account not only of current data but also of future trends in labour supplies, technological developments, and people's tastes for various goods and services. Doing so involves the planners in the notoriously difficult business of forecasting the future.

A decade ago over one-third of the world's population lived in countries that relied heavily on central planning to deal with the basic economic questions. Today the number of such countries is small. Even in countries where planning is the proclaimed system, as in China, increasing amounts of market determination are being accepted, even encouraged.

MIXED SYSTEMS

Economies that are fully traditional, or fully centrally controlled, or wholly free-market are pure types that are useful for studying basic principles. When we look in detail at any real economy, however, we discover that its economic behaviour is the result of some mixture of central control

and market determination, with a certain amount of traditional behaviour as well.

In practice, every economy is a mixed economy in the sense that it combines significant elements of all three systems—traditional, command, and market—in determining economic behaviour.[4]

Furthermore, within any economy, the degree of the mix will vary from sector to sector. For example, in most planned economies the command principle was used more often to determine behaviour in heavy goods industries, such as steel, than in agriculture. Farmers were often given substantial freedom to produce and sell what they wished in response to varying market prices.

When we speak of a particular economy as being 'centrally planned', we mean only that the degree of the mix is weighted heavily towards the command principle. When we speak of an economy as being a 'market' economy, we mean only that the degree of the mix is weighted heavily towards decentralized decision-taking in response to market signals. Although no country offers an example of either system working alone, some economies, such as those of the United Kingdom, Germany, and Hong Kong, rely much more heavily on market decisions than others, such as China, North Korea, and Cuba. Although the United Kingdom is primarily a market economy, the command principle still has some significant sway. Some examples are minimum prices on many agricultural products, fixed charges for medical prescriptions, and university fees, all set by law rather than demand and supply. Other examples are rules and regulations for environmental protection, quotas on some agricultural outputs, and restrictions on the import of items such as textiles, cheap shoes, and cars.

OWNERSHIP OF RESOURCES

We have seen that economies differ as to the principles used for co-ordinating their economic decisions. They also differ as to who owns their productive resources. Who owns a nation's farms and factories, its coal mines and forests? Who owns its railways, streams, and golf courses? Who owns its houses and hotels?

In a private-ownership economy, the basic raw materials, the productive assets of the society, and the goods produced in the economy are predominantly privately owned. By this standard, the United Kingdom has primarily a private-ownership economy. However, even in the United Kingdom, public ownership extends beyond the usual basic services such as schools, hospitals, and roads to include such other activities as council housing, forest and national

---

[4] Although tradition influences behaviour in all societies, we shall have little to say about it in the rest of this chapter because we are primarily interested in the consequences of making economic decisions through the market and the command principles.

park land, the coal mines, and the Post Office.

In contrast, a public-ownership economy is one in which the productive assets are predominantly publicly owned. This was true of the former Soviet Union, and it is true to a great extent in present-day China. In China, however, private ownership exists in many sectors—including the rapidly growing part of the manufacturing sector that is foreign owned, mainly by Japanese and by Chinese from Taiwan, Hong Kong, and Singapore.

THE CO-ORDINATION–OWNERSHIP MIX

Leaving aside tradition, because it is not the predominant co-ordinating method in any modern market economy, there are four possible combinations of co-ordination and ownership principles. Of the two most common combinations, the first is the private-ownership market economy, in which the market principle is the main co-ordinating mechanism and the majority of productive assets are privately owned. The second most common combination during the twentieth century has been the public-ownership planned economy, in which central planning is the primary means of co-ordinating economic decisions and property is primarily publicly owned.

The two other possible combinations are a market economy in which the resources are publicly owned, and a command economy in which the resources are privately owned. No modern economy has achieved either of these two hybrid types. Nazi Germany from 1932 to 1945 went some way towards combining private ownership with the command principle; and the United Kingdom from 1945 to 1980 went quite a way towards a public-ownership market economy, because many industries and much housing were publicly owned. On balance, however, Germany and the United Kingdom were still best described as private-ownership market economies. (The United Kingdom's privatization programme, which began in the early 1980s, has returned most publicly owned industries to private ownership, thus returning that country more fully to the ranks of private-ownership market economies. In 1995 the two major industries (apart from health and education) remaining in public ownership were coal and the railways—but privatization of both was planned.)

Command versus market determination

For over a century, a great debate raged on the relative merits of the command principle versus the market principle for co-ordinating economic decisions in practice. The Soviet Union, the countries of Eastern Europe, and China were command economies for much of this century. The United States and most of the countries of Western Europe were, and are, primarily market economies. The successes of the Soviet Union and China in the early stages of indus-

trialization suggested to many observers earlier in this century that the command principle was at least as good for organizing economic behaviour as the market principle, if not better. In the long haul, however, planned economies proved unable to raise living standards at anything approaching the pace in market economies. By the end of the 1980s, this was obvious to most ordinary citizens in the planned economies of Eastern Europe.

Rarely in human history has such a decisive verdict been delivered on two competing systems. Box 1.1 gives some of the reasons why central planning was a failure in Eastern Europe and the Soviet Union. The discussion is of more than purely historical interest, because the reasons for the failure of planned economies give insight into the reasons for the relative success of free-market economies.

THE LESSONS FROM THE FAILURE OF COMMAND SYSTEMS

The failure of planned economies suggests that mixed economies, with substantial elements of market determination, are superior to command economies. The reason is that markets provide a better and more flexible device for co-ordinating decisions than does government central planning. The failure does *not* demonstrate, as some have asserted, the superiority of completely free market economies over mixed economies.

There is no guarantee that free markets will handle, on their own, such urgent matters as pollution control and prevention of the overfishing that depletes fishing grounds. (Indeed, as we shall see in later chapters, much economic theory is devoted to explaining why free markets often fail to do these things.) Governments may, for example, wish to provide income support for those who would be unable to survive in a totally free market. Mixed economies, with significant degrees of government intervention, are needed to do these jobs.

It follows that there is still room for disagreement about the *degree* of the mix of market and government determination in any modern mixed economy—room enough to accommodate such divergent views as could be expressed by the range of major political parties found in the United Kingdom and most other advanced market economies. People can accept the free market as an efficient way of organizing economic affairs and still disagree over the degree of the government's presence in the market to fulfil such functions as preserving the environment, controlling pollution, producing goods and services such as defence and traffic control that private firms have no motive to produce, and helping those in need.[5]

[5] The first two of these examples come under the heading of dealing with externalities. The next two are providing public goods, and the final one is an example of redistribution policy. All of these are discussed in detail in Part Six.

BOX 1.1

The failure of central planning

The year 1989 signalled to the world what many economists had long argued: the superiority of a market-oriented price system over central planning as a method of organizing economic activity. The failure of central planning had many causes, but four were particularly significant.

The failure of co-ordination

In centrally planned economics, a body of planners tries to co-ordinate all the economic decisions about production, investment, trade, and consumption that are likely to be made by the producers and consumers throughout the country. This proved impossible to do with any reasonable degree of efficiency. Bottlenecks in production, shortages of some goods, and gluts of others plagued the Soviet economy for decades. For example, in 1989 much of a bumper harvest rotted on the farm because of shortages of storage and transportation facilities, and for years there was an ample supply of black-and-white television sets and severe shortages of toilet paper and soap.

Friedrich von Hayek (1899–1992), a persistent critic of central planning, suggests a battle analogy to compare markets to central planning. In one army soldiers can only move exactly in the direction and amount they are ordered by some general operating at the centre; in the other army, soldiers are given the general objectives and told to respond as fits the situation as it develops. It is clear who will win the battle.

Failure of quality control

Central planners can monitor the number of units produced by any factory and reward those who over-fulfil their production targets and punish those who fall short. It is much harder, however, for them to monitor quality. A constant Soviet problem, therefore, was the production of poor-quality products. Factory managers were concerned with meeting their quotas by whatever means were available, and once the goods passed out of their factory, what happened to them was someone else's headache. The quality problem was so serious that very few Eastern European-manufactured products were able to stand up to the newly permitted competition with superior goods produced in the advanced market societies.

In market economies, poor quality is punished by low sales, and retailers soon give a signal to factory managers by shifting their purchases to other suppliers. The incentives that obviously flow from such private-sector purchasing discretion are generally absent from command economies, where purchases and sales are planned centrally.

Misplaced incentives

In market economies, relative wages and salaries provide incentives for labour to move from place to place, and the possibility of losing one's job provides an incentive to work diligently. This is a harsh mechanism that punishes losers with loss of income (although social programmes provide floors to the amount of economic punishment that can be suffered). In planned economies, workers usually have complete job security. Industrial unemployment is rare, and even when it does occur, new jobs are usually found for those who lose theirs. Although the high level of security is attractive to many, it proved impossible to provide sufficient incentives to work reasonably hard and efficiently under such conditions. In the words of Oxford historian Timothy Garton Ash, who wrote eyewitness chronicles of the developments in Eastern Europe from 1980 to 1990, the social contract between the workers and the government in the Eastern countries was 'We pretend to work, and you pretend to pay us.'

Because of the absence of a work-oriented incentive system, income inequalities do not provide the normal free-market incentives. Income inequalities were used instead to provide incentives for party members to toe the line. The major gap in income standards was between party members on the one hand and non-party members on the other. The former had access to such privileges as special stores where imported goods were available, special hospitals providing sanitary and efficient medical care, and special resorts where holidays could be taken. In contrast, non-members had none of these things.

Environmental degradation

Fulfilling production plans became the all-embracing incentive in planned economies, to the exclusion of most other considerations, including the environment. As a result, environmental degradation occurred in all the countries of Eastern Europe on a scale unknown in advanced Western nations. A particularly disturbing example occurred in central Asia, where high quotas for cotton output led to indiscriminate use of pesticides and irrigation. Birth defects are now found there in nearly one child in three, and the vast Aral Sea has been half drained, causing incalculable environmental effects.

The failure to protect the environment stemmed from a combination of pressure to fulfil plans and lack of a political marketplace. The democratic process allows citizens to express views on the use of scarce resources for environmental protection. Imperfect though the system may be in democratic market economies, their record of environmental protection has been vastly better than that of command economies.

The price system

In contrast to the failures of command economies, the performance of the free-market price system is impressive. One theme of this book is *market success*: how the price system works to co-ordinate with relative efficiency the decentralized decisions

BOX 1.1 *(continued)*

made by private consumers and producers, providing the right quantities of relatively high-quality outputs and incentives for efficient work. It is important, however, not to conclude that doing things better means doing things perfectly. Another

theme of this book is *market failure*: how and why the unaided price system sometimes fails to produce efficient results and fails to take account of social values that cannot be expressed through the market-place.

The evolution of market economies

THE great seventeenth-century philosopher Thomas Hobbes described life in a state of nature as 'nasty, brutish and short'. Modern study of the several surviving hunter–gatherer societies suggests that Hobbes's ideas were wide of the mark. In fact, societies in the pre-agricultural stage are characterized by a

relative simplicity of the material culture (only 94 items exist among Kung bushmen); the lack of accumulation of individual wealth [and mobility] . . . Subsistence requirements are satisfied by only a modest effort—perhaps two or three days' work a week by each adult; they do not have to struggle over food resources; the attitudes towards ownership are flexible and their living groups open.[6]

Such features set hunters and gatherers apart from more technologically developed societies whose very survival depends upon their ability to maintain order and to control property.

Many of the characteristic problems of modern economies do not arise in these primitive societies. Indeed, most of the economic problems that we know today have been with us only ten thousand or so years—little more than an instant compared with the tens of millions of years that hominid creatures have been on earth. It began with the original agricultural revolution, dated somewhere this side of 10,000 BC, when people first found it possible to stay in one place and survive. Gradually abandoning the old nomadic life of food gathering, people began to settle down, tending crops that they themselves had learned to plant and animals that they had learned to domesticate. Since that time, societies have faced the all-pervading problem of choice under conditions of scarcity.

Specialization, surplus, and trade

Along with permanent settlement, the agricultural revolu-

tion brought surplus production: farmers could produce substantially more than they needed to survive. The agricultural surplus led to the appearance of new occupations, such as artisans, soldiers, priests, and government officials. Freed from having to grow their own food, these people turned to producing specialized services and goods other than food. They too produced more than they themselves needed, so they traded the excess to obtain whatever else they required.

Economists call this allocation of different jobs to different people **specialization of labour**. There are two fundamental reasons why specialization is extraordinarily efficient compared with universal self-sufficiency.

First, individual abilities differ, and specialization allows each person to do what he or she can do relatively well while leaving everything else to be done by others. Even when people's abilities are unaffected by the act of specializing, production is greater with specialization than with self-sufficiency. This, which is one of the most fundamental principles in economics, is called the *principle of comparative advantage*. An example is given in Box 1.2 and a much fuller discussion is found in Chapter 25.

The second reason concerns changes in people's abilities that occur *because* they specialize. A person who concentrates on one activity becomes better at it than could a jack-of-all-trades. This is called *learning by doing*. It was a factor much stressed by early economists. Modern research into what are called *learning curves* shows that learning by doing is important in many modern industries.

Probably much of the exchange of goods and services in early societies took place by simple, mutual agreement among neighbours. In the course of time, however, trading became centred in particular gathering places called *mar-*

---

[6] *The Times Atlas of World History*, ed. G. Barraclough (London: Times Books, 1978), p. 35. See also Roland Oliver, *The African Experience* (London: Weidenfeld & Nicolson), 1991. Roland observes (p. 12) that people in these societies 'enjoyed better health, a more balanced diet and more leisure than many agricultural populations do today'.

BOX 1.2

Absolute and comparative advantage

A simple case will illustrate the important principles involved in the gains from specialization.

Absolute advantage

Suppose that, working full time on his own, Jacob can produce either 100 pounds of potatoes *or* 40 sweaters per year, whereas Maria can produce 400 pounds of potatoes *or* 10 sweaters. These productive abilities are shown in the first column of Table (i). Maria has an absolute advantage in producing potatoes because she can make more per year than Jacob. However, Jacob has an absolute advantage over Maria in producing sweaters for the same reason. If they both spend *half* their time producing each commodity, the results will be as given in the second column of Table (i).

Now let Jacob specialize in sweaters, producing 40 of them, and Maria specialize in potatoes, producing 400 pounds. The final column of Table (i), labelled 'Full specialization', shows that production of both commodities has risen because each person is better than the other person at his or her speciality. Sweater production rises from 250 to 400, while potato production goes from 25 to 40.

Comparative advantage

Now make things a little less obvious by giving Maria an absolute advantage over Jacob in both commodities. We do this by making Maria more productive in sweaters, so that she can produce 48 of them per year, with all other productivities remaining the same. This gives us the new data for productive

Table (i)

		Time spent fully producing one product or the other		Time divided equally between producing the two products		Full specialization	
		Sweaters	Potatoes	Sweaters	Potatoes	Sweaters	Potatoes
Jacob	either ——— 100	or ——— 40	50	20	—	40
Maria	either ——— 400	or ——— 10	200	5	400	—
Total			250	25	400	40

Table (ii)

		Time spent fully producing one product or the other		Time divided equally between producing the two products		Jacob is fully specialized; Maria divides her time 25% and 75% between sweater and potato production	
		Sweaters	Potatoes	Sweaters	Potatoes	Sweaters	Potatoes
Jacob	either ——— 100	or ——— 40	50	20	—	40
Maria	either ——— 400	or ——— 48	200	24	300	12
Total			250	44	300	52

BOX 1.2 *(continued)*

abilities shown in the first column of Table (ii). Now, compared with Jacob, Maria is four times (400 per cent) more efficient at producing potatoes and 20 per cent more efficient at producing sweaters. The second column of Table (ii) gives the outputs when Jacob and Maria each divide their time equally between the two products.

It is possible to increase their combined production of both commodities by having Maria increase her production of potatoes and Jacob increase his production of sweaters. The third column of Table (ii) gives an example in which Jacob specializes fully in sweater production and Maria spends 25 per cent of her time on sweaters and 75 per cent on potatoes. (Her outputs of sweaters and potatoes are thus 25 and 75 per cent of what she could produce of these commodities if she worked full time on one or the other.) Total production of sweaters rises from 250 to 300, while total production of potatoes goes from 44 to 52.

In this latter example, Maria is absolutely more efficient than Jacob in both lines of production, but her margin of advantage is greater in potatoes than in sweaters. Economists say that Maria has a **comparative advantage** over Jacob in the line of production in which her margin of advantage is greatest (potatoes, in this case), and that Jacob has a comparative advantage over Maria in the line of production in which his margin of disadvantage is least (sweaters, in this case). This is only an illustration; the principles can be generalized in the following way.

- Absolute efficiencies are not necessary for there to be gains from specialization.
- Gains from specialization occur whenever there are *differences* in the margin of advantage one person enjoys over another in various lines of production.
- Total production can always be increased when each person specializes in the production of the commodity in which he or she has a comparative advantage.

A more detailed study of the important concept of comparative advantage and its many applications to international trade and specialization must await the chapter on international trade (which is sometimes studied in courses on microeconomics and sometimes in courses on macroeconomics). In the meantime, it is worth noting that the comparative advantage of individuals and of whole nations may change. Maria may learn new skills and develop a comparative advantage in sweaters that she does not currently have. Similarly, whole nations may develop new abilities and know-how that will change their pattern of comparative advantage.

---

kets. The French markets or trade fairs of Champagne were well known throughout Europe as early as the eleventh century AD. Even now, many towns in Britain have regular market days. Today, however, the term 'market' has a much broader meaning. We use the term **market economy** to refer to a society in which people specialize in productive activities and meet most of their material wants through exchanges voluntarily agreed upon by the contracting parties.

Specialization must be accompanied by trade. People who produce only one thing must trade most of it to obtain all of the other things they require.

Early trading was by means of **barter**, the trading of goods directly for other goods. But barter is costly in terms of time spent searching out satisfactory exchanges. If a farmer has wheat but wants a hammer, he must find someone who has a hammer and wants wheat. A successful barter transaction thus requires what is called a *double coincidence of wants.*

Money eliminates the cumbrous system of barter by separating the transactions involved in the exchange of products. If a farmer has wheat and wants a hammer, he does not have to find someone who has a hammer and wants wheat: he merely has to find someone who wants wheat. The farmer takes money in exchange, then finds a person who wishes to trade a hammer, and gives up the money for the hammer.

Money greatly facilitates specialization and trade.

Although most transactions in the modern world make use of money, Box 1.3 shows that barter is not unknown in the modern economy.

Factor services and the division of labour

In early economies, producers specialized in making some product and then traded it for the other products they needed. The labour services required to make the product would usually be provided by the makers themselves, by apprentices who were learning to become craftsmen, or by slaves. Over the last several hundred years, many technical advances in methods of production have made it efficient to organize agriculture and manufacturing into large-scale firms. These technical developments have made use of what

BOX 1.3

Barter in the modern world

Although barter is the dominant form of exchange only in very primitive societies, barter transactions are not unknown in modern societies. When you agree to do a job for your neighbour in return for a job your neighbour does for you, the two of you are bartering.

More sophisticated barter transactions also occur. In the 1970s, for example, many chemical plants were built in the Soviet Union by contractors based in Western countries. The contracting firms were paid not in money, but by a promise of some proportion of the output of those plants for a number of years after they first became productive. This had two advantages for the Soviets: it gave the contractors an incentive to ensure that the plant would produce the desired chemicals to the full design capacity; it also conserved the Soviet Union's scarce supplies of Western currencies.

Since 1983, the Saudi Arabian government has been buying American jumbo jets, British Rolls-Royce engines, and French military aircraft, each time paying in oil. As another example,

the British car manufacturer Talbot agreed in early 1985 to supply Iran with kits for the construction of its cars, with payment to be made in oil.

In the same year the South American country of Guyana struck agreements to use rice to pay for spare parts from East Germany and oil from Trinidad. It also paid for Japanese lorries with bauxite (the ore from which aluminium is made). Guyana had other barter arrangements with the governments of Yugoslavia, China, and Brazil.

Until February 1986, barbers in Warsaw, Poland, obtained modern equipment from firms in West Germany, in return for hair cuttings which were made into West German wigs.

What all of these examples have in common is that they involve *international* trade, so that two currencies would be involved if the transaction used money; and that the government of at least one of the countries does not (perhaps cannot) allow its currency to be freely traded for the other currency involved.

---

is called the **division of labour**. This term refers to specialization within the production process of a particular product. The labour involved is divided into specialized tasks, and each individual repeatedly does one task that is a small fraction of those necessary to produce the product.

Today's typical workers do not earn their incomes by selling products they have produced by themselves; rather, they sell their labour services to firms and receive money wages in return.

Two very recent changes have significantly altered the degree of specialization found in many modern production processes. First, individual artisans have recently reappeared in some lines of production. They are responding to a revival in the demand for individually crafted, rather than mass-produced, products. Second, many manufacturing operations are being reorganized along new lines called 'lean production' or 'flexible manufacturing' which was pioneered by Japanese car manufacturers. It has led back to a more craft-based form of organization within the factory. In this technique, which is discussed in Chapter 11, employees work as a team; each employee is able to do every team member's job rather than one very specialized task at one point on the assembly line.

Recent origins

The modern market economies that we know today first arose in Europe out of the ashes of the feudal system. As we have already mentioned, the feudal system was a traditional one in which people did jobs based on heredity (the miller's son became the next generation's miller) and received shares of their village's total output that were based on custom. Peasants were tied to the land. Much land was owned by the Crown and granted to the lord of the manor in return for military services. Some of it was made available for the common use of all villagers. Establishments such as the village mill and blacksmith's shop rarely belonged to those who worked there and could therefore never be bought and sold by them.

In contrast, modern market economies are based on market transactions between people who voluntarily decide whether or not to engage in them. They have the right to buy and sell what they wish, to accept or refuse work that is offered to them, and to move to where they want when they want.

Key institutions are private property and freedom of contract, both of which must be maintained by active government policies. The government creates laws of ownership and contract and then provides the courts to enforce these laws.

Performance of the UK economy

THROUGHOUT this book we study the functioning of a modern, market-based, mixed economy, such as is found in the United Kingdom today. By way of introduction, this section introduces a few salient aspects that should be kept in mind from the outset.

Living standards

The material living standards of any society depend on how much it can produce. What there is to consume depends on what is produced. If the productive capacity of a society is small, then the living standards of its typical citizen will be low. Only by raising that productive capacity can average living standards be raised.

No society can generate increased real consumption merely by voting its citizens higher money incomes.

How much a society can produce depends both on how many of its citizens are at work producing things and on their productivity in their work. How well has the UK economy performed in each of these dimensions?

JOBS

The trend in employment in the United Kingdom has been positive throughout the twentieth century. However, the rise was rapid in the first half of the century and only gradual in the second half. While employment increased by nearly 50 per cent between 1900 and 1945, it rose by only 10

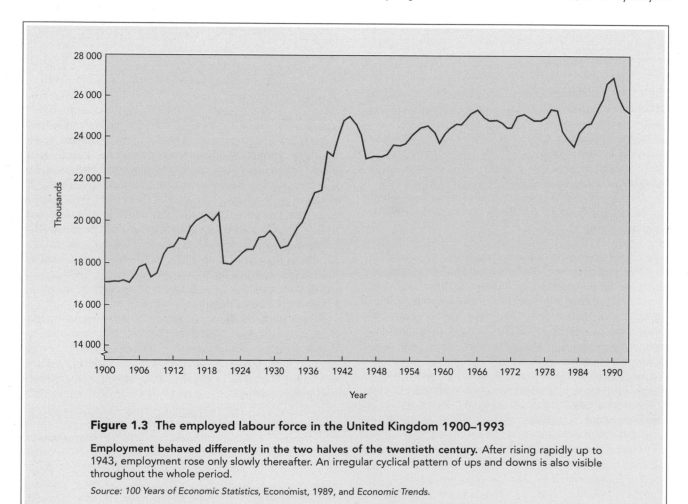

Figure 1.3 The employed labour force in the United Kingdom 1900–1993

Employment behaved differently in the two halves of the twentieth century. After rising rapidly up to 1943, employment rose only slowly thereafter. An irregular cyclical pattern of ups and downs is also visible throughout the whole period.

Source: 100 Years of Economic Statistics, Economist, 1989, and Economic Trends.

per cent between 1946 and 1993. It is clear from Figure 1.3 that the two world wars each produced a temporary surge in employment, but it is noticeable that employment stayed high after the Second World War. This can largely be attributed to the greater participation of females in the labour force that was encouraged by the war and was only slightly reversed afterwards.

The slow growth in employment since 1945 is broadly in line with the slow growth in total population, which increased by only 15 per cent between 1946 and 1990. Two other factors explain why total employment has grown slightly less than total population in the period following the Second World War. First, there has been a rise in unemployment; this affected only 1.7 per cent of the labour force in 1946, whereas it was over 10 per cent at the end of 1992. Secondly, the proportion of the population over the age of 65 rose from 10 per cent in 1946 to over 15 per cent in 1990.

Another notable feature of the UK employment figure is its cyclical behaviour. Although it is irregular, this cycle seems to be getting more volatile in the sense that the swings in employment in the 1980s and 1990s have been greater than at any time since 1945. The causes and possible cures for these swings in employment will be a key issue studied in the second half of this book.

LABOUR PRODUCTIVITY

Labour productivity refers to the amount produced per hour of work. Rising living standards are closely linked to the rising productivity of the typical worker.

If each worker produces more, then (other things being equal) there will be more production in total, and hence more for each person to consume on average.

In the period from 1750 to 1850, the market economies in Europe and the United States became industrial economies. With industrialization, modern market economies have raised ordinary people out of poverty by raising productivity at rates that appear slow from year to year but that have dramatic effects on living standards when sustained over long periods of time.

Over a year, or even over a decade, the economic gains [of the late eighteenth and the nineteenth centuries], after allowing for the growth of population, were so little noticeable that it was widely believed that the gains were experienced only by the rich, and not by the poor. Only as the West's compounded growth continued through the twentieth century did its breadth become clear. It became obvious that Western working classes were increasingly well off and that the Western middle classes were prospering and growing as a proportion of the whole population. Not that poverty disappeared. The West's achievement was not the abolition of poverty but the reduction of its incidence from 90 per cent of the population to 30 per cent, 20 per

cent, or less, depending on the country and one's definition of poverty. . .[7]

Figure 1.4 shows the rise in labour productivity from 1920 to 1993. For the economy as a whole, labour productivity doubled between 1920 and 1970, and then increased by a further 70 per cent by 1993. Even more spectacular has been the increase in productivity in the manufacturing sector. This doubled between 1920 and 1953 and then more than trebled between 1953 and 1993. It has increased by 80 per cent since 1980 (up to 1993).

The growth in labour productivity is especially important as a determinant of real output growth in the United Kingdom, because, as we have seen, both population and employment have grown very slowly since the Second World War. So increases in production must be associated with greater output per worker. During the post-war period, output per worker for the whole UK economy has grown at an annual rate of 2.1 per cent. Although this may seem rather slow when viewed from one year to the next, it leads to a *doubling* of output in about 34 years. (A helpful device is the rule of 72: divide 72 by the annual growth rate, and the result is approximately the number of years required for output to double.)[8]

In fact, a productivity growth of 2.1 per cent is high by the standards of Britain's own history. Even during the 'industrial revolution' between 1760 and 1860, labour productivity is now thought to have grown at an annual average rate of under 0.7 per cent. With a growth rate of 0.7 per cent, it takes 100 years to double output. However, even this 'slow' rate causes dramatic changes in life styles. It means that in each century the average citizen has twice the material living standards as his counterpart a mere 100 years previously.

The long period of sustained productivity growth in the twentieth century, and especially since the Second World War, has caused British citizens to expect to be substantially better off than their parents and grandparents. Indeed, if output per person continues to double every 34 years or so, the average citizen will be nearly twice as well off as his or her parents. Figure 1.5 shows average weekly wages since 1940 in real terms (at 1992 prices). It shows that real wages doubled between 1940 and 1973, exactly in line with the increase implied by productivity growth. However, real wages rose by only 20 per cent between 1974 and 1993, indicating a much slower rate of increase during that period. Real wages actually fell in the periods 1974–77 and 1979–81.

[7] N. Rosenberg and L. E. Birdzell, Jr, *How the West Grew Rich* (New York: Basic Books, 1986).

[8] The rule of 72 is an approximation, derived from the mathematics of compound interest. Any variable X with an initial value of X_0 will have the value $X_t = X_0 e^{rt}$ after t years at a continuous growth rate of r per cent per year. Because $X_t/X_0 = 2$ requires $r \times t = 0.69$, a 'rule of 69' would be correct for continuous growth. The rule of 72 was developed in the context of compound interest, and if interest is compounded only once a year, the product of r times t for X to double is approximately 0.72.

Between 1970 and 1980, productivity in the United Kingdom grew by only 1.4 per cent per annum. At this diminished rate, the time taken to double output increased from 34 years to over 50. Fortunately, this slowdown does not appear to have been permanent. The economy returned to its trend productivity growth in the 1980s and, despite the setbacks of the 1970s, real wages exactly doubled in the 34 years from 1959 to 1993. Indeed, one important sector of the UK economy had a spectacular increase in productivity in the 1980s. This was the manufacturing sector. Productivity growth in this sector was 4.6 per cent per annum from 1980 to 1993, which was well above its postwar average of 2.9 per cent. Productivity increases at the rate of 4.6 per cent will double output every 16 years! Unfortunately, not all of this increase was accounted for by increased output of each person who remained in a job. Instead, a large number of firms closed down in the 1980s,

and the ones that closed tended to have lower-than-average productivity. As a result, total productivity in manufacturing rose to some extent because lower-productivity jobs were eliminated, not because those in high-productivity jobs raised their productivity by 4 per cent per year. In the later part of the period, however, most of the increase was accounted for by rising output of people who continued to work in that part of the economy.

Ongoing change

The growth in incomes over the centuries since market economies first arose has been accompanied by continual technological change. Our technologies are our ways of doing things. New ways of doing old things, and new things to do, are continually being invented and brought into use.

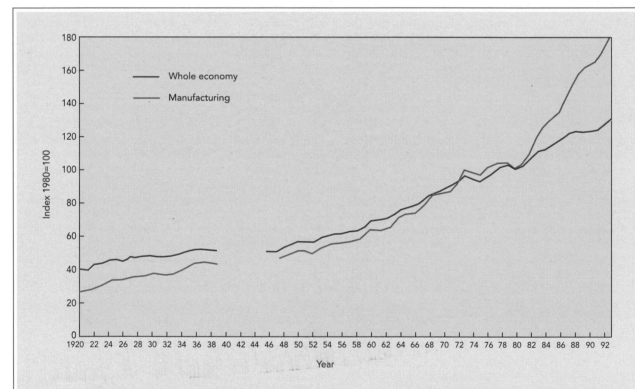

Figure 1.4 Output per person employed in the UK 1920–1993.

Productivity rose steadily throughout the 20th century. The two lines show the course of output per head in the whole economy, and in the manufacturing sector, since the end of the First World War. Each chart shows an index of real per capita output (with 1980 set at 100). Notice the steady rise across the whole economy through the 1980s and the dramatic rise in manufacturing productivity during the same period. Notice, also, the slowdown in productivity growth that occurred in the recessions of 1974–5, 1980–1, and 1990–1. (No data are available for the period of World War II, (1939–1945 for the whole economy, and 1939–48 for manufacturing.))

Source: 100 Years of Economic Statistics, Economist, 1989, and Economic Trends.

These technological changes make labour more productive, and they are constantly changing the nature of our economy. Old jobs are destroyed and new jobs are created as the technological structure slowly evolves.

JOB STRUCTURE

Not only has output per worker changed over time; the pattern of work has also changed. In traditional economies, a high proportion of employment tends to be in agriculture. Great Britain, as the first industrial nation, was also the first to exhibit a sharp decline in agricultural employment. In 1840, only 25 per cent of its employment was in agriculture, and this had declined to 13.3 per cent by 1901 and 1.0 per cent by 1993. As recently as 1900, 40 per cent of the US population was engaged in agriculture. This figure has now fallen to under 3 per cent.

The other clear structural change in employment has been the shift from manufacturing to services. Manufacturing employment peaked in Britain in the mid-1950s at around 38 per cent of total employment. This declined steadily thereafter, but the fall accelerated sharply in the early 1980s. Employment in services displayed a contrasting pattern. Only 15.5 per cent of employment was in services in 1955, but by the late 1980s this proportion had more than doubled to over 35 per cent. The trends for this century are shown in more detail in Table 1.1.

Services in manufacturing The enormous growth in what are recorded as service jobs overstates the decline in the

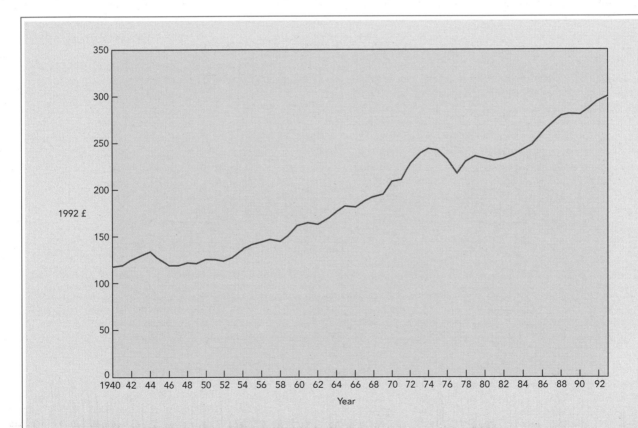

Figure 1.5 Average weekly wages at 1992 prices in the UK 1940–1993.

The trend of average real wages has been upward over the period shown. The chart shows wages, defined as average weekly earnings for the whole economy, converted to 1992 prices which allows us to see how the purchasing power of wages has changed over the years. For example, in the early 1950s, average weekly wages were sufficient to buy what £120 would buy in 1992, while in 1993 they were sufficient to buy about £300 worth of goods and services. Although the overall trend has been upward, real wages fell significantly during three periods, 1944–46, 1974–77, and 1979–81. Notice that real wages doubled (from £150 to £300 at 1992 prices) in the 34 years from 1959 to 1993, as discussed in the text.

Source: 100 Years of Economic Statistics, Economist, 1989, and Economic Trends.

importance of the manufacturing of goods in our economy. This is because many of the jobs recorded as service jobs are integral parts of the production of manufactured goods.

First, some of the growth has occurred because services that used to be provided within the manufacturing firms have now been contracted out to specialist firms. These often include design, quality control, accounting, legal services, and marketing. Indeed, one of the most significant of the new developments in manufacturing is the breakdown of the old hierarchical organization of firms (sometimes called 'delayering') and the development of a flexible, core–team of employees who run the business but purchase many of its labour and material inputs from other independent firms.

A quaint but dramatic example of this point concerns shepherds and oil wells! In the 1970s Esso Petroleum had as an employee a full-time shepherd. This was because one of their oil storage facilities had a significant area of grass, so the company decided to put sheep on it. To look after the sheep they hired a shepherd. This shepherd would have been classified as a worker in the petrochemical industry. In the 1980s Esso decided to contract out the maintenance of their facilities to another company. This other company is classified as providing 'services', so the shepherd's income is now recorded as being earned in a service industry.

Second, as a result of the rapid growth of international trade, production and sales have required growing quantities of service inputs for such things as transportation, insurance, banking, and marketing.

Third, as more and more products become high-tech, increasing amounts are spent on product design at one end and customer liaison at the other end. These activities, which are all related to the production and sale of goods, are often recorded as service activities.

Services for final consumption   As personal incomes have risen over the decades, consumers have spent a rising proportion of their incomes on services rather than manufactured goods. Today, for example, eating out is common; for our grandparents, it was a luxury. This does not mean, however, that we spend more on food. The extra expenditure goes to pay for the services of those who prepare and serve in restaurants the same ingredients that our grandparents prepared for themselves at home. Young people spend far more on attending live concerts than they used to, and all of us spend vastly more on travel. In 1890 the salesman in a small town was likely to be *the* well-travelled citizen because he had travelled 50 miles by train to the county town. Nowadays, many people travel greater distances just commuting to work every day.

NEW PRODUCTS

When we talk of each generation having more real income than previous generations, we must not think of just having more of the same products that our parents or grandparents consumed. In fact, we consume very few of the products that were the mainstays of expenditure for our great-grandparents.

Table 1.1 Percentage of UK employment in major sectors, 1901–1993

	Agriculture forestry, and fishing	Manufacturing	Construction	Transportation and communication	Distribution	Services	Public administration and defence	Other*
1901	13.3	33.1	6.0	8.0	11.0	19.8	4.9	3.9
1938	5.9	32.5	5.9	7.9	14.4	21.9	3.7	7.8
1955	2.8	38.0	5.7	7.0	9.8	15.5	5.5	15.7
1970	1.9	33.7	5.4	6.4	10.8	23.4	6.0	12.4
1987	1.3	20.3	4.0	5.3	12.1	35.8	6.5	14.7
1993	1.0	16.8	3.2	5.0	13.1	35.5	7.3	18.1

* 'Other' includes: mining and quarrying; gas, water, and electricity; and self-employment

The distribution of employment among the various sectors has changed dramatically over the century. The figures give the percentage of total employment accounted for by each sector in each year. Note among other things the following changes in the percentages of the labour force employed by sector: the dramatic fall in agriculture, forestry, and fishing; the peaking of manufacturing in the mid-1950s followed by a steady fall; the reductions in construction and transportation and communications; the dramatic rise in services and public administration. The very large rise in the 'other' category is accounted for mainly by a rise in self-employment, which made up 14.4 per cent of the labour force in 1993.

Source: Monthly Digest of Statistics, CSO.

One of the most important aspects of the change that permeates market economies is the continual introduction of new products. Most of the myriad instruments and tools in a modern dentist's office, doctor's office, and hospital did not exist 50 years ago. Penicillin, painkillers, bypass operations, films, stereos, television, videocassettes and recorders, pocket calculators, computers, ballpoint pens, compact discs, mobile phones, and fast, safe travel by jet aircraft have all been introduced within the lifetimes of people still alive today. So also have the products that have eliminated much of the drudgery formerly associated with housework. Dishwashers, detergents, disposable nappies, washing machines, vacuum cleaners, microwave ovens, refrigerators, deep freezers, and their complement, the supermarket, were not there to help your great-grandparents when they first set up house.

GLOBALIZATION

Another aspect of the constant change that occurs in evolving market economies is the globalization that has been occurring at an accelerating rate over the last two decades. At the heart of globalization lies the rapid reduction in transportation costs and the revolution in information technology. The cost of moving products around the world has fallen greatly in recent decades. More dramatically, our ability to transmit and to analyse data has been increasing dramatically, while the costs of doing so have been decreasing, equally dramatically. For example, today £1,000 buys a computer that fits into a suitcase and has the same computing power as one that in 1970 cost £5 million and filled a large room.

Many *markets* are globalizing; for example, as some tastes become universal to young people, we can see the same designer jeans and leather jackets in virtually all big cities. Many *corporations* are globalizing, as they increasingly become what are called **transnationals**. These are massive firms with a physical presence in many countries and an increasingly decentralized management structure. MacDonald's restaurants are as visible in Moscow or Beijing as in London or New York. Many other brands are also virtually universal, such as Coca Cola, Kelloggs, Heinz, Nestlé, Guinness, Mercedes Benz, Rolls-Royce, Sony, and Hoover. Many *labour markets* are globalizing, as the revolutions in communications and transportation allow the various components of any one product to be produced all over the world. A typical compact disc player, TV set, or car will contain components made in literally dozens of different countries. We still know where a product is assembled, but it is becoming increasingly difficult to say where it is *made*.

On the investment side, the most important result of globalization is that large firms are seeking a physical presence in many major countries. In the 1950s and 1960s most foreign investment was made by US firms investing abroad to establish a presence in foreign markets. Today, most developed countries see major flows of investment in both directions, inward as foreign firms invest in their markets, and outward as their own firms invest abroad.

In 1967, 50 per cent of all outward-bound foreign investment came from the United States and went to many foreign countries. In 1991, according to United Nations figures, the United States accounted for just under 25 per cent of all outward-bound foreign investment. In that year Japan was the largest single foreign investor, with just over 25 per cent of the total, while other major investors were France with 19 per cent, Germany with 17 per cent, and the United Kingdom, with 15 per cent of the total amount of new foreign investment.

On the inward-bound side, the change is even more dramatic. In 1967 the United States attracted only 9 per cent of all foreign investment made in that year. By the late 1980s, however, the United States attracted close to 30 per cent. The year 1992 saw another reversal, with a significant exodus of foreign investment from the United States.

Although these flows are volatile from year to year, the total stocks of foreign investment remain large. Not only do US firms hold massive foreign investments in foreign countries, but foreign firms now hold massive investments in the United States. As a result, many US citizens work for British, Japanese, German, Dutch, and French firms—just as many of the citizens of these other countries work for US firms. The same can be said of most other countries, particularly the United Kingdom, Germany, France, and Japan. Around the world many people work for German, French, British, and Japanese firms, just as many British, Germans, and French (but not Japanese) work for foreign owned firms.

An important push to the globalization of investment was given by the freeing of investment flows from government regulation. Serious regulations on funds flowing abroad were never present in the United States—which is a major reason why it was the world's leading foreign investor from 1945 through the 1980s. In the United Kingdom and Europe, however, there were major restrictions on individuals and firms wishing to invest abroad. These controls came off in 1979 in the United Kingdom, and they were eliminated in the late 1980s and early 1990s in Japan and Europe. In the European Union (EU), this liberalization was enforced on the laggards by the EC Capital Liberalization Directive. This required all member-states to abolish exchange and capital controls by June 1990; Greece, Spain, Ireland, and Portugal had until 1992, and all have now complied. Greece still has more to do but the others have opened up totally. France and Italy were forced down this road by the Directive. Without this liberalization of capital flows, the pattern of globalization would have been significantly different and much more dominated by US foreign investment.

It is also interesting to note that globalization of investment had big effects on what 'national interest' means. The pension funds and personal savings of most UK citizens are now internationally diversified, making them less dependent upon the future success of Britain. Instead, the citizens of most advanced industrialized countries are accumulating shares in the world economy.

The world is truly globalizing in both its trade and investment flows.

Today no country can take an isolationist economic stance and hope to take part in the global economy where an increasing share of jobs and incomes are created.

Conclusion

In this last part of the chapter, we have briefly considered how people's living standards are affected by the availability of jobs, the productivity of labour in those jobs, and the distribution of the income produced by those jobs. Our discussion reveals an economy characterized by ongoing change in the structure of jobs, in the production techniques used by the workers, and in the kinds of goods and services produced. The issues discussed here arise again at many places throughout this book. Because most of them are interrelated, it helps to know the basic outlines of all of them before studying any one in more depth.

Summary

1 Scarcity is a fundamental problem faced by all economies because not enough resources—land, labour, capital, and entrepreneurship—are available to produce all the goods and services that people would like to consume. Scarcity makes it necessary to choose among alternative possibilities: what products will be produced and in what quantities.

2 The concept of opportunity cost emphasizes scarcity and choice by measuring the cost of obtaining a unit of one product in terms of the number of units of other products that could have been obtained instead.

3 A production-possibility boundary shows all of the combinations of goods that can be produced by an economy whose resources are fully employed. Movement from one point to another on the boundary shows a shift in the amounts of goods being produced which requires a re-allocation of resources.

4 Three pure types of economy can be distinguished: traditional, command, and free market. In a free-market economy the allocation of resources is determined by the production, sales, and purchase decisions made by individual firms and consumers, each acting in response to such market signals as prices and profits. In practice, all economies are mixed economies in that their economic behaviour responds to mixes of tradition, government command, and price incentives.

5 Modern economies are based on the specialization and division of labour, which necessitate the exchange of goods and services. Exchange takes place in markets and is facilitated by the use of money. Much of economics is devoted to a study of how markets work to co-ordinate millions of individual, decentralized decisions.

6 Modern economies are based on private property and freedom of contract. They have generated sustained growth, which, over long periods, has raised material living standards massively.

7 Modern market economies are characterized by constant change in such things as the structure of jobs, the structure of production, the technologies in use, and the types of product produced.

8 Driven by the revolution in transportation and communications, the world economy is rapidly globalizing. National and regional boundaries are becoming less important as transnational corporations locate the production of each component part of a product in the country that can produce it at the best quality and the least cost.

Topics for review

- Factors of production
- Goods and services
- Scarcity, choice, and opportunity cost
- Production-possibility boundary
- Resource allocation
- Growth in productive capacity
- Specialization and the division of labour
- Price system as a social-control mechanism
- Command, traditional, market, and mixed economic systems
- Globalization

CHAPTER 2

Economics as a social science

POETRY is an art; nuclear physics is a science. By classifying economics as a social science, economists place their subject in the category of science rather than art.

Calling economics a science implies a claim that the truth and applicability of economic theories can be supported or challenged by the test that all sciences accept: the degree to which theories correspond to observations of the real world. Calling economics a science does *not*, however, imply a claim for the universal truth of its current theories.

The claim that economics is scientific stands or falls on the ability of economists to understand and predict events in the real world by stating theories, subjecting the theories to the test of real-world observations, and improving the theories in the light of what has been learned.

In this chapter we look at economics as a social science. We start by distinguishing between positive and normative statements—a distinction that is basic to all scientific enquiry. We then go on to consider whether or not it is possible to conduct a scientific study of *any* aspect of human behaviour. Finally, we look at the structure of *economic theories* and *economic models*.

The main questions dealt with in this chapter, 'What can we hope to learn?' and 'How can we go about learning it?', are fundamental to the whole subject.

Positive and normative statements

A KEY contributor to the success of modern science is its ability to separate views on *what actually happens* from views on *what one would like to happen*. For example, until recent times virtually all Christians, Jews, and Muslims believed that the earth was only a few thousand years old. A few hundred years ago, evidence began to accumulate that some existing rocks were millions of years old. Most people found this hard to accept; it would force them to rethink their religious beliefs and abandon many of those that were based on a literal reading of the Old Testament. They wanted rocks to be only a few thousand years old. By the beginning of the nineteenth century, however, the age of the earth came to be dated in thousands of millions of years. This advance in our knowledge came because the question 'How old are rocks?' could be separated from the feelings of scientists (many of them devoutly religious) about the age they would have liked the rocks to be.

Definitions and illustrations

Distinguishing what is from what we feel ought to be[1] depends partly on knowing the difference between **positive** and **normative** statements.

Positive statements concern what is, was or will be; they assert alleged facts about the universe in which we live. **Normative statements** concern what ought to be; they depend on our value judgements about what is good or bad. As such, they are inextricably bound up with our philosophical, cultural, and religious positions.

To illustrate the distinction, consider some assertions, questions, and hypotheses which can be classified as positive or normative. The statement 'It is impossible to break up atoms' is a positive one which can quite definitely be (and of course has been) refuted by empirical experimentation; while the statement 'Scientists ought not to break up atoms' is a normative statement that involves ethical judgements, and cannot be proved right or wrong by any evidence. In economics, the questions 'What policies will reduce unemployment?' and 'What policies will prevent inflation?' are positive ones, while the question 'Ought we to be more concerned about unemployment than about inflation?' is a normative one.

As an example of the importance of this distinction in the social sciences, consider the question 'Does watching violence on TV encourage violent behaviour among children?' Many people abhor TV violence, particularly in programmes watched by children; some of these will be inclined to answer the question with a yes, hoping to provide a reason for legislating a reduction in TV violence. Others do not disapprove of violence on TV; some of these will be inclined to answer the question in the negative because they do not wish to control violence on TV. Both are examples of letting one's value judgements influence the answer to positive questions. Examining the possible link between what children see on TV and how they behave in the real world requires a careful study of large numbers

---

[1] The word 'ought' has two distinct meanings: the 'logical ought' and the 'ethical ought'. The logical ought refers to the consequences of certain things, e.g. 'you ought to leave now if you wish to arrive on time'. The ethical ought refers to the desirability of certain things, e.g. 'arriving late is impolite and you ought to be polite'. The text refers to the ethical ought.

of children exposed to different degrees of TV violence over extended periods of time. Determining the existence and strength of such a link depends on evidence that is separate from our normative feelings of approval or disapproval of TV violence.

Positive statements, such as the one just considered, assert things about the world. If it is possible for a statement to be proved wrong by empirical evidence, we call it a *testable statement*. Many positive statements are testable, and disagreements over them are appropriately handled by an appeal to the facts.

In contrast to positive statements, which are often testable, normative statements are never testable. Disagreements over such normative statements as 'It is wrong to show excessive violence on TV' or 'It is immoral for someone to have sexual relations with another person of the same sex' cannot be settled by an appeal to empirical observations. Normative questions can be discussed rationally, but doing so requires techniques that differ from those required for rational decisions on positive questions. For this reason, it is convenient to separate normative from positive enquiries. This is done not because the former are less important than the latter, but merely because they must be investigated by different methods.

Some points of possible confusion

Having made the basic distinction between positive and normative, a number of related points require attention. Although we deal with them only briefly, any one of them could be the subject of extended discussion.

The classification is not exhaustive. A classificatory system is exhaustive if every item can be placed in one or another of the defined classes. All statements cannot, however, be classed as either 'positive' or 'normative'. For example, there is an important class, called *analytic statements*, whose truth or falsehood depends only on the rules of logic. Such statements are thus neither positive nor normative. Consider the single sentence: 'If every X has the characteristic Y, and if this item Z is in fact an X, then it has the characteristic Y.' This sentence is true by the rules of logic, and its truth is independent of what particular items we substitute for X, Y, and Z. Thus, the sentence 'If all people are immortal, *and if* you are a person, *then* you are immortal' is a true analytic statement. It tells us that *if* two things are true *then* a third thing must be true. The truth of the whole statement is not dependent on whether or not its individual parts are factually correct. Indeed, the sentence 'All people are immortal' is a positive statement which has been refuted by countless deaths. Yet no amount of empirical evidence on mortality can upset the truth of the sentence 'If all people are immortal, *and if* you are a person, *then* you are immortal.'

Not all positive statements are testable. A positive statement may be empirically true or false in the sense that what it

---

BOX 2.1

....

Positive and normative ideas in physics

Distinguishing how the world is from how we would like it to be is at the basis of a scientific approach to the study of any issue. Nowhere was the issue more starkly presented than with the development of the quantum theory of light, earlier in this century. The 4,000-year-old dream of science, that the world was like a machine in which given causes always had given effects, was upset within a generation and replaced by a statistical view of the universe in which given causes are followed by results that occur only with given levels of probability. In such a world, it is never possible to know everything with certainty.

Albert Einstein could not bring himself to accept quantum theory, although his early work had pioneered its development. His intuition told him that, as he put it in his famous saying, 'God does not play dice with the universe.' As always, however, it was observation of what is, rather than feelings about what ought to be, that settled the issue—in this case against Einstein and in favour of the 'ridiculous' quantum theory.

Here is how a famous physicist, the late Richard Feynman, described the issue in his lectures on quantum electrodynamics.*

'I'm going to describe to you how Nature is—and if you don't like it, that's going to get in the way of your understanding it. It's a problem that physicists have learned to deal with: They've learned to realize that whether they like a theory or they don't like a theory is *not* the essential question. Rather, it is whether or not the theory gives predictions that agree with experiment. It is not a question of whether or not the theory is philosophically delightful, or easy to understand, or perfectly reasonable from the point of view of common sense. The theory of quantum electrodynamics described Nature as absurd from the point of view of common sense. And it agrees fully with experiment. So I hope you can accept Nature as She is—absurd.

I'm going to have fun telling you about this absurdity, because I find it delightful. Please don't turn yourself off because you can't believe Nature is so strange. Just hear me all out, and I hope you'll be as delighted as I am when we're through.'

* Richard P. Feynman, *QED: The Strange Theory of Light and Matter* (Princeton University Press, 1985), p. 10.

asserts may or may not be true of reality. Many positive statements are refutable: if they are wrong, this can be ascertained (within a margin for error of observation) by checking them against data. For example, the positive statement that the earth is less than five thousand years old was tested and refuted by a mass of evidence which was accumulated in the eighteenth and nineteenth centuries. The statement 'Angels exist and occasionally visit the earth in visible form' is also a positive statement. However, we cannot refute it with evidence because, no matter how hard we search, believers can argue that we have not looked in the right places or in the right way, or that angels won't reveal themselves to non-believers, or any one of a host of other alibis. Thus, statements that could conceivably be refuted by evidence if they are wrong are a subclass of positive statements; other positive statements cannot be refuted by evidence.

The distinction is not unerringly applied.   Because the positive–normative distinction helps the advancement of knowledge, it does not follow that all scientists automatically and unerringly apply it. Scientists often have strongly held views and they sometimes let their value judgements get in the way of their assessment of evidence. For example, many scientists are not even prepared to consider evidence

that there may be differences in intelligence among races because as good liberals they feel that all races ought to be equal. None the less, the desire to separate *what is* from *what we would like to be* is the guiding light of science. The ability to do so, even if imperfectly, is attested to by the final acceptance of many ideas that were initially extremely unpalatable—ideas such as the extreme age of the earth and the evolution of man from other animal species. Another case in point is described in Box 2.1.

Ideals can be important even though they are not universally applied. However, many critics of the idea of positive science have argued otherwise. They feel that, because no person can be perfectly objective about other people, the idea of an objective, fact-guided science of human behaviour is a contradiction. Fortunately, science based on the testing of positive hypotheses is possible even though individuals are not always able to separate their judgements of what the facts are from their wishes of what they would like the facts to be. Box 2.2 discusses this matter further.

Economists need not confine their discussions to positive statements.   Some critics have mistakenly assumed that economists must try to deal only in statements that are positive and testable. In practice, economists must frequently consider the correctness of analytic statements: 'Is a certain

---

BOX 2.2
....

Can economics be made value-free?

We have made two key statements about the positive–normative distinction. First, the ability to distinguish positive from normative questions is a key part of the foundation of science. Second, economists, in common with all scientists, seek to answer positive questions.

Some people who have accepted these points have gone on to argue that there can be a completely value-free inquiry into any branch of science, including economics. After long debate over this issue, the conclusion that most people seem to accept is that a *completely* value-free inquiry is impossible.

Our values become involved at all stages of any inquiry. For example, we must allocate our scarce time. This means that we choose to study some problems rather than other problems. This choice is often influenced by our value judgements about the relative importance of various problems. The choice is also influenced by available funding, and those who allocate funds among disciplines and subdisciplines are no doubt at least partially influenced by their values. Also, evidence is never conclusive and so is always open to more than one interpretation. It is difficult to assess such imperfect evidence without giving some play to our values. Further, when reporting the results of our studies, we must use words that we know will arouse various emotions in those who read them. So the words we choose and the emphasis we give to the available evidence (and to the uncer-

tainties surrounding it) will influence the impact that the study has.

For these and many other reasons, most people who have discussed this issue believe that there can be no totally value-free study of economics.

This does not mean that economists and other scientists should conclude that *everything* is a matter of subjective value judgements. The very real advancements of knowledge in all sciences, natural and social, show that science is not just a matter of opinion or of deciding between competing value judgements.

Science has been successful in spite of the fact that individual scientists have not always been totally objective. Individual scientists have sometimes passionately resisted the apparent implications of evidence. *The rules of the scientific game—that facts cannot be ignored and must somehow be fitted into the accepted theoretical structure—tend to produce scientific advance in spite of what might be thought of as unscientific, emotional attitudes on the part of many scientists.*

But if those engaged in scientific debate, in economics or any other science, ever succeed in changing the rules of the game to allow inconvenient facts to be ignored or defined out of existence, a major blow would be dealt to scientific inquiry in economics.

prediction actually implied by a certain set of assumptions?' Furthermore, theories from which positive, testable statements are deduced often contain some untestable assumptions. Nor need economists shrink from discussing value judgements, as long as they know what they are doing.

This last point is important. Just because positive economics does not seek to answer normative questions (because its tools are inappropriate to them), economists need not stop their enquiry as soon as someone says the word 'ought'. The pursuit of what appears to be a normative statement will often turn up positive hypotheses on which our *ought* conclusion depends. For example, although many people have strong emotional feelings about government control of industry, few probably believe that such control is good or bad in itself. Their advocacy or opposition will be based on certain beliefs about relations which can be stated as positive rather than normative hypotheses; e.g.: 'Government control reduces (or increases) efficiency, changes (or does not change) the distribution of income, leads (or does not lead) to an increase in state control in other spheres.'

The nature of positive economics

WE begin this section by summarizing the above discussion. Positive economics is concerned with the development of knowledge about the behaviour of people and things. This means that its practitioners are concerned with developing propositions that fall into the positive, testable, class. This does not mean, however, that every single statement and hypothesis to be found in positive economics will actually be positive and testable.

Some time ago a philosophy of knowledge called *logical positivism* was popular. It held that every single statement in the theory had to be positive and testable. This proved to be a harmful and unnecessary straitjacket.

All that positive economists ask is that something that is positive and testable should emerge from their theories somewhere—for if it does not, their theories will be unrelated to the real world.

The use of evidence

Scientists seek to answer positive questions by relating them to evidence. This approach is one of the characteristics that distinguish scientific enquiries from other types of enquiry.[2] Experimental sciences, such as chemistry and some branches of psychology, have an advantage because they can produce relevant evidence through controlled laboratory experiments. Other sciences, such as astronomy and most of economics, must wait for evidence to be produced in the natural course of events.

The ease with which one can collect evidence does not determine whether a subject is scientific, although many people have thought otherwise.[3] The techniques of scientific enquiry do, however, differ radically between fields in which laboratory experiment is possible and those in which it is not. In this chapter we consider general problems more or less common to all sciences. Later we deal with problems peculiar to the non-experimental sciences.

Stability in human behaviour?

To be able to conduct a scientific study involving human behaviour, it is necessary that human beings show stable response patterns to various stimuli. Is it reasonable to expect such stability in human behaviour?

Stability only in the natural sciences? It is sometimes argued that natural sciences deal with inanimate matter that is subject to natural 'laws', while the social sciences deal with people, who have free will and cannot, therefore, be made the subject of such (inexorable) laws. Such an argument, however, concentrates on the physical sciences; it omits biology and the other life sciences which deal successfully with animate matter.

---

[2] Other approaches might be to appeal to authority, for example to Aristotle or the Scriptures, to appeal by introspection to some inner experience (to start off, 'all reasonable people will surely agree'), or to proceed by way of definitions to the 'true' nature of the problem or concepts under consideration.

[3] It is often thought that scientific procedure consists of grinding out answers by following blind rules of calculation, and that only in the arts is the exercise of real imagination required. This view is misguided. What the scientific method gives is an impersonal set of criteria for answering some questions. What questions to ask, exactly how to ask them, and how to obtain the evidence are difficult problems for which there are no rules. They often require great imagination and ingenuity.

Stability only in non-human behaviour?   When this point is granted, it may then be argued that the life sciences deal with simple living material, while only the social sciences deal with human beings, who are the ultimate in complexity and who alone possess free will. Today, when we are increasingly aware of our common heritage with primates in general, and apes in particular, an argument that human behaviour is totally different from the behaviour of other animals finds few adherents among informed students of animal behaviour.

None the less, many social observers, while accepting the success of the natural and the life sciences, hold that there cannot be a successful social science. Stated carefully, this view implies that inanimate and non-human animate matter will show stable responses to certain stimuli, while humans will not. For example, if you put a match to a dry piece of paper, the paper will burn; while if you try to extract vital information from unwilling human beings by torture, some will yield while others will not, and, more confusingly, the same individual will react differently at different times. Whether or not human behaviour shows sufficiently stable responses to be predictable within an acceptable margin of error is a positive question. It can only be settled by an appeal to evidence, and not by *a priori* speculation.[4]

If group human behaviour were in fact random and capricious, orderly living would be impossible. Neither law nor justice nor airline timetables would be more reliable than the outcome of a single spin of a roulette wheel; a kind remark could as easily provoke fury as sympathy; your landlady might put you out tomorrow or forgive you the rent. One cannot really imagine a society of human beings that could work like this. Indeed, a major part of brainwashing techniques is to mix up rewards and punishments until victims genuinely do not know 'where they are': unpredictable pressures drive human beings mad. In fact, we live in a world that is a mixture of the predictable, or average, or 'most of the people most of the time', and of the haphazard, contrary, or random.

When we try to analyse our world, and apply our orderly models to it, we need help from statisticians, specialists in probability; but we have not yet found that we need the advice of experts in the study of systems whose underlying behaviour is purely random.

THE 'LAW' OF LARGE NUMBERS

How is it that group human behaviour can show stable responses even though we can never be quite sure what each single individual will do? As a first step, we must distinguish between deterministic and statistical hypotheses. *Deterministic hypotheses* permit no exceptions. An example would be the statement 'If you enforce a reduction in the speed limit from 70 mph to 60 mph, there will be no acci-

dents.' *Statistical hypotheses,* however, permit exceptions and purport to predict the probability of certain occurrences. An example would be 'If you enforce a reduction in the speed limit from 70 mph to 60 mph, any individual driver will be less likely to have an accident; in fact, if you survey many people, the average number of accidents per driver will fall.' Such an hypothesis does not predict what each driver will *certainly* do, but only what each will *probably* do. This does allow us, however, to predict within a determinable margin of error what a large group of drivers will do.

Successful predictions about the behaviour of large groups are made possible by the statistical 'law' of large numbers. Very roughly, this 'law' asserts that random movements of a large number of items tend to offset one another. The law is based on one of the most beautiful constants of behaviour in the whole of science, the *normal distribution of error,* which you will encounter in elementary statistics.

Let us consider what is implied by the law of large numbers. When the speed limit is lowered, it will be almost impossible to predict in advance what changes will occur in any single individual's driving record. One individual whose record had been good may have a series of accidents after the speed limit is lowered because of a deterioration in her physical or emotional health. Another person may have an improved accident record for reasons also unassociated with the alteration in the speed limit, for example the purchase of a more reliable car. Yet others may have altered driving records for no reason that we discern—we may have to put it down to an exercise of unpredictable free will.

If we study only a few individuals, we will learn nothing about the effects of the speed limit since we will not know the importance of all the other causes that are at work. But if we observe 1,000 individuals, the effects of the change in the speed limit—if such effects exist at all—will tend to show up in the average. If a lowered speed limit does discourage accidents, the group as a whole will have fewer accidents even though some individuals have more. Individuals may do peculiar things which, as far as we can see, are inexplicable, but the group's behaviour will none the less be predictable, *precisely because the odd things that one individual does will tend to cancel out the odd things that some other individual does.*

The precise conditions under which we can observe the effects of one common cause that acts on all individuals are studied in statistics courses. Loosely speaking, the requirement is that changes in the other causes that affect accident rates should be randomly distributed among individuals. In the case of the reduction in the speed limit, the other causes include the type of car being driven and the state of

---

[4] *A priori* is a phrase commonly used by economists. It is defined as that which is prior to actual experience, i.e. is innate or assumed rather than acquired by evidence.

the driver's health. While some people buy cars that are more accident-prone, others buy cars that are less accident-prone; and while changes in the health of some drivers make them more accident-prone, changes in the health of others encourage safer driving. These and many other causes make it impossible to predict with certainty how one individual's driving record will change after the new speed limit is enforced. But the more drivers we study, the greater is the chance that these other effects will cancel out, and any common influence exerted by the change in the speed limit will show up in a change in the average accident rate among all the drivers studied.

So, given the appropriate conditions, which can be specified exactly in theory and are often found approximately in practice, we can determine the effect of a common cause that acts on a large group of people. Having determined the effect, we can then predict in advance the outcome of a further similar change in the common cause.

The structure of theories

A THEORY consists of (1) a set of definitions that clearly describe the *variables* to be used, (2) a set of *assumptions* about the behaviour of these variables, and outlining the conditions under which the theory is to apply, (3) a set of *predictions* that are deduced from the assumptions of the theory, and a set of *tests* against actual data, to which the predictions can be subjected. We consider these four constituents in the following four sections.

VARIABLES

A **variable** is a magnitude that can take on different possible values. Variables are the basic elements of theories, and each one needs to be carefully defined.

Price is an example of an important economic variable. The price of a product is the amount of money that must be given up to purchase one unit of that product. To define a price, we must first define the product to which it attaches. Such a product might be one dozen free-range eggs. The price of these eggs when they are sold in a supermarket in Newmarket is an economic variable. The particular values taken on by that variable might be £1.80 on 1 July 1994, £2.00 on 8 July 1995, and £1.90 on 15 July 1996.

There are many distinctions between kinds of variables; two of the most important are discussed below.

Endogenous and exogenous variables　An **endogenous variable** is a variable that is explained within a theory. An **exogenous variable** influences endogenous variables but is itself determined by factors outside the theory.

To illustrate, consider this theory: the price of apples in Glasgow on a particular day depends on several things, one of which is the weather in southern England during the previous apple-growing season. We can safely assume that the state of the weather is not determined by economic conditions. In this theory, the price of apples is an endogenous variable—something determined within the framework of the theory. The state of the weather in southern England is an exogenous variable: the weather influences apple prices (by affecting the output of apples), but the state of the weather is not influenced by apple prices.

Other words are sometimes used to make the same distinction. One frequently used pair is **induced** for endogenous and **autonomous** for exogenous. ('Autonomous' means self-governing or independent.)

Stock and flow variables　A **flow variable** has a time dimension; it is so much per unit of time. The quantity of free-range eggs purchased in Glasgow is a flow variable. No useful information is conveyed if we are told that the number purchased was 2,000 dozen eggs unless we are also told the period of time over which these purchases occurred—2,000 dozen per hour would indicate an active market in eggs, while 2,000 dozen per month would indicate a sluggish market.

A **stock variable** has no time dimension; it is just so much. Thus, the number of eggs in an egg producer's warehouse—for example, 20,000 dozen eggs—is a stock variable. All those eggs are there at one time, and they remain there until something happens to change the stock held by the producer. The stock variable is just a number, not a rate of flow of so much per day or per month.

Economic theories use both flow variables and stock variables, and it takes a little practice to keep them straight. The amount of income earned is a flow—so much per year or per month or per hour. The amount of a consumer's expenditure is also a flow—so much spent per week or per month. The amount of money in a student's bank account is a stock—just so many pounds sterling. The key test for a variable being a flow is that a time dimension is required to give the variable meaning. Other variables are just numbers, for example the price of eggs.

ASSUMPTIONS

Assumptions are essential to theorizing and they can take many forms. The most important types of assumption concern (1) the motives of those who take decisions (called *agents*), (2) certain physical relations, and (3) the conditions under which the theory is meant to apply.

On motives, standard economic theory (sometimes called neoclassical theory) is based on the fundamental assumption that all people taking economic decisions pursue their self-interest in a fully informed manner. Consumers are assumed to seek to maximize their well-being, or *utility,* as it is often called, while firms seek to maximize their profits.

On physical relations, the most important assumptions concern how the quantities of the outputs of goods and services are related to the quantities of factors of production or inputs used to produce them. For example, as more factors are used, how much more output results?

Assumptions are also used to outline the conditions under which a theory is meant to hold. For example, a theory that assumes there is 'no government' does not mean literally the absence of government, but only that the theory is meant to hold only when governments are not significantly affecting the process being studied.

Assessing 'unrealistic assumptions' People studying economic theories are often greatly concerned about the justification of assumptions, particularly if the assumptions seem unrealistic.

An example will illustrate some of the issues involved in this question of realism. Much of the theory that we are going to study in this book uses the assumption that firms try to make as much money as they possibly can; as economists put it, firms are assumed to *maximize their owners' profits.* The assumption of profit maximization allows economists to make predictions about the behaviour of firms. They study the effects that alternative choices would have on profits, and then predict that the alternative selected will be the one that produces the most profits.

But profit maximization may seem a rather crude assumption. Surely the managers of firms sometimes have philanthropic or political motives. Does this not discredit the assumption of profit maximization by showing it to be unrealistic?

To make successful predictions, however, the theory does not require that managers are solely and always motivated by the desire to maximize profits. All that is required is that profits are a sufficiently important consideration that a theory based on the assumption of profit maximization will produce predictions that are substantially correct. Indeed, we are normally concerned with the behaviour of the *average* firm, not just of one particular firm.

This illustration shows that it is not always appropriate to criticize a theory because its assumptions seem unrealis-

tic. *All theory is an abstraction from reality.* If it were not, it would merely duplicate the world and would add nothing to our understanding of it. A good theory abstracts in a useful way; a poor theory does not. If a theory has ignored really important factors, then some of its predictions will be contradicted by the evidence.

PREDICTIONS

A theory's predictions are the propositions that can be deduced from that theory. Here is an example: *if* firms maximize their profits, and *if* certain other assumptions of the theory hold true, *then* a rise in the rate of corporation tax will cause a reduction in the amount of investment that firms make in new plant and equipment; in short, a rise in the tax rate will be accompanied by a fall in investment. The forces that lie behind the prediction are contained in the assumptions that constitute the theory in question.

For a second example, the theory of consumer behaviour predicts that, if people seek to maximize their own well-being and are faced with given money incomes, they will buy less of any product whose price rises. The assumption of maximizing well-being concerns the behaviour of individuals, while the assumption of a fixed money income gives the conditions under which the theory is meant to apply. The negative relation between a product's price and the amount people buy is a prediction of the theory.[5]

Predictions versus prophecy It should be apparent from this discussion that a scientific prediction is not the same thing as a prophecy.

A scientific prediction is a conditional statement that takes the form: *If* something is done, *then* such and such will follow.

For example, *if* the government cuts taxes, *then* investment will increase. It is most important to realize that this prediction is very different from the statement: 'I prophesy that in two years' time there will be a large increase in investment because I believe the government will decide to cut tax rates.' The government's decision to cut tax rates in two years' time will be the outcome of many influences, both economic and political. If the economist's prophecy about investment turns out to be wrong because in two years' time the government does not cut tax rates, then all that has been learned is that the economist is not good at guessing the behaviour of the government. However, *if* the

---

[5] One possible terminological confusion should be noted. So far, we have not used the word 'hypothesis'. Unfortunately, this term is commonly used to refer both to important assumptions, such as the maximization 'hypothesis', and to important predictions, such as the 'hypothesis' of the negative relation between a commodity's price and the demand for it. This is unfortunate, but it will usually be clear from the context whether hypothesis refers to an assumption or a prediction.

government does cut tax rates (in two years' time or at any other time) and *then* investment does not increase, a conditional scientific prediction in economic theory will have been contradicted.

Prediction versus forecasting   Conditional prediction should not be confused with forecasting. Forecasting attempts to predict the future by discovering relations between economic variables of the sort that the value of Y at some future date depends primarily on the value of X today, in which case future Y can be predicted by observing present X. Many conditional predictions are not of this form. First, those that relate the Y today to the value of X today provide significant and useful relations that allow us to predict 'if you now do this to X, Y will change now in some specified way', without allowing us to forecast the future. Second, relations predicting that the value of X today is *one* important determinant of the future value of Y allow us to influence Y in the future without being able to forecast its precise value (because we cannot predict the changes in all the other forces that influence Y).

The analogy often drawn between economics and weather forecasting relates to economic forecasting rather than to the wider class of conditional economic predictions.

TESTS

A theory is tested by confronting its predictions with evidence. Are events of the type contained in the theory followed by the consequences predicted by the theory? For example, is an increase in the rate of corporation tax followed by a decline in business investment? Sometimes economists try to test theories directly. More often, however, theories get tested indirectly when they are used to predict the outcomes of changes occurring either naturally or because of government policy. For example, government economists use economic theories to predict the consequences of specific changes in government policies such as a rise in taxes on business profits. If these predicted consequences repeatedly failed to occur, economists would quickly stop using the theories. The theories would then fall out of use, having been tested in practice and found to be inaccurate.

Generally, theories tend to be abandoned when they are no longer useful. A theory ceases to be useful when it cannot predict better than an alternative theory. When a theory consistently fails to predict better than an available alternative, it is either modified or replaced.[6]

Refutation or confirmation   The scientific approach to any phenomenon consists in setting up a theory that will explain it and then seeing if that theory can be refuted by evidence. If the theory is not refuted when confronted with new evidence it has passed a test. Repeated success in passing tests when a genuine chance of refutation exists generates confidence in the usefulness of a theory.

The alternative to testing theories where there is a real chance of finding conflicting evidence is to set up a theory and then look for confirming evidence. Such an approach is hazardous because the world is sufficiently complex for *some* confirming evidence to be found for almost any theory, no matter how unlikely the theory may be.

An example of the unfruitful approach of seeking confirmation is frequently seen when a leader—be it the British prime minister or a foreign dictator—is surrounded by flatterers who filter out evidence that conflicts with the leader's existing views. This approach is usually a road to disaster, because the leader's decisions become more and more out of touch with reality. A wise leader adopts a scientific approach instinctively, constantly checking the validity of his or her views by encouraging subordinates to criticize them. This tests how far the leader's existing views correspond to all available evidence and encourages amendment in the light of conflicting evidence.

Theory and evidence: which came first?   The old question of the chicken and the egg is often raised when discussing economic theories. In the first instance, it was observation that preceded economic theories. People were not born with economic theories embedded in their minds; instead, economic theories first arose when people observed certain market behaviour and asked themselves why such behaviour occurred. But, once economics had begun, theories and evidence interacted with each other, and it has become impossible to say that one now precedes the other. In some cases, empirical evidence may suggest inadequacies that require the development of better theories. In other cases, an inspired guess may lead to a theory that has little current empirical support but is subsequently found to explain many observations.[7]

Economic models

Economists often proceed by way of constructing what they

---

[6] The development of a new theory to account for existing observations is often the result of creative genius of an almost inspired nature. This step in scientific development is the exact opposite of the popular conception of the scientist as an automatic rule-follower. One could argue for a long time whether there was more original creative genius embodied in a first-class symphony or a new theory of astronomy. Fascinating studies of the creative process may be found in A. Koestler, *The Sleep Walkers* (London: Hutchinson, 1959), especially the section on Kepler, and J. D. Watson, *The Double Helix* (London: Weidenfeld & Nicolson, 1968).

[7] This latter procedure is quite common these days in physics, where theories that are put forward to explain known facts gain wide acceptance mainly because of their elegance and aesthetic appeal. Experimentalists often spend years looking for some new particle or other phenomenon predicted by the theory. In the end, however, the theory stands or falls on the balance of evidence between it and competing theories.

call *economic models*. When they do this, they talk of *model building*. Because the term 'economic model' is used in several different contexts, it is important to gain some understanding of the range of meanings.

First, the term 'model' is sometimes used merely as a synonym for a theory, as when economists speak of the *model* of the determination of national income. Sometimes it may refer to a particular subset of theories, such as the Keynesian model or the neoclassical model.

Second, model sometimes means a specific quantitative formulation of a theory. In this case, specific numbers are attached to the mathematical relationships implied by the theory, the numbers often being based on empirical evidence. The theory in its specific form can then be used to make precise predictions about, say, the behaviour of prices in the potato market, or the course of national income and total employment. Forecasting models used, for example, by H.M. Treasury are of this type.

Third, a model is often an application of a general theory in a specific context. The successful model may then explain behaviour that previously seemed inexplicable or even downright perverse. An example is provided by a branch of economics called principal-agent theory. The *principal* is the person who wants something done, and the *agent* is the person she hires to do it for her. For example, managers of firms may be thought of as agents while the owners are principals. Both principal and agent are assumed to wish to maximize their own well-being, and the principal's problem is to design a set of incentives that give the agent a self-interest in doing what the principal requires.

Specific models of principal-agent behaviour have been successful in two ways. First, they have explained why conflicts between principals and agents arise in certain situations by showing that the incentives push the agent to do things other than what the principal desires. Second, they have provided a rational explanation of what at first sight seemed to be perverse behaviour by showing that this behaviour was designed to create incentives for the agent to act in the principal's interest. For example, people put in positions of trust are often paid much more than is needed to induce them to take these jobs. Why should principals pay their agents more than they need to pay to fill the jobs? The explanation is that, if the agent is paid much more than he could earn in another job, he has an incentive not to violate the trust placed in him. If he does violate the trust and is caught, he loses the premium attached to the job. The model can then be used to work out the exact premium needed to give the agent a self-interest in doing what the principal requires rather than violating the trust placed in him.

The general principal-agent theory predicts co-operation and conflict between principals and agents depending on whether the incentive structure creates a harmony or a conflict between the self-interest of the two types of person. A specific principal-agent *model* fills in the details of specific cases and predicts the existence of co-operation or conflict in those specific cases.

Fourth, a model may be just an illustrative abstraction, not meant to be elaborate enough for testing as such. For example, we may wish to gain insight into the consequences of the observation that the amount of research that goes into developing a new product often depends on the product's current sales (since the profits that finance research and development are generated by sales). To do this, we may build a very simple model in which the amount of current research is positively related to the amount of current sales. This creates what is called a *positive feedback*: the larger are current sales, the more research is done; the more research is done, the more rapidly does the product improve; the more rapidly the product improves, the more current sales rise. We could then elaborate the model by adding a second product which competes with the first one. The model will then show that the product that gets the larger sales initially (for whatever reason) will attract more R&D, and hence will be improved more rapidly than the product with the smaller initial sales. This model will reveal one key tendency of positive feedback systems: initial advantages tend to be reinforced, making it more and more difficult for competitors to keep up. No one believes that this simple model catches everything about the complex interactions when various new products compete with each other in the early stages of their development. But it does alert us to certain forces to watch for when we build more complex models or create more general theories of competition among new products and new technologies.

Interestingly, these self-reinforcing characteristics have been observed in many circumstances, such as the competition to be the power source of the first motor cars early in this century, the competition among alternative technologies to produce nuclear power after the Second World War, and the recent competition to produce the operating system of personal computers (which was won by Microsoft).

While the final test of the value of theories lies in their ability to pass empirical tests, economists spend much of their time constructing models that give specific forms to general theories, or show how puzzling observations may be explained by existing theories, or display and illustrate how various assumed forces work in highly simplified environments.

In some ways, a model is like a political caricature: its value is in the insights it provides by helping us to understand key features of a complex world.

Because the world is complex, and because no issue can be settled beyond any doubt, economists are never in unanimous agreement on any issue. None the less, the methods we have been discussing in this chapter have produced an impressive amount of agreement on many aspects of how the economy works and what happens when governments intervene to alter its workings. Examples of these areas of agreement will be given in countless places throughout this book. In the meantime, Box 2.3 further discusses the reasons for disagreement among economists.

The state of economics

On the one hand, any developing science will be continually finding conflicts between new evidence and some of its existing theories; it will also be cataloguing observations that cannot be explained by any existing theory or explained by models based on those theories. These observations indicate the direction required for the development of new theories and models or for the extension of existing ones. On the other hand, there will be many implications of existing theories that have not yet been tested, either because no one has yet figured out how to test them, or merely because no one has got around to doing the job. These untested predictions provide an agenda for new empirical studies.

Economics provides no exception. On the one hand, there are many observations for which no fully satisfactory theoretical explanation exists. On the other hand, there are many predictions that have not been satisfactorily tested. Thus, serious students of economics must not expect to find a set of answers to all possible questions as they progress in their study. Sometimes you will encounter nothing more than a set of problems requiring further theoretical or empirical research. Even when they do find answers to problems, they should accept these answers as tentative and ask, even of the most time-honoured theory, 'What observations might we make that would be in conflict with this theory?' Economics is still a very young science with many issues remaining almost untouched. Those of you who venture further than this book may well, only a few years from now, publish a theory to account for some of the problems mentioned herein, or you may make a set of observations that will conflict with some time-honoured theory described within these pages.

Having counselled disrespect for the authority of accepted theory, it is necessary to warn against adopting an approach that is too cavalier. To criticize a theory on logical grounds (economists sometimes say 'on theoretical grounds'), one must show that it contains some internal

---

BOX 2.3

Why economists disagree

If you hear a discussion among economists on *Newsnight* or *The Money Programme*, or if you read about their debates in the daily press or weekly magazines, you will find that economists frequently disagree with each other. Why do economists disagree, and what should we make of this fact?

A *Newsweek* columnist recently suggested four reasons. (1) Different economists use different benchmarks (e.g., inflation is down compared with last year but up compared with the 1950s). (2) Economists fail to make it clear to their listeners whether they are talking about short-term or long-term consequences (e.g., tax cuts will stimulate consumption in the short run and investment in the long run). (3) Economists often fail to acknowledge the full extent of their ignorance. (4) Different economists have different values, and these normative views play a large part in most public discussions of policy.

There is surely some truth in each of these assessments, but there is also a fifth reason: the public's *demand for disagreement*. For example, suppose that most economists were in fact agreed on some proposition such as the following: unions are not a major cause of inflation. This view would be unpalatable to some individuals. Those who are hostile to unions, for instance, would like to blame inflation on them and would be looking for an intellectual champion. Fame and fortune would await the economist who espoused their cause, and a champion would soon be found.

Notice also that any disagreement that does exist will be exaggerated, possibly unintentionally, by the media. When the media cover an issue, they naturally wish to give both sides of it. Normally, the public will hear one or two economists on each side of a debate, regardless of whether the profession is divided right down the middle or is nearly unanimous in its support of one side. Thus, the public will not know that in one case a reporter could have chosen from dozens of economists to present each side, whereas in another case the reporter had to spend three days finding someone willing to take a particular side because nearly all the economists contacted thought it was wrong. In their desire to show both sides of all cases, however, the media present the public with the appearance of a profession equally split over all matters.

Thus, anyone seeking to discredit some particular economist's advice by showing that there is disagreement among economists will have no trouble finding evidence of some disagreement. But those who wish to know if there is a majority view or even a strong consensus will find one on a surprisingly large number of issues. For example, a survey published in the *American Economic Review* showed strong agreement among economists on many propositions, including 'Rent control leads to a housing shortage' (85 per cent yes).

These results illustrate that economists do agree on many issues—where the balance of evidence seems strongly to support certain predictions that follow from economic theories.

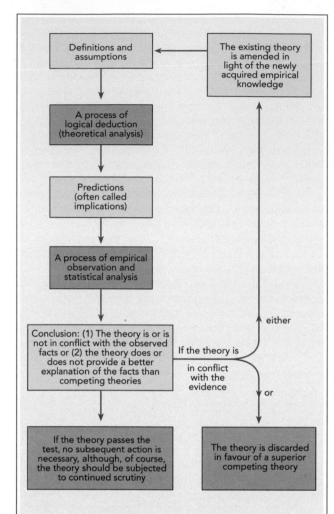

Figure 2.1   The interaction of deduction and measurement in theorizing

Theory and observation are in continuous interaction. Start at the top left, because description must start somewhere. Using the theory's definitions of relevant terms, and its assumptions, the theorist deduces the theory's implications, which are the predictions of the theory. The theory is tested by confronting its predictions with evidence, using factual observations and the techniques of statistical analysis. If the theory is in conflict with the evidence, it will usually be amended to make it consistent with those facts (thereby making it a better theory); in extreme cases it will be discarded, to be replaced by a superior alternative. The process then begins again: the new or amended theory is subjected first to logical analysis and then to empirical testing.

made set of observations, that some aspect of the theory is contradicted by the facts. Rarely are these tasks easily accomplished.

Figure 2.1 provides a summary of the discussion of theories. It shows a closed circuit, because theory and observation are in continuous interaction with each other.

Scientific crises

Sciences often evolve through a series of stages. At first, an existing theory seems to be working well and the main scientific tasks are to extend it in various directions. Then, gradually, observations begin to accumulate that conflict with the theory. For a long time these exceptions are explained away on an *ad hoc* basis, but eventually the weight of conflicting evidence causes a crisis for the theory. Finally a breakthrough occurs, and some genius develops a new theory that comprehends both what still seems right in the older theory *and* the observations that were not accounted for. Once the new theory is accepted, often after an interlude of uncertainty and heated controversy, another period of consolidation and extension occurs until new conflicts between theory and observation emerge.

Periods of scientific crisis, whether in the natural or the social sciences, can be profoundly disturbing to the scientists who become involved in them, to say nothing of those who depend on the scientists for answers to practical questions. What is true of science in general is true of economics in particular. Economics is valuable in so far as it helps us to understand and predict what we observe, and it progresses by resolving conflicts between theory and observations when these arise. Such resolutions are seldom easy and are often accompanied by heated debate. Many economists are so committed to particular theories that they will never be convinced by new evidence. It is important, however, that one of the rules of debate should be: 'Try to show that your theory fits the evidence better than do competing theories.' Although the most committed protagonists may never change their minds, a new generation, not so committed to old and outdated positions, may be able to judge the issues more dispassionately and be able to decide which of various competing theories conforms more closely with the evidence.

Science has been successful even though individual scientists have not always been completely objective. Individuals may passionately resist the apparent implications of evidence. But the rules of the game—that facts cannot be ignored, and must somehow be fitted into the accepted theoretical structure—tend to produce scientific

contradictions,[8] or that alleged predictions do not follow from its assumptions. To criticize a theory effectively on empirical grounds, one must demonstrate, by a carefully

[8] This is what Einstein did in his famous thought experiment, in which he imagined what would happen, according to Newtonian physics, if a particle were to be accelerated to the speed of light.

advance in spite of what might be thought of as unscientific, emotional attitudes on the part of many scientists, particularly at times of scientific crisis.[9]

Summary

1 A key to the success of scientific inquiry lies in separating positive questions about the way the world works from normative questions about how one would like the world to work, formulating positive questions precisely enough so that they can be settled by an appeal to evidence, and then finding means of gathering the necessary evidence.

2 Some people argue that, although natural phenomena can be subject to scientific inquiry and 'laws' of behaviour, human phenomena cannot. The evidence, however, is otherwise. Social scientists have observed many stable human behavioural patterns. These form the basis for successful predictions of how people will behave under specified conditions.

3 The fact that people sometimes act strangely, even capriciously, does not destroy the possibility of scientific study of group behaviour. The odd and inexplicable things that one person does will tend to cancel out the odd and inexplicable things that another person does. As a result, systematic patterns can often be seen in the behaviour of large groups of individuals.

4 Theories are designed to give meaning and coherence to observed sequences of events. A theory consists of a set of definitions of the variables to be employed, a set of assumptions about how things behave, and the conditions under which the theory is meant to apply.

5 A theory provides conditional predictions of the type 'if one event occurs, *then* another event will also occur'. An important method of testing theories is to confront their predictions with evidence. The progress of any science lies in finding better explanations of events than are now available. Thus, in any developing science, one must expect periodically to discard present theories, replacing them with demonstrably superior alternatives.

6 The term 'model' has a number of meanings, including (*a*) a synonym for theory, (*b*) a precise realization of a general theory, with a specific numerical relation in place of each general relation posited by the theory, (*c*) an application of a general theory to a specific case, and (*d*) a simplified set of relations designed to study one specific force in isolation.

Topics for review

- Positive and normative statements
- Testable statements
- The law of large numbers and the predictability of human behaviour
- Endogenous and exogenous variables
- Stock and flow variables
- Negative and positive relations between variables
- Variables, assumptions, and predictions

[9] One of the best introductions to methodology for economists is Mark Blaug, *The Methodology of Positive Economics: Or How Economists Explain* (Cambridge University Press, second edition 1992), which is, however, probably better read after one has studied a certain amount of economics.

✎ CHAPTER 3

The tools of economics

THE formulation of economic theories and models requires, as in most other sciences, that explicit relations be specified among a theory's variables. How, for example, is spending related to income, and how is production related to price? The relationships that are assumed to hold in theories are set out as equations, and simple ones can also be shown on graphs. To test whether these equations fit the facts, we then need to use statistical techniques. This chapter is designed to make you feel comfortable with the use of relationships expressed in mathematical form and to introduce the idea of testing whether or not theories are supported by evidence. Readers who already have a good training in mathematics and statistics can safely skip this chapter. Readers with little training in maths, or who have not done maths for a long time, might first read the Appendix to this chapter, which gives details of some elementary concepts in algebra and geometry that are used throughout any economics textbook.

Economists usually start with some problem. Perhaps we want to explain the amount people spend on consumption. We then develop a theory to deal with that problem. In this case it would be a theory concerning the determinants of consumption. The theory may come from a hunch, or from inspection of some data, or we may deduce it from some more basic assumptions about how people behave. In the present simple example, we merely assume that people's total spending on consumption is related to their after-tax income.

Now we have three things to do. First, we need to write this assumed relation in some explicit form—we speak of *formalizing* the relation. Second, we need to see what follows from our assumed relation. Can we deduce other things that must be true if our basic assumption is true? We speak of deducing the theory's implications or predictions. Third, we wish to see if the assumed relation, and any predictions that follow from it, fit the facts. When we do this we are making statistical tests of our theory.

In this chapter we look at each of these procedures in turn. Notice before we start that these three steps correspond to what we saw in Figure 2.1 on p. 36: we lay out our assumptions; we see what follows from them; we test the relations that we assume, or deduce, against the facts.

Formalizing relations

THEORIES are built on assumptions about how variables are related to each other. How shall we express these relations? When one variable is related to another in such a way that to every value of one variable there is only one possible value of the second variable, we say that the second variable is a **function** of the first.[1] When we write this relation down, we are expressing a functional relation between the two variables.

Let us do this for the example of consumption and income. Two steps are needed in order to express this functional relation in symbols. First, each variable needs to be given a symbol. We let C stand for the individual's expenditure on goods and services, and Y stand for her after-tax income, which economists call *disposable* income. Second, we designate a symbol, in this case the letter f, to express the dependence of one variable on another. We can now write:

$$C = \mathrm{f}(Y). \qquad (1)$$

This is read 'consumption is a function of income'. The variable on the left-hand side is called the *dependent variable*, since its value depends on the value of the variable on the right-hand side. The variable on the right-hand side is called the *independent variable*, since it can take on any value whatsoever. The letter f tells us that a functional relation is involved. This means that a knowledge of the value of the variable (or variables) within the parentheses on the right-hand side allows us to determine the value of the variable on the left-hand side. Although in this case we have used 'f' (a memory-aid for 'function'), any convenient symbol can be used to denote the existence of a functional relation. (Greek letters are often used.)

Functional notation can seem intimidating. But it *is* helpful. Since the functional concept is basic to all science, the notation is worth mastering.

The expression $C = \mathrm{f}(Y)$ states that C is related to Y; it says nothing about the *form* that this relation takes. The term *functional form* refers to the specific nature of the rela-

---

[1] When two variables, X and Y, are related in some way, mathematicians say that there is a *correspondence* between them. When the relationship is such that to any value of the variable X there corresponds one and only one value of the variable Y, then Y is said to be a *function* of X. For example, in the relation, $Y = a + bX + cX^2$, Y is a function of X because each value of X gives rise to one and only one value of Y. In the text, we confine ourselves to functions. It is worth noting that Y being a function of X does not necessarily imply that X is a function of Y. For example, in the equation given in this footnote, X cannot be expressed as a function of Y because for many values of Y there correspond not one, but two values of X.

tion between the variables in the function. The following is one possible form of the general relation between consumption and income:

$$C = 0.75Y. \qquad (2)$$

Equation (1) expresses the general assumption that a person's consumption depends upon his or her disposable income. Equation (2) expresses the more specific assumption that expenditure on consumption will be three-quarters of the individual's disposable income. There is no reason why either of these assumptions *must* be true; indeed, neither may be consistent with the facts. But those are matters for testing. What we do have in each equation is a concise statement of a particular assumption.

Thus, the existence of some relation between any two variables, Y and X, is denoted by $Y = f(X)$, whereas any precise relation may be expressed by a particular form such as $Y = 2X$, $Y = 4X^2$, or $Y = X + 2X^2 + 0.5X^3$.

If Y increases as X increases (e.g., $Y = 10 + 2X$), Y and X are said to be **positively related** to each other. If Y decreases as X increases (e.g., $Y = 10 - 2X$), Y and X are said to be **negatively related** to each other.[2]

The error term

The functional relation in equation (2) is *deterministic* in the sense that, given the value of Y, we know the value of C exactly. Relations in economics are seldom of this sort, except where definitions are being expressed. When an economist says that the world behaves so that $Y = f(X)$, he does not expect that knowing X will tell him *exactly* what Y will be, but only that it will tell him what Y will be *within some margin of error*.

The error in predicting Y from a knowledge of X arises for two quite distinct reasons. First, there may be other variables that also affect Y. Although we may say that the quantity of butter purchased is a function of the price of butter, $q_b = f(p_b)$, we know that other factors will also influence these purchases. A change in the price of margarine will certainly affect the demand for butter, even though the price of butter does not change. Thus, we do not expect to find a perfect relation between q_b and p_b that will allow us to predict q_b exactly, from a knowledge of p_b. Second, we can never measure our variables exactly, so that, even if p_b were the only cause of q_b, our measurements will give various values of q_b corresponding to the same value of p_b. In the case of the demand for butter, the errors of measurement might not be so large. In other cases, errors can be substantial. In the relation between spending on consumption goods and disposable income, the measurements of both C and Y can be subject to quite significant errors. As a result, we may observe various measured values of C associated with the same measured value of Y, not because C is varying independently of Y, but because the error of measurement is itself varying from one individual to another.

If all the factors other than Y that affect the measured value of C are summarized into an *error term*, ε (the Greek letter epsilon), we write $C = f(Y, \varepsilon)$. This says that the observed value of C is related to the observed value of Y as well as to a lot of other things, both observational errors and other causal factors, all of which will be lumped together and called ε. In economic theory this error term is almost always suppressed, and we proceed as if our functional relations were deterministic. (When we come to test our theories, however, some very serious problems arise because functional relations do not hold exactly.)

It is important to remember, both when interpreting a theory in terms of the real world and when testing a theory against facts, that the deterministic formulation is a simplification. The error term is really present in all the functional relations dealt with in economics.

Alternative representations

A functional relation can be expressed in words, in graphs, or in mathematical equations. (It can also be illustrated by displaying specific values in a *table* or, as it is sometimes called, a *schedule*.) In the following simple example, we consider another specific form of the general relation between C and Y given in (1) above. Equation (2) gave one specific form of the relation; now we consider a second specific form whose alternative expressions are as follows.

1. *Verbal statement.* When income is zero, the consumer will spend £800 a year (either by borrowing the money or by consuming past savings), and for every £1 of disposable income that he obtains, he will increase his expenditure by £0.80.

2. *Mathematical (algebraic) statement.* $C = 800 + 0.8Y$ is the equation of the relation just described in words. As a check, you can substitute any two values of Y that differ by £1, multiply each by 0.80, and add 800, and then satisfy yourselves that the corresponding two values of consumption differ by £0.80.

3. *Geometrical (graphical) statement.* Figure 3.1 shows the same relation on a graph. Comparison of the values on the graph with the values derived from the equation just stated shows that these are two alternative expressions of the same relation between C and Y. Box 3.1 gives some further discussion of the ways in which such functions can be graphed.

---

[2] The terms 'directly related' and 'inversely related' are sometimes used instead of 'positively related' and 'negatively related'. These alternative terms can, however, be ambiguous. 'Direct' might be taken to mean the opposite of 'indirect', and 'inverse' might be taken to refer to the specific inverse relation $Y = 1/X$. To avoid these possible ambiguities, we usually use the terms 'positively related' and 'negatively related' in the text.

Deriving Implications

AFTER laying out the functional relations that express the theory's assumptions, the next step is to discover their implications. To do this, economists can employ verbal, geometrical, or mathematical reasoning. At this stage there are two main concerns. The first is to ensure that the reasoning process is correct, so that deductions are actually implied by the theory. The second is to ensure that the reasoning process is efficient, so that everything that is implied by the theory is discovered.

The assumptions of any theory may be described in words, formulated mathematically, or illustrated graphically. Once they are expressed in a precise way, their implications may also be derived by verbal, mathematical, or geometrical analysis.[3]

To a great extent, these three methods are interchangeable. Any piece of logical reasoning that can be done verbally or geometrically can also be done mathematically. Some pieces of logical reasoning that can be done mathematically, however, are too complex to be done verbally or geometrically. The worries that many people have about the use of mathematical analysis in economics are further discussed in Box 3.2.

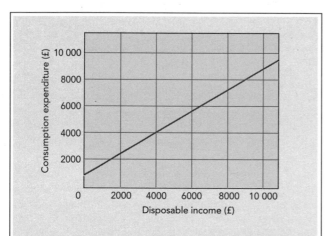

Figure 3.1 The relation between a household's expenditure and its income

The graph shows consumption expenditure as an increasing function of income. Plotting income on one axis and consumption expenditure on the other produces a visual representation of the assumed relation between the two variables.

Examples of theoretical reasoning

In later chapters, you will encounter many interesting examples of the process of logical deduction in economics. In the meantime, we can illustrate the procedure by seeing what we can discover about the behaviour of an individual who has the 'consumption function'

$$C = 800 + 0.8Y. \qquad (3)$$

Implication 1 When her income is zero, the individual is using up past savings or going into debt at the rate of £800 per year. This result is discovered by setting $Y = 0$ in equation (3) above.

Implication 2 An increase in income of £1 leads to an increase in consumption of 80p. This result takes a little more proving. First, we might check an example by substituting $Y = 100$ and $Y = 101$ into (3). The equation then tells us that $C = 880$ in the first case and 880.80 in the second, making C rise by 0.80 when Y rises by 1. More generally, we prove this by taking any two values of Y that differ by one unit:

$$C_1 = 800 + 0.80Y. \qquad (4)$$
$$C_2 = 800 + 0.80(Y + 1). \qquad (5)$$

Now if we multiply out the bracket in (5), we get

$$C_2 = 800 + 0.80Y + 0.80. \qquad (5')$$

Now all we need to do is subtract (4) from (5') to get: $C_2 - C_1 = 0.80$ which is what we wanted to prove.

Of course, the algebra involved in the above proof is trivial, but if you have followed it you have taken a big step. You have actually followed a formal proof of an elementary proposition in economics. Indeed, this is a numerical illustration of an important proposition that we will meet in macroeconomics later in this book.

Implication 3 There will be a level of income at which the individual is neither running into debt nor saving anything out of income. This is called the *break-even level of income*, and it is easily discovered by finding the level of Y such that C and Y are equal. To do this, we need to solve the two simultaneous equations $C = 800 + 0.8Y$ and $C = Y$. The first tells us how the individual's consumption expenditure varies with its income, and the second imposes the condition that consumption expenditure should equal disposable income. If you solve these two equations, you will

[3] Geometry is, of course, a branch of mathematics, but it is convenient to distinguish between 'geometrical' and 'mathematical' methods—meaning by the latter term mathematical *other than* the geometrical.

BOX 3.1

Graphing functional relations

The consumption function given in the text is $C = 800 + 0.8Y$. Let us start by taking five different levels of income, £0, £2,500, £5,000, £7,000, and £10,000, and calculating the level of consumption expenditure that would be associated with each. The table shows these values and, for further reference, assigns a letter to each pair of values.

Part (i) of the figure plots these data on a co-ordinate grid.

Part (ii) plots not only these five points, but a line relating C to every value of Y in the range covered by the graph. You should take the equation $C = 800 + 0.8Y$, and calculate then plot as many points as are needed to satisfy yourself that all points generated by the equation lie on this straight line.

Once we have plotted this line, we have no further need for the co-ordinate grid, and the figure will be less cluttered if we suppress it, as in part (iii).

For some purposes we do not really care about the specific numerical values of the function; we are content merely to represent it as a positively sloped, straight line. This is done in part (iv). We have now replaced the specific numerical values of the variables C and Y with the letters C_1, C_2, Y_1, and Y_2, each of which indicates some specific value. For example, part (iv) tells us that, if we increase the quantity of disposable income from OY_1 to OY_2, consumption expenditure will increase from OC_1 to OC_2.

In speaking of the quantity of Y as OY_1 or OY_2, we are follow-ing good geometric practice and recognizing that a *value* of Y is a *distance* on the Y axis. For brevity, we will usually use a shorter notation and speak of the quantity of Y as Y_1 or Y_2 to stand for a specific value of the variable. It is the value that would occur on the axis at that point. This is less cumbrous, but it is important to remember that *any point on the axis represents the distance from the origin to that point*. For example, Y_1 stands geometrically for the distance from O to Y_1.

The beginning student may feel that we have lost ground by omitting so much in moving from part (ii) to part (iv). It is in the form of (iv), however, that most diagrams appear in economics texts. The great advantage of illustrating functional relations graphically is that we can easily compare different relations without specifying them in precise numerical form.

Selected values of the function

Y (£)	C (£)	Reference letter
0	800	A
2,500	2,800	B
5,000	4,800	C
7,500	6,800	D
10,000	6,800	E

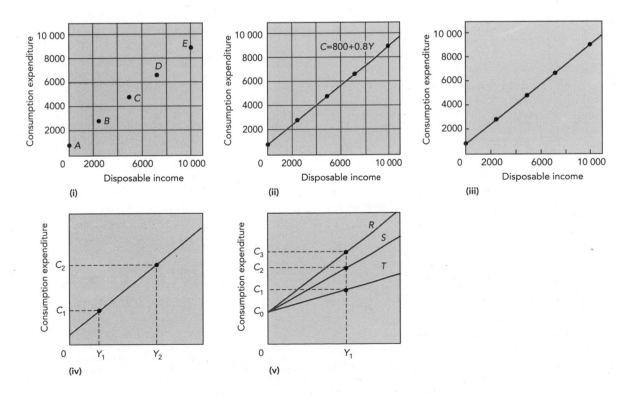

(i)   (ii)   (iii)   (iv)   (v)

BOX 3.1 *(continued)*

Suppose, for example, that we wish to compare and contrast three households, *R*, *S*, and *T*, whose consumption functions are shown in part (v) of the figure. All three consumption functions have the same intercept, C_0, indicating that they all have the same level of consumption when their incomes are zero. The function for *R* is steeper than that for *S*, which in turn is steeper than that for *T*. This shows that *R*'s consumption responds more to a change in income than does *S*'s, which in turn responds more than does *T*'s. Thus, for example, when the incomes of all three households rise from zero to Y_1, their respective levels of consumption rise from C_0 to C_1 for *T*, to C_2 for *S*, and to C_3 for *R*. Note that all these comparisons have been made without specifying the precise numerical values of any of the three households' consumption functions.

discover that the break-even level of income for this person is £4,000.[4] A little further experimentation will show that at any level of income less than £4,000 expenditure exceeds income, while at any income level over £4,000 expenditure is less than income. The graphical determination of the break-even level of income is shown in Figure 3.2.

Implication 4   As a final example of elementary theoretical reasoning, let us ask by how much the break-even level of income will increase if the individual's behaviour changes so that, at each level of income, consumption expenditure is £800 higher than before, i.e. £1,600 instead of £800. The changed behaviour is described by the new equation: $C = 1,600 + 0.8Y$. To find the new break-even level of income, we solve this simultaneously with $C = Y$ and find the solution to be £8,000. Thus, when consumption is increased by £800 at each level of income, the break-even level of income rises by £4,000. This result, which is illustrated in Figure 3.2, is perhaps a little less obvious than the previous ones.

Is this an accident depending upon the numbers chosen, or is there some more general relation being illustrated by this particular example? To deal with this question, we replace the numbers in our specific example with letters that can take on any specific values: $C = a + bY$. These letters are called *parameters*. They are constant for any one consumption function but vary from one consumption function to another. Thus, in both cases considered above, the parameter *b* took on the value 0.8, while in the first case the parameter *a* had a value of £800 and in the second case it had a value of £1,600.

A bit of experimentation with the algebra or geometry of this case should allow you to prove that any change in the constant *a* by an amount Δa will change the break-even level of income by $\Delta a / (1 - b)$. This is a general result that holds for any straight-line consumption function.[5] Notice that Δ, the Greek letter delta, is used to denote a *change*, so Δa means a change in *a*, which in the numerical case just considered is £800 because the value of *a* rises from £800 to £1,600.

The power of theorizing

Notice how far we have come. We began with a very simple economic hypothesis relating two variables, consumption expenditure and disposable income. We took a numerical

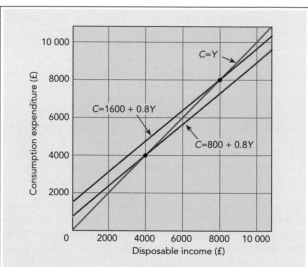

Figure 3.2   The determination of the break-even level of income

The graph shows pictorially the solution of two simultaneous equations. The lines graphing the consumption function $C = 800 + 0.8Y$ and the condition $C = Y$ intersect at income £4000. This is the solution to the two equations.
The lines graphing the consumption function $C = 1600 + 0.8Y$ and the condition $C = Y$ intersect at income £8000. This tells us that, when this consumption function shifts upwards by £800, the break-even level of income rises by £4000.

---

[4]   Substituting $C = Y$ into $C = 800 + 0.8Y$ yields $Y = 800 + 0.8Y$. Subtracting $0.8Y$ from both sides of the equation yields $0.2Y = 800$. Dividing both sides by 0.2 solves for $Y = 4,000$.

[5]   This last result can be taken on trust for the moment since we will study it in some detail later in the book. You can, however, prove it with simple algebra, using the Δ notation for changes explained in more detail in the appendix to this chapter on p. 52. We have two equations: the first expresses the consumption function, and the second expresses the condition for the break-even level, i.e. that consumption should equal income: $C = a + bY$; and $C = Y$. To solve for *Y*, substitute the second into the first to get $Y = a + bY$; subtract *bY* from both sides to get $Y - bY = a$; factor out the *Y* to get $Y(1 - b) = a$, and divide through by $1 - b$ to obtain $Y = a/(1 - b)$. First differencing for *Y* and *a* yields $\Delta Y = \Delta a/(1 - b)$.

BOX 3.2

......

The use of mathematics in theoretical reasoning

Many people — not just beginning students — are disturbed by the use of mathematics in economic reasoning. 'Surely,' they argue, 'human behaviour is too subtle and complex to be reduced to mathematical formulae.' At least four issues can be distinguished here.

First, we might wonder if we can ever understand enough about human behaviour to be able to build useful theories about it. This has to do with our ability to understand, not with the language we should use to express what we do understand.

Second, we might wonder if it is possible to express assumptions about human behaviour in mathematical terms. If such assumptions can be stated at all, they can be stated mathematically, since mathematics is just another language like English or Polish — albeit more precise than any of the languages of common speech. Any hypothesis about how two or more things are related can be expressed mathematically.

Third, we might wonder if the subtlety and complexity of human behaviour make mathematics less appropriate than a verbal language such as English for expressing our assumptions. Verbal expression may sometimes be so vague as to *hide* our ignorance, but verbal expression can never *overcome* our ignorance. Mathematical expression is more precise than verbal expression. Not only can a relation between two or more things be stated mathematically, but any qualifications to that relation can also be stated mathematically, if it is clearly understood. It is

an advantage, not a disability, of mathematical formulation that it exposes what is being said and what is left unsaid, and that it makes it hard to employ imprecise qualifications.

Fourth, we might worry about the application of long chains of mechanical, mathematical deductions to our theories. Once the assumptions of a theory have been fully stated, the theorist must discover their implications. This stage simply requires logical deduction. It is not a criticism to say that a technique is mechanical if by 'mechanical' we mean that it allows us to discover efficiently and accurately what is, and is not, implied by our assumptions. It is never an advantage to use a technique that leaves us in doubt on this. If we accept the view that, somehow, verbal analysis (or 'judgement') can solve problems, even though we are unable to state clearly how we have reached the solutions, then we are involved not in a science but in a medieval mystery, in which the main problem is to be able to distinguish between the true and the false prophet.

Mathematics is neither the maker nor the destroyer of good economic theory. It is merely a precise and compact means of expression and an efficient tool for deriving implications from assumptions. Irrelevant or factually incorrect assumptions will yield irrelevant or factually incorrect implications, whatever logical tools are used to derive them.

---

example and expressed it algebraically and geometrically. We then made certain simple logical deductions about what was implied by the hypothesis. At first these deductions were obvious, but the last one—that if £800 more is spent at each level of income the break-even level of Y rises by £4,000—was not quite so obvious. We then wondered if this not-quite-so-obvious result was an accident depending on the particular numbers we chose. Experimentation showed that there was a single general result for all linear consumption functions: break-even Y rises by $1/(1 - b)$ every time the constant a rises by one unit.

All of this illustrates how the tools of theoretical analysis do allow us to discover what is implied by our assumptions. It

also shows how theorizing tends to become cumulative: we obtain one result, possibly quite an obvious one, and this suggests another possible result to us; we check this and find that it is true, and this suggests something else. Then we wonder if what we have discovered applies to cases other than the one we are analysing. Before we know it, we are led off on a long chase that ends only when we think we have found all of the interesting implications of the theory. Of course, when we say the chase ends, we mean it ends for the particular investigator, for he is usually wrong when he thinks he has found all the implications of a complex theory. Some new and ingenious investigator is likely to discover new implications or generalizations, and so, for her, the chase begins again.

......

Testing theories

HAVING got a theory, the next step is to test it. This requires statistical analysis. (See the second of the two dark blue rectangles in Figure 2.1.) In practice, statistical

analysis is used for two related purposes: first, to test the predictions of theories against evidence, and, second, to estimate the magnitude of relations among variables. For example, statistical analysis has been used not only to test the prediction that people spend more when their after-tax incomes rise, but also to measure by how much expenditure rises for each rise in income. This second use is estimating the specific form of the functional relation from observed data.

An understanding of the intricacies of statistical analysis when used for either of these purposes can be gained only from a detailed study of statistical theory. Here we take a brief look at how statistical analysis is used in economics. Because this is a book about economic theory, we concentrate on the use of statistics in testing theories. Later, however, we shall often refer to statistical estimates of the magnitude of specific relations.

Kinds of sciences

In order to determine whether or not predictions are correct within some acceptable margin of error, they are tested against evidence. This is not a task that is easily accomplished (or briefly described), particularly in non-laboratory sciences.

Laboratory sciences In some sciences, it is possible to obtain all necessary observations from controlled experiments made under laboratory conditions. In such experiments, all the factors that are thought to affect the outcome of the process being studied can be controlled. They are varied one by one, while all other factors are held constant so that the influence of each factor can be studied one at a time.

Non-laboratory sciences In other sciences, such as astronomy and much of economics, controlled laboratory experiments are usually impossible. (In recent years, however, some economists have conducted controlled experiments to observe people's behaviour with respect to many of the choices that are studied in economic theory.)

Although economics is mainly a non-laboratory science, a mass of data is being generated continually by the economy. Every day, for example, consumers are comparing prices and deciding what to buy; firms are comparing prices and deciding what to produce and offer for sale; and governments are intervening with taxes, subsidies, and regulations. All of these acts can be observed and recorded to provide empirical observations against which theories can be tested. Given the complexity of data generated under non-experimental conditions, casual observation is insufficient for testing economic hypotheses.[6] Modern statistical analysis was developed to test hypotheses rigorously in situations in which many things were varying at once.

An example of statistical testing

To illustrate how data may be used to test theories even

while other things are not held constant, we take the very simple, and intuitively plausible, hypothesis that the personal income taxes paid by UK households increase as their incomes increase.[7]

A SAMPLE

To begin with, observations must be made of household income and tax payments. It is not practical to do so for all households, so a small number (called a sample) is studied on the assumption that those included in the sample will be typical of the entire group.

It is important that the sample is what is called a random sample. A *random sample* is chosen according to a rigidly defined set of conditions guaranteeing, among other things, that every member of the group from which we are selecting the sample has an equal chance of being selected. Choosing the sample in a random fashion has two important consequences.

First, it reduces the chance that the sample will be unrepresentative of the entire group from which it is selected. Second, and more important, it allows us to calculate just how likely it is that the sample is unrepresentative by any specified amount. For example, if the average amount of income tax paid by the households in a sample is £400, then it is most likely that the average tax paid by all households in the country is close to £400. But that is not necessarily so. The sample might be so unrepresentative that the actual figure for average tax paid by all households is £2,000. We can never be certain that we will avoid such misleading results. However, if the sample is random, we can calculate the probability that the actual data for the whole population differ from the data in our sample by any stated amount.

That chance events are predictable may sound surprising, but consider these questions. If you pick a card from a deck of ordinary playing cards, how likely is it that you will pick a heart? An ace? An ace of hearts? You play a game in which you pick a card and win if it is a heart and lose if it is anything else; a friend offers you £3 if you win against £1 if you lose. Who will make money if the game is played a large number of times? The same game is played again, but now

---

[6] Often in ordinary conversation a person advances a possible relation (e.g. between unemployment and crime), while someone else will 'refute' this theory by citing a single counter-example (e.g. 'My friend was unemployed and did not take to crime'). It is a commonplace in everyday conversation to dismiss a hypothesis with some such remark as 'Oh, that's just a generalization.' All interesting hypotheses are generalizations, and it will always be possible to notice some real or apparent exceptions. What we need to know is whether or not the mass of evidence supports the hypothesis as a statement of a general tendency for two or more things to be related to each other. This issue can never be settled one way or the other by the casual quoting of a few bits of evidence that just happened to be readily available.

[7] So far we have spoken of individuals. Most empirical work on spending behaviour is, however, based on households, which are defined as individuals living in the same dwelling and taking (or being subject to others taking for them) joint financial decisions. See Chapter 4 p. 62 for further discussion of this distinction between individuals and households.

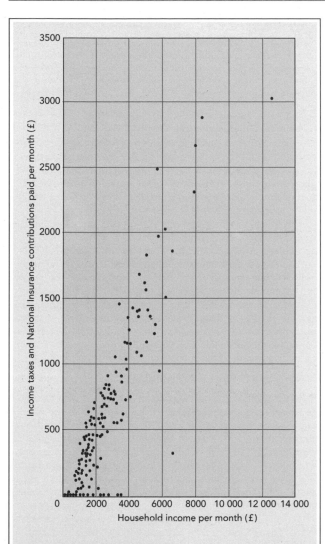

Figure 3.3 Monthly income and taxes paid for 250 British households in 1991

Taxes paid clearly rise as income rises. Each dot shows, for one household, its monthly income and its monthly tax payments. The positive association is clear to the eye and statistical analysis shows that, on average across all of these households, an increase of £1 in monthly income is associated with an increase of about 30p in monthly tax payments. The marginal tax rate in 1991 was 25p up to about £21 000 of taxable income and 40p above that. National Insurance contributions also affect the observed outcome.

Source: British Household Panel Study, Essex University

you get £5 if you win and pay £1 if you lose. Who will make money when the game is played many times? That these questions can be answered tells us that chance events are in some sense predictable.

ANALYSIS OF THE DATA

To test the hypothesis about taxes, a random sample of 250 households was chosen and its income and the taxes it paid were recorded for each family.[8] There are several ways in which the data may be used to evaluate the hypothesis. Box 3.3 discusses graphical presentations of data in more general terms; the text that follows uses the particular technique that is relevant to the problem at hand.

Scatter diagram   Figure 3.3 is a *scatter diagram* that relates family income to income-tax payments. The pattern of the dots suggests that there is a strong tendency for tax payments to be higher when family income is higher. It thus supports the hypothesis.

There is some scattering of the dots because the relationship is not 'perfect'; in other words, there is some variation in tax payments that cannot be associated with variations in family income. As we saw in our earlier discussion of the error term, these variations in tax payments occur mainly for two reasons. First, factors other than income influence tax payments, and some of these other factors will undoubtedly have varied among the households in the sample. Second, there will inevitably be some errors in measurement. For example, a family might have incorrectly reported its tax payments to the person who collected the data.

Regression analysis   The scatter diagram shows the general relationship between income tax payments and family income; it does not, however, characterize the precise relationship. Regression analysis does this by calculating a regression equation, which is the best estimate of the average relationship between the variables. The equation can be used in the present example to describe the tendency for higher family income to be associated with higher tax payments.

How closely are tax payments related to household income? This question is answered by a measure called the *coefficient of determination* (r^2), which tells us the percentage of the variance in the dependent variable (tax payments in this case) that can be accounted for by variations in the independent variable (household income in this case). For our sample, $r^2 = 0.84$. This number tells us that 84 per cent of the variance in tax payments can be 'explained' by associating it with variations in family incomes.

A *significance test* can be applied to determine the odds that the relation discovered in the sample does not exist for the whole population but has arisen by chance because the households selected happen not to be representative of the entire set of households in the country. It turns out that in this example there is less than one chance in a million that the rising pattern of dots shown in Figure 3.3 would have

[8] The data were provided by Essex University British Household Panel Study. We are grateful to Mark Taylor for his assistance.

BOX 3.3

Graphing economic data

Economic data may be collected, and presented, in many ways. This box mentions a few of the key distinctions.

Types of data

Economic data come in two basic forms. The first is called *cross-sectional data,* which means a number of different observations all taken at the same point in time. For example, the data on tax payments considered in the text are cross-section data. They show how monthly wages, number of persons, and tax payments vary across households in one specific year.

The second type of data is called *time-series data.* They refer to observations taken on the same variable, or variables, at successive points in time. For example, the data used to plot Figure 1.4 on page 20 are time-series data. They show the level of productivity for successive years from 1920 to 1993.

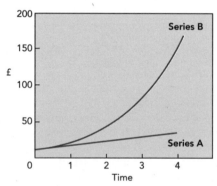

(i) A natural scale

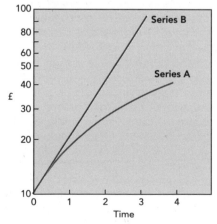

(ii) A ratio scale

Graphing data

Two main forms in which data may be graphed are the time-series graph and the scatter diagram. A *time-series graph* plots data for a single series at successive points of time. Each point on a time-series chart gives the value of the variable at the time indicated. Examples of time-series charts are shown on pages 18, 20 and 21, and it would be a good idea to glance at these now.

Another way in which data can be presented is in a *scatter diagram.* This type of diagram is designed to show the relation between two different variables, such as income and taxes paid. To plot a scatter diagram, values of one variable are measured on the horizontal axis and values of the second variable are measured on the vertical axis. Any point on the diagram relates a specific value of one variable to a specific value of the other. An example of a scatter diagram is given in Figure 3.3, where taxes paid by households are related to household income. Each dot represents one household's income and its tax payments.

Ratio (logarithmic) scales and graphs

All the foregoing graphs use axes that plot numbers on a natural, arithmetic scale. On a **natural scale** the distance between numbers is proportionate to the absolute difference between those numbers. Thus, 200 is placed halfway between 100 and 300. If *proportionate* rather than *absolute* changes in variables are important, it is more revealing to use a ratio scale. On a **ratio scale**, the distance between numbers is proportionate to the percentage difference between the two numbers (which can also be measured as the absolute difference between their logarithms). Equal distances anywhere on a ratio scale represent equal percentage changes rather than equal absolute changes. On a ratio scale, the distance between 100 and 200 is the same as the distance between 200 and 400, between 1,000 and 2,000, and between any two numbers that stand in the ratio 1:2 to each other. A ratio scale is also called a **logarithmic scale**. When a time series is plotted with a natural scale on the horizontal axis (i.e., each year is the same distance apart) but with a ratio scale on the vertical axis — it is said to be plotted on a *semi-log* scale.

The table shows two series, one growing at a constant absolute amount of 8 units per period and the other growing at a constant

Time period	Series A	Series B
0	£10	£10
1	£18	£20
2	£26	£40
3	£34	£80
4	£42	£160

Series A shows constant absolute growth (£8 per period) but declining percentage growth. Series B shows constant percentage growth (100% per period) but rising absolute growth.

BOX 3.3 (*continued*)

rate of 100 per cent per period. In the figure, the series are plotted first on a natural scale and then on a ratio scale.

The natural scale makes it easy for the eye to judge absolute variations, and the logarithmic scale makes it easy for the eye to judge proportionate variations. Series A, which grows at a constant absolute amount, appears as a straight line on a natural scale but as a curve of diminishing slope on a ratio scale because the same absolute growth represents a decreasing percentage growth. Series B, which grows at a rising absolute rate but a constant percentage rate, appears as a curve of increasing slope on a natural scale but *as a straight line on a ratio scale*. This is an important relation: when any economic variable is plotted on a semi-log scale, a constant slope (a straight line) indicates a constant rate of growth; an increasing or a decreasing slope indicates a rising or a falling rate of growth, respectively.

---

been observed if there were no positive association between income and tax payments for all households. We therefore conclude, with less than one chance in a million of being wrong, that the hypothesis that tax payments and family income are positively related is correct. Statistically, the relationship is said to be significant.

EXTENDING THE ANALYSIS TO THREE VARIABLES

The scatter diagram and the regression equation show that not all the variation in income tax payments can be accounted for by observed variations in household income. If it could, all the dots would lie on a line. Since they do not, some other factors must influence tax payments.

Why might one household with an income of £10,000 pay 20 per cent more in income taxes than another household with the same income? One reason is that tax laws provide exemptions based on the number of dependants in each household. (There will be other reasons too, such as differences in deductions for allowable expenses). Fortunately, the survey also collected data on household size. This gives us three observations for each of the 227 households: annual income, income tax payments, and number of persons in the household.

How should these data be handled? The scatter diagram technique is not available because the relation between three sets of data cannot conveniently be shown on a two-dimensional graph. A technique called *multiple regression analysis* can, however, be used to estimate the numerical relation among household income, family size, and tax payments. This type of analysis allows estimation of both the separate and joint effects on tax payments of variations in size and variations in income by fitting to the data an equation that 'best' describes them. It also permits the measurement of the proportion of the total variation in tax payments that can be explained by associating it with variations in both income and household size. In this case, multiple regression analysis shows that, on average, each additional family member lowers the amount of taxes paid by £48 per month. Finally, multiple regression analysis permits the use of significance tests to determine how likely it is that the relations found in the sample are the result of

chance and thus do not reflect a similar relationship for all households. Chance plays a role, because by bad luck an unrepresentative sample of households might have been chosen.

Testing and measurement

Statistical techniques allow us to judge the *probability* that any particular prediction is false. They cannot, however, prove with certainty that a prediction is either true or false.

CAN WE PROVE THAT A PREDICTION IS TRUE?

Most predictions in economics are universal. They state that, whenever certain conditions are fulfilled, cause X always produces effect Y.

Universal predictions cannot be proved to be correct because we can never rule out the possibility that we shall in the future make observations that conflict with the theory.

CAN WE PROVE THAT A PREDICTION IS FALSE?

Predictions are either deterministic or statistical. A *deterministic prediction* admits no exceptions. For example, an increase in a household's income will always lead to increased spending. A *statistical prediction* describes a general tendency and so admits exception. For example, an increase in a household's income will 'normally' (or 'typically' or 'usually') be observed to lead to an increase in expenditure.

We cannot hope to refute statistical predictions with certainty. Consider, for example, the prediction: most people who receive more income will spend more. Assume that we observe 50 people, all of whom get more income and 49 of whom *reduce* their expenditures. Have we disproved the prediction? The answer is no, for it is possible that the individuals we observed were untypical and, if we could observe all the people in the country, most would spend more when their incomes rose.

What, then, is required if we are to be able to refute any

prediction with finality? First, the prediction must be deterministic, admitting of no exceptions; it must say, for example, that each and everyone who gets more income will increase their spending. Second, we must be certain that any apparently refuting observations are not mistaken. The observation of one person who spends less when her income increases does not refute the hypothesis that all persons do otherwise unless we are sure of our conflicting observation. But are we sure that the person really got more income? Perhaps we made a mistake. Are we sure she did not spend more? Perhaps she made some black market expenditures which escaped our notice.[9] Errors in observation may always be present. Thus:

A statistical prediction cannot be refuted on the basis of a single conflicting observation, and indeed it can never be categorically refuted, no matter how many conflicting observations we make.

If we observe 49 people who spend less when their incomes rise and only one who spends more, our faith in the prediction that all people who gain more income spend more may well be shaken and, as a practical matter, we may choose to abandon the theory that leads to it (see below). We can never be certain, however, that all 49 cases were not due to errors of observation, and had we persisted we might have ended up observing 999,951 people who spent more and 49 who spent less. (This would make the prediction look pretty good, since an observational error on only 0.005 per cent of all cases observed might not seem at all improbable.)

RULES FOR DECISION-TAKING

Although we can neither prove nor refute a prediction conclusively, no matter how many observations we make,[10] we do have to make decisions. We act as if some predictions were refuted by rejecting them, and we act as if some were proved by accepting them. Such decisions are always subject to error and hence are tentative ones. Fortunately, statistical analysis allows us to calculate and control the chance of making errors even if we cannot eliminate them.

Consider an example. When studying taxes, our hypothesis might have been the opposite of the one we have been considering: the taxes paid by households *fall* as their incomes rise. We would then ask what the chances were of making the conflicting observations shown in Figure 3.3 if this new hypothesis were correct. There is always some chance that our sample was untypical of all households in the country or that the relationship appears as it is because of measurement errors. We calculate, however, (using the tools taught in courses on statistics) that there is less than one chance in one million of making the observations of the positively sloped pattern of dots in Figure 3.3 *if* the hypothesized relation were correct, i.e., if tax payments are negatively related to income for all households. We would

then abandon the hypothesis and regard it as refuted for all practical purposes.

Typically, economists accept a hypothesis if there is less than one chance in 20 that the observations supporting it could have arisen by chance. It is important, however, to understand, first, that we can never be certain that we are right in rejecting a statistical prediction and, second, that there is nothing magical about our arbitrary cut-off points. The cut-off point (less than one chance in 100 of being wrong in this case) is used because some decision has to be made. Notice also that decisions can always be reversed should new evidence come to light.

JUDGING AMONG THEORIES

Some methodologies emphasize the testing of theories one at a time. As it has become clearer that theories in economics can be neither confirmed nor refuted with finality, other methodologies have emphasized the use of statistical analysis to choose among two or more competing theories. Although we can never be absolutely sure of two theories that one is right and the other is wrong, we can hope to show that the data favour one over the other.

To make such tests, we must first establish where theories A and B make predictions that conflict with each other. Theory A might, for example, predict a close relation between variables X and Y because, according to it, X causes Y; theory B might predict no strong relation between the two variables because, according to it, X has no effect on Y one way or the other. The empirical relation between X and Y can then be studied and conclusions reached about the probability that what we saw could have happened if theory A were correct or if theory B were correct.

QUANTITATIVE MEASUREMENT OF ECONOMIC RELATIONS

Economic theories are seldom of much use until we are able to give quantitative magnitudes to our relations. For esti-

[9] Even if we satisfy ourselves that we saw one person who spent less when her income rose, future generations may not accept our evidence unless they go on observing the occasional exception of this sort. After all, we no longer accept the mass of well-documented evidence accumulated several centuries ago on the existence and power of witches, even though it fully satisfied most contemporary observers. Clearly, the existence of observational errors on a vast scale has been shown to be possible even though it may not be frequent.

[10] This is because we take all hypotheses about observable events to be statistical ones due to unavoidable errors of observation. We do, of course, make arbitrary decisions to reject statistical hypotheses, but so also do we make arbitrary decisions to accept them. These rules of thumb for taking decisions have nothing to do with the methodological questions of whether any hypothesis can be conclusively refuted and whether any hypothesis can be conclusively proved. Our answer to both of these questions is no. Those who are not convinced by our arguments may proceed with the text as long as they are prepared to accept that most hypotheses in economics are statistical hypotheses.

mating such magnitudes, our common sense and intuition do not get us very far. Common sense might well have suggested that people's expenditures would rise rather than fall when their incomes rose, but only careful observation is going to show by *how much* it typically rises. One of the major uses of statistical analysis is to quantify the general relations suggested by theory. In practice, we can use actual observations both to test the hypothesis that two things are related and to estimate the numerical values of the relations that do exist.

Although theories can never be accepted or rejected with finality, statistical analysis can be used, first, to establish the probability that observations are consistent with some specific theory; second, to establish the balance of probabilities between two competing theories; and, third, to measure the quantitative relations among variables in the theory.

WORDS OF WARNING

Chapters 2 and 3 have made a case that economics can be a scientific inquiry. Some words of caution are now in order.

Early statistical techniques were first developed to analyse data from controlled experiments in agricultural research. They were then used with some success in economics. In more recent times, they have given rise to a whole new subject called *econometrics*. This subject has been developed to handle the special problems that arise when the available data do not come from controlled experiments. These modern statistical techniques go way beyond those mentioned in this chapter. They are often difficult to apply, and many pitfalls can trap the unwary user of inappropriate methods.

To test our theories against facts, we need reliable facts. Because this is not a textbook in economic statistics, we do not stress the problems involved in collecting reliable observations. Such problems can, however, be formidable, and there is always the danger of rejecting a theory on the basis of mistaken observations. Unreliable observations are all too frequently encountered. If we think that *all* our observations are totally unreliable, we have nothing to explain and, hence, no need for any economic theory. In contrast, if we believe that we do have observations reliable enough to require explanation, then we must also believe that we have observations reliable enough to provide tests for the predictive powers of our theories.

Because there are major differences among the sciences, methods that work well in one may not be suitable in another. In particular, what works in physics, the queen of sciences, may not work well in a social science such as economics. What unites all sciences is the attempt to explain and predict observed phenomena. The successes and failures of all sciences are judged by their abilities to further these objectives.

Summary

1 Economic theory is based on relations among specific variables. Because all such relations can be expressed mathematically, mathematics is important in economics. Once hypotheses have been written down as algebraic expressions, mathematical manipulation can be used to discover their implications.

2 A functional relation can be expressed in words, in a graph, or in a mathematical equation. Deducing the consequences of assumptions is a logical process that can often be done verbally, geometrically, or mathematically.

3 In non-laboratory sciences where controlled experiments are impossible, statistical techniques are used to examine the influence of each independent variable *ceteris paribus*.

4 Empirical observations can neither prove nor refute hypotheses with absolute finality. Hypotheses can never be proven to be true because the possibility of making conflicting observations in the future can never be entirely ruled out. Hypotheses can never be shown to be certainly false since the possibility of errors of observation—sometimes on a massive scale—cannot be totally ruled out.

5 None the less, practical decisions to accept some hypotheses and to reject others are made all the time. Statistical analysis allows the possibility of errors in making such decisions to be controlled even though they cannot be eliminated.

Topics for review

- Functional relations
- Ways of expressing a relation between two variables
- Laboratory and non-laboratory sciences
- A sample
- Scatter diagrams
- Proof and refutation of hypotheses

APPENDIX TO CHAPTER 3

Some common techniques

CERTAIN graphical and mathematical concepts are frequently encountered in economic analysis. In this appendix we deal briefly with the ones most frequently used in this book.

Every student needs to master the elementary techniques described in this appendix before completing his or her study of introductory economics. Those who find they can manage it at this stage should study the appendix carefully now. Those who had difficulty with simple mathematics at school should skim through the appendix now, making a list of the concepts discussed. When these concepts are encountered later in the text, they should be reviewed again carefully here.

THE FUNCTION AS A RULE

Using functional notation, we write $Y = f(X)$, and we read it, 'Y is a function of X'. The letter 'f' stands for a rule which we use to go from a value of X to a value of Y. The rule tells us how to operate on X to get Y. Consider, for example, the specific function

$$Y = 5X - 3.$$

The rule here is 'take X, multiply it by 5, and substract 3'; this then yields the value of Y. In another case we may have

$$Y = X^2/2 + 6.$$

This rule says 'take X, square it, divide the result by 2, then add 6'; again, the result is the value of Y. If, for example, X has a value of 2, then the first rule yields $Y = 7$, while the second rule yields $Y = 8$.

(Notice that the expression $X^2/2 + 6$ means: first square X, then divide X^2 by 2 and *then* add 6; it does not mean add 2 and 6 to get 8 and divide X^2 by 8. If we had wanted you to do that we would have written $X^2/(2 + 6)$.)

The equations displayed above describe two different rules. We may confuse these if we denote both by the same letter. To keep them separate, we can write

$$Y = f(X)$$

for the first and

$$Y = g(X)$$

for the second.

Since the choice of symbols to designate different rules *is* arbitrary, we can use any symbols that are convenient. In the above examples we had $Y = 5X - 3$ and $Y = X^2/2 + 6$, and

we chose to indicate these rules by 'f' and 'g'. If we wanted to indicate that these were rules for yielding Y we could use that letter, and then use subscripts to indicate that there were two different rules. Thus we would write

$$Y = Y_1(X)$$

and

$$Y = Y_2(X),$$

where Y_1 and Y_2 stand for two different rules for deriving Y from any given value of X.

Suppose now that we have two different variables Y and Z both related to X. A specific example would be

$$Y = 3 + 10X$$

and

$$Z = 28 - 2X.$$

Again we have two different rules for operating on X; the first rule yields Y and the second yields Z. We could denote these rules $f(X)$ and $g(X)$ but, since the choice of a letter to denote each rule is arbitrary, we could also write

$$Y = Y(X)$$

and

$$Z = Z(X).$$

In this case the choice of letters is a memory device which reminds us that the first rule, $3 + 10X$, yields Y, while the second rule, $28 - 2X$, yields Z.

SOME CONVENTIONS IN FUNCTIONAL NOTATION

Assume we are talking about some sequence of numbers, say, 1, 2, 3, 4, 5, . . . If we wished to talk about one particular item in this series without indicating which one, we could talk about the ith term, which might be the 5th or the 50th. If we now want to indicate terms adjacent to the ith term, whatever it might be, we talk about the $(i - 1)$th and the $(i + 1)$th terms.

By the same token, we can talk about a series of time periods, say, the years 1900, 1901, and 1902. If we wish to refer to three adjacent years in any series without indicating which three years, we can talk about the years $(t - 1)$, t, and $(t + 1)$.

Consider a functional relation, between the quantity produced by a factory and the number of workers employed. In general, we can write $Q = Q(W)$, where Q is the amount of production and W is the number of workers. If we wished to refer to the quantity of output where 10 workers were employed, we could write $Q_{10} = Q(W_{10})$, whereas, if we wished to refer to output when some particular, but unspecified, number were employed, we would write $Q_i = Q(W_i)$. Finally, if we wished to refer to output when the number of workers was increased by one above the previous level, we could write $Q_{i+1} = Q(W_{i+1})$. This use of subscripts to refer to particular values of the variables is a useful notion, and one that we shall use at various points in this book.

We may use time subscripts to date variables. If, for example, the value of X depends on the value of Y three months ago, we write this as $X_t = f(Y_{t-3})$. Another convention is the use of '. . .' to save space in functions of many variables. For example, $f(X_1, . . ., X_n)$ indicates a function containing n (some unspecified number of) variables.

GRAPHING FUNCTIONS

A coordinate graph divides space into four quadrants, as shown in Figure 3A.1. The upper right-hand quadrant, which is the one in which both X and Y are positive, is usually called the *positive quadrant*. Very often in economics we are concerned only with the positive values of our variables, and in such cases we confine our graph to the positive quadrant. Whenever we want one or both of our variables to be allowed to take on negative values, we must include some or all of the other quadrants. For example, one of the functions in Figure 3A.2(ii) is extended into the quadrant in which X is positive and Y is negative, while the remain-

ing two functions are not extended beyond the positive quadrant.

STRAIGHT LINES AND SLOPES

Consider the following functional relations:

$$Y = 0.5X,$$
$$Y = X,$$
$$Y = 2X.$$

These are graphed in Figure 3A.2(i). You will see that they all pass through the origin. This is also obvious from the fact that, if we let $X = 0$ in each of the above relations, Y also

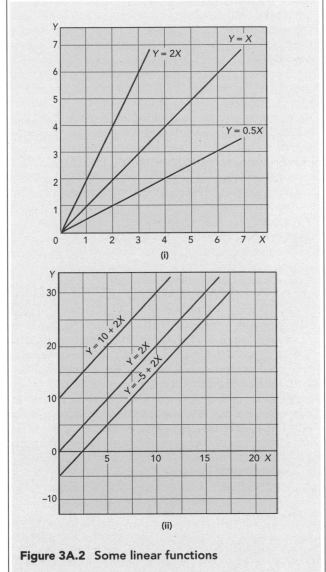

Figure 3A.2 Some linear functions

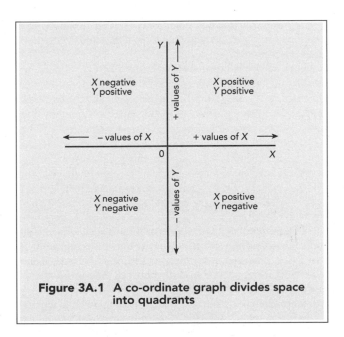

Figure 3A.1 A co-ordinate graph divides space into quadrants

becomes 0. In the first equation, Y goes up half a unit every time X goes up by one unit; in the second equation, Y goes up one unit every time X goes up one unit; and in the third equation, Y goes up two units every time X goes up one unit.

We now introduce the symbol Δ to indicate a change in a variable. Thus, ΔX means the value of the change in X and ΔY means the value of the change in Y. In the first equation, if $X = 10$ then Y is 5, and, if X goes up to 16 Y goes up to 8. Thus, in this exercise, $\Delta X = 6$ and $\Delta Y = 3$.

Next consider the ratio $\Delta Y/\Delta X$. In the above example it is equal to 0.5. In general, it will be noted that, for any change we make in X in the first equation, $\Delta Y/\Delta X$ is always 0.5. In the second $\Delta Y/\Delta X$ is unity, and in the third the ratio is always 2. In general, if we write $Y = bX$, then, as is proved below, the ratio $\Delta Y/\Delta X$ is always equal to b.

We now define the slope, or gradient, of a straight line to be the ratio of the distance moved up the Y axis to the distance moved along the X axis. Start at the point (X_1, Y_1) and move to the point (X_2, Y_2). The change in X is $X_2 - X_1$ or ΔX. The change in Y is $Y_2 - Y_1$ or ΔY. The ratio $\Delta Y/\Delta X$ is the slope of the straight line. It tells us the ratio of a change in Y to a change in X.

In trigonometry the tangent of an angle is defined as $\Delta Y/\Delta X$; thus, the slope of the line is equal to the tangent of the angle between the line and any line parallel to the X axis. Given the scale on any diagram, the larger the ratio $\Delta Y/\Delta X$, the steeper the graph of the relation. Figure 3A.2(i) shows three lines corresponding to $\Delta Y/\Delta X = 0.5$, 1, and 2. Clearly, the steeper the line, the larger the change in Y for any given change in X.

Now consider the following equations:

$$Y = 2X$$

$$Y = 10 + 2X$$

$$Y = -5 + 2X,$$

which are graphed in Figure 3A.2(ii). All three lines are parallel. In other words, they have the same slope. In all three $\Delta Y/\Delta X$ is equal to 2. Clearly, the addition of a (positive or negative) constant does not affect the slope of the line. This slope is influenced only by the number attached to X. When that number is positive, X and Y are positively related: an increase in one variable is associated with an increase in the other, and a decrease in one with a decrease in the other. When the number is negative, the two variables are negatively related: an increase in either variable is associated with a decrease in the other.

FIRST-DIFFERENCING LINEAR EQUATIONS

In national income theory we make much use of linear equations. A typical equation relates consumption expenditure, C, to income, Y.

$$C = a + cY,$$

where a is any positive constant and c is positive but less than unity.

We can now first-difference this equation to get an expression relating changes in C to changes in Y. To do this let Y take on some specific value, Y_1, multiply it by c and add a to obtain C_1:

$$C_1 = a + cY_1.$$

Now do the same thing for a second value of Y called Y_2:

$$C_2 = a + cY_2.$$

Next, subtract the second equation from the first to obtain

$$C_1 - C_2 = a - a + cY_1 - cY_2$$

$$= c(Y_1 - Y_2).$$

Now use the delta notation for changes to write

$$\Delta C = c\Delta Y.$$

The constant a disappears, and we see that the change in C is c times the change in Y, and also that the ratio of the changes is c, i.e.

$$\Delta C/\Delta Y = c.$$

Thus, whenever we see a linear relation of the form $Y = a + bX$, we know immediately that

$$\Delta Y/\Delta X = b.$$

NONLINEAR FUNCTIONS

All of the examples used so far in this appendix and most of the examples in the text of Chapter 3 concern *linear relations* between two variables. A linear relation is described graphically by a straight line, and algebraically by the equation $Y = a + bX$. It is characteristic of a linear relation that the effect on Y of a given change in X is the same everywhere on the relation.

Many of the relations encountered in economics are *nonlinear*. In these cases the relation will be expressed graphically by a curved line and algebraically by some expression more complex than the one for a straight line. Two common examples are:

$$Y = a + bX + cX^2$$

and

$$Y = a/X^b$$

The first example is a *parabola*. It takes up various positions and shapes depending on the signs and magnitudes of a, b, and c. Two examples of parabolas are given in Figure 3A.3 and 3A.4. The second example becomes a *rectangular hyperbola* if we let $b = 1$, and then the position is determined by the value of a. Three examples where $a = 0.5$, 2.5, and 5 are shown in Figure 3A.5.

There are, of course, many other examples of nonlinear

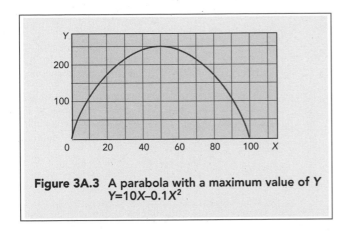

Figure 3A.3 A parabola with a maximum value of Y
$Y = 10X - 0.1X^2$

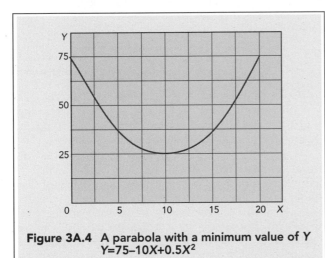

Figure 3A.4 A parabola with a minimum value of Y
$Y = 75 - 10X + 0.5X^2$

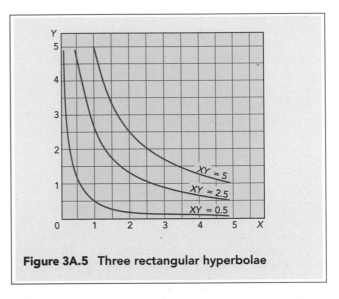

Figure 3A.5 Three rectangular hyperbolae

relations between variables. In general, whatever the relation between X and Y, as long as it can be expressed on a graph it can also be expressed by means of an algebraic equation.

MARGINAL VALUES AND INCREMENTAL RATIOS

Economic theory makes much use of what are called 'marginal' concepts. Marginal cost, marginal revenue, marginal rate of substitution, and marginal propensity to consume are a few examples. 'Marginal' means on the margin or border, and the concept refers to what would happen if there were a small change from the present position.

Marginals refer to functional relations: the independent variable X is determining the dependent variable Y, and we wish to know what would be the change in Y if X changed by a small amount from its present value. The answer is referred to as the marginal value of Y and is given various names depending on what economic variables X and Y stand for.

There are two ways of measuring the marginal value of Y. One is exact and the other is an approximation. Because the exact measure uses differential calculus, introductory texts in economics usually use the approximation which depends only on simple algebra. Students are often justifiably confused, because the language of economic theory refers to the exact measure while introductory examples use the approximation. For this reason it is worth explaining each at this time.

Consider the example shown in Figure 3A.6 in which a firm's output, Q, is measured on the X axis and the total revenue earned by selling this output, R, is measured on the Y axis. Thus, we have the function $R = R(Q)$. (We shall see later that the graph corresponds to the shape of a monopolist's revenue function, but right now we may take its shape as given.)

The marginal concept that corresponds to this function is *marginal revenue*. It refers to the change in the firm's revenue when sales are altered slightly from their present level. But what do we mean by 'altered slightly'? The answer depends on which marginal concept we use.

The approximation to marginal revenue is called the **incremental ratio**. Let sales in Figure 3A.6(i) be 6, with a corresponding revenue of £70. Now increase sales to 8, so that revenue rises to £100. The increase in sales is 2 and the increase in revenue is £30. Using the Δ notation for changes, we can write this as

$$\Delta R / \Delta Q = £30/2 = £15.$$

Thus, incremental revenue is £15 per unit when sales change from 6 to 8. This means that sales are increasing at an average rate of £15 *per unit of commodity sold* over the range from 6 to 8 units. We may call this the marginal revenue at 6 units of output but, as we shall see, it is only an approximation to the true marginal revenue at that output.

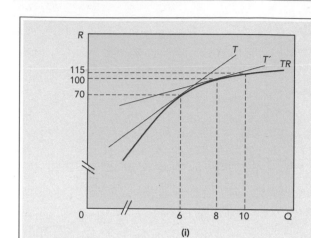

Figure 3A.6(i) The revenue function of a firm

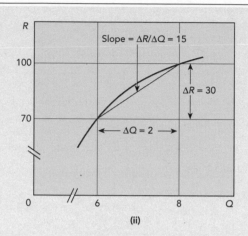

Figure 3A.6(ii) Enlargement of a section of the firm's revenue function

Graphically, incremental revenue is the slope of the line joining the two points in question. In this case they are the two points on the revenue function corresponding to outputs of 6 and 8. This is shown in Figure 3A.6(ii), which is an enlargement of the relevant section of the function graphed in 3A.6(i). Look at the small triangle created by these points. Its base is 2 units long and its vertical side is 30 units in height. The slope of the hypotenuse of the triangle is 30/2 = 15, which is the incremental revenue. Visually it is clear that this slope tells us the average gradient or steepness of the revenue function over the range from $Q = 6$ to $Q = 8$. It thus tells us how fast revenue is changing on average as output changes over the range of Q.

Incremental revenue will be different at different points on the function. For example, when output goes from 8 to 10, revenue goes from 100 to 115 and this gives us an incremental revenue of

$$\Delta R / \Delta Q = £15/2 = £7.50.$$

This calculation confirms what visual inspection of the figure suggests: the larger is output (at least over the ranges graphed in the figure), the less is the response of revenue to further increases in output.

The incremental ratio is an approximation to the true marginal concept, which is based on the derivative of differential calculus. The derivative is symbolized in general by dY/dX, and in the case of the function $R = R(Q)$, by dR/dQ. It measures the tendency for R to change as Q changes *at a precise point on the curve*. (Whereas the incremental ratio measures the average tendency *over a range of the curve*.) The value of the derivative is given by the slope of the tangent at the point on the function in which we are interested. Thus, 'true' marginal revenue at 6 units of output is given by

the slope of the tangent, T, to the curve at that point.[1] This slope measures the tendency for R to change *per unit change in Q* at the precise value at which it is evaluated (i.e. the point on the function at which the tangent is drawn).[2]

We saw in the example of Figure 3A.6 that, on the particular function being considered, the incremental ratio declines as we measure it at larger and larger values of Q. It should be visually obvious that this is also true for marginal revenue: the slope of the tangent to the function is smaller the larger is the value of Q at which the tangent is taken. Two examples are shown in Figure 3A.6(i); one, T, for $Q = 6$ and the other, T', for $Q = 8$.

Now try measuring the incremental ratio starting at 6 units of output but for smaller and smaller changes in output. Instead of going from 6 to 8, go, for example, from 6 to 7. This brings the two points in question closer together and, in the present case, it steepens the slope of the line joining them. It is visually clear in the present example that, as ΔQ is made smaller and smaller, the slope of the line corresponding to the incremental ratio starting from $Q = 6$ gets closer and closer to the slope of the tangent corresponding to the true marginal value evaluated at $Q = 6$.

Let us now state our conclusions in general for the function $Y = Y(X)$.

---

[1] Because of the thickness of the lines, the tangents in the figures seem to coincide with the curve over a range. It is of course impossible for a curve and a straight line to do this. The true tangents T and T' touch the curve TR at $Q = 6$ and $Q = 8$ respectively, and *lie above the curve for all other values of Q.*

[2] The text discussion refers to functions of a single variable. Where Y is a function of more than one variable, $X_1, \ldots, X_n$, then the marginal concept refers to a *partial* derivative: $\partial Y/\partial X_1$ etc. There is then a marginal value of Y with respect to variations in *each* of the independent variables, $X_1, \ldots, X_n$.

1. The marginal value of Y at some initial value of X is the rate of change of Y per unit change in X as X changes from its initial value.

2. The marginal value is given by the slope of the tangent to the curve graphing the function at the point corresponding to the initial value of X.

3. The incremental ratio $\Delta Y/\Delta X$ measures the average change in Y per unit change in X over a range of the function starting from the initial value of X.

4. As the range of measurement of the incremental ratio is reduced (i.e. as ΔX gets smaller and smaller), the value of the incremental ratio eventually approaches the true marginal value of Y. Thus, the incremental ratio may be regarded as an approximation to the true marginal value, the degree of approximation improving as ΔX gets very small.[3]

MARGINAL AND TOTAL VALUES

We saw in a previous section that marginal revenue refers to the change in the total revenue as output changes. Figure 3A.7(i) draws a new total revenue curve. Figure 3A.7(ii) gives the corresponding marginal revenue curve. (The equation of the plotted curve is $R = 100q - 0.50q^2$.)

From totals to marginals

Let us now assume that we have only the curve in part (i) of Figure 3A.7, and that we wish to obtain the curve in part (ii). (Note that the two parts are not plotted on the same scales).

Graphically, the marginal curve is derived by measuring the slope of the tangent to the TR curve at each level of output and plotting the value of that slope against the same level of output in part (ii) of the figure. One example is shown in the figure. When output is 60 in part (i), the slope of the tangent to the curve is 40. This value of 40 is then plotted against output 60 in part (ii) of the figure. Looked at either as the slope of the tangent to the TR curve in part (i), or as the height of the MR curve in part (ii), this value tells us that revenue increases at a rate of *£40 per unit increase in output* when output is 60 units.

Mathematically, the procedure is to differentiate the function showing the dependence of total revenue on output. So, on the function $R = R(q)$, we calculate the derivative dR/dq. If you know the calculus, you can make this simple operation; if not, you know from the previous section what concepts are involved. (In the case plotted, the equation of the marginal revenue curve is $MR = dR/dq = 100 - q$.)

From marginals to totals

Now let us assume that we have only the curve in part (ii)

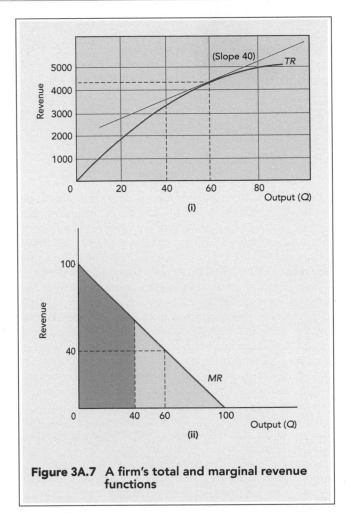

Figure 3A.7 A firm's total and marginal revenue functions

of the figure, and that we wish to derive the curve in part (i). In other words, we know that marginal revenue associated with any specific output and we wish to deduce the corresponding total revenue.

If we had a schedule of incremental ratios, all we would have to do is to add up the necessary marginal values. This is illustrated in Table 3A.1. For example, the total revenue when output is three units is calculated in the table as the sum of the contributions to total revenue of the first, the second, and the third units. This illustrates that, if we know what each unit adds to total revenue, we can calculate the total revenue associated with any amount of output, say q_0, by summing the separate contributions to revenue of each of the q_0 units.

[3] This footnote need only concern those who already know some calculus. We must be careful how we state conclusion 4 since, on a wavy function, the degree of approximation may alternately improve and worsen as ΔX gets smaller; but, provided the conditions for a derivative to exist are met, there *must* be a small neighbourhood around the point in question within which the degree of approximation improves as ΔX gets smaller, with the 'error' going to zero as ΔX goes to zero.

Table 3A.1 Total and marginal revenues associated with various levels of output

Output	Marginal revenue	Total revenue
1	99.5	99.5
2	98.5	198.0
3	97.5	295.5
4	96.5	392.0

Graphically, the same operation is done on a continuous curve by calculating the area under the marginal curve from zero to any given level of output. For example, at output 40 in part (ii) of Figure 3A.7, total revenue is given by the shaded area under the *MC* curve, which is 3,600. The value of this area is the height of the *TR* curve in part (i) at output 40.

The common sense of this relation is that the height of the *MR* curve at any given output tells us how much is being added to revenue by a change in output when output has the value in question. Adding all these heights, from zero to the output in question, means summing all the contributions to revenue from each unit of output from zero to the amount in question. On a continuous curve, this summation yields the area under the curve between zero and that output.

Mathematically, going from the marginal to the total revenue curve is merely a matter of integrating the marginal revenue function. Since differentiation derives the marginal function from the total function, and since integration reverses the process of differentiation, integrating the marginal function gets back to the total function.[4]

MAXIMUM AND MINIMUM VALUES

Consider the function

$$Y = 10X - 0.1X^2,$$

which is plotted in Figure 3A.3. *Y* at first increases as *X* increases, but after a while *Y* begins to fall as *X* goes on rising. We say that *Y* rises to a *maximum*, which is reached in this case when $X = 50$. Until $X = 50$, *Y* is rising as *X* rises, but after $X = 50$, *Y* is falling as *X* rises. Thus, *Y* reaches a maximum value of 250 when *X* is 50.

A great deal of economic theory is based on the idea of finding a maximum (or a minimum) value. Since *Y* is a function of *X*, we speak of *maximizing the value of the function*, and by this we mean that we wish to find the value of *X* (50 in this case) for which the value of *Y* is at a maximum (250 in this case).

Now consider the function

$$Y = 75 - 10X + 0.5X^2,$$

which is graphed in Figure 3A.4. In this case, the value of *Y*

falls at first while *X* increases, reaches a *minimum*, and then rises as *X* goes on increasing. In this case, *Y* reaches a minimum value of 25 when *X* is 10. Here we speak of *minimizing the value of the function*, by which we mean finding the value of *X* for which the value of *Y* is at a minimum.

FUNCTIONS OF MORE THAN ONE VARIABLE

In most of the examples used so far, *Y* has been a function of only one variable, *X*. In many cases, however, the dependent variable is a function of more than one independent variable. The demand for a good might depend, for example, on the price of that good, on the prices of a number of competing products, on the prices of products used in conjunction with the product with which we are concerned, and on consumers' incomes.

When we wish to denote the dependence of *Y* on several variables, say, *V*, *W*, and *X*, we write $Y = Y(V, W, X)$, which is read *Y* is a function of *V*, *W*, and *X*.

In mathematics and in economics we often wish to discover what happens to *Y* as *X* varies, assuming meanwhile that the other factors that influence *Y* are held constant at some stated level. The result is often phrased '*Y* varies in such and such a way with *X*, *other things being equal*' or '*Y* varies with *X* in such and such a way, *ceteris paribus*'.

Students who do not know mathematics are often disturbed by the frequent use in economics of arguments that depend on the qualification 'other things being equal' (for which we often use the Latin phrase *ceteris paribus*). Such arguments are not peculiar to economics. They are used successfully in all branches of science and there is an elaborate set of mathematical techniques available to handle them.

When mathematicians wish to know how *Y* is changing as *X* changes when other factors that influence *Y* are held constant, they calculate what is called the *partial derivative of Y with respect to X*. This is written symbolically as $\partial Y/\partial X$. We cannot enter here into a discussion of how this expression is calculated. We only wish to note that finding $\partial Y/\partial X$ is a well recognized and very common mathematical operation, and the answer tells us approximately how *Y* is affected by small variations in *X*, *when all other relevant factors are held constant*.

---

[4] If we differentiate a function with a specific constant term and then integrate the resulting function, we get back to the original function but with the specific constant replaced by the undetermined constant of integration. In the case of the total revenue function, we know that the constant on the original function is zero since, when output is zero, nothing is earned from selling output. In other cases, however, adding up the area under the marginal curve gets the total curve except for an undetermined constant of integration.

✌ PART TWO

The elementary theory of demand and supply

❧ CHAPTER 4

Demand, supply, and price

THE preliminaries of Part One are now completed, and we are ready to study one of the most important questions in the whole of economics: how do individual markets work? The answer comes in the form of what are called the laws of supply and demand. They provide a *formalization* of Chapter 1's intuitive discussion of the potato and beef markets. Chapter 4 is a key chapter. Here we look first at the determinants of demand, then of supply, and then at how demand and supply interact to determine market price. Finally, we discuss the various types of markets and the concept of a market economy together with its various sectors.

Demand

Agents

Economics is about the behaviour of people. Much that we observe in the world, and that we assume in our theories, can be traced back to decisions taken by millions of individuals. Any person who makes decisions relevant to our theory is called an **agent**.

To make the study of their behaviour more manageable, agents are consolidated into three groups: individuals, firms, and government. These are the *dramatis personae* of economic theory, and the stage on which their play is enacted is the market. In this chapter you will encounter both individuals (here) and firms (later); while in Chapter 6 you will first meet the government.

INDIVIDUALS

Individuals play two major roles in economic theory. First, those who are employed sell their services to employers and receive incomes in return. Others, such as spouses and children who do not work, share in the incomes of those members of their household who do work. Yet others receive income transfers from the government in such forms as unemployment benefits, student grants, and old age pensions. Second, individuals spend their incomes purchasing goods and services. In this capacity they are often referred to as **consumers**.

Microeconomic theory is inhabited by adult individuals who earn income by selling factor services (the services of their labour, land, or capital) and spend this income purchasing goods and services. When one applies the theory to real-world observations, however, the spending unit that can be studied is often not the individual but the household.

A **household** is defined as all the people who live under one roof and who make joint financial decisions or are subject to others who make such decisions for them. Some economists have studied resource allocation within households. This field of study was pioneered by University of Chicago economist and Nobel Prize winner Gary Becker, and is covered in specialized labour economics courses. For purposes of developing the elementary theory of market behaviour, however, we stick to individuals, who obtain income through their own work or the work of others and who spend that income purchasing goods and services for consumption.

MOTIVATION

Economists assume that each individual consumer seeks maximum *satisfaction*, or *well-being*, or *utility*, as the concept is variously called. The consumer does this within the limits set by his or her available resources.

The nature of demand

The amount of a product that consumers wish to purchase is called the **quantity demanded**. Notice two important things about this concept. First, quantity demanded is a *desired* quantity. It is how much consumers *wish* to purchase, not necessarily how much they actually succeed in purchasing. We use phrases such as **quantity actually purchased**, or **quantity actually bought and sold**, to distinguish actual purchases from quantity demanded. Second, note that quantity demanded is a *flow*. (See p. 31 for the distinction between stocks and flows.) We are concerned not with a single isolated purchase, but with a continuous flow of purchases, and we must, therefore, express demand as so much per period of time—e.g. one million oranges *per day*, or seven million oranges *per week*, or 365 million oranges *per year*.

The concept of demand as a flow appears to raise difficulties when we deal with the purchases of durable consumer goods (often called consumer durables). It makes obvious sense to talk about a person consuming oranges at the rate of 30 per month, but what can we say of a consumer that buys a new television set every five years? This apparent difficulty disappears if we measure the demand for the *services* provided by the consumer durable. Thus, at the rate of a new set every five years, the television purchaser is using the service (viewing TV programmes) at the rate of 1/60 of a set per month.

The determinants of quantity demanded: the demand function

Five main variables influence the quantity of each product that is demanded by each individual consumer:

1. The price of the product
2. The prices of other products
3. The consumer's income and wealth
4. Various 'sociological' factors
5. The consumer's tastes

Making use of the functional notation that was introduced in Chapter 3, the above list is conveniently summarized in what is called a **demand function**:

$$q_n^d = D(p_n, p_1, ..., p_{n-1}, Y, S),$$

In the above expression, q_n^d stands for the quantity that the consumer demands of some product, which we call product n; p_n stands for the price of this product, where $p_1, ...,$ p_{n-1} is a shorthand notation for the prices of all other products; Y is the consumer's income; S stands for a host of sociological (and other) factors such as number of children, place of residence (e.g. big city, small town, country), and the state of the weather; and the form of the function D is determined by the tastes of the members of the consumer.[1] The demand function is just a shorthand way of saying that quantity demanded depends on the variables listed on the right-hand side, while the form of the function determines the sign and the magnitude of that dependence.

We will not be able to understand the separate influences of each of the above variables if we ask what happens when everything changes at once. To avoid this difficulty, we consider the influence of the variables one at a time. To do this, we use a device that is frequently employed in economic theory. We assume that all except one of the variables in the right-hand side of the above expression are held constant; we then allow this one variable, say p_n, to change, and we consider how the quantity demanded (q_n^d) changes. This means we study the effect of changes in one influence on quantity demanded, *assuming that all other influences remain unchanged*, or, as economists are fond of putting it, *ceteris paribus* (which means 'other things being equal').

We can do the same for each of the other variables in turn, and in this way we can come to understand the effect of each variable. Once this is done, we can add up the separate influences of each variable to discover what will happen when several variables change at the same time—as they usually do in practice.

Demand and price

We are interested in developing a theory of how products get priced. To do this, we need to study the relation between the quantity demanded of each product and that product's own price. This requires that we hold all other influences constant and ask: how will the quantity of a product demanded vary as its own price varies?

A basic economic hypothesis is that the lower the price of a product, the larger the quantity that will be demanded, other things being equal.[2]

Why might this be so? A major reason is that there is usually more than one product that will satisfy any given desire or need. Hunger may be satisfied by meat or vegetables; a desire for green vegetables may be satisfied by broccoli or spinach. The need to keep warm at night may be satisfied by several woollen blankets, or one electric blanket, or a sheet and a lot of oil burned in the boiler. The desire for a holiday may be satisfied by a trip to the Scottish Highlands or to the Swiss Alps, the need to get there by an aeroplane, a bus, a car, or a train; and so on. Name any general desire or need, and there will usually be several products that will satisfy it.

Now consider what happens if we hold income, tastes, population, and the prices of all other products constant and vary the price of only one product.

First, let the price of the product rise. The product then becomes a more expensive way of satisfying a want. Some consumers will stop buying it altogether; others will buy smaller amounts; still others may continue to buy the same amount; but no rational consumer will buy more of it. Because many consumers will switch wholly, or partially, to other products to satisfy the same want, less will be bought of the product whose price has risen. For example, as meat becomes more expensive, consumers may switch some of their expenditure to meat substitutes; they may also forgo meat at some meals and eat less meat at others.

---

[1] Where these other factors are important, they are often included explicitly in empirical measurements. For example, equations predicting the monthly demand for fuel oil usually contain a term for the state of the weather. In other cases, they will be included in the error term, which covers 'all other unmeasured influences'. In theoretical work, no harm is done by including these other factors under tastes and thinking of them as determining the form of the function. When this is done, however, tastes are exogenous, in the sense that they are not determined by economic variables but are subject to change when any of these other influencing forces, such as weather, changes.

[2] In this chapter we introduce the hypothesis as an assumption; in Chapters 7 and 8 we derive it from more basic assumptions.

Second, let the price of a product fall. This makes the product a cheaper method of satisfying any given want. Consumers will thus buy more of it. Consequently, they will buy less of similar other products whose prices have not fallen and which, as a result, have become expensive *relative to* the product in question. When a bumper tomato harvest drives prices down, shoppers buy more tomatoes and fewer alternative vegetables, which are now relatively more expensive.

THE DEMAND SCHEDULE AND THE DEMAND CURVE

An individual's demand   A **demand schedule** is one way of showing the relationship between quantity demanded and price. It is a numerical tabulation that lists some selected prices and shows the quantity that will be demanded at each.

Table 4.1 is an individual's hypothetical demand schedule for carrots. It shows the quantity of carrots that the individual would demand at six selected prices. For example, at a price of £0.40 per kilogram, the quantity demanded is 10.25 kg per month. Each of the price–quantity combinations in the table is given a letter for easy reference. We can now plot the data from Table 4.1 in Figure 4.1, with price on the vertical and quantity on the horizontal axis.[3]

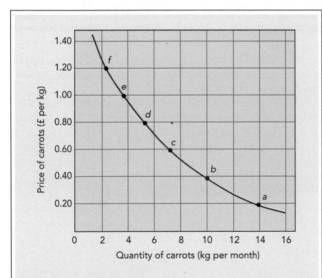

Figure 4.1 An individual consumer's demand curve

An individual consumer's demand curve relates the price of a commodity to the amount that the consumer wishes to purchase. The curve is drawn from the data in Table 4.1, each point on the figure relating to a row on the table. For example, when price is £1.20, 2.5 kg are bought per month (point *f*), while when the price is £0.20, 14 kg are bought each month (point *a*).

Table 4.1 An individual consumer's demand schedule for carrots

Reference letter	Price (£ per kg)	Quantity demanded (kg per month)
a	0.20	14.0
b	0.40	10.25
c	0.60	7.5
d	0.80	5.25
e	1.00	3.5
f	1.20	2.5

The table shows the quantity of carrots that one consumer would demand at each selected price, *ceteris paribus*. For example, at a price of £0.20 per kilogram the consumer demands 14 kg per month, while at a price of £1.20 per kilogram he demands only 2.5 kg.

Next, we draw a smooth curve through these points. This curve, also shown in Figure 4.1, is called the **demand curve** for carrots. It shows the quantity of carrots that the consumer would like to buy at every possible price; its *negative slope* indicates that the quantity demanded increases as the price falls.[4]

A single point on the demand curve indicates a single price–quantity relation. *The whole demand curve shows the complete relation between quantity demanded and price.* Economists often speak of the conditions of demand in a particular market as 'given' or as 'known'. When they do so they are referring not just to the particular quantity that is being demanded at the moment (i.e. not just to a particular point on the demand curve); they are referring rather to the

---

[3] Readers trained in other disciplines often wonder why economists plot demand curves with price on the vertical axis. The normal convention, which puts the independent variable (the variable that does the explaining) on the horizontal axis and the dependent variable (the variable that is explained) on the vertical axis, calls for price to be plotted on the horizontal axis and quantity on the vertical axis.

The axis reversal—now enshrined by a century of usage—arose as follows. The analysis of the competitive market that we use today stems from the French economist Leon Walras (1834–1910), in whose theory quantity was the dependent variable. Graphical analysis in economics, however, was popularized by the English economist Alfred Marshall (1842–1924), in whose theory *price* was the dependent variable. Economists continue to use Walras's theory and Marshall's graphical representation, and thus draw the diagram with the independent and dependent variables reversed—to the everlasting confusion of readers trained in other disciplines. In virtually every other graph in economics the axes are labelled conventionally, with the dependent variable on the vertical axis.

[4] Mathematicians refer to the slopes of curves as *positive* if both variables change in the same direction along the curve (i.e. if either they both increase or they both decrease) and as *negative* if the variables change in opposite directions along the curve (i.e. if one increases while the other decreases). Economists often read curves from left to right, calling negatively sloped curves 'downward-sloping' and positively sloped curves 'upward-sloping'. We stick mainly to the unambiguous terminology of positive and negative slopes.

whole demand curve, to the complete functional relation whereby desired purchases are related to all possible alternative prices of the product.

The market demand curve   So far we have discussed how the quantity of a product demanded by one consumer depends on the product's price, other things being equal. To explain market behaviour, we need to know the total demand of all consumers. To obtain a market demand schedule, we sum the quantities demanded by each consumer at a particular price to obtain the total quantity demanded at that price. We repeat the process for each price to obtain a schedule of total, or market, demand at all possible prices. A graph of this schedule is called the *market demand curve*. Figure 4.2 shows the summation geometrically. It illustrates the proposition that the market demand curve is the horizontal sum of the demand curves of all the individual consumers in the market.[5]

We have illustrated the market demand curve by summing the demands for only two consumers. An actual market demand curve will represent the demands of all the consumers who buy in that market. In practice, our knowledge of market curves is usually derived by observing total quantities directly. The derivation of market demand curves by summing individual curves is a theoretical operation. We do it to understand the relation between curves for individual consumers and market curves.

In Table 4.2 we assume we have data for the market demand for carrots. The schedule tells us the total quantity that will be demanded by all buyers in that market at a selected set of market prices. The data are plotted in Figure 4.3, and the curve drawn through these points is the market demand curve.

Table 4.2 A market demand schedule for carrots

Reference letter	Price (£ per kg)	Quantity demanded ('000 kg per month)
U	0.20	110.0
V	0.40	90.0
W	0.60	77.5
X	0.80	67.5
Y	1.00	62.5
Z	1.20	60.0

The table shows the quantity of carrots that would be demanded by all consumers at various prices, *ceteris paribus*. For example, row *W* indicates that if the price of carrots were £0.60 per kilogram consumers would desire to purchase 77,500 kg of carrots per month, given the values of the other variables that affect quantity demanded, including average consumers' income.

[5] When summing curves, students sometimes become confused between vertical and horizontal summation. Such a confusion can only result from the application of memory rather than common sense to one's economics. *Consider what would be meant by vertical summation*: measure off equal quantities, say 2 kg in parts (i) and (ii) of Figure 4.2. Now add the price on each household's demand curve to which this quantity corresponds. This is £0.50 + £0.60 = £1.10. If we now plot the point corresponding to £1.10 and 2 kg, we have related a given quantity of the commodity to the sum of the prices which the households are separately prepared to pay for this commodity. Clearly, this information is of no interest to us in the present context. *Every graphical operation can be translated into words*. The advantage of graphs is that they make proofs easier; the disadvantage is that they make it possible to make silly errors. To avoid error, you should always translate into words any graphical operation you have performed and ask yourself: 'Does this make sense and is this what I meant to do?'

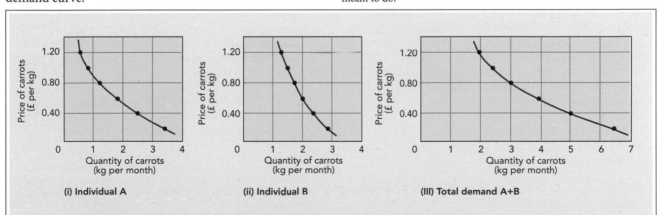

(i) Individual A   **(ii) Individual B**   **(III) Total demand A+B**

Figure 4.2 The relation between individual and market demand curves

The market demand curve is the horizontal sum of the individual demand curves of all consumers in the market. The figure illustrates aggregation over two individuals. For example, at a price of £0.80 per kilogram, consumer A purchases 1.2 kg and consumer B purchases 1.8 kg. Thus, together they purchase 3 kg. No matter how many individuals are involved, the process is the same.

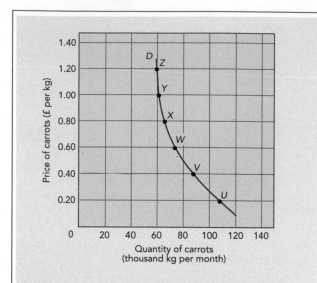

Figure 4.3   A market demand curve for carrots

This demand curve relates quantity of carrots demanded to their price; its negative slope indicates that quantity demanded increases as price falls. The six points correspond to the price–quantity combinations shown in Table 4.2. Each row in the table defines a point on the demand curve. The smooth curve drawn through all of the points and labelled *D* is the demand curve.

DETERMINANTS OF DEMAND ONCE AGAIN

When we go from the individual consumer's demand curve to the market demand curve, we must reconsider item 3 in our list of the determinants of demand. 'Consumer income' now refers to *the total income of all consumers*. If, for example, the population increases as a result of immigration and each new immigrant has an income, the demands for most products will rise even though existing consumers have unchanged incomes and face unchanged prices.

When we take total income of all consumers as our income variable, we must add another factor to the major determinants of demand.

A sixth determinant: income distribution among individuals
Consider two societies with the same total income. In one society there are some rich people, many poor people, but only a few in the middle-income range. In the second society, most of the people have incomes that do not differ much from the average income for all consumers. Even if all other variables that influence demand are the same, the two societies will have quite different patterns of demand. In the first there will be a large demand for Mercedes-Benz and Rolls-Royce cars and also for baked beans, bread, and

chips. In the second, there will be a smaller demand for these products, but a large demand for ski holidays, medium-sized cars, and other middle-income consumption goods. Clearly, the distribution of income is a major determinant of market demand.

MARKET DEMAND: A RECAPITULATION

The total quantity demanded in any market depends on the price of the product being sold, on the prices of all other products, on the income of the individuals buying in that market, on the distribution of that income among the individuals, and on tastes.

To obtain the market demand curve, we hold constant all the factors that influence demand, other than the product's own price.

The market demand curve relates the total quantity demanded of a product to its own price on the assumption that all other prices, total income, its distribution among individuals, and tastes are held constant.

SHIFTS IN THE DEMAND CURVE

The demand schedule and the demand curve are constructed on the assumption of *ceteris paribus*. But what if other things change, as surely they must? What, for example, if consumers find themselves with more income? If they spend their extra income, they will buy additional quantities of many products *even though market prices are unchanged,* as shown in Table 4.3. But if consumers increase their purchases of any product whose price has not changed, the new purchases cannot be represented by the original demand curve. Thus, the rise in consumer income *shifts* the demand curve to the right as shown in Figure 4.4.[6] This shift illustrates the operation of an important general rule.

A demand curve shifts to a new position in response to a change in any of the variables that were held constant when the original curve was drawn.

---

[6] The conventions used throughout this book for shifts in curves are as follows. The initial position of the curve is indicated by a solid curve labelled with the subscript 0 where necessary. All shifted curves are drawn as broken lines and indicated by a subscript 1 for the first shift, 2 for the second shift, and so on. The equilibrium price and quantity associated with the initial curve are indicated by p_0 and q_0, those associated with the curve after one shift by p_1 and q_1, and so on. When there is no curve shift, and hence no room for ambiguity, the subscripts are often dropped. Thus, for example, there are no subscripts in Figure 4.3, but in Figure 4.4 the initial curve is labelled D_0 and the shifted curve D_1.

Where we wish to indicate two alternative curves rather than a shift of a curve, we use prime (') marks. Thus, for example, D_0 and D_1 refer to the curve that starts at D_0 and shifts to D_1 while D, D', and D'' refer to three alternative curves, any one of which might actually exist at any one time.

Table 4.3 Two alternative market demand schedules for carrots

(1)	Price of carrots (£ per kg) (2)	Quantity of carrots demanded at original level of personal income ('000 kg per month) (3)	Quantity of carrots demanded when personal income rises to new level ('000 kg per month) (4)	(5)
U	0.20	110.0	140.0	U'
V	0.40	90.0	116.0	V'
W	0.60	77.5	100.8	W'
X	0.80	67.5	90.0	X'
Y	1.00	62.5	81.3	Y'
Z	1.20	60.0	78.0	Z'

An increase in total consumers' income increases the quantity demanded at each price. When income rises, quantity demanded at a price of £0.60 per kilogram rises from 77,500 kg per month to 100,800 kg per month. A similar rise occurs at every other price. Thus, the demand schedule relating columns (2) and (3) is replaced by the one relating columns (2) and (4). The graphical representations of these two schedules are labelled D_0 and D_1 in Figure 4.4.

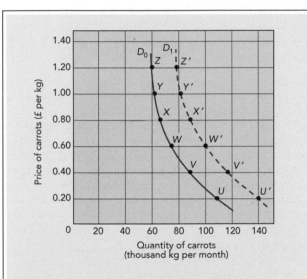

Figure 4.4 Two demand curves for carrots

The rightward shift in the demand curve from D_0 to D_1 indicates an increase in the quantity demanded at each price. The lettered points correspond to those in Table 4.3. A rightward shift in the demand curve indicates an increase in demand in the sense that more is demanded at each price and that a higher price would be paid for each quantity. For example at price £0.60, quantity demanded rises from 77.5 thousand kilograms (point *W*) to 100 (point *W'*); while the quantity of 90 thousand kilograms, which was formerly bought at a price of £0.40 (point *V*), will be bought at a price £0.80 after the shift (point *X'*).

and any change that decreases the amount consumers wish to buy at each price will shift the demand curve to the left.

Changes in other prices We saw that demand curves have negative slopes because the lower a product's price, the cheaper it becomes relative to other products that can satisfy the same needs. Those other products are called **substitutes**. A product becomes cheaper relative to its substitutes if its own price falls. This also happens if the substitute's price rises. For example, carrots can become cheap relative to cabbage, either because the price of carrots falls or because the price of cabbage rises. Either change will increase the amount of carrots consumers are prepared to buy.

A rise in the price of a product's substitute shifts the demand curve for the product to the right. More will be purchased at each price.

For example, a rise in the price of cabbage could shift the demand curve for carrots from D_0 to D_1 in Figure 4.4, just as did a rise in income.

Products that tend to be used jointly with each other are called **complements**. Cars and petrol are complements; so are golf clubs and golf balls, electric cookers and electricity, an aeroplane trip to Austria and lift tickets at St Anton. Since complements tend to be consumed together, a fall in the price of either will increase the demand for both. For example, a fall in the price of cars that causes more people to become car owners will, *ceteris paribus*, increase the demand for petrol.

A fall in the price of one product that is complementary to a second product will shift the second product's demand curve to the right. More will be purchased at each price.

Any change that increases the amount consumers wish to buy at each price will shift the demand curve to the right,

Changes in total income If consumers receive more income, they can be expected to purchase more of most products even though product prices remain the same. Such a shift is illustrated in Table 4.3 and Figure 4.4. A product whose demand increases when income increases is called a **normal good**.

A rise in consumers' incomes shifts the demand curve for normal products to the right, indicating that more will be demanded at each possible price.

For a few products, called **inferior goods**, a rise in consumers' income leads them to reduce their purchases (because they can now afford to switch to a more expensive, but superior, substitute).

A rise in income will shift the demand for inferior goods to the left, indicating that less will be demanded at each price.

The distribution of income If total income and all other determinants of demand are held constant while the distribution of income changes, the demands for normal goods will rise for consumers gaining income and fall for consumers losing income. If both gainers and losers buy the good in similar proportions, these changes will tend to cancel out. This will not, however, always be the case.

When the distribution of income changes, demands will rise for those goods favoured by those gaining income and fall for those goods favoured by those losing income.

Sociological variables Changes in the many sociological variables that influence demand will cause demand curves to shift. For example, a reduction in the typical number of children per consumer, as has happened in this century, will reduce the demands for many of the things used by children. If the typical age of retirement falls significantly, there will be a rise in the demands for goods consumed during leisure times and a fall in the demands for goods required while working.

Changes in tastes If there is a change in tastes in favour of a product, more will be demanded at each price, causing the demand curve to shift to the right. In contrast, if there is a change in tastes away from a product, less will be demanded at each price, causing the entire demand curve to shift to the left.

Figure 4.5 summarizes our discussion of the causes of shifts in the demand curve. Notice that, since we are generalizing beyond our example of carrots, we have relabelled our axes 'price' and 'quantity', dropping the qualification 'of carrots'. The term *quantity* should be understood to mean quantity per period in whatever units the goods are measured. The term *price* should be understood to mean the price measured as £ per unit of quantity for the same product.

MOVEMENTS ALONG DEMAND CURVES VERSUS SHIFTS

Suppose you read in today's newspaper that carrot prices have soared because more carrots are being demanded. Then tomorrow you read that the rising price of carrots is greatly reducing the typical consumer's demand for carrots as shoppers switch to potatoes, courgettes, and peas. The two statements appear to contradict each other. The first associates a rising price with a rising demand; the second associates a rising price with a declining demand. Can both statements be true? The answer is that they can be, because they refer to different things. The first refers to a *shift* in the

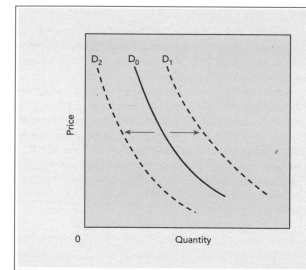

Figure 4.5 Shifts in the demand curve

A shift in the demand curve from D_0 to D_1 indicates an increase in demand; a shift from D_0 to D_2 indicates a decrease in demand. An increase in demand means that more is demanded at each price. Such a rightward shift can be caused by a rise in the price of a substitute, a fall in the price of a complement, a rise in income, a redistribution of income toward groups who favour the commodity, or a change in tastes that favours the commodity.

A decrease in demand means that less is demanded at each price. Such a leftward shift can be caused by a fall in the price of a substitute, a rise in the price of a complement, a fall in income, a redistribution of income away from groups who favour the commodity, or a change in tastes that disfavours the commodity.

demand curve; the second refers to a movement *along a* demand curve in response to a change in price.

Consider first the statement that the increase in the price of carrots has been caused by an increased demand for carrots. This statement refers to a shift in the demand curve for carrots. In this case, the demand curve must have shifted to the right, indicating more carrots demanded at each price. This shift will, as we shall see later in this chapter, increase the price of carrots.

Now consider the statement that fewer carrots are being bought because carrots have become more expensive. This refers to a movement along a given demand curve and reflects a change between two specific quantities being bought, one before the price rose and one afterwards.

So what lay behind the two stories might have been something like the following.

1. A rise in the population shifts the demand curve for carrots to the right as more and more are demanded at each price. This in turn is raising the price of carrots (for reasons we will soon study in detail). This was the first newspaper story.
2. The rising price of carrots is causing each individual consumer to cut back on his or her purchase of carrots. This causes a movement upward to the left along any particular demand curve for carrots. This was the second newspaper story.

To prevent the type of confusion caused by our two newspaper stories, economists have developed a specialized vocabulary to distinguish shifts of curves from movements along curves. **Demand** refers to one *whole* demand curve. **Change in demand** refers to a *shift* in the whole curve, that is, a change in the amount that will be bought at *every* price.

An increase in demand means that the whole demand curve has shifted to the right; a decrease in demand means that the whole demand curve has shifted to the left.

Any one point on a demand curve represents a specific amount being bought at a specified price. It represents, therefore, a particular quantity demanded. A movement along a demand curve is referred to as a **change in the quantity demanded**.[7]

A movement down a demand curve is called an increase (or a rise) in the quantity demanded; a movement up the demand curve is called a decrease (or a fall) in the quantity demanded.

To illustrate this terminology, look again at Table 4.3. First, at the original level of income, a decrease in price from £0.80 to £0.60 increases *the quantity demanded* from 67.5 to 77.5 thousand kilograms a month. Second, the increase in average consumer income *increases demand*

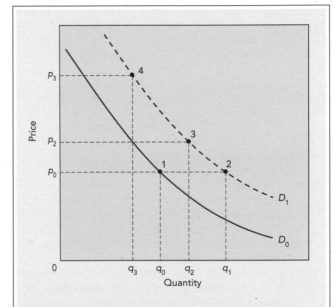

Figure 4.6 Shifts of and movements along the demand curve

A rise in demand means that more will be bought at each price, but it does not mean that more will be bought under all circumstances. The demand curve is originally D_0 and price is p_0, at which q_0 is bought (point 1). Demand then increases to D_1. At the old price of p_0, the quantity demanded is now q_1 (point 2). Next, assume that the price rises to above p_0. This causes quantity demanded to be reduced to below q_1. The net effect of these two shifts can be either an increase or decrease in the quantity demanded. If the price rises to p_2, the quantity demanded of q_2 still exceeds the original quantity q_0 (point 3); while a rise in price to p_3 leaves the final quantity of q_3 (point 4) below the original quantity of q_0.

from what is shown by column (3) to what is shown by column (4). The same contrast is shown in Figure 4.4, where a fall in price from £0.80 to £0.60 increases the quantity demanded from the quantity shown by point x to the quantity shown by point w. An increase in total consumers' income increases demand from curve D_0 to curve D_1.

Figure 4.6 illustrates the combined effect of (1) a rise in demand, and (2) a fall in the quantity demanded. The first of these is shown by a rightward shift in the whole demand curve. The second is shown by a movement upward, along a given demand curve.

[7] Sometimes a movement along a demand curve is referred to as an *expansion* or a *contraction* of demand, an expansion referring to what we have called an increase in the quantity demanded and a contraction to a decrease in the quantity demanded.

Supply

AS with demand, we first need to meet the agents that are responsible for the behaviour we are going to study.

Firms

A **firm** is the agent on the supply side of the theory of market price. It is defined as the unit that employs factors of production to produce products that it sells to other firms, to consumers, or to government. For obvious reasons, a firm is often called a producer. Elementary economic theory gives firms several attributes.

First, each firm is assumed to make consistent decisions, as though it were composed of a single individual. This strand of theory ignores the internal problems of how particular decisions are reached by assuming that the firm's internal organization is irrelevant to its decisions. This allows the firm to be treated, at least in elementary theory, as the individual unit of behaviour on the production or supply side of product markets, just as the consumer is treated as the individual unit of behaviour on the consumption or demand side.[8]

Second, economists assume that, in their role as producers, firms are the principal users of the services of factors of production. In 'factor markets' where factor services are bought and sold, the roles of firms and consumers are thus reversed from what they are in product markets: in factor markets, firms do the buying and consumers do the selling.

Motivation   Economists assume that most firms make their decisions with a single goal in mind: to make as much profit as possible. This goal of *profit maximization* is analogous to the consumer's goal of utility maximization.

The nature of supply

The amount of a product that firms are able and willing to offer for sale is called the **quantity supplied**. Supply is a desired flow: how much firms are willing to sell per period of time, not how much they actually sell.

We make a brief study of supply in this chapter, establishing only what is necessary for a theory of price. In later chapters we study the determinants of supply in some detail. In those chapters we first study the behaviour of individual firms, and then aggregate individual behaviour to obtain the behaviour of market supply. For present purposes, however, it is sufficient to go directly to market supply, the collective behaviour of all the firms in a particular market.

The determinants of quantity supplied: the supply function

Four major determinants of the quantity supplied in a particular market are

1. The price of the product
2. The prices of factors of production
3. The goals of producing firms
4. The state of technology

This list can be summarized in a **supply function**:

$$q_n^s = S(p_n, F_1, \ldots, F_m) ,$$

where q_n^s is the quantity supplied of product n; p_n is the price of that product; $F_1, \ldots, F_m$ is shorthand for the prices of all factors of production; and the goals of producers and the state of technology determine the form of the function S. (Recall, once again, that the form of the function refers to the precise quantitative relation between the variable on the left-hand side and the variables on the right-hand side.)

Supply and price

For a simple theory of price, we need to know how quantity supplied varies with a product's own price, all other things being held constant. We are only concerned, therefore, with the *ceteris paribus* relation, $q_n^s = S(p_n)$. We will have much to say in later chapters about the relation between quantity supplied and price. For the moment, it is sufficient to state the hypothesis that, *ceteris paribus, the quantity of any product that firms will produce and offer for sale is positively related to the product's own price, rising when price rises and falling when price falls.*[9]

The reasons for this relation are fully laid out in Chapter 12. In the meantime, all we need to note is that the costs of increasing output by another unit tend to be higher, the higher is the existing rate of output. So, for example, if the firm is already producing 100 units per week, the cost of increasing output to 101 per week might be £1, while if 200

---

[8] At the more advanced level, many studies look within the firm to ask questions such as: does the firm's internal organization affect its behaviour? We briefly consider such questions in Chapter 17.

[9] As we did with demand, we introduce the relation between price and quantity supplied as an assumption in this chapter. In Chapter 12 we derive it as a prediction from more basic assumptions about the behaviour of firms.

units were already being produced, the cost of increasing output to 201 units might be £2. Clearly, the firm will not find it profitable to increase output if it cannot at least cover the additional costs that are incurred. As the price of the product rises, the firm can increase its output until the cost of producing an additional unit rises to the level where it is just covered by the price at which that unit can be sold. In summary, because the cost of raising output increases the more is being produced already, higher and higher prices are needed to induce firms to make successive increases in output. The result is a positively sloped supply curve indicating that the higher the price the more will be produced. Do not worry if this does not seem obvious; it will become so after Chapter 12 has been studied.

We now extend the numerical example of the carrot market to include the quantity of carrots supplied. The **supply schedule** given in Table 4.4 is analogous to the demand schedule in Table 4.2, but it records the quantities all producers wish to produce and sell at a number of alternative prices, rather than the quantities consumers wish to buy.

Next, the six points corresponding to each price–quantity combination shown in the table are plotted in Figure 4.7. When we draw a smooth curve through the six points, we obtain a **supply curve** for carrots. The curve shows the quantity produced and offered for sale at each price. Since we are not considering individual firms in this chapter, all

Table 4.4 A market supply schedule for carrots

Reference letter	Price (£ per kg)	Quantity demanded ('000 kg per month)
u	0.20	5.0
v	0.40	46.0
w	0.60	77.5
x	0.80	100.0
y	1.00	115.0
z	1.20	122.5

The table shows the quantities that producers wish to sell at various prices, *ceteris paribus*. For example, row *y* indicates that if the price were £1.00 per kilogram, producers would wish to sell 115,000 kg of carrots per month.

supply curves are market curves showing the aggregate behaviour of all firms in the market. Where that is obvious from the context, the adjective 'market' is usually omitted.

The supply curve in Figure 4.7 has a positive slope. This is a graphical expression of the following assumption:

The market price and the quantity supplied are positively related to each other.

SHIFTS IN THE SUPPLY CURVE

A shift in the supply curve means that, at each price, a different quantity will be supplied. An increase in the quantity supplied at each price is illustrated in Table 4.5 and plotted in Figure 4.8. This change appears as a rightward shift in the supply curve. A decrease in the quantity supplied at each price would appear as a leftward shift.

For supply-curve shifts, there is an important general rule similar to the one stated earlier for demand curves:

When there is a change in any of the variables (other than the product's own price) that affect the amount of a product that firms are willing to produce and sell, the whole supply curve for that product will shift.

The major possible causes of such shifts are summarized in the caption of Figure 4.9 and are considered briefly below.

Prices of inputs All things that a firm uses to produce its outputs—such as materials, labour, and machines—are called the firm's *inputs*. Other things being equal, the higher the price of any input used to make a product, the less will be the profit from making that product. Thus, the higher the price of any input used by a firm, the lower will be the amount that the firm will produce and offer for sale at any given price of the product.

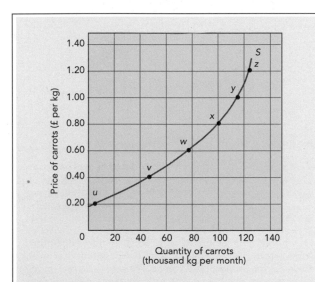

Fig 4.7 A supply curve for carrots

This supply curve relates quantity of carrots supplied to the price of carrots; its positive slope indicates that quantity supplied increases as price increases. The six points correspond to the price–quantity combinations shown in Table 4.4. Each row in the table defines a point on the supply curve. The smooth curve drawn through all of the points, labelled *S*, is the supply curve.

Table 4.5 Two alternative market supply schedules for carrots

	Price of carrots (£ per kg)	Original quantity supplied ('000 kg per month)	New quantity supplied ('000 kg per month)	
(1)	(2)	(3)	(4)	(5)
u	0.20	5	28	u'
v	0.40	46	76	v'
w	0.60	77.5	102	w'
x	0.80	100	120	x'
y	1.00	115	132	y'
z	1.20	122.5	140	z'

An increase in supply means a larger quantity is supplied at each price. For example, the quantity that is supplied at £1.00 per kilogram rises from 115,000 to 132,000 kg per month. A similar rise occurs at every price. Thus, the supply schedule relating columns (2) and (3) is replaced by one relating columns (2) and (4).

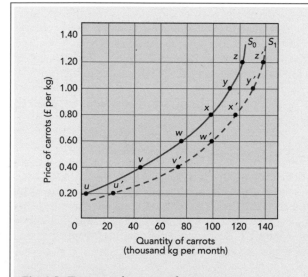

Fig 4.8 Two supply curves for carrots

The rightward shift in the supply curve from S_0 to S_1 indicates an increase in the quantity supplied at each price. The lettered points correspond to those in Table 4.5. A rightward shift in the supply curve indicates an increase in supply in the sense that more carrots are supplied at each price.

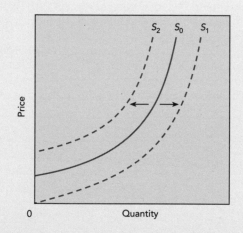

Figure 4.9 Shifts in the supply curve

A shift in the supply curve from S_0 to S_1 indicates an increase in supply; a shift from S_0 to S_2 indicates a decrease in supply. An increase in supply means that more is supplied at each price. Such a rightward shift can be caused by some changes in producers' goals, improvements in technology, or decreases in the costs of inputs that are important in producing the commodity. A decrease in supply means that less is supplied at each price. Such a leftward shift can be caused by some changes in producers' goals, or increases in costs of inputs that are important in producing the commodity.

A rise in the price of any input shifts the supply curve to the left, indicating that less will be supplied at any given price; a fall in the cost of inputs shifts the supply curve to the right.

Goals of the firm   In elementary economic theory, firms are usually assumed to have a single goal: profit maximization. Firms could, however, have other goals, either in addi-

tion to, or as substitutes for, profit maximization. If firms worry about risk, they will pursue safer lines of activity even though these lines promise lower probable profits. If firms value size, they may produce and sell more than the profit-maximizing quantities. If they worry about their image in society, they may forsake highly profitable activities when there is major public disapproval.

As long as firms prefer higher to lower profits, they will respond to changes in the profitabilities of alternative lines of action, and supply curves will have positive slopes. But if the importance that firms give to other goals changes, the supply curve will shift, indicating a changed willingness to supply the quantity at each given price.

Technology At any time, what is produced and how it is produced depends on the technologies in use. Over time, knowledge and production technologies change; so do the quantities of individual products supplied.

A technological change that decreases costs will increase the profits earned at any given price of the product. Since increased profitability leads to increased production, this change shifts the supply curve to the right, indicating an increased willingness to produce the product and offer it for sale at each possible price.

MOVEMENTS ALONG SUPPLY CURVES VERSUS SHIFTS

As with demand, it is essential to distinguish between a movement along the supply curve (caused by a change in the product's own price) and a shift of the whole curve (caused by a change in something other than the product's own price). We adopt the same terminology as with demand: **supply** refers to the whole relation between price and quantity supplied, and quantity supplied refers to a particular quantity actually supplied at a particular price of the product. Thus, when we speak of an *increase* or a *decrease in supply*, we are referring to shifts in the supply curve such as the ones illustrated in Figures 4.8 and 4.9. When we speak of a *change in the quantity supplied*, we mean a movement from one point on the supply curve to another point on the same curve.[10]

The determination of price

SO far, demand and supply have been considered separately. We now come to a key question: how do the two forces of demand and supply interact to determine price in a competitive market?

The concept of a market

Markets are basic concepts in economics. Originally the term designated a physical place where products were bought and sold. Once developed, however, theories of market behaviour were easily extended to cover products such as wheat, which can be purchased anywhere in the world at a price that tends to be uniform the world over. Thus, the concept of 'the wheat market' extends our viewpoint well beyond the idea of a single place to which the consumer goes to buy something.

For present purposes, a **market** may be defined as an area over which buyers and sellers negotiate the exchange of some product or related group of products. It must be possible, therefore, for buyers and sellers to communicate with each other and to make meaningful deals over the whole market.

Individual markets differ in the degree of competition among the various buyers and sellers. In the next few chapters we shall confine ourselves to markets in which the number of buyers and sellers is sufficiently large that no one of them has any appreciable influence on price. This is a very rough definition of what economists call *perfectly competitive markets*. Starting in Chapter 13, we will consider the behaviour of markets that do not meet this competitive requirement.

The graphical analysis of a market

Table 4.6 brings together the demand and supply schedules from Tables 4.2 and 4.4. Figure 4.10 shows both the demand and the supply curves on a single graph; the six points on the demand curve are labelled with upper-case letters, while the six points on the supply curve are labelled with lower-case letters, each letter referring to a common price on both curves.

QUANTITY SUPPLIED AND QUANTITY DEMANDED AT VARIOUS PRICES

Consider first the point at which the two curves in figure

---

[10] As with demand, an alternative terminology refers to an increase in the quantity supplied as an **expansion of supply** and a reduction in the quantity supplied as a **contraction of supply**.

Table 4.6 Demand and supply schedules for carrots and equilibrium price

Price per kg (£)	Quantity demanded ('000 kg per month)	Quantity supplied ('000 kg per month)	Excess demand (quantity demanded minus quantity supplied) ('000 kg per month)
0.20	110.0	5.0	105.0
0.40	90.0	46.0	44.0
0.60	**77.5**	**77.5**	**0.0**
0.80	67.5	100.0	−32.5
1.00	62.5	115.0	−52.5
1.20	60.0	122.5	−62.5

Equilibrium occurs where quantity demanded equals quantity supplied so that there is neither excess demand nor excess supply. These schedules are repeated from Tables 4.2 and 4.4. The equilibrium price is £0.60. For lower prices, there is excess demand; for higher prices, there is excess supply, which is shown as negative excess demand.

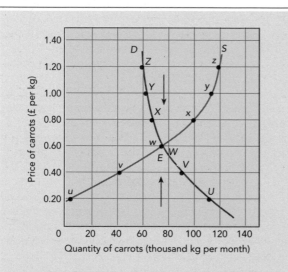

Figure 4.10 Determination of the equilibrium price of carrots

The equilibrium price corresponds to the intersection of the demand and supply curves. Point *E* indicates the equilibrium. At a price of £60, quantity demanded (point *W*) equals quantity supplied (point *w*). At prices above equilibrium, there is excess supply and downward pressure on price. At prices below equilibrium, there is excess demand and upward pressure on price. The pressures on price are represented by the vertical arrows.

4.10 intersect. Both the figure and Table 4.6 show that the market price is £0.60, the quantity demanded is 77.5 thousand kilograms, and the quantity supplied is the same. At that price consumers wish to buy exactly the same amount as producers wish to sell. Provided that the demand curve is negatively sloped and the supply curve positively sloped throughout their entire ranges, there will be no other price at which the quantity demanded equals the quantity supplied.

Now, consider prices below £0.60. At these prices, consumers' desired purchases exceed producers' desired sales. It is easily seen, and you should again check one or two examples, that, at all prices below £0.60, the quantity demanded exceeds the quantity supplied. Furthermore, the lower the price, the larger the excess of the one over the other. The amount by which the quantity demanded exceeds the quantity supplied is called the **excess demand**, which is defined as quantity demanded *minus* quantity supplied ($q^d - q^s$). This is shown in the last column of Table 4.6.

Finally, consider prices higher than £0.60. At these prices consumers wish to buy less than producers wish to sell. Thus, quantity supplied exceeds quantity demanded. It is easily seen, and again you should check a few examples, that, for any price above £0.60, quantity supplied exceeds quantity demanded. Furthermore, the higher the price, the larger the excess of the one over the other. In this case there is negative excess demand ($q^d - q^s < 0$). This is also shown in the last column of Table 4.6.

Note that negative excess demand is usually referred to as **excess supply**, which measures the amount by which supply exceeds demand ($q^s - q^d$).

CHANGES IN PRICE WHEN QUANTITY DEMANDED DOES NOT EQUAL QUANTITY SUPPLIED

Where there is excess demand, consumers will be unable to buy all they wish to buy; when there is excess supply, firms will be unable to sell all they wish to sell. In both cases some people will not be able to do what they would like to do, and we might expect some action to be taken as a result.

To develop a theory about how the market does behave in the face of excess demand or excess supply, we now make two further assumptions. First, we assume that, *when there is excess supply, the market price will fall.* Producers, unable to sell some of their goods, may begin to offer to sell them at lower prices; purchasers, observing the glut of unsold output, may begin to offer lower prices. For either or both of these reasons, the price will fall.

Second, we assume that, *when there is excess demand, market price will rise.* Individual consumers, unable to buy as much as they would like to buy, may offer higher prices in an effort to get more of the available goods for themselves; suppliers, who could sell more than their total production, may begin to ask higher prices for the quantities that they have produced. For either or both of these reasons, prices will rise.

THE EQUILIBRIUM PRICE

For any price above £0.60, according to our theory, the price tends to fall; for any price below £0.60, the price tends to rise. At a price of £0.60, there is neither excess demand creating a shortage, nor excess supply creating a glut; quantity supplied is equal to quantity demanded and there is no tendency for the price to change. The price of £0.60, where the supply and demand curves intersect, is the price towards which the actual market price will tend. It is called the **equilibrium price**: the price at which quantity demanded equals quantity supplied. The amount that is bought and sold at the equilibrium price is called the **equilibrium quantity**. The term 'equilibrium' means a state of balance; it occurs when desired purchases equal desired sales.

When quantity demanded equals quantity supplied, we say that the market is in **equilibrium**. When quantity demanded does not equal quantity supplied we say that the market is in **disequilibrium**. We may now summarize our theory.

Assumptions concerning a competitive market:

1. All demand curves have negative slopes throughout their entire range.

2. All supply curves have positive slopes throughout their entire range.

3. Prices change if, and only if, there is excess demand; rising if excess demand is positive and falling if excess demand is negative.

Implications:

1. There is no more than one price at which quantity demanded equals quantity supplied: equilibrium is unique.

2. Only at the equilibrium price will the market price be constant.

3. If either the demand or the supply curve shifts, the equilibrium price and quantity will change.

The laws of demand and supply

Earlier in this chapter, we studied shifts in demand and supply curves. Recall that a rightward shift in the relevant curve means that more is demanded or supplied *at each market price*, while a leftward shift means that less is demanded or supplied *at each market price*. How does a shift in either curve affect price and quantity?

The answers to this question are called the 'laws' of supply and demand. Each of the laws summarizes what happens when an initial position of equilibrium is upset by some shift in either the demand or the supply curve, and a new equilibrium position is then established. The sense in which it is correct to call these propositions 'laws' is discussed in Box 4.1.

To discover the effects of each of the curve shifts that we wish to study, we use the method known as **comparative statics.**[11] We start from a position of equilibrium and then introduce the change to be studied. The new equilibrium position is determined and compared with the original one. The differences between the two positions of equilibrium must result from the change that was introduced, for everything else has been held constant.

The four laws of demand and supply are derived in Figure 4.11, the caption of which must be carefully studied. The analysis of that figure generalizes our specific discussion about carrots. Because it is intended to apply to any product, the horizontal axis is simply labelled 'quantity' and the vertical axis 'price'.

The laws of supply and demand are:

1. A rise in the demand for a product (a rightward shift of the demand curve) causes an increase in both the equilibrium price and the equilibrium quantity bought and sold.

2. A fall in the demand for a product (a leftward shift of the demand curve) causes a decrease in both the equilibrium price and the equilibrium quantity bought and sold.

3. A rise in the supply of a product (a rightward shift of the supply curve) causes a decrease in the equilibrium price and an increase in the equilibrium quantity bought and sold.

4. A fall in the supply of a product (a leftward shift of the supply curve) causes an increase in the equilibrium price and a decrease in the equilibrium quantity bought and sold.

The Appendix to this chapter provides an algebraic treatment to finding equilibrium prices and quantities and to deriving these four laws of supply and demand.

---

[11] The term 'static' is used because we are not concerned about the actual path by which the market goes from the first equilibrium position to the second. Analysis of that path would be described as *dynamic analysis.*

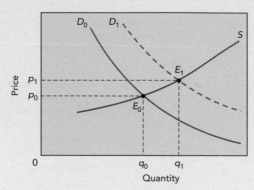
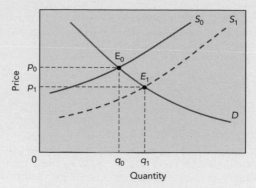

(i) The effect of shifts in the demand curve

(ii) The effect of shifts in the supply curve

Figure 4.11   The 'laws' of demand and supply

The effects on equilibrium price and quantity of shifts in either demand or supply are called the laws of demand and supply. *An increase in demand.* In part (i), assume that the original demand and supply curves are D_0 and S, which intersect to produce equilibrium at E_0, with a price of p_0 and a quantity of q_0. An increase in demand shifts the demand curve to D_1, taking the new equilibrium to E_1. Price rises to p_1 and quantity rises to q_1.
A decrease in demand. In part (i), assume that the original demand and supply curves are D_1 and S, which intersect to produce equilibrium at E_1, with a price of p_1 and a quantity of q_1. A decrease in demand shifts the demand curve to D_0, taking the new equilibrium to E_0. Price falls to p_0 and quantity falls to q_0.
An increase in supply. In part (ii), assume that the original demand and supply curves are D and S_0, which intersect to produce an equilibrium at E_0, with a price of p_0 and a quantity of q_0. An increase in supply shifts the supply curve to S_1, taking the new equilibrium to E_1. Price falls to p_1 and quantity rises to q_1.
A decrease in supply. In part (ii), assume that the original demand and supply curves are D and S_1, which intersect to produce an equilibrium at E_1, with a price of p_1 and a quantity of q_1. A decrease in supply shifts the supply curve to S_0, taking the new equilibrium to E_0. Price rises to p_0, and quantity falls to q_0.

In Figures 4.5 and 4.9 we summarized the many events that cause demand and supply curves to shift. Using the four 'laws' derived in Figure 4.11, we can understand the link between these events and changes in market prices and quantities. To take one example, a rise in the price of butter will lead to an increase in both the price of margarine and the quantity bought (because a rise in the price of one product causes a rightward shift in the demand curves for its substitutes, and 'law' 1 tells us that such a shift causes price and quantity to increase).

We shall see in subsequent chapters that the theory of the determination of price by demand and supply is beautiful in its simplicity and yet powerful in its range of applications. In the meantime, Box 4.2 suggests some simple applications.

Prices in inflation

Up to now we have developed the theory of the prices of individual products under the assumption that all other prices remain constant. Does this mean that the theory is inapplicable during an inflationary period when almost all prices are rising? Fortunately, the answer is no.

We have mentioned several times that what matters for demand and supply is the price of the product in question relative to the prices of other products. The price of the product expressed in money terms is called its **money price** or its **absolute price**; the price of a product expressed as a relation to other prices is called a **relative price**.

In an inflationary world, a product's relative price can be measured by changes in the product's own price relative to changes in the average of all other prices, which is called the *general price level*. If, during a period when the general price level rose by 40 per cent, the price of oranges rose by 60 per cent, then the price of oranges rose relative to the price level as a whole. Oranges became *relatively* expensive. However, if the price of oranges had risen by only 30 per cent when the general price level had risen by 40 per cent, then their relative price would have fallen. Although the money price of oranges rose, oranges became *relatively* cheap.

In Lewis Carroll's famous story *Through the Looking Glass*, Alice finds a country where everyone has to run in order to stay still. So it is with inflation. A product's price

BOX 4.1

The 'laws' of demand and supply

As with all theories, the implications of the theory of demand and supply may be looked at in two quite distinct ways. First, they are logical deductions from a set of assumptions about behaviour. When we consider the truth of the implications, we are concerned with whether or not they are logically correct deductions. If we discovered that we made mistakes in our reasoning process, then we would conclude that the alleged implications are false in the sense that they do not follow from the assumptions of the theory. Second, the implications are predictions about real-world events. When we consider the truth of the implications, we are concerned with whether or not they are empirically correct. If one or more of the assumptions are empirically incorrect, the predictions of the theory are likely to be found to be at variance with the facts. In this case, we would conclude that the predictions are false in the sense that they are contradicted by real-world observations.

Consider an example. The sentence '*If* the demand curve for cars is negatively sloped, and *if* the supply curve is positively sloped, *then* an increase in demand for cars will raise their equilibrium price' is logically correct in the sense that the 'then' statement follows logically from the two 'if' statements. The single statement 'A rise in the demand for motor cars will increase the price of motor cars' is one that may or may not be empirically true. If any one of the assumptions of the theory is not empirically correct for motor cars, the statement may be found to be empirically false, even though it is a correct logical deduction from the theory's assumptions. If, for example, the

market for cars does not respond to excess demand with a rise in price, the statement may be empirically false: even though a rise in demand for motor cars does create excess demand, market price will not rise.

Economists are concerned with developing implications that are correct in both senses: that they follow logically from the assumptions of a theory, and that they are factually correct.

Use of the term 'laws' in the popular phrase 'the laws of supply and demand' implies that the four implications have been shown to be true in the empirical sense. We must remember, however, that these 'laws' are nothing more than predictions that are always open to testing. There is considerable evidence that the predictions are consistent with the facts in many markets. In other markets, especially those for durable consumer goods such as cars and TV sets, it is not so clear that they are fully consistent with all relevant empirical observations.

Strictly, the theory of demand and supply applies only to cases in which no single buyer or seller has any influence over the market price. In Chapter 6, however, we will learn to extend demand and supply analysis to situations in which those price-taking assumptions are not true for suppliers. The theory may still generate useful predictions, but the proof of the value of these extensions is an empirical one: does the theory generate predictions that agree with the facts?

must rise as fast as the general level of prices just to keep its relative price constant.

It has been convenient in this chapter to analyse a change in a particular price in the context of a constant price level. The analysis is easily extended, however, to an inflationary period by remembering that any force that raises the price of one product when other prices remain constant will, given general inflation, raise the price of that product relative to all other prices. Consider the example of a change in tastes in favour of carrots that would raise their price by 20 per cent when other prices were constant. If, however, the

general price level goes up by 10 per cent, then the price of carrots will rise by 32 per cent.[12] In each case the price of carrots rises 20 per cent *relative to the average of all prices*.

In price theory, whenever we talk of a change in the price of one product, we mean a change relative to the general price level.

[12] Let the price level be 100 in the first case and 110 in the second. Let the price of carrots be 120 in the first case and x in the second. To preserve the same relative price, we need x such that $120/100 = x/110$, which makes $x = 132$.

Individual markets, sectors, and the economy

IN this final section, we start with the concept of an economy as a whole and then consider various subdivisions of the economy, which are called *sectors*.

The concept of an economy

An **economy** is a rather loosely defined term for any broad

---

BOX 4.2

Demand and supply: what really happens

'The theory of supply and demand is neat enough,' said the sceptic, 'but tell me what really happens.'

'What really happens,' said the economist, 'is that demand curves have negative slopes; supply curves have positive slopes; prices rise in response to excess demand and fall in response to excess supply.'

'But that's theory,' insisted the sceptic. 'What about reality?'

'That is reality as well,' said the economist.

'Show me,' said the sceptic.

The economist produced the following passages from the press:

How deep is the art market's recession? . . . in today's unforgiving economic climate, the sales of contemporary, impressionist and modern works of art took hits at this week's auctions. Sales totalled just under £60 million compared with £500 million just one year ago. Many paintings on offer went unsold, and those that did sell went for well under their predicted price.

Coffee prices at the London Commodity Exchange staged another spectacular rise, putting them above their level at the start of the year. . . . Mr Barbosa (President of the Association of Coffee Producing Countries) said that the supply shortages that are underpinning prices would last quite some time.

Japan's six leading electronics companies plan to increase investment in semiconductor making capacity by 15.3 per cent to a combined ¥461 billion (£2.93 billion) in the year to March 1995 in response to a surge in demand for personal computers in the United States and Japan.

Increased demand for macadamia nuts causes price to rise above competing nuts. A major producer now plans to double the size of its orchards during the next five years.

OPEC countries once again fail to agree on output quotas. Output soars and prices plummet.

Fish which were once the poor people's staple in Mediterranean countries are now eaten almost exclusively by rich tourists. Over-fishing is blamed.

The effects of [the first year of] deregulation of US airlines were spectacular: cuts in air fares of up to 70 per cent in some cases, record passenger jam-ups at the airports, and a spectacular increase in the average load factor [the proportion of occupied seats on the average commercial flight].

The sceptic's response is not recorded, but you should be able to tell which clippings illustrate which of the economist's four statements about 'what really happens'.

---

collection of interrelated productive activities. It may refer to productive activity in a region of one country, such as *the economy of eastern Canada*; it may refer to one country, such as *the UK economy*, or it may refer to a group of countries, such as *the economy of Western Europe.*

A typical economy consists of thousands and thousands of markets. There are markets for wheat, strawberries, steel, cement, coal, oil, new cars, used cars, TVs, shirts, skis, compact discs, haircuts, video rentals, air travel, financial consulting, accounting services, consumer loans, mortgages, foreign currencies, and the myriad other goods and services that are found in a modern economy. Each is produced and sold in its own individual market.

Goods and factor markets

For many purposes, it is useful to group these markets into two types. **Goods markets** are those where goods and services are bought and sold.[13] The sellers in such markets are usually firms; the buyers may be consumers, other firms, or the central authorities. **Factor markets** are those where factor services are bought and sold. The sellers in such markets are the owners of factors of production (usually individuals, but sometimes firms); the buyers are usually firms and governments. As we shall see many times throughout this book, demand and supply analysis helps us to understand the operation of both goods markets and factor markets. The latter determine how much we earn, while the former determine how much our income will buy.

Relations among markets

Although each of the individual markets referred to above is distinct, all are interrelated and we need to see why.

[13] Since these markets include both goods and services, it might seem better to refer to them as *commodity markets*. Unfortunately, this term is in common use in the business world to refer to markets where basic commodities such as rubber, tin, and jute are sold. To avoid confusion, economists often speak of 'goods markets' where, in their own terminology, 'commodity markets' would be better.

The Separation of Individual Markets Markets are separated from each other by the product sold, by natural economic barriers, and by barriers created by the governments. To illustrate, consider one example of each type of separation. First, the market for men's shirts is different from the market for refrigerators because different products are sold in each. Second, the market for cement in the United Kingdom is distinct from the market for cement in the western United States. The costs of transporting cement are so high that UK purchasers would not buy American cement even if its market price in the western United States were very much lower than its market price in Britain. Third, the market for textiles is separated among many countries since government-imposed quotas severely limit the amount that firms in one country can sell to consumers in another.

Because markets are distinct, we can use demand and supply analysis to study the behaviour of markets one at a time, as we have done in this chapter and will do in much more detail in Chapter 6.

The interlinking of individual markets Although all markets are to some extent separated, most are also interrelated. Consider again the three causes of market separation: different products, spatial separation, and government intervention. First, the markets for different kinds of products are interrelated because all products compete for consumers' income. Thus, if more is spent in one market, less will be available to spend in other markets. Second, the geographical separation of markets for similar products depends on transport costs. Products whose transport costs are high relative to their production costs tend to be produced and sold in geographically distinct markets. Products whose transport costs are low relative to their production costs tend to be sold in what amounts to one world market. But whatever the transport costs, there will be some price differential at which it will pay someone to buy in the low-priced market and ship to the high-priced one. Thus, there is always some potential link between geographically distinct markets, even when shipping costs are high. Third, markets are often separated by policy-induced barriers, such as tariffs (which are taxes paid when goods come into a country from abroad). Although high tariffs tend to separate markets, they do not do so completely because, if price differences become large enough, it will pay buyers in the high-cost market to import from the low-cost one and producers in the low-cost market to export to the high-cost one, even though they have to pay the tariff as a result.

Because markets are interrelated, we must treat them as a single interrelated system for many purposes. *General equilibrium analysis* studies markets as such a system in which demands and supplies depend on all prices, and what happens in any one market will affect many other markets—and in principle could affect all other markets.

Sectors of an economy

Markets are often conceptually aggregated into various groups called *sectors*. Each of these is an aggregation of the individual markets contained within it. Three of the most common types of aggregation are used to distinguish: various physical types of production, the public and private sectors, and the marketed and non-marketed sectors.

Types of production It is often useful to aggregate the production that passes through the nation's markets into various types. One broad classification divides primary, secondary, and tertiary. *Primary* consists of all economic activity that is a first step in the productive process, i.e. the harvesting of the natural resources of the world, especially agricultural crops and minerals, and sources of energy such as coal oil and natural gas. These provide foodstuffs, basic raw materials, and power on which other production depends. *Secondary* production is concerned with the later stages in the production of finished goods. It comprises all of manufacturing and construction. The *tertiary* sector covers the production of all services, such as transport, entertainment, personal services, commerce, retailing, government, finance, and professions.

The overall sizes of these three broad sectors as well as the details for the manufacturing sector are given in Box 4.3.

The public and private sectors The productive activity of a country is often aggregated in a different way to obtain the private and the public sectors. The **private sector** refers to all production that is in private hands; the **public sector** refers to all production that is in public hands. The distinction between the two sectors depends on the legal distinction of ownership. In the private sector, the organization that does the producing is owned by individuals or other firms; in the public sector, it is owned by the state. The public sector includes all production of goods and services by government agencies, plus all production by nationalized industries that is sold to consumers through ordinary markets.

In both the public and the private sectors, demand and supply analysis is useful. For example, whether privately or publicly owned, the consequences of pricing a product at a price that differs from the equilibrium value will be the same—excess demand or excess supply. Furthermore, both publicly and privately owned firms in secondary industries must usually buy their primary products in competitive markets. Both will suffer similar consequences if alterations in the market conditions cause large changes in primary product prices.

Market and non-market sectors The third type of aggregate which we consider distinguishes the two basic ways in which products may pass from those who make them to those who use them. First, products may be sold by pro-

BOX 4.3

Size of production sectors

The charts show the relative sizes of some UK sectors classified by types of production. In these charts size is gauged by employment, not value of output. The left-hand pie shows that primary production—agriculture, mining, fishing, energy, and water production—is a small sector. The secondary sector—manufacturing and construction—although much larger, is still small (at least in terms of employment) relative to the tertiary sector.

The middle bar shows the relative employment of the major UK industries across all three of these sectors. While manufacturing is one of the largest single sectors, it only accounts for about 20 per cent of all employment—down from figures in the mid-30s which were typical of the first eight decades of the twentieth century.

The right-hand pie shows the relative sizes of the various manufacturing industries. Engineering is the largest manufacturing industry, employing one in every four factory workers. Food, drink, and tobacco, paper and printing, and vehicles (including shipbuilding) are the next largest groups. Together with engineering, these industries account for the employment of well over half the manufacturing work-force. Among others, chemicals, metal goods (a miscellaneous category including tools, cutlery, and metal containers), clothing, timber and furniture, textiles, and metal manufacture (mainly iron and steel) are sufficiently important to be separately distinguished.

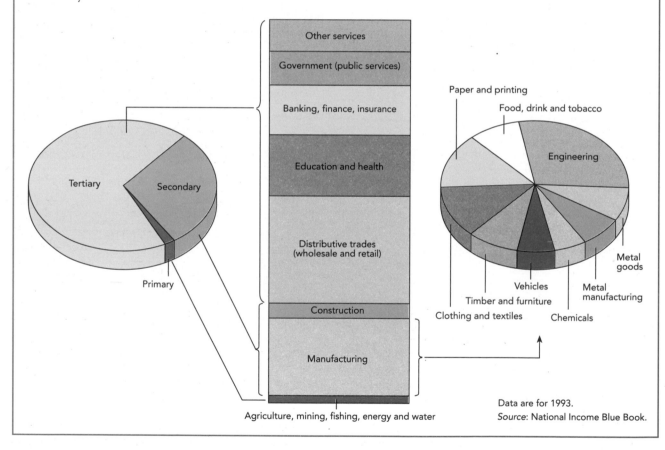

Data are for 1993.
Source: National Income Blue Book.

ducers and bought by consumers. When this happens, the producers must cover their costs by the revenues they obtain from the sale of the product. Such production is called *marketed production,* and this part of the country's activity belongs to the **market sector**. Second, the product

may be given away. In this case the costs of production must be covered by some means other than sales revenues. This production is called *non-marketed production* and belongs to the **non-market sector**. In the case of private charities, the money required to pay for factor services may be raised from the public by voluntary subscriptions. In the case of production by the government—which accounts for the great bulk of non-marketed production—the money is provided from government revenue, which in turn comes mainly from taxes levied on firms and consumers. Government production is discussed in Chapter 42.

Supply and demand analysis is directly applicable to marketed goods whose prices tend to fluctuate with changing market conditions. It is also useful, although in less obvious ways, in studying non-market production. For instance, if a good is supplied free of charge, the quantity demanded will be determined at the point where the demand curve cuts the quantity axis. If the government is unwilling to supply everything that is demanded at that price, as is often the case, then the government must find some way of rationing the supply that it does make available—since price is prevented from doing this job.

Whatever the market in which we are interested, whatever the level of aggregation that we wish to study, and whatever the method by which production is financed, the theory of market price is an invaluable tool. Eventually, we will need to expand our theory to consider new situations—particularly where there are only a few buyers or sellers. But, as we shall soon see, we can understand much economic behaviour, and make sense of much seemingly peculiar behaviour, using nothing more than the simple theoretical tools now at our command—plus just one more: the concept of elasticity, which we study in the next chapter.

Summary

1 The decision-taking units in economic theory are: (*a*) individuals, for demand in goods markets and for supply in factor markets; (*b*) firms, for supply in goods markets and demand in factor markets; and (*c*) governments, for supply of some goods and for regulation and control of the private sector (see Chapter 6). Given the resources at their command, each individual is assumed to maximize his or her satisfaction, and each firm is assumed to maximize its profit.

2 An individual consumer's demand curve shows the relation between the price of a product and the quantity of that product the consumer wishes to purchase per period of time. It is drawn on the assumption that all other prices, income, and tastes remain constant. Its negative slope indicates that the lower the price of the product, the more the consumer wishes to purchase.

3 The market demand curve is the horizontal sum of the demand curves of all the individual consumers. The demand curve for a normal good shifts to the right when the price of a substitute rises, or when the price of a complement falls, total income rises, the distribution of income changes in favour of those with large demands for the product, or tastes change in favour of the product. It shifts to the left with the opposite changes.

4 A movement along a demand curve indicates a change in quantity demanded in response to a change in the product's own price; a shift in a demand curve indicates a change in the quantity demanded at each price in response to a change in one of the conditions held constant along a demand curve.

5 The supply curve for a product shows the relationship between its price and the quantity of it that producers wish to produce and offer for sale per period of time. It is drawn on the assumption that all other forces that influence quantity supplied remain constant, and its positive slope indicates that the higher the price, the more producers wish to sell.

6 A supply curve shifts in response to changes in the prices of the inputs used by producers, and to changes in technology. The shift represents a change in the amount supplied at each price. A movement along a supply curve indicates that a different quantity is being supplied in response to a change in the product's own price.

7 At the *equilibrium price* the quantity demanded equals the quantity supplied. Graphically, equilibrium occurs where the demand and the supply curves intersect. At any price below equilibrium there will be excess demand and price will tend to rise; at any price above equilibrium there will be excess supply and price will tend to fall.

8 A rise in demand raises both equilibrium price and quantity; a fall in demand lowers both. A rise in supply raises equilibrium quantity but lowers equilibrium price; a fall in supply lowers equilibrium quantity but raises equilibrium price. These are the so-called 'laws' of supply and demand.

9 Price theory is most simply developed in the context of a constant price level. Price changes discussed in the theory are changes relative to the average level of all prices. In an inflationary period, a rise in the *relative price* of one product means that its price rises by more than the rise in the general price level; a fall in its relative price means that its price rises by less than the rise in the general price level.

10   Individual markets are partially separated from each other because different products are sold in each, and because of barriers to the movement of products among markets such as transport costs (a natural barrier) and tariffs (a policy-induced barrier). In spite of a substantial degree of separation, most individual markets are more or less interlinked.

11   For various types of study, data for individual markets are aggregated into sectors. Examples are primary, secondary, and tertiary, a distinction depending on the types of goods produced; private and public sectors, a distinction depending on ownership; and market and non-market, a distinction depending on whether or not the costs of producing products are recovered by selling them to their users.

Topics for review

- Quantity demanded and the demand function
- The demand schedule and the demand curve for an individual and for the market
- Shifts in the demand curve and movements along the curve
- Substitutes and complements
- Quantity supplied and the supply function
- The supply schedule and the supply curve
- Shifts in the supply curve and movements along the curve
- Excess demand and excess supply
- Equilibrium and disequilibrium prices
- The 'laws' of demand and supply
- Money prices and relative prices
- Goods and factor markets
- Sectors of the economy

APPENDIX TO CHAPTER 4

An algebraic treatment of demand and supply theory

WE observed in Chapter 3 that economic reasoning could be conducted using words, geometry, or mathematics, the comparative advantage of mathematics growing enormously as the theory becomes more complex. The interchangeability between geometric and algebraic treatments is clearly visible in the theory of the determination of price by demand and supply. This theory is composed of a system of three equations, one for the demand curve, one for the supply curve, and one for the condition that quantity demanded should equal quantity supplied. The first two are called behavioural relations and the third, an equilibrium condition.

In the text we have used a geometric approach. If we are willing to assume that these curves are linear, we can handle them using simple algebra.

A numerical example

First, consider a simple numerical example:

$$q^d = 100 - 2p \qquad (1)$$
$$q^s = 3p \qquad (2)$$
$$q^d = q^s \qquad (3)$$

Equation (1) is an example of a linear demand curve in which 100 units are consumed at a zero price and quantity falls by 2 units for every one unit increase in price. Equation (2) is an example of a linear supply curve in which quantity supplied starts at zero and rises by 3 units for every one-unit increase in price. These are the behavioural equations. Equation (3) expresses the equilibrium condition that quantity demanded should equal quantity supplied. We solve the system by substituting (1) and (2) into (3):

$$100 - 2p = 3p$$

or

$$5p = 100$$

or

$$p = 20$$

and substituting the equilibrium price into (1) and (2) tells us that $q^d = q^s = 60$.

If we let the demand curve shift to the right so that 60 more units are bought at each price, (1) becomes

$$q^d = 160 - 2p. \qquad (1')$$

Substituting (1') and (2) into (3) yields $p = 32$ and $q^d = q^s = 96$.

This is an elementary example of comparative statics, whereby we show that in the market under consideration a rightward shift in the demand curve by 60 units increases price by 12 and quantity by 36.

A general solution to the linear system

We could solve the equations every time we have a specific example. Algebra allows us, however, to find the solution to any linear demand–supply system once and for all. To do this, we substitute letters, called *parameters,* for the numbers in the above system:

$$q^d = a + bp \qquad a > 0, 0 < b \qquad (4)$$
$$q^s = c + dp \qquad c < a, d > 0 \qquad (5)$$
$$q^d = q^s. \qquad (6)$$

The restrictions on the parameters ensure that a positive amount is demanded at a zero price ($a > 0$), that the demand curve has a negative slope ($b < 0$), and the supply curve has a positive slope ($d > 0$). The restriction on c is a little more complex. If c is less than zero a positive price is required to call forth any supply, while if c exceeds zero some amount is supplied at a zero price. In that case, we need less to be supplied than demanded at a zero price ($c < a$) if we are to get a positive equilibrium price. If $c > a$, supply exceeds demand at zero price and the linear model solves for a negative price. To avoid this, we need the added condition that $p = 0$ *whenever c > a.*

Once again, we solve by substituting the behavioural equations (4) and (5) into the equilibrium condition (6). This gives $a + bp = c + dp$. Simple manipulation produces

$$p = \frac{a-c}{d-b}. \qquad (7)$$

Now, whenever we encounter a numerical example, we can substitute the numbers directly into (7) and obtain the answer. You should check that substituting into (7) the values $a = 100$, $b = -2$, $c = 0$, and $d = 3$ from the above numerical example gives the result we obtained earlier.

Equation (7) also allows us to prove the laws of demand as they relate to price for any linear system. If you know calculus, you can differentiate p with respect to a and to c to find out what happens to price when either the demand or the supply curve shifts. If you do not know calculus, you can accomplish the same thing by first-differencing equation (7). (If this procedure bothers you, see the discussion of first-differencing on p. 54 in the Appendix to Chapter 3.) We write (7) out in full as

$$p = \frac{a}{d-b} - \frac{c}{d-b}$$

and first-difference it to get

$$\Delta p = \frac{\Delta a}{d-b} - \frac{\Delta c}{d-b}. \qquad (8)$$

Now all we need to do is to check the sign of $d - b$. We know from our initial restrictions that d, the slope of the supply curve, is positive and b, the slope of the demand curve, is negative, so $d - b > 0$. It follows immediately that a rightward shift in the demand curve ($\Delta a > 0$) raises price while a rightward shift in the supply curve ($\Delta c > 0$) lowers price.

The generalizing power of even very simple mathematics is readily apparent from this example. If you have read this far, you should try to prove for yourself the laws of demand with respect to quantity. This requires you to get an explicit expression, parallel to (7), for the equilibrium quantity.

∿ CHAPTER 5

Elasticity of demand and supply

N this chapter, we develop and apply measures of the responses of the quantity demanded and the quantity supplied to changes in the variables that determine them, particularly prices and incomes. These measures are called *elasticities*, and we need to learn how to calculate and interpret them.

To illustrate why we want to have such a measure, consider the effects of a new government subsidy on each kilogram of carrots grown. This will shift the supply curve of carrots to the right because more will be produced at each price. If the demand for carrots is as shown in part (i) of Figure 5.1, the effect of the government's policy will be to reduce carrot prices slightly, while greatly increasing the quantity grown and consumed. If, however, the demand is as shown in part (ii) of Figure 5.1, the effect of the policy will be to reduce carrot prices greatly but to increase carrot

production and consumption by only a small amount. If the purpose of the subsidy is to increase the quantity that is produced and consumed, then the policy will be a great success when the demand curve is similar to the one shown in part (i), but a failure when the demand curve is similar to that shown in part (ii). If, however, the main purpose of the subsidy is to achieve a large reduction in the price of carrots, the policy will be a failure when demand is as shown in part (i) but a great success when demand is as shown in part (ii).

This example illustrates that it is often not enough to know whether quantity rises or falls in response to some changes; it may be important to know by how much. To measure this in a useful way, we use the concept of *elasticity*.

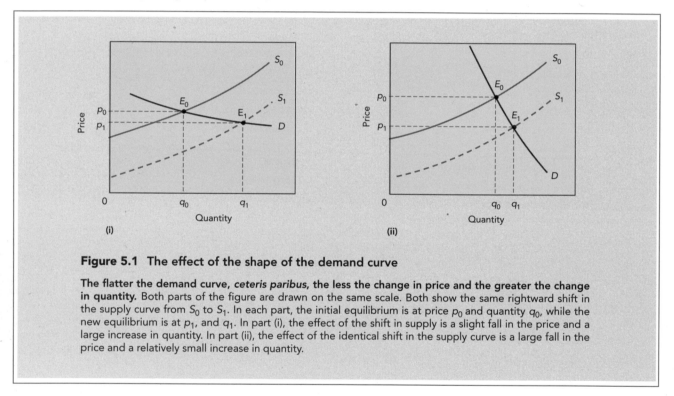

Figure 5.1 The effect of the shape of the demand curve

The flatter the demand curve, *ceteris paribus*, the less the change in price and the greater the change in quantity. Both parts of the figure are drawn on the same scale. Both show the same rightward shift in the supply curve from S_0 to S_1. In each part, the initial equilibrium is at price p_0 and quantity q_0, while the new equilibrium is at p_1, and q_1. In part (i), the effect of the shift in supply is a slight fall in the price and a large increase in quantity. In part (ii), the effect of the identical shift in the supply curve is a large fall in the price and a relatively small increase in quantity.

Demand elasticity

N the first part of this chapter, we deal with quantity demanded and start by considering its response to changes in the product's own price.

Price elasticity of demand

The degree to which quantity demanded responds to

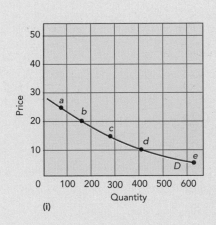
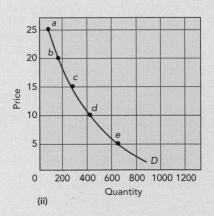

Figure 5.2 The same demand curve drawn on two different scales

Suitable choice of scale can make any demand curve appear steep or flat. The curves in parts (i) and (ii) are the same demand curve, as can easily be checked by noting that each lettered point in part (ii) measures the same price–quantity relation as part (i). Because the same distance on the quantity axes stands for twice as much in part (ii) as in part (i), and the same distance on the price axes stands for half as much, the curve is steeper when plotted in graph (ii) than when plotted in graph (i).

changes in the product's own price is called the *responsiveness of demand*. Sometimes we wish to know how the responsiveness of one product changes over time, or we may wish to compare the responsiveness of several products or several alternative demand curves for one product. In Figure 5.1, we were able to compare the responsiveness of quantity demanded along the two demand curves because they were drawn on the same scale. But you should not try to compare two curves without making sure that the scales are the same. Also, you must not leap to conclusions about responsiveness of quantity demanded on the basis of the apparent steepness of a single curve. The hazards of so doing are illustrated in Figure 5.2. Both parts of the figure plot the same demand curve, but the choice of scale on the 'Quantity' axis serves to make one curve look steep and the other flat.

MEASURING THE RESPONSIVENESS OF DEMAND TO PRICE

In order to get a measure of responsiveness that is independent of the scale we use, and that can be compared across products, we need to deal in percentage changes. A given percentage change in the quantity of carrots will be the same whether we measure it in tonnes, kilograms, or pounds. Similarly, although we cannot easily compare the absolute changes in tonnes of carrots and barrels of oil, we can compare their two percentage changes.

These considerations lead us to the concept of the **price elasticity of demand**, which is defined as the percentage change in quantity demanded *divided by* the percentage change in price that brought it about.[1] This elasticity is usually symbolized by the Greek letter eta, η:

$$\eta = \frac{\text{percentage change in quantity demanded}}{\text{percentage change in price}}. \quad (1)$$

Many different elasticities are used in economics. To distinguish η from the others, the full term 'price elasticity of demand' can be used. Since η is by far the most commonly used elasticity, economists often drop the adjective 'price' and refer to it merely as *elasticity of demand*, or sometimes just *elasticity*. When more than one kind of elasticity could be involved, however, η should be given its full title.

The sign of the measure Because of the negative slope of the demand curve, the price and the quantity will always change in opposite directions. One change will be positive and the other negative, making the measured elasticity of demand negative. This would pose no problem except for two unfortunate habits of economists. First, sometimes, either by carelessness or by design, the minus sign is dropped and elasticity is reported as a positive number.

---

[1] Elasticity is an example of what mathematicians call a *pure number*, which is a number whose value is independent of the units in which it is calculated. Slope, $\Delta p / \Delta q$, is not a pure number. For example, if price is measured in pence, $\Delta p / \Delta q$ will be 100 times as large as $\Delta p / \Delta q$ along the same demand curve where price is measured in pounds sterling.

Table 5.1   Calculation of two demand elasticities

	Original	New	% change	Elasticity
Good A				
Quantity	100	95	–5%	$\frac{-5}{10} = -0.5$
Price	£1	£1.10	10%	
Good B				
Quantity	200	140	–30%	$\frac{-30}{20} = -1.5$
Price	£5	£6	20%	

Elasticity is calculated by dividing the percentage change in price by the percentage change in quantity. With good A, a rise in price of 10p on £1, or 10 per cent, causes a fall in quantity of 5 units from 100, or 5 per cent. Dividing the 5 per cent reduction in quantity by the 10 per cent increase in price gives an elasticity of –0.5. With good B, a 30 per cent fall in quantity is caused by a 20 per cent rise in price making elasticity –1.5.

Second, it is almost universal practice when comparing two elasticities to compare their absolute, not their algebraic, values. For example, if product *X* has an elasticity of –2 while product *Y* has an elasticity of –10, economists will say that *Y* has a greater elasticity than *X* (in spite of the fact that –10 is *less than* –2). As long as it is understood that absolute and not algebraic values are being compared, this usage is acceptable.[2] After all, the demand curve with the larger absolute elasticity *is* the one where quantity demanded is more responsive to price changes. For example, an elasticity of –10 indicates greater response of quantity to price than does an elasticity of –2.

This need not cause us trouble as long as we remember the basics:

Demand elasticity is measured by a ratio: the percentage change in quantity demanded divided by the percentage change in price that brought it about; for normal, negatively sloped demand curves, elasticity is negative, but two elasticities are compared by comparing their absolute values.

Table 5.1 shows the calculation of two demand elasticities, one that is quite large and one that is quite small. The larger elasticity indicates that quantity demanded is highly responsive to a change in price. The smaller elasticity indi-

[2] The absolute value is the magnitude without the sign. Thus, for example, –2 and +2 have the same absolute value of 2.

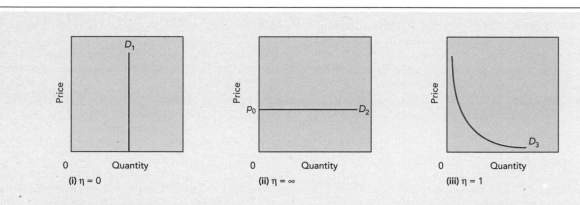

Figure 5.3   Three constant-elasticity demand curves

Each of these demand curves has a constant elasticity. D_1 has *zero elasticity*: the quantity demanded does not change at all when price changes. D_2 has *infinite elasticity at the price p_0*: a small price increase from p_0 decreases quantity demanded from an indefinitely large amount to zero. D_3 has *unit elasticity*: a given percentage increase in price brings an equal percentage decrease in quantity demanded at all points on the curve; it is a rectangular hyperbola for which price *times* quantity is a constant.

cates that the quantity demanded is relatively unresponsive to a change in price.

INTERPRETING PRICE ELASTICITY

The value of price elasticity of demand ranges from zero to minus infinity. In this section, however, we concentrate on absolute values, and so ask by how much the absolute value *exceeds zero*. It is zero if there is no change in quantity demanded when price changes, i.e. when quantity demanded does not respond to a price change. A demand curve of zero elasticity is shown in Figure 5.3(i). It is said to be *perfectly* or *completely* inelastic.

As long as there is some positive response of quantity demanded to a change in price, the absolute value of elasticity will exceed zero. The greater the response, the larger the elasticity. Whenever this value is less than one, however, the percentage change in quantity is less than the percentage change in price and demand is said to be **inelastic**.

When elasticity is equal to one, the two percentage changes are then equal to each other. This case, which is called **unit elasticity**, is the boundary between elastic and inelastic demands. A demand curve having unit elasticity over its whole range is shown in Figure 5.3(iii).[3]

When the percentage change in quantity demanded exceeds the percentage change in price, the elasticity of demand is greater than one and demand is said to be **elastic**. When elasticity is infinitely large, there exists some small price reduction that will raise demand from zero to infinity. Above the critical price, consumers will buy nothing. At the critical price, they will buy all that they can obtain (an infinite amount, if it were available). The graph of a demand curve having infinite price elasticity is shown in Figure 5.3(ii). Such a demand curve is said to be *perfectly* or *completely elastic*. (This unlikely looking case will turn out to be important later when we study the demand for the output of a single firm with many competitors.)

Box 5.1 summarizes the discussion of this and subsequent sections. The terminology in the table is important, and you should become familiar with it.

ELASTICITY AND TOTAL REVENUE

How does consumers' total expenditure react when the price of a product is changed? Notice that the total expenditure of the product's buyers is equal to the revenues of the firm's sellers plus any taxes that the government levies on the product. The simplest example will show that buyers' expenditure and sellers' revenue may rise or fall in response to a decrease in price. Suppose 100 units of a product are being sold at a unit price of £1. The price is then cut to £0.90. If the quantity sold rises to 110, the total expenditure falls from £100 to £99. But if quantity sold rises to 120, total expenditure rises from £100 to £108.

The change in total expenditure brought about by a change in price is related to the elasticity of demand. If elasticity is less than unity, the percentage change in price will exceed the percentage change in quantity. The price change will then be the more important of the two changes, so that total expenditure will change in the same direction as the price changes. If, however, elasticity exceeds unity, the percentage change in quantity will exceed the percentage change in price. The quantity change will then be the more important change, so that total expenditure will change in the same direction as quantity changes (that is, in the opposite direction to the change in price).

1. If elasticity of demand exceeds unity (demand elastic), a fall in price increases total expenditure on the good and a rise in price reduces it.
2. If elasticity is less than unity (demand inelastic), a fall in price reduces total expenditure on the good and a rise in price increases it.
3. If elasticity of demand is unity, a rise or a fall in price leaves total expenditure on the good unaffected.[4]

You should now return to the example in Table 5.1 and calculate what happens to total revenue when price changes in each case. In the case of product A, whose demand is inelastic, you will see that a rise in price raises the revenue of sellers from £100 to £104.50. In contrast, the rise in the price of good B, whose demand is elastic, lowers revenue from £1,000 to £840.

SOME COMPLICATIONS

We now need to look a little more closely at the elasticity measure. Let us first write out in symbols the definition we

---

[3] The curve is called a rectangular hyperbola. Any rectangular hyperbola has the formula *x* times *y* equals a constant. In this case, the two variables are price, p, and quantity, q, so the formula of the unit-elastic demand curve is $pq = C$. Beginners are often confused by the fact that any demand curve having a constant elasticity other than zero or infinity is a curve and *not* a straight line. In Figure 5.3(iii), as we move down on the price axis, equal *absolute* changes in price (say, continuous price cuts of 10p) represent larger and larger *percentage* changes. But as we move outwards on the quantity axis, equal *absolute changes* represent smaller and smaller *percentage changes* in quantity, because the quantity from which we start is becoming larger and larger. If the ratio, *percentage change in quantity/percentage change in price*, is to be kept constant, equal absolute cuts in price must be met with larger and larger absolute increases in quantity. Thus, geometrically, the curve must get flatter as price becomes lower and lower. This increasing flatness of the demand curve indicates an increasing responsiveness of the absolute quantity demanded to any given absolute price change.

[4] Algebraically, total revenue is price *times* quantity. If, for example, the equilibrium price and quantity are p_1 and q_1, then total revenue is $p_1 q_1$. On a demand-curve diagram, price is given by a vertical distance and quantity by a horizontal distance. It follows that on such a diagram total revenue is given by the *area* of a rectangle the length of whose sides represent price and quantity. Total revenue to the supplier and total expenditure by consumers are identical in these examples.

BOX 5.1

··

The terminology of elasticity

TERM	SYMBOL	NUMERICAL MEASURE OF ELASTICITY	VERBAL DESCRIPTION
Price elasticity of demand (supply)	$\eta\ (\varepsilon_s)$		
Perfectly or completely inelastic		Zero	Quantity demanded (supplied) does not change as price changes
Inelastic		Greater than zero, less than one	Quantity demanded (supplied) changes by a smaller percentage than does price
Unit elasticity		One	Quantity demanded (supplied) changes by exactly the same percentage as does price
Elastic		Greater than one, but less than infinity	Quantity demanded (supplied) changes by a larger percentage than does price
Perfectly, completely, or infinitely elastic		Infinity	Purchasers (sellers) are prepared to buy (sell) all they can at some price and none at all at an even higher (lower) price
Income elasticity of demand	η_y		
Inferior good		Negative	Quantity demanded decreases as income increases
Normal good		Positive	Quantity demanded increases as income increases:
Income-inelastic		Less than one	less than in proportion to income increase
Income-elastic		Greater than one	more than in proportion to income increase
Cross-elasticity of demand	η_{xy}		
Substitute		Positive	The quantity demanded of some good and the price of a substitute are positively related
Complement		Negative	The quantity demanded of some good and the price of a complement are negatively related

---

have been using, which is percentage change in quantity divided by percentage change in price:

$$\eta = \frac{\dfrac{\Delta q}{q}.100}{\dfrac{\Delta p}{p}.100}.$$

We can cancel out the 100s and multiply the numerator and denominator by $p/\Delta p$ to get

$$\eta = \frac{\Delta q}{q}.\frac{p}{\Delta p}.$$

Since it does not matter in which order we do our multiplication (i.e. $q.\Delta p \equiv \Delta p.q$), we may reverse the order of the two terms in the denominator and write

$$\eta = \frac{\Delta q}{\Delta p}.\frac{p}{q}. \tag{2}$$

We have now split elasticity into two parts: $\Delta q/\Delta p$, the ratio of the change in quantity to the change in price, which is related to the slope of the demand curve; and p/q, which is related to the place on the curve at which we made our measurement.

Figure 5.4 shows a straight-line demand curve. If we wish to measure the elasticity at a point, we take our p and q at that point and consider a price change, taking us to another point, and measure our Δp and Δq between those two points. The slope of the straight line joining the two points is $\Delta p/\Delta q$. (If you have forgotten this, refer to the appendix to Chapter 3, pp. 53–4.) The term in equation (2), however, is $\Delta q/\Delta p$, which is the reciprocal of $\Delta p/\Delta q$. Thus, the first term in the elasticity formula (2) is the reciprocal of the

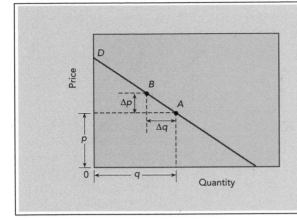

Figure 5.4 Elasticity measured on a linear demand curve

Elasticity depends on the slope of the demand curve and the point at which the measurement is made. Starting at point A and moving to point B, the ratio $\Delta p/\Delta q$ is the slope of the line, while its reciprocal $\Delta q/\Delta p$ is the first term in the percentage definition of elasticity. The second term is p/q, which is the ratio of the coordinates of the point A. Since the slope $\Delta p/\Delta q$ is constant, it is clear that the elasticity along the curve varies with the ratio p/q, which is zero where the curve intersects the quantity axis and 'infinity' where it intersects the price axis.

slope of the straight line joining the two price–quantity positions under consideration.[5] The second term is the ratio of price to quantity at the point where elasticity is measured.

Now we can use the expression in (2) to discover a number of things about our elasticity measure.

First, *the elasticity of a downward-sloping straight-line demand curve varies from infinity (∞) at the price axis to zero at the quantity axis.* We first notice that a straight line has a constant slope, so that the ratio $\Delta p/\Delta q$ is the same anywhere on the line. Therefore, its reciprocal, $\Delta q/\Delta p$, must also be constant. We can now infer the changes in η by inspecting changes in the ratio p/q as we move along the demand curve. At the price axis, $q = 0$ and p/q is undefined. However, if we let q approach zero, without ever quite reaching it, we see that the ratio p/q increases without limit. Thus, elasticity increases without limit as q approaches zero. Loosely, we say elasticity is infinity when q is zero. Now move the point at which elasticity is being measured down the demand curve. As this happens, p falls and q rises steadily; thus the ratio p/q is falling steadily, so that η is also falling. At the q axis, the price is zero, so the ratio p/q is zero. Thus, elasticity is zero.

The second point to make is that, *with a straight-line demand curve, the elasticity measured from any point (p, q), according to equation (2) above, is independent of the direction and magnitude of the change in price and quantity.* This follows immediately from the fact that the slope of a straight line is a constant. If we start from some point (p,q) and then change price, the ratio $\Delta q/\Delta p$ will be the same whatever the direction or the size of the change in p.

Our third point takes us back to the beginning of this chapter, where we warned against judging elasticity from the apparent shape of a demand curve. Since we frequently need to compare elasticities on two curves, it is fortunate that there is a way in which this can be done in one key situation: the elasticities of two intersecting straight-line demand curves can be compared *at the point of intersection* merely by comparing slopes, the steeper curve being the less

elastic. Figure 5.5 shows two intersecting curves and proves that the steeper curve is less elastic than the flatter curve when elasticity is measured at the point where the two curves intersect. The intuitive reason is that at the point of intersection p and q are common to both curves, so all that differs in the elasticity formula is their relative slopes. This is a valuable result, which we will use many times in later chapters.

Measured at the point of intersection of two demand curves, the steeper curve has the lower elasticity.

Our final point is that, *when equation (2) is applied to a nonlinear demand curve, the elasticity measured at any one point varies with the direction and magnitude of the change in price and quantity.* Figure 5.6 shows a nonlinear demand curve with elasticity being measured at one point. The figure makes it apparent that the ratio $\Delta q/\Delta p$, and hence the elasticity, will vary according to the size and the direction of the price change. This result is very inconvenient. It happens because the ratio $\Delta q/\Delta p$ gives the average reaction of q to a change in p over a section of the demand curve, and, depending on the range that we take, the *average reaction* will be different.

A MORE PRECISE MEASURE

The measure defined in (2) gives the elasticity over some range, or *arc*, of the demand curve. This measure is sometimes used in empirical work where elasticity is measured between two observed price–quantity situations. In theoretical work, however, it is normal to use a concept of elasticity that gives a unique measure of the elasticity at each specific point on the demand curve. Instead of using the changes in price (Δp) and quantity (Δq) over some range of

---

[5] If economists followed normal mathematical practice of plotting the demand curve with the dependant variable (quantity in this case) on the vertical axis, the ratio in (2) would be the slope of the demand curve rather than its reciprocal.

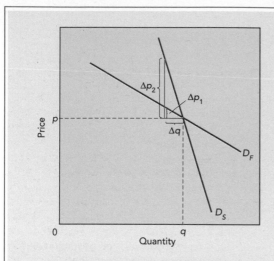

Figure 5.5 Two intersecting demand curves

At the point of intersection of two demand curves, the steeper curve has the lower elasticity. At the point of intersection, p and q are common to both curves, and hence the ratio p/q is the same. Therefore, elasticity varies only with $\Delta q/\Delta p$. The absolute value of the slope of the steeper curve, $\Delta p_2/\Delta q$, is larger than the absolute value of the slope $\Delta p_1/\Delta q$, of the flatter curve. Thus, the absolute value of the ratio $\Delta q/\Delta p_2$ is smaller on the steeper curve than the ratio $\Delta q/\Delta p_1$ on the flatter curve, so that elasticity is lower.

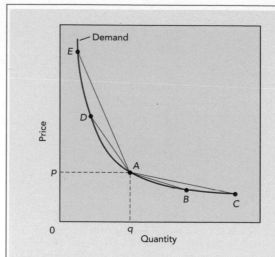

Figure 5.6 Elasticity measured on a nonlinear demand curve

Elasticity, measured from one point on a nonlinear demand curve and using the percentage formula, varies with the direction and magnitude of the change being considered. Elasticity is to be measured from point A, so the ratio p/q is given. The ratio $\Delta p/\Delta q$ is the slope of the line joining point A to the point reached on the curve after the price has changed. The smallest ratio occurs when the change is to point C and the highest ratio when it is to point E. Since the term in the elasticity formula, $\Delta q/\Delta p$, is the reciprocal of this slope, measured elasticity is largest when the change is to point C and smallest when it is to point E.

the curve, this elasticity measure uses the concept of how quantity is *tending to* change as price changes at each specific point on the curve.

If we wish to measure the elasticity in this way, we need to know the reaction of quantity to a change in price at each point on the curve, not over a whole range on the curve. We use the symbols dq/dp to refer to the reaction of quantity to a change in price at a specific point on the curve. We define this to be *the reciprocal of the slope of the straight line (i.e. $\Delta q/\Delta p$) that is tangent to the demand curve at the point in question*. In Figure 5.7, the elasticity of demand at a, calculated according to this measure, is the ratio p/q (as it has been in all previous measures) now multiplied by the ratio of $\Delta q/\Delta p$ measured along the straight line that is tangent to the curve at a. This definition may now be written as

$$\eta = \frac{\mathrm{d}q}{\mathrm{d}p} \cdot \frac{p}{q}. \tag{3}$$

The expression dq/dp, as we have defined it, is in fact the differential-calculus concept of the derivative of quantity with respect to price evaluated at the point p,q.

This elasticity measure is the one normally used in economic theory. Elasticity measured by the percentage for-

mula $(\Delta q/\Delta p)(p/q)$ may be regarded as an approximation to this expression. It is obvious from inspecting Figure 5.7 that the elasticity measured from $(\Delta q/\Delta p)(p/q)$ will come closer and closer to that measured by $(\mathrm{d}q/\mathrm{d}p)(p/q)$, the smaller the price change used to calculate the value of $\Delta q/\Delta p$.[6] Thus, if we consider the percentage definition of elasticity as an approximation to the precise definition, the approximation improves as the size of Δp diminishes. Box 5.2 further investigates some of the properties of the percentage definition and shows a practical way of avoiding some of its undesirable aspects.

WHAT DETERMINES ELASTICITY OF DEMAND?

The main determinant of elasticity is the availability of substitutes. Some products, such as margarine, cabbage, lamb, and Ford Escorts, have quite close substitutes—butter,

---

[6] Those who know calculus may notice that, if the curve is 'wiggly', this statement will not be true over *any* range of the curve; but, as long as the derivative is defined at the point in question, the statement must be true for a finite range around that point.

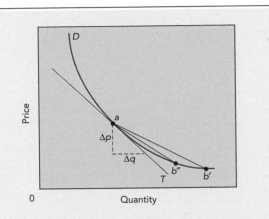

Figure 5.7 Elasticity measured by the exact method

When elasticity is related to the slope of the tangent to the demand curve at some point, there is one and only one measured value of elasticity at that point. In this method, the ratio $\Delta q/\Delta p$ is taken as the reciprocal of the slope of the line that is tangent to point a. Thus, there is only one measured elasticity at point a: it is p/q multiplied by $\Delta q/\Delta p$ measured along the tangent T. There is no averaging of changes in p and q in this measure because only one point on the curve is used.

The percentage formula can be thought of as an approximation to the exact method. Starting from a, change the price so that we move to some point b'; the ratio $\Delta q/\Delta p$ is the reciprocal of the slope of the straight line joining a and b'. Next, let the price change take us to b''. The ratio $\Delta p/\Delta q$ is now the reciprocal of the slope of the line joining a and b''. The smaller the price change that we make, the closer the point representing the new price–quantity combination comes to point a, and the closer the slope of the line joining the two points comes to the slope of the line tangential to the curve at a. If the slopes of those two lines get closer together, so also do the reciprocals of the slopes, and thus, so do the elasticities as measured by the formula involving $\Delta q/\Delta p$ and the formula dq/dp.

other green vegetables, beef, and Vauxhall Astras. A change in the price of any one of these products, *the prices of the substitutes remaining constant,* will lead consumers to substitute one product for another. A fall in price leads consumers to buy more of the product and less of its substitutes; and a rise in price leads consumers to buy less of the product and more of its substitutes. More broadly defined products, such as all foods, all clothing, cigarettes, and petrol, have few if any satisfactory substitutes. A rise in their price can be expected to cause a smaller fall in quantity demanded than would be the case if close substitutes were available.

A product with close substitutes tends to have an elastic demand; one with no close substitutes tends to have an inelastic demand.

Closeness of substitutes—and thus measured elasticity—depends both on how the product is defined and on the time-period under consideration. This is explored in the following sections. One common misconception about demand elasticity is discussed in Box 5.3.

Definition of the product Food is a necessity of life; there is no substitute for food. Thus, for food taken as a whole, demand is inelastic over a large price range. It does not follow, however, that any one food, such as Weetabix or Heinz tomato soup, is a necessity in the same sense; each of these has close substitutes, such as Kelloggs cornflakes and Campbells tomato soup. Individual food products can have quite elastic demands, and they frequently do.

Durable goods provide a similar example. Durables as a whole have less elastic demands than do individual kinds of durable goods. For example, when the prices of television sets rise, many consumers may replace their lawnmower or their vacuum cleaner instead of buying a new television set. Thus, although their purchases of television sets will fall, their total purchases of durables may fall by much less.

Because most specific manufactured goods have close substitutes, they tend to have price-elastic demands. Hats, for example, have been estimated to have an elasticity of −3.0. In contrast, all clothing taken together tends to be inelastic.

Any one of a group of related products will tend to have an elastic demand, even though the demand for the group as a whole may be inelastic.

Long-run and short-run elasticity of demand Because it takes time to develop satisfactory substitutes, a demand that is inelastic in the short run may prove elastic when enough time has passed. For example, when cheap electric power was first brought to rural areas of the United States in the 1930s, few houses were wired for electricity. The initial measurements showed demand for electricity to be very inelastic. Gradually, however, houses became electrified and households then purchased electric appliances, while new industries moved into the area to take advantage of the cheap electric power. Thus, when measured over several years, the response of quantity demanded to the fall in price was quite large, even though, when measured over a short period, the response was quite small.

Petrol provides a similar, more recent, example. Before the first OPEC price shocks of the mid-1970s, the demand for petrol was thought to be highly inelastic because of the absence of satisfactory substitutes. But the large price increases over the 1970s led to the development of smaller, more fuel-efficient cars and to less driving. The most recent

BOX 5.2

Measuring elasticity over a range

We have seen that the percentage formula gives different answers for the elasticity at any point on a nonlinear demand curve depending on the size and the direction of the change being considered. Many textbooks just give the percentage elasticity formula, without warning the reader of this property. Inquisitive students usually discover this property with a shock the first time they try to calculate some elasticities from numerical data.

One way in which the problem is often discovered is when elasticity on a unit elasticity curve is calculated as not being unity. For example, the demand curve

$$p = £100/q \qquad (1)$$

is a unit-elastic curve because expenditure, pq, remains constant at £100 whatever the price. But if you substitute any two prices into the above equation and calculate the elasticity according to the percentage formula, you will never get an answer of unity, whatever two prices you take. For example, the equation tells us that, if price rises from £2 to £3, quantity falls from 50 to 33⅓. If we take the original price as £2, we have a price change of 50 per cent and a quantity change of −33 per cent, making an elasticity of −0.66. If we take the original price as £3, the elasticity comes out to be −1.5.

This is unsatisfactory. The problem can be avoided when measuring elasticity between two separate points on the curve by taking p and q as the average values between the two points on the curve. This measure has two convenient properties. First, it is independent of the direction of the change and, second, it gives a value of unity for any point on a demand curve whose true value is unity.

In the above example, the average p is £2.5 and the average q is 41.666. This makes the percentage change in price 40 per cent $((1/2.5)×100)$ and the percentage change in quantity also 40 per cent $((16.667/41.667)×100)$. So elasticity is correctly measured as one. Whatever two prices you put into equation (1), you will always get a value of unity for the elasticity, provided you use the average of the two prices and of the two quantities when calculating the elasticity. Readers who enjoy playing with algebra can have fun proving this proposition.*

The best approximation to the correct measure when elasticity is measured between two separate points on a demand curve is obtained by defining p and q as the average of the prices and quantities at the two points on the curve.

The above is the best way to measure elasticities given readings from any two points on a curve when that is all that is known. As we have seen in the text, for theoretical purposes, the way out of the problem is to measure the ratio $\Delta q/\Delta p$ as the slope of the tangent to one point on the curve rather than between two points on the curve. To do this, we need to know a portion of the demand curve around the point in question.

In practice, economists do not usually estimate elasticity on the basis of only one observation. In such cases, it is common to report an elasticity measure that is valued at the mean of two p and q data points. This is analogous to the averaging we suggest here.

---

* What you need to prove is that
$$\frac{q_2 - q_1}{p_2 - p_1} \cdot \frac{(p_1 + p_2)/2}{(q_1 + q_2)/2} = 1.$$

---

estimates of elasticity of demand for petrol have risen from around 0.6 to around unity. Given another decade in which to develop substitutes, petrol demand might have proved elastic had the real, inflation-corrected price not fallen back towards its earlier level. Each of these measures relates the change in price at one point in time to the change in quantity over time. What is found is that, the larger the time-period over which the change in quantity is measured, the larger the elasticity tends to be.

The response of quantity demanded to a given price change, and thus the measured price elasticity of demand, will tend to be greater the longer the time-span considered.

The different quantity responses can be shown by different demand curves. Every demand curve shows the response of consumer demand to a change in price. For such products as cornflakes and ties, the full response occurs quickly and there is little reason to worry about longer-term effects. For these products a single demand curve will suffice. Other products are typically used in connection with highly durable appliances or machines. A change in price of, say, electricity or petrol may not have its major effect until the stock of appliances and machines using these products has been adjusted. This adjustment may take a long time. It is useful to identify two kinds of demand curve for such products. A *short-run demand curve* shows the response of quantity demanded to a change in price, *given* the existing quantities of the durable goods that use the product, and *given* existing supplies of substitute products. A different short-run demand curve will exist for each such structure of durable goods and substitute products.

The *long-run demand curve* shows the response of quantity demanded to a change in price after enough time has passed to allow all adjustments to be made. The relation

BOX 5.3

Elasticity and income

It is often argued that the demand for a product will be more inelastic the smaller the proportion of income spent on it. The argument runs as follows. When only a small proportion of income is spent on some product, consumers will hardly notice a price rise. Hence they will not react strongly to price changes one way or the other. The most commonly quoted example of this alleged phenomenon is salt.

Salt is, however, a poor example for the argument being advanced. Not only does it take up a very small part of consumers' total expenditure, it also has few close substitutes. Consider another product, say one type of mints. These mints no doubt account for only a small portion of the total expenditure of mint-suckers, but there are many close substitutes—other types of mints and other sucking sweets. The makers of Polo mints know, for example, that if they raise Polo prices greatly, mint-suckers will switch to other brands of mints and to other types of sucking sweets. They thus face an elastic demand for their product.

Similar considerations apply to any one brand of matches. If the makers of Swan Vesta matches raise their prices significantly, people will switch to other brands of matches rather than pay the higher price.

What this discussion shows is that: *goods with close substitutes will tend to have elastic demands whether they account for a large or a small part of consumers' incomes.*

There is, however, another aspect of the influence of income. To see this, consider any good that has an inelastic demand. A rise in its price causes more to be spent on it. If consumers spend more on that product, they must spend less on all others taken as a group. But the higher is the proportion of income spent on the product, the less likely are they to spend more on it when its price falls. After all, if a consumer spends all of his or her income on potatoes, demand must have a unit elasticity. As price rises, purchases must fall in proportion since the consumer has only a given income to spend. Thus, *for a good to have a highly inelastic demand it must have few good substitutes, and it must not take up too large a proportion of consumers' total expenditure.*

---

between long-run and short-run demand curves is shown in Figure 5.8. Assume for example that there is a large rise in the price of electricity. The initial response will be along the short-run demand curve. There will be some fall in quantity demanded, but the percentage drop is likely to be less than the percentage rise in price, making short-run demand inelastic. Over time, however, many people will replace their existing electric cookers with gas cookers as they wear out. New homes will be equipped with gas rather than electric appliances more often than they would have been before the price rise. Over time, factories will switch to relatively cheaper sources of power. When all these types of long-run adaptations have been made, the demand for electricity will have fallen a great deal. Indeed, over this

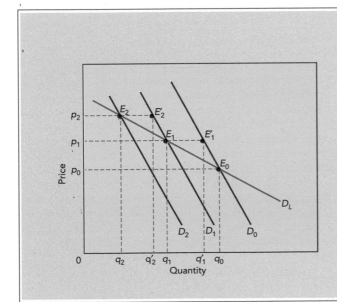

Figure 5.8 Short-run and long-run demand curves

The long-run demand curve is more elastic than the short-run curves. D_L is a long-run demand curve. Suppose consumers are fully adjusted to price p_0. Equilibrium is then at E_0, with quantity demanded q_0. Now suppose price rises to p_1. In the short run, consumers will react along the short-run demand curve D_0 and reduce consumption to q'_1. Once enough time has passed to permit the full range of adjustments to the new price, p_1, a new equilibrium at E_1 will be reached with quantity at q_1.

Now that all adjustments have been made, there will be a new short-run demand curve, D_1, passing through point E_1. A further rise in price to p_2 would lead first to a short-run equilibrium at E'_2 with quantity q'_2, but eventually to a new long-run equilibrium at E_2 with quantity q_2. The blue long-run demand curve is more elastic than the short-run curves where they intersect.

longer period of time, the percentage reduction in quantity demanded may exceed the percentage increase in price. If so, the long-run demand for electricity will be elastic.

The principal conclusion in the discussion of elasticity is:

The long-run demand curve for a product that is used in conjunction with durable products will tend to be substantially more elastic than any of the short-run demand curves.

This distinction will prove valuable in several of the chapters that follow.

Other demand elasticities

So far we have discussed *price elasticity of demand*, the response of the quantity demanded to a change in the product's own price. The concept of demand elasticity can, however, be broadened to measure the response to changes in *any* of the factors that influence demand. How much, for example, do changes in income and the prices of other products affect quantity demanded?

INCOME ELASTICITY

The reaction of demand to changes in income is an important economic variable. In many economies, economic growth has been doubling real national income every twenty or thirty years. This rise in income is shared by most people. As they find their incomes increasing, people increase their demands for many products. In the richer countries the demand for food and basic clothing does not increase with income nearly so much as does the demand for many other products. In many of these richer countries, the demands that are increasing most rapidly as incomes rise are the demands for durable goods. In an increasing number of the very richest of the Western countries, however, the demand for services is rising even more rapidly than the demand for durables as income rises.

The responsiveness of demand for a product to changes in income is termed **income elasticity of demand**, and is defined as

$$\eta_y = \frac{\text{percentage change in quantity demanded}}{\text{percentage change in income}}.$$

For most products, increases in income lead to increases in quantity demanded, and income elasticity is therefore positive. For such products, we have the same subdivisions of income elasticity as for price elasticity. If the resulting percentage change in quantity demanded is larger than the percentage increase in income, η_y will exceed unity. The product's demand is then said to be **income-elastic**. If the percentage change in quantity demanded is smaller than the percentage change in income, η_y will be less than unity. The product's demand is then said to be **income-inelastic**. In the boundary case, the percentage changes in income and quantity demanded are equal, making η_y unity. The product is said to have a *unit income elasticity of demand*.

Virtually all products have negative price elasticities. Both positive and negative income elasticities, are, however, commonly found.

We have already encountered these relations on pages 66–9, where we argued that a change in income would shift the demand curve for a product. If the product is a normal good, a rise in income causes more of it to be demanded, other things being equal, which means a rightward shift in the product's demand curve. If the product is an inferior good, a rise in income causes less of it to be demanded, which means a leftward shift in the product's demand curve. So normal goods have positive income elasticities while inferior goods have negative income elasticities. Finally, the boundary case between normal and inferior goods occurs when a rise in income leaves quantity demanded unchanged, so that income elasticity is zero.

The important terminology of income elasticity is summarized in Figure 5.9 and in Box 5.1 on page 90. You should spend time studying this terminology and committing it to memory. Figure 5.9 shows a product with all types of income elasticity—positive, zero, and negative. This is to illustrate all of the possible reactions. Specific goods do not need to show all of these. For example, a good may have a positive income elasticity at all levels of income. (You should be able to explain, however, why no good can have a negative income elasticity at *all* levels of income.) A graph that directly relates quantity demanded to income, such as Figure 5.9, is called an *Engel curve* after Ernst Engel (1821–1896), the German economist who used this device to establish a systematic relationship between household income and expenditure on necessities.

CROSS-ELASTICITY

The responsiveness of quantity demanded of one product to changes in the prices of other products is often of considerable interest. Producers of, say, beans and other meat substitutes find the demands for their products rising when cattle shortages force the price of beef up. Producers of large cars found their sales falling when the price of petrol rose dramatically after the 1973 and 1979 oil price rises.

The responsiveness of demand for one product to changes in the price of another product is called **cross-elasticity of demand**. It is defined as

$$\eta_{xy} = \frac{\substack{\text{percentage change in quantity demanded} \\ \text{of one commodity}}}{\text{percentage change in price of another commodity}}.$$

Cross-elasticity can vary from minus infinity to plus infin-

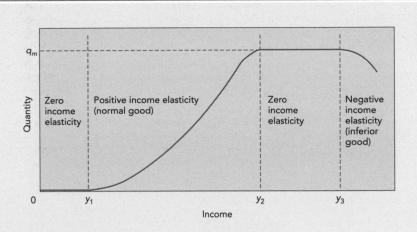

Figure 5.9 The relation between quantity demanded and income

Normal goods have positive income elasticities; inferior goods have negative elasticities. The graph relates the quantity of some good demanded to income. Nothing is demanded at income less than y_1, so for incomes between 0 and y_1 income elasticity is zero. Between incomes of y_1 and y_2, quantity demanded rises as income rises, making income elasticity positive. Between incomes of y_2 and y_3, quantity demanded stays constant at q_m, making income elasticity once again zero. At incomes above y_3, increases in income cause reductions in quantity demanded, making income elasticity negative.

ity. Complementary goods have negative cross-elasticities and substitute goods have positive cross-elasticities.

Bread and butter, for example, are complements: a fall in the price of butter causes an increase in the consumption of both products. Thus, changes in the price of butter and in the quantity of bread demanded will have opposite signs. In

contrast, butter and margarine are substitutes: a fall in the price of butter increases the quantity of butter demanded, but reduces the quantity of margarine demanded. Changes in the price of butter and in the quantity of margarine demanded will, therefore, have the same sign. The terminology of cross-elasticity is also summarized in Box 5.1.

Elasticity of supply

WE have seen that elasticity of demand measures the response of quantity demanded to changes in any of the factors that influence it. Similarly, elasticity of supply measures the response of quantity supplied to changes in any of the factors that influence it. Because we wish to focus on the product's own price as a factor influencing its supply, we shall be concerned with *price elasticity of supply*. We shall follow the usual practice of dropping the adjective 'price', and will refer simply to 'elasticity of supply' whenever there is no ambiguity in this usage.

Supply elasticities are important in economics. Our

treatment is brief for two reasons: first, much of what has been said about demand elasticity carries over to the case of supply elasticity and does not need repeating; second, we will have more to say about the determinants of supply elasticity later in this book.

A DEFINITION

The **price elasticity of supply**, which is often shortened to *supply elasticity*, is defined as the percentage change in quantity supplied divided by the percentage change in

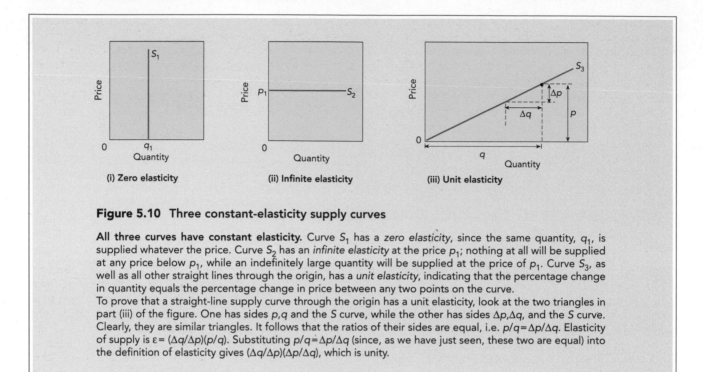

Figure 5.10 Three constant-elasticity supply curves

All three curves have constant elasticity. Curve S_1 has a *zero elasticity*, since the same quantity, q_1, is supplied whatever the price. Curve S_2 has an *infinite elasticity* at the price p_1; nothing at all will be supplied at any price below p_1, while an indefinitely large quantity will be supplied at the price of p_1. Curve S_3, as well as all other straight lines through the origin, has a *unit elasticity*, indicating that the percentage change in quantity equals the percentage change in price between any two points on the curve.

To prove that a straight-line supply curve through the origin has a unit elasticity, look at the two triangles in part (iii) of the figure. One has sides p,q and the S curve, while the other has sides $\Delta p, \Delta q$, and the S curve. Clearly, they are similar triangles. It follows that the ratios of their sides are equal, i.e. $p/q = \Delta p/\Delta q$. Elasticity of supply is $\varepsilon = (\Delta q/\Delta p)(p/q)$. Substituting $p/q = \Delta p/\Delta q$ (since, as we have just seen, these two are equal) into the definition of elasticity gives $(\Delta q/\Delta p)(\Delta p/\Delta q)$, which is unity.

price that brought it about. Letting the Greek letter epsilon, ε, stand for this measure, its formula is

$$\varepsilon = \frac{\text{percentage change in quantity supplied}}{\text{percentage change in price}} .$$

Supply elasticity is a measure of the degree of responsiveness of quantity supplied to changes in the product's own price.

Since supply curves normally have positive slopes, supply elasticity is normally positive.[7]

INTERPRETING SUPPLY ELASTICITY

Figure 5.10 illustrates three cases of supply elasticity. The case of zero elasticity is one in which the quantity supplied does not change as price changes. This would be the case, for example, if suppliers persisted in producing a given quantity and dumping it on the market for whatever it would bring. Infinite elasticity occurs at some price if nothing is supplied at lower prices, but an indefinitely large amount will be supplied at that price. Any straight-line supply curve drawn through the origin, such as the one shown in part (iii) of the figure, has an elasticity of unity. The proof is given in the figure caption. The reason is that, for any positively sloped straight line, the ratio of p/q at any point on the line is equal to the ratio $\Delta p/\Delta q$ that defines the

slope of the line. Thus, in the formula $(\Delta q/\Delta p)(p/q)$, the two ratios cancel each other out.

The case of unit supply elasticity illustrates that the warning given earlier for demand applies equally to supply: do not confuse geometric steepness of supply curves with elasticity. Since *any* straight-line supply curve that passes through the origin has an elasticity of unity, it follows that there is no simple correspondence between geometrical steepness and supply elasticity. The reason is that varying steepness (when the scales on both axes are unchanged) reflects varying *absolute* changes, while elasticity depends on *percentage* changes. For two supply curves that intersected (other than at the origin) the steeper curve is less elastic (more inelastic) than the flatter curve, at the point of intersection. The terminology of supply elasticity is summarized in Box 5.1 on page 90.

WHAT DETERMINES ELASTICITY OF SUPPLY?

What determines the response of producers to a change in the price of the product that they supply? First, the size of the response depends in part on how easily producers can shift from the production of other products to the one

---

[7] As with demand elasticity, the unique measure of supply elasticity at any point on a supply curve as given by the formula $(\mathrm{d}q/\mathrm{d}p)(p/q)$ where $\mathrm{d}q/\mathrm{d}p$ is the reciprocal of the slope of the tangent to the supply curve at the point p,q—which is the same thing as the calculus concept of the *derivative* of quantity supplied with respect to price.

whose price has risen. If agricultural land and labour can be readily shifted from one crop to another, the supply of any one crop will be more elastic than if labour cannot easily be shifted. Here also, as with demand, length of time for response is critical. It may be difficult to change quantities supplied in response to a price increase in a matter of weeks or months, but easy to do so over a period of years. An obvious example concerns the planting cycle of crops. Also, new oilfields can be discovered, wells drilled, and pipelines built over a period of years, but not in a few months. Thus, the elasticity of supply of oil is much greater over five years than over one year. Second, elasticity is strongly influenced by how costs respond to output changes. This issue will be treated at length in later chapters.

Measurement of demand and supply

MUCH of what economists do to earn a living uses measurements of demand and supply elasticities. Will a fare increase help to ease the deficit of London Underground or the Panama Canal? The answer requires a knowledge of price elasticity of demand. The United Nations Food and Agricultural Organization (FAO), and producers' co-ops, use income elasticities of demand to predict future changes in demand for food. Over the past decade, many industries have estimated their products' cross-elasticities of demand with petroleum in order to predict the effects of sharply changing petroleum prices. Members of the Organization of Petroleum Producing Countries (OPEC) wish to know supply elasticities in non-member countries in order to predict the reaction to price increases manipulated by OPEC. The methods for obtaining this information are dealt with in econometrics courses. Solutions to two of the most troubling problems concerning measurement are discussed below. All of these issues relate to both demand and supply, but we can illustrate what is involved by concentrating mainly on demand.

Problems of demand measurement

The explosion of knowledge of elasticities in recent decades came about when econometricians overcame major problems in measuring demand (and supply) relationships. A full discussion must be left to a course in econometrics, but some aspects of such measurements are sufficiently troubling to most students to make them worth mentioning here.

EVERYTHING IS CHANGING AT ONCE

When quantity demanded changes over time, it is usually because *all* of the influences that affect demand have been changing at the same time. How, then, can the separate influence of each variable be determined?

What, for example, is to be made of the observation that the quantity of butter consumed per capita rose by 10 per cent over a period in which average consumer income rose by 5 per cent, the price of butter fell by 3 per cent, and the price of margarine rose by 4 per cent? How much of the change is due to income elasticity of demand, how much to price elasticity, and how much to the cross-elasticity between butter and margarine? If this is all we know, the question cannot be answered. If, however, there are many observations showing, say, quantity demanded, income, price of butter, and price of margarine every month for four or five years, it is possible to discover the separate influence of each of the variables. The standard technique for doing so is called *multiple regression analysis*.

SEPARATING THE INFLUENCES OF DEMAND AND SUPPLY

A second set of problems concerns the separate estimation of demand and supply curves. We do not observe directly what people wish to buy and what producers wish to sell. Rather, we see what they do buy and what they do sell. The problem of how to estimate both demand and supply curves from observed market data on prices and quantities actually traded is called the **identification problem**.

To illustrate the problem, we assume in Figure 5.11 that all situations observed in the real world are equilibrium ones, in the sense that they are produced by the intersection of demand and supply curves. The first two parts of the figure show cases where only one curve shifts. Observations made on prices and quantities then trace out the curve that has not shifted. The third part of the figure, however, shows that, when both curves are shifting, observations of prices and quantities are not sufficient to identify the slope of either curve.

The identification problem is surmountable. The key to identifying the demand and supply curves separately is to bring in variables other than price, and then to relate

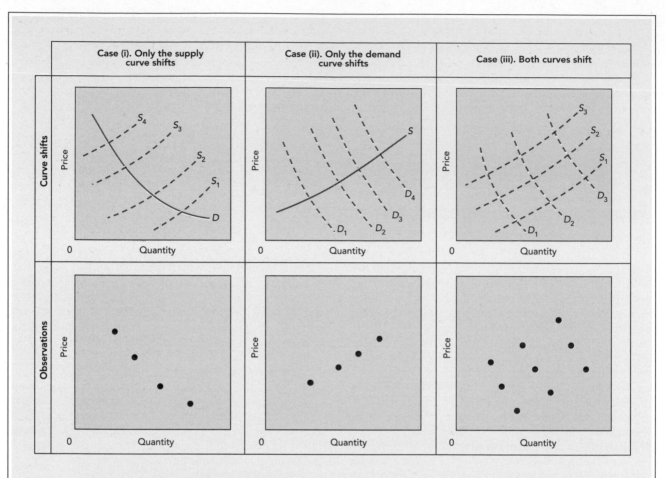

Figure 5.11 The identification problem

Observations on prices and quantities are sufficient to identify the slope of one of the curves only when it is stationary while the other shifts. In each case, the curves in the top row shift randomly from one numbered position to another. All that one sees, however, are the observations indicated by each of the points in the corresponding bottom row. The problem is to identify the slope of one of the curves in the top row given only the observations in the corresponding bottom row. In case (i) the observations trace out the shape of the demand curve. In case (ii) they trace out the supply curve. In case (iii) neither curve can be identified from the observed prices and quantities.

demand to one set and supply to *some other* set. For example, supply of the product might be related not only to the price of the product but also to its cost of production, and demand might be related not only to the price of the product but also to consumers' incomes. Provided that these other variables change sufficiently, it is possible to determine the relation between quantity supplied and price as well as the relation between quantity demanded and price. The details of how this is done will be found in a course on econometrics.

In serious applied work, concern is usually given to the identification problem. In more popular discussions, however, the problem is sometimes ignored. Whenever you see an argument such as, 'We know that the foreign elasticity of demand must be very low because the price of whisky rose by 10 per cent last year while whisky exports hardly changed at all', you should ask if the author has really identified the demand curve. If the rise in price was due to a rise in foreign demand for whisky, we may actually have discovered that the short-run *supply curve* of whisky is very inelastic (since whisky takes several years to manufacture). The general proposition to keep in mind is:

Unless we know that one curve has shifted while the other has not, price and quantity data alone are insufficient to reveal anything about the shape of either the demand or the supply curve.

Measurements of specific elasticities

The solution of the statistical problems associated with demand measurement has led to a large accumulation of data on demand elasticities. The value of these data to the applied economist shows the usefulness of demand theory.

PRICE ELASTICITIES

Much of the early work on demand measurement concentrated on the agricultural sector. Large fluctuations in agricultural prices provided both the incentive to study this sector and the data on which to base estimates of price elasticities of demand. Nobel laureate Professor Richard Stone in the United Kingdom, and Professor Henry Schultz (1893–1938) in the United States, did much of the pioneering work. Many agricultural research centres extended their work, and even today are making new estimates of the price elasticities of foodstuffs. The resulting data mostly confirm the existence of low price elasticities for food products as a whole, as well as for many individual products. The policy pay-off of this knowledge in terms of understanding agricultural problems has been enormous; it represents an early triumph of empirical work in economics. (See the discussion in Chapter 6.)

Although the importance of the agricultural problem led early investigators to concentrate on the demand for foodstuffs, modern studies have expanded to include virtually the whole range of products on which consumers spend their incomes. The demands for consumer durables such as cars, radios, refrigerators, television sets, and houses are of particular interest because they constitute a large fraction of total demand, and because they can vary markedly from one year to the next. A durable product can usually be made to last for another year; thus, purchases can be postponed with greater ease than can purchases of non-durables such as food and services. If enough consumers decide simultaneously to postpone purchases of durables for even six months, the effect on the economy can be enormous.

Durables as a whole have an inelastic demand, while many individual brands of durables have elastic demands. This is another example of the general proposition that the broader the category, the lower the elasticity because the fewer the close substitutes. Indeed, whether durable or non-durable, most specific manufactured goods have close substitutes, and studies show that they tend to have price-elastic demands.

Table 5.2 shows some recent measures of price elasticity for food products.

Table 5.2 Estimated price and income elasticities of demand for selected foods in the United Kingdom, 1989

Product	Price elasticity	Income elasticity
Carcass meats	−1.37	−0.01*
Cheese	−1.20	0.19
Frozen peas	−1.12	0.15*
Cereals	−0.94	0.03*
Fruit juices	−0.80	0.94
Bacon and ham	−0.70	−0.28
Fresh green vegetables	−0.58	0.13
Other fresh vegetables	−0.27*	0.35
Fresh potatoes	−0.21	−0.48
Bread	−0.09*	−0.25

*Indicates not significantly different from zero at the 5% probability level.

Source: Ministry of Agriculture, Food, and Fisheries, *Household Food Consumption and Expenditure, 1992*. London: HMSO.

Most foodstuffs have very low income elasticities while price elasticities cover a wider range. Notice that, although carcass meats have a zero income elasticity, they have a high price elasticity of 1.37. Cheese is an inferior good, yet it has a strong price elasticity. All demands are measured as being negatively related to price, as theory predicts. Three of the products—bread, potatoes, and cheese—show statistically significant negative income elasticities which classify them as inferior goods.

INCOME ELASTICITIES

Table 5.2 shows some measured income elasticities for the United Kingdom. Note the low income elasticities for all of the food products consumed by consumers that are listed in the table.

Note also the interesting contrast between the data for price and income elasticities. The meat products that are price elastic none the less have zero income elasticities. This tells us that changes in relative prices will cause substantial substitution among different types of meat—hence the greater-than-unity price elasticities—but that increases in incomes cause almost no increases in overall meat consumption—hence the low income elasticity. Of the products shown, cheese, potatoes, and bread have negative income elasticities, indicating that they are inferior goods at current levels of consumer incomes. Thus, although reductions in relative prices lead to increased purchases—normal price elasticities—the goods are inferior with respect to increases in income.

CROSS-ELASTICITIES

In many countries monopoly is illegal. Measurement of cross-elasticities has helped courts to decide on the allega-

---

BOX 5.4

....

Are elasticity measurements part of economic science?

Many years ago the late Lord Robbins had this to say about empirical measures of demand:*

'Suppose we are confronted with an order fixing the price of herrings at a point below the price hitherto ruling in the market. Suppose we are in a position to say, 'According to the researches of Blank . . . the elasticity of demand for common herring (*Clupea harengus*) is 1.3; the present price-fixing order therefore may be expected to leave an excess of demand over supply of two million barrels.

But can we hope to attain such an enviable position? Let us assume that . . . Blank had succeeded in ascertaining that, with a given price change in some year, the elasticity of demand was 1.3 . . . But what reason is there to suppose that he was unearthing a constant law? . . . Is it possible reasonably to suppose that coefficients derived from the observation of a particular herring market at a particular time and place have any *permanent* significance—save as Economic History?'

This is a bit of Robbins's argument that measurement of elasticities is not a valid part of economics. Several criticisms can be made of this position. First, although *a priori* arguments may strongly suggest that certain relationships will not be stable, they can never establish this. Even if the *a priori* arguments turn out to be correct most of the time, they may be wrong in a few cases. Only observation can reveal the cases in which the *a priori* argument is wrong.

The second major criticism is that the variability of any given relationship is an important matter. If, for example, tastes were so variable that demand curves shifted violently from day to day, then all of the comparative-static equilibrium analysis of the previous chapters would be useless. Only by accident would any market be near its equilibrium, and this would occur only momentarily. If, instead, tastes changed extremely slowly, then we might do very well to regard the relation between demand and price as being stable over long time-periods. Even if we could show, on *a priori* grounds, that every relation between two or more variables used in economic theory was necessarily not perfectly stable, it would be critical for purposes of theory to know the quantitative amount of the lack of stability. Only observation can show this, and such observations are thus important for economic theory as well as for economic history.

The third criticism is that, even if we find substantial variations in our relations, we want to know if these variations appear capricious or if they display a systematic pattern that might lead us to suspect that herring demand is related to other factors. We might, for example, find a strong but sometimes interrupted tendency for the elasticity of demand for herrings to fall over time. We might then find that this systematic variation in price elasticity could be accounted for by income variations. (As the population gets richer, its demand for herrings is less and less affected by price variations and so the demand becomes more and more inelastic.) We might now find that a high proportion of the changes in herring demand could be accounted for by assuming a *stable relation* between demand on the one hand, and price *and* income on the other. In general, what looked like an unstable relation between two variables might turn out to be only part of a more stable relation among three or more variables. All of this leads us to the following conclusion:

Empirical measurements are critical to economics. Without some quantitative evidence of the magnitude and the stability of particular relations, we cannot use economic theory to make useful predictions about the real world.

  * L. Robbins, *An Essay on the Nature and Significance of Economic Science* (London: Macmillan, 1932), pp. 98–101; final italics added.

---

tion that a monopoly exists. To illustrate, assume that the government of a particular country brings suit against a company for buying up all the firms making aluminium cable, claiming the company has created a monopoly of the product. The company replies that it needs to own all the firms in order to compete efficiently against the several firms producing copper cable. It argues that these two products are such close substitutes that the firms producing each are in intense competition, so that the sole producer of aluminium cable cannot be said to have an effective monopoly over the market for cable. Measurement of cross-elasticity can be decisive in such a case. A cross-elasticity of 10, for example, would support the company by showing that the two products were such close substitutes that a monopoly of either would not be an effective monopoly of the cable market. A cross-elasticity of 0.5, on the other hand, would support the government's contention that the monopoly of aluminium cable *was* a monopoly over a complete market.

OTHER VARIABLES

Modern studies show that demand is often influenced by a wide variety of socio-economic factors—family size, age, geographical location, type of employment, wealth, and income expectations—not included in the traditional theory of demand. Although significant, the total contribution of all these factors to changes in demand tends to be small. Typically, less than 30 per cent of the variations in demand are accounted for by these 'novel' factors and a much higher proportion is explained by the traditional variables of current prices and incomes.

Why the measurement of demand is important

The empirical measurements of demand elasticity help to provide the theory of price with empirical content. If we knew *nothing* about demand elasticities, then all of the exercises we have gone through in previous chapters would have very little application to the real world. A different view of the importance of empirical measures of demand, made many years ago by Lionel (later Lord) Robbins (1898–1984), is discussed in Box 5.4.[8]

Since the time when Robbins made his criticism, modern research has gone a long way in establishing quantitative demand relations. As time goes by, further evidence accumulates, and economists are far beyond merely wondering if demand curves have negative slopes. Not only do we now know the approximate shape of many demand curves, we also have information about how demand curves shift. Our knowledge of demand relations increases significantly every year.

....

Summary

1 *Elasticity of demand* (also called *price elasticity of demand*) is defined as the percentage change in quantity divided by the percentage change in price that brought it about.

2 When the percentage change in quantity is less than the percentage change in price that brought it about, demand is said to be *inelastic* and a fall in price lowers the total amount spent on the product. When the percentage change in quantity is greater than the percentage change in price that brought it about, demand is said to be *elastic* and a fall in price raises total revenue.

3 A more precise measure that gives a unique value for elasticity on any point on any demand curve replaces $\Delta q/\Delta p$ measured between two points on the curve with $\Delta q/\Delta p$ measured along the tangent to the curve at the point in question (symbolized by dq/dp).

4 The main determinant of the price elasticity of demand is the availability of substitutes for the product. Any one of a group of close substitutes will have a more elastic demand than the group as a whole.

5 Elasticity of demand tends to be greater the longer the time over which adjustment occurs. Items that have a few substitutes in the short run may develop ample substitutes when consumers and producers have time to adapt.

6 *Income elasticity* is the percentage change in quantity demanded divided by the percentage change in income that brought it about. The income elasticity of demand for a product will usually change as income varies.

7 *Cross-elasticity* is the percentage change in quantity demanded divided by the percentage change in the price of some other product that brought it about. It is used to define products that are substitutes for one another (positive cross-elasticity) and products that complement one another (negative cross-elasticity).

8 *Elasticity of supply* is an important concept in economics. It measures the ratio of the percentage change in the quantity supplied of a product to the percentage change in its price.

9 Over the years, economists have measured many price, income, and cross-elasticities of demand. Being able to do so requires the use of statistical techniques to measure the separate influences of each of several variables when all are changing at once. It also requires a solution of the identification problem, which refers to measuring the separate shapes of the demand and the supply curves. This cannot be done from price and quantity data alone.

....

Topics for review

• Price, income, and cross-elasticity of demand

• Zero, inelastic, unitary, elastic, and infinitely elastic demand

• The relation between price elasticity and changes in total expenditure

• Determinants of demand elasticity

• Income elasticities for normal and inferior goods

• Cross-elasticities between substitutes and complements

• Long- and short-run elasticity of demand

• Elasticity of supply and its determinants

[8] L. Robbins, *An Essay on the Nature and Significance of Economic Science* (London: Macmillan, 1932). This provocative work contains classic statements of many views still held by economists. It also states a view on the nature of economic theory and its relation to empirical observations that is contradictory to the one presented in this book. Many other economists of Lord Robbins's time shared this view. For a similar statement, see L. von Mises, *Human Action* (New Haven, Conn.: Yale University Press), Ch. 2. For a view much closer to the one presented in this book, however, see L. Robbins, 'The Present Position of Economics', *Rivista Di Economica*, September 1959.

❧ CHAPTER 6

Demand and supply in action

DEMAND and supply analysis provides a powerful tool for understanding the world around us. It is an apparatus that economists use frequently in their professional lives. Although there is more to be learned, especially about how the behaviour of firms affects supply, we have already come a long way. This chapter provides some payoff. Its purpose is to show you how to use demand and supply to deal with real-world problems. Learning how to use these tools is more important than memorizing the results in the illustrative cases we study.

In the first part of this chapter, we look at how the tools of demand and supply can be used to understand two real-world situations. One is based upon an unusual price war in the UK quality newspaper market. The other is an example of how to anticipate the effects of major supply innovations, in this case as a result of the opening of the Channel Tunnel. In the rest of the chapter, we concentrate on what demand and supply can tell us about the effects of various attempts by governments to intervene in markets.

Keeping up with *The Times*: demand analysis in action

IN September 1993, the owners of *The Times* newspaper launched what was expected to be a price war. They unilaterally lowered the price of *The Times* from 45p to 30p, a price reduction of one-third. The other broadsheet newspapers responded not by matching the price cut, as often happens when a price war breaks out, but by doing absolutely nothing. All the major competing newspapers kept their prices constant and carried on as if nothing had happened. The price war broke out much later.

This is an excellent case to analyse precisely because only one price changed and then nothing else happened for some time. In many real-world situations a lot of variables move together, so that it is hard to disentangle the individual effects without using formal statistical analysis. In this case, not only was there just one discrete price change, but it also occurred in a market where total demand for all newspapers was approximately constant.

THE EFFECTS OF THE PRICE CUT

Table 6.1 provides price and sales figures for the five major national broadsheet newspapers: *The Times*, the *Guardian*, the *Daily Telegraph*, the *Financial Times*, and the *Independent*.

The sales figures reported are average daily sales on weekdays for the four-month period after the price cut by *The Times*, compared with the same four-month period in the previous year. (Comparing the same months in two years removes any seasonal effects.) Notice that the total market size, i.e. the total sales of all these newspapers combined, was virtually constant at around 2.5 million copies. Hence the existing suppliers were fighting for a share of a stable market. If one of them gained more customers, it had to be mainly at the expense of rival suppliers. Since average consumers' incomes changed only slightly over the period

and newspapers have a low income elasticity (most people only buy one newspaper, however rich they are), we would expect total sales to be nearly constant, unless there were a major change in tastes over the period in question. The data suggest that tastes did not change significantly.

Table 6.1 shows us that the 33.33 per cent price reduction of *The Times* led to a 19.14 per cent increase in sales of *The Times* itself. This indicates a price elasticity of demand for *The Times* of -0.57 (calculated as the percentage change in quantity divided by percentage change in price, or 19.14/−33.3). Hence, although there was a clear sales increase, it was proportionately smaller than the reduction in price. As a result, the total daily sales revenue received by *The Times* fell, from £169,576 (376,836 × £0.45) to £134,688 (448,962 × £0.30). Only if the price elasticity had been greater than one would total revenue have increased. We shall enquire shortly why *The Times* might have persisted with its price cut despite the fall in revenue. However, let us first look at the effect on other papers.

The *Independent* suffered most, with a 14.1 per cent loss of sales. This would suggest that the *Independent* was the closest substitute for *The Times*. The cross-elasticity of demand implied by these figures was −14.1/−33.3 = 0.42. (This is positive as both the sales and the price changes were negative.) The cross-elasticity for the *Guardian* was −4.39/−33.3 = 0.13, and the cross-elasticity for the *Daily Telegraph* was −1.93/−33.3 = 0.06.

The *Financial Times* had a small increase in sales over this period. Its cross-elasticity was 0.58/−33.3 = −0.017. Taken at face value, this means that the *Financial Times* is (very weakly) complementary to *The Times*. However, the change is very small, and it is more likely that the two papers serve different markets (and hence have a cross-elasticity of zero) while the slight rise in sales of the *Financial Times* was for reasons unrelated to the fall in the price of

Table 6.1 Changes in demand for newspapers

	Price		Average daily sales		Percentage change	
	Before Sept. '93	After Sept. '93	Pre-Sept. '93	Post-Sept. '93	Price	Sales
The Times	45p	30p	376,836	448,962	−33.3	+19.14
Guardian	45p	45p	420,154	401,705	0	−4.39
Daily Telegraph	45p	45p	1,037,375	1,017,326	0	−1.93
Independent	50p	50p	362,099	311,046	0	−14.10
Financial Times	65p	65p	289,666	291,119	0	+0.58
			2,486,130	2,470,158		

The Times led but no one followed. The table shows the fall in the price of *The Times* and the less-than-proportionate increase in sales. It also shows the constant prices of the other papers, with declining sales (except for the *Financial Times*) as they lost readers to *The Times*.

Source: The Audit Bureau of Circulation. The sales figures are daily average circulation for September 1992 to February 1993 and for September 1993 to February 1994.

The Times. The demand for the *Financial Times* could, for example, be driven more by the demands of business readers, while the other broadsheets are read by ordinary consumers with little interest in business. Further study of the demand for the *Financial Times* would be required to settle this issue.

DEMAND AND SUPPLY AT WORK

So far we have looked at the demand for these newspapers. Can we use the theory of market price which we developed in Chapter 4 to study this case? The theory in Chapter 4 assumes that there are many buyers and many sellers, each one of whom must accept the price that is determined by overall demand and supply. Newspapers fit this theory on the demand side since there are tens of thousands of buyers each of whom can do nothing to affect the price. On the supply side, however, there are only a few newspapers, each of which sets the price of its product. Since our interest is mainly with the demand side of the market, we can use our demand-supply theory. We fit in the supply side by assuming a perfectly elastic supply of each newspaper: each sets its price and then sells all the copies that are demanded at that price.

Figure 6.1 illustrates the effect of *The Times*'s price cut, both on its own quantity demanded and on the demand for the *Independent*. Notice that, since each newspaper is a distinct product, there is no industry supply curve for newspapers. Each supplier simply sets a price and lets demand determine the level of its sales.

Our observation that the demand for *The Times* is price-inelastic may explain why the rival newspapers did not cut their prices. If their demands were also inelastic, they would

have lost more revenue by cutting their prices than they did by leaving them unchanged. As it was, the *Independent* suffered a daily loss of revenue of a little over £25,000 per day (just over 50,000 sales at 50p each).

The puzzle is why *The Times* persisted with its price drop even though it ended up losing revenue. We can only speculate at the answer since we have no knowledge of what the managers at *The Times* were thinking.

One possibility is that the increased circulation of *The Times*, as a result of its price cut, led to an increase in advertising revenue. Newspapers are able to charge advertisers rates for space that are related to circulation. Hence revenue from selling the paper on the street is not the only source of income to the publishers. (Many towns in the UK have free newspapers which make all their revenue from advertising.) If *The Times* were able to increase its advertising revenue by more than about £35,000, the price reduction might be understood as a move that increased profit.

A second possibility is that the managers of *The Times* thought that their price cut might force the *Independent* out of business—a strategy sometimes referred to as *predatory pricing* (see Chapter 14). The *Independent* was known to be in financial difficulty through the winter of 1993/94 and doubts about its survival persisted until March 1994; at that time it was taken over by another company (the Mirror Group) which had more financial resources. Hence if *The Times* was adopting a predatory price, its strategy failed. However, had it succeeded, it is likely that a high proportion of *Independent*'s readers would have moved over to *The Times* since the sales data suggest that the *Independent* was the closest substitute for *The Times*.

We cannot analyse what happened next in detail, since it was in the future at our time of writing. What we know is

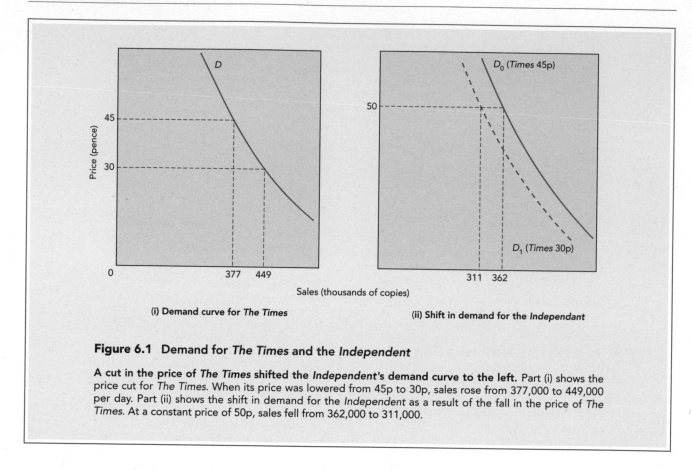

Figure 6.1   Demand for *The Times* and the *Independent*

A cut in the price of *The Times* shifted the *Independent*'s demand curve to the left. Part (i) shows the price cut for *The Times*. When its price was lowered from 45p to 30p, sales rose from 377,000 to 449,000 per day. Part (ii) shows the shift in demand for the *Independent* as a result of the fall in the price of *The Times*. At a constant price of 50p, sales fell from 362,000 to 311,000.

that a price war broke out in the summer of 1994, when the *Telegraph* and the *Independent* both cut their prices to 30p and *The Times* further cut its price to 20p. The effects of this later price war are not known yet. However, we can say that the tools of demand and supply will be just as helpful in interpreting these events, as they unfold, as they were in giving us some insight into the newspaper market in the first place.

The Channel Tunnel

WE now use the tools of demand and supply to analyse what is likely to happen in the market for cross-Channel journeys between England and mainland Europe once the Channel Tunnel comes into full operation. Readers will be able to compare our expectations with reality. The tunnel opened shortly before this book went to press, and was expected to be operating at its full level of service by the spring of 1995.

We confine ourselves to the market in cross-Channel journeys, though there will undoubtedly be other economic effects—such as on the location of industry and on property values in Kent and north-western France—and there is also the market for freight which we do not discuss.

Once again, we have to stretch things a bit to use demand and supply curves to study this issue. The demand curve is for cross-Channel trips of all sorts. Although things other than price, such as speed and convenience, will affect the division of demand between the various types of travel, we hold these factors constant so that the overall quantity demanded varies with the price. The supply comes from the tunnel, several shipping firms, hovercraft, and airlines. Although firms operating each of these types of travel have power over price, it is

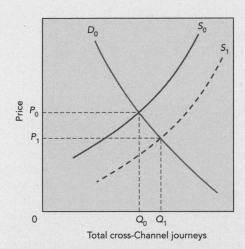

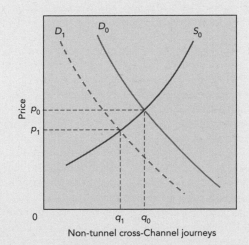

Figure 6.2 The market for cross-Channel journeys

The opening of the tunnel adds to total supply but reduces demand for non-tunnel travel. Part (i) shows demand and supply curves for all cross-Channel journeys. The opening of the tunnel shifts the supply curve to the right from S_0 to S_1. With a given demand curve D_0, this lowers price and increases quantity from P_0 and Q_0 to P_1 and Q_1. Part (ii) shows the demand and supply curves for non-tunnel journeys (air and ferry). The fall in price of a substitute (tunnel travel has fallen from an infinite price to a finite one) shifts the demand curve for other forms of travel to the left from D_0 to D_1. The price and quantity, accordingly, fall from p_0 and q_0 to p_1 and q_1. Notice that before the tunnel opened the original demand and supply curves were the same in both diagrams (so P_0 and Q_0 were equal to p_0 and q_0). Total tunnel journeys after opening will be measured by Q_0Q_1, which is the extra journeys created by the tunnel, plus q_1q_0, which is those trips that would have gone by air or ferry before, but now shift to the tunnel.

safe to assume that the total amount they will all supply will vary directly with the price they end up charging.

Before the tunnel, the main suppliers of cross-Channel journeys were the airlines and ferry operators. The question to be answered is: what is likely to happen when a major new source of supply opens up? Figure 6.2 analyses the problem with demand and supply curves. The opening of the tunnel is represented by a rightward shift of the supply curve. Part (i) of the figure shows the total demand and supply for cross-Channel journeys. Part (ii) shows the demand for airline and ferry journeys. Initially, the demand curve facing ferry and airline operators is the same as the total market demand curve. The opening of the tunnel shifts the market supply curve to the right in part (i). However, while the market demand curve remains unchanged after the tunnel opens, the demand curve facing ferry and air companies falls.[1] (One way to think of the effect on demand for air and ferry journeys is that the price of a substitute—tunnel journeys—has fallen from infinity to some positive number.)

Notice that it does not matter for the general analysis whether tunnel journeys are cheaper or more expensive than existing methods of travel, although the quantitative

effects will depend on this. All that matters is that they are cheap enough so that some passengers travel by the tunnel who might otherwise have gone by another route—a condition that will certainly be met. Notice also that for this purpose we can lump together all forms of transport that are alternatives to the tunnel (and assume an average price). If we wanted to do a more detailed study we could, for example, separate airlines from ferries. Or we could look at each air and ferry route individually. If you were in the airline or ferry business this might be necessary, but we can draw interesting conclusions even for an aggregate of all suppliers. Also, dealing with suppliers in the aggregate makes the use of a supply curve safer (because, as we shall discover in Chapter 13, monopolists do not have supply curves).

The first prediction implied by Figure 6.2(i) is that the result of opening the tunnel will be a fall in the average price of cross-Channel journeys and an increase in the quantity purchased. The increase in the total market size results (at

[1] There may be some increase in demand as people who did not travel because they were averse to air and sea transport now decide to travel. This shift is probably small enough to ignore in a broad-brush study, although a fuller analysis would have to allow for it.

least in the short term when incomes are constant) from the rise in quantity demanded in response to the fall in price. How big this rise will be depends entirely on the size of the price reduction and the elasticity of demand.

Figure 6.2(ii) shows that the air and ferry operators will experience a fall in demand. (Price of a substitute falls.) Initially, this will be felt entirely in empty seats and car decks, because prices are set in advance (though there may be some anticipation of a demand fall in price-setting). Very soon, however, this is likely to lead to special cut-price deals, and eventually to sustained price-cutting even for regular fares. Only if the supply curve of air and ferry services were totally inelastic (vertical) would there be no fall in air and ferry journeys, but in that case there would be a sharp fall in revenue and an even larger fall in price. This could happen in the very short term if the air and ferry operators were determined to keep seats full and followed an aggressive price-cutting strategy. In this event, however, the revenue loss would likely cause airlines to shift some of their airplanes to other routes and ferry owners to decommission or sell some of their ferries. Hence, the supply

curve of air and ferry services would become less inelastic over time.

In the longer term, the only factor that could save the airlines and ferries from the sales decline would be income growth, causing a growth in demand for travel. This is likely, since travel typically increases more than in proportion to income. But we cannot say how long it will take.

Quantitative predictions in this area are difficult because we cannot observe an event like the Channel Tunnel opening elsewhere. However, it has been estimated that after the tunnel opens there will be an approximate market size of 70 million journeys per year in the year 2003. Of these, the tunnel may take a market share of about 35 per cent, or about 25 million passenger journeys. Up to about half of these 25 million journeys may be diverted from air and ferries, and the rest will be new journeys stimulated by the new lower prices.

Further analysis will have to wait until we see what actually happens. However, readers can check for themselves the clear predictions of price-cutting by airline and ferry operators and of increased travel.

Government intervention in markets

BEFORE we continue with this chapter, we need to introduce a third set of players on the economic stage. We have called decision-takers *agents*, and in Chapter 4 we introduced two sets of agents: consumers and firms. The third set is most accurately called the *central authorities* but is more commonly, if loosely, referred to as the **government** or the state. This broad class of agents includes all public agencies, government bodies, and other organizations belonging to, or owing their existence to, either central or local governments. This includes such institutions as the central bank, the civil service, commissions and regulatory agencies, the cabinet, the police force, the judiciary, and all other authorities that can exercise control over the behaviour of producers and consumers. It is not important to draw up a comprehensive list of all central authorities; just keep in mind the general idea of a group of organizations that exist at the centre of legal and political power and exert some control over the rest of us.[2]

The dominant form of economic organization in the world today is the market economy. (See Chapter 1 for a discussion of alternative structures.) However, there are many current, or recent, examples of attempts by governments to alter market outcomes. Although this is often done for the best of motives, demand and supply analysis

helps us to see how and why the intended effects are not always achieved.

If, for example, the government wishes to influence the price at which some product is bought and sold, it has two main alternatives. First, it may change the equilibrium price by altering the product's demand or supply. Second, it may enact legislation that regulates the price. **Price controls** refer to the latter alternative: influencing price by laws, rather than by market forces.

If controls are used to hold price at a disequilibrium level, what determines the quantity actually traded on the market? Any voluntary market transaction requires both a willing buyer and a willing seller. Thus, if quantity demanded is less than quantity supplied, demand will determine the amount actually traded, and the excess supply will remain in the hands of the unsuccessful sellers. If quantity supplied is less than quantity demanded, however, supply will determine the amount actually traded and the excess

---

[2] It is *not* a basic assumption of economics that the central authorities always act in a consistent fashion as if they were a single individual. Indeed, conflict among different central-authority agencies is often an important component in theories that analyse government intervention in the economy.

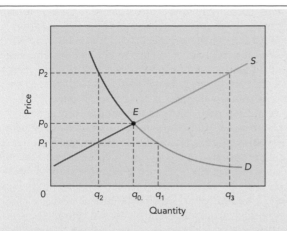

Figure 6.3 Disequilibrium quantity

In disequilibrium, quantity exchanged is determined by the lesser of quantity demanded or quantity supplied. When the market is in equilibrium at point E, price is p_0, while quantity demanded equals quantity supplied at q_0. For prices below p_0, the quantity exchanged will be determined by the supply curve. For example, the quantity q_2 will be exchanged at the disequilibrium price p_1 in spite of the excess demand of q_1-q_2. For prices above p_0, the quantity exchanged will be determined by the demand curve. For example, the quantity q_2 will be exchanged at the disequilibrium price p_2, in spite of the excess supply of q_3-q_2. Thus, the dark blue and dark red portion of the S and D curves show the actual quantities exchanged at each price.

demand will take the form of desired purchases by unsuccessful buyers. This is shown graphically in Figure 6.3.

At any disequilibrium price, quantity exchanged is determined by the lesser of quantity demanded or quantity supplied.

This result is often expressed by the maxim: *in disequilibrium, the short side of the market dominates* (i.e. determines what is bought and sold).

Maximum-price legislation

Since the dawn of history, governments have passed laws regulating the prices at which certain products could be sold. In this section we concentrate on laws setting *maximum* permissible prices, which are often called 'price ceilings'. Such laws have had many purposes. Governments of medieval cities sometimes sought to protect their citizens from the consequences of crop failures by fixing a maximum price at which bread could be sold. In modern times,

many governments have employed rent controls in an attempt to make housing available at a price that could be afforded by lower-income groups.

The effects on price and quantity Although frequently referred to as *fixed* or *frozen prices*, most price ceilings actually specify the highest permissible price that producers may legally charge. If the ceiling is set above the equilibrium price, it has no effect, since the equilibrium remains attainable. If, however, the ceiling is set below the equilibrium price, it determines the price—in which case it is said to be *binding*. The key consequences of price ceilings are shown in Figure 6.4.

The setting of a maximum price either will have no effect (maximum price set at or above the equilibrium) or will cause a shortage of the product (maximum price set below the equilibrium), thereby reducing the quantity actually bought and sold below its equilibrium value.

Allocation of available supply In the case of a binding price ceiling, production is insufficient to satisfy everyone who wishes to buy the product. Since price is not allowed to rise

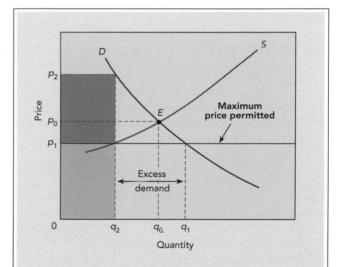

Figure 6.4 Black market pricing

A price ceiling set below the equilibrium price causes excess demand and invites a black market. Equilibrium price is at p_0. If a price ceiling is set at p_1, the quantity demanded will rise to q_1 and the quantity supplied will fall to q_2. Quantity actually exchanged will be q_2. Although excess demand is q_1-q_2, price may not legally rise to restore equilibrium. Black marketeers would buy q_2 at the controlled price of p_1, paying the amount shown by the light blue area p_1q_2. They would sell at the price p_2, earning profits shown by the dark blue area between p_1 and p_2.

so as to allocate the available supply among the would-be purchasers, some other method of allocation must be found. Theory does not predict what this other method will be, but experience has shown several possibilities.

If shops sell to the first customers who arrive, people are likely to rush to those stores that are rumoured to have any stocks of the scarce product. Long queues will develop, and allocation will be on the basis of luck, or to those knowing enough to gain from the principle of 'first come, first served'. This system was commonly found in the command economies of Eastern Europe, where queuing was a way of life.

Sometimes shopkeepers themselves decide who will get the scarce products and who will not. They may keep products under the counter and sell only to regular customers, or only to people of a certain colour or religion. Such a system is called allocation by **sellers' preferences**.

If the central authorities dislike the allocation system that results from price ceilings, they can ration the goods, giving out ration coupons sufficient to purchase the available supply. The authorities then determine, as a conscious act of policy, how the available supply is to be allocated. The coupons might be distributed equally, or on such criteria as age, sex, marital status, or number of dependants. Rationing by coupons was used in Britain during, and immediately after, the Second World War. During the oil crisis of 1973/4, some US states introduced 'odd–even' rationing schemes for petrol, to prevent prices from rising to market-clearing levels; car owners with number plates ending in an odd number could buy petrol on one particular day and those with even number plates could buy on the next day. Road congestion can be thought of as a rationing mechanism. Box 6.1 discusses use of the price mechanism to solve the congestion problem.

Any official rationing scheme substitutes the government's preferences for the sellers' preferences in allocating a product that is in excess demand because of a binding price ceiling.

Black markets A binding price ceiling, with or without rationing, is likely to give rise to a **black market**. This is a market in which goods are sold illegally at prices that violate the legal restrictions. Many products have only a few manufacturers but many retailers. Although it is easy to police the producers, it is difficult even to locate, much less control, all those who are, or could be, retailing the product.

Figure 6.4 illustrates the case where the central authorities can fix the price that producers get, but are unable to control the price at which retailers sell to the public. Output is restricted by the low price received by producers, while consumers must pay the high price that equates demand to the available supply. The difference between what consumers pay and what producers get goes as profits to the black marketeers.

The theory predicts that the potential for a profitable black market will exist whenever effective price ceilings are imposed. The actual growth of such a market depends on there being a few people willing to risk heavy penalties by running a black market supply organization, and a reasonably large number of persons prepared to purchase goods illegally on such a market.

It is unlikely that all of the output will be sold on the black market—both because there are many honest people in every society, and because the central authorities usually have some power to enforce their price laws. Thus, the normal case is not the extreme result mentioned above. Instead, some of the limited supplies will be sold at the controlled price and some at the black market price.

Economists can evaluate a black market situation only when the central authorities' objectives are known. If the authorities are concerned mainly with an equitable distribution of a scarce product, effective price control on manufacturers, plus a largely uncontrollable black market at the retail level, may produce the worst possible result. If, however, they are interested mainly in restricting production in order to release resources for other more urgent needs, such as war production, the policy works effectively, if somewhat unfairly. Where the purpose is to keep prices down, the policy is a failure to the extent that black marketeers succeed in raising prices, and a success to the extent that sales actually occur at the controlled prices.

Empirical evidence There is much evidence confirming these predictions. In the First and Second World Wars, governments set binding ceilings on many prices. The legislation of maximum prices was always followed by shortages, then by either the introduction of rationing or the growth of some private method of allocation (such as sellers' preferences), and then by the rise of some sort of black market. The ceilings were more effective in limiting consumption than in controlling prices, although they did restrain price increases to some extent. Until recently, many of the former socialist countries of Eastern Europe followed a policy of controlling food prices at levels that were below the equilibrium prices. Chronic shortages, queues, allocation by sellers' preferences, and black markets were the result.

Rent controls

Our study of the consequences of maximum-price legislation has an important application in rent-control legislation. Although there have been debates on the desirability of rent-controls, there is little doubt about its major consequences. They can all be observed in the United Kingdom, where rent control was first introduced in 1914 and gradually extended to cover the entire rental market. Over a period of sixty years, the market for privately owned

BOX 6.1

Road pricing

Some products are provided free, but this does not mean that everyone can have as much as they like all the time. Unless provision expands to equal the quantity demanded at zero price, excess demand will develop and will be handled by some other non-price allocation mechanism. Examples include waiting lists for health services and congestion on the roads.

Economists have long argued that efficient road use requires that it be priced. Indeed, in the seventeenth and eighteenth centuries many main roads in Britain were 'turnpikes' and travellers had to pay a fee to travel on them. This fee was used to maintain the road surface. Throughout the twentieth century, road provision in the United Kingdom has been paid by the state out of the revenue from general taxation. (Specific taxes on cars such as the road fund licence have not been linked directly to expenditure on roads.) Some other countries have charges on some major roads, such as the autostrada of Italy, the autoroutes of France, some turnpikes in the United States, and new motorways in Mexico.

The current problem is that the growth of car ownership has been such that demand for road use continually outstrips supply; for example, the orbital motorway around London has had frequent jams from the day it opened. Also, many town centres suffer severe traffic congestion during rush hours, and, in some cases, for most of the day.

The economics of demand and supply suggests that the problem of congestion will be common if we let people use roads free. At zero price, the demand for road use exceeds the supply, so congestion will result at busy periods—in effect, there will be rationing by queuing. This creates an economic loss for those whose time is valuable. By introducing a positive price which reduces quantity demanded to the market-clearing price, all users will be able to use road services without congestion. Travellers with essential business will be happy to pay, while those who could easily take another route, use public transport, or postpone a journey will be encouraged to do so.

Pricing of specific bits of road with limited access presents no technical problem. Hence, for example, we already have tolls on the Severn Bridge, the Dartford Crossing, the Forth Bridge, and the Mersey Tunnel. Although the pricing of road use in, say, central London presents greater problems, these will soon be solved by the electronic tagging of cars, now in the experimental stage. An electronic meter will soon be able to record the identity of each car passing over city streets and motorways. Drivers can then be billed for miles travelled just as householders are now billed for gas or electricity used. This may seem futuristic, but the UK government announced in 1993 that it intended to introduce electronic road pricing by 1998. Although that timetable may not be met, road pricing seems inevitable at some time in the not-too-distant future.

The price set for road use will be higher in periods of peak demand and lower in off-peak periods. This will tend to even out the flow compared with the zero price situation in which the road is congested at peak periods but has excess capacity during the off-peak times. A form of this type of pricing has been operating for some time in Singapore—a country with many people but little space. Licences to drive only at weekends are considerably cheaper than licences to drive at any time, and there is a surcharge for driving in the central area during peak traffic times. Also, the number of licences issued is limited. As a result of this and other supporting measures, such as a first-class public transport system, Singapore has one of the few urban road systems in the whole of South-East Asia that is not heavily congested and polluted. In contrast, Bangkok and Manila are suffering near traffic paralysis from road congestion.

The lesson of this example is that the economics of markets has important applications even in areas where there is not an obvious market structure at present. Free goods can be consumed without restriction only if the supply continues to equal (or exceed) demand at zero price. Where the free good is a gift of nature, pricing soon appears when a resource becomes scarce. Where the free good is provided by the state, pricing is often preferable to other rationing mechanisms, for at least, it provides a potential solution to the allocation problem.

---

unfurnished rental accommodation was largely eliminated! From 45 per cent of households in privately owned rental accommodation in 1945, the figure fell steadily, until, by the end of the 1980s, it was only 8 per cent. Finally, in 1989 the British government announced measures to phase out rent controls. They also encouraged (subsidized) the formation of housing associations, which are non-profit-making providers of rental accommodation. However, the long-term consequences of rent controls will affect the UK housing market well into the twenty-first century.

In other countries, rent control has caused severe housing shortages. In the United States, rent control is in the hands of individual cities. The existence of controlled markets in some cities and uncontrolled markets in others facilitates the testing of predictions about rent controls. For example, rent control in the Queens borough of New York City was accompanied by severe housing shortages; whole blocks of buildings were abandoned because the controlled rent did not even cover operating costs, although they could have lasted for decades. Uncontrolled markets in the south-western United States have seen supplies increase rapidly to meet the growing demands for housing as more people moved there. Rent control over lower-rent properties was introduced in the Canadian province of Ontario in

1975, and extended to all rental accommodation in 1985. Since that time the construction of rental accommodation has halted, except where it is subsidized. Conversions to owner-occupancy soared and were then made illegal, entrance fees and subletting have become common, and would-be renters have resorted to increasingly desperate measures, ranging from bribes to searching out the families of newly deceased tenants.

Economic theory predicts that these consequences always follow, sooner or later, from the imposition of *effective* rent controls. Rent controls are just a special case of price ceilings. They are usually imposed to freeze rents at their current levels at times when equilibrium rents are rising either because demand is shifting rightward (due to forces such as rising population and income) or because supply is shifting leftward (due to forces such as rising costs). The result is that the controlled rents are soon well below the free-market equilibrium level, and excess demand appears. The further the controlled price falls below the free-market price, the stronger are the consequences. (The discrepancy often grows in periods of inflation, because the controlled price is not increased as much as the price level is rising.)

The following predictions about rent controls are simply applications to the housing market of the results concerning binding price controls in any competitive market.

1. There will be a shortage of rental accommodation; quantity demanded will exceed quantity supplied.

2. The quantity of accommodation occupied will be less than if free-market rents had been charged.

3. Black markets will appear. Landlords may require large lump-sum entrance fees from new tenants, and may evict existing tenants so as to collect this fee. Existing tenants may sublet their accommodation, charging the market price while themselves paying only the controlled price.

4. As a political response to the forces just outlined, governments typically pass security-of-tenure laws, which protect the tenant from eviction and thus give existing tenants priority over potential new tenants. By making it harder to evict undesirable tenants, these laws reduce the expected return from any given rental price. Landlords may resort to illegal harassment to evict tenants.

FURTHER ANALYSIS OF THE RENTAL MARKET

We can say more about the effects of rent controls if we take a closer look at the specific supply and demand conditions in the rental housing market.

Supply The supply of accommodation depends on the *stock* of rental housing available, and in any year it is composed mainly of buildings built in earlier years. The stock is added to by conversions of owner-occupied housing into rental accommodation and the construction of new buildings. It is diminished by conversions to other uses, and the demolition or abandonment of existing buildings whose economic life is over.

These considerations mean that we can draw more than one supply curve for rental accommodation depending on how much time is allowed for reactions to occur to any given level of rents. We shall distinguish just two such curves.

The *long-run supply curve* relates rents to the quantity of rental accommodation that will be supplied after sufficient time has passed for all adjustments to be made. If the expected return from investing in new rental units rises significantly above the return on comparable other investments, there will be a flow of investment funds into the building of new flats. It may take several years for this adjustment to be completed.

If the return from rental accommodation falls significantly below that obtainable on comparable investments, investment will go elsewhere. Old flats will not be replaced as they wear out, so the quantity available will fall drastically. Existing flats may be removed from the rental market as their freeholds, or leaseholds, are sold. Depletion of the housing stock, as old flats wear out and are not replaced, can take many decades.

The *short-run supply curve* relates rents to quantity supplied when only a short time—say, a few months—is allowed for immediate adjustments to be made in response to a change in rents. Because adjustments to the stock of rental accommodation take a long time, the short-run supply curve tends to be quite inelastic. The reaction of the quantity supplied to price changes in the short run is limited mainly to conversions. Rental accommodation will be converted into alternative uses when price falls, and accommodation now in other uses will be converted into rental accommodation when price rises.

The long-run supply of rental accommodation is responsive to changes in market conditions, making the long-run supply curve quite *elastic*. The short-run supply curve that relates rentals to the quantity supplied tends to be quite *inelastic* at the level of the quantity currently supplied.

Demand Although accommodation may be a necessity, *rental* accommodation is not. As rents rise in a particular area, each of the following trends will occur:

1. Some people will stop renting and will buy instead.

2. Some will move to where rental accommodation is cheaper.

3. Some will economize on the amount of housing they use by renting smaller, cheaper accommodation (or renting out a room or two in their present accommodation).

4. Some will double up, and others will not 'undouble' (for example, young adults will not move out of parental homes as quickly as they might otherwise have done).

Such behaviour contributes to a substantial elasticity of the demand for rental housing.

These special features of the housing market allow us to be more specific about the effects of controls that keep the price of rental accommodation below its equilibrium value.

As shown in Figure 6.5, most of the initial effects of rent controls are on the demand side. A shortage is caused mainly because quantity demanded exceeds the equilibrium quantity supplied, with only a small shortfall of quantity supplied below its equilibrium value as a secondary cause of the shortage. Over the long term, however, supply falls greatly, and the main cause of the shortage of rental accommodation comes from the supply side. Under free-market conditions, rents would rise and quantity demanded would shrink as people economized on housing.

Rent controls prevent such increases in rents from occurring. Thus, even while the quantity of rental accommodation is contracting for the reasons discussed above, the signal to economize on rental accommodation is *not* given through rising rents. The housing shortage grows as the stock of rental accommodation shrinks while nothing decreases the demand for it.

The long lag helps to explain why rent controls are so often tolerated in spite of the harm that they do in the long run. The first generation of tenants gains from controlled rents, while future generations suffer from a drastically reduced supply of rental accommodation.

The growing housing shortage puts pressure on the state to build the accommodation that private investors will not supply at controlled rents. In the United Kingdom local authorities did so for decades, supplying large quantities of council housing. In response to financial stringency in the late 1970s and 1980s, however, the construction of new council housing was curtailed and much of the existing stock was sold to occupiers.

The shortage of rental accommodation makes existing occupiers reluctant to move from areas of high unemployment to areas where, although unemployment is low, rent-controlled accommodation is hard to find. People are also reluctant to move out of accommodation that is no longer suitable because families have grown up and moved away.

Effective rent control leads to housing shortages, black market prices, security-of-tenure laws, pressure for public housing, and a reluctance of sitting tenants to move from their present accommodation, even when this is no longer suitable.

Rent controls are an example of a price ceiling. Governments sometimes legislate a 'price floor', which states the minimum price at which some good or service may be sold. The most topical example in Europe is minimum wage legislation. The Maastricht Treaty of 1992, creating the EU out of the EC, included a provision for a minimum wage. However, the United Kingdom negotiated an opt-out from the so-called Social Chapter. None the less, the Labour Party proposed to introduce a national minimum wage in its 1992 election manifesto and made it clear that it would opt back into the EU Social Chapter. Hence minimum wages are likely to be a very hotly debated topic in Britain over the next few years. Readers might like to use the tools of demand and supply at this stage to anticipate what problems might arise if a minimum wage is set above the market-clearing wage level. We, however, postpone further discussion of this topic until Chapter 18, where we look at labour markets in more detail.

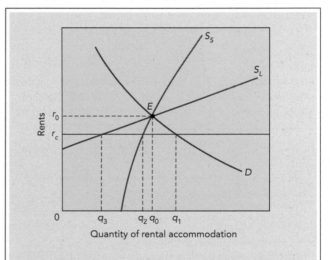

Figure 6.5 Rent control in the short and long run

Rent control causes housing shortages that worsen as time passes. The controlled rent of r_c forces rents below their free-market equilibrium value of r_0. The short-run supply of housing is shown by the rather inelastic curve S_S. The controls reduce quantity supplied to q_2 in the short run, and the housing shortage becomes q_1–q_2. Over time, supply falls, as shown by the long-run supply curve S_L. In long-run equilibrium, there are only q_3 units of rental accommodation. Since the long-run supply is quite elastic, the shortage of rental accommodation of q_1–q_3 that occurs after supply has fully adjusted ends up being much larger than the initial shortage q_1–q_2.

The problems of agriculture

TO the casual observer, the agricultural sector of almost any advanced Western economy presents a series of apparent paradoxes. Food is a basic necessity of life. Yet, over the last century, agricultural sectors have been declining in relative importance. The number of farmers and farmworkers in the original six EC member-states fell (from nearly 10.5 million in 1960 to under 5 million in 1990), and many of those persons who have remained on the land have been receiving incomes well below national averages.

Governments of many countries have felt it expedient to intervene, and have resorted to a bewildering array of controls and subsidies. These have often led to the accumulation of vast surpluses which have sometimes rotted in storage and sometimes been sold abroad at subsidized prices. The theory of demand and supply can help us gain some insight into these, and other, agricultural problems.

Short-term fluctuations in prices and incomes: supply-side influences

Agricultural production is subject to large variations resulting from factors beyond human control; for example, bad weather reduces output below that planned by farmers, while exceptionally good weather pushes production above planned levels. What are the effects of these unplanned fluctuations?

A supply curve shows desired output and sales at each market price. If there are unplanned variations in output, then actual output will diverge from its planned level.

The basic predictions about the consequences of such fluctuations are derived in Figure 6.6. Variations in farm output cause prices to fluctuate in the opposite direction to crop sizes. A bumper crop sends prices down; a poor crop sends them up. The price changes will be larger the less elastic is the demand curve.

Because farm products often have inelastic demands, price fluctuations tend to be large in response to unplanned changes in production.

Now consider the effects of the expenditures on purchasing farm products and hence on the revenues that farmers earn by selling their products.[3] Here the relations are a bit more complex, but they all follow immediately from the results established on p. 89.

---

[3] While we can make predictions in this section only about their revenues, such receipts are closely related to farmers' incomes. We can, therefore, without risk of serious error, extend these predictions to incomes.

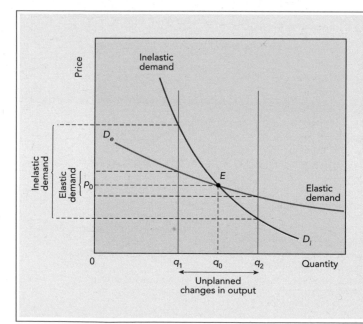

Figure 6.6   Unplanned fluctuations in output

Unplanned fluctuations in output lead to much sharper fluctuations in price if the demand curve is inelastic than if it is elastic. Suppose that the expected price is p_0 and the planned output is q_0. The two curves D_i and D_e are alternative demand curves. If actual production always equalled planned production, the equilibrium price and quantity would be p_0 and q_0 with either demand curve. Unplanned fluctuations in output, however, cause quantity to vary year by year between q_1 (a bad harvest) and q_2 (a good harvest). When demand is inelastic (shown by the red curve), prices will show large fluctuations. When demand is elastic (shown by the blue curve), prices will show much smaller fluctuations. (In both cases, elasticity is measured around the point E.)

Unplanned variations in output will cause producers' revenues:

1. to vary in the same direction as output varies whenever demand for the product is elastic;
2. to vary in the opposite direction as output varies whenever demand for the product is inelastic;
3. to be unchanged whenever the demand for the product is of unit elasticity;
4. to fluctuate more, the further the elasticity of demand diverges from unity in either direction.

Since many agricultural products have inelastic demands, farmers often see their incomes dwindling when nature is unexpectedly kind in producing a bumper crop, while their incomes rise when crops are poor.[4]

_____

[4] It does not follow that every individual farmer's income must rise (after all, some farmers may have nothing to harvest); it follows only that the aggregate revenue earned by *all* farmers must rise.

Cyclical fluctuations in prices and incomes: demand-side influences

Agricultural markets are subject not only to short-run instabilities arising from uncontrollable changes in output, but also to cyclical instability resulting from shifts in demand. In periods of prosperity, employment and wages are high, which implies a strong demand for most products. In periods of depressed business activity, employment and wages are diminished, which implies a weaker demand for most products. Thus, the demand curves for most products rise and fall as business activity ebbs and flows.

The effects on product prices are analysed in Figure 6.7. Industrial products typically have rather elastic supply curves, so that demand shifts tend to cause large changes in outputs but small changes in prices. Agricultural products tend to have rather inelastic supplies. Thus, when demand falls because of a decline in general business activity, prices tend to fall drastically in agriculture but to remain fairly

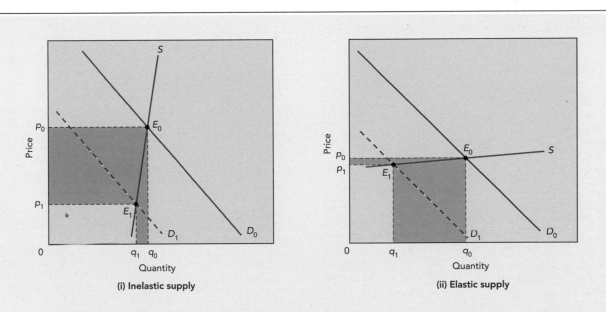

Figure 6.7 The effect on receipts of a shift in demand

When demand falls, both inelastic and elastic supply curves can lead to a sharp decrease in receipts, but the effect on price is very different in the two cases. In each part of the diagram, when demand decreases from D_0 to D_1, price and quantity decrease from p_0 and q_0 to p_1 and q_1. Total receipts decline by the shaded area. In (i), which is typical of many agricultural markets, the result is mainly a sharp decrease in price. Output and employment remain high, but the drastic fall in price will reduce or eliminate profits and put downward pressure on wages. In (ii), which is typical of the markets for many manufactured goods, the result is primarily a sharp decrease in quantity. Employment and total profits earned fall drastically, though wage rates and profit margins on what is produced may remain close to their former levels.

The effects of an increase in demand are merely the reverse of those just studied. They can be seen by letting the initial demand curve be D_1, while the shift takes it to D_0.

stable in manufacturing. In both cases, revenues fluctuate cyclically.

When demand falls and the supply is very inelastic, revenue falls because price falls a great deal; when demand falls and the supply is very elastic, revenue falls because quantity falls a great deal.

Agricultural stabilization programmes

In free-market economies, agricultural incomes often tend to fluctuate around a low *average* level. As a result, agricultural stabilization programmes often have two goals: to reduce the fluctuations, and to raise the average level of farm incomes. We shall see that these two goals of stable incomes and high incomes often conflict with each other.

Stabilization schemes can be illustrated by considering those designed to lessen the effect of unplanned fluctuations in supply. A similar analysis could be carried out for schemes designed to lessen the effects of fluctuations in demand.

Market stabilization by a producers' association   One method of preventing fluctuations in prices and incomes for non-perishable agricultural products is for the individual farmers to form a producers' association which stabilizes the quantity coming on to the market, in spite of variations in production. Under the conditions shown in Figure 6.8, a producers' association can stabilize price and income in spite of year-to-year fluctuations in output. It does this by selling the same quantity every year, adding to its stocks when output exceeds that quantity and selling from its stocks when output falls short. Farmers are paid when output is sold, not when it is delivered to the storehouses. Provided that the level of sales to be maintained is equal to the *average* level of production over good and bad years, the policy can be carried on indefinitely. If, however, the producers attempt to keep the price too high, sales will be less than *average* production. Then, taken over a number of years, additions to stocks will exceed sales from stocks, and the association's stockpile will grow.

Market stabilization by government sales and purchases What will happen if a producers' association is not formed but the government itself attempts to stabilize the incomes of farmers, as so often occurs? To do this, the government buys and adds to its own stockpile when there is a surplus, and sells when there is a shortage. The government is assumed not to consume any of the product but only to hold stocks. If it wishes to stabilize farmers' incomes, should it aim, like the producers' association, at keeping price constant at all times?

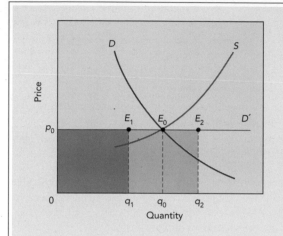

Figure 6.8   Alternative schemes for price stabilization

Stabilizing quantity sold stabilizes income, though stabilizing price does not. The curve S shows planned supply at each price; p_0 and q_0 are the equilibrium price and quantity, respectively. Actual production is assumed to vary in an unplanned manner between q_1 and q_2.

(i) *A producers' association.* When production is q_2, the producers' association sells q_0 and stores q_2-q_0. When production is q_1, it still sells q_0, supplementing the current production by selling q_0-q_1 from its stocks. Producers' revenue is stabilized at p_0q_0.

(ii) *Government purchases and sales at a stabilized price.* The quantity sold to the public is always q_0, and this stabilizes price at p_0. Producers sell their whole crop every year. When production is q_2, the government buys q_2-q_0 and stores it. When production is q_1, the government sells q_0-q_1 from storage. The government policy converts the demand curve facing farmers from the negatively sloped curve D to the perfectly elastic curve D'. Farmers' revenue varies from p_0q_1 (the dark blue area), when production is q_1, to p_0q_2 (the entire medium and dark blue areas), when production is q_2.

The answer is no: this policy will not stabilize farmers' incomes. Farmers are now faced with an infinitely elastic demand at a stabilized price. They are able to sell any amount at that price; whatever the public will not buy, the government will purchase. (To put upper limits on their purchases, governments often combine price support with quotas.) The second part of the caption to Figure 6.8 shows that, if prices are held constant and farmers sell their whole production each year, farmers' incomes will fluctuate in proportion to fluctuations in production. This government policy, therefore, will not eliminate income fluctuations, but will simply reverse their direction. Now, good crops will be associated with high incomes, while poor crops will be associated with low incomes.

What, then, must a government's policy be if it wishes to

stabilize farmers' revenues through its own purchases and sales in the open market? Too much price stability causes revenues to vary directly with production, as in the case just considered, while too little price stability causes them to vary inversely with production, as in the free-market case shown in Figure 6.6. It appears that the government should aim at some intermediate degree of price stability. In fact, if it allows prices to vary in inverse proportion to variations in production, revenues will be stabilized. A 10 per cent rise in production should be met by a 10 per cent fall in price, and a 10 per cent fall in production by a 10 per cent rise in price.

Figure 6.9 analyses this policy. Farmers sell their whole crop each year. When production unexpectedly exceeds normal output, the government buys in the market. It allows price to fall, but only by the same proportion that production has increased. When production unexpectedly falls short of normal output, the government enters the market and sells some of its stocks. It allows price to rise, but only by the same proportion that production has fallen below normal. Thus, as farmers encounter unplanned fluctuations in their output, they encounter exactly offsetting fluctuations in prices so that their revenues are stabilized.

This policy has the following results. First, price fluctuations are smaller than they would be on a completely free market. Second, total revenues of the producers are stabilized in the face of fluctuations in production. Finally, the government scheme is self-financing. In fact, if we ignore costs of storage, the scheme will show a profit, for the government will be buying at low prices—the lower the price, the more it buys—and selling at high prices—the higher the price, the more it sells.

PROBLEMS WITH STABILIZATION POLICIES

The above analysis illustrates some of the many types of stabilization schemes and shows how the theory of price can be used to predict their consequences. If such schemes have all the advantages outlined above, why is there so much trouble with most actual stabilization programmes?

Choosing the proper price   One of the major problems arises from uncertainty, combined with political pressure applied by farmers. Demand and supply curves are never known exactly, so the central authorities do not know average production over a number of years at each possible price. They do not know, therefore, exactly what level of income they can try to achieve while also keeping average sales from stocks equal to average purchases for stocks. Since farmers have votes, there is strong pressure on any government to be over-generous. If the price, and hence the level of income, is fixed too high, then the government will

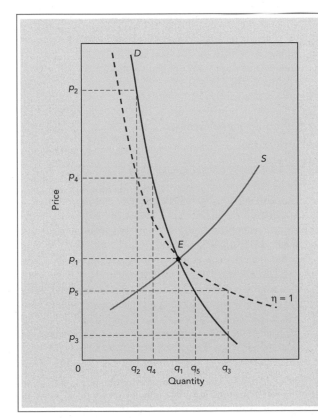

Figure 6.9 Government income stabilization with variable price

Income stabilization is obtained by allowing prices to fluctuate in inverse proportion to output. D is demand, S is planned supply, and equilibrium is at E. However, actual production fluctuates between q_2 and q_3, and these fluctuations cause the free-market price to fluctuate between p_2 and p_3.

A curve of unit elasticity through its whole range is drawn through E and labelled $\eta=1$. To stabilize income, any given output must be sold at a price determined by the curve labelled $\eta=1$. To achieve that price, the government buys or sells from its stocks an amount equal to the horizontal distance between the $\eta=1$ curve and the demand curve.

When production is q_3, market price must be held at p_5 if income is to be unchanged. But at market price p_5, the public wishes to purchase only q_5 and the government must buy up the remaining production, q_3-q_5, and add it to its stocks. Farmers' total sales are q_3 at price p_5, and since the broken red curve is a rectangular hyperbola, income $p_5 \times q_3$ is equal to income $p_1 \times q_1$.

When production is equal to q_2, price must be allowed to rise to p_4 (by construction, the area $p_4 q_2$ is equal to the area $p_1 q_1$). But at price p_4 the public will wish to buy q_4, so that the government must sell q_4-q_2 out of its stocks.

have to buy unsold crops in most years. Thus, stocks will build up more or less continuously (forming 'butter mountains' and 'wine lakes', in well known EU terminology), and sooner or later they will have to be destroyed, given away, or dumped on the market for what they will bring, thus forcing the market price down, defeating the purpose for which the crops were originally purchased. If they are dumped on foreign markets, they will lower the return to foreign producers.

The government's plan will now show a deficit, which will have to be covered by taxation. This means that people in cities will be paying farmers for producing goods that cannot be sold at a price covering their costs of production. The next step is often to try to limit the production of each farmer. Quotas may be assigned to individual farmers, and penalties imposed for exceeding them, or bonuses may be paid for leaving land idle. Such measures attempt to avoid the consequence of there being too many resources allocated to the agricultural sector by preventing these resources from producing all that they could.

Government policies that stabilize prices at too high a level will cause excess supply, a rising level of unsold stocks, and pressure for further government intervention to restrict output.

The long-term problem of resource allocation   Even if the temptation to set too high a price is avoided, there is still a formidable problem facing the managers of agricultural stabilization programmes. Output and real incomes have been rising at an average rate of about 2 per cent per year over the last 100 years in the countries that now form the European Union. Low income elasticities of demand for agricultural products have caused the demands for these goods to rise only slowly—while the demands for other goods with high income elasticities have risen rapidly. If the allocation of resources had remained unchanged, the production of each product would have risen in proportion to the rise of productivity in the industry producing that product. This would have caused shortages and surpluses.

Assume for simplicity that productivity expands more or less uniformly in all industries. The demand for products with low income elasticities will be expanding more slowly than output; excess supplies will develop, prices and profits will be depressed, and it will be necessary for resources to move out of these industries. Exactly the reverse will happen for products with high income elasticities: demand will expand faster than supply, prices and profits will tend to rise, and resources will move into those industries.

With continuous productivity increases, there will be a continuous tendency towards excess supply of products with low income elasticities and excess demand for products with high income elasticities. Adjustment to these changes requires a continuous movement of resources out of industries producing the former type of products into industries producing the latter.

In a free-market economy, this reallocation will take place under the incentives of low prices, wages, and incomes in the declining sector and high prices, wages, and incomes in the expanding sector. Because of the tendency towards excess supply in the agricultural sector, prices will fall, taking producers' incomes down with them. There will be a decline in the demand for farm labour and the other factors of production used in agriculture, and the earnings of these factors will also decline. At the same time, the opposite tendencies will be observed in sectors with high income elasticities. Here demand is expanding faster than supply; prices will rise; incomes and profits of producers will be rising. There will be a large demand for the factors of production used in these industries, so that the price of these factors, and consequently the incomes that they earn, will be bid upwards.

Stabilization schemes that guarantee a 'reasonable' income to farmers remove the incentive for resources to transfer out of the agricultural sector. Unless some other means are found to persuade resources to transfer, a larger and larger proportion of the resources currently devoted to agriculture will become redundant. Productivity growth will be raising quantity supplied faster than income growth is raising quantity demanded.[5] If, however, the government does not intervene at all, leaving the price mechanism to accomplish the resource allocation, a more or less permanently depressed agricultural sector must be accepted.

Economists cannot prove that governments ought, or ought not, to interfere with the price mechanism. However, by providing some insight into the workings of the price mechanism, economics can predict some of the gains and losses. It can also point out problems that must be solved if intervention is to be successful.

The EU's agricultural policy

The Common Agricultural Policy of the European Union, nicknamed the CAP, amply illustrates the applicability of the theories just outlined. The policy has held agricultural prices well above their market equilibrium values within the EU. To prevent the flood of imports that would have been attracted by these high prices, all imported agricultural goods that receive EU price support[6] have been subject to a tariff. The high European prices cause production

---

[5] Between 1970 and 1990, cereal yields per acre nearly doubled in the EU. Milk yields in France and the Netherlands, sugar yields in Italy, and rape yields in Germany increased by almost 50 per cent over the same period. In France and Italy, the potato yield doubled between 1960 and 1985.

[6] The EU imports more than it exports by value, but its imports are many tropical fruits, such as bananas, or those that are out of season in Europe.

BOX 6.2

The EU's common agricultural policy

The following discussion is an excerpt from *The Economist*.[*] Such is the power of farmers that the only change needed to make it fully applicable in 1995 would be to increase the quoted US dollar values (which we have not done).

'Farming in most rich countries is in a classic mess. As food prices have tumbled on world markets, subsidies to farmers (paid through taxes or propped-up food prices) have spiralled to more than $100 billion a year. Such protectionism only sharpens the appetite for more; it never achieves its proclaimed goals. Farmers' incomes and land prices are falling, bankruptcies are rising. Now the Americans have urged the EC to agree to abolish all subsidies and barriers to agricultural trade within ten years. The Americans have good reasons for wanting a change: their own spending on farm support has trebled in the past three years. The main way in which the EU's common agricultural policy supports farmers is by Eurocrats setting guaranteed prices for dairy products, beef, cereals, sugar. If market prices fall below the floor, intervention agencies buy the surpluses. This rigged system is buttressed by import levies and export subsidies, and its benefits go mainly to the wrong people. Three-quarters of EU farm support reaches the biggest and richest 25% of farmers, concentrated in the wealthier northern countries. They get nearly $10,000 a year each from Europe's taxpayers. The other quarter goes to the poorer, southern 75% of farmers. They get about $1,000 a year each. Because German and French politicians want their farmers to have average German and French incomes, the EU pays Karl and Jacques to produce butter at five times the price at which New Zealanders can do it; some of this butter is dumped on world markets at under one-fifth of its true cost, making economic New Zealand butter unsaleable.

Europe's farm ministers recognize some of these absurdities, but prefer to tackle the symptoms (eg, through curbing surpluses of milk and sugar by imposing production quotas) rather than the cause (which is the gap between Community prices and world prices). Quotas have sometimes made the gap worse, because farmers have received higher prices to compensate them for not being allowed to produce so much of what is not wanted. Quotas also freeze market shares. Trading in quotas mitigates this, but creates nonsense of its own. In parts of Britain a farmer's milk quotas are now worth more than his land. Curbs on milk output can just mean more beef or cereals. When everything is in surplus, quotas are a nightmare of red tape, with each farmer having to account for his production down to the last bunch of radishes.

Every statesman knows that a better solution would be sharp cuts in support prices, but these are called politically impossible.'

Since this passage was written, the problems facing the European Union's agricultural policy have not lessened. Overproduction is unabated, and payments to farmers continue to take up the majority of the EU's entire budget. One of the latest measures is 'the set-aside policy', under which farmers are paid for not producing. The more they do not produce, the more they earn! The day has not yet come when a new entrant can earn a large income by setting up a farm designed to non-produce a range of agricultural commodities, but that nightmare vision is only an exaggeration of trends visible in the European Union's current policies.

* Source: *The Economist*, 3 October 1987, pp. 18–19.

to exceed consumption. Surpluses pile up, only to be destroyed or sold abroad at a fraction of their production costs. EU farmers gain, while taxpayers, consumers, and efficient foreign producers are the losers. The payments to farmers have risen so much over the years that they put serious strain on the EU budget. Expenditure on agriculture in 1992 was ECU36.4 billion (about £27.6 billion at April 1994 exchange rates), which is just under 60 per cent of the entire EU budget. In contrast, agriculture in 1990 produced only 2.4 per cent of total EU production of all goods and services (down from 4.8 per cent in 1973).

Efficient agricultural producers in the developed and developing countries have found their livelihoods threatened by subsidized exports of surplus EU products. The attempt to restrain these subsidized exports has caused great strains on the relations between the EU and other agricultural producing countries. These were focused in the long-running Uruguay Round of trade negotiations,[7] as a result of which the EU has agreed to relatively minor alterations in its agricultural intervention policy. A phased reduction in intervention prices started in 1993. However, the ability to subsidize farmers was only modestly curtailed. (The planned cost on the CAP in 1997 was ECU39.2 billion and it may turn out to be larger.) Rather, it seems likely that price supports will be replaced by direct subsidies. In many cases these subsidies will be payments for non-production. For example, the new 'set-aside' policy pays farmers to keep some of their land idle. Thus, while the nature of intervention in the EU is changing, it is not disappearing. Consumers may gain from the price reductions planned (over time), but taxpayers may stand to take an even greater share of the burden of intervention.

[7] These negotiations took place under the auspices of an international organization called the GATT. These and related trade matters are discussed in Chapter 26.

Box 6.2 presents a brief report on EU farm policy taken from *The Economist*. Readers should determine what pieces of analysis given earlier in this chapter explain the economic forces lying behind the various issues raised in the article.

Some general lessons about the price system

IN this chapter we have examined examples of demand and supply forces at work and of government intervention in markets that might have been left unregulated. Our discussion suggests four widely applicable lessons.

Costs may be shifted, but they cannot be avoided

Production, whether in response to free-market signals or to government controls, uses resources; thus, it involves costs to members of society. If it takes 5 per cent of the nation's resources to provide housing at some stated average standard, those resources will not be available to produce other products. If resources are used to produce unwanted wheat, those resources will not be available to produce other products. For society, there is no such thing as free housing or free wheat.

The average standard of living depends on the amount of resources available to the economy and on the efficiency with which these resources are used. It follows that *costs are real*, and are incurred no matter who provides the goods. Rent controls or subsidies to agriculture can change the share of the costs paid by particular individuals or groups, lowering the share for some and raising the share for others, but they cannot make the costs go away.

Different ways of allocating the costs may also affect the total amount of resources used and thus the amount of costs incurred. For example, controls that keep prices and profits of some product below free-market levels will lead to increased quantities demanded and decreased quantities supplied. Unless government steps in to provide additional supplies, fewer resources will be allocated to producing the product. If government chooses to supply all the demand at the controlled prices, more resources will be allocated to it, which means that fewer resources will be devoted to other kinds of goods and services.

Free-market prices and profits encourage efficient use of resources

Prices and profits in a market economy provide signals to both demanders and suppliers. Prices that are high and rising (relative to other prices) provide an incentive to purchasers to economize on the product. They may choose to satisfy the want in question with substitutes whose prices have not risen so much (because they are less costly to provide) or to satisfy less of that want by shifting expenditure to the satisfaction of other wants.

On the supply side, rising prices tend to produce rising profits. High profits attract further resources into production. Short-term profits that bear no relation to current costs repeatedly occur in market economies. They cause resources to move into those industries with profits until profits fall to levels that can be earned elsewhere in the economy.

Falling prices and falling profits provide the opposite motivations. Purchasers are inclined to buy more; sellers are inclined to produce less and to move resources out of the industry and into more profitable undertakings.

The price system responds to a need for change in the allocation of resources, say, in response to an external event such as the loss of a source of a raw material or the outbreak of a war. Changing relative prices and profits signal the need for change to which consumers and producers respond.

Government intervention affects resource allocation

Governments intervene in the price system sometimes to satisfy generally agreed-upon social goals and sometimes to help politically influential interest groups. Government intervention changes the allocation of resources that the price system would achieve.

Interventions have allocative consequences because they inhibit the free-market allocative mechanism. Some controls, such as rent controls, prevent prices from rising (in response, say, to an increase in demand with no change in supply). If the price is held down, the signal is not given to consumers to economize on a product that is in short supply. On the supply side, when prices and profits are prevented from rising, the profit signals that would attract new resources into the industry are never given. The shortage continues, and the movements of demand and supply that would resolve it are not set in motion.

Other controls, such as agricultural price supports, prevent prices from falling (in response, say, to an increase in supply with no increase in demand). This leads to excess supply, and the signal is not given to producers to produce less or to buyers to increase their purchases. Surpluses continue, and the movements of demand and supply that would eliminate them are not set in motion.

Intervention requires alternative allocative mechanisms

Intervention typically requires alternative allocative mechanisms. During times of shortages, allocation will be by sellers' preferences, on a first-come, first-served basis, or by some system of government rationing. During periods of surplus, there will be unsold supplies unless the government buys and stores the surpluses. Because long-run changes in demand and costs do not induce resource reallocations through private decisions, the government will have to step in. It will have to force resources out of industries in which prices are held too high, as it has tried to do in agriculture, and into industries in which prices are held too low, as it can do, for example, by providing public housing.

Intervention almost always has both benefits and costs. Economics cannot answer the question of whether a particular intervention with free markets is desirable, but it can clarify the issues by identifying benefits and costs and who will enjoy or bear them. In doing so, it can identify the competing values involved. This matter will be discussed in detail in Chapters 23 and 24.

4 Rent control does not assure a secure supply of cheap housing for lower-income people; it redistributes incomes from landlord to tenant, but not necessarily from richer to poorer people.

5 On the free market, many agricultural prices are subject to wide fluctuations as a result of weather-induced, year-to-year fluctuations in supply operating on inelastic demand curves, and cyclical fluctuations in demand operating on inelastic supply curves.

6 Governments can stabilize agricultural incomes by reducing price fluctuations through purchases in times of surplus and sales in times of shortage.

7 The long-term problems of agriculture arise from productivity growth on the supply side combined with low income elasticity on the demand side. This means that, unless many resources are being transferred out of agriculture fairly rapidly, quantity supplied tends to increase faster than quantity demanded year after year.

8 Stabilization schemes that hold prices above their free-market levels on average, over short-term and cyclical swings, frustrate the long-term adjustment process and lead to ever-growing surpluses—as has the EU's Common Agricultural Policy (the CAP).

9 Major lessons about the price system are: costs may be shifted, but they cannot be avoided; free-market prices and profits encourage economical use of resources; government intervention affects resource allocation; and intervention requires alternative allocative mechanisms.

Summary

1 Changes in market conditions on either the demand or the supply side can be analysed using demand and supply curves adapted to the specific market circumstances.

2 Effective price ceilings lead to excess demand, black markets and non-price methods of allocating the scarce supplies among would-be purchasers.

3 Rent controls are a form of price ceiling. Their major consequence is a shortage of rental accommodation that gets worse because of a slow but inexorable decline in the quantity of rental accommodation.

Topics for review

- Maximum, or ceiling, prices
- Alternative allocation systems under excess demand
- Short- and long-run effects of rent controls
- Minimum, or floor, prices
- Causes of fluctuations in agriculture prices and incomes
- Schemes for price and income stabilization
- The CAP

PART THREE

The intermediate theory of demand

❧ CHAPTER 7

Marginal utility

IN Chapter 4 we said just enough about the determinants of market demand and market supply curves to enable us to develop the theory of the determination of prices in competitive markets. Now we need to study both the consumer behaviour that lies behind demand curves and the firm behaviour that lies behind supply curves.

The theory of demand will occupy us for only two chapters, because we do not need to depart from our assumption that each consumer is a price-taker, unable to influence by any action of his or her own the market prices of the products purchased.

The theory of supply requires more space. This is because a large proportion of production is carried on by firms that are able to exert a significant influence on the market prices of the products they sell. Therefore, although we do not need to alter any of the assumptions about demand introduced in Chapter 4, we must amend the assumption that there *always* exists a simple relation between market price and firms' supply. Before we come to these supply complications, however, we must turn our attention to the theory of demand.

The history of demand theory has seen two major breakthroughs. The first was the marginal utility theory, which assumed that the utility that people got from consuming products could be measured quantitatively. By distinguishing total and marginal utilities, this theory showed that what seemed like a paradox—necessary goods that cannot be dispensed with often have low market values, while luxury goods that could easily be dispensed with often have high market values—was not a paradox at all.

The second breakthrough came with indifference theory, which allowed demand theory to dispense with the dubious assumption of quantitatively measurable utility on which marginal utility theory was based. In this new theory, all that was needed was the assumption that consumers could say which of two consumption bundles they preferred without having to say by how much.

The utility theory of demand

WE deal with these two theories in their historical order. In this chapter we will distinguish marginal from total utility, see that the shape of the demand curve depends on the former, and then go on to see how the individual consumer maximizes utility by equating marginal utility to price. From this insight, it is an easy step to derive the negative slope of the demand curve from utility theory and to resolve the paradox of value.

Marginal and total utility

Let us confine our attention for the moment to the consumption of a single product. The satisfaction a consumer receives from consuming that product is called his or her **utility**. **Total utility** refers to the *total satisfaction* from the amount of that product consumed. **Marginal utility** refers to the change in satisfaction resulting from consuming a little more or a little less of that product. For example, the total utility of consuming 14 eggs a week is the total satisfaction that those 14 eggs provide. The marginal utility of the fourteenth egg consumed is the additional satisfaction provided by the consumption of that unit. Thus, marginal utility of the fourteenth egg is the difference in total utility gained from consuming 13 eggs per week and from consuming 14 per week.

THE ASSUMPTION OF DIMINISHING MARGINAL UTILITY

The basic assumption of utility theory, sometimes called the *law of diminishing marginal utility*, is as follows:

The utility that any consumer derives from successive units of a particular product diminishes as total consumption of the product increases while the consumption of all other products remains constant.

Consider water. Some minimum quantity is essential to sustain life, and a person would, if necessary, give up all his or her income to obtain that quantity of water. Thus, the marginal utility of that much water is extremely high. More than this bare minimum will be drunk, but the marginal utility of successive glasses of water drunk over a period will decline steadily.

You can convince yourself that diminishing marginal utility is not an unreasonable assumption by asking a few questions. How much money would have to be paid to persuade you to cut your consumption of water by one glass per week? The answer is very little. How much would you need if you were to cut it by a second glass? By a third glass? Down to only one glass consumed per week? The answer to the last question is quite a bit. The fewer glasses you are consuming already, the higher the marginal utility of one more or one less glass of water.

But water has many uses other than for drinking. A fairly high marginal utility will be attached to some minimum quantity for bathing, but much more than this minimum will be used only for more frequent baths or for having a water level in the tub higher than is absolutely necessary. The last weekly gallon used for bathing is likely to have a low marginal utility. Again, some small quantity of water is necessary for tooth brushing, but many people leave the water running while they brush. The water going down the drain between wetting and rinsing the brush surely has a low utility. When all the extravagant uses of water by the modern consumer are considered, it is certain that the marginal utility of the last, say, 30 per cent of all units consumed is very low, even though the total utility of *all* the units consumed is extremely high.

UTILITY SCHEDULES AND GRAPHS

The economists who developed marginal utility theory assumed that utility could be measured in some abstract unit called **utils**. The problem with this approach is that no one has ever succeeded in defining such a unit in terms that could be explained to consumers, let alone in measuring it. The way around this difficulty was to use money as a measure of utils. Many elementary textbooks still use this approach.

Modern economists argue that there is no point inventing a hypothetical measure called utils, which lies behind money measures but adds nothing to what can be established by starting with a money measure in the first place. In the modern view, the total utility a consumer derives from consuming 10 units of eggs is measured by the largest amount of money he or she would pay for 10 eggs if the alternative were no eggs. The total utility of 11 eggs is measured by the total amount of money the consumer would give up to get 11 eggs rather than no eggs.

In contrast, the marginal utility of a single egg is measured by the amount of money the consumer would give up to get *that* egg. This depends on the number of eggs already being consumed. According to the assumption of diminishing marginal utility, the more of any product the person is already consuming, the less he or she would pay to increase consumption by one more unit.

The schedule in Table 7.1 illustrates the assumptions that have been made about utility, using the number of cinema attendances as an example. The table shows the total utility rising as the number of films attended each month rises. Everything else being equal, the more films the consumer attends each month, the more satisfaction she gets—at least over the range shown in the table. But the marginal utility of each additional film per month is less than that of the previous one, even though each film adds something to the consumer's satisfaction. The schedule shows that marginal

Table 7.1 Total and marginal utility schedules

Number of films attended per month	Total utility	Marginal utility
0	0	
1	15	15
2	25	10
3	31	6
4	35	4
5	37.50	2.50
6	39.00	1.50
7	40.25	1.25
8	41.30	1.05
9	42.20	0.90
10	43.00	0.80

Total utility rises, but marginal utility declines as this consumer's consumption increases. The marginal utility of 10, shown as the second entry in the last column, arises because, with attendance at the second film, total utility increases from 15 to 25, a difference of 10. Although total utility rises with more attendance, each additional visit adds less to the total.

utility declines as quantity consumed rises. The same data are shown graphically in the two parts of Figure 7.1.

Maximizing utility

We saw in Chapter 4 that a basic assumption of the theory of consumer behaviour is that consumers try to make themselves as well off as they possibly can in the circumstances in which they find themselves. In other words, consumers seek to maximize their total utility.

EQUILIBRIUM FOR ONE PRODUCT

If we hold the consumption of all but one product constant, we can study the consumer's maximizing behaviour and derive his demand curve from a marginal utility schedule such as the one shown in Figure 7.1.

Let the consumer be faced with a given market price of some product. The price shows what he must sacrifice to obtain each unit of the product. The marginal utility schedule, or graph, shows the value he places on each unit of the product. Clearly, the consumer can increase his utility by adding to his purchases as long as the value he places on each additional unit exceeds the amount he must pay for that unit. It follows that the utility-maximizing consumer will adjust his purchases of a product until the marginal utility of the last unit purchased (measured in money units) is equal to the price of a unit of that product.

For example, at a price of £6, the consumer will make

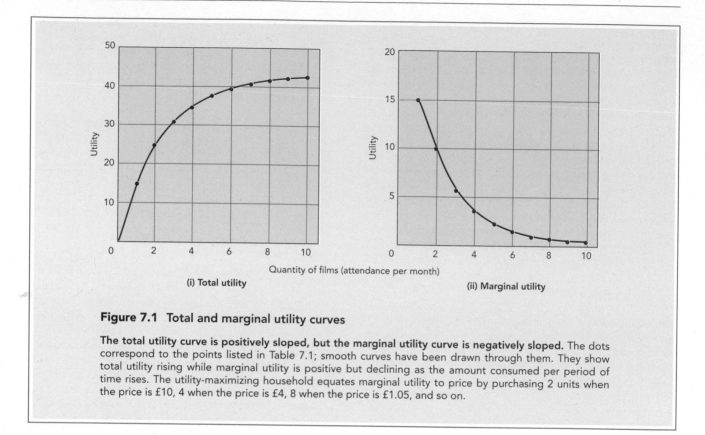

Figure 7.1 Total and marginal utility curves

The total utility curve is positively sloped, but the marginal utility curve is negatively sloped. The dots correspond to the points listed in Table 7.1; smooth curves have been drawn through them. They show total utility rising while marginal utility is positive but declining as the amount consumed per period of time rises. The utility-maximizing household equates marginal utility to price by purchasing 2 units when the price is £10, 4 when the price is £4, 8 when the price is £1.05, and so on.

three visits per month, since the first and second attendance are valued more highly than the price that must be paid for them. This is shown in part (ii) of the figure .

When the consumption of all but one product is held constant, the marginal utility schedule for the variable product is that product's demand curve.

EQUILIBRIUM FOR MANY PRODUCTS

The assumption that the consumption of all other products is held constant is not satisfactory, since it must be violated if the demand for the quantity in question has any elasticity other than unity. If the demand is elastic, more is spent on it when its price falls and less *must* be spent on all other products in total. If the demand is inelastic, less is spent on it when its price falls and more is available to spend on all other products.

How can a consumer adjust her expenditure among more than one product so as to maximize her total utility? Should she go to the point at which the marginal utility of each product is the same, that is, the point at which she would value equally the last unit of each product consumed? This would make sense only if each product had the same price per unit. But if a consumer must spend £3 to

buy an additional unit of one product and only £1 for a unit of another, the first product would represent a poor use of her money if the marginal utility of each were equal. The consumer would be spending £3 to get satisfaction she could have acquired for only £1.

The consumer maximizing his or her utility will allocate expenditure among products so that the utility derived from the last unit of money spent on each is equal.

Imagine that the consumer is in a position in which the utility of the last £ spent on carrots yields three times the utility of the last £ spent on Brussels sprouts. In this case total utility can be increased by switching £1 of expenditure from sprouts to carrots and gaining the difference between the utilities of £1 spent on each.[1]

The utility-maximizing consumer will continue to switch expenditure from sprouts to carrots as long as £1 spent on carrots yields more utility than £1 spent on sprouts. But this switching reduces the quantity of sprouts consumed and, given diminishing marginal utility, raises

---

[1] By the 'last unit' we do not refer to money spent over successive time periods. Instead, we refer to buying more or fewer units at one point in time. We refer, that is, to alternative allocations of expenditures at a moment of time, not to successive allocations over time.

the marginal utility of sprouts; at the same time the switching increases the quantity of carrots consumed and thereby lowers the marginal utility of carrots.

Eventually the marginal utilities will have changed enough so that the utility of £1 spent on carrots is just equal to the utility of £1 spent on sprouts. At this point there is nothing to be gained by a further switch of expenditure from sprouts to carrots. If the consumer persists in reallocating her expenditure, this will further reduce the marginal utility of carrots (by consuming more of them) and raise the marginal utility of sprouts (by consuming less of them). Total utility will no longer be at its maximum because the utility of £1 spent on sprouts will exceed the utility of £1 spent on carrots.

Let us now consider the conditions for maximizing utility in a more general way. Denote the marginal utility of the last unit of product X by MU_x and its price by p_x. Let MU_y and p_y refer, respectively, to the marginal utility of a second product Y and its price. The marginal utility per pound spent on X will be MU_x/p_x. For example, if the last unit adds 30 units to utility and costs £2, its marginal utility per pound is 30/2 = 15.

The condition required for a consumer to maximize utility is, for any pair of products,

$$\frac{MU_x}{p_x} = \frac{MU_y}{p_y}. \qquad (1)$$

This says that the consumer will allocate expenditure so that the utility gained from the last £1 spent on each product is equal.

This is the fundamental equation of the utility theory of demand. Each consumer demands each good (for example, film attendance) up to the point at which the marginal utility per pound spent on it is the same as the marginal utility of a pound spent on another good (for example, water). When this condition is met, the consumer cannot shift a pound of expenditure from one product to another and increase total utility.

AN ALTERNATIVE VIEW

If we rearrange the terms in equation (1), we can gain additional insight into consumer behaviour.

$$\frac{MU_x}{MU_y} = \frac{P_x}{P_y}. \qquad (2)$$

The right-hand side of this equation states the *relative* price of the two goods. It is determined by the market and is outside the control of the individual consumer; the consumer reacts to these market prices but is powerless to change them. The left-hand side of the equation states the relative ability of the goods to add to the consumer's satisfaction, and is within the control of the consumer. In determining the quantities of different goods she buys, the consumer determines also what her marginal utilities of the goods will be. Looking at Table 7.1, we see, for example, that if the consumer attends three cinema performances a month the marginal utility of the last performance to her will be 6, while if she attends six performances her marginal utility for the last performance attended will be 1.5.

If the two sides of equation (2) are not equal, the consumer can increase total satisfaction by rearranging purchases. Assume, for example, that the price of a unit of X is twice the price of a unit of Y ($p_x/p_y = 2$), while the marginal utility of a unit of X is three times that of a unit of Y ($MU_x/MU_y = 3$). Under these conditions it pays the consumer to buy more X and less Y. For example, reducing purchases of Y by two units frees enough purchasing power to buy a unit of X. Since one extra unit of X bought yields 1.5 times the satisfaction of two units of Y forgone, the switch is worth making. What about a further switch of X for Y? As the consumer buys more X and less Y, the marginal utility of X falls and the marginal utility of Y rises. The consumer will go on rearranging purchases—reducing Y consumption and increasing X consumption—until, in this example, the marginal utility of X is only twice that of Y. At this point total satisfaction cannot be further increased by rearranging purchases between the two products.

Consider what the consumer is doing. She is faced with a set of prices that she cannot change. She responds to these prices and maximizes her satisfaction by adjusting the things that can be changed—the quantities of the various goods purchased—until equation (2) is satisfied for all pairs of products.

This sort of equation—one side representing the choices the outside world gives decision-makers and the other side representing the effect of those choices on their welfare—occurs frequently in economics. It reflects the equilibrium position reached when decision-makers have made the best adjustment they can to the external forces that limit their choices.

When they enter the market, all consumers face the same set of market prices. When they are fully adjusted to these prices, each one of them will have identical ratios of their marginal utilities for each pair of goods. Of course, a rich consumer may consume more of each product than a poor consumer. However, the rich and the poor consumers (and every other consumer) will adjust their *relative* purchases of each product so that the relative marginal utilities are the same for all. Thus, if the price of X is twice the price of Y, each consumer will purchase X and Y to the point at which his or her marginal utility of X is twice the marginal utility of Y. Consumers with different tastes will, however, have different marginal utility schedules and so may consume differing relative quantities of products, even though the ratios of their marginal utilities are the same for all consumers.

The consumer's demand curve

To derive the consumer's demand curve for some product, say sugar, take equation (2) and let X stand for sugar and Y for all other products. What will happen if, with all other prices constant, the price of sugar rises?

We start by observing that for most consumers sugar absorbs only a small proportion of total expenditure. If, in response to a change in its price, expenditure on sugar changes by, say, £2 per month, this represents a large change in sugar consumption but would require only a negligible change in the consumption of each of many other products. Hence we proceed in the text by assuming that the marginal utilities of other products do not change when the price and consumption of sugar change. The appendix to this chapter gives the major alternative treatments.

The consumer starts from a position of equilibrium in which

$$\frac{MU\ of\ sugar}{MU\ of\ Y} = \frac{price\ of\ sugar}{price\ of\ Y}. \qquad (3)$$

When the price of sugar rises, the consumer will now be in a position in which

$$\frac{MU\ of\ sugar}{MU\ of\ Y} < \frac{price\ of\ sugar}{price\ of\ Y}. \qquad (4)$$

To restore equilibrium, the consumer must buy less sugar, thereby raising her marginal utility until once again equation (2) (where X is sugar) is satisfied. The common sense of this is that the marginal utility of sugar *per £* falls when its price rises. The consumer began with the utility of the last £ spent on sugar equal to the utility of the last £ spent on all other goods, but the rise in sugar prices changes this. The consumer buys less sugar (and more of other goods) until the marginal utility of sugar rises enough to make the utility of a £ spent on sugar the same as it was originally.

This analysis leads to the basic prediction of demand theory.

A rise in the price of a product (with income and the prices of all other products held constant) will lead to a decrease in the quantity of the product demanded by each consumer.

If this is what each consumer does, it is also what all consumers taken together do. Thus, the theory predicts a negatively sloped market demand curve.

Consumers' surplus

The concept

The negative slope of demand curves has an interesting consequence:

All consumers pay less than they would be *willing* to pay for the total amount of any product that they consume.

The difference between what they would be willing to pay—which is the value of the total utility that they derive from consuming the product—and what they do pay—which is their total expenditure on that product—is called **consumers' surplus**.

For example, in Table 7.1 the consumer attends the cinema five times a month when the price is £2.50 per visit and hence spends £12.50 per month on the cinema. However, the total value placed on these attendances, i.e. the maximum the consumer would pay rather than forgo *all* attendances, is £37.50. So the consumers' surplus is £25.

This concept is important enough to deserve further elaboration. Table 7.2 gives hypothetical data for the weekly consumption of milk by some consumer. The second column, labelled 'Total utility', tells the total value placed on consumption of so many glasses per week (when the alternative is zero). The third column, labelled marginal utility, gives the amount the consumer would pay to add the last glass indicated to weekly consumption. Thus, for example, the marginal utility of £0.80 listed against four glasses gives the value the consumer places on increasing consumption from three to four glasses. It is the difference between the total utilities attached to consumption levels of three and four glasses per week.

If the consumer is faced with a market price of £0.30, he will maximize utility by consuming eight glasses per week because he values the eighth glass just at the market price, while valuing all earlier glasses at higher amounts. Because he values the first glass at £3.00 but gets it for £0.30, he makes a 'profit' of £2.70 on that glass. Between his £1.50 valuation of the second glass and what he has to pay for it, he clears a 'profit' of £1.20. He clears £0.70 on the third

Table 7.2 Consumers' surplus

Glasses of milk consumed per week (1)	Total utility (2)	Marginal utility (3)	Consumers' surplus on each glass if milk costs £0.30 per glass (4)
1	£3.00	£3.00	£2.70
2	£4.50	£1.50	£1.20
3	£5.50	£1.00	£0.70
4	£6.30	£0.80	£0.50
5	£6.90	£0.60	£0.30
6	£7.40	£0.50	£0.20
7	£7.80	£0.40	£0.10
8	£8.10	£0.30	£0.00
9	£8.35	£0.25	—
10	£8.55	£0.20	—

Consumers' surplus on each unit consumed is the difference between the market price and the maximum price the consumer would pay to obtain that unit. The table shows the value that one consumer puts on successive glasses of milk consumed each week. His negatively sloped demand curve shows that he would be willing to pay progressively smaller amounts for each additional glass of milk consumed. As long as he would be willing to pay more than the market price for any glass, he obtains a consumers' surplus on it when he buys it. The marginal glass of milk is the eighth, the one valued just at the market price and on which no consumers' surplus is earned.

glass; and so on. These 'profits', which are called his consumers' surpluses on each unit, are shown in the final column of the table. The total surplus is £5.70 per week. In the table, we arrive at the consumers' surplus by summing the surpluses on each glass. We arrive at the same total, however, by first summing what the consumer would pay for all the glasses bought (which is £8.10 in this case) and then subtracting the £2.40 that he does pay.

The value placed by each consumer on his or her total consumption of some product can be estimated in at least two ways: the valuation that the consumer places on each successive unit may be summed, or the consumer may be asked how much he or she would pay to consume the amount in question if the alternative were to have none.[2]

While other consumers would put different numerical values into Table 7.2, diminishing utility implies that the figures in the final column would be declining for each person. Since a consumer will go on buying further units until the value placed on the last unit equals the market price, it follows that there will be a consumers' surplus on every unit consumed except the last one.

The data in columns (1) and (3) of Table 7.2 give the consumer's demand curve for milk. It is his demand curve because he will go on buying glasses of milk as long as he values each glass at least as much as the market price he

must pay for it. When the market price is £3.00 per glass he will buy only one glass; when it is £1.50 he will buy two glasses; and so on. The total consumption value is the area below his demand curve, and consumers' surplus is that part of the area that lies above the price line. This is shown in Figure 7.2.

Figure 7.3 shows that the same relation holds for the smooth market demand curve that indicates the total amount all consumers would buy at each price.[3]

Applications

In subsequent chapters we will find many uses for the concept of consumers' surplus. In this chapter we show how it can be used to resolve some very old problems.

[2] This is only an approximation, but it is good enough for our purposes. More advanced theory shows that the calculations presented here overestimate consumers' surplus because they ignore the income effect. Although it is sometimes necessary to correct for this bias, none of the corrections that are called for would upset our basic conclusion: *when consumers can buy all units they require at a single market price, they pay much less than they would be willing to pay if faced with the choice between having the quantity they consume and having none.*

[3] Figure 7.2 is a bar chart because we allowed the consumer to vary his consumption only in discrete units, one at a time. Had we allowed him to vary his consumption continuously, we could have traced out a continuous curve for the consumer similar to the one shown in Figure 7.3.

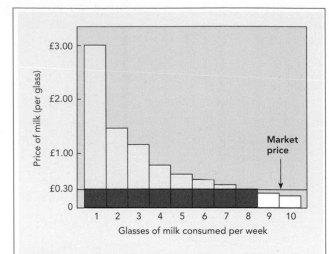

Figure 7.2 Consumers' surplus for an individual

Figure 7.2 **Consumers' surplus is the sum of the extra valuations placed on each unit above the market price paid for each.** This figure is based on the data in Table 7.2. The consumer will pay the red area for the 8 glasses of milk he will consume per week when the market price is £0.30 a glass. The total value he places on these 8 glasses of milk is the entire shaded area. Hence his consumers' surplus is the light green area.

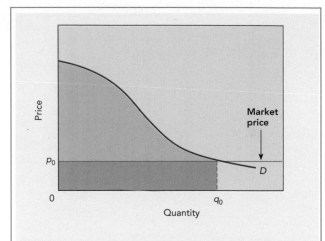

Figure 7.3 Consumers' surplus for the market

Total consumers' surplus is the area under the demand curve and above the price line. The area under the demand curve shows the total valuation that consumers place on all units consumed. For example, the total value that consumers place on q_0 units is the entire light and dark blue shaded area under the demand curve up to q_0. At a market price of p_0, the amount paid for q_0 units is the dark blue area. Hence consumers' surplus is the medium blue area.

THE PARADOX OF VALUE

Early economists, struggling with the problem of what determines the relative prices of products, encountered what they called the *paradox of value*: many necessary products, such as water, have prices that are low compared with the prices of luxury products, such as diamonds. Does it not seem odd, these economists asked, that water, which is so important to us, has such a low market value while diamonds, which are much less important, have a much higher market value? It took a long time to resolve this apparent paradox, so it is not surprising that, even today, similar confusions persist and cloud many policy discussions.

The key to resolving the 'paradox' lies in the distinction between total and marginal utility. We have already seen in the previous section that the area under the demand curve measures the *total utility* that consumers place on *all* of the units consumed. In Figure 7.3 the total consumption value of q_0 units is the entire shaded area (light and dark blue) under the demand curve.

What about the value that the consumer places on having *one more*, or *one less*, than the q_0 units she is currently consuming? Faced with a market price of p_0, the consumer buys all units that she values at p_0 or greater, but she does not purchase any units that she values at less than p_0. It follows that the value consumers place on the last unit con-

sumed of any product, its marginal utility, is equal in equilibrium to the product's price.

Now look at the total amount spent to purchase the product—the price paid for it multiplied by the quantity bought and sold—which we can call its *total market value* or *sale value*. In Figure 7.3 this is shown by the dark blue rectangle with sides p_0 and q_0.

We have seen that the total utility consumers derive from a given amount of a product exceeds its total market value. The two values do not, however, have to bear any constant relation to each other. Figure 7.4 shows two goods, one where total market value is a very small fraction of its total utility and another where total market value is a much higher fraction of total utility.

The resolution of the paradox of value is that a good that is very plentiful, such as water, will have a low price and will thus be consumed to the point where all consumers place a low value on the last unit consumed, whether or not they place a high value on their total consumption of the product; i.e. marginal utility will be low whatever the value of total utility. On the other hand, a product that is relatively scarce will have a high market price and consumption will, therefore, stop at a point at which consumers place a high value on the last unit consumed whatever value they place on their total consumption of the good; i.e. marginal utility will be high whatever the value of total utility.

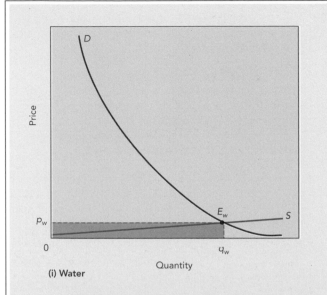
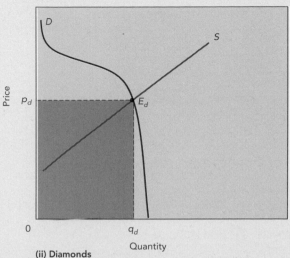

(i) Water

(ii) Diamonds

Figure 7.4 Total utility versus market value

The market value of the amount of some commodity bears no necessary relation to the total utility that consumers derive from that amount. The two parts of the diagram present hypothetical demand curves for water and diamonds that are meant to be stylized versions of the real curves. The total utility that consumers derive from water, as shown by the area under the demand curve, is great—indeed, we cannot possibly show the curve for very small quantities, because people would pay all they had rather than be deprived completely of water. The total utility that consumers derive from diamonds is shown by the area under the demand curve for diamonds. This is less than the total utility derived from water. The supply curve of diamonds makes diamonds scarce and keeps diamonds high in price. Thus, when equilibrium is at E_d the total market value of diamonds sold, indicated by the dark blue area of $p_d q_d$, is high. The supply curve of water makes water plentiful and makes water low in price. Thus, when equilibrium is at E_w, the total market value of water consumed, indicated by the dark blue area of $p_w q_w$, is low.

We have now reached an important conclusion:

The market price of a product depends on demand and supply. Hence no paradox is involved when a product on which consumers place a high total utility sells for a low price, and hence has only a low total market value (i.e. a low amount spent on it).

TOTAL UTILITY, MARGINAL UTILITY, AND ELASTICITY

In ordinary discussion, people often distinguish between products that are difficult to do without, such as food and water, and products that can be fairly easily dispensed with, such as camembert cheese, electric curtain openers, and diamond rings. In the previous section we learned to measure these total utilities by the areas under demand curves. Using this terminology, we could say that an indispensable product has a very large total utility as measured by the area

under its demand curve; a dispensable one has a smaller total utility.

A frequent error occurs when people try to use knowledge of total values to predict demand elasticities. It is sometimes argued that, since dispensables can be given up, they have highly elastic demands; when their prices rise, consumers can stop purchasing them. Conversely, it is argued that indispensable products have highly inelastic demands because, when prices rise, consumers have no choice but to continue to buy them.

But elasticity of demand depends on marginal utilities, not total utilities. The relevant question for predicting the response to a price change is 'how much do consumers value a bit more of the product?', not 'how much do they value *all* that they are consuming?'

When the price of a product rises, each consumer will reduce his or her purchase of that product until he or she values the last unit consumed at the price that must be paid for that unit.

Elasticity of demand depends on the value consumers place on having a bit more or a bit less of the product (marginal utility); it bears no necessary relation to the value they place on total consumption of the product (total utility).

ATTITUDE SURVEYS

Attitude surveys often ask people which of several alternatives they prefer. Such questions *measure total rather than marginal utilities.*[4] Where the behaviour being predicted involves an either–or decision, such as to vote for the Labour or the Conservative candidate, the total utility that is attached to each party or candidate will indeed be what matters, because the voter must choose one and reject the other. Where the decision is a marginal one regarding a little more or a little less, however, total utility is not what will determine behaviour. If one attempts to predict behaviour in these cases from a knowledge of total utilities, even if the information is correct, one will be hopelessly in error.

Here are two examples of how surveys can be misleading. A market research survey asked people to name the household device they thought was most important. Suppliers of a new version of this device used the survey to predict demand but subsequently found that it had failed to do so. A post-mortem revealed that most people did not respond to the sales promotion because they already had the product and were unwilling to pay the advertised price for a second one. In other words, although the total utility they got from the device was high, the marginal utility they attached to another unit of it was low.

For a second example, a political party conducted a survey to determine what types of public expenditure people thought most valuable. Unemployment benefits rated very high. The party was subsequently surprised when it aroused great voter hostility by increasing unemployment benefits. Although the party was surprised, there was nothing inconsistent or irrational in the voters' feeling that protection of the unemployed was a very good thing, providing a high total utility, but that additional payments were unnecessary, and therefore had a low marginal utility.

Summary

1 Marginal utility theory distinguishes between the total utility that each consumer gets from the consumption of all units of some product and the marginal utility each consumer obtains from the consumption of one more unit of the product.

2 The basic assumption in utility theory is that the utility the consumer derives from the consumption of successive units of a product diminishes as the consumption of that product increases.

3 Consumers are assumed to maximize utility. Each consumer reaches equilibrium when the utility he or she derives from the last £1 spent on each product is equal. Another way of putting this is that the marginal utilities derived from the last unit of each product consumed will be proportional to their prices.

4 Demand curves have negative slopes because, when the price of one product, X, falls, each consumer restores equilibrium by increasing his or her purchases of X sufficiently to restore the ratio of X's marginal utility to its new lower price (MU_x/p_x), to the ratio that has been achieved for all other products.

5 Consumers' surplus is the difference between the value a consumer places on his total consumption of some product, as measured by the maximum he would pay for the amount consumed rather than go without it completely, and the actual amount paid, as measured by market price times quantity consumed.

6 It is important to distinguish between total and marginal values because choices concerning a bit more and a bit less cannot be predicted from a knowledge of total values. The paradox of value involves a confusion between total and marginal values.

7 Elasticity of demand is related to the marginal value that consumers place on having a bit more or a bit less of some product; it bears no necessary relationship to the total value that consumers place on all of the units consumed of that product.

Topics for review

- Marginal and total utility
- Diminishing marginal utility
- Derivation of a demand curve
- Consumers' surplus
- Paradox of value

[4] I am indebted to Professor G. C. Archibald for making this penetrating point when we were discussing the practical value of a particular attitude survey.

APPENDIX TO CHAPTER 7

Derivation of a demand curve from marginal utility theory further considered

Marginal utility theory can derive the negatively sloped demand curve for one product only by making some key simplifying assumptions. In this appendix we investigate some of the alternative assumptions that can be used. To begin, we consider deriving the demand curve for some product, say sugar.

Case 1

In the simplest case we hold the consumption of all other products constant and the equilibrium is given by

$$p_s = MU_s. \tag{A1}$$

Diminishing marginal utility then yields a negatively sloped demand curve. The problem here is that, if demand has any elasticity other than unity, adjusting sugar purchases to a change in the price of sugar implies altering purchases of other products as well.

Case 2

To deal with the problem just mentioned, we allow for n products. First we divide (A1) by MU_s to get

$$\frac{p_s}{MU_s} = 1. \tag{A2}$$

Then we observe that there will be a similar equation for each product. Since the right-hand sides of each are all unity, we can equate the left-hand sides to get the following:

$$\frac{p_1}{MU_1} = \frac{p_2}{MU_2} = \frac{p_3}{MU_3} = \ldots = \frac{p_n}{MU_n}. \tag{A3}$$

Sugar is now product one and n is a very large number. The dots indicate the equivalent ratios for all goods other than the four listed.

Since the consumption of each of the goods from 2 to n will change only a little when sugar purchases are altered in response to a change in its price, we can *assume* their marginal utilities are constant. In this case, when p_1 changes, MU_1 must change in the opposite direction to keep the ratio of the two values equal to the *unchanged* ratios of all other MUs to their respective prices.

Case 3

Next, we let money stand for all other goods since money is general purchasing power. This reduces (A3) to:

$$\frac{MU_1}{p_1} = \frac{MU_m}{p_m}. \tag{A4}$$

MU_m is the marginal utility of money, which is the additional utility derived from spending £1 of additional purchasing power distributed optimally among all products. Since the price of £1 of money is by definition £1, cross-multiplication reduces (A4) to:

$$MU_1 = p_1 MU_m. \tag{A5}$$

This is the same as (A1) except for the multiple MU_m, the marginal utility of money. If the marginal utility of each and every product declines as more is consumed, then the marginal utility of money must decline as more income is received. Each increment of income permits an increment of consumption of all products, and the utility of this increment must be declining since the utility of successive units of each product that make it up is declining. A problem arises because a fall in the price of sugar makes it possible to buy more of all products and hence will reduce the marginal utility of money. This is why, when equations (A1) or (A3) are used, it is necessary to assume that the product in question only takes up a small part of total expenditure so that the change in MU_m caused by a change in p_1 is negligible.

Case 4

Finally, all *ceteris paribus* assumptions on consumption can be dropped. In equation (A3), p_1 can be changed with all other prices held constant while the consumer adjusts her consumption of *all* products and while *all* associated changes in MUs are taken into account. The problem now is that MU_1 depends on the amounts consumed of all other products. For example, the marginal utility of sugar depends on the amount of tea, coffee, and breakfast cereal being consumed; the marginal utility of petrol depends on the amount and types of cars available; while the marginal utility of margarine depends on the amount of bread and butter being consumed. When the price of sugar falls, the consumption of all other products alters. When the effects of those alterations on sugar are explicitly allowed for, we cannot be sure which way the *MU* curve for sugar will shift. This problem is analysable using the indifference curves to be studied in the next chapter, but little can be said about it using marginal utility theory.

In marginal utility theory, the negative slope of the demand curve is derived using *ceteris paribus* assumptions about the marginal utilities of all other goods or, equivalently, about the marginal utility of money.

These have the effect of eliminating (by assumption) what we will learn in Chapter 8 to call the income effect. There we will see that it is the income effect which prevents us from being able to show that the demand curve for each and every product must be negatively sloped.

❧ CHAPTER 8

Indifference preference theory

THIS chapter deals with the second major theory of consumer behaviour. It was originated by the Italian economist Vilfredo Pareto (1848–1923) and introduced to the English speaking world (and greatly elaborated) by two British economists, John Hicks (1904–1989) and R. G. D. Allen (1906–1983). This theory dispenses with the questionable assumption that the utility people obtain from consuming a good can be directly measured, and that various changes in utility can be compared.

In this chapter we will first use indifference curves to describe the consumers' tastes and then introduce a budget line to describe the consumption possibilities open to them. After that, we show how consumers reach equilibrium by consuming the bundle that allows them to reach the highest possible levels of satisfaction. We can then see how any consumer alters behaviour when income or prices change, and we go on to derive the negative slope of the demand curve in a more satisfactory fashion than is done with marginal utility theory.

There are two great advantages of this approach to consumer behaviour. First, it allows us to distinguish between two effects of a change in price which are called the income and the substitution effects. Second, it allows us to understand the rare but interesting exception to the prediction that all demand curves are negatively sloped, which arises with a so-called Giffen good.

Utility and indifference theory contrasted

To explain the difference between the two theories, think of a consumer comparing alternative amounts of several goods. A given amount of each good is called a *bundle* of goods. For example, bundle one (signified by b_1) might have 6 apples, 3 oranges, and 5 lemons, while bundle two (signified by b_2) might contain 8 apples, 2 oranges, and 4 lemons. Each different collection of goods is called a different *bundle*.

In utility theory, the consumer is assumed not only to be able to say that she is better or worse off when her consumption bundle changes, say, from bundle b_1 to b_2 to b_3, but also to be able to compare the magnitudes of these changes. The consumer might say, for example, that the increase in utility in going from b_1 to b_2 exceeded the increase in utility in going from b_2 to b_3. When this can be done, utility is said to be *cardinally measurable*.

Indifference theory uses a much weaker assumption. The consumer is only assumed to be able to *order* various consumption bundles, saying for example that b_3 is preferred to b_2 which is preferred to b_1, but not to be able to say *by how much* each bundle is preferred to the other. When this assumption is made, utility is said to be only *ordinally measurable*. In this case, one needs to resort to the concepts of increasing or diminishing marginal utility.[1]

Consider for example, Table 7.1 on p. 129. In marginal utility theory, the consumer is assumed not only to say that she prefers three cinema attendances to two and two to one, but that the increase in utility in going from one to two (10 units on the table) exceeds the increase in going from two to three (6 units on the table), *which is the meaning of diminishing marginal utility*. In indifference theory, the consumer is assumed to be able to say *only* that she prefers two to one and three to two cinema attendances per month. This is a much weaker assumption, but it is all that is needed to develop demand theory.

How the consumer reaches equilibrium

OUR first task is to discover the consumer's equilibrium in this new theory. Once that is done, we will be able to study consumers' responses to changes in such things as prices and incomes.

The consumer's preferences

In utility theory, the consumer's tastes or preferences are shown by the total and marginal utility curves. In indifference preference theory, they are shown by indifference curves.

A SINGLE INDIFFERENCE CURVE

We start by developing a single indifference curve. To do this we give our imaginary consumer some quantities of each of two products, say 18 units of clothing (C) and 10

[1] Under ordinal measurability, the consumer can order bundles, saying for example that $b_2 > b_1 > b_0$ where the > sign indicates the bundle on the left has a larger utility and hence is preferred to the bundle on the right. Under cardinal measurement, the consumer can *order first differences*, saying, for example, $b_2 - b_1 > b_1 - b_0$; that is, in this example the change in utility in going from b_1 to b_2 *exceeds* the change in going from b_0 to b_1.

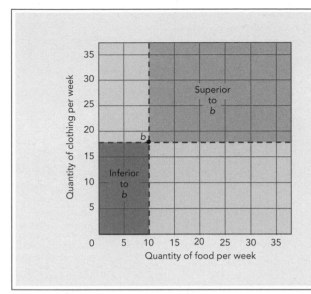

Figure 8.1 A comparison of consumption bundles containing more or less of everything

According to assumption 1, bundle *b* is superior to all bundles that have less of both goods and inferior to all bundles that have more of both goods. A vertical and a horizontal line drawn through *b* divides the graph into four areas. The consumer will regard all points within the dark blue area as inferior to bundle *b* because they contain less of both commodities (except on the boundaries, where they have less of one and the same amount of the other). The consumer will regard all points within the medium blue shaded area as superior to bundle *b* because they contain more of both commodities (except the boundaries, where they have the same amount of one and more of the other). Points within the two light blue areas have more of one commodity and less of the other than bundle *b*.

units of food (*F*). This bundle is plotted as point *b* in Figure 8.1. We first consider points in the two shaded areas defined by a vertical and a horizontal line drawn through *b*. To do so, we introduce our first assumption about tastes:

Assumption 1: *Ceteris paribus*, the consumer always prefers more of any product to less of that product.

This is sometimes referred to as *the non-satiation assumption*. The reason for using this term is that, if the consumer is to prefer more to less of any product, he must not have so much of it that no satisfaction is gained from having any more.

As the figure shows, assumption 1 implies that the consumer will prefer bundle *b* to any point in the dark blue area, which has less of both products, and will prefer all points in the medium blue area to *b*, because they have more of both products. But what about points in the two light blue areas? Compared with bundle *b*, the points within these areas have more of one good and less of the other. Further assumptions about the consumer's tastes are needed if points in these areas are to be ranked against point *b*.

To develop a view of the consumer's preferences in these two areas, we imagine offering the consumer an alternative bundle—say, 13 units of clothing and 15 units of food. This alternative has 5 units fewer of clothing and 5 units more of food than bundle *b*. Whether the consumer prefers this bundle depends on the relative value that he places on 5 units more of food and 5 units less of clothing. If he values the extra food more than the forgone clothing, he will prefer the new bundle to the original one. If he values the food less than the clothing, he will prefer the original bundle. There is a third alternative: if the consumer values the extra food the same as he values the forgone clothing, he would

gain equal satisfaction from the two alternative bundles. In this case the consumer is said to be *indifferent* between the two bundles.

Assume that we have identified a number of bundles, shown in Table 8.1, each of which gives equal satisfaction. There will, of course, be other bundles that yield the same level of satisfaction. All of these that lie within the confines of Figure 8.2 are shown by the smooth curve passing through the points plotted from the table. This curve is an indifference curve.

In general, an **indifference curve** shows combinations of products that yield the same satisfaction to the consumer.

Table 8.1 Alternative bundles conferring equal satisfaction

Bundle	Clothing	Food
a	30	5
b	18	10
c	13	15
d	10	20
e	8	25
f	7	30

Since each of these bundles gives the consumer equal satisfaction, he is indifferent among them. These hypothetical data illustrate an indifference relation. The consumer is assumed to be indifferent among all of these bundles of the two goods. None of the bundles contains more food *and* more clothing than any of the other bundles. The consumer's indifference among these bundles is not, therefore, in conflict with the assumption that the consumer prefers more to less of each product.

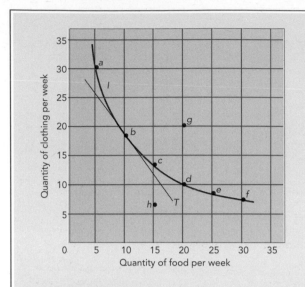

Figure 8.2   An indifference curve

This indifference curve shows combinations of food and clothing that yield equal satisfaction and among which the consumer is indifferent. Points *a* to *f* are plotted from Table 8.2. The smooth curve through them is an indifference curve; each combination on it gives equal satisfaction to the consumer. Point *g* above the line is a preferred combination to any point on the line; point *h* below the line is an inferior combination to any point on the line.

The slope of the line *T* gives the marginal rate of substitution at point *b*. Moving down the curve from *b* to *f*, the slope flattens, showing that, the more food and the less clothing the consumer has, the less willing he will be to sacrifice further clothing to get more food.

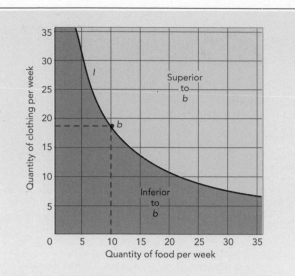

Figure 8.3   One consumption bundle compared with all others

The indifference curve allows any bundle such as *b* to be compared with all other bundles. The consumer regards all bundles in the dark blue area as inferior to *b*. He regards all bundles in the light blue area as superior to *b*. The indifference curve is the boundary between these two areas. The consumer regards all points on it as conferring equal satisfaction and is, therefore, indifferent among all such points.

A consumer is *indifferent* between the combinations indicated by any two points on one indifference curve.

Now we can rate bundles in the two unshaded portions of Figure 8.1. Any points above and to the right of the curve in Figure 8.2 show combinations of food and clothing that the consumer would prefer to combinations indicated by points on the curve. Consider, for example, the combination of 20 food and 20 clothing, which is represented by point *g* in the figure. Although it might not be obvious that this bundle is preferred to bundle *a* (which has more clothing but less food), assumption 1 tells us that *g* is preferred to bundle *c*, because *g* has more clothing *and* more food than *c*. Inspection of the graph shows that *any* point above the curve will be obviously superior to *some* points on the curve in the sense that it will contain both more food and more clothing than those points on the curve. But since all points on the curve are equal in the consumer's eyes, the point above the curve must therefore be superior to *all* points on the curve. By a similar argument, points such as *h*, which are below and to the left of the curve, represent bundles of goods that are inferior to all bundles represented by points on the curve. These comparisons are summarized in Figure 8.3.

DIMINISHING MARGINAL RATE OF SUBSTITUTION

We now make a second assumption:

Assumption 2: **The less of one product that is presently being used by a consumer, the smaller the amount that the consumer will be willing to forgo in order to increase his or her consumption of a second product by one unit.**

This assumption is usually referred to as **diminishing marginal rate of substitution**. It is illustrated in Table 8.2, which is based on the example of food and clothing shown in Table 8.1. As we move down the table through points *a* to *f*, the consumer is consuming bundles with less and less clothing and more and more food. In accordance with the hypothesis of diminishing marginal rate of substitution, the consumer is willing to give up smaller and smaller amounts of clothing to further increase his consumption of food by one unit. When the consumer moves from *c* to *d*, for ex-

Table 8.2 Diminishing marginal rate of substitution

Movement	Change in clothing (1)	Change in food (2)	Marginal rate of substitution (3)
From a to b	– 12	5	2.4
From b to c	– 5	5	1.0
From c to d	– 3	5	0.6
From d to e	– 2	5	0.4
From e to f	– 1	5	0.2

The marginal rate of substitution measures the amount of one product the consumer must be given to compensate for giving up one unit of the other. This table is based on the data in Table 8.2. When the consumer moves from a to b, he gives up 12 units of clothing and gains 5 units of food; he remains at the same level of overall satisfaction. The consumer at point a was prepared to sacrifice 12 units of clothing for 5 of food (i.e. 12/5 = 2.4 units of clothing per unit of food obtained). When the consumer moves from b to c, he sacrifices 5 units of clothing and gains 5 of food (a rate of substitution of 1 unit of clothing for each unit of food). Note that the marginal rate of substitution (MRS) is the absolute value of the ratio $\Delta C/\Delta F$, which always have opposite signs. Hence the MRS is obtained by multiplying this ratio by –1.

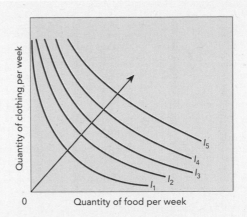

Figure 8.4 An indifference map

An indifference map consists of a set of indifference curves. All points on a particular curve indicate alternative combinations of food and clothing that give the consumer equal satisfaction. The further the curve from the origin, the higher the level of satisfaction it represents. For example, I_5 is a higher indifference curve than I_4, which means that all points on I_5 yield a higher level of satisfaction than do the points on I_4. If the consumer moves along the arrow, he is climbing a 'utility mountain', moving to ever-higher utility levels and crossing ever-higher equal-utility contours, which we call indifference curves.

ample, the table tells us that he is prepared to give up 6/10 of a unit of clothing to get a further unit of food; while when he moves from e to f, he will give up only 2/10 of a unit.

The geometrical expression of this hypothesis is found in the shape of the indifference curve. Look closely, for example, at the slope of the curve in Figure 8.2. Its downward slope indicates that, if the consumer is to have less of one product, he must have more of the other to compensate. Diminishing marginal rate of substitution is shown by the fact that the curve is convex viewed from the origin: moving down the curve to the right, its slope gets flatter and flatter. The absolute value of the slope of the curve is the marginal rate of substitution, the rate at which the consumer is willing to reduce his consumption of the product plotted on the vertical axis in order to increase his consumption of the product plotted on the horizontal axis.

Geometrically, the slope of the indifference curve at any point is indicated by the slope of the tangent to the curve at that point. The slope of tangent T drawn to the curve at point b shows the marginal rate of substitution at that point. It can be seen that, moving down the curve to the right, the slope of the tangent, and hence the marginal rate of substitution at that point, gets flatter and flatter.[2]

THE INDIFFERENCE MAP

So far we have constructed only a single indifference curve.

There must, however, be a similar curve through other points in Figures 8.2 and 8.3. Starting at any point, such as g, there will be other combinations that will yield equal satisfaction to the consumer, and, if the points indicating all of *these* combinations are connected, they will form another indifference curve. This exercise can be repeated as many times as we wish, generating a new indifference curve each time.

It follows from the comparisons given in Figure 8.3 that the farther away any indifference curve is from the origin, the higher is the level of satisfaction given by the consumption bundles that it indicates. We refer to a curve that confers a higher level of satisfaction as a *higher curve*.

A set of indifference curves is called an **indifference map**. An example is shown in Figure 8.4. It specifies the consumer's tastes by showing his or her rate of substitution between the two products for every level of consumption of

---

[2] Table 8.2 calculates the rate of substitution between distinct points on the indifference curve. Strictly speaking, these are the incremental rates of substitution between the two points. Geometrically, this incremental rate is given by the slope of the chord joining the two points. The marginal rate refers to the slope of the curve at a single point and is given by the slope of the tangent to the curve at the point. The discussion of the relation between marginal and incremental rates given on p. 55 in the appendix to Chapter 3 should be read, or reread, at this point.

these products. When economists say that a consumer's tastes are *given*, they do not mean merely that the consumer's current consumption pattern is given: rather, they mean that the consumer's entire indifference map is given.

Of course, there must be an indifference curve through *every* point in Figure 8.4. To graph them we only show a few, but all are there. Thus, as the consumer moves upwards to the right starting from the origin, her utility is rising continuously. As she follows a route such as the one shown by the arrow, consuming ever more of both products, she can be thought of as climbing a continuous utility mountain. We show this 'mountain' by selecting a few equal-utility contours, labelled I_1 to I_5. But every point between each of the contours shown must also have a curve of equal utility passing through it.

If we assume cardinal (i.e. measurable) utility, we could attach a specific utility number to each curve. Perhaps every point on I_1 would confer 50 utils, every bundle on I_2 100 utils, on I_3 140 utils, on I_4 170 utils, etc. In this case, we could say by how much utility was increasing as we moved from I_1 through to I_5. As we have chosen the numbers, utility would be rising at a diminishing rate as utility rose by 50, 40, and 30 between the curves I_1, I_2, I_3, and I_4.

In indifference theory, we do not make such a strong assumption. Instead, all we say is that the utility attached to I_5 exceeds that attached to I_4 which in turn exceeds the utility attached to I_3, and so on. We can say that the consumer is climbing a utility hill as he moves along the arrow starting from the origin, but we cannot say if the hill is gentle or steep.

Box 8.1 shows some specific shapes of indifference curves that correspond to some specific taste patterns.

BOX 8.1

Shapes of indifference curves

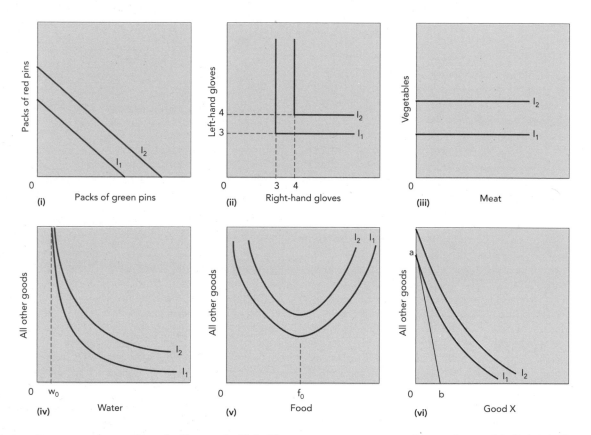

Any taste pattern we care to specify can be illustrated with indifference curves. Here are a few examples of extreme cases that help you to understand how indifference curves work. In each case, two curves are drawn, the one labelled I_2 indicating a higher utility than the one labelled I_1.

BOX 8.1 *(continued)*

Perfect substitutes

Drawing pins that came in red packages of 100 would be perfect substitutes for identical pins that came in green packages of 100 for a colour-blind consumer. He or she would be willing to substitute one type of package for the other at a rate of one for one. The indifference curves would thus be a set of parallel lines with a slope of –1, as shown in part (i) of the figure.

Indifference curves for perfect substitutes are straight lines, the slopes of which indicate the rate at which one good can be substituted for the other.

Perfect complements

Left- and right-hand gloves are perfect complements, since one of them is of no use without the other. This gives rise to the indifference curves shown in part (ii) of the figure. There is no rate at which the consumer will substitute one kind of glove for the other when she starts with equal numbers of each. Of course, she prefers more pairs to fewer, so the curve I_2 represents a higher level of satisfaction than does curve I_1.

Indifference curves for perfect complements are 'L-shaped'.

A good that gives zero utility

When a good gives no satisfaction at all, a person would be unwilling to sacrifice even the smallest amount of other goods to obtain any quantity of the good in question. Such would be the case for meat for a vegetarian consumer, whose indifference curves are horizontal straight lines indicating a marginal rate of substitution of zero for meat (part iii). Since the consumer likes vegetables, the curve I_2 indicates a higher level of satisfaction than does I_1, but in both cases her satisfaction is not affected by the amount of meat she has (since, no matter how much she is given, she will eat none of it).

Indifference curves for a product yielding zero satisfaction are parallel to that product's axis.

An absolute necessity

In part (iv) of the figure, there is some minimum quantity of water, w_0, that is necessary to sustain life. No amount of other goods will persuade any consumer to cut his water consumption below that amount. As consumption of water falls towards w_0, increasingly large amounts of other goods are necessary to persuade the consumer to cut down on his water consumption. Thus, each indifference curve becomes steeper and steeper as it approaches w_0, and the marginal rate of substitution increases.

The marginal rate of substitution for an absolute necessity reaches infinity as consumption falls towards the amount that is absolutely necessary.

A good that confers a negative utility after some level of consumption

Beyond some point, further consumption of many foods, beverages, movies, plays, or cricket matches would reduce satisfaction. Beyond that point, the indifference curves begin to slope upwards, because the consumer would be willing to sacrifice some amount of other goods to be allowed to reduce his or her consumption of the offending product.

Part (v) of the figure shows a consumer who is *forced* to eat more and more food. At the amount f_0, she has all the food she could possibly want. Beyond f_0, her indifference curves have positive slopes, indicating that she gets *negative* value from consuming the extra food, and so would be willing to sacrifice some amount of other products to avoid consuming it.

When, beyond some level of consumption, the consumer's utility is reduced by further consumption, the indifference curves have positive slopes.

This case does not arise if the consumer can dispose of the extra unwanted units at no cost. The indifference curves then become horizontal.

A good that is not consumed

Typically, a consumer will consume only one or two of all of the available types of cars, TV sets, dishwashers, or tennis rackets. If a consumer is in equilibrium consuming a zero amount of say, green peas, she will be in what is called a *corner solution*, where (as shown in part (vi) of the figure) her indifference curve cuts the axis of the non-consumed good with a slope flatter than the budget line (shown by the straight line *ab* in the figure).

The choices available to the consumer

The indifference map tells us what the consumer *would like* to do: reach the highest possible indifference curve, i.e. climb as high up the utility mountain as possible. To see what the consumer *can* do, we need another construction called the budget line.

We start by considering a single consumer who is allocating the whole of her money income between two goods, called food and clothing.[3]

THE BUDGET LINE

The **budget line** shows all those combinations of the goods

[3] These assumptions are not as restrictive as they at first seem. Two goods are used so that the analysis can be handled geometrically; the argument can easily be generalized to any number of goods with the use of mathematics. Savings are ignored because we are interested in the allocation of expenditure between commodities for current consumption. The possibilities of saving or borrowing (or using up past savings) can be allowed for, but they affect none of the results in which we are interested here.

that are just obtainable, given the consumer's income and the prices of the products that she buys.[4]

Assume, for example, that the consumer's income is £120 per week, that the price of clothing is £4 per unit, and the price of food is £2 per unit. As in the earlier discussion, we denote food by F and clothing by C so that, for example, 20 units of food and 10 units of clothing is written as $20F$ and $10C$. We have noted that an amount of both goods consumed by a consumer is called a **bundle** or a **combination** of these goods. Table 8.3 lists a few of the bundles of food and clothing available to this consumer, while the line ab in Figure 8.5 shows all the possible bundles. Point b, for example, indicates all the consumer's income spent buying $60F$ and no clothing, while point a indicates all income spent on buying $30C$ and no food. Points on the line between a and b indicate how much the consumer could buy of both products.

THE SLOPE OF THE BUDGET LINE

Figure 8.5 highlights two points from Table 8.3. It is clear from the figure that the absolute value of the slope of the budget line measures the ratio of the change in C to the change in F as we move along the line. This ratio, $\Delta C/\Delta F$, is 0.5 in our present example (10/20).

How does the slope of the budget line relate to the prices of the two goods? This question is easily answered if we remember that all points on the budget line represent bun-

---

[4] A budget line is analogous to the production-possibility boundary shown in Figure 1.1 on p. 7. The budget line shows the combinations of commodities available to one consumer given her income and prices, while the production-possibility curve shows the combination of commodities available to the whole society given its supplies of resources and techniques of production.

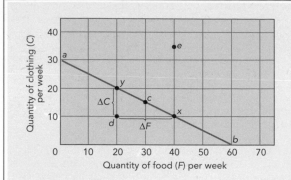

Figure 8.5 A budget line

The budget line shows the quantities of goods available to a consumer given her money income and the price of the goods she buys. Any point indicates a bundle of so much food and so much clothing; point c, for example, indicates 15 units of clothing and 30 units of food consumed per week. With an income of £120 a week and prices of £2 per unit for food and £4 per unit of clothing, line ab is the consumer's budget line showing all combinations of F and C that are obtainable.

Bundle d ($10C$ and $20F$) does not use all of the consumer's income. Bundle e ($35C$ and $40F$) is not available because it would require more than the consumer's present income. Points x and y are both on the budget line and indicate bundles consisting of $40F$ and $10C$ (point x) and $20F$ and $20C$ (point y). If the consumer moves from point y ($20F$ and $20C$) to point x ($40F$ and $10C$), she consumes 20 more F and 10 fewer C, which amounts are indicated by ΔF and ΔC in the figure. Thus, the opportunity cost of each unit of F added to consumption is 10/20=0.5 units of clothing forgone. In the figure this is $\Delta C/\Delta F$, which is the slope of the budget line ab.

Table 8.3 Data for a budget line

Quantity of food	Value of food	Quantity of clothing	Value of clothing	Total expenditure
60	£120	0	£0	£120
50	100	5	20	120
40	80	10	40	120
30	60	15	60	120
20	40	20	80	120
10	20	25	100	120
0	0	30	120	120

The table shows combinations of food and clothing available to a consumer with an income of £120 and facing prices of £4 for clothing and £2 for food. Any row in this table indicates a bundle of given amounts of food and clothing. The quantities in each row exactly exhaust the consumer's income of £120 when the prices are £2 for a unit of food and £4 for a unit of clothing.

dles of goods that just exhaust the consumer's whole income. It follows that, when the consumer moves from one point on the budget line to another, the change in expenditure on *C* must be of equal value, but opposite sign, to the change in expenditure on *F*. Letting ΔC and ΔF stand for the changes in the quantities of clothing and food respectively, and p_c and p_f stand for the money prices of clothing and food respectively, we can write this relation as follows:

$$\Delta C p_c = - \Delta F p_f.$$

There is nothing at all difficult in this. All it says is that, if any amount more is spent on one product, the same amount less must be spent on the other. A given income imposes this discipline on the consumer.

If we divide the above equation through, first by ΔF, and then by p_c, we get the following:

$$\frac{\Delta C}{\Delta F} = - \frac{p_f}{p_c}.$$

So the slope of the budget line is the negative of the ratio of the two prices (with the price of the good that is plotted on the horizontal axis appearing in the numerator).

Notice that the slope of the budget line depends only on the relation between the two prices, not on their absolute values. To check this, consider an example. If clothing costs £4 and food costs £2, then 0.5 unit of clothing must be forgone in order to be able to purchase one more unit of food; if clothing costs £8 and food costs £4, it is still necessary to forgo 0.5 unit of clothing to be able to purchase one more unit of food. As long as the price of clothing is twice the price of food, it will be necessary to forgo half a unit of clothing in order to be able to purchase one more unit of food.

More generally, the amount of clothing that must be given up to obtain another unit of food depends only on *the relation between the price of clothing and the price of food*. If we take the money price of food and divide it by the money price of clothing, we have the opportunity cost of food in terms of clothing (the quantity of clothing that must be forgone in order to be able to purchase one more unit of food). This may be written:

$$\frac{p_f}{p_c} = \text{opportunity cost of food in terms of clothing.}$$

It is apparent that changing income and/or changing both prices in the same proportion leaves the ratio p_f/p_c unchanged.[5]

This discussion helps to clarify the distinction between money prices and relative prices introduced in Chapter 4.

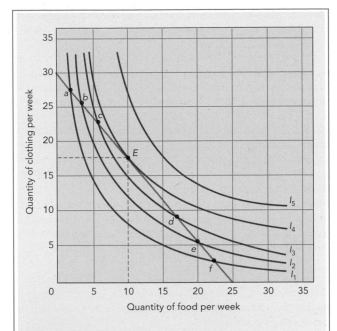

Figure 8.6 The equilibrium of a consumer

Equilibrium occurs at *E*, where an indifference curve is tangent to the budget line. The consumer has an income of £150 a week and faces prices of £5 a unit for clothing and £6 a unit for food. A bundle of clothing and food indicated by point *a* is attainable, but by moving along the budget line higher indifference curves can be reached. The same is true at *b* and *c*. At *E*, however, where the indifference curve I_4 is tangent to the budget line, it is impossible to reach a higher curve by moving along the budget line. If the consumer did alter her consumption bundle by moving from *E* to *d*, for example, she would move to the lower indifference curve I_3 and thus to a lower level of satisfaction.

Both p_f and p_c are money prices, while the ratio p_f/p_c is a relative price.[6]

The equilibrium of the consumer

The budget line tells us what the consumer *can do*: she can

[5] Those who prefer an algebraic derivation may refer now to the proof of this proposition on pp. 159–60, in the appendix to this chapter.

[6] The concepts introduced in this section can be tricky, and readers are encouraged to experiment with some examples. For example, if the prices of food and clothing are £2 and £6 respectively, what are the values of: (i) the relative price of food? (ii) the relative price of clothing? (iii) the opportunity cost of food measured in units of clothing? (iv) the opportunity cost of clothing measured in units of food? (v) the slope of the budget line drawn with food on the horizontal and clothing on the vertical axis? and (vi) the slope of the budget line drawn with the two commodities on the opposite axes?

select any consumption bundle on, or below, the line, but not above it. To see what the consumer *wants to do*, we introduce our third assumption:

Assumption 3: The consumer seeks to maximize total satisfaction, which means reaching the highest possible indifference curve.

We have now developed representations of the consumer's tastes and the choices open to her. Figure 8.6 brings together the budget line and the indifference curves. Any point on the budget line can be attained. Which one will the consumer actually choose?

Since the consumer wishes to maximize satisfaction, she wishes to reach her highest attainable indifference curve. Inspection of the figure shows that, if the consumer is at a point where an indifference curve cuts her budget line, a higher indifference curve can be reached by moving along the line. When the consumer is at a point of tangency between the indifference curve and the budget line, it is impossible to reach a higher indifference curve by varying the bundle consumed.

Satisfaction is maximized at the point where an indifference curve is tangent to a budget line. At that point, the slope of the indifference curve (the marginal rate of substitution of the goods in the consumer's preferences) is equal to the slope of the budget line (the opportunity cost of one good in terms of the other as determined by market prices).

Notice that a consumer is presented with market prices that she cannot change. She adjusts to these prices by choosing a bundle of goods such that, at the margin, her own relative valuation of the two products conforms with the relative valuations given by the market. The consumer's relative valuation is given by the slope of her indifference curve, while the market's relative valuation is given by the slope of the budget line.

When the consumer has chosen the consumption bundle that maximizes her satisfaction, she will go on consuming that bundle unless something changes. The consumer is thus in equilibrium.

How the consumer responds to changes

WE are now ready to consider how consumers respond to various changes in their incomes and the prices that they face.

Parallel shifts in the budget line

A change in money income A change in the consumer's money income will, *ceteris paribus*, shift his budget line. For example, if the consumer's income is doubled, he will be able to buy twice as much of both goods compared with any combination on his previous budget line. The budget line will therefore shift out parallel to itself to indicate this expansion in the consumer's consumption possibilities. (The fact that it will be a parallel shift is established by our demonstration on p. 147 that the slope of the budget line depends only on the relative price of the two products.) This illustrates the result that is proven (as proposition 1) in the appendix to this chapter:

A change in the consumer's income shifts the budget line parallel to itself, outwards when income rises and inwards when income falls.

The effect of income changes is shown in Figure 8.7. For each level of income, there will, of course, be an equilibrium position at which an indifference curve is tangent to the relevant budget line. Each such equilibrium position means that the consumer is doing as well as he possibly can for that level of income. If we join up all the points of equilibrium, we trace out what is called an **income–consumption line**. This line shows how the consumption bundle changes as income changes, with prices held constant.[7]

A proportionate change in all prices Now consider what happens when all prices change in the same proportion. For example, a halving of all prices allows the consumer to buy twice as much of both products as was bought at any point on his previous budget line. This is exactly the same shift in the budget line as when the consumer's income doubled

---

[7] This income–consumption line can be used to derive the curve relating quantity demanded to income that was introduced on p. 97. This is done by plotting the quantity of one of the goods consumed at the equilibrium position against the level of money income that determined the position of the budget line. Repeating this for each level of income produces the required curve.

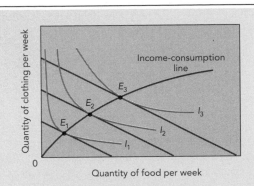

Figure 8.7 An income–consumption line

The income–consumption line shows how the consumer's purchases react to changes in income with relative prices held constant. Increases in income shift the budget line out parallel to itself, moving the equilibrium from E_1 to E_2 to E_3. By joining up all the points of equilibrium, an income–consumption line (in blue) is traced out.

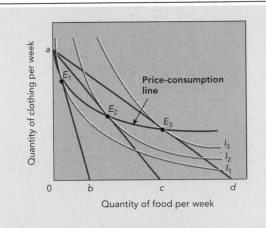

Figure 8.8 The price–consumption line

The price–consumption line shows how the consumer's purchases react to a change in one price with money income and other prices held constant. Decreases in the price of food (with money income and the price of clothing constant) pivot the budget line from ab to ac to ad. The equilibrium position moves from E_1 to E_2 to E_3. By joining up all the points of equilibrium, a price–consumption line (in blue) is traced out.

with prices held constant. On the other hand, a doubling of all prices will cause the budget line to shift inwards in exactly the same way as if his money income had halved with prices held constant.

This illustrates the following general result (which is also proven as proposition 2 in the appendix to this chapter):

An equal proportionate change in all money prices, with money income held constant, shifts the budget line parallel to itself, towards the origin when prices rise and away from the origin when prices fall.

From this point on, the analysis is the same as in the previous section, since changing money prices proportionately has the identical effect as changing money income.

Offsetting changes in money prices and money incomes The results in the last two sections suggest that we can have offsetting changes in money prices and money incomes. Consider a doubling of money income that shifts the budget line outwards. Let this be accompanied by a doubling of all money prices that shifts the budget line inwards. The net effect is to leave the budget line where it was before income and prices changed. This illustrates the general result (which is proven as proposition 3 in the appendix to this chapter):

Multiplying money income by some constant, λ, and simultaneously multiplying all money prices by λ leaves the budget line unaffected and hence leaves consumer purchases unaffected.[8]

Changes in the slope of the budget line

A change in relative prices We already know that a change in the relative price of the two goods changes the slope of the budget line. At a given price of clothing, the consumer has an equilibrium consumption position for each possible price of food. Connecting these positions traces out a **price–consumption line**, as is shown in Figure 8.8. Notice that, as the relative price of food and clothing changes, the relative quantities of food and clothing purchased also change. In particular, as the price of food falls, the consumer buys more food.

Real and money income[9]

The preceding analysis suggests an important distinction between two concepts of income. **Money income** measures a consumer's income in terms of some monetary unit; for example, so many pounds sterling or so many dollars. **Real income** measures the *purchasing power* of the consumer's money income. A rise in money income of x per cent com-

[8] The symbol λ is the Greek letter lambda, which is often used for some constant multiple.
[9] Now that we have developed the appropriate theoretical tools, this discussion can go further and deeper than the discussion of the same issue at the end of Chapter 4.

bined with an x per cent rise in all money prices leaves a consumer's purchasing power, and hence his or her real income, unchanged. When we speak of the real value of a certain amount of money, we are referring to the goods and services that can be bought with the money, that is, to the purchasing power of the money.

ALLOCATION OF RESOURCES: THE IMPORTANCE OF RELATIVE PRICES

Price theory predicts that the allocation of resources depends on the structure of relative prices. If the money value of all prices, incomes, debts, and credits were doubled, there would, according to our theory, be no noticeable effect. The economy would function as before. The same set of relative prices and real incomes would exist, and there would be no incentive for any reallocation of resources.

This prediction is an implication of the theories of the behaviour of consumers and firms. We have already seen that doubling all money prices, and money income, leaves the consumer's budget line unchanged and so, according to the theory of consumer behaviour, gives the consumer no incentive to vary the quantity of each product that he or she purchases. As far as producers are concerned, if the prices of all outputs and inputs double, the relative profitabilities of alternative lines of production will be unchanged. Thus, producers will have no incentive to alter production rates so as to produce more of some things and less of others.

If *relative* prices change, however, then our theory predicts that resources will be reallocated. Consumers will buy more of the relatively cheaper products and less of the relatively expensive ones, and producers will increase production of those products whose prices have risen relatively, and reduce production of those whose prices have fallen relatively (since the latter will be relatively less profitable lines of production).

The theory of price and resource allocation is a theory of relative, not absolute, prices.

INFLATION AND DEFLATION: THE IMPORTANCE OF ABSOLUTE PRICES

The average level of all money prices is called the general price level, or more usually just the **price level**. If all money prices double, we say that the price level has doubled. An increase in the price level is called an **inflation**, a decrease is called a **deflation**. If a rise in all money prices and incomes has little or no effect on the allocation of resources, it may seem surprising that so much concern is expressed over inflation. Clearly, people who spend all their incomes, and whose money incomes go up at the same rate as money prices, lose nothing from inflation. Their real income is unaffected.

Inflation, while having no effect on consumers whose incomes rise at the same rate as prices, does none the less have many serious consequences. These are studied in detail later in this book; for present purposes *we shall assume that the price level is constant.*

Under these circumstances, a change in one money price necessarily changes that price *relative* to the average of all other prices. The theory can easily be extended to situations in which the price level is changing. Under inflationary conditions, whenever shifts in demand or supply require a change in a product's relative price, its price rises *faster* (its relative price rising) or *slower* (its relative price falling) than the general price level is rising. Explaining this each time can be cumbersome. It is, therefore, simpler to deal with relative prices in a theoretical setting in which the price level is constant. It is important to realize, however, that, even though we develop the theory in this way, it is not limited to such situations. The propositions we develop can be applied to changing price levels merely by making explicit what is always implicit: in the theory of relative prices, 'rise' or 'fall' *always* means rise or fall *relative to the average of all other prices.*

....

The consumer's demand curve[10]

TO derive the consumer's demand curve for any product, we need to depart from the world of two products. We are now interested in what happens to the consumer's demand for some product, say petrol, as the price of that product changes, *all other prices being held constant.*

Derivation of the demand curve

In part (i) of Figure 8.9 a new type of indifference map is

[10] The rest of this chapter can be skipped without loss of continuity as long as one is willing to accept the negative slope of demand curves on the basis of the intuitive arguments given in Chapter 4.

The slope of the demand curve

The price–consumption line in part (i) of Figure 8.9 indicates that, as price decreases, the quantity of petrol demanded increases. But one can draw the indifference curves in such a way that the response to a given decrease in price is for less to be consumed rather than more. This possibility gives rise to the positively sloped demand curve, referred to as a **Giffen good** after the Victorian economist Sir Robert Giffen (1837–1910), who is reputed to have documented a case of such a curve. Let us see how the conditions leading to this case are analysed using indifference curves.

Income and substitution effects   The key is to distinguish between what is called the income effect and the substitution effect of a change in price. The separation of the two effects according to indifference theory is shown in Figure 8.10. We can think of the separation occurring in the following way. After the price of the good has fallen, we reduce money income *until the original indifference curve can just be obtained*. The consumer is now on his original indifference curve but facing the new set of relative prices. His response is defined as the **substitution effect**: the response of quantity demanded to a change in relative price, real income being held constant (meaning staying on the original indifference curve). Then, to measure the income effect, we restore money income. The consumer's response is defined as the **income effect**: the response of quantity demanded to a change in real income, relative prices being held constant. The distinction between income and substitution effects is one of the most tricky bits of basic economic theory. Readers are advised, therefore, to study Figure 8.10 with great care. Box 8.2 discusses one of the many practical applications of this concept.

In Figure 8.10, the income and substitution effects work in the same direction, both tending to increase quantity demanded when price falls. Is this necessarily the case? The answer is no. It follows from the convex shape of indifference curves that the substitution effect is always in the same direction: more is consumed of a product whose relative price has fallen. The income effect, however, can be in either direction: it can lead to more or less being consumed of a product whose price has fallen. The direction of the income effect depends on the distinction we drew earlier between normal and inferior goods.

The slope of the demand curve for a normal good   For a normal good, an increase in consumer's real income, arising from a decrease in the price of the product, leads to increased consumption, reinforcing the substitution effect. Because quantity demanded increases, the demand curve has a negative slope. This is the case illustrated in Figure 8.10.

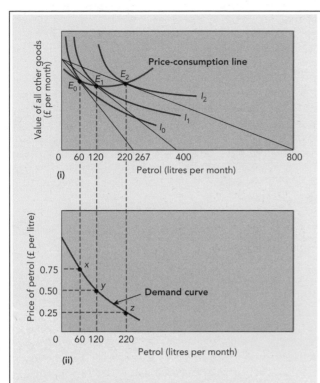

Figure 8.9 Derivation of an individual's demand curve

Every point on the price–consumption line corresponds to both a price of the commodity and a quantity demanded; this is the information required for a demand curve. In part (i) the consumer has an income of £200 per month, and alternatively faces prices of £0.75, £0.50, and £0.25 per litre of petrol, choosing positions E_0, E_1, and E_2. The information for litres demanded at each price is then plotted in part (ii) to yield the consumer's demand curve. The three points x, y, and z in (ii) correspond to the three equilibrium positions E_0, E_1, and E_2 in (i).

plotted in which the horizontal axis measures litres of petrol and the vertical axis measures the value of all other goods consumed. We have in effect used *everything but petrol* as the second product. The indifference curves now give the rate at which the consumer is prepared to substitute petrol for money (which allows him to buy all other goods).

The derivation of a demand curve is illustrated in Figure 8.9. For a given income, each price of petrol gives rise to a particular budget line, and a particular equilibrium position. Plotting the quantity of petrol consumed against the price that determined the position of the budget line yields one point on the demand curve. Each such price yields a different point, and taken together gives the whole demand curve.

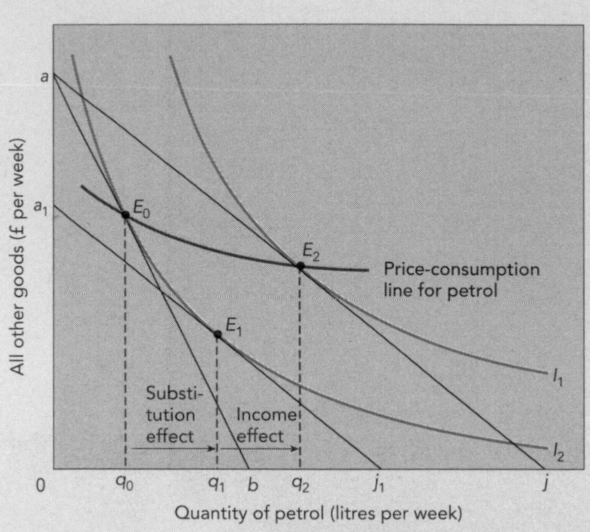

Figure 8.10 The income effect and the substitution effect

The substitution effect is defined by sliding the budget line around a fixed indifference curve; the income effect is defined by a parallel shift of the budget line. The original budget line is at ab and a fall in the price of petrol takes it to aj. The original equilibrium is at E_0 with q_0 of petrol consumed, and the final equilibrium is at E_2 with q_2 of petrol consumed. To remove the income effect, imagine reducing the consumer's income until she is just able to attain her original indifference curve at the new price. We do this by shifting the line aj to a parallel line nearer the origin until it just touches the indifference curve that passes through E_0. The intermediate point E_1 divides the quantity change into a substitution effect q_1–q_0 and an income effect q_2–q_1. This point can also be obtained by sliding the original budget line ab around the indifference curve until its slope reflects the new relative prices.

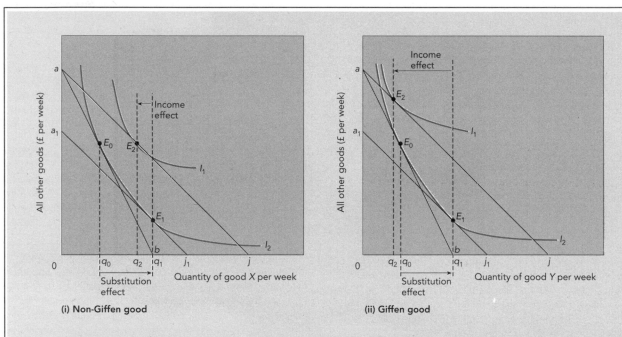

Figure 8.11 Income and substitution effects for inferior goods

Inferior goods have negative income effects; a large enough negative income effect can outweigh the substitution effect and lead to a decrease in consumption in response to a fall in price. In each part of the diagram, the individual is in equilibrium at E_0, consuming a quantity q_0 of the good in question. The price then decreases and the budget line shifts to aj, with a new equilibrium at E_2 and quantity consumed q_2. In each case the substitution effect is to increase consumption from q_0 to q_1. In (i) there is a negative income effect of q_1–q_2. Because this is less than the substitution effect, the latter dominates, so good X has a normal, negatively sloped demand curve. In (ii) the negative income effect q_1–q_2 is larger than the substitution effect, and quantity consumed actually decreases. Good Y is then a Giffen good.

BOX 8.2

....

Income and substitution effects in practice

Although they sound highly abstract and 'theoretical' when first encountered, the income and substitution effects turn out to be useful tools. They help us to deal with many problems such as: Do high rates of income tax act as disincentives to work? Would cutting the rate of income tax increase the amount of work people do? Would raising the wage rate of workers in some industry lead to a reduction in absenteeism?

Many such questions frequently face decision-takers and they are often surprised at the results that the market produces. For example, many years ago the National Coal Board (as British Coal was then called) raised miners' wages in an attempt to boost coal production and was surprised to find miners working fewer rather than more hours. In several countries, increases in rates on income tax (within a moderate, not a confiscatory, range), were found to be associated with people working more rather than less; at other times, reductions in tax rates seemed to cause people to work less.

The surprise in all these cases was the same. Intuition suggests that if you pay people more they will work more; experience shows that the result is often the opposite: more pay, less work; less pay, more work.

The explanation of this surprising behaviour lies in distinguishing the income from the substitution effect of a change in the reward for work.

To see how this works, we must think of a worker starting with an endowment of 24 hours per day and deciding to consume some of it as 'leisure' (including sleeping time) and trading the rest for income by working. So a person who works 9 hours a day at an after-tax rate of £10 per hour is consuming 15 hours a day of leisure and trading the other 9 for £90 worth of income which can be used to buy goods and services.

Now let the after-tax wage rate rise to £12 an hour, either because the wage rate rises by £2 or because the rate of personal income tax falls to produce that increase in after-tax earnings. The response to this change will have an income and a substitution component.

The substitution effect works the way intuition suggested: more wages, more work. Gaining income is now cheaper in terms of the leisure that must be sacrificed per pound sterling worth of income gained. At the new wage rate, 1/12 of an hour (i.e. 5 minutes) of work earns £1 worth of income while before

it took 1/10 of an hour (6 minutes). Looked at the other way around, consuming leisure is now more expensive per amount of income that must be given up. An extra hour of leisure consumed requires sacrificing £12 worth of income instead of £10 worth. The substitution effect leads to an increased consumption of the thing whose relative price has fallen—income in this case—and a reduced consumption of the thing whose relative price has risen—leisure.

So far so good. The surprise lies in the income effect. The rise in the after-tax wage rate has an income effect in the sense that the worker can have more goods *and* more leisure. He could, for example, consume an extra hour of leisure by cutting his hours worked from 9 to 8 while at the same time raising his income from £90 a day (9 hours @ £10) to £96 a day (8 hours @ £12). The income effect leads him to consume more goods and more leisure, i.e. to work fewer hours.

Only if the substitution effect is strong enough to overcome the income effect will the rise in the wage rate lead the person to want to work more. If the substitution effect is strong enough, the worker might for example work 9½ hours instead of 9 and increase income from £90 to £114 a day. This means, however, choosing this combination of income and leisure in preference to all combinations that give more income and more leisure, such as 8¾ hours work (down from 9) and £105 of income (up from £90).

So we should not be surprised if increases in the after-tax hourly wage lead to less work; this merely means that the income effect is stronger than the substitution effect.

The above analysis helps to explain why employers separate higher overtime rates from normal rates of pay. If the normal rate of pay is increased, the income effect is quite large, while if only the overtime rate is raised, the income effect is much smaller but the substitution effect is unchanged. In the above example, raising the normal wage rate from £10 to £12 increases income by £18 for a person who continues to work an unchanged 9 hours a day. But introducing an overtime rate has an income effect only in so far as overtime hours are already being worked. If, in the previous example, the employer introduced a £15 hourly rate for work of over 9 hours a day, the income effect would be zero; the employee must work more in order to gain any benefit from the higher overtime rate.

The slope of the demand curve for an inferior good Figure 8.11 shows indifference curves for inferior goods. The income effect is negative in each part of the diagram. This follows from the nature of an inferior good: as income rises, less of the good is consumed. In each case, the substitution effect serves to increase the quantity demanded as price decreases and is offset to some degree by the negative income effect. The final result depends on the relative

strengths of the two effects. In part (i), the negative income effect only partially offsets the substitution effect, and thus quantity demanded increases as a result of the price decrease, though not as much as for a normal good. This is the typical pattern for inferior goods, and it too leads to negatively sloped demand curves, often relatively inelastic ones.

In part (ii), the negative income effect actually outweighs

the substitution effect and thus leads to a positively sloped demand curve. This is the Giffen case. For this to happen the good must be inferior. But that is not enough; the change in price must have a negative income effect *strong enough* to offset the substitution effect. Most economists believe that these circumstances are unusual ones; they believe that a positively sloped market demand curve is a rare exception to the general rule that demand curves have negative slopes.

Box 8.3 gives an alternative definition of the income effect that is used in empirical applications of demand theory.

Criticisms of demand theory

STUDENTS often find demand theory excessively abstract and feel that it is unrealistic. Some very senior critics have often felt more or less the same way. In this section we first consider the charge that demand theory is unrealistic and then consider some alleged exceptions to the law of demand.

Is demand theory in conflict with everyday experience?

It is easy to prove that people do not *always* behave in the manner assumed by demand theory. Does that make the theory inapplicable? The answer depends on what we want demand theory to accomplish. Three uses may be distinguished. First, we may be interested in the aggregate behaviour of all consumers, as shown by the market demand curve for a product. Second, we may want to make probabilistic statements about the actions of individual consumers. Third, we may want to make statements about what *all* consumers *always* do.

The aggregate use of the theory of demand is the most common one in economics. All of the predictions developed in Chapter 6 depend on having some knowledge of the shape of the relevant market demand curves, yet they do not require that we be able to predict the behaviour of each individual consumer. The second use, though much less common than the first, is important; we do sometimes want to be able to say what a single consumer will probably do. The third use of demand theory is by far the least important of the three. Rarely do we wish to make categorical statements about what all consumers will always do.

Fortunately, the observation that consumers occasionally behave in ways not predicted by demand theory would, if carefully documented, refute only the assertion that the theory's predictions *always* applied to *all* consumers.

Neither the existence of a relatively stable negatively sloped market demand curve nor our ability to predict what a single consumer will probably do requires that all consumers invariably behave in the manner assumed by the theory. Such fully consistent behaviour on the part of everyone at all times is sufficient but not necessary for a stable market demand curve. Consider two other possibilities. First, some consumers may always behave in a manner contrary to the theory. Consumers whose members are handicapped or emotionally disturbed are obvious possibilities. The erratic behaviour of such consumers will not cause market demand curves for normal goods to depart from their downward slope, provided that the consumers account for a small part of purchases of any product. Their behaviour will be swamped by the normal behaviour of the majority of the consumers. Second, an occasional irrationality on the part of every consumer will not upset the downward slope of the market demand curve for a normal good. As long as these are unrelated across consumers, occurring now in one and now in another, their effect will be swamped by the normal behaviour of most consumers most of the time.

The negative slope of the demand curve requires only that at any moment of time most consumers are behaving as is predicted by the theory. This is quite compatible with behaviour contrary to the theory by some consumers all of the time and by all consumers some of the time. Thus, we cannot test the theory of market demand by observing the behaviour of *a few* isolated consumers.

Demand and taste changes

Some critics have argued that the inclusion of changes in tastes as a cause of shifts in demand make demand theory untestable. The proposition that demand and tastes are related is not really testable unless we have some way of measuring a change in tastes. Since we do not have an independent measure of taste changes, what we usually do is infer them from the data for demand. We make such state-

BOX 8.3

The income effect according to Slutzky

In indifference theory, the income effect of a price change is removed by reducing income to the initial level of satisfaction shown by the initial indifference curve. An alternative approach to distinguishing income and substitution effects is based on the 'Slutzky definition'. In this alternative, the income effect of a price change is removed by altering income *until the initial bundle of goods can just be purchased.*

Say, for example, that we were interested in the income effect that would arise from ending the European Union's Common Agricultural Policy. Careful studies could estimate quite closely the effect on retail food prices, and there is no doubt that there would be substantial decreases. Let us say that food prices were estimated to fall by 30 per cent. When this price cut occurs, what is the income effect? In indifference theory, we let food prices fall by 30 per cent and then reduce income until the initial level of satisfaction is obtained. But if we do not know people's indifference curves, we cannot conduct that operation. However, we can easily calculate how much incomes would have to fall to allow consumers to purchase their original bundle of goods. For a consumer who was spending 20 per cent of her income on food, this would require an income cut of 6 per cent (30 per cent of 20 per cent). Put the other way around, the consumer could buy the initial bundle of goods and now have 6 per cent of her income left to spend on new purchases. So in this hypothetical example the income effect of the elimination of the CAP would be 6 per cent of existing income. To do a similar calculation for the economy as a whole, all we need is the percentage of disposable income that all consumers spend on food products, which is well known.

The Slutzky measure could be shown graphically in Figure 8.10 (on p. 152). In that figure, the reduction in the price of petrol pivots the budget line from *ab* to *aj* and the income effect was removed by sliding *aj* inwards and parallel to itself until it was just tangent to the initial indifference curve at E_1 (budget line a_1j_1). In the Slutzky approach, the budget line is shifted inwards until it goes through the initial consumption position. That would slide *aj* inwards parallel to itself until it passes through E_0. If you draw such a line on Figure 8.10, it will be clear that the consumer can reach a higher level of satisfaction by substituting along this new budget line in the direction of consuming more petrol and less of everything else.

From a theoretical point of view, the disadvantage of the Slutzky measure is that it leaves the consumers with an increased level of satisfaction when the 'income effect' is removed and they adjust to the new relative prices. From an empirical point of view, the disadvantage of the indifference measure is that it is non-operational: we cannot use it unless we know the shape of indifference curves, which requires more knowledge than we usually have.

In summary, in indifference theory the income effect is removed by holding satisfaction constant, while in the Slutzky approach it is removed by holding purchasing power constant, in the sense of adjusting income so that the initial bundle of goods can just be purchased.

Not surprisingly, empirical work that seeks to measure the income and substitution effects typically uses the Slutzky approach, while theorists seeking to study the effects on consumer welfare of a particular change typically use the indifference approach.

---

ments as: ' In spite of the rise in price, quantity purchased increased, so there must have been a change in tastes in favour of this product.' More generally, we are likely to use prices and incomes to account for as many changes in demand as possible, and then assert that the rest must be due to changes in tastes (and to errors of measurement). This does not concern us unduly because we are not particularly interested in establishing precise relations between tastes and demand.

The fact that we cannot identify those changes in demand that are due to changes in tastes does, however, cause trouble when we come to consider the relation between demand and other factors. Anything that does not seem to agree with our theory can be explained away by saying that tastes must have changed. Say, for example, *incomes and other prices were known to be constant*, while the price of some product X rose and, at the same time, more X was observed to be bought. This gives us observations such

as the two illustrated in Figure 8.12(i). The demand curve for X might be positively sloped in this case, but another explanation is that the rise in price coincided with a change in tastes, so that the demand curve shifted just as price changed. These possibilities are analysed in Figure 8.12. With only two observations, we are unable to distinguish between these possibilities, since we have no independent way of telling whether or not tastes changed. If, however, we have many observations, we can get some idea of where the balance of probabilities lies between the two explanations. If, *after using appropriate statistical procedures to remove the effects due to changes in income and other prices*, we have the 26 observations illustrated in Figure 8.13 (say the product's own price changed each week over a period of six months), we will be hard-pressed to avoid the conclusion that the evidence conflicts with the hypothesis of a negatively sloping demand curve.

Of course, we can always explain away these observations

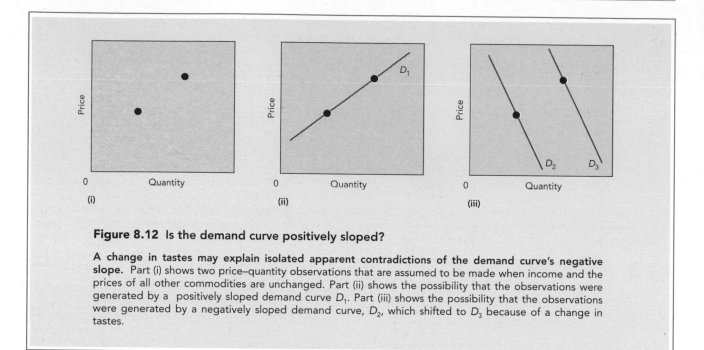

Figure 8.12 Is the demand curve positively sloped?

A change in tastes may explain isolated apparent contradictions of the demand curve's negative slope. Part (i) shows two price–quantity observations that are assumed to be made when income and the prices of all other commodities are unchanged. Part (ii) shows the possibility that the observations were generated by a positively sloped demand curve D_1. Part (iii) shows the possibility that the observations were generated by a negatively sloped demand curve, D_2, which shifted to D_3 because of a change in tastes.

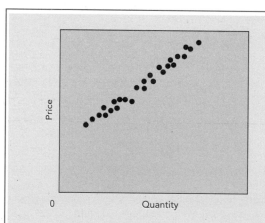

Figure 8.13 The demand curve appears to be positively sloped

Repeated changes in tastes are unlikely to be a satisfactory explanation of repeated contradictions of the demand curve's negative slope. Each of the 26 dots shows a price–quantity combination. All observations are assumed to be taken over a 26-week period when incomes and other prices did not change. The explanation that the demand curve is positively sloped is more likely to be correct than the explanation that a negatively sloped demand curve had shifted each week so as to generate the data showing a positive association between price and quantity.

by saying that tastes must have changed in favour of this product each time its price rose and against the product each time its price fell. This 'alibi' can certainly be used with effect to explain away a single conflicting observation, but we would be uncomfortable using the same alibi 26 times in six months. Indeed, we should begin to suspect a fault in the hypothesis that demand and price vary inversely with each other.

We now have a problem in statistical testing of the sort described in Chapter 3. We are not prepared to throw away a theory after only one or two conflicting observations, but we are prepared to abandon it once we accumulate a mass of conflicting observations that were very unlikely to have occurred if the theory was correct.[11] Thus, statistically, the theory is testable. Fortunately, there is, as we have seen, a great deal of evidence that most demand curves do have negative slopes. With a few possible exceptions, the predictions of the theory have been found to be in agreement with the facts.

[11] If changes in tastes are not related to changes in price, we can easily calculate the odds that the observations in Figure 8.13 are consistent with a negatively sloped, but continually shifting, demand curve. If tastes changed randomly each week, there is a 50–50 chance that tastes changed in the direction needed to offset the first week's price change. In the second week there is also a 50–50 chance. The chances that they changed the 'right' way in both weeks are $(1/2)\,(1/2) = 1/4$, and the chance that they changed the right way for 25 successive weeks is $(1/2)^{25} = 1/33{,}544{,}432$!

Alleged exceptions to the law of demand

The prediction that demand curves have negative slopes has long been known as *the law of demand*. Over the years, a number of exceptions to this law have been alleged.

GIFFEN GOODS AND THE LAW OF DEMAND

Great interest attached to a refutation of the law of demand, supposedly made by Sir Robert Giffen. He was reputed to have observed that an increase in the price of wheat led to an increase in the consumption of bread by nineteenth-century English peasants. If this observation is correct, it does refute the hypothesis that all demand curves always have negative slopes. Does it refute the modern theory of demand? The answer is No, because that is just the type of rare exception to the normal case that is envisaged by the modern indifference preference theory and studied earlier in this chapter.

Thus, the modern theory of demand makes an unequivocal prediction only when we have extraneous information about income elasticities of demand. Since incomes change continuously as a result of economic growth, we do have such information about many products. When we know that the income effect is positive (income elasticity of demand exceeds zero), as it is for most products, we can predict in advance that the quantity demanded will be negatively related to its price. When we know the income effect is negative (i.e. the good is inferior), we cannot be sure of the result. The only thing we can then say is that, the smaller is the proportion of total expenditure accounted for by this product, the less important the income effect will be, and, hence, the more likely we are to get the normal result of price and quantity varying negatively with each other. Finally, if we have no knowledge about the income effect, we can still hazard a probabilistic statement.

The great weight of existing evidence suggests that, if we had to guess with no prior knowledge whether the demand for some product *X* was negatively or positively related to price, the former choice would be the odds-on favourite.

ALTERNATIVE THEORIES OF THE SOURCES OF CONSUMER SATISFACTION

The only exception to the law of demand admitted within indifference preference theory is the Giffen good. Further exceptions all arise from making assumptions that contradict those of indifference theory.

Assume, for example, that a consumer's satisfaction depends not only on the quantities of the various products that she consumes but also on the prices she has to pay for them. The consumer may, for example, buy diamonds not because she particularly likes diamonds *per se*, but because she wishes to show off her wealth in an ostentatious but socially acceptable way. The consumer values diamonds precisely because they are expensive; thus, a fall in price might lead her to stop buying diamonds and switch to a more satisfactory object of ostentatious display. Such consumers will have positively sloping demand curves for diamonds: the lower the price, the fewer they will buy. If enough consumers act similarly, the *market* demand curve for diamonds could be positively sloped as well.

Does this mean that, if a salesman offers a discount to a rich purchaser of diamonds, she would be less likely to buy? Not necessarily. The ostentatious value depends on the price others *think* she paid for the diamonds. Thus, although the demand may be positively associated with published price, it may also be negatively associated with the price as known only to the buyer and seller.

But a positively sloping market demand curve for diamonds and other similar products has never been observed. Why? A moment's thought about the industrial uses of diamonds, and the masses of lower-income consumers who would buy diamonds only if they were sufficiently inexpensive, suggests that positively sloping demand curves for some individual consumers are much more likely than a positively sloping market demand curve for the same product. Recall the discussion earlier in the chapter about the ability of the theory of the negatively sloping demand curve to accommodate odd behaviour on the part of a small group of consumers. (This time the 'odd' group is the rich, rather than the handicapped or the emotionally disturbed.)

Conclusion

Today we not only believe that most demand curves have negative slopes, we also have a good idea of the elasticity in many cases. Reasonably precise knowledge about demand curves is needed if we are to make real-world applications of price theory. If we knew nothing at all empirically about these curves, the theory would be devoid of real-world applications. Since we do have this knowledge, we can predict in advance the effects of changes in many factors such as taxes, costs, the amount of competition in a particular market, and so forth. The more accurate our knowledge of the shape of demand curves, the smaller will be the margin of error in such predictions. Fortunately, as we have seen earlier, economists have accumulated a great store of the requisite empirical knowledge.

Summary

1 Indifference theory assumes only that individuals can order alternative consumption bundles, saying which bundles are preferred to which but not by how much.

2 A single indifference curve shows combinations of products that give the consumer equal satisfaction, and among which he or she is therefore indifferent. An indifference map is a set of indifference curves. The basic assumption about tastes in indifference curve theory is that of a diminishing marginal rate of substitution: the less of one good and the more of another good the consumer has, the less willing he or she will be to give up some of the first good to get a further unit of the second. This means that indifference curves are negatively sloped and convex to the origin.

3 While indifference curves describe the consumer's tastes and, therefore, refer to what he or she *would like* to purchase, the budget line describes what the consumer *can* purchase.

4 Each consumer achieves an equilibrium that maximizes his or her satisfaction at the point at which an indifference curve is tangent to his or her budget line.

5 The income–consumption line shows how quantity consumed changes as income changes with relative prices constant.

6 The price–consumption line shows how quantity consumed changes as relative prices change. The consumer will normally consume more of the product whose relative price falls.

7 The price–consumption line relating the purchases of one particular product to all other products contains the same information as an ordinary demand curve. The horizontal axis measures quantity, and the slope of budget line measures price. Transferring this price–quantity information to a diagram whose axes represent price and quantity leads to a conventional demand curve.

8 The effect of a change in price of one product, all other prices and money income constant, is to change both relative price and real income. The effect of each of these changes on consumption is measured by the substitution effect and the income effect.

9 Demand curves for normal goods have negative slopes because both income and substitution effects work in the same direction, a decrease in price leading to increased consumption.

10 For an inferior good, a decrease in price leads to more consumption via the substitution effect and less consumption via the income effect. In the exceptional case of a Giffen good, the negative income effect more than offsets the substitution effect, causing the product's demand curve to have a positive slope.

11 Observed demand curves are negatively sloped in spite of odd behaviour on the part of some people some of the time. Such behaviour tends to cancel out as long as individuals behave independently of each other.

12 The Giffen good, although a genuine exception to the law of demand, is consistent with indifference theory. Other exceptions, based on such things as snob appeal, are not consistent with indifference theory because they assume that people value goods for reasons other than the utility they get from consuming them. All these exceptions are rarely if ever observed in practice.

Topics for review

- An indifference curve and an indifference map
- Slope of an indifference curve and diminishing marginal rate of substitution
- Budget line
- Absolute and relative prices, and the slope of the budget line
- Response of a consumer to changes in income and prices
- Derivation of the demand curve from indifference curves
- Income and substitution effects
- Normal goods, inferior goods, and Giffen goods

APPENDIX TO CHAPTER 8

The algebra of the budget line

In this appendix we use simple algebra to prove the propositions asserted in the chapter.

Let the consumer's money income be M. Let p_x and p_y be the prices of food and clothing, and let X and Y be the quantities of food and clothing purchased by the consumer. Total expenditure is thus $p_x X + p_y Y$. If we assume, as we did in the text, that the consumer spends all his income on these two goods, we have the following equation:

$$p_x X + p_y Y = M. \qquad (A1)$$

Rearrangement of terms yields the equation of the budget line as it is plotted in Figure 8.5. To do this, we subtract $p_x X$ from both sides, and then divide through by p_y to obtain

$$Y = \frac{M}{p_y} - \frac{p_x}{p_y} X. \qquad (A2)$$

Equation (A1) is a linear equation of the form

$$Y = a - bX, \qquad (A3)$$

where $a = M/p_y$ and $b = p_x/p_y$. The intercept a is the number of units of Y that can be purchased by spending all of M on Y, i.e. money income divided by the price of Y. The slope b depends on the relation between p_x and p_y.

We first prove that the opportunity cost, the slope of the budget line, and the relative price are identical. If we take first differences representing changes in quantities, with prices constant, we get from (A1):

$$p_x \Delta X + p_y \Delta Y = \Delta M.$$

This says that the sum of any changes in the value of purchases of X and the value of purchases of Y must be equal to the change in income (since income determines the total value of purchases).

Along a budget line expenditure is constant, so we can write

$$p_x \Delta X + p_y \Delta Y = 0,$$

which says that if income does not change the change in the total value of purchases must be zero. Simple manipulation of the above equation yields

$$p_x/p_y = -\Delta Y/\Delta X. \qquad (A4)$$

Now $-\Delta Y/\Delta X$ is the change in Y per unit change in X. It is thus the opportunity cost of X measured in units of Y: the amount of Y sacrificed (gained) per unit of X gained (sacrificed). From (A4) this is equal to the relative price of X, which, from (A2), is the slope of the budget line.

We may now prove the five propositions used in the text.

Proposition 1 A change in money income, with money prices (and thus, necessarily, relative prices) constant, shifts the budget line parallel to itself, inwards towards the origin when income falls, and outwards away from the origin when income rises.

Proof. If we change the value of M in (A2), we change the value of a in (A3) in the same direction: $\Delta a = \Delta M/p_y$, but b is unaffected since M does not appear in that term; thus, changing M shifts the budget line inwards ($\Delta M < 0$) or outwards ($\Delta M > 0$) but leaves the slope unaffected.

Proposition 2 An equal percentage change in all absolute prices leaves relative prices unchanged. If money income remains unchanged, it will shift the budget line parallel to itself, inwards towards the origin when prices rise, and outwards away from the origin when prices fall.

Proof. Multiplying both prices in (A2) by the same constant λ gives

$$Y = \frac{M}{\lambda p_y} - \frac{\lambda p_x}{\lambda p_y} X.$$

Since the λ cancel out of the slope term, b is unaffected; the a term however is changed. If $\lambda > 1$, then a is diminished, while if $\lambda < 1$ then a is increased.

Proposition 3 Multiplying all money prices by the same constant, λ, while holding money income constant has exactly the same effect on the budget line as multiplying money income by $1/\lambda$ while holding money prices constant.

Proof. Multiply both money prices in (A2) by λ:

$$Y = \frac{M}{\lambda p_y} - \frac{\lambda p_x}{\lambda p_y} X.$$

Cancelling the λ from the slope term gives

$$Y = \frac{M}{\lambda p_y} - \frac{p_x}{p_y} X.$$

Finally, bringing the λ from the denominator to the numerator of the constant term gives

$$Y = \frac{(1/\lambda)M}{p_y} - \frac{p_x}{p_y} X.$$

Proposition 4   A change in relative prices causes the budget line to change its slope.

Proof. The relative price p_x/p_y in (A2) is the slope term, b, in (A3). Thus, changing the relative price is necessary and sufficient for changing the slope of the budget line.

Note that to pivot the budget line, keeping its Y intercept (and money income) constant as in Figure 8.8, it is necessary to change the relative price by changing p_x only. This can be seen algebraically by inspection of (A2), since p_x does not appear in the constant term. If the relative price change is accomplished solely, or partly, by changing p_y, then both the slope and the Y intercept change. This is because in (A2) p_y appears in both the a and the b term. The common sense of these results is that the Y intercept measures the quantity of Y that can be consumed by buying only Y, and this obviously depends on money income and the price of Y.

We conclude that any change in the relative price necessarily changes the slope of the budget line; while, with money income constant, a change in p_y changes the Y intercept, and (by analogous reasoning) a change in p_x changes the X intercept of the budget line.

Proposition 5   Equal percentage changes in all absolute prices and in money income leave the budget line unaffected.

Proof. Multiply M and both prices in (A2) by λ:

$$Y = \frac{\lambda M}{\lambda p_y} - \frac{\lambda p_x}{\lambda p_y} X.$$

Cancel out the λ from the intercept and the slope terms to obtain

$$Y = \frac{M}{p_y} - \frac{p_x}{p_y} X.$$

Which is equation (A2) once again.

CHAPTER 9

Decision-taking in the presence of risk

THIS chapter deals with issues involving risk. Since nothing is certain, all economic transactions carry some element of risk and often quite substantial amounts. It is necessary, therefore, to consider the important topic of decision-taking in the presence of risk. We first consider how to characterize and measure risk. We then go on to consider two important issues that involve risk: insurance and gambling. We ask why there are markets in each of these services with people willingly supplying and demanding both insurance and gambling. We also look at some of the problems that arise when the existence of insurance influences how people behave and when the buyers and sellers of insurance have different amounts of information about the risks that are being insured against. Later in the chapter, we consider the problems of investing in financial assets which carry different amounts and types of risk. This leads to the important issue of portfolio diversification.

In some areas of economics, it is important to distinguish between risk and uncertainty—a distinction that was originally made by the American economist Frank Knight (1885–1973) in his pathbreaking study of the causes of profits. Risk refers to situations in which the probabilities of particular occurrences can be calculated. Consider, for example, a purchaser who pays now for a commodity that is to be delivered in the future. There is some chance that she may not get what she had paid for. For example, the company may default on its agreement, or go into liquidation before she gets her purchase. To make the situation easy to understand, assume that the outcome is determined by randomly drawing one card from a normal pack of playing cards. If an ace is drawn, the customer does not receive what she paid for; if any other card is drawn, she does get her purchase. In this case, the customer is purchasing under conditions of risk and has 1 chance in 13 of not getting what she paid for. Knowing the chances, she can make a calculation of what price it is worth paying to get 12 chances out of 13 of receiving the good.

In contrast, uncertainty refers to situations in which the decision-taker does not know the probability of various possible outcomes. For example, he may not know the type of pack from which the draw is being made. Not knowing the proportion of the cards in the pack that are aces, he can have no idea of the probability of getting what he pays for. If, for example, the pack is half aces, he has a 50 per cent chance of losing out on the deal; if the pack has 50 cards and only 1 ace, he has only 1 chance in 50 of being disappointed.

As we shall see in this chapter, rational calculation of choices among alternatives is possible under conditions of risk. Rational choice among alternatives is not possible, however, under conditions of uncertainty; when uncertainty is present, one just does not know enough to make a fully rational decision about the best course of action. Fortunately, uncertainty does not typically arise in the situations in which we are interested in this chapter, so we can confine our discussion to situations involving risk. (Some uncertainty is often present, and is a source of profit for those who guess right, when entrepreneurs make decisions to introduce new products, or a new, untried production process, whose performance and acceptability cannot be predicted in advance.)

The behaviour of the consumer under risk

SO far, we have studied the behaviour of consumers when they are presented with choices that involve outcomes that are certain. We asked, for example, if the consumers would prefer bundle A, containing 10 units of food and 5 units of clothing, to bundle B, containing 6 units of food and 12 units of clothing. In so doing, we assumed implicitly that the bundle chosen could be obtained with certainty. What happens, however, if the consumer is faced with only a *probability* of obtaining each bundle?

For example, the consumer might be told that she must choose between two alternatives. Course A gives her 5 chances out of 6 of getting bundle A and 1 chance out of 6 of getting nothing. Course B gives her 4 chances out of 6 of getting bundle B and 2 chances out of 6 of getting nothing.

This is not the type of choice that normally faces a consumer in a shop. Usually, the shopper knows that if he pays his money, he will get what he has paid for with certainty. Sometimes, however, the consumer is uncertain about the quality of the products among which selection is made. The buyer may think that the more expensive brand X will last longer and require less maintenance expenditure than the cheaper brand Y. He may not, however, be sure of how *much* longer it will last, and how *much* less maintenance will be involved.

Other types of choices involve more serious kinds of risk. Buying a flat in area A rather than area B may reduce the chances of being burgled, as may installing a burglar alarm or bars on the ground-floor windows. But by how much?

This part is about consumers, so we concentrate on how consumers behave when their decisions involve risk. Note, however, that all of the economy's decision-takers operate in risky situations much of the time. For example, since production takes time, firms must spend money now to produce goods to be sold in a future that can never be foreseen with certainty.

Many of the principles discussed in this chapter were first developed by analysing games of chance such as roulette or coin-tossing. The same principles arise in consumption and production decisions involving risk, but it is often easier to appreciate them in the kind of games that the early theorists studied. The reader is warned at the outset that many of the ideas are quite subtle. To handle them rigorously requires careful definitions and some complex analysis. This chapter gives only an intuitive overview.

The characterization of risk

Much of what is involved in risky choices can be captured in two measures: the most likely outcome if the choice is repeated over and over again, which is called the **expected value** of the choice, and the dispersion of possible outcomes, which is called the **degree of risk** attached to making that choice. We now need to consider each of these two concepts in some detail.

Expected value   Say you play a game in which a coin is tossed once every minute. The coin is fair in that there is an equal chance of throwing a head or a tail. The probability of throwing a head is said to be 0.5 or 1/2, and the probability of throwing a tail is also 0.5 or 1/2.[1] You win £1 if the result is a head and lose £1 if the result is a tail. If you play the game for 10 minutes, you may have a lucky run and win £10 in 10 minutes. There is an equal chance that you will have an unlucky run and lose £10. It is much more likely, however, that you will get some heads and some tails and end up winning or losing a sum much smaller than £10. The single most likely outcome is that you will exactly break even. This is because there are more sequences of 10 tosses that will end up with 5 heads and 5 tails than any other single combination of heads and tails. For the same reason, the two next most likely results are that you will win £1 (6 heads and 4 tails) or that you will lose £1 (6 tails and 4 heads). Outcomes with larger gains and larger losses become less and less likely, until one gets to the two least likely results of winning £10 or losing £10.[2]

Now consider playing the game repeatedly day after day. It is still quite possible that you will end up winning £10 or losing £10. After all, if you have broken even after many days of play, the chance that you will now encounter 10 heads in a row is the same as it was on your first ten tosses of the coin. But as you go on playing, the average return *per minute spent playing the game* gets smaller and smaller. This return can be expressed as $(H - T)/n$, where H is the number of heads, T is the number of tails, and n is the number

of minutes you have spent playing the game which is the same as the number of tosses. Every time the game is played, n increases by one; the only way the numerator can increase by the same amount is if *every* toss is an H, or every toss is a T. So if your sequence of losses contains a mixture of heads and tails, the average gain or loss per play will tend to decline. Indeed, it can be shown that, as you go on playing for longer and longer periods of time, so that n increases without limit, the value of $(H - T)/n$ tends to zero. This is the expected value of the game. It tells you the most likely outcome for a small number of tosses, and what you can expect to earn as an average per toss if you play the game for a long time—in this case, zero.

Another way of calculating the expected value of the outcome of any game is to add up the various outcomes, each multiplied by its probability of occurrence. The game we are considering has two outcomes on each toss: either you win £1 with probability 0.5 or you lose £1 with probability 0.5. The expected value of the outcome is £1(0.5) − £1(0.5) = £0.5 − £0.5 = 0.

Risk   In the above game you stood to win £1 per toss or lose £1 per toss. If you contract to play for 10 minutes, your maximum possible loss is £10. Now suppose you play the same game but you win £100 on a head and lose £100 on a tail. The expected value of the outcome is still zero. But you risk more if you play it for any given amount of time. There is the same chance that you will encounter an unlucky run of 10 tails, but now you stand to lose £1,000 in this event. Clearly there is more risk attached to the second game than to the first. Risk refers to the dispersion of the possible results. In the first game the possible results from 10 minutes play are dispersed over a range running from +£10 to −£10; in the second game the possible results are dispersed over a range running from +£1,000 to −£1,000.

The risk attached to any choice refers to the variation in the possible outcomes resulting from making that choice.[3]

Fair and unfair games

The penny-toss games that we have considered so far are

---

[1] These are equivalent expressions. The first 0.5 is the ratio of the expected number of heads to the expected number of tails. The second 1/2 says there is one chance in two of throwing a head (since there are two equally likely outcomes on any one toss).

[2] This game is called a *zero-sum game,* which is defined as any game in which the sum of the winnings and losses of all the players is always zero. In other words, what someone in the game wins, someone else in the game must have lost.

[3] For many purposes, the variation can be satisfactorily measured by what is called the *variance* of the possible results, which is the sum of the squares of the deviations of each result from the average, or most likely, result. It is also often measured by the standard deviation, which is the square root of the variance.

fair games in the sense that, if you play them, you have just as much chance of winning as of losing. A lottery, in which all of the ticket money is paid out, is also a fair game. Say, for example, that 100 lottery tickets are sold for £1 each, and a draw then determines which one of the ticket-holders wins £100. This is a fair game because each ticket-holder has 1 chance in 100 of winning £99 (the person's own £1 back and £99 of winnings) and 99 chances out of 100 of losing £1. To find the expected value of this gamble, we multiply the winning of £99 by the chance of winning it (1 chance in 100) and subtract the loss multiplied by the chance of losing it (99 chances in 100). This gives:

$$£99(1/100) - £1(99/100) = £0.99 - £0.99 = 0.$$

A mathematically fair game is one for which the expected value of the outcome is zero.

If you play a fair game repeatedly, you may end up winning or losing, depending on the 'luck of the toss', but the *average gain or loss per play* calculated over all plays will tend towards zero as time passes.

Now consider playing the coin-tossing game under the rules that heads you win £2, tails you lose £1. The expected value of the outcome of this game is £2(0.5) – £1(0.5) = £1 – £0.50 = £0.50. If you play the game only once, you will either win £2 or lose £1. If you play it repeatedly, however, your average gain will tend towards £0.50 per toss. This is not a fair game. Instead it is biased in your favour (and hence biased *against* whomever you are playing with).[4]

Finally, consider the kind of lottery that typically exists. The organizers—be they a firm or, as in many countries, the government—take a proportion of the ticket revenue as their profit and distribute the rest as prize money. All such lotteries are not fair games. They are biased against the participants in the sense that the expected value of participating in the game is negative.[5]

To illustrate, take our previous lottery where 100 tickets are sold at £1 each. Now, however, assume that the organizers take £50 as their profit and pay out the other £50 to the winning ticket. The expected value of a lottery ticket is now £49(1/100) – £1(99/100) = £0.49 – £0.99 = –£0.50. The negative value shows that this is not a fair game; instead, it is biased against anyone who plays it.

Another way of seeing this is to ask yourself what would happen if you bought all the tickets. You would spend £100 and win back £50, thus making a loss of £50. This is a loss of £0.50 per ticket, which, we have already seen, is the expected value of each ticket. (What do you now think about someone who buys two tickets instead of one and tells you he does this in order 'to increase my chances of coming out a winner'?)

Consumers' tastes for risk

Economists distinguish three kinds of decision-takers when risk is involved. Those who are **risk-neutral** will be indifferent about playing a fair game, will willingly play one that is biased in their favour, but will not play one that is biased against them. Those who are **risk-averse** will only play games that are sufficiently biased in their favour to overcome their aversion to risk, but will be unwilling to play fair games, let alone ones that are biased against them. Finally, people who are **risk-lovers** are willing to play games even when they are biased against them, the extent of the love of risk being measured by the degree of bias that a person is willing to accept. (No one would knowingly buy a ticket on a lottery in which the prize was zero, but some extreme risk-lovers might enter a lottery in which only 10 per cent of the ticket money was paid out as prize money.)

Let us start by assuming that people are risk-neutral.

Consumers' valuation of income

We can get quite some way in explaining consumer behaviour with respect to risk if we use a second assumption.

According to the *assumption of diminishing marginal utility of income*, individuals get less and less satisfaction from successive, equal increases in their income and wealth.

The argument is that, if you only have £1,000 per year, you will spend it satisfying your most urgent wants. The next £1,000 will also go for quite important needs, but they will be a little less urgent than those satisfied by the first £1,000. If your income is increased progressively by £1,000 increments, less and less urgent needs will be satisfied by each additional £1,000 of income. The general idea, therefore, is that people can arrange their wants in order and will satisfy the ones that give them most utility first, and then, as their incomes increase, those wants that give them progressively less and less utility. It follows from this assumption that the utility each consumer will attach to successive equal increments of income will decrease steadily as income increases;[6] or, put the other way around, the utility attached to succes-

---

[4]   However, it is still a zero-sum game since your gain is exactly equal to the other player's loss.

[5]   They are not zero-sum games, since the losses of those whose tickets are not selected exceed the gains for those whose tickets are winners.

[6]   This proposition may seem obvious to you. Indeed, it is possible to define terms in such a way that it is true by definition. If we want the proposition to be useful in a theory designed to predict behaviour, it must not be made true by definition. It is worth noting that, when stated in the form of a testable prediction derived from the theory of diminishing marginal utility of each individual commodity, it is not obviously supported by the evidence.

sive equal reductions of income will increase steadily as income is decreased.

Let us accept the hypothesis of diminishing marginal utility of income, and the assumption that all consumers are risk-neutral, and study two cases, insurance and gambling. Each of these cases is typical of other similar ones. They differ from each other in that, with insurance, one pays a smaller sum for certain to avoid a small chance of a larger loss, while, with gambling, one pays a smaller sum to obtain the chance of a larger gain.

The demand for insurance

Say that you feel there is 1 chance in 100 of some unfavourable outcome in which you will lose some asset (possibly your house) which you value at £100,000 and 99 chances in 100 that nothing will happen at all with respect to this asset. The most likely outcome is that nothing will happen at all, but there is a small chance of a really big loss. Say that someone now offers you a mathematically fair insurance policy which avoids this big loss. The policy costs you £1,000 paid now. If nothing else happens, you have given up £1,000. However, if the disaster occurs and you suffer the loss of £100,000, you will be fully compensated.

So you have two possible choices. Choice *A*: you buy the policy, giving up £1,000 for certain, but you avoid the 1 chance in 100 of losing £100,000. The 'expected value' of *A* is −£1,000, i.e. −£1,000(100/100) − £100,000(0). Choice B: you reject the policy, and the expected value of your choice is 1 chance in 100 of losing £100,000 and 99 chances out of 100 of losing nothing, i.e. −£100,000(1/100) − 0(99/100) = −£1,000. The insurance policy represents a fair bargain because the expected values of both courses of action are the same: a loss of £1,000.

Not buying the insurance is, however, a much riskier course than buying it. If you are lucky, you save the £1,000 insurance premium; if you are unlucky, you lose £100,000. Clearly, someone who is risk-averse would buy the policy. But what about someone who is risk-neutral? Both courses have the same expected value so, if there were no other considerations, the risk-neutral person would be indifferent between buying this insurance policy and not buying it.

This is where the hypothesis of diminishing marginal utility of income comes into play. If we think of reducing the consumer's income by successive units of £1,000, the loss attached to each unit will grow as income is reduced. Thus, the utility forgone if £100,000 is lost will be more than 100 times the utility forgone if £1,000 is lost. It is now rational for a risk-neutral person to prefer the insurance policy. The key is that the utility attached to each £1 lost is not the same. Larger losses of money result in utility forgone that is more than in proportion to the utility forgone as a result of smaller losses. As a result, the expected utility is greater with the policy than without it, even though the

expected monetary loss is the same in either case.

There is one further complication that needs to be mentioned. Since insurance companies must themselves make money, they do not offer their policy-holders mathematically fair policies such as the one just described. In the above case, where the risk was 1 chance in 100 of losing £100,000, an insurance company would charge a premium of more than £1,000. Say it was £1,200. The insurance company expects to pay out an average of £1,000 per policy, so the £200 goes to cover its costs and to earn a profit.

For the purchaser, the expected value of buying the policy is now −£1,200. But the expected value of not buying remains at −£1,000. If nothing else intervened, a risk-neutral person would not buy the policy, which requires spending £1,200 to avoid a situation (no insurance) whose expected value is −£1,000.

If risk-neutral people buy insurance, diminishing marginal utility of income must be strong enough to make an unfair gamble appear attractive to them.

Risk-neutral people are willing to pay more than £1,000 to avoid the 1 chance in 100 of losing £100,000 because they rate the utility they would sacrifice because of a £100,000 loss at more than 100 times the utility they would sacrifice because of a loss of £1,000.

The demand to gamble

Now let us consider any situation where one can either do nothing or pay money to purchase the chance of a gain. This could be a lottery ticket, a coupon on the football pools, a bet on the horse races, a firm investing money in future output, or a person purchasing a share in a firm.

Consider first a mathematically fair possibility. You are offered a ticket on a lottery consisting of 100 tickets sold for £1 each, with a single prize of £100 going to the winning ticket. Now you have 99 chances out of 100 of losing £1 and 1 chance in 100 of winning £99. (If you win, you get your £1 back and £99 more.) This is a fair game, since the expected value of a ticket is zero (£99(1/100) − £1(99/100)). But, given diminishing marginal utility of income, the utility a person will get from winning £100 will be less than 100 times the utility sacrificed by the loss of £1. Thus, because the expected value of the ticket measured in money is zero, the expected value of the ticket measured in utility is negative. Thus, if you are risk-neutral, and have diminishing marginal utility of income, you would not buy a ticket.

So far we have considered a fair gamble. Most gambling games, however, are not mathematically fair. Instead they are biased against the player. The proprietor of the game takes out some of the money wagered to cover costs and provide a profit (the government may also take some as a betting tax); what is left is distributed as prize money. This is true of lotteries, pools, dog and horse races, casino gambling and every commercial gambling function. (When individuals play games of pure chance with each other, such as a friendly Saturday night poker game, the games are usually fair in the sense that the value of what is won is equal to the value of what is lost, so that the expected value of playing the game is zero.)

Gambling on any event in which the organizers take a profit, and/or on which the government levies a tax, has a negative expected value and is thus inconsistent with risk-neutral participants who are subject to constant, let alone diminishing, marginal utility of income.

Yet we observe such behaviour every day. How can we explain it? At least four possibilities suggest themselves.

One possibility is that people have increasing marginal utilities of income. This could explain why they gamble on games that have negative expected values. It would, however, be inconsistent with their buying insurance policies with negative expected values. So this explanation would work only if there were one class of people who gambled (those with increasing marginal utility of income) and another class who bought insurance (those with decreasing marginal utility of income). The common observation that there are many people who do both rules out this possibility as a general explanation.

A second possibility is that people are risk-lovers. This would explain why they took part in mathematically unfair gambling games whenever the extra utility from the gambling overcame the diminishing marginal utility attached to the income to be won. This would also be consistent with buying insurance as long as the marginal utility of the income to be lost was a stronger force than the utility attached to taking a risk.

A third possibility is that, although people are not risk-lovers in general, they get utility out of the dreams attached to even a remote possibility of winning a vast sum on the pools or some similar bet. In this case, the gamblers know that the average player will lose money over his or her lifetime, but that does not matter. The gamblers are sustained by the mere thought that, against all the odds, they might win a sum large enough to transform an otherwise hard life, in the same way that Cinderella's fairy godmother transformed her life. This may go a long way towards explaining why people take part in gambling games where a few very large prizes are to be won. It seems less satisfactory as an explanation of why people bet on horses or dogs where winnings, although more frequent, are not enough to change one's whole lifestyle. Here the answer seems to be a more conventional enjoyment of small risks.

A fourth possibility, of course, is that people are just badly informed. They may not know the expected value of the gamble that they take. It is probably true that many people do not realize the magnitude of the negative expected value of many gambles. (The smaller the *payout ratio*—the ratio of money paid out to money taken in—the larger the magnitude of the negative expected value of the game.)

The supply of gambling

This chapter is mainly about consumers and their demands for various goods and services. It is, however, convenient at this point to complete the story of gambling and insurance by explaining why firms are willing to supply these services to consumers who demand them. We first consider the easy case of gambling, and then go on to the more difficult, but also more interesting, case of insurance.

There is no difficulty in understanding why firms are willing to provide such gambling opportunities as the pools or betting on horse or dog races. If firms make their own odds after they know the amounts bet, they are on the right side of a mathematically unfair game from which they must win. Assume, for example, that you run a lottery and are free to take for yourself what you wish from the funds raised and then distribute the rest as prizes. You cannot lose.

Firms providing this type of gambling service sometimes have a government monopoly and sometimes are subject to competition from other firms. If there is competition, then there will be pressure to keep the payout ratio (what is paid out divided by what is taken in) high, provided that ticket purchasers are aware of the prizes given out by competing lotteries. If the lottery has a monopoly, there will be an optimum payout ratio that will maximize the profits of the firm running the game. As the payout ratio goes to one, profits go to zero, since all money taken in is paid out. As the payout ratio goes to zero, profits will also go to zero, since fewer and fewer people will be willing to wager money as the size of the winnings and/or the number of winners get smaller.

Somewhere in between a ratio of zero and one will be the optimum payout ratio that maximizes the profits of a monopoly firm running a lottery or other betting game.

The supply of insurance

In the gambling case, the firm could decide how much to pay out after it knew how much it had taken in. Insurance is a different matter. The insurance firm takes your money and agrees to pay out a certain sum if the unlucky event strikes you. Conceivably the insurance firm could have an unlucky run of luck in which, in the limit, all of the people it insures suffer loss at the same time. The basis for profitable insurance firms is not, therefore, being on the right side of an unfair game. Instead, it lies in the mathematics of what are called *pooled risks*.

RISK-POOLING

To see what is involved in the pooling of risks, consider two individuals who get an income which varies according to the toss of a coin. (Once again, the coin toss stands for any source of risk.) Each individual tosses a coin each month. If a head comes up, John gets £500; if a tail, he gets nothing. The same applies to June: she gets £500 if she tosses a head and nothing if a tail comes up. The expected value of each person's income is £500(0.50) = £250 per month. Over a long period of time, each person's monthly income will indeed average close to £250. But neither of them may like the possibility of going from £500 to nothing on the toss of a coin each month. Suppose they decide to pool their incomes each month and each take half of the resulting amount. The expected value of the pooled income is £500 and of each person's income is £250 per month.[7]

Importantly, however, the variation from month to month in each person's income will be diminished. The result is shown in Table 9.1. When they were operating on their own, each person's income deviated from its expected value by £250 each month; in good months it was £250 over, and in bad months it was £250 below. When the two incomes are pooled, the expected value is reached whenever one is lucky and the other unlucky, which will tend to be about half the time. Only in one-quarter of the outcomes will income be £250 above, and in one-quarter will it be £250 below. These two results require that both be lucky at the same time or both be unlucky.

If three people pool their incomes, the extreme cases of £500 each and zero each occur only when all three are lucky

or unlucky at the same time. These cases each occur with a probability of 1 chance in 8. (There is 1 chance in 2 that any one person will get a head, and (1/2)(1/2)(1/2) = 1/8 that all three will get heads at once.) So the extreme cases in which everyone gets *either* £500 *or* zero occur only one-quarter of the times. If four people pool their incomes, the extreme cases of *either* £500 *or* £0 income per person will occur only with probability 2/16. By the time ten people are involved, the two extreme cases will occur only twice in two raised to the tenth power (2^{10}) times, which is a very small fraction indeed.

The larger the number of independent events that are pooled, the less and less likely is it that extreme results will occur.

The key to this proposition is that the events must be independent; the result of John's coin toss must not be in any way related to the result of June's. In the unpooled case, the extreme result occurs to one of them when one of them is unlucky or lucky. The probability of the extreme result is less likely when they pool their incomes because it requires that both be unlucky or lucky at the same time.

The same reasoning applies to all kinds of events that may be regarded as chance occurrences, as long as they are independent of each other. There is some probability that any given house in the country will burn down in any given year; let us say it is 1 in 1,000. An insurance company takes a premium from house-owners and offers them full compensation if their house burns down. If the company is so small that it insures only ten houses, it may be unlucky in having ten owners who just happen to be careless at the same time and burn their houses down accidentally. This is unlikely, but not impossible. A bad bit of luck over all ten houses insured will ruin the company, which could not meet all of its insured risks at the same time. But let the company be large enough to insure 100,000 houses. Now it is pooling risk over a large number, and the chances are that very close to 1 house in every 1,000 insured houses will burn down. With 100,000 houses insured, the most likely outcome is that 100 houses will burn down. The company might be unlucky and have 110 burn down, or lucky and have only 90 burn down. But to have 200 burn down is very unlikely indeed, as long as a fire in one house is independent of a fire in another.

This requirement of independence explains why insur-

Table 9.1 Incomes of two persons when risks are and are not pooled

	Risks are not pooled		Risks are pooled:
	John	June	both get
T–T	0	0	0
T–H	0	500	250
H–T	500	0	250
H–H	500	500	500

Pooling of independent risks reduces risk. Each person gets an income of £500 if he or she tosses a head (H) and nothing if a tail (T). There are four possible results, in two of which one head and one tail occurs. In the other two, there are either two tails or two heads. When each accepts his or her own risks, each expects an income of £500 half the time and zero the other half. When the incomes are pooled then split, only one combination in four gives them zero income while half of the time they will get £250. The deviations of their monthly incomes from the expected value of £250 is decreased by pooling.

[7] This can be seen in a number of ways. First, sum the expected values of each person's income, £250 + £250 = £500, and divide it between the two to get £250 each. Second, evaluate the four possible outcomes: there is a 0.25 chance of the pool being £1,000; there is a 0.25 chance that John will get £500 and June zero and the same chance that June will get £500 and John zero, making a 0.5 chance that the pool will be £500; and a 0.25 chance of the pool being £0. This sums to £1,000(0.25) + £500(0.5) + 0(0.25) = £250 + £250 = £500 as an expected value for the pool and, hence, £250 for each of the participants.

ance policies normally exclude wars and other situations where some common cause acts on all the insured units. A war may lead to a vast number of houses being destroyed. Since the cause of the loss of one house is not independent of the cause of the loss of another, the insurance company has a high probability, should a war break out, of suffering ruinous losses.

The basic feature of insurance is the pooling of independent events, which is what makes extreme outcomes unlikely. A common cause that seriously affects all insured items in the same way defeats the principle on which insurance is based.

The typical insurance company, therefore, deals with repeated events such as fires or death in which the probability of each insured item becoming a claimant is independent of the probability of any other item becoming a claimant.

RISK-SHARING

A further practice of insurance companies allows them to extend their coverage to events that are not repeated and where the loss might be large enough to ruin any one company.

Say that a famous pianist wants to insure her hands against any event that would stop her from playing the piano. The amount insured would be colossal, amounting to all the income she would earn over her lifetime if her hands stayed unharmed. The company can calculate the chances that any randomly chosen female in the population will suffer such a loss to her hands. But it is not insuring the whole population. Only one person is involved. If there is no catastrophe, the company will gain its premium. If there is a catastrophe, the company will suffer a large loss.

The trick in being able to insure the pianist, or any single person or thing where the loss would be large, lies in what is called *risk-sharing* (or re-insurance, as it is sometimes called). One company writes a policy for the pianist and then breaks the policy up into a large number of sub-policies. Each sub-policy carries a fraction of the payout and earns a fraction of the premium. The company then sells each sub-policy to many different firms.

Assume, for illustration, that 100 firms each write one such primary policy—one on a pianist's hands, one on a footballer's legs, one on a rare treasure being flown to Japan for exhibit, etc. Each then breaks its primary policy up into 100 sub-parts and sells each part to the other 99 firms. Each firm ends up holding risks that are independent of each other, no one of which is large enough to threaten the firm should it give rise to a claim. This is what Lloyd's of London does. It is a syndication of a large number of insurance underwriters. Each one is prepared to insure almost anything as long as a claim would not break all of the firms

when the risk is spread over a large number of them.[8]

We return to risk in the context of financial investments later in this chapter.

Problems with insurance

Economists have been prominent in helping us to understand two major problems with insurance, called moral hazard and adverse selection.

MORAL HAZARD

If the contents of your flat are valuable but are not insured for theft, you are likely to be careful in locking your door every time you leave and will take other sensible, anti-break-in precautions. If you take out an insurance policy, you may be less careful. Say, for example, that you get three minutes down the road and realize that you forgot to lock up. You may decide to press on, reasoning that you cannot afford the time you would lose in returning to lock up, that being visited by burglars on any particular day is unlikely, and that anyway you are insured against burglary.

The existence of the insurance policy has altered your behaviour. You take more risks, making a loss from burglary more likely than if you were uninsured.

This behaviour, called **moral hazard**, is defined as an insurance-induced alteration of behaviour that makes the event insured against more likely to occur.

Moral hazard occurs in many lines of insurance. For example, people are observed to be more careless about fire prevention when they are insured than when they are not. Fire insurance is clearly socially beneficial in allowing people to pool risks, thus avoiding the chances of a large loss in return for a relatively small payment. However, there is an offsetting social loss if the very existence of fire insurance leads to more destruction by fire than would occur without it.

ADVERSE SELECTION

When the person on one side of a bargain knows more about what is being bought and sold than the person on the other side, we have a situation of *asymmetrical information*. This can lead to undesirable consequences.

For example, a person who is considering taking out life insurance may know more about her health than the insurance company can find out in one medical examination and a few lifestyle questions. The insurance company will

---

[8] This is also what bookmakers do when they cannot control the odds themselves. When they take bets at odds set by others, one large bet could ruin them by requiring a payout greater than their current assets. To avoid such risks, they lay off part of the bet with other bookmakers. In this way no one ends up holding bets that are big enough to threaten their solvency if they suffer an unlucky run of payouts.

quote a rate that covers the average risk for all persons in some category, such as middle-aged, female, non-smokers, in apparent good health. Those who believe they are in better than average health know they are being asked for a premium that is high relative to their individual risk. In contrast, those who know they are less healthy than the average in their group know they are being offered a bargain: insurance at a rate that is low relative to their own individual risk. As a result, a higher proportion of people who are above the average risk will insure themselves than those who are below the average risk.

Adverse selection refers to the tendency for people who are more at risk than the average to choose to be insured while people who are less at risk are less likely to choose to be insured. It occurs whenever individuals within a group that is offered a common insurance rate know that their own risk deviates significantly from the average risk within the group. Those at high risk relative to the average are offered a bargain; those at low risk are offered expensive insurance.

This problem would be serious if all people were charged the same rate that covered the average risk. Young, healthy, non-smokers in good health would be heavily penalized and much less inclined to take out insurance. In contrast, older smokers with chronic ailments would be subsidized and have a strong inducement to insure themselves.

The result would be that the average risk of the group who took out insurance would rise above the average risk in the whole population. Rates would then have to be raised to cover the average risk of the insured groups, and this would put an even stronger disincentive on those who have below- average risks to go uninsured.

Insurance companies try to cope with this problem by defining a number of groups distinguished from each other by characteristics that affect their risk. They then charge each group a different rate based on the average risk of that group. For example, rates for theft insurance in London vary with the postal code. This certainly helps, but it is always true that there will be variations within any one group. Those who know they are more at risk than the average in their group are offered a bargain, while those who know they are less at risk than the average are offered what is, for them, expensive insurance.

The objective of insurance companies is to strike a balance between the increasing costs and complexity of defining and administering more and more groups, and the decreasing adverse selection that results from reducing the amount of variation within each group (by having more groups).

One strategy is to target large groups rather than self-selecting individuals, i.e. all AA members or all Natwest account holders or all ICI employees. These are likely to be an average cross-section of the population rather than an especially high-risk group.

Adverse selection also applies in banking. Banks tend to expand by merger or acquisition, not by organic growth. The reason is that marginal customers are not the ones banks want to lend to. They are riskier than average. If one

---

BOX 9.1

Used-car prices: the problem of 'lemons'

It is common for people to regard the large loss of value of a new car in the first year of its life as a sign that consumers are overly style-conscious and will always pay a big premium for the latest in anything. Professor George Akerlof of the University of California at Berkeley suggests a different explanation, based on the proposition that the flow of services expected from a one-year-old car that is *purchased on the used-car market* will be lower than those expected from an *average* one-year-old car on the road. Consider his theory.

Any particular model year of motor cars will include a certain proportion of 'lemons'—cars that have one or more serious defects. There were faults in their assembly, or in the parts assembled, that went undetected. Purchasers of new cars of a certain year and model take a chance on their car turning out to be a lemon. Those who are unlucky and get a lemon are more likely to resell their car than those who are lucky and get a well functioning car. Hence, in the used-car market there will be a disproportionately large number of lemons for sale. (Also, not all cars are driven in the same manner; those that are driven for long distances or under bad conditions are much more likely to be traded in or sold as used cars than those that are driven on good roads and for moderate distances.)

Thus, buyers of used cars are right to be on the lookout for low-quality cars, while salespeople are quick to invent reasons for the high quality of the cars they are selling. ('It was owned by a little old lady who drove it only on Sundays.') Because it is difficult to identify a lemon or a badly treated used car before buying it, the purchaser is prepared to buy a used car only at a price that is low enough to offset the increased probability that it is of poor quality.

This is a rational consumer response to asymmetric knowledge between the seller of a car and its eventual buyer. It helps to explain why one-year-old cars typically sell for a discount that is somewhat larger than can be explained by the physical depreciation that occurs in one year in the *average* car of that model. The larger discount reflects the lower services that the purchaser can expect from a used car because of the higher probability that it will be a lemon.

bank buys a whole set of existing customers of some other bank, it knows their average characteristics and it picks up good ones as well as bad.

All the large UK banks have grown up from mergers of existing banks. None of their major components is less than 150 years old. (NatWest, Lloyds, Barclays, and Midland all fit this story.)

Box 9.1 outlines a different case of moral hazard; in this case it is the sellers that know more about the product than the buyers.

Financial choices and risk

GAMBLING and insurance are not the only areas in which an analysis of attitudes towards risk and return provides insights into individual (and institutional) behaviour. The ideas that we have introduced have wide applications in the financial system as a whole.

Much of what any financial system does can be explained in terms of channelling surplus funds from one set of agents through financial institutions or markets to another set of agents who wish to borrow. Savers are investing their own money in the hope of receiving a return on that investment (interest) but they also have to consider risk, because there is often a possibility that borrowers may default and that the savers' money would be lost. Even if default is not likely, many forms of investment involve risks of capital gains and losses which occur when the market value of the investment changes. Accordingly, all investors have to take into consideration not just the expected return on their investment, but also the risks involved.

The analysis of risk and return as applied to finance has created a vast literature. Here we can develop only a few of the key ideas. However, a few simple ideas take us a long way in the understanding of a wide range of financial behaviour.

Portfolio diversification

'Don't put all your eggs in one basket' is a well-known proverb which summarizes the message that there may be benefits to diversification. If you carry your breakable items in several baskets, there is a chance that one will be dropped, but you are unlikely to drop all your baskets on the same trip. Similarly, if you invest all your wealth in the shares of one company, there is a chance that the company will go bust and you will lose all your money. Since it is unlikely that all companies will go bust at the same time, a portfolio of shares in several companies will be less risky.

This may sound like the idea of risk-pooling which we discussed earlier in this chapter, and risk-pooling is certainly an important reason for many elements of diversification. We will use the notion of risk-pooling to explain some forms of financial behaviour, but a full understanding of portfolio diversification involves a slightly wider knowledge of the nature of risk than what is involved in coin-tossing.

The key difference about risk in the real world of finance, as opposed to coin-tossing, is that many of the potential outcomes are not independent of other outcomes. If you and I toss a coin, the probability of yours turning up heads is independent of the probability of my throwing a head. However, the return on an investment in, say, BP is not independent of the return on an investment in Shell. This is because these two companies both compete in the same industry. If BP does especially well in attracting new business, it may be at the expense of Shell. So high profits at BP may be associated with low profits at Shell, or vice versa.

The fact that risks of individual investments may not be independent has important implications for investment allocations, or what is now called *portfolio theory*. Investments can be combined in different proportions to produce risk and return characteristics which cannot be achieved through single investments, although institutions have grown up to take advantage of the benefits of diversification, as we shall see below.

Diversified portfolios may produce combinations of risk and return which dominate non-diversified portfolios.

This is a very important statement which requires a little closer investigation. It will help to identify the circumstances under which diversification is beneficial. It will also clarify what we mean by the word 'dominate'.

Table 9.2 sets out two simple examples. There are two assets that an investor can hold, and there are two possible outcomes, which are equally likely to arise. Thus, there is a probability of 0.5 attached to each state and the investor has no advanced knowledge of which is going to happen.

Consider part (i) of the table. In this case both assets have the same expected return (20 per cent) and both have the same degree of risk. (The possible range of outcomes is between 10 and 30 per cent on each asset.) If all that mattered in investment decisions was the risk and return of individual shares, the investor would be indifferent between asset A and asset B. Indeed, if the choice were between holding only A or only B, all investors should be indifferent (whether they were risk-averse, risk-neutral, or risk-loving) because the risk and expected return would be identical for both assets. However, this is not the end of the story because the returns on these assets are not independent. Indeed, there is a perfect negative correlation between them: when one is high the other is low and vice versa.

What would a sensible investor do if permitted to hold some combination of the two assets? Clearly, there is no possible combination that will change the overall expected return because it is the same on both assets. However, the risk can be reduced by holding some of each asset. If the investor holds half his wealth in asset A and half in asset B, risk will be reduced to zero—the return will be 20 per cent whatever state of the world results. This diversified portfolio will clearly be preferred to either asset alone by risk-averse investors. The risk-neutral investor is indifferent to all combinations of A and B because they all have the same expected return, but the risk-lover may prefer not to diversify. This is because, by picking one asset alone, the risk-lover still has a chance of getting a 30 per cent return and the extra risk gives positive pleasure.

Risk-averse investors will choose the diversified portfolio which gives them the lowest risk for a given expected rate of return, or the highest expected return for a given level of risk.

Diversification does not always reduce the riskiness of a portfolio, so we need to be clear what conditions matter.

Table 9.2 Combinations of risk and return

	State 1	State 2
(i) Returns are negatively correlated		
Asset A	10%	30%
Asset B	30%	10%
(ii) Returns are positively correlated		
Asset A	10%	30%
Asset B	0%	40%

Assets differ in expected return and variability in returns. Part (i) illustrates the return on two assets in two different states of the world. In this case, asset A has a high return in state 2 and low return in state 1. The reverse is true for asset B. A portfolio of both assets has the same expected return but lower risk than a holding of either asset on its own. In (ii) both assets have a high return in state 2 and low return in state 1. For the risk-averse investor, asset A dominates asset B.

Consider the example in part (ii) of Table 9.2. As in part (i), both assets have an expected return of 20 per cent. However, now asset B is riskier than asset A and it has returns that are positively correlated with A. Does portfolio diversification reduce risk in this case? Clearly not. Risk-averse investors would be likely to invest only in asset A, while risk-lovers might invest only in asset B. Combinations of A and B are always riskier than holding A alone. Thus, we could say that for the risk-averse investor asset A dominates asset B, as asset B will never be held so long as asset A is available.

The key difference between the example in part (ii) of Table 9.2 and that in part (i) is that in the second example returns on the two assets are positively correlated while in the former they are negatively correlated.[9]

The risk attached to a combination of two assets will be smaller than the sum of the individual risks if the two assets have returns that are negatively correlated.

DIVERSIFIABLE AND NON-DIVERSIFIABLE RISK

Not all risk can be eliminated by diversification. The specific risk associated with any one company can be diversified away by holding large numbers of other companies' shares. But even if you held shares in every available traded company, you would still have some risk, because the stock market as a whole tends to move up and down over time. Hence we talk about market risk and specific risk. *Market risk* is non-diversifiable, whereas *specific risk* is diversifiable through risk-pooling.

Beta It is now common to measure the relationship between how a specific company share moves and movements in the market as a whole in terms of a coefficient called Beta. A share that is perfectly correlated with the stock market index will have a Beta of 1. A Beta higher than 1 means that the share moves in the same direction as the market but with amplified fluctuations. A Beta between 1 and 0 means that the share moves in the same direction as the stock market but is less volatile. A negative Beta indicates that the share moves in opposite direction to the market in general. Clearly, a share with a negative Beta would be in high demand by investment managers as it would reduce a portfolio's risk .

A well known theory of asset pricing called the *capital asset pricing model*, or CAPM, suggests that shares will be priced in the market in such a way that shares with higher Betas must offer higher average returns in order to com-

---

[9] Readers who have studied statistics will recall that, if two statistical series *A* and *B* are added together, the variance of the combined series is equal to the variance of *A* plus the variance of *B* plus twice the covariance of *A* and *B*. The covariance of *A* and *B* will be negative if *A* and *B* are negatively correlated, hence the combined variance will be less than the sum of its parts.

pensate investors for the higher risk that they carry. Empirical evidence supports this general proposition.

For any given market conditions, there is a trade-off between risk and return. Investments offering higher expected returns will, on average, also be associated with higher risk.

MUTUAL FUNDS

Many small investors do not have enough wealth to invest in company shares to gain the benefits of a diversified portfolio. Yet the average returns on investing in shares are higher than those on safe assets, such as National Savings Certificates or bank and building society deposits. Hence there is a role for institutions that sell to small investors a share in a much bigger and more diversified portfolio.

Such institutions are generally known as mutual funds. They are like clubs in which savers pool their funds and then jointly own a much bigger diversified set of investments. There are two potential benefits from such an organization. The first is the gain from diversification. The second is the fact that the combined fund can afford to have a professional manager. (Although there is no clear evidence that professional managers do better at stock picking than the market average, they probably do better than would many less informed individual investors.)

There are two types of mutual funds. *Unit trusts* are open-ended funds which buy more shares when investors buy more units (i.e. deposit more money in the fund) and sell shares when investors want their money back. *Investment trusts* are quoted companies whose only business is investing in other company shares. Investment trusts are themselves companies whose shares can be bought and sold on the stock exchange. Once they are set up, their capital is locked in. An investor trying to get her money back must sell her shares in the investment trust on the stock exchange, but the trust itself would not have to sell any of its investments. For this reason, investment trusts are referred to as closed-end mutual funds.

Mutual funds play an especially important role in helping small investors to achieve international diversification. Just as diversification across UK companies is beneficial in improving the risk–return trade-off, so international diversification improves it still further. Small investors find it very difficult and costly to buy and sell foreign shares, but mutual funds are able to access foreign markets and spread the costs over large numbers of investors. Investment opportunities for small investors are thereby greatly enhanced.

Financial intermediaries

Mutual funds are a form of financial intermediary. They take in money from investors and invest the money in company shares. Banks and building societies are even more important financial intermediaries in terms of the scale of the funds they handle. Their existence can also be explained to some degree by the benefits of risk-pooling and portfolio diversification. Some financial instruments which help companies or individuals to manage risk are discussed in Box 9.2. We shall have more to say in Chapter 35, which deals with banks and their role in the monetary system. Here we make the simple point that the very existence of some of our major financial institutions arises, in part, as a way of coping with risk.

The easiest example to think of is of the traditional building society, which takes in deposits from savers and makes loans to house purchasers (mortgages) to help them buy a house. Why is the intermediary there at all? Why do savers not lend directly to house buyers? After all, the building societies' costs could be avoided and lenders and borrowers could, perhaps, get better terms. (The spread between deposit rates and loans rates could be split between the lender and the borrower.)

There are several reasons why both lender and borrower prefer to deal with an intermediary rather than with each other directly.

First, there are transaction or search costs for lender and borrower before they can meet. The intermediary provides a 'trading post' where depositors know they can find a willing borrower at all times and home buyers know they find a potentially willing lender.

Second, the characteristics of the loan that a saver wants to make may differ from those the ultimate borrower would be happy with. A typical saver may want to get money back at short notice; a typical house buyer wants to borrow money for 20 or 25 years. The building society can make a long-term loan by taking in a whole series of different short-term deposits.

Third, a typical saver would be unlikely to be able to lend to more than one or two house buyers. Any single house may collapse, or the borrower may default. A building society can spread the risk over a wide range of different borrowers and a wide range of different types of house. Nationwide building societies (such as the Halifax) have grown up to take advantage of the fact that wide diversification of loans across different industries and regions is safer than, say, lending only to coal miners in South Yorkshire. Hence, minimizing overall risk is a central part of any financial intermediary's *raison d'être*.

A fourth reason for the existence of financial intermediaries applies rather more to banks than to building societies. The latter make loans secured upon a house, while banks make many loans that are not secured on any asset. When lending, therefore, banks must make judgements about who is likely to pay them back and who is not. Banks are well placed to do this because they will normally lend only to people with whom they have an ongoing banking

BOX 9.2

Derivatives: dealing with risk in financial markets

Many modern financial instruments help to create markets in various aspects of risk. Agents who wish to avoid or reduce risk can deal on these markets with others who are willing to accept the risk (for a price). The many financial firms that operate in these markets are dealing in risk, even though they would not normally be classified as insurance companies. We discuss below some of the financial products that are most commonly used. As they are themselves not primary loans or securities, but can be used to change the risk characteristics of some underlying asset or liability position, they are often referred to as 'derivatives'.

Futures and forward contracts

These enable agents to buy, at a price agreed today, some product or asset which will be delivered and paid for at some time in the future. Thus, a farmer might sell his wheat crop six months before it is harvested in order to hedge the risk of the price falling at harvest time. A tyre manufacturer might buy rubber ahead of production needs either to lock in a particularly favourable supply price or just to have the security of knowing what the price will be when the rubber is needed. An importer of American jeans who will have to pay the producer in dollars in nine months time may buy the dollars with pounds sterling in the forward foreign exchange market in order to avoid the risk that the dollar might appreciate against the pound in the meantime. *Futures contracts* are contracts traded in standard sizes on organized exchanges (such as the London International Financial Futures Exchange, LIFFE). *Forward contracts* are contracts that are typically made between a customer and a bank and are custom made in terms of characteristics (hence they are said to be traded in the Over-the-Counter market, or OTC).

Swaps

Interest rate swaps involve the exchange of the *difference* in the payment streams on two different assets or liabilities calculated on the basis of a notional principle sum. Typically, it is the difference between fixed- and floating-rate interest streams. They are used to manage interest rate risk. Agents who hold fixed interest rate assets and floating interest rate liabilities will be exposed to losses if interest rates rise, because the cost of borrowing will rise while the return on assets will not. Hence, swapping either the fixed asset rate into floating, or the floating liability rate into fixed will reduce risk. The principle involved here is referred to as 'matching' because it creates assets and liabilities that will move up or down together.

Foreign exchange swaps involve two simultaneous forward transactions in which the second transaction reverses the first. They are widely used by banks as a way of closing 'exposure gaps'. Consider for example, a bank that has sold $1 million for sterling to one customer for future settlement on 30 September and agreed to buy $1 million for sterling from another customer on 20 October. Assume that a second bank has done the reverse, agreeing to buy $1 million for sterling on 30 September and to sell $1 million for sterling on 20 October. Both banks are at risk because the exchange rate may change unexpectedly at any time between now and 20 October. Because they are on opposite sides of these two transactions, if one loses the other will gain. They can remove their risk by arranging a swap. The first bank would simultaneously buy the sterling with dollars for 30 September (the second bank sells sterling) and sell it back again for 20 October (the second bank buys sterling) at a predetermined price. Thus the banks, which have made price commitments to their customers, are guaranteed to be able to deliver the currency at the right time at a price that is also fixed. The banks have hedged their own positions and will gain only their fees or commissions on the deals.

Options

Options come in two varieties. A *call option* is the right (but not the obligation) to buy some commodity or security at a specific price called the *exercise price*. A *put option* is the right (but not the obligation) to sell some commodity or security at a specific price. With a forward or futures contract, you are committed to a future transaction; with an option, you have the right to go ahead but you can walk away from the deal if you prefer. A wheat farmer who has sold his crop on the futures market must fulfil the contract (even if his crop falls short of what he has sold, in which case he would have to buy to the market price to fulfil the contract). With a put option, however, he could choose not to deliver if the market price turned out to be much higher than the exercise price of his contract. Options thus have favourable characteristics. They limit the downside of risk without limiting the upside. Naturally, there is a price which has to be paid for this one-way bet which is known as the option premium. Those who sell options must charge a premium high enough to cover their losses when options are exercised at prices that are much better than the existing market price.

Students will encounter many other varieties of derivatives in courses on finance. However, most of them are variations on those discussed above.

relationship. They can see how much money a customer is earning because it passes through a bank account. They therefore have better information about the creditworthiness of a potential borrower than any other potential lender would have.

Banks have superior information about the risks involved, and they are in a good position to monitor the financial progress of their customers over time.

Thus, again, the existence of risk is central to the need for banks to play this role, and the nature of their relationship with customers puts them in an ideal position to monitor (and possibly control) those risks.

Financial intermediaries allow savers to find relatively safe outlets for their savings which pay a competitive rate of interest. (Financial intermediaries compete for business just like the other firms that we will discuss below.) Those who wish to borrow are also able to do so in a well developed market for loans. Such savings-and-loans markets are important for the functioning of a market economy. In particular, they enable consumers to move consumption either forward or backward in time, thereby greatly enhancing the range of choices available. Saving postpones consumption for the future. Borrowing permits consumption today that will be paid for in future, or the purchase of large durable product like a house or a car, the services of which will be consumed over future periods.

Conclusion

All economic activity is inherently risky. Goods are produced or bought today for sale in the future. Contracts commit producers, customers, and borrowers to exchanging goods and services in the future, and lenders to various actions in the future. Because the future can never be known with certainty, these essential economic activities all carry risks.

One of the triumphs of markets in action has been their ability to permit a specialization of tasks where specialists in risk assume (for a fee) the risks that others must take and, in the process, reduce the total amount of risk because of risk-sharing and their own specialized knowledge of risky situations. Insurance grew up when overseas trade became important in the post-medieval world. It allowed merchants who were specialists in markets to pass the risks of the voyage on to insurers who were specialists in marine risks. The joint stock company grew up in the post-industrial period as a way of allowing vast amounts of capital to be accumulated with acceptable risks to the individual investors.

Today's specialists in risks are many and varied. They often act as financial intermediaries, standing between savers and borrowers. They facilitate complex transactions which, among other things, allow many economic agents to specialize in what they can best do while allowing others to assume the risks that are inherent in these activities.

Summary

1 Many economic decisions taken by firms and consumers involve risky choices which can often be characterized by the expected value of the outcome and the degree of risk as measured by the dispersion of the possible outcomes.

2 Because those providing the insurance, or gambling games, must make profits, those gambling or taking out insurance do not take mathematically fair gambles. Diminishing marginal utility explains why risk-neutral people would buy such insurance policies but predicts that such people would not gamble. Gambling where there is a small chance of a very large gain may be explained by the value placed on the hope (however small) of transforming one's life. Gambling where small gains and losses are involved may be explained by risk-loving, while taking out insurance may be explained by increasing marginal utility of units of forgone income.

3 From the firm's point of view, providing gambling games where the odds can be set endogenously is a no-lose situation. Providing insurance is risky, but the risk is minimized by the pooling of independent risks.

4 Two problems with insurance are moral hazard, when the existence of insurance alters people's behaviour in a socially costly way, and adverse selection, which arises under conditions of asymmetric information.

5 Portfolio diversification is a method of reducing an investor's risk by holding a broad spectrum of financial assets. This is partly the pooling of the return on assets whose risks are independent of each other and partly the pooling of assets whose risks are correlated with each other but of different magnitude. Optimum portfolio diversification allows investors to choose a bundle of assets that minimizes the risk on any given expected rate of return.

6 Mutual funds allow even small investors to hold highly diversified portfolios.

7 Financial intermediaries are institutions that stand between savers and borrowers. Their specialized knowledge and large volume of transactions reduces the transaction costs of matching savers and lenders and reduces risk.

Topics for review

- Expected value and risk
- Fair and unfair games
- Attitudes to risk
- Risk-sharing and risk-pooling
- The demand for insurance
- Portfolio diversification
- The Beta coefficient
- Mutual funds—unit trusts, and investment trusts
- Financial intermediaries

✌ PART FOUR

The intermediate theory of supply

CHAPTER 10

The firm, production, and cost

IN Chapter 4 we assumed the existence of a supply curve relating the price of a product to the quantity firms would be willing to produce and offer for sale. We now go behind the supply curve to explain how its shape results from the decision of individual firms. Thus, Chapters 10–12 do for the supply curve what Chapters 7 and 8 did for the demand curve. These chapters are also a first step towards dealing with a host of interesting policy questions, such as: What is the effect of various forms of competition or monopoly on the production of an industry? Why do firms combine? What are the causes and consequences of takeover bids? Will taxing the domestic consumption of a product encourage its export?

In this, the first chapter of the Part, we begin by considering the firm as it appears in practice. It is important to know some outlines of the organization and financing of firms in order to know what the subsequent theory is abstracting from. Furthermore, many terms that will be used throughout the rest of the book are introduced. We then go on to compare the treatment of the firm in economic theory with what we have just studied about the firm in practice. Finally, we introduce the concepts of costs revenues and profits and conclude by outlining the key place played by profits in determining the allocation of the nation's resources.

The firm in practice

WE start by taking a brief look at the basic unit of production, the firm. After briefly studying firms as we see them in the real world, we go on to see how firms are treated in economic theory.

Forms of business organization[1]

There are five main ways of organizing the production of goods and services that are sold on markets. With a **single proprietorship**, or sole trader, one owner is personally responsible for everything that is done. The firm may or may not have employees, but it has just one owner-manager. In an ordinary **partnership** there are two or more joint owners, each of whom is personally responsible for all of the partnership debts. The **limited partnership**, which is less common than ordinary partnerships,[2] provides for two types of partner. *General partners* take part in the running of the business and have unlimited liability. *Limited partners* take no part in the running of the business, and their liability is limited to the amount they actually invest in the enterprise. A **joint-stock company** (called a *corporation* in the United States) is a firm regarded in law as having an identity of its own; its owners are not personally responsible for anything that is done in the name of the firm, though its directors may be. In the United Kingdom joint-stock companies are indicated either by the initials PLC after the firm's name, standing for *public limited company*, or Ltd (limited) which indicates a *private* limited liability company. Private in this context means that its shares are not traded on the London Stock Exchange or in any other market, while 'public' means that their shares are traded on some public exchange. A **public corporation** is set up to run

a nationalized industry. It is owned by the state but is usually under the direction of a more or less independent, state-appointed board. Although its ownership differs, the organization and legal status of such a public corporation is similar to that of a joint-stock company.

A sixth method of organizing production differs from all the others in that the output is not sold. Instead, it is provided to consumers free (or at a nominal price), while costs of production are paid from tax revenue (in the case of government production) or charitable donations (in the case of private production). Important examples found in all countries are government agencies providing defence, roads, and education, as well as private charities. In the United Kingdom we must also add the National Health Service to this list. (In countries without nationalized medical services, hospitals and doctors behave just as other firms do: they purchase factors of production on the open market and gain revenue by selling their services to people who wish to, and can afford to, purchase them.)

The first five types of organizations comprise what in Chapter 4 we called the market sector of the economy. The sixth type comprises the non-market sector.

Joint-stock companies that have locations in more than one country are often called **multinational enterprises (MNEs)**, although the United Nations officially designates them as **transnational corporations (TNCs)**. Their num-

---

[1] For a detailed discussion of the types of business organization, their finance, and other related issues, see C. Harbury and R. G. Lipsey, *An Introduction to the UK Economy*, 4th edn. (Oxford: Basil Blackwell, 1993).

[2] Limited partnerships are mainly used for high-tech start ups, where the inventor has unlimited liability and the backer limited liability. However, it is in the interest of the general partner (inventor) to convert to 'Ltd' fairly quickly.

BOX 10.1

*Transnational corporations**

Over the past half century, the concept of a *national* economy has become less precise as a growing portion of production has been undertaken by firms with production facilities in more than one country. Such firms used to be called *multinational corporations*, but they are now officially designated by the United Nations as *transnational corporations* (TNCs). TNCs encourage global competition as well as the transfer of technological know-how among countries.

The number of TNCs has been increasing steadily over the years. In 1969 there were about 7,000 TNCs headquartered in the 14 major developed countries; in 1990 there were about 24,000. Firms in these developed countries dominate the TNC scene, although in the last decade there has been a rise in TNCs located in Eastern Europe and the developing countries, particularly the NICs. Although large firms still dominate the TNC scene, the role of medium-sized and small TNCs is significant and growing.

The 1980s saw many changes in the behaviour of TNCs. The United States changed from being the leading provider of foreign investment through its TNCs to being the world's leading recipient of investment from foreign TNCs. Japan has become a leading foreign investor through TNCs. The Japanese transnationals have demonstrated a superior ability to innovate in high-tech activities such as the application of microelectronics-based technologies to manufacturing systems and to the handling of information in the service sector. Finally, the less developed countries (LDCs) have suffered large reductions in the amount of foreign capital that they import through foreign TNCs. (As a result, most of the LDCs have ended their anti-foreign-capital rhetoric and instead have adopted policies designed to attract such investment.)

The world is still in the phase of what the United Nations calls the 'continuing transnationalization of world economic activity'. TNCs in the United States now seem to have reached a plateau of size after strong expansion in earlier decades. However, rapid expansion of TNCs from Japan, Western Europe, Australia, Canada, and Korea suggests that, although the location of expanding TNCs may have changed, the overall expansion continues.

At the beginning of the 1990s there were about 37,000 TNCs in the world and they controlled about 170,000 foreign affiliates. Ninety per cent of these TNCs are headquartered in developed countries. The five major home countries of France, Germany, Japan, the United Kingdom and the United States are home for over half of the developed country total. About 60 per cent of all parent TNCs are in manufacturing, 37 per cent are in services, and 3 per cent are in primary production such as forestry and mining. Ranked by size of foreign assets (and excluding banking and finance), the largest 100 TNCs had about US$3,200 billion in global assets of which an estimated US$1,200 billion was outside of the parent firm's home country. About three-quarters of these very large firms are headquartered in the five major investor countries of France, Germany, Japan, the United Kingdom and the United States.

The TNCs' primary instrument for developing foreign operations has been foreign direct investment (FDI)—acquiring the controlling interest in foreign production facilities either by purchasing existing facilities or by building new ones. During the 1980s, however, FDI fell dramatically, and other instruments have become more common. The most important of these are joint ventures with domestic firms located in countries where the TNCs wish to develop an interest, and licensing arrangements whereby a domestic firm produces a TNC's product locally.

There are many reasons for a company to transfer some of its production beyond its home base (thus becoming a TNC) rather than producing everything at home and then exporting the output. First, local conditions matter. As products become more sophisticated and differentiated, locating production in large local markets allows more flexible responses to local needs than can be achieved through centralized production 'back home'. Second, non-tariff barriers to trade make location in large foreign markets, such as the United States and the European Community, less risky than sending exports from the home base. Third, many of the TNCs are now in rapidly developing service industries such as advertising, marketing, public management, accounting, law, and financial services, where the option of producing everything at home and then exporting the output does not exist: to produce a service in some country, a physical presence is needed in that country. Fourth, the computer and communications revolutions have allowed production to be 'disintegrated' on a global basis. Components of any one product are often manufactured in many countries, each component being made where its production is cheapest. This globalization of production has been a boon to many less developed countries, which have gained increasing employment at wages that are low by world standards but high by their own. In contrast, however, some TNCs that transferred assembly operation abroad in the 1970s have recently been repatriating them to the home country, particularly in North America. This follows from a trial and error procedure where some movements offshore proved not to lower costs in spite of the lower wages that were attained. Costs, after all, depend on wages paid to workers, worker productivity, *and* all the other costs of doing business in various locations.

As a result of 'transnationalization', TNCs account for a large proportion of the foreign trade of many developed countries. This has long been so for the United States and is now becoming true for several other countries, particularly Japan. Although all types of TNCs have grown, much of the growth in recent years has been concentrated in small and medium-size TNCs, including some based in less developed countries. As the United Nations puts it, 'This dynamic aspect of the growth of TNCs is one of the major channels by which economic change is spread throughout the world.'

---

* The material in this box draws on *Transnational Corporations in World Development: Trends and Prospects* (New York: United Nations, 1988).

bers and importance have increased greatly over the last few decades. They are discussed in more detail in Box 10.1.

The financing of firms

The money a firm raises for carrying on its business is sometimes called its **financial capital** (or its *money capital*), as distinct from its **real capital** (or *physical capital*), which are the firms physical assets such as factories, machinery, offices, office equipment, and stocks of material and finished goods.

The use of the term 'capital' to refer to both an amount of money and a quantity of goods can be confusing, but which is being referred to is usually made clear by the context. The two uses are not independent, for much of the financial capital raised by a firm will be used to purchase the capital goods that the firm requires for production.

There are two basic types of financial capital used by firms: equity, funds provided by the owners, and debt, funds borrowed from outside the firm.

OWNERS' CAPITAL

The first main source of funds is the firm's owners. In individual proprietorships and partnerships, one or more owners will put up much of the required funds. A joint-stock company acquires funds from its owners by selling **stocks, shares,** or **equities** (as they are variously called) to them. These are basically ownership certificates. The money goes to the company and the purchasers become owners of the firm, risking the loss of their money, and gaining the right to share in the firm's profits. Profits that are paid out to shareholders are called **dividends.**

One easy way for an established firm to raise money is to retain current profits rather than paying them out to shareholders. Financing investment from *undistributed profits* has become an important source of funds in modern times. Reinvested profit adds to the value of the firm, and hence raises the market value of existing shares; it is capital provided by owners.

DEBT

The firm's creditors are not owners; they have loaned money in return for some form of loan agreement, or IOU.

There is a bewildering array of such agreements, which are collectively called **debt instruments.** Each has its own set of characteristics and its own name. The two characteristics that are common to all instruments issued by firms are, first, an obligation to repay the amount borrowed, called the **principal** of the loan, and, second, an obligation to make some form of payment to the lender called **interest.** The time at which the principal is to be repaid is called the **redemption date** of the debt. The amount of time between the issue of the debt and its redemption date is called its **term.**

Most debt instruments can be grouped into three broad classes. First, some debt is in the form of *loans* from financial institutions. These are private agreements between the firm and the institution usually calling for the periodic payment of interest and repayment of the principal, either at a stipulated future date or 'on demand', meaning whenever the lending institution requests repayment.

Second, *bills* and *notes* are commonly used for short-term loans of up to a year. They carry no fixed interest payments, only a principal value and a redemption date. Interest arises because the borrowing firm sells the new bills that it issues at a price below their redemption value. If, for example, a bill promising to pay £1,000 in one year's time is sold to a lender for £950, this gives the lender an interest payment of £50 in one year's time when the bill that he bought for £950 is redeemed for £1,000. This makes an interest rate of 5.26 per cent per year ($(50/950)100$). Bills are *negotiable,* which means they can be bought and sold. So if I buy a 90-day bill from some firm and want my money back 30 days later, I can sell the bill on the open market to someone else who is prepared to assume the loan to the firm for the 60 days that it still has to run.

The third type of instrument carries a fixed redemption date, as does a bill, and the obligation to make periodic interest payments, as do most loans. These are commonly used for long-term loans—up to 20 or 30 years. A firm that issues a 7 per cent 30-year instrument of this sort with redemption value of £1,000 is borrowing money now and promising to pay £70 a year for 30 years and then to pay £1,000. These instruments have many different details and correspondingly many different names, such as *bonds, stocks,* and *debentures.* They are all negotiable. This is important, because few people would be willing to lend money for such long periods of time if there were no way to get their money back before redemption date.

Firms' debt falls into three main classes: loans, which are non-negotiable agreements to pay interest and repay the principal either at a stated time or on demand; bills, which are negotiable promises to pay a stated sum, usually within a year's time; and bonds, which are negotiable promises to pay interest periodically and repay the principal sum at some redemption date, usually many years later than the date of issue.

In economic theory, the term **bond** is used to refer to any piece of paper that provides evidence of a debt carrying a legal obligation to repay the principal at some stated future time and an actual (as with bonds) or implicit (as with bills) payment of interest (though in reality bonds are long-term debt instruments). Hereafter we refer to all debt instruments as 'bonds', except where we need to distinguish among the various types.

The firm in economic theory

IN Chapter 4 we defined the firm as the unit that takes decisions with respect to the production and sale of goods and services. This concept of the firm covers a variety of business organizations, from the single proprietorship to the joint-stock company, and a variety of business sizes, from the single inventor operating in his garage and financed by whatever he can extract from a reluctant bank manager, to vast undertakings with many thousands of shareholders and creditors.

Why are there firms?

In previous chapters (and in many that follow) we have studied the role of markets in allocating resources. As we have seen, markets work through the forces of supply and demand; people with a particular good or service to sell, and people who wish to purchase that good or service, satisfy their mutual desires by exchanging with each other.

However, not all mutually advantageous trade occurs through markets; often it occurs within institutions, and, in particular, within firms. As we will see in this chapter, there are many kinds and sizes of firms. Economists, like most other people, are inclined to take the existence of firms for granted. But in a famous article published in 1937, the British-born economist Ronald Coase, recipient of the 1991 Nobel Prize in Economic Science, took up the question of why firms should exist at all.[3]

The key to Coase's analysis is the recognition that there are costs associated with transactions. When a firm purchases some good or service, it must identify the market and then find what different quantities and qualities are available at what prices. This takes time and money, and it usually involves some uncertainty. When the firm decides instead to produce the good or service itself, it uses the *command principle*: it orders the product to be made to its desired specifications. The transaction costs may be lower, but the advantage of buying in a competitive market are lost. Furthermore, as the firm gets larger, the inefficiencies of the command system tend to become large compared with the efficiencies involved in decentralizing through the market system.

The firm must choose when to transact internally and when to transact through the market. For example, a car manufacturer must decide whether to purchase a certain component by contracting with a parts manufacturer to supply it, or to 'supply the component to itself' by producing it. Coase viewed the firm as an institution that economizes on transaction costs. He argued that the market works best when transaction costs are low, and that when transaction costs are high there is an incentive for the firm to use internal mechanisms in place of market transactions.

Coase's insights have stimulated much further research by economists such as Professor Oliver Williamson of the University of California at Berkeley. This research has contributed to the understanding of the interaction of institutions and markets. Organization theorists have stressed that firms sometimes require less information than markets do for certain types of transaction; for example, transactions within firms do not require that decision-makers be fully informed on market prices. Some research even shows that transactions within firms sometimes *generate* information that is useful to the firm. For example, close relationships between the producer of a particular component and the user often lead to improvements in its design. Another consideration is that when firms internalize a production process they use one type of contract (say, with their employees) to replace a set of often more complicated contracts with external suppliers.

Coase's analysis has proven remarkably robust over the years, and its influence has spread throughout economics. As economic historian and 1993 Nobel Prize winner Douglass North recently put it, 'Whenever transactions costs are high, institutions become important.'

Profit maximization

We know that the decisions taken by large firms are actually taken by many different individuals. None the less, the firm can be regarded as a single, consistent, decision-taking unit because of the assumption that all its decisions are taken in order to maximize its profits. This assumption is critical to what is called the *neoclassical theory of the firm*, and we may state it formally as follows:

The desire to maximize profits is assumed to motivate all decisions taken within a firm, and such decisions are uninfluenced by who takes them. Thus, the theory abstracts from the peculiarities of the persons taking the decisions and from the organizational structure in which they work.

The assumption of profit maximization allows economists to predict firm behaviour. Economists do this by studying the effect that each of the choices available to the firm would have on its profits. They then predict that the

[3] 'The Nature of the Firm', *Economica* 4 (1937), pp. 386–405.

BOX 10.2

Worries about the assumption of profit maximization

Two criticisms are commonly made of the traditional theory of the firm: first, profit maximization is too crude an assumption about motivation, and, second, the firm's organizational structure must affect its decisions.

The motivation of the firm

Many critics have argued that it is unrealistic to build an elaborate theory on such a crude assumption as profit maximization. It is well known that some businessmen are not inspired by the desire to make as much money as possible. Some pursue political influence, while others may be influenced by philanthropic urges. Should we not, therefore, say that the assumption that firms seek to maximize profits is refuted by empirical evidence?

The real world is complex. A theory selects certain factors which are assumed to be the most important ones, while those that are ignored are assumed to be relatively unimportant. If it is true that the key factors have been included, then the theory's predictions will be supported by the facts. It follows that it is not an important criticism to point out that a theory ignores some factors known to be present in the world; this tells us nothing more than that we are dealing with a theory rather than a photographic reproduction of reality. If the theory has ignored some really important factors, its predictions will be contradicted by the evidence.

How do these considerations relate to theories based on the assumption of profit maximization? First, such a theory does not require that profit is the only factor that ever influences firms. What it requires is that profits are an important consideration, important enough that assuming profit maximization to be the firm's sole motive will produce predictions that are substantially correct. Thus, pointing out that businessmen are sometimes motivated by considerations other than profits does not constitute a relevant criticism. It may well be that the theory is substantially wrong, but if so, the way to demonstrate this is to show that its predictions are in conflict with the facts. We cannot, of course, even consider such a possibility until we know what the theory does and does not predict. Accordingly, we shall press on

to develop the theory. When we have completed this task, we shall study relevant criticisms.

Organizational structure

In the neoclassical theory of the firm, it does not matter whether a decision is taken by a small independent proprietor, a plant manager, or the board of directors. As far as the theory is concerned, the decision-taker *is* the firm. This is an assumption of heroic proportions. It amounts to saying that we can treat the farm, the corner greengrocer, the large department store, and the giant chemical company all under the umbrella of a single theory of the behaviour of the firm. Even if this is only partially correct, it represents an enormously valuable simplification. It also illustrates the power of theory in revealing unity of behaviour where to the casual observer there is only a bewildering diversity.

Do not be surprised, therefore, if the theory seems rather abstract and out of touch with reality at first encounter. Because it does generalize over such a wide variety of behaviour, it must ignore those features with which we are most familiar, and which, in our eyes, distinguish the grocer from Royal Dutch Shell. Any theory that generalizes over a wide variety of apparently diverse behaviour necessarily has this characteristic, because it ignores those factors that are most obvious to us and which create in our minds the appearance of diversity.

The final test of whether or not organizational factors can be legitimately ignored is an empirical one: if the theory that we develop by ignoring these factors is successful in predicting the outcome of the kind of events in which we are interested, then we can conclude that we were correct in assuming that these factors could be safely ignored.

Criticisms of the neoclassical theory for ignoring the importance of the firm's institutional structure are discussed in Chapter 17, at which point competing hypotheses about business behaviour are also discussed.

firm will select the alternative that will produce the largest profits. Box 10.2 deals with some common worries about the assumptions of profit maximization. Chapter 17 con-

siders some limitations of all theory that is based on this simple but powerful assumption.

Production, costs, and profits

A FIRM'S profits are the difference between the revenues it received from selling its output and its costs of producing that output. This simple-sounding concept turns out to be a tricky one because, as we shall see later in this chapter, costs of production involve some rather subtle notions.

Firms seek profits by producing and selling products. The materials and factor services used in the production process are called **inputs**, and the products that emerge are called **outputs**. One way of looking at the process is to regard the inputs as being combined to produce the output. One might also regard the inputs as being used up, or sacrificed, to gain the output.

Types of input

Hundreds of inputs enter into the output of a specific good or service. Among the many inputs entering into car production are sheet steel, rubber, spark plugs, electricity, the site of the factory, the carpark for its employees, machinists, cost accountants, spray-painting machines, forklift trucks, managers, and painters. These inputs can be grouped into four broad classes: (1) those that are inputs to the car firm but outputs to some other firm, such as spark plugs, electricity, and sheet steel; (2) those that are provided directly by nature, such as land; (3) those that are provided directly by people, such as the services of workers and managers; and (4) those that are provided by the factories and machines used for manufacturing cars.

The first class of inputs is made up of goods produced by other firms. They are called *intermediate products*. For example, one firm may mine iron ore and then sell this ore to be used as an input by a second firm which produces steel. Iron ore is thus an intermediate product which is an output of the first firm and an input of the second. Intermediate products thus appear as inputs only because the stages of production are divided among different firms. At any one stage of production, a firm is using as inputs goods produced by other firms at an earlier stage. If these intermediate products are traced back to their sources, all production can be accounted for by the services of the three kinds of input which we first discussed in Chapter 1, and which are called *factors of production*. These are the gifts of nature, such as soil and raw materials, called *land*; physical and mental efforts provided by people, called *labour*; and factories, machines, and other man-made aids to production, called *capital*.

Evaluating costs

We have said that profit is the difference between revenue and cost. Any rate of output will have a set of inputs associated with it. To arrive at the cost of producing this output, a value must be put on each of the separate inputs used. The assignment of monetary values to physical quantities of inputs is easy in some cases and difficult in others. All economic costing is, however, governed by a common principle, which is sometimes called user cost but is more commonly called *opportunity cost*:

The cost of using something in a particular use is the benefit forgone by (or opportunity cost of) not using it in its best alternative use.

If the firm is a profit-maximizer, it must—either explicitly or implicitly—evaluate its costs according to the opportunity cost principle.

In principle, measuring opportunity cost is easy. The firm must assign to each factor of production it uses a monetary value equal to what it sacrifices in order to have the use of that factor.

PURCHASED AND HIRED INPUTS

Assigning costs is straightforward when the firm buys a factor on a competitive market and uses up the entire quantity purchased during the period of production. Materials purchased by the firm fall into this category. If the firm pays £10,000 for electricity used by its factory, it has sacrificed its claims to whatever else that £10,000 can buy, and thus the purchase price is a reasonable measure of the opportunity cost of using that electricity.

The situation is the same for hired factors of production. Most labour services are hired, but typically the cost is more than the wages paid because employers have to contribute to such things as national insurance and pension funds. The cost of these must be added to the direct wage in determining the opportunity cost of labour.

IMPUTED COSTS

A cost must also be assigned to factors of production that the firm neither purchases nor hires because it already owns them. The costs of using such factors are called **imputed costs**. They are reckoned at values reflecting what the firm could earn if it shifted these factors to their next best use. Important imputed costs arise from the use of owners' money, the use of the firm's own capital equipment, the need to compensate risk-taking, and the need to value any special advantages (such as franchises or patents) that the firm may possess. Correct cost imputation is needed if the firm is to discover the most profitable lines of production.

The firm's own funds   What is the opportunity cost to a firm of the financial capital it has tied up in its operations of, say, £100,000? The answer can best be broken into two parts. First, ask what the firm could earn by lending its £100,000 on a riskless loan to someone else, e.g. by purchasing a government bond which has no significant risk of not being repaid. Say this is 8 per cent per annum. This amount is called the **pure return on capital**. It is clearly a cost to the firm, since the firm could close down operations, lend out its money, and earn an 8 per cent return. Next, ask what the firm could earn in addition to this amount by lending its money to another firm where the risk of default was equal to the risk of loss in the firm itself. Say this is an additional 6 per cent. This is called the **risk premium** and it is clearly also a cost. If the firm does not expect to earn this much in its own operations, it will pay it to close down and lend its money out to some other equal-risk use earning 14 per cent (8 per cent pure return plus 6 per cent risk premium).[4]

Special advantages   Suppose a firm owns a valuable patent or a highly desirable location, or produces a product with a popular brand name such as Guinness, Tizer, Triumph, or Player's. Each of these involves an opportunity cost to the firm in production (even if it was acquired free), because if the firm did not choose to use the special advantage itself, *it could sell or lease it to others*. The firm must, therefore, charge itself for using the special advantage if it chooses to do so.

The use of the firm's own capital equipment   The cost of using the capital equipment the firm owns, such as buildings, machinery, and office equipment, consists of the loss in the value of the asset, called **depreciation**, caused by its use in production. Accountants use various conventional methods of calculating depreciation based on the price originally paid for the asset. While such historical costs are often useful approximations, they may, in some cases, seriously differ from the depreciation required by the opportunity-cost principle. Two examples of possible errors are given in the paragraphs that follow.

Example 1. The owner of a firm buys a £12,000 car that she intends to use for six years for business purposes and then discard. She may think this will cost her £2,000 per

year. But if after one year the value of her car on the used-car market is £9,000, it has cost her £3,000 to use the car during the first year. Why should she charge herself £3,000 depreciation during the first year? After all, she does not intend to sell the car for six years. The answer is that one of her alternatives is to buy a one-year-old car and operate it for five years. Indeed, that is the very position she is in after the first year. Whether she likes it or not, she has paid £3,000 for the use of the car during the first year of its life. If the market had valued her car at £11,000 after one year (instead of £9,000), the correct depreciation charge would have been only £1,000.

Example 2. A firm has just purchased a set of machines for £100,000. The machines have an expected lifetime of ten years and the firm's accountant calculates the 'depreciation cost' of these machines at £10,000 per year. The machines can be used to make only one product, and, since they are installed in the firm's factory, they can be leased to no one else. They have a negligible second-hand or scrap value. Assume that, if the machines are used to produce the firm's product, the cost of all other factors utilized will amount to £25,000 per year. Immediately after purchasing the machines, the firm finds that the price of the product in question has unexpectedly fallen, so that the output can now be sold for only £29,000 per year instead of the £35,000 that had originally been expected. What should the firm do?

If in calculating its costs the firm adds in the historically determined 'depreciation costs' of £10,000 a year, the total cost of operation comes to £35,000; with the revenue at £29,000 this makes a loss of £6,000 per year. It appears that the product should not be made. But this is not correct. Since the machines have no alternative use, their opportunity cost to the firm (which is determined by what else the firm could do with them) is zero. The total cost of producing the output is thus only £25,000 per year, and the whole current operation shows a return over cost of £4,000 per year rather than a loss of £6,000. (If the firm did not produce the goods, in order to avoid expected losses, it would earn £4,000 per year less than if it carried on with production.)

Of course, the firm would not have bought the machines had it known that the price of the product was going to fall, but once it has bought them, the cost of using them is zero, and it is profitable to use them as long as they yield any net revenue whatsoever over all other costs.

The principle illustrated by both of these examples may be stated in terms of an important maxim:

---

[4] Owner-managed firms must also include an imputed cost for the owner's time.

Bygones are bygones and should have no influence in deciding what is currently the most profitable thing to do.[5]

The definition of profits

We have earlier defined profits as the difference between the revenue the firm gains from selling its output minus the costs of producing that output. Different definitions of profits are in use because of different definitions of costs.

The accounting definition   When firms report their profits, they use the accounting definition of costs which excludes both the opportunity cost of the firm's own financial capital and any risk premium. According to this definition, the firm's 'profits' are the return on its capital.

The calculation of profits according to the accounting definition is done in a profit and loss statement, a simplified version of which is shown in Table 10.1. Notice that this statement divides the firm's costs between those that vary with output, called *variable costs,* and those that do not, called *fixed costs.* To get from the accountant's definition to the economist's definition of profits, the opportunity cost of capital must be deducted, as shown in Table 10.2.

The economist's definition   What the economists call

Table 10.1 Profit and loss account for XYZ Company for the year ending 31 December 1995

Expenditure		Income
Variable costs		
Wages	£200,000	Revenue from sales £1,000,000
Materials	300,000	
Other	100,000	
Total VC	600,000	
Fixed costs		
Rent	50,000	
Managerial salaries	60,000	
Interest on loans	90,000	
Depreciation allowance	50,000	
Total FC	250,000	
Total cost	850,000	
Profit		150,000

The profit and loss account shows profits as defined by the firm. The table gives a simplified version of a real profit and loss statement. The total revenue earned by the firm, minus what it regards as costs, yields profits. Since firms do not count the opportunity cost of capital, this is included in profits as calculated by the firm. (Note that costs are divided into those that vary with output, called variable costs, and those that do not, called fixed costs. This distinction is discussed in detail in Chapter 11.)

Table 10.2 Calculation of pure profits

Profit as reported by the firm	£150,000
Opportunity cost of capital	
Pure return on the firm's capital	– 100,000
Risk premium	– 40,000
Pure or economic profit	10,000

The economist's definition of profit excludes the opportunity cost of capital. To arrive at the economist's definition of profit, the opportunity cost of capital—the pure return on a riskless investment plus any risk premium—must be deducted from the firm's definition of profit. What is left is called profit by economists, but the terms 'pure' or 'economic' are sometimes added to distinguish it from the firm's more inclusive definition of profit.

profit is the excess of revenue over all opportunity costs including those of capital. To discover whether pure profit exists, take the revenue of the firm and deduct the costs of all factors of production other than capital, which gives the accountant's definition of profits. Then deduct the pure return on capital and any risk premium necessary to compensate the owners of capital for the risks associated with its use in this firm and industry. Anything that remains is profit according to the definition used by economists. It belongs to the owners of the firm and, therefore, may be regarded as an additional return on their capital, over and above its opportunity cost. Profit in the sense just defined is variously called **pure profit**, **economic profit,** or, where there is no room for ambiguity, just **profit**.

Alternative terminology in economics   The opportunity cost of capital is defined by economists as part of total cost. Profits are thus defined in economics as what is left after deducting this cost from what the businessman calls profits. An alternative terminology, still used in some elementary textbooks but seldom in advanced theory, calls the opportunity cost of capital *normal profits.* Any excess of

[5] This is an important principle that extends well beyond economics. In many poker games, for example, the cards are dealt a round at a time and betting occurs each time the players have been given an additional card. Players who bet heavily on early rounds because their hands looked promising often stay in through later rounds on indifferent hands because they 'already have such a stake in the pot'. The professional players know that, after each round of cards has been dealt, their bet should be made on the probability that the hand currently held will turn into a winner when all the cards have been dealt. If the probabilities look poor after the fourth card has been dealt (five usually constitutes a complete hand), the player should abandon the hand whether he or she has put 5p or £5 into the pot already. Amateurs who base their current decisions on what they have put into the pot in earlier rounds of betting, will be long-term losers if they play in rational company. In poker, war and economics, bygones *are* bygones, and to take account of them in current decisions is to court disaster!

Table 10.3   Alternative terminology of profits

Accounting definition	Economic definitions	
	Standard usage	Alternative usage
Profits	Opportunity cost of capital =	Normal profits
	Pure profits =	Supernormal profits

Economists count the opportunity cost of capital as a cost; accountants include it as part of profits. The distinctions are clear; it is only the words used to describe them that can be confusing.

revenue over normal profits is then called *supernormal profits*. Since you may encounter this alternative terminology, the equivalents are laid out in Table 10.3.

Clear distinctions, confusing terminology   The distinctions we have been considering are clear enough; the only problem is that the same word, 'profits', is used to describe one thing by firms and another thing by economists. Firms are interested in the returns that they earn on their investment and they call these profits. Economists are interested in the role played in the allocation of resources by the returns that firms made *over and above* the opportunity cost of their capital, and they call this smaller amount profits.

In everything that follows, we use the economist's definition of costs and profits unless we explicitly say otherwise. For us, *costs* include the opportunity costs of capital and *profits* mean pure or economic profits, which are earnings in excess of *all* opportunity costs. The alternative usages are summarized in Table 10.3.[6]

Profits and resource allocation

When resources are valued by the opportunity-cost principle, their costs show how much these resources would earn if used in their best alternative uses. If there is an industry in which all firms' revenues exceed opportunity costs, all the firms in the industry will be earning pure profits. Thus, the owners of factors of production will want to move resources into this industry because the earnings potentially available to them are greater there than in alternative uses of the resources. If in some other industry firms are incurring losses, some or all of this industry's resources are more highly valued in other uses, and owners of the resources will want to move them to those other uses.

Profits and losses play a crucial signalling role in the workings of a free-market system.

Profits in an industry are the signal that resources can profitably be moved into the industry. Losses are the signal that the resources can profitably be moved elsewhere. Only if there are zero economic profits is there no incentive for resources to move into or out of an industry.

A preview

We have seen that firms are assumed to maximize their profits (π), which are the difference between the revenues derived from the sale of their output (R) and the cost of producing that output (C):

$$\pi = R - C.$$

Thus, what happens to profits depends on what happens to revenues and costs.

We already explained the special meaning that economists give to the concept of costs. In Chapter 11 we develop a theory of how costs vary with output. This theory is common to all firms. We then consider how revenues vary with output and find that it is necessary to deal separately with firms in markets that are competitive (Chapter 12) and monopolistic (Chapters 13 and 14). Costs and revenues are then combined to determine the profit-maximizing behaviour for firms in various market situations. This theory can then be used to predict the outcome of changes in such things as demand, costs, taxes, and subsidies, which we do in Chapter 15.

Summary

1 Production is organized either by private-sector firms, which take four main forms—sole traders, with one owner–manager; ordinary partnerships, with several fully liable owners; limited partnerships, with some ordinary partners and some non-active partners who have limited liability; or joint-stock companies, with limited liability for their many owners who are not usually the firms' managers—or by state-owned enterprises called public corporations.

[6] A little symbolism can help a lot in this case. Let R stand for the firm's total revenue; let D stand for the direct costs of production (labour, materials, power, etc.): let r be the opportunity cost of £1 worth of capital and K be the firm's total capital, so that rK is the total opportunity cost of the firm's capital; and let π_e be pure or economic profits. Then we can write the economist's definition of profits as $\pi_e = R - D - rK$, the accountant's definition of profits as $\pi_a = R - D$, and 'normal profits' as rK. In the equation that follows in the text, C corresponds to $D + rK$ in this footnote.

2 Firms comprise the production side of the market sector. The non-market sector consists of organizations that do not seek to cover their costs of production by revenue gained from selling that production.

3 Modern firms finance themselves by obtaining money from their owners by selling them shares or by reinvesting their profits, and by borrowing from both the public and various financial institutions.

4 Neoclassical economic theory treats all types of firms under one umbrella by assuming that all firms make consistent decisions designed to maximize their profits. The theory thus assumes that the organizational structure of firms, and objectives other than profits, do not exert significant influences on situations whose outcomes are predicted by economic theory.

5 Costs in economic theory refer to opportunity costs. These are correctly measured by the price paid for hired factors, but they must be imputed for the costs of using factors owned by the firm. The cost of firms' own capital includes the pure return—what could be earned on a riskless investment—and a risk premium—what could be earned over the pure return elsewhere in the economy on an equally risky investment. Profits are the difference between revenues and costs.

6 Accountants do not deduct the cost of the firm's own capital when calculating what they call profits, which thus include the pure return on capital as well as the risk premium. When these two amounts are also deducted from revenues, the result is the economist's definition of profit, which is sometimes called pure, or economic, profit, to distinguish it from what firms call profits.

7 Pure profits play a key role in resource allocation. Positive pure profits attract resources into an industry; negative pure profits induce resources to move elsewhere.

Topics for review

- Forms of business organization
- Methods of financing modern firms
- Loans, bills, and bonds
- Profit maximization
- The definition of costs
- The measurement of opportunity costs for hired and for owned factors
- Imputed costs
- The principle of 'bygones are bygones'
- Alternative definitions of profits

❧ CHAPTER 11

Cost and output

WE now know how to calculate cost, revenue, and profit. To discover which rate of output is the most profitable, firms need to know the cost and revenue associated with each rate of output. This tells them how profit relates to output. Selecting the profit-maximizing output is then a simple matter. This chapter deals with costs; subsequent chapters consider revenues.

This chapter is divided into three main parts. The first part deals with the short run, when a firm can vary only some of its inputs. The relation between these variable inputs and outputs is governed by a famous relation called the law of diminishing returns. Having discovered how inputs and outputs are related, we need only to put prices on the inputs and see how the firm's costs vary with its output. We then go on to see how costs vary with output in the long run. Here we pay special attention to economies of scale, where increases in the scale of output result in falling costs per unit of output. In the third and final section, we study how firms may seek to alter their production functions by their own research and development, in response to such changes in economic signals as rising costs of particular inputs.

The production function

THE **production function** relates inputs to outputs. It describes the technological relation between what is fed into the productive apparatus by way of materials and the inputs of factor services and what is turned out by way of product. When using this function, remember that production is a flow: it is so many units *per period of time*. If we speak of raising the production from, say, 100 to 101 units, we do not mean producing 100 units this month and one unit next month, but going from a rate of production of 100 units *each month* to a rate of 101 units *each month*.

Using functional notation, the production function is written as

$$q = q(f_1, \ldots, f_m), \qquad (1)$$

where q is the quantity of output of some good or service and $f_1, \ldots, f_m$ are the quantities of m different inputs used in its production, everything being expressed as rates per period of time.[1]

For the rest of this chapter, we shall consider a very simple example relating to the production of some industrial product. We can best focus on essentials by dealing with only two inputs: labour, to which we give the symbol L, and capital, to which we give the symbol K. This means that we are ignoring land and all intermediate inputs (see Chapter 10, p. 185) to deal with the simplified production function:

$$q = q(L, K), \qquad (2)$$

where q is quantity of output per period of time, L is labour employed in production, K is units of capital services used, and q stands for the relation that links q to K and L. For example, q might be measured in tonnes per day while L and K were measured in labour and machine days—i.e. the amount of labour and machines used per day. Confining attention to two inputs simplifies without obscuring the essence of the problem.

Suppose that a firm wishes to increase its rate of output. To do so, it must increase the inputs of one or both factors of production. But the firm cannot vary all of its factors with the same degree of ease. It can vary labour on short notice, but time is needed to install more capital.

To capture the fact that different inputs can be varied with different speeds, we abstract from the more complicated nature of real decisions and think of each firm as making three distinct types of decisions: (1) how best to employ its existing plant and equipment; (2) what new plant, equipment, and production processes to select, within the framework of existing technology; and (3) what to do about encouraging the development of new technology. The first set of decisions is said to be made over the short run; the second, over the long run; the third, over the very long run.

The short run   The **short run** is defined as the period of time over which the inputs of some factors, called **fixed factors**, cannot be varied. The factor that is fixed in the short run is usually an element of capital (such as plant and equipment), but it might be land, or the services of management, or even the supply of skilled, salaried labour. What matters is that at least one significant factor is fixed.

In the short run, production can be changed only by using more or less of those inputs that can be varied. These inputs are called **variable factors**. In our example, the vari-

---

[1] If you have any trouble with this form of expression, you should review the first part of the Appendix to Chapter 3 at this time.

able factor is labour services. Thus, in the short run, q is varied by varying L, with K held fixed (see equation (2)).

The short run is not of the same duration in all industries. In the electric power industry, for example, where it takes three or more years to build new power stations, an unforeseen increase in demand must be served as well as possible with the existing capital equipment for several years. At the other end of the scale, a machine shop can acquire new equipment in a few weeks, and thus the short run is correspondingly short. The length of the short run is influenced by technological considerations such as how quickly equipment can be manufactured and installed. These things may also be influenced to some extent by the price the firm is willing to pay to increase its capacity *quickly*.

The long run The **long run** is defined as the period long enough for the inputs of all factors of production to be varied, but not so long that the basic technology of production changes. Again, the long run is not a specific period of time, but varies among industries.

The special importance of the long run in production the-

ory is that it corresponds to the situation facing the firm when it is *planning* to go into business, or to expand or contract the scale of its operations. The planning decisions of the firm are made from among fixed technical possibilities but with freedom to choose whatever techniques, and hence factor inputs, seem most desirable. Once these planning decisions are carried out—once a plant is built, equipment purchased and installed, and so on—these factors are fixed and the firm makes its operating decisions in the short run.

The very long run Unlike the short and the long run, the **very long run** is concerned with situations in which the *technological possibilities* open to the firm are subject to change, leading to new and improved products and new methods of production. In the very long run, the production function itself changes so that *given* inputs of K and L will be associated with *different* amounts of output. The firm may bring about some changes itself, through its research and development; other changes may come from outside.

We shall now study the firm's production possibilities, and its costs, under each of these 'runs'.

The short run

IN the short run, we are concerned with what happens to output and costs as more, or less, of the variable factor is applied to a given quantity of the fixed factor. To illustrate, we use the simplified production function of (2) above, and assume that capital is fixed and labour is variable.

Short-run variations in output

Our firm starts with a fixed amount of capital (say 10 units) and contemplates applying various amounts of labour to it. Table 11.1 shows three different ways of looking at how output varies with the quantity of the variable factor. As a preliminary step, some terms must be defined.

Total product (TP) means just what it says: the total amount produced during some period of time by all the factors of production that the firm uses. If the inputs of all but one factor are held constant, the total product will change as more or less of the variable factor is used. This variation is illustrated in column (2) of Table 11.1, which gives a total product schedule. Figure 11.1(i) shows such a schedule graphically. (The shape of the curve will be discussed shortly.)

Average product (AP) is merely the total product per unit of the variable factor, which is labour in the present illustration:

$$AP = \frac{TP}{L}.$$

Average product is shown in column (3) of Table 11.1. Notice that as more of the variable factor is used, average product first rises and then falls. The point where average product reaches a maximum is called the *point of diminishing average productivity*. In the table, average product reaches a maximum when 7 units of labour are employed.

Marginal product (MP) is the change in total product resulting from the use of one more (or one less) unit of the variable factor:[2]

---

[2] Strictly speaking, the text defines what is called 'incremental product', that is the rate of change of output associated with a discrete change in an input. Marginal product refers to the rate at which output is tending to vary as input varies at a particular output. Students familiar with elementary calculus will recognize the marginal product as the partial derivative of the total product with respect to the variable factor. In symbols, $MP = \partial q/\partial L$. In the text we refer only to finite changes, ΔL and ΔTP, but the phrase 'a change of one unit' should read 'a very small change'. At this time it would be helpful to read, or reread, the discussion of the marginal concept given on pp. 55–57 in the Appendix to Chapter 3.

Table 11.1 Total, average, and marginal products in the short run

(1) Quantity of labour L	(2) Total product TP	(3) Average product AP	(4) Marginal product MP
1	43	43	
			43
2	160	80	
			117
3	351	117	
			191
4	600	150	
			249
5	875	175	
			275
6	1,152	192	
			277
7	1,372	196	
			220
8	1,536	192	
			164
9	1,656	184	
			120
10	1,750	175	
			94
11	1,815	165	
			65
12	1,860	155	
			45

The relation of output to changes in the quantity of the variable factor can be looked at in three different ways. Capital is assumed to be fixed at 10 units. As the quantity of labour increases, the rate of output (the total product) increases, as shown in column (2). The average product in column (3) is found by dividing the total product figure in column (2) by the amount of labour required to produce that product—as shown by the figure in the corresponding row of column (1).

The marginal product is shown between the rows because it refers to the *change* in output from one level of labour input to another. When graphing the schedule, *MP*s of this kind should be plotted at the midpoint of the interval. Thus, graphically, for example, the marginal product of 249 would be plotted to correspond to the quantity of labour of 3.5. This is because it refers to the increase in output when labour inputs rise from 3 to 4 units.

$$MP = \frac{\Delta TP}{\Delta L},$$

where ΔTP stands for the change in the total product and ΔL stands for the change in labour input that caused TP to change. In everything that follows in the text of this chapter, we assume that output is varied in the short run by combining different amounts of the variable factor with a *given* quantity of the fixed factor.

Computed values of the marginal product appear in column (4) of Table 11.1. *MP* in the example reaches a maximum between $L = 5$ and $L = 6$ and thereafter declines. The level of output where marginal product reaches a maximum is called the *point of diminishing marginal returns*.

Figure 11.1(ii) shows the average and marginal product curves plotted from the data in Table 11.1. Notice, first, that *MP* reaches its maximum at a lower level of L than does *AP*, and, second, that $MP = AP$ when AP is a maximum. These

relations are discussed in more detail below.

Finally, bear in mind that the schedules of Table 11.1, and the curves of Figure 11.1, all assume a specified quantity of the fixed factor. If the quantity of capital had been, say, 14 instead of the 10 units that were assumed, there would be a different set of total, average, and marginal product curves. The reason is that, if any specified amount of labour has more capital to work with, it can produce more output: its total, average, and marginal products will be greater.

THE LAW OF DIMINISHING RETURNS

We now consider the variations in output that result from applying different amounts of a variable factor to a given quantity of a fixed factor. These variations are the subject of a famous hypothesis called the **law of diminishing returns**.

The law of diminishing returns states that, if increasing quantities of a variable factor are applied to a given quantity of a fixed factor, the marginal product, and the average product, of the variable factor will eventually decrease.

As illustrated in Figure 11.2, the law of diminishing returns is consistent with marginal and average product curves that decline over the whole range of output (part (i) of the figure), or that increase for a while and only later diminish (part (ii) of the figure). The latter case arises when it is impossible to use the fixed factor efficiently with only a small quantity of the variable factor (if, say, one man were trying to farm 1,000 acres). In this case, increasing the quantity of the variable factor makes possible more efficient division of labour, so that the addition of another unit of the variable factor would make all units more productive than they were previously. According to the hypothesis of diminishing returns, the scope for such economies must eventually disappear, and sooner or later the marginal and average product of additional workers must decline.

Notice that, when various amounts of labour are applied to a fixed quantity of capital, the proportions in which the two factors are used is being varied. For this reason,

The law of diminishing returns is also called the 'law of variable proportions', because it predicts the consequences of varying the proportions in which factors of production are used.

The common sense of diminishing marginal product is that the fixed factor limits the amount of additional output that can be realized by adding more of the variable factor. Were it not for the law of diminishing returns, there would be no need to fear that rapid population growth will cause food crises in poorer countries. If the marginal product of additional workers that were employed on a fixed quantity of land were constant, then a country's food production could be expanded in proportion to the increase in popula-

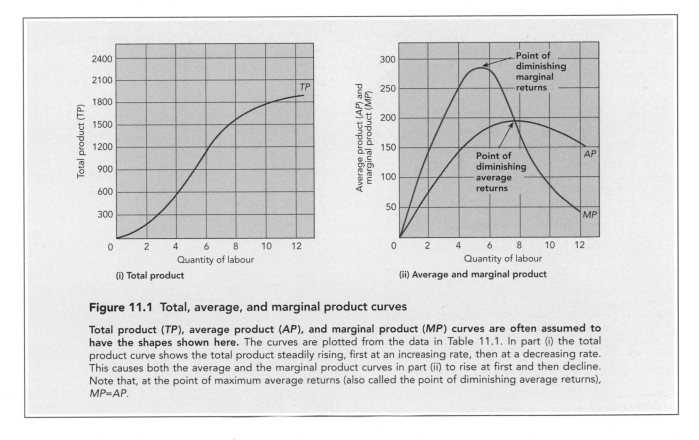

Figure 11.1 Total, average, and marginal product curves

Total product (TP), average product (AP), and marginal product (MP) curves are often assumed to have the shapes shown here. The curves are plotted from the data in Table 11.1. In part (i) the total product curve shows the total product steadily rising, first at an increasing rate, then at a decreasing rate. This causes both the average and the marginal product curves in part (ii) to rise at first and then decline. Note that, at the point of maximum average returns (also called the point of diminishing average returns), MP=AP.

tion merely by keeping the same proportion of the population on farms. As it is, diminishing returns means an inexorable decline in the marginal product of each additional labourer as an expanding population is applied, with static techniques, to a fixed supply of agricultural land. Thus, unless there is a continual and rapidly accelerating improvement in the techniques of production, a population explosion among subsistence farmers in a poor country must bring with it declining living standards.[3]

The relation between marginal and average product curves Notice that in Figure 11.2(ii) the MP curve cuts the AP curve at the latter's maximum point. It is important to understand why. The key is that the average product curve slopes upward as long as the marginal product curve is above it; it makes no difference whether the marginal curve is itself sloping upwards or downwards. The common sense of this relation is that, if an additional worker is to raise the average product of all workers, the worker's output must be greater than the average output of all existing workers. It is immaterial whether his contribution to output is greater or less than the contribution of the worker hired immediately before him; all that matters is that his contribution to output exceeds the average output of *all* the workers hired before him.[4] Since AP slopes upwards or downwards depending on whether MP is above or below AP, it follows

that MP must equal AP at the highest point on the AP curve.[5]

Short-run variations in cost

We have now learned how, according to economic theory, output varies with factor inputs in the short run, and we know from Chapter 10 how to value the firm's inputs. By combining

---

[3] This has not happened throughout the world because rapid technological advances have increased productivity in agriculture faster than population has increased. However, in many poorer countries, farmers subsist mainly on what they themselves grow and use relatively static techniques. For them, rising population in combination with the law of diminishing returns means declining output per person and hence declining living standards.

[4] To check your understanding, try an example in which five workers produce 50 units of output. In the first case a sixth worker adds 16 units and a seventh worker adds 14 to total output. In the second case, the sixth worker adds 14 and the seventh worker adds 16 to total output. When you do the calculations, you will find that AP is rising in both cases, although MP is declining in the first case and rising in the second.

[5] This is easily proved for those who know elementary calculus. Our definitions are: $TP = q(n)$, $AP = q(n)/n$, and $MP = q'(n)$, where the single prime mark indicates the first derivative and n is the quantity of the variable factor employed. A necessary condition for the maximum of the AP curve is that its first derivative, $[nq'(n) - q(n)]/n^2$, be equal to zero. Setting the above expression equal to zero, adding $q(n)/n^2$ to both sides, and multiplying through by n yields: $q'(n) = q(n)/n$, which is to say $MP = AP$.

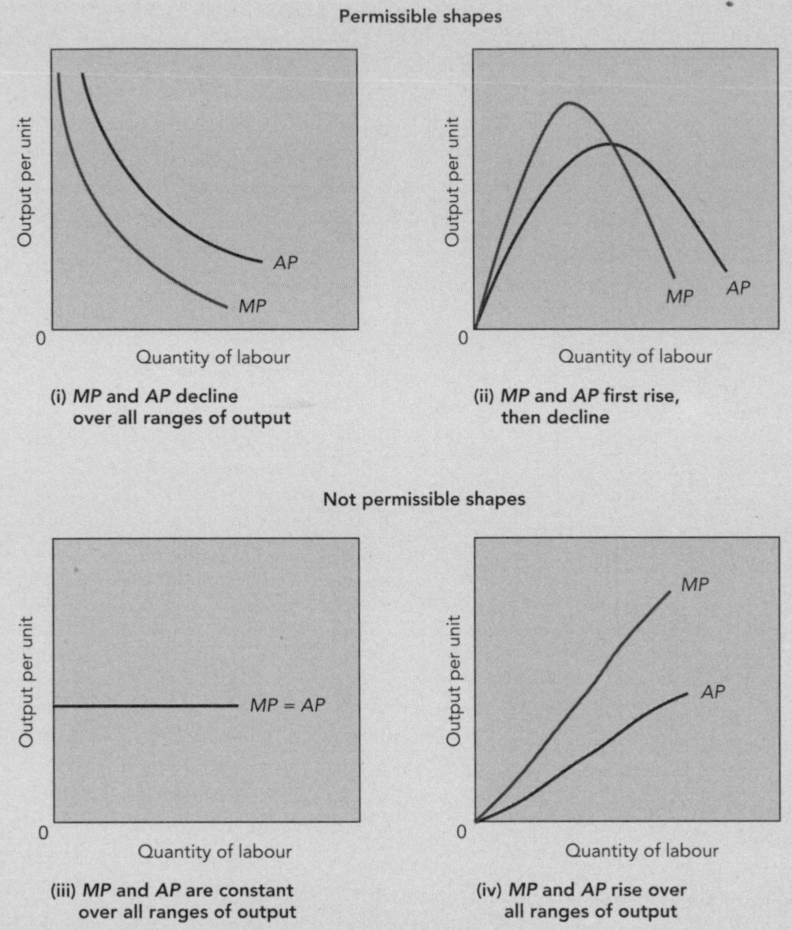

Permissible shapes

(i) *MP* and *AP* decline
over all ranges of output

(ii) *MP* and *AP* first rise,
then decline

Not permissible shapes

(iii) *MP* and *AP* are constant
over all ranges of output

(iv) *MP* and *AP* rise over
all ranges of output

Figure 11.2 Alternative average and marginal product curves

According to the law of diminishing returns, average and marginal product must decline sooner or
later as output increases. The law of diminishing returns permits the average and marginal product curves
to decline at all positive levels of output, as shown in part (i). The law also allows the average and marginal
products to rise over an initial range of output and only then decline, as shown in part (ii). This is the case
where the fixed factor cannot be efficiently used when combined with very small amounts of the variable
factor.

The law does *not* permit average and marginal products that are constant (part (iii)) or that rise over the
entire range of output (part (iv)).

these two pieces of knowledge, we can discover how a firm's
output is related to its cost of production. For the time being,
we consider firms that are not in a position to influence the
prices of the factors of production that they employ.

The following brief definitions of several cost concepts
are closely related to the product concepts defined earlier in
this chapter.

Total cost (TC) means just what it says: the total cost of
producing any given rate of output. Total cost is divided

into two parts, total fixed costs (*TFC*) and total variable
costs (*TVC*). **Fixed costs** are those costs that do not vary
with output; they will be the same if output is 1 unit or 1
million units. These costs are also often referred to as 'overhead costs' or 'unavoidable costs'. All of those costs that
vary positively with output, rising as more is produced and
falling as less is produced, are called **variable costs**. In our
present example, since labour is the variable factor of production, the wage bill would be a variable cost. Variable

costs are often referred to as 'direct costs' or 'avoidable costs'. The latter term is used because the costs can be avoided by not hiring the variable factor.[6]

Average total cost (ATC) is the total cost of producing any given output divided by the number of units produced, or the cost per unit. *ATC* may be divided into **average fixed costs (AFC)** and **average variable costs (AVC)** in just the same way as total costs were divided.

Marginal cost (MC) is the increase in total cost resulting from raising the rate of production by one unit. The marginal cost of the tenth unit, for example, is the change in total cost when the rate of production is increased from nine to ten units per period.

These three measures of cost are merely different ways of looking at a single phenomenon, and they are mathematically interrelated.[7] Sometimes it is convenient to use one, and sometimes another.

SHORT-RUN COST CURVES

The relations just outlined are most easily understood if we show them as cost curves. To illustrate how this is done, we take the production relationships in Table 11.1 and assume that the price of labour is £20 per unit and the price of capital is £10 per unit. In Table 11.2, we present the cost schedules computed for these values. (It is important that you see

[6] This twofold division of costs is sufficient for an introductory treatment. More detailed study of the firm requires the use of further categories of costs. For example, what we have called fixed costs can be divided into those that cannot be avoided as long as the firm stays in existence, such as the costs of the firm's fixed capital, and those that do not vary with output but can be avoided by shutting down a plant's operations, such as the salaries of management and supervisory staff.

[7] Mathematically, average total cost is total cost divided by output while marginal cost is the first derivative of total cost with respect to output.

Table 11.2 Variation of costs with capital fixed and labour variable

(1) Capital	(2) Labour (L)	(3) Output (q)	(4) Fixed (TFC)	(5) Variable (TVC)	(6) Total (TC)	(7) Fixed (AFC)[a]	(8) Variable (AVC)[b]	(9) Total (ATC)[c]	(10) (MC)[d]
10	1	43	£100	£20	£120	£2.326	£0.465	£2.791	£0.465
10	2	160	100	40	140	0.625	0.250	0.875	0.171
10	3	351	100	60	160	0.285	0.171	0.456	0.105
10	4	600	100	80	180	0.167	0.133	0.300	0.080
10	5	875	100	100	200	0.114	0.114	0.228	0.073
10	6	1,152	100	120	220	0.087	0.104	0.191	0.072
10	7	1,372	100	140	240	0.073	0.102	0.175	0.091
10	8	1,536	100	160	260	0.065	0.104	0.169	0.122
10	9	1,656	100	180	280	0.060	0.109	0.169	0.167
10	10	1,750	100	200	300	0.057	0.114	0.171	0.213
10	11	1,815	100	220	320	0.055	0.121	0.176	0.308
10	12	1,860	100	240	340	0.054	0.129	0.183	0.444

[a] Col. (4) ÷ col. (3). [c] Col. (6) ÷ col (3) = col. (7) + col. (8).
[b] Col. (5) ÷ col. (3). [d] Change in col. (6) from one row to the next ÷ corresponding change in col. (3)

The relation of cost to the rate of output can be looked at in several different ways. These cost schedules are computed from the product curves of Table 11.1, given the price of capital of £10 per unit and the price of labour of £20 per unit. Marginal cost (in column (10)) is shown between the lines of total cost because it refers to the *change* in cost divided by the *change* in output that brought it about. Marginal cost is calculated by dividing the increase in costs by the increase in output when one additional unit of labour is used. This gives the increase in cost per unit of output over that range of output. For example, the *MC* of £0.08 is the increase in total cost of £20 (from £160 to £180) divided by the 249-unit increase in output (from 351 to 600). This tells us that, when output goes from 351 to 600 (because labour inputs go from 3 to 4), the increase in costs is £0.08 per unit of output. In constructing a graph, marginal costs should be plotted midway in the interval over which they are computed. The *MC* of £0.08 would thus be plotted at output 475.5.

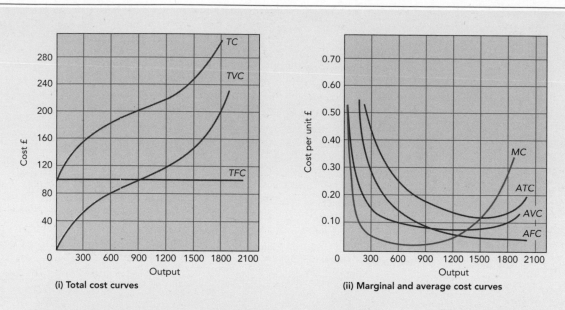

Figure 11.3 Total cost, average cost, and marginal cost curves

Total cost (*TC*), average cost (*AC*), and marginal cost (*MC*) curves often have the shapes shown here.
These curves are plotted from Table 11.2. Total fixed cost does not vary with output. Total variable cost and the total of all costs (*TC=TVC+TFC*) rise with output, first at a decreasing rate, then at an increasing rate. The total cost curves in (i) give rise to the average and marginal curves in (ii). Average fixed cost (*AFC*) declines as output increases. Average variable cost (*AVC*) and average total cost (*ATC*) fall and then rise as output increases. Marginal cost (*MC*) does the same, intersecting the *ATC* and *AVC* curves at their minimum points. Capacity output is at the minimum point of the *ATC* curve, which is an output of 1500 in this example.

where the numbers come from;[8] if you do not, review Table 11.1 and the definitions of cost just given.) Figure 11.3(i) shows the total cost curves; Figure 11.3(ii) plots the marginal and average cost curves.

HOW COST VARIES WITH OUTPUT

Since total fixed costs (*TFC*) do not, by definition, vary with output, average fixed cost (*TFC/q*) is negatively related to output while marginal fixed cost is zero. Variable cost is positively related to output, since to produce more requires more of the variable factor, which in turn entails spending more to buy the factor. Average variable cost may, however, be negatively or positively related to output. If output rises faster than variable costs, average variable costs will be falling as output rises; if output rises less fast than costs rise, average variable cost will be rising. Marginal variable cost is always positive, indicating that it costs something to increase output, but, as we shall soon see, marginal cost may rise or fall as output rises.

Notice that the marginal cost curve cuts the *ATC* and

AVC curves at their lowest points. This is another example of the relation (discussed above) between a marginal and an average curve. The *ATC* curve, for example, slopes downwards as long as the marginal cost curve is below it; it makes no difference whether the marginal cost curve is itself sloping upwards or downwards.

In Figure 11.3 the average variable cost curve reaches a minimum and then rises. With fixed factor prices, when average product per worker is at a maximum, average variable cost is at a minimum. The common sense is that each new worker adds the same amount to cost but a different amount to output, and when output per worker is rising the cost per unit of output must be falling, and vice versa.

---

[8] There is one problem associated with our numerical example that has not so far been discussed. We have derived the data in Tables 11.1 and 11.2 by letting inputs of labour vary one unit at a time. This gives rise to variation in output of more than one per unit of time. Marginal cost is defined as the change in cost when output varies one unit at a time. To calculate marginal cost, we divide the *increase in costs when labour inputs rise by one unit* by the *increase in output*. This gives us the increase in costs *per unit of output* over that range of output. This, and similar, problems do not arise when all marginal concepts are defined as derivatives.

The law of diminishing returns implies eventually increasing marginal and average variable cost.

Short-run *AVC* curves are often drawn U-shaped. This reflects the assumptions that (1) average productivity is increasing when output is low, but that (2) eventually average productivity begins to fall fast enough to cause average total cost to increase.[9]

The definition of capacity   The output that corresponds to the minimum short-run average total cost is very often called **capacity**. Capacity in this sense is not an upper limit on what can be produced, as you can see by looking again at Table 11.2. In the example, capacity output is between 1,536 and 1,656 units, but higher outputs can be achieved. A firm producing *below capacity* is producing at a rate of output less than the one for which average total cost is a minimum. A firm producing *above capacity* is producing more than this amount. It is thus incurring costs per unit of output that are higher than the minimum achievable.

In this section we have implicitly assumed that all of the fixed factor must be used. However, firms often have the opportunity of leaving some of their fixed factor unused when they reduce output. The consequences of this possibility are discussed in Box 11.1.

A family of short-run cost curves   A short-run cost curve shows how costs vary with output for a given quantity of the fixed factor—say, a given size of plant.

There is a different short-run cost curve for each quantity of the fixed factor.

A small plant for manufacturing nuts and bolts will have its own short-run cost curve. A medium-size and a very large-size plant will each have their own short-run cost curves. If a firm expands by replacing its small plant with a medium-size plant, it will move from one short-run cost curve to another. This change from one size of plant to another is a long-run change. We now study how short-run cost curves of different size plants are related to each other.

The long run

IN the short run, with only one factor variable, there is only one way to produce a given output: by adjusting the input of that factor until the desired rate of output is achieved. Thus, once the firm has decided on a rate of output, there is only one technically possible way of achieving it.

By contrast, in the long run, all factors are variable. The firm must decide both on a level of output *and* on how to produce that output. Specifically, this means that firms in the long run must choose the nature and amount of plant and equipment, as well as the size of their labour force.

In making this choice, the firm will wish to avoid being technically inefficient, which means using more of *all* inputs than are necessary. Being technically efficient is not enough, however. To be economically efficient, the firm must choose, from among the many technically efficient options, the one that produces a given level of output at the lowest possible cost. (The distinction between various types of efficiency sometimes causes confusion, particularly when engineers and economists are involved in the same decision-making process.)

Long-run planning decisions are important. A firm that decides to build a new steel mill and to invest in machinery that will go into it will choose among many alternatives.

Once installed, that equipment is fixed for a long time. If the firm makes a wrong choice, its survival may be threatened; if it estimates shrewdly, it may be rewarded with large earnings.

Long-run decisions are risky because the firm must anticipate what methods of production will be efficient, not only today, but also for many years in the future, when the costs of labour and raw materials will no doubt have changed. The decisions are also risky because the firm must estimate how much output it will want to produce. Is the industry to which it belongs growing or declining? Will new products emerge to render its existing products less useful than an extrapolation of past sales suggests?

---

[9] This point is easily seen if a little algebra is used. (The only new symbols used here are w, which stands for the price of a unit of labour and a dot to indicate multiplication.) By definition, $AVC = TVC/q$. But $TVC = L \cdot w$, and $q = AP \cdot L$ (since $AP = q/L$). Therefore

$$AVC = (L \cdot w)/(AP \cdot L)$$
$$= w/AP.$$

In other words, average variable cost equals the price of the variable factor divided by the average product of the variable factor. Since w is constant, it follows that AVC and AP vary inversely with each other, and when AP is at its maximum value AVC must be at its minimum value.

BOX 11.1

Saucer-shaped industry cost curves

Ever since economists began measuring the cost curves of manufacturing firms more than half a century ago, they have reported flat, short-run variable cost curves. The evidence is now clear that in most manufacturing industries, and in some others, cost curves are shaped like the *AVC* curve shown in the figure, with a long, flat portion in the middle and sharply rising sections at each end. For such a 'saucer-shaped' curve, there is a large range of output over which average variable costs are constant. Over this range, marginal costs are equal to average variable costs, and thus they, too, are constant per unit of output.

Why are many cost curves saucer-shaped rather than U-shaped? The answer is that firms design plants to have this property so that they can accommodate the inevitable seasonal and cyclical swings in demand for their products.

To see why a firm can choose the shape of its short-run average cost curve, consider again the law of diminishing returns. The U-shaped, short-run cost curve arises when a variable amount of one factor, say, labour, is applied to a fixed amount of a second factor, say, capital. Imagine starting from zero output and zero use of the variable factor and then increasing output. As more of the variable factor is used, a more nearly optimal combination with the fixed factor is achieved. Once the optimal combination obtains, the use of further units of the variable factor leads to too much of that factor being used in combination with the fixed factor. This causes average variable costs to begin to rise. Only one quantity of labour leads to the least-cost factor proportions.

These changing combinations of fixed and variable factors must occur in the short run whenever all of the fixed factor must be used all of the time; in other words, when the fixed factor is *indivisible*. This, however, is not usually the case. Even though the firm's plant and equipment may be fixed in the short run, so that *no more* than what exists is available, it is often possible to use *less* than this amount.

Consider, as a simple example, a factory that consists of 10 sewing machines in a shed, each of which has a productive capacity of 20 units per day when operated by 1 operator for 1 shift. If 200 units per day are required, then all 10 machines would be operated by 10 workers on a normal shift. If demand falls to 180, then 1 operator could be laid off. There is no need, however, to have the 9 remaining operators dashing about trying to work 10 machines. Clearly, 1 machine could be 'laid off' as well, leaving constant the ratio of *employed* labour to *employed* machines.

Production could go from 20 all the way to 200 units per day without any change in the proportions in which the employed factors are used. In this case, we would expect the factory to have constant marginal and average variable costs from 20 to 200 units per day. Only beyond 200 units per day would it begin to encounter rising costs, because production would have to be extended by overtime and other means of combining more labour with the maximum available supply of 10 machines.

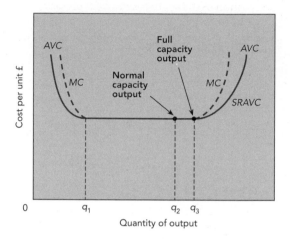

In such a case, the fixed factor is *divisible*. Because some of it can be left unemployed, there is no need to depart from the most efficient ratio of *labour used* to *capital used* as production is decreased. The *divisibility* of the fixed factor means that diminishing returns does not apply, because variations in output below full capacity are accomplished by reducing the input of both labour and capital. Thus, average variable costs can be constant over a large range, up to the point at which all of the fixed factor is used.*

A similar situation occurs when a firm has many plants. For example, a manufacturer with 10 plants may choose to reduce its output by temporarily closing one or more plants (or operating them on a limited-time basis) while operating the rest at normal-capacity output. Another firm can choose to put its factory on short time, working 6 hours a day or 4 days a week, thus reducing its use of both capital and labour. In such cases the *firm's* short-run variable costs tend to be constant over a large range of output because there is no need to depart from the optimal combination of labour and capital in the plants that are kept in operation.

The figure shows the type of cost curve that is observed when the fixed factor is divisible. At outputs between q_1 and q_3, the *AVC* curve is flat because output is varied by using more or less labour *and* capital in constant proportions. Normal-capacity output is q_2 and full-capacity output is q_3. When output reaches q_3, the fixed stock of capital is fully employed, and further increases in output can be achieved only at rising cost as more labour is applied to a fixed quantity of capital.

* Let K stand for the amount of capital used by the firm and K_0 for the fixed amount available in the short run. The constraints governing the use of capital are $K = K_0$ for indivisible capital and $K \leq K_0$ for divisible capital.

Profit maximization and cost minimization

Any firm seeking to maximize its profits in the long run must select the economically efficient method, which is the method that produces its output at the lowest possible cost. This implication of the hypothesis of profit maximization is called **cost minimization**: from the alternatives open to it, the profit-maximizing firm will choose the least costly way of producing whatever specific output it chooses.

CHOICE OF FACTOR MIX

If it is possible to substitute one factor for another to keep output constant while reducing total cost, the firm is not using the least costly combination of factors. In such a situation, the firm should substitute one factor for another factor, as long as the marginal product of the one factor *per pound sterling* expended on it is greater than the marginal product of the other factor *per pound* expended on it. The firm cannot minimize its costs as long as these two magnitudes are unequal. For example, if an extra pound spent on labour produces more output than an extra pound spent on capital, the firm can reduce costs by spending less on capital and more on labour.

If we use K to represent capital, L to represent labour, and p to represent the price of a unit of the factor, the necessary condition for cost minimization is as follows:

$$\frac{MP_K}{p_K} = \frac{MP_L}{p_L}. \qquad (3)$$

Whenever the two sides of equation (3) are not equal, there are possibilities for factor substitutions that will reduce costs.

To see why this equation must be satisfied if costs of production are to be minimized, consider a situation where the equation is not satisfied. Suppose, for example, that the marginal product of capital is 20 and its price is £2, making the left side of equation (3) equal to 10. Suppose that the marginal product of labour is 32 and its price is £8, making the right side of equation (3) equal to 4. Thus, the last pound spent on capital adds 10 units to output, whereas the last pound spent on labour adds only 4 units to output. In such a case, the firm could maintain its output level and reduce costs by using £2.50 less of labour and spending £1.00 more on capital. Making such a substitution of capital for labour would leave output unchanged and reduce costs by £1.50 Thus, the original position was not cost-minimizing.[10]

We can take a different look at cost minimization by multiplying equation (3) by p_K/MP_L:

$$\frac{MP_K}{MP_L} = \frac{P_K}{p_L}. \qquad (4)$$

The ratio of the marginal products on the left-hand side of the equation compares the contribution to output of the last unit of capital and the last unit of labour. If the ratio is 4, this means that 1 unit more of capital will add 4 times as much to output as 1 unit more of labour. The right-hand side of the equation shows how the cost of 1 unit more of capital compares with the cost of 1 unit more of labour. If the ratio is also 4, the firm cannot reduce costs by substituting capital for labour or vice versa. Now suppose that the ratio on the right-hand side of the equation is 2. Capital, which is four times as productive as labour, is now only twice as expensive. It will pay the firm to switch to a method of production that uses more capital and less labour. If, however, the ratio on the right-hand side is 6 (or *any* number more than 4), it will pay to switch to a method of production that uses more labour and less capital.

We have seen that, when the ratio MP_K/MP_L exceeds the ratio p_K/p_L, the firm will substitute capital for labour. This substitution is measured by changes in the **capital–labour ratio**—the amount of capital per worker used by the firm.

How far does the firm go in making this substitution? There is a limit, because the law of diminishing returns tells us that, as the firm uses more capital, the marginal product of capital falls, and as it uses less labour, the marginal product of labour rises. Thus, the ratio MP_K/MP_L falls. When it reaches 2, the firm need substitute no further. The ratio of the marginal products is equal to the ratio of the prices.

Equation (4) shows how the firm can adjust the elements over which it has control (the quantities of factors used, and thus the marginal products of those factors) to the prices of the factors given by the market.

LONG-RUN EQUILIBRIUM OF THE FIRM

The firm will have achieved its equilibrium capital–labour ratio when there is no opportunity for cost-reducing substitutions. This occurs when the marginal product per pound spent on each factor is the same (equation (3)) or, equivalently, when the ratio of the marginal products of factors is equal to the ratio of their prices (equation (4)).

The principle of substitution

Suppose that a firm is meeting the cost-minimizing conditions shown in equations (3) and (4) and that the cost of labour increases while the cost of capital remains unchanged. The least-cost method of producing any out-

---

[10] The argument in this paragraph assumes that the marginal products do not change when expenditure changes by a small amount.

put will now use less labour and more capital than was required to produce the same output before the factor prices changed.

Methods of production will change if the relative prices of factors change. Relatively more of the cheaper factor and relatively less of the more expensive factor will be used.

This is called the **principle of substitution,** and it follows from the assumption that firms minimize their costs.

The principle of substitution plays a central role in resource allocation, because it relates to the way in which individual firms respond to changes in relative factor prices that are caused by the changing relative scarcities of factors in the economy as a whole. When a factor becomes more scarce to the economy as a whole, its price will tend to rise. This motivates individual firms to use less of that factor. When some other factor becomes more plentiful to the economy as a whole, its price will tend to fall. This motivates individual firms to use more of it. Firms need never know the relative scarcities of the various factors. As long as relative factor prices reflect relative scarcities, firms will tend to substitute plentiful factors for scarce factors through their own cost-minimizing responses to the changes in the prices of their inputs.

The Appendix to this chapter gives a formal analysis of the firm's choice of factor proportions and of its factor substitution in response to changes in relative factor prices. The analysis uses the concept of isoquants, which are the firms' equivalent of consumers' indifference curves: an indifference curve shows all those combinations of products that give the consumer the same satisfaction, while an isoquant shows all those combinations of factor inputs that give the firm the same output. Those who wish to study this formal analysis of the subject matter of this section should read the Appendix now. Those who are content with the intuitive discussion in the text can read on in the text.

Box 11.2 discusses the broader significance of the principle of substitution.

BOX 11.2

The economy-wide significance of the principle of substitution

In free markets, relative factor prices reflect the relative scarcities (in relation to demand) of different factors of production: abundant factors have prices that are low relative to the prices of factors that are scarce. Firms seeking their own private profit will be led to use much of the factors with which the whole country is plentifully endowed, and to economize on the factors that are in scarce supply.

In a country with a great deal of land and a small population, for example, the price of land will be low while, because labour is in short supply, the wage rate will be high. In such circumstances firms producing agricultural goods will tend to make lavish use of (cheap) land and to economize on (expensive) labour; a production process will be adopted that is labour-extensive and land-intensive. On the other hand, in a small country with a large population, the demand for land will be high relative to its supply. Thus, land will be very expensive, and firms producing agricultural goods will tend to economize on it by using a great deal of labour per unit of land. In this case production will tend to be labour-intensive and land-extensive.

In recent decades, construction workers' wages have risen sharply relative to the wages of factory labour and the cost of machinery. In response, many home builders have shifted from on-site construction to panelization, a method of building that uses standardized modules. The wiring, plumbing, insulation, and painting of these standardized modules are all done at the factory. The bulk of the factory work is performed by machinery and by assembly-line workers whose wages are only half those of on-site construction workers.

These are examples of the price system as an automatic control system. No single firm need be aware of national factor surpluses and scarcities. Since they are reflected in market prices, individual firms that never look beyond their own private profits are led to economize on factors that are scarce in the nation as a whole. We should not be surprised, therefore, to discover that methods of producing the same product differ in different countries. In Europe, where labour is highly skilled and very expensive, a steel company may use very elaborate equipment to economize on labour. In China, where labour is abundant and capital scarce, a much less mechanized method of production may be appropriate. The Western engineer who feels that the Chinese are behind because they are using methods abandoned in the West as inefficient long ago, may be missing the significance of economic efficiency.

In spite of the price system's ability to induce profit-maximizing firms to take account of the nation's relative factor scarcities when choosing among possible methods of production, one must avoid jumping to the conclusion that whatever productive processes are adopted are the best possible ones and should never be interfered with. There is, however, a strong common-sense appeal in the idea that:

Any society interested in getting the most out of its resources needs to take account of their relative scarcities in deciding what productive processes to adopt, which is what the price system leads individual firms to do.

Cost curves in the long run

When all factors can be varied, there is a least-cost method of producing each possible level of output. Thus, with given factor prices, there is a minimum achievable cost for each level of output; if this cost is expressed as a quantity per unit of output, we obtain the long-run average cost of producing each level of output. When this least-cost method of producing each output is plotted on a graph, the result is called a **long-run average cost (*LRAC*) curve**. Figure 11.4 shows one such curve.

This cost curve is determined by the technology of the industry (which is assumed to be fixed) and by the prices of the factors of production. It is a 'boundary' in the sense that points below it are unattainable; points on the curve, however, are attainable if sufficient time elapses for all inputs to be adjusted. To move from one point on the *LRAC* curve to another requires an adjustment in all inputs, which may, for example, require building a larger, more elaborate factory.

The *LRAC* curve is the boundary between cost levels that are attainable, with known technology and given factor prices, and those that are unattainable.

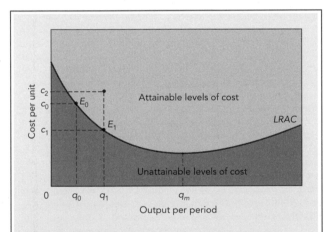

Figure 11.4 A long-run average cost curve

The long-run average cost (*LRAC*) curve provides a boundary between attainable and unattainable levels of cost. If the firm wishes to produce output q_0, the lowest attainable cost level is c_0 per unit. Thus, point E_0 is on the *LRAC* curve. E_1 represents the least-cost method of producing q_1. Suppose a firm is producing at E_0 and desires to increase output to q_1. In the short run it will not be able to vary all factors, and thus costs above c_1, say c_2, must be accepted. In the long run, a plant that is the optimal size for producing output q_1 can be built and costs of c_1 can be attained. At output q_m the firm attains its lowest possible per unit cost of production for the given technology and factor prices.

Just as the short-run cost curves discussed earlier in this chapter are derived from the *production function* describing the physical relationship between factor inputs and output, so is the *LRAC* curve. The difference is that in deriving the *LRAC* curve there are no fixed factors, so all factors are treated as variable. Because all input costs are variable in the long run, we do not need to distinguish between average variable cost (*AVC*), *average fixed cost (AFC)*, and average total cost (*ATC*), as we did in the short run. In the long run, there is only one long-run average cost (*LRAC*) for any given set of input prices.

THE SHAPE OF THE LONG-RUN AVERAGE COST CURVE

The *LRAC* curve shown in Figure 11.4 first falls and then rises. This curve is often described as U-shaped, although 'saucer-shaped' might be a more accurate description of the evidence from many empirical studies.

Decreasing costs   Over the range of output from zero to q_m, the firm has falling long-run average costs: an expansion of output permits a reduction of costs per unit of output. Technologies with this property are referred to as exhibiting **economies of scale**. (Of course, when output is increased, such economies of scale will be realized only after enough time has elapsed to allow changes in all factor inputs.) The prices of factors are assumed to be constant, and thus the decline in long-run average cost occurs because output is increasing *more than* in proportion to inputs as the scale of the firm's production expands. Over this range of output, the decreasing-cost firm is often said to enjoy long-run **increasing returns**. This is an extremely important phenomenon, and its sources are discussed in the section below.

Increasing costs   Over the range of outputs greater than q_m, the firm encounters rising long-run costs. An expansion in production, even after sufficient time has elapsed for all adjustments to be made, will be accompanied by a rise in average costs per unit of output. If costs per unit of input are constant, the firm's output must be increasing *less than* in proportion to the increase in inputs. When this happens, the increasing-cost firm is said to encounter long-run **decreasing returns**.[11] Decreasing returns imply that the firm suffers some diseconomy of scale. As its scale of operations increases, diseconomies are encountered that increase its per-unit cost of production.

---

[11] Long-run decreasing returns differ from short-run diminishing returns. In the short run at least one factor is fixed, and the law of diminishing returns ensures that returns to the variable factor will eventually diminish. In the long run all factors are variable, and it is possible that physically diminishing returns would never be encountered—at least as long as it was genuinely possible to increase inputs of all factors.

These diseconomies may be associated with the difficulties of managing and controlling an enterprise as its size increases. For example, planning problems do not necessarily vary in direct proportion to size. At first, there may be scale economies as the firm grows, but sooner or later, planning and co-ordination problems may multiply more than in proportion to the growth in size. If so, management costs per unit of output will rise. These things are part of the more general phenomenon of rising transactions cost. After some optimum size is reached, the costs of making transactions of all sorts within the boundaries of the firm may increase more than in proportion to the increase in the firm's size. Other sources of scale diseconomies concern the possible alienation of the labour force as size increases and the difficulties of providing appropriate supervision as more and more tiers of supervisors and middle managers come between the person at the top and the workers on the shop floor. Control of middle-range managers may also become more difficult. As the firm becomes larger, managers may begin to pursue their own goals rather than devote all of their efforts to making profits for the firm. (This is the principal–agent problem that is discussed in detail in Chapter 17.)

Constant costs   In Figure 11.4 the firm's long-run average cost falls until output reaches q_m and rises thereafter. Another possibility should be noted. The firm's *LRAC* curve might have a flat portion over a range of output

---

BOX 11.3

Economies of scale in the electricity industry

In the 1940s, 1950s and 1960s, major economies of scale in electricity generation came from the use of larger and larger generators: from 30 MW (= 30,000 kilowatt) generating sets in 1948 to 100 MW sets in 1956, 200 MW sets in 1959, and 500 MW sets in 1966.

Since the 1970s, there has been little increase in the size of generators, with the largest now being installed at 660 MW. Furthermore, total generating capacity has been declining since 1980. The cause is a decline in the demand for energy, because of (1) the decline of British manufacturing and (2) the superior energy efficiency of newer technologies such as chips and fibre optics

In spite of the absence of further economies in the size of generators after 1970, and in spite of the decline in overall capacity after 1980, methods of gaining scale economies were still being found! The new method was to reduce the *number* of power stations, each station having several generators. As a result, the average capacity of each power station has continued to rise significantly, bringing a different type of economy of scale. From 233 power stations with an average capacity of 147 MW in March 1965, the Central Electricity Generating Board (which was responsible for the generation of all the electricity supplied by area electricity boards in England and Wales until the industry was privatized in 1989–90) reduced the number of stations to 174 with an average capacity of 324 MW by March 1974 and to 78 stations with an average capacity of 671 MW by March 1987. It is interesting to note that the 'energy crisis' starting in 1973–4 brought a stop to the rapid growth in demand for electricity in Britain, so the overall generating capacity is now *smaller* than it was 15 years ago. Nevertheless, the adoption of larger generating units and their concentration in larger and larger power stations brought significant scale economies over the period.

The CEGB has also benefited from economies of scale in bulk transmission of electricity. In the mid-1960s, the Board began construction of a 'Supergrid' of 400 KV (= 400,000 volt) transmission lines, based on the knowledge that such a line could replace 3 lines operating at 275 KV or 18 lines operating at 132 KV, without a corresponding increase in costs.

Economies of scale have allowed the industry to cope with rising *real* prices of its main inputs—coal and labour—without raising the real price of electricity. During the 1960s, when the real price of the major alternative fuel—oil—was falling (this fall itself being the result of the increasing exploitation of economies of scale in oil tankers delivering crude oil from the Middle East), the UK electricity industry was actually able to reduce the real price of electricity, which is one of the reasons why electricity was adopted more and more widely in preference to other fuels.

Strictly speaking, scale economies refer to the effects of increasing output *along* a negatively sloped *LRAS* curve as a result of rising output within the confines of known technology, while changes in technological knowledge *shift* the *LRAS* curve. As this example shows, the two forces usually become mixed in most real-world applications. The rise in demand for electricity in the three decades of the 1950s, 1960s, and 1970s required an increase in output. The rise in output made the use of higher-capacity equipment possible and thus provided an incentive for the development of such equipment. No fundamental new knowledge was required, but the details of the technology of larger generators had to be developed through research rather than being taken from already existing blueprints.

Privatization did not change the cost structure of the industry significantly. It did, however, lock the generating companies into coal contracts for three years, after which shifts in energy sources began once again. Shifts were made when possible to cheaper imported coal and, where new capacity was warranted, to the adoption of the cheaper technology called combined cycle gas turbines (CCGT).

Competitive forces continue to put pressure on producers to reduce costs. The main pressures now are on cutting costs through productivity gains rather then exploiting further economies of even larger-scale production.

around q_m. With such a flat portion, the firm would be encountering constant costs over the relevant range of output. This means that the firm's long-run average costs per unit of output do not change as its output changes. Because factor prices are assumed to be fixed, the firm's output must be increasing *exactly in proportion to* the increase in inputs. A firm in this situation is said to be encountering **constant returns**.

SOURCES OF INCREASING RETURNS

Whenever a firm finds that it can increase its output per unit of input, that firm is enjoying economies of large-scale production. These economies are important, and wherever they exist they encourage large plants and/or large firms. We mention three important sources of scale economies: geometrical relations, one-time costs, and the technology of large-scale production.

Geometrical relations   One important source of scale economies lies in the geometry of our three-dimensional world. To illustrate how geometry matters, consider a firm that wishes to store a gas or a liquid. The firm is interested in the *volume* of storage space. However, the amount of material required to build the container is related to the *area* of its surface. When the size of a container is increased, the storage capacity, which is determined by its volume, increases faster than its surface area.[12] This is a genuine case of increasing returns—the output, in terms of storage capacity, increases proportionately more than the increase in the costs of the required construction materials. Here is another of the many other similar effects. The heat loss in a smelter is proportional to its surface area, while the amount of ore smelted depends on its volume. Thus, there is a scale economy in heat needed per tonne of ore smelted as smelters get larger. The size of the smelter is limited, however, by the need to deliver a smooth flow of air to all the molten ore. Thus, when improved forced air pumps were invented in the nineteenth century, smelters could be built larger and unit costs fell.

One-time costs   A second source of increasing returns consists of inputs that do not have to be increased as the output of a product is increased, even in the long run. For example, there are often large fixed costs in developing new products, such as a new generation of airplanes or a more powerful computer. These research and development (R&D) costs have to be incurred only once for each product, and hence are independent of the scale at which the product is subsequently produced. Even if the product's *production costs* increase in proportion to output in the long run, average total costs, including *product development costs*, will fall as the scale of output rises. The influence of such once-and-for-all costs is that, other things being equal, they cause average total costs to be falling over the

entire range of output. (The significance of such once-and-for-all costs is further discussed in Chapter 14.)[13]

The technology of large-scale production   A third and very important source lies in technology. Large-scale production can use more specialized and highly efficient machinery than smaller-scale production. It can also lead to more specialization of human tasks with a resulting increase in human efficiency.

Even the most casual observation of the differences in production techniques used in large and small plants will show that larger plants use greater specialization. An example, drawn from the electricity industry, is discussed in Box 11.3.

These differences arise because large, specialized equipment is useful only when the volume of output that the firm can sell justifies employment of that equipment. For example, assembly-line techniques, body-stamping machinery, and multiple-boring engine-block machines in car production are economically efficient only when individual operations are repeated thousands of times. Use of elaborate harvesting equipment (which combines many individual tasks that would otherwise be done by hand and by tractor) provides the least-cost method of production on a big farm but not on a few acres.

Typically, as the level of planned output increases, capital is substituted for labour and complex machines are substituted for simpler ones. Robotics is a contemporary example. Electronic devices can handle huge numbers of operations quickly, but unless the level of production requires such a large volume of operations, robotics or other forms of automation will not provide the least-cost method of production.

Until very recently, large-scale production meant mass production, sometimes referred to as 'Fordism', a system that was introduced early in the twentieth century. It was based on a very detailed division of jobs, often on a production line, in which each person did one repetitive task in co-operation with such very specialized machinery (called dedicated machinery). In this technology size was very important. Very high rates of output were required in order

---

[12] For example, consider a cubic container with metal sides, bottom, and lid, all of which measure 1 foot by 1 foot. To build this container, 6 square feet of metal is required (six sides, each 1 square foot), and it will hold 1 cubic foot of gas or liquid. Now increase all of the lengths of each of the container's sides to 2 feet. Now 24 square feet of metal is required (six sides, each 4 square feet), and the container will hold 8 cubic feet of gas or liquid (2 feet times 2 feet times 2 feet). So increasing the amount of metal in the container's walls fourfold has the effect of increasing its capacity eightfold.

[13] This phenomenon is popularly referred to as 'spreading one's overhead'. It is similar to what happens in the short run when averaged fixed costs fall with output. The difference is that fixed short-run production costs are variable long-run production costs. If the firm increases its scale of output for some product, it will incur more capital costs in the long run as a larger plant is built. However, its costs of developing that product are not affected.

BOX 11.4

*The lean production revolution**

Production techniques are currently being revolutionized by the introduction, in many industries and in many countries, of *lean production techniques,* or, as they are sometimes called, *flexible manufacturing.* This is the most fundamental change to occur since mass production was brought to full development by Henry Ford early in the twentieth century.

To understand the 'lean production revolution' pioneered by the Japanese, we distinguish three methods of production used today.

Craft methods employ highly skilled workers to make non-standardized products that are often tailor-made for individual purchasers. The result is usually an expensive product of high quality, made by artisans who get considerable job satisfaction.

Mass-production methods are based on specialization and division of labour, as first analysed by Adam Smith in the eighteenth century. They entail the use of skilled personnel to design products and production methods, and then the employment of relatively unskilled labour to produce standardized parts and to assemble them using highly specialized, single-purpose machines. The parts are usually manufactured in separate locations, often by distinct companies, and then assembled on a central production facility, often called an *assembly line.* The design of the product is centralized, and manufacturers bid competitively to produce parts to the stated specifications. The result is a standardized product, made in a fairly small number of variants and produced at low cost with moderate quality. The work is repetitive, and workers are regarded as variable costs to be laid off or taken on as the desired rate of production varies.

Lean production methods combine the flexibility and high-quality standards of craft production with the low cost of mass-production techniques. They are lean because they use fewer of all inputs, including time, labour, capital, and inventories, compared with either of the other techniques. They are flexible because the costs of switching from one product line to another are minimized.

In lean production, workers are organized as teams; each worker is encouraged to do all of the tasks assigned to the team, using equipment that is less highly specialized than that used in mass production techniques. This emphasizes individuality and initiative rather than a mind-numbing repetition of one unskilled operation. It also helps workers to identify places where improvements can be made and encourages them to follow up on these. Finally, it reduces the costs of switching equipment from production of one product variant to another.

In mass-production plants, stopping an assembly line to correct a problem at one point stops work at all points. So stopping the line is regarded as a serious matter, and keeping the assembly line running is the sole responsibility of a senior line manager. To reduce stoppages, large stocks of each part are held, and defective parts are discarded. Faults in assembly, which are treated as random events, are left to be corrected after the product has been assembled—often an expensive procedure. Stops

are none the less frequent to correct materials-supply and co-ordination problems. In lean production, every worker has the ability to stop production whenever a fault is discovered. Parts are delivered by the suppliers to the work stations 'just in time'. Defective parts are put aside for their source to be identified, and any defects are treated as events with patterns of causes that need to be understood. When lean methods are first introduced, stoppages are frequent as problems are identified and investigated. As the sources are found and removed, work stoppages diminish, and the typical mature lean production line—wherein any worker can stop the line—stops much less frequently than the typical mass-production assembly line, where only the line foreman can press the stop button. The result for labour is much more worker identification with the job and much more worker satisfaction than under mass-production techniques.

Product design is expensive. Mass-production firms try to reduce the costs by using specialist designers which creates problems both in co-ordinating the work of various designers and in getting good feedback from parts producers and assembly-line workers to designers. Lean producers use design teams that work closely with production engineers and parts producers. This creates more flexibility and better feedback, from the practical problems that arise in production to the basic design of products. It also allows parts producers to be presented with broad specifications of the required parts while they carry out their own R&D to develop the detailed specifications.

In the specialized design techniques, the designing must be done in a linear manner: the product design must be worked out in detail before the machine makers begin to design the specialized equipment needed to do the work. In the lean design team, everyone is working together. As the new product begins to take shape, the tool designers can begin to work on their outline plans; as the product design becomes better specified, the design of the tools can likewise be more fully developed.

Although lean production methods still have scale economies—unit costs fall as the volume of output increases—their main effect is to shift the whole long-run cost curve dramatically downward. Lean methods are also effective in the very long run, especially in developing successful new products that can be produced efficiently and cheaply. Japanese motor car manufacturers using these methods have been able to achieve unit costs of production below those of mass-production-based North American and European car factories that have twice their volume of output. They have also been able to lead in international competition to design new products efficiently and rapidly. The ability of firms in other countries to compete successfully with these Japanese firms may depend on the speed with which they can institute lean methods in their own production processes.

* The material in this box is adapted from J. P. Womack, D. T. Jones, and D. Roos, *The Machine That Changed the World* (New York: Maxwell Macmillan, 1990).

to reap all the scale economies available to this type of production.

In recent decades, production technology has been revolutionized by what is called *lean production* or *flexible manufacturing*. This is a much less specialized type of production, in which workers do many tasks in co-operation with machinery that is also less specialized. One of its most important characteristics is its ability to achieve maximum efficiency with low average costs at much smaller rates of output than are required for mass production techniques. This is further discussed in Box 11.4.

RELATIONSHIP BETWEEN LONG-RUN AND SHORT-RUN COSTS

The short-run cost curves and the long-run cost curves are all derived from the same production function. Each curve assumes given prices for all factor inputs. In the long run, all factors can be varied; in the short run, some must remain fixed. The long-run average cost (*LRAC*) curve shows the lowest cost of producing any output when all factors are variable. Each short-run average total cost (*SRATC*) curve shows the lowest cost of producing any output when one or more factors are held constant at some specific level.

No short-run cost curve can fall below the long-run curve, because the *LRAC* curve represents the lowest attainable cost for each possible output. As the level of output is changed, a different-size plant is normally required to achieve the lowest attainable cost. This is shown in Figure 11.5, where the *SRATC* curve lies above the *LRAC* curve at all outputs except q_0.

As we observed earlier in this chapter, a short-run cost curve such as the *SRATC* curve shown in Figure 11.5 is one of many such curves. Each curve shows how costs vary as output is varied from a base output, holding the fixed factor at the quantity most appropriate to that output. Figure 11.6 shows a family of short-run average total cost curves along with a single long-run average cost curve. The long-run average cost curve sometimes is called an **envelope** because it encloses a series of short-run average total cost curves by being tangent to them. Each *SRATC* curve *is tangent to* (touches) the long-run average cost curve at the level of output for which the quantity of the fixed factor is optimal, and lies above it for all other levels of output.

Shifts in cost curves

The cost curves derived so far show how cost varies with output, given constant factor prices and fixed technology. Changes in either technological knowledge or factor prices will cause the entire family of short-run and long-run aver-

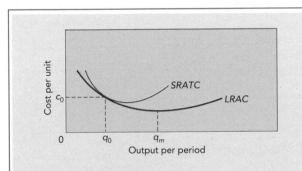

Figure 11.5 Long-run average cost and short-run average cost curves

The short-run average total cost (*SRATC*) curve is tangent to the long-run average cost (*LRAC*) curve at the output for which the quantity of the fixed factors is optimal. Assume that output is varied with plant and equipment fixed at the level that is optimal for producing q_0. Costs will then follow the short-run cost curve shown in the figure. The curves *SRATC* and *LRAC* coincide at output q_0, where the fixed plant is optimal for that level of output. For all other outputs, there is too little or too much plant and equipment, and *SRATC* lies above *LRAC*. If some output other than q_0 is to be sustained, costs can be reduced to the level of the long-run curve when sufficient time has elapsed to adjust the size of the firm's plant and equipment. The output q_m is the lowest point on the firm's long-run average cost curve. It is called the firm's *minimum efficient scale* (MES), and it is the output at which long-run costs are minimized.

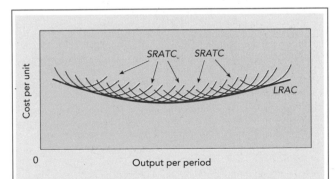

Figure 11.6 The envelope long-run average cost curve

To every point on the long-run average cost (*LRAC*) curve there is an associated short-run average cost (*SRAC*) curve tangent at that point. Each short-run curve shows how costs vary if output varies, with the fixed factor held constant at the level that is optimal for the output at the point of tangency. As a result, each *SRATC* curve touches the *LRAC* curve at one point and lies above it at all other points. This makes the *LRAC* curve the envelope of the *SRATC* curves.

age cost curves to shift. Loss of existing technological knowledge is rare, so technological change normally causes change in only one direction, shifting cost curves downward. Improved ways of producing existing products make lower-cost methods of production available. (Technological change will be discussed in more detail later in this chapter.)

Changes in factor prices can exert an influence in either direction. If a firm has to pay more for any factor that it uses, the cost of producing each level of output will rise; if the firm has to pay less for any factor that it uses, the cost of producing each level of output will fall.

A rise in factor prices shifts the family of short-run and long-run average cost curves upward. A fall in factor prices, or a technological advance, shifts the entire family of average cost curves downward.

Although factor prices usually change gradually, sometimes they change suddenly and drastically. For example, in the mid-1980s oil prices fell dramatically; the effect was to shift downward the cost curves of all users of oil and oil-related products.

The very long run: endogenous technical change

IN the long run, profit-maximizing firms do the best they can to produce known products with the techniques and the resources currently available. This means being *on*, rather than above, their long-run cost curves. In the very long run, production techniques change. This means that the production function itself alters so that the same inputs produce more output. This in turn causes long-run cost curves to shift.

The decrease in costs that can be achieved by choosing from among available factors of production, known techniques, and alternative levels of output is necessarily limited. Improvements by invention and innovation are potentially limitless, however, and hence sustained growth in living standards is critically linked to *technological change*.

Technological change was once thought to be mainly a

BOX 11.5

Endogenous materials design: a new industrial revolution?

Some experts in the science of materials believe that a new industrial revolution has been in progress since the mid-1980s. Many call it the 'Materials Revolution'.

Throughout history, an important element of technical change has been associated with advances in people's understanding of how to produce the physical materials used to make things. Indeed, we label stages of history by the materials that were used to make tools—the stone age, the bronze age, the iron age. Many key twentieth-century advances in manufacturing would not have been possible without materials such as steel and hydrocarbons. Today, important technical progress is built upon silicon chips and fibre optics.

Economic history used to be taught as though 'inventions' were random events which then had unforeseen implications. The modern view is that these inventions are an endogenous product of economic activity which is motivated by solving problems that have already been to some extent defined. For example, the depletion of the supply of wood in the late Middle

Ages led to a long sustained drive to find methods of smelting iron with coal.

Previous materials advances were usually the outcome of a process of trial and error—Edison allegedly tried many thousands of different materials and designs before he 'invented' the light bulb. From now on, however, the new materials will themselves be the product of an ongoing process of manufacture. Modern materials science is able to use knowledge of the microstructure of matter, combined with advanced computing power, to design the materials to be used in production, simultaneously with the engineering of production itself.

There are potentially profound implications of this revolution for industry. For example, more and more types of manufacturing will not migrate to areas of 'cheap labour'. Rather, they will be linked to the 'high-tech' design skills which are currently located in Japan, the United States, and, to a lesser extent, Europe.

random process, brought about by inventions made by crackpots and eccentric scientists working in garages and scientific laboratories. As a result of much recent research, we now know better. Many scholars on both sides of the Atlantic have been influential in establishing this key result.[14]

Changes in technology are often *endogenous responses* to changing economic signals; that is, they result from responses by firms to the same things that induce the substitution of one factor for another within the confines of a given technology.

In our discussion of long-run demand curves in Chapter 5, we looked at just such technological changes in response to rising relative prices when we spoke of the development of smaller, more fuel-efficient cars in the wake of rising petrol prices. Similarly, much of the move to substitute capital for labour in manufacturing, transportation, communications, mining, and agriculture in response to rising wage rates has taken the form of inventing new labour-saving methods of production.

Most microeconomic theory analyses only the short- and long-run responses of the firm to various changes that affect incentives faced by firms. Whenever technological change is an endogenous response to economic signals, such an analysis may be seriously misleading. Consider, for example, a rise in the price of an important input in one country. In the short run, firms that use the input will cut back production in response to the rise in costs. In the long run, they will substitute capital for labour. When all adjustments have been made, however, they will still find themselves at a cost disadvantage compared with competitors in other countries who have not suffered the rise in the price of their inputs. In the very long run, these firms may engage in research and development designed to reduce further the inputs of the costly factor. If the firms succeed, they may develop processes that allow them to lower costs below those of their competitors.

The rise in input prices that began by conferring a competitive disadvantage may end up by causing a competitive advantage, if it induces research and development that is more successful than was expected.

Many such instances have been documented by modern researchers into induced technological development. As a result, the response of firms to changes in such economic signals as output price and input costs must be seen in three steps:

1. the short-run response that consists of altering the variable factor;
2. the long-run response that consists of adjusting *all* factors;

3. induced research and development that seeks to innovate the firm out of difficulties caused by reductions in its product prices and/or increases in its input prices.

Studies that ignore the third response ignore what are often the most important responses, once several years have elapsed.

In this context, it is interesting to note that the techniques of lean production and flexible manufacturing (see Box 11.4 on p. 206), which are revolutionizing production all over the advanced countries, were first developed by the Japanese car producers in response to a scale disadvantage. They were unable to reach the efficient scale of production when they were selling only in their small, protected, home market. In response, they innovated their way out of these difficulties. They developed techniques that allowed them to produce a superior product at lower prices than their American and European competitors and so turned a long-run disadvantage into a very-long-run advantage.

Box 11.5 deals with another revolutionary change, the ability of modern science to design new materials that are appropriate for newly designed products. This links technological change even more closely to economic incentives than it has been in the past.

Summary

1 The production function relates inputs of factor services to outputs.

2 In the short run at least one important input is fixed. In the long run all inputs can be varied. In the very long run the production function itself changes, so that given amounts of inputs produce an increased amount of output.

3 Short-run variations in a variable input with another input fixed are subject to the law of diminishing returns: equal increments of the variable input sooner or later produce smaller and smaller additions to total output and, eventually, a reduction in average output per unit of variable input.

4 Short-run average and marginal cost curves are U-shaped, the rising portion reflecting diminishing average and marginal returns. The marginal cost curve intersects the average cost curve at the latter's minimum point, which is called the firm's capacity output.

---

[14] One of the most important books on this issue is N. Rosenberg, *Inside the Black Box: Technology and Economics* (Cambridge University Press, 1982).

5 There is a family of short-run average and marginal cost curves, one for each amount of the fixed factor.

6 In the long run, the firm will adjust all factor inputs to minimize the cost of producing any given level of output. This requires that the ratio of a factor's marginal product to its price be the same for all factors.

7 The principle of substitution states that, when relative factor prices change, firms will substitute relatively cheaper factors for relatively more expensive ones.

8 Long-run cost curves are often assumed to be U-shaped, indicating decreasing average costs (increasing returns to scale) followed by increasing average costs (decreasing returns to scale). The long-run cost curve may be thought of as the envelope of the family of short-run cost curves, all of which shift when factor prices shift.

9 In the very long run, innovations introduce new methods of production that alter the production function. These innovations respond to changes in economic incentives such as variations in the prices of inputs and outputs. They cause cost curves to shift downwards.

Topics for review

- The production function
- The short, long, and very long run
- The law of diminishing returns
- Short-run average, marginal, fixed, and total cost
- Capacity and minimum efficient scale (MES)
- Conditions for cost minimization
- The principle of substitution
- The long-run envelope cost curve
- Constant, increasing, and decreasing long-run costs
- Inventions and innovations in the very long run

APPENDIX TO CHAPTER 11

Isoquants: an alternative analysis of the firm's long-run input decisions

THE long-run choices of factor proportions that we have just studied can be shown graphically by using a new concept. This concept, which is called an *isoquant*, is defined below.

A SINGLE ISOQUANT

Table 11A.1 gives a hypothetical illustration of those combinations of two inputs (labour and capital) that will produce a given quantity of output. The data from Table 11A.1 are plotted in Figure 11A.1. A smooth curve is drawn through the points to indicate that there are additional ways, not listed in the table, of producing 6 units. The curve is called an **isoquant**. It shows the set of technologically efficient possibilities for producing a given level of output— here, it is 6 units. The isoquant in this example is analogous to an indifference curve that shows all combinations of commodities that yield a given utility. It is derived from the production function in equation (2) of the text, by altering L and K in such a way as to keep q constant.

As we move from one point on an isoquant to another, we are *substituting one factor for another* while holding output constant. The **marginal rate of substitution (MRS)** measures the rate at which one factor is substituted for another with output held constant. Graphically, this is measured by the absolute value of the slope of the isoquant at a particular point. The table shows the calculation of some rates of substitution between various points of the isoquant.[1]

[1] The table calculates the incremental rate of substitution between distinct points on an isoquant. The marginal rate of substitution refers to substitutability at a particular point on the isoquant. Graphically, the incremental rate of substitution is related to the slope of the chord joining the two points in question, while the marginal rate of substitution is given by the slope of the tangent to the curve at one particular point. See pp. 56–58 of the Appendix to Chapter 3.

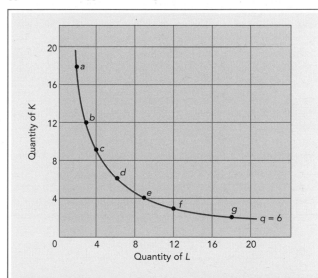

Figure 11A.1 An isoquant for output of six units

Isoquants are negatively sloped and convex. The lettered points are plotted from the data in Table 11A.1. The convex shape of the isoquant reflects a diminishing marginal rate of substitution; moving along the isoquant to the right, its slope becomes flatter. Starting from point *a*, which uses relatively little labour and much capital, and moving to point *b*, 1 additional unit of labour can substitute for 6 units of capital (while holding production constant); but from *b* to *c*, 1 unit of labour substitutes for only 3 units of capital; and so on.

Table 11A.1 Alternative methods of producing six units of output: points on an isoquant

Method	K	L	ΔK	ΔL	Rate of substitution ΔK/ΔL
a	18	2			
b	12	3	–6	1	–6.0
c	9	4	–3	1	–3.0
d	6	6	–3	2	–1.5
e	4	9	–2	3	–0.67
f	3	12	–1	3	–0.33
g	2	18	–1	6	–0.17

An isoquant describes the firm's alternative methods for producing a given output. The table lists some of the methods indicated by a production function as being available to produce six units of output. The first combination uses a great deal of capital (*K*) and very little labour (*L*). As we move down the table, labour is substituted for capital in such a way as to keep output constant. Finally, at the bottom, most of the capital has been replaced by labour. The rate of substitution between the two factors is calculated in the last three columns of the table. Note that, as we move down the table, the absolute value of the rate of substitution declines.

Let us now see how the marginal rate of substitution is related to the marginal products of the factors of production. An example will illustrate this relation. Assume that, at the present level of inputs of labour and capital, the marginal product of a unit of labour is 2 units of output while the marginal product of capital is 1 unit of output. If the firm reduces its use of capital and increases its use of labour so as to keep output constant, it needs to add only ½ unit of labour for 1 unit of capital given up. If, at another point on the isoquant with more labour and less capital, the marginal products are 2 for capital and 1 for labour, then the firm will have to add 2 units of labour for every unit of capital it gives up. The general proposition this example illustrates is:

The magnitude of the marginal rate of substitution between two factors of production is equal to the ratios of their marginal products.

Isoquants satisfy two important conditions: they are negatively sloped, and they are convex viewed from the origin. What is the meaning of each of these conditions?

The negative slope indicates that each factor of production has a positive marginal product. If the input of one factor is reduced and that of the other is held constant, output must fall. Thus, if one input is reduced, production can be held constant only if the other input is increased. This gives the marginal rate of substitution a negative value: decreases in one factor must be balanced by increases in the other factor if output is to be held constant.

Now consider what happens as the firm moves along the isoquant of Figure 11A.1 downwards and to the right. This movement means that labour is being added and capital reduced so as to keep output constant. If capital is cut by successive increments of exactly one unit, how much labour must be added each time? The key to the answer is that both factors are assumed to be subject to the law of diminishing returns. Thus, the gain in output associated with each additional unit of labour added is *diminishing*, while the loss of output associated with each additional unit of capital forgone is *increasing*. It therefore takes ever larger increases in labour to offset equal reductions in capital in order to hold production constant. This implies that the isoquant is convex viewed from the origin.

AN ISOQUANT MAP

The isoquant drawn in Figure 11A.1 referred to 6 units of output. There is another isoquant for 7 units, and for every other output. Each isoquant refers to a specific output; it connects alternative combinations of factors that are technologically efficient methods of achieving that output. If we plot a representative set of these isoquants on a single graph, we obtain an **isoquant map**. Such a map is shown in Figure 11A.2. The higher the level of output along a particular isoquant, the further away from the origin it will be.

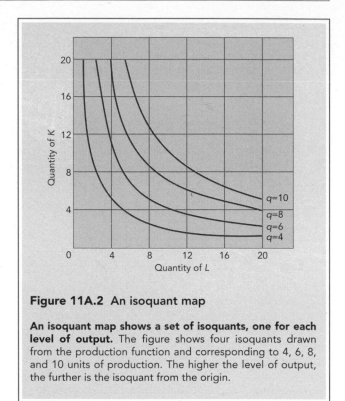

Figure 11A.2 An isoquant map

An isoquant map shows a set of isoquants, one for each level of output. The figure shows four isoquants drawn from the production function and corresponding to 4, 6, 8, and 10 units of production. The higher the level of output, the further is the isoquant from the origin.

ISOQUANTS AND THE CONDITIONS FOR COST MINIMIZATION

Finding the efficient way of producing any output requires finding the least-cost factor combination. To do this when both factors are variable, factor prices need to be known. Suppose, to continue the example, that capital is priced at £4 per unit and labour at £1. We can now draw what are called **isocost lines**, each one of which shows all of the combinations of the two factors that can be purchased for a given outlay. Four such lines are shown in Figure 11A.3. For given factor prices, the parallel isocost lines reflect alternative levels of expenditure on factors. The higher the expenditure, the farther from the origin is the isocost line. Note that the isocost line is similar to the budget line introduced in Chapter 8, which shows all the combinations of two goods that can be bought with a given income.

In Figure 11A.4 the isoquant and isocost maps are brought together. A careful study of that figure reveals the following important results. If the isoquant cuts the isocost line, it is possible to move along the isoquant and reach a lower level of cost. Where the isoquant is tangent to the isocost line, however, a movement in either direction along the isoquant is a movement to a higher level of cost. Thus:

The least-cost method of producing any given output is shown graphically by the point of tangency between the relevant isoquant and an isocost line.

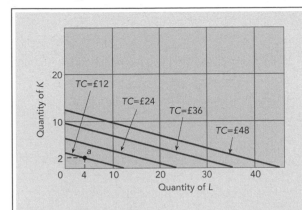

Figure 11A.3 Isocost lines

An isocost line shows alternative factor combinations that can be purchased for a given outlay. The graph shows the four isocost lines that result when labour costs £1 a unit and capital £4 a unit, and expenditure is held constant at £12, £24, £36, and £48 respectively. The line labelled *TC* = £12 represents all combinations of the two factors that the firm could buy for £12. Point *a* represents 2 units of *K* and 4 units of *L*.

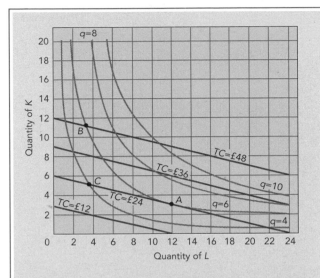

Figure 11A.4 The determination of the least-cost method of output

Least-cost methods are represented by points of tangency, such as A, between isoquant and isocost lines. The isoquant map of Figure 11A.2 and the isocost map of Figure 11A.3 are brought together in Figure 11A.4. Consider point A. It is on the 6-unit isoquant and the £24 isocost line. Thus, it is possible to achieve an output of 6 units for a total cost of £24. There are, however, other ways to achieve this output. For example, at point B 6 units are produced, but at a total cost of £48.

Now consider moving along the isocost line, say from point A to point C. Although costs are held constant, output falls from 6 to 4 units.

Point A thus shows both the least-cost method of producing 6 units of output and the maximum output that can be produced for an outlay of £24. Moving along the isoquant from point A in either direction clearly increases cost.

Notice that point *A* in Figure 11A.4 indicates not only the lowest level of cost for 6 units of output but also the highest output for £24 of cost.[2]

The absolute value of the slope of the isocost line is given by the ratio of the prices of the two factors of production.[3] The slope of the isoquant is given by the ratio of their marginal products. (Both statements refer to absolute values.) When the firm reaches its least-cost position, it has equated the price ratio (which is given to it by the market prices) with the ratio of marginal products (which it can adjust by varying the proportions in which it hires the factors). In symbols,

$$\frac{MP_K}{MP_L} = \frac{p_K}{p_L}.$$

This is equation (4) on p. 201. We have now derived this result by use of the isoquant analysis of the firm's decisions.

ISOQUANTS AND THE PRINCIPLE OF SUBSTITUTION

Suppose that with technology unchanged—that is, with the isoquant map fixed—the price of one factor changes. Figure 11A.5 shows why the change in price changes the least-cost method of producing a given output. An increase in the price of one factor pivots the isocost line inwards and thus increases the cost of producing any output. It also changes the slope of the isocost line and thus changes the least-cost method of production. Costs at the new least-

cost point *C* are higher than they were before the price increase, but not as high as if the factor substitution had not occurred. The slope of the isocost line has changed, making it efficient to substitute the now relatively cheaper capital for the relatively more expensive labour.

This result illustrates the principle of substitution.

Changes in relative factor prices will cause a partial replacement of factors that have become relatively more expensive by factors that have become relatively cheaper.

---

[2] Thus, we find the same solution if we set out *either* to minimize the cost of producing 6 units of output *or* to maximize the output that can be obtained for £24. One problem is said to be the *dual* of the other.

[3] The isocost line's equation is $Lp_L + Kp_K = t$, where *t* is total cost. Taking first differences yields $\Delta Lp_L + \Delta Kp_K = \Delta t = 0$, since *t* is held constant. Thus, $\Delta K/\Delta L = -p_K/p_L$.

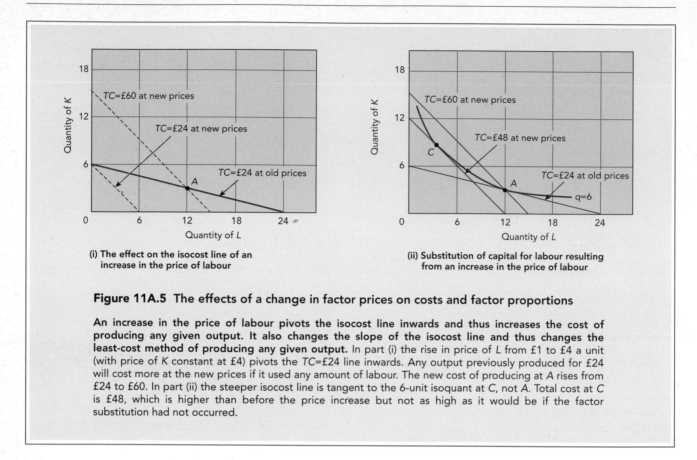

(i) The effect on the isocost line of an increase in the price of labour

(ii) Substitution of capital for labour resulting from an increase in the price of labour

Figure 11A.5 The effects of a change in factor prices on costs and factor proportions

An increase in the price of labour pivots the isocost line inwards and thus increases the cost of producing any given output. It also changes the slope of the isocost line and thus changes the least-cost method of producing any given output. In part (i) the rise in price of L from £1 to £4 a unit (with price of K constant at £4) pivots the TC=£24 line inwards. Any output previously produced for £24 will cost more at the new prices if it used any amount of labour. The new cost of producing at A rises from £24 to £60. In part (ii) the steeper isocost line is tangent to the 6-unit isoquant at C, not A. Total cost at C is £48, which is higher than before the price increase but not as high as it would be if the factor substitution had not occurred.

Of course, substitution of capital for labour cannot fully offset the effects of a rise in the cost of labour, as Figure 11A.5(i) shows. This means that if production is to be held constant, higher costs must be accepted—but because of substitution it is not necessary to accept costs as high as would be needed to accompany an unchanged factor proportion.

This leads to the following prediction

A rise in the price of one factor with all other factor prices constant will (1) shift upwards the cost curves of commodities that use that factor, and (2) lead to a substitution of factors that are now relatively cheaper for the factor whose price has risen.

Both of these predictions were stated in this chapter; they have now been derived formally using the isoquant technique.

CHAPTER 12

Perfect competition

WE now know how each firm's costs vary with its output. Once we know how each firm's revenue varies with its output, we can put the two together and see the relation between its output and its profits. The assumption of profit maximization then allows us to determine the firm's output. Taking the step of relating revenue to output proves complicated because the relation differs with the competitive situation in which the firm operates. Our first step in this chapter, therefore, is to ask what we mean by 'competitive situation'. We then go on to study the firm's short- and long-run price and output decisions in a situation called 'perfect competition'. This allows us to study the reaction of an industry first to a stream of new technological improvements and then to a long-term decline in the demand for its product. In the following two chapters we study the behaviour of the firm in less competitive situations.

Market structure and firm behaviour

DOES Shell compete with British Petroleum in the sale of petrol? Does Lloyds Bank compete with Barclays? Does a wheat farmer from Yorkshire compete with a wheat farmer from Somerset? If we use the ordinary meaning of the word 'compete', the answer to the first two questions is plainly yes, and the answer to the third is probably no.

The Shell Oil Company and British Petroleum both advertise extensively to persuade car drivers to buy *their* products. Gimmicks such as new mileage-stretching additives and free dishes are used to tempt drivers to buy one brand of petrol rather than another. Most town centres in England and Wales have not only Barclays and Lloyds Banks but also Midland and National Westminster. They all provide similar services but work hard to attract customers from each other. For example, they all offer incentives for students to open bank accounts in the hope that they will stay with that bank for life.

When we shift our attention to firms producing wheat, however, we see that there is nothing that the Yorkshire farm family can do to affect either the sales or the profits of the Somerset farm family. There would be no point in doing so even if they could, since the sales and profits of the Somerset farm have no effect on those of the Yorkshire farm.

To sort out the questions of who is competing with whom and in what sense, it is useful to distinguish between the behaviour of individual firms and the *type of market* in which they operate. In everyday use, the word 'competition' usually refers to competitive behaviour. Economists, however, are interested both in the competitive behaviour of individual firms and in a quite distinct concept: competitive market structure.

Market structure and behaviour

The term **market structure** refers to all the features that may affect the behaviour and performance of the firms in a market (for example, the number of firms in the market, or the type of product that they sell).

Competitive market structure   The competitiveness of the market refers to the extent to which individual firms have power to influence market prices or the terms on which their product is sold. *The less power an individual firm has to influence the market in which it sells its product, the more competitive that market is.*

The extreme form of competitiveness occurs when each firm has zero market power. In such a case, there are so many firms in the market that each must accept the price set by the forces of market demand and market supply. The firms perceive themselves as being able to sell as much as they choose at the prevailing market price and as having no power to influence that price. If the firm charged a higher price, it would obtain no sales; so many other firms would be selling at the market price that buyers would take their business elsewhere.

This extreme is called a *perfectly competitive market structure.* (Usually the term 'structure' is dropped and economists speak of a *perfectly competitive market.*) In it, there is no need for individual firms to compete actively with one another, since none has any power over the market. One firm's ability to sell its product does not depend on the behaviour of any other firm. For example, the Yorkshire and Somerset wheat farmers operate in a perfectly competitive market over which they have no power. Neither can change the market price for its wheat by altering its own behaviour.

Competitive behaviour   In everyday language, the term 'competitive behaviour' refers to the degree to which individual firms actively compete with one another. For example, Shell and BP certainly engage in competitive behaviour. It is also true, however, that both companies have some real power over their market. Either firm could raise its prices and still continue to attract customers. Each has the power to decide, within limits set by buyers' tastes and the prices of competing products, the price that people will pay for their petrol and oil. So even though they actively compete with each other, they do so in a market that does not have a perfectly competitive structure.

In contrast, the Yorkshire and Somerset wheat farmers do not engage in competitive behaviour, because the only way they can affect their profits is by changing their outputs of (or their costs of producing) wheat.

Behaviour versus structure   The distinction that we have just made explains why firms in perfectly competitive markets (e.g. the Yorkshire and the Somerset wheat producers) do not compete actively with each other, whereas firms that do compete actively with each other (e.g. Shell and BP) do not operate in perfectly competitive markets.

The significance of market structure

Shell and BP are two of several large firms in the oil *industry*. They produce petroleum products and sell them in various *markets*. The terms 'industry' and 'market' are familiar from everyday use. However, economists give them precise definitions, which we need to understand.

We noted earlier that a *market* consists of an area over which buyers and sellers can negotiate the exchange of some product. The firms that produce a well-defined product, or a closely related set of products, constitute an **indus**-try. In earlier chapters we developed and used market demand curves; here we note that the market demand curve for any particular product is the demand curve facing the *industry* that produces the product.

When the managers of a firm make their production and sales decisions, they need to know what quantity of a product their firm can sell at various prices. Their concern is, therefore, not with the *market* demand curve for their industry's product, but rather with the demand curve for their firm's own output of that product. If they know the demand curve that their own firm faces, they know the sales that their firm can make at each price it might charge, and thus they know its potential revenues. If they also know their firm's costs for producing the product, they can calculate the profits that would be associated with each rate of output. With this information, they can choose the output that maximizes profits.

Recall that economists define market structure as the characteristics that affect the behaviour and performance of firms that sell in that market. These characteristics determine, among other things, the relationship between the market demand curve for the industry's product and the demand curve facing each firm in that industry.

To reduce the analysis of market structure to manageable proportions, economists focus on four theoretical market structures that cover most actual cases. These are called perfect competition, monopoly, monopolistic competition, and oligopoly. Perfect competition will be dealt with in the rest of this chapter; the others will be dealt with in the chapters that follow.

Elements of the theory of perfect competition

THE perfectly competitive market structure—usually referred to simply as *perfect competition*—applies directly to a number of real-world markets. It also provides an important benchmark for comparison with other market structures.

Assumptions of perfect competition

The theory of **perfect competition** is built on a number of key assumptions relating to the firm and to the industry.

- *Assumption 1.* All the firms in the industry sell an identical product. Economists describe this by saying that the firms sell a **homogeneous product.**

- *Assumption 2.* Customers know the nature of the product being sold and the prices charged by each firm.

- *Assumption 3.* The level of a firm's output at which its long-run average total cost reaches a minimum is small relative to the industry's total output.

- *Assumption 4.* The firm is a **price-taker.** This means that the firm can alter its rate of production and sales without significantly affecting the market price of its product. This is why a firm operating in a perfectly competitive market has no power to influence that market through its own individual actions. It must passively accept whatever happens to be the ruling price, but it can sell as much as it wants at that price.[1]

- *Assumption 5.* The industry is assumed to be characterized by *freedom of entry and exit;* that is, any new firm is free to enter the industry and start producing if it so wishes, and any existing firm is free to cease production and leave the industry. Existing firms cannot bar the entry of new firms, and there are no legal prohibitions or other artificial barriers to entering or exiting the industry.

An illustration   The Yorkshire and the Somerset wheat farmers that we considered earlier provide us with good illustrations of firms that are operating in a perfectly competitive market.

Because each individual wheat farmer is just one of a very large number of producers who are all growing the same product, one firm's contribution to the industry's total production is only a tiny drop in an extremely large bucket. Each firm will correctly assume that variations in its output have no significant effect on the price at which it sells its wheat. Thus each firm, knowing that it can sell as much or as little as it chooses at that price, adapts its behaviour to a given market price of wheat. Furthermore, anyone

---

[1] To emphasize its importance, we identify price-taking as a separate assumption, although, strictly speaking, it is implied by the first three assumptions.

BOX 12.1

Demand under perfect competition: firm and industry

Because all products have negatively sloped market demand curves, *any* increase in the industry's output will cause *some* fall in the market price. The calculations given below show, however, that any conceivable increase that one wheat farm could make in its output has such a negligible effect on the industry's price that the farmer correctly ignores it. (For our purposes, the farm is a firm producing wheat.)[*]

The calculations given below arrive at the elasticity of demand facing one wheat farmer in two steps. Step 1 shows that a 200 per cent variation in the farm's output leads to only a very small percentage variation in the world price. Thus, as step 2 shows, the elasticity of demand for the farm's product is very high: 71,428!

Although the arithmetic used in reaching these measures is unimportant, understanding why the wheat farmer is a price-taker in these circumstances is vital.

Here is the argument that the calculations summarize. The market elasticity of demand for wheat is approximately 0.25. This means that, if the quantity of wheat supplied in the world increased by 1 per cent, the price would have to fall by 4 per cent to induce the world's wheat buyers to purchase the extra wheat.

Even huge farms produce a very small fraction of the total world crop. In a recent year, one large farm produced 1,750 metric tonnes of wheat; this was only 0.0035 per cent of the world production of 500 million metric tonnes. Suppose that the farmer decided in one year to produce nothing and in another year managed to produce twice the normal output of 1,750 metric tonnes; this is an extremely large variation in one farm's output. The increase in output from zero to 3,500 metric tonnes represents a 200 per cent variation measured around the farm's average output of 1,750 metric tonnes. Yet the percentage increase in world output is only $(3,500/500,000,000)100 = 0.0007$ per cent. The calculations show that this increase would lead to a decrease in the world price of 0.0028 per cent (2.8p in £1,000) and give the farm's own demand curve an elasticity of over 71,000! This is an enormous elasticity of demand. The farm would have to increase its output by over 71,000 per cent to bring about a 1 per cent decrease in the price of wheat! It is not

surprising, therefore, that the farmer regards the price of wheat as unaffected by any change in output that his one farm could conceivably make. For all intents and purposes, the wheat-producing firm faces a perfectly elastic demand curve for its product; *it is a price-taker.*

We shall now proceed with the calculation of the firm's elasticity of demand (η_F) from market elasticity of demand (η_M), given the following figures:

World elasticity of demand (η_M) = 0.25
World output = 500,000,000 metric tonnes

A large farm with an average output of 1,750 metric tonnes varies its output between 0 and 3,500 tonnes. The variation of 3,500 tonnes represents 200 per cent of the farm's average output of 1,750 metric tonnes. This causes world output to vary by only $(3,500/500,000,000)100 = 0.0007$ per cent.

Step 1: Find the percentage change in world price. We know that the market elasticity is 0.25. This means that the percentage change in quantity must be one-quarter as big as the percentage change in price. Put the other way around, the percentage change in price must be four times as large as the percentage change in quantity. We have just seen that world quantity changes by 0.0007 per cent, so world price must change by $(0.0007)(4) = 0.0028$ per cent.

Step 2: Find the firm's elasticity of demand. This is the percentage change in its *own output* divided by the resulting percentage change in the world price. This is 200 per cent divided by 0.0028 per cent. Clearly, the percentage change in quantity vastly exceeds the percentage change in price, making elasticity very high. Its precise value is 200/0.0028 or 2,000,000/28, which is 71,429.

---

[*] Strictly speaking, this box applies to wheat farmers outside of the EU. It will apply directly when the EU lowers its support price to the world price or removes it altogether. In the meantime, EU wheat farmers do face a perfectly elastic demand curve because the Commission stands ready to buy all the wheat that is legally produced at its support price.

who has enough money to buy or rent the necessary land, labour, and equipment can become a wheat farmer.[2]

There is nothing that existing farmers can do to stop another farmer from growing wheat, and there are no legal deterrents to becoming a wheat farmer.

The difference between the wheat farmers and the Shell Oil Company is in *degree of market power*. Each firm that is producing wheat is an insignificant part of the whole market and thus has no power to influence the price of wheat. The oil company does have power to influence the price of petrol because its own sales represent a significant part of the total sales of petrol.

Box 12.1 explores further the reasons why each firm producing wheat finds the price of wheat to be beyond its influence.

Demand and revenue for a firm in perfect competition

A major distinction between firms operating in perfectly competitive markets and firms operating in any other type of market is in the shape of the firm's own demand curve.

The demand curve facing each firm in perfect competition is horizontal, because variations in the firm's output over the range that it needs to consider have no noticeable effect on price.

The horizontal (perfectly elastic) demand curve does not mean that the firm could actually sell an infinite amount at the going price. It means, rather, that the variations in production *that it will normally be possible for the firm to make* will leave price virtually unchanged because their effect on total industry output will be negligible.

Figure 12.1 contrasts the demand curve for the product of a competitive industry with the demand curve facing a single firm in that industry.

To study the revenues that firms receive from the sales of their products, economists define three concepts called total, average, and marginal revenue. These are the revenue counterparts of the concepts of total, average, and marginal cost that we considered in Chapter 10.

Total revenue (TR) *is the total amount received by the seller from the sale of a product.* If q units are sold at p dollars each,[3] $TR = p \cdot q$.

Average revenue (AR) *is the amount of revenue per unit sold.* This is equal to the price at which the product is sold.

Marginal revenue (MR), *sometimes called incremental revenue,* is the change in a firm's total revenue resulting from a change in its rate of sales by one unit. Whenever output changes by more than one unit, the change in revenue must be divided by the change in output to calculate mar-

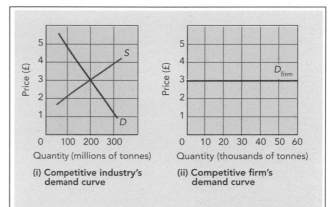

Figure 12.1 The demand curve for a competitive industry and for one firm in the industry

The industry's demand curve is negatively sloped; the firm's demand curve is virtually horizontal. Notice the difference in the quantities shown on the horizontal scale in each part of the figure. The competitive industry has output of 200 million tonnes when the price is £3. The individual firm takes that market price as given and considers producing up to, say, 60,000 tonnes. The firm's demand curve in part (ii) appears horizontal because of the change in quantity scale compared with the industry's demand curve in part (i). The firm's output variation has only a tiny percentage effect on industry output. If we plotted the industry demand curve from 199,970,000 to 200,030,000 tonnes on the scale used in part (ii), the D curve would appear virtually horizontal.

ginal revenue. For example, if an increase in output of three units per month is accompanied by an increase in revenue of $1,500, the marginal revenue resulting from the sale of *one extra unit* per month is $1,500/3, or $500. At any existing level of sales, marginal revenue shows what revenue the firm would gain by selling one unit more and what revenue it would lose by selling one unit less.[4]

---

[2] Most of the world's wheat growers sell at a price determined in the world wheat market. However, in 1995 farmers in the European Union faced a price above the world price because of EU price supports. These price supports are being phased out and replaced by other measures to help farmers at the expense of consumers. When this is done, EU farmers may face the world price. In the meantime, there are so many farmers within the EU that no one of them could affect the EU price even if that price were not set wholly on the world market.

[3] Four common ways of indicating that any two variables such as p and q are to be multiplied are $p \cdot q$, $p \times q$, $(p)(q)$, and pq.

[4] Total revenue is a function of, i.e. varies with, output. Because we use numerical examples in the text, we are, strictly speaking, using the concept of *incremental revenues*, $\Delta TR/\Delta q$. Marginal revenue is defined formally as the first derivative of total revenue with respect to output, dTR/dq. For small changes, incremental revenue may be regarded as an approximation of marginal revenue, which we do in the text. The material in the Appendix to Chapter 3 is once again relevant at this point.

Table 12.1 Revenue concepts for a price-taking firm

Quantity sold (units) q	Price p	TR = p·q	AR = TR/q	MR = ΔTR/Δq
10	£3.00	£30.00	£3.00	
11	3.00	33.00	3.00	£3.00
12	3.00	36.00	3.00	3.00
13	3.00	39.00	3.00	3.00

When price is fixed, average revenue, marginal revenue and price are all equal to each other. The table shows the calculation of total (*TR*), average (*AR*), and marginal revenue (*MR*) when market price is £3.00 and the firm varies its quantity over the range from 10 to 13 units. Marginal revenue is shown between the lines because it represents the change in total revenue in response to a change in quantity. For example, when sales rise from 11 to 12 units, revenue rises from £33 to £36, making marginal revenue (36 − 33)/(12 − 11) = £3 per unit.

To illustrate each of these revenue concepts, consider a firm that is selling an agricultural product in a perfectly competitive market at a price of £3 per tonne. Total revenue rises by £3 for every tonne sold. Because every tonne brings in £3, the average revenue per tonne sold is clearly £3. Furthermore, because each *additional* tonne sold brings in £3, the marginal revenue of an extra tonne sold is also £3. Table 12.1 shows calculations of these revenue concepts for a range of outputs between 10 and 13 tonnes.

The important point illustrated in Table 12.1 is that, as long as the amount of the firm's output does not significantly affect the price at which that output sells, marginal revenue is equal to average revenue (which is *always* equal to price). Graphically, as shown in part (i) of Figure 12.2, average revenue and marginal revenue are the same horizontal line drawn at the level of market price. Because the firm can sell any quantity it chooses at this price, the horizontal line is also the *firm's demand curve;* it shows that any quantity the firm chooses to sell will be associated with this same market price.

If the market price is unaffected by variations in the firm's output, then the firm's demand curve, its average revenue curve, and its marginal revenue curve all coincide in the same horizontal line.

This result can be stated in a slightly different way, which turns out to be important for our later study:

For a firm in perfect competition, price equals marginal revenue.

This means, of course, that total revenue rises in direct proportion to output, as shown in part (ii) of Figure 12.2.

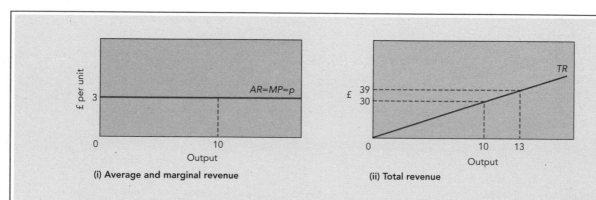

Figure 12.2 Revenue curves for a firm in perfect competition

The demand curve for a perfectly competitive firm is a horizontal straight line. The lines graph the data from Table 12.1. Because price does not change, neither marginal nor average revenue varies with output—both are equal to price. When price is constant, total revenue is a rising straight line from the origin whose slope is given by the price.

Short-run equilibrium

WE learned in Chapter 11 how each firm's costs vary with its output. In the short run, the firm has one or more fixed factors, and the only way in which it can change its output is by using more or fewer of the factor inputs that it can vary. Thus, the firm's short-run cost curves are relevant to its decision regarding output.

We have just learned how the revenues of each price-taking firm vary with its output. The next step is to combine information about the firm's costs and revenues to determine the level of output that will maximize its profits. We start by stating three rules that apply to *all* profit-maximizing firms, whether or not they operate in perfectly competitive markets.

Rules for all profit-maximizing firms

SHOULD THE FIRM PRODUCE AT ALL?

The firm always has the option of producing nothing. If it exercises this option, it will have an operating loss that is equal to its fixed costs. If it decides to produce, it will add the variable cost of production to its costs and the receipts from the sale of its product to its revenue. Therefore, it will be worth while for the firm to produce as long as it can find some level of output for which revenue exceeds variable cost. However, if its revenue is less than its variable cost at *every* level of output, the firm will actually lose more by producing than by not producing.

Rule 1: **A firm should not produce at all if, for *all* levels of output, the total variable cost of producing that output exceeds the total revenue derived from selling it or, equivalently, if the average variable cost of producing the output exceeds the price at which it can be sold.**

The shut-down price   The price at which the firm can just cover its average variable cost, and so leaves it indifferent between producing and not producing, is often called the **shut-down price.** At any price below this price, the firm will shut down. Such a price is shown in part (i) of Figure 12.6 on page 224. At the price of £2 the firm can just cover its average variable cost by producing q_0 units. Any other output would not produce enough revenue to cover variable costs. For any price below £2 there is no output at which variable costs can be covered. The price £2 in part (i) is thus the shut-down price.

HOW MUCH SHOULD THE FIRM PRODUCE?

If a firm decides that (according to rule 1) production is

worth undertaking, it must decide how much to produce. Common sense dictates that, on a unit-by-unit basis, if any unit of production adds more to revenue than it does to cost, producing and selling that unit will increase profits. However, if any unit adds more to cost than it does to revenue, producing and selling that unit will decrease profits. Using the terminology introduced earlier, a unit of production raises profits if the marginal revenue obtained from selling it exceeds the marginal cost of producing it; it lowers profits if the marginal revenue obtained from selling it is less than the marginal cost of producing it.

Now let a firm with some existing rate of output consider increasing or decreasing that output. If a further unit of production will increase the firm's profits, the firm should expand its output. However, if the last unit produced reduced profits, the firm should contract its output. From this it follows that the only time the firm should leave its output unaltered is when the last unit produced adds the same amount to costs as it does to revenue. The results just obtained can be combined in the following rule:

Rule 2: **Assuming that it is worth while for the firm to produce, the firm should produce the output at which marginal revenue equals marginal cost.**

MAXIMIZATION NOT MINIMIZATION

Figure 12.3 shows that it is possible to fulfil rule 2 and have profits at a minimum rather than a maximum.

In the figure there are two outputs where marginal cost equals marginal revenue. Rule 3 is needed to distinguish minimum-profit positions from maximum-profit positions:

Rule 3: **For an output where marginal cost equals marginal revenue to be profit-maximizing rather than profit-minimizing, it is sufficient that marginal cost be less than marginal revenue at slightly lower outputs and that marginal cost exceed marginal revenue at slightly higher outputs.**

The geometric statement of this condition is that, at the profit-maximizing output, the marginal cost curve should intersect the marginal revenue curve from below. This ensures that *MC* is less than *MR* to the left of the profit-maximizing output and greater than *MR* to the right of the profit-maximizing output.[5]

---

[5] Those students who are familiar with elementary calculus can follow the formal derivations of these three rules given in the Appendix to this chapter.

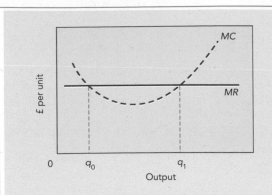

Figure 12.3 Two outputs where marginal cost equals marginal revenue

The equality of marginal cost and marginal revenue is necessary, but not sufficient, for profit maximization. The firm is assumed to be able to sell any output at the going market price, so that the market price is the firm's marginal revenue. (If all units can be sold at the prevailing market price, then each unit adds that price to the firm's total revenue.) $MC=MR$ at outputs q_0 and q_1. Output q_0 is a minimum-profit position because a change of output in either direction would increase profit: for outputs below q_0, marginal cost exceeds marginal revenue and profits can be increased by *reducing* output, while for outputs above q_0, marginal revenue exceeds marginal cost and profits can be increased by *increasing* output. Output q_1 is a maximum-profit position, since at outputs just below it marginal revenue exceeds marginal cost and profit can be increased by *increasing* output towards q_1; while at outputs just above it marginal cost exceeds marginal revenue and profit can be increased by *reducing* output towards q_1.

THE OPTIMUM OUTPUT

The above three rules determine the output that will be chosen by any firm that maximizes its profits in the short run. This output is called the firm's **profit-maximizing output**, and sometimes its **optimum output**:

- The firm's optimum output is zero if total revenue is less than total variable cost at all levels of output; the optimum output is positive if there is any output for which total revenue exceeds total variable cost.

- When the firm's optimum output is positive, it is where marginal cost equals marginal revenue.

- If output is reduced slightly from the optimum level, marginal cost must be less than marginal revenue; if output is increased slightly from the optimum level, marginal cost must exceed marginal revenue.

RULE 2 APPLIED TO PRICE-TAKING FIRMS

Rule 2 tells us that any profit-maximizing firm that pro-

duces at all will produce at the point where marginal cost equals marginal revenue. However, we have already seen that, for price-taking firms, marginal revenue is the market price. Combining these two results gives us an important conclusion:

A firm that is operating in a perfectly competitive market will produce the output that equates its marginal cost of production with the market price of its product (as long as price exceeds average variable cost).

In a perfectly competitive industry, the market determines the price at which the firm sells its product. The firm then picks the quantity of output that maximizes its profits. We have seen that this is the output for which price equals marginal cost.

When the firm has reached a position where its profits are maximized, it has no incentive to change its output. Therefore, unless prices or costs change, the firm will continue to produce this output because it is doing as well as it can do, given the market situation. The firm is in *short-run equilibrium*, as illustrated in Figure 12.4. (The long run is considered later in this chapter.)

In a perfectly competitive market, each firm is a price-taker and a quantity-adjuster. It pursues its goal of profit maximization by increasing or decreasing quantity until it equates its short-run marginal cost with the price of its product that is given to it by the market.

Figure 12.4 shows the equilibrium of the firm using average cost and revenue curves. We can, if we wish, show the same equilibrium using total cost and revenue curves. Figure 12.5 combines the total cost curve first drawn in Figure 11.3 with the total revenue curve first shown in Figure 12.2. It shows the profit-maximizing output as the output with the largest positive difference between total revenue and total cost. This must of course be the same output as we located in Figure 12.4 by equating marginal cost and marginal revenue.

Short-run supply curves

We have seen that in a perfectly competitive market the firm responds to a price that is set by the forces of demand and supply. By adjusting the quantity it produces in response to the current market price, the firm helps to determine the market supply. The link between the behaviour of the firm and the behaviour of the competitive market is provided by the *market supply curve*.

The supply curve for one firm   The firm's supply curve is derived in part (i) of Figure 12.6, which shows a firm's marginal cost curve and four alternative prices. The horizontal

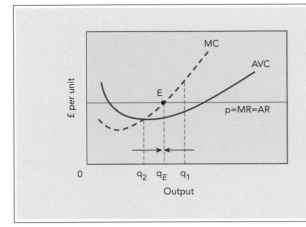

Figure 12.4 The short-run equilibrium of a firm in perfect competition

The firm chooses the output for which *p=MC* above the level of *AVC*. When price equals marginal cost, as at output q_E, the firm loses profits if it either increases or decreases its output. At any point left of q_E, say q_2, price is greater than the marginal cost, and it pays to increase output (as indicated by the left-hand arrow). At any point to the right of q_E, say q_1, price is less than the marginal cost, and it pays to reduce output (as indicated by the right-hand arrow).

line at each price is the firm's demand curve when the market price is at that level. The firm's marginal cost curve gives the marginal cost corresponding to each level of output. We require a supply curve that shows the quantity that the firm will supply at each price. For prices below average variable cost, the firm will supply zero units (rule 1). For prices above average variable cost, the firm will equate price and marginal cost (rule 2, modified by the proposition that $MR = p$ in perfect competition). This leads to the following conclusion:

In perfect competition, the firm's supply curve is its marginal cost curve for those levels of output for which marginal cost is above average variable cost.

The supply curve of an industry   To illustrate what is involved, Figure 12.7 shows the derivation of an industry supply curve for an industry containing only two firms. The general result is as follows:

In perfect competition, the industry supply curve is the horizontal sum of the marginal cost curves (above the level of average variable cost) of all firms in the industry.

The reason for this is that each firm's marginal cost curve shows how much that firm will supply at each given market price, and the industry supply curve is the sum of what each firm will supply.

This supply curve, based on the short-run marginal cost curves of all the firms in the industry, is the industry's supply curve that was first encountered in Chapter 4. We have now established the profit-maximizing behaviour of individual firms that lies behind that curve. It is sometimes called a **short-run supply curve** because it is based on the short-run, profit-maximizing behaviour of all the firms in the industry. This distinguishes it from a *long-run supply curve*, which relates quantity supplied to the price that rules in long-run equilibrium (which we will study later in this chapter).

Short-run equilibrium price

The price of a product sold in a perfectly competitive market is determined by the interaction of the industry's short-run supply curve and the market demand curve. Although no one firm can influence the market price significantly, the collective actions of all firms in the industry (as shown by the industry supply curve) and the collective actions of con-

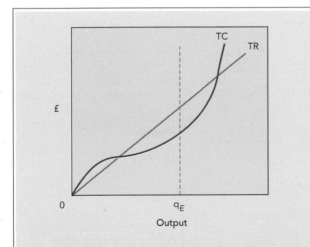

Figure 12.5 Total cost and revenue curves

The firm chooses the output for which the gap between the total revenue and the total cost curves is the largest. At each output, the vertical distance between the *TR* and the *TC* curves shows by how much total revenue exceeds or falls short of total cost. In the figure, the gap is largest at output q_E, which is thus the profit-maximizing output.

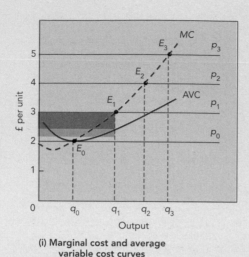

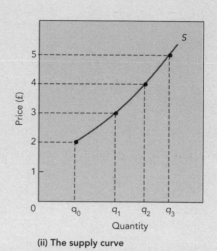

(i) Marginal cost and average variable cost curves

(ii) The supply curve

Figure 12.6 The supply curve for a price-taking firm

For a price-taking firm, the supply curve has the same shape as its *MC* curve above the level of *AVC*. The point E_0, where price p_0 equals *AVC*, is the shutdown point. For prices below £2 optimum output is zero, because the firm is better off if it produces nothing. As prices rise from £2 to £3 to £4 to £5, the firm increases its production from q_0 to q_1 to q_2 to q_3. If, for example, price were £3, the firm would produce output q_1 rather than 0 because it would be earning the contribution to fixed costs shown by the dark blue rectangle.

The firm's supply curve is shown in part (ii). It relates market price to the quantity the firm will produce and offer for sale. It has the same shape as the firm's *MC* curve for all prices above *AVC*.

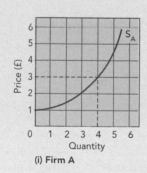

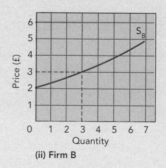

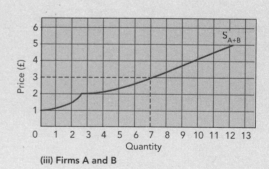

(i) Firm A

(ii) Firm B

(iii) Firms A and B

Figure 12.7 The supply curve for a group of firms

The industry supply curve is the horizontal sum of the supply curves of each of the firms in the industry. At a price of £3, firm A would supply 4 units and firm B would supply 3 units. Together, as shown in part (iii), they would supply 7 units. In this example, because firm B does not enter the market at prices below £2, the supply curve S_{A+B} is identical to S_A up to price £2 and is the sum of $S_A + S_B$ above £2.

If there are hundreds of firms, the process is the same: each firm's supply curve (which is derived in the manner shown in Figure 12.6) shows what that firm will produce at each given price. The industry supply curve shows the sum of the quantities produced by all firms at each given price.

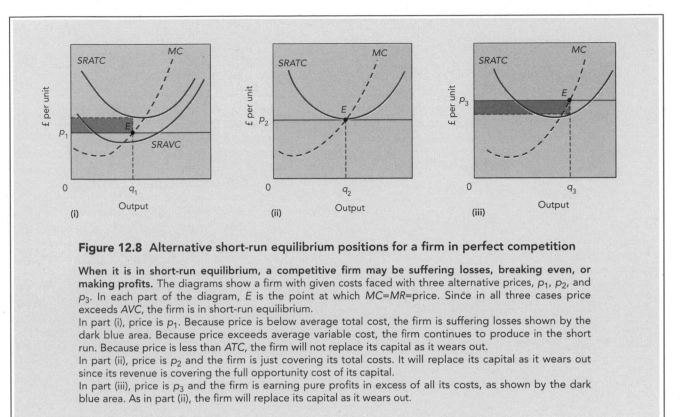

Figure 12.8 Alternative short-run equilibrium positions for a firm in perfect competition

When it is in short-run equilibrium, a competitive firm may be suffering losses, breaking even, or making profits. The diagrams show a firm with given costs faced with three alternative prices, p_1, p_2, and p_3. In each part of the diagram, E is the point at which $MC = MR = $ price. Since in all three cases price exceeds AVC, the firm is in short-run equilibrium.

In part (i), price is p_1. Because price is below average total cost, the firm is suffering losses shown by the dark blue area. Because price exceeds average variable cost, the firm continues to produce in the short run. Because price is less than ATC, the firm will not replace its capital as it wears out.

In part (ii), price is p_2 and the firm is just covering its total costs. It will replace its capital as it wears out since its revenue is covering the full opportunity cost of its capital.

In part (iii), price is p_3 and the firm is earning pure profits in excess of all its costs, as shown by the dark blue area. As in part (ii), the firm will replace its capital as it wears out.

sumers (as shown by the market demand curve) together determine the equilibrium price. This occurs at the point where the market demand curve and the industry supply curve intersect.

At the equilibrium price, each firm is producing and selling a quantity for which its marginal cost equals price. No firm is motivated to change its output in the short run. Because total quantity demanded equals total quantity supplied, there is no reason for market price to change in the short run; the market and all the firms in the industry are in short-run equilibrium.

Short-run profitability of the firm

We know that when an industry is in short-run equilibrium, each firm is maximizing its profits. However, we do not know *how large* these profits are. It is one thing to know that a firm is doing as well as it can, given its particular circumstances; it is another thing to know how well it is doing.

Figure 12.8 shows three possible positions for a firm in short-run equilibrium. In all cases the firm is maximizing its profits by producing where price equals marginal cost, but in part (i) the firm is suffering losses, in part (ii) it is just covering all of its costs (breaking even), and in part (iii) it is making profits because average revenue exceeds average total cost. In part (i) we could say that the firm is minimizing its losses rather than maximizing its profits, but both statements mean the same thing. In all three cases, the firm is doing as well as it can, given its costs and the market price.

Long-run equilibrium

ALTHOUGH Figure 12.8 shows three possible short-run equilibrium positions for the firm in perfect competition, not all of them are possible long-run equilibrium positions.

The effect of entry and exit

The key to long-run equilibrium under perfect competition is entry and exit. We have seen that when firms are in *short-run equilibrium* they may be making profits, suffering losses, or just breaking even. Because costs include the opportunity cost of capital, firms that are just breaking even are doing as well as they could do by investing their capital elsewhere. Thus, there will be no incentive for such firms to leave the industry. Similarly, if new entrants expect just to break even, there will be no incentive for firms to enter the industry, because capital can earn the same return elsewhere in the economy. If, however, existing firms are earning revenues in excess of all costs, including the opportunity cost of capital, new capital will enter the industry to share in these profits. If existing firms are suffering losses, capital will leave the industry because a better return can be obtained elsewhere in the economy. Let us now consider this process in a little more detail.

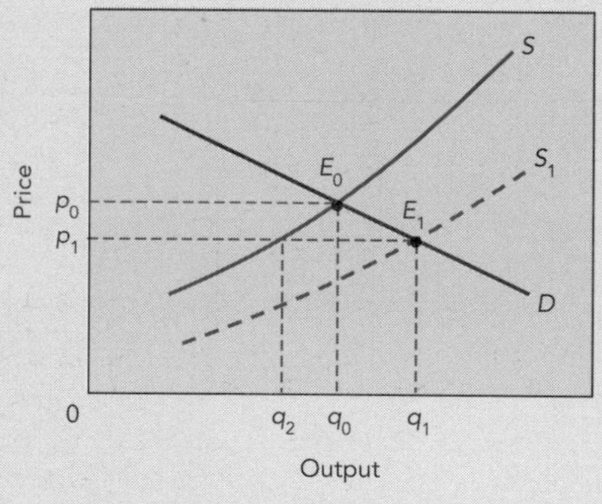

An entry-attracting price   First, let all firms in the competitive industry be in the position of the firm shown in part (iii) of Figure 12.8. New firms, attracted by the profitability of existing firms, will enter the industry. Suppose that, in response to the high profits that the 100 existing firms are making, 20 new firms enter. The market supply curve that formerly added up the outputs of 100 firms must now add up the outputs of 120 firms. At any price, more will be supplied because there are more producers.

With an unchanged market demand curve, this shift in the short-run industry supply curve means that the previous equilibrium price will no longer prevail. The shift in supply will lower the equilibrium price, and both new and old firms will have to adjust their output to this new price. This is illustrated in Figure 12.9. New firms will continue to enter, and the equilibrium price will continue to fall, until all firms in the industry are just covering their total costs. Firms will then be in the position of the firm shown in part (ii) of Figure 12.8, which is called a *zero-profit equilibrium*.

Profits in a competitive industry are a signal for the entry of new firms; the industry will expand, pushing price down until the profits fall to zero.

An exit-inducing price   Now let the firms in the industry be in the position of the firm shown in part (i) of Figure 12.8. Although the firms are covering their variable costs, the return on their capital is less than the opportunity cost of capital. They are not covering their total costs. This is a signal for the exit of firms. Old plants and equipment will not be replaced as they wear out. As a result, the industry's short-run supply curve shifts leftward, and the market price rises. Firms will continue to exit, and the market price will continue to rise, until the remaining firms can cover their total costs, that is, until they are all in the zero-profit equilibrium illustrated in part (ii) of Figure 12.8. The exit of firms then ceases.

Losses in a competitive industry are a signal for the exit of firms; the industry will contract, driving the market price up until the remaining firms are covering their total costs.

The break-even price   Because firms exit when they are motivated by losses and enter when they are motivated by profits, this conclusion follows:

Figure 12.9 The effect of new entrants on the supply curve

New entrants shift the supply curve to the right and lower the equilibrium price. Initial equilibrium is at E_0 with price p_0 and output q_0. The entry of new firms shifts the supply curve to S_1, the equilibrium price falls to p_1, while output rises to q_1. At this price, before entry only q_2 would have been produced. The extra output is supplied by the new firms.

The long-run equilibrium of a competitive industry occurs when firms are earning zero profits.

The firm in part (ii) of Figure 12.8 is in a zero-profit, long-run equilibrium. For that firm, the price p_0 is sometimes called the **break-even price**. It is the price at which all costs, including the opportunity cost of capital, are being covered. The firm is just willing to stay in the industry. It has no incentive to leave, nor do other firms have an incentive to enter.

In the preceding analysis, we see profits serving the function of providing signals that guide the allocation of scarce resources among the economy's industries. It is also worth noting that freedom of entry will tend to push profits towards zero in any industry, whether or not it is perfectly competitive.

Marginal and intra-marginal firms When considering possible exit from an industry, it is sometimes useful to distinguish marginal from intra-marginal firms. The marginal firm is just covering its full costs and would exit if price fell by even a small amount. The intra-marginal firm is earning profits and would require a larger fall in price to persuade it to exit. In the pure abstract model of perfect competition, however, all firms are marginal firms in long-run equilibrium. All firms have access to the same technology, and all, therefore, will have identical cost curves when enough time has passed for full adjustment of all capital to be made.[6] In long-run industry equilibrium, all firms are thus in position (ii) in Figure 12.6. If price falls below £2 in that figure, all firms wish to withdraw. Exit must then be by some contrived process, such as random lot, since there is nothing in the theory to explain who will exit first.

In real-world situations, firms are not identical, since technology changes continually and different firms have different histories. A firm that has recently replaced its capital is likely to have more efficient, lower-cost plant and hence lower cost curves than a firm whose capital is ageing. The details of each practical case will then determine the identity of the marginal firm that will exit first when price falls. For one example, assume that all firms have identical costs and differ only in the date at which they entered the industry. In this case, the firm whose capital comes up for replacement first will be the marginal firm. It will exit first because it will be the first to confront the long-run decision about replacing its capital in a situation where no firms are covering long-run opportunity costs.

Two applications

To illustrate the value of long-run analysis, we use it to shed light on two situations: an industry in which technical change is lowering costs, and an industry in which falling demand is causing a long-term decline.

CHANGES IN TECHNOLOGY

As an illustration of the use of long-run analysis, consider the effects of technological progress on a competitive industry. Initially, the industry is in long-run equilibrium where each firm is earning zero profits. Now assume that some technological development lowers the cost curves of newly built plants. The technology cannot be used by old plants because it must be *embodied* in new plants and equipment. Since price is just equal to the average total cost for the old plants, new plants will now be able to earn profits and they will be built immediately. But this expansion in capacity shifts the short-run supply curve to the right and drives price down. The expansion in capacity and the fall in price will continue until price is equal to the *ATC* of the *new* plants. At this price, old plants will not be covering their long-run costs. As long as price exceeds their average variable cost, however, such plants will continue in production. As the outmoded plants wear out, they will gradually disappear. Eventually a new long-run equilibrium will be established in which all plants use the new technology.

What happens in a competitive industry in which this type of technological change occurs not as a single isolated event but more or less continuously? Plants built in any one year will tend to have lower costs than plants built in any previous year. Figure 12.10 illustrates such an industry. It will exhibit a number of interesting characteristics.

One is that plants of different ages and different levels of efficiency will exist side by side. This is dramatically illustrated by the variety of types and vintages of generator found in any long-established electricity industry. Critics who observe the continued use of older, less efficient plants and urge that the industry be modernized miss the point of economic efficiency. If the plant is already there, it can be operated profitably as long as it can cover its variable costs. As long as a plant can produce goods that are valued by consumers at an amount above the value of the resources currently used up by its operation (variable costs), the value of society's total output is increased by producing these goods.

A second characteristic of such an industry is that price will be governed by the minimum *ATC* of the most efficient plants. Entry will continue until plants of the latest vintage are just expected to cover the opportunity cost of capital over their lifetimes. The benefits of the new technology are passed on to consumers because all units of the product, whether produced by new or old plants, are sold at a price that is related solely to the *ATC*s of the new plants. Owners of older plants find their returns over variable costs falling

---

[6] If one firm has some special advantage, such as a patented production process or an unusually good manager, the principle of imputed opportunity cost requires that the extra revenues attributable to such advantages be included as a cost—since the patent or manager could be leased to other firms. This emphasizes once again that all firms have the same costs in long-run perfectly competitive equilibrium.

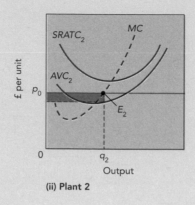

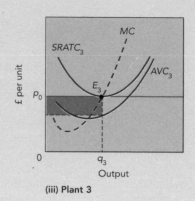

Figure 12.10 Plants of different ages in an industry with continual technical progress

Entry of progressively lower-cost firms forces price down, but older plants with higher costs remain in the industry as long as price covers average variable cost. Plant 3 is the newest plant with the lowest costs. Long-run equilibrium price will be determined by the average total costs of plants of this type, since entry will continue as long as the owners of the newest plants expect to earn profits from them. Plant 1 is the oldest plant in operation; it is just covering its AVC, and if the price falls any further it will be closed down. Plant 2 is a plant of intermediate age; it is covering its variable costs and earning some contribution towards its fixed costs. In (ii) and (iii), the dark blue areas show the excess of revenues over variable costs.

steadily as increasingly efficient plants drive the price down.

A third characteristic is that old plants will be discarded when the price falls below their AVC. This may occur well before the plants are physically worn out. In industries with continuous technical progress, capital is usually discarded because it is economically obsolete, not because it has physically worn out. This illustrates the economic meaning of obsolete:

Old capital is obsolete when its average variable cost exceeds the average total cost of new capital.

DECLINING INDUSTRIES

What happens when a competitive industry in long-run equilibrium begins to suffer losses owing to a permanent and continuing decrease in the demand for its products? As market demand declines, market price falls, and firms that were previously covering average total costs are no longer able to do so. They find themselves in the position shown in part (i) of Figure 12.8. Firms suffer losses instead of breaking even; the signal for the exit of capital is given, but exit takes time.

The response of firms The economically efficient response to a steadily declining demand is to continue to operate with existing equipment as long as its variable costs of production can be covered. As equipment becomes obsolete

because it cannot cover even its variable cost, it will not be replaced unless the new equipment can cover its total cost. As a result, the capacity of the industry will shrink. If demand keeps declining, capacity must keep shrinking.

Declining industries typically present a sorry sight to the observer. Revenues are below long-run total costs, and as a result, new equipment is not brought in to replace old equipment as it wears out. The average age of equipment in use thus rises steadily. The untrained observer, seeing the industry's plight, is likely to blame it on the old equipment.

The antiquated equipment in a declining industry is often the effect rather than the cause of the industry's decline.

Box 12.2 covers an interesting illustration of the above point that had profound effects on British economic policy some fifty years ago.

The response of governments Governments are often tempted to support declining industries because they are worried about the resulting job losses. Experience suggests, however, that propping up genuinely declining industries only delays their demise—at significant national cost. When the government finally withdraws its support, the decline is usually more abrupt and hence more difficult to adjust to than it would have been had the industry been allowed to decline gradually under the market force of steadily declining demand.

Once governments recognize the decay of certain indus-

BOX 12.2

The economics of declining industries

The view that public control was needed to save an industry from the dead hand of third-rate, unenterprising private owners was very commonly held about the British coal industry in the period between the First and Second World Wars. It was undoubtedly a factor leading to the nationalization of coal in 1946.

The late Sir Roy Harrod argued, however, that the run-down state of the industry in South Wales and Yorkshire, and the advanced state of the pits in Nottinghamshire and Derbyshire, represented the correct response of the owners to the signals of the market. He wrote:

'The mines of Derbyshire and Nottinghamshire were rich, and it was worth sinking capital in them. If similar amounts of capital were not sunk in other parts of the country, this may not have been because the managements were inefficient, but simply because it was known that they were not worth these expenditures. Economic efficiency does not consist in always introducing the most up-to-date equipment that an engineer can think of but rather in the correct adaptation of the amount of new capital sunk to the earning capacity of the old asset. In not introducing new equipment, the managements may have been wise, not only from the point of view of their own interest, but from that of national interest, which requires the most profitable application of available capital . . . it is right that as much should be extracted from the inferior mines as can be done by old-fashioned methods (i.e. with equipment already installed), and that they should gradually go out of action.'*

Declining industries always present a sorry sight to the observer. Because revenues have fallen below long-run costs, new equipment is not installed to replace old equipment as it wears out. The average age of equipment in use thus rises steadily. A declining industry will *always* display an old age-structure of capital, and thus 'antiquated' methods. The superficial observer, seeing the industry's very real plight, is likely to blame the antiquated equipment, which is actually the effect, not the cause, of the industry's decline.

To modernize at high capital costs merely makes the plight worse, since output and costs will rise in the face of declining demand and prices. To nationalize a declining industry, as was done with coal, in order to install new plant and equipment which privately owned firms were unwilling to install (at least in some areas) was to use the nation's scarce resources inefficiently. Capital resources are scarce: if investment occurs in mines, there is less for engineering, schools, roads, computer research, and a host of other things. To re-equip a declining industry that cannot cover its capital costs is to use scarce resources where, by the criterion of the market, their product is much less valuable than it would be in other industries. The efficient response to a steadily declining demand is not to replace old equipment, but to continue to operate existing equipment as long as it can cover its variable costs of production.

* Roy Harrod, *The British Economy* (New York: McGraw-Hill, 1963), p. 54.

---

tries and the collapse of certain firms as an inevitable aspect of economic growth, a more effective response is to provide welfare and retraining schemes that cushion the impacts of change. These can moderate the effects on the incomes of workers who lose their jobs and make it easier for them to transfer to expanding industries. Intervention that is intended to increase mobility while reducing the social and personal costs of mobility is a viable long-run policy; trying to freeze the existing industrial structure by shoring up an inevitably declining industry is not.

A more detailed analysis of the long run

For some purposes it is important to understand some complications omitted from the foregoing broad treatment. The rest of this chapter will be devoted to a more detailed examination of the long-run behaviour of a perfectly competitive industry. It can, however, be omitted without loss of continuity.

Consider the position of the firms and the industry when both are in long-run equilibrium. There is no change that any firm could make, over the short or the long run, that would increase its profits. This requirement can be stated as three distinct conditions.

1. *No firm will want to vary the output of its existing plants.* Short-run marginal cost ($SRMC$) must equal price.

2. *Profits earned by existing plants must be zero.* This implies that short-run ATC must equal price—that is, firms must be in the position of the firm in Figure 12.8(ii).

3. *No firm can earn profits by building a plant of a different size.* This implies that each existing firm must be producing at the lowest point on its long-run average cost curve.

We have already seen why the first two conditions must hold. The reasoning behind the third condition is shown in Figure 12.11. Although the firm with average cost curve $SRATC$ is in short-run equilibrium, it is not in long-run equilibrium because its $LRAC$ curve lies below the market

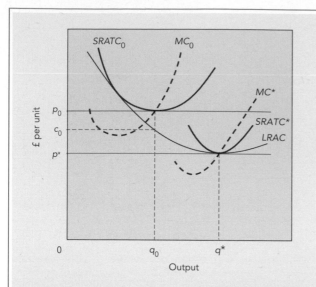

Figure 12.11 Short-run and long-run equilibrium of a firm in perfect competition

A perfectly competitive firm that is not at the minimum point on its _LRAC_ curve cannot be in long-run equilibrium. Let the firm have short-run cost curves $SRATC_0$ and MC_0 and let it face a market price of p_0. The firm produces q_0 where MC_0 equals price and total costs are just being covered. Since the firm's long-run curve lies below its short-run curve at output q_0, it could produce output q_0 at cost c_0 by building a larger plant which could take advantage of scale economies. Profits would rise because average total costs of c_0 are less than price p_0. Thus, the firm cannot be in long-run equilibrium at any output below q^*, because with any such output average total costs can be reduced by building a larger plant. If all firms do this, industry output will increase and price will fall until long-run equilibrium is reached at price p^*.

In long-run industry equilibrium, each firm is at the minimum point on its short- and long-run cost curves. The market price is p^* and each firm is in short-run equilibrium with a plant whose average cost curve is $SRATC^*$ and whose short-run marginal cost curve, MC^*, intersects the price line p^* at an output of q^*. Because the _LRAC_ lies above p everywhere except at q^*, the firm has no incentive to move to another point on its _LRAC_ curve by altering the size of its plant. The output q^* is the _minimum efficient scale_ of the firm.

All three of the conditions listed above are fulfilled when each firm in the industry is in the position shown in Figure 12.11 by the short-run cost curve $SRATC$.[8]

LONG-RUN RESPONSE TO A CHANGE IN DEMAND

Now suppose that the demand for the product increases. Price will rise to equate demand with the industry's short-run supply. Each firm will expand output until its short-run marginal cost once again equals price. Each firm will earn profits as a result of the rise in price, and the profits will induce new firms to enter the industry. This will shift the short-run supply curve to the right and force down the price. Entry will continue until all firms are once again just covering average total costs.

Now consider a fall in demand. The industry starts with firms in long-run equilibrium as shown in Figure 12.11, and the market demand curve shifts left and price falls. There are two possible consequences.

First, the decline in demand forces price below _ATC_ but leaves it above _AVC_. Firms are then in the position shown in Figure 12.8(i). They can cover their variable costs and earn some return on their capital, so they remain in production for as long as their existing plant and equipment lasts. Exit will occur, however, as old capital wears out and is not replaced. As firms exit, the short-run supply curve shifts left and market price rises. This continues until the remaining firms in the industry can cover their total costs. At this point, it will pay to replace capital as it wears out, and the industry will stop declining. This adjustment may take a long time, for the industry shrinks in size only as existing plant and equipment wears out.

The second possibility is that the decline in demand is large enough to push price below the level of _AVC_. Now firms cannot even cover their variable costs, and some will shut down immediately. Reduction in capital devoted to production in the industry occurs rapidly because some existing capacity is scrapped or shifted to other uses. The decline in the number of firms reduces supply and raises the equilibrium price. Once the price rises enough to allow the remaining firms to cover their variable costs, the rapid withdrawal of capital ceases. Further exit occurs more slowly, as described in the previous paragraph.

[7] Because all costs are variable in the long run, there is no need to distinguish long-run average variable cost from long-run average total cost. They are identical, and we refer to them, as we learned to do in Chapter 11, merely as long-run average costs (_LRAC_).

[8] The text discussion implies that all existing firms and all new entrants face identical _LRAC_ curves. This means that all firms face the same set of factor prices and have the same technology available to them. Do not forget that we are in the long run, _where technological knowledge is given and constant_, and where all firms have had a chance to adjust their capital to the best that is available. This is a theoretical construction designed to analyse tendencies. In any industry in which technological change is continuous, the long run will never occur and a wide variety of different technologies will be used by different firms (as is typically observed).

price at some higher levels of output.[7] The firm can, therefore, increase its profits by building a plant of larger size, thereby lowering its average total costs. Since the firm is a price-taker, this change will increase its profits.

A price-taking firm is in long-run equilibrium only when it is producing at the minimum points on its _LRAC_ curve.

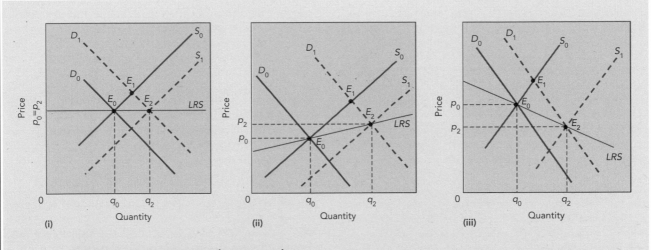

Figure 12.12 Long-run industry supply curves

The long-run industry supply curve may be horizontal, or positively or negatively sloped. In all three parts the initial curves are at D_0 and S_0, yielding equilibrium at E_0 with price p_0 and quantity q_0. A rise in demand shifts the demand curve to D_1, taking the short-run equilibrium to E_1. New firms now enter the industry, shifting the supply curve outwards and pushing price down until pure profits are no longer being earned. At this point the supply curve is S_1 and the new equilibrium is E_2 with price at p_2 and quantity q_2. In part (i) price returns to its original level, making the long-run supply curve horizontal. In part (ii) profits are eliminated before price falls to its original level, giving the *LRS* curve a positive slope. In part (iii) the price falls below its original level before profits return to normal, giving the *LRS* curve a negative slope.

Entry of new capital into a profitable industry can take place only as fast as new plants can be built and new equipment installed. Exit of existing capital from an unprofitable industry with losses will occur very quickly when price is less than average variable cost, but only at the rate at which old plant and equipment wears out when price exceeds average variable cost.

This adjustment process is examined in greater detail in the following section.

THE LONG-RUN INDUSTRY SUPPLY CURVE

Possible adjustments of the industry to the kinds of changes in demand just discussed are shown by the **long-run industry supply (*LRS*) curve.** This curve shows the relation between equilibrium price and the output that firms will be willing to supply after all desired entry or exit has occurred.

The long-run supply curve connects positions of long-run equilibrium after all demand-induced changes have occurred.

When induced changes in factor prices are considered, it

is possible for the *LRS* curve to be horizontal or to be positively or negatively sloped. The various cases are illustrated in Figure 12.12.

In Figure 12.12(i) the long-run supply curve is horizontal. This indicates that, given time, the industry will adjust its size to provide whatever quantity is demanded at a constant price equal to the lowest possible average total costs. An industry with a horizontal long-run supply curve is said to be a *constant-cost industry.*

While conditions of constant *LRS* may exist, such conditions are not necessary. This case occurs when the expansion of the industry leaves the long-run cost curves of existing firms unchanged, which requires that the industry's input prices do not change as the whole industry's output expands or contracts. Since new firms have access to the same technology and face the same factor prices, their cost curves will not be higher than those of existing firms. Under these circumstances, the long-run equilibrium with price equal to minimum long-run average total cost can be re-established only when price returns to its original level.

Changing factor prices and rising long-run supply curves
When an industry expands its output, it needs more inputs.

The increase in demand for these inputs may bid up their prices.[9]

If costs rise with increasing levels of industry output, so too must the price at which the producers are able to cover their costs. As the industry expands, the short-run supply curve shifts outwards but the firms' $SRATC$ curves shift upwards because of rising factor prices. The expansion of the industry comes to a halt when price is equal to minimum $LRAC$ for existing firms. This must occur at a higher price than ruled before the expansion began, as illustrated in part (ii) of Figure 12.12. A competitive industry with rising long-run supply prices is often called a *rising-cost industry*.

Can the long-run supply curve decline?   So far we have suggested that the long-run supply curve may be horizontal or positively sloped. Could it ever decline, thereby indicating that higher outputs are associated with lower prices in long-run equilibrium?

It is tempting to answer yes, because of the opportunities of more efficient scales of operation using greater mechanization and more effective specialization of labour. But this answer would not be correct for perfectly competitive industries, because each firm in long-run equilibrium must already be at the lowest point on its $LRAC$ curve. If a firm could lower its costs by building a larger, more mechanized plant, it would be profitable to do so without waiting for an increase in demand. Since any single firm can sell all it wishes at the going market price, it will be profitable to expand the scale of its operations as long as its $LRAC$ is falling.

The scale economies that we have just considered are within the control of the firm; they are said to be **internal economies**. A perfectly competitive industry might, however, have falling long-run costs if industries that supply its inputs have increasing returns to scale. Such effects are outside the control of the perfectly competitive firm and are called **external economies**. Whenever expansion of an industry leads to a fall in the prices of some of its inputs, the firms will find their cost curves shifting downwards as they expand their outputs.

As an illustration of how the expansion of one industry could cause the prices of some of its inputs to fall, consider the early stages of the growth of the car industry. As the output of cars increased, the industry's demand for tyres grew greatly. This, as suggested earlier, increased the demand for rubber and tended to raise its price, but it also provided the opportunity for tyre manufacturers to build larger plants which exploited some of the economies available in tyre production. These economies were large enough to offset any factor-price increases, and tyre prices charged to car manufacturers fell. Thus, car costs fell, because of lower prices of an important input. This case is illustrated in part (iii) of Figure 12.12. An industry that has a negatively sloped long-run supply curve is often called a *falling-cost industry*.

Notice that, although the economies were external to the car industry, they were internal to the tyre industry. This in turn requires that the supplying industry not be perfectly competitive. If it were, all its scale economies would already have been exploited. So this case refers to a perfectly competitive industry that uses an input produced by a non-competitive industry, whose own scale economies have not yet been fully exploited because demand is insufficient. An example is provided by perfectly competitive agricultural industries buying their farm machinery from the farm implement industry, which is dominated by a few large firms.

Is perfect competition compatible with long-run equilibrium?[10]

The key to answering the question posed in this heading lies in the size of the firm relative to the size of the market.

A competitive firm will never be in equilibrium on the falling part of its $LRAC$—if price is given and costs can be reduced by increasing the scale of output, profits can also be increased by doing so. Thus, firms will grow in size until all scale economies are exhausted. Provided that the output that yields the minimum $LRAC$ for each firm is small relative to the industry's total output, the industry will contain a large number of firms and will remain competitive. If, however, reaching the minimum $LRAC$ makes firms so large that each one has significant market power, they will cease to be price-takers and perfect competition will also cease to exist. Indeed, if scale economies exist over such a large range that one firm's $LRAC$ would still be falling if it served the entire market, a single firm may come to monopolize the market. This is what economists call the case of a *natural* monopoly; it is considered further in later chapters.

A necessary condition for a long-run perfectly competitive equilibrium is that any scale economies that are within the firm's control should be exhausted at a level of output that is small relative to the whole industry's output.

Is the size of the firm determinate?

Only if the firm's $LRAC$ curve is U-shaped will there be a

---

[9] In a fully employed economy, the expansion of one industry implies the contraction of some other industry. What happens to factor prices depends on the proportions in which the expanding and the contracting industries use the factors. The relative price of the factor used intensively by the expanding industry will rise, causing the costs of the expanding industry to rise relative to those of the contracting industry. In a two-sector, two-factor model, a rising long-run industry supply curve is normal because of the effect that changes in industry outputs have on relative factor prices.

[10] This section deals with a topic that is often postponed until more advanced courses; it may be skipped without loss of continuity.

determinate size of the firm in a competitive industry. To see why, assume instead that *LRAC* falls to a minimum at some level of output and then remains constant for all larger outputs. All firms will have to be at least the minimum size, but they can be just that size or much larger, since price will equal *LRAC* for any output above the minimum efficient size. In other words, there will then be no unique size for the firm.

There are very good reasons why the *LRAC* curve for a single plant may be U-shaped. Modern technology often results in lower average costs for large, automated factories compared with smaller factories in which a few workers use relatively unsophisticated capital equipment. As a single plant becomes too large, however, costs rise because of the sheer difficulty of planning for, and controlling the behaviour of, a vast integrated operation. Thus, we have no problem accounting for a U-shaped cost curve for the *plant*.

What of the U-shaped cost curve for the *firm*? A declining portion will occur for the same reason that the *LRAC* for one plant declines when the firm is so small that it operates only one plant. Now, however, let the firm be operating one plant at the output where its *LRAC* is a minimum. (Call that output q^*.) What if the firm decides to double its output to $2q^*$? If it tries to build a vast plant with twice the output of the optimal-size plant, the firm's average total cost of production may rise (because the vast plant has higher costs than a plant of the optimal size). But the firm has the option of *replicating* its first plant in a physically separate location. If the firm obtains a second parcel of land, builds an identical second plant, staffs it identically, and allows its production to be managed independently, there seems no reason why the second plant's minimum *LRAC* should be different from that of the first plant. *Because the firm can replicate plants and have them managed independently, there seems no reason why any firm, faced with constant factor prices, should have a rising LRAC, at least for integer multiples*[11] *of the output produced by the optimal-sized plant.*

In the modern theory of perfect competition, a U-shaped cost curve for a *firm* is merely assumed. Without it—although a competitive equilibrium may exist for an arbitrary number of firms—there is nothing to determine the equilibrium size of the firm and hence the number of firms in the industry. If all firms have constant *LRAC*s, then equilibrium requires that price equals *LRAC*, but the equilibrium output can just as well be produced by a large number of firms each producing a small output or a small number of firms each producing a large output.

[11] This means multiplying the output of the optimal-sized plant by any whole number, i.e. building and fully utilizing that number of complete new plants. It rules out multiplying it by some fractional number such as 7/2, which would mean either building one plant smaller than the optimal size or only partially utilizing one optimal-sized plant.

Summary

1 Competitive *behaviour* refers to the extent that individual firms compete with each other to sell their products. Competitive *market structure* refers to the power that individual firms have over the market—perfect competition occurring where firms have no market power and hence no need to react to each other.

2 Perfect competition requires price-taking behaviour and freedom of entry and exit.

3 Any firm maximizes profits by producing the output where the marginal cost curve cuts the marginal revenue from below or by producing nothing if average variable cost exceeds price at all outputs.

4 A perfectly competitive firm is a quantity adjustor, facing a perfectly elastic demand curve at the given market price and maximizing profits by equating its marginal cost to that price.

5 The supply curve of a firm in perfect competition is its marginal cost curve, and the supply curve of a perfectly competitive industry is the sum of the marginal cost curves of all its firms. The intersection of this curve with the market demand curve for the industry's product determines market price.

6 Long-run industry equilibrium requires that each individual firm be producing at the minimum point of its *LRAC* curve and be making zero profits.

7 The long-run industry supply curve for a perfectly competitive industry may be (i) positively sloped, if input prices are driven up by the industry's expansion, (ii) horizontal, if plants can be replicated and factor prices remain constant, or (iii) negatively sloped, if some other industry that is not perfectly competitive produces an input under conditions of falling long-run costs.

Topics for review

- Competitive behaviour and competitive market structure
- Behavioural rules for the profit-maximizing firm
- Price-taking and a horizontal demand curve

- Average revenue, marginal revenue, and price under perfect competition
- Relation of the industry supply curve to its firms' marginal cost curves
- The role of entry and exit in achieving equilibrium
- Short-run and long-run equilibrium of firms and industries

APPENDIX TO CHAPTER 12

A mathematical derivation of the rules of profit maximization

I N this brief appendix we provide formal derivations of the three rules for profit maximization. The first derivation uses only algebra and can be read by anyone. The second and third use elementary calculus and should not be attempted by those who are unfamiliar with simple derivatives.

Condition 1   Profits, π, are defined as follows:

$$\pi = R - (F + V),$$

where R is total revenue, F is total fixed cost, and V is total variable cost. Now let subscript n stand for a state where there is no production and p for one where there is production. It pays the firm to produce if there is at least one level of production for which

$$\pi_p \geq \pi_n.$$

When the firm does not produce, R and V are zero, so the above condition becomes

$$R - F - V \geq -F$$

or

$$R \geq V.$$

Dividing both sides by output, q, we get:

$$\text{price} \geq AVC.$$

Condition 2

$$\pi = R - C,$$

where C is total cost $(F + V)$. Both revenues and costs vary with output, i.e. $R = R(q)$ and $C = C(q)$. Thus, we may write

$$\pi = R(q) - C(q).$$

A necessary condition for the maximization of profits is[1]

$$\frac{d\pi}{dq} = R'(q) - C'(q) = 0$$

or

$$R'(q) = C'(q).$$

But these derivatives define marginal revenue and marginal cost, so we have

$$MR = MC.$$

Condition 3   To ensure that we have a maximum and not a minimum for profits, we require

$$\frac{d^2\pi}{dq^2} = R''(q) - C''(q) = \frac{dMR}{dq} - \frac{dMC}{dq} < 0$$

or

$$\frac{dMR}{dq} < \frac{dMC}{dq},$$

which means that the algebraic value of the slope of the marginal cost curve must exceed, at the point of intersection, the algebraic value of the slope of the marginal revenue curve. This translates into the geometric statement that the marginal cost curve should cut the marginal revenue curve from below.

---

[1] Note the convenient use of a prime for a derivative. Thus, for the function $F(X)$, the two notations d/dX and $F'(X)$ mean the same thing as do d^2/dX^2 and $F''(X)$.

❧ CHAPTER 13

Monopoly

IN this chapter we study the market structure called monopoly which is at the opposite extreme from perfect competition. A **monopoly** occurs when the output of an entire industry is produced and sold by a single firm, called a **monopolist** or a *monopoly firm.*

In the case of perfect competition, there are so many individual producers that no one of them has any power whatsoever over the market; any one firm can vary its production without affecting the market price significantly. In contrast, a monopoly firm has the power to set its market price. In this chapter we see that a monopoly firm will produce less, charge a higher price, and earn greater profits than do firms operating under perfect competition. We also see that monopoly profits provide a strong incentive for new firms to enter the industry and that this will happen unless there are effective barriers to entry of either a natural or a man-made variety. Finally, we find that all monopoly firms have an incentive to engage in price discrimination, which they can succeed in doing only under certain specific circumstances.

A single-price monopolist

THE first part of this chapter deals with a monopoly firm that charges a single price for its product. The firm's profits, like those of all firms, will depend on the relationship between its production costs and its sales revenues.

Cost and revenue in the short run

We saw in Chapter 11 that U-shaped short-run cost curves are a consequence of the law of diminishing returns. Because this law applies to the conditions under which goods are produced rather than to the market structure in which they are sold, monopoly firms have U-shaped short-run cost curves just as perfectly competitive firms do.

Because a monopoly firm is the sole producer of the product that it sells, its demand curve is identical with the market demand curve for that product. The market demand curve, which shows the total quantity that buyers will purchase at each price, also shows the quantity that the monopoly firm will be able to sell at each price. Thus, the monopoly firm, unlike the perfectly competitive firm, faces a negatively sloped demand curve. This means that it faces a trade-off between the price it charges and the quantity it sells. Sales can be increased only if price is reduced, and price can be increased only if sales are reduced.

AVERAGE AND MARGINAL REVENUE

Starting with the market demand curve, the monopoly firm's average and marginal revenue curves can be readily derived. When the monopoly firm charges the same price for all units sold, average revenue per unit is identical with price. Thus, the market demand curve is also the firm's *average revenue curve.*

Now consider the monopoly firm's *marginal revenue* resulting from the sale of an additional (or marginal) unit of production. Because its demand curve is negatively sloped, the monopoly firm must lower the price that it charges on *all* units in order to sell an *extra* unit.

It follows that the addition to its revenue resulting from the sale of an extra unit is less than the price that it receives for that unit (less by the amount that it loses as a result of cutting the price on all the units that it was selling already).

The monopoly firm's marginal revenue is less than the price at which it sells its output.

This proposition is illustrated in Figure 13.1.

To clarify these relations, we consider a numerical example of a specific, straight-line demand curve. Some points on this curve are shown in tabular form in Table 13.1 while the whole curve is shown in Figure 13.2. Notice in the table that the change in total revenue associated with a change of £1 in price, and the change in total revenue associated with a change of one unit of output, are both recorded between the rows that refer to specific prices. This is done because the data refer to what happens when the price is changed from the value shown in one row to the value shown in the adjacent row.

Notice also that, when price is reduced starting from £10, total revenue rises at first and then falls. The maximum total revenue is reached in this example at a price of £5. Because marginal revenue gives the change in total revenue resulting from the sale of one more unit of output, marginal revenue is positive whenever total revenue is increased by selling more, but it is negative whenever total revenue is reduced by selling more.[1]

The proposition that marginal revenue is always *less than*

---

[1] Notice that the marginal revenue shown in the table is obtained by subtracting the total revenue associated with one price from the total revenue associated with another, lower, price and then apportioning the change in revenue among the extra units sold. In symbols, it is $\Delta TR / \Delta q$.

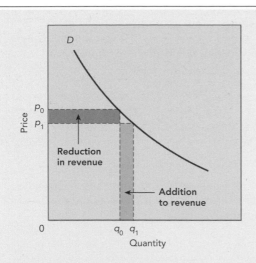

Figure 13.1 The effect on revenue of an increase in quantity sold

Because the demand curve has a negative slope, marginal revenue is less than price. A reduction of price from p_0 to p_1 increases sales by one unit from q_0 to q_1 units. The revenue from the extra unit sold is shown as the medium blue area. But to sell this unit, it is necessary to reduce the price on each of the q_0 units previously sold. The loss in revenue is shown as the dark blue area. Marginal revenue of the extra unit is equal to the *difference* between the two areas.

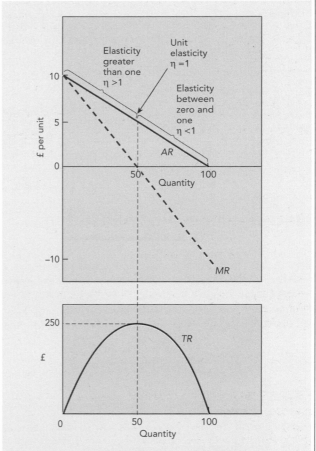

Figure 13.2 Total, average, and marginal revenue curves and the elasticity of demand

When *TR* is rising, *MR* is positive and demand is elastic. When *TR* is falling, *MR* is negative and demand is inelastic. In this example, for outputs from 0 to 50 marginal revenue is positive, elasticity is greater than unity, and total revenue is rising. For outputs from 50 to 100 marginal revenue is negative, elasticity is less than unity, and total revenue is falling.

Table 13.1 Total, average, and marginal revenue illustrated

Price $p = AR$	Quantity q	Total revenue $TR = p \cdot q$	Marginal revenue $MR = \Delta TR/\Delta q$
£9.10	9	£81.90	
£9.00	10	£90.00	£8.10
£8.90	11	£97.90	£7.90

Marginal revenue is less than price because price must be lowered to sell an extra unit. Consider, for example, the marginal revenue of the eleventh unit. This is total revenue when 11 units are sold minus total revenue when 10 units are sold. The result is £7.90, which is less than the price of £8.90 at which all 11 units are sold. To see why, notice that, to increase sales from 10 to 11 units, the price on all units sold must be reduced from £9.00 to £8.90. The net addition to revenue is the £8.90 gained from selling the extra unit minus £0.10 lost on each of the 10 units already being sold: £8.90 − (£0.10 × 10) = £7.90.

Marginal revenue is shown displaced by half a line to emphasize that it represents the effect on revenue of the *change* in sales.

average revenue, which has been illustrated numerically in Table 13.1 and graphically in Figure 13.2, provides an important contrast with perfect competition. You will recall that in perfect competition the firm's marginal revenue from selling an extra unit of output is *equal to* the price at which that unit is sold. The reason for the difference is not difficult to understand. The perfectly competitive firm is a price-taker; it can sell all it wants at the given market price. The monopoly firm faces a negatively sloped demand curve; it must reduce the market price in order to increase its sales.

MARGINAL REVENUE AND ELASTICITY

In Chapter 5 we discussed the relationship between the elasticity of the market demand curve and the total revenue derived from selling the product. Figure 13.2 summarizes this earlier discussion and extends it to cover marginal revenue.[2]

Over the range in which the demand curve is elastic, total revenue rises as more units are sold; marginal revenue must therefore be positive. Over the range in which the demand curve is inelastic, total revenue falls as more units are sold; marginal revenue must therefore be negative.

Short-run monopoly equilibrium

To show the profit-maximizing equilibrium of a monopoly firm, we bring together information about its revenues and its costs and then apply the two rules developed in Chapter 12. Recall that these two rules are: (1) the firm should not produce at all unless there is some level of output for which price is at least equal to average variable cost; and (2) if the

firm does produce, its output should be set at the point where marginal cost equals marginal revenue.

When the monopoly firm equates marginal cost with marginal revenue, it reaches the equilibrium shown in Figure 13.3. The output is found as the quantity for which marginal cost equals marginal revenue. The price is read off the demand curve, which shows the price corresponding to that output.

Notice that, because marginal revenue is always less than price for the monopoly firm, when it equates marginal revenue to marginal cost, both are less than price.

When a monopoly firm is in profit-maximizing equilibrium, its marginal cost is always less than the price it charges for its output.

Competition and monopoly compared   The comparison with firms in perfect competition is important. In perfect competition, firms face perfectly elastic curves, so that price and marginal revenue are the same. Thus, when they equate marginal cost to marginal revenue, they ensure that marginal cost also equals price. In contrast, a monopoly firm faces a negatively sloped demand curve for which marginal revenue is less than price. Thus, when it equates marginal cost to marginal revenue, it ensures that marginal cost will be less than price.

The relationship between elasticity and revenue discussed above has an interesting implication for the monopoly firm's equilibrium. Because marginal cost is always greater than zero, a profit-maximizing monopoly (which produces where $MR = MC$) will always produce where marginal revenue is positive, that is, where demand is elastic. If the firm were producing where demand was inelastic, it could reduce its output, thereby increasing its total revenue and reducing its total costs. No such restriction applies to firms in perfect competition. Each reacts to its own perfectly elastic demand curve, not to the market demand curve. Thus, the equilibrium can occur where the market demand curve is either elastic or inelastic.

A profit-maximizing monopoly will never sell in the range where the demand curve is inelastic.

Monopoly profits   The fact that a monopoly firm produces the output that maximizes its profits tells us nothing about how large these profits will be or even whether there will be any profits at all. Figure 13.4 illustrates this by showing

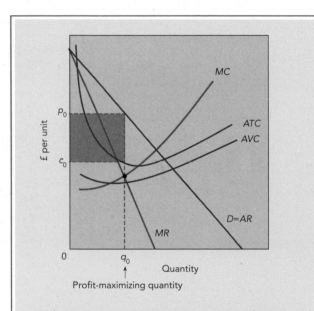

Figure 13.3 The equilibrium of a monopoly

The monopoly maximizes its profits by producing where marginal cost equals marginal revenue. The monopoly produces the output q_0 for which marginal revenue equals marginal cost (rule 2). At this output, the price of p_0—which is determined by the demand curve—exceeds the average variable cost (rule 1). Profits per unit are the difference between the average revenue of p_0 and the average total cost of c_0. Total profits are the profits per unit of $p_0 - c_0$ multiplied by the output of q_0, which is the dark blue area.

---

[2] It is helpful when you are drawing these curves to remember that, if the demand curve is a negatively sloped straight line, the MR curve is also negatively sloped and exactly twice as steep. Its price intercept (where $q = 0$) is the same as that of the demand curve, and its quantity intercept (where $p = 0$) is one-half of that of the demand curve. This is easily established for those who know calculus. A linear demand curve is $p = a - bq$. Total revenue (TR) is $pq = aq - bq^2$. Marginal revenue is $\mathrm{d}TR/\mathrm{d}q = a - 2bq$, which is a straight line of twice the slope of the demand curve.

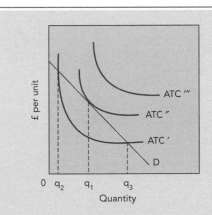

Figure 13.4 Alternative profit possibilities for a monopolist

Profit maximization means that the monopoly is doing as well as it can do, given the cost and demand curves that it faces; it does not mean that profits are being earned. The monopolist faces a demand curve of D. Three alternative cost curves are considered. With the curve ATC''', there is no positive output at which the monopolist can avoid making losses. With the curve ATC'', the monopolist covers all costs at output q_1, where the ATC curve is tangent to the D curve. With the curve ATC', profits can be made by producing at any output between q_2 qnd q_3. (The profit-maximizing output will be some point between q_2 and q_3, where $MR=MC$, which is not shown on the diagram.)

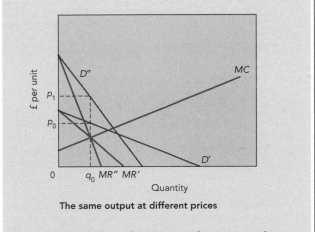

The same output at different prices

Figure 13.5 No supply curve under monopoly

When a firm faces a negatively sloped demand curve, there is no unique relation between the price that it charges and the quantity that it sells. The demand curves D' and D'' both have marginal revenue curves that intersect the marginal cost curve at output q_0. But because the demand curves are different, q_0 is sold at p_0 when the demand curve is D', and at p_1 when the demand curve is D''.

three alternative average total cost curves: one where the monopolist can earn pure profits, one where it can just cover its costs, and one where it makes losses at any level of output.

No supply curve for a monopoly In describing the monopolist's profit-maximizing behaviour, we did not introduce the concept of a supply curve, as we did in the discussion of perfect competition. In perfect competition the industry short-run supply curve depends only on the marginal cost curves of the individual firms. This is true because, under perfect competition, profit-maximizing firms equate marginal cost with price. Given marginal costs, it is possible to know how much will be produced at each price. This is not the case, however, with a monopoly.

As with all profit-maximizing firms, the monopolist equates marginal cost to marginal revenue; but marginal revenue does not equal price. Hence the monopoly does *not* equate marginal cost to price. In order to know the amount produced at any given price, we need to know the demand curve as well as the marginal cost curve. Under these circumstances, it is possible for different demand conditions to cause the same output to be sold at different prices. This is illustrated in Figure 13.5 by an example in which two monopolists facing the same marginal cost curves but different demand curves sell identical outputs at different prices.

For a monopoly firm, there is no unique relationship between market price and quantity supplied.

Box 13.1 deals with an interesting variation of monopoly theory, the pricing of limited editions.

Firm and industry Because the monopolist is the only producer in an industry, there is no need for separate theories about the firm and the industry, as is necessary with perfect competition. The monopoly firm *is* the industry. Thus, the short-run, profit-maximizing position of the firm, as shown in Figure 13.3, is also the short-run equilibrium of the industry.

A multi-plant monopoly

So far we have implicity assumed that the monopoly firm produces all of its output in a single plant. Fortunately, the analysis easily extends to multi-plant monopolists. Assume, for example, that the firm has two plants. How will it allocate production between them? The answer is that any given output will be allocated between the two plants so as to equate their marginal costs. Assume for example that plant A was producing 30 units per week at a marginal cost of £20, while plant B was producing 25 units at a marginal

BOX 13.1

Demand for once-off production

An interesting case of monopoly pricing occurs with 'limited editions'. These are works of art—sometimes lithographs, etchings, and woodcuts by famous artists and sometimes products with less artistic merit, as in the following examples.

Not long ago one had only to pick up a London telephone directory to see the words 'Limited Edition Print Offer: See inside back cover' in the bottom right-hand corner of a coloured sketch (portraying Buckingham Palace, the Tower of London, St Paul's Cathedral, or the Houses of Parliament) which decorated the front cover of each of the four volumes of the directory. Information on the inside cover revealed that the four water-colours were 'specially commissioned' and will be reproduced 'in a limited edition of 500 prints' to be sold at £25 each or £85 for the set of four. 'Only 500 prints will be made of each image following which the plates will be destroyed.' This suggested that British Telecom felt that limiting the quantity supplied to 500 was necessary to make £25 a reasonable price, in the sense that the quantity demanded at £25 would be around 500, and that making the prints more plentiful would require a significantly lower price in order to 'clear the market'. Of course, the estimates of market demand are slightly complicated by the possibility of buying individual prints *or* a set of four prints, but the same principle applies.

Similar examples can be seen in the booklets sent to credit-card users with their monthly statements. A Wedgwood 'collector's plate produced on fine bone china' and depicting 'Meadows of Wheatfields' was offered in March 1987 (with a statement 'Offer closes 15th May 1987') to holders of Midland Bank's Access card, with the promise that production would be 'limited to 150 firing days' and that a numbered certificate would accompany the plate. In fact, the sellers must have over-estimated the quantity that would be demanded at their price of £16.65 (including postage and packing), as the offer was repeated in October 1987 ('Offer closes 7th December 1987').

Analysing this case helps to illustrate the flexibility of theory when used imaginatively. The normal demand curve is for a repeated flow of purchases, period after period. In this case, the demand is for a stock to be produced and purchased once only. Presumably, however, the smaller the total number of items produced, the more people will value each item and the higher the price that can be charged. This gives rise to a negatively sloped demand curve.

If producers know the curve exactly and know their marginal cost of production, choosing the profit-maximizing price–quantity combination is simple. They equate marginal cost with marginal revenue. But since production and sales are not repeated period after period, producers have no chance to learn the shape of the demand curve. They must guess on the basis of the sales of earlier, more or less similar, limited editions.

What if they guess wrong? If they set the price too low, they will sell all their output but not at its profit-maximizing price. If they set the price too high, they will be left with unsold output which they must destroy or readvertise at some considerable expense. Solution to the problem of choosing the best price then becomes a more complex problem in the economics of uncertainty which would take us much further along the road of the analysis of uncertainty than we went in Chapter 9.

cost of £17. Plant A's production could be reduced by one unit, saving £20 in cost, while plant B's production was increased by one unit, adding £17 to cost. Overall output is held constant while costs are reduced by £3. The generalization is that, whenever two plants are producing at different marginal costs, the total cost of producing their combined output can be reduced by reallocating production from the plant with the higher marginal cost to the plant with the lower marginal cost.

A multi-plant, profit-maximizing monopolist will always operate its plants so that their marginal costs are equal.

How does the multi-plant monopolist determine its overall marginal cost? Assume, for example, that both plants are operating at a marginal cost of £10 per unit and one is producing 14 units per week while the other is producing 16. The firm's overall output is 30 units at a marginal cost of £10. This illustrates the following general proposition:

The monopoly firm's marginal cost curve is the horizontal sum of the marginal cost curves of its individual plants.

For each marginal cost, this sum tells us the total output of all the firm's plants *when* each is operating at that marginal cost.

It follows that the analysis in the chapter applies to any monopolist, no matter how many plants it operates. The marginal cost curve we have used is merely the sum of the marginal cost curves of all the plants. In the special case in which there is only one plant, the *firm's MC* curve is that *plant's MC* curve.

Long-run monopoly equilibrium

In both monopolized and perfectly competitive industries, losses and profits provide incentives for exit and entry.

If the monopoly firm is suffering losses in the short run, it will continue to operate as long as it can cover its variable costs. In the long run, however, it will leave the industry unless it can find a scale of operations at which its full opportunity costs can be covered.

If the monopoly firm is making profits, other firms will wish to enter the industry in order to earn more than the opportunity cost of their capital. If such entry occurs, the equilibrium position shown in Figure 13.3 will change, and the firm will cease to be a monopolist.

Entry barriers

Impediments that prevent entry are called **entry barriers;** they may be either natural or created.

If a monopoly firm's profits are to persist in the long run, the entry of new firms into the industry must be prevented by effective entry barriers.

BARRIERS DETERMINED BY TECHNOLOGY

Natural barriers most commonly arise as a result of economies of scale. When the long-run average cost curve is negatively sloped over a large range of output, big firms have significantly lower average total costs than small firms.

You will recall from Chapter 12 that perfectly competitive firms cannot be in long-run equilibrium on the negatively sloped segment of their long-run average cost curve (see Figure 12.11 on p. 230).

Now suppose that the technology of an industry is such that any firm's minimum achievable average cost is £10 which is reached at an output of £10,000 units per week. Further, assume that at a price of £10 the total quantity demanded is 11,000 units per week. Under these circumstances, only one firm can operate at or near its minimum costs.

A **natural monopoly** occurs when, given the industry's current technology, the demand conditions allow no more than one firm to cover its costs while producing at the minimum point of its long-run cost curve. In a natural monopoly, there is no price at which two firms can both sell enough to cover their total costs.

Another type of technologically determined barrier is *set-up cost*. If a firm could be catapulted fully grown into the market, it might be able to compete effectively with the existing monopolist. However, the cost to the new firm of entering the market, developing its products, and establishing such things as its brand image and its dealer network may be so large that entry would be unprofitable.

POLICY-CREATED BARRIERS

Many entry barriers are created by conscious government action and are, therefore, officially condoned. Patent laws, for instance, may prevent entry by conferring on the patent holder the sole legal right to produce a particular product for a specific period of time.

Patent protection has led to a major and prolonged battle among nations fought out in international organizations that seek to enforce conditions for fair trade and investment. The major developed countries, where most of the world's research and development is done, have sought to extend patent rights to other countries. They argue that, without the temporary monopoly profits that a patent creates, the incentive to develop new products and new production processes will be weakened. The less developed countries have sought to maintain weak or non-existent patent laws. This allows them to produce new products under more competitive conditions and so avoid paying monopoly profits to the original patent-holders in developed countries.[3]

A firm may also be granted a charter or a franchise that prohibits competition by law. Regulation and licensing of firms, often in service industries, can restrict entry severely. For example, the 1979 Banking Act requires all banks in the United Kingdom to be authorized by the Bank of England. The 1986 Financial Services Act requires all sellers of investment products to be authorized by the Securities and Investment Board (SIB) or some other recognized regulatory body.

Other barriers can be created by the firm or firms already in the market. In extreme cases, the threat of force or sabotage can deter entry. The most obvious entry barriers of this type are encountered in the production and sale of illegal goods and services, where operation outside of the law makes available an array of illegal but potent barriers to new entrants. The drug trade is a current example. In contrast, legitimate firms must use legal tactics intended to increase a new entrant's set-up costs. Examples are the threat of price-cutting, designed to impose unsustainable losses on a new entrant, and heavy brand-name advertising. (These and other created entry barriers will be discussed in much more detail in Chapter 14.)

THE SIGNIFICANCE OF ENTRY BARRIERS

Because there are no entry barriers in perfect competition, profits cannot persist in the long run.

Profits attract entry, and entry erodes profits.

In monopoly, however, profits can persist in the long run whenever there are effective barriers to entry.

Entry barriers frustrate the adjustment mechanism that would otherwise push profits towards zero in the long run.

[3] This so-called intellectual property trade is covered by the GATT agreement on the Uruguay Round and is discussed in Chapter 25.

'CREATIVE DESTRUCTION'

In the very long run, technology changes. New ways of producing old products are invented, and new products are created to satisfy both familiar and new wants. What has this to do with entry barriers? The answer is that a monopoly that succeeds in preventing the entry of new firms capable of producing its product will sooner or later find its barriers circumvented by innovations. One firm may be able to use new processes that avoid some patent or other barrier that the monopolist relies on to bar entry of competing firms. Another firm may compete by producing a new product that, although somewhat different, still satisfies the same need as the monopoly firm's product. Yet another firm might get around a natural monopoly by inventing a technology that produces the good at a much lower cost than the existing monopoly firm's technology. The new technology may subsequently allow several firms to enter the market and still cover costs.

One distinguished economist, the late Joseph Schumpeter (1883–1950), took the view that entry barriers were not a serious problem in the very long run. He argued that monopoly profits provide one of the major incentives for people who risk their money by financing inventions and innovations. In his view, the large, short-run profits of a monopoly provide a strong incentive for others to try to usurp some of these profits for themselves. If a frontal attack on the monopolist's barriers to entry is not possible, the barriers will be circumvented by such means as the development of similar products against which the monopolist will not have entry protection.

Schumpeter called the replacing of an existing monopoly by one or more new entrants through the invention of new products or new production techniques the *process of creative destruction*. He argued that this process precludes the very long-run persistence of barriers to entry into industries that earn large profits.

He pushed this argument further and argued that, because creative destruction thrives on innovation, the existence of monopoly profits is a major incentive to economic growth. A key part of his argument can be found in the following words:

'What we have got to accept is that it [monopoly profit] has come to be the most powerful engine of progress and in particular of the long-run expansion of total output not only in spite of, but to a considerable extent through, this strategy [i.e. creating monopolies], which looks so restrictive when viewed in the individual case and from the individual point of time.

In this respect, perfect competition is not only impossible but inferior, and has no title to being set up as a model. It is hence a mistake to base the theory of government regulation of industry on the principle that big business should be made to work as the respective industry would work in perfect competition.'[4]

Schumpeter was writing at a time when the two dominant market structures studied by economists were perfect competition and monopoly. His argument easily extends, however, to any market structure that allows profits to exist in the long run. Today there are few examples of pure monopolies, but there are many industries in which profits can be earned for long periods of time. Such industries, which are called *oligopolies*, are candidates for the operation of the process of creative destruction. We study these industries in detail in Chapter 14.

Cartels as monopolies

U NTIL now a monopoly has meant that there is only one firm in an industry. A second way in which a monopoly can arise is for many firms in an industry to agree to co-operate with one another, to behave as if they were a single seller, in order to maximize joint profits, eliminating competition among themselves. Such a group of firms is called a **cartel**, or sometimes just a producers' association. A cartel that includes *all* firms in the industry can behave in the same way as a single-firm monopoly that owned all of these firms. The firms can agree among themselves to restrict their total output to the level that maximizes their joint profits.[5]

The effects of cartelization

Because perfectly competitive firms are price-takers, they

[4] Joseph Schumpeter, *Capitalism, Socialism, and Democracy*, 3rd edn. (New York: Harper & Row, 1950), p. 106.
[5] In this chapter we deal with the simple case in which *all* of the firms in a perfectly competitive industry form a cartel in order to act as if they were a monopoly. Cartels are sometimes formed by a group of firms that account for a significant part, but not all, of the total supply of some commodity. The effect is to create what is called an *oligopoly*. The most famous example of this type is the Organization of Petroleum Exporting Countries, best known as OPEC. We shall return to this type of cartel in Chapter 14.

accept the market price as given and increase their output until their marginal cost equals price. In contrast, a monopoly firm knows that increasing its output will depress the market price. Taking account of this, the monopolist increases its output only until marginal revenue is equal to marginal cost. If all the firms in a perfectly competitive industry form a cartel, they too will be able to take account of the effect of their *joint output* on price. They can agree to restrict industry output to the level that maximizes their joint profits (where the industry's marginal cost is equal to the industry's marginal revenue). The incentive for firms to form a cartel lies in the cartel's ability to restrict output, thereby creating profits.

When a perfectly competitive industry is cartelized, the firms can agree to restrict their joint output to the profit-maximizing level. One way to do this is to establish a quota for each firm's output. Say that the profit-maximizing output is two-thirds of the perfectly competitive output. When the cartel is formed, each firm could be given a quota equal to two-thirds of its competitive output.

The effect of cartelizing a perfectly competitive industry and of reducing its output through production quotas is shown in more detail in Figure 13.6.

Problems facing cartels

Cartels encounter two characteristic problems. The first is ensuring that members follow the behaviour that will maximize the industry's *joint* profits, and the second is preventing these profits from being eroded by the entry of new firms.

Enforcement of output restrictions   The managers of any cartel want the industry to produce its profit-maximizing output. Their job is made more difficult if individual firms either stay out of the cartel or enter and then cheat on their output quotas. Any one firm, however, has an incentive to do just this: to be either the one that stays out of the organization, or the one that enters and then cheats on its output quota. For the sake of simplicity, assume that all firms enter the cartel, so enforcement problems are concerned strictly with cheating by its members.

If Firm *X* is the only firm to cheat, it is in the best of all possible situations. All other firms restrict output and hold the industry price near its monopoly level. They earn profits, but only by restricting output. Firm *X* can then reap the full benefit of the other firms' output restraint and sell some additional output at the high price that has been set by the cartel's actions. However, if all of the firms cheat, the price will be pushed back to the competitive level, and all of the firms will return to their zero-profit position.

This conflict between the interests of the group and the interests of the individual firm is the cartel's dilemma. Provided that enough firms co-operate in restricting out-

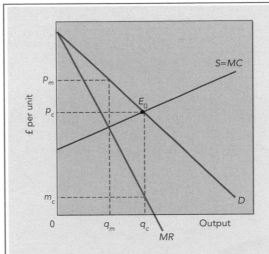

Figure 13.6 Effect of cartelizing an industry in perfectly competitive equilibrium

Cartelization of a perfectly competitive industry can always increase that industry's profits. Equilibrium for a perfectly competitive industry occurs at E_0, where the supply and the demand curves intersect. Equilibrium price and output are p_c and q_c. Because the industry demand curve is negatively sloped, the industry's marginal revenue is less than price. In the graph, marginal revenue is m_c at the competitive equilibrium output of q_c.

If the industry is cartelized, profits can be increased by reducing output. All units between q_m and q_c add less to revenue than to cost—the marginal revenue curve lies below the marginal cost curve. (Recall from Figure 12.7 that the industry's supply curve is the sum of the supply curves, and hence of the marginal cost curves, of each of the firms in the industry.) If the units between q_m and q_c are not produced, output is reduced to q_m and price rises to p_m. This price–output combination maximizes the industry's profits because it is where industry marginal revenue equals industry marginal cost.

put, all firms are better off than they would be if the industry remained perfectly competitive. Any one firm, however, is even better off if it remains outside, or enters and cheats. However, if all firms act on this incentive, all will be worse off than if they had joined the cartel and restricted output.

Cartels tend to be unstable because of the incentives for individual firms to violate the output quotas needed to enforce the monopoly price.

The conflict between the motives for co-operation and for independent action is analysed in more detail in Figure 13.7.

Cartels and similar output-restricting arrangements have a long history. For example, schemes to raise farm incomes by limiting crops bear ample testimony to the

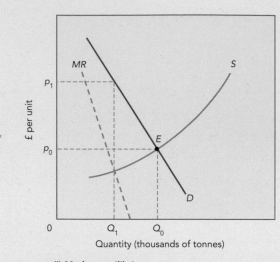

(i) Market equilibrium

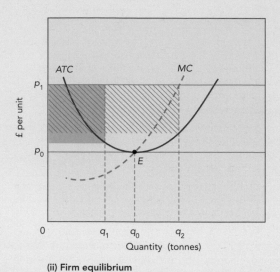

(ii) Firm equilibrium

Figure 13.7 Conflicting forces affecting cartels

Co-operation leads to the monopoly price, but individual self-interest leads to production in excess of the monopoly output. Market conditions are shown in part (i), and the situation of a typical firm is shown in part (ii). (Note the change of scale between the two graphs.) Initially, the market is in competitive equilibrium, with price p_0 and quantity Q_0. The individual firm is producing output q_0 and is just covering its total costs.

The cartel is formed and then enforces quotas on individual firms that are sufficient to reduce the industry's output to Q_1, the output where the supply curve cuts the marginal revenue curve. Q_1 is thus the output that maximizes the joint profits of the cartel members. Price rises to p_1 as a result. The typical firm's quota is q_1. The firm's profits rise from zero to the amount shown by the dark blue area in part (ii). Once price is raised to p_1, however, the individual firm would like to increase output to q_2, where marginal cost is equal to the price set by the cartel. This would allow the firm to earn profits, shown by the blue hatched area. However, if all firms increase their outputs above their quotas, industry output will increase beyond Q_1, and the profits earned by all firms will fall.

accuracy of the predicted instability of cartels. Industry agreements concerning crop restriction often break down, and prices fall as individual farmers exceed their quotas. This is why most crop restriction plans are now operated by governments rather than by private cartels. Production quotas backed by the full coercive power of the state can force monopoly behaviour on existing producers and can effectively bar the entry of new ones, as discussed in Chapter 6.

Restricting entry   A cartel must not only police the behaviour of its members, but must also be able to prevent the entry of new producers. An industry that can support a number of individual firms must have no overriding natural entry barriers. Thus, if it is to maintain its profits in the long run, a cartel of many separate firms must create barriers that prevent the entry of new firms that are attracted by the cartel's profits. Successful cartels are often able to license the firms in the industry and to control entry by restricting the number of licences. At other times the government has operated a quota system and has given it the force of law. If no one can produce without a quota and the quotas are allocated among existing producers, entry is precluded.

A multi-price monopolist: price discrimination

SO far in this chapter we have assumed that the monopoly firm charges the same price for every unit of its product, no matter where or to whom it sells that product. A monopoly firm will also, as we shall soon see, find it profitable to sell different units of the same product at different prices whenever it gets the opportunity.[6] Because this is also prevalent in oligopolistic markets, the range of examples quoted covers both types of market structure.

Raw milk is often sold at one price when it is to be used as fluid milk but at a lower price when it is to be used to make ice cream or cheese. Doctors in private practice often charge for their services according to the incomes of their patients. Cinemas often have lower admission prices for children than for adults. Railroads charge different rates per ton per mile for different products. Electricity producers sell electricity at one rate to homes and at a lower rate to firms. Airlines often charge less to people who stay over a Saturday night than to those who come and go within the week.

Price discrimination occurs when a producer charges different prices for different units of the same product for reasons not associated with differences in cost. Not all price *differences* represent price *discrimination*. Quantity discounts, differences between wholesale and retail prices, and prices that vary with the time of day or the season of the year may not represent price discrimination, because the same product sold at a different time, in a different place, or in different quantities may have different costs. If an electric power company has unused capacity at certain times of the day, it may be cheaper for the company to provide service at those hours than at peak demand hours. If price differences reflect cost differences, they are not discriminatory.

When a price difference is based on different buyers' valuations of the same product, it is discriminatory. It does not cost a cinema operator less to fill seats with children than with adults, but it may be worth while for the cinema to let the children in at a discriminatory low price if few of them would attend at the full adult fare and if they take up seats that otherwise would be empty.

Why price discrimination is profitable

Why should a firm want to sell some units of its output at a price that is well below the price that it receives for other units of its output? The simple answer is because it is profitable to do so.

Why should it be profitable? Persistent price discrimination is profitable either because different buyers are willing to pay different amounts for the same product or because one buyer is willing to pay different amounts for different units of the same product. The basic point about price discrimination is that, in either of these circumstances, sellers may be able to capture some of the consumers' surplus that would otherwise go to buyers.

Discrimination among units of output   Look back to Table 7.2 on p. 133, which showed the consumers' surplus received by one consumer when she bought eight glasses of milk at a single price. If the supplier could sell each glass separately to the consumer, it could capture this consumers' surplus. It would sell the first unit for £3.00, the second unit for £1.50, the third unit for £1.00, and so on until the eighth unit was sold for £0.30. The firm would get total revenues of £8.10 rather than the £2.40 obtained from selling eight units at the single price of £0.30 each. In this example, the firm is able to discriminate perfectly and to extract the entire consumers' surplus.

Perfect price discrimination occurs when the entire consumers' surplus is obtained by the firm. This usually requires that each unit be sold at a separate price. In practice, perfect discrimination is seldom possible. Suppose, however, that the firm could charge two different prices, one for the first four units sold and one for the next four units sold. If it sold the first four units for £0.80 and the next four units for £0.30, it would receive £4.40—less than it would receive if it could discriminate perfectly but more than it would receive if it sold all units at £0.30.

Discrimination among buyers in one market   Think of the demand curve in a market that is made up of individual buyers, each of whom has indicated the maximum price that he or she is prepared to pay for the single unit each wishes to purchase. Suppose, for the sake of simplicity, that there are only four buyers, the first of whom is prepared to pay any price up to £4, the second of whom is prepared to pay £3, the third, £2, and the fourth, £1. Suppose that the product has a marginal cost of production of £1 per unit for all units. If the selling firm is limited to a single price, it will maximize its profits by charging £3, thereby selling two units, and earning profits of £4. If the seller can discriminate among each of the buyers, it could charge the first buyer £4 and the second £3, thus increasing its profits from

---

[6] Although multiple price systems are found among many monopolists, such as electricity and water supply firms, they are also found in industries that contain several large firms. Thus, we could discuss such practices under monopoly in this chapter or under oligopoly in Chapter 14. We deal with it here because it naturally arises whenever monopoly is discussed.

the first two units to £5. Moreover, it could also sell the third unit for £2, thus increasing its profits to £6. It would be indifferent about selling a fourth unit because the price would just cover marginal cost.

Discrimination among markets Let the monopoly firm sell in two different markets. For example, the firm might be the only seller in a tariff-protected home market while in foreign markets it sells in competition with so many other firms that it is a price-taker. In this case, the firm would equate its marginal cost to the price in the foreign market but to marginal revenue in the domestic market. As a result, it would charge a higher price on sales in the home market than on sales abroad. This case is elaborated in the Appendix to this chapter.

Price discrimination more generally Demand curves have a negative slope because different units are valued differently, either by one individual or by different individuals. This fact, combined with a single price for a product, gives rise to consumers' surplus.

The ability to charge multiple prices gives a seller the opportunity to capture some (or, in the extreme case, all) of the consumers' surplus.

In general, the larger the number of different prices that can be charged, the greater is the firm's ability to increase its revenue at the expense of consumers. This is illustrated in Figure 13.8.

It follows that, if a selling firm is able to discriminate through price, it can increase revenues received (and thus also profits) from the sale of any given quantity. However, price discrimination is not always possible, even if there are no legal barriers to its use.

When is price discrimination possible?

Discrimination among units of output sold to the same buyer requires that the seller be able to keep track of the units that a buyer consumes in each period. Thus, the tenth unit purchased by a given buyer in a given month can be sold at a price that is different from the fifth unit *only* if the seller can keep track of who buys what. This can be done by an electric company through its meter readings or by a magazine publisher by distinguishing between renewals and new subscriptions. It can also be done by distributing certificates or coupons that allow, for example, a car wash at a reduced price on a return visit.

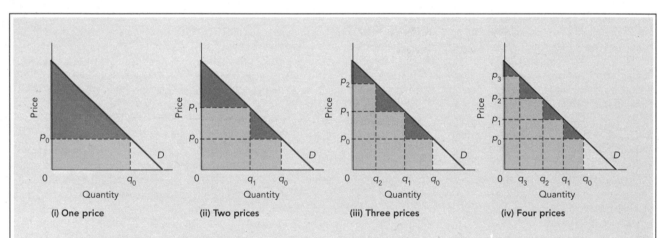

Figure 13.8 Price discrimination

Price discrimination turns consumers' surplus into producers' revenue. In each of the four parts of the figure, a monopolist faces the same demand curve, D, and the total quantity sold is assumed to be q_0. Each firm is assumed to be allowed to do a different amount of price discrimination, and in each case the firm's revenue is shown by the light blue area while consumers' surplus is shown by the dark blue area.
In part (i) a single price p_0 is charged.
In part (ii) the first q_1 units are sold at p_1 and the next q_0–q_1 are sold at p_0.
In part (iii) the first q_2 are sold at p_2; the next q_1–q_2 are sold at p_1, and last q_0–q_1 at p_0.
In part (iv) the first q_3 units are sold at p_3; the next q_2–q_3, at p_2, the next q_1–q_2 at p_1, and the last q_0–q_1 at p_0.
As the amount of price discrimination increases, consumers' surplus diminishes and producers' revenue increases.

Discrimination among buyers is possible only if the buyers who face the low price cannot resell the goods to the buyers who face the high price. However, even though the local butcher might like to charge the banker twice as much for buying his steak as he charges the taxi driver, he cannot succeed in doing so. The banker can always shop for meat in the supermarket, where her occupation is not known. Even if the butcher and the supermarket agreed to charge her twice as much, she could hire the taxi driver to shop for her. The surgeon, however, may succeed in discriminating (especially if other reputable surgeons do the same) because it will not do the banker much good to hire the taxi driver to have her operation for her.

Price discrimination is possible if the seller can either distinguish individual units bought by a single buyer or separate buyers into classes such that resale among classes is impossible.

The ability to prevent resale tends to be associated with the character of the product or the ability to classify buyers into readily identifiable groups. Services are less easily resold than goods; goods that require installation by the manufacturer (e.g., heavy equipment) are less easily resold than movable goods such as household appliances.

An interesting example of non-resaleability occurs in the case of plate glass. Small pieces of plate glass are much cheaper to buy per square foot than bigger pieces, but the person who needs glass for a picture window that is 6 feet by 10 feet cannot use four pieces of glass that are 3 feet by 5 feet. Transportation costs, tariff barriers, and import quotas separate classes of buyers geographically and may make discrimination possible.

Of course, it is not enough to be able to separate different buyers or different units into separate classes. The seller must also be able to control the supply going to each group. There is no point, for example, in asking more than the competitive price from some buyers if they can simply go to other firms who sell the good at the competitive price.

Consequences of price discrimination

In the Appendix to this chapter, we show that a monopolist who is able to discriminate between two markets will allocate any level of production between those two markets so as to equate the marginal revenues in the two. This is fairly obvious since, if this is not done, total revenue can always be increased by reducing sales by one unit in the market with the lower marginal revenue and raising sales by one unit in the market with the higher marginal revenue. This reallocation of sales raises total revenue by the difference between the two marginal revenues. If the demand curves are different in the two markets, having the same marginal revenues means charging different prices.

Two important consequences of price discrimination follow from this result.

Proposition 1: **For any given level of output, the most profitable system of discriminatory prices will provide higher total revenue to the firm than the profit-maximizing single price.**

This proposition, which was illustrated in Figure 13.8, requires only that the demand curve have a negative slope. To see that the proposition is plausible, remember that a monopolist with the power to discriminate could produce exactly the same quantity as a single-price monopolist and charge everyone the same price. Therefore, it need never receive *less* revenue, and it can do better if it can raise the price on even one unit sold, as long as the price need not be lowered on any other.

Proposition 2: **Output under price discrimination will generally be larger than under a single-price monopoly.**

Remember that a monopoly firm that must charge a single price for a product will produce less than would all the firms in a perfectly competitive industry because it knows that selling more depresses its price. Price discrimination allows the firm to avoid this disincentive. To the extent that the firm can sell its output in separate blocks, it can sell another block without spoiling the market for the block that is already being sold. In the case of perfect price discrimination, in which every unit of output is sold at a different price, the profit-maximizing monopolist will produce every unit for which the price charged is greater than or equal to its marginal cost. It will therefore produce the same quantity of output as does the firm in perfect competition.

Normative aspects of price discrimination

The predicted combination of higher average revenue and higher output does not in itself have any *normative* significance. It will typically lead to a different distribution of income and a different level of output than when the seller is limited to a single price. The ability of the discriminating monopolist to capture some of the consumers' surplus will seem undesirable to consumers but not to the monopolist. How outsiders view the transfer may depend on who gains and who loses. Box 13.2 gives some illustrative examples.

There are two quite separate issues involved in evaluating any particular example of price discrimination. One concerns the effect of discrimination on the level of output, and the other concerns the effect of discrimination on the distribution of income. Discrimination usually results in a

BOX 13.2

Examples of discriminatory pricing

British Rail

Some years ago British Rail was not allowed to discriminate among passengers in different regions. To prevent discrimination, a fixed fare per passenger-mile was laid down and had to be charged on all lines whatever the density of their passenger traffic and whatever the elasticity of demand for their services. In the interests of economy, branch lines that could not cover costs were often closed down. This meant that some lines closed even though the users preferred rail transport to any of the available alternatives and the strength of their preference was such that they would voluntarily have paid a price sufficient for the line to have covered its costs. The lines were none the less closed because it was thought inequitable to charge the passengers on such lines more than the passengers on other lines. Subsequently, British Rail was allowed to charge prices that did take some account of market conditions, and the effect was an increase in revenues.

Air fares

In June 1994, a standard fare on British Airways from London Heathrow to Rome was £445. This fare covered return the same day or within the week. However, if you stayed over Saturday night, the fare was only £176! This difference for the same class of fare on the same planes is meant to discriminate between the business traveller and the tourist. Such discrimination is profitable if the elasticity of demand for these two types of travel are different and higher for business. Indeed, the Minister of Transport has recently quoted figures of −1.25 for the elasticity of demand of leisure travel and −0.3 for business travel. If these are the facts, the only puzzle is why British Airways does not raise business class fares more since, as we saw in the chapter, no monopolist would ever be in profit-maximizing equilibrium with an elasticity of demand less than unity. Presumably, the answer here is that the quoted elasticity is for business travel in general, not for business travel on one airline such as British Airways. If all airlines raised business class fares, demand elasticity might prove to be only 0.3, but if one airline raises fares on

its own, it will lose customers to other airlines and might encounter an elasticity greater than one.

Making unprofitable production profitable

A product that a number of people want has cost and demand curves such that there is no single price at which costs can be covered (i.e. the average cost curve lies everywhere above the demand curve). However, if a monopoly is allowed to charge discriminatory prices, it will make a profit.

A monopolist selling at a single price (illustrated in the above figure) and producing output q would make a loss. Total cost is given by the rectangle $0cbq$ while total revenue is $0feq$, leaving losses of $fcbe$. However, a monopolist with the same demand and cost structure could increase total revenue by the area fde, if it could price discriminate perfectly. This means that it would make profits so long as the dark blue area cda were greater than the area abe.

higher output than would occur if a single price were charged. Often, however, it is the effect of discrimination on income distribution that accounts for people's strong emotional reactions to it. By increasing the monopoly firm's profits, price discrimination transfers income from buyers to sellers. When buyers are poor and sellers are rich, this may seem undesirable. However, as in the case of doctors' fees and senior citizens' discounts, discrimination sometimes allows lower-income people to buy a product that they would be unable to afford if it were sold at the single price that maximized the producers' profits.

Summary

1 A monopoly is an industry containing a single firm. The monopoly firm maximizes its profits by equating marginal cost to marginal revenue which is less than price. Production under monopoly is less than it would be under perfect competition where marginal cost is equated to price.

2 The monopoly can earn positive profits in the long run if there are barriers to entry. These may be man-made, such as patents or exclusive franchises, or natural, such as sufficiently large-scale economies.

3 If a monopolist can discriminate among either different units or different customers, it will always sell more and earn greater profits than if it must charge a single price.

4 For price discrimination to be possible, the seller must be able to distinguish individual units bought by a single buyer or to separate buyers into classes among whom resale is impossible.

5 No simple judgement that price discrimination is either always beneficial or always harmful to the interests of consumers seems justified. Each case needs to be evaluated on its own merits.

Topics for review

- Relationship between price and marginal revenue for a monopolist
- Relationships among marginal revenue, total revenue, and elasticity for a monopolist
- Short- and long-run monopoly equilibrium
- Natural and created entry barriers
- Price discrimination among different units and different buyers

APPENDIX TO CHAPTER 13

A formal analysis of price discrimination among markets

Consider a monopoly firm that sells a single product in two distinct markets, A and B, whose demand, marginal revenue and cost curves are shown in Figure 13A.1. Resale among customers is impossible and a single price must be charged in each market.

What is the best price for the firm to charge in each market? The simplest way to discover this is to imagine the firm deciding how best to allocate any given total output Q^*, between two markets. Since output is fixed arbitrarily at Q^*, there is nothing the monopolist can do about costs. The best thing it can do, therefore, is to maximize the revenue that it gets by selling Q^* in the two markets. *To do this it will allocate its sales between the markets until the marginal revenues are the same in each market.* Consider what would happen if the marginal revenue in market A exceeded the marginal revenue in market B. The firm could keep its overall output constant at Q^* but reallocate a unit of sales from B to A, gaining a net addition in revenue equal to the difference between the marginal revenues in the two markets. Thus, it will always pay a monopoly firm to reallocate a given total quantity between its markets as long as marginal revenues are not equal in the two markets.

If we assume that marginal cost is constant, we can determine the profit-maximizing course of action from Figure

13A.1. The MC curve in both figures shows the constant marginal cost. The firm's total profits are maximized by equating MR in each market to its constant MC, thus selling q_A at p_A in market A and q_B at p_B in market B. Marginal revenue is the same in each market $(c_A = c_B)$ so that the firm has its total output correctly allocated between the two markets, and marginal costs equals marginal revenue, showing that the firm would lose profits if it produced more or less total output.

Next, assume that marginal cost varies with output, being given by MC' in Figure 13A.2(iii). Now we cannot just put the MC curve on to the diagram for each market, since the marginal cost of producing another unit for sale in market A will depend on how much is being produced for sale in market B and vice versa. To determine what overall production should be, we need to know overall marginal revenue. To find this, we merely sum the separate quantities in each market that correspond to each particular marginal revenue. If, for example, the 10th unit sold in market A and the 15th unit sold in market B each have a marginal revenue of £1 in their separate markets, then the marginal revenue of £1 corresponds to overall sales of 25 units (10 units in A and 15 in B). This example illustrates the general principle: the overall marginal revenue curve to

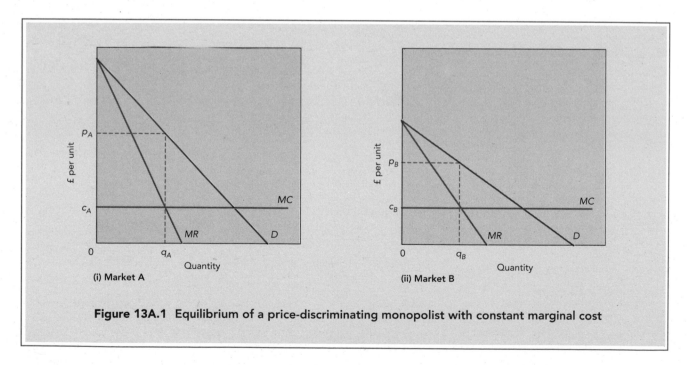

Figure 13A.1 Equilibrium of a price-discriminating monopolist with constant marginal cost

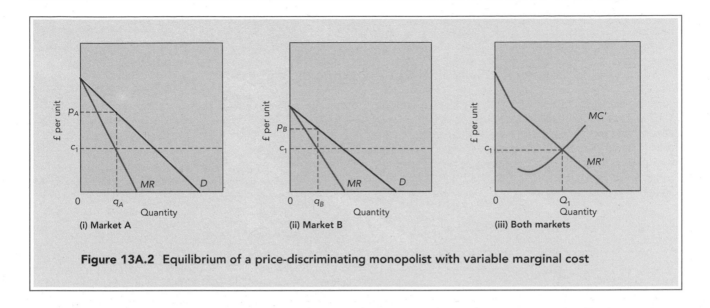

Figure 13A.2 Equilibrium of a price-discriminating monopolist with variable marginal cost

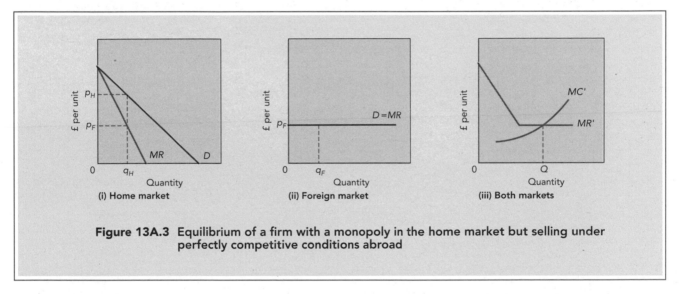

Figure 13A.3 Equilibrium of a firm with a monopoly in the home market but selling under perfectly competitive conditions abroad

a discriminating monopolist is the horizontal sum of the marginal revenue curves in each of its markets. This overall curve shows the marginal revenue associated with an increment to production on the assumption that sales are divided between the two markets so as to keep the two marginal revenues equal.

This overall MR curve is shown in Figure 13A.2(iii) and is labelled MR'. The firm's total profit-maximizing output is at Q_1, where MR' and MC' intersect (at a value of c_1). By construction, marginal revenue is c_1 in each market although price is different. To find the equilibrium price and quantity in each market, find the quantities, q_A and q_B, that correspond to this marginal revenue; then find the

prices in each market that correspond to q_A and q_B. All of this is illustrated in parts (i) and (ii) of the figure.

AN APPLICATION

In some industries firms sell competitively on international markets while enjoying a home market that is protected from foreign competition by tariffs or import quotas. To illustrate the issues involved, consider the following extreme case. A firm is the only producer of product X in country A. There are thousands of producers of X in other countries, so that X is sold abroad under conditions of perfect competition. The government of country A grants the firm a monopoly in the home market by prohibiting imports of X. The firm is now faced with a negatively sloped demand curve at home and a perfectly elastic demand curve abroad at the prevailing world price of X.

What will it do? To maximize profits, the firm will divide its sales between the foreign and the home markets so as to equate marginal revenues in the two. On the world market its average and marginal revenues are equal to the world price. Thus, the firm will equate marginal revenue in the home market with the world price, and since price exceeds marginal revenue at home (because the demand curve slopes downwards), price at home must exceed price abroad.

The argument is illustrated in Figure 13A.3. The home market is shown in (i), the foreign market in (ii), and the sum of the marginal revenue curves in (iii). Provided that the marginal cost curve cuts the marginal revenue curve to the right of the kink (i.e. MC does not exceed the world price when only the home market is served), both markets will be served at prices of p_H at home and p_F abroad. The total quantity sold will be Q, of which q_H is allocated to the home market and the rest ($q_F = Q - q_H$) is sold abroad.[7]

[7] It is an interesting exercise to consider the effect on the firm's exports of a tax on the sale of X in the home market.

CHAPTER 14

Imperfect competition

THE two extreme market structures of perfect competition and monopoly cover only a small fraction of modern economic activity. Most firms involved in the production, distribution, and retailing of consumer goods and services, as well as capital goods, come under intermediate market structures. On the one hand, they are not monopolies because their industries contain several firms which often compete actively against each other. Firms manufacturing cars, refrigerators, TV sets, breakfast cereals, and just about any other consumers' good operate in industries containing several close rivals (often foreign as well as domestic). Even in small towns, residents find more than one chemist, garage, hairdresser, and supermarket competing for their patronage. On the other hand, they do not operate in perfectly competitive markets because the number of competing firms is often small, and, even when the number is large, *the firms are not price-takers.*

In this chapter we study firm behaviour in two intermediate market structures called monopolistic competition and oligopoly. The former is close to perfect competition with the major difference that firms do not sell a homogeneous product. The latter deals with industries that typically contain a few large firms which compete actively with each other.

Patterns of concentration in manufacturing

One measure of the extent to which the individual firms in an industry have potential market power is called a **concentration ratio**. This measures the fraction of total sales in the nation that are controlled by some specified number of the industry's largest sellers. Common types of concentration ratios cite the share of an industry's total market sales made by the largest three or five firms, but it could be any other number of firms, such as two or ten. For example, the UK five-firm concentration ratio for soaps and toilet preparations is 53.5 per cent. This means that the largest five firms in that industry account for 53.5 per cent of the industry's total sales.

Table 14.1 gives the distribution of five-firm concentration ratios across UK manufacturing industries. They suggest that in most industries the largest five firms control too many of the sales to be price-takers and too few to be monopolists.

Using national concentration ratios to measure market power raises a number of problems. For example, most large firms sell products in several different industries.

Table 14.1 UK selected concentration ratios, 1990 (% of total industry value added produced by largest five enterprises)

Industry	Concentration ratio
Tobacco	99.3
Motor vehicles	87.7
Cycles and motor cycles	76.7
Domestic electric appliances	61.2
Ice cream and sweets	58.8
Spirit distilling	56.1
Pharmaceuticals	55.8
Soap and toilet preparations	53.5
Rubber products	49.5
Brewing	43.0
Paints, varnishes, and ink	31.9
Toys and sports goods	24.7
Leather goods	12.4

Source: CSO Census of Production, published in *Business Monitor* (PA1002).

UK concentration ratios vary greatly across manufacturing industries. The largest five firms account for virtually all of the output of tobacco products but only 12 per cent of the output of leather products.

More importantly, markets may occasionally be smaller than the whole nation and often are larger. A single firm operating in the United Kingdom does not have a monopoly if it is competing in the UK market against products imported from several foreign producers. Indeed, the globalization of competition brought about by the falling costs of transportation and communication has been one of the most significant developments in the world economy in recent decades. As a result, the UK economy, like the economies of all other countries, is much more open than it was even a few decades ago. Global competition has greatly reduced the number of secure monopolies that exist in national markets. These highly important developments are further considered in Box 14.1.

To measure potential market power appropriately, concentration ratios need to measure the fraction of sales made in the relevant market—which is usually larger than the entire United Kingdom—by the largest firms operating in that market, whether they are located at home or abroad.

Imperfectly competitive market structures

THE market structures that we are now going to study are called *imperfectly competitive*, which refers to *rivalrous competitive behaviour among firms that have a significant degree of market power*. The word 'competitive' emphasizes that we are not dealing with monopoly, and the word 'imperfect' emphasizes that we are not dealing with perfect competition.

We first note patterns of firm behaviour that are typical of all imperfectly competitive market structures.

Firms select their products

If a new farmer enters the wheat industry, the full range of products that can be produced is already in existence. In contrast, if a new firm enters the computer software industry, that firm must decide on the characteristics of the new computer programs that it is to produce. It will not produce programs that are identical to those already in production. Rather, it will develop, at substantial cost, one or more new programs, each of which will have its own distinctive characteristics. As a result, firms in this industry sell an array of differentiated products, no two of which are identical. This is true of firms in virtually all consumer and capital goods industries.

The term **differentiated product** refers to a group of products that are similar enough to be considered variations on one generic product but dissimilar enough that they can be sold at different prices. For example, although one brand of toilet soap is similar to most others, soaps differ from each other in their chemical composition, colour, smell, softness, brand name, reputation, and a host of other characteristics that matter to customers. So all toilet soaps taken together are one differentiated product.

Most firms in imperfectly competitive market structures sell differentiated products. In such industries, the firm itself must decide on the characteristics of the products it will sell.

Firms choose their prices

In perfect competition, firms are price-takers and quantity-adjusters. In all other market structures, firms face negatively sloped demand curves and thus face a trade-off between the price that they charge and the quantity that they sell.

Because firms' products are not perfect substitutes for each other, each firm must quote a price. Any one manufacturer will typically have several product lines that differ more or less from each other and from the competing product lines of other firms. No market sets a single price for razor blades, television sets, word processing packages, or any other differentiated product by equating overall demand with overall supply. Instead, each type of the differentiated product has a price that must be set by its maker. Of course, a certain amount of haggling is possible, particularly at the retail level; but this is usually within well-defined limits set by the price charged by the manufacturer.

In such circumstances, economists say that firms *administer* their prices and are **price-makers** rather than price-takers. An **administered price** is a price set by the conscious decision of an individual firm rather than by impersonal market forces.

Each firm has expectations about the quantity it can sell at each price that it might set for each of its product lines. *Unexpected* market fluctuations then cause unexpected variations in the quantities that are sold at the administered prices.

In market structures other than perfect competition, firms set their prices and then let demand determine sales. Changes in market conditions are signalled to the firm by changes in the quantity that the firm sells at its current administered price.

The changed conditions may or may not then lead firms to change their prices.

Short-run price stability   In perfect competition, prices change continually in response to changes in demand and supply. In markets for differentiated manufactured products, prices often change less frequently. Manufacturers' prices for motor cars, computers, television sets, and men's suits do not change with anything like the frequency that prices change in markets for basic materials or stocks and bonds. (Retail mark-ups are, however, varied more often in response to short-term fluctuations in market conditions.)

Modern firms that sell differentiated products typically have hundreds, or even thousands, of distinct products on their price lists. Changing such a long list of administered prices at the same frequency that competitive market prices change would be physically impossible. Changing them at all involves costs. These include the costs of printing new list prices and notifying all customers, the difficulty of keeping track of frequently changing prices for purposes of accounting and billing, and the loss of customer and retailer goodwill owing to the uncertainty caused by frequent

BOX 14.1

Globalization of production and competition

A mere 100 years ago, people and news travelled by sailing ship, so that it took months to communicate across various parts of the world. Advances in the first 60 years of the twentieth century sped up both communications and travel. In the past three decades, the pace of change in communications technology has accelerated. The world has witnessed a communications revolution that has dramatically changed the way business decisions are made and implemented.

Three decades ago, telephone links were laboriously and unreliably connected by operators; satellites were newfangled and not especially useful toys for rocket scientists; photocopying and telecopying were completely unknown; mail was the only way to send hard copy, and getting it to overseas destinations often took weeks; computers were in their infancy; and jets were just beginning to replace the much slower and less reliable propeller aircraft. Today direct dialing is available to most parts of the world, at a fraction of what long-distance calls cost 30 years ago, and faxes, satellite links, fast jet travel, computer networks, cheap courier services, and a host of other developments have made communication that is reliable, and often instantaneous, available throughout the world.

The communications revolution has been a major contributor to the development of what has become known as the 'global village'. Three important characteristics of the global village are a *disintegration* of production, an increase in competition, and a decline in the power of the nation-state.

Production

The communications revolution has allowed many large international companies, known as transnational corporations (TNCs), to decentralize their production process (see Box 10.1). They are now able to locate their research and development (R&D) where the best scientists are available. They can produce various components in dozens of places, locating each activity in a country where costs are cheapest for that type of production. They can then ship all the parts, as they are needed, to an assembly factory where the product is 'made'.

The globalization of production has brought employment, and rising real wages, to people in many less developed countries. At the same time, it has put less skilled labour in the developed countries under strong competitive pressures.

Competition

The communications revolution has also caused an internationalization of competition in almost all industries. National markets are no longer protected for local producers by high costs of transportation and communication or by the ignorance of foreign firms. Walk into a local supermarket or department store today, and you will have no trouble in finding products representing most of the UN member-states.

Consumers gain by being able to choose from an enormous range of well-made, low-priced goods and services. Firms that are successful gain worldwide sales. Firms that fall behind even momentarily may, however, be wiped out by competition coming from many quarters. Global competition is fierce competition, and firms need to be fast on the uptake—either of other people's new ideas or of their own—if they are to survive.

Economic policy

The international character of TNCs means that national economic policies have been seriously constrained. Much international trade takes place between segments of single TNCs. This gives them the chance, through their accounting practices, to localize their profits in countries where corporate taxes are lowest and their costs in countries where cost write-offs are highest.

The globalization of production also allows TNCs to shift production around the world. So tough national policies that reduce profitability may be self-defeating as firms move production elsewhere. Generous policies that seek to attract production may succeed only in attracting small and specialized parts of it. For example, Sweden has given generous tax treatment to R&D expenditures, seeking to attract firms to do their high-tech, high-wage production in that country. Instead, however, many firms have come to Sweden to do their R&D and then have transferred the knowledge to countries where production costs are lower. The net result is that Swedish taxpayers are subsidizing world consumers by paying for R&D that is generating production in other countries.

The examples given here illustrate an important development: globalization of production, and consequently of competition, means a great reduction in the scope for individual countries to implement distinctive economic policies.

---

changes in prices. These costs are often a significant consideration to multi-product manufacturing firms.

Because producers of differentiated products must administer their own prices, firms must decide on the *frequency* with which they change these prices.

In making this decision, the firm will balance the cost of making price changes against the revenue lost by not mak-

ing price changes. Clearly, the likelihood that the firm will make costly price changes rises with the size of the disturbance to which it is adjusting and the probability that the disturbance will not be reversed.

Thus, transitory fluctuations in demand may be met by changing output with prices constant, while changes in costs that are thought to be permanent are passed on

BOX 14.2

Oligopolistic price stickiness in the market for a primary product

Price stickiness is common in manufactured goods, most of which are produced under conditions of oligopoly. Primary products are usually produced and sold under conditions that come closer to those of perfect competition. An interesting exception occurs in the case of germanium, a rare metal which is used to make semiconductors. One source said that there were 13 producers in 1977/8, with the top five accounting for nearly 80 per cent of world output. A reference book published in 1985 listed five suppliers of germanium dioxide, one in each of five countries, and nine suppliers of the metal itself (in a total of six countries). This material can thus be regarded as the product of an oligopolistic industry.

The first source mentioned above shows absolute stability for the price of germanium from 1970 until 1976. More recently,

the periodical *Metal Bulletin*, which publishes current prices in each issue, showed the price as BFr 13,075 (Belgian francs) from March 1979 until January 1980, price rises in January, March and July and then a price of BFr 22,275 from July 1980 until April 1981. The new price, of BFr 31,200, lasted for five months, and a price of BFr 38,900 for a further five-and-a-half months. The price set in February 1982— BFr 42,100—lasted until April 1986, and the prices of two grades of germanium oxide were similarly unchanged: completely stable prices for about four years (at the end of which the prices fell by a mere 1 per cent). This is quite unlike the behaviour of most mineral prices, which fluctuate continuously in response to changes in both demand and supply.

---

through price increases. An example of such price 'stickiness' is given in Box 14.2.[1]

Other aspects of the behaviour of firms

Several other important aspects of the observed behaviour of firms in imperfect competition could not occur under either perfect competition or monopoly.

Nonprice competition   Many firms spend large sums of money on advertising. They do so in an attempt both to shift the demand curves for the industry's products and to attract customers from competing firms. Many firms engage in a variety of other forms of nonprice competition, such as offering competing standards of quality and product guarantees. Any kind of sales promotion activity undertaken by a single firm would not happen under perfect competition since each firm can sell any amount at the going market price. Any such scheme directed at competing firms in the same industry is, by definition, inconsistent with monopoly.

Unexploited scale economies   Many firms in industries that contain more than one firm appear to be operating on the downward-sloping portions of the long-run average cost curves for many of the individual product lines that they produce. Although this is possible under monopoly, firms in perfect competition must, in the long run, be at the minimum point of their long-run average cost curves (see Figure 12.11 on p. 230).

One set of reasons for this is found in high development costs and short product lives. Many modern products involve huge development costs. For example, roughly US$1 billion was recently spent just to *design the wing* of the new McDonnell Douglas airliner! Today, many products are only sold for a few years before being replaced by a new, superior product. For example, the manager of a large telecommunications firm recently stated that 80 per cent of the products his firm sells today did not exist five years ago! In such cases, firms face steeply falling long-run average total cost curves. The more units that are sold, the lower are the fixed development costs per unit. Given perfect competition, these firms would go on increasing outputs and sales until rising marginal costs of production just balanced the falling fixed unit costs, bringing their average total cost to a minimum. As it is, they often face falling average total cost curves all through each product's life-cycle.

Entry prevention   Firms in many industries engage in activities that appear to be designed to hinder the entry of new firms, thereby preventing existing pure profits from being eroded by entry. We will consider these activities in much more detail later in the chapter.

---

[1] Over 50 years ago, the British economist Paul Sweezy offered an explanation of oligopolistic price stickiness called the 'kinked demand curve'. This explanation has long since been discredited on both empirical grounds (no evidence for it) and theoretical grounds (the behaviour it assumes can be shown to be inconsistent). It will not be found in any modern textbook on industrial organization, although it still survives in a few elementary textbooks and the occasional examination paper.

Imperfect competition among the many

The development of monopolistic competition

Dissatisfaction with the two polar market structures of perfect competition and monopoly because of observations such as those just discussed, led the American economist Edward Chamberlin (1899–1967) to develop the theory of a market structure called **monopolistic competition**. The dissatisfaction that motivated his theorizing lay in these conflicts between theory and evidence.[2]

ASSUMPTIONS

The theory of monopolistic competition is based on four key assumptions.

1. *Each firm produces one specific variety, or brand, of the industry's differentiated product.* Each firm thus faces a demand curve that, although it is negatively sloped, is highly elastic, because other varieties of the same product that are sold by other firms provide many close substitutes.

2. *The industry contains so many firms that each one ignores the possible reactions of its many competitors when it makes its own price and output decisions.* There are too many firms for it to be possible for any one firm to try to take the other firms' separate reactions into account. In this way, firms in monopolistic competition are similar to firms in perfect competition. They make decisions based on their own demand and cost conditions and do not consider interdependence between their own decisions and those of the other firms in the industry. This is the key aspect that distinguishes the market structure of monopolistic competition from the market structure of oligopoly, which we discuss later in the chapter.

3. *There is freedom of entry and exit in the industry.* If profits are being earned by existing firms, new firms have an incentive to enter. When they do, the demand for the industry's product must be shared among more brands, and this is assumed to take demand equally from all existing firms.

4. *There is symmetry.* When a new firm enters the industry selling a new version of the differentiated product, it takes custom equally from all existing firms. For example, a new entrant that captured 5 per cent of the existing market would do so by capturing 5 per cent of the sales of each existing firm.

The theory was an important step in the development of models of intermediate market structures, and its main predictions are outlined below.

EQUILIBRIUM

Short-run equilibrium   Because each firm has a monopoly over its own product, each firm faces a negatively sloped demand curve. But the curve is rather elastic because similar products sold by other firms provide many close substitutes. The negative slope of the demand curve provides the potential for monopoly profits in the short run, as illustrated in part (i) of Figure 14.1.

Long-run equilibrium   Freedom of entry and exit forces profits to zero in the long run. If profits are being earned by existing firms, new firms will enter. Their entry will mean that the demand for the product must be shared among more and more brands. Thus, the demand curve for each existing firm's brand shifts to the left.[3] Entry continues until profits fall to zero as shown in part (ii) of Figure 14.1.

EXCESS CAPACITY

The absence of positive profits requires that each firm's demand curve be nowhere above its long-run average cost curve. The absence of losses, which would cause exit, requires that each firm be able to cover its costs. Thus, average revenue must equal average cost at some output. Together these requirements imply that, when a monopolistically competitive industry is in long-run equilibrium, each firm will be producing where its demand curve is tangent to (i.e. just touching at one point) its average total cost curve.

Two curves that are tangent at a point have the same slope at that point. If a negatively sloped demand curve is to be tangent to the *LRAC* curve, the latter must also be negatively sloped at the point of tangency. This situation is

---

[2] Another attempt to reconcile theory with the same evidence was made by the British economist Joan Robinson (1903–1983). She assumed that each industry was monopolized. Although her work led to important clarifications of the theory of monopoly, it proved a dead end in explaining the behaviour of manufacturing industries. Instead, it was Chamberlin's work that set the direction that more modern explanations have successfully followed.

[3] The shift in the demand curve is determined by Chamberlin's critical *symmetry assumption*: a new entrant takes sales in equal proportions from all existing firms.

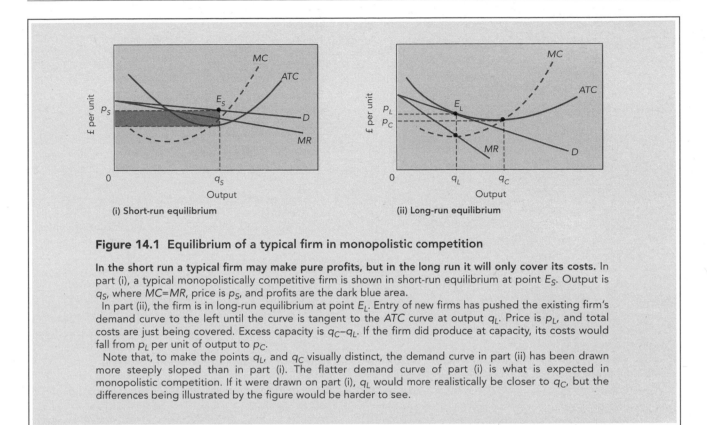

Figure 14.1 Equilibrium of a typical firm in monopolistic competition

In the short run a typical firm may make pure profits, but in the long run it will only cover its costs. In part (i), a typical monopolistically competitive firm is shown in short-run equilibrium at point E_S. Output is q_S, where $MC=MR$, price is p_S, and profits are the dark blue area.

In part (ii), the firm is in long-run equilibrium at point E_L. Entry of new firms has pushed the existing firm's demand curve to the left until the curve is tangent to the ATC curve at output q_L. Price is p_L, and total costs are just being covered. Excess capacity is q_C-q_L. If the firm did produce at capacity, its costs would fall from p_L per unit of output to p_C.

Note that, to make the points q_L, and q_C visually distinct, the demand curve in part (ii) has been drawn more steeply sloped than in part (i). The flatter demand curve of part (i) is what is expected in monopolistic competition. If it were drawn on part (i), q_L would more realistically be closer to q_C, but the differences being illustrated by the figure would be harder to see.

shown in Figure 14.1(ii): the typical firm is producing an output less than the one for which its *LRAC* reaches its minimum point.

This is the famous **excess capacity theorem** of monopolistic competition. Each firm is producing its output at an average cost that is higher than it could achieve by producing its capacity output. In other words, each firm has *unused* or *excess* capacity. So:

The theory of monopolistic competition shows that an industry can be competitive, in the sense of containing numerous competing firms, and yet contain unexploited scale economies, in the sense that each firm is producing on the negatively sloped portion of its average cost curve.

The explanation, however, seemed to imply waste and inefficiency. Production was at higher cost than was necessary, and firms typically invested in capacity that was not fully utilized.

Is excess capacity wasteful? The excess capacity theorem aroused passionate debate for decades. Was it really true that the free-market system necessarily caused waste and inefficiency whenever an industry produced differentiated products?

The debate was finally resolved with a negative answer in the 1960s by considering the question: what is the optimal number of differentiated products that should be produced?

People clearly have different tastes. For example, each brand of breakfast food, hi-fi set, car, word processing package, and watch has its sincere devotees. Increasing the number of differentiated products has two effects. First, it increases the amount of excess capacity in the production of each product because the total demand must be divided among more products. Second, the increased diversity of available products will better satisfy diverse tastes.

Now consider how to maximize consumers' satisfactions in these circumstances. The correct policy is *not* to reduce the number of differentiated products until each remaining product can be produced at its least-cost output. Instead:

To maximize consumers' satisfaction, the number of differentiated products should be increased until the marginal gain in consumers' satisfaction from an increase in diversity equals the loss from having to produce each existing product at a higher cost.

For this reason, among others, the charge that large-group monopolistic competition would lead to a waste of resources is no longer accepted as necessarily, or even probably, true.[4]

The empirical relevance of large-group monopolistic competition

A long controversy raged over several decades as to the empirical relevance of monopolistic competition. Of course, product differentiation is an almost universal phenomenon in industries producing consumers' goods and capital goods. None the less, many economists maintained that the monopolistically competitive market structure was almost never found in practice.

To see why, we need to distinguish between products and firms. Single-product firms are extremely rare in manufacturing industries. Typically, a vast array of differentiated products is produced by each of the few firms in the industry. Most of the vast variety of breakfast foods, for example, is produced by a mere three firms. Similar circumstances exist in soap, chemicals, cigarettes, and numerous other industries where many competing products are produced by a few very large firms. These industries are clearly not perfectly competitive and neither are they monopolies. Are they monopolistically competitive? The answer is no, because they contain few enough firms for each to take account of the others' reactions when determining its own behaviour. Furthermore, these firms often earn large profits without attracting new entry. In fact, they operate under a market structure called oligopoly, which we consider in the next section.

While accepting that many differentiated products are produced by industries that are not monopolistically competitive, some economists feel that the theory is useful in analysing industries that contain many relatively small firms producing differentiated products.[5] Others agree with the views expounded by the British economist Nicholas Kaldor (1908–1986) in his long debate with Chamberlin. Kaldor maintained that, because every variety of a differentiated product was not an equally good substitute for every other variety, even differentiated-product industries with many firms were better studied in a model of overlapping oligopolies.[6]

The 1980s witnessed a great outburst of theorizing concerning all aspects of product differentiation. The newer theories are consistent with Chamberlin's famous proposition that it pays firms to differentiate their products, to advertise heavily, and to engage in many other forms of competitive behaviour. These are characteristics to be found in the world, but not in perfect competition. Most modern industries that sell differentiated products, however, contain only a few firms. This is the market structure of oligopoly that is discussed in the next section.

Imperfect competition among the few

AN **oligopoly** is an industry that contains only a few competing firms. Each firm has enough market power to prevent its being a price-taker, but each firm is subject to enough inter-firm rivalry to prevent it considering the market demand curve as its own. In most modern economies this is the dominant market structure for the production of consumers' and capital goods as well as many basic industrial materials such as steel and aluminium. Services, however, are often produced under somewhat more competitive conditions.

In contrast to a monopoly (which has no competitors) and to a monopolistically competitive firm (which has many competitors), an oligopolistic firm faces a few competitors. *The number of competitors is small enough for each firm to realize that its competitors may respond to anything that it does and that it should take such possible responses into account.* In other words, oligopolists are aware of the interdependence among the decisions made by the various firms in the industry, and they engage in the type of rivalrous behaviour discussed on pp. 216–17.

This is the key difference between oligopolists on the one

[4] Important demonstrations of this result were given by several economists, including Kelvin Lancaster, formerly of the London School of Economics and now at Columbia University in New York.

[5] At first sight, retailing may appear to be closer to the conditions of large-group monopolistic competition than is manufacturing. Every city has many retailers selling any one commodity, each of them differentiated from the others mainly by its geographical location. Each firm, however, tends to have only a few close neighbours and many more distant ones. Thus, a model of interlocking oligopolies, with every firm in strong competition with only a few close neighbours, seems to be a better model for retailing than the model of large-group monopolistic competition, in which every firm competes directly, and equally, with all other firms in the industry.

[6] The symmetry assumption implies, unrealistically, that all differentiated products in an industry are equally good substitutes for each other; if they were not, a new product would not take sales equally from all existing products.

hand and perfect or monopolistic competitors, and monopolies, on the other hand. We say that oligopolists' behaviour is **strategic,** which means that they take explicit account of the impact of their decisions on competing firms and of the reactions they expect competing firms to make. In contrast, firms in perfect and monopolistic competition engage in **non-strategic** behaviour, which means they make decisions based on their own costs and their own demand curves without considering any possible reactions from their large number of competitors. Monopolists do not engage in strategic behaviour, either; this, however, is because they have no competitors rather than too many.

Oligopolistic industries are of many types. In some industries there are only a few firms (three, in the case of cigarettes). In others there are many firms, but only a few dominate the market. Oligopoly is also consistent with a large number of small sellers, called a 'competitive fringe', as long as a 'big few' dominate the industry's production. For example, about 500 banks operate in the United Kingdom, but the big four—Barclays, Lloyds, Natwest, and Midland—dominate the industry.

In oligopolistic industries, prices are typically administered. Products are usually differentiated. Firms engage in the type of rivalrous behaviour described on p. 216, although its intensity varies greatly across industries and over time. This variety has invited extensive theorizing and empirical study.

Why bigness?

Several factors contribute to explaining why so many industries are dominated by a few large firms. Some of these factors are 'natural', and some are created by the firms themselves.

NATURAL CAUSES OF BIGNESS

Economies of scale Much factory production uses the principle of the division of labour that we first studied in Chapter 1. The production of a product is broken up into hundreds of simple, repetitive tasks. This type of division of labour is the basis of the assembly line, which revolutionized the production of many goods in the early twentieth century, and it still underlies economies of large-scale production in many industries. Such division of labour is, as Adam Smith observed long ago, dependent on the size of the market. If only a few units of a product can be sold each day, there is no point in dividing its production into a number of tasks, each of which can be done in a few minutes. So big firms with large sales have an advantage over small firms with small sales whenever there is great potential for economies based on an extensive division of labour.

Economies of scope Modern industries produce many differentiated products that give rise to a different type of large-scale advantage. To develop a new product is costly, and it may be a matter of only a few years before it is replaced by some superior version of the same basic product. These fixed costs of product development must be recovered in the revenues from sales of the product. The larger the firm's sales, the lower the cost that has to be recovered from each unit sold. Consider a product that costs £1 million to develop and to market. If 1 million units can be sold before the product is replaced by a superior version, £1 of the selling price of each unit must go towards recovering the development costs. If, however, the firm expects to sell 10 million units, each unit need contribute only 10 pence to these costs, and the market price can be lowered accordingly. With the enormous development costs of some of today's high-tech products, firms that can sell a large volume have a distinct pricing advantage over firms that sell a smaller volume.

Other scope economies are related to financing and to marketing. It is costly to enter a market, to establish a sales force, and to make consumers aware of a product. These costs are often nearly as high when a small volume is being marketed as when a large volume is being marketed. Thus, the smaller the volume of the firm's sales, the higher the price must be if the firm is to cover all of these costs. Notice that these economies, which are related to the size of the firm, are related neither to the amount the firm produces of any one of its differentiated products, nor to the size of any one of its plants. Economies that depend on the overall size of the *firm* rather than on the size of its *plants* or the volume of production of any one product are called the **economies of scope.**

Where size confers a cost advantage, through economies either of scale or of scope, there may be room for only a few firms, even when the total market is quite large. This cost advantage of size will dictate that the industry be an oligopoly, unless government regulation prevents the firms from growing to their efficient size.

FIRM-CREATED CAUSES OF BIGNESS

The number of firms in an industry may be decreased while the average size of the survivors rises, due to *strategic* behaviour of the firms themselves. Firms may grow by buying out rivals (acquisitions), or merging with them (mergers), or by driving rivals into bankruptcy through predatory practices. This process increases the size and market shares of the survivors and may, by reducing competitive behaviour, allow them to earn larger profit margins.

The surviving firms must then be able to create and sustain barriers to entry where natural ones do not exist. The industry will then be dominated by a few large firms only when they are successful in preventing the entry of new firms that would lower the industry's concentration ratio.

IS BIGNESS NATURAL OR FIRM-CREATED?

Most observers would agree that the general answer to the question posed in the heading to this section is 'some of both'. Some industries have high concentration ratios because the efficient size of the firm is large relative to the overall size of the industry's market. Other industries may have higher concentration ratios than efficiency considerations would dictate because the firms are seeking enhanced market power through large size plus entry restriction. The issue that is debated is the relative importance of these two forces, the one coming from the efficiencies of large scale and scope, and the other coming from the desire of firms to create market power by growing large.

Harvard economist Alfred D. Chandler, Jr is a champion of the view that the major reason for the persistence of oligopolies in the manufacturing sector is the efficiency of large-scale production. His monumental work *Scale and Scope*[7] argues this case in great detail for the United States, the United Kingdom, and Germany.

The basic dilemma of oligopoly

Oligopoly behaviour is necessarily *strategic* behaviour. In deciding on strategies, oligopolists face a basic dilemma between competing and co-operating.

The firms in an oligopolistic industry will make more profits as a group if they co-operate; any one firm, however, may make more profits for itself if it defects while the others co-operate.

This result is similar to the one established in Chapter 13 for the cartelization of a perfectly competitive industry.[8] In a perfectly competitive industry, however, there are so many firms that they cannot reach the co-operative solution unless some central governing body is formed, by either themselves or the government, to force the necessary behaviour on all firms. In contrast, the few firms in an oligopolistic industry will themselves recognize the possibility of co-operating to avoid the loss of profits that will result from competitive behaviour.

THE CO-OPERATIVE SOLUTION

If the firms in an oligopolistic industry co-operate, either overtly or tacitly, to produce among themselves the monopoly output, they can maximize their joint profits. If they do this, they will reach what is called a **co-operative solution,** which is the position that a single monopoly firm would reach if it owned all the firms in the industry.

THE NON-COOPERATIVE EQUILIBRIUM

In Chapter 13, our analysis of a cartel showed that, if all the firms in an oligopolistic industry are at the co-operative solution, it will be profitable for any one of them to cut its price or to raise its output, as long as the others do not do so. However, if everyone does the same thing, they will be worse off as a group and may all be worse off individually. An equilibrium that is reached by firms when they proceed by calculating only their own gains, without co-operating with others, is called a **non-cooperative equilibrium.**

AN EXAMPLE FROM GAME THEORY

The **theory of games** is a study of rational decision-making in situations in which a number of players compete, knowing that other players will react to their moves, and taking account of their expected reactions when making moves. For example, firm A asks: 'Shall I raise or lower my price or leave it unchanged?' Before arriving at an answer, it asks: 'What will the other firms do in each of these cases, and how will their actions affect the profitability of whatever decision I make?'

When game theory is applied to oligopoly, the players are firms, their game is played in the market, their strategies are their price or output decisions, and the payoffs are their profits.

A game-theory illustration of the basic dilemma of oligopolists, to co-operate or to compete, is shown in Figure 14.2 for the case of a two-firm oligopoly, called a **duopoly.** The simplified game, adopted for the purposes of illustration, allows only two strategies for *each firm*: produce an output equal to one-half of the monopoly output, or two-thirds of the monopoly output. Even this simple game, however, is sufficient to illustrate several key ideas in the modern theory of oligopoly.

Figure 14.2 presents what is called a *payoff matrix*. The data in the matrix show that if both sides co-operate, *each producing* one-half of the monopoly output, they achieve the co-operative solution and jointly earn the monopoly profits by *jointly producing* the output that a monopolist would produce. As a group, they can do no better.

Nash equilibrium   The non-cooperative equilibrium shown in Figure 14.2 is called a *Nash equilibrium*, after the US mathematician John Nash, who developed the concept in the 1950s. A **Nash equilibrium** is one in which each firm's best strategy is to maintain its present behaviour, *given the present behaviour of the other firms*.

---

[7] A. D. Chandler, Jr, *Scale and Scope: The Dynamics of Industrial Capitalism* (Cambridge, Mass.: Harvard University Press, 1990).

[8] The basic reason is that, when only one firm increases its output by 1 per cent, the price falls by less than when all firms do the same. Thus, when the point is reached at which profits will be *reduced* if all firms expand output together, it will still pay one firm to expand output *if the* others do not do the same.

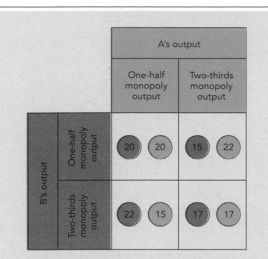

Figure 14.2 The oligopolist's dilemma: to co-operate or to compete

Co-operation to determine the overall level of output can maximize joint profits, but it leaves each firm with an incentive to alter its production. The figure gives what is called a payoff matrix for a two-firm duopoly game. Only two levels of production are considered in order to illustrate the basic problem. A's production is indicated across the top, and its profits (measured in millions of pounds) are shown in the blue circles within each square. B's production is indicated down the left side, and its profits (in millions of pounds) are shown in the red circles within each square. For example, the top right square tells us that if B produces one-half, while A produces two-thirds, of the output that a monopolist would produce, A's profits will be £22 million, while B's will be £15 million.

If A and B co-operate, each produces one-half the monopoly output and earns profits of £20 million, as shown in the upper left box. However, at that position, known as the 'co-operative solution', each firm can raise its profits by producing two-thirds of the monopoly output, provided that the other firm does not do the same.

Now assume that A and B make their decisions non-cooperatively. A reasons that, whether B produces either one-half or two-thirds of the monopoly output, A's best output is two-thirds. B reasons similarly. In this case they reach the 'non-cooperative equilibrium', where each produces two-thirds of the monopoly output, and each makes less than it would if the two firms co-operated.

BOX 14.3

The prisoner's dilemma

The game shown in Figure 14.2 is often known as a prisoner's dilemma game. This is the story that lies behind the name:

Two men, John and William, are arrested for jointly committing a crime and are interrogated separately. They know that if they both plead innocent they will get only a light sentence. Each is told, however, that if either protests innocence while the other admits guilt, the one who claims innocence will get a severe sentence while the other will be let off. If they both plead guilty, they will both get a medium sentence.

Here is the payoff matrix for that game:

		John's plea	
		Innocent	Guilty
William's plea	Innocent	J light sentence W light sentence	J no sentence W severe sentence
	Guilty	J severe sentence W no sentence	J medium sentence W medium sentence

John reasons as follows: 'William will either plead guilty or innocent. First, assume he pleads innocent. I get a light sentence if I also plead innocent but no sentence at all if I plead guilty, so guilty is my better plea. Second, assume he pleads guilty. I get a severe sentence if I plead innocent and a medium sentence if I plead guilty. So once again guilty is my preferred plea.' William reasons in the same way, and, as a result, they both plead guilty and get a medium sentence, whereas if they had been able to communicate, they could both have agreed to plead innocent and get off with a light sentence.

Another example of a prisoner's dilemma can arise when two firms are making sealed bids on a contract. For simplicity, assume that only two bids are permitted, either a high or a low price. The high price yields a profit of £10 million, whereas the low price yields a profit of £7 million. If they put in the same price, they share the job and each earns half the profits. If they give different bids, the firm submitting the lower bid gets the job and all the profits. You should have no trouble in drawing up the payoff matrix and determining the outcomes under strategic and co-operative behaviour.

It is easy to see that there is one Nash equilibrium in Figure 14.2. In the bottom-right cell, the best decision for each firm, given that the other firm is producing two-thirds of the monopoly output, is to produce two-thirds of the monopoly output itself. Between them they produce a joint output of one-and-a-third times the monopoly output. Neither firm has an incentive to depart from this position, except through co-operation with the other. In any other

cell, each firm has an incentive to alter its output, *given the output of the other firm.*

The basis of a Nash equilibrium is rational decision-making in the absence of co-operation. Its particular importance in oligopoly theory is that it is the only type of equilibrium that is *self-policing.* It is self-policing in the sense that there is no need for group behaviour to enforce it. Each firm has a self-interest to maintain it because no move that it can make on its own will improve its profits, given what other firms are currently doing.

If a Nash equilibrium is established—by any means whatsoever—no firm has an incentive to depart from it by altering its own behaviour. It is self-policing.

Strategic behaviour   The Nash equilibrium will be attained if each firm behaves strategically, by choosing its optimal strategy taking into account what the other firm may do. Let us see how this works.

Suppose that firm A reasons as follows: 'B can do one of two things; what is the best thing for me to do in each case? First, what if B produces one-half of the monopoly output? If I do the same, I receive a profit of 20, but if I produce two-thirds of the monopoly output, I receive 22. Second, what if B produces two-thirds of the monopoly output? If I produce one-half of the monopoly output, I receive a profit of 15, whereas if I produce two-thirds, I receive 17. Clearly, my best strategy is to produce two-thirds of the monopoly output in either case.'

B will reason in the same way. As a result, they end up producing one-and-a-third times the monopoly output between themselves, and each earns a profit of 17.

This type of game, where the non-cooperative equilibrium makes both players worse off than if they were able to co-operate, is called the prisoner's dilemma. The reason for this curious name, and some further applications, are discussed in Box 14.3.

Breakdown of co-operation   The Nash equilibrium is attained by the strategic reasoning just outlined. It can however be used to give an intuitive argument for why oligopolistic co-operation tends to break down.

Assume that the co-operative position has been attained. The data in Figure 14.2 show that, if A cheats and produces more, its profits will increase. However, B's profits will be reduced: A's behaviour drives the industry's prices down, so B earns less from its unchanged output. Because A's cheating takes the firms away from the joint profit-maximizing monopoly output, their joint profits must fall. This means that B's profits fall by more than A's rise.

Figure 14.2 shows that similar considerations also apply to B. It is worth while for B to depart from the joint maximizing output, as long as A does not do so. So both A and B have an incentive to depart from the joint profit-maximizing level of output.

Finally, Figure 14.2 shows that, when either firm does depart from the joint-maximizing output, the other has an incentive to do so as well. When each follows this 'selfish' strategy, they reach a non-cooperative equilibrium at which they jointly produce one-and-a-third times as much as the monopolist would. Each then has profits that are lower than at the co-operative solution.[9]

Game theory is an extremely flexible tool that has been applied to many branches of economics. Box 14.4 elaborates on some of the theory's basic concepts.

The Appendix to this chapter deals with a different approach to analysing the competition among oligopolists in the short run. This analysis, which is often reserved for more specialized courses in industrial organization, treats a special case of two firms competing to sell an identical product. Although these are very special circumstances, the theories are interesting, both in showing how different types of competition may lead to very interesting results, and in providing an early demonstration of a Nash equilibrium a century before that concept was formulated and analysed in general terms. Those who want to take this further step in the study of the theory of oligopoly might read the Appendix at this point.

TYPES OF CO-OPERATIVE BEHAVIOUR

We have seen that, although oligopolists have an incentive to co-operate, they may be driven, through their own individual decisions, to produce more and earn less than they would if they co-operated. Our next step is to look in more detail at the types of co-operative and competitive behaviour that oligopolists may adopt. We can then go on to study the forces that influence the balance between co-operation and competition in actual situations.

When firms agree to co-operate in order to restrict output and to raise prices, their behaviour is called **explicit collusion**. Collusive behaviour may occur with or without an actual agreement to collude. Where explicit agreement occurs, economists speak of *overt* or *covert collusion*, depending on whether the agreement is open or secret. Where no explicit agreement actually occurs, economists speak of **tacit collusion.**

Explicit collusion   The easiest way for firms to ensure that they will all maintain their joint profit-maximizing output is to make an explicit agreement to do so. Such collusive agreements have occurred in the past, although they have been illegal for a long time in the United Kingdom. When they are discovered today, they are prosecuted. We shall see, however, that such agreements are not illegal everywhere in the world, particularly when they are supported by national governments.

When a group of firms gets together to act in this way in international markets, it is called a cartel. Cartels, which we first met in Chapter 12, show in stark form the basic conflict between co-operation and competition that we just discussed. Full co-operation always allows the industry to achieve the result of monopoly. It also always presents individual firms with the incentive to cheat. The larger the

---

[9] This is why we do not speak of the co-operative *equilibrium*. It is a solution to the problem of finding the best co-operative behaviour; but it is not an equilibrium, since, once achieved, each firm has an incentive to depart from it.

BOX 14.4

Strategies and equilibrium concepts in game theory

A *dominant strategy* occurs when there is one best choice for A to make whatever B does, and one best choice for B to make whatever A does. The equilibrium in Figure 14.2 is a dominant strategy since it is always best for each to produce two-thirds of the monopoly output whatever the other produces. The prisoner's dilemma game in Box 14.3 also has a dominant strategy which is for each to confess no matter what the other does.

All dominant strategies are Nash equilibria, but not all Nash equilibria are dominant strategies. Consider, for example, a hypothetical payoff matrix which arises when two firms, A and B, are trying to decide which independent R&D laboratory to employ to develop some new technology that they both want to use. (In each cell in Table (i), A's payoff is written before the comma and B's payoff after it.) When both firms employ the same laboratory, there is a much bigger payoff than when the research funds are divided between the two laboratories, neither of which may have enough funding to develop the best new technique.

Table (i)

	Firm A employs	
	Lab. Q	Lab. R
Firm B employs		
Lab. Q	20, 20	5, 8
Lab. R	8, 5	15, 15

If A chooses to employ laboratory Q, the best thing B can do is also to employ Q. But if A chooses to employ laboratory R, B should also employ R. The difference between this game and the one in the text is that the biggest payoffs come when both make the same choice and the smallest payoffs when they make different choices. In such cases, each person's best choice depends on the choice made by the other. There are two Nash equilibria in which both firms make the same choice. Although the choice of laboratory Q is better for both than the choice of R, if either firm chooses R, the best the other can do is also to choose R.

There are two problems with Nash equilibria. First, there are games, including the one just considered, with more than one Nash equilibrium (equilibrium is not unique). Second, there may exist no Nash equilibrium, as in the payoff matrix in Table (ii). In this game, if A chooses *U*, B wants to choose *T*, but if B chooses *T*, A wants to choose *V*; but if A does choose *V*, B wants to choose *S*, and if B does choose *S*, A wants to choose *U*. There is no combination of choices where each will be satisfied with his or her own choice given the other player's choice.

So far, we have implicitly assumed that the game is played only once. In *repeated games* the players play the same game many times, and we need to distinguish between *pure strategies*, which means a strategy that does not change, and *mixed strate-*

Table (ii)

	Player A chooses	
	U	*V*
Player B chooses		
S	10, 10	2, 10
T	10, 20	30, 2

gies, which means that each player alternates randomly between each of the available choices with pre-assigned probabilities. In the game of Figure 14.2, one player might choose half the monopoly output with probability 5/6 and two-thirds the monopoly output with probability 1/6. (She could roll a die and choose half the monopoly output if any number from 1 to 5 turned up and two-thirds the monopoly output if a 1 turned up.) The other might choose either output with a probability of 1/2. It is an interesting theorem in game theory that, whatever the payoff matrix, there always exists a Nash equilibrium in mixed strategies for a wide class of games. There is some set of probabilities for making choices among the alternatives by each player that leaves *each player* satisfied with his or her choice of strategy, given the other player's current choice of strategy.

The important insight following from prisoner's dilemma games is that individual maximization does not always lead to a Pareto optimum. In the Nash equilibria of the prisoner's dilemma games shown in Table 14.2 and Box 14.3, both players can be made better off if they co-operate and so move to the top left-hand box. But if both make individual maximizing decisions, they end up in the bottom right-hand box.

Repeated games give a possibility of avoiding the non-optimal prisoner's dilemma solution. In a game that is repeated for ever, called an *infinite game*, one can establish a reputation by punishing a person who does the 'wrong thing' and rewarding him if he does the 'right thing'. In Figure 14.2, call half the monopoly output the 'right choice'. A can adopt the strategy that if B makes the right choice A will make the right choice the next time the game is played; but if B makes the wrong choice A will punish B by also making the wrong choice on the next round of play. This strategy is called *tit for tat*. On computer experiments, this simple strategy outperforms many other, more complex, strategies. The moral is that both players can learn that co-operation pays if the game is played long enough for them to discover that non-cooperation is followed by a competitive reaction that hurts both players.

Perhaps surprisingly, a repeated game that is played for only a finite number of moves provides no such simple resolution to the prisoner's dilemma. The last move of any finite repeated game is exactly the same as a one-time game, since there are no reputation effects to worry about in a game that will not be

---

BOX 14.4 *(continued)*

....

played again. Thus, the best strategy for either player on the last play of the game is to sell two-thirds of the monopoly output. But if that is so, then the second-to-last move also carries no penalty for non-cooperation. And so, by what is called backward induction, we conclude that, as long as co-operation cannot be

ensured by some binding agreement, there is no incentive to co-operate at any point in a finite repeated game.

Game theory has been used in many contexts in economics. It is rich in its applications and ability to explain phenomena that are observed and which seem otherwise inexplicable.

---

number of firms, the greater the temptation for any one of them to cheat. After all, the cheating of one small firm may not be noticed, because it will have a negligible effect on price. This is why, as we saw in Chapter 12, cartels that involve firms in industries that would otherwise be perfectly competitive tend to be unstable.

Cartels may also be formed by a group of firms that would otherwise be in an oligopolistic market. The smaller the group of firms that forms a cartel, the more likely that the firms will let their joint interest in co-operating guide their behaviour. Although cheating may still occur, the few firms in the industry can easily foresee the outcome of an outbreak of rivalry among themselves.

The most famous modern example of a cartel that encourages explicit co-operative behaviour among oligopolists is the Organization of Petroleum Exporting Countries (OPEC). This cartel is discussed in more detail in Chapter 15.

Tacit co-operation While collusive behaviour that affects prices is illegal, a small group of firms that recognize the influence that each has on the others may act without any explicit agreement to achieve the co-operative equilibrium. In terms of Figure 14.2, Firm A decides to produce one-half of the monopoly output, hoping that Firm B will do the same. Firm B does what A expects, and they achieve the co-operative equilibrium without ever explicitly co-operating.

In such *tacit* agreements, the two forces that push towards co-operation and competition are still evident. First, firms have a common interest in co-operating to maximize their joint profits at the co-operative solution. Second, each firm is interested in its own profits, and any one of them can usually increase its profits by behaving competitively.

TYPES OF COMPETITIVE BEHAVIOUR

Although the most obvious way for a firm to violate the co-operative solution is to produce more than its share of the joint profit-maximizing output, there are other ways in which rivalrous behaviour can break out.

Competition for market shares Even if *joint* profits are maximized, there is the problem of market shares. How is the profit-maximizing level of sales to be divided among the competing firms? Competition for market shares may

upset the tacit agreement to hold to joint maximizing behaviour. Firms often compete for market shares through various forms of nonprice competition, such as advertising and variations in the quality of their product. Such costly competition may reduce industry profits.

Covert cheating In an industry that has many differentiated products and in which sales are often by contract between buyers and sellers, covert rather than overt cheating may seem attractive. Secret discounts and rebates can allow a firm to increase its sales at the expense of its competitors while appearing to hold to the tacitly agreed monopoly price.

Very-long-run competition As we first discussed in Chapter 11, very-long-run considerations may also be important. When technology and product characteristics change constantly, there may be advantages to behaving competitively. A firm that behaves competitively may be able to maintain a larger market share and earn larger profits than it would if it co-operated with the other firms in the industry, even though all the firms' joint profits are lower. In our world of constant change, a firm that thinks it can *keep* ahead of its rivals through innovation has an incentive to compete even if that competition lowers the joint profits of the whole industry. Such competitive behaviour contributes to the long-run growth of living standards and may provide social benefits over time that outweigh any losses arising from the restriction of output at any point in time.

For these and for other reasons, there are often strong incentives for oligopolistic firms to compete rather than to maintain the co-operative solution, even when they understand the inherent risks to their joint profits.

Long-run behaviour: the importance of entry barriers

Suppose that firms in an oligopolistic industry succeed in raising prices above long-run average total costs and earn substantial profits that are not completely eliminated by nonprice competition. In the absence of significant barriers to entry, new firms will enter the industry and erode the profits of existing firms, as they do in monopolistic competition. Natural barriers to entry were discussed in Chapter 13. They are an important part of the explanation of the persistence of profits in many oligopolistic industries.

Where such natural barriers do not exist, however, oligopolistic firms can earn profits in the long run only if they can create entry barriers. To the extent to which this is done, existing firms can move towards joint profit maximization without fear that new firms, attracted by the high profits, will enter the industry. We discuss next some types of created barriers.

BRAND PROLIFERATION

By altering the characteristics of a differentiated product, it is possible to produce a vast array of variations on the general theme of that product. Think, for example, of cars with a little more or a little less acceleration, braking power, top speed, cornering ability, petrol mileage, and so on, compared with existing models.

Although the multiplicity of existing brands is no doubt partly a response to consumers' tastes, it can have the effect of discouraging the entry of new firms. To see why, suppose that the product is the type for which there is a substantial amount of brand-switching by consumers. In this case, the larger the number of brands sold by existing firms, the smaller the expected sales of a new entrant.

Say, for example, that an industry contains three large firms, each selling one brand of cigarettes, and say that 30 per cent of all smokers change brands in a random fashion each year. If a new firm enters the industry, it can expect to pick up 25 per cent of the smokers who change brands. (The smoker has available one out of the new total of four brands). This would give the new firm 7.5 per cent (25 per cent of 30 per cent) of the total market the first year merely as a result of picking up its share of the random switchers, and it would keep increasing its share for some time thereafter. If, however, the existing three firms have five brands each, there would be 15 brands already available, and a new firm selling one new brand could expect to pick up only one-sixteenth of the brand switchers, giving it less than 2 per cent of the total market the first year, with smaller gains also in subsequent years. This is an extreme case, but it illustrates a general result:

The larger the number of differentiated products that are sold by existing oligopolists, the smaller the market share available to a new firm that is entering with a single new product.

BOX 14.5

Brand proliferation in alcoholic drinks

What used to be Allied–Lyons PLC and is now Allied–Domecq PLC is one of Britain's largest companies. This is partly because of the diversity of its activities—manufacturing and selling beers and other alcoholic drinks, producing a wide variety of food products, and operating restaurants including Baskin Robins and Dunkin Donuts which are big sellers in North America.

Even within a limited field like alcoholic drinks, the range of apparently competing brands for which the company is responsible is staggering. In addition to the beers produced by the original Ind Coope group and Benskins in the South of England, Allied is responsible for Tetley Bitter, Ansells Bitter, John Bull Bitter, and Draught Burton Ale, all of which originated in the North of England or the Midlands but are increasingly being found in the South. It also produces Double Diamond beer. Even if the Scottish brewers in the group—Drybrough Brewery and Alloa Brewery Company—do not compete much with those further south, there is a wealth of lager brands from which to choose: Lowenbrau, Castlemaine XXXX, Skol, and Oranjeboom. If you want to encourage competition in the cider field, it's no good switching from Gaymer's Olde English to Whiteways: they're both made by Allied. Of course, you could ponder the situation while sipping a whisky: Allied won't mind whether you choose Ballantine's or Teacher's as they own both, while having a 50 per cent share in Grant's Steadfast and Glenfiddich. Switch to Hiram Walker, Irish Mist, or Laphroaig, and you are still drinking Allied. Try a Lamb's Navy Rum for a change, or Courvoisier brandy or Kahlua and Tia Maria liqueurs, and you're still buying from Allied. You may prefer fortified wines like Harvey's sherries or Cockburn's ports; your sophisticated friends go for Tico mixer sherry; your less sophisticated acquaintances for British wines like VP or Rougemont Castle—you're all drinking Allied products.

Of course, Allied is not the only multi-brand producer; most of Allied's few competitors are also very large firms. For another, Guinness own Dimple, Black and White, Vat 69, Gordons, I. W. Harper, Rebel Yell, Tanqueray, Johnnie Walker, Old Parr, White Horse, Harp, Kaliber, Guinness, Hennessy, Moet and Chandon, Hine, Cossack Vodka, Pimm's, Booths, Haig, Dewar's, Bell's, Cardhu, Oban, Talisker, Glen Ord, Glen Elgin, Ushers, Canadian LTD, Mercier, Glenkinchie, and Lagavulin.

The production of such a wide range of differentiated products helps to satisfy consumers' clear demand for diversity. It also has the effect of making it more difficult for a new firm to enter the industry. If the new firm wishes to compete over the whole range of differentiated products, it must enter on a massive scale. If it wishes to enter on only a small scale it faces a formidable task of establishing brand images and customer recognition with only a few products over which to spread these expenses of entry.

An example of brand proliferation drawn from the alcoholic drinks industry is given in Box 14.5.

SET-UP COSTS

Existing firms can create entry barriers by imposing significant fixed costs on new firms that enter their market. This is particularly important if the industry has only weak natural barriers to entry because the minimum efficient scale occurs at an output that is low relative to the total output of the industry.

Advertising is one means by which existing firms can impose heavy set-up costs on new entrants. Advertising, of course, serves purposes other than that of creating barriers to entry. Among them, it performs the useful function of informing buyers about their alternatives, thereby making markets work more smoothly. Indeed, a new firm may find that advertising is essential, even when existing firms do not advertise at all, simply to call attention to its entry into an industry in which it is unknown.

None the less, advertising can also operate as a potent entry barrier by increasing the set-up costs of new entrants. Where heavy advertising has established strong brand images for existing products, a new firm may have to spend heavily on advertising to create its own brand images in consumers' minds. If the firm's sales are small, advertising costs *per unit sold* will be large, and price will have to be correspondingly high to cover those costs.

Figure 14.3 illustrates how heavy advertising can shift the cost curves of a firm with a low minimum efficient scale (MES) to make it one with a high MES. In essence, what happens is that a high MES of advertising is added to a low MES of production, with the result that the overall MES is raised.

A new entrant with small sales but large set-up costs finds itself at a substantial cost disadvantage relative to its established rivals.

Any once-and-for-all cost of entering a market has the same effect as a large initial advertising expenditure. For example, with many consumer goods, the cost of developing a new product that is similar, but not identical, to existing products may be quite substantial. Even if there are few economies of scale in the *production* of the product, its large fixed *development cost* can lead to a falling long-run average total cost curve over a wide range of output.

AN APPLICATION

The combined use of brand proliferation and advertising as an entry barrier helps to explain one apparent paradox of everyday life—that one firm often sells multiple brands of the same product, which compete actively against one another as well as against the products of other firms.

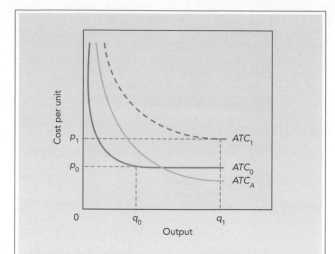

Figure 14.3 Advertising cost as a barrier to entry

Large advertising costs can increase the minimum efficient scale (MES) of production and thereby increase entry barriers. The ATC_0 curve shows that the MES without advertising is at q_0. The curve ATC_A shows that advertising cost per unit falls as output rises. Advertising increases total cost to ATC_1, which is downward-sloping over its entire range. Advertising has given a scale advantage to large sellers and has thus created a barrier to entry.

The soap and cigarette industries provide classic examples of this behaviour. Because all available scale economies can be realized by quite small plants, both industries have few natural barriers to entry. Both contain a few large firms, each of which produces an array of heavily advertised products. The numerous existing products make it harder for a new entrant to obtain a large market niche with a single new product. The heavy advertising, although it is directed against existing products, creates an entry barrier by increasing the set-up costs of a new product that seeks to gain the attention of consumers and to establish its own brand image.

PREDATORY PRICING

A firm will not enter a market if it expects continued losses after entry. One way in which an existing firm can create such an expectation is to cut prices below costs whenever entry occurs and to keep them there until the entrant goes bankrupt. The existing firm sacrifices profits while doing this, but it sends a discouraging message to potential future rivals, as well as to present ones. Even if this strategy is costly in terms of lost profits in the short run, it may pay for itself in the long run by creating *reputation effects* that deter the entry of new firms at other times or in other markets that the firm controls.

Predatory pricing is controversial. Some economists argue that pricing policies that appear to be predatory can be explained by other motives and that existing firms only hurt themselves when they engage in such practices instead of accommodating new entrants. Others argue that predatory pricing has been observed and that it is in the long-run interests of existing firms to punish the occasional new entrant even when it is costly to do so in the short run.

CONTESTABLE MARKETS AND POTENTIAL ENTRY

The theory of contestable markets, developed by the American Professors Baumol, Panzar, and Willig, holds that markets do not have to contain many firms or to experience actual entry for profits to be held near the competitive level. *Potential* entry can do the job just as well as actual entry, as long as (1) entry can be easily accomplished and (2) existing firms take potential entry into account when making price and output decisions.

The theory   Entry is usually costly to the entering firm. It may have to build a plant, it may have to develop new versions of the industry's differentiated product, or it may have to advertise heavily in order to call attention to its product. These and many other initial expenses are often called *sunk costs of entry*. A sunk cost of entry is a cost that a firm must incur to enter the market and that cannot be recovered if the firm subsequently exits. For example, if an entering firm builds a product-specific factory that has no resale value, this is a sunk cost of entry. However, the cost of a factory that is not product-specific and that can be resold for an amount that is close to its original cost is not a sunk cost of entry.

A market in which new firms can enter and leave without incurring any sunk costs of entry is called a perfectly **contestable market**. A market can be perfectly contestable even if the firm must pay some costs of entry, as long as these can be recovered when the firm exits. Because all markets require at least some sunk costs of entry, contestability must be understood as a variable. The lower the sunk costs of entry, the more contestable the market.

In a contestable market, the existence of profits, even if they are due to transitory causes, will attract entry. Firms will enter to gain a share of these profits and will exit when the transitory situation has changed.

Consider, for example, the market for air travel on the lucrative London–Paris route. This market would be quite contestable if it were not regulated, as are all air routes in the EU—and as long as counter and loading space were available to new entrants at the two cities' airline terminals. An airline that was not currently serving the cities in question could shift some of its existing planes to the market with small sunk costs of entry. Some training of personnel would be needed for them to become familiar with the route and the airport. This is a sunk cost of entry that cannot be recovered if the cities in question are no longer to be served. However, most of the airline's costs are not sunk costs of entry. If it subsequently decides to leave a city, the rental of terminal space will stop, and the airplanes and the ground equipment can be shifted to another location. The former head of the American Civil Aeronautics Board, and architect of airline deregulation, captured this point by referring to commercial aircraft as 'marginal cost with wings'.

Sunk costs of entry constitute a barrier to entry, and the larger they are, the larger the profits of existing firms can be without attracting new entrants. The flip side of this coin is that firms operating in markets without large sunk costs of entry will not earn large profits. Strategic considerations will lead them to keep prices near the level that would just cover their total costs. They know that, if they charge higher prices, firms will enter to capture the profits while they last and then exit.

Contestability, where it is possible, is a force that can limit the profits of existing oligopolists. Even if entry does not occur, the ease with which it could be accomplished may keep existing oligopolists from charging prices that would maximize their joint profits.

Contestability is just another example, in somewhat more refined form, of the key point that the possibility of entry is the major force preventing the exploitation of market power to restrict output and to raise prices.

Empirical relevance   Most economists take the view that, although contestable markets are an elegant extension of competitive markets in theory, there are at least *some* barriers to entry in almost all real markets—and very large barriers in many markets. Setting up an effective organization to produce or to sell almost anything incurs fixed costs. In the case of airlines, for instance, a new entrant at a given airport must hire and train staff, advertise extensively to let customers know that it is in the market, set up baggage-handling facilities, and overcome whatever loyalties customers have to the pre-existing firms. New firms in almost all industries face entry costs that are analogous to these. Entering a manufacturing industry usually requires a large investment in industry-specific, and sometimes product-specific, plants and equipment.

These considerations suggest that contestability, in practice, is something to be measured, rather than simply asserted. The higher the costs of entry, the less contestable is the market, and the higher the profits that existing firms can earn without inducing entry. Current evidence suggests that, in practice, a high degree of contestability is quite rare in purely domestic markets. However, the threat of potential entry may come from existing foreign firms rather than new domestic ones. They may have lower set-up costs.

Oligopoly and the functioning of the economy

Oligopoly is found in many industries and in all advanced economies. It typically occurs in industries where both perfect and monopolistic competition are made impossible by the existence of major economies of scale or of scope (or both). In such industries, there is simply not enough room for a large number of firms, all operating at or near their minimum efficient scales.

Three questions are important for the evaluation of the performance of the oligopolistic market structure. First, do oligopolistic markets allocate resources very differently from perfectly competitive markets? Second, in their short-run and long-run price–output behaviour, where do oligopolistic firms typically settle between the extreme outcomes of earning zero profits and earning the profits that would be available to a single monopolist? Third, how much do oligopolists contribute to economic growth by encouraging innovative activity in the very long run? We consider each of these questions in turn.

THE MARKET MECHANISM UNDER OLIGOPOLY

We have seen that under perfect competition prices are set by the impersonal forces of demand and supply, whereas firms in oligopolistic markets administer their prices. The market signalling system works slightly differently when prices are administered rather than being determined by the market. Changes in the market conditions for both inputs and outputs are signalled to the perfectly competitive firm by changes in the prices of its inputs and its outputs. Changes in the market conditions for inputs are signalled to oligopolistic firms by changes in the prices of their inputs. However, changes in the market conditions for the oligopolist's output are typically signalled by changes in the volume of sales at administered prices.

Increases in costs of inputs will shift cost curves upward, and oligopolistic firms will be led to raise prices and lower outputs. Increases in demand will cause the sales of oligopolistic firms to rise. Firms will then respond by increasing output, thereby increasing the quantities of society's resources that are allocated to producing that output. They will then decide whether or not to alter their administered prices.

The market system reallocates resources in response to changes in demands and costs in roughly the same way under oligopoly as it does under perfect competition.

PROFITS UNDER OLIGOPOLY

Some firms in some oligopolistic industries succeed in coming close to joint-profit maximization in the short run. In other oligopolistic industries, firms compete so intensely among themselves that they come close to achieving competitive prices and outputs.

In the long run, those profits that do survive competitive behaviour among existing firms will tend to attract entry. These profits will persist only in so far as entry is restricted either by natural barriers, such as large minimum efficient scales for potential entrants, or by barriers created, and successfully defended, by the existing firms.

VERY-LONG-RUN COMPETITION

Once we allow for the effects of technological change, we need to ask which market structure is most conducive to the sorts of very-long-run changes that we discussed in Chapter 11. These changes are the driving force of the economic growth that has so greatly raised living standards over the last two centuries. They are intimately related to Schumpeter's concept of creative destruction, which we first encountered in our discussion of entry barriers in Chapter 13 (on pp. 243–4).

Examples of creative destruction abound. In the nineteenth century, railways began to compete with wagons and barges for the carriage of freight. In the twentieth century, lorries operating on newly constructed highways began competing with rail. During the 1950s and 1960s, airplanes began to compete seriously with lorries and rail.

In recent years the development of facsimile transmission and electronic mail has eliminated the monopoly of the Post Office in delivering hard-copy (as opposed to oral) communications. In their myriad uses, microcomputers for the home and the office have swept away the markets of many once-thriving products and services. For instance, in-store computers answer customer questions, decreasing the need for salespeople. Aided by computers, 'just in time' inventory systems greatly reduce the investment in inventories required of existing firms and new entrants alike. Computer-based flexible manufacturing systems allow firms to switch production easily and inexpensively from one product line to another, thereby reducing the minimum scale at which each can be produced profitably. One day computers may even displace the textbook.

An important defence of oligopoly relates to this process of creative destruction. Some economists have adopted Schumpeter's concept of creative destruction to develop theories that intermediate market structures, such as oligopoly, lead to more innovation than would occur in either perfect competition or monopoly. They argue that the oligopolist faces strong competition from existing rivals and cannot afford the more relaxed life of the monopolist. At the same time, however, oligopolistic firms expect to keep a good share of the profits that they earn from their innovative activity.

The empirical evidence is broadly consistent with this view. Professor Jesse Markham of Harvard University concluded a survey of empirical findings thus:

If technological change and innovational activity are, as we generally assume, in some important way a product of organized R&D activities financed and executed by business companies, it is clear that the . . . payoffs that flow from them can to some measurable extent be traced to the doorsteps of large firms operating in oligopolistic markets.[10]

Everyday observation provides some confirmation of this finding. Leading North American firms that operate in highly concentrated industries, such as Kodak, IBM, Du Pont, Xerox, General Electric, and 3M, have been highly innovative over many years. UK examples include Rolls-Royce, Glaxo, Wellcome, and GEC.

A FINAL WORD

Oligopoly is an important market structure in modern economies because there are many industries in which the minimum efficient scale is simply too large to support many competing firms. The challenge to public policy is to keep oligopolists competing, rather than colluding, and using their competitive energies to improve products and lower costs, rather than merely erect entry barriers.

Summary

1 Firms in market structures other than perfect competition face negatively sloped demand curves and must administer their prices.

2 In the theory of large-group monopolistic competition, many firms compete to sell differentiated products. Each may make pure profits in the short run, but in the long run freedom of entry shifts its demand curve until it is tangent to the *ATC* curve, leading to excess capacity and production at average costs above the minimum possible level.

3 Competitive behaviour among oligopolists may lead to a non-cooperative equilibrium which is self-policing in the sense that no one has an incentive to depart from it unilaterally. The prisoner's dilemma case of game theory is a case in point.

4 Oligopolistic profits can persist only if there are entry barriers. Natural barriers include economies of large-scale production and large fixed costs of entering the market. Artificial barriers include brand proliferation and high levels of advertising.

5 In qualitative terms, the workings of the allocative system under oligopoly is similar (but not identical) to what it is under perfect competition. Whether oligopoly or perfect competition is more conducive to long-run growth of productivity is an open question.

Topics for review

• The assumptions of monopolistic competition

• Excess capacity under monopolistic competition

• The co-operative solution and the non-cooperative equilibrium

• Entry barriers

• Resource allocation under oligopoly

[10] J. Markham, 'Market Structure and Innovation', *American Economic Review*, May 1966.

APPENDIX TO CHAPTER 14

Cournot and Bertrand on oligopoly

COMPETITION among oligopolists is an important economic phenomenon. Because the group of firms is small enough for each firm to consider how other firms will react to what it does, the possible patterns of behaviour are enormous. This makes the theory of oligopoly much more complex than the theories of perfect or monopolistic competition, where the large number of competitors precludes strategic behaviour.

The path-breaking study of competitive (non-cooperative) behaviour among oligopolists was made by the French economist A. A. Cournot (1801–77). The non-cooperative equilibrium that he demonstrated in 1838 has become one of the basic tools in the recent development of modern oligopoly theory known as 'the new industrial organization' (or the 'new IO' for short). It is indeed an early example of what is now called a Nash equilibrium.

Cournot confined his attention to the special case of an industry containing only two firms, called a **duopoly**. He then assumed that the two firms sold an identical product which was produced at zero marginal cost.[11] Each chose its profit-maximizing output *on the assumption that the other firm would hold its output constant.*

COURNOT EQUILIBRIUM

Figure 14A.1 shows the situation as it looks to either firm when Cournot's assumptions are made. Let us call the firm we are looking at firm 1, and its rival firm 2. For any given quantity produced by firm 2, call it q_2, firm 1 needs only to subtract that quantity from the market demand curve to obtain its own demand curve. Firm 1 can then calculate its profit-maximizing output by equating its marginal cost to its marginal revenue in the usual way.[12] Call this output q_1. Repeating this process for each given q_2 yields a set of corresponding q_1's. We now have what is called firm 1's **reaction curve**. It shows firm 1's profit-maximizing output for each given quantity sold by firm 2. Such a curve is shown in Figure 14A.2.

The whole procedure can now be repeated for firm 2. For each given output for firm 1, q_1, that output can be subtracted from the market demand curve to obtain firm 2's

own demand curve. Firm 2's profit-maximizing output, q_2, can then be calculated. Repeating the procedure for each possible output of firm 1 yields a set of corresponding profit-maximizing outputs for firm 2. This gives us firm 2's reaction curve, showing its profit-maximizing output for each given output by firm 1. This curve is also shown in Figure 14A.2.

Inspection of Figure 14A.2 shows the Cournot equilib-

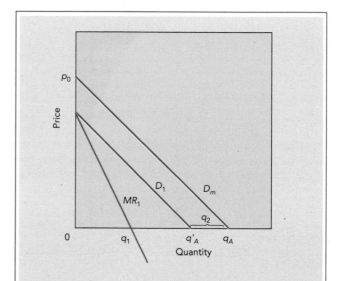

Figure 14A.1 Calculation of a firm's own demand curve in Cournot's model

If one firm's output is given, the other firm's demand curve is easily calculated. The market demand curve is D_m. On that curve, quantity demanded is q_A when price is zero, and it falls to zero when price reaches p_0. Firm 1 assumes that firm 2 will hold its output constant at q_2. Subtracting this fixed quantity from the market demand curve yields firm 1's demand curve which tells firm 1 what it can sell at each price. This curve, labelled D_1 in the diagram, is the market demand curve shifted to the left by the amount q_2, which is the distance q_A–q'_A in the figure. Firm 1's marginal revenue curve, MR_1, is derived from its own demand curve. Equating MR to zero (since marginal cost is zero in this example) yields firm 1's profit-maximizing output, q_1, *given firm 2's output of q_2.*

Firm 1 has its own demand curve, its own marginal cost curve, and its own desired output for each given quantity that it assumes firm 2 will produce.

---

[11] The simplifying assumption of zero marginal cost does not restrict the usefulness of the conclusions, none of which are changed in any important way, if marginal costs are assumed positive.

[12] Since we have simplified by assuming marginal cost to be zero, the firm will produce at the point where its MR curve cuts the quantity axis, i.e. the output for which marginal revenue is zero.

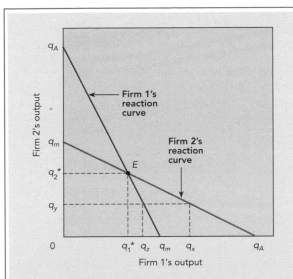

Figure 14A.2 Cournot equilibrium

Cournot equilibrium occurs when, given each firm's present output, the other firm's profit-maximizing output is its present output. The figure shows each firm's reaction curve. Firm 1's curve shows its profit-maximizing output for each *given* output of firm 2. Firm 2's reaction curve shows its profit-maximizing output for *given* outputs of firm 1. The quantity q_m is the monopoly output measured on both axes because it shows what each firm would like to produce if the other's production were zero. The quantity q_A, measured on both axes, is equal to the quantity-axis intercept of the market demand curve in Figure 14.A1 because, when its competitor sells that quantity, the firm in question can sell nothing.

The outputs where the two reaction curves intersect (at E) are the equilibrium outputs. At that point, given q_2^*, firm 1's desired output is q_1^*; and given q_1^*, firm 2's desired output is q_2^*.

No other combination of outputs is an equilibrium. For example, if firm 1 produces output q_x, firm 2 will want to produce q_y; but if firm 2 produces q_y, firm 1 will want to change its output to q_z.

rium. There is the pair of outputs, call them q_1^* and q_2^*, such that, *if firm 1 produces q_1^*, then firm 2 will wish to produce q_2^*; and if firm 2 produces q_2^*, then firm 1 will wish to produce q_1^**. This is a Nash equilibrium: if these outputs are established, neither firm will wish to depart from them, given the assumptions made about their behaviour.

In the Cournot equilibrium, the two firms are making profits that exceed those earned under perfect competition but are less than those that would be earned by a monopoly. They earn less than a monopoly would earn because their joint outputs exceed the monopoly output. They earn more than perfectly competitive firms would make since each is aware that it drives the price down when it increases its own output. Thus, even if each takes its competitor's output as given, the demand curve that they both assume they are facing is negatively sloped; so each stops short of the output for which marginal cost equals price.

BERTRAND EQUILIBRIUM

Some fifty years after Cournot's book was published (and largely ignored), it was reviewed by the French mathematician Bertrand (1822–1900). He argued that Cournot's analysis was unrealistic because each firm determined its own best quantity *on the assumption that the other would hold its quantity constant*. Instead, Bertrand had each firm assume that the other would hold its *price* constant, and then ask itself what is the best *price* for it to charge.

The result was destructive competition which drove price to the level of short-run marginal cost, so that firms would not be covering their fixed costs. To see why, assume that firms start in the Cournot equilibrium as shown in Figure 14A.2. Firm 1 then follows Bertrand's reasoning and asks: 'If firm 2 holds its price constant, what is my best price?' The answer is to undercut firm 2's price by a marginal amount. Firm 1 then gains the whole market in return for a small price cut. For example, if each firm were selling 1,000 units at a price of £1, and firm 1 cut its price to £0.99, it would sell 2,000 units and increase its total revenue from £1,000 (1,000 units at £1) to £1,980 (2,000 units at £0.99). But firm 2 will now reason in the same way. At a price of £1 its sales are now zero, but at a price of £0.98 it could capture the entire market and earn £1,960 (2,000 units at £0.98).[13]

The incentive for price-cutting is always present as long as each firm can increase its profits by capturing the whole market. The only stable position is when price has been driven to short-run marginal cost (which is zero in the present case). At this price, neither firm has any incentive to cut price. Although it would gain the entire market, selling at a price below the marginal cost of production is never profitable.

DO THE THEORIES EMPLOY UNREALISTIC ASSUMPTIONS?

For many years, it was popular to criticize both Cournot's and Bertrand's theories on the grounds that they employed unrealistic assumptions. Surely, it was argued, each firm would learn that its competitors did not sit idly by, holding their prices, or their outputs, constant, while the firm adopted its own best strategy. Indeed, if these theories were

[13] The figures in this paragraph imply a completely inelastic market demand, since 2,000 units are sold whatever the price. If the demand curve has the normal negative slope, the incentive to undercut the competitor becomes even stronger. The undercutting strategy then increases the firm's sales by the amount that it takes from the other firm, plus the amount that market quantity demanded increases as a result of a fall in the market price.

meant to explain how equilibrium was reached, the theories would be naive. As the process of price or quantity undercutting continued, each firm would learn that it was wrong to assume that the other firm would not react. But the theories are not meant to be about the process by which equilibrium is reached, although many critics have thought otherwise. Instead, they are about the existence of an equilibrium which, if reached by any means, will be self-perpetuating.

The great significance of both Cournot's and Bertrand's equilibria is that they are self-policing.

If firms compete actively with each other by varying the quantities that they sell, and if they reach Cournot's equilibrium by any path whatsoever, they will tend to stay there. Any other combination of outputs is not self-policing in the sense that each firm will be tempted to vary its *output*. The same is true of Bertrand's equilibrium. If firms compete with each other by varying prices, and if price is at marginal cost, there is no incentive for any one firm to depart from this *price*. Raising price will reduce sales to zero, while cutting price will capture the entire market but at a price that does not even cover variable costs.

CONSEQUENCES

Intense price competition tends to produce an equilibrium in which firms are not covering their full costs, while intense quantity competition tends to produce an equilibrium in which firms are earning profits that exceed the perfectly competitive result, but are less than the monopoly result.

These two theories left economists in what seemed an unsatisfactory situation. Many of them felt that it was more realistic to assume that firms competed by setting prices rather than quantities. Bertrand's equilibrium, however, could not be a typical one, because if firms reached it in the short run, they would exit from the industry in the long run —the reason being that, if short-run marginal costs are constant and equal to price, firms cannot be covering their fixed costs and so will exit in the long run.[14]

Examples of Bertrand-style price competition do seem to occur from time to time. In unusually bad recessions, price competition sometimes drives prices well below average total costs. Similar behaviour is sometimes found in the aircraft industry even in good times. When the major aircraft companies are competing to sell a new generation of aircraft, most of the development costs have already been incurred. Although direct production costs are not zero, they are a small part of average total costs because the costs of developing a new line of aircraft are enormous. Under these circumstances, the few major aircraft companies compete to sell their similar planes to the world's major air-

lines. If an order is lost, nothing is earned. If an order is gained at any price above variable costs, it contributes something to fixed costs. The resulting competition to obtain large orders can lead to something close to Bertrand's equilibrium. Rather than lose an order, price is sometimes cut well below average total cost and little more than marginal production cost is covered. Such competition is harmful to firms in the long run, but once the fixed costs have been incurred it is hard to prevent price-cutting when large orders can be won or lost.

PRICE OR QUANTITY COMPETITION?

Until recently, economists were left to choose between Cournot's quantity competition and Bertrand's price competition by arguing on intuitive grounds which theory made the more reasonable assumptions—a most unsatisfactory way of choosing between two competing theories. More recently, however, economists, developing what is called *the new theories of industrial organization (the new IO)*, have investigated circumstances under which each type of competition is more likely to occur. For example, in the aircraft case, where fixed costs are all paid before sales take place and the firms have capacity to fill many more orders than they may get, price competition is likely. In other cases, where the production process takes a long time, firms may commit themselves to some level of output, and then sell it for what they can get. In this case, competition is in quantities.

The most important result of these studies, however, concerns capacity.

One firm's temptation to undercut its rival's price and capture all the market, which underlies Bertrand's model, is present only when that firm has the capacity to serve the whole market.

To see this, assume that two firms are in a Cournot equilibrium such as is shown in Figure 14A.2. Now assume also that both firms' plants are operating at maximum capacity; they cannot produce any larger output. Under these circumstances, there is no reason to cut price, since output cannot be increased beyond its present levels in either firm.

An important result using this insight has recently been established by two American economists, D. Kreps and J. Scheinkman.[15] They study a case in which firms first decide how much capacity to install. (How large a plant should I

---

[14] Under perfect competition in the long run, price is equal to short-run marginal cost and to long-run average total cost because the firms' cost curves are U-shaped (see Figure 12.11 on p. 230). If short-run marginal costs are constant, and equal to short-run average variable costs as in the Figure in Box 11.1 marginal cost will be less than average total cost. For example, if *every* unit produced costs £5 in direct production costs, and is sold for £5, there is no revenue available to cover fixed costs.

[15] D. M. Kreps and J. A. Scheinkman, 'Quantity Precommitment and Bertrand Competition yield the same results', *Bell Journal*, 11:326–37.

build?) Having built their plants, firms then compete with each other to sell their outputs. When firms decide on their own best capacity, they know whether the subsequent competition will be in prices (Bertrand) or quantities (Cournot). Under these circumstances, profit-maximizing firms build plants just big enough to supply the output that would occur in Cournot equilibrium. Then, whether they subsequently compete by deciding on quantities, as in Cournot's theory, or on prices, as in Bertrand's theory, they end up in Cournot's equilibrium. They cover their total costs and make profits that are less than a monopoly but more than a perfectly competitive industry. When they do reach the Cournot equilibrium, they are not tempted to cut prices because they are already producing at full capacity.[16]

The intuitive reason for this result is as follows.

Firms often recognize the self-destructive nature of the price competition that was analysed by Bertrand. Having recognized it, they take steps to avoid it. They do this by limiting their capacity to produce.

This very suggestive theory leads us to expect Cournot's results when demand is such that firms can just use their capacity, and Bertrand's results when firms unexpectedly find themselves with large quantities of unused capacity. Thus, for example, when demand persists at unexpectedly low levels, firms will have excess capacity and will be tempted to engage in price competition that may drive price below average total costs. But when demand is at its expected level, firms will not find themselves with the excess capacity that tempts them to undercut their competitors, thereby driving price below Cournot's equilibrium level. This is no accident; firms will have planned it that way.

[16] The firms are engaged in what is called a two-stage game that uses the equilibrium concept of subgame perfection. The two stages are the decision on plant size and the competition between the firms once their plants are built. Subgame perfection means that, in making its first decision on capacity, each firm understands the kind of competitive game it will be playing in the second stage when it competes to sell its output. Recent research has focused on the conditions for Cournot's equilibrium to be the outcome of this two-stage game. The important result, however, is that Bertrand's equilibrium is never the outcome if demand is correctly foreseen.

~ CHAPTER 15

The theory of the firm and industry in action

THIS chapter is in two parts. In the first section, we use our theory to predict how industries will react to both natural and policy-induced changes in the incentives that affect their behaviour. In the second section, we use the theory to understand the effects of the Organization of Petroleum Exporting Countries (OPEC). This provides a case study that uses much of the theory we have learned so far in this book. Although understanding the behaviour of OPEC is important in itself, what really matters is that you get practice in using economic theory to understand real-world events on your own.

Predictions of the theory of the firm and industry

IN this part of this chapter, we use economic theory to predict how firms and industries will react to changes in demand, costs, and taxes. These predictions can be viewed in two different ways. First, they are logical implications of the theory's assumptions. From this point of view, the truth of a certain proposition is a matter of logic: the proposition either is, or is not, implied by the theory. Second, the predictions may be regarded as empirical hypotheses. Their consistency with the facts is then a matter for testing.

Whether or not a given proposition is implied by some theory is a question that can be settled definitely without reference to facts; whether or not a given proposition that follows from a theory is consistent with the facts can be settled only by observation.

Changes in demand

How do markets respond to changing demands and costs? The analysis of this question is important because it sets the stage for a study of the effects of taxes, subsidies, innovations, and a host of other things, all of which affect either the revenues or the costs of firms. As in any study using comparative statics, we must start at an equilibrium. (Appropriate corrections can be made if one wishes to apply the results to cases in which the initial position is one of disequilibrium.)

COMPETITION

The effects of shifts in demand in perfect competition have been analysed on pp. 230–1 of Chapter 12. For completeness, we summarize these results here.

In the short run, a rise in demand in a competitive industry will cause:

1. price to rise;

2. an increase in the quantity supplied by each firm and hence by the industry;

3. each firm to earn profits.

The long-run effects follow from the third prediction. Profits will attract new investment. New entry will cause an increase in supply that will force the price below the previously established, short-run equilibrium. This will continue until profits have returned to zero.

In the long run, a rise in demand in a competitive industry will cause:

1. the scale of industry to expand;

2. profits to return to zero;

3. the new equilibrium price to be above, below, or equal to the original price; but (i) constant factor prices and (ii) identical, and unchanged, cost curves for new and old firms ensure that price returns to its original level.

Now consider the effects of a fall in demand.

In the short run, a fall in demand in a competitive industry will cause:

1. price to fall;

2. a decrease in the quantity supplied by each firm and hence by the industry;

3. each firm to make losses;

4. firms to cease production immediately if they are unable to cover their variable costs of production.

The long-run effects follow from the third prediction. Losses make the industry an unattractive place in which to invest. No new capital will enter; as old plant and equipment wear out, it will not be replaced. As the supply diminishes, the price of the product will rise until the remaining firms can cover their total costs.

In the long run, a fall in demand in a competitive industry will cause:

1. the scale of the industry to contract;

2. losses to be eliminated eventually;

3. price to be above, below or equal to its original level; but (i) constant factor prices and (ii) identical, and unchanged, cost curves for all firms ensure that price returns to its original level.

OLIGOPOLY

When we consider market structures other than perfect competition, we must distinguish short-run cyclical fluctuations in demand from changes that are perceived to be longer-lasting. We observed in Chapter 14 that oligopolies tend to adjust quantity rather than price when demand fluctuates in the short term (see p. 257). Thus, cyclical fluctuations in demand cause output to change at a (more or less) constant price in oligopolistic industries.

Long-term changes in demand lead to more familiar adjustments. Permanent decreases in demand cause capital to leave the industry. Price then rises or falls depending on what happens to the costs of the remaining firms, and to their degree of competition. Permanent increases in demand cause capital to enter the industry. Price rises or falls depending on what happens to firms' costs and to the degree of competition. Even if the number of firms does not change, existing firms will alter their outputs. They will then wish to move to a different point on their *LRAC* curves by altering their plant size. (Recall that perfect competition is the only market structure in which firms must be on the lowest point of their *LRAC* curve in equilibrium.)

MONOPOLY

Short-term cyclical fluctuations have the same effect as in oligopoly and for the same reasons: it does not always pay the monopolist to vary price in response to shifts in demand that are expected to be transitory.

Now consider a shift in demand that is assumed to be long-lasting. In the section on the absence of a supply curve under monopoly (see Figure 13.5 on p. 241), we saw that a rise in demand need not always cause an increase in a monopolist's price and output, even in the short run. It is possible, provided that the elasticity of demand changes sufficiently, for a rise in demand to cause a fall either in price or in output.

At this level of generality, we are left with the implication that a rise in demand for a monopoly can cause both its price and its output to rise, but that either price or output might fall. This may seem a disappointingly vague conclusion, but it is all that the theory implies. In order to get a more specific prediction, we need to know more about the precise shape of the demand curve.

There are some cases in which predictions are possible. Two are of particular interest. In the first case, every point on the demand curve shifts by the same amount. This case applies to a *per-unit* tax or subsidy on the monopolist's output. A specific tax can be shown as a shift of the firm's demand curve vertically downwards by the amount of the tax, since for any given market price the firm receives the price *minus* the tax. A specific subsidy shifts it upwards in the same way.

In the second case the demand curve pivots through its point of intersection on the price axis. This case applies when the market expands because of the addition of new customers with the same tastes as those initially in the market. In this case, if the number of customers increases by x per cent, the quantity demanded also increases by x per cent at each price.

Figure 15.1 shows that, in each of these cases, both price and quantity rise when demand rises, and fall when demand falls.

Changes in costs

COMPETITION

Figure 15.2 analyses the effects of a reduction in the costs of production in a competitive industry. The short-run supply curve shifts downwards by the amount of the downward shift in the firms' marginal cost curves. This leads to a higher output and a lower price. The price will fall, however, by less than the fall in costs, while profits will now be earned because of the lower costs of production.

In the short run under perfect competition, a fall in variable cost causes price to fall but by less than the reduction in marginal cost. The benefit of the reduction in cost is thus shared between consumers, in terms of lower prices, and producers, in terms of higher profits.

In the long run, however, profits cannot persist in an industry having freedom of entry. New firms will enter the industry, increasing output and reducing price until all profits are eliminated.

In the long run under perfect competition, all of the benefits of lower costs are passed on to consumers in terms of higher output and lower prices.

The case of a rise in costs is just the reverse. In the short run, the effects will be shared between consumers, in terms of higher prices, and producers, in terms of losses. In the long run, however, firms will leave the industry until those remaining can cover all their costs. Therefore, the effects of higher costs are fully borne by consumers in terms of lower output and higher prices.

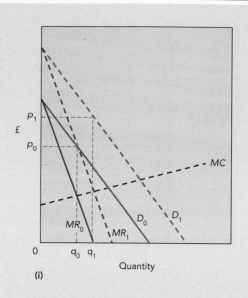
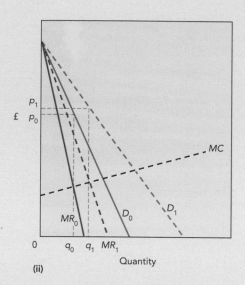

(i)   (ii)

Figure 15.1 Shifts in a monopolist's demand curve

When a monopolist's demand curve either shifts parallel to itself or pivots through the price intercept, both price and quantity change in the same direction. In both parts of the figure, the original demand curve is D_0. The marginal revenue curve MR_0 and the marginal cost curve intersect at output q_0, which is sold at price p_0. The demand curve then shifts outwards to D_1. The new marginal revenue curve, MR_1, intersects the unchanged MC curve to produce a new equilibrium price and quantity of p_1 and q_1. Both price and quantity rise. (Both fall if the shift is a fall in demand from D_1 to D_0). The difference between the two parts is in the nature of the demand shift.

In part (i) the demand curve shifts parallel to itself, indicating the same *absolute change* in quantity demanded at each price, and the same *absolute change* in price at which each quantity will be bought.

In part (ii) the demand curve pivots through the price intercept, indicating the same *percentage change* in quantity demanded at each price.

OLIGOPOLY

In oligopoly, a fall in costs yields a fall in the profit-maximizing price at normal-capacity output. Therefore, price will fall and output will rise. Also, profits will rise so that, once again, pressure will occur for new entry. A battle may then ensue between new firms desiring entry and existing firms pursuing entry-barring strategies.

MONOPOLY

A fall in marginal costs will cause a reduction in price and an increase in output. (You should draw your own figure to illustrate this.) Thus, the direction of the change in price and output, in response to a change in costs, is the same in monopoly as in perfect competition. But the magnitude of the change will be less in monopoly than in competition. Since a monopoly firm necessarily has barriers to entry (or it would not be a monopoly), the higher profit that it earns as a result of a fall in its costs does *not* attract new entrants.

Thus, there is no long-run force to drive profits back to their original level.

In monopoly, in both the short run and the long run, the effects of rising or falling costs are shared between the consumers, in terms of price and output variations, and the firm, in terms of profit variations.

We now have a powerful tool at our command: once we can relate anything in which we are interested to change in either costs or revenues, we have a series of predictions already worked out. We shall see examples of how this can be done in the next section of this chapter, and later in this book.

The effect of taxes on price and output

There are many kinds of taxes that affect the costs of firms. We shall consider three of them here: a tax that is a fixed

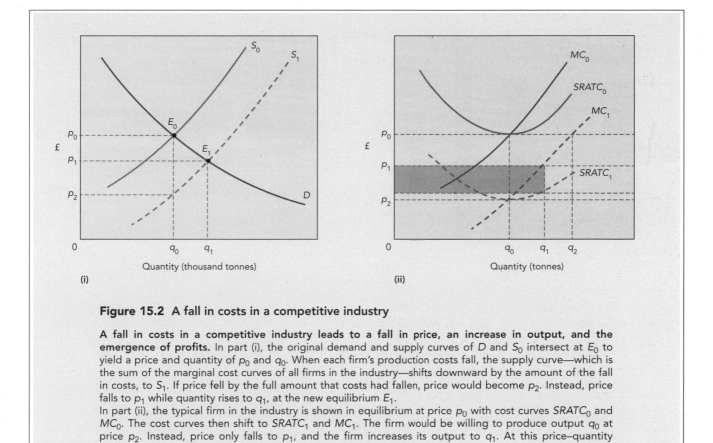

Figure 15.2 A fall in costs in a competitive industry

A fall in costs in a competitive industry leads to a fall in price, an increase in output, and the emergence of profits. In part (i), the original demand and supply curves of D and S_0 intersect at E_0 to yield a price and quantity of p_0 and q_0. When each firm's production costs fall, the supply curve—which is the sum of the marginal cost curves of all firms in the industry—shifts downward by the amount of the fall in costs, to S_1. If price fell by the full amount that costs had fallen, price would become p_2. Instead, price falls to p_1 while quantity rises to q_1, at the new equilibrium E_1.

In part (ii), the typical firm in the industry is shown in equilibrium at price p_0 with cost curves $SRATC_0$ and MC_0. The cost curves then shift to $SRATC_1$ and MC_1. The firm would be willing to produce output q_0 at price p_2. Instead, price only falls to p_1, and the firm increases its output to q_1. At this price–quantity combination, it earns profits shown by the dark blue area.

amount per unit produced; a tax that is a fixed amount; and a tax that is a fixed percentage of profits. The first is called a per-unit tax, the second a lump-sum tax, and the third a profits tax.

PER-UNIT TAX

Box 15.1 shows two methods of analysing the effects of a per-unit tax. The method that we use in what follows is to observe that, with a per-unit tax, the firm must pay the tax to the government on each unit that it produces. Thus, the tax may be thought of as increasing the costs associated with producing each unit. The marginal cost curve of every firm shifts vertically upwards by the amount of the tax, where marginal cost now refers to the total outlay—factor payments and taxes—associated with each additional unit of production.

Perfect competition In perfect competition, the upward shift in marginal cost curves means that the industry supply curve shifts upward by the amount of the tax. Now we can

refer to the results of our previous study of cost changes in order to obtain the required predictions.

The effects of a per-unit tax on the output of a competitive industry are as follows:

1. in the short run, the price will rise but by less than the amount of the tax, so that the burden will be shared by consumers and producers;

2. in the long run, the industry will contract, profits will return to normal, and the whole burden will fall on consumers;

3. if cost curves of firms remaining in the industry are unaffected by the contraction in the size of the industry, price will rise in the long run by the full amount of the tax.

The second of the above predictions is an example of a most important general proposition: *in an industry with freedom of entry or exit and where there is room for a large number of firms, profits will always be pushed to zero in the*

BOX 15.1

···

Alternative methods of analysing a sales tax

The two parts of the figure show a competitive market in equilibrium with the demand and supply curves D and S intersecting at E_0 to produce equilibrium price and output of p_0 and q_0. A tax of T pence per unit is then placed on the product.

Part (i) analyses the effect of the tax by adding it to the supply curve. The 'costs' of the firm now include production costs plus the tax that must be paid to the government. Every point on the supply curve shifts vertically upwards by the amount of the tax. The intersection of the new curve S_T and the demand curve D yields the new quantity and market price of q_1 and p_1. Producers'

after-tax receipts are read for the original supply curve, S, and are p_2 ($= p_1 - T$) per unit.

Part (ii) analyses the same tax by subtracting it from the demand curve. The new curve D_T tells us the after-tax receipts of producers. Its intersection with the supply curve, S, yields the after-tax equilibrium. The new equilibrium quantity is q_1, producers get after-tax receipts of p_2 per unit, while the market price is p_1.

These are two alternative ways of studying the same tax and they give identical results, as can be seen by comparing the two figures.

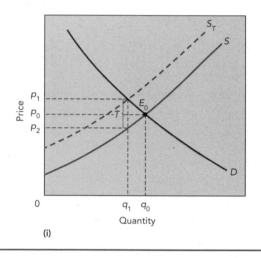

(i)

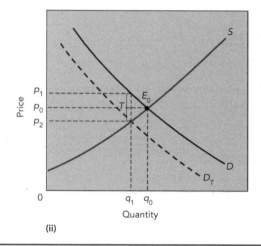

(ii)

---

long run. Thus, any temporary advantage or disadvantage given to the industry by any public policy or private action must be dissipated in the long run—free entry and exit always ensures that surviving firms earn zero profits.

Government intervention in an industry with freedom of entry and exit can influence the size of the industry, the total volume of its sales, and the price at which its goods are sold; but intervention cannot influence the long-run profitability of the firms that remain in the industry.

Many a government policy has started out to raise the profitability of a particular industry, and ended up only increasing the number of firms operating at an unchanged level of profits. A further illustration of this important point is given in Box 15.2.

Monopoly   Although the monopoly firm has no supply curve, the tax does shift its marginal cost curve. The analysis of the previous section on cost shifts allows us to state that:

In the short run, and in the long run, the burden of a per-unit tax placed on a monopoly that is earning profits will be shared between consumers, in terms of lower output and higher prices, and the producer, in terms of lower profits.

LUMP-SUM TAX

Lump-sum taxes increase the fixed costs of the firm but do not increase marginal costs. As long as a firm is able to cover its variable costs, it will remain in production. Since both marginal costs and marginal revenues are unaffected by the taxes, the profit-maximizing level of output must be unchanged.

A lump-sum tax leaves the short-run equilibrium price and output unchanged in all market structures, unless the tax is so high that it causes firms to abandon production at once.

This result is shown in Figure 15.3(i). The long-run effects

BOX 15.2

....

The price of haircuts and the profits of hairdressers

Suppose that there are many hairdressers and freedom of entry into the industry: anyone can set up as a hairdresser. Assume that the going price for haircuts is £5 and that at this price all hairdressers believe their incomes are too low.

The hairdressers hold a meeting and decide to form a trade association. The purpose of the association is to impose a price of £10 for haircuts. What is the result?

We need to distinguish between the short-run and the long-run effects of an increase in the price of haircuts. In the short run the number of hairdressers is fixed. Thus, in the short run the answer depends only on the elasticity of the demand for their services. If demand elasticity is less than 1, total expenditure will rise and so will the incomes of hairdressers; if demand elasticity exceeds 1, the hairdressers' revenues will fall. Thus, to answer the question we need some knowledge about the size of the elasticity of demand for haircuts.

Suppose we estimate the elasticity of demand over the relevant price range to be 0.45. We then predict that hairdressers will be successful in raising incomes in the short run. A 40 per cent rise in price will be met by an 18 per cent fall in quantity, so the total revenue of the typical hairdresser will rise by about 15 per cent.*

Now what about the long run? If hairdressers were just covering costs before the price change, they will now be earning economic profits. Hairdressing will become an attractive trade relative to others requiring equal skill and training, and there will be a flow of new entrants into the industry. As the number of hairdressers rises, the same amount of business must be shared among more and more of them, so the typical hairdresser will find business—and thus earnings—decreasing.

Profits may also be squeezed from another direction. With fewer customers coming their way, hairdressers may compete against one another for the limited number of customers. Their agreement does not allow them to compete through price cuts, but they can compete in service. They may spruce up their shops, offer their customers expensive magazines to read, and so forth. This kind of non-price competition will raise operating costs.

These changes will continue until hairdressers are just covering their opportunity costs, at which time the attraction for new entrants will vanish. The industry will settle down in a new long-run equilibrium in which individual hairdressers make incomes only as large as they did before the price rise. There will be more hairdressers than there were in the original situation, but each one will be working for a smaller fraction of the day and will be idle for a larger fraction. (The industry will have excess capacity.) Customers will have shorter waits even at peak periods, and they will get to read a wide choice of magazines, but they will be paying £10 for haircuts.

If the association adopted the plan in order to raise the average income of hairdressers, it will have failed. It has created more jobs for hairdressers, but not a higher income for each.

The general lesson is clear: one cannot raise income by raising price above the competitive level *unless* one can prevent new entry or otherwise reduce the quantity of the product or service provided.

* Let p and q be the price and quantity before the price increase. Total revenue after the increase is $TR = (1.4p)\,(0.82q) = 1.148pq$.

---

of a lump-sum tax differ between monopolistic and competitive industries.

Perfect competition   If a perfectly competitive industry is in equilibrium with zero profits before the tax is instituted, then the tax will cause losses. Although nothing will happen in the short run to price and output, equipment will not be replaced as it wears out. Thus, in the long run the industry will contract, and price will rise until the *whole tax* has been passed on to consumers and the firms remaining in the industry are again covering total costs.

A lump-sum tax will have no effect on a competitive industry in the short run, but in the long run it will cause the exit of firms; output will fall and price will rise until the whole of the tax is borne by consumers.

Monopoly   Assuming that the firm was previously making

profits, the tax merely reduces the level of these profits. But, since the tax reduces the profit associated with every output by the same amount, it does not change the profit-maximizing output. Therefore, the tax leaves the monopoly's price and output unchanged.

In the long run, the lump-sum tax that does not drive a monopolist out of business has no effect on its price and output; hence the whole tax is paid by the monopolist.

Of course, if the tax is so large that, even at the profit-maximizing output, profits become negative, the monopolist will cease production in the long run.

PROFITS TAX

A famous prediction is that a tax levied as a percentage on what economists call profits will have no effect on price and

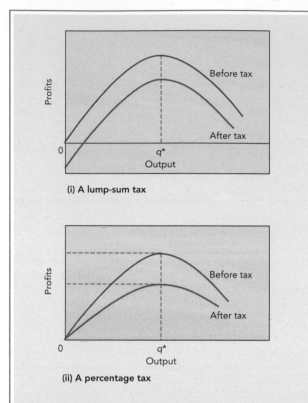

(i) A lump-sum tax

(ii) A percentage tax

Figure 15.3 A tax on pure profits

A tax on pure profits leaves equilibrium price and output unchanged. In both parts of the diagram, the upper curve shows how profits vary with output in the absence of a tax. The profit-maximizing output is q^*. The lower curve shows how profits vary with output after a tax is imposed on profits.

In part (i) the tax is a lump sum. Every point on the upper curve shifts down by the same amount. The profit-maximizing output remains at q^*.

In part (ii) the tax is 20 per cent of profits. Every point on the lower curve is 20 per cent less than the corresponding point on the upper curve. The profit-maximizing output remains at q^*.

output under any market structure. Let us first see how the prediction is derived, and then consider its application to real-world situations.

Perfect competition In perfect competition, there are no profits in long-run equilibrium. Thus, the firms in a perfectly competitive industry will pay no profit tax in the long run. (x per cent of zero is zero.) It follows that the tax does not affect the firm's long-run behaviour.

Monopoly A monopoly firm usually earns profits in the long run and, therefore, would pay a profits tax. The tax would reduce its profits but would not cause the firm to alter its quantity produced nor (hence) its price. Since the firm's previous output yields higher profits than any other output, taxing away a percentage of the firm's profits cannot make any other output yield more profits than the previous profit-maximizing output. This result is illustrated in Figure 13.3 on p. 240. A tax which is a proportion of the profit (shaded) will not change the optimal price and output, as it does not shift the MC, MR or D curves, so post tax profits are still maximized at the existing output and price.

A tax on profit, as defined in economics, affects neither price nor output in perfect competition and in monopoly. Hence it does not affect the allocation of resources.

A qualification Does this prediction apply to taxes on firms' profits that are actually levied in many countries? The answer is no, because profits are defined in tax law according to accountants' rather than economists' usage. In particular, the tax-law definition includes the opportunity cost of capital and the reward for risk-taking. To economists, this is a cost; for tax purposes, it is profit. (The discussion on p. 187 is relevant to this point.)

Consider some of the consequences of a tax on the return to capital. First, perfectly competitive firms will pay such taxes even in long-run equilibrium, since they use capital and must earn enough money to pay a return on it. Second, the tax will affect costs differently in different industries. To see this, compare two industries. One is very labour-intensive, so that 90 per cent of its costs of production go to wages and only 10 per cent to capital and other factors. The other is very capital-intensive, so that fully 50 per cent of its costs (in the economists' sense) are a return to capital. The tax on the return to capital will take a small part of the total earnings of the first industry and a large part of those of the second industry. If the industries were equally profitable (in the economists' sense) before the tax, they would not be afterwards, and producers would be attracted into the first industry and out of the second one. This would cause prices to change until both industries became equally profitable, after which no further movement would occur.

A tax on profits as they are defined in tax law does affect the allocation of resources.

Other ways in which 'profit taxes' influence the allocation of resources could be mentioned. Enough has been said, however, to show the importance of distinguishing between taxes levied on what economists mean by profits, and taxes levied on what accountants and the firm define as profits.

OPEC: a case study of a cartel

COCOA producers in West Africa, farmers in the European Union, coffee growers in Brazil, oil producers in the OPEC countries, taxi drivers in many cities, and labour unions throughout the world have all sought to obtain, through collective action, some of the benefits of departing from the price-taking aspects of perfect competition. Although no real-world industry is exactly described by the assumptions of perfect competition, the theory is useful because it captures some characteristic of real-world market structures. In all of the cases mentioned above, the sellers were so numerous that they had no individual market power; acting individually, they had to accept the market price that was determined by forces beyond their control. In short, they were similar to the firms in the theory of perfect competition in that they were price-takers.

In Chapter 13 we studied the behaviour of perfectly competitive firms that organized themselves into a cartel. We reached two important conclusions:

1. **It always pays the producers in a perfectly competitive industry to enter into an output-restricting agreement.**
2. **Each individual cartel member can increase its profits by violating the output restrictions, provided that the other members do not violate theirs.**

These two predictions highlight the dilemma of any cartel, composed of firms which, acting individually, would be price-takers, whether it be OPEC or a local producers' association. Each firm is better off if the cartel is effective in restricting output and so raising price. But each is even better off if everyone else co-operates while it cheats. Yet if all cheat, all will be worse off.

The behaviour of the Organization of Petroleum Exporting Countries (OPEC) provides an example of the cartelization of an industry that contained a large number of competing firms, most of which were price-takers. It created an oligopoly rather than a monopoly. Its behaviour illustrates both the problems of oligopolistic industries and the general functioning of the price system in all the runs—short, long, and very long.

Early success

Before 1973, the oil industry was not perfectly competitive. There were so many oil-producing countries, however, that no one country could significantly influence the price of oil by withholding its own output from the market. Thus, at least in the price-taking aspect, the various oil-producing countries sold their oil in a perfectly competitive market. There was large unused productive capacity in the OPEC countries, making the short-run world supply highly elastic at a world price that was close to OPEC's production costs.

OPEC did not attract world attention until 1973, when for the first time its members voluntarily agreed to restrict their outputs by negotiating quotas. At the time, OPEC countries accounted for about 70 per cent of the world's supply of crude oil and 87 per cent of world oil exports. So, although it was not quite a complete monopoly, the cartel had substantial monopoly power. As a result of the output restrictions, the world price of oil nearly quadrupled within a year. What happened is analysed in more detail in Figure 15.4.[1]

OPEC's policy succeeded for several reasons. First, the member-countries provided a large part of the total world supply of oil; second, other producing countries could not quickly increase their outputs in response to price increases; and third, the world demand for oil proved to be highly inelastic in the short run.

OPEC's exports were about 31 million barrels per day in 1973. In order to raise prices within a year from an average of $3.37 per barrel to an average of $11.25 a barrel, exports had only to be restricted to 28.5 million barrels per day. A reduction in OPEC's exports of less than 10 per cent was sufficient to more than triple the world price! (Note that oil prices are usually expressed in terms of US dollars.)

The higher prices were maintained for the remainder of the decade, as shown in Figure 15.5. As a result, OPEC countries found themselves suddenly enjoying vast wealth,

---

[1] In this chapter, we are concerned mainly with the direct impact of OPEC on micro markets for petroleum. It is worth noticing, however, that the OPEC price shock had massive, world-wide effects on many of the macroeconomic variables. Petroleum is used for a wide range of products beyond the fuels we most associate with it. For example, it is also used for fertilizers and as the basis for many plastics and other chemical products. Its use as a fuel is so widespread that, when its price rose dramatically, the costs of producing many manufactured products, and hence their prices, also rose. For all of these reasons, many countries suffered modern history's first 'stagflation'—a rising general price level combined with falling output and employment. For those of the world's poorer countries who were also oil-importers, the OPEC price shock was little short of a disaster. Unable to pay the current prices for their oil imports, and unwilling to suffer the drastic fall in economic activity that would have been the consequence of curtailing oil imports to what could currently be paid for, these countries borrowed heavily to pay for the imports. A vicious circle then arose, with OPEC countries earning vast profits and depositing the money with banks and other financial institutions, which lent it to the poorer countries, which spent it on oil, which created yet more profits for OPEC countries and yet more borrowing. Although it was not the only reason, the OPEC price shock was one of the major causes of the build-up of the vast stock of debt that still hampers many poorer countries in their attempts to encourage economic development.

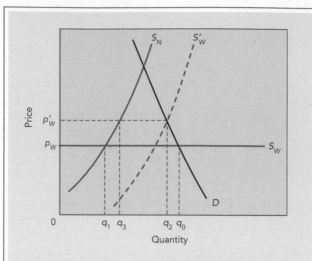

Figure 15.4 OPEC as a successful cartel

Given a rising, non-OPEC supply curve of oil, OPEC could determine equilibrium price by choosing its contribution to total supply. The curve S_N represents the non-OPEC supply curve of oil. When the OPEC countries were prepared to supply all that was demanded at the world price p_W, the world supply curve was S_W. At that price, production was q_1 in non-OPEC countries, and q_0-q_1 in OPEC countries.

By fixing its production, OPEC shifted the world supply curve S'_W, where the horizontal distance between S_N and S'_W is OPEC's production. The world price rose to p'_W. Production became q_3 in non-OPEC countries, and q_2-q_3 in the OPEC countries.

OPEC increased its oil revenues because, although sales fell, the price rose more than in proportion. Non-OPEC countries gained doubly because they were free to produce more, and to sell it at the new, higher world price.

while oil-importing countries found their real incomes substantially diminished.

So great was the increase in the wealth of the member-countries that the temptation to cheat, in order to gain even more, was small during the rest of the 1970s. Indeed, the development programmes of many OPEC countries were constrained not by funds, but by physical limits to their growth. For example, there was a great need for roads, warehouses, and other basic facilities to be constructed. Ships carrying supplies often lay in harbour for months because of insufficient port facilities. Even when they were unloaded, supplies often sat at the harbour side for further months because of inadequate internal transport facilities. Because further funds were not urgently needed by OPEC members, the temptation to cheat was weak, making the enforcement of OPEC's output quotas an easy matter.

By the end of the 1970s, however, the OPEC countries had become used to their vast wealth and were spending more and more on arms, as well as on economic development. Eager for yet more income, they engineered a second output restriction that pushed prices (measured in current dollars) from the $10–$12 range to over $30 a barrel. New income poured in, and OPEC's power to hold the oil consuming world to ransom seemed limitless.

Longer-term market forces, however, were inexorably working against OPEC.

Pressure on the cartel

Monopolistic producers always face a dilemma. The closer are their prices to the profit-maximizing level, the greater their short-term profits, but also the greater the incentive for market reactions that will reduce their profits in the longer term. In OPEC's case, the market reactions came from both the demand and the supply sides of the market.

INCREASING WORLD SUPPLY

The high prices and high profits achieved by the OPEC cartel spurred major additions to the world's oil supply by non-OPEC producers. This was, in effect, new entry. In 1973 OPEC produced more than 70 per cent of the world's oil; by 1979 its share was less than 60 per cent, and by 1985 it was only 30 per cent. North Sea oil, Mexican oil, Soviet oil, and increased American and Canadian production gradually replaced output that had been withdrawn from the market by OPEC. Higher prices encouraged new exploration and induced the oil companies to produce more from already proven reserves. The increased supply of non-OPEC oil tended to drive the world price down. To maintain the price, OPEC had to reduce its own output so as to hold world output constant. The OPEC countries would lose revenue if they held their output constant because their prices fell; if they took steps to maintain prices, outputs and shares of the world market would have to be reduced.

DECLINING WORLD DEMAND

The market demand curve for oil shows how the purchases of oil will vary as price varies, *other things being equal*. But, other things being equal, there was little that users could do to reduce their consumption of petroleum products in response to the price rise. Car drivers could take fewer Sunday trips, and some took a train or bus to work when petrol prices soared. Householders and office managers turned their heating down a bit. Factories tried to economize on their fuel consumption. But, overall, the response of world demand to the initial price increase was modest. The market demand curve was thus highly inelastic.

Over a longer period of time, however, major economies proved possible—as they almost always do for any product whose relative price rises greatly. When it came time to

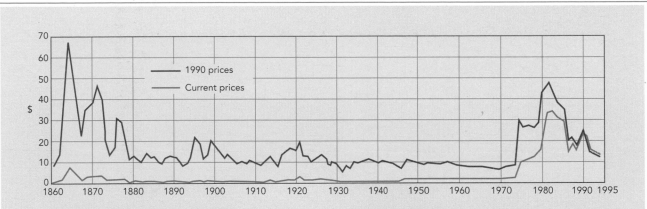

Figure 15.5 Oil prices 1860–1994 (current and constant US$ per barrel)

Oil prices have now almost returned to their pre-OPEC shock level in real terms. The blue line gives average oil prices in current dollars for each year from 1860 to date. These are the prices quoted in the text. The red line gives oil prices in constant 1990 dollars. This corrects oil prices for the changes in the price level and expresses them in 1990 prices relative to the average level of prices in 1990. Oil was a rare commodity with few uses in 1860, and its small demand and even smaller supply produced a very high price. By 1890 oil had many uses and was being produced in quantity at a low and stable price. The first OPEC shock is seen pushing up prices to the $25–$30 range, while the second shock pushed them to the $40–$45 range (expressed in 1990 prices). Since then, the decline in OPEC's market power has been manifest in a gradual fall of prices back nearly to their pre-1973 level in real terms.

Source: BP Statistical Review of World Energy, 1994.

replace the family car, many people responded to the high price of petrol by buying smaller, more fuel-efficient cars. Householders and office managers found that they could greatly reduce their fuel bills by properly insulating their buildings or by turning to such alternative sources of heating as natural gas. New factories were able to use newly designed power plants that used alternative fuels or were much more economical in their use of oil. A host of longer-term adaptations economized on petroleum products within known technology. The long-run demand curve proved to be much more elastic than the short-run demand curve. (See Figure 5.8 on p. 95, for an elaboration of the distinction between short- and long-run demand curves.)

Very-long-run forces were also unleashed. The high price of petroleum led to a burst of scientific research to develop more petroleum-efficient technologies, and alternatives to petroleum. Solar-heating technology was advanced, as was technology concerning many longer-term alternatives such as tidal power and heat from the interior of the earth. Had the price of petroleum remained at its 1980 peak, this research would have continued at an intense pace, and would have borne increasing fruits in the decades that followed.

As a result of the long- and very-long-run reactions, other things did *not* remain equal over the period of a decade. Instead, the market demand curve for oil began to shift to the left.[2]

The combined effect of decreasing demand and increasing supply is illustrated in Figure 15.6. The shrinking market for OPEC oil at the high OPEC price necessitated ever stiffer production limitations if the cartel was to maintain its prices. By 1981 OPEC exports were only 18 million barrels per day, two-thirds of the 1973 level, and by 1985 maintaining prices required that production be cut to only 15 million barrels per day.

THE PRESSURE TO CHEAT

We have seen that, as world output of oil grew, OPEC output had to be reduced substantially to hold prices high. As a result, incomes in OPEC countries declined sharply. Many oil-producing countries had become used to their new wealth, and thus the instabilities inherent in any cartel

---

[2] One reason why these demand reactions took so long to develop was that government policies in many countries were designed to hold domestic prices far below world prices in order to cushion the blow on domestic consumers. This delayed many of the reactions on both the demand and the supply sides. Governments exhorted people to economize on petrol and fuel oil, but the response was slight until the incentive of higher domestic prices was allowed to operate.

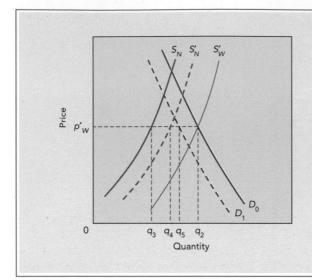

Figure 15.6 OPEC in trouble

As demand declined and non-OPEC oil supply increased, declining OPEC production was required to maintain the world price. The figure repeats the post-OPEC equilibrium from figure 15.4. The world demand curve is D_0, and the non-OPEC supply curve is S_N. OPEC's production is q_2–q_3, making the world supply curve S'_W, and the world price p'_W. Over time, the discovery and development of new oil sources shifted the supply curve of the non-OPEC countries to S'_N. At the same time, long-term economizing, and adoption of other energy sources, shifted the market demand curve for oil to D_1. At the world price p'_W, non-OPEC production rises to q_4. To maintain that price, OPEC production must be contracted to q_5–q_4.

began to be felt seriously from within OPEC. In 1981 the cartel price reached its peak of US$35 per barrel. In real terms, this was about five times as high as the 1972 price, but production quotas were less than half of OPEC's capacity. Anxious to increase their oil revenues, many individual OPEC members gave in to the pressures that were analysed in Figure 13.7 on p. 246—they began to exceed their production quotas.

OPEC members met every few months to debate quotas, deplore cheating, and argue about strategy. But the agreements that were reached proved impossible to enforce, and in December 1985 OPEC decided to eliminate production quotas. The price fluctuated considerably and then settled down near $18 a barrel, which is a little higher than the price before OPEC's restrictions began (allowing for inflation)—the slightly higher price being accounted for by modest output restrictions that OPEC is still able to enforce.

Since that time, increased needs for revenues, particularly because of arms buildups, wars, and lower revenues because of falling real prices, have increased the pressure to cheat. Attempts to re-establish severe production cuts through new quota restrictions have failed. By 1994, the price of crude oil was $13–$15 per barrel, which was very close to the real price that held before OPEC first began its market interventions.[3]

The relevance of the OPEC experience

OPEC's experience illustrates some basic problems of monopolies and of cartels.

Restriction of output below the competitive level can lead to immense profits in the short term.

This is particularly so if the short-run market demand curve turns out to be inelastic. There is thus substantial incentive for an industry to be monopolized, or for a group of producers to co-operate in exercising their collective market power.

Maintaining market power becomes increasingly difficult as time passes.

Supply is likely to increase when, as Schumpeter long ago predicted, new producers find ways of overcoming entry barriers in order to share in the large profits. Furthermore, demand is likely to decrease as new substitutes are invented and produced. These long-term adjustments limit the market power of monopolies and cartels, but only with a significant time-lag.

Producers with market power face a basic trade-off between profits in the short term and profits in the longer term.

The closer does the single producer, or a cartel, push price to the monopoly level, the higher are the short-run profits, but the greater is the incentive for longer-term, profit-reducing reactions from both the supply side and the demand side of the market.

Output restriction by voluntary agreement among several firms is difficult to maintain over any long period of time.

[3] The real price of oil is the money price corrected for inflation. Doing this expresses the price *relative to* the general level of all prices. Since the general level of all dollar prices has risen by about fourfold since 1970, a nominal price of $3.40 in 1970 and $15 in 1994 indicates an approximately unchanged real price—i.e. oil prices are unchanged relative to the average level of all prices.

When there are many producers, the price-taking equilibrium is the self-policing, non-cooperative equilibrium. The monopoly position is a co-operative solution and, because it is not self-policing, it is hard to maintain. This is particularly so if declining demand and increasing competition from new sources, or new products, leads to a steadily shrinking share of the market and falling profits for the members of the cartel.

Predictions of the theory of supply

IN this chapter we have developed a number of quite general predictions of the theory of the firm and industry, and we have also illustrated the use of the theory in yielding predictions after certain specific information has been added to its general assumptions. The theory is an outstanding intellectual achievement.

The theory of perfect competition shows in a quite general way how a large number of separate profit-maximizing firms can, with no conscious co-ordination, produce an equilibrium which depends only on the 'technical data' of demand and costs. Individual idiosyncracies of producers, and a host of other factors, are ignored, and an equilibrium is shown to follow solely from the conditions of costs and demand.

The analysis extends, with necessary corrections, to the cases of monopolistic competition and monopoly. It does not extend so easily, however, to oligopoly. It is here that the traditional theory has had the least success. A great burst of recent theorizing on oligopoly has yielded some advances in this area. Non-cooperative equilibria are relatively easy to analyse and have important applications. In dynamic adjustments, however, strategies matter and the number of possible cases proliferates.

The consumer goods with which the ordinary citizen is most familiar—motor cars, radios, TV sets, washing machines, cookers, etc.—are produced mostly by oligopolistic industries. This has led many superficial observers to conclude that the perfectly competitive model is totally irrelevant to the modern economy. This is emphatically not so. Markets where buyers and sellers adjust quantities to a given price which they cannot change by their own individual efforts abound in the economy. Foreign exchange markets, markets for raw materials, markets for many agricultural products, real estate, most futures markets, the markets for gold and other precious metals, and securities markets are but a few whose behaviour is comprehensible with the basic model of perfect competition (usually augmented by one or two specific additional assumptions to catch the key institutional details of each case).

Manufactured consumer goods are, as already mentioned, dominated by oligopolistic industries. Retail trades and many other service industries were once thought to come close to the conditions of monopolistic competition in that there is free entry, a large number of competing firms, and product differentiation. (The person who provides the service matters, and each person is different.) Because of the nature of spatial differentiation, however, a model of overlapping oligopolies seems closer to the mark than does that of monopolistic competition, at least for many service industries.

Many market structures are relevant to our economy. Happily, as illustrated in this chapter, existing theories do make many useful predictions about how our economy behaves. However, economics is still a young subject, and there are many problems that remain to be solved, particularly in respect to oligopoly behaviour. As a result, there are still many situations for which current theory does not provide clear predictions, particularly in oligopolistic markets.

Summary

1 In perfectly competitive industries, shifts in demand and cost cause changes in the prices paid by consumers and the profits earned by producers in the short run. In the long run, however, free entry and exit ensure that profits will not be affected, so that all gains and losses are passed on to consumers.

2 In monopoly, the gains and losses arising from shifts in demand and costs will be shared between the firm and its customers.

3 Under perfect competition, taxes and subsidies will affect profits in the short run. In the long run, they will affect price and output, but will not affect profits.

4 Under monopoly, lump-sum taxes and taxes on economic profits will affect profits, but will not affect either price or output (provided they are not so high as to drive the firm out of business). Taxes on output and on the return to capital (called profit taxes) will affect price, output, and profits in a monopoly industry.

5 An industry's profits can always be increased if firms co-operate to depart from a perfectly competitive equilibrium and reduce output until marginal cost equals the industry's marginal revenue. At this co-operative solution, each firm can increase its profits by increasing its output. If all try to do this simultaneously, price will be driven back to its perfectly competitive level.

6 The OPEC experience shows the value to producers of restricting output below the perfectly competitive level, as well as the difficulties of maintaining the co-operative solution for a long time. It also shows the economy's powerful response to price signals: high relative prices and profits call forth increased supplies and long-term reductions in demand.

Topics for review

- The effect of changes in demand and in costs under competition, oligopoly, and monopoly

- The effect of taxes on output and profits under competition, oligopoly, and monopoly

- The gains from monopolizing a perfectly competitive industry

- OPEC

- The incentives to cheat on a cartel

✺ CHAPTER 16

Public policy towards monopoly and competition

I N this chapter, we first consider what economic theory has to say about the relevant advantages of the two polar market structures of monopoly and perfect competition. Part of the appeal of competition and the distrust of monopoly is non-economic, being based on a fear of concentration of power. This was discussed in Chapter 12. Much of the attraction of competition and the dislike of monopoly, however, has to do with the understanding that we develop in this chapter that competition is efficient in ways that monopoly is not. After developing this case, we go on to examine intermediate market forms such as monopolistic competition and oligopoly and then go on to study public policies that are directed at encouraging competition and discouraging monopoly. Monopoly has long been regarded with suspicion. In *The Wealth of Nations* (1776), Adam Smith developed a stinging attack on monopolists. Since then, most economists have criticized monopoly and advocated competition.

Economic efficiency

E CONOMIC efficiency requires avoiding the waste of resources. When labour is unemployed and factories lie idle (as occurs in serious recessions), their potential output is lost. If these resources were employed, total output would be increased and hence everyone could be made better off. However, the full employment of resources is not by itself enough to prevent the waste of resources. Even when resources are being fully used, they may be used inefficiently. Let us look at three examples of inefficiency in the use of fully employed resources.

1. If firms do not use the least costly method of producing their chosen outputs, they waste resources. For example, a firm that produces 30,000 pairs of shoes at a resource cost of £400,000 when it could have produced them at a cost of only £350,000 is using resources inefficiently. The lower-cost method would allow £50,000 worth of resources to be transferred to other productive uses.

2. If, within an industry, the cost of producing the last unit of output is higher for some firms than for others, the industry's overall cost of producing its output is higher than necessary.

3. If too much of one product and too little of another product are produced, resources are being used inefficiently. To take an extreme example, suppose that so many shoes are produced that every consumer has all the shoes he or she could possibly want and so places a zero value on obtaining an additional pair of shoes. Further, assume that fewer coats are produced relative to demand, so that each consumer places a positive value on obtaining an additional coat. In these circumstances, each consumer can be made better off if resources are reallocated from shoe production, where the last shoe produced has a low value in the eyes of each consumer, to coat production, where one more coat produced would have a higher value to each consumer.

These examples suggest that we must refine our ideas of the waste of resources beyond the simple notion of ensuring that all resources are employed. The sources of inefficiency just outlined suggest important conditions that must be fulfilled if economic efficiency is to be attained. These conditions are conveniently collected into two categories, called *productive efficiency* and *allocative efficiency*, which were studied long ago by the Italian economist Vilfredo Pareto (1848–1923). Indeed, efficiency in the use of resources is often called Pareto optimality or Pareto efficiency in his honour.

PRODUCTIVE EFFICIENCY

Productive efficiency refers to the efficient production of any bundle of products that is being produced. It occurs when it is *impossible* to reallocate resources so as to produce more of some product *without* producing less of some other product. Watch the double negative! An allocation of resources is productively *inefficient* when it is *possible* to produce more of some product without producing less of any other product, and *efficient* when this cannot be done, in other words, when the only way to produce more of one product is to produce less of some other product.

Productive efficiency has two aspects, one concerning the allocation of resources within each firm, and one concerning the allocation of resources among the firms in an industry. The first condition for productive efficiency is that each firm should produce any given output at the lowest possible cost. In the short run, with only one variable factor, the firm has no problem of choice of technique: it merely uses enough of the variable factor to produce the desired level of output. In the long run, however, more than one method of production is available. Productive efficiency requires that the firm use the least costly of the available methods of producing any given output. This means that firms will be located on, rather than above, their long-run average cost curves.

In Chapter 11 we studied the condition for long-run productive efficiency within the firm.

Productive efficiency requires that each firm produce its given output by combining factors of production in such a way that the ratio of the marginal products of each pair of factors is made equal to the ratio of their prices.

This is the same thing as saying that £1 spent on every factor should yield the same output. If this is not so, the firm can reduce the resource costs of producing its given output by altering the inputs it uses. It should substitute the input for which £1 of expenditure yields the higher output for the input for which £1 of expenditure yields the lower output.

Any firm that is not being productively efficient is producing at a higher cost than is necessary. This must reduce its profits. It follows that any profit-maximizing firm will seek to be productively efficient no matter which market structure—perfect competition, monopoly, oligopoly, or monopolistic competition—it operates within.

There is a second condition for productive efficiency. This ensures that the total output of each industry is allocated among its individual firms in such a way that the total cost of producing the industry's output is minimized.

Productive efficiency requires that the marginal cost of producing its last unit of output must be the same for each firm in any industry.

If an industry is productively inefficient, it is possible to reduce the industry's total cost of producing any given total output by reallocating production among the industry's individual firms. To illustrate, suppose that the Jones Brothers shoe manufacturing firm has a marginal cost of £70 for the last shoe of some standard type that it produces, while Campbell Ltd has a marginal cost of only £65 for the same type of shoe. If the Jones plant produces one less pair of shoes while the Campbell plant produces one more, total shoe output is unchanged, but total industry costs are reduced by £5. Thus, £5 worth of resources will be freed to increase the production of other products.

Clearly, this cost saving can go on as long as the two firms have different marginal costs. However, as the Campbell firm produces more shoes, its marginal cost rises, and as the Jones firm produces fewer shoes, its marginal cost falls. (By producing more, the Campbell firm is moving upward to the right along its given *MC* curve, whereas by producing less, the Jones firm is moving downward to the left along its given *MC* curve.) Say, for example, that after Campbell Ltd increases its production by 1,000 shoes per month its marginal cost *rises* to £67, whereas when Jones Brothers reduces its output by the same amount its marginal cost *falls* to £67. Now there are no further cost savings to be obtained by reallocating production between the two firms.

Figure 16.1 shows a production possibility curve of the sort that was first introduced in Figure 1.1 on p. 7. Productive *inefficiency* implies that the economy is at some point inside the curve. In such a situation it is possible to produce more of some goods without producing less of others.

Productive efficiency implies being on, rather than inside, the economy's production possibility curve.

Box 16.1 deals with two other efficiency concepts that are often confused with the economic concept of production efficiency.

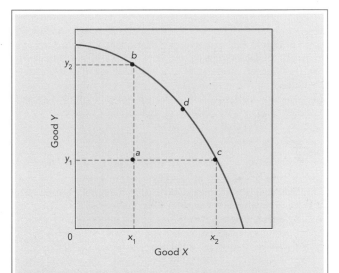

Figure 16.1 Productive and allocative efficiency

Any point on the production possibility curve is productively efficient; not all points on this curve are allocatively efficient. The curve shows all combinations of two goods X and Y that can be produced when the economy's resources are fully employed and being used with productive efficiency.

Any point inside the curve, such as *a*, is productively inefficient. If the inefficiency exists in industry X, production could be reallocated among firms in that industry in such a way as to raise production of X from x_1 to x_2. This would take the economy from point *a* to point *c*, raising production of X without any reduction in production of Y. Similarly, if the inefficiency exists in industry Y, production of Y could be increased from y_1 to y_2, which would take the economy from point *a* to point *b*. If both industries are allocatively inefficient, production can be increased to take the economy to some point on the curve *between b* and *c*, thus increasing the production of *both* products.

Allocative efficiency is concerned with being at the most efficient point on the production possibility curve. Assessing allocative efficiency means judging among points on the curve, such as *b*, *c*, and *d*. Usually only one such point will be allocatively efficient, while all others will be inefficient.

BOX 16.1

....

Various concepts of productive efficiency

In popular discussion, in business decision-making, and in government policies, three different types of productive efficiency concepts are encountered. These are engineering, technical, and economic efficiency. Each is a valid concept, and each conveys useful information. However, the use of one concept in a situation in which another is appropriate is a potential source of error and confusion.

Engineering efficiency refers to the *physical* amount of some *single key input* that is used in production. It is measured by the ratio of that input to output. For example, the engineering efficiency of an engine refers to the ratio of the amount of energy in the fuel burned by the engine to the amount of usable energy produced by the engine. The difference goes in friction, heat loss, and other unavoidable sources of waste. Saying that a steam engine is 60 per cent efficient means that 60 per cent of the energy in the fuel that is burned in the boiler is converted into work that is done by the engine, while the other 40 per cent is lost.

Technical efficiency is related to the *physical* amount of *all factors* used in the process of producing some product. A particular method of producing a given output is technically inefficient if there exist other ways of producing the output that will use less of at least one input while not using more of any others. (Economists often call technical inefficiency *X-inefficiency,* and it is discussed in more detail in Chapter 34.)

We have seen in the text that economic efficiency is related to the *value* of *all inputs* used in producing a given output. The production of a given output is economically efficient if there is no other way of producing the output that will use a smaller total value of inputs.

What is the relationship between economic efficiency and these other two concepts?

We have seen that engineering efficiency measures the efficiency with which a single input is used. Although knowing the efficiency of any given petrol-driven, electric, or diesel engine is interesting, increasing this efficiency is not necessarily economically efficient, because doing so usually requires the use of other valuable resources. For example, the engineering efficiency of a gas turbine engine can be increased by using more and stronger steel in its construction. Raising the engineering efficiency of an engine saves on fuel, but at the cost of using more of other inputs. To know whether this is worth doing, the firm must compare the value of the fuel saved with the value of the other inputs used. The optimal level of engineering efficiency is achieved by increasing efficiency where the value of the input saved exceeds the value of the extra resources used, but not into the range where the costs exceed the value of the input saved.

The existence of technical inefficiency means that costs can be cut by reducing some inputs and not increasing any others. If a technically inefficient process is replaced by a technically more efficient process, there is a saving. Avoiding technical inefficiency is therefore a necessary condition for producing any output at the least cost. Avoiding technical efficiency is not, however, a sufficient condition for producing at lowest possible cost. The firm must still ask which of the many technically efficient methods it should use. This is where the concept of economic efficiency comes in. The appropriate method is the one that uses the smallest value of inputs. This ensures that the firm spends as little as possible to produce any given output.

ALLOCATIVE EFFICIENCY

Allocative efficiency concerns the allocation of resources among products; in other words:

Allocative efficiency concerns the choice among alternative points on the production possibility curve.

For example, it relates to which bundle of outputs should be produced, such as those indicated by the points *b, c,* or, *d* in Figure 16.1.

Allocative efficiency is defined as a situation in which it is impossible to change the allocation of resources in such a way as to make some person better off without making some other person worse off. Changing the allocation of resources implies producing more of some goods and less of others, which in turn means moving from one point on the production possibility curve to another. This is called changing the *mix* of production.

From an allocative point of view, resources are said to be used *inefficiently* when using them to produce a different bundle of goods makes it possible for at least one person to be better off while making no other person worse off. Conversely, resources are said to be used *efficiently* when it is impossible, by using them to produce a different bundle of goods, to make any one person better off without making at least one other person worse off.

This tells us what is meant by allocative efficiency, but how do we find the efficient point on the production possibility curve? For example, how many shoes, dresses, and hats should be produced to achieve allocative efficiency? The answer is as follows:

The economy's allocation of resources is efficient when, for each good produced, its marginal cost of production is equal to its price.

To understand the reasoning behind this answer, we

need to recall a point that was established in our discussion of consumers' surplus in Chapter 7. The price of any product indicates the value that each consumer places on the last unit consumed of that product. Faced with the market price of some product, the consumer goes on buying units until the last one is valued exactly at its price. Consumers' surplus arises because the consumer would be willing to pay more than the market price for all but the last unit that is bought. On the last unit bought (i.e. the marginal unit), however, the consumer only 'breaks even', because the valuation placed on it is just equal to its price.

Now assume that some product, say, shoes, sells for £60 per pair but has a marginal cost of £70. If one less pair of shoes were produced, the value that all consumers would place on the pair of shoes not produced would be £60. Using the concept of opportunity cost, however, we see that the resources that would have been used to produce that last pair of shoes could instead produce another good (say, a coat) valued at £70. If society can give up something that its members value at £60 and get in return something that its members value at £70, the original allocation of resources is inefficient. Someone can be made better off, and no one need be worse off.

This is easy to see when the same consumer gives up the shoes and gets the coat, but it follows even when different consumers are involved. In this case, the market value of the gains to the consumer who gets the coat exceeds the market value of the loss to the consumer who gives up the shoes. The gaining consumer *could* afford to compensate the losing consumer and still come out ahead.

Assume next that shoe production is cut back until the price of a pair of shoes rises from £60 to £65, while its marginal cost falls from £70 to £65. Efficiency is achieved in shoe production because $p = MC = £65$. Now if one less pair of shoes were produced, £65 worth of shoes would be sacrificed, while, at most, £65 worth of other products could be produced with the freed resources.

In this situation the allocation of resources to shoe production is efficient because it is not possible to change it to make someone better off without making someone else worse off. If one consumer were to sacrifice the pair of shoes, it would give up goods worth £65 and would then have to obtain for itself all of the new production of the alternative product produced just to break even. It cannot gain without making another consumer worse off. The same argument can be repeated for every product, and it leads to the conclusion that we have stated already: The allocation of resources is efficient when each product's price equals its marginal cost of production.

Efficiency and inefficiency in perfect competition and monopoly

We now know that for productive efficiency marginal cost should be the same for all firms in any one industry, and that for allocative efficiency marginal cost should be equal to price in each industry. Do the market structures of perfect competition and monopoly lead to productive and allocative efficiency?

PERFECT COMPETITION

Productive efficiency We saw in Figure 12.11 that in the long run, under perfect competition, each firm produces at the lowest point on its long-run average cost curve. Therefore, no one firm could lower its costs by altering its own production.

We also know that in perfect competition all firms in an industry face the same price of their product and that they equate marginal cost to that price. It follows immediately that marginal cost will be the same for all firms. Because all firms in the industry have the same cost of producing their last unit of production, no reallocation of production among the firms could reduce the total industry cost of producing a given output.

Productive efficiency is achieved under perfect competition because all firms in an industry have identical marginal costs and identical minimum costs in long-run equilibrium.

Allocative efficiency We have seen already that perfectly competitive firms maximize their profits by equating marginal cost to price. Thus, when perfect competition is the market structure for the whole economy, price is equal to marginal cost in each line of production.

Allocative efficiency is achieved when perfect competition prevails throughout the economy because price will be equal to marginal cost for all products.

MONOPOLY

Productive efficiency Monopolists have an incentive to be productively efficient because their profits will be maximized when they adopt the lowest-cost method that can be used to produce whatever level of output they choose. Thus, profit-maximizing monopolists will operate on their *LRAC* curves. Furthermore, when they have more than one plant producing the same product, they will allocate production among those plants so that the cost of producing the last unit of output is the same in all plants.

Allocative efficiency Although a monopoly firm will be productively efficient, it will choose a level of output that is too low to achieve allocative efficiency. This follows from what we saw in Chapter 13 (p. 240) that the monopolist chooses an output at which the price charged is *greater than* marginal cost. This violates the conditions for allocative efficiency because the amount that consumers pay for the last unit of output exceeds the opportunity cost of producing it.

Consumers would be prepared to buy additional units for an amount that is greater than the cost of producing these units. Some consumers could be made better off, and none need be made worse off, by shifting extra resources into production of the monopolized product, thus increasing the production of the product. From this follows the classic efficiency-based preference for competition over monopoly:

Monopoly is allocatively inefficient, because the monopolist's price always exceeds its marginal cost.

This result has important policy implications for economists and for policy-makers, as we shall see later in this chapter.

EFFICIENCY IN OTHER MARKET STRUCTURES

Note that the result just stated extends beyond the case of a simple monopoly. Whenever a firm has any power over the market, in the sense that it faces a negatively sloped demand curve rather than one that is horizontal, its marginal revenue will be less than its price. Thus, when it equates marginal cost to marginal revenue, as do all profit-maximizing firms, marginal cost will also be less than price, which is inefficient. Thus, strictly speaking, both oligopoly and monopolistic competition are allocatively inefficient, too.

Oligopoly is an important market structure in today's economy because in many industries the minimum efficient scale is simply too high to support a large enough number of competing firms to make each a price-taker. Although oligopoly does not achieve the conditions for allocative efficiency, it nevertheless may produce more satisfactory results than monopoly. We observed one reason why this might be so in Chapter 14: competition among oligopolists may encourage very-long-run innovations, which result in both new products and cost-reducing methods of producing old ones.

An important defence of oligopoly as an acceptable market structure is that it may be the best of the available alternatives when minimum efficient scale is large. As we observed at the end of Chapter 14, the challenge to public policy is to keep oligopolists competing and using their competitive energies to improve products and lower costs rather than to restrict interfirm competition and erect entry barriers. As we shall see later in this chapter, much public policy has just this purpose. What economic policy-makers call *monopolistic practices* include not only output restrictions operated by firms with complete monopoly power, but also anti-competitive behaviour among firms that are operating in oligopolistic market structures.

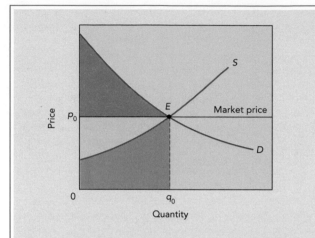

Figure 16.2 Consumers' surplus and producers' surplus

Consumers' surplus is the area under the demand curve and above the market price line. Producers' surplus is the area above the supply curve and below the market price line. The equilibrium price and quantity in this competitive market are p_0 and q_0, respectively. The total value that consumers place on q_0 of the product is given by the sum of the dark red, light red, and dark blue coloured areas. The amount that they pay is p_0q_0, the rectangle that consists of the light red and dark blue areas. The difference, shown as the dark red area, is *consumers' surplus*.

The receipts to producers from the sale of q_0 units are also p_0q_0. The area under the supply curve, the blue shaded area, is total variable cost, the minimum amount that producers require to supply the output. The difference, shown as the light red shaded area, is *producers' surplus*.

Allocative efficiency: an elaboration[1]

We have already established the basic points of productive and allocative efficiency. However, fuller interpretation of the normative significance of allocative efficiency can be given by using the concepts of consumers' and producers' surplus.

CONSUMERS' AND PRODUCERS' SURPLUS

We saw in Chapter 7 that consumers' surplus is the difference between the total value that consumers place on all the units consumed of some product and the payment that they actually make for the purchase of that product. Consumers' surplus is shown once again in Figure 16.2.

Producers' surplus is analogous to consumers' surplus. It occurs because all units of each firm's output are sold at the

---

[1] The section from here to p.300 can be skipped without loss of continuity.

same market price, while, given a rising supply curve, each unit except the last is produced at a marginal cost that is less than the market price.

Producers' surplus is defined as the amount that producers are paid for a product less the total variable cost of producing the product. The total variable cost of producing any output is shown by the area under the supply curve up to that output.[2] Thus, producers' surplus is the area above the supply curve and below the line giving market price. Producers' surplus is also shown in Figure 16.2.

THE ALLOCATIVE EFFICIENCY OF PERFECT COMPETITION REVISITED

If the total of consumers' and producers' surplus is not maximized, the industry's output could be altered to increase that total. The additional surplus could then be used to make some consumers better off without making any others worse off.

Allocative efficiency occurs where the sum of consumers' and producers' surplus is maximized.

The allocatively efficient output occurs under perfect competition where the demand curve intersects the supply curve, that is, the point of equilibrium in a competitive market. This is shown graphically in Figure 16.3. For any output that is less than the competitive output, the demand curve lies above the supply curve, which means that the value consumers put on the last unit of production exceeds its marginal cost of production. Suppose, for example, that the current output of shoes is such that consumers value at £70 an additional pair of shoes that adds £60 to costs. If it is sold at any price between £60 and £70, both producers and consumers gain; there is £10 of potential surplus to be divided between the two groups. In contrast, the last unit produced and sold at competitive equilibrium adds nothing to either consumers' or producers' surplus, because consumers value it at exactly its market price, and it adds the full amount of the market price to producers' costs.

If production were pushed beyond the competitive equilibrium, the sum of the two surpluses would fall. Assume, for example, that firms were forced to produce and sell further units of output at the competitive market price and that consumers were forced to buy these extra units at that price. (Note that neither group would do so voluntarily.) Firms would lose producers' surplus on those extra units because their marginal costs of producing the extra output would be above the price that they received for it. Purchasers would lose consumers' surplus because the valuation that they placed on these extra units, as shown by the demand curve, would be less than the price that they would have to pay.

The sum of producers' and consumers' surplus is maxi-

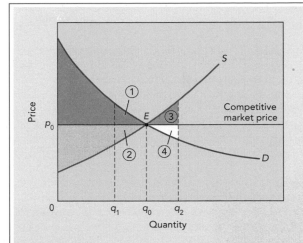

Figure 16.3 The allocative efficiency of perfect competition

Competitve equilibrium is allocatively efficient because it maximizes the sum of consumers' and producers' surplus. The competitive equilibrium occurs at the price–output combination p_0q_0. At this equilibrium, consumers' surplus is the dark red area above the competitive market price line, while producers' surplus is the grey area below the competitive market price line.

For any output that is less than q_0, the sum of the two surpluses is less than it is at q_0. For example, reducing the output to q_1 but keeping price at p_0 lowers consumers' surplus by area 1 and lowers producers' surplus by area 2. For any output that is greater than q_0, the sum of the surpluses is also less than at q_0. For example, if producers are forced to produce output q_2 and to sell it to consumers, who are in turn forced to buy it at price p_0, producers' surplus is reduced by area 3 (the amount by which variable costs exceed revenue on those units), while the amount of consumers' surplus is reduced by area 4 (the amount by which expenditure exceeds consumers' satisfactions on those units). Only at competitive output, q_0, is the sum of the two surpluses maximized.

mized only at the perfectly competitive output, which is thus the only level of output that is allocatively efficient.

---

[2] The marginal cost shows the addition to total cost caused by producing one more unit of output. Summing these additions over each unit of output, starting with the first, yields the total variable cost of output. For example, the sum of the marginal costs of producing the first 10 units of output is the total variable cost associated with 10 units of output. Graphically, this process of summation is shown by the whole area under the marginal cost curve. Because, as we have already seen, the industry supply curve under perfect competition is merely the sum of the marginal cost curves of all the firms in the industry, the area under that supply curve up to some given output is the total of all the firms' variable costs of producing that output. Similarly, the area under a monopolist's marginal cost curve up to some given output is the total of the monopolist's variable costs of producing that output.

THE ALLOCATIVE INEFFICIENCY OF MONOPOLY REVISITED

We have just seen in Figure 16.3 that the output in perfectly competitive equilibrium maximizes the sum of consumers' and producers' surpluses. It follows that the lower monopoly output must result in a smaller total of consumers' and producers' surpluses.

The monopoly equilibrium is not the outcome of a voluntary agreement between the one producer and the many consumers. Instead, it is imposed by the monopoly firm by virtue of the power it has over the market. When the monopoly chooses an output below the competitive level, market price is higher than it would be under perfect competition. As a result, consumers' surplus is diminished, and producers' surplus is increased. In this way, the monopoly firm gains at the expense of consumers. This is not the whole story, however.

When output is below the competitive level, there is always a *net* loss of surplus. More is given up by consumers than is gained by the monopolist. Some surplus is lost by society, because output between the monopolistic and the competitive levels is not produced. This loss of surplus is called the *deadweight loss of monopoly*. It is illustrated in Figure 16.4.

It follows that there is a conflict between the private interest of the monopoly producer and the public interest of all the nation's consumers. This creates a rational case for government intervention to prevent the formation of monopolies if possible, and if not then to control their behaviour.

Public policy towards monopoly and competition

MONOPOLIES, cartels, and price-fixing agreements among oligopolists, whether explicit or tacit, have met with public suspicion and official hostility for over a century. These, and other non-competitive practices, are collectively referred to as *monopoly practices*. Note that such practices are not just what *monopolists* do; they include non-competitive behaviour of firms that are operating in other market structures such as oligopoly. The laws and other instruments that are used to encourage competition and discourage monopoly practices make up **competition policy** and are used to influence both the market structure and the behaviour of individual firms. By and large, UK competition policy has sought to create more competitive market structures where possible, to discourage monopolistic practices, and to encourage competitive behaviour where competitive market structures could not be established. In addition, the government employs *economic regulations,* which prescribe the rules under which firms can do business, and in some cases determine the prices that businesses can charge for their output.

The goal of economic efficiency provides rationales both for competition policy and for economic regulation. Competition policy is used to promote efficiency by increasing competition in the market-place. Where effective competition is not possible (as in the case of a natural monopoly, such as an electric power company), economic regulation of privately owned firms or public ownership can be used as a substitute for competition. The purpose is to protect consumers from the high prices and reduced output that result from the exercise of monopoly power.

Public policies are indeed used in these ways, but they are also often used in ways that reduce economic efficiency. One reason is that efficiency is not the only thing that policy-makers have been concerned with in the design and implementation of competition policy. Most public policies have the potential to redistribute income and people often use them for private gain, regardless of their original public purpose. This is studied more generally in Chapter 23.

We have seen that competition policy refers to public policy designed to encourage competition and discourage monopoly practices. This can be done by influencing either the market structure or the behaviour of individual firms. By and large, UK competition policy has sought to create more competitive market structures where possible, to discourage monopolistic practices, and to encourage competitive behaviour where competitive market structures could not be established.

We shall study three aspects of competition policy: first, the direct control of natural monopolies; second, the direct control of oligopolies; and, third, the creation of competitive conditions. The first is a necessary part of any competition policy, the second has been important in the past but is less so now, and the third constitutes the main current thrust of UK competition policy.

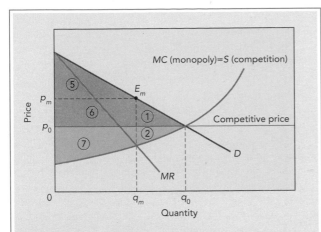

Figure 16.4 The allocative inefficiency of monopoly

Monopoly is allocatively inefficient because it produces less than the competitive output and thus does not maximize the sum of consumers' and producers' surpluses. If this market were perfectly competitive, price would be p_0, output would be q_0, and consumers' surplus would be the sum of areas 1, 5, and 6 (the red shaded areas). When the industry is monopolized, price rises to p_m, and consumers' surplus falls to area 5. Consumers lose area 1 because that output is not produced; they lose area 6 because the price rise has transferred it to the monopolist. Producers' surplus in a competitive equilibrium would be the sum of areas 7 and 2 (the dark blue shaded areas). When the market is monopolized and price rises to p_m, the surplus area 2 is lost because the output is not produced. However, the monopolist gains area 6 from consumers. (6 is known to be greater than 2 because p_m maximizes profits.) While area 6 is transferred from consumers' to producers' surplus by the price rise, *areas 1 and 2 are lost*. They represent the deadweight loss resulting from monopoly and account for its allocative inefficiency.

For all output between q_m and q_0, the value of the output to consumers, given by D, exceeds the cost of production, given by MC. Thus, failure to produce this output reduces consumers' plus producers' surpluses.

Direct control of natural monopolies

The clearest case for public intervention arises with a natural monopoly, an industry in which scale effects are so dominant that there is room for only one firm to operate at the minimum efficient scale. UK policy-makers have not wanted to *insist on* the establishment of several smaller, less efficient producers whenever a single firm would be much more efficient; neither have they wanted to give a natural monopolist the opportunity to restrict output, raise prices, and reap monopoly profits.

One response to natural monopoly is for government to *assume ownership* of the single firm, setting it up as a nationalized industry. The government appoints managers who are supposed to set prices guided by their understanding of the national interest. Another response has been to allow private ownership but to *regulate* the monopoly firm's behaviour. Earlier in this century, UK policy favoured public ownership. Recently, such industries have been privatized—i.e., sold to members of the public—and then to some extent regulated. Examples are telecommunications, gas, water, and electricity.

SHORT-RUN PRICE AND OUTPUT

Whether the state nationalizes or merely regulates privately owned, natural monopolies, the industry's pricing policy is determined by the government. Usually, the industry is asked to follow some policy other than profit maximization.

Marginal cost pricing Sometimes the government dictates that the natural monopoly should try to set price equal to short-run marginal cost in an effort to maximize consumers' plus producers' surpluses in that industry. According to economic theory, this policy, which is called **marginal cost pricing**, provides the efficient solution.

Marginal cost pricing does, however, create some problems. The natural monopoly may still have unexploited economies of scale and may hence be operating on the falling portion of its average total cost curve. In this case, marginal cost will be less than average total cost, and pricing at marginal cost will lead to losses. This is shown in part (i) of Figure 16.5.

A falling-cost, natural monopoly that sets price equal to marginal cost will suffer losses.

Demand, however, may be sufficient to allow the firm to produce on the rising portion of its average total cost curve, that is, where output exceeds what is needed to achieve the minimum efficient scale. At any such output, marginal cost exceeds average total cost. If the firm is directed to equate marginal cost to price, it will earn profits. This is shown in part (ii) of the figure.[3]

When a rising-cost, natural monopoly sets price equal to marginal cost, it will earn profits.

Average cost pricing Sometimes natural monopolies are

---

[3] Sometimes a natural monopoly is defined as one where long-run costs are falling when price equals marginal cost. This, however, is only *sufficient* for a natural monopoly; it is not *necessary*. Demand may be such that one firm is producing, when price equals marginal cost, on the rising portion of its long-run cost curve, while there is no price at which two firms could both cover their costs. For example, if a firm's minimum efficient scale (MES) is 1 million units of output and demand is sufficient to allow the firm to cover costs at 1.2 million units, there may be no price at which two firms, with their combined MES of 2 million units, can cover their full costs.

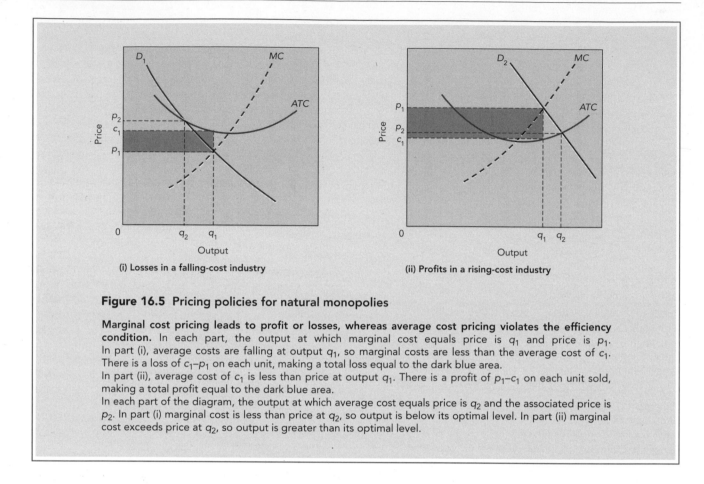

(i) Losses in a falling-cost industry

(ii) Profits in a rising-cost industry

Figure 16.5 Pricing policies for natural monopolies

Marginal cost pricing leads to profit or losses, whereas average cost pricing violates the efficiency condition. In each part, the output at which marginal cost equals price is q_1 and price is p_1. In part (i), average costs are falling at output q_1, so marginal costs are less than the average cost of c_1. There is a loss of c_1–p_1 on each unit, making a total loss equal to the dark blue area.

In part (ii), average cost of c_1 is less than price at output q_1. There is a profit of p_1–c_1 on each unit sold, making a total profit equal to the dark blue area.

In each part of the diagram, the output at which average cost equals price is q_2 and the associated price is p_2. In part (i) marginal cost is less than price at q_2, so output is below its optimal level. In part (ii) marginal cost exceeds price at q_2, so output is greater than its optimal level.

directed to produce the output that will just cover total costs, thus earning neither profits nor losses. This means that the firm produces to the point where average revenue equals average total cost, which is where the demand curve cuts the average total cost curve. Part (i) of Figure 16.5 shows that, for a falling-cost firm, this pricing policy requires producing at less than the optimal output. The losses that would occur under marginal cost pricing are avoided by producing less than the efficient output.[4] Part (ii) shows that, for a rising-cost firm, the policy requires producing at more than the optimal output. The profits that would occur under marginal cost pricing are dissipated by producing more than the efficient output.

Generally, average cost pricing will not result in allocative efficiency.

LONG-RUN INVESTMENT POLICIES

The optimal pricing policy makes price equal to short-run marginal cost. However, the position of the short-run marginal cost curve (as well as the short-run average cost curve) depends on the amount of fixed capital that is currently available to be combined with the variable factor. What should determine the long-run investment decision to accumulate fixed capital?

The efficient answer, if marginal cost pricing is being followed, is to compare the current market price with the long-run marginal cost. The former expresses the value consumers place on one additional unit of output. The latter expresses the full resource cost of providing an extra unit of output including capital costs.[5] If price exceeds long-run marginal cost, capacity should be expanded; if it is less, capacity should be allowed to decline as capital wears out.

The efficient pricing system rations the output of existing capacity by setting price equal to the short-run resource cost of producing another unit. It also adjusts capacity in

---

[4] Note that the losses are financial losses, not social welfare losses. Every unit produced between the points where AC equals price and MC equals price adds to consumers' surplus but brings private financial loss to the producer.

[5] To make the correct comparison, the cost of capital must be expressed at its current rental price so that it can be added to such other costs as wages and fuel.

the long run until the full marginal cost of producing another unit of output is equal to the price.

THE VERY LONG RUN

Natural monopoly is a long-run concept, meaning that, *given existing technology,* there is room for only one firm to operate profitably. In the very long run, however, technology changes. Not only does today's competitive industry sometimes become tomorrow's natural monopoly, but today's natural monopoly sometimes becomes tomorrow's competitive industry.

A striking example is the telecommunications industry. Twenty years ago, message transmission was a natural monopoly. Now technological developments such as satellite transmission, electronic mail, and fax machines have made this activity highly competitive. Also, new firms can be given access to existing infrastructure such as cables, thus greatly lowering set-up costs and encouraging competition from new entrants. In many countries, an odd circumstance then arose: nationalized industries, such as the Post Office, sought to maintain their profitability by prohibiting entry into what would otherwise become a fluid and competitive industry. Since it has the full force of the legal system behind it, the public firm may be more successful than the privately owned firm in preserving its monopoly long after technological changes have destroyed its 'naturalness'.

Market economies change continually under the impacts of innovation and growth; to be successful, government policy must also be adapted continually to keep it relevant to the ever-changing situation.

REGULATION OF NATURAL MONOPOLIES

Now that many UK nationalized industries have been privatized with, presumably, most of the rest to follow soon, those that are natural monopolies are being regulated by newly formed public, regulatory authorities, such as OFTEL (telephones), OFGAS (gas), and OFWAT (water). In the United States, these regulatory bodies were often captured by the firms they were supposed to regulate (see Box 16.2) and ended up working against the interests of consumers. An opposite pitfall that some worry about in the United Kingdom is that prices will be pushed so far down in the short-term interests of consumers that the regulated industries will have little incentive to spend money on technological innovations. In today's world of rapid technological change, this could work to the long-term disadvantage of consumers and place firms in such industries at a disadvantage compared with their foreign competitors.

This worry is often raised in connection with the so-called RPI – X formula, which is used to regulate the prices charged by several privatized firms. The permitted price increase is the increase in the retail price index (RPI) minus some amount designed to pass on some of the firm's cost reductions to its customers. For example, if X is 2 per cent and the price index rises by 5 per cent, the firm can raise its prices by 3 per cent. This is all very well, provided X is not set too high or adjusted too rapidly whenever the firm succeeds in cutting its costs. Large profits provide the incentive to spend money and take risks in developing new cost-cutting innovations. If prices are forced down as soon as the cost reductions are effective, the incentive to innovate will quickly be dissipated.

The UK water industry is being regulated under an RPI+K formula, rather than RPI – X. This is to allow for the fact that the water companies have an obligation to undertake significant expenditures on capital projects, both to improve the reliability and quality of tap water, and to reduce pollution of rivers and beaches. The 'K' factor, announced by Ian Byatt, head of OFWAT, in July 1994, for the rest of the decade, was an average of 1.5 per cent. (It was different for each company.) This means that water companies will be permitted to raise the price charged to consumers each year by an average of 1.5 per cent above the rate of increase of retail prices.

UK regulation is in its early days. One can only hope that the regulators will remain flexible as experience accumulates and will avoid, as far as possible, excessively favouring either firms or consumers at the expense of the other.

Direct control of oligopolies

Governments have from time to time intervened in industries that were oligopolies, rather than natural monopolies, seeking to enforce the type of price and entry behaviour that was thought to be in the public interest. Such intervention has typically taken two distinct forms. In the United Kingdom from 1945 to 1980, it was primarily nationalization of whole oligopolistic industries such as airlines, railways, steel, and coal mining, which were then to be run by government-appointed boards. In the United States, firms in such oligopolistic industries as airlines, railways, and electric power were left in private hands, but their decisions were regulated by government-appointed bodies that set prices and regulated entry.

SCEPTICISM ABOUT DIRECT CONTROL

In recent times, policy-makers have become increasingly sceptical of their ability to improve the behaviour of oligopolistic industries by having the state control the details of their behaviour either through ownership or regulation. Several experiences have been important in determining this scepticism.

First, oligopolistic market structures have provided much of the economic growth since the Second World

War. New products, and new ways of producing old products, have followed each other in rapid succession, all leading to higher living standards and higher productivity. Many of these innovations have been provided by firms in oligopolistic industries such as motor cars, agricultural implements, steel, petroleum refining, chemicals, and telecommunications. As long as governments can keep oligopolists competing with each other, rather than co-operating to produce monopoly profits, most economists see no need to regulate such things as the prices at which oligopolists sell their products and the conditions of entry into oligopolistic industries.

Second, many regulatory bodies had imposed policies that were not related to the cost of each of the services being priced. These prices involved what is called *cross-subsidization*, whereby profits that are earned in the provision of one service are used to subsidize the provision of another at a price below cost.

Third, the record of postwar government intervention into regulated industries seemed poorer in practice than its supporters had predicted. After industries were *nationalized*, antagonism often persisted between management, concerned with financial viability, and workers, concerned

with take-home pay. As a result, it was not long before the unexpected became commonplace: strikes against the industries that the British people themselves owned. On the other hand, when industries were *regulated*, as was common in the United States, the results again were often less beneficial to consumers than had been expected. Research by economists slowly established that in many industries regulatory bodies were captured by the very firms that they were supposed to be regulating. As a result, the regulatory bodies that were meant to ensure competition often acted to enforce monopoly practices that would have been illegal if instituted by the firms themselves.

This last point, which entails the use of regulatory policy to protect firms from too much competition rather than to protect consumers from too little, has a long history in North America. Regulation of newly privatized industries in Britain is too recent to tell if UK regulators will fall into the patterns established earlier in North America of protecting sellers rather than buyers.

North American experience, which certainly provides a cautionary tale for UK policy-makers and consumers, is briefly discussed in Box 16.2.

BOX 16.2

Regulation as protection against *competition*

North American regulatory bodies have all too frequently protected firms rather than consumers. For example, Canadian and American railroad rates were originally regulated in order to keep profits down by establishing schedules of *maximum* rates. By the 1930s, however, concern had grown over the depressed economic condition of the railroads and the emerging vigorous competition from lorries and barges. The regulators then became the protectors of the railroads, permitting them to establish *minimum* rates for freight of different classes, allowing price discrimination and encouraging other restrictive practices. Moreover, the regulators became leading advocates of including road haulage under the regulatory umbrella. Restricting entry into road haulage and setting minimum rates for lorries was unmistakably protectionist. The only reason for regulating the large carriers was to control their competition with the railroads. The big road carriers were limited in where they could go and how low a price they could quote. As a result, they became targets for small, unregulated road haulage firms, who could cut rates and thus draw away customers without fear of retaliation. To eliminate the rate competition, regulation was extended to such small road haulage firms.

Airline regulation provided another example. When airline routes and fares were first regulated, there was arguably so little demand that competition could not have been effective. By the mid-1960s, however, the regulation was plainly protectionist

and was designed to shield the major North American carriers from competition. (Unlike Europe, where most carriers are government-owned, North America is served by many competing privately owned airlines.) Supporters of regulation argued that unrestricted competition would be so intense that it might ruin the industry and even invite cost-cutting practices that endangered public safety. Critics argued that competition might destroy some existing airlines but would prepare the ground for an efficient industry, while regulation could still be used to enforce such things as minimum safety standards on private airline firms.

Why did regulatory bodies shift from protecting consumers to protecting firms? One thesis, championed by the American professor George Stigler (1911–1991), is that the regulatory commissions were gradually captured by the firms they were supposed to regulate. In part, this capture was natural enough. When regulatory bodies were hiring staff, they needed people who were knowledgeable in the industries they were regulating. Where better to go than to people who had worked in these industries? Naturally, these people tended to be sympathetic to firms in their own industries. Also, since many of them aspired to go back to those industries once they had gained experience within the regulatory bodies, they were not inclined to arouse the wrath of industry officials by imposing policies that were against the firms' interests.

DEREGULATION AND PRIVATIZATION

The 1980s witnessed a movement in virtually all advanced industrial nations and the vast majority of less developed nations to reduce the level of government control over industry.

Figure 16.6 shows the extent of this movement worldwide. The last great wave of nationalizations began in the mid-1960s and reached a peak in the early 1970s. It was inspired by the twin beliefs that control over natural resources and key industries was a prerequisite to growth and that such control was best exercised through public ownership. By the 1980s these beliefs were fading. As a result, publicly owned activities throughout the world were being transferred to private ownership. This shift of resources from the public to the private sector was still occurring at an increasing rate at the time of the latest available data in 1992. No doubt, privatization activity will fall off sometime in the 1990s, for the simple reason that very few publicly owned industries remain to be transferred to the private sector.

Causes A number of forces had been pushing in this direction: (1) the experience that regulatory bodies often sought to reduce, rather than increase, competition; (2) the realization that replacing a private monopoly with a publicly owned one would not greatly change the industry's performance, and that replacing privately owned oligopolists by a publicly owned monopoly often worsens the industry's performance; (3) the dashing of the unreasonable hopes that nationalized industries would work better than private firms in the areas of efficiency, productivity growth, and industrial relations; and (4) the awareness that falling transportation costs and revolutions in data processing and communications were exposing local industries to much more widespread international competition than they had previously experienced domestically.

More generally, the worldwide movement towards privatization and deregulation is part of a growing belief among policy-makers that markets are more efficient allocators of resources than governments. This change of view spreads beyond the advanced industrial nations to most of the poorer developing nations who had tried heavy government intervention for decades and concluded that market determination is on balance superior.

The call is for a diminished role of government in resource allocation—but not for a zero role. Although there is a strong, almost worldwide, belief that there has been too much government intervention in the recent past, there are many reasons why the public interest may require significant intervention into the workings of the price system. We will see this with respect to advanced countries in Chapter 23 and developing countries in Chapter 34.

Privatization and deregulation reflect a new belief in the efficiency of a market-oriented economy, but still leave a

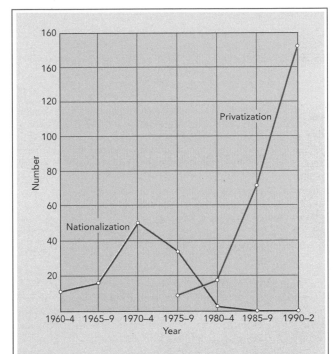

Figure 16.6   Nationalization and privatization, 1960–1992

The last wave of nationalization in the 1960s gave way to a wave of privatization that had not yet crested by 1992. The nationalization data refer to the average number of acts of nationalization in each period. There were earlier peaks not shown in the figure, such as 1945–50, when most UK nationalization occurred. The latest recorded peak occurred in the late 1960s and early 1970s and is shown in the figure. The privatization data refer to the average number of firms privatized during each period. Starting from a low in the 1970s, privatization has been rising dramatically right through the early 1990s.

Source: World Investment Report, 1993 (New York: UN, UNCTAD Programme on TNCs), p.17.

major role for government to intervene to improve the operation of the free market.

The natural outcome of these revised views was the privatization of nationalized industries and the deregulation of privately owned ones. This latter policy was intended, among other things, to return price-setting and entry decisions to market determination.

Privatization has gone a long way in the United Kingdom. The majority of the nationalized industries, both those containing a few large firms and those containing many smaller firms, have been returned to private ownership. Some details are given in Box 16.3.

BOX 16.3

Privatization in the United Kingdom

Privatization has been a complex development in the United Kingdom. Some nationalized industries were sold outright; in others, the government maintained substantive holdings while selling off the rest of its shares. In yet other cases, profitable parts of unprofitable enterprises were separated off and sold. In still other cases, the government sold shares that it held in private companies that had never been nationalized.

The first step towards United Kingdom privatization was the sale of council houses, which began in 1979. Over the succeeding decade there was a major reduction in the stock of publicly owned housing, with almost 700,000 dwellings being sold to their occupiers.

The next phase covered a number of relatively small operations in markets where competition was strong. These included the British Sugar Corporation, British Rail Hotels, Sealink Ferries, British Ports, Jaguar, British Aerospace, and several others. These companies have operated successfully, under relatively competitive conditions, since their privatization.

The third phase covers the great industrial giants. It began with British Telecom in 1984 and continued with British Gas in 1986, British Airways in 1987, and British Steel in 1988. Sale of shares in the publicly owned electricity industry began in 1990, with water following soon thereafter. Sale of the remaining coal pits was completed in 1994. British Rail has already had a significant infusion of private capital since much of its rolling stock is now leased from private owners.

It is too early to say whether privatization has been unambiguously beneficial for the performance of all the companies involved, though there is no ambiguity about the financial benefits received by those who subscribed to privatization share issues. (These ranged up to an 80 per cent premium for buyers of BT shares on the first day of trading.) However, it is clear that some former state-owned companies have become world leaders in a manner that would have been unlikely under state control. The most obvious examples are BT, Cable and Wireless, and British Airways.

In the early 1980s it could have been argued that privatization was just a product of the political agenda of the government of Mrs Thatcher. However, this does not fit with the recent evidence that privatization has spread to countries with governments of widely differing ideologies. It is happening even in countries with left-of-centre governments. This suggests that it is being driven partly by fundamental economic forces. In short, private ownership may facilitate more efficient management of rapidly changing globalized business. Of course, this argument does not apply with equal force to all of those industries privatized in the United Kingdom.

Criticisms Only a minority of economists today support public over private ownership in industries that can support several competing firms. Those who do, oppose most privatization, in principle.

There is more disagreement over natural monopolies such as gas and electricity. Supporters of privatization argue that there are no natural monopolies in the very long run and that private ownership will encourage the technological dynamism that will erode the natural monopoly. They argue that, in the meantime, the private firms can be prevented from charging monopoly prices by effective regulation. Opponents argue that a privately owned monopoly will not be more technologically progressive and will behave more like a profit-maximizer than would a publicly owned firm. There is no simple resolution to this part of the debate, and the behaviour probably depends on the managements of the publicly owned and privately owned firms and on the nature of the regulation to which they are subjected.

A more widely accepted criticism concerns the way in which privatization has been conducted. When selling off its industrial giants, the government faced a dilemma:

The government's sale price is maximized by selling an industry as a single unit, but this also maximizes the industry's subsequent allocative inefficiency.

The government could sell off a giant, such as British Airways or British Gas, as a single unit; this maximizes the monopoly power of its private owners, and hence maximizes the price that will be paid for it. Alternatively, the giant could be broken up and sold in separate units as far as is feasible. This could have been possible, for example, in the sale of British Gas and British Telecom. While this minimizes the monopoly power of the private purchasers (which would still be substantial), it also minimizes the price that will be paid for the industry by private investors.

Up until 1990, the government appeared to have succumbed to the temptation to maximize the sale price by selling off each giant as a single unit. This policy is likely to create more regulatory problems a decade from now than would have arisen if the government had sacrificed some short-term financial gain for the long-term advantages of enhanced competition.

In later cases of privatization, the government seems to

have responded to its critics by breaking up the monopoly before selling it to the public. This was the case, for example, of the electricity industry, which was broken up into many constituent parts before being privatized in 1990 (distribution) and 1991 (generation).

Intervention to keep firms competing

The least stringent form of government intervention is designed neither to force firms to sell at particular prices nor to regulate the conditions of entry and exit: it is designed to create conditions of competition by preventing firms from merging unnecessarily or from engaging in certain anti-competitive practices such as colluding to set monopoly prices. Here the policy seeks to create the most competitive market structure possible and then to prevent firms from reducing competition by engaging in certain forms of co-operative behaviour.

Industrial concentration has been increasing in Britain over many years, with the percentage of industrial production accounted for by the five largest firms growing steadily. Much of this has been the result of the growth of large firms at the expense of smaller ones, but much has also been the result of mergers of existing firms. Should one be alarmed over the growing concentration of UK industries? The main reason why many economists answer this question in the negative is the growing internationalization of competition that we observed at the beginning of Chapter 14. The absence of trade barriers within the European Union, and the decline in world transportation costs, has extended the size of most markets well beyond the boundaries of single nations. An apparent monopoly in the United Kingdom may well be operating in a highly competitive market that includes German, French, and even Japanese firms.

UK POLICIES

Ultimate responsibility for competition policy in the United Kingdom lies with the Secretary of State for Trade and Industry. However, key elements of monitoring and enforcement are delegated to three important institutions: the Restrictive Practices Court (RPC), the Office of Fair Trading (OFT), and the Monopolies and Mergers Commission (MMC).

There is an important difference in the legislation affecting *restrictive practices* from that affecting the potential creation of a monopoly by a *merger*. Restrictive practices must be registered and demonstrated to be in the public interest. The OFT can investigate cases that are not already approved and refer them to the RPC for judgement. By contrast, the onus is entirely on the authorities to prove that a merger is not in the public interest; otherwise it must be permitted to proceed. Here decisions are made by the Secretary of State on the basis of recommendations made by the MMC.

Restrictive practices Restrictive practices involve, for example, agreements between firms over the prices they will charge or the way in which they will divide up the market in some way (by, perhaps, not competing in specific locations). In the United Kingdom, a restrictive practice must pass through one of eight 'gateways' to establish that it is in the public interest, as defined by the 1956 Restrictive Trades Practices Act. (Originally there were seven gateways, but one more was added in 1968; also, the Act was extended to cover services as well as goods.) The gateways for a restrictive practice to be in the public interest are that:

1. It protects the public from physical injury.
2. Consumers gain identifiable benefits from it.
3. Employment is protected as a result of it.
4. It counteracts other restrictions to competition.
5. It is necessary to support other acceptable restrictive practices.
6. Its existence supports greater exports.
7. Its existence enhances a fair market for suppliers of inputs.
8. The restrictive practice does not deter competition.

In the last forty years, over 10,000 restrictive agreements have been registered, but many of these have been ended voluntarily without requiring a judgement from the RPC.

The EU Commission can intervene in restrictive agreements affecting trade between EU member-states. Article 85 of the Treaty of Rome prohibits anti-competitive agreements, such as market-sharing, price-fixing, and supply restrictions. The Treaty also prohibits the use of monopoly power to exploit consumers, and distortions to competition resulting from government subsidies.

Mergers All companies involved in a merger must submit notification to the OFT. The Director-General of Fair Trading must then decide if the creation of a monopoly is involved. In such cases, the OFT will recommend to the Secretary of State that the merger be referred to the MMC. The MMC then has to decide if the merger is against the public interest. The final decision is referred back to the Secretary of State, who may decide to accept or reject the MMC recommendation.

Under current UK legislation, a merger potentially creates a monopoly if the merging firms together control 25 per cent or more of the market, though a merger involving significant assets may also be referred. Only about one in fifty mergers, over the last thirty years, has been referred to the MMC, and less than half of those were ruled to be against the public interest.

The OFT may recommend an MMC investigation in

BOX 16.4

The MMC in action

The Monopolies and Mergers Commission gets into the head-line news when a large and controversial takeover bid is referred to it, such as the 1992 bid by Lloyds Bank for the Midland Bank (which was abandoned because of the MMC referral, long before the inquiry could be concluded). However, the MMC reports on many specific potential instances of monopoly behaviour, not all resulting from merger proposals. In this box we outline six recent MMC inquiries, out of dozens produced in the last few years. Dates in brackets are the publication dates of the MMC reports.

British Aerospace and Thomson-CSF (January 1991)

In 1990, these two companies proposed to merge their guided weapons businesses into a company to be known as Eurodynamics, which would be 50 per cent owned by each. The Secretary of State referred the proposal to the MMC to deter-mine whether they would operate against the public interest, given the concerns that arose because of the ownership of Thomson-CSF's parent, Thomson SA, by the French govern-ment, and the latter's control or influence over other defence companies, as well as the pure competitive threat from greater concentration of production.

The MMC report concludes:

'We have considered the proposed merger against the back-ground of current trends in the defence industry: falling demand and growing overcapacity; increasingly sophisticated and expensive technologies; breakdown of national markets and internationalisation of procurement through consortia; intro-duction of competitive procedures for the award of contracts by the Ministry of Defence (MOD) in the United Kingdom . . . the major participants in the industry will increasingly have to join together to compete. Eurodynamics is a response to these trends. . . . We conclude that the proposed arrangements would not be against the public interest.'

Allied–Lyons PLC and Carlsberg A/S (July 1992)

Allied–Lyons (as we saw in Box 14.5) is a major force in the UK brewing and pub business. It concluded an agreement with Danish brewer, Carlsberg, to merge their brewing and whole-saling activities into a new jointly owned company, Carslberg–Tetley Brewing Ltd (CTL). Under the agreement, Allied–Lyons would continue to own its public houses, but would enter into a seven-year supply contract to buy all of its beer from CTL, up to 15 per cent of which could be third-party brands stocked by CTL.

The MMC recommended (with one member dissenting) that the merger should not proceed unless: (1) CTL undertook not to raise prices charged to Carlsberg's existing customers (regional brewers or independent wholesalers); (2) the supply agreement between CTL and Allied–Lyons was reduced from seven to five years; and (3) Allied–Lyons permitted its tenants (publicans) freedom, after two years, to purchase half their lager from other suppliers.

Notice that tied sales is the key issue here. If publicans have to buy from one distributor, they cannot seek alternative supplies if prices are raised.

Acquisition of Parker Pen Holdings Ltd by Gillette (February 1993)

The sole business of Parker is the manufacture of writing instru-ments. Competition issues arose from the fact that Gillette already owned two suppliers of writing instruments, Papermate and Waterman. The MMC concluded that 'any attempt by a merged company to exploit its market position would be held in check by the bargaining strength of retailers and the existence of both actual and potential competitors to which they could turn'. So it was judged that the proposed merger would not adversely affect competition, price, or choice in the retail market.

Networking Arrangements for Channel 3 TV (April 1993)

Following the 1990 Broadcasting Act, new licences were awarded to 15 regional television companies (including Carlton, Central, and Anglia). A Network Centre was set up to draw up the net-work schedule and to acquire and commission programmes from the licensed TV companies and from independent pro-ducers. Independent producers were precluded from entering a supply contract with the Network Centre, but, rather, had to do so with the TV companies with whom they could be competing to supply programmes. The TV companies, however, could con-tract directly with the Network Centre.

The OFT concluded that these arrangements failed the com-petition test under the Broadcasting Act. The issue was referred to the MMC, which proposed a new contracting arrangement involving tripartite agreements between independent produc-ers, the Network Centre, and a TV company (with the latter's role being strictly limited). This was intended to ensure that the TV companies could not unfairly block access to the network for independent programme producers.

Contact Lens Solutions (May 1993)

Over 2 million people in the United Kingdom wear contact lenses, and the market for contact lens solutions (CLS) is about £90 million per annum. Suppliers have to obtain a product licence from the Medicines Control Agency (MCA) of the Department of Health, and CLS may be sold at retail level only by opticians and pharmacists, because the MCA thinks expert advice should be available at the point of sale.

BOX 16.4 *(continued)*

The MMC estimated that opticians have about 60 per cent of the sales (with Dollond and Aitchison PLC (DA) and Boots Opticians Ltd (BOL) taking 10 and 5 per cent respectively) and pharmacists 40 per cent (with Boots the Chemist Ltd (BTC) alone having 31 per cent). The leading suppliers are Allergan Ltd, with 38 per cent of the market, and CIBA Vision (UK) Ltd, with 34 per cent.

The MMC concluded that Allergan's pricing policy exploited its monopoly position and that it had made excessive profits. It also concluded that Boots (BTC and BOL together) had enjoyed substantial margins and that its pricing policy was contrary to the public interest. DA and CIBA were not found to be behaving against the public interest.

Notice that this situation was not created by a merger, but, rather, was the outcome of a restrictive regulatory regime. Accordingly, the MMC recommended changes in regulation that would permit the entry of new products, and permit sales through a wider range of retailers. In the absence of such changes, the MMC recommended that direct price controls be placed on Allergan and Boots.

Southdown Motor Services Ltd (June 1993)

In September 1992 the OFT asked the MMC to investigate the registration, operation, and charging of uneconomic fares by Southdown (bus company), now called Sussex Coastline Buses Ltd, on routes 262 and 242 in Bognor Regis, Sussex.

Deregulation of the bus industry had occurred in the late 1980s. Southdown had been the main bus operator in Bognor, but after deregulation a new company, Easy Rider, started up. Southdown started to run a new 262 service just ahead of the buses on one of Easy Rider's routes. This was withdrawn after a while, but then it started the 242 services, again just ahead of an Easy Rider service, and at a revenue that did not even cover the cost of the driver's wage. The 242 made a substantial loss, but caused financial problems for Easy Rider, which eventually sold out to Southdown.

This is an example of *predatory pricing*, which was discussed on p. 270. Predatory pricing involves selling goods or services at a loss in order to drive a rival out of business, and then resorting to monopolistic behaviour. The MMC concluded that the loss of competition could be expected to lead to higher fares and poorer service in the areas previously served by Easy Rider. It recommended that fare increases be limited to the rate of RPI inflation for two years, and that there should be no reduction in the level of service for the same period, compared with that existing before the introduction of the 242. Further monitoring by the OFT was also recommended.

---

cases of suspected monopoly behaviour, even where this does not result from merger. Box 16.4 contains a summary of six recent MMC investigations. These cases do not cover all possible types of investigation. The MMC has, for example, recently investigated the monopoly position of British Gas, a natural monopoly privatized in the mid-1980s but regulated by OFGAS. It recommended the splitting off of some of British Gas's activities and the ending of its monopoly supply position within four years. MMC investigations have even been directed at institutions still in public ownership, such as London Underground and the UK Atomic Energy Authority. Privatized water companies that do not accept the *K* factor imposed on them by OFWAT have the right of appeal to the MMC, which would then conduct its own inquiry. South West Water was threatening just such an appeal in July 1994.

The EU Commission also has a role in monitoring mergers that affect more than one EU country simultaneously, that is, where the companies involved have a significant cross-border presence. There are two criteria, either of which could trigger investigation of a merger by the Commission: first, the companies involved must have a global turnover exceeding ECU 5 billion; second, each company involved has an EU-wide turnover of at least ECU 250 million. However, if both merging companies have at least two-thirds of their combined turnover in only one member-state, then the merger will be subject to vetting in that member-state, and not by the Commission. Thus, as UK companies become more international, it is likely that a higher proportion of merger activity will be monitored by the EU Commission rather than by the MMC.

In the following chapter merger activity is discussed from the perspective of the direct interests of those involved rather than from the perspective of monopoly policy.

Summary

1 Resources are said to be used efficiently when it is impossible, by using them differently, to make any one consumer better off without making at least one other consumer worse off. Economists distinguish two main kinds of efficiency: productive and allocative.

2 Productive efficiency exists for a given technology when whatever output is being produced is being produced at the lowest attainable cost for that level of output. This requires, first, that firms be on, rather than above, their relevant cost curves and, second, that all firms in an industry have the same marginal cost.

3 Allocative efficiency is achieved when it is impossible to change the mix of production in such a way as to make someone better off without making someone else worse off. The allocation of resources will be efficient when each product's price equals its marginal cost.

4 Perfect competition achieves both productive and allocative efficiency. Productive efficiency is achieved because the same forces that lead to long-run equilibrium lead to production at the lowest attainable cost. Allocative efficiency is achieved because in competitive equilibrium, price equals marginal cost for every product. The economic case against monopoly rests on its allocative inefficiency, which arises because price exceeds marginal cost in equilibrium.

5 Very-long-run considerations, such as the effect of market structure on innovation and the incentive effects of monopoly profits, are important in evaluating market structures. Joseph Schumpeter advocated the view that the incentive to innovate is so much greater under monopoly that monopoly is to be preferred to perfect competition, despite its allocative inefficiency. Though few modern economists go that far, the empirical evidence suggests that technological change and innovation can to a measurable extent be traced to the efforts of large firms operating in oligopolistic industries.

6 Government policy is designed to encourage competitive practices and discourage monopolistic ones. It seeks to regulate natural monopolies either by running them as nationalized industries (the UK solution in the past) or putting them in private hands and regulating them (the typical UK solution today). Regulation of oligopolistic industries involves controlling their prices and conditions of entry. Competition policy has two goals: to prohibit combines where scale economies do not require them, and to control their behaviour when scale economies make combines efficient.

7 Efficiency of natural monopolies requires that price be set equal to short-run marginal cost and that investment be undertaken whenever that price exceeds the full long-run marginal cost of providing another unit of output. Average cost pricing results in too much output in the short run and too much investment in the long run in rising-cost industries and too little output and too little investment in falling-cost industries.

8 Direct control of pricing and entry conditions of some key oligopolistic industries has been common in the past, but deregulation is reducing such control. The move to deregulation was largely the result of the experiences that oligopolistic industries are a major engine of growth, as long as their firms are kept competing; that direct control of such industries has produced disappointing results in the past; and that forced cross subsidization can have serious consequences for some users.

Topics for review

- Productive and allocative efficiency
- Consumers' and producers' surplus
- Classical preference for competition over monopoly
- Pareto optimality
- Economies of scale and of scope
- Effect of cost on market structure
- Effect of market structure on costs
- Marginal and average cost pricing
- Privatization

❧ CHAPTER 17

Takeovers, foreign investment, and profit maximization

PROFIT maximization is a critical assumption of the theory of the firm and the industry. Predictions about how firms will respond to any change that affects them are derived by discovering the profit-maximizing response and then predicting that the response will occur. In this chapter, we first study takeovers and related phenomena which often seem to imply an absence of profit maximization. After extending this study to cover foreign investment, we pass on to the key question: is the theory of profit maximization supported by the evidence?

Takeovers, mergers, and buyouts

A TAKEOVER occurs when company A buys company B (which then becomes a part of A). A **merger** occurs when companies A and B join together, often combining even their names. A **buyout** occurs when a group of investors (often including existing managers), rather than an existing firm, buys up a firm.

Three types of takeover and merger are commonly distinguished: horizontal, vertical, and conglomerate. When takeovers or mergers are among companies producing similar products, they are termed *horizontal.* Recent UK examples are the mergers of the computer firms Amstrad and Sinclair, and of the food and drink firms Allied-Lyons and Domecq to make Allied–Domecq. An earlier example was the merger of the National Provincial and Westminster Banks to make National Westminster, known as NatWest.

Takeovers or mergers among businesses producing in different stages of the production process are termed *vertical,* which may be 'forward' or 'backward'. A forward takeover or merger involves moving towards the market in which the product is sold—for example, the acquisition of retail filling stations by the oil refining companies, or of public houses by breweries. A backward takeover or merger involves one firm's acquisition of other firms that supply its inputs—for example, the purchase of a printing company by a publishing company.

A *conglomerate takeover or merger* takes place between firms without obvious common interests in production, such as the takeover of the flour and baking firm Rank Hovis MacDougall by the predominantly engineering firm, Tomkins. In so far as lower costs result from conglomerate mergers, they are usually associated with managerial, marketing, or financial economies or with risk reduction through diversification.

Buyouts, mergers, and takeovers can be interpreted as transactions in a **market for corporate control.** This market, like any other, has both buyers (those who would acquire the rights to control a firm) and sellers (the current owners of stock in the firm). As in other markets, the expected outcome is that the assets being bought and sold will wind up in the hands of those who value them most. These will tend to be those who can come closest to maximizing the firm's profits.

A *takeover* begins when the management of the acquiring firm makes a **tender offer** to the stockholders of the target firm. Tender offers are promises to purchase stock at a specified price for a limited period of time, during which the acquiring firm hopes to gain control of the target company. Typically, the prices offered are considerably higher than the prevailing stock market price. The takeover is called a *hostile takeover* when the current management of the target firm opposes it.

The effects of takeovers

Takeovers, mergers, and buyouts seem to come in waves. Some are driven by technological changes that increase the minimum efficient scale of firms in many industries. They tend to have long-lasting effects. Such was the merger wave at the beginning of this century. Some are based on experiments that prove to be either outright failures or far less valuable than originally thought. Such was the wave of conglomerate mergers in the 1970s which often involved firms selling widely different products in widely different markets. Although some of the conglomerates formed in that period survived, many were dismantled in the wave of buyouts that occurred in the 1980s.

Do takeovers improve economic efficiency? In this section we consider the takeover of one domestic firm by another. The main argument in favour is that, after a takeover, the new management can make more efficient use of the target firm's assets. The acquiring firm should be able to exploit profit opportunities that the target management has not been exploiting. This can be done by such means as operating the target firm more efficiently, providing funds that the target firm could not obtain, or providing access to markets that would be too expensive for the target firm to access on its own. If this is true, the value of the target firm will rise in response to a takeover, reflecting the expectation of increased future profits. Further, if the *acquiring* firm's managers are acting in the best interest of *their* shareholders, the value of the acquiring firm should also rise when it is successful in a takeover bid.

RETURNS TO SHAREHOLDERS OF TARGET COMPANIES

Evidence on the effects of takeovers strongly supports the proposition that they benefit the shareholders of target firms. Estimates of the magnitude of the gains for UK and US firms exceed 20 per cent of pre-takeover share value during the period from the early 1960s to the late 1980s.

RETURNS TO SHAREHOLDERS OF ACQUIRING COMPANIES

The benefits to shareholders in the acquiring firms vary greatly from takeover to takeover. Sometimes the benefit is large; at other times it is negative. (The takeover *lowers* the acquiring firm's profits.) One example of an unprofitable takeover was the Midland Bank's purchase of the Crocker Bank in California. Midland was once Britain's largest bank (indeed, earlier this century it was the world's largest bank), but it ended up being taken over by the Hong Kong and Shanghai Banking Corporation (HSBC). In fact, the evidence is that the *average benefit* to the acquiring firms in both the United States and the United Kingdom is insignificantly different from zero. How could this be?

One answer is that this is what we would expect if the market for corporate control were competitive. A typical takeover starts when an existing firm is perceived to be operating at well below its potential profitability. Other firms will want to take the firm over and will bid up the value of its shares to reflect the potential they see to raise the firm's profits once they own it. The result is a large rise in the price of the target firm's shares to the benefit of the owners, whereas the firm that finally makes the successful takeover pays about the price that makes its investment yield a normal return (plus a risk premium to cover the possibility that it may have guessed wrong about the potential of the target firm). Because expectations about the potential profitability of the target firm are subject to a wide margin of error, some takeovers will turn out to be more valuable than expected and the acquiring firm will gain, while others will turn out to be less valuable than expected and the acquirer will lose. If, however, the market judges correctly on average, takeovers will produce only a normal rate of return on average for the firm making the takeover.

BENEFITS TO THE ECONOMY

What is the effect of takeovers on the whole economy?

Takeovers provide a useful discipline that help to restrain managers from acting in non-maximizing ways.

Each new bout of takeovers and mergers helps to chart new waters. As technology changes, there are changes in the advantages of scale and scope resulting from changes in production techniques, market demand, and market boundaries. To meet the new circumstances, new forms of organization are often necessary and are sometimes effected through mergers, takeovers, and buyouts (and sometimes through the downsizing of firms). When firms react to rapidly changing circumstances, they must learn by experience. It is not surprising that, even though people generally move in the right direction, some make mistakes. In particular, a merger movement may go too far, so that, among the profit-*increasing* mergers, takeovers, or buyouts, there are also some profit-*reducing* ones. Over time, the successful ones will be solidified and the unsuccessful ones abandoned.

This is what we would expect in a world of rapidly changing circumstances where people must learn appropriate responses through experience. It makes an assessment of any current wave of mergers, buyouts, or takeovers difficult until the whole process is completed. Before then, it is hard to distinguish between some spectacular, attention-getting failures that are an inevitable part of the learning process and a more general failure of the concept behind the wave.

In the absence of strong evidence to show that a particular wave of takeovers was efficiency-decreasing, most economists would probably favour leaving the market for corporate control free from major government intervention. However, some commentators argue that the threat of takeover gives managers too short-term a focus when it comes to investment decisions. This is known as *short-termism*; but, again, there is no conclusive evidence of its existence.

Leveraged buyouts

A **leveraged buyout (LBO)** refers to the buying of a firm by new owners where the required funds are raised by bonds sold to the public. ('Leverage' refers to the ratio of a firm's debt to its equity, so a 'highly leveraged firm' is one that has much debt relative to equity.) The group wishing to take over the firm borrows most of the money needed to buy up the existing shares. When the deal is completed, a public company, owned by many shareholders, has been turned into a private one, owned by a few buyers who financed their purchase by issuing debt.

Leveraged buyouts are often financed by some combination of bank loans and junk bonds—which are high-risk bonds rated below the investment grade.[1] UK buyouts have tended to rely more on bank finance, while US buyouts have made more use of junk bonds (since there is a more

---

[1] Bonds are rated for their riskiness by investment grading agencies. Many institutional investors cannot, or will not, invest in bonds rated more risky than the investment grade.

active market for low-grade, i.e. high-risk, debt in the United States than in Britain).

Leveraged buyouts are risky because the buyers may have been mistaken in believing that the acquired firm could be made to yield much higher profits under their management. Furthermore, the new management must make profits sufficient to meet the large interest payments on the debt they incur to finance their purchases in bad times as well as in good times. In contrast, when finance is by equities, a year of low profits can be a year of low dividend payments without threatening the financial solvency of the firm. Junk bonds and bank debt carry high interest rates, and the amounts by which these exceed the interest on a safe government bond reflect the market's assessment of the risks involved in the newly financed enterprises.

DISMANTLING CONGLOMERATES

The 1970s saw a wave of what were called **conglomerate mergers.** These occurred when several firms producing quite different products and operating in quite different industries were merged into a single conglomerate firm. Examples of such conglomerates in the United Kingdom are Hanson and BTR. One important idea behind these mergers was risk-sharing. Typically, as economic growth proceeds, some industries decline while others grow. If a firm is in an industry that is declining, there may be little it can do to stem its own decline no matter how progressive its management. But if a firm straddles many industries, so went the argument, it may spread its risks among them.

Another reason for many of these takeovers was to gain economies of scope. For example, a large conglomerate might find it easier to raise cash from outside lenders, or to move cash from one enterprise to another within its structure; or it might be able to share its marketing expertise across its firms.

In retrospect, many conglomerate mergers proved to be ill-conceived. In an impressive demonstration of the efficiency of the division of labour, management based in one industry proved to be poorly equipped to assist in the management of firms based in other industries. Neither did the expected economies of scope emerge in any large way. Much marketing and financial expertise proved to be industry-specific, and any gains that could be realized often turned out to be smaller than the losses stemming from the inefficiencies involved in uniting firms across industries. (To the extent that the separate units of the conglomerate were left to behave completely independently, there was no advantage in having the conglomerate in the first place.)

Investors also found problems with conglomerates. By buying the stock of a conglomerate, they were forced to take a stake in *all* of its enterprises. They could not sell off their ownership in one of the conglomerate's parts whose performance they disliked, while holding on to a share of another part whose performance they liked.

For these and other reasons, many of the conglomerates formed in the 1970s were judged to be failures by the mid-1980s. The result of this failure was that the current value of the whole firm was less than the potential value of the sum of its individual parts, if they were operated independently. In some cases, existing management saw the problem and split their firms themselves; for example, ICI created Zeneca to take over its pharmaceutical business. Where existing management did not perceive the possibilities, smart outsiders often did. They decided to buy up the conglomerates, break them up into their constituent parts, allow them to operate long enough so that their profits would rise, and then sell the parts for more in total than they had paid for the whole firm.

When buyers made the correct assessment, they paid off the junk bonds or bank debt out of the proceeds of the sales and pocketed the balance as a return for perceiving that efficiency could be increased by breaking up the conglomerates. The new purchasers financed much of their acquisition by issuing equities, so that the firm was no longer heavily debt-financed.

When buyers guessed wrong, either because there was no advantage in breaking up the conglomerate or, more usually, because the advantage was smaller, or establishing it took longer than expected, they might default on their junk bond or bank debt payments. The investors would then lose their money.

Someone who perceives that a firm's current management practices, or its internal organization, are inefficient can make a gain by buying the firm at its current value and then selling at an increased value after the firm's efficiency has been increased.

When a leveraged buyout turns sour, forcing the firm into bankruptcy, investors lose much of their money. But the real assets of the firm continue to exist and, if they can be operated profitably, it will pay someone to do so. The result is that many of its investors and creditors lose their money, but the physical capital continues to be operated, possibly under some reorganized structure of firms.

Foreign investment

WHEN takeovers, buyouts, and mergers involve firms of two different nationalities, a further consideration is added: how much should citizens worry about the nationality of the owners of firms that operate in their country? This question arises most dramatically when a foreign takeover occurs. It pertains more generally with all **foreign direct investment (FDI)**, that is investment which gives foreign owners control over the behaviour of firms in which the investment is made. In the case of the United Kingdom, FDI gives foreign owners control over the decisions of producers located in Britain (just as British FDI made abroad gives British citizens control over the decisions of producers located in foreign countries). In contrast, the other major category of foreign investment, called **portfolio investment**, involves no control. Major components of portfolio investment are foreign holdings of government and private-sector debt, often in the form of bonds and Treasury bills. (A Treasury bill is short-term government debt, repayable in up to six months.)

Portfolio investment does not usually arouse the popular concerns that sometimes occur over FDI. FDI often causes interest and concern, whether it is the formation of a new foreign-owned firm in the United Kingdom, new investment by an existing foreign-owned firm such as the construction of a factory (called 'greenfield investment'), or a takeover of a British-owned firm by a foreign-owned firm (called 'brownfield investment').

In the past, the major form of foreign investment was greenfield investment, and it is still important, for instance, in the establishment of Japanese car factories in England. In the last decade or so, more and more foreign direct investment has taken the form of mergers or acquisitions of domestically owned firms by foreign-owned firms. For example, UK firms have become major investors in the United States over the last 15 years, mainly by takeover of US firms. Two of the many examples are Grand Metropolitan's purchase of Pillsbury (Burger King, Haagen Dazs, etc.) and Allied–Lyons' purchase of Baskin Robins and Dunkin Donuts.

Motives for FDI

One motive for FDI is just an international extension of what we have already discussed. If a firm in country A is the first to perceive that some firm in country B is not maximizing its profits, country B's firm may take over country A's firm.

A second key motive is to globalize production and competition. At several points in the book we have noted the globalization of the world's economy. In the last 15 years, large companies in Europe, Japan, and North America have been moving to develop presences in all three of these major market areas. This has been done largely with takeovers of, and mergers with, firms located in foreign countries.

A third reason is to move some production to more profitable locations. Firms in advanced countries have moved much of their labour-intensive production to developing nations where wages are lower. Japanese firms have built factories in the United Kingdom partly to get inside the EU market and partly to take advantage of some local conditions in Britain.

These motives have existed for a long time. Until 1979, however, the ability to respond to profitable opportunities was restricted by significant controls over outward-bound UK foreign investment. In that year, the new Conservative government eliminated all controls over capital flows and established a free market for UK foreign investment, both inward- and outward-bound.

World attitudes to transnationals

World attitudes towards foreign investment have been fairly tolerant throughout most of the period since the Industrial Revolution. Most people saw such investment as a benign force leading to more rapid growth, both in total output and in output per person, than could be financed through domestic savings alone. Britain was the major supplier of foreign investment right up to the beginning of the First World War in 1914. Recently, it has once again become an important, although by no means the largest, supplier of FDI. The United States was a major recipient of foreign investment all through the nineteenth and early twentieth centuries. After 1945 it became the world's largest supplier of new investment in foreign countries.

In the late 1950s and the 1960s, many countries became more hostile to foreign investment. The change in attitude was partly the result of the growth of what is variously called the *multinational enterprise (MNE)*, or the *transnational corporation (TNC)*. (See Box 10.1 on p. 181.) These are firms that have locations in many countries. A domestic firm may engage in international trade by selling in many countries; a transnational has production facilities in many countries. In the 1960s the vast majority of the world's TNCs were US-owned.

In the 1950s and 1960s the rise of TNCs was seen in many parts of the world as an ominous development. People correctly perceived that TNCs would make it more difficult for individual countries to maintain economic policies that differed from those of their trading partners. For example, TNCs have the ability, through internal accounting, to shift costs to areas where local tax laws permit the greatest cost write-offs and to shift profits to areas where profit taxes are lowest. They can also shift research and development (R&D) to where tax advantages or subsidies are largest and then make the results of this R&D available throughout their entire organization—which often means throughout the entire world.

This ability represents an inevitable weakening of the power of the individual state. It also provides a pressing reason for the creation of larger political units such as the European Union to provide the political scope necessary to exercise some control over TNCs.

In the 1960s, the rise of TNCs aroused worldwide concern over what was perceived by many as US economic imperialism. Because many of the most successful early TNCs were US-owned, many observers in other countries feared the spread of US economic dominance and cultural influence sometimes referred to as 'Coca Colanization'. Influential books in Europe decried the growth of US economic and cultural imperialism and urged that TNCs be kept out as a defence. Today, with North American firms often on the defensive against Japanese and European TNCs, the fear of US dominance seems but a quaint reminder of the human tendency to think that whatever is now happening will always happen.

TNCs have become increasingly important over the years and now account for the majority of international trade and foreign investment. Indeed, much international trade is between different units of the same TNC (intra-firm trade). Also, the typical organization of a TNC has undergone changes. The typical form in earlier times was a highly centralized firm. Today, with the demands for specialized products carefully tailored to the specific needs of each country, and with the ability to produce small runs of each product variation efficiently, thanks to computer-assisted production, internationally decentralized organizations are becoming increasingly prevalent.

By the 1980s, world attitudes towards TNCs had become tolerant again. Several developments were responsible. First, it was clear to industrial nations that TNCs were here to stay. As world trade became more and more globalized under the impact of the communications and computer revolutions, TNCs became increasingly important until it became apparent that no advanced country could do without them. Second, less developed countries came to the same realization and put out a welcome mat. As the executive director of the United Nations Center on TNCs recently said,

'The 1980s have witnessed major changes in the world production system, with TNCs being the principal forces shaping the future of technological innovation. At the same time, a more pragmatic and businesslike relationship between host governments and TNCs has emerged within the past decade. Many developing countries, burdened by debt and economic stagnation, have liberalized their policies towards TNCs while these corporations have displayed greater sensitivity to the development and economic goals of host countries. The era of confrontation has receded and been replaced by a practical search for a meaningful and mutually beneficial accommodation of interests.'[2]

Do firms maximize profits?

ONE reason why a firm may be taken over by another domestic or foreign firm is that the first firm is not maximizing its profits. The new management may believe that, after the takeover, it can exploit profitable opportunities that are being ignored by the present management. In this section, we discuss a number of alternative theories which all suggest that firms do not routinely succeed in maximizing their profits. Box 17.1 outlines some approaches to testing such theories.

Alternative maximizing theories

The view that many firms may systematically maximize something other than profits is made plausible by the nature of the modern corporation. One hundred years ago the small firm, whose manager was its owner, was common in many branches of industry. In such firms the single-minded pursuit of profits would be expected. Today, however, ownership is commonly diversified among thousands of shareholders, and the firm's managers are rarely its owners. Arranging matters so that managers always act in the best interests of shareholders is, as we shall see, anything but straightforward. Thus, there is potential for managers to maximize something other than profits.

[2] UN Center on Transnational Corporations, *Transnational Corporations in World Development: Trends and Prospects* (New York: United Nations, 1988), p. iii.

BOX 17.1

Approaches to testing the theory

Formulate an alternative theory

Given two alternative theories, we can derive their conflicting predictions, and choose to accept the one that comes closer to predicting what is observed. One competing theory hypothesizes, for example, that firms choose to maximize their sales rather than their profits. A valid way of testing between profit- and sales-maximizing theory is to identify those predictions of each theory that conflict with each other, and confront them with the evidence. This way of choosing between two theories is satisfactory—although it is seldom easy to carry out.

Ask decision-takers how they behave

Another approach to testing the theory of profit-maximizing is to ask businessmen: 'Do you seek to maximize profits?' This approach has from time to time been tried, and it will not surprise you to learn that, when asked if their sole motive was to make as much money as possible, businessmen replied that it was not; that they sought instead to charge a 'fair price', to make only a reasonable profit, and generally to conduct their affairs in a manner conducive to the social good.

One needs only a nodding acquaintance with elementary psychology to realize that we are not likely to discover very much about human motivation by asking people what motivates them. They may have either no idea at all, or else only a pleasantly acceptable rationalization. At best (assuming the subject tries to be scrupulously honest), direct questioning tells us what the people who are questioned think they are doing. Such information can never refute an hypothesis about what people are actually doing. To challenge such an hypothesis, we must observe what they do, not ask them what they *think* they do.

Observe decision-takers within the firm

Carefully conducted case studies can reveal much about behaviour. For example, the management of a firm may be observed consistently to reject alternatives that would increase profits. Such studies can cover only a small sample of firms, and worries naturally arise about the representativeness of the firms that are studied and about comparability between studies made by different researchers.

In spite of such doubts, case studies are fruitful in suggesting new theories. If studies show, for example, that firms habitually follow certain procedures that lead them away from profit maximization, we can formulate a new theory in which these procedures play a prominent role. We would then have two conflicting theories, and we could proceed to test between them in the manner discussed in the earlier section.

Observe decision-takers under laboratory conditions

Economists have only recently begun to use the methods of behavioural psychologists. Several centres of experimental economics now exist, and increasing numbers of researchers are studying economic decisions taken under controlled conditions. It is too early to evaluate the success of this work, although some very suggestive results have been obtained. It will be a long time, however, before economists will be willing to discard theories solely as a result of tests taken under what many would regard as artificial conditions. What is more likely is that some of the results that persist under laboratory conditions will be used to formulate new theories of behaviour—theories that will then be subjected to conventional testing.

The separation of ownership from control

In corporations the shareholders elect directors, who appoint managers. Directors are supposed to represent shareholders' interests and to determine the broad policies that the managers will carry out. In order to conduct the complicated business of running a large firm, a full-time professional management group must be given broad powers of decision. Although managerial decisions can be reviewed from time to time, they cannot be supervised in detail. The links between the directors and the managers are typically weak enough so that it is often top management that really controls the corporation over long periods of time.

As long as the directors have confidence in the man-

agerial group, they accept and ratify their proposals. Shareholders in turn elect and re-elect the directors who are proposed to them. If the managerial group does not satisfy the directors' expectations, it may be replaced, but this is a disruptive and drastic action that is seldom employed.

Within wide limits, then, effective control of the corporation's activities resides with the managers. Although the managers are legally employed by the shareholders, they remain largely independent of them. Indeed, the management group typically asks for, and gets, the *proxies* of enough shareholders to elect directors who will reappoint it, and thus it perpetuates itself in office. (A **proxy** authorizes a person who is attending a shareholders' meeting to cast a shareholder's vote.) In the vast majority of cases, nearly all votes cast are in the form of proxies.

None of this matters unless the managers pursue different interests from those of the shareholders. Do the interests of the two groups diverge? To study this question, we need to look at what is called *principal–agent theory*.

PRINCIPAL–AGENT THEORY

If you (the *principal*) hire a gardener (your *agent*) to mow your lawn while you are away, all you can observe is how the lawn looks when you come back. He *could* have mowed it every 10 days, as you agreed, or he could have waited until two days before you were due home and mowed it only once. By prevailing on a friend or a neighbour to *monitor* your employee's behaviour, you could find out what he actually did, but only at some cost.

When you hire a solicitor to prepare a case against someone against whom you have a grievance, it is almost impossible for you to monitor the solicitor's effort and diligence on your behalf. You have not studied law, and much of what the solicitor does will be a mystery to you.

This latter situation is close to the relationship that exists between shareholders and managers. The managers have information and expertise that the shareholders do not have—indeed, that is *why* they are the managers. The shareholders can observe profits, but they cannot directly observe the managers' efforts. To complicate matters further, even when the managers' behaviour can be observed, the shareholders do not generally have the expertise to evaluate whether that behaviour was as good as it might have been. Everyone can see the firm's revenues, but it takes very detailed knowledge of the firm and the industry to know how large those revenues *could* have been. Boards of directors, who represent the firm's shareholders, can acquire some of the relevant expertise and monitor managerial behaviour, but, again, this is costly.

These examples illustrate the **principal–agent problem**: the problem of designing mechanisms that will induce *agents* to act in their *principals'* interests. In general, unless there is costly monitoring of the agent's behaviour, the problem cannot be completely solved. Hired managers (like hired gardeners) will generally wish to pursue their own goals. They cannot ignore profits because if they perform badly enough they will lose their jobs. Just how much latitude they have to pursue their own goals at the expense of profits will depend on many things, including the degree of competition in the industry and the possibility of takeover by more profit-oriented management.

Principal–agent analysis shows that, when ownership and control are separated, the self-interest of agents will tend to make profits lower than in a 'perfect', frictionless world in which principals act as their own agents.

We know that in the case of firms, the principals, i.e. the shareholders, are interested in maximizing profits. What different motives might their agents, i.e. the managers, have?

SALES MAXIMIZATION

If agents do not maximize profits on behalf of the principals, what do they do? One possibility is that they seek to maximize sales. Suppose that the managers need to make some minimum level of profits to keep the shareholders satisfied; beyond this they are free to maximize their firm's sales revenue. This is a sensible policy on the part of management, the argument runs, because salary, power, and prestige all rise with the size of a firm as well as with its profits. Generally, the manager of a large, normally profitable corporation will earn a salary that is considerably higher than the salary earned by the manager of a small but highly profitable corporation.

The sales maximization hypothesis says that managers of firms seek to maximize their sales revenue, subject to a profit constraint.

As shown in Figure 17.1, sales maximization subject to a profit constraint leads to the prediction that a firm's managers will sacrifice some profits by setting price below and output above their profit-maximizing levels.

Non-maximizing theories

Some critics argue that firms do not know enough to maximize anything. These rather crude criticisms are outlined

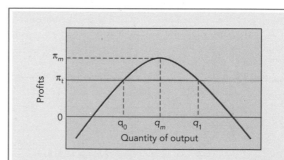

Figure 17.1 Output of the firm under profit maximizing, sales maximizing, and satisficing

The 'best' level of output depends on the motivation of the firm. The curve shows the level of profits associated with each level of output. A profit-maximizing firm produces output q_m and earns profit π_m. A sales-maximizing firm, with a minimum profit constraint of π_t, produces the output q_1.

A satisficing firm with a target level of profits of π_t is willing to produce any output between q_0 and q_1. Thus, satisficing allows a range of outputs on either side of the profit-maximizing level, whereas sales maximization results in a higher output than does profit maximization.

BOX 17.2

Non-maximization due to ignorance?

One group of critics says that profit-maximizing theory is inadequate because firms, however hard they may try, cannot reach decisions in the way the theory predicts. This criticism has several aspects, some crude and some quite sophisticated.

Businessmen do not understand marginal concepts

One of the crudest criticisms is based on the observation that businessmen do not calculate in the manner assumed by the theory. Sometimes when businessmen are interviewed it is discovered (apparently to the surprise of the interviewer) that many have never heard of the concepts of marginal cost and marginal revenue. It is then argued that maximizing theory is refuted because businessmen cannot be employing concepts of which they are unaware.

This observation, assuming it to be correct, does refute the theory that firms take decisions by calculating marginal values and consciously equating them. But it does not refute the theory that firms maximize profits. The mathematical concepts of marginal cost and marginal revenue are used by economic theorists to discover what will happen as long as, by one means or another —be it guess, hunch, clairvoyance, luck, or good judgement— the firms do approximately succeed in maximizing their profits. The constructs of the theory are not meant to be descriptions of *how* firms reach their decisions. If firms are maximizing their profits, then the tools of economic theory allow us to predict how they will react to certain changes, such as the introduction of a new tax. The methods used to derive these predictions have no necessary connection with the thought process by which firms actually reach their decisions.

Business calculations are cruder than assumed by profit-maximizing theory

A similar argument stems from the observation that firms do not calculate down to a single unit with such a nice degree of accuracy as is assumed in profit-maximizing theory. In the verbal presentation of the theory of the firm, it is usually stated that firms will increase production until the cost of producing the very last unit is just equal to the revenue gained from its sale. This is merely a verbal statement of the mathematical conditions for the maximization of the profit function. The observation that firms do not calculate down to single units is not of itself relevant as a test of the theory. Marginal analysis allows us to predict how firms will respond to certain changes that affect them. If they are maximizing their profits, they will respond in the predicted manner even though they calculate in a much cruder fashion than mathematicians do.

Firms have inadequate information

More sophisticated critics argue that the information available to decision-takers is simply not adequate to permit them to reach the decisions that economists predict they will reach. This argument generally takes one of three forms: that firms base their decisions on accounting concepts, which differ from economic ones; that the natural lag between accumulating and processing data is such that important decisions must be made on fragmentary and partially out-of-date information; or that firms cannot afford to acquire as much information as economists assume them to have. All of this suggests that, although firms may be profit-seekers, they may not be profit-maximizers.

in Box 17.2. Other students of corporate behaviour, particularly economists based in business schools, criticize the profit maximization assumption from a perspective different from that given by principal–agent theory. They argue that there are other reasons for doubting that modern corporations are 'simple profit-maximizing computers'. They believe that corporations are *profit-oriented* in the sense that, other things being equal, more profits are preferred to less profits. They do not believe, however, that corporations are profit-maximizers.

FAILURE TO MINIMIZE COSTS

The sales maximization hypothesis implies that the firm's managers will choose to produce more than the profit-maximizing level of output. It is also possible that firms will produce their chosen output at greater than minimum cost. Why would a firm's managers fail to minimize costs?

There are many possible answers, but the most straightforward one is that minimizing costs can demand a great deal of detailed managerial attention, and if management can avoid doing so, it would prefer not to make the effort. Moreover, it is usually costly for a firm to change its routine behaviour. If this is so, one firm may operate at a higher cost than another, but it will still not be worth while for the first firm to copy the behaviour of the second firm. The *transaction costs* of making the change could outweigh the benefits. As with sales maximization, pressure from shareholders, competition from other firms, and threat of takeover will limit the extent to which economic or technological inefficiency can survive, but they may not eliminate inefficiency.

FULL-COST PRICING

Most manufacturing firms are price-setters: they must

quote a price for their products rather than accept a price set on some impersonal competitive market. Simple profit-maximizing theory predicts that these firms will change their prices in response to every change in demand and cost that they experience. In the short run, prices of manufactured goods do not vary in response to every shift in the firm's demand. Instead, they appear to change rather sluggishly.

This short-run behaviour is consistent with the hypothesis of **full-cost pricing**, which was first advanced following a series of detailed case studies of actual pricing decisions made in Oxford in the 1930s. Case studies in the intervening decades have continued to reveal the widespread use of full-cost pricing procedures.

The full-cost pricer, instead of equating marginal revenue with marginal cost, sets price equal to average cost at normal-capacity output, plus a conventional mark-up.

The firm changes its prices when its average costs change substantially (as a result of such events as a new union contract or a sharp change in the prices of key raw materials), and it may occasionally change its mark-up. However, its short-run pricing behaviour appears conventional rather than profit-maximizing.

Modern critics of profit-maximizing theory accept the evidence that full-cost prices are sometimes changed in the profit-maximizing direction. They hold, however, that the prevalence of conventional full-cost practices shows that prices are typically not at their profit-maximizing level. They also hold that the prevalence of full-cost pricing shows that firms are creatures of custom that at most make profit-oriented changes at infrequent intervals.

We have seen in Chapter 14 that the short-term stickiness of oligopolistic prices can be accounted for under profit-maximizing theory by the fact that it is costly for a multi-product firm to change its list prices. If so, the possible conflict between full-cost and profit-maximizing theory concerns only the setting of the mark-up that relates prices to costs. If mark-ups are conventional, and are only rarely revised, then there is a conflict. If, however, the mark-up is the profit-maximizing one for normal-capacity output, full-cost pricing is consistent with profit maximization when it is costly to change prices.

SATISFICING THEORY

A major group of critics of profit maximization develop their argument as follows. Firms operate in highly uncertain environments. Their long-term success or failure is determined largely by their ability to administer innovation and change. But the risks of innovation are large, and the outcomes are highly uncertain. Rational firms tend, therefore, to be quite risk-averse. They develop routines of behaviour that they follow as long as they are successful.

Only when profits fall low enough to threaten their survival do they adopt risky courses of action.

Supporters of this view are economists such as Michael Porter,[3] who argues on the basis of considerable evidence that firms react to the stick of threatened losses of existing profit more than to the carrot of possible increases in profit. Other supporters of this view, such as Richard Nelson and Sidney Winter,[4] argue that firms simply cannot handle the task of scrutinizing all possibilities, calculating the probable outcomes, and then choosing among these so as to maximize their expected profits. Instead, in their view firms carry on with existing routines as long as these produce satisfactory profits, and only when profits fall to unacceptably low levels do the firms search for new ways of doing old things or new lines of activity.

One way of formalizing these views is the theory of **satisficing**. It was first put forward by Professor Herbert Simon of Carnegie-Mellon University in Pittsburgh, Pennsylvania, who in 1978 was awarded the Nobel Prize in economics for his work on the behaviour of firms. He wrote: 'We must expect the firm's goals to be not maximizing profits but attaining a certain level or rate of profit, holding a certain share of the market or a certain level of sales.' In general, a firm is said to be satisficing if it does not change its behaviour, provided that a *satisfactory* (rather than optimal) level of performance is achieved.

According to the satisficing hypothesis, firms could produce any one of a range of outputs that produce profits at least equal to the target level. This contrasts with the unique output that is predicted by profit-maximizing theory. Figure 17.1 on p. 318 compares satisficing behaviour with sales- and profit-maximizing behaviour.

The theory of satisficing predicts not a unique equilibrium output but a range of possible outputs that includes the profit-maximizing output.

EVOLUTIONARY THEORIES

The modern evolutionary theories advanced by economists such as Nelson and Winter build on the earlier theories of full-cost pricing and satisficing. Evolutionary theorists have gathered much evidence to show that tradition often dominates firms' planning. The basic effort at the early stages of planning is directed, they argue, towards the problem of performing reasonably well in established markets and maintaining established market shares. They quote evidence to show that suggestions made in preliminary planning documents to do radically new things are usually weeded out in the reviewing process. They believe that

---

[3] M. Porter, *The Competitive Advantage of Nations* (New York: Macmillan, 1990).

[4] R. Nelson and S. Winter, *The Evolutionary Theory of the Firm* (New Haven, Conn.: Yale University Press, 1984).

most firms spend very little effort on *planning* to enter entirely new markets, and still less on direct efforts to leave, or even reduce, their share in long-established markets. These attitudes were illustrated by one firm which, although faced with obviously changing circumstances, reported to the economists surveying it that 'We have been producing on the basis of these raw materials for more than 50 years with success, and we have made it a policy to continue to do so.'

The evolutionary theory of the firm draws many analogies with the biological theory of evolution. Here are two of the most important.

The genes In biological theory, behavioural patterns are transmitted over time by genes. Rules of behaviour fulfil the same function in the evolutionary theory of the firm. In Nelson and Sidney Winter's words, 'That a great deal of firm decision behaviour is routinized . . . is a "stylized fact" about the realities of firm decision process. Routinized . . . decision procedures . . . cover decision situations from pricing practices in retail stores to such "strategic" decisions as advertising or R and D effort, or the question of whether or not to invest abroad.' Nelson and Winter talk of firms 'remembering by doing' according to repetitive routines. They add that government policy-makers tend to have unrealistic expectations about firms' flexibility and responsiveness to changes in market incentives. These expectations arise from the maximizing model, whose fatal flaw, Nelson and Winter allege, is to underestimate the importance, and the difficulty, 'of the task of merely continuing the routine performance, i.e. of preventing undesired deviations'.

The mutations In the theory of biological evolution, mutations are one vehicle of change. In the evolutionary theory of the firm, this role is played by innovations. The most common innovation concerns the introduction of new products and new production techniques. However, a further important class of innovations in evolutionary theory is the introduction of new rules of behaviour. Sometimes innovations are thrust on the firm; at other times the firm consciously plans for, and creates, this type of innovation.

According to maximizing theory, innovations are the result of incentives—the 'carrot' of new profit opportunities. In evolutionary theory, the firm is much more of a satisficer. It usually innovates only under the incentive of the 'stick', either of unacceptably low profits or of some form of external prodding. Firms change routines when they get into trouble, not when they see a chance to improve an already satisfactory performance. For example, in the growing markets of the 1960s and 1970s, many firms adopted wasteful practices which they shed fairly easily when their profits were threatened in the more difficult economic climate of the 1980s.

FIRMS CONTROL THE MARKET

An even more basic criticism of standard theory was levied some time ago by the American professor John Kenneth Galbraith. He argued that firms were able to manipulate markets largely in their own interests by creating demands for their products through advertising. No one doubts that firms can have some influence on their markets through advertising but the major problems that have beset firms in recent decades have largely discredited Galbraith's once-popular views that firms can effectively control their markets. In today's world of fierce global competition, firms have trouble even surviving, let alone making large profits by manipulating markets. Even the great computer giant IBM got into serious trouble in the early 1990s because it failed to keep up with the rapidly changing patterns of market demand. These are troubles that firms never would have encountered if they had had the market power that Galbraith thought they had.

The importance of non-maximizing theories

An impressive array of empirical and theoretical evidence can be gathered in support of non-maximizing theories. What would be the implications if they were accepted as being better theories of the behaviour of the economy than the 'standard model', which is based on the assumption of profit maximization?

To the extent that existing non-profit-maximizing theories are correct, the economic system does not perform with the delicate precision that follows from profit maximization. Firms will not always respond quickly and precisely to small changes in market signals from either the private sector or government policy. Nor are they certain to make radical changes in their behaviour even when the profit incentives to do so are large.

The non-maximizing theories imply that in many cases firms' responses to changes in market signals will be of uncertain speed and direction.

According to all existing theories, both maximizing and non-maximizing, firms will tend to sell more when demand increases and less when it decreases. They will also tend to alter their prices and their input mixes when they face sufficiently large changes in input prices. Moreover, there are limits to the extent to which the non-maximizing behaviour can survive in the market-place. Failure to respond to profit opportunities can lead to takeover by a more profit-oriented management. Although this does not mean that profits are being precisely maximized at all times, it does put real limits on the extent to which firms can ignore profits.

Profits are a potent force in the life and death of firms. The resilience of profit-maximizing theory and its ability to predict the economy's reactions to many major changes (such as the dramatic variations in energy prices that have occurred since 1973) suggest that firms are at least strongly motivated by the pursuit of profits.

Three key points are at issue here:

1. the extent to which firms respond predictably to changes in such economic signals as output and input prices, taxes, and subsidies;

2. the extent to which non-maximizing behaviour provides scope for profit-oriented takeovers, mergers, and buyouts;

3. the way in which firms manage very-long-run change.

One of the most important lessons learned by economists in the last decade is that much oligopolistic competition takes place in product or process innovation. How firms perform relative to their domestic or foreign competitors with respect to innovation is a major determinant of their competitive performance over the period of a decade or so. These matters require making decisions on highly uncertain issues relating to the very long run. Many investigators argue that the innovative performance of firms is best understood by theories that take account of firms' organizational structures and the routines that they use to guide their decision-making.

In the 1980s and 1990s, the question of how firms behave in detail has received renewed attention from both economists and organization theorists. Almost everyone in the field agrees that firms do not exactly maximize profits at all times and in all places. At the same time, almost everyone agrees that firms cannot stray too far from the goal of profit maximization. Just how far is too far depends on the circumstances in which firms operate and on the mechanisms that firms' owners can use to influence managers. Just how much firms' non-maximizing behaviour influences how they manage change is another important unsettled issue. These areas are at the frontier of current economic research.

PROFIT MAXIMIZATION AS AN EVOLUTIONARY EQUILIBRIUM

US economist Armen Alchian has suggested that, in long-run equilibrium, firms will evolve to become profit-maximizers. His argument is based on the principle of 'survival of the fittest'. In a competitive environment, firms that pursue goals or adopt rules that are inconsistent with profit maximization will be unable to stay in business; firms that either choose or happen upon rules that are closer to profit maximization will undersell and displace those that do not. Eventually, only the profit-maximizing firms will survive in the market-place.

A similar kind of argument can be applied to firms that operate in oligopolistic or monopolistic markets. Here it is not competition that forces the firm towards profit maximization in the long run but the possibility of a takeover. A firm that does not maximize profits will be less valuable than one that does maximize profits. Thus, the non-maximizing firm can be bought by maximizing managers, who will increase its value as they increase its profits, as described earlier in this chapter.

Alchian's argument suggests the following conclusion:

Even if no firm starts out with the intention of maximizing profits, in the long run, the firms that survive in the market-place will tend to be those that come closest to profit maximization.

This view provides an apparent synthesis of maximizing and evolutionary theories of the firm, suggesting that the distinction between the theories is not so stark as it might seem.

In contrast, many organization theorists point out that evolutionary equilibrium is unlikely ever to be achieved. As technology and tastes change over time, so too does the behaviour that will maximize profits. Without a fixed target, a firm's behaviour will continually evolve (generally towards profit maximization), but it will never reach an equilibrium. The target refuses to stay put.

Summary

1 In the market for corporate control, would-be buyers of firms deal with would-be sellers (in friendly takeovers, mergers, and buyouts) as well as with reluctant sellers (in hostile takeovers). Buyers who believe that they can operate a firm more profitably than its present management or its present organization allows can afford to pay more than the present market value of the firm's equities to acquire it. The possibility of such purchases provides an incentive for current managers to come close to maximizing the firm's profits and encourages their replacement by new buyers when they do not.

2 Leveraged buyouts, financed by junk bonds, have been a means of buying out firms whose organization is too large and cumbersome—often as a result of conglomerate mergers of earlier decades. If the deal is successful, the firm is broken up into its constituent parts, which are sold for a total exceeding the purchase price of the whole. The bank debt or junk bonds are then retired, with a profit left over for the purchasers. This is the

market system working to undo an earlier experiment (conglomerate mergers) that often proved to be a failure.

3 Another major reason for a takeover of a domestic firm by a foreign TNC is to integrate the local firm into the large multinational organization.

4 Foreign direct investment has played a large part in opening up less developed countries over the past two centuries. In their time, Canada and the United States were less developed than the United Kingdom and some other European countries and were the recipients of foreign investment that flowed from Europe to the New World.

5 The growth of transnational corporations means that no country can hope to own a majority of the capital that is devoted to the production, within its borders, of internationally traded products. The TNCs also have the power to arbitrage national policies, thereby reducing the effectiveness of many policies designed to give advantages to the initiating country.

6 Principal–agent theory gives support to the idea that corporate managers will not always operate in the best interests of the shareholders; that is, the managers may pursue their own interests rather than simply maximizing profits. Sales maximization is an example of such a pursuit.

7 Another class of theories claims that firms are not *maximizers* of anything. This may be because they lack sufficient knowledge, or because they choose not to do so.

8 Full-cost pricing with conventional mark-ups makes firms creatures of convention. The same theory, with mark-ups determined at the profit-maximizing level for normal-capacity output (plus the assumption that changing prices is costly), is consistent with profit maximization.

9 Organization theory assumes that the firm satisfices—which means that it is satisfied with any level of output and prices that meets its minimum-profit constraint.

10 Evolutionary theories see firms as profit-oriented but not profit-maximizing. Firms follow rules of behaviour that have been shown to work and change these only when forced to by major changes in market conditions.

11 Even if individual firms do not always maximize profits, it is possible that the industry will be characterized by behaviour that is approximately profit-maximizing. The reason is that those firms that come closest to maximizing profits will prosper and grow while those further away from profit maximization will shrink or fail altogether.

Topics for review

- Mergers, takeovers, and buyouts
- Transnational corporations
- Foreign direct investment
- Portfolio investment
- Leveraged buyouts
- Junk bonds
- Sales maximization
- Satisficing
- Evolutionary theories
- Takeovers as a constraint on non-maximizing behaviour

PART FIVE

The theory of distribution

~ CHAPTER 18

Factor pricing and factor mobility

IN this chapter, we will study the determination of the distribution of income in competitive markets, those in which individual buyers and sellers have no market power over prices. We will study first the forces that determine the demand for factors, then the forces that influence supply, and finally how these interact to determine both the prices of factors of production and the share of the nation's total income going to each factor. In subsequent chapters we will amend our analyses to allow for market power exercised in factor markets by a few larger sellers and/or buyers.

The neoclassical theory of distribution in outline

WHY does the market system reward some people with high incomes, while others earn very little? It is tempting to give superficial answers such as: 'People are paid what they are worth.' But we may wonder: worth what, and to whom? What gives them value? Sometimes it is said that people earn according to their ability. But note that incomes are distributed in a very much more unequal fashion than any measured index of ability such as IQ or physical strength. In what sense is Anthony Hopkins twenty times as able as a promising new actor? He earns twenty times as much. In what sense is someone working on a North Sea oil rig more able than a schoolteacher? If answers couched in terms of worth and ability seem superficial, so are answers such as 'It's all a matter of luck', or 'It's just the system'.

Functional distribution and size distribution

The founders of classical economics, Adam Smith and David Ricardo, were concerned with the distribution of income among what were then the three great social classes: workers, capitalists, and landowners. They defined three factors of production: labour, capital, and land. The return to each factor was treated as the income of the respective social class. This is why the theory of factor prices is also called the theory of distribution. Debate ensued about how the progress of society, particularly in terms of rising population, accumulation of capital, and technological change, would influence the distribution of income among these three great social classes.

These nineteenth-century debates focused on what is now called the **functional distribution of income,** defined as the distribution of total income among the major factors of production. Modern economists have, however, shifted much of their emphasis to another way of looking at differences in incomes, called the **size distribution of income.** This term refers to the distribution of income among dif-

ferent households without reference to the source of the income or the social class of the household. Figure 18.1 shows the functional distribution by income class. It includes cash benefits received from the government and pension income as well as incomes received in return for the current sale of factor services in such forms as wages and salaries, income from self-employment, and investment and rental income.

Table 18.1 shows the size distribution of disposable income (incomes after taxes and cash benefits) for the years 1979 and 1991. The growing inequality in the size distribution is readily apparent from the table.

The current inequality in the size distribution of disposable income is shown graphically in Figure 18.2. This curve is called a **Lorenz curve** and it shows how much of total income is accounted for by given proportions of the nation's households. (The farther the curve bends away from the diagonal, the more unequal is the distribution of

---

Table 18.1 Distribution of disposable UK household income, 1979–1991

	1979	1991
Bottom fifth	10	7
Next fifth	14	12
Middle fifth	18	17
Next fifth	23	23
Top fifth	35	41

Source: Social Trends (CSO), 1994.

Inequalities in disposable income have increased between 1979 and 1991. The data give the percentage distribution of household incomes after taxes and benefits from 1979 to 1991. In 1979 the bottom 20 per cent in the size distribution of income received 10 per cent of total income; in 1991 they received only 7 per cent. In 1979 the top 20 per cent of income recipients received 35 per cent of all income; in 1991 they received 41 per cent.

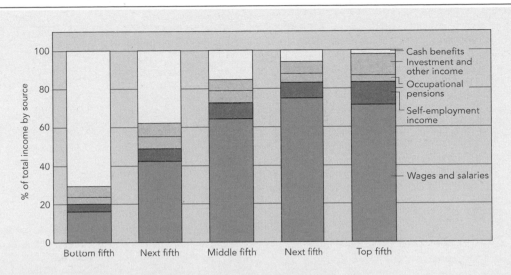

Figure 18.1 Sources of income by income classes, UK, 1991

Wages are by far the largest source of income for all but the poorest fifth of households. The figure divides households into five groups classified by the size of their income. It then shows the proportion of income coming from each income source for each of the five groups. The bottom one-fifth of income receivers get most of their incomes from cash benefits from the government, and this is also a major source for those in the second fifth. Wages and salaries are seen to be the most important income source for all but those in the bottom fifth. Income from self-employment is significant for all income levels as is investment income, but both become relatively more important as the size of overall income is increased.

Source: Social Trends, CSO, 1994.

income.) The curve shows, for example, that the bottom 20 per cent of all UK households receive only 7 per cent of all income earned, while the bottom 80 per cent receive only 59 per cent of total disposable income—the remaining 41 per cent goes to the top 20 per cent of income-earners.

Today most economists devote more attention to the size distribution of income than to the functional distribution. After all, some capitalists (such as the owners of small retail stores) are in the lower part of the income scale, and some wage-earners (such as professional athletes) are at the upper end of the income scale. Moreover, if someone is poor, it matters little whether that person is a landowner or a worker.

The link between output and input decisions

In Chapters 10 and 11, we saw how firms' costs varied with their outputs and how they could achieve cost minimization by finding the least costly combination of factors to produce any given output. In Chapter 12 we saw that firms in perfect competition decided how much to produce by equating their marginal costs to given market prices. We

also saw how the market supply curve interacted with the market demand curve in each goods market. This interaction determines the market price as well as the quantity that is produced and consumed.

These events in goods markets have implications for factor markets. The decisions of firms on how much to produce and how to produce it imply specific demands for various quantities of the factors of production. These demands, together with the supplies of the factors of production (which are determined by the owners of the factors), come together in factor markets. Together they determine the quantities of the various factors of production that are employed, their prices, and the incomes earned by their owners.

The above discussion shows that there is a close relationship between the production and pricing of the goods and services produced by firms on the one hand and the pricing, employment, and incomes earned by the factors of production they hire on the other hand. These are two aspects of a single set of economic activities relating to the production of goods and services and the allocation of the nation's resources among their various possible uses. This discussion provides a brief introduction to one of the great insights of economics:

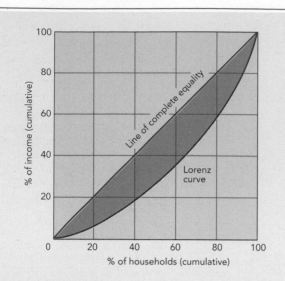

Figure 18.2 A Lorenz curve of household income in the UK

The size of the shaded area between the Lorenz curve and the diagonal is a measure of the inequality of income distribution. If there were complete income equality, the bottom 20 per cent of income receivers would get 20 per cent of the total income, the bottom 40 per cent would receive 40 per cent of the income, and so forth. The Lorenz curve would then coincide with the diagonal line. Because of income inequality (e.g. the lower 20 per cent receive only 7 per cent of the income), the Lorenz curve lies below the diagonal. The extent to which it bends away from the straight line indicates the amount of inequality in the distribution of income. The income measured is disposable income, which is income *after* taxes and after cash benefits. The pre-tax and –benefit income is more unevenly distributed than the disposable income shown in the figure. For example, while the bottom fifth of households receive only 7 per cent of total disposable income, fully 70 per cent of that comes, as shown in Figure 18.1, from cash benefits.

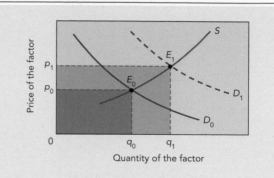

Figure 18.3 Factor income determined in competitive markets

The interaction of demand and supply in competitive factor markets determines a factor's equilibrium price and quantity, and hence its income. The original demand and supply curves are D_0 and S. Equilibrium is at E_0, with price p_0 and quantity employed q_0. The factor's income is its price times its quantity, which is shown by the dark blue area in the figure. When the demand curve shifts to D_1, equilibrium shifts to E_1, with price p_1 and quantity q_1. The factor's income rises by the amount of the medium blue area.

When demand and supply interact to determine the allocation of resources among various lines of production, they also determine the incomes of the factors of production that are used in making the outputs.

This insight is the basis of the neoclassical theory of distribution. According to this theory, the distribution of income is nothing more than a special case of price theory. The way this works can be summarized in the following three points.

1. The income of any factor of production (and hence the amount of the national product that it is able to command) depends on the price that is paid for the factor and the amount that is used.

2. Factor prices and quantities are determined by demands and supplies in factor markets in exactly the same way that the prices and quantities of commodities are determined in product markets.

3. To explain distribution through price theory, all that is needed, therefore, is to identify the main determinants of the demand for, and supply of, factors of production and allow for any intervention into free markets caused by governments, unions, or other similar institutions.

Figure 18.3 illustrates the neoclassical theory by showing how competitive market forces determine one factor's income. The rest of this chapter is an elaboration of this important theme. We first study the demand for factors, then their supply, and finally how they come together to determine factor prices and quantities.

Two assumptions

Before we begin, we need to make two assumptions designed to facilitate the analysis.

Other prices constant In order to ensure that we are speaking of relative and not just absolute prices and quantities, we assume that, when the changes studied in Figure 18.3 occur, *the price of all other factors of production, the prices of all goods, and the level of national income are given and con-*

stant.[1] Under these circumstances, fluctuations in a factor's equilibrium price and quantity cause fluctuations (1) in the money earnings of that factor, (2) in its earnings relative to other factors, and (3) in the share of national income going to the factor. Assume, for example, that the money price of one factor changes from some value p_0 to a higher value p_1, while the quantity employed changes the amount from q_0 to q_1. This means that (*a*) the factor's *relative price* rises from p_0/F to p_1/F, where F is the constant, average price of *all* other factors; and (*b*) because the factor's total earnings change from p_0q_0 to p_1q_1, the share of income going to this factor changes from p_0q_0/Y to p_1q_1/Y, where Y is the constant total national income.

Competitive markets In this chapter we confine ourselves to goods and factor markets that are perfectly competitive. This means that individual firms are price-takers in both markets. On the one hand, they face a given price for the product they produce, and that price is both their average and marginal revenue. On the other hand, they face a given price of each factor that they buy, and that price is both the average and marginal cost of the factor.

Dealing first with firms that are price-takers in product and factor markets allows us to study the principles of factor price determination in the simplest context. Once these are understood, it is relatively easy to allow for monopolistic elements in either or both types of markets. This is done in Chapter 19.

The demand for factors

FIRMS require the services of land, labour, capital, and natural resources[2] to be used as inputs. They also use as their inputs intermediate products, such as steel, plastics, and electricity, that are produced by other firms.

If we investigate the production of these produced inputs, we will find that they, too, are made by using land, labour, capital, natural resources, and other produced inputs. If we continue following through the chain of outputs used as inputs, we can account for all of the economy's output in terms of inputs of the basic factors of production—land, labour, and capital, and natural resources. The theory of factor pricing applies to *all* inputs used by a firm. The theory of distribution explains the division of total national income among the owners of the basic factors: land, labour, capital, and natural resources.

Firms require inputs not for their own sake but as a means to produce goods and services. For example, the demand for computer programmers and technicians is growing as more and more computers are used. The demand for carpenters and building materials rises and falls as the amount of housing construction rises and falls. Thus, demand for any input is derived from the demand for the goods and services that it helps to produce; for this reason, the demand for a factor of production is called a **derived demand.**

Derived demand provides a link between the markets for output and the markets for inputs.

The quantity of a factor demanded

We start by deriving a famous relation that holds in equi-

librium for every factor employed by a wide class of firms. In Chapter 12, we established the rules for the maximization of a firm's profits in the short run. When one factor is fixed and another is variable, the profit-maximizing firm increases its output until the last unit produced adds just as much to cost as to revenue, that is, until marginal cost equals marginal revenue. Another way of stating that the firm maximizes profits is to say that *the firm will increase production up to the point at which the last unit of the variable factor employed adds just as much to revenue as it does to cost.*

The addition to total cost resulting from employing one more unit of a factor is its price. (Recall that the firm is assumed to buy its factors in competitive markets.) So if one more worker is hired at a wage of £15 per hour, the addition to the firm's costs is £15.

The amount that a unit of a variable factor adds to revenue is the amount that the unit adds to total output multiplied by the change in revenue caused by selling an extra unit of output.

In Chapter 11 we called the variable factor's addition to total output its *marginal product.* When dealing with factor markets, economists use the term **marginal *physical* product** *(MPP)* to avoid confusion with the revenue concepts that they also need to use.

---

[1] We make these assumptions because we are concerned with a factor's relative share of total national income. As we observed in the texts these assumptions are only a simplifying device for our analysis; they do not prevent it from being applied to inflationary situations.

[2] Although natural resources are often included with land as a single factor of production, they have so many important special characteristics that it is sometimes worth while treating them as a separate factor. Some of the issues involved with pricing natural resources are discussed in Chapter 20.

The change in revenue caused by selling one extra unit of output is just the price of the output, p (since the firm is a price-taker in the market for its output).

The resulting amount, which is $MPP \times p$, is called the factor's **marginal revenue product** and given the symbol MRP.

For example, if the variable factor's marginal physical product is two units per hour and the price of a unit of output is £7.50, then the factor's marginal revenue product is £15 (£7.50 × 2).

We can now restate the equilibrium condition for a firm to be maximizing its profits in two ways. First:

Addition to total costs caused by hiring another unit of the variable factor	=	The factor's marginal revenue product (MRP) (1)

Because the firm is a price-taker in both its input and output markets, we can restate equation (1) by noting that the left-hand side is just the price of a unit of the variable factor, which we call w, while the right-hand side is the factor's marginal physical product, MPP, multiplied by the price at which the output is sold, which we call p. In words, this gives us

Price of a unit of the variable factor	=	The factor's marginal physical product multiplied by its market price (2a)

and in symbols,

$$w = MPP \times p. \qquad (2b)$$

To check your understanding of equation (2), consider an example. Suppose that the variable factor is available to the firm at a cost of £10 a unit ($w = £10$). Suppose also that employing another unit of the factor adds three units to output ($MPP = 3$). Suppose further that output is sold for £5 a unit ($p = £5$). Thus, the additional unit of the variable factor adds £15 to the firm's revenue and £10 to its costs. Hiring one more unit of the factor brings in £5 more than it costs. *The firm will take on more of the variable factor whenever its marginal revenue product exceeds its price.*

Now alter the example so that the last unit of the variable factor taken on by the firm has a marginal physical product of one unit of output—it adds only one extra unit to output—and so adds only £5 to revenue. Clearly, the firm can increase profits by cutting back on its use of the factor, since laying off one unit reduces revenues by £5 while reducing costs by £10. *The firm will lay off units of the variable factor whenever its marginal revenue product is less than its price.*

Finally, assume that another unit of the factor taken on, or laid off, has an MPP of two units, so that it increases revenue by £10. Now the firm cannot increase its profits by altering its employment of the variable factor in either direction. *The firm cannot increase its profits by altering*

employment of the variable factor whenever the factor's marginal revenue product equals its price.

This example illustrates what was said earlier. We are doing nothing that is essentially new; instead, we are merely looking at the firm's profit-maximizing behaviour from the point of view of its inputs rather than its output. In Chapters 12 and 13, we saw the firm varying its output until the marginal cost of producing another unit was equal to the marginal revenue derived from selling that unit. Now we see the same profit-maximizing behaviour in terms of the firm varying its inputs until the marginal cost of another unit of input is just equal to the revenue derived from selling the unit's marginal product.

The firm's demand curve for a factor

We now know what determines the quantity of a variable factor a firm will buy when faced with some specific price of the factor and some specific price of its output. Next, we wish to derive the firm's whole demand curve, which tells us how much the firm will buy at *each* price of the variable factor.

To derive a firm's demand curve for a factor, we start by considering the right-hand side of equation (2b), which tells us that the factor's marginal revenue product is composed of a physical component and a value component.

The physical component of MRP   As the quantity of the variable factor varies, output will vary. The hypothesis of diminishing returns, first discussed in Chapter 10, predicts what will happen: as the firm adds further units of the variable factor to a given quantity of the fixed factor, the additions to output will eventually get smaller and smaller. In other words, the factor's marginal physical product will decline. This is illustrated in part (i) of Figure 18.4, which uses hypothetical data that have the same general characteristics as the data in Table 11.1 on p. 194. The negative slope of the MPP curve reflects the operation of the law of diminishing returns: each unit of labour adds less to total output than the previous unit.

The value component of MRP   To convert the marginal physical product curve of Figure 18.4(i) into a curve showing the marginal revenue product of the variable factor, we need to know the value of the extra physical product. As long as the firm sells its output in a competitive market, this value is simply the marginal physical product multiplied by the market price at which the firm sells its product.

This operation is illustrated in part (ii) of Figure 18.4, which shows a marginal revenue product curve for labour on the assumption that the firm sells its product in a competitive market at a price of £5 a unit. This curve shows how much would be added to revenue by employing one more unit of the factor *at each level of total employment of the factor.*

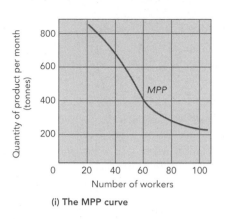
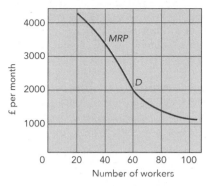

(i) The MPP curve

(ii) The MRP and demand curve

Figure 18.4 From marginal physical product to demand curve

Each additional unit of the factor employed adds a certain amount to total product (part (i)) and hence a certain amount to total revenue (part (ii)), and this determines the amount of the factor that firms will demand at each price. Part (i) assumes data that are consistent with marginal productivity theory; it shows the addition to the firm's *output* produced by additional units of labour hired. The curve is negatively sloped because of the law of diminishing returns.

Part (ii) shows the addition to the firm's *revenue* caused by the employment of each additional unit of labour. It is the marginal physical product from part (i) multiplied by the price at which that product is sold. In this case the price is assumed to be £5. (The multiplication is by market price because the firm is assumed to be a price-taker in the market for its output.)

Since the firm equates the price of the variable factor, which in this case is labour, to the factor's marginal revenue product, it follows that the *MRP* curve, in part (ii), is also the demand curve for labour, showing how much will be employed at each price.

The basic principle is that firms should equate the addition to cost of buying another unit of a variable factor with the addition to revenue caused by selling the output of that unit, which we call the factor's marginal revenue product, *MRP*. The *MRP* is always composed of a physical component, which is the factor's *MPP*, and a value component, which is the marginal revenue of selling those extra physical units of output. Because in this chapter our firms are price-takers in their output markets, the marginal revenue is just the price that they face in that market. If the firm faces a negatively sloped demand curve, we know from Chapter 13 that the addition to the revenue from selling further units is not the market price because marginal revenue is less than price.

From MRP to the demand curve   Equation (2a) states that the profit-maximizing firm will employ additional units of the factor up to the point at which the *MRP* equals the price of the factor. If, for example, the price of the variable factor were £2,000 per month, then it would be most profitable to employ 60 workers. (There is no point in employing a sixty-first, since that would add just less than £2,000 to revenue but a full £2,000 to costs.) So the profit-maximizing firm

hires the quantity of the variable factor that equates the marginal revenue product with the price of the variable factor. Thus, the curve that relates the quantity of the variable factor employed to its *MRP* is also the curve that relates the quantity of the variable factor the firm wishes to employ to its price.

The *MRP* curve of the variable factor is the same as the demand curve for that variable factor.

The slope of an industry's demand curve for a factor

So far we have seen how a single firm that takes its market price as given will vary its quantity demanded for a factor as that factor's price changes. But when a factor's price changes and *all firms* in a competitive industry vary the amount of the factor that they demand in order to vary their output, the price of the industry's product changes. That change will have repercussions on desired output and the quantity of the factor demanded.

For example, a fall in carpenters' wages will reduce the cost of producing houses, thus shifting the supply curve of houses to the right. Price-taking construction firms would plan to increase construction, and hence increase the quantity of carpenters demanded, by some specific amount if the price of houses does not change. Because the demand curve for houses is negatively sloped, however, the increase in output leads to a fall in the market price of houses. As a result, each individual firm will increase its desired output *by less* than it had planned to do before the market price changed.

An increase in carpenters' wages has the opposite effect. The cost of producing houses rises; the supply curve shifts to the left; and the price of houses rises. As a result, the individual firm will cut its planned output and employment of factors of production by less than it would have done if market price had not changed.

The industry's demand curve for a factor, relating the quantity demanded to the factor's price, is steeper when the reaction of market price is allowed for than it would be if firms faced an unchanged product price.

It may be useful to summarize the reasoning used so far.

1. The derived demand curve for a factor of production on the part of a *price-taking* firm will have a negative slope because of the law of diminishing returns. As more of the factor is employed in response to a fall in its price, its marginal product falls. No further units will be added once its marginal revenue product falls to the factor's new price.

2. An industry's demand curve for a factor is less elastic than suggested by point 1. As the industry expands output in response to a fall in a factor's price, the price of the firm's output will fall, causing the final increase in each firm's output, and hence employment of factors, to be less than would occur if the output price remained unchanged.

Elasticity of factor demand

The elasticity of demand for a factor measures the *degree* of the response of the quantity demanded to a change in its price. The influences that were discussed in the preceding sections explain the *direction* of the response; that is, the quantity demanded is negatively related to price. You should not be surprised, therefore, to hear that the amount of the response depends on the strength with which these influences operate. This section gives the four principles of derived demand that come from the work of the English economist Alfred Marshall (1842–1924).

DIMINISHING RETURNS

The first influence on the slope of the demand curve is the diminishing marginal productivity of a factor. If marginal productivity declines rapidly as more of a variable factor is employed, a fall in the factor's price will not induce many more units to be employed. Conversely, if marginal productivity falls only slowly as more of a variable factor is employed, there will be a large increase in quantity demanded as price falls.

The faster the marginal productivity of a factor declines as its use rises, the lower is the elasticity of each firm's demand curve for the factor.

For example, both labour and fertilizers are used by market gardeners who produce vegetables for sale in nearby cities. For many crops, additional doses of fertilizers add significant amounts to yields over quite a wide range of fertilizer use. Although the marginal product of fertilizer does decline, it does so rather slowly as more and more fertilizer is used. In contrast, although certain amounts of labour are needed for planting, weeding, and harvesting, there is only a small range over which additional labour can be used productively. The marginal product of labour, although high for the first units, declines rapidly as more and more labour is used.

Under these circumstances, market gardeners will have an elastic demand for fertilizer and an inelastic demand for labour.

SUBSTITUTION

In the long run, all factors are variable. If one factor's price rises, firms will try to substitute relatively cheaper factors for it. For this reason, the slope of the demand curve for a factor is influenced by the ease with which other factors can be substituted for the factor whose price has changed.

The greater the ease of substitution, the greater is the elasticity of demand for the factor.

The ease of substitution depends on the substitutes that are available and on the technical conditions of production. It is often possible to vary factor proportions in surprising ways. For example, in car manufacturing and in building construction, glass and steel can be substituted for each other simply by varying the dimensions of the windows. Another example is that construction materials can be substituted for maintenance labour in the case of most durable consumer goods. This is done by making the product more or less durable and more or less subject to breakdowns by using more or less expensive materials in its construction.

Such substitutions are not the end of the story. Plant and equipment are being replaced continually, which allows

---

BOX 18.1

More than one variable factor

When a firm can vary the amounts of several factors that it uses, profit maximization requires that the last pound it spends on each factor brings in the same amount of revenue.

To see how this works out for two factors, call their prices p_A and p_B and their marginal revenue products MRP_A and MRP_B. The amount of extra revenue per pound spent on factor A is MRP_A/p_A and per pound spent on factor B is MRP_B/p_B. For example, if one more unit of A costs £3 and adds £6 to revenue, it yields £2 of revenue per pound spent on it. If one more unit of B cost £5 and adds £10 to revenue, it too yields £2 of revenue per pound spent on it. If the firm wants to equate these MRPs per pound spent on the factor, it must set

$$\frac{MRP_A}{p_A} = \frac{MRP_B}{p_B}. \qquad \text{(i)}$$

We know that the marginal revenue product is $MPP \times P$ for firms that are price-takers in their output markets. So we can rewrite equation (i) as:

$$\frac{MPP_A \times P}{p_A} = \frac{MPP_B \times P}{p_B}. \qquad \text{(ii)}$$

If we eliminate the common P term, we have

$$\frac{MPP_A}{p_A} = \frac{MPP_B}{p_B}. \qquad \text{(iii)}$$

This is equation (3) on p. 201, except that we are now calling the factor's marginal product MPP (to distinguish it from MRP), whereas we called it MP in the earlier treatment, because there was no possibility of confusion there.

Equation (i) can be rewritten as follows:

$$\frac{MRP_A}{MRP_B} = \frac{p_A}{p_B}. \qquad \text{(iv)}$$

Equation (iv) should be compared with the equation (2) on p. 131 of Chapter 7. In equation (iv) the firm is given prices of the two factors, and it adjusts to these by altering the quantities of the two inputs until it has the profit-maximizing amount of each. This behaviour is similar to that of the consumer described on p. 131. The consumer is given the prices of two commodities and she adjusts her consumption until her utility is maximized (which she does by making the ratios of the marginal utilities equal the ratio of their prices).

Those who have studied the Appendix to Chapter 11 have seen the analysis of this box carried out with isoquants.

---

more or less capital-intensive methods to be built into new plants in response to changes in factor prices. Similarly, engines that use less petrol per mile tend to be developed when the price of petrol rises severely.

Box 18.1 provides an optional treatment of the argument just given, while Box 18.2 provides an example drawn from the electricity industry.

IMPORTANCE OF THE FACTOR

Other things being equal, the larger the fraction of the total costs of producing some product that are made up of payments to a particular factor, the greater is the elasticity of demand for that factor.

To see this, suppose that wages account for 50 per cent of the costs of producing a good and raw materials account for 15 per cent. A 10 per cent rise in the price of labour raises the cost of producing the product by 5 per cent (10 per cent of 50 per cent), but a 10 per cent rise in the price of raw materials raises the cost of the product by only 1.5 per cent (10 per cent of 15 per cent). The larger the increase in the cost of production, the larger is the shift in the product's supply curve, and hence the larger the decreases in quantities demanded both of the product and of the factors used to produce it.

ELASTICITY OF DEMAND FOR THE OUTPUT

The fourth, and last, principle of derived demand is as follows:

Other things being equal, the more elastic the demand for the product that the factor helps to make, the more elastic is the demand for the factor.

If an increase in the price of the product causes a large decrease in the quantity demanded—that is, if the demand for the product is elastic—there will be a large decrease in the quantity of a factor needed to produce it in response to

---

BOX 18.2

Electricity generation: substitution in practice

One field in which the principle of substitution has been important, but has not always worked in the same direction, is the choice of fuels used to generate electricity.

During the 1950s and 1960s, economies of scale in shipping crude oil from the Middle East to Western Europe made oil-based fuels more and more competitive. The relative price of fuels for industrial use fell by even more than the production cost of petrol, as it was the demand for petrol that was mainly responsible for the derived demand for crude oil. Other outputs of the oil-refining process were by-products. The Central Electricity Generating Board, as it was then called (it has since been privatized as National Power and Powergen), responded to the falling relative price of 'bunker' oil by building more and more oil-fired power stations and gradually closing down (or converting) the older coal-fired stations. From 85–7 per cent of electricity generated from coal and 11–14 per cent from oil in 1962–5, the CEGB steadily changed the 'mix', so that by 1971–4 it was generating 63–6 per cent from coal and 24–6 per cent from oil.

Then came the 'oil shocks' of 1973/4 and 1979/80, when the

OPEC countries dramatically raised the price of crude oil, leading to correspondingly dramatic increases in the prices of all oil products. Even though people in coal-mining saw an opportunity to raise coal prices substantially, the *relative* price of oil was significantly higher in the 1980s than it had been in the 1960s and early 1970s. The CEGB accordingly switched back to increasing reliance on coal-firing, generating 77–81 per cent of its electricity from coal and only 5–7 per cent from oil in 1982–4.

Nevertheless, the CEGB clearly retained the ability to switch back to oil rapidly if required: in 1984/5, the coal miners' strike which lasted almost the whole year led to an amazing 41 per cent of electricity being generated from oil (with total output slightly higher than the previous year) and only 42 per cent from coal. After the strike, the figures quickly returned to their 1982–4 levels. However, the proportion of coal used declined again in the late 1980s and early 1990s due to the growing use of natural gas and nuclear power. By 1993 the percentages of fuels used in electricity generation were: coal 53, oil 8, gas 9, nuclear 26 and hydro 1.8.

---

a rise in the factor's price. However, if an increase in the price of a product causes only a small decrease in the quantity demanded—that is, if the demand for the product is inelastic—there will be only a small decrease in the quantity of the factor required in response to a rise in its price.

In Box 18.3 the forces affecting the elasticity of the derived demand curves that have just been discussed are related more specifically to the market for the industry's output.

The supply of factors

WHEN we consider the supply of any factor of production, we must consider the amount supplied to the economy as a whole, to each industry and occupation, and to each firm. The elasticity of supply of a factor will normally be different at each of these levels of aggregation. We start with the highest level of aggregation, the total supply of each factor to the economy as a whole.

The total supply of factors

At any one time, the total quantity of each factor of production is given. For example, in each country the labour force is of a certain size, there is so much arable land available, and there is a given supply of discovered petroleum. However, these supplies can and do change in response to both economic and non-economic forces. Sometimes the change is very gradual, as when a climatic change slowly turns arable land into desert or when a medical discovery lowers the rate of infant mortality and hence increases the rate of population growth, thereby eventually increasing the supply of adult labour. Sometimes the changes can be quite rapid, as when a boom in business activity brings retired persons back into the labour force or a rise in the price of agricultural produce encourages the draining of marshes to add to the supply of arable land.

BOX 18.3

The principles of derived demand

This box demonstrates two of the four principles of derived demand using demand and supply curves.

1. The larger the proportion of total costs accounted for by a factor, the more elastic is the demand for it.

Consider the left-hand figure shown. The demand curve for the *industry's product* is D and, given the factor's original price, the *industry supply curve* is S_0. Equilibrium is at E_0 with output at q_0.

Suppose that the factor's price then falls. If the factor accounts for a small part of the industry's total costs, each firm's marginal cost curve shifts downward by only a small amount. So also does the industry supply curve, as illustrated by the supply curve S_1. Output expands only a small amount to q_1, which implies only a small increase in the quantity of the variable factor demanded.

If the factor accounts for a large part of the industry's total costs, each firm's marginal cost curve shifts downward a great deal. So also does the industry supply curve, as illustrated by the

curve S_2. Output expands greatly to q_2, which implies a large increase in the quantity of variable factor demanded.

2. The more elastic the demand curve for the product made by a factor, the more elastic is the demand for the factor.

Consider the right-hand figure. The original demand and supply curves for the industry's product intersect at E_0 to produce an industry output of q_0. A fall in the price of a factor causes the industry's supply curve to shift downward to S_1.

When the demand curve is relatively inelastic, as shown by the curve D_i, the industry's output increases by only a small amount, to q_1. The quantity of the variable factor demanded will increase by a correspondingly small amount.

When the demand curve is relatively elastic, as shown by the curve D_e, the industry's output increases by a large amount to q_2. The quantity of the variable factor demanded will then increase by a correspondingly large amount.

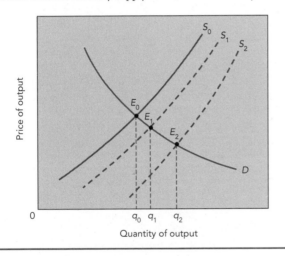
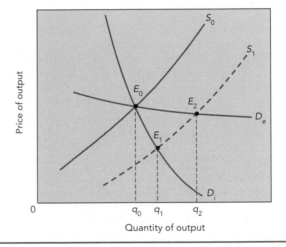

TOTAL SUPPLY OF CAPITAL

The supply of capital in a country consists of the stock of existing machines, plants, equipment, and so on. Capital is a manufactured factor of production, and its total quantity is in no sense fixed, although it changes only slowly. Each year the stock of capital goods is diminished by the amount that becomes physically or economically obsolete and is increased by the amount that is newly produced. The difference between these is the net addition to, or net subtraction from, the capital stock. On balance, the trend has been for the capital stock to grow from decade to decade over the past few centuries. In Chapter 20 we shall consider in some detail the determinants of investment in capital.

TOTAL SUPPLY OF LAND

The total area of dry land in a country is almost completely fixed, but the supply of *fertile* land is not fixed. Considerable care and effort are required to sustain the productive power of land. If farmers earn low incomes, they may not provide the necessary care and the land's fertility may be destroyed within a short time. In contrast, high earnings from farming may provide the incentive to increase the supply of arable land by irrigation and other forms of reclamation.

TOTAL SUPPLY OF LABOUR

The number of people willing to work is called the *labour force;* the total number of hours they are willing to work is called the **supply of effort** or, more simply, the **supply of labour.** The supply of effort depends on three influences: the size of the population, the proportion of the population willing to work, and the number of hours worked by each individual. Each of these is partly influenced by economic forces.

Population   Populations vary in size, and these variations are influenced to some extent by economic forces. There is some evidence, for example, that the birth rate and the net immigration rate (immigration minus emigration) is higher in good times than in bad. Much of the variation in population is, however, explained by factors outside economics.

The labour force   The proportion of the total population, or of some subgroup such as men, women, or teenagers, that is willing to work is called that group's **labour force participation rate.** This rate varies in response to many influences, for example changes in attitudes and tastes. The enormous rise in female participation rates in the last three decades is a case in point. A force that is endogenous to the economic system is the demand for labour. Generally, a rise in the demand for labour, and an accompanying rise in earnings, will lead to an increase in the proportion of the population willing to work. More married women and elderly people enter the labour force when the demand for labour is high. For the same reasons, the labour force tends to decline when earnings and employment opportunities decline.

Hours worked   Not only does the wage rate influence the number of people in the labour force (as we observed earlier), it is also a major determinant of hours worked. Workers trade their leisure for incomes; by giving up leisure (in order to work), they obtain income with which to buy goods. They can, therefore, be thought of as trading leisure for goods.

A rise in the wage rate implies a change in the relative price of goods and leisure. Goods become cheaper relative to leisure, since each hour worked buys more goods than before. The other side of the same change is that leisure becomes more expensive, since each hour of leisure consumed is at the cost of more goods forgone.

This change in relative prices has both the income and the substitution effects that we studied on pp. 151–4. The substitution effect leads the individual to consume more of the relatively cheaper goods and *less* of the relatively more expensive leisure—that is, to trade more leisure for goods. The income effect, however, leads the individual to consume more goods and *more* leisure. The rise in the wage rate makes it possible for the individual to have more goods and more leisure. For example, if the wage rate rises by 10 per cent and the individual works 5 per cent fewer hours, more leisure and more goods will be consumed.

Because the income and the substitution effects work in the same direction for the consumption of goods, we can be sure that a rise in the wage rate will lead to a rise in goods consumed. Because, however, the two effects work in the opposite direction for leisure,

A rise in the wage rate leads to less leisure being consumed (more hours worked) when the substitution effect is the dominant force and to more leisure consumed (fewer hours worked) when the income effect is the dominant force.

Box 18.4 provides an optional analysis of these two cases using indifference curves.

Much of the long-run evidence tends to show that, as real hourly wage rates rise for the economy as a whole, people wish to reduce the number of hours they work.

The supply of factors for a particular use

Most factors have many uses. A given piece of land can be used to grow any one of several crops, or it can be subdivided for a housing development. A computer programmer in Oxford can work for one of several firms, for the government, or for the University. A lathe can be used to make many different products, and it requires no adaptation when it is turned for one use or another. Plainly, it is easier for any one user to acquire more of a scarce factor of production than it is for all users to do so simultaneously.

One user of a factor can bid resources away from another user, even though the total supply of that factor may be fixed.

When we are considering the supply of a factor for a particular use, the most important concept is *factor mobility.* A factor that shifts easily between uses in response to small changes in incentives is said to be *mobile.* Its supply to any one of its uses will be elastic, because a small increase in the price offered will attract many units of the factor from other uses. A factor that does not shift easily from one use to another, even in response to large changes in remuneration, is said to be *immobile.* It will be in inelastic supply in any one of its uses, because even a large increase in the price offered will attract only a small inflow from other uses. Often a factor may be immobile in the short run but mobile in the long run.

An important key to factor mobility is time. The longer the time interval, the easier it is for a factor to convert from one use to another.

BOX 18.4

The supply of labour

The discussion in the text can be formalized using indifference curves. The key proposition is the following:

Because a change in the wage rate has an income effect and a substitution effect that pull in opposite directions, the supply curve of labour may have a positive or a negative slope.

Part (i) of the figure plots leisure on the horizontal axis and the consumption of goods (measured in pounds) on the vertical axis. The budget line always starts at 24, indicating that everyone is endowed with 24 hours a day that may either be consumed as leisure or traded for goods by working.

At the original wage rate, the individual could obtain q_a of goods by working 24 hours (i.e. the hourly wage rate is $q_a/24$). Equilibrium is at E_0, where the individual consumes l_0 of leisure and works $24 - l_0$ hours in return for q_0 of goods.

The wage rate now rises, so that q_b becomes available if 24 hours are worked (i.e. the hourly wage rate is $q_b/24$). Equilibrium shifts to E_1. Consumption of leisure falls to l_1, and

the individual works $24 - l_1$ hours in return for a consumption of q_1 goods. The rise in wages increases hours worked.

The hourly wage rate now rises further to $q_c/24$, and equilibrium shifts to E_2. Consumption of leisure rises to l_2, whereas $24 - l_2$ hours are worked in return for an increased consumption of q_2 goods. This time, therefore, the rise in the wage rate lowers hours worked.

Part (ii) of the figure shows the same behaviour as in part (i), using a supply curve. It plots the number of hours worked against the wage rate. At wage rates of up to w_1, the individual is not in the labour force, since no work is offered. As the wage rate rises from w_1 to w_2, more and more hours are worked so the supply curve of effort has the normal, positive slope. The wage rates that result in E_0 and E_1 in part (i) of the figure lie in this range. Above w_2 and q_2, the quantity of effort falls as wages rise, so that the supply curve has a negative slope. This latter case is often referred to as a *backward-bending supply curve of labour*. The wage that gives rise to equilibrium E_2 in part (i) lies in this range.

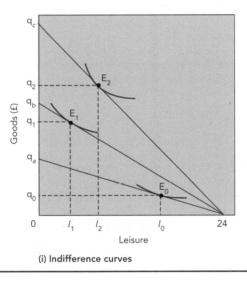

(i) Indifference curves

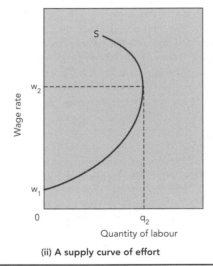

(ii) A supply curve of effort

Consider the factor mobility among particular uses of each of the three key factors of production.

Capital   Some kinds of capital equipment—lathes, lorries, and computers, for example—can be shifted readily among uses; many others are comparatively unshiftable. A great deal of machinery is quite specific: once built, it must be used for the purpose for which it was designed, or it cannot be used at all. (It is the immobility of much fixed capital equipment that makes the exit of firms from declining

industries the slow and difficult process described in Chapter 12.)

In the long run, however, capital is highly mobile. When capital goods wear out, a firm may simply replace them with identical goods, or it may exercise other options. It may buy a newly designed machine to produce the same goods, or it may buy machines to produce totally different goods. Such decisions lead to changes in the long-run allocation of a country's stock of capital among various uses.

Land   Land, which is physically the least mobile of factors, is one of the most mobile in an economic sense. Consider agricultural land. Within one year, one crop can be harvested and a totally different crop can be planted. A farm on the outskirts of a growing city can be sold for a housing development at short notice—as long as planning permission is forthcoming. Once land is built on, its mobility is much reduced. A site on which a hotel has been built can be converted into a warehouse site, but it takes a large differential in the value of land use to make that transfer worth while, because the hotel must be torn down.

Although land is highly mobile among alternative uses, it is completely immobile as far as location is concerned. There is only so much land within a given distance of the centre of any city, and no increase in the price paid can induce further land to be located within that distance. This locational immobility has important consequences, including high prices for desirable locations and the tendency to build tall buildings to economize on the use of scarce land, as in the centre of large cities.

Labour   Labour is unique as a factor of production in that the supply of the service often requires the physical presence of the person who supplies it.[3]

Absentee landlords, while continuing to live in the place of their choice, can obtain income from land that is located in remote parts of the world. Investment can be shifted from iron mines in South Africa to mines in Labrador, while the owners move between London and San Francisco. However, when a worker who is employed by a firm producing men's ties in York decides to supply labour service to a firm producing women's shoes in Northampton, the worker must physically travel to Northampton. This has an important consequence.

Because of the need for labour's physical presence when its services are provided for the production of many commodities, non-monetary considerations are much more important for the supply of labour than for other factors of production.

People may be satisfied with, or frustrated by, the kind of work that they do, where they do it, the people with whom they do it, and the social status of their occupations. Since these considerations influence their decisions about what they will do with their labour services, they will not always move just because they could earn a higher wage.

Nevertheless, labour does move among industries, occupations, and areas in response to changes in the signals provided by wages and opportunities for employment. The ease with which movement occurs depends on many forces. For example, it is not difficult for a secretary to shift from one company to another in order to take a job in Cheltenham, instead of in Hull, but it can be difficult for a secretary to become an editor, a model, a machinist, or a doctor within a short period of time. Workers who lack ability, training, or inclination find certain kinds of mobility to be difficult or impossible.

Some barriers to movement may be virtually insurmountable once a person's training has been completed. It may be impossible for a farmer to become a surgeon or for a lorry-driver to become a professional athlete, even if the relative wage rates change greatly. However, the *children* of farmers, doctors, lorry-drivers, and athletes, when they are deciding how much education or training to obtain, are not nearly as limited in their choices as their parents, who have already completed their education and are settled in their occupations.

In any year, some people enter the labour force directly from school or further education, and others leave it through retirement or death. The turnover in the labour force owing to these causes is 3 or 4 per cent per year. Over a period of 10 years, the allocation of labour can change dramatically merely by directing new entrants to jobs other than the ones that were left vacant by workers who left the labour force.

The role of education in helping new entrants adapt to available jobs is important. In a society in which education is provided to all, it is possible to achieve large increases in the supply of any needed labour skill within a decade or so. These issues are discussed at greater length in the first part of Chapter 19.

The labour force as a whole is mobile, even though many individual members in it are not.

The supply of factors to individual firms

Most firms usually employ a small proportion of the total supply of each factor that they use. As a result, they can usually obtain their factors at the going market price. For example, a firm of management consultants can usually augment its clerical staff by placing an advert in the local paper and paying the going rate for clerks. In doing so, the firm will not affect the rate of pay earned by clerks in its area. Thus, most individual firms are price-takers in factor markets.

---

[3] Labour must be physically present if it is helping in the direct production of most goods, such as cars, and of some services, such as haircuts. In other cases, however, labour services, such as consulting, designing a product, or writing advertising copy, can be supplied at a distance and its product communicated to the purchaser by such means as phone, fax, or mail.

The operation of factor markets

THE determination of the price, quantity, and income of a factor in a single market poses no new problem. Figure 18.3 on p. 330 has already shown a competitive market for a factor in which the intersection of the demand and supply curves determines the factor's price and the quantity of it that is employed. As we saw at that time, the factor's price times its quantity employed is its total income, and that amount, divided by the total income earned by all factors in the economy (so-called national income), represents that factor's share of the nation's total income.

Factor-price differentials

First consider labour. If every labourer were the same, if all benefits were monetary, and if workers moved freely among markets, then the price of labour would tend to be the same in all uses. Workers would move from low-priced jobs to high-priced ones. The quantity of labour supplied would diminish in occupations in which wages were low, and the resulting labour shortage would tend to force those wages up; the quantity of labour supplied would increase in occupations in which wages were high, and the resulting surplus would force wages down. The movement would continue until there were no further incentives to change occupations, that is, until wages were equalized in all uses.

In fact, however, wage differentials commonly occur. These differentials may be divided into two distinct types: those that exist only in disequilibrium situations, and those that persist in equilibrium.

As it is with labour, so it is with other factors of production. If all units of any factor of production were identical and moved freely among markets, all units would receive the same remuneration in equilibrium. In fact, however, different units of any one factor receive different remunerations.

DISEQUILIBRIUM DIFFERENTIALS

Some factor-price differentials reflect a temporary state of disequilibrium. They are brought about by circumstances such as the growth of one industry and the decline of another. The differentials themselves lead to reallocation of factors, and such reallocations in turn act to eliminate the differentials.

Consider the effect on factor prices of a rise in the demand for air transport and a decline in the demand for rail transport. The airline industry's demand for factors increases while the railroad industry's demand for factors decreases. Relative factor prices will go up in airlines and down in railroads. The differential in factor prices causes a net movement of factors from the railroad industry to the airline industry, and this movement causes the differentials to lessen and eventually to disappear. How long this process takes will depend on how easily factors can be reallocated from one industry to the other, that is, on the degree of factor mobility.

EQUILIBRIUM DIFFERENTIALS

Some factor-price differentials persist in equilibrium, without generating any forces that will eliminate them. These **equilibrium differentials** can be explained by intrinsic differences in the factors themselves and, for labour, by differences in the cost of acquiring skills and by different non-monetary advantages of different occupations. They are also called *compensating differentials,* and were introduced into economics more than two hundred years ago by Adam Smith.

Intrinsic differences If various units of a factor have different characteristics, the price that is paid may differ among these units. If intelligence and dexterity are required to accomplish a task, intelligent and manually dexterous workers will earn more than less intelligent and less dexterous workers. If land is to be used for agricultural purposes, highly fertile land will earn more than poor land. These differences will persist even in long-run equilibrium.

Acquired differences If the fertility of land can be increased by costly methods, then more fertile land must command a higher price than less fertile land. If it did not, landlords would not incur the costs of improving fertility. The same holds true for labour. It is costly to acquire most skills. For example, a mechanic must train for some time, and unless the earnings of mechanics remain sufficiently above what can be earned in less skilled occupations, people will not incur the cost of training.

Non-monetary advantages Whenever working conditions differ among various uses for a single factor, that factor will earn different equilibrium amounts in its various uses. The difference between a test pilot's wage and a chauffeur's wage is only partly a matter of skill; the rest is compensation to the worker for facing the higher risk of testing new planes as compared with driving a car. If both were paid the same, there would be an excess supply of chauffeurs and a shortage of test pilots.

Academic researchers commonly earn less than they could earn in the world of commerce and industry because of the substantial non-monetary advantages of academic employment, such as long holidays from teaching, which can be devoted partly to research and partly to leisure. If chemists were paid the same in both sectors, many chemists would prefer academic to industrial jobs. Excess demand for industrial chemists and excess supply of academic chemists would then force chemists' wages up in industry and down in academia until the two types of jobs seemed equally attractive on balance.

The same forces account for equilibrium differences in regional earnings of otherwise identical factors. People who work in remote logging or mining areas are paid more than people who do jobs requiring similar skills in large cities. Without higher pay, not enough people would be willing to work at sometimes dangerous jobs in unattractive or remote locations.

DIFFERENTIALS AND FACTOR MOBILITY

The distinction between equilibrium and disequilibrium differentials is closely linked to factor mobility.

Disequilibrium differentials lead to, and are eroded by, factor movements; equilibrium differentials are not eliminated by factor mobility.

The behaviour that causes the erosion of disequilibrium differentials is summarized in the assumption of the *maximization of net advantage:* the owners of factors of production will allocate them to uses that maximize the net advantages to themselves, taking both monetary and non-monetary rewards into consideration. If net advantages were higher in occupation A than in occupation B, factors would move from B to A. The increased supply in A and the lower supply in B would drive factor earnings down in A and up in B until net advantages were equalized, after which no further movement would occur. This analysis gives rise to the prediction of *equal net advantage:* in equilibrium, units of each kind of factor of production will be allocated among alternative possible uses in such a way that the net advantages in all uses are equalized.

Although non-monetary advantages are important in explaining differences in levels of pay for labour in different occupations, they tend to be quite stable over time. As a result, monetary advantages, which vary with market conditions, lead to changes in *net advantage.*

A change in the relative price of a factor between two uses will change the net advantages of the uses. It will lead to a shift of some units of that factor to the use whose relative price has increased.

This implies a positively sloped supply curve for a factor in any particular use. When the price of a factor rises in that use, more will be supplied to that use. This factor supply curve (like all supply curves) can also *shift* in response to changes in other variables. For example, an improvement in the safety record in a particular occupation will shift the labour supply curve to that occupation.

Pay equity

The distinction between equilibrium and disequilibrium factor-price differentials raises an important consideration for policy. Trade unions, governments, and other bodies often have explicit policies about earnings differentials, sometimes seeking to eliminate them in the name of equity. The success of such policies depends to a great extent on the kind of differential that is being attacked. Policies that attempt to eliminate equilibrium differentials will encounter severe difficulties.

Some government legislation seeks to establish *equal pay for work of equal value,* or *pay equity.* These laws can work as intended whenever they remove pay differentials that are due to prejudice. They run into trouble, however, whenever they require equal pay for jobs that have different non-monetary advantages.

To illustrate the problem, say that two jobs demand equal skills, training, and everything else that is taken into account when deciding what is work of equal value but that, in a city with an extreme climate, one is an outside job and the other is an inside job. If some pay commission requires equal pay for both jobs, there will be a shortage of people who are willing to work outside and an excess of people who want to work inside. Employers will seek ways to attract outside workers. Higher pensions, shorter hours, longer holidays, overtime paid for but not worked, and better working conditions may be offered. If these are allowed, they will achieve the desired result but will defeat the original purpose of equalizing the monetary benefits of the inside and outside jobs; they will also cut down on the number of outside workers that employers will hire, since the total cost of an outside worker to an employer will have risen. If the authorities prevent such 'cheating', the shortage of workers for outside jobs will remain.

In Chapter 19, we discuss the effects of discrimination on wage differentials. Although discrimination is often important, it remains true that many factor-price differentials are a natural market consequence of supply and demand conditions that have nothing to do with inequitable treatment of different groups in society.

Policies that seek to eliminate factor-price differentials without considering what caused them or how they affect the supply of the factor are likely to have perverse results.

Economic rent

One of the most important concepts in economics is that of

BOX 18.5

Origin of the term 'economic rent'

In the early nineteenth century, there was a public debate about the high price of wheat in England. The price was causing great hardship because bread was a primary source of food for the working class. Some people argued that wheat had a high price because landlords were charging high rents to tenant farmers. In short, it was argued that the price of wheat was high because the rents of agricultural land were high. Some of those who held this view advocated restricting the rents that landlords could charge.

David Ricardo, a great British economist who was one of the originators of classical economics, argued that the situation was exactly the reverse. The price of wheat was high, he said, because there was a shortage, which was caused by the Napoleonic Wars. Because wheat was profitable to produce, there was keen competition among farmers to obtain land on which to grow wheat. This competition in turn forced up the rent of wheat land. Ricardo advocated removing the tariff so that imported wheat could come into the country, thereby increasing its supply and lowering both the price of wheat and the rent that could be charged for the land on which it was grown.

The essentials of Ricardo's argument were these. The supply of land was fixed. Land was regarded as having only one use, the growing of wheat. Nothing had to be paid to prevent land from transferring to a use other than growing wheat because it had no other use. No landowner would leave land idle as long as some

return could be obtained by renting it out. Therefore, all the payment to land—that is, rent in the ordinary sense of the word—was a surplus over and above what was necessary to keep it in its present use.

Given a fixed supply of land, the price of land depended on the demand for land, which depended on the demand for wheat. *Rent,* the term for the payment for the use of land, thus became the term for a surplus payment to a factor over and above what was necessary to keep it in its present use.

Later, two facts were realized. First, land often had alternative uses, and, from the point of view of any one use, part of the payment made to land would necessarily have to be paid to keep it in that use. Second, factors of production other than land also often earned a surplus over and above what was necessary to keep them in their present use. Television stars and great athletes, for example, are in short and fairly fixed supply, and their potential earnings in other occupations often are quite moderate. However, because there is a huge demand for their services as television stars or athletes, they may receive payments greatly in excess of what is needed to keep them from transferring to other occupations. This surplus is now called *economic rent,* whether the factor is land, labour, or a piece of capital equipment.

economic rent. A factor must earn a certain amount in its present use to prevent it from moving to another use.[4] If there were no non-monetary advantages in alternative uses, the factor would have to earn its opportunity cost (what it could earn elsewhere) to prevent it from moving elsewhere. This is usually true for capital and land. Labour, however, gains important non-monetary advantages in various jobs, and it must earn in one use enough to equate the two jobs' total advantages—monetary and non-monetary.

Any excess that a factor earns over the minimum amount needed to keep it at its present use is called its **economic rent.** Economic rent is analogous to economic profit as a surplus over the opportunity cost of capital. The concept of economic rent is crucial in predicting the effects that changes in earnings have on the movement of factors among alternative uses. However, the terminology of rent is confusing because economic rent is often called simply *rent,* which can of course also mean the full price paid to hire something, such as a machine or a piece of land. How the same term came to be used for these two different concepts is explained in Box 18.5.

THE DIVISION OF FACTOR EARNINGS

In most cases, economic rent makes up part of the actual

earnings of a factor of production. The distinction is most easily seen, however, by examining two extreme cases. In one, everything a factor earns is rent; in the other, none is rent.

The possibilities are illustrated in Figure 18.5. When the supply curve is perfectly inelastic (vertical), the same quantity is supplied, whatever the price. Evidently, there is no minimum that the factor needs to be paid to keep it in its present use, since the quantity supplied does not decrease, no matter how low the price goes. In this case, the whole of the payment is economic rent. The price actually paid allocates the fixed supply to those who are most willing to pay for it.

When the supply curve is perfectly elastic (horizontal), none of the price paid is economic rent. If any lower price is offered, nothing whatsoever will be supplied. All units of the factor will transfer to some other use.

The more usual situation is that of a gradually rising supply curve. A rise in the factor's price serves the allocative function of attracting more units of the factor into the market in question, but the same rise provides additional economic rent to all units of the factor that are already employed. We know that the extra pay that is going to the

---

[4] Alfred Marshall called this amount the factor's *transfer earnings.*

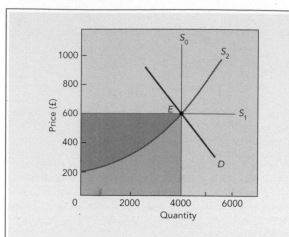

Figure 18.5 The determination of rent in factor payments

The amount of rent in factor payments depends on the shape of the supply curve. A single demand curve is shown with three different supply curves. In each case the competitive equilibrium price is £600, and 4,000 units of the factor are hired. The total payment (£2.4 million) is represented by the entire dark and medium blue areas. When the supply curve is vertical (S_0), the whole payment is economic rent, because a decrease in price would not lead any units of the factor to move elsewhere.
When the supply curve is horizontal (S_1), none of the payment is rent, because even a small decrease in price offered would lead all units of the factor to move elsewhere.
When the supply curve is positively sloped (S_2) part of the payment is rent. As shown by the height of the supply curve, at a price of £600 the 4000th unit of the factor is receiving just enough to persuade it to offer its services in this market, but the 2000th unit, for example, is earning well above what it requires to stay in this market. The aggregate of economic rents is shown by the dark blue area, and the aggregate of what must be paid to keep 4000 units in this market is shown by the light blue area.

nomic rent varies from situation to situation. We cannot point to a factor of production and assert that some fixed fraction of its income is always its economic rent. The proportion of its earnings that is rent depends on the alternatives that are open to it.

Focus first on a narrowly defined use of a given factor, say, its use by a particular firm. From that firm's point of view, the factor will be highly mobile, since it could readily move to another firm in the same industry. The firm must pay the going wage or risk losing that factor. Thus, from the perspective of the single firm, a large proportion of the payment made to a factor is needed to prevent it from transferring to another use.

Focus now on a more broadly defined use, for example the factor's use in an entire industry. From the industry's point of view, the factor is less mobile, because it would be more difficult for it to gain employment quickly outside the industry. From the perspective of the particular *industry* (rather than the specific *firm* within the industry), a larger proportion of the payment to a factor is economic rent.

From the even more general perspective of a particular *occupation*, mobility is likely to be less, and the proportion of the factor payment that is economic rent is likely to be more. It may be easier, for example, for a carpenter to move from the construction industry to the furniture industry than to retrain as a computer operator.

These distinctions are illustrated by the often controversial large salaries that are received by some highly specialized types of labour, such as superstar singers and professional athletes. These performers have a style or a talent that cannot be duplicated, whatever the training. The earnings that they receive are mostly economic rent from the viewpoint of the occupation: these performers enjoy their occupations and would pursue them for much less than the high remuneration that they actually receive. For example, Ryan Giggs would choose football over other alternatives even at a much lower salary than he was earning in 1994. However, because of Giggs's skills as a football player, most teams would pay handsomely to have him, and he is able to command a high salary from the team he does play for. From the perspective of the firm, Manchester United, most of Giggs's salary is required to keep him from switching to another team and hence is not economic rent. From the point of view of the 'football industry', however, much of his salary is economic rent.

Similar arguments apply to famous entertainers such as Phil Collins, who earned over £5 million in 1993 from record sales and concerts.

units already employed is economic rent because the owners of these units were willing to supply them at the lower price. The general result for a positively sloped supply curve is stated as follows.

If there is an upward shift in the demand for a factor in any sector, its price will rise. This will serve the allocative function of attracting additional units into that sector. It will also increase the economic rent going to all units of the factor already employed in that sector.[5]

DETERMINANTS OF THE DIVISION

The proportion of a given payment to a factor that is eco-

[5] In this context, the term 'sector' can stand for occupation, industry, or geographic area.

Summary

1 The functional and size distributions of income refer, respectively, to the shares of total national income going to each of the major factors of production, and to various groups of individuals. One focuses on the source of income, the other on its size.

2 The income of a factor of production depends on the price paid per unit of the factor, and the quantity of the factor used.

3 The firm's decisions on how much to produce and how to produce it imply demands for factors of production, which are said to be *derived* from the demand for goods that they help to produce.

4 A profit-maximizing firm equates a factor's marginal cost to its marginal revenue product, which is its marginal physical product multiplied by the marginal revenue associated with the sale of another unit of output. When the firm is a price-taker in input markets, the marginal cost of the factor is its price per unit. When the firm sells its output in a competitive market, the marginal revenue product is the factor's marginal physical product multiplied by the market price of the output.

5 A price-taking firm's demand for a factor is negatively sloped because the law of diminishing returns implies that the marginal physical product of a factor declines.

6 The industry's demand for a factor will be more elastic: (*a*) the faster that the marginal physical product of the factor declines as more of the factor is used, (*b*) the easier it is to substitute one factor for another, (*c*) the larger is the proportion of total variable costs accounted for by the cost of the factor in question, and (*d*) the more elastic is the demand for the good that the factor helps to make.

7 The total supply of each factor is fixed at any moment but varies over time. The supply of labour depends on the size of the population, the participation rate, and hours worked. A rise in the wage rate has a substitution effect, which tends to induce more work, and an income effect, which tends to induce less work (more leisure consumed).

8 The supply of a factor to a particular use is more elastic than its supply to the whole economy because one user can bid units away from other users. The elasticity of supply to a particular use depends on factor mobility, which tends to be greater the longer the time allowed for a reaction to take place.

9 Disequilibrium factor price differentials induce factor movements that eventually remove the differentials. Equilibrium differentials persist indefinitely.

10 According to the theory of equal net advantage, owners of factors will choose the use that produces the greatest net monetary and non-monetary advantage. In so doing, they will cause disequilibrium factor-price differentials to be eliminated.

11 Whenever the supply curve is positively sloped, part of the total pay going to a factor is needed to prevent it from transferring to another use, and the rest is rent. The proportion of each depends on the mobility of the factor.

Topics for review

• Functional distribution and size distribution of income

• Derived demand

• Marginal physical product

• Marginal revenue product

• Factor mobility

• Disequilibrium and equilibrium differentials

• Equal net advantage

• Economic rent

∾ CHAPTER 19

The income of labour

IN this chapter,[1] we look specifically at labour markets. Do not forget that by 'labour' we mean all human resources of both workers and management, and by 'labour income', or 'wages', we mean all income earned from work, whether in the form of wages or salaries. Most of the chapter is devoted to explaining wage differentials between different types of labour. We see that these are due partly to different skills and educational attainments, to some extent to age and sex, and to a great extent to the type of market in which labour services are supplied. Labour does best when it is organized as a single seller dealing with a large number of buyers and worst when its services are sold by many sellers to a single buyer. Cases in which both sides are competitive fall in between these two extremes. We then go on to consider unions which, although much less important in the United Kingdom than they were twenty years ago, are still an important part of the economic landscape. We are able to use our economic theory to understand quite a bit about union behaviour.

In this chapter we deal with what can be called market-clearing theories of wage determination. In them, we assume that wages are set in such a way that markets clear in the sense that there is neither excess demand nor excess supply in equilibrium—unless some exercise of market power by strong buyers or seller prevents this from occurring. These models can tell us quite a bit about the behaviour of wages in the real world, particularly about some of the forces that create wage differentials. But they are not the whole story.

A persistent feature of labour markets is significant amounts of what looks like involuntary unemployment: there are unemployed workers who would like to work at the prevailing wage rates for their skills and occupations but cannot get jobs. In fully competitive markets, wage rates would fall until such involuntary unemployment had been eliminated. This does not appear to happen. A full story of the operation of labour markets must explain the influence that these phenomena have on wage differentials and, more interestingly, on the total amount of unemployment that exists at various points of time. This story will be postponed until Chapter 41. In the meantime, we will be able to get quite a long way by using market-clearing theories that analyse the influence that aggregate market forces have on wage differentials. This is an important beginning of our development of an understanding of behaviour on the market of labour.

Wage differentials

WE noted in the previous chapter that, if labour were a homogeneous factor of production, and were sold in perfectly competitive markets, every person would earn the same income in equilibrium. Disequilibrium differentials in wages would arise whenever demand or supply curves shifted, but workers would move from the lower-income to the higher-income jobs until the differentials had disappeared. In reality, however, some workers scrape out a bare living, others earn modest but adequate incomes, while yet others earn enough to afford many of life's luxuries.

- *Incomes vary with the type of job.* Dustmen and charwomen earn less than electricians and computer operators.

- *Incomes vary with education.* Average earnings of people with university degrees exceed the average earnings of those with only A-levels, which in turn exceed the average earnings of those with only O-levels.

- *Incomes vary with age.* Average earnings rise until a person's mid-40s and fall thereafter.

- *Incomes vary with years on the job.* Generally, the longer one stays with one firm, the higher the income one earns.

- *Incomes vary with sex and race.* On average, men earn more than women, and members of some minority ethnic groups earn less than members of majority groups—even when differences in education and experience are allowed for.

- *Incomes vary with the type of market in which labour sells its services.* Workers who sell their labour in markets dominated by unions often earn more than similar persons who sell their labour in more competitive markets.

In what follows, we study some of the major causes of these equilibrium differentials in earnings of various types of labour.

Differentials due to basic differences: non-competing groups

More highly skilled jobs pay better wages than less highly

---

[1] The descriptive and institutional background to this chapter is outlined in Chapter 4 of C. Harbury and R. G. Lipsey, *An Introduction to the UK Economy,* 4th edn. (Oxford: Basil Blackwell, 1993).

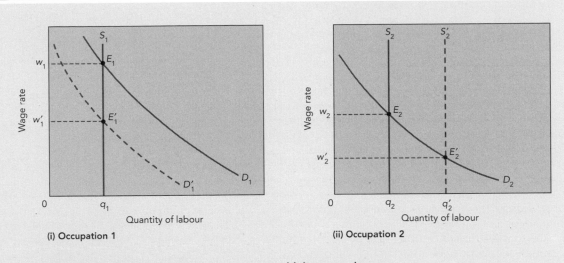

Figure 19.1 Wage differentials in segmented labour markets

If labour cannot move from one market to another because of an inability to acquire the necessary qualifications, wage differentials of any size can persist. Because of assumed basic differences in abilities, the supply of labour is fixed at q_1 in occupation 1, and at q_2 in occupation 2. Demand and supply curves intersect at E_1 and E_2 to produce the high wage of w_1 in occupation 1, and the low wage of w_2 in occupation 2.

A fall in demand from D_1 to D_1' in occupation 1 takes equilibrium to E_1', lowering the equilibrium wage to w_1'.

An exogenous rise in supply in occupation 2, to q_2', takes equilibrium to E_2' and lowers the wage in occupation 2 to w_2'.

skilled jobs. Why does a movement from the latter to the former not erode these differentials?

One obvious answer lies in human differences that are either innate or acquired so early in life as to be beyond each individual's personal control. Some people are brighter than others, some people are more athletic, while some people are better endowed with manual skills.

Some of the earliest theories of the labour market dealt with income differentials among *non-competing groups*. These groups were assumed to sell their services in *segmented labour markets* which were separated by insurmountable barriers caused by basic human differences.

Figure 19.1 shows that wage differentials among non-competing groups arise from the positions of both the demand and the supply curves. One non-competing group will earn higher incomes than another only if its supply is low *relative to the demand for it*. It is not good enough to have a rare skill; that skill must be rare in relation to the demand for it.

Over time, wage differentials change. On the demand side, economic growth constantly alters the derived demand for many specific groups of labour, creating new differentials and eroding old ones. On the supply side, there may be exogenous shifts. For example, a new group of

immigrants may alter the mix of skills available in the local market. Furthermore, human differences notwithstanding, substantial mobility between groups does occur—particularly in the long run, when older people with specific skills leave the labour force and young people with different skills enter.

The shorter the period of time under consideration, the more useful is the hypothesis of zero labour mobility between markets. Over time, supplies of different kinds of labour change endogenously as labour moves between markets in response to changing economic incentives.

None the less, the lesson of the simple theory of non-competing groups is important:

Some income differentials arise because basic human characteristics cause the supply of some types of labour to remain low relative to the demand for it, even in the long run.

Differentials due to human capital

The key to mobility among occupations is education. Many skills are learned rather than inherited. These may be thought of as a stock of personal capital acquired by each worker.

A machine is physical capital. It requires an investment of time and money to create it and, once built, it yields valuable services over a long time. In the same way, labour skills require an investment of time and money to acquire and, once acquired, they yield an increased income to their owner over a long time. Since investment in labour skills is similar to investment in physical capital, acquired skills are called **human capital**.

Because human capital can be acquired, groups distinguished by such capital do not constitute non-competing groups over any long period of time. Instead, the supply of some particular skill increases when more people find it worth while to acquire the necessary human capital, and decreases when fewer do so. Because acquiring human capital is costly, the more highly skilled the job, the more it must pay if enough people are to be attracted to train for it.

The stock of skills acquired by individual workers is called human capital; investment in this capital is usually costly, and the return is usually in terms of higher labour productivity and hence higher earning power.

The two main ways in which human capital is acquired are through formal education and on-the-job training.

FORMAL EDUCATION

Compulsory education is an attempt to provide some minimum human capital for all citizens. Some people, either through luck in the school they attend, or through their own efforts, profit more from their early education than do others. They acquire more human capital than their less fortunate contemporaries. Subsequent income differentials reflect these differences in human capital acquired in the early stages of education. Those who decide to stay in school beyond the years of compulsory education are deciding to invest voluntarily in acquiring further human capital.

Costs and benefits   The cost is in terms of the income that could have been earned if the person had entered the labour force immediately, plus any out-of-pocket costs for such things as fees and equipment minus any student grant received from the state. The return is the higher income to be earned when a better job is obtained than is available to an early school-leaver. (There is also a consumption return whenever higher education is something that students enjoy more than work.) These costs and benefits are analysed in Figure 19.2.

Changes in costs and benefits   If the demand for labour with low amounts of human capital falls off, the earnings of such persons will fall. This will lower the costs of staying on

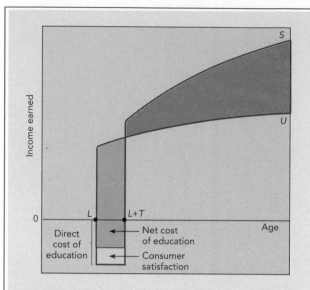

Figure 19.2   The costs and benefits of human capital acquired through formal education

Acquiring human capital through formal education beyond minimum school-leaving age implies costs now and benefits later. Age is plotted on the horizontal axis and income earned on the vertical axis. Income is zero until age L, which is the minimum school-leaving age. After that, the red line U shows the income of a typical person who leaves school at age L and takes the relatively unskilled job for which his or her human capital is suitable.

The blue line, S, shows the more complicated stream of payments and income receipts of someone who stays on for T years of formal training after age L. At first receipts are negative, reflecting the net out-of-pocket expenses related to attending school and university. Deducting the consumption value placed on being at school rather than at work (light red area) yields the net cost associated with being in school. Adding this to the income that could have been earned by going directly into the labour force at age L yields the total cost of the education, which is the medium red area.

The benefit is shown by the dark red area, representing the difference between the income earned in the skilled job that is acquired at year $L+T$ (line S) and the income that would have been earned if the labour force had been entered at age L (line U). The investment in human capital could not possibly be worth while unless the dark red benefit area exceeds the medium red cost area. The net benefit to a particular individual depends on how much he or she discounts the more distant gain in order to compare it with the more immediate costs.

in school and acquiring more capital, since the earnings forgone by not going to work are reduced. A rise in unemployment will also lower the costs, because the probability of earning a steady income will be reduced, and this will reduce the expected loss from not entering the labour force early. If the demand for labour having more human capital rises, the earnings of such labour will rise. This will raise the expected return to those currently deciding whether to make the investment themselves.

Individual decisions For any *given* state of these incentives, why do some people decide to acquire human capital while others do not?

First, there are differences among individuals. For reasons related to genetics or to early educational experience, some people at the age of 16 correctly decide that they have a low chance of profiting from further formal education. For them, the return from such education is lower than for others who have the necessary aptitudes.

Second, some people have special talents for types of work that do not require further human capital. For them, the cost of acquiring more human capital is higher than it is for others; the earnings they would forgo by not entering the labour force are higher than the earnings that would be forgone by the average school-leaver.

Third, different people have different time preferences. The cost of acquiring human capital is forgone income *now*, and the return is a *probability* of higher income *later*. Tastes differ. Some people put a high value on income now, and are not willing to pay the cost of postponing it. Others place a higher value on income to be earned later in life, and are willing to have less now in return for the chance of much more later.

Fourth, different people put different values on the consumption aspects of education. Those who enjoy the experience find the costs of acquiring human capital lower than those who do not. Those who would prefer to be at work rather than at school find the cost increased by the negative value they place on the educational experience.

Market forces adjust the overall costs and benefits of acquiring human capital, while individuals respond according to their varying personal assessments of costs and benefits.

In the long run, decisions to acquire human capital help to erode disequilibrium differentials in incomes. Market signals change the costs and benefits of acquiring human capital in such specific forms as skill in electronics, accountancy, law, or medicine. By reacting to these signals, young people increase the supplies of high-income workers and reduce the supplies of low-income workers, thus eroding existing disequilibrium differentials.

ON-THE-JOB EDUCATION

Differentials according to age are readily observable in most firms and occupations. To a significant extent, these differentials are a response to human capital acquired on

the job. This type of human capital falls into two types.

Firm-specific human capital This term refers to skills acquired on the job that are specific to that firm. Learning how one firm does such things as recording and retrieving its information, how it makes decisions, and how the personal relations among its employees are to be used to advantage are all firm-specific. As employees acquire this knowledge, they become more valuable to the firm. But the knowledge is not valuable to other firms; workers who move to similar jobs with other firms will have to learn the new firm-specific characteristics of their jobs.

Firms do not want to lose long-term employees with large amounts of firm-specific human capital since other employees will then have to be trained. But, being firm-specific, the capital is of no value to other firms. So if the firm pays the employee a wage that reflects the productivity conferred by this capital, employees have an incentive to stay in the job, rather than to move to another firm where their value would be much less.

In jobs where all the necessary firm-specific capital can be learned quickly, differences in human capital account for differences in earnings between the relatively new employees and all the rest. In jobs where employees go on acquiring firm-specific human capital over many years, differences in human capital account for income differentials among employees with many different lengths of employment.

General human capital If a firm trains a junior secretary through various ranks up to a senior secretary, able to run the life of its general manager, the secretary's skills will be useful to other firms. Some of the secretary's human capital can be acquired only through on-the-job training, hence it must be acquired within the firm. However, unlike the firm-specific capital, a secretary who is paid the value of his or her marginal product at all times has no monetary incentive to stay with the firm that taught these general skills. The same is true of any non-specific human capital acquired through on-the-job experience by any of the firm's employees.

Firms have no incentive to provide freely what can immediately be transferred to another firm. The solution is to pay each worker less than his or her marginal product in the early years, and more later. The low pay can be seen as the employees' payment to the firm for helping them to acquire marketable human capital. The high pay later in life is a return on that capital.

Human capital acquired through on-the-job experience provides a reason why earnings rise with the length of time spent with a firm. Firms tend to pay employees the value of their current marginal products for firm-specific capital, but for general human capital they pay less than the marginal products early in life, and more later in life.

Another reason for the same pattern of lifetime wages is that competition tends to be strongest at the initial point of entry into the firm and to weaken thereafter, when promotion posts typically go to internal candidates. This will tend to hold wages down to competitive levels at entry points but allow them to drift above those levels for personnel with years of seniority and experience.

Market solutions   The above analysis shows the subtlety of market solutions to the issues posed by the human capital acquired through on-the-job experience. What looks arbitrary, or unfair, to the casual observer is often a rational response that has evolved to handle some aspect of the market—such as the fact that on-the-job training creates capital that is sometimes firm-specific and sometimes general.

To illustrate the significance of this lesson, consider two jobs that employ persons with equal initial requirements.

One provides on-the-job training that is mainly firm-specific, and the wage follows the time-path of the employee's evolving marginal product fairly closely. The second job provides general training, and the wage paid is less than marginal product for younger employees and greater for older ones. Now assume that government policy-makers get worried about the discrimination among workers in different jobs and introduce legislation requiring equal pay for 'work of equal value'. Both types of employees must now be paid the value of their marginal products. Firms then become reluctant to invest in helping their employees acquire general human capital, because it is now illegal to use a time-pattern of wages that allows the firm to cover the cost of providing this capital. However fair it may appear to some, this government policy, designed to enhance equity, may not be in the interests of the workers affected by it.

BOX 19.1

Why are women paid less than men?

Discrimination can affect women (or any other group that is discriminated against) in at least two ways. They may earn less than men when doing the same job, or they may be forced into jobs that typically pay lower wages than the jobs from which they are excluded. Non-discriminatory wage differentials arise when men and women differ on average in relevant labour-market characteristics. For example, men and women differ significantly in their average educational qualification and in their labour-market experience, with women, typically, spending somewhere between five and ten years out of the labour market raising children.

Across the whole economy, the average pay of women is less than that of men. This has been known since at least the 1880s, when reliable records started. Indeed, at the Trade Union Congress of 1888, a motion was passed stating that where men and women do the same jobs they should get the same pay. However, it was 1970 before the Equal Pay Act finally legislated that pay must be the same 'for the same or broadly similar work'.

Up to 1970, the data show that on average women were paid just over 60 per cent of the average male wage. However, by the late 1970s this had narrowed to a little over 70 per cent. Researchers have been unable to explain this narrowing in any other way than as a result of the legislation. This suggests that some previously existing discrimination has been eliminated.

Further research has looked at the remaining differentials. Correcting for differing lengths of labour-market experience would increase female pay to almost 80 per cent of male. Other differences between the sexes, such as years of schooling, accounted for another 8 percentage points, leaving 12 percentage points (or about one third of the differential) unexplained. This could be due to discrimination.

On a narrow interpretation, the pay differentials according to

different labour-market experiences is a reflection of the resulting lower marginal products. On a wider view of discrimination, however, these different experiences are merely convenient excuses for paying women less. This wider view is given some plausibility by the fact that in Sweden, the most egalitarian country in Europe, female earnings average fully 90 per cent of male earnings.

The effects of discrimination in crowding women into acceptable jobs is harder to estimate. Studies suggest, however, that, if the discrimination in type of employment were eliminated, wages in currently female-dominated occupations would rise significantly (up to 50 per cent!) while wages in currently male-dominated jobs would fall by only a few percentage points.

These estimates put *upper bounds* on the effects of discrimination. To some extent, the crowding of women into certain types of jobs may reflect their own preferences for these types of jobs, and the amount of human capital that they are willing to acquire. To the extent that this is true, the crowding into certain occupations and the resulting lower female earnings represent the outcome of female preferences. However, to the extent that crowding is due to discriminatory practices on the part of employers, the wage differentials are not an efficient market outcome.

All of the research results reported here are tentative, since this type of estimation is no easy matter. However, the evidence does suggest two things. First, there is almost certainly some discrimination against women remaining in labour markets today. Second, we have to be very careful in interpreting the raw data. The measured average differentials have to be adjusted for labour-force characteristics in order to identify any residual that is due to discrimination.

Differentials due to sex and race

Crude statistics show that incomes vary by race and sex. More detailed studies suggest that much of these differences can be explained by such influences as amount of human capital acquired through both formal education and on-the-job experience. When these influences are taken into account, however, a core of difference remains that is consistent with discrimination based on race and sex. This is further discussed with respect to male–female earnings differentials in Box 19.1.

Some forms of discrimination make it difficult, or impossible, for certain groups to take certain jobs, even if they are equipped by skill and education for these jobs. Until very recently, non-whites and women found many occupations closed to them. Even today, when overt discrimination in hiring is illegal, many feel that more subtle forms of discrimination are applied.

* To the extent that such discrimination occurs, it reduces the supply of labour in the exclusive jobs—by keeping out the groups who are discriminated against. It also increases the supply in non-exclusive jobs, which are the only ones open to the groups subject to discrimination. This raises the wages in the exclusive jobs and lowers them in the non-exclusive jobs. Since discrimination prevents movement from the lower- to the higher-wage jobs, the resulting wage differences are equilibrium, not disequilibrium, differentials.

A MODEL OF LABOUR-MARKET DISCRIMINATION

To isolate the effects of discrimination, we begin by considering a non-discriminating labour market and then introduce discrimination between two groups of equally qualified workers called *group X* and *group Y*. The analysis, however, applies generally to situations in which workers are distinguished on grounds other than their ability, such as female and male, black and white, alien and citizen, Catholic and Protestant.

Suppose that, except for the fact that half of the people are marked with X and the other half are marked with Y, the groups are the same; each has the same number of members, the same proportion who are educated to various levels, identical distributions of talent, and so on. Suppose also that there are two occupations. Occupation E (for elite) requires people of above-average education and skills, and

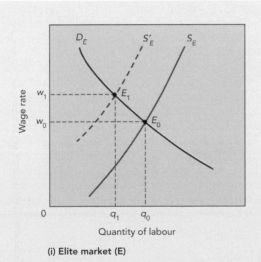
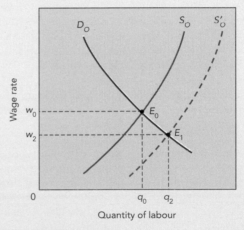

(i) Elite market (E) (ii) Ordinary market (O)

Figure 19.3 Economic discrimination: wage level effects

If market E discriminates against one group and market O does not, the supply curve will shift to the left in E and to the right in O. Market E requires above-average skills, while market O requires only ordinary skills. When there is no discrimination, demands and supplies are D_E and S_E in market E, and D_O and S_O in market O. Initially, the wage rate is w_0 and employment is q_0 in each market. (The actual wage in market E will be slightly higher than the wage in market O.) When all Ys are barred from E occupations, the supply curve shifts to S'_E, and the wage earned by the remaining workers, all of whom are Xs, rises to w_1. Ys put out of work in the E occupations now seek work in the O occupations. The resulting shift in the supply curve to S'_O brings down the wage to w_2 in the O occupations. Because all Ys are in O occupations, they have a lower wage rate than many Xs. The average X wage is higher than the average Y wage.

occupation O (ordinary) can use anyone. If wages in the two occupations are the same, employers in occupation O will prefer to hire the above-average worker. Finally, suppose that the non-monetary advantages of the two occupations are equal.

In the absence of discrimination, the labour markets that we are studying are competitive. The theory of competitive factor markets that we developed in Chapter 18 suggests that the wages in E occupations will be bid up above those in O occupations in order that the E jobs attract the workers of above-average skills. Xs and Ys of above-average skill will take the E jobs, while the others, both Xs and Ys, will have no choice but to seek O jobs. Because skills are equally distributed, each occupation will employ one-half Xs and one-half Ys.

Now discrimination enters in an extreme form. All E occupations are hereafter open only to Xs; all O occupations are hereafter open to either Xs or Ys. The immediate effect is to reduce by 50 per cent the supply of job candidates for E occupations; candidates must now be *both* Xs and above average. The discrimination also increases the supply of applicants for O jobs by 50 per cent; this group now includes all Ys and the below-average Xs.

Wage-level effects   Suppose that labour is perfectly mobile among occupations, that everyone seeks the best job for which he or she is eligible, and that wage rates are free to vary so as to equate supply and demand. The analysis is shown in Figure 19.3. Wages rise in E occupations and fall in O occupations. The take-home pay of those in O occupations falls, and the O group is now approximately two-thirds Ys.

Discrimination, by changing supply, can decrease the wages and incomes of a group that is discriminated against.

In the longer run, further changes may occur. Notice that total employment in the E industries falls. Employers may find ways to utilize slightly below-average labour and thus lure the next best qualified Xs out of O occupations. Although this will raise O wages slightly, it will also make these occupations increasingly 'Y occupations'. If discrimination has been in effect for a sufficient length of time, Ys will learn that it does not pay to acquire above-average skills. Regardless of ability, Ys are forced by discrimination to work in unskilled jobs.

Now suppose that a long-standing discriminatory policy is reversed. Because they will have responded to discrimination by acquiring fewer skills than Xs, many Ys will be locked into the O occupations, at least for a time. Moreover, if both Xs and Ys come to expect that Ys will have less education than Xs, employers will tend to look for Xs to fill the E jobs. This will reinforce the belief of Ys that education does not pay. This, and other kinds of subtle discrimination, can persist for a very long time, making the

supply of Ys to O jobs higher than it would be in the absence of the initial discrimination, thus depressing the wages of Ys and poor Xs.

Employment effects   Labour-market discrimination may have serious adverse employment effects. Labour is not perfectly mobile; wages are not perfectly flexible downward; and not everyone who is denied employment in an E occupation for which he or she is trained and qualified will be willing to take a 'demeaning' O job. We continue the graphical example in Figure 19.4.

If wages do not fall to the market-clearing level, possibly because of minimum wage laws, the increase in the supply of labour to O occupations will cause excess supply, which will result in unemployment in O occupations. Because Ys dominate these occupations, Ys will bear the brunt of the extra unemployment, as illustrated in Figure 19.4(i).

A similar result will occur if labour is not fully mobile between occupations. For example, many of the O jobs might be in places to which the Ys are unable or unwilling to move (see Figure 19.4(ii)). (Discrimination in housing markets may be one reason for this.) Potential O workers who cannot move to places where jobs are available become unemployed or withdraw from the labour force. Quite apart from any discrimination, long-term technological changes tend to decrease the demand for less skilled labour of the kind that is required in O occupations. Occupation O then becomes increasingly oversupplied. This possibility is outlined in Figure 19.4(iii).

The kind of discrimination that we have considered in our model is extreme. It is similar to South Africa's former apartheid system (which was eliminated by 1994), in which blacks were excluded by law from prestigious and high-paying occupations. In most Western countries, labour-market discrimination against a specific group usually occurs in somewhat less obvious ways. First, it may be difficult (but not impossible, as in our model) for members of the group to get employment in certain jobs. Second, members of groups subject to discrimination may receive lower pay for a given kind of work than members of groups not subject to discrimination.

Is discrimination rational?   There has been a long debate among economists about whether discrimination is rational and would persist in highly competitive markets. The answer depends partly on the source of the discrimination. To see this, let firms consider hiring members of a majority and a minority ethnic group.

First, assume that the discrimination stems from the prejudices of employers. They hire only members of the majority group, even though the majority group are paid the value of their marginal products while the minority group are paid less than the value of theirs. If every employer has the same strong prejudices, the discrimination may persist. But there are profits to be made by hiring

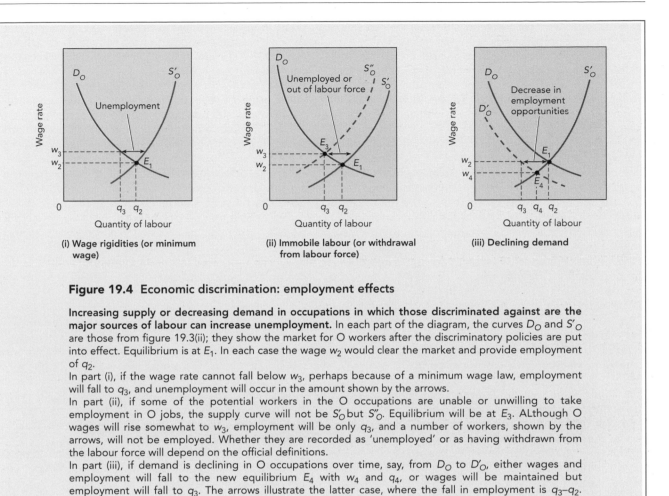

Figure 19.4 Economic discrimination: employment effects

Increasing supply or decreasing demand in occupations in which those discriminated against are the major sources of labour can increase unemployment. In each part of the diagram, the curves D_O and S'_O are those from figure 19.3(ii); they show the market for O workers after the discriminatory policies are put into effect. Equilibrium is at E_1. In each case the wage w_2 would clear the market and provide employment of q_2.

In part (i), if the wage rate cannot fall below w_3, perhaps because of a minimum wage law, employment will fall to q_3, and unemployment will occur in the amount shown by the arrows.

In part (ii), if some of the potential workers in the O occupations are unable or unwilling to take employment in O jobs, the supply curve will not be S'_O but S''_O. Equilibrium will be at E_3. ALthough O wages will rise somewhat to w_3, employment will be only q_3, and a number of workers, shown by the arrows, will not be employed. Whether they are recorded as 'unemployed' or as having withdrawn from the labour force will depend on the official definitions.

In part (iii), if demand is declining in O occupations over time, say, from D_O to D'_O, either wages and employment will fall to the new equilibrium E_4 with w_4 and q_4, or wages will be maintained but employment will fall to q_3. The arrows illustrate the latter case, where the fall in employment is q_3–q_2.

members of the minority group and, sooner or later, someone may just do this. When this happens, the non-prejudiced employer will outperform the prejudiced employers. More competitive situations with many firms and easy entry make it more likely that this anti-discrimination tactic will be tried by someone and will eventually force non-prejudiced behaviour on competing firms. In contrast, if there are only a few firms and entry is difficult, the prejudices of existing hirers may persist unchallenged for a long time—but only in so far as the firms themselves are not profit-maximizers, preferring to sacrifice profits in order to indulge their prejudices.

Other types of discrimination may have their source in the tastes of agents other than the owners and managers of firms, in particular in those of customers and workers. In these cases, it may pay profit-maximizing firms to discriminate. If customers care about who makes the product they consume, profit-maximizing employers will hire the preferred workers. (Although the two groups may have the same physical marginal products, the market values of these products will be lower for the minority workers than for the majority ones.) After all, the market is a relatively efficient way of responding to consumers' tastes, not of imposing some standards of morality on society. It is unlikely, however, that customers know, or care, about the colour or race of the hand that makes most of the manufactured products they consume today—although exceptions may be found in the case of small firms serving local markets where everyone knows all of the firm's employees. But customers can, and often do, care about these matters in the case of personal services, because close physical proximity, and even contact, is required to deliver many of these. In societies where racial feelings are very strong, such as the South of the United States a few decades ago, personal services that are regarded as demeaning have often been reserved for the minority group while others, in which the served and server meet more on terms of equality, have been reserved for the majority group—and the source of the discrimination seems to be the tastes of customers rather than the prejudices of employers.

The second source of this type of pressure comes from workers themselves. If members of the majority group find it sufficiently upsetting to work alongside the minority group, their marginal physical products may be lower in mixed working situations than in homogeneous ones. In this case, it is again rational for profit-maximizing firms to hire homogeneous labour forces. Now non-prejudiced employers can profit from their lack of prejudice only if they can set up a minority-only plant. However, just because its members have been discriminated against in the past, the minority group may not have the full range of human capital needed to fill all of the jobs efficiently. The other alternative is to take production to another geographical area where workers are not so prejudiced.

In summary, competitive pressures put limits on employers' non-maximizing behaviour motivated by their own prejudices, and its persistence is less likely the more competitive the situation and the less universal are the prejudices.

The market, however, leads profit-maximizing firms to respond to prejudices originating in the tastes of customers or of workers in the majority group.

It is interesting to note, however, that falling transport and communication costs over the twentieth century have expanded firms' choice of location for the production of goods, from local markets, to national markets, to wider regional markets, and now often to global markets. This has greatly reduced the power of local prejudices to impose discrimination on maximizing firms. If firms give in to local pressure, the production can be transferred to other sites and the customers will quickly lose any concern about, or even awareness of, the nature of the far-distant work-force that makes the products they consume.

Differentials due to labour market structures

Evidence suggests that wages are higher in many markets dominated by unions than in more competitive markets. In this section, we see how differences among markets in the degree of competition can contribute to income differentials. We then go on to study unions in a little more detail.

THE DETERMINATION OF WAGES WITHOUT UNIONS

We first look at the determination of wages in an individual labour market when labour is supplied competitively. Each individual worker must take the existing wage rate as given, and decide how much labour services to supply at that wage. We have seen that each worker has a supply curve showing how much effort he or she will supply at each wage (see p. 338). The sum of these curves yields a market supply curve showing the total supply of effort to this market as a function of the real wage rate. The determination of wages under competitive supply now falls into three cases, distinguished by whether labour is bought by competitive purchasers, a single-wage monopsonist, or a discriminating monopsonist.

Case 1: A competitive market   We first assume that there are so many purchasers of labour services that no one of them can influence the market wage rate. Instead, each merely decides how much labour to hire at the current rate. Since both demanders and suppliers are price-takers and quantity-adjusters, this labour market is perfectly competitive. The wage rate and volume of employment is then determined by demand and supply as shown in Figure 18.3 on p. 330.

Case 2: A single wage monopsonist: a single purchaser   In cases 2 and 3, we consider a labour market containing so few firms that each one realizes it can influence the wage rate by varying the amount of labour that it employs. For simplicity, we deal with a case in which the few purchasers form an employers' association and act as a single decision-taking unit in the labour market. In this section, the single buyer is restrained to pay a single wage to all workers of one type that it employs.

When there is a single purchaser in any market, that purchaser is called a **monopsonist**. A monopsonist can offer any wage rate it chooses, and workers must either work for that wage or move to other markets (i.e. change occupation or location).

Suppose that the monopsonist decides to hire some specific quantity of labour. The labour supply curve shows the wage that it must offer. To the monopsonist, this wage is the *average cost curve* of labour. In deciding how much labour to hire, however, the monopsonist firm is interested in the marginal cost of hiring additional workers. It wants to know how much its costs will rise if it takes on more labour.

Whenever the supply curve of labour has a positive slope, the marginal cost of employing extra units will exceed the average cost. It exceeds the wage paid (the average cost) because the increased wage rate necessary to attract an extra worker must also be paid to *everyone already employed*.

Consider an example. If 100 workers are employed at £2 per hour, then total cost is £200 and average cost per worker is £2. If an extra worker is employed and this drives the wage rate up to £2.05, then total cost becomes £207.05 (101 × £2.05); the average cost per labourer is £2.05, but the total cost has increased by £7.05 as a result of hiring one more labourer.

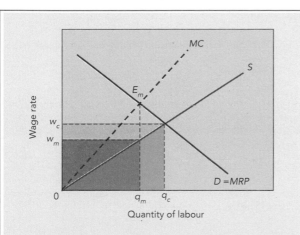

Figure 19.5 A monopsonist facing many sellers

Under monopsony, employment and wages are less than under competition. The competitive wage and employment are w_c and q_c where the demand and supply curves intersect. The monopsonist that must pay the same wage to all equates the marginal cost of hiring labour with labour's marginal revenue product, which occurs at point E_m. The firm hires q_m workers at a wage of w_m. (According to the supply curve, w_m is the wage at which q_m workers will be supplied.) Labour's income is shown by the dark red and dark blue areas enclosed by q_m and w_m.

A perfectly discriminating monopsony can pay each worker his or her supply price so the S curve is also its marginal cost curve. It will hire q_c labour and pay labour a total income equal to the dark and medium blue areas *under* the S curve. The light red area between the S curve and the competitive wage, w_c, is now part of the monopsonists' profits as is the dark red area between w_m and the S curve (whereas under perfect competition it is part of labour's income).

Monopsony results in a lower level of employment and a lower wage rate than when labour is purchased competitively.

The reason is that the monopsonistic purchaser is aware that, by trying to purchase more units of the factor, it is driving up the price against itself. It will, therefore, stop short of the point that is reached when the factor is purchased by many different firms, none of which can exert an influence on its price.

Case 3: A discriminating monopsonist   What happens if the monopsonist can discriminate among different units of a single type of labour that it hires? As with the discriminatory monopolists that we studied in Chapter 13, the ability to discriminate has two effects:

A discriminating monopsonist will hire more labour and

earn more profits than will a monopsonist who must pay the same wage to everyone.

The monopsonist in Figure 19.5 did not hire more labour because doing so drove up the wage of its existing workers. For this reason the monopsonist's marginal cost of hiring labour exceeds the average costs. If the monopsonist can split its labour into groups, it can hire a second group without driving up the price of the first group. Consider the extreme case in which the monopsonist can make a separate bargain with each worker, paying just what is needed to persuade that person to accept a job. The supply curve is then the marginal cost curve of labour and the monopsonist employs the same amount of labour as would a perfectly competitive industry.

In Figure 19.5 the perfectly competitive employment is q_c with a wage of w_c, so that labour earns $w_c q_c$.

A perfectly discriminating monopsonist will also employ q_c of labour, but, by paying each worker his or her supply price, the total wage bill is reduced to the area under the supply curve. Thus, the area between the supply curve and the perfectly competitive wage is added to the monopsonist's profits.

This is the extreme case. As long, however, as the monopsonist can discriminate between two or more groups, employment and profits will be higher than when a single wage must be paid.

THE DETERMINATION OF WAGES WITH UNIONS

Unions affect wages and employment. There are two cases, depending on whether labour is hired competitively or monopsonistically.[2]

Case 4: Monopsony (a single seller)   Suppose a union enters a competitive labour market and raises the wage above its equilibrium level. By so doing, it is establishing a minimum wage below which no one will work. This changes the supply curve of labour. The industry can hire as many units of labour as are prepared to work at the union wage, but none at a lower wage. Thus, the industry (and each firm) faces a supply curve that is horizontal at the level of the union wage up to the quantity of labour willing to work at that wage.

This is shown in Figure 19.6. The intersection of this horizontal supply curve and the demand curve establishes a higher wage rate, and a lower level of employment, than would occur at the competitive equilibrium.

---

[2] For simplicity, we deal here with only the single-wage monopsonist. Combining a union with a discriminating monopsonist complicates the analysis substantially without adding any new insights. Theoretically inclined readers may, none the less, like to do this for themselves as an exercise.

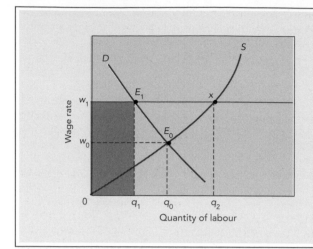

Figure 19.6 A single union facing many buyers of labour

A union that faces many employers can raise wages above the competitive level. Competitive equilibrium is at E_0. When the union sets the wage at w_1, it creates a perfectly elastic supply curve of labour up to the quantity q_2, which is the amount of labour willing to work at the wage w_1. The supply curve follows the blue line running from w_1 to x and then rises along the remainder of the supply curve, S. Equilibrium is at E_1, with q_1 workers employed, and $q_2–q_1$ willing to work at the going wage rate but unable to find employment. Labour income is shown by the dark blue area.

There will be a group of workers who would like to obtain work in the industry or occupation but cannot. This presents a problem for the union if it seeks to represent *all* the employees in the industry or occupation. A conflict has been created between serving the interests of the union's employed and unemployed members. Pressure to cut the wage rate may develop among the unemployed, but the union must resist this pressure if the higher wage is to be maintained.

A union can raise wages above the competitive-market level, but only at the costs of lowering employment and creating an excess supply of labour with its consequent pressure for wage-cutting.

Case 5: A monopsony versus a monopoly We now consider the effects of introducing a union into the monopsonistic labour market first illustrated in Figure 19.5.

The monopsonistic employer's organization now faces a monopoly union, and the two sides will settle the wage through collective bargaining. The outcome of this bargaining process will depend on the objective that each side sets and on the skill that each has in bargaining for its objective. We have seen that, left to itself, the employer's organization will set the monopsonistic wage shown in Figure 19.5. To understand the range over which the wage may be set after the union enters the market, let us ask what the union would do if it had the power to set the wage unilaterally. The result will give us insight into the union's objectives in the actual collective bargaining that does occur.

Suppose, then, that the union can set a wage below which its members will not work. There is now no point in the employer's holding off hiring for fear of driving the wage up or of reducing the quantity demanded in the hope of driving the wage rate down. Here, just as in the case of a wage-setting union in a competitive market, the union pre-sents the employer with a horizontal supply curve (up to the maximum number of workers who will accept work at the union wage). As demonstrated in Figure 19.7, the union can raise wages *and employment* above the monopsonistic level.

Because the union turns the firm into a price-taker in the labour market, it can stop a firm from exercising its monopsony power and thus raise both wages and employment to the competitive level.

The union may not be content merely to neutralize the monopsonist's power. It may choose to raise wages further. If it does, the outcome will be similar to that shown in Figure 19.6. If the wage is raised above the competitive level, the employer will no longer wish to hire all the labour that is offered at that wage. The amount of employment will fall, and unemployment will develop. This is also shown in Figure 19.7. Notice, however, that the union can raise wages substantially above the competitive level before employment falls to a level as low as it was in the pre-union monopsonistic situation.

So now we know that the employer would like to set the monopsonistic wage and that the union would not want a wage below the competitive wage. The union may target for a still higher wage depending on how it trades off employment for its members and the wage they earn. If the union is happy with an amount of employment as low as would occur at the monopsonistic wage, it could target for a wage substantially higher than the competitive wage.

Simple demand and supply analysis can take us no further. The actual outcome will, as we have already observed, depend on such other things as what target wage the two sides actually set for themselves, their relative bargaining skills, how each side assesses the costs of concessions, and how serious a strike would be for each.

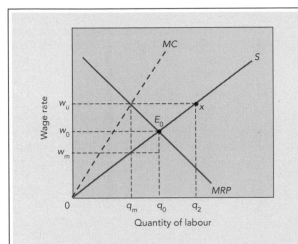

Figure 19.7 A single union facing a single buyer of labour

By presenting the monopsonist with a fixed wage, a union can raise both the wage and employment above their monopsonistic levels. The monopsonist facing competitively supplied labour is in the equilibrium analysed in Figure 19.5 with q_m workers employed at a wage of w_m. If a newly entering union sets its wage at w_0, the supply curve follows the horizontal line from w_0 to E_0, and then rises along the line S. Equilibrium is E_0 with employment at q_0.

If the union seeks a wage higher than w_0, it must accept a lower level of employment than q_0. The union can, for example, set a wage of w_u, creating a supply curve that runs from w_u to x, then up the S curve. This yields the same level of employment, q_m, as when the monopsonist dominated the market, but at the much higher wage of w_u. At that wage rate, there are q_2–q_m people who would like to work but who are unable to find employment.

Differentials due to product market structures

The ability of a union to raise wages above the competitive level depends partly on the profitability of the industry in which it is operating. Some industries are highly competitive because they contain a large number of small firms and entry and exit is easy. Typically, firms in such industries will be earning enough to cover the opportunity cost of their capital, but no pure profits. In other industries, scale economies allow only a few firms, each one of which may earn significant pure profits. (In the limit, there will be only one firm.) Government regulation that restricts competitive behaviour can also create economic profits over and above the opportunity cost of capital.

Evidence suggests that unions can appropriate a share of these profits through aggressive collective bargaining. This was particularly clear in the United States when a large number of industries were deregulated, subjecting their firms to greatly increased competitive pressures. Wages fell significantly in most of these industries, showing that their employees had succeeded in obtaining significant rents in excess of what they could have earned elsewhere.

In a competitive industry, where only the opportunity cost of capital is being earned, there is no pool of pure profits for employers and employees to share out between themselves. A strong union might still raise wages in such an industry. This would increase costs and lead to exit until prices rose sufficiently for the remaining firms fully to cover their now-higher costs. Thus, the rise in wages would be accompanied by a fall in output. However, even this limited gain may not be possible. If the union does not have a closed shop, new firms may enter, with lower costs achieved by hiring non-union labour. Also, if there is competition from foreign firms that do not face strong unions, the domestic industry may suffer a drastic contraction. So ability to raise wages above their competitive levels tends to be higher the less competitive is the industry and the more difficult is new entry into it.

Minimum wage laws

When unions set wages for their members, they are in effect setting a minimum wage. Governments can cause similar effects by legislating specific *minimum wages*, which define the lowest wage rates that may legally be paid. Such minimum wages are common in the United States and Canada and are a part of the European Union's Social Chapter. One of the reasons why the United Kingdom opted out of this part of the Maastricht agreement was to avoid having minimum wage laws in Britain.

Although minimum wages are an accepted part of the labour scene in some countries, economists view their effects as less obviously beneficial than do many other observers. To the extent that they are effective, they raise the wages of employed workers. However, as our analysis in Chapter 6 indicated, an effective floor price (which is what a minimum wage is) may well lead to a market surplus—in this case, unemployment. Thus, minimum wages benefit some groups of workers while hurting others.

The problem is more complicated than the analysis of Chapter 6 would suggest, both because not all labour markets are competitive and because minimum wage laws do not cover all employment. Moreover, some groups in the labour force, especially youth and minorities, are affected more than the average worker.

A COMPREHENSIVE MINIMUM WAGE

Suppose that minimum wage laws apply uniformly to all occupations. The occupations and the industries in which minimum wages are effective will be the lowest-paying in the country; they will usually involve unskilled or, at best, semi-skilled labour. In most of them, the workers are not members of unions. Thus, the market structures in which minimum wages are likely to be effective include both those in which competitive conditions pertain and those in which employers exercise monopsony power. The effects on employment are different in the two cases.

Competitive labour markets   The consequences for employment of an effective minimum wage are unambiguous when the labour market is competitive. By raising the wage that employers must pay, minimum-wage legislation leads to a reduction in the quantity of labour that is demanded and an increase in the quantity of labour that is supplied. As a result, the actual level of employment falls, and unemployment is generated. This situation is exactly analogous to the one that arises when a union succeeds in setting a wage above the competitive equilibrium wage, as illustrated in Figure 19.6. The excess supply of labour at the minimum wage also creates incentives for people to evade the law by working below the legal minimum wage.

In competitive labour markets, effective minimum wage laws raise the wages of those who remain employed but also create some unemployment.

Monopsonistic labour markets   By effectively flattening out the labour supply curve, the minimum wage law can simultaneously increase both wages and employment in monopsonistic labour markets. The circumstances in which this can be done are the same as those in which a union that is facing a monopsonistic employer succeeds in setting a wage above the wage that the employer would otherwise pay, as shown in Figure 19.7. Of course, if the minimum wage is raised above the competitive wage, employment will start to fall, as in the union case. When it is set at the competitive level, however, the minimum wage can protect workers against monopsony power *and* lead to increases in employment.

EVIDENCE FROM NORTH AMERICA

Empirical work on the effects of minimum wage laws in North America, where they are commonly used, reflects these mixed theoretical predictions. There is some evidence that those who keep their jobs gain when the minimum wage is raised. There is also evidence that some groups suffer a decline in employment consistent with raising the wage in a fairly competitive market. At other times and places, there is evidence that both wages earned and employment rise when the minimum wage rises, as is consistent with monopolistic labour markets.

Recent empirical work on the subject also tends to suggest that the distributional effects of the minimum wage, like the employment effects, are fairly small. When reviewing the literature on minimum wages, US economist Charles Brown concludes that 'the minimum wage is overrated: by its critics as well as its supporters'.[3]

Given its mixed economic effects, support for and opposition to the minimum wage might be understood as arising largely from political and sociological motives. Organized labour has consistently pressed for a broad, relatively high minimum wage. There is some economic reason for this, in that there is evidence that the minimum wage 'trickles up' to higher-wage workers, both unionized and not. Arguably, however, the support dates back to the 1930s, when organized labour was still fighting to establish its position. Enactment of a minimum wage was then a great political victory, and the minimum wage still has symbolic significance.

Unions

HAVING concluded our discussion of the causes of equilibrium wage differentials with a study of the influence of unions, it is appropriate to raise some further issues related to unions. We begin by discussing the rise of unions.

The rise of unions

One reason for the rise of unions was to be able to turn cases 1, 2, and 3 that we studied above into cases 4 and 5. Another was to provide the many workers with a collective, and hence an effective, voice in dealing with the few employers on such other conditions of work as safety, hours, holidays, and non-wage benefits.

Since early unions did not have large resources, employ-

---

[3] For more information, see Charles Brown, 'Minimum Wage Laws: Are They Overrated?' *Journal of Economic Perspectives* (Summer 1988).

ers had to be attacked where they were weakest. The unions that succeeded first were those that covered skilled artisans rather than semi-skilled or unskilled workers. Economic theory provides reasons that help to explain their success—reasons coming from both the demand and the supply side of the market.

Demand forces Highly skilled specialists usually faced quite inelastic demands for their services, and thus could raise wages without facing major losses of employment. Inelastic demands are explained by two of the principles outlined in Chapter 17. First, these specialists were difficult to dispense with since their services had no real substitutes (see the substitution rule on p. 334). Second, labour in any one skilled occupation usually accounted for a very small proportion of total production costs, since large quantities of unskilled labour were employed in most production processes (see the importance rule on p. 335).

Supply forces We have seen that one of the problems of

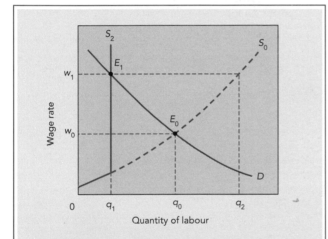

Figure 19.8 Raising wages by restricting supply

If wages are raised by restricting supply, any given target wage can be maintained without creating a pool of workers who are available to work at the going wage rate but are unable to find employment. With free entry into the occupation, the supply curve S_0 and the demand curve D intersect at E_0 to produce an equilibrium wage of w_0 with employment of q_0. If entry is restricted to the quantity q_1, the supply curve follows the curve S_0 up to that quantity and then becomes vertical (the blue supply curve in the figure labelled S_1). The competitive market now reaches equilibrium at E_1, determining the wage rate at w_1. There is no excess supply.

If instead the wage had been fixed at w_1 without controlling entry, the supply of persons willing to work at that wage, but unable to find employment, would have been q_2-q_1.

raising wages above their competitive levels is the emergence of a supply of workers who would like to work at the going wage rate, but cannot find employment. These would-be employees are tempted to work for less than the union wage, and thus can undercut the union's ability to maintain a high wage rate.

The skilled workers normally had guilds, and other associations, that controlled entry into their profession. Thus, they did not have to rely on the strategy of fixing the wage and letting the employer decide quantity. Instead, they could restrict supply by restricting entry into their trade, and then accept the free-market wage rate. This method of raising wages, which is studied in Figure 19.8, had the advantage of avoiding a pool of unemployed workers ready to undercut the prevailing wage. Such a method was not, however, available to the semi-skilled and unskilled workers.

This is a method that has been used at many times and in many places. The key requirement is that the supply of persons offering themselves for employment can be controlled. This can be done by unions that can restrict membership and have closed-shop agreements preventing non-members from being employed. It can also be done by professional associations that license those allowed to practise the profession; entry can then be reduced by raising standards for entry. This makes it difficult to decide whether the public is being protected by ensuring that practitioners are of a reasonable standard, or is being exploited by restricting entry through the imposition of unnecessarily high standards.

Unions today

Table 19.1 shows the wide variations in union membership among advanced industrial countries. Although union membership has been falling in the United Kingdom, as discussed in Box 19.2, it is currently close to the average for all of these countries.

INSTITUTIONS

Modern unions are organized throughout the world along two main principles. In **trade (or craft) unions**, workers with a common set of skills are joined in a common association, no matter where, or for whom, they work. In **industrial unions**, all workers in a given plant, or a given industry, are collected into a single union, whatever their skills.

Industrial unions are common in the United States. Because of them, many firms, including the great American automobile companies, deal with one union. So also do American steel companies. A single agreement over wages, working conditions, or union practices is sufficient to change the situation throughout the entire industry.

Table 19.1 Percentage of the labour force in trade unions, OECD countries, 1985

Country	%
Sweden	87.7
Denmark	78.2 (1983)
Belgium	75.8
Norway	65.1 (1984)
Austria	58.2 (1984)
New Zealand	56.0
Australia	51.2
Ireland	46.2
UK	43.3
Italy	40.0
West Germany	36.7
Switzerland	32.5
Canada	30.5
Netherlands	29.1
Japan	28.9
France	18.2 (1982)
USA	15.7

Source: R. Bean and K. Holden, 'Cross sectional differences in trade union membership in OECD countries', *Industrial Relations Journal*, 1992.

The importance of trade unions varies greatly across the advanced industrial countries. The authors of the article quoted in the source study the reasons for these large differences and conclude that 'higher density of membership is . . . associated with a higher degree of centralisation of wage bargaining, higher percentage of employees covered by collective bargaining, a larger public sector and a more leftist party of government'.

A single union covering an entire industry is less common in the United Kingdom (and in many other countries) because the main basis of organization is the trade union. As a result, a typical employer has to deal with many unions—twenty or more within a single firm is not uncommon in the United Kingdom. Under these circumstances, agreement between labour and management can be hard to reach.

Unions do many things designed to influence the wages and conditions of work of their members. What they are able to accomplish depends partly on the institutional setting within which they operate.

Modern unions bargain under two basic types of arrangements: the open shop and the closed shop. In an **open shop** a union represents its members, but does not have exclusive negotiating rights for all the workers of one kind; membership in the union is not a condition of getting or keeping a job. Unions usually oppose such an arrangement, and it is easy to see why. Consider an open-shop negotiating situation. If, on the one hand, employers

accede to union demands, the non-members achieve the benefits of the union without paying dues or sharing the risks. If, on the other hand, employers choose to fight the union, they can run their plants with the non-union members, thus weakening the power of the union.

The desire to avoid the open shop leads to other union arrangements. In a **closed shop**, only union members can be employed. (Closed shops may be either 'pre-entry', where the worker must be a member of the union before being employed, or 'post-entry', where the worker must join the union on becoming employed.) These were once common in the United Kingdom, but under the 1980 Employment Act they were virtually abolished.

Box 19.2 discusses the dramatic decline in the importance of unions that has been going on in the 1980s and 1990s.

COLLECTIVE BARGAINING

In collective bargaining between firms and unions, there is usually a substantial range over which wages may be set. An example is shown in Figure 19.9.

Economic theory can put limits on the outcome, but where it settles within those limits may depend on a host of considerations. Just as in oligopolistic competition between firms, the outcome may be significantly influenced by such political and psychological factors as skill in bargaining, ability to bluff, and one side's assessment of the other side's reactions to its own moves. For example, the employers will ask, 'How much can we resist without provoking the unions into calling a costly strike?' and the union will ask, 'Will the employers force us to strike only for a token period so they can tell their shareholders they *tried* to resist, or do they think this is a really serious matter so that they intend to hold out to the bitter end against any strike that we might call?' It is because monopoly versus monopsony allows more than one acceptable economic solution that these non-economic factors become so important.

WAGES VERSUS EMPLOYMENT

We have already seen that in many situations the union faces a trade-off between wages and employment: an increase in wages can be obtained only at the cost of lowered employment. In some cases, however, it is possible to avoid the conflict between wages and unemployment by bargaining with the employer about both wages and employment. This can sometimes be accomplished in one small sector of the economy by manning agreements, forcing employers to use more labour than they need for a given level of output; such agreements were common in the United Kingdom from 1945 to 1980, but most had disappeared by 1990.

The demand curve shows for each wage rate the amount of labour a firm would like to hire. But a firm may prefer to

BOX 19.2

The decline of trade union membership

UK trade union membership peaked in 1978. At that time, 53 per cent of the civilian work-force were union members. By the beginning of 1994, that number had declined to around 30 per cent. The main factors behind this decline are the changes in industrial structure and in employment patterns.

Trade unions had their roots in primary and secondary industries, especially coal mining and such 'metal bashing' industries as steel, shipbuilding, and metal manufacturing. They had also been strong in the public-sector industries, such as gas, electric, water, and public transport. Unions have always had a much smaller role in the tertiary sector, where virtually all the job growth of the 1980s and 1990s has been located.

The traditional 'heavy' industries have suffered dramatic falls in employment. These have been especially large in coal mining, shipbuilding, and steel, though manufacturing in general has exhibited a declining share of total employment over the last forty years.

These declines in the potential demand for union membership have been exacerbated by three other factors. First, technology has broken the ability of some traditional 'craft' unions to control their employment contracts. One example was in the printing industry, where computer composition made old type-setting skills redundant; another was on the docks, where containers made redundant most dockworkers who loaded and unloaded boats by hand. Second, privatization of many former public-sector industries (steel, telephones, electricity, water, gas) has led both to job losses and new conditions of employment. Third, women and part-time workers have accounted for a rising proportion of employment while self-employment has also increased. Members of all of these groups are historically less likely to join unions than are full-time male employees.

The decline in trade union membership is not necessarily irreversible. It is clear, however, that if unions are to attract new members they will have to adjust to modern employment structures. They will also have to redefine their 'product' in ways that will attract more 'customers'. In other words, they will have to drop some of their old class-war attitudes and accept that employers and employees have a common stake in keeping firms successful in a fiercely competitive world.

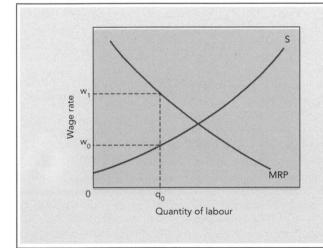

Figure 19.9 Collective bargaining between one union and one employer

There is often more than one mutually acceptable outcome to the bargaining process. The supply curve of persons who would like to work in the job in question is given by S, but the union is assumed to have restricted entry to q_0. The single employer (one firm or an employers' association) has a marginal revenue product curve for this labour of MRP. The supply curve indicates that q_0 workers would be willing to work for w_0. The MRP curve indicates that the employer would be willing to employ q_0 workers at any wage up to w_1. Both sides would prefer any wage between w_0 and w_1 rather than have no agreement at all.

hire some other amount rather than go without labour altogether. A union may offer the firm the alternative of employing more labour than the firm would choose to hire at a given wage rate, or facing a strike. If the firm accepts the former option, it will move to a point off its demand curve.

The union's ability to raise the wage rate, and increase the employment of its members, will depend partly on the size of the profits in the industry (i.e. on the extent to which the industry departs from the perfectly competitive equilibrium), and partly on the current state of the firm's market.

The current market conditions will determine the relation between the losses resulting from hiring more than the desired quantity of labour at the agreed wage rate, and the expected losses resulting from a strike. Under boom conditions, when profits are high, the union may succeed in holding firms off their demand curves for a long time. Under less buoyant conditions, when there may be no pure profits, firms may exit from the industry because their total costs now exceed their total revenues. Furthermore, employers are given a strong incentive to develop new technology that will eliminate the unneeded workers by replacing their jobs with machines.

The workers may fight the introduction of the new technology, but they cannot resist it indefinitely. When it is introduced, the demand curve shifts left and employment may be less than it would have been if employers had not been pushed off their demand curves in the first place. This is a reasonable description of the battle between printers' unions and newspaper owners, in which unions forced the owners off their demand curves for years while they successfully held off the introduction of new technology. Finally, when the new technology was introduced, many of the union members lost their jobs. (The full story is of course more complex, but the economic analysis needed to understand it is what has been outlined above.)

Where it is not possible to push employers off demand curves, unions will be more aware of the wage–employment trade-off the more centralized is the bargaining process. In firm-by-firm bargaining unions know that, if they push wages up high enough to reduce employment, the displaced workers can get jobs elsewhere. However, a single-union bargaining with an employers' federation over the whole economy would be aware that there was no 'elsewhere'. They would thus be much more restrained by the wage–employment trade-off than the small unions. In their book *The Unemployment Crisis* (Oxford University Press, 1994), three British economists—Richard Layard, Stephen Nickell, and Richard Jackman—present data for several countries that seem to support this view that wage bargaining is more likely to create unemployment the more decentralized it is.

UNIONS AND THE STRUCTURE OF RELATIVE WAGES

So far we have considered the influence of one particular union, operating in a small section of the total labour market, on the wages of its members. Our theory predicts that a powerful union can in such circumstances raise the wages earned by its members, possibly at the expense of increased unemployment. This prediction seems to be supported by substantial empirical evidence that unions do influence the structure of relative wages by raising wages in some industries and occupations where they are particularly strong, without a corresponding rise in wages elsewhere.

Research suggests that in the past British unions were able to raise wages on average around 10 per cent above what they would have been if the occupation had not been unionized. If one group got a larger share of total national income, some other groups must have got less, but the identities of the other groups were not always obvious. A substantial amount of the extra earnings of unionized labour appears to have been at the expense of lower wages for some groups of unorganized workers, as well as lower incomes for others who were unemployed but would have had jobs if wages had not been raised above their competitive levels.

There are several reasons for believing that by the early 1990s the union-induced wage differentials reported above had all but disappeared. First, union power had been broken in those industries where unions had been powerful. For example, computer-based composition finally destroyed the power of the old printers' union, which had been able to hold wages substantially above competitive levels (and in the process made it more difficult for UK publishing firms to compete with foreign rivals). Second, many of the industries in which unions were strong, such as coal, steel, and the docks, are all in decline, employing small and shrinking numbers of workers. Third, in the one place where unions may still be maintaining a major wage differential which would not exist in their absence—the public sector—contracting out is becoming common (usually to non-union firms). Over time, therefore, unions in that sector can be expected to become less and less effective in imposing large average wage differentials between their workers and those in the private sector.

Unions were effective in many ways, but whenever they did succeed in establishing large wage differentials over what market forces would have determined, these set up forces of Schumpeterian creative destruction which in the end eroded the differentials. It took time, but in the end economic forces of substitution, international competition, and induced technological innovation eroded both the wage differentials and the union power that created them.[4]

Summary

1 Equilibrium wage differentials can arise among jobs because: (*a*) each requires different degrees of physical or mental abilities, (*b*) each requires different amounts of human capital acquired through costly formal education or on-the-job training, (*c*) some jobs are closed to some who could fill them, as a result of discrimination, and (*d*) the factor markets related to different jobs have different competitive structures.

2 In perfectly competitive factor markets, wages are set by demand and supply and there is no unemployment in equilibrium. In monopsonistic markets, wages and employment are less than their competitive levels, but there is no unemployment in equilibrium.

[4] Notice that these last two paragraphs give positive statements about what happened and why it happened. These do not imply any normative judgement about whether the reported changes were desirable or undesirable (which will, to a great extent, depend on the point of view of the person making the judgement).

3   If a union enters a perfectly competitive market, it can raise wages above the competitive level at the cost of lowering employment and creating a pool of persons who would like to work at the union wage but cannot. If a union enters a monopsonistic labour market, it can raise wages *and* employment to the competitive level. If it raises wages beyond that point, employment will fall.

4   Unions and professional associations can sometimes restrict the supply of labour and thereby achieve wages above the competitive equilibrium without creating a pool of unemployed.

5   Modern unions are organized either on trade or on industrial lines and they bargain either in open or closed shops. Collective bargaining between a union with monopoly power and firms with monopsony power can lead to a wide range of possible outcomes depending on factors other than demand and supply.

Topics for review

- Causes of equilibrium wage differentials
- Human capital
- Formal education and on-the-job training
- Wage differentials due to departure from perfect competition on the demand and the supply sides of labour markets
- The significance of unions

❧ CHAPTER 20

Non-renewable natural resources and capital

IN this chapter we discuss the two important cases of non-renewable resources and physical capital. These are similar factors of production in that each is a stock of valuable things that gets used up in the process of producing goods and services. They are different in that physical capital can be replaced while non-renewable natural resources cannot. A new machine can always be created to replace one that wears out, but a barrel of oil used represents a permanent reduction in the total stock of oil in the world—no more natural oil can be created to replace what we use.

Resources that can be replaced, either by being made by man as with machines or by reproducing themselves as with people or fish, are called **renewable resources**. Resources that cannot be renewed, as with fossil fuels, are called **non-renewable or exhaustible resources**.

The economics of non-renewable resources

THE world's minerals and fossil fuels are examples of non-renewable resources. However, since some of the stock is as yet undiscovered, the *known* supply of each is not fixed over time. New discoveries add to the known stock, and use subtracts from it. It is, however, possible to imagine exhausting all of the world's supplies of oil, natural gas, coal, or any one mineral. In this sense, they are non-renewable.

Are we exhausting our supply of non-renewable resources too quickly? Some people ask: 'Should we not save more of them for our children and grandchildren?' Others are willing to let future generations take care of themselves. 'After all,' they argue, 'they will be richer than we are in any case.'

In the first part of this chapter, we deal with questions such as: How does the price system regulate the use of a non-renewable resource? Does it lead to overly rapid exploitation? Does it lead to too much conservation of a resource, which may in any case be rendered less useful by future technological change?

Determining the rate of extraction

To focus on the basic issues, it is easiest to consider at the outset a non-renewable resource whose total supply is known. Suppose for the moment that all the petroleum in existence has been discovered, so that every unit that is used permanently diminishes the known stock by one unit.

Many different firms own the land that contains the oil supply. They have invested money in discovering the oil, drilling wells, and laying pipelines. Assume that their current extraction costs are virtually zero—all they have to do is turn their taps on, and the oil flows at any desired rate to the petroleum markets.[1]

OPTIMAL FIRM BEHAVIOUR

What should each firm do? It could extract all of its oil in a great binge of production this year, or it could husband the resource for some future rainy day and produce nothing this year. In practice, it is likely to adopt some intermediate policy, producing and selling some oil this year and holding stocks of it in the ground for extraction in future years. But *how much* should it extract this year and *how much* should it carry over for future years? What will the decision imply for the price of oil over the years?

The firms that own the oil land are holding a valuable resource. Holding it, however, imposes an opportunity cost: the oil could have been extracted and sold this year, yielding revenue to the firms (and value to consumers) in the same year. A firm will be willing to leave the resource in the ground only if it earns a return equal to what it can earn in other investments. This is measured by the interest rate.

First, suppose the price of oil is expected to rise by less than the interest rate. Oil extracted and sold now will have a higher value than oil left in the ground. Firms will, therefore, extract more oil this year. Because the demand curve for oil has a negative slope, raising the extraction rate will lower this year's price. Production will rise, and the current price will fall until the expected price rise between this year and next year is equal to the interest rate.[2] The firms will then be indifferent at the margin between producing

---

[1] It is, of course, a simplification of the real case to assume that current production costs are actually zero. The assumption, however, is not too far from reality in the case of such a resource as oil, where the fixed costs of discovery, extraction (e.g. drilling wells), and distribution (e.g. laying pipelines) account for the bulk of total costs. When the variable extraction costs are not zero, all statements about prices in the text refer to the margin by which price *exceeds* the current variable costs of extraction.

[2] The discussion is simplified by assuming next year's expected price to be given. The decision to produce more this year may also affect next year's price. If the total supplies are small, next year's expected price may rise. The argument proceeds exactly as in the text, except that the equilibrium gap between two prices is achieved by the present price falling and the expected future price rising, rather than by having next year's expected price remaining constant and all the adjustment coming through this year's price.

another barrel this year and holding it for production next year.

Second, suppose that the price is expected to rise by more than the interest rate. Firms will prefer to leave their oil in the ground, where they earn a higher return than could be earned by selling the oil this year and investing the proceeds at the current interest rate. Thus, firms will cut their rate of production for this year, which will raise this year's price. When the current price has risen so that the gap between the current price and next year's expected price is equal to the interest rate, firms will value equally a barrel of oil extracted and one left in the ground.

In a perfectly competitive industry, the profit-maximizing equilibrium for a non-renewable resource occurs when the last unit currently produced earns just as much for each firm as it would if it had been left in the ground for future use.

To illustrate these important relations, assume that next year's price is expected to be £1.05 and that the rate of interest is 5 per cent.

First, suppose the current price is £1.04 per barrel. Clearly, it pays to produce more now, since the £1.04 that is earned by selling a barrel now can be invested to yield approximately £1.09 (£1.04 × 1.05), which is more than the £1.05 that the oil would be worth in a year's time if it is left in the ground. Second, suppose that the current price is £0.90 per barrel. Now it pays to reduce production, since oil left in the ground will be worth 16.66 per cent more next year ((1.05/0.90) × 100). Extracting it this year and investing the money will produce a gain of only 5 per cent. Finally, let the current price be £1.00. Now oil producers make the same amount of money whether they leave £1.00 worth of oil in the ground to be worth £1.05 next year or sell the oil for £1.00 this year and invest the proceeds at a 5 per cent interest rate.

MARKET PRICING

What we have established so far determines the pattern of prices over time: if stocks are given and unchanging, prices should rise over time at a rate equal to the rate of interest. But what about the level of prices? Will they start low and rise to only moderate levels over the next few years, or will they start high and then rise to even higher levels? The answer depends on the total stock of the resource that is available (and, where some new discoveries are possible, on the expected additions to that stock in the future). The scarcer is the resource relative to the demand for it, the higher its market price will be at the outset.

The optimal profile of the resource's price over time is to rise at a rate equal to the rate of interest, while the height of that price profile will depend on the resource's scarcity relative to current demand.

OPTIMAL SOCIAL BEHAVIOUR

Petroleum is a valuable social resource. The value to consumers of one more barrel produced now is the price that they would be willing to pay for it, which is the current market price of the oil (in this example assumed to be £1.00). If the oil is extracted this year and the proceeds are invested at the rate of interest (the proceeds might be used to buy a new capital good), they will produce £1.05 worth of valuable goods next year. If that barrel of oil is not produced this year and is left in the ground for extraction next year, its value to consumers at that time will be next year's price of oil. It is not socially optimal, therefore, to leave the oil in the ground unless it will be worth £1.05 to consumers next year. More generally, society obtains increases in the value of what is available for consumption by conserving units of a non-renewable resource to be used in future years only if the price of the units is expected to rise at a rate that is at least as high as the interest rate.

This answer to the question 'How much of a non-renewable resource should be consumed now?' was provided many years ago by the US economist Harold Hotelling (1895–1973). His answer is very simple, yet it specifically determines the optimal profile of prices over the years. It is interesting that the answer applies to all non-renewable resources. It does not matter whether there is a large or a small demand or whether that demand is elastic or inelastic. In all cases the answer is the same:

The rate of extraction of any non-renewable resource should be such that its price increases at a rate equal to the interest rate.

For example, if the rate of interest is 4 per cent, then the price of the resource should be rising at 4 per cent per year. If it is rising by more, there is too much current extraction; if it is rising by less, then there is not enough current extraction. We have already seen that this is the rate of extraction that will be produced by a competitive industry.

THE ACTUAL RATE OF EXTRACTION

What about the actual rate at which the resource will be extracted *if the competitive market fulfils Hotelling's rule for optimal extraction rates*? The answer to this question *does* depend on market conditions. Specifically, it depends on the position and the slope of the demand curve. If the quantity demanded at all prices is small, the rate of extraction will be small. The larger the quantity demanded at each price, the higher the rate of extraction will tend to be.

Now consider the influence of the demand elasticity. A highly inelastic demand curve suggests that there are few substitutes and that purchasers are prepared to pay large sums rather than do without the resource. This will produce a relatively even rate of extraction, with small reductions in each period being sufficient to drive up the price at the required rate. A relatively elastic demand curve suggests that people can easily find substitutes once the price rises. This will encourage a great deal of consumption now and a rapidly diminishing amount over future years, since large reductions in consumption are needed to drive the price up at the required rate.

Figure 20.1 illustrates this working of the price mechanism with a simple example in which the whole stock of oil must be consumed in only two periods, this year and next year. The general point is as follows:

The more inelastic the demand curve, the more even the rate of extraction (and hence the rate of use) will be over the years; the more elastic the demand curve, the more uneven the rate of extraction will be over the years.

An elastic demand curve will lead to a large consumption now and a rapid fall in consumption over the years. An inelastic demand curve will lead to a smaller consumption now and a less rapid fall in consumption over the years. In each case, quantities consumed are varying over time in such a way as to equate the rate of price increase with the rate of interest. The difference between the two lies in the different patterns of quantity variation that are required along demand curves of different slopes if prices are to rise at the same rate.

RENTS TO NATURAL RESOURCES

The incomes earned by the owners of the oil resources are *rents* in the sense defined in Chapter 18: the owners would be willing to produce the oil at any price that covers the direct costs of extraction, which in this example is zero.[3] Although these incomes serve no function in getting the product produced, since any non-zero price would do that, they do fulfil the important function of determining the extraction rate, and hence the use of the resource, *over time*. As we have seen, the price profile determines the use of the resource and hence the amount of resources allocated to its production *over time*.

---

[3] In real cases, the direct cost of extracting the resource is positive, and the rent is the income earned above that amount.

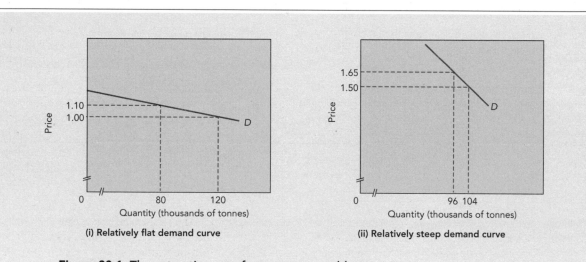

Figure 20.1 The extraction rate for a non-renewable resource

The shape of the demand curve determines the extraction profile over time. In the example illustrated, the interest rate is assumed to be 10 per cent, and there is a fixed supply of 200,000 tonnes of oil that can be extracted from the ground at zero variable cost. (All costs are fixed costs.) The oil is available for extraction either in the current period or in the next period, after which it spoils.

In part (i) the demand curve is relatively flat. The two conditions—that the whole supply be used over two periods and that the price rise by 10 per cent between the two periods—dictate that the quantities must be 120,000 tonnes in the first period, with a price of £1.00 per tonne, and 80,000 tonnes in the second period, with a price of £1.10 per tonne.

In part (ii) the demand curve is rather steep. The same two conditions now dictate that the quantities be 104,000 tonnes in the first period, with a price of £1.50 per tonne, and 96,000 tonnes in the second period, with a price of £1.65 per tonne.

The price system as a conservation mechanism

In the above discussion we see the price system playing its now familiar role of co-ordinator. By following private profit incentives, firms are led to conserve the resource in a manner that is consistent with society's needs.

THE ROLE OF RISING PRICES

From society's viewpoint, the optimal extraction pattern of a totally non-renewable resource occurs when its price rises each year at a rate equal to the interest rate. If the price is prevented from rising, the resource is depleted much too rapidly. The rising price fulfils a number of useful functions.

First, the rising price encourages conservation. As the resource becomes scarcer and its price rises, users will be motivated to be more and more economical in its use. Uses with low yields may be abandoned altogether, and uses with high yields will be pursued only as long as their value at the margin is enough to compensate for the high price.

Second, the rising price encourages the discovery of new sources of supply—at least in cases in which the world supply is not totally fixed and already known. Unlike our simple example given above, the world's supply of petroleum is not completely known. High prices, when they do occur, encourage exploration which adds to known reserves; low prices discourage it.

Third, the rising price encourages innovation. New products that will do the same job may be developed, as well as new processes that use alternative resources.

HOW MIGHT THE PRICE SYSTEM FAIL?

We will discuss three basic ways in which the price system might fail to produce the optimal rate of resource extraction: first, private owners may not have sufficient information to determine the optimal extraction rate; second, deficiencies in property rights may result in firms having incentives to extract the resource too fast; and third, markets may not correctly reflect social values. We look at examples of each of these and ask if they justify government intervention.[4]

Ignorance Private owners might not have sufficient knowledge to arrive at the best estimate of the rate at which prices will rise. If they do not know the world stocks of their commodity and the current extraction rate, they may be unable to estimate the rate of the price rise and thus will not know when to raise or lower their current rates of extraction. For example, if all firms mistakenly think that prices will not rise greatly in the future, they will all produce too much now and conserve too little for future periods.

There is no reason to think that the government could do better, unless it has access to some special knowledge that private firms do not possess. If it does have such knowledge, the government can make it public; further intervention is unnecessary as long as a competitive industry is maximizing profits on the basis of the best information available to it. In practice, what knowledge does exist about both the proven reserves of non-renewable resources and their current extraction rates is usually freely and openly available.

Inadequate property rights Some non-renewable resources have the characteristics of what is called a **common property resource**. Such property cannot be exclusively owned and controlled by one person or firm. For example, one person's oil-bearing land may be adjacent to another person's, and the underground supplies may be interconnected; if one firm holds off producing now, the oil may end up being extracted by the neighbour. In such cases, which are sometimes encountered with petroleum, there is a tendency for a firm to extract the resource too fast, because a firm's oil that has been left in the ground may not be available to that firm at a future date. (Similar issues arise with any common property resource such as fishing grounds, and they are discussed in more detail in Chapter 23.)

This problem arises because of inadequate property rights. Since the resource will be worth more in total value when it is exploited at the optimal extraction rate than when small firms exploit it too quickly, there will be an incentive for individual owners to combine until each self-contained source of supply is owned by only one firm. After that, the problem of over-exploitation will no longer arise. Government ownership is not necessary to achieve this result. What is needed, at most, is intervention to ensure that markets can work to provide the optimal size of individual units so that proper extraction management can be applied by the private owners.

Political uncertainty can provide another source of inadequate property rights. For example, the owners of the resource may fear that a future election or a revolution will establish a government that will confiscate their property. They will then be motivated to exploit the resource too quickly, on the grounds that certain revenue now is more valuable than highly uncertain revenue in the future. The current rate of extraction will tend to increase until the expected rate of price rise exceeds the interest rate by a sufficient margin to compensate for the risks of future confiscation of supplies left in the ground. The problem arises here because property rights are insecure over time.

Unequal market and social values Normally in a competi-

---

[4] This discussion partly anticipates the analysis in Part Six, which investigates market successes and market failures in more general terms.

tive world, the real interest rate indicates the rate at which it is optimal to discount the future over the present. Society's investments are valuable if they earn the market rate of return, and are not valuable if they earn less (because the resources could be used in other ways to produce more value to consumers). In certain circumstances, however, the government may have reasons to adopt a different rate of discount. It is then said that the *social rate of discount*—the discount rate that is appropriate to the society as a whole—differs from the private rate, as indicated by the market rate of interest. In such circumstances, there is reason for the government to intervene to alter the rate at which the private firms would exploit the resource. If the government owns the resources, it must be careful to use the social rate of discount in all of its decisions about exploiting the resource.

Critics are often ready to assume that profit-mad producers will despoil most non-renewable resources by using them up too quickly. They argue for government intervention to conserve the resource by slowing its rate of extraction. Yet unless the social rate of discount is *below* the private rate, there is no clear social gain in investing by holding resources in the ground where they will yield only, say, a 2 per cent return when, say, 5 per cent can be gained on other investments.

Since governments must worry about their short-term popularity and their chances of re-election, there is no presumption that government intervention will slow down the rate of extraction, even if the social discount rate is below the private rate. Instead, governments often extract resources faster than would free markets. This is because governments, being concerned primarily with the next election, may have a rate of discount much higher than either the social or the market rate.

A good example is provided by the Hybernia oil field that lies off the Newfoundland coast of Canada. The costs of developing the field and extracting the oil exceed its current market value. It would thus not be developed under free-market conditions. Instead, Canadian taxpayers' money is being used to produce oil whose market value is less than its costs of production. If left in the ground, the field would one day develop a positive value, if either the price of oil rose or the costs of production fell.

ACTUAL PRICE PROFILES

Many non-renewable resources do not seem to have the steadily rising profile of prices that the theory predicts. The price of petroleum, having been raised artificially by the OPEC cartel (see Figure 15.5 on p. 289), returned in the late 1980s to an inflation-adjusted level that was not far from where it was in 1970, and has remained there ever since. Indeed, it has since been held somewhat above that price only in so far as the producing countries have succeeded in intermittently enforcing some monopolistic output restrictions. The price of coal has not soared; nor has the price of iron ore.

In many cases, the reason lies in the discovery of new supplies, which have prevented the total known stocks of many resources from being depleted. In the case of petroleum, for example, the ratio of known reserves to one year's consumption is no lower now than it was two or even four decades ago. Furthermore, most industry experts believe that large quantities of undiscovered oil still exist under both the land and the sea.

In other cases, the invention of new substitute products has unexpectedly reduced the demand for some of these resources. For example, plastics have replaced metals in many uses, fibre optics have replaced copper wire in many types of message transmission, and newer fuels have replaced coal in many of its uses. The interesting case of the coal industry's decline in the face of massive unused resources is discussed in Box 20.1.

In yet other cases, the reason is to be found in government pricing policy. An important example of this type is the use of *non-renewable* water for irrigation in much of the United States. Vast underground reserves of water lie in aquifers beneath many areas of North America. Although these reserves were accumulated over millennia, they are being used up at a rate that will exhaust them in a matter of decades. The water is often supplied by government water authorities at prices that cover only a small part of total costs and that do not rise steadily to reflect the dwindling stocks.

Such a constant-price policy for *any* non-renewable resource creates three characteristic problems. First, the resource will be exhausted much faster than if price were to rise over time; a constant price will lead to a constant rate of extraction to meet the quantity demanded at that price until the resource is completely exhausted. Second, no signals go out to induce conservation, innovation, and exploration. Third, when the supply of the resource is finally exhausted, the adjustment will have to come all at once. If the price had risen steadily each year under free-market conditions, adjustment would have taken place little by little each year. The controlled price, however, gives no signal of the ever-diminishing stock of the resource until all at once the supplies run out. The required adjustment will then be much more painful than it would have been if it had been spread over time in response to steadily rising prices.

BOX 20.1

The abdication of king coal

The British coal industry has witnessed a dramatic decline in output and employment stretching over most of this century. This has occurred despite the often-quoted fact that there is enough coal under Britain to satisfy all domestic needs, at least to the middle of the twenty-first century. Many have argued that this decline must be the outcome of a political decision designed to reduce the power of the National Union of Mineworkers. However, the underlying economics of the industry has rather more influence on events than have political vendettas.

Peak output for the coal industry was achieved immediately before the First World War, when 290 million tonnes were produced and over 1 million workers were employed. About a third of this output was exported. A significant decline in production during the inter-war period resulted from the loss of export markets. However, in 1955 output was still 225 million tonnes; there were 850 working collieries and nearly 750,000 miners.

Substitution in favour of oil and natural gas, combined with a sharp decline in demand for coal for domestic heating (following the Clean Air Act of 1956), caused coal output to decline to 125 million tonnes, produced in 133 pits by just over 150,000 workers in 1975. Substitution towards cheaper imported coal, combined with greater use of other energy sources, including electricity imported from France and hydroelectric power, meant that by 1991/2 coal output was down to just over 30 million tonnes, produced by only 50 pits, employing less than 50,000 workers.

In October 1992 the government announced that a further 31 pits were to close, with a loss of 30,000 jobs. This announcement was precipitated by the impending expiry of contracts to sell coal to the privatized electricity generating companies, PowerGen and National Power. They had been obliged to buy 70 million tonnes of coal in 1990/1 and 1991/2, and 65 million tonnes in 1992/3; but they were expected to demand no more than 30 million tonnes beyond 1994/5, when the restrictions imposed at the time of privatization had expired.

The main driving force behind this decline in demand for British coal was price. Imported coal could be obtained at a delivered cost to most power stations of around £1.33 per GJ (at 1992 prices). The figure shows the costs of domestic production. It is derived by showing the industry output accumulated over each mine plotted at each mine's cost of production. Thus, for example, the five most efficient UK mines can produce about 10 million tonnes per year all operating at a cost of under £1.50 per GJ. This curve is very flat (elastic) in the price range just above the ruling world market price. While around 60 million tonnes could be produced at £2 per GJ, only about 25 million tonnes would be supplied at £1.50 per GJ.

This is not all. Coal is a greater producer of harmful gases (CO_2, N_2O, and SO_2) than most alternative fuels. Even worse, British coal has nearly twice the acid-rain-producing sulphur content of imported coal. Britain is committed to reducing its SO_2 emissions 40 per cent by 1998 and 60 per cent by 2003 (compared with 1980 levels). It is also committed to limiting the emission of CO_2 (greenhouse gases) to the 1990 level by 2000. Gas turbine generation produces about half the greenhouse gas emissions of coal. The high costs of building clean coal technology (such as flue gas desulphurization) will induce a continued drift away from reliance on British coal.

Thus, the decline in the British coal industry seems irreversible. It is the result of fundamental economic and environmental pressures, rather than of the arbitrary decisions of politicians.

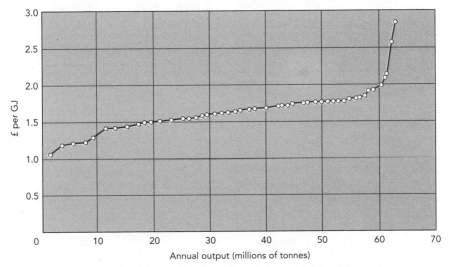

Source: House of Commons Trade and Industry Select Committee, *Report on Coal Industry*, HMSO (1993).

Capital

CAPITAL is a produced factor of production and hence it is renewable. The nation's capital stock consists of all those produced goods that are used in the production of other goods and services. Factories, machines, tools, computers, roads, bridges, houses, and railroads are but a few of the many examples.

The pure return on capital

To calculate the income going to capital, which we call the *return on capital*, we take the receipts from the sale of the output that the capital helps to make and subtract all variable costs of production. This gives us the **gross return on capital**.[5] It is convenient to divide this gross return into four components using concepts defined in Chapter 10 (see pp. 187–88).

1. *Depreciation* is an allowance for the decrease in the value of a capital good over time resulting from its use in production and its obsolescence. Most theories take depreciation to occur at a constant rate, independent of use.

2. The *pure return on capital* is the amount that capital could earn in a riskless investment in equilibrium. When expressed as a return per £1 worth of capital invested, the result is called the **pure rate of interest**.

3. The *risk premium* compensates the owners for the actual risks of the enterprise.

4. *Pure* or *economic profit* is the residual after all other deductions have been made from the gross return. It may be positive, negative, or zero.

The *gross return* on capital is the sum of these four items. The *net return* is the sum of the last three—i.e. the gross return minus depreciation.

In a competitive economy, positive and negative pure profits are a signal that resources should be reallocated, because earnings exceed opportunity costs in some lines of production and fall short of costs elsewhere. Economic profits are thus a product of disequilibrium.

To study the return to capital in its simplest form, we consider an economy that is in equilibrium with respect to the allocation of existing factors of production among their possible uses. Thus, economic profits are zero in every productive activity. This does not mean that the owners of capital get nothing; it means only that the gross return to capital does not include an element signalling the need to reallocate resources. The *equilibrium* net return on capital is composed of components 2 and 3 minus 1.

To simplify things further at the outset, we deal with a world of perfect certainty: everyone knows what the return to an existing new unit of capital will be in any of its possible uses. Since there is no risk, the gross return to capital does not include a risk premium.

We have now simplified to the point where the net return to capital is all pure return (item 2 on the above list), while the gross return is pure return plus depreciation (items 1 and 2). Our study is directed at understanding what determines this pure return on capital.

Do we now have a case that is too unrealistic to be interesting? The answer is No. All we have done is to focus on the pure return to capital. This is the return that varies from time to time and from place to place under the influences of economic forces. Risk and disequilibrium differentials are merely additions to that pure return.[6]

Implications of durability

Next we must consider an important complication that arises because factors of production are durable—a machine lasts for years, a labourer for a lifetime, and land more or less for ever. *It is convenient to think of a factor's lifetime as being divided into the shorter periods that we refer to as production periods, or rental periods.* The present time is the current period. Future time is one, two, three, and so on, periods hence.

The durability of factors makes it necessary to distinguish between the factor itself and the flow of services that it provides in a given production period. We can, for example, rent the use of a piece of land for some period of time, or we can buy the land outright. This distinction is just a particular instance of the general distinction between flows and stocks that we first encountered in Chapter 2 (p. 31).

Although what follows applies to any durable factor, applications to capital are of most importance, so we limit the discussion to capital. Box 20.2 discusses some of these issues as they apply to labour.

If a firm hires the use of a piece of capital equipment for some period of time—for example, one lorry for one month—it pays a price for the privilege of using that piece of capital equipment. If the firm buys the lorry outright, it pays a different (and higher) price for the purchase. Consider in turn each of these prices.

[5] This simplified example assumes that capital is the only fixed factor of production.

[6] We are implicitly assuming a constant price level. Under inflationary conditions, we need to distinguish the nominal return on capital, where everything is measured in nominal monetary units, from the real return, where nominal values are deflated by a price index. This distinction is considered in detail in Chapter 4.

BOX 20.2

The rental and purchase price of labour

If you wish to farm a piece of land, you can buy it yourself, or you can rent it for a specific period of time. If you want to set up a small business, you can buy your office and equipment, or you can rent them. The same is true for all capital and all land; a firm often has the option of either buying or renting.

Exactly the same would be true for labour if we lived in a slave society. You could buy a slave to be your assistant, or you could rent the services either of someone else's slave or of a free person. Fortunately, slavery is illegal throughout most of today's world. As a result, the labour markets that we know deal only in the services of labour; we do not go to a labour market to buy a worker, only to hire his or her services.

You can, however, buy the services of a labourer for a long period of time. In professional sports, multi-year contracts are common, and 10-year contracts are not unknown. The late Herbert von Karajan was made conductor for life of the Berlin Philharmonic Orchestra. Publishers sometimes tie up their authors in multi-book contracts, and movie and television production firms often sign up their actors on long-term contracts. In all cases of such *personal services contracts,* the person is not a slave, and his or her personal rights and liberties are protected by law. The purchaser of the long-term contract is none the less buying ownership of the factor's services for an extended period of time. The price of the contract will reflect the person's expected earnings over the contract's lifetime. If the contract is transferable, the owner can sell these services for a lump sum or rent them out for some period. As with land and capital goods, the price paid for this *stock* of labour services depends on the expected rental prices over the contract period.

RENTAL PRICE

The *rental price of capital* is the amount that a firm pays to obtain the services of a capital good for a given period of time. The rental price of one week's use of a piece of capital is analogous to the weekly wage rate that is the price of hiring the services of labour.

Just as a profit-maximizing firm operating in competitive markets continues to hire labour until its marginal revenue product (MRP) equals its wage, so will the firm go on hiring capital until its MRP equals its rental price, which we call R. Since in a competitive market all firms will face the same rental price, all firms that are in equilibrium will have the same MRP of capital.

A capital good may also be used by the firm that owns it. In this case the firm does not pay out any rental fee. However, the rental price is the amount that the firm could charge if it leased its capital to another firm. It is thus the *opportunity cost* to the firm of using the capital good itself. This rental price is the *implicit* price that reflects the value to the firm of the services of its own capital that it uses during the current production period.

Whether the firm pays the rental price explicitly or calculates it as an implicit cost of using its own capital, the profit-maximizing firm equates the rental price of a capital good over the current production period to its marginal revenue product.

PURCHASE PRICE

The price that a firm pays to buy a capital good is called the *purchase price of capital.* When a firm buys a capital good outright, it obtains the use of the good's services over the whole of that good's lifetime. What the capital good will contribute to the firm is a flow that is equal to the expected marginal revenue product of the good's services over the good's lifetime. The price that the firm is willing to pay is, naturally enough, related to the total value that it places now on this stream of *expected* receipts over future time periods.

The term 'expected' emphasizes that the firm is usually uncertain about the prices at which it will be able to sell its outputs in the future. For the sake of simplicity, we assume that the firm knows the future MRPs.

Present value of future returns

Consider the stream of future income that is provided by a capital good. How much is that stream worth *now*? How much would someone be willing to pay now to buy the right to receive that flow of future payments? The answer is called the good's *present value.* In general, **present value (PV)** refers to the value *now* of one or more payments to be received *in the future*.

PRESENT VALUE OF A SINGLE FUTURE PAYMENT

One period hence To learn how to find the present value, we start with the simplest possible case. How much would a firm be prepared to pay *now* to purchase a capital good that will produce a single marginal physical product valued at £100 in one year's time, after which time the good will be useless? One way to answer this question is to discover how much the firm would have to lend out in order to have £100 a year from now. Suppose for the moment that the interest rate is 5 per cent, which means that £1.00 invested today will be worth £1.05 in one year's time.[7]

If we use *PV* to stand for this unknown amount, we can write $PV(1.05) = £100$. (The left-hand side of this equation means *PV* multiplied by 1.05.) Thus, $PV = £100/1.05 = £95.24$. This tells us that the present value of £100, receivable in one year's time, is £95.24 when the interest rate is 5 per cent. Anyone who lends out £95.24 for one year at 5 per cent interest will get back £95.24 plus £4.76 in interest, which makes £100 in total. When we calculate this present value, the interest rate is used to *discount* (i.e. reduce to its present value) the £100 to be received one year hence. The maximum price that a firm would be willing to pay for this capital good is £95.24 (assuming that the interest rate relevant to the firm is 5 per cent).

To see why, let us start by assuming that firms are offered the capital good at some other price. Say that the good is offered at £98. If, instead of paying this amount for the capital good, a firm lends its £98 out at 5 per cent interest, it would have at the end of one year more than the £100 that the capital good will produce. (At 5 per cent interest, £98 yields £4.90 in interest, which, together with the principal, makes £102.90.) Clearly, no profit-maximizing firm would pay £98—or, by the same reasoning, any sum in excess of £95.24—for the capital good. It could do better by using its funds in other ways.

Now say that the good is offered for sale at £90. A firm could borrow £90 to buy the capital good and would pay £4.50 in interest on its loan. At the end of the year, the good yields £100. When this is used to repay the £90 loan and the £4.50 in interest, £5.50 is left as profit to the firm. Clearly, it would be worth while for a profit-maximizing firm to buy the good at a price of £90 or, by the same argument, at any price less than £95.24.

The actual present value that we have calculated depended on our assuming that the interest rate is 5 per cent. What if the interest rate is 7 per cent? At that interest rate, the present value of the £100 receivable in one year's time would be £100/1.07 = £93.46.

These examples are easy to generalize. In both cases we have found the present value by dividing the sum that is receivable in the future by 1 plus the rate of interest.[8] In general, the present value of £R one year hence at an interest rate of *i* per year is

$$PV = \frac{R}{(1 + i)}. \qquad (1)$$

Several periods hence   Now we know how to calculate the present value of a single sum that is receivable one year hence. The next step is to ask what would happen if the sum were receivable at a later date. What, for example, is the present value of £100 to be received *two* years hence when the interest rate is 5 per cent? This is £100/(1.05)(1.05) = £90.70. We can check this by seeing what would happen if £90.70 were lent out for two years. In the first year the loan would earn an interest of (0.05)(£90.70) = £4.54, and hence after one year the firm would receive £95.24. In the second year the interest would be earned on this entire amount; interest earned in the second year would equal (0.05)(£95.24) = £4.76. Hence, in two years the firm would have £100. (The payment of interest in the second year on the interest income earned in the first year is known as *compound interest*.)

In general, the present value of £R after *t* years at *i* per cent is

$$PV = \frac{R}{(1 + i)^t}. \qquad (2)$$

All that this formula does is discount the sum, *R*, by the interest rate, *i*, repeatedly, once for each of the *t* periods that must pass until the sum becomes available. If we look at the formula, we see that the higher *i* or *t* is, the higher is the whole term $(1 + i)^t$. This term, however, appears in the denominator, so *PV* is *negatively* related to both *i* and *t*.

The formula $PV = R/(1 + i)^t$ shows that the present value of a given sum payable in the future will be smaller the more distant the payment date and the higher the rate of interest.

PRESENT VALUE OF A STREAM OF FUTURE PAYMENTS

Now consider the present value of a stream of receipts that continues indefinitely, as might the *MRP* of a very long-lived piece of capital. At first glance that *PV* might seem very high, because the total amount received grows without reaching any limit as time passes. The previous section suggests, however, that people will not value the far-distant money payments very highly.

To find the *PV* of £100 a year, payable for ever, we ask: how much would you have to invest now, at an interest rate of *i* per cent per year, to obtain £100 each year? This is simply $iPV = £100$, where *i* is the interest rate and *PV* the sum required. Dividing through by *i* shows the present value of the stream of £100 a year for ever:

$$PV = \frac{£100}{i}.$$

---

[7] The analysis in the rest of this chapter assumes *annual* compounding of interest.

[8] Notice that in this type of formula the interest rate, *i*, is expressed as a decimal fraction; for example, 7 per cent is expressed as 0.07, so $(1 + i)$ equals 1.07.

BOX 20.3

The future value of a present sum

In the text, we have concentrated on the present value of amounts to be received in the future. We can, however, turn the question around and ask: what is the future value of an amount of money that is available in the present?

Assume that you have £100 available to you today. What will that sum be worth next year? If you lend it out at 5 per cent, you will have £105 in one year. Letting *PV* stand for the sum you have now and *FV* for the value of the sum in the future, we have *FV* = *PV*(1.05) in this case. Writing the interest rate as we have in the text, we get

$$FV = PV(1 + i).$$

If we divide through by (1 + *i*), we get equation (1) in the text.

Next, if we let the sum build up by reinvesting the interest each year, we get

$$FV = PV(1 + i)^t.$$

If we divide both sides by (1 + *i*)^t, we get equation (2) in the text.

This tells us that what we did in the text is reversible. If we have an amount of money today, we can figure out what it will be worth if it is invested at compounded interest for some number of future periods. Similarly, if we are going to have some amount of money at some future date, we can figure out how much we would need to invest today to get that amount at the specified date in the future.

Our argument tells us that the two sums, *PV* and *FV*, are linked by the compound interest expression (1 + *i*)^t. To go from the present to the future, we *multiply PV* by the interest expression, and to go from the future to the present we *divide FV* by the interest expression.

The rule of 72 that we first introduced in Chapter 1 (see p. 19) is a convenient way of going from *PV* to *FV* by finding out how long it takes for *FV* to become twice the size of *PV* at any given interest rate. According to that rule, the time it takes for *FV* to become twice *PV* is given approximately by 72/100*i*. So, for example, if *i* is 0.1 (an interest rate of 10 per cent), any present sum doubles in value in 72/10 = 7.2 years.

For example, if the interest rate is 10 per cent, the present value would be £1,000. This merely says that £1,000 invested at 10 per cent yields £100 per year, for ever. Notice that, as in the previous sections, *PV* is negatively related to the rate of interest: the higher the interest rate, the less is the present value of the stream of future payments.

In the text, we have concentrated on finding the present value of amounts available in the future. Box 20.3 reverses the process and discusses the future value of sums available in the present.

CONCLUSIONS

From the foregoing discussion, we can put together the following important propositions about the rental and purchase prices of capital.

1. The rental price of capital paid in each period is the flow of net receipts that the capital good is expected to produce during that period, that is, the marginal revenue product of the capital good.

2. The maximum purchase price that a firm would pay for a capital good is the discounted present value of the flow of net receipts, that is rental values, that the good is expected to produce over its lifetime.

3. The maximum purchase price that a firm would pay for

a capital good is positively associated with its rental price and negatively associated with both the interest rate and the amount of time that the owner must wait for payments to accrue.

Equilibrium of the firm

When putting a present value on future income flows, each firm will discount them at a rate that reflects its own opportunity cost of capital, often called its *internal rate of discount*. With perfect capital markets in which the firm can borrow all that it needs, the internal rate of discount will equal the market rate of interest (suitably adjusted for risk in each case). The evidence suggests, however, that most firms do not face perfect capital markets and have internal rates of return that exceed market rates. They thus have internal rates of discount that exceed the relevant market rate of interest. The general points made in the text are not affected by this complication, as long as *i* is interpreted in each case to mean the 'appropriate rate of discount'. In what follows we assume, for simplicity, that firms face perfect capital markets so that the internal rate of discount is equal to the market rate of interest.

In adjusting to market forces, an individual firm faces a given interest rate and a given purchase price of capital goods. The firm can vary the quantity of capital that it employs, and, as a result, the marginal revenue product of its capital varies. The law of diminishing returns tells us that the more capital the firm uses, the lower is its *MRP*.

THE DECISION TO PURCHASE CAPITAL

Consider a firm deciding whether or not to add to its capital stock and facing an interest rate of 10 per cent at which it can borrow (and lend) money. The first thing the firm needs to do is to estimate the expected marginal revenue product of the new piece of capital over its lifetime. Then it discounts this at the appropriate rate, 10 per cent in this example, to find the present value of that stream of receipts the machine will create.[9] Let us say it is £5,000.

The present value, by its construction, tells us how much any flow of future receipts is worth now. If the firm can buy the machine for less than its *PV*, this is a good buy. If it must pay more, the machine is not worth its price.

It is always worth while for a firm to buy another unit of capital whenever the present value of the stream of future *MRP*s that the capital provides exceeds its purchase price.

THE SIZE OF THE FIRM'S CAPITAL STOCK

Since the *MRP* declines as the firm's capital stock rises, the firm will eventually reach an equilibrium with respect to the size of its capital stock. The firm will go on adding to its capital until the *present value* of the flow of *MRP*s conferred by the last unit added is equal to the purchase price of that unit.

The equilibrium capital stock of the firm is such that the present value of the stream of net income that is provided by the marginal unit of capital is equal to its purchase price.

Now let the firm be in equilibrium with respect to its capital stock and ask what would lead the firm to wish to increase that stock. Given the price of the machines, anything that increases the present value of the flow of income that the machines produce will have that effect. Two things will do this job. First, the *MRP*s of the capital may rise. That would happen, for example, if technological changes make capital more productive so that each unit produces more than before. (This possibility is dealt with later in the chapter.) Second, the interest rate may fall, causing an increase in the present value of any given stream of future *MRP*s. For example, suppose that next year's *MRP* is £1,000. This has a *PV* of £909.09 when the interest rate is 10 per cent and £952.38 when the interest rate falls to 5 per cent.

So when the interest rate falls, the firm will wish to add to its capital stock. It will go on doing so until the decline in the *MRP*s of successive additions to its capital stock, according to the law of diminishing returns, reduces the

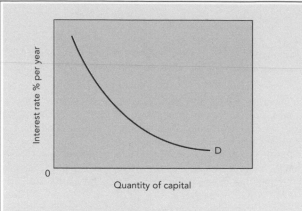

Figure 20.2   The firm's demand for capital

The lower the rate of interest, the larger is the firm's desired capital stock. A firm will go on adding to its capital stock until the discounted present value of the stream of marginal revenue products equals the cost of a unit of capital. The lower the interest rate, the higher is the present value of any given stream of marginal revenue products, and hence the more capital the firm will wish to use.

present value of the *MRP*, at the new lower rate of interest, to the purchase price of the capital.

The size of a firm's desired capital stock increases when the rate of interest falls, and it decreases when the rate of interest rises.

This relationship is shown in Figure 20.2. It can be considered as the firm's demand curve for capital plotted against the interest rate. It shows how the desired stock of capital varies with the interest rate. (It is sometimes called the *marginal efficiency of capital curve*.)

Equilibrium for the whole economy

The term **capital stock** refers to some aggregate amount of capital. The *firm's capital stock* has an *MRP*, showing the net increase in the firm's revenue when another unit of capital is added to its existing capital stock. The *economy's capital*

[9] Suppose that the machine has an *MRP* of £1,000 each period. First, suppose the machine only lasts this period. The present value is then £1,000. Next, suppose it lasts two periods. The *PV* is then £1,000 + £1,000/1.10 = £1,909.09. If it lasts three periods, the *PV* is £1,000 + £1,000/1.10 + £1,000/(1.10)² = £2,735.53, and so on. Each additional period that it lasts produces an *MRP* of £1,000, but at a more and more distant date, so that the *present value* of that period's revenue gets smaller due to more heavy discounting. The details of the calculation do not need to concern us. We only need to know that such a present value can be calculated.

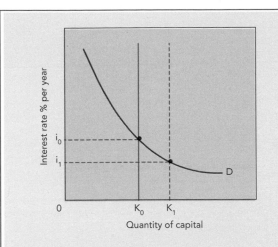

Figure 20.3 The equilibrium interest rate

In the short run the interest rate fluctuates to equate the demand and supply of capital; in the long run the interest rate falls, *ceteris paribus*, as more capital is accumulated. The economy's desired capital stock is negatively related to the interest rate, as shown by the curve D. In the short run the capital stock is given. When the stock is K_0 the equilibrium interest rate is i_0, because above that rate people will not want to hold all the available capital and below it people will want to borrow and add to capital. In the long run, as the capital stock grows to K_1, the equilibrium interest rate falls to i_1.

stock also has a marginal revenue product; this is the addition to total national output (GDP) that is caused by adding another unit of capital to the economy's total stock. This capital stock also has an average product, which is total output divided by the total capital stock (i.e. the amount of output per unit of capital).

The same analysis that we used for one firm in the previous section applies to the whole economy. The lower the rate of interest, the higher is the desired stock of capital that all firms will wish to hold. Such a curve is shown as the economy's demand curve in Figure 20.3.

SHORT-RUN EQUILIBRIUM

In the short run the economy's capital stock is given, but for the economy as a whole, the interest rate is variable. Whereas the firm reaches equilibrium by altering its capital stock, the whole economy reaches equilibrium through variations in the interest rate.

For the economy as a whole, the condition that the present value of the *MRP*s should equal the price of capital goods determines the equilibrium interest rate.

Let us see how this comes about. If the price of capital is less than the present value of its stream of future *MRP*s, it would be worth while for all firms to borrow money to invest in capital. For the economy as a whole, however, the stock of capital cannot change quickly, so the effect of this demand for borrowing would be to push up the interest rate until the present value of the *MRP*s equals the price of a unit of capital goods. Conversely, if the price of capital is above its present value, no one would wish to borrow money to invest in capital, and the rate of interest would fall. This is illustrated in Figure 20.3.

ACCUMULATION OF CAPITAL IN THE LONG RUN

In an economy with positive saving, more capital is accumulated over time and the stock of capital grows slowly. As this happens, the *MRP* falls. This will cause the equilibrium interest rate to fall over time, as is also shown in Figure 20.3.

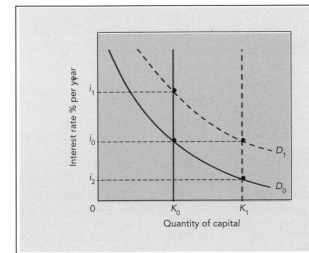

Figure 20.4 The effect of changing technology and capital stock

Increases in technological knowledge and the capital stock have opposite effects on the equilibrium interest rate. The original capital stock is K_0, and the original state of technology gives rise to a relation between the desired capital stock and the interest rate D_0. Thus, the equilibrium interest rate is i_0. Technological improvements shift the desired capital stock curve to D_1 and, with a constant stock of capital, raise the interest rate to i_1. Suppose that in addition the capital stock increases to K_1. If the curve had remained at D_0, the equilibrium interest rate would have fallen to i_2. In the figure, the two effects exactly offset each other, and i remains unchanged at i_0, where K_1 and D_1 intersect.

BOX 20.4

Questions about capital and investment

Is capital itself either a villain or a dispensable drone in the productive process?

None but the most extreme back-to-nature advocates would answer Yes to either of these suggestions. A primitive society in which there are no capital goods—not a spear, a lever, a washing tub, or even a stone axe—is almost impossible to imagine.

Is a charge for the use of capital necessary?

Early communist societies thought not. Such charges were officially barred during the early years after the Russian Revolution of 1917. The trouble with doing this, however, is that capital is scarce; all producers would like to have more of it than they now have. If it does not have a price, how is the available supply to be allocated among the virtually limitless demands for it? Of course the state could allocate it. But how? Any state that is interested in maximizing production will want to allocate its scarce capital to its most productive uses. For this reason, virtually all communist states soon came to assign a price to capital. They allowed firms to use more of it only if the capital would earn enough to cover its costs. Furthermore, the planners in these societies worried about setting the right price of capital. The answer to this question is therefore Yes.

Does capital need to be in private hands so that the price of capital becomes an income for its private owners?

This time the answer is clearly No. In many socialist countries, capital is owned by the state, and the payments made for its use go to the state rather than to private 'capitalists'. People have differing views on the advantages of private versus public ownership of the 'means of production' (the term often used in socialist and communist literature to describe capital), but either arrangement is possible.

Capital is indispensable, and its efficient use requires that it be priced. When capital is privately owned, its price becomes the income of its owners; when it is publicly owned, its price goes to the state.

Notice that, if nationalized industries raise their capital by selling bonds to the public, much of the return on capital goes to private bond-holders, even though the capital is owned by the state.

CHANGING TECHNOLOGY IN THE VERY LONG RUN

In the very long run, technology changes. As a result, the capital stock becomes more productive as the old, obsolete capital is replaced by newer, more efficient capital. This shifts the *MRP* curve outward, which in turn tends to increase the equilibrium interest rate associated with any particular size of the capital stock. This, of course, is also the equilibrium return on capital. However, the accumulation of capital moves the economy downward to the right along any given *MRP* curve, and that tends to lower the return on capital associated with any one *MRP* curve. The net effect on the return on capital of both of these changes may be to raise it, to lower it, or to leave it unchanged, as shown in Figure 20.4. The very-long-run effects of changing technology, combined with a growing capital stock, are studied further in Chapter 33.

So we see that the income going to capital is the pure rate of return (multiplied by the amount of capital in use), plus a risk premium, plus any pure profits or minus any pure losses. The pure return serves to allocate capital to its most productive uses. All uses that yield more than the pure rate of return (plus any necessary risk premium) will be ex-

ploited; all uses that earn less than the pure rate will not be taken up. Box 20.4 deals with some broader issues that are often raised about capital and its owners (who are often called capitalists).

Summary

1 The socially optimal rate of exploitation for a completely non-renewable resource occurs when its price rises at a rate that is equal to the rate of interest. This is also the rate that will be established by a profit-maximizing, competitive industry.

2 Resources for which the demand is highly elastic will have a high rate of exploitation in the near future and a fairly rapid fall-off over time. Resources for which the demand is highly inelastic will have a lower rate of exploitation in the near future and a smaller fall-off over time.

3 Rising prices act as a conservation device by rationing the consumption over time according to people's preferences. As prices rise, conservation, discovery of new sources of supply, and innovation to reduce demand are all encouraged.

4 The price system can fail to produce optimal results if (*a*) people lack the necessary knowledge, (*b*) property rights are inadequate to protect supplies left for future use by their owners, or (*c*) the social rate of discount differs significantly from the market rate.

5 Controlling the price of a non-renewable resource at a constant level speeds up the rate of exploitation and removes the price incentives to react to the growing scarcity.

6 Because capital goods are durable, it is necessary to distinguish between the stock of capital goods and the flow of services provided by them, and thus between their purchase price and their rental price. The linkage between them relies on the ability to assign a present value to future returns. The present value of a future payment will be lower when the payment is more distant and the interest rate is higher.

7 The rental price of capital in each period equals its marginal revenue product in that period. It is the amount that is paid to obtain the flow of services that a capital provides for a given period. The purchase price is the amount that is paid to acquire ownership of the capital, and in equilibrium it is equal to the present value of the future net income stream generated by the capital. This is the present value of capital's future stream of marginal revenue products.

8 An individual firm will invest in capital goods as long as the present value of the stream of future net incomes that are provided by another unit of capital exceeds its purchase price. For a single firm and for the economy as a whole, the size of the total capital stock demanded varies negatively with the rate of interest.

Topics for review

- Hotelling's rule
- The role of rising prices of non-renewable resources
- Rental price and purchase price of capital
- Present value
- The interest rate and the capital stock

❧ CHAPTER 21

Distribution theory in action

IN this chapter, we consider the explanatory power of the theory of factor pricing, or distribution theory, as it is variously called. We start by restating the basic outlines of the theory. We then go on to outline the impressive evidence, first, that market conditions do strongly influence factor prices and, second, that factor prices do influence the allocation of factors among various possible alternative uses. In the last part of the chapter we illustrate the power of the theory by applying it to an important issue concerning wage differentials among advanced and developing nations and within advanced nations themselves.

The theory restated

THE previous chapters developed the neoclassical theory of distribution in several contexts, repeating what is basically the same analysis in applications to land, labour, and capital. This repetition helps to develop a 'feel' for the workings of the price system that is very important to the economist. It has the disadvantage, however, of making the theory appear to be more complex than it actually is. In fact, the whole of distribution theory depends on a very few basic hypotheses about the behaviour of factor owners and firms. Before going on, it will be useful to repeat its underlying structure.

The neoclassical theory of distribution maintains that factor prices can be explained by supply and demand. The theory of factor supply is based on the assumption that factors will move among occupations, industries, and places in search of the highest net advantage, taking both monetary and non-monetary rewards into account, until the net advantages in all possible uses are equalized. Because there are impediments to the mobility of factors, there may be lags in their response to changes in prices. The elasticity of supply will depend on what factor is being discussed and what time-horizon is being considered.

The demand side of the neoclassical theory is based on profit maximization and is called the *marginal productivity theory* (of factor demand). The demand for a factor is a derived demand. It depends for its existence on the demand for the product made by the factor. The elasticity of an industry's demand curve for a factor is higher in the long run than in the short run, since more substitution is possible the longer the time considered. Also, as we saw in Chapter 5, the demand for any product made by the factor will itself be more elastic in the long run than in the short run—thus making the derived demand for the factors that it uses correspondingly more elastic.

In equilibrium, *all* profit-making firms will employ *all* variable factors up to the point at which the marginal unit of each type of factor adds as much to revenue as to costs. All profit-maximizing firms that are price-takers in factor markets will employ factors up to the point at which the price paid for the last unit of each factor equals the increase in revenue resulting from the sale of the additional output produced when that unit is employed. For firms selling goods in competitive markets, the increase in revenue is the marginal physical product *times* the price; for firms facing negatively sloped demand curves for their products, the increase in revenue is marginal physical product *times* marginal revenue.

The relations described in the above paragraphs all hold in equilibrium. They apply to all firms that succeed in maximizing their profits and can be stated in two equivalent ways. First, the firm that is not equating the marginal revenue product of each of its factors with that factor's price is not maximizing its profits. Second, a firm that is maximizing its profits is necessarily equating each factor's price to its marginal revenue product, whether or not it knows it is doing so. The theory thus stands or falls with the theory of profit maximization. It is merely an implication of profit maximization, and the only reason for spelling it out in detail is that this helps us to develop interesting and useful insights into the effects of various changes in the economy on the markets for factors of production.

When one thinks of all the heated arguments over the neoclassical theory of distribution, and of all the passionate denunciations and defences that it has occasioned over more than a century, it is surprising to observe how uncontroversial most of its predictions seem today. These propositions, which are supported by much evidence, do not on the surface seem the sort that would create heated debate. They are important since they frequently apply to practical issues of policy. Box 21.1 deals with some misconceptions about the theory that are commonly found in debate about its relevance and validity. The last item in the box may have accounted for the feeling that the theory aroused among past supporters and critics: some supporters argued that distributing income according to marginal product created a just distribution of income. There may also have been a feeling, no longer a real worry today, that there was something highly suspect, possibly demeaning, about reducing

BOX 21.1

Some fallacious criticisms of marginal productivity theory

This box deals with four common misconceptions, all of which have been drawn from real sources.

1. *The theory assumes perfect competition in all markets (which is sometimes called 'pluperfect competition').* This is incorrect. The relationship between the marginal physical product and the marginal revenue product will be altered if the degree of competition alters, but the marginal revenue product will be equated with the price of a factor in perfect competition, imperfect competition, oligopoly, and monopoly, provided only that firms are price-takers in factor markets.

2. *The theory assumes that the amount and the value of the marginal product of a factor are known to the firm.* The theory assumes no such thing! Critics argue that firms will not pay factors the value of their marginal product because firms will usually have no idea what that marginal product is. It has already been pointed out, however, that payment according to marginal revenue product occurs *automatically* whenever firms are maximizing profits. It does not matter *how* firms succeed in doing this—by guess, luck, skill, or calculating marginal quantities. The theory does not purport to describe *how* firms calculate; it merely predicts how they will react to various situations, on the assumption that they are maximizers. The marginal productivity curve is a tool of analysis used by economists; it is not necessarily a tool for decision-taking by firms.

3. *The theory is inhuman because it treats labour in the same way as it treats an acre of land or a wagonload of fertilizer.* One must be careful to distinguish one's emotional reaction to a procedure that treats human and non-human factors alike from one's evaluation of it in terms of positive economics. Those who accept this criticism must explain carefully why separate theories of the pricing of human and non-human factors are needed. Marginal productivity theory is only a theory of the *demand* for a factor. It predicts that firms' desired purchases of labour (and all other factors) depend on the price of the factor in question, the technical conditions of production, and the demand for the product made by labour. No evidence has yet been gathered to indicate that it is necessary to have separate theories of the *demand* for human and non-human factors of production. *Supply* conditions will differ between human and non-human factors, but these differences are accommodated within the theory. Indeed, one of the important insights of the theory of net advantage is that non-monetary considerations are more important in allocating labour than other factors. Non-monetary considerations do sometimes matter, even with land and capital. For instance, concern over the former racial policies of the South African government led some firms to reduce their investments in that country, even where they were highly profitable. Now that these policies have ended, trade and investment has returned to normal.

4. *The theory purports to demonstrate that when all factors are paid according to their marginal products, the resulting distribution of income will be a just distribution.* Some supporters of the theory of marginal productivity have argued that the theory describes an *equitable* distribution of income. It is just, they assert, that factors be rewarded according to the values of their contributions to the national product. Critics of the low levels of wages generally prevailing in the nineteenth century, and even in some sectors today, reacted with passion against a theory that claimed to provide moral justification for such wages.

The normative question of what constitutes a just distribution of income cannot be decided on the basis of economic analysis alone. It is, however, worth getting the facts straight. According to marginal productivity theory, each labourer (or each unit of any other factor) does *not* receive the value of what he or she personally contributes to production. Instead, each labourer receives the value of what the last labourer employed would add to production *if all other factors of production were held constant.* Whatever the justice of the matter, it is not correct to say that each factor receives the value of *its own* contribution to production. Indeed, where many factors co-operate in production, it is generally impossible to divide up the *total production* into amounts contributed by each.

human behaviour to theories that can be expressed in impersonal mathematics. One of the present authors recalls hearing, when he was a graduate student, a paper denouncing marginal productivity theory for reducing glorious and diverse human behaviour to two mere curves: the labour supply curve and the marginal revenue curve. In the text we deal with more serious issues.

Do factor markets allocate resources?

PEOPLE sometimes advocate government intervention to determine factor prices such as wages in specific jobs, industries, or parts of the country. When critics reply that the intervention will prevent the price mechanism from satisfactorily allocating resources, the advocates reply that the price system is ineffective in doing that job anyway. This debate involves a basic criticism that factor markets do not work as described by the theory. To make that case, one of two allegations must be established: *either* the theory does not explain relative factor earnings, *or* factors do not move in response to relative earnings. Conversely, if the theory is to stand up to this criticism, *both* of these allegations must be shown to be substantially incorrect. We shall consider them in turn.

Do market conditions determine factor prices?

FACTORS OTHER THAN LABOUR

Most non-human factors are sold on competitive markets. The overwhelming preponderance of evidence supports the hypothesis that changes in the earnings of these factors are associated with changes in market conditions. Consider just a few examples.

Raw materials   The prices of copper, tin, rubber, and hundreds of other basic commodities fluctuate daily in response to changes in their demand and supply. Current shortages of certain key raw materials are almost always signalled by price increases. These prices also show a strong cyclical component. They rise on the upswing of the trade cycle, when their (derived) demand rises, and fall on the downswing, when their (derived) demand falls.

The theory of factor pricing in competitive markets successfully explains raw material prices and the incomes earned by their producers.

Of course, if monopoly elements arise, the theories of factor pricing under monopoly or monopsony need to be applied. OPEC's escalation of prices in the 1970s and early 1980s, for example, led to a large rise in the prices of the petroleum-based inputs in many production processes and to increases in the profits of the owners of oilfields.

Land values   Values of land in the hearts of growing cities rise in response to increasing demand. Often it is even worth while to destroy buildings to convert land to more profitable uses. The London and New York skylines are monuments to the high value of urban land. The increase in the price of land on the periphery of every growing city is another visible example of the workings of the market.

Agricultural land appears at first glance to provide counter-evidence. The classical economists predicted 150 years ago that, as population and the demand for agricultural products grew, the price of the fixed supply of land would rise enormously. The price of agricultural land, however, has *not* skyrocketed throughout the world. Although the demand for agricultural produce did expand in the predicted fashion because of the rise in population, the *productivity* of agricultural land has increased in quite unexpected ways with the invention of the vast range of machines and techniques that characterize modern agriculture. The prediction was falsified, not because the price of agricultural land is not determined by market forces, but because some of the market forces were incorrectly foreseen.

The experience of the European Union's Common Agricultural Policy (CAP) provides another example. This policy has insulated the European market from cheap foreign imports and has held up food prices. As a result, prices of agricultural land in Europe, and the incomes of landowners, have been much higher than prices and incomes for comparable land in such other food-producing countries as Australia and Canada. When Ireland entered the European Union, prices of various types of agricultural land increased by between 100 and 500 per cent, a strong testimony both of the power of the CAP and to the applicability of the theory of derived demand.

Legal right to produce   In many instances, the right to produce is restricted by regulations enforced either by governments or by private organizations. Many governments, faced with agricultural surpluses due to over-generous price supports, restrict output by issuing production quotas. The number of taxis operating in many cities is restricted by the local authorities who issue a fixed number of licences to operate. Also, some products and production processes are controlled by patent.

In such cases, the quota, licence, or patent become factors of production: without them, production is impossible. Whenever the right to produce is saleable, the market value of the right becomes the present value of the monopoly profits that arise from the output restriction. Suppose, for example, that each unit of a good that is produced under quota restriction earns £1,000 of pure profit, i.e. £1,000 of revenue in excess of what it would have to yield to persuade firms to go on producing it. People who obtain a quota to produce a unit of the product can thus make £1,000 per year more than they could by producing in some other industry where freedom of entry and exit forces profits to zero. The quota will thus sell in the open market for the present value of a flow of £1,000 per year, 1,000/i, which for example is £10,000 at a 10 per cent rate of interest.[1] As the demand for the product fluctuates and the supply restriction is held constant, the profits, and hence the present value of the quota, will fluctuate.

Various forms of output restrictions are found throughout the world, and the evidence supports the theory that the market determines their values.

Where output restrictions create monopoly profits, the market value of the instrument that confers the right to produce a unit of output equals the present value of the flow of monopoly profits earned by a unit of output.

LABOUR

When we apply the theory of factor pricing to labour, we encounter two important sets of complications: first, labour markets are a mixture of competitive and non-competitive elements, the proportions of the mixture differing from market to market; second, labour being the human factor of production, non-monetary considerations loom large in its incentive patterns. These complications help to make labour economics one of the most difficult, and interesting, fields of economics.

Nevertheless, we do have a mass of evidence to go on. We do have cases in which a strong union—one able to bargain effectively and to restrict entry of labour into the field—has caused wages to rise well above the competitive level. Unions can and do succeed in raising wages and incomes when they operate in small sections of the whole economy; the high earnings do attract others to enter the occupation or industry; and the privileged position can be maintained only if entry can be effectively restricted. Closed-shop laws are one obvious way of doing this.

Not only can monopoly elements raise incomes above their competitive levels, they can also prevent incomes from falling and reflecting decreases in demand. Of course, if demand disappears more or less overnight (as it did for silent-film stars and carriage-makers), there is nothing any union can do to maintain incomes. But the story may be different if, as is more usual, demand shrinks slowly over a few decades. In this case, unions that are powerful enough virtually to prohibit new entry of labour into the industry can often hold wages up in the face of declining demand. The industry's labour force thus declines, through death and retirement, in spite of the relatively high wage being paid to the employees who remain.

Wages also respond to fluctuations in competitive conditions of demand and supply. Consider some examples. With the advent of the motor car, many skilled carriage-

makers found the demand for their services declining rapidly. Earnings fell, and many craftsmen who were forced to leave the industry found that they had been earning substantial rents for their scarce, but highly specific, skills. When the demand for silent films grew, music-hall stars whose talents did not project on to the flat, flickering screen of the early silent films suffered disastrous cuts in income and sank into oblivion. A similar fate later hit many silent-screen actors whose voices were unsuitable for the 'talkies'. Later still, falling incomes beset many radio personalities who were unable to make the transition to television and had to compete in a greatly reduced market for radio talent.

These variations in factor earnings are caused by changes in market conditions, not by changes in our notions of the intrinsic merit of various activities. To illustrate, ask yourself why, if you have the ability, you can make a lot of money writing copy for a London advertising agency, whereas even if you have great talent you are unlikely to make a lot of money writing books of poetry. This is not because any economic dictator or group of philosophers has decided that advertising is more valuable than poetry, but because there is a large demand for advertising and only a tiny demand for poetry. A full citing of all such evidence would cover many pages, and it would point to the following conclusion.

Earnings of labour do respond to changes in market forces. Some factor markets are competitive and some are monopolistic or monopsonistic, and the evidence is that the theory of competitive, monopolistic, and monopsonistic market behaviour helps to explain factor incomes.

Do factors move in response to changes in factor prices?

In the previous section we saw that earnings do tend to change in response to changes in the conditions of demand and supply. Changes in earnings are signals that attract resources into those lines of production in which more are needed and out of lines in which less are needed. But do changes in factor prices produce the supply responses predicted by the theory?

Land   In the case of land, there is strong evidence that the theory is able to predict the actual course of events quite accurately. Land is transferred from one crop to another in response to changes in the relative profitabilities of the crops. Land on the edge of town is transferred from rural to urban uses as soon as it can earn substantially more as a

---

[1] Where, as we saw in Chapter 20, i is the rate of interest expressed as a decimal fraction; for example, $i = 0.1$ means a 10 per cent rate of interest. In practice, there will be a further discounting of more distant profits because of the risk that government policy will change.

building site than as a corn field (and provided planning permission can be obtained). Although physically immobile, land is constantly transferred among its possible uses as the relative profitabilities of these uses change. Little more needs to be said here; the most casual observation will show the allocative system working with respect to land just as the theory predicts.

Capital   The location of, and products produced by, the nation's factories have changed greatly over the last two centuries. Over a period of, say, fifty years, the change is dramatic; from one year to the next, it is small. Most plant and machinery is relatively specific. Once installed, it will be used for the purpose for which it was designed as long as the variable costs of production can be covered. But if full, long-run opportunity costs are not covered, the capital will not be replaced as it wears out. Investment will take place in other industries instead.

Long-run movements in the allocation of physical capital clearly occur in response to market signals.

The mechanism works as long as there is freedom of entry and exit. Exit is difficult to prevent (other than by government legislation and subsidy), but monopolies and oligopolies, government regulations, and nationalized industries do erect barriers to entry. Where entry is blocked, profits of monopolists or oligopolists do not induce flows of new investment, and therefore such barriers serve no apparent long-run allocative function.

Although the profits that arise from market power do not cause capital to move when entry is blocked in the long run, we cannot be so sure about this in the very long run. These profits may cause other firms to develop competing products and to innovate in other ways so as to attack the firms with market power in a process of what Schumpeter called 'creative destruction' (see p. 244). If so, then monopoly profits do influence the allocation of capital in the very long run.

Labour   Countless studies of labour mobility show that labour moves in response to monetary incentives. High relative wages do attract and hold labour in such unattractive parts of the world as the North Sea oilfields, the Canadian North, Siberia, and the Amazon jungles, while occupations with much leisure and pleasant working conditions pay lower wages, *ceteris paribus*. There is a supply as well as a demand element at work here. Unpleasant but unskilled jobs are often poorly paid because anyone can do them, but, even so, dustmen in the frozen Canadian North are paid more than dustmen in Toronto because otherwise they would not stay in the unattractive climate.

At the risk of grossly oversimplifying a complex situation, the following generalizations seem consistent with the evidence:

1. There exists a fairly mobile component of labour in any group. It tends to consist of the younger and more adaptable members of the group.

2. This mobile group can be attracted from one area, occupation, or industry to another by relatively small changes in economic incentives.

3. Provided that the pattern of demand for resources does not shift too quickly, most of the necessary reallocation can be accomplished by movements of this mobile group. Of course, the same individual need not move over and over again. The group is constantly replaced by new entrants into the labour force.

4. As we go beyond these very mobile persons, we get into ranges of lower and lower mobility until, at the very bottom, we find those who are completely immobile. The most immobile are the old, those with capital sunk in non-marketable assets, the timid, the weak, and those who receive high rents in their present occupation or location. In extreme cases, even the threat of starvation may not be enough to induce movement since some people believe they will starve even if they do move.

Thus, shifts in earnings may create substantial inflows of workers into an expanding occupation, industry, or area and an outflow of workers from a depressed occupation, industry, or area. Over long periods of time, outflows have been observed from depressed areas such as Ireland, the Highlands of Scotland, the former Welsh mining areas, the Appalachian region in the United States, the Maritime Provinces of Canada, southern Italy, and the rural parts of central France. Although *some* out-migration occurs readily, it is difficult for large transfers to take place in short periods of time. When demand falls rapidly, pockets of poverty tend to develop. Workers have been leaving each of the geographical areas mentioned above, but poverty has increased too. The reason is that the rate of exit has been slower than the rate of decline of the economic opportunities in the area. Indeed, the exit itself causes further decline, because when a family migrates all the locally provided goods and services that it once consumed suffer a reduction in demand, leading to a further decline in the demand for labour.

The modern non-market theories of wage determination suggest an additional force. According to these theories, wages reflect the long-term value of labour to the firm but do not fluctuate with every change in labour's short-term value. This leaves employment and unemployment to do much of the short-term equilibrating. Assume, for example, a fairly rapid fall in the demand for labour in area A and a rise in demand in area B. If wages, being responsive to long-term considerations, do not respond quickly, employment will. There will be unemployment in region A and a labour shortage in region B. Labour may then move from A to B not in response to a differential in current wages, but to a differential in the probability of obtaining employment which implies a differential in lifetime earnings expected by people located in the two areas. Indeed, there is some substantial evidence that, at some times and places, differences in the probability of finding a job motivate the movement of labour at least as much as differences in current wage rates.

Factor movements can to a great extent be explained by demand-and-supply theory, using mixtures of competitive and market forces and the assumption that factors do move in response to changes in relative factor prices and expected factor earnings.

HOW FAST?

It is one thing to say that factors move in response to price signals, for which there is much evidence; it is quite another thing to say that they always move fast enough that equilibrium theory is all we need. There is also much evidence that factors' movements are quite sluggish at various times and in various markets. When this happens, there are many more possibilities, many of which come under the heading

---

BOX 21.2

Distribution theory and the macro-distribution of income

Questions of the macro-distribution of income among the main social classes of society—labourers, landlords, and capitalists—were central issues to classical economics. With the development of marginal analysis in the last half of the nineteenth century, emphasis shifted to the determination of factor prices and quantities in millions of individual markets.

The theory that grew out of this development (often called 'marginal productivity theory' after its demand half) offers few general predictions about the macro-distribution of income. It holds that, to discover the effect of some change—say, a tax or a new trade union—on the macro-distribution between wages, profits, and rent, we would need to be able to discover what would happen in each individual market of the economy and then aggregate to find the macro-result. To do this, we would need to know the degree of monopoly and monopsony power exercised in each market, we would need to be able to predict the effect on oligopolists' prices and outputs of changes in their costs, and we would need to have a theory of the outcome of collective bargaining in situations of monopoly and monopsony. We would also need to know how much factor substitution would occur in response to any resulting change in relative factor prices. Finally, we would need a general equilibrium theory linking all these markets together.

In recent years the development of *computable general equilibrium models* has gone a long way towards doing just this! None the less, with our present state of knowledge, marginal productivity theory provides few if any predictions about the effects on macro-distribution of such changes as shifts in total factor supplies, taxes on one factor, and the rise of trade unions.

This conclusion is not necessarily a criticism of the theory. It may well be that relative shares are determined by all the detailed interactions of all the markets in the economy, and that general predictions about the effects of various events on macro-distribution can be obtained only after we have enough knowledge to solve the general equilibrium problem outlined in the previous paragraph. Nor does this conclusion mean that we can never identify forces that will affect the macro-distribution in a pre-dictable way. If some common cause, such as a new employment tax, were to act on the demands for labour in all individual markets, then the average return to all labour, and hence labour's share in total national income, would be significantly affected in predictable ways.

Some economists argue that we should not expect to get further than this. They hold that the great macro-questions on the scale of *labour versus capital* are largely unanswerable. The ability of the traditional theory to deal with micro-questions is none the less a remarkable triumph—although, they admit, it is much less dramatic than would be 'solutions' to the great macro-'puzzles'.

One reason advanced for the view that the great macro-distribution questions are unanswerable is that it makes sense to talk about laws governing macro-distribution only if labour, capital, and land are each relatively homogeneous and are each subject to a common set of influences not operating on the other two factors, whereas in fact (so goes the view) there is likely to be as much difference in demand and supply conditions between two kinds of labour as between one kind of labour and one kind of machine. On the one hand, the micro-distribution of income can be thought of as subject to understandable influences because it deals with innumerable relatively homogeneous factors.

On the other hand, macro-distribution is nothing more than the aggregate of the micro-distributions, and there is no more reason to expect that there should be simple laws governing the macro-distribution among land, labour, and capital than to expect that there should be simple laws governing the macro-distribution between blondes and brunettes.

As we shall see in the next section of the text, however, the theory can successfully account for distributional shares going to quite large groups of labour. When we divide labour into just two groups, skilled and unskilled, we find that the wage differential between these groups varied across countries as the demands and supplies for each type of labour varied.

of what is called 'hysteresis'. For example, the amount of human capital that workers acquire depends, among other things, on the time that they are unemployed. Long bouts of unemployment not only may reduce their accumulated experience but also may create attitudes that lower their future abilities to get work and to command high wages even if they do find employment. It is quite possible for factor markets to work qualitatively in the directions that we have discussed above while in many cases working slowly enough that their behaviour can be regarded as less than satisfactory. Quantitative studies of how well factor markets work are an important research area in modern labour economics. This problem is briefly discussed in Chapter 41, and is discussed in detail in books and courses devoted to labour economics.

The functional distribution of income

The neoclassical theory of distribution concentrates on the pricing of factors in each of the many markets of the economy. The theory has little to say about the determinants of the functional distribution of income among land, labour, and capital. Questions of distribution at the level of aggregation of whole factors are often referred to as questions about *macro-distribution* (as opposed to *micro-distribution*, which refers to such questions as what determines the share of total income going to some small group of labour operating in a single labour market). This issue is briefly discussed in Box 21.2.

International trade and relative wages

IN this section, we show factor-price theory in action by using it to study an important development in international trade and observe how this may have impacted on the differentials between wages for skilled and unskilled workers in both the developed and the developing nations.

Background

International trade in goods and services has grown rapidly ever since the end of the Second World War in 1945. Trade has risen in each decade much faster than incomes have risen. Two important implications are, first, that consumers in all countries have satisfied an increasing proportion of their needs by buying goods made in other countries and, second, that employment in all countries has moved increasingly to export industries and away from those satisfying home demand. In the first post-war decades, most of the new trade in manufactured goods and services took place between the advanced industrial countries, often referred to as 'the North', which may be taken to include mainly the countries of the European Union, North America, Australia, New Zealand, and Japan. At that time, the North exported manufactured goods to the developing world, often called 'the South', which can be taken to include the countries of South America, Asia (except Japan), and Africa. In return, the North imported raw materials, energy products, and semi-finished products from the South.

As time went on, however, the South became a major exporter of manufactured goods to the North. If we consider all the South's non-fuel exports to the North, manufactured goods accounted for only 6 per cent of the total in 1955, 23 per cent in 1970, 45 per cent in 1980, and 71 per cent in 1989![2] The manufactured products exported by the South have been those made mainly with low-skilled labour. In return, the North has progressively reduced its production of goods requiring mainly low-skilled labour and has increasingly concentrated on exporting to the South manufactured products (and a wide range of services) produced with high-skilled labour.

The average citizen in both the North and the South has benefited from these developments. A widening range of goods has become available at falling cost, and both imports and exports have risen steadily. (The reasons why a large and rising volume of trade is beneficial to the average citizen of a country are analysed in detail in Chapter 25.)

An important concern, however, has been the effect of this increase in globalized trade on the unskilled workers who occupy the lower end of the size distribution of income in both the North and the South. Demand and supply analysis of factor markets can shed light on what is

---

[2] Fuel exports, which are mainly oil, come from a few countries that are not major manufacturing exporters. In dealing with the South, it is best to exclude trade in fuel and omit those, mainly Middle Eastern, countries whose exports are heavily specialized in oil.

at issue.[3] In doing this, we simplify by following many current studies of these issues in treating the South as a single unit. For present purposes, it includes all those countries that constituted the less developed world in the mid-1950s and that subsequently became exporters of manufactured goods to the North. This excludes much of Africa, which did not develop sufficiently to take part in this trade. It includes countries, such as the Philippines, that still have relatively low incomes today, and countries, such as Singapore and Taiwan, that have caught up to the living standards in many countries of the European Union. The common characteristic of these countries at the outset of the period under study was that their ratios of unskilled to skilled labour were much higher than was typical in the North.[4]

Trade in manufactures

As a first step in understanding what has happened, we must account for this rapid increase in trade in manufactured goods between the North and the South. The most important causes were as follows.

First, the countries of the North have progressively reduced their trade restrictions that took the form of exchange controls and import tariffs. This process was started soon after the end of the Second World War and continues to this day. (The latest reductions in trade restrictions were negotiated in the so-called Uruguay round, which was concluded in 1994 and which is discussed in more detail in Chapter 26.)

Second, in the immediate post-war period, most developing countries sought to induce domestic growth by protecting the domestic industries that replaced imports. This 'import substitution policy' is no longer regarded as appropriate. It has been replaced in country after country by the view that the best policy is open international trade with domestic growth being created by exports. With this change of view, most of the countries of the South are now on a path of continued reductions of their trade barriers.

Third, transport costs have fallen dramatically with a number of technological improvements in ocean transport.

Fourth, the on-going revolution in communication has allowed parts required for Northern-based assembly plants to be produced anywhere in the world and then transported to the North, arriving where and when they are needed. This requires a degree of worldwide co-ordination that was just not possible 20 or 30 years ago.

Finally, many of the developing nations have invested heavily in education and infrastructure so that they now have labour forces with the minimum education needed to perform modern manufacturing processes as well as the background conditions needed for efficient manufacturing.

THE TYPES OF LABOUR

To understand the directions that trade took once it was opened up, we need to look at labour markets. For simplicity, we can divide labour into three groups: skilled labour (S), which has acquired considerable amounts of human capital, less skilled labour (L), which has the basic skills needed for modern manufacturing—which usually means completion of a reasonable amount of good secondary education, and non-educated labour (N), which means labour that has not acquired the minimum skills needed for employment in modern manufacturing.

Some poor countries that have not invested heavily in education have labour forces that are mainly in the N class. Modern manufacturing industries do not locate in such countries and there is no demand for the services of their N-type labour in manufacturing, except from local producers of products for sale in the domestic market. This is the case in many (but not all) African countries that have low, static, or sometimes falling national incomes. They play no further part in the present story. Much of the rest of the South has a labour force mainly concentrated in the L rather than the S class. The North, in contrast, has abundant supplies of S labour and relatively smaller supplies of L labour.

WAGE DIFFERENTIALS

We can now use demand and supply analysis to study what has happened. First, consider the pre-trade situation. Since overall productivity is lower in the South than in the North, the average level of wages is much lower. However, the South's relatively plentiful L labour had a wage well below the South's average, while its very scarce S labour commanded a well-above-average wage. Thus, the differential between L and S wages was large. In contrast, the wage differential between the S and L groups was less marked in the North because of a larger supply of S labour relative to L labour. Both wages are, however, higher than in the South, because average productivity is higher in the North than in the South. As shown in parts (i) and (ii) of Figure 21.1, demand-and-supply analysis of factor markets predicts

---

[3] Our treatment is based on the analyses of C. Freeman and L. Soete (*Information Technology and Employment*, Brighton, Sussex: SPRU, 1994) and Adrian Wood (*North–South Trade, Employment and Inequality*, Oxford: Clarendon Press, 1994). Even if their estimates of the strength of the forces at work are wrong, there is no disagreement among researchers about the qualitative nature of the predictions. The only major debate is whether the tendencies discussed here are large, as the above writers argue, or small, as many others have argued.

[4] A fuller study of this remarkable period of development, that brings out many of the details that are suppressed here, is given in Chapter 34. Do not forget that at this point our main concern is to use the theory of factor pricing to shed some light on real world events rather than to tell the story of the extraordinary development of many of the nations that were included in the South at the end of World War II.

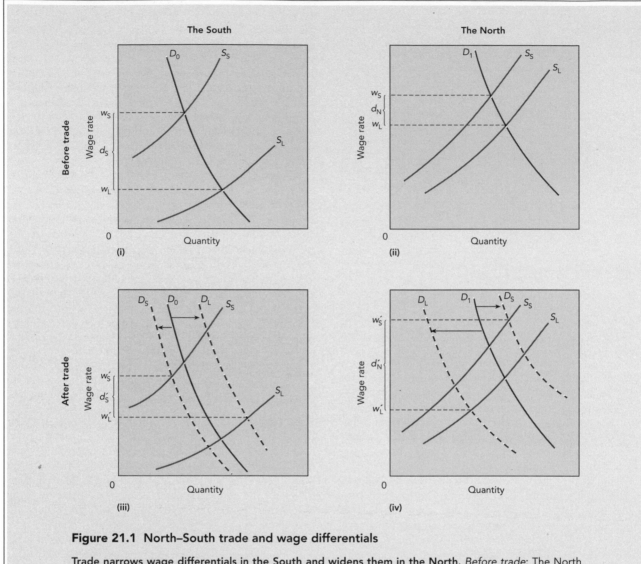

Figure 21.1 North–South trade and wage differentials

Trade narrows wage differentials in the South and widens them in the North. *Before trade*: The North has a larger supply of S labour and a smaller supply of L labour than the South. This makes the differential between L and S wages smaller in the North (shown by d_N) than in the South (shown by d_S). Because productivity is eveywhere higher in the North than the South, both skilled and unskilled wages are higher in the North. (For simplicity, the demand for each type of labour is assumed to be the same, D_0 in the South and D_1 in the North.)

After trade: In the South, the opening of trade in manufactured goods reduces the demand for skilled labour to D_S and increases the demand for unskilled labour to D_L in part (iii), causing the wage differential, shown by d_S', to narrow. In the North, the demand for S labour rises to D_S while the demand for L labour falls to D_L in part (iv). This widens the wage differential, as shown by d_N'.

that the differential between S and L labour will be less in the North than in the South, as indeed was the case before the new trade became important.

DIRECTION OF TRADE FLOWS

Next, we look at the effect of these wage differentials on the direction of the trade flows once trade in manufactured goods was liberalized. In the South, unskilled wages were very low—low enough to compensate for the lower levels of productivity so that goods requiring mainly less skilled labour could be produced at a lower price in the South than in the North. In contrast, the North could make goods requiring S labour cheaper than the South. Although wages for skilled workers were higher in the North than in the South, the higher productivity of that kind of labour meant that products using skilled labour could be produced at a lower price in the North than in the South.

As trade opened up for all the reasons described above, the South expanded its exports of products that required mainly L labour and the North expanded its exports of goods that required mainly S labour. Some consumer's goods that are made mainly with L labour, such as cheap shoes, shirts, and carpets, were made wholly in the South. Components of complex goods assembled in the North were also made in the South wherever a particular component required mainly L labour. (This could not have happened without the vast increase in the ability to co-ordinate complex production activities across the world brought on by the modern revolution in information and communication techniques.) Not only did the countries of the South expand their own industries, but many L-using Northern-based firms moved to the South because the labour they needed was much cheaper there.

CHANGING WAGE DIFFERENTIALS

As already mentioned, this great increase in trade worked to the benefit of the average person in both the North and the South—but it did not work to everyone's benefit. To see why, we must ask what the new trade did to wage differentials in the two areas.

The expansion of the L-using industries in the South raised the demand for L workers relative to the demand for S workers and narrowed the wage differential to the benefit of the mass of L workers. Income inequalities shrank as average incomes rose, as shown in parts (iii) and (iv) of Figure 21.1.

The opposite occurred in the North, where the demand for S labour rose while the demand for L labour fell. Most investigators agree that this is what happened, but there is debate about the magnitude of these shifts. Adrian Wood, of the Science Policy Research Unit (SPRU) in Sussex, estimates that the fall in demand was large enough to have had a major depressing effect on the equilibrium wage of L workers as shown in Figure 21.1.

DIFFERING RESPONSES IN THE EUROPEAN UNION AND THE UNITED STATES

What happened next differed between the United States, and the European Union. In the United States, unions are weak and decentralized while government income support

policies are too small in size and spotty in application to put a significant floor on people's disposable incomes. There, the market was allowed to determine the outcome. Equilibrium was established with more or less full employment of L workers but with low L wages. Because L workers' wages fell to the full extent needed to clear the market, the differential between S and L workers widened dramatically, as shown in part (i) of Figure 21.2.

In the European Union, trade unions are much stronger and were able to resist major declines in L wages. Also, government income support measures are more widespread and more generous than in the United States. These measures put a floor on wages, because if they fall too far people will elect to live on government support. This is to some extent what happened in the European Union. All through the 1980s and 1990s, unemployment remained high, as is shown in part (ii) of Figure 21.2, so that the differential between L and S workers did not widen anything like as much as in the United States

To summarize, the relative supplies of L and S workers in the North and South initially determined different wage differentials. Major reductions in natural and policy-created barriers to trade then opened trade between the North and South. The different wage differentials then determined that the North exported goods that required mainly S workers, while the South exported goods that required mainly L workers. The opening of such trade thus raised the demand for L workers and raised their wages relative to S wages in the South; in contrast, it raised the demand for S workers and hence raised S wages relative to L wages in the North. In the United States, where markets were allowed to clear, these growing discrepancies increased income inequalities. In the European Union, where markets were prevented from clearing, the effect was high unemployment without a major increase in the S/L wage differential.

This is an impressive amount of understanding of one of the most pressing problems facing EU and US policy-makers that can be conveyed by the elementary theory of factor pricing, and it is as far as simple economic analysis can take us.[5]

Conclusion

This concludes our study of the theory of factor pricing. In the first part of this chapter, we reviewed the evidence, first, that factor prices respond to variations in the conditions of demand and supply and, second, that factors move among uses in response to changing differentials in factor prices. In the second part of the chapter, we showed the theory at work in explaining differentials between skilled and unskilled wages in the North and the South, how these have

[5] For a full story we need a little international trade theory, which is given in Part Seven of this book.

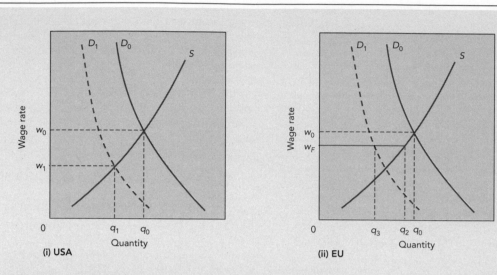

Figure 21.2 Falling wages versus rising unemployment

The decline in demand for less skilled labour causes unemployment in the European Union and low wages in the United States. In each panel the original curves are S and D_0, giving a wage rate of w_0 and employment q_0. The demand for less skilled labour then falls to D_1.
In the United States the market is allowed to clear. Employment and wages fall to q_1 and w_1 but there is no unemployment.
In the European Union, there is a floor on wages of w_F. Employment falls sharply to q_3, and unemployment of q_2–q_3 develops for less skilled labour.

changed as new trading opportunities have altered the demands for various types of labour in both areas, and how market rigidities in the European Union altered the outcome compared with the free-market determination that occurred in the United States.

Summary

1   The neoclassical theory of distribution is an implication of profit maximization. Each factor is paid the value of its marginal revenue product and units of the factor move among uses to equalize net advantages, taking monetary and non-monetary rewards into account.

2   The satisfactory working of factor markets to allocate resources depends on two conditions: that factor prices reflect market conditions, and that factors move in response to changes in relative factor prices.

3   Both of the above conditions are clearly fulfilled in those competitive markets in which most non-human factors are bought and sold. It is not so obvious that they are fulfilled for labour, since many labour services are traded in markets that have monopolistic elements on the demand and/or the supply side, and because non-monetary aspects are an important part of labour's remuneration. The evidence suggests, however, that long-term changes in wage rates do occur in response to changing market conditions, and that the allocation of labour does respond to market signals at least over the long run.

4   In the early decades following the Second World War, plentiful unskilled and scarce skilled labour caused a large differential in the wages going to these two groups in the South. More plentiful supplies of skilled labour gave rise to smaller differentials in the North.

5   The growth of North–South trade in manufactures led the South to produce goods made mainly with its plentiful supplies of less skilled labour and the North to produce goods made mainly with its plentiful supplies of skilled labour.

CHAPTER 21 DISTRIBUTION THEORY IN ACTION 395

6 As a result, the demand for less skilled labour grew greatly in the South, narrowing its wage differential, while the demand for skilled labour grew greatly in the North, widening its wage differential.

7 In the United States, markets were allowed to clear, creating full employment and a large wage differential. In the European Union, wages were more rigid, so the differential did not widen greatly but unemployment among the unskilled became chronic.

Topics for review

- The effect of market conditions on factor prices
- The effect of factor prices on the allocation of factors among uses
- Wage differentials between skilled and unskilled labour in the North and the South
- The effect of growing North–South trade on wage differentials

PART SIX

Microeconomic policy

∾ CHAPTER 22

The case for free-market economies

THOSE who have read this far understand that markets are impressive institutions. Consumers' tastes and producers' costs help to generate price signals. These signals co-ordinate decisions taken by millions of independent agents, all pursuing their own self-interest and oblivious of national priorities. The power of this automatic co-ordinating function is painfully obvious to any central planner who has sought to co-ordinate a modern command economy by consciously calculating all of its needs, directing its allocation of resources, and determining its distribution of income.

In this chapter, we first summarize some of the key aspects of market economies, drawing together what we have learned in earlier chapters. Then we lay out the explicit arguments that have been made for 'letting the market do it'. We do this, first, for the broad intuitive set of arguments in favour of the market and, second, for the formal arguments which are based on the proof that perfect competition leads to an optimal allocation of resources. Finally, we go beyond efficiency considerations to deal with some broader issues of the behaviour of markets in the long and very long runs.

Characteristics of market economies

MARKETS co-ordinate decentralized decision-taking; markets function without conscious central direction; in allocating resources, markets also determine the distribution of income; the long-term behaviour of markets often exhibits a cycle in which products are born, grow to maturity, pass into old age, and eventually die.

Understanding these four points is a key to understanding the functioning of any market economy.

A co-ordinator of decisions

Every day millions of people make millions of independent decisions concerning production and consumption. These decisions are usually motivated by fairly immediate considerations of personal or family self-interest, rather than by a desire to contribute to the social good. The price system co-ordinates these decisions.

When a product such as oil becomes scarce, its free-market price rises. Firms and households that use it are led to economize on it and look for alternatives. Firms that produce it are led to produce more of it. This system works best when prices are determined on free markets in which there are many buyers and many sellers. Scarcities and surpluses are then signalled through prices that are set by the impersonal, aggregate forces of demand and supply.

Prices convey information. Furthermore, they convey an enormous amount of information about constantly changing market conditions. As the central planners of the former Soviet Union found, trying to generate this information by conscious central planning is a horrendous task. The Soviet Gosplan authorities had to generate prices for over 5 million items—and this in an economy that was vastly simpler than a Western economy because it sup-

pressed most of the vast range of product differentiation that is available in the West.

Administered prices   Since oligopolistic industries have administered prices set by firms, rather than impersonal market forces, their prices do not fluctuate continually in response to ever-changing market conditions. The price system still works under oligopoly, but it works slightly differently (and possibly less efficiently) than when prices are determined on competitive markets. Oligopolistic firms respond to price signals on the input side, since the prices of their inputs are usually determined on competitive markets. On the output side, however, these firms respond to quantity signals. Firms adjust their outputs in response to changes in their sales and inventories, rather than in response to changes in market prices. What matters, however, is that markets co-ordinate decisions even when prices are administered.

Profits and losses   The basic engine that drives the adaptations of the economy is variations in the earnings of factors of production. A rise in demand, or a fall in costs, produces economic profits for producers, while a fall in demand, or a rise in costs, produces economic losses. Profits signal that there are too few resources devoted to that industry. In search of these profits, more resources will enter, increasing output and driving down price, until the economic profits fall to zero. Economic losses signal the reverse. Resources leave the industry until those left behind are no longer making losses. If the government taxed away *all* such profits and replaced by subsidy *all* such losses, it would effectively destroy the market economy by removing its driving force.

A similar mechanism works for other factors of production. A rise in wages in one industry or occupation above wages that are earned in other similar industries or occupations signals the need for labour to move into that industry or occupation; a fall in wages signals the need for labour to leave.

An illustration of market co-ordination Say, for example, that every family in the Greater London area decides that it wants to own a detached house with a garden. This would be physically impossible, because there is not nearly enough land to house London's population in such a manner. If the entire populace tried to move to such dwellings, the prices of land and existing detached houses would rise enormously, while the prices of multiple-unit dwellings would plummet. Reacting to these signals, many people would decide that, although they would have preferred to live in single-family dwellings at the *original* prices, they prefer to live in multi-family units at the *new* prices. With a price system, no central administrator has to calculate scarcities and decide what proportion of the population must live in multi-family dwellings, or has the unenviable task of saying which individuals must live in each type of dwelling. If there is excess demand for one type and excess supply of the other, the relative price will change. As this happens, some people will switch from demanding the type that is becoming more expensive to demanding the type that is becoming relatively cheaper. Once the excess demand and supply are eliminated, the relative prices of the two will be in equilibrium.

No need for conscious direction

The market economy fulfils its function of co-ordinating decisions without anyone having to understand how it works. As Professor Tom Schelling puts it

'The dairy farmer doesn't need to know how many people eat butter and how far away they are, how many other people raise cows, how many babies drink milk, or whether more money is spent on beer or milk. What he needs to know is the prices of different feeds, the characteristics of different cows, the different prices . . . for milk . . . the relative cost of hired labour and electrical machinery, and what his net earnings might be if he sold his cows and raised pigs instead'.[1]

By responding to such public signals as the costs and prices of what he buys and sells, the dairy farmer helps to make the whole economy fit together, to produce more or less what people want, and to provide it more or less where, and when, they want it.

It is, of course, an enormous advantage that all the citizens of a country can collectively make the system operate without any one of them having to understand how it

works. This becomes a disadvantage, however, when they are asked, as voters or as legislators, to pass judgement on schemes for consciously intervening to improve the economy's operation. *Ignorance of how the system works then becomes a serious drawback.*

The distribution of income

The third important characteristic of a market economy is that it determines a *distribution* of the total income that it generates. People whose services are in heavy demand relative to supply, such as TV comedians and football players, earn high incomes, while people whose services are not in heavy demand relative to supply, possibly because they have low IQs or are unskilled, earn low incomes.

The distribution of income produced by the market can be looked at in equilibrium or in disequilibrium. In equilibrium, similar efforts by similar people will be similarly rewarded everywhere in the economy. In disequilibrium, however, similar people making similar efforts of work, or investment, will not be similarly rewarded. People in declining industries, areas, and occupations will have earnings below the going rate elsewhere in the economy through no fault of their own. Those in expanding sectors will achieve earnings above the going rate elsewhere in the economy for no extra effort of their own. These rewards and punishments serve an important function of causing decentralized decision-takers to respond appropriately to changes in demands and costs. The advantage is that individuals can take their own decisions about how to alter their behaviour when market conditions change. The disadvantage is that temporary rewards and punishments are dealt out for reasons that are beyond the control of the individuals affected.

The product cycle

The motto of a market economy might be 'Nothing is permanent'. New products appear continually, while others disappear. At the early stage of a product, total demand is low and costs of production are high. Many small firms are each trying to get ahead of their competitors by discovering the variations in the product's specifications that most appeal to consumers, or the technique that slashes costs. Sometimes new products never get beyond that phase; they prove to be passing fads, or else they remain as high-priced items catering to a small demand. Others, however, do become items of mass consumption. Successful firms in growing industries buy up, merge with, or otherwise eliminate their less successful rivals. Simultaneously their costs fall, owing to scale economies. Competition drives prices

[1] T. C. Schelling, *Micromotives and Macrobehavior* (New York: W. W. Norton, 1978).

down along with costs. Eventually at the mature stage, the industry is often dominated by a few giant firms. They become large, and conspicuous, parts of the nation's economy. Sooner or later, however, new products are introduced to erode the position of the established giants. Demand falls off, and unemployment occurs as the few remaining firms run into financial difficulties. A large but declining industry appears to many as a national disgrace. People ask themselves if the market system has failed because yesterday's healthy giants have become today's ailing firms. Large declining industries are, however, as much a natural part of a healthy changing economy as are small, growing ones and large, healthy mature ones.

The intuitive case for market economies

ECONOMISTS have used two types of argument to demonstrate the advantages of a market system. The first, which can be called the intuitive case, is as old as economics itself. The case is intuitive in the sense that it is not laid out in equations leading to some mathematical, maximizing result. But it does follow from some hard reasoning, and it has been subjected to some searching intellectual probing. (What follows seeks to *present* the intuitive case, *not* to evaluate it.)

The best co-ordinator

The market system co-ordinates economic decisions better than any known alternative. Compared with the alternatives, the decentralized market system is more flexible and leaves more scope for personal adaptation at any moment in time, and for quick adjustment to change over time. If, for example, a scarcity of oil raises its price, one individual can elect to leave her heating on full and economize on her driving (petrol consumption), while another may wish to do the opposite. In order to obtain the same overall effect by non-price rationing, the authorities must force the same reduction in heating and driving on both individuals, independent of their tastes, doctor's advice, and other perceived needs.

Furthermore, as conditions change over time, prices change, and decentralized decision-takers can react continuously, whereas government quotas, allocations, and rationing schemes are slower to adjust. The market provides automatic signals *as a situation develops*, so that all the adjustments to some major economic shock do not have to be anticipated and allowed for by a body of central planners. Millions of adaptations to millions of changes in tens of thousands of markets are required every year; and it would be a Herculean task to anticipate these and plan the necessary adjustments.

Relative prices reflect relative costs

A market system tends to drive prices towards the average total costs of production. When markets are close to perfectly competitive, this movement occurs quickly and completely; but even where there is substantial market power, new products and new producers respond to the lure of profits, and their output drives prices down towards the costs of production.

The advantage of having relative prices reflect relative costs was discussed in Chapter 15. When prices are equal to marginal costs, there will be allocative efficiency, because market choices are then made in the light of opportunity costs.[2] Firms will choose methods that minimize their own cost of producing output, and in so doing will automatically minimize the opportunity cost of the resources that they use. Similarly, when consumers choose to fly to Paris rather than to take the train, even though flying uses more resources per person transported than does rail, they have to pay the price. They will do so only when they value flying correspondingly more than rail at the margin. As it is with rail and air, so it is with any two products that consumers choose between: they will choose the one that requires more resources to produce only if they value that one over its competitor as much as the difference in the production costs.

When relative prices reflect relative costs, producers and consumers use the nation's resources in a manner that is consistent with allocative efficiency.

---

[2] The mechanism in the text ensures only that prices tend to equal average costs, not marginal costs. Except when there is natural monopoly, long-run average costs will be near long-run marginal costs, and the mechanism in the text will generate allocations that are near to being efficient.

Decentralization of power

Another important part of the case for a market economy is that it tends to decentralize power and thus requires less coercion of individuals than does any other type of economy. Of course, even though markets tend to diffuse power, they do not do so completely; large firms and large unions clearly have and exercise substantial economic power.

While the market power of large corporations and unions is not negligible, it tends to be constrained both by the competition of other large entities and by the emergence of new products and firms. This is the process of creative destruction that was described by Joseph Schumpeter (see p. 244). In any case, say defenders of the free market, even such aggregations of private power are far less substantial than government power.

Governments must coerce if markets are not allowed to allocate people to jobs and products to consumers. Not only will such coercion be regarded as arbitrary (especially by those who do not like the results), but the power surely creates major opportunities for bribery, corruption, and allocation according to the tastes of the central administrators. If, at the going prices and wages, there are not enough flats or coveted jobs to go around, the bureaucrats can allocate some to those who pay the largest bribe, some to those with religious beliefs, hairstyles, or political views that they like, and only the rest to those whose names come up on the waiting list.[3]

Stimulus to innovation and growth

Technology, tastes, and resource availability are changing all the time, in all economies. Thirty years ago there was no such thing as a personal computer or a digital watch. Front-wheel drive was a curiosity. Students carried their books in briefcases or in canvas bags that were anything but waterproof. Manuscripts existed only as hard copy, not as files in a computer. In order to change one word in a manuscript, one often had to retype every word on a page. Videocassettes did not exist. The next 30 years will surely also see changes great and small. New products and techniques will be devised to adapt to shortages, gluts, and changes in consumer demands, and to exploit new opportunities made available by new technologies. Fibre optics, for example, will radically change the nature of communication, permitting general availability of inexpensive, two-way video transmission.

In a market economy, individuals risk their time and money in the hope of earning profits. While many fail, some succeed. New products and processes appear and disappear. Some are fads or have little impact; others become items of major significance. The market system works by trial and error to sort out the successes from the failures and allocates resources to what prove to be successful innovations.

In contrast, planners in more centralized systems have to guess which innovations will be productive and which products will be strongly demanded. Planned growth may achieve wonders by permitting a massive effort in a chosen direction, but central planners also may guess wrong about the direction and put far too many eggs in the wrong basket, or reject as unpromising something that will turn out to be vital.

Probably the biggest failure of centrally planned economies was their inability to encourage the experimentation and innovation that has proved to be the driving force behind long-run change and growth in all advanced market economies. It is striking that the last decade has seen most centrally planned economies abruptly abandon their system in favour of a price system, while the only remaining large, planned economy—China—is slowly introducing more and more market determination into most aspects of its economy.

The formal case for market economies: general equilibrium welfare economics

WHILE accepting the intuitive defence just outlined, professional economists wanted to be more precise about just what the market economy did so well. To do so, they developed the proof that an idealization of the market economy (perfect competition) would lead, in equilibrium, to an *optimum* allocation of resources. This is an equilib-

[3] This line of reasoning has been articulated forcefully by the Nobel Prize winner Milton Friedman, who argues that economic freedom—the ability to allocate resources through private markets—is essential to the maintenance of political freedom. While many economists and social theorists have challenged this proposition, most agree that a centrally controlled economy requires more coercion and hence gives more opportunities for corruption, than a decentralized market economy.

rium situation that is *efficient* in the sense that it is impossible to make anyone better off without simultaneously making someone else worse off. This analysis of the optimality of perfect competition has already been given in Chapter 16. There we used the tools of consumers' and producers' surpluses to show that a perfectly competitive market economy produces allocative efficiency by maximizing the sum of these surpluses. That demonstration used demand and supply curves. These are tools of *partial equilibrium analysis* because each demand curve is based on *ceteris paribus* assumptions; in particular, when a product's price varies, the prices of all other products do not change. The following section provides an alternative demonstration in terms of transformation and indifference curves. These are tools of general equilibrium analysis because they allow all quantities and all prices to vary simultaneously.[4] Those who wish to skip this alternative treatment can jump immediately to the next major heading on p. 408.

An alternative approach to allocative efficiency

MARKET EQUILIBRIUM

The analysis of allocative efficiency using indifference curves and transformation curves comes from the field of study called general equilibrium welfare economics. We look first at producers and then at consumers.

Producers' equilibrium   To begin, consider an economy in which *n* different products are produced under conditions of perfect competition. Look first at any two, which we call products *a* and *b*. Because these are produced under perfectly competitive conditions, we know that in equilibrium each good's marginal cost will equal its price:

$$MC_a = p_a \qquad (1)$$

and

$$MC_b = p_b \qquad (2)$$

where MC_a and MC_b are marginal costs of *a* and *b* respectively, and p_a and p_b are the market prices of these two products. The same relation will, of course, hold for every product.

The next step is to divide equation (1) by equation (2) to obtain

$$\frac{MC_a}{MC_b} = \frac{p_a}{p_b} . \qquad (3)$$

This says that the ratio of the marginal costs in the two industries is equal to the ratio of the two prices—i.e. the rel-

ative price. Similar ratios apply to every pair of products.

What does the ratio of the marginal costs, shown on the left-hand side of (3), tell us? To illustrate, assume that the marginal cost of good *a* is £16, while that of good *b* is £4. Let the production of good *a* be reduced by one unit, and the resources that are freed be used to produce more of good *b*. Then £16 worth of resources are freed from production of *a*, and, at *b*'s marginal cost of £4 per unit, these can produce 4 units of good *b*. Using these illustrative figures, the ratio in the left-hand side of (3) above takes on a value of 4 (£16/£4). This is the extra amount of good *b* that can be obtained by giving up one unit of good *a*.

This ratio is called the **marginal rate of transformation**. The word 'transformation' is not to be taken literally. We do not take units of good *a* and magically transform them into units of good *b* (as the ancient alchemists wished to transform base metals into gold). Instead, the 'magic' is performed by reallocating resources, so that the production of good *a* falls by one unit, and the production of good *b* rises by whatever amount the freed resources can produce.

Now we can rewrite (3), replacing the ratio of the marginal costs with the term 'marginal rate of transformation', which we abbreviate *MRT*:

$$MRT = \frac{p_a}{p_b} . \qquad (4)$$

Figure 22.1 shows the graphical interpretation of this result for an economy with only two products.

In perfect competition, the marginal rate of transformation between any pair of products is equal to the ratio of their market prices.

This result is important. Be sure that you understand the reasoning behind it.

Consumers' equilibrium   We saw in Chapter 8 that each consumer is in equilibrium when the marginal rate of substitution between each pair of products is equal to those products' relative price (see Figure 8.6 on p. 147). The marginal rate of substitution shows the amount of good *b* that a consumer must be given to compensate for sacrificing one unit of good *a*. Using the abbreviation *MRS* for this concept, we can write the consumers' equilibrium as

$$MRS = \frac{p_a}{p_b} . \qquad (5)$$

Although different consumers have different incomes and

---

[4] To convey the analysis graphically, we must confine ourselves to economies that produce and consume only two commodities. Mathematical tools easily extend the analysis to economies with any number of products.

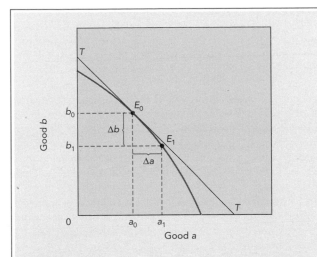

Figure 22.1 The marginal rate of transformation

The slope of the production possibility curve is the _MRT_, and it equals the relative price of the good under perfect competition. The graph illustrates the case of an economy that produces only two goods, _a_ and _b_. The curve is the economy's production possibility curve showing all the combinations of _a_ and _b_ that can be produced. It is also called a transformation curve. When production is at E_0, output is a_0 of product _a_ and b_0 of product _b_. Production then moves to a point E_1 with a_1 and b_1 of the two products being produced. The changes are shown by Δa and Δb, in the figure. The marginal rate of transformation is the ratio of Δb to Δa, which is the amount of _b_ that can be obtained per unit of _a_ given up.

The line _TT_ is drawn tangent to the curve at the point E_0. (Technical limitations in the artwork make tangents hard to draw, but the line _TT_ is supposed to touch the production possibility curve at E_0 and lie above it everywhere else.) When the changes in _a_ and _b_ are very small, the ratio $\Delta b/\Delta a$ along the production possibility curve is approximately equal to the slope of the tangent to the curve at the point from which changes are being measured. _Graphically, the slope of the tangent to the curve at any point measures the MRT at that point._ In the figure, therefore, the slope of _TT_ measures the _MRT_ at E_0.

hence achieve different levels of total satisfaction, all face the same set of relative prices so all will achieve the same set of _MRS_s.

THE CONDITION FOR ALLOCATIVE EFFICIENCY

The condition for allocative efficiency is that the marginal rate of substitution should equal the marginal rate of transformation:

$$MRS = MRT. \qquad (6)$$

To understand why this is the efficiency condition, we will study a numerical example which involves changing the economy's allocation of resources and hence the bundle of goods produced. While this is being done, we will hold constant the bundle of goods consumed by all consumers except one. Then all the changes in total output will be reflected in changes in the consumption of this one consumer. Since, in equilibrium, all consumers have the same _MRS_, it does not matter which consumer we choose; the argument applies to each of them. This simple device allows us to see whether or not a reallocation of resources allows one consumer to be made better off while no other consumer is made worse off.[5]

We assumed in the previous section that the _MRT_ between goods _a_ and _b_ was 4. Now let us assume that the _MRS_ for consumers is only 2. The _MRT_ tells us that we can get 4 units of _b_ by giving up 1 unit of _a_. The _MRS_, however, tells us that consumers will be satisfied if they receive only 2 units of _b_ for every 1 unit of _a_ given up. Now let the production of _a_ fall by 1 unit and the production of _b_ rise by 4 units. The consumer that we have chosen can be given 2 units of _b_ to compensate it for the loss of a unit of _a_, according to her _MRS_. There are now 2 further units of _b_ left over. This can be used to make someone better off while no one else is made worse off.

Now take the opposite case, by letting the _MRS_ be 6, while the _MRT_ remains at 4. In these circumstances, more of _b_ cannot be produced while fully compensating consumers for the loss of _a_. But resources could be reallocated in the other direction. The _MRT_ tells us that, in order to produce 1 more unit of _a_, 4 units of _b_ must be sacrificed. But the _MRS_ tells us that consumers would be willing to sacrifice 6 units of _b_ to get 1 unit of _a_. If 1 more unit of _a_ is produced, the sacrifice is only 4 units of _b_. Since our consumer is willing to give up 6 units of _b_, she can be given the unit of _a_ and only 4 units of _b_ taken away, leaving her better off while all other consumers are in an unchanged position.

Finally, let the _MRS_ and the _MRT_ be equal at 4. In this case, it is necessary to produce 4 fewer units of _b_ to get 1 more unit of _a_, and that is the amount consumers are prepared to give up. So if the change is made, there is just enough extra _a_ to compensate for the forgone _b_. So the consumer is neither better nor worse off. Now consider a change in the other direction. Producing 1 less unit of _a_ allows 4 more units of _b_ to be produced. 4 units of _b_, however, is what any consumer requires as compensation for giving up one unit of _a_. So, if the change is made, no one can be made better off while keeping everyone else in an unchanged position.

---

[5] An alternative device is to assume that the changes in output are shared out _equally_ among all _m_ consumers in the economy. Thus, each change of one unit in the _production_ of a commodity changes each consumer's _consumption_ of that commodity by $1/m$ of a unit.

Whenever the *MRS* does not equal the *MRT*, it is possible to reallocate resources and make someone better off without making anyone else worse off.

Above we have illustrated this proposition with an example. Figures 22.1 and 22.2 show the same result graphically for a two-product example.[6] The common sense of the result is that, if people are willing to trade one good for another at a rate different from that at which these goods can be substituted for each other in production, there must be room for gain. More should be produced of the good that people value more highly than its opportunity cost in production. For example, if people are willing to give up

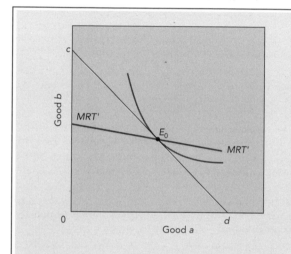

Figure 22.2 The conditions for allocative effiency

For allocative effiency the **MRS** must equal the **MRT**. The diagram shows a typical consumer in equilibrium at point E_0 on the budget line *cd*. Although different consumers have different incomes, and hence have budget lines that are different distances from the origin, all face the same prices and so all have budget lines with the same slope, and hence the same *MRS*.

Because each consumer faces the same prices as do producers, the slope of the budget line is equal to the *MRT* (which is the slope of the line *TT* in Figure 22.1). Because the consumer reaches a tangency with the budget line, the *MRS* at E_0 must be equal to the *MRT*.

If producers face a relative price *different* from that faced by consumers, the *MRT* will have a slope different from the budget line. An example is shown in the figure by the line *MRT'*, whose slope does not equal that of the budget line *cd*. Consumers remain in equilibrium at E_0. However, by altering the allocation of resources, holding the consumption of all other consumers constant, production—and hence this consumer's consumption—could, by assumption, be moved along the line *MRT'*. In this case, higher indifference curves could be attained by moving to the right along *MRT'*. Hence the equilibrium at E_0 is not efficient when *MRT* does not equal *MRS*.

more *a* to get a unit of *b* than it is necessary to sacrifice when resources are reallocated, there is room to make someone better off without making anyone else worse off.

ACHIEVING ALLOCATIVE EFFICIENCY

The condition for allocative efficiency is that *MRS* = *MRT*. We already know that consumers equate their *MRS*s between pairs of products to the ratio of those products' relative prices (equation (5) above). We also know that in perfect competition the marginal rate of transformation between any pair of products will equal the ratio of their prices (equation (4)). Since both consumers and producers face the same set of relative prices, it follows (by equating (4) and (5)) that in perfect competition the *MRS* will equal the *MRT* and the condition for allocative efficiency given in (6) will be established.

This is the key result. It is also an example of a chain of reasoning referred to in the Foreword. Each step is obvious enough, but the cumulative effect of several steps, built one on the other, can seem forbidding on first encounter. The ideas involved are not difficult, but to reinforce them we now review the entire argument in summary form.

RECAPITULATION

1. The efficiency condition is that the marginal rate of substitution in consumption (*MRS*) should equal the marginal rate of transformation in production (*MRT*). This is the type of condition we have encountered on several previous occasions. If goods can be transformed into each other at a rate that differs from the rate consumers are willing to trade one for the other, there is room for profitable substitution. More of the goods that consumers value (in terms of the quantities of other goods they are willing to forgo) more highly than their opportunity cost can be produced to everyone's gain. Only when consumers value goods at their opportunity cost is there no room for further gain.

2. Under perfect competition, each product is produced where its marginal cost equals its price.

---

[6] You may be tempted to put the two figures together, plotting the indifference curve from 22.2 against the production possibility curve in 22.1. Indeed, some elementary books do just that. But remember that Figure 22.1 refers to a whole economy while Figure 22.2 refers to a single consumer. We could combine the two diagrams only if the economy contained but one consumer—in which case we could not have price-taking behaviour. To be able to combine indifference curves with production possibility curves on a single diagram, we need to construct what are called *community indifference curves*. This requires procedures well beyond the scope of an introductory textbook. In the meantime, by comparing the production equilibrium in Figure 22.1 with the equilibrium for a single consumer in Figure 22.2, which must hold for each and every consumer, we are able to show the efficiency of perfect competition without needing to combine these two figures.

3. For any pair of products produced under perfect competition, therefore, the ratio of their marginal costs will equal the ratio of their prices.

4. The ratio of two products' marginal costs is equal to the marginal rate of transformation of one into the other.

5. In consumption, each consumer equates his or her marginal rate of substitution between any pair of goods to the slope of his or her budget line. The slope equals the ratio of the prices of the two goods.

6. Since under perfect competition both the *MRT* and the *MRS* between any pair of products are made equal to the ratio of these products' prices, it follows that the *MRS* must equal the *MRT*. Thus, the condition for allocative efficiency is fulfilled under perfect competition.

Feasibility?

Can an optimum, i.e. a Pareto-efficient, allocation of resources be achieved in the real world? Achieving it requires, among other things, that the following conditions be met.

1. *For an optimal allocation of resources, there should be perfect competition in all sectors of the economy, therefore ensuring that marginal cost will equal price everywhere.* This condition is sometimes called *pluperfect* competition. If it does not exist, we cannot be sure what the effect will be of making marginal cost equal marginal revenue somewhere in the economy. Specifically, if in a world of mixed-market structures we break up one monopoly and make it into a competitive industry, we have no general presumption, even in a theoretical

model, that this will move us closer to an optimum position. This important issue, which comes under the heading of 'the theory of the second best', is discussed further in the Appendix to this chapter.

2. *For an optimal allocation of resources under perfect competition, there should be no external economies or diseconomies of scale.* An external economy or diseconomy is beyond the influence of a single firm, and thus does not enter into the firm's calculations, even though it may be important for society. These are studied in detail in Chapters 23 and 24.

3. *For perfect competition to produce an optimal allocation of resources, there should be no divergence between private and social cost anywhere in the economy.* From society's point of view, it pays to maximize consumers' plus producers' surplus only if the demand curve indicates the value that society places on output of each product and if the marginal cost curve represents the opportunity cost to society of the resources used in production. We will see in the next chapter that social and private costs often diverge.

It is clear that these conditions for an optimal allocation of resources are not fulfilled in any modern economy. In particular, perfect competition does not prevail in many sectors since the producers of most manufactured goods, and many services, administer their own prices rather than facing prices set for them on impersonal, perfectly competitive markets. Since these firms face negatively sloped demand curves, they will not take production to the point where marginal cost equals price.

The theory of the optimal allocation of resources under perfect competition provides uncertain guidance to practi-

---

BOX 22.1

The political appeal of perfect competition

A long time ago, the English historian, Lord Acton, said something that is no less true today than it was in his own time: 'Power tends to corrupt and absolute power corrupts absolutely.' To anyone who fears concentrations of power, the perfectly competitive model is almost too good to be true. In it, no single firm, and no single consumer, has any power over the market. Individually, they are passive quantity-adjusters. If we add to this the assumption that firms are profit-maximizers, all firms become passive responders to market signals, doing what is most desirable from society's point of view. The great impersonal force of the market produces an appropriate response to every important change. For example, if tastes change, prices will change, and the allocation of resources will move in the appropriate direction.

In perfectly competitive markets, countless firms react to the same price changes. If one refuses to react, others will be eager to make the appropriate changes. If one firm refuses to hire employees from minority ethnic groups, or takes any other decision based on prejudice, thousands of other firms will recognize that profit maximization is not consistent with discrimination on the basis of race, colour, sex, creed, or anything other than how hard a person works.

It is a noble model: no one has power over anyone, and yet the system behaves in a co-ordinated way. Many will feel that it is a pity that it corresponds so imperfectly to reality as we know it today. Not surprisingly, some people still cling tenaciously to the belief that the perfectly competitive model describes the world in which we live; so many problems would disappear if only it did.

cal policies of market intervention by governments. Economic theory does not predict that in our societies of mixed-market structures *every* increase in the degree of competitiveness will always increase the efficiency of resource allocation. To evaluate current policy, we need to know the effects on the efficiency of resource allocation of interventions designed to produce a little more or a little less competition in some sectors of the economy. Unfortunately, this is just what we cannot do in general, and every case must be studied and evaluated in terms of its own specific circumstances.

This important proposition upsets much of the basis of piecemeal welfare economics. We know how to identify the best of all possible worlds (from the limited point of view of the optimum we are discussing), but we have a less clear idea of how to order two states of the very imperfect world in which we live. If this were not so, economists could not disagree as much as they do about specific policy measures.[7]

The theory of the optimal allocation of resources under perfect competition also has a substantial political appeal, which is briefly discussed in Box 22.1.

Unsettled questions

THE classical condemnation of non-competitive forms of behaviour was based on the belief that the alternative to monopoly was perfect competition. Today we realize that the effective choice is often not between monopoly and perfect competition, but between more or less oligopoly, so that we are not sure what effects a specific intervention will have on price and output. Thus, even if we accept the perfectly competitive result as being more desirable than a completely monopolistic one, this does not in itself tell us much about the real decisions that face us. In this section, we discuss competitive and monopolistic situations in general terms. We do this because we wish to study and evaluate the effects of encouraging a little more or less competition than we now have.

The given-cost assumption

The classical predictions about monopoly depend critically on the assumption that costs are unaffected when an industry is monopolized. If any savings are effected by combining numerous competing groups into a single integrated operation, then the costs of producing any given level of output will be lower than they were previously. If this reduction does occur, then it is possible for output to be raised and price to be lowered as a result of the monopolization of a perfectly competitive industry. Such a case is shown in Figure 22.3.

The monopolization of an industry, combined with a sufficiently large consequent increase in efficiency, can result in a fall in price and a rise in quantity produced, as compared with the competitive industry.[8]

Of course, the monopolization of an industry might reduce the efficiency of production and so shift the marginal cost curve upwards. In this case, monopolization will obviously raise price and lower output as compared with the competitive industry. You should draw your own diagram, showing the effects of a monopolization that caused costs to rise above those ruling under competition. Notice, however, that if this happened smaller, more efficient firms could enter and undersell the inefficient large firm. (This is what happens when mergers that were thought to be cost-reducing turn out to be cost-increasing and new smaller firms enter to challenge the inefficient, merger-created, large firm.)

The influence of market structure in the very long run

The classical case against monopoly concerns the allocation of resources within the context of a fixed technology. In the very long run, however, the production function is changing, as a result of both the discovery of lower-cost methods of producing old products and the introduction of new and improved products. Does market structure affect the rate of innovation in the very long run?

[7] More advanced students may wish to consult one of the early demonstrations of this proposition given in R. G. Lipsey and K. J. Lancaster, 'The General Theory of Second Best', *Review of Economic Studies*, vol. 24 (1956–7).

[8] You should be able to show for yourself that, if the elasticity of demand were less than one at the competitive price, the monopolist would reduce output and raise price, no matter how large the reduction in its costs.

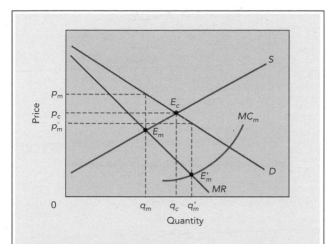

Figure 22.3 A Monopoly that reduces costs

If a monopoly reduces cost sufficienctly, it may result in a lower price and higher output than would perfect competition. The competitive equilibrium is at E_c, with price p_c and quantity q_c. Monopolization with unchanged costs raises price to p_m and lowers output to q_m. If the integration of the industry reduces costs to MC_m, equilibrium shifts to E'_m with an output q'_m and price p'_m.

THE INCENTIVE TO INNOVATE

Both the monopolist and the perfect competitor have a profit incentive to introduce cost-reducing innovations. A monopoly can always increase its profits if it can reduce costs. Furthermore, since it is able to prevent the entry of new firms into the industry, these additional profits will persist into the long run. Thus, a monopoly has both a short- and a long-run incentive to reduce its costs.

Firms in perfect competition or in monopolistic competition have the same incentive in the short run, but not in the long run. In the short run, a reduction in costs will allow a firm that was just covering costs to earn profits. In the long run, other firms will be attracted into the industry by these profits. Existing firms will copy the cost-saving innovation, and new firms will enter the industry using the new techniques. This will go on until the profits of the innovator have been eliminated.

Monopolies have both a short- and a long-run incentive to innovate; perfectly competitive firms have only a short-run incentive.

The effectiveness of profits as an incentive for a firm in perfect competition to develop cost-reducing innovations will thus depend on the magnitude of the extra profits, and on how long they persist. For example, if an innovation can be copied in a few months, the profits earned over that per-

iod may not be sufficient to compensate the innovating firm for the risks involved in making the innovation.

Funds for research and development   So far, we have looked at the profit incentive to innovate. Another consideration is the availability of the resources needed to finance research to develop new methods and new products. The large profits available to oligopolistic firms provide a ready fund out of which research and development can be financed. The typical perfectly competitive firm, however, is earning only enough to cover all its costs, and it will have no funds to spare for research and development.[9] As an empirical illustration, the innovations that have vastly raised agricultural productivity over the last century were not developed by farmers producing under perfect competition; rather, they were developed by a few oligopolistic manufacturers of farm equipment and by researchers in universities and in government-financed research institutions.

Penalties for not innovating   A common argument is that competitive firms *must* innovate or they will lose out to their competitors, while, although firms with monopoly power have an incentive to innovate, they do not need to do so because they are insulated from potential competition by their barriers to entry. Those who do not accept this argument offer two counter arguments. First, they say that it is wrong to think of a monopolist or oligopolist as shielded from all competition. It is always possible that some new firm will break into the market by developing some new, similar but superior, product that evades existing patents and other barriers to entry. Furthermore, the larger the monopoly profits of the existing firm(s), the larger the incentive for new firms to break into the market. Thus, it is argued, all monopoly and oligopolistic firms are in *potential* competition with possible new entrants, and the firm that sits back and does not innovate will not long remain profitable.

A second argument that opponents advance is that the penalty for not innovating is not always high in perfect competition. If innovations are hard to copy, then there *is* a strong incentive for a competitive firm to innovate, and a big penalty for firms who do not innovate, because a long time will be needed before other firms can copy and catch up with the innovator. In contrast, if innovations are easy to copy, there is a smaller incentive for the competitive firm to innovate and a smaller penalty for the firm that fails to innovate, since it is easy for it to copy and catch up with the innovator.

The above discussion may be summarized as follows.

All firms have an incentive to innovate since they can increase their profits with a successful innovation. The

[9] In perfect competition, when factors are paid the values of their marginal products this exhausts the entire value of the firm's output, leaving nothing to pay for research and development.

greater the barriers to entry and the harder it is for other firms already in the industry to copy the innovation, the longer will the profits of innovating persist and, thus, the larger will be the incentive to innovate. In competitive industries without barriers to entry, there will be little incentive to make innovations that are very easily copied, since both the profits of innovating and the losses from not innovating ahead of other firms will be very short-lived.

Schumpeter's defence of oligopoly and monopoly   We have already considered at several earlier points in this book the writings of the greatest opponent of the classical preference for perfect competition, Joseph Schumpeter. His theory relies on many of the forces just discussed, and his basic argument has two main parts.

The first part is that innovations that lower costs of production—by increasing output per head and creating economic growth—have a much larger effect on living standards than any 'misallocation' of resources which causes too much production of one kind of product and too little of another at any one time. Modern measures made since Schumpeter wrote have tended to support his contention. It appears unlikely that the losses due to monopolistic and oligopolistic misallocations are more than 2 or 3 per cent of a country's national income. But the national income of most advanced countries grows between 2 and 4 per cent *each year*, and a growth rate of 3 per cent per year doubles material living standards in under 25 years.

The second part of Schumpeter's argument is that monopolistic and oligopolistic market structures are more conducive to growth than perfect competition. He claimed that only the incentive of profits leads people to take the great risks of innovation, and that market power is much more important than competition in providing the climate under which innovation occurs. The large short-run profits of the firms with market power provide the incentive for others to try to usurp some of these for themselves. If a frontal attack on the major barriers to entry is not possible, then the barriers will be circumvented by such dodges as the development of similar products against which the established firms will not have entry protection. Schumpeter called the replacing of one entrenched position of market power by another through the invention of new products or new production techniques the *process of creative destruction.*

Since, in Schumpeter's theory, monopoly and oligopoly are more conducive to growth-creating innovations than is perfect competition, it follows that a 'bad' allocation of resources at any moment of time, such as results from much oligopoly and little perfect competition, is more conducive to a rapid rate of innovation and growth than a 'good' allocation, such as results from little oligopoly and much perfect competition. This important hypothesis cannot be handled with normal long-run theory, because long-run theory *assumes* constant technology.

Schumpeter's theory is not easy to test. Empirical work does suggest, however, that there may be more to his argument when it is applied to oligopolies than to textbook monopolies. Business school studies of firm behaviour show that much, possibly most, interfirm competition is in product and process innovation. Firms rarely fail because they set the wrong prices—for one reason, it is easy to alter prices that turn out to be uncompetitive. Firms do fail, however, when they fall behind their competitors in the constant battle to produce new and better products by ever more cost-efficient methods. Box 22.2 gives an example of the kind of creative destruction that does occur in oligopolistic industries.

THE EFFECT OF MARKET STRUCTURE ON CONSUMERS' RANGE OF CHOICE

It is sometimes argued that one of the virtues of competition among several producers is that it presents consumers with a wide range of differentiated products, while complete monopoly tends towards uniformity of product. This is a very-long-run problem because we are concerned with changing the number of products to be produced.

An example from radio and television   An interesting case, in which competition tends to produce a nearly uniform product while profit-maximizing monopoly tends to produce widely differentiated ones, is drawn from radio and television. Consider an example in which there are two potential radio audiences: one group, comprising 80 per cent of the total audience, wishes to hear rock, while the other group, comprising 20 per cent, wishes to hear classical music. Each individual radio station seeks to maximize its own listening audience.

If there is only the one station, it will produce rock. If a second competing station is now opened up, its most profitable policy will be to produce a similar rock programme because half of the large audience is better than all of the small one. A third station would also prefer a third of the large audience to all of the small one. Indeed, four stations would be needed (each hoping to attract one-fourth of the larger audience, or 20 per cent of the total audience) before it would be profitable for any one station to produce classical music. Thus, competition between a few stations tends to produce two or three almost identical rock programmes, each competing for a share of the larger audience.

A profit-maximizing monopoly controlling two stations would not, however, pursue this policy. To maximize its total listening audience, it would produce rock on one station and classical music on the other. The monopoly might spend more money on preparing the programme for the larger audience, but it would not spend money to produce a similar programme on its second station—the optimal

---

BOX 22.2

Creative destruction in action

Creative destruction, the elimination of one product by a superior product and/or of one production process by a superior process, is a major characteristic of all advanced countries. It eliminates the strong market position of the firms and workers who make the threatened product or operate the threatened process.

The steel nibbed pen eliminated the quill pen with its sharpened bird's feather nib. The fountain pen eliminated the steel pen and its accompanying ink-well. The ball point pen or 'biro' virtually eliminated the fountain pen. The rolling-ball and fibre-tipped pens have partly replaced the biro. Who knows what will come next in writing implements?

The hand-cranked adding machine replaced the Dickensian clerk adding up long columns of figures in his head. (This was an all-male occupation.) The electrically driven, mechanical desk calculator eliminated the hand-cranked version. The electronic desk calculators eliminated the mechanical calculator, while the pocket calculator eliminated the slide rule (which was a device for doing calculations based on logarithms). The mainframe computer largely replaced the electronic calculator during the 1960s and 1970s (except for pocket use). In the late 1980s and early 1990s, the increasingly powerful PC (personal computer) largely replaced the mainframe (with disastrous consequences for what was the world's largest producer of computer equipment, IBM). Each step vastly increased the speed and accuracy with which calculations could be completed. A modern PC will do in a fraction of a second what the Dickensian clerk did in a week, and what a desk calculator could do in half a day.

The silent films eliminated vaudeville. The 'talkies' eliminated the silent film, and colour largely eliminated black and white films. The TV seriously reduced the demand for films (and radio) while not eliminating either of them. Satellites reduced the demand for direct TV reception by offering better pictures and a more varied selection, and cable may do the same to satellite transmission.

In the 1920s and 1930s, the American supermarket threatened the small grocery store as the main shopping point for the typical family. The small store fought back with assistance from the courts and the regulators, and was able to slow the advance of the supermarkets. But in the end, the big stores were seen to offer a superior product and they pushed the small operations into the niche of the convenience store or corner shop. In the 1960s, supermarkets spread throughout Britain. In the 1980s and 1990s, town-centre supermarkets were threatened by out-of-town shopping malls and hypermarkets.

For long-distance passenger travel by sea, the steamship eliminated the sailing vessel around the turn of the twentieth century. The airplane eliminated the ocean liner in the 1950s and 1960s. For passenger travel on land, the train eliminated the stage coach, while the bus competed with the train without eliminating it. The airplane wiped out the passenger train in most of North America while leaving the bus still in a low-cost niche used mainly for short and medium distances. In Europe distances are such that bus, train, and plane all compete over many routes while air transport dominates the longer trips.

The above are all product innovations. Production processes also undergo the same type of creative destruction. The laborious hand-setting of metal type for printing was replaced by the linotype, which allowed the type to be set by a keyboard operator but which still involved a costly procedure for making corrections. The linotype was swept away by computer typesetting, and much of the established printing shop operations have recently been replaced by desktop publishing.

Masses of assembly-line workers, operating highly specialized and inflexible machines, replaced the craftsman when Henry Ford perfected the techniques of mass production. A smaller number of less specialized flexible manufacturing workers, operating sophisticated and less specialized machinery, have now replaced the assembly line workers that operated the traditional factory in many industries.

The cases can be extended almost indefinitely, and they all illustrate the same general message. Creative destruction transforms the products we consume, how we make those products, and how we work. It continually sweeps away positions of high income and economic power established by firms that were in the previous wave of technological change and by those who work for them. It is an agent of dynamism in our economy, an agent of change and economic growth; but it is not without its dark side in terms of the periodic loss of privileged positions on the part of the replaced firms and their workers.

---

policy for its second station is to go after the other 20 per cent of potential listeners so that, between the two channels, the monopoly would have the maximum audience.

In cases of both monopoly and competition, each individual firm tries to maximize its own listening audience, but two competing stations will both go after the same large audience, ignoring the minority group, while two stations owned by one monopoly will go after both audiences, one for each station. Under these circumstances, competition produces a uniformity of product which ignores the desires of the minority, while monopoly produces a varied product catering to the desires of both the majority and the minority group.

Product selection   The above example illustrates the problem of product choice that has recently concerned theorists of industrial organization. The standard neoclassical theory of the firm takes the number of products as given. With differentiated products, however, the number of conceivable products is infinite and the firm must *choose* which products to develop and then market. Think, for example, of the endless alternative types of car that could be produced by varying the characteristics of existing cars. How do firms decide which of the many possible products to produce? Why do competing firms sometimes choose very similar products and at other times seek to establish substantial differences from competitors' products? These are interesting issues on which modern industrial organization theory has shed substantial light.[10]

Conclusion

The theory of the optimality of perfect competition is an intellectual triumph in providing an abstract demonstration of how markets co-ordinate decentralized decision-taking. It shows what seems counterintuitive to many non-economists:

Conscious co-operation is not always the best route to desirable social outcome; the atomistic pursuit of self-interest can sometimes produce a better outcome than the co-operative route.

The analysis of efficiency is also an important aid to understanding the real world. Most economists who have spent time in countries where price signals have been seriously distorted—by such policy interventions as price controls, subsidies, import restrictions, state trading boards, and profit restraints—do not doubt the power of major inefficiencies to reduce living standards.

The intuitive defence for placing significant reliance on the price system to influence the nation's allocation of resources is a very strong one. The world over, governments of the left and the right have been accepting that message more and more during the last few decades. As a result, governments of all political persuasions have been placing more reliance on decentralized decision-taking, operating through markets. An understanding of how such decision-taking works, and why it tends to produce an effective use of the society's resources, is one of economists' most important insights.

Another great insight concerns the power of competitive behaviour to protect consumers from exploitation in the short and the long run, and to produce increases in living standards via profit-seeking, innovative behaviour in the very long run. The other side of this pro-competitive coin is the classical mistrust of monopoly. Schumpeter's support of profits as an engine of creative destruction can be applied to oligopoly, without having to embrace textbook monopoly as a desirable market structure. Ever since Adam Smith, economists have repeated the warning that the behaviour of established monopolists is usually not in the social interest. Many Marxists have seen good and bad social behaviour as being the prerogative of particular

classes. The classical economists' message, however, was that *any monopoly* is against the social interest. Adam Smith observed that businessmen rarely got together without plotting some new action to raise prices or otherwise exploit consumers. The same might be said for monopolies of trade unions and government bodies.

The classical prescription is that monopoly should be avoided whenever possible; it should be discouraged in any form in which it might arise in both the private and the public sectors. The Schumpeterian prescription is that market forces will break up monopoly power provided that governments do not support that power by taking action to restrict entry—which they often do.

All of these insights are powerful and valuable. Problems arise, however, when attempts are made to prove the *perfection* of any real market economy. Does the economy, as we know it, produce an optimal allocation of resources? Economic theory answers this question with a clear 'no', since many of the conditions needed for Pareto optimality are absent from any modern economy. Consider, for example, the many giant manufacturing firms which sell in oligopolistic markets and the many service firms who sell distinct services. Whatever else they may be, such firms are certainly not price-takers. The attempt to defend the *perfection* of the price system is doomed to failure by the economists' own analysis of the necessary conditions for optimality.

Pluperfect competition, defined as universal perfect competition, is unattainable. A mixture of competitive, oligopolistic, and monopolistic markets *is* attainable. Furthermore, most economists agree that oligopolies are preferable to monopolies. As we observed in Chapter 14,

The defence of oligopoly is that, given the efficiency of large-scale production, oligopoly may be the most competitive system that is available in the real world. The challenge to policy-makers is to keep oligopolists competing with each other, rather than co-operating to obtain monopoly results.

The realistic defence of the price system, then, has to be that it is better than any known alternative for making the majority of decisions concerning the allocation of resources. Those who accept this position are still free to disagree on the extent that government intervention is needed to alter the results that would be achieved by unhindered markets. After all, virtually everyone agrees that some intervention is desirable. Most debates among most social observers, therefore, concern the degree of government

---

[10] For further discussion, advanced students may wish to consult B. C. Eaton and R. G. Lipsey, 'Product Differentiation', in R. Schmalensee and R. Willig (eds.), *Handbook of Industrial Organization* (Amsterdam: Elsevier Science Publishers, 1989).

Now assume that the government considers removing the distorting tax on M but feels it cannot remove it from S. Surely this will improve matters because one of the tax distortions is removed? The answer is that there is no assurance that removing one distortion will make things better.

Consider the new situation, with only S subject to a sales tax (Table 22A.3). The removal of the tax on M makes consumers and producers see the same relative price of M and F (the two untaxed goods) and so equates MRS_{FM} with MRT_{FM}. This is an improvement. It leaves the distortion on the relative price of F and S unchanged. So there is a standoff. However, it now causes consumers and producers to face a different relative price of untaxed M and taxed S

whereas previously they had each seen the same relative price (since both M and S were taxed at an equal rate). This introduces a new distortion where none had existed before. This makes things worse.

So nothing can be said in general about the removal of one distorting factor. It improves things in some directions by allowing consumers and producers now to see the same relative prices, but it worsens things in other dimensions by introducing differences in the relative prices seen by the two groups where none had existed before.

As it was with the removal of one tax, so it is with the removal of some but not all tariffs, or the establishment of price-taking behaviour in some but not all sectors of the economy.

Fulfilling one optimal condition where others are not fulfilled removes some distortions but introduces (or increases) others and overall may either raise or lower consumers' welfare.

This is the main message of second best theory. However, it is possible, using more mathematics than is assumed in this book, to calculate the optimum amount of any 'distortion' in one sector *given that distortions in other sectors cannot be changed*. In the above example, the problem would be: given that S must keep its 10 per cent tax and that F remains untaxed, what is the optimum tax to levy on M? If all three goods are substitutes, the second-best optimum tax on M turns out to be greater than zero but less than the tax on S.

Table 22A.3 A 10 per cent sales tax on S only

Consumers		Relative price facing consumers		Relative prices facing producers	
MRS_{FM}	$=$	$\dfrac{p_F}{p_M}$	$=$	$\dfrac{p_F}{p_M}$	$= MRT_{FM}$
MRS_{FS}	$=$	$\dfrac{p_F}{1.1p_S}$	$\neq$	$\dfrac{p_F}{p_S}$	$= MRT_{FS}$
MRS_{MS}	$=$	$\dfrac{p_M}{1.1p_S}$	$\neq$	$\dfrac{p_M}{p_S}$	$= MRT_{MS}$

✍ CHAPTER 23

The case for government intervention

AN unkind critic of economics once said that economists have two great insights: *markets work,* and *markets fail.* An unkind critic of politics once added that economics was thus a step ahead of both the political left and the political right, each of which accepts only one of these insights. Whatever may be true of others, economists do try to take the critical step of showing when each of these insights applies, and why.

We have seen that the general case for reliance on free markets lies in the belief that decentralized decision-taking is more efficient than fully centralized decision-taking. We have also seen that the general case for some government intervention is that most people wish to mitigate the disastrous results that the market produces for some people, and to improve the functioning of those markets that they believe do not work well. Thus, the practical issue is not to choose between unhampered free-market economies and fully centralized, command economies: it is, instead, to choose the mix of market and government determination that best suits the objectives of public policy.

In this chapter, we study the reasons for government intervention. The first set of reasons relates to situations in which free markets will not produce efficient results because of monopoly power, externalities, public goods, and asymmetric information. The second set relates to objectives other than efficiency, such as distributive justice and the need to protect some individuals from decisions taken on their behalf by others. Next, we study the main tools of government intervention, rules and regulations, expenditures, and taxes. After that, we study the many costs, both direct and indirect, that are associated with government intervention. Finally, we see that the optimal type and amount of government intervention arises from balancing the costs of such interventions against the benefits, proceeding when the benefits exceed the costs, and pulling back when the costs exceed the benefits.

The case against completely free markets

THE term **market failure** describes any market performance that is judged to be less good than the best possible performance. The word 'failure' in this context may convey the wrong impression.

Market failure means that the *best attainable outcome* has not been achieved; it does not mean that nothing good has happened.

The phrase 'market failure' applies to two quite different sets of circumstances. One is the failure of the market system to achieve efficiency in the allocation of society's resources. The other is the failure of the market system to serve social goals other than efficiency, such as achieving some desired distribution of income or preserving our value systems. We treat each in turn.

Failure to achieve efficiency

There are five broad types of phenomenon that lead to inefficient market outcomes: *monopoly power, externalities, absence of property rights, public goods* (sometimes called *collective consumption goods*), and *information asymmetries.* We consider each of these in a separate section below.

MONOPOLY POWER

As we discussed in Chapter 15, firms that face negatively sloped demand curves will maximize profits at an output where price exceeds marginal cost, leading to inefficiency. Although some market power is maintained through artificial barriers to entry, such power often arises naturally because in many industries the least costly way to produce a good or a service is to have few producers relative to the size of the market. The standard government remedies are anti-monopoly policy and public service regulation, which, as discussed in Chapter 16, present problems of their own. We do not consider these issues further here because they received a full treatment in Chapter 16.

EXTERNALITIES

Costs, as economists define them, involve the value of resources used in the process of production. According to the opportunity-cost principle, value is the benefit that resources would produce in their best alternative use. But who decides what resources are used when and what their opportunity cost is?

Consider the case of a selfish student who is thinking of extending a party for one more hour at 1.00 a.m. For this student, the opportunity cost includes the psychological value of an extra hour of sleep, as well as the money cost of whatever will be eaten and drunk, the value of any repairs to the bedsitter, and so forth. However, there is another resource used when the party runs for an extra hour—the neighbours' sleep—and the student need not consider it when she makes her decision to keep the stereo blasting.

Private and social costs   The difference in the viewpoint of the selfish party-thrower and the neighbours illustrates the important distinction between **private cost** and **social cost.** Private cost measures the best alternative use of the resource available to the private decision-maker. The party-thrower incurs private costs equal to her best alternative use of the resources that go into an extra hour of partying. The party-thrower cannot make any use of the neighbours' sleep and so values their sleep at zero. The *social cost* includes the private cost but also the best use of *all* resources available to society. In this case, social cost includes the cost imposed on the neighbours by an extra hour of partying.

Discrepancies between social and private cost occur when there are **externalities,** which are the costs or benefits of a transaction that are incurred or received by other members of the society but not taken into account by the parties to the transaction. They are also called *third-party effects,* because parties other than the two primary participants in the transaction (the consumer and the producer) are affected. Externalities arise in many different ways, and they may be beneficial or harmful.

A harmful externality occurs, for example, when a factory generates smoke. Individuals who live and work in the neighbourhood bear real costs arising from the factory's production: the disutility of enduring the smoke, of adverse health effects, and of clean-up costs. These effects will not be taken into account by the factory owners when they decide how much to produce. The element of social cost that they ignore is external to their decision-making process. Producers who create harmful externalities will produce more than the socially optimal level of output.

Beneficial externalities occur, for example, when I paint my house and enhance my neighbours' view and the value of their property, or when an Einstein or a Rembrandt gives the world a discovery or a work of art whose worth is far in excess of what he was paid to produce it. Firms will tend to produce less than the socially optimal level of output whenever their products generate beneficial externalities, because they bear all of the costs while others reap part of the benefits.

Externalities, whether harmful or beneficial, cause market failures: marginal private revenue differs from marginal social cost, causing output to diverge from its socially optimal level.

This is illustrated in Figure 23.1 for the case of a harmful externality.

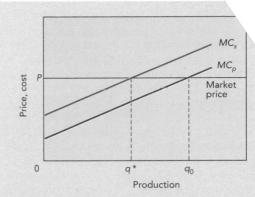

Figure 23.1 Private and social cost

A competitive firm will produce output to the point where its private marginal cost equals the market price. In this case, every unit of output produced imposes *external* costs, equal to the distance between MC_p (private marginal cost—the marginal cost curve that is faced by the firm) and MC_s (social marginal cost).

The profit-maximizing, competitive firm produces q_0, the output where price equals private marginal cost. If the full social costs of production were taken into account, only q^* would be produced. Notice that, for each unit of output between q^* and q_0, the cost borne by all members of society exceeds the value to consumers, which is the market price. Over this range, social cost exceeds private revenue, implying allocative inefficiency.

COMMON PROPERTY RESOURCES

A common property resource is a resource that is owned by no one and may be used by anyone. No one owns the ocean's fish until they are caught. No one owns common grazing land. The world's international fishing grounds are common property for all fishermen, as is common grazing land for all livestock owners. If, by taking more fish, one fisherman reduces the catch of other fishermen, he does not count this as a cost, although it is a cost to society. If, by grazing his own goat, he reduces the feed available for other people's goats, he does not count this as a cost.

It is socially optimal to add to a fishing fleet until the last boat increases the *value of the fleet's total catch* by as much as it costs to operate the boat. Similarly, it is optimal to add another goat to the herd grazing on the common as long as the total supply of meat (or milk) is increased. This is the size of fishing fleet and goat herd that a social planner or a private monopolist would choose.

The free market will not, however, produce that result. Potential new entrants will judge entry to be profitable if the *value of their own catch* is equal to the costs of operating their boats, or if the value of their own goat meat is equal to their costs. But a new entrant's catch is *partly* an addition to total catch, and *partly* a reduction of the catch of other fishermen—because of congestion, each new boat reduces the catch of all other boats. Similarly, a new goat reduces the feed available to add weight to the existing goats. Thus, under competitive free entry there will be too many boats in the fleet and too many goats on the common. Indeed, boats will continue to enter until there are no longer any profits for the marginal boat. In other words, boats will enter until the *average* value of the catch of a typical boat is equal to the cost of running that boat. At this point, however, the *net* addition to the *total* catch brought about by the last boat will be substantially less than the cost of operating the boat and it may be negative. Similarly, farmers will go on adding goats to the herd until the average value of a goat so pastured equals its costs. This will be long after the net addition to the village's meat supply has been reduced by successive additions of more and more goats.

With common property resources, the level of activity will be too high because each new entrant will not take account of the cost that he or she imposes on existing producers by reducing their outputs.

Fishing grounds, common pastures, and other common property resources often show a typical pattern of overexploitation. Most of the world's fishing grounds do so today, except where the catch is effectively regulated by government intervention. Box 23.1 discusses this case in more detail.

PUBLIC GOODS

A **public good**, which is sometimes called a **collective consumption good**, is one for which the total cost of produc-

---

BOX 23.1

....

Endangered fish

The fish in the ocean are a common property resource and theory predicts that such a resource will be overexploited if a high enough demand for the product and the supplier's ability to meet such a demand are both present. In past centuries, there were not enough people eating fish, or fishermen catching fish, to endanger stocks. Over the last fifty years, however, the population explosion has added to the demand for fish and advances in technology have vastly increased fishermen's ability to catch fish. As a result, the overfishing prediction has been amply born out. Today fish are a common property resource; tomorrow, they could become no one's property.

Overfishing

Since 1950, the world's fish catch has increased fivefold. Although the catch grew until the 1980s, it did so because smaller, less desirable, fish were substituted for diminishing stocks of the more desirable fish and because fishing boats penetrated ever further into remote oceans. Today, all available stocks are being exploited, and now even the total tonnage is beginning to fall. The UN estimates that the total value of the world's catch could be increased by nearly $30 billion if fish stocks were properly managed by governments interested in the total catch, rather than exploited by individuals interested in their own catch!

The developed countries have so overfished their own stocks that Iceland and the European Union could cut their fleets by 40 per cent and catch as much fish as they do today. This is because more fish would survive to spawn, allowing each boat in a smaller fleet to catch about 40 per cent more than does each boat in today's large fishing fleet.

The problem has become so acute that Canada shut down its entire Atlantic cod fishing industry. Tens of thousands of Newfoundland residents lost their livelihoods in the demise of

what had been the province's largest industry—the catching, freezing, and canning of fish. Canada and the European Union have since been in conflict over what Canada claims is predatory overfishing by EU boats just outside Canadian territorial waters.

The Mediterranean has been so overfished that a product that was once the staple for poorer persons is now an expensive luxury eaten mainly by rich tourists.

Policy response

The European Union has a common fishing policy covering the Atlantic territorial waters of its member-countries which, since the 1970s, have extended 200 metres offshore. Since 1983, total allowable catches for all main species have been set annually and divided up into catch quotas for each member-country. Minimum mesh size and other ways of protecting young fish are also imposed. Inspection and monitoring measures are rigorously applied to give force to the regulations. So far, however, the regulations apply only to the Atlantic. In 1994, there was still no equivalent set of policies to protect the seriously overfished Mediterranean.

Some developing countries are following similar lines, but the majority are encouraging rapid expansion of their own fishing fleets with the all-too-predictable results that their domestic waters will soon be seriously overfished.

Worldwide action saved most species of whales, and just in time for many species. It remains to be seen how many types of fish will be caught to extinction and how many will recover as the nations of the world slowly learn the lesson of economic theory: common property resources need central management if they are not to be overexploited to an extent that risks extinction.

tion does not increase as the number of consumers increases. The classic case is national defence: an army of a given size protects all the nation's citizens, whether these number 25 million, 50 million, or 100 million. Another important case is police protection: a visitor benefits from the city's crime-free streets just as much as its residents do. Information is also a public good. Suppose a certain food additive causes cancer. The cost of discovering this needs to be borne only once. The information is then of value to everyone who might have used the additive, and the cost of making the information available to one more consumer is essentially zero. Other public goods include lighthouses, weather forecasts (a type of information), the provision of clean air, and outdoor band concerts. Importantly, once a public good is produced, it is available to everyone; its use cannot be restricted to those who are willing to pay for it.

For this reason, the private market will not produce efficient amounts of the public good, because, once the good is produced, it is either inefficient or impossible to make people pay for its use. Indeed, markets may fail to produce public goods at all whenever non-payers cannot be made non-users. The obvious remedy in these cases is government provision of the good, paid for by taxes.

The above discussion illustrates the two key characteristics of a pure public good: it must be non-rivalrous, and it must be non-excludable. By **non-rivalrous** we mean that the amount that one person consumes should not affect the amount that other people can consume. For example, if ten boats enter a channel guided by a lighthouse, this does not reduce the benefit that the eleventh boat can get from the light when entering the channel. In contrast, a normal private good is rivalrous in the sense that, if one person consumes some amount of it, that amount is not available for anyone else to consume. By **non-excludable** we mean that, once produced, there is no way to stop anyone from consuming it. Once the lighthouse casts its light on the harbour entrance, all passers-by can use its services. National defence is an even better example. An army that protects a country from invasion protects all citizens. If some of its citizens do not pay their share, they cannot be denied protection as long as they continue to live in the country.

In practical situations, pure public goods do exist, and defence is the best example. In many other cases, however, a good has some mixture of 'publicness' and 'privateness'. For example, a good that is subject to congestion may be non-rivalrous up to the congestion point but rivalrous thereafter. A motorway that is operated under capacity has the non-rivalrous characteristic of a public good. If one more person elects to use it, that does not in any way reduce the benefit that the existing users get from the road. But once the motorway is used to normal capacity, each new person who elects to use it reduces the benefit obtained by existing users. For a while, as use continues to increase, no existing users need to be squeezed out; they each merely get less benefit as congestion builds up. Eventually, however, the upper limit to capacity may be reached and the motorway then behaves like a private good: each new user must force out some existing user since the total number of possible users is fixed. This is also a characteristic of public parks and a host of other goods whose services are non-rivalrous up to capacity, partially rivalrous over a range of use in excess of normal capacity, and fully rivalrous at absolute capacity utilization.

Similar considerations apply to excludability. Defence is completely non-excludable as long as one resides in the country being defended. But the owners of the lighthouse might be able to exclude those who did not pay for its services if they could police the harbour entrance and prevent entry. This example shows two further aspects of excludability. It is partly a matter of property rights, and partly a matter of technology.

The lighthouse owners probably could not prevent non-payers from entering the harbour because the state would not give them a property right over the water around the harbour entrance. Even if they did have such a property right, they would have to enforce it. This is where technology comes in. In the case of the harbour, if the entrance is narrow enough, a single patrol boat could police the entrance. This would be easy with today's radar and other modern detection devices, but might have been difficult 200 years ago in the days of sail. Non-payers might have slipped in unnoticed during the hours of darkness. Usually technology is not just a matter of making something possible or impossible; more often, it is a matter of 'at what cost?' It would be possible, for example, to build a fence around the Yorkshire moors and prevent anyone who did not pay a user fee from entering them. But the cost in terms of miles of fencing and required watch-persons would vastly exceed any user fees that could be charged. In that case, 'non-excludability' does not mean being technically impossible to exclude but impossible to exclude at an economic cost.

One final point follows from the above. Since what is or is not excludable is partly a matter of technology, and since technology changes over time, what was not excludable in the past may become excludable in the future. For example, over most of the twentieth century it has been impracticable to charge tolls for use of urban roads and exclude non-payers because of excessive costs in terms of money and time (delay at toll booths). Today it is possible to implant a device on each car that allows its location to be continuously tracked at very small cost. Fees for use of urban roads can then be assessed and non-payers denied use of the roads by cancelling drivers' licences or denial of road licences or other fully practicable means.

A pure public good such as defence is completely non-rivalrous and non-excludable. In practice, for any given state of technology many goods are partially rivalrous and not economically excludable.

ASYMMETRIC INFORMATION

The role of information in the economy has received increasing attention from economists in recent years. Information is, of course, a valuable product, and markets for information and expertise are well developed, as every university student is aware. Although markets for expertise are conceptually identical to markets for any other valuable service, they do pose special problems. We have already considered one of these: information is often a public good because once the information is known to anyone it is often easily available to others; this makes it difficult to charge users enough to cover the costs of production and causes the private sector to produce too little.

Even where information is not a public good, markets for expertise are prone to market failure. The reason for this is that one party to a transaction often can take advantage of special knowledge in ways that change the nature of the transaction itself. The two important sources of market failure that arise when privately held information is bought and sold are *moral hazard* and *adverse selection*. These were discussed in Chapter 9 and so we need say no more here except to observe, first, that when insurance leads people to engage in more risky behaviour, social costs are unnecessarily high and, second, when buyers and sellers have unequal knowledge about their transaction, the outcome can be less efficient than if they were equally well informed.

The principal–agent problem once again   Asymmetric information is involved in many situations of market failure. The *principal-agent* problem, which was first discussed in Chapter 16, is an example. In its classic form, the firm's managers act as agents for the stockholders, who are the legal principals of the firm. The managers are much better informed than the principals are about what they actually do and what they could do. Indeed, the managers are hired for their special expertise. Given that it is expensive for the shareholders (principals) to monitor what the managers (agents) do, the managers have latitude to pursue goals other than the firm's profits. The private costs and benefits of their actions thus will be different from the social costs and benefits, with the usual consequences for the efficiency of the market system.

Missing markets   Another reason for inefficiency is that some needed markets do not exist. This point, which follows from some rather advanced general equilibrium theory, is discussed briefly in Box 23.2.

Failure to achieve other social goals

The great strength of the market system is its ability to generate reasonably efficient outcomes in a great many cases, using a decentralized organization. Markets do this well because, most of the time, the information that they need to perform well is derived from individuals' desires to improve their private circumstances. It should not be sur-

---

BOX 23.2

Missing markets as a source of market failure

For complete optimality, there has to be a market in which each good and service can be traded to the point where the marginal benefit equals the marginal cost. Missing markets for such things as public goods are a source of inefficiency.

One important set of missing markets are those covering most risks. You can insure your house against its burning down. This is because your knowledge of the probability of this occurrence is not much better than your insurance company's, and because the probability of your house burning down is independent of the probability of other houses burning down.

If you are a farmer, however, you cannot usually insure your crop against bad weather. This is because the probability of you and your neighbour's crop suffering from bad weather are interrelated. If the insurance company has to pay you, the probabilities are it will also have to pay your neighbour, and everyone else in the county—perhaps even throughout the country. An insurance company survives by pooling independent risks. It cannot survive if the same event affects all its clients in the same way. (This is why, although you can insure your house against a fire from ordinary causes, you cannot insure it against fires caused by war.)

If you are in business, you cannot insure against bankruptcy. Here the problem is adverse selection. You know much better than your would-be insurance company the chances that your business will fail. If insurance was offered against such failure, it would be taken out mainly by people whose businesses had recently developed a high chance of failure.

For these and other reasons, many risks cannot be insured against. Optimality cannot occur because these markets are not there.

Another set of missing markets are many futures markets. You can buy certain well-established and unchanging products, such as corn or pigs, on futures markets. But you cannot do so for most manufactured products, such as cars and TV sets, because no one knows the precise specifications of future models. Because these markets are missing, there is no way that the costs and benefits of planned future expenditure on these products can be equated by economic transactions made today.

prising that markets do not always perform well in fostering broader social goals such as achieving an 'equitable' distribution of income or promoting shared community values. Markets are not effective in fostering these goals, precisely because individuals do not pursue these goals by purchasing goods and services in markets.

INCOME DISTRIBUTION

An important characteristic of a market economy is the *distribution* of the income that it determines. People whose services are in heavy demand relative to supply earn large incomes, whereas people whose services are not in heavy demand relative to supply earn much less.

As we have seen in earlier chapters, differentials in earnings serve the important function of motivating people to adapt. The advantage of such a system is that individuals can make their own decisions about how to alter their behaviour when market conditions change; the disadvantage is that temporary rewards and penalties are dealt out as a result of changes in market conditions that are beyond the control of the affected individuals. The resulting differences in incomes will seem unfair to many—even though they are the incentives that make markets work.

Because the workings of the market may be stern, even cruel, society often chooses to intervene. Should heads of households be forced to bear the full burden of their misfortune if, through no fault of their own, they lose their jobs? Even if they lose their jobs through their own fault, should they and their families have to bear the whole burden, which may include starvation? Should the ill and the aged be thrown on the mercy of their families? What if they have no families? Both private charities and a great many government policies are concerned with modifying the distribution of income that results from such things as where one starts, how able one is, how lucky one is, and how one fares in the labour market.

Problems arise when our measures designed to improve equity seriously inhibit the efficient operation of the price system.

Often the goal of a more equitable distribution conflicts with the goal of a more efficient economy.

Say that we were so extreme as to believe that equity demanded that everyone received the same income. All incentives to work hard and to move from job to job would be eliminated. Some command economies came close to these extreme positions, and the results were predictably disastrous. Suppose that, to be less extreme, we believed that factor earnings should not reflect short-term fluctuations in demand and supply. The UK controls on rents of living accommodation did just that in the 1960s and 1970s, and current controls in several other countries do that

today. The problem then is that the whole incentive system for resource allocation is removed if such intervention is effective. A rise in demand creates extra earnings which attract resources to meet the demand. Remove the price reaction and there is no reason for the resource reallocation to occur.

Some of the problems that this conflict between efficiency and equity can create in policy debates are further discussed in Box 23.3.

PROTECTING INDIVIDUALS FROM OTHERS

People can use and even abuse other people for economic gain in ways that the members of society find offensive. Child labour laws and minimum standards of working conditions are responses to such actions. Yet direct abuse is not the only example of this kind of market failure. In an unhindered free market, the adults in a household would usually decide how much education to buy for their children. Selfish parents might buy no education, while egalitarian parents might buy the same education for all of their children, regardless of their abilities. The members of society may want to interfere in these choices, both to protect the child of the selfish parent and to ensure that some of the scarce educational resources are distributed according to ability rather than the family's wealth. All households are forced to provide a minimum of education for their children, and a number of inducements are offered—through public universities, scholarships, and other means—for talented children to consume more education than they or their parents might choose if they had to pay the entire cost themselves.

PATERNALISM

Members of society, acting through the state, often seek to protect adult (and presumably responsible) individuals, not from others but from themselves. Laws prohibiting the use of heroin, crack, cocaine, and other drugs, and laws prescribing the installation and use of seat belts, are intended primarily to protect individuals from their own ignorance or shortsightedness. This kind of interference in the free choices of individuals is called **paternalism.** Whether such actions reflect the wishes of the majority in society or whether they reflect the actions of overbearing governments, there is no doubt that the market will not provide this kind of protection. Buyers do not buy what they do not want, and sellers have no motive to provide it.

Protection and paternalism are often closely related to **merit goods.** Merit goods are goods that society deems to be especially important and that those in power feel individuals should be required or encouraged to consume. Housing, education, and health care are often cited as merit goods.

BOX 23.3

Distribution versus efficiency—the 'leaky bucket'

Economists recognize that government actions can affect both the allocation of resources and the distribution of income. Resource allocation is easier to talk about, simply because economists have developed precise definitions of *efficient* and *inefficient* allocations. Distribution is more difficult, because we cannot talk about *better* or *worse* distributions of income without introducing normative considerations. Partly because of this, much of economics concerns efficiency and neglects effects on the distribution of income. Many disagreements about economic and social policy can be understood in terms of differences in emphasis on efficiency and distribution. Distribution, of course, is often more important as a political matter, because it is distribution (especially one's own share) that people care about most, not the overall efficiency with which the economy is operating.

Moreover, to the extent that society chooses to redistribute income, it is generally the case that economic efficiency will be reduced. The image of the 'leaky bucket' summarizes the problem. Suppose we have a well-supplied reservoir of water, and we wish to get some water to a person who is not able to come to the reservoir. The only vessel available for transporting the water is a leaky bucket; it works, in that water is deliverable to the intended location, but it works at cost, in that some of the water is lost on the trip. Thus, in order to get a gallon of water to its destination, more than a gallon of water has to be removed from the reservoir. It may be possible to design better or worse buckets, but all of them will leak somewhat.

The analogy to an economy is that the act of redistributing income (carrying the water) reduces the total value of goods and services available to the economy (by the amount of 'water' that 'leaks' on the trip). Getting a dollar to the poor reduces the resources available to everyone else by more than a dollar.

Why is the bucket always leaky? Because there is no way to redistribute income without changing the incentives faced by consumers and producers. Generally, a programme that takes from the rich and gives to the poor will reduce the incentives of both the rich and the poor to produce income. A policy of subsidizing goods that are deemed to be important—goods such as food, shelter, or oil—will cause the market prices of those goods to be lower than marginal costs, implying that resources used to produce those goods could be used to produce goods of higher value elsewhere in the economy. (This is the basic efficiency argument that we first discussed in Chapter 16.)

Measuring the efficiency costs of redistribution is an important area of economic research. Most economists would agree that programmes that directly redistribute income are more efficient (per pound of resources made available to a given income group) than programmes that subsidize the prices of specific products. One reason for this is that price subsidies apply even when high-income people purchase the products in question.

Although redistribution almost always entails some efficiency loss, this *does not imply* that redistribution should not be undertaken. (That buckets leak surely does not imply that they should not be used to transport water, given that we want to transport water and that buckets are the best available tools.) Whatever the social policy regarding the redistribution of income, economics has an important role to play in measuring the efficiency costs and distributional consequences of different programmes of redistribution. Put another way, it has useful things to say about the design and deployment of buckets.

SOCIAL OBLIGATIONS

In a free-market system, if you can pay another person to do things for you, you may do so. If you persuade someone else to clean your house in return for £20, presumably both parties to the transaction are better off: you prefer to part with £20 rather than to clean the house yourself, and the person you hire prefers £20 to not cleaning your house. Normally, society does not interfere with people's ability to negotiate mutually advantageous contracts.

Most people do not feel this way, however, about activities that are regarded as social obligations. For example, during major wars when military service is compulsory, contracts similar to the one between you and a housekeeper could also be negotiated; some persons, faced with the obligation to do military service, could no doubt pay enough to persuade others to do their tour of service for them. By exactly the same argument as we just used, we can presume that both parties will be better off if they are allowed to negotiate such a trade. Yet such contracts are usually prohibited. They are prohibited because there are values to be considered other than those that can be expressed in a market. In times when it is necessary, military service by all healthy males is usually held to be a duty that is independent of an individual's tastes, wealth, influence, or social position. It is felt that everyone *ought* to do this service, and exchanges between willing traders are prohibited.

Military service is not the only example of a social obligation. Citizens are not allowed to buy their way out of jury duty or to sell their votes, even though in many cases they could find willing trading partners.

Even if the price system allocated goods and services with complete efficiency, members of a society might not wish to rely solely on the market since they have other goals that they wish to achieve.

The tools of government intervention

THE main sets of tools available to governments to deal with market failure are rules, public ownership, expenditure, and taxation.

Rules and regulations

Rules and regulations are potent tools for redressing market failures. Governments use rules both to set the framework within which market forces operate and to alter the workings of unhindered markets. Rules pervade economic activities. Shop hours and working conditions are regulated. Rules govern the circumstances under which various types of unions can be formed and operated. Discrimination between labour services provided by males and females is illegal in Britain and in many other countries. Children cannot be served alcoholic drinks. They must attend school in most countries, and be inoculated against communicable diseases in many. Laws prohibit people from selling or using certain drugs. Prostitution is prohibited in many societies even though it usually involves a willing buyer and a willing seller. In many countries, you are forced to purchase insurance for the damage you might do to others with your private motor car. In some countries, people who offer goods for sale cannot refuse to sell them to someone just because they do not like the customer's colour or religion. There are rules against fraudulent advertising and the sale of substandard, adulterated, or poisonous food. In some countries, such as the United States, anyone can purchase a variety of firearms ranging from pistols to machine-guns; in other countries, such as the United Kingdom, it is difficult for a private citizen to obtain a handgun.

Most business practices are controlled by rules and regulations. In many countries, agreements among oligopolistic firms to fix prices, or divide up markets, are illegal. The mere existence of monopoly is outlawed in some countries. When the cost advantages of monopoly resulting from scale economies are considerable, the prices a monopolistic firm can charge, and the return it can earn on its capital investment, are often regulated.

Public ownership

Assume the government feels that, under free-market conditions, the firms in some industry would charge an 'excessive' price and earn 'unnecessary' profits. The government could nationalize the industry and then instruct the managers to follow the desired pricing policy. Government ownership is thus a tool for exerting control over production and distribution. It brings the production in question under public ownership as an alternative to using regulations to control the behaviour of private owners. Alternatively, the government could use rules and regulations to force the firms in that industry to charge a 'reasonable' price and so eliminate the 'unnecessary' profits. The recent trend in Britain has been to move from the first to the second type of solution. State-owned industries have been privatized and put under the control of regulatory bodies such as OFTEL for telecommunications and OFWAT for water. These important developments and the experience behind them were discussed in detail in Chapter 16 and so need no further attention here.

Expenditure

Some government expenditures are in return for goods and services that count as part of current output. When the government buys the services of factors of production and uses them to produce goods and services in the public sector of the economy, the factors are unavailable to produce private-sector output. This type of expenditure is sometimes called **exhaustive expenditure**. Among their many uses, exhaustive expenditures are the tool for filling in gaps in what the free market provides. For example, public goods, such as national defence, the legal system, and coastal navigation aids, must be produced by the government or not at all. In those cases, the failure of the free market, and the potential for a remedy by government action, are obvious.

The remainder of government expenditure consists of **transfer payments**, which are payments *not* made in return for any contribution to current output. Old-age pensions, unemployment insurance and supplementary benefits, welfare payments, disability payments, and a host of other expenditures made by the modern welfare state are all transfer payments. They do not add to current marketable output; they merely transfer the power to purchase output from those who provide the money (usually taxpayers) to those who receive it. Their main purpose, therefore, is to alter the *distribution* of income. Transfer payments do not represent a claim by the government on real productive resources. Revenue must none the less be raised to finance them.

Taxation

Taxes are of major importance in the pursuit of many government policies. They provide the funds to finance expenditure, but they are also used as tools in their own right for a wide range of purposes. They are used to alter the incentives to which private maximizing agents react, and to alter the distribution of income.

INDIRECT TAXES

Taxes are divided into two broad groups, depending on whether persons or transactions are taxed. An **indirect tax** is levied on a transaction, and is paid by an individual by virtue of his or her association with that transaction. Taxes and stamp duties on the transfer of assets from one owner to another are indirect taxes, since they depend on the assets being transferred. Inheritance taxes, which depend on the size of the estate being inherited and not on the circumstances of the beneficiaries, are also an indirect tax.

The most important indirect taxes in today's world are those on the sale of currently produced products. These taxes are called excise taxes when they are levied on manufacturers, and sales taxes when they are levied on the sale of goods from retailer to consumer. The EU countries levy a comprehensive tax of this sort on all transactions, whether at the retail, wholesale, or manufacturer's level, called the **value added tax** (VAT). Value added is the difference between the value of factor services and materials that the firm purchases as inputs and the value of its output. It therefore represents the value that a firm adds by virtue of its own activities. The VAT is an indirect tax because it depends on the value of what is made and sold, not on the wealth or income of the maker or seller. Thus, two self-employed fabric designers, each with a 'value added' of £50,000 in terms of designs produced and sold, would pay the same VAT even if one had no other source of income while the other was independently wealthy.

Indirect taxes may be levied in two basic ways. An **ad valorem tax** is a percentage of the value of the transaction on which it is levied. An 8 per cent retail sales tax would mean, for example, that the retail firm had to charge a tax of 8 per cent of the value of everything it sold. A **specific** or **per-unit tax** is a tax expressed as so many pence (say) per unit, independent of its price. Taxes on cinema and theatre tickets, and on each litre of petrol or alcohol, and on each packet of cigarettes independent of the price at which they are produced or sold, are specific, indirect taxes.

DIRECT TAXES

The second broad group of taxes are called **direct taxes**. These are levied on persons, and vary with the status of the taxpayer. The most important direct tax is the income tax. The personal income tax falls sometimes on the income of households and sometimes separately on each member of the household. It varies with the size and source of the taxpayer's income and various other characteristics laid down by law, such as marital status and number of dependants.

Firms also pay taxes on their incomes. This is a direct tax, both in the legal sense that the company is an individual in the eyes of the law, and in the economic sense that the company is owned by its shareholders so that a tax on the company is a tax on them. An expenditure tax (as advocated some years ago for the United Kingdom by the Royal Commission headed by Nobel-prize-winning economist James Meade) is also a direct tax. It is based on what a person spends, rather than on what he or she earns, and has exemptions that are specific to the individual taxpayer. A poll tax, which is simply a lump-sum tax levied on each person, is also a direct tax.

The rate of tax is the tax expressed as a percentage of the base on which it is levied. The rate of income tax, for example, is the tax paid expressed as a percentage of the income on which it is levied. It is important in the discussion to distinguish average from marginal rates. The *average rate* of income tax paid by a person is that person's total tax divided by his or her income. The *marginal rate* of tax is the rate he or she would pay on another unit of income.

Progressivity   The general term for the relation between income and the percentage of income paid as a tax is **progressivity**. A **regressive tax** takes a *smaller percentage* of people's incomes the larger is their income. A **progressive tax** takes a *larger percentage* of people's incomes the larger is their income. A **proportional tax** is the boundary case between the two: it takes the *same percentage* of income from everyone. Taxes on food, for example, tend to be regressive because the proportion of income spent on food tends to fall as income rises. Taxes on alcoholic spirits tend to be progressive, since the proportion of income spent on spirits tends to rise with income. Taxes on beer, on the other hand, are regressive. Different progressivities are shown in Figure 23.2.

Progressivity can be defined for any one tax, or for the tax system as a whole. Different taxes have different characteristics. Inevitably, some will be progressive and some regressive. The impact of a tax system as a whole on high-, middle-, and low-income groups is best judged by looking at the progressivity of the whole set of taxes taken together. For example, income taxes are progressive in the United Kingdom, rising to a maximum marginal rate of 40 per cent. The overall tax system is also progressive, but much less so than one would guess from studying only the income tax rates. This is because much revenue is raised by indirect taxes, all of which are less progressive than income taxes, and some of which are regressive.

Conclusion

Almost all government actions, including the kinds that we have discussed above, change the incentives facing con-

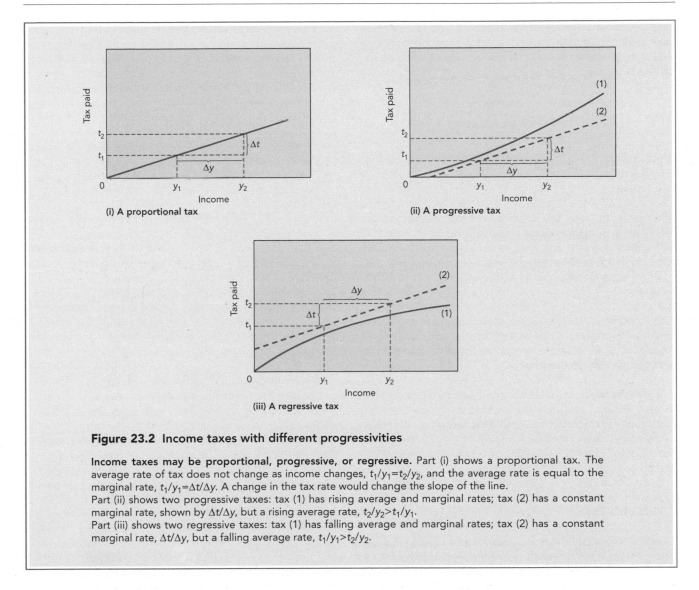

Figure 23.2 Income taxes with different progressivities

Income taxes may be proportional, progressive, or regressive. Part (i) shows a proportional tax. The average rate of tax does not change as income changes, $t_1/y_1 = t_2/y_2$, and the average rate is equal to the marginal rate, $t_1/y_1 = \Delta t/\Delta y$. A change in the tax rate would change the slope of the line.
Part (ii) shows two progressive taxes: tax (1) has rising average and marginal rates; tax (2) has a constant marginal rate, shown by $\Delta t/\Delta y$, but a rising average rate, $t_2/y_2 > t_1/y_1$.
Part (iii) shows two regressive taxes: tax (1) has falling average and marginal rates; tax (2) has a constant marginal rate, $\Delta t/\Delta y$, but a falling average rate, $t_1/y_1 > t_2/y_2$.

sumers and producers. If the government provides a park, people will have a weakened incentive to own large plots of land of their own. Fixing minimum or maximum prices (as we saw in the discussion of rent control and agriculture in Chapter 6) affects privately chosen levels of output.

The government can adjust the tax system to provide subsidies to some kinds of behaviour and penalties to others. In some countries, deductible mortgage interest makes owner-occupied housing relatively more attractive than other assets that a person might purchase. Such tax treatment sends the household different signals from those sent by the free market. Grants enabling students to become nurses or teachers may offset barriers to mobility into those occupations.

Fines and criminal penalties for violating the rules that are imposed are another part of the incentive structure. By providing direct or indirect fines or subsidies, the government can (in principle) correct externalities, induce private production of public goods, change the income distribution, and encourage behaviour that is deemed socially valuable. However, as we shall see, interventions of this kind are not always successful, and they can do as much (or more) harm as good.

It is clear that the government controls a wide variety of instruments that might be used to reduce market failures. For example, it can alter the distribution of income by raising money through a progressive income tax and spending the money on services used mainly by people with low incomes. As another example, it can try to move a natural monopoly's output towards the optimal level by rules and regulations governing privately owned firms, by nationalizing the industry, or by levying taxes and subsidies that provide an incentive for profit-maximizing firms to produce the socially optimal output.

We shall consider such policies in greater detail in the next chapter. In the meantime, we go on to our next question: given that government action could alleviate some market failures, what are the costs of doing so?

The costs of government intervention

SO far in this chapter we have seen that market failures provide scope for governments to intervene and that governments have many tools to use in such interventions. This, however, is not the end of the story. To evaluate government intervention, we need to consider costs as well as benefits.

Large potential benefits do not necessarily justify government intervention, nor do large potential costs necessarily make it unwise. What matters is net benefits—the balance between benefits and costs.

Three types of costs of government intervention are considered below: costs that are internal to the government, costs that are external to the government but directly paid by others in the sector where the intervention occurs, and costs that are external to the government and felt more generally throughout the entire economy.

Internal costs

When government inspectors visit plants to check on compliance with government-imposed health standards, industrial safety or environmental protection, costs are incurred in such forms as the salaries and expenses of the inspectors. When the government solicitors spend time on an anti-monopoly case, they are incurring costs. The costs of the judges, the clerks, and the court reporters who are needed when the case is heard are likewise costs imposed by regulation. All these activities use valuable resources, resources that could have been used to produce other goods and services.

Everything the government does uses resources. Armies of clerks, backed up by computers and other modern equipment, keep track of income tax and VAT receipts. Inspectors take the field to enforce compliance, and the courts deal with serious offenders. Unemployment and supplementary benefits must be administered. The size of the body of public employees at the national and local level (see Box 23.3 on p. 424) attests to the significant resource costs of government activity, costs that need to be set against the benefits produced.

Direct external costs

External costs are costs that the government's action imposes on others. Direct external costs are those directly associated with the government's actions.

Increases in production costs   Regulation and control often add directly to the costs of producing goods. For example, firms must inspect machinery to ensure that it meets government safety standards.

Costs of compliance   Much business activity is devoted to understanding, reporting, and contesting regulatory provisions. Occupational safety and environmental control have increased the number of employees not working on the shop floor. The legal costs of a large company can run into large sums each year.

The same can be said of the costs of complying with tax laws. Firms, and wealthy individuals, spend substantial sums on lawyers and accountants. These advisers help them to comply with tax laws. They also assist in choosing tax-minimizing courses of action. These resources have alternative uses. So do firms' time and planning energies, whose social product might be higher if devoted to maximizing growth potential rather than minimizing their tax payments.

Losses in productivity   Quite apart from the actual expenditures, government intervention may reduce the incentive for experimentation, innovation, and the introduction of new products. Requiring advance government clearance before introducing a new method, or product (on grounds of potential safety hazards or environmental impact) can reduce the incentive to develop it. New lines of investment may be chosen more for their tax implications than for their potential for reducing production costs and so contributing to productivity growth.

Indirect external costs

Indirect external costs are costs of the government's action that spread beyond those immediately affected by it—sometimes covering the entire economy. There are many such costs and we give a sampling of some of them.

EXTERNALITIES

Ironically, government intervention to offset adverse externalities can create new adverse externalities. For example, government regulations designed to ensure the safety of new drugs delay the introduction of all drugs, including those that are safe. The benefits of these regulations are related to the unsafe drugs kept off the market. The cost includes the delayed availability of new safe drugs.

Tax shifting   Major externalities are often caused by tax shifting. The **shifting** of a tax refers to the passing of its incidence from the person who initially pays it to someone else. The **incidence** refers to who bears it. One major problem with the use of taxes as a means of redistributing income is that market forces may shift the burden of the tax from the person who initially pays it to others. The major conclusion that follows from studying the effects of a tax levied in a single market (see Chapter 15, pp. 282–6) is as follows:

If the supply curve is positively sloped, and the demand curve negatively sloped, the burden of a tax is shared between producers and consumers.

There will, however, be repercussions in other markets. As the price of one product rises, the demand curves for substitutes will shift to the right, while the demand curves for complements will shift to the left. The resulting changes in their market prices will induce changes in other related markets. The effects of a tax on one market will thus spread throughout the economy, making the final distribution of the burden difficult to ascertain.

INEFFICIENCIES

Almost all government interventions have some adverse efficiency effects. These have played an important part in the so-called supply-side criticisms of government policy, and we need to look at them in some detail.

Taxation   First, consider a sales tax on one specific good. The tax raises the relative price of that good faced by consumers, so they will buy less of it, and more of other products. Production falls below the competitive equilibrium level, which is the one that maximizes the sum of consumers' and producers' surplus. The result, as shown in Figure 23.3, is a loss of consumers' surplus exactly analogous to the deadweight loss of monopoly.

This result applies to any taxes that affect the prices of products in different proportions and hence change rela-

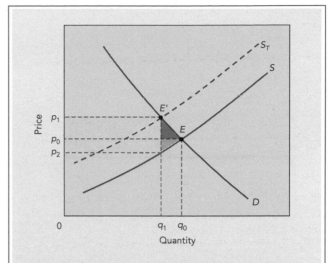

Figure 23.3 The efficiency loss of an indirect tax

An indirect tax lowers output and causes a deadweight loss of consumers' surplus. The original demand and supply curves are D and S. Equilibrium is at E, with q_0 bought at a price of p_0. A tax is added to producers' costs, whose supply curve now shifts upwards to S_T. Equilibrium then shifts to E'. The quantity sold falls to q_1 while the market price rises to p_1. This is the price that purchasers pay. Producers, however, receive only p_2 per unit, net of tax.

As a result of the fall in consumption from q_0 to q_1, purchasers suffer a loss of consumers' surplus. This is the amount shown by the dark red area between the demand curve and the original price over the range of the reduction in consumption.

As a result of the same fall in production, producers suffer a loss of producers' surplus. This is shown by the medium red area between the supply curve and the original equilibrium price. Because these areas look like triangles (they are not, unless the demand and supply curves are straight lines), they are often referred to as the 'triangles of surplus'.

The government gains the tax revenue given by the light red area, whose height is p_1–p_2, and whose length is q_1. This revenue is raised partly at the expense of the consumers, and partly at the expense of the producers. But no one gains the lost consumers' and producers' surpluses between q_1 and q_0. These lost-surplus triangles constitute the *deadweight* loss from the tax.

tive prices. It thus applies to VAT whenever different products are taxed at different rates. The key is that:

Consumers adjust their marginal rates of substitution to prices including tax, while producers adjust their marginal costs, and hence their marginal rates of transformation, to the prices excluding tax. Any set of taxes that alters relative prices will cause inefficiency by confronting producers and consumers with different relative prices.

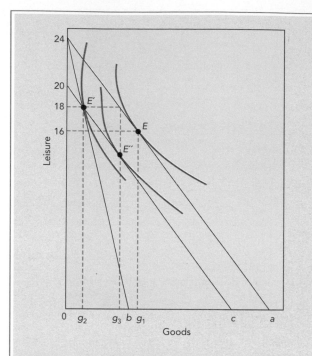

Figure 23.4 The distortion of the work–leisure choice by an income tax

An income tax upsets the optimum condition between work and leisure. An individual faces a pre-tax wage rate shown by the slope of the budget line running from 24 to a. Equilibrium is at E, where g_1 of goods and 16 hours of leisure are consumed. This individual can be thought of as starting with 24 hours of leisure and no goods, then trading down the budget line to reach E by giving up 8 hours of leisure to gain g_1 of goods.

An income tax is now levied at the rate $(a-b)/a$. The pre-tax budget line is unchanged but the after-tax budget line shifts to the line running from 24 to b. The horizontal distance between the two lines shows the amount of the tax at each amount of work. For example, if 24 hours a day were worked, pre-tax income would be a, but the tax would be $a-b$, making after-tax income b. Equilibrium now shifts to E', where g_2 of goods and 18 hours of leisure are consumed. When the individual works 6 hours, the pre-tax income is g_3 along the original budget line. But $g_3 - g_2$ is paid in taxes, leaving after-tax consumption at g_2.

The budget line running from 20 to c corresponds to a poll tax that takes the same amount from the individual as did the income tax. (It goes through the point E'.) This line has the same slope as the pre-tax budget line, but it is shifted inwards horizontally by the amount of the poll tax which is $a-c = g_3 - g_2$. After paying the poll tax, the consumer's budget line runs from 20 to c. Equilibrium is now at E'', where, compared with the income tax, the same tax is paid, but a higher indifference curve is reached.

Next consider the income tax. It creates an inefficiency by distorting the work–leisure choice. Each individual,

reacting to after-tax wage rates, sees a rate of substitution between work and leisure that differs from the rate implied by the pre-tax wage the employer is prepared to pay.

To understand the source of the inefficiency, compare the income tax with a **poll tax**, which takes the same lump sum from everyone. Because it is not related to income, a poll tax leaves the marginal rate of substitution between goods and leisure unaffected. Employees see a wage rate that correctly reflects the wage the employers are ready to pay. The tax exerts no disincentive to work at the margin, and thus is more efficient than the income tax.

Figure 23.4 demonstrates the inefficiency of the income tax. It shows that each individual achieves a higher indifference curve when he or she is forced to pay a given amount of tax revenue through a poll tax, rather than through an income tax. The poll tax is more efficient because it leaves each person facing a choice at the margin that reflects the wage rate actually paid in the market.

The importance of the figure lies in its demonstration that any practical tax does have negative efficiency effects, because it distorts relative price signals. The only tax that does not do so, under normal conditions, is the poll tax. It has no negative efficiency effects because the amount paid does not vary with any of the taxpayer's economic decisions. It is precisely for this reason that most people find it unacceptable (on equity grounds) as anything other than a minor source of revenue.[1]

Exceptional circumstances Two extreme circumstances provide exceptions to the rule that all taxes upset efficiency conditions. These occur, as shown in Figure 23.5, where either the demand or the supply curve is perfectly inelastic. In either case, the same amount will be bought and sold both before and after the tax. Because the quantity is insensitive to the price changes caused by the tax, it does not have adverse efficiency effects. If decisions do not respond to changes in the price signals, then these changes have no effects, unfavourable or favourable.

There are few, if any, markets where these extreme conditions are met. It is sometimes alleged that taxes on cigarettes and alcohol come close because demand is highly inelastic. But there is plenty of room for substitution among types of alcohol, with people shifting to cheaper sources as prices rise. Furthermore, there is international substitution whenever tax rates differ among countries. In the European Union, for example, consumers take day trips to buy from adjacent countries with lower taxes on specific

---

[1] The argument in the text assumes a closed economy in which everyone actually pays the tax. In practice, however, even the poll tax will have some efficiency effects. A large enough poll tax will cause people to emigrate. It will also cause some people to choose jobs, and lifestyles, that facilitate evasion. People with no fixed addresses, and no regular jobs, find evasion easier than people who are stuck with one job and own their own houses or flats. Thus, at the margin, the poll tax will influence some people's job and residence decisions, which means it does have some adverse efficiency effects.

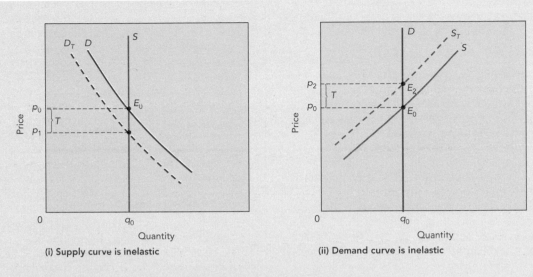

Figure 23.5 Taxes that do not cause inefficiencies

Any tax that does not alter economic behaviour will not cause economic inefficiency. In both parts of the figure a demand curve, D, and supply curve, S, intersect at E_0 to produce equilibrium price and quantity of p_0 and q_0. A tax of T per unit is then placed on the sale of the product.

In part (i), the supply curve is completely inelastic and the market equilibrium remains at E_0. The after-tax receipts of suppliers are shown by the curve D_T, and their after-tax price by p_1. The quantity produced, and hence the allocation of resources, is unaffected by the tax, all of which is paid by suppliers.

In part (ii), the demand curve is perfectly inelastic. The after-tax supply curve shifts to S_T and market equilibrium goes to E_2, taking market price to p_2. Once again, the allocation of resources is unaffected. This time, however, the whole tax is paid by consumers.

products such as alcohol and tobacco. This has become a major phenomenon since the Single Market rules permitted unlimited purchases 'for personal use' and created a new blue channel for passengers returning from other EU countries.

For these and other similar reasons, although elasticities of demand for alcohol and tobacco may be less than unity, they are not zero. Thus, taxes on these products have efficiency effects. The very high rates charged on them may be justified on grounds of negative externalities, since a significant proportion of medical and hospital care goes to treat alcohol- and tobacco-related ailments. They may also be explained, however, by a government seeking to maximize its tax revenue from products which, although inelastic in demand, are not regarded socially as necessities.

DISINCENTIVE EFFECTS

The disincentive effects of high marginal rates of income tax are still a subject of debate. If we consider a 'closed economy' where there is no possibility of emigration, then marginal rates of up to 40 or 50 per cent do not seem to have strong disincentive effects. Some people work less

hard, but others work harder in order to restore their after-tax incomes to what they would have been if tax rates had been lower. At some point, however, high marginal tax rates begin to have more serious disincentive effects. As marginal rates approach 100 per cent, the disincentive effect becomes absolute.

Steeply progressive rates also have efficiency-reducing allocative effects among types of employment. People whose incomes are high for a few years and low thereafter pay high taxes, relative to others who have the same lifetime incomes but have them spread more evenly over the years. People with high incomes spend much time and expense on lawyers and accountants to shield their incomes from taxes. Such activities produce no other net output for society.

In an open society where emigration is possible, very high marginal rates of tax have major effects. Authors, artists, pop groups, and others who 'strike it rich' are strongly tempted to emigrate to countries that will allow them to keep a higher proportion of their incomes. The temptation is particularly strong when there are countries with common linguistic and cultural environments and substantially lower tax rates. Emigration of successful people of this type from the United Kingdom to the United States was significant between 1945 and 1980, when UK marginal rates of income tax were often double those in the United States.

From the point of view of maximizing tax revenues, and reducing tax burdens on middle- and lower-income groups, it would be better to have high-income people still in the country paying tax rates of 40–50 per cent than out of the country, avoiding higher tax rates.

Income taxes and the supply of effort Do high rates of income tax cause people to work less? Would a reduction of income tax rates cause people to work more?

Economic theory makes no general prediction about the effect on the supply of effort of raising or lowering the rates of income tax. On p. 338 and in Box 18.4, we showed that a rise in the wage rate might increase, or decrease, the supply of effort, and, similarly, a fall in the wage rate might have either effect. Now observe that the after-tax wage rate is lowered by a rise in the rate of income tax, and raised by a fall in the rate. It follows immediately that any given change

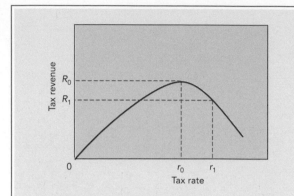

Figure 23.6 The Laffer curve

Increases in tax rates beyond some level will decrease rather than increase tax revenue. The curve relates the government's tax revenue to the tax rate. As drawn, revenue reaches a maximum level of R_0 at average tax rate r_0. If tax rates were at r_1, *reducing* them to r_0 would increase revenue to the government.

BOX 23.4

....

The Laffer curve 600 years before Laffer

In the fourteenth century, the Arabic philosopher Ibn Khaldun wrote:

It should be known that at the beginning of the dynasty, taxation yields a large revenue from small assessments. At the end of the dynasty, taxation yields a small revenue from large assessments. . . .

When the dynasty follows the ways of group feeling and (political) superiority, it necessarily has at first a desert attitude. The desert attitude requires kindness, reverence, humility, respect for the property of other people, and disinclination to appropriate it, except in rare instances. Therefore, the individual imposts and assessments, which together constitute the tax revenue, are low. When tax assessments and imposts upon the subjects are low, the latter have the energy and desire to do things. Cultural enterprises grow and increase, because the low taxes bring satisfaction. When cultural enterprises grow, the number of individual imposts and assessments mounts. In consequence, the tax revenue, which is the sum total of [the individual assessments], increases.

When the dynasty continues in power and their rulers follow each other in succession, they become sophisticated. The Bedouin attitude and simplicity lose their significance, and the Bedouin qualities of moderation and restraint disappear.

As a result, the individual imposts and assessments upon the subjects, agricultural labourers, farmers and all the other tax-

payers, increase. Every individual impost and assessment is greatly increased, in order to obtain a higher tax revenue. Customs duties are placed upon articles of commerce. Gradual increases in the amount of assessments succeed each other regularly, in correspondence with the gradual increase in the luxury customs and many needs of the dynasty, and the spending required in connection with them. Eventually, the taxes will weigh heavily upon the subjects and overburden them. Heavy taxes become an obligation and tradition, because the increases took place gradually, and no one knows specifically who increased them or levied them. They lie upon the subjects like an obligation and tradition.

The assessments increase beyond the limits of equity. The result is that the interest of the subjects in cultural enterprises disappears, since when they compare expenditures and taxes with their income and gain and see the little profit they make, they lose all hope. Therefore, many of them refrain from all the activity. The result is that the total tax revenue goes down.

Finally, civilization is destroyed, because the incentive for cultural activity is gone. It is the dynasty that suffers from the situation, because it [is the dynasty that] profits from cultural activity.*

* *From the Muqaddimah: An Introduction to History*, translated from the Arabic by Franz Rosenthal (Bollingen Series **XLIII**. Copyright 1958 and 1967 by Princeton University Press. Reprinted by permission of Princeton University Press.)

in the rate of income tax may either raise or lower the supply of effort.

The Laffer curve   The possibility that a cut in the rate of tax might increase the supply of effort so much that tax collections increased is illustrated in a famous curve called the **Laffer curve**, named after an American exponent of supply-side economics, Professor Arthur Laffer.

The general shape of the curve, which is shown in Figure 23.6, is argued as a matter of simple logic. At a zero tax rate, no revenue will be collected. Similarly, at an average tax rate of 100 per cent, revenues will again be zero because no one would bother to earn taxable income just to support the government. At intermediate rates, people will earn taxable income and pay taxes. Government tax revenues will reach a maximum value at some rate of taxation between zero and 100 per cent. For rates higher than the rate that produces this maximum, every increase in tax rates will lead to a decrease in tax revenues. The curve cannot be a guide to practical policy, however, until we know where this maximum occurs. An interesting early precursor of Laffer's curve is discussed in Box 23.4.

Welfare measures and the supply of effort   Payments designed to help certain low-income groups are often means-tested. Sometimes the welfare payments are reduced by £1 for every £1 of income received by welfare recipients. The person in effect faces a marginal tax rate of 100 per cent on every unit of income earned up to the level of the benefit payments. This introduces a severe disincentive to work, and we should not be surprised when people respond rationally to these market signals.

Say, for example, benefit payments are £50 a week and are cut by £1 for every £1 of income earned. If the person makes £10 a week, benefits fall to £40; if £20 is earned, benefits fall to £30, and so on. Only when more than £50 per week is earned will the person's disposable income begin to rise. Even if the benefits are reduced at a less sharp rate, say 50p per £1 earned, the disincentive of the high implicit tax rate is strong. Figure 23.7 illustrates this disincentive effect by showing how such schemes induce many people to reject employment that they would have accepted if the schemes were not there.

Benefit payments are required to help those in real need. If they are income-related, however, they tend to discourage rational recipients from working.

This does not argue against welfare payments, but it does suggest the desirability of designing schemes to minimize their effects on efficiency.

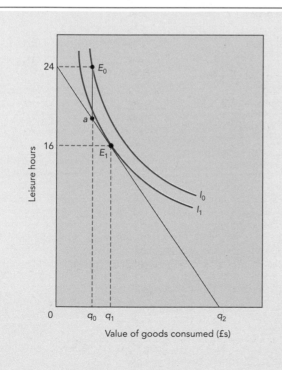

Figure 23.7   Work disincentives of welfare schemes

Income-tested benefits provide disincentives for work. The individual is not employed but is receiving benefits from some welfare scheme of q_0. Consumption is at point E_0, with 24 hours of leisure and q_0 of goods.

The opportunity for work now arises. The wage is $q_2/24$ per hour. (Twenty-four hours' work earns q_2 of goods.) If the welfare scheme did not exist, the budget line would be the line from 24 to q_2. Equilibrium would be at E_1 on indifference curve I_1 with 8 hours being worked in return for q_1 income.

For the individual at E_0, however, the benefits are reduced £1 for every £1 of income earned. The effective budget line thus starts at E_0 and is vertical down to a, where q_0 is earned by work rather than being received as benefits. (As the individual moves down the segment from E_0 to a, more of q_0 is being earned by work and less received as benefits, but total consumption remains fixed at q_0.) The budget line then runs from a to q_2, indicating that all income comes from work with no benefits being received.

Faced with these choices, a rational person will reject the work offer and remain at E_0 on indifference curve I_0, even though he or she would have worked if the benefits had been unavailable.

Optimal government intervention

WE have seen that government intervention can have benefits in removing market failure, but that it also has costs of many sorts. Government intervention is justified when the benefits exceed the costs. Consideration of this issue leads us into the question: how much government intervention is optimal? We illustrate how to handle this question by studying pollution prevention. We start by assuming that the only costs are the direct production costs of reducing the pollution.

Reducing pollution

Suppose a factory is emitting noxious sulphur dioxide (SO_2) and the government wishes to correct this externality. How much of the pollution should be eliminated? Suppose that simple recirculation of the gases through the chimney filters would reduce the discharge of SO_2 by 50 per cent; after that, the cost would double for each further 10 per cent reduction in the remaining SO_2. At most, it would be possible to eliminate 99.44 per cent of all SO_2, but the cost would be vast. The marginal costs of removal rise sharply as the amount of SO_2 eliminated rises from 50 per cent to 99.44 per cent.

The optimal amount of SO_2 reduction occurs, as is shown in Figure 23.8, where the marginal costs of further prevention equals the marginal benefits in terms of the avoidance of external effects.

The optimal amount of pollution prevention will be less than the maximum possible when pollution is costly to prevent.

We know that government intervention brings with it enforcement costs—costs to the government, to the firm, and to third parties—as well as possible inefficiencies introduced elsewhere in the economy. These direct and indirect costs have to be added to the extra production costs we have just considered. Suppose, for simplicity, that these further costs are variable and rise with the level of pollution to be eliminated.

These new costs add to the marginal cost of reducing pollution and, as shown in Figure 23.8, decrease the amount of prevention that is optimal. If the costs are large enough, they may even make any prevention uneconomical.

The optimal amount of government intervention to avoid market failure will be lower, the greater are the costs of prevention and intervention.

Government failure

Governments are far from perfect. This is not because bureaucrats and politicians are worse than other people, more stupid, more rigid, or more venal. Instead, it is because they are like others, with flaws as well as virtues. So, having found potential net benefits from perfect but costly government intervention, the final issue is, would the imperfect governments that we encounter in the real world achieve some of these benefits? Where they do not succeed in achieving potential benefits, we speak of **government failure**.

Governments may sometimes make isolated mistakes

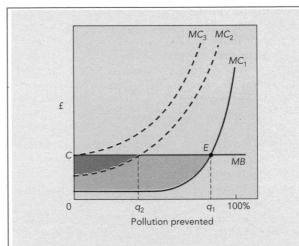

Figure 23.8 The optimal amount of pollution prevention

The optimal amount of pollution control occurs when the marginal cost of prevention equals the marginal benefit. *MB* represents the marginal benefit achieved by pollution prevention, assumed in this example to be constant at £*C* per percentage point. MC_1 represents the marginal cost of preventing pollution. For all units up to q_1, marginal benefits from pollution prevention exceed marginal costs. For all units beyond q_1, marginal costs exceed marginal benefits. The optimal level of pollution control is thus q_1, where $MB = MC_1$. Total net benefits are shown by the area that is medium- and dark blue.

If the marginal cost curve shifts to MC_2, say, owing to the addition of enforcement and other external costs, the optimal quantity of prevention will decrease to q_2. The net benefits are then reduced to the dark blue area.

If costs increase to MC_3, the optimal amount of prevention becomes zero.

just as private decision-makers do. What is interesting, however, are reasons why governments may tend, under certain circumstances, to be more systematically in error than would unhindered markets. Here are a few of the many possible causes of systematic government failure.

RIGIDITIES

Rules and regulations, tax rates, and expenditure policies are hard to change. Market conditions, however, change continually and often rapidly. A rule requiring the use of a certain method to reduce pollution may have made sense when the cost of that method was low. It may, however, become a wasteful rule when some alternative becomes the least costly method.

Today's natural monopolies are often made into tomorrow's competitive industries by technological innovations. For example, the near monopoly of the early railways was eliminated by the development of cheap road transport, and the falling cost of air transport is currently providing potent competition for surface transport in the movement of many products. One danger of government intervention is that it will be too slow in adapting to a constantly changing environment.

A centralized decision-taking body has difficulty in reacting to changing conditions as fast as decentralized decision-takers react to market signals.

As well as rigidities in reacting to changing market conditions, governments are often slow to admit mistakes even when they are aware of them. It is often politically easier to go on spending money on a project that has turned sour, than to admit fault. A classic example was the development of Concorde. Successive governments realized it was an enormous money-loser, but went on supporting it long after any chance of commercial success was gone.

Markets are much harsher in judging success. When people are investing their own money, the principle that bygones are bygones is usually followed. No firm could raise fresh financial capital for what was currently a poor prospect just because the prospects had seemed good in the past, or because much money had already been spent on it.

DECISION-MAKERS' OBJECTIVES

By far the most important cause of government failure arises from the nature of the government's own objectives. Until recently, economists did not concern themselves greatly with the motivation of government. The theory of economic policy implicitly assumed that governments had no objectives of their own. As a result, it was thought that economists needed only to identify places where the market was best left on its own, and places where government intervention could improve the market's functioning.

Governments would then stay out of the former markets, and intervene as necessary in the latter.

This model of government behaviour never fitted reality, and economists were gradually forced to think more deeply about the motivation of governments. Why was economists' advice followed closely in some cases, while it was systematically ignored in others? Today, economists no longer assume that governments are faceless robots doing whatever economic analysis shows to be in the social interest. Instead, they are modelled just as are producers and consumers—as units with their own objectives which they seek to maximize.

Governments undoubtedly do care about the social good to some extent, but public officials have their careers, their families, and their prejudices as well. Public officials' own needs are seldom wholly absent from their consideration of the actions they will take. Similarly, their definition of the public interest is likely to be influenced heavily by their personal views of what policies are best. The resulting problems are similar to the principal–agent issues mentioned earlier as a source of market failure. In the present case, the *principals* are the public; they want policies that contribute to the public good. However, their *agents*—elected and appointed—are motivated by considerations that sometimes pull against the public good.

Modelling governments as maximizers of their own welfare, and then incorporating them into theoretical models of the working of the economy, was a major breakthrough. One of the pioneers of this development was the American economist, James Buchanan, who was awarded the 1986 Nobel Prize in economics for his work in this field. The theory that he helped to develop is called *public choice theory*.

The key breakthrough was to view the government as just another economic agent engaging in its own maximizing behaviour. When this view is adopted, there is still room for many competing theories, depending on what variables are in the government's preference function (i.e. what things the government cares about). Consider the other two main decision-taking bodies in orthodox economics. Firms have only profits in their utility functions, and they seek to maximize these. Consumers have only goods and services in their utility functions, and they seek to maximize their satisfactions from consuming them. An analogous theory of the government allows only one variable in its utility function, the variable being votes! Such a government takes all its decisions with a view to maximizing its votes at the next election.

Of course, real government behaviour is more complex, just as real firm and consumer behaviour is more complex than simple theory assumes. For one thing, some government decisions are genuinely intended to improve people's welfare, even when those decisions reduce the government's popularity. But, crude though it is, a surprising amount of behaviour can be understood by using the assumption that governments care only about votes, and that they operate to increase social welfare only when such action also happens to be vote-maximizing. An example will illustrate the power of this hypothesis.

Why, in spite of strong advice from economists, have governments persisted in subsidizing agriculture for decades, until many governments now have major farm crises on their hands? Public choice theory looks at the gainers and the losers among the voters.

The gainers from agricultural supports are farmers. They are a politically powerful group, who are aware of what they will lose if farm supports were reduced. They would show their disapproval of such action by voting against any government that even suggests it. The losers are the entire group of consumers. Although they are more numerous than farmers, and although their total loss is large, each individual consumer suffers only a small loss. For example, a policy that gives £50 million a year to British farmers need only cost each citizen £1 per year.[2] Citizens have more important things to worry about, and so do not vote against the government because it supports farmers. As long as the average voters are unconcerned and often unaware of the losses they suffer, the vote-maximizing government will ignore the interests of the many, and support the interests of the few. Only when the cost of agricultural support becomes so large that ordinary taxpayers begin to count the cost, does the vote-maximizing government consider changing the agricultural policy. What is required for a policy change, according to this theory, is that those who lose become sufficiently aware of their losses for this awareness to affect their voting behaviour.

INEFFICIENT PUBLIC CHOICES

At the core of most people's idea of democracy is that each citizen's vote should have the same weight. One of the insights of public choice theory is that resource allocation, based on the principle of one-person–one-vote, will often be inefficient because it fails to take into account the *intensity of preferences*.

To illustrate this problem, consider three farmers, Abraham, Bob, and Charles. Farmers Abraham and Bob want the government to build an access road to each of their farms, each road to cost £6,000. Suppose that the road to Abraham's farm is worth £7,000 to Abraham and that the road to Bob's farm is worth £7,000 to Bob. (Charles's farm is on the main road and so requires no new access road.) Suppose that, under the current taxing rules, the cost of building each road would be shared equally among the three farmers—£2,000 each. It is efficient to build both roads, since each generates net benefits of £1,000 (£7,000 gross benefits to the farmer helped, less £6,000 total cost). But each would be defeated 2–1 in a simple majority vote. (Bob and Charles would vote against Abraham's road; Abraham and Charles would vote against Bob's road.)

Now suppose that we allow Abraham and Bob to make a deal: 'I will vote for your road if you will vote for mine.' Although such deals are often decried by political commentators, the deal enhances efficiency. Both roads now get 2–1 majorities, and both roads get built. However, such deals can just as well reduce efficiency. If we make the gross value of each road £5,000 instead of £7,000 and let Abraham and Bob make their deals, each road will still command a 2–1 majority because the total cost is £4,000 to each farmer while Abraham and Bob each gain £5,000 worth of road. It is, however, socially inefficient to build the roads, since the gross value of each road is now only £5,000, while the cost is still £6,000. Abraham and Bob will be using democracy to appropriate resources from Charles while reducing economic efficiency.

This case can be interpreted in a different way. Instead of being the third farmer, Charles might be all of the other voters in the county. Instead of bearing one-third of the costs, Abraham and Bob each might bear only a small portion of the costs. To the extent that Abraham and Bob are able to go to the local government and forcefully articulate the benefits that they would derive from the roads, they may be able to use democracy to appropriate resources from taxpayers in general. Much of the concern with the power of 'special interests' stems from the fact that the institutions of representative democracy tend to be responsive to benefits (or costs) that focus on particular, identifiable, and articulate groups. Often, costs that are borne diffusely by taxpayers or voters in general are hardly noticed.

This potential bias applies to regulations as well as to direct government provisions. Chapter 16 discussed a number of cases in which economic regulations are used to benefit the affected industry. Similarly, as we saw in Chapter 6, rent control can be interpreted, at least in part, as benefiting existing tenants at the expense of future potential tenants; the latter group tends to have no political power at all.

THE EFFECTS OF GOVERNMENT FAILURE

Suppose that, for any of the reasons discussed above, the government makes a mistake in regulation. Say it mistakenly specifies a method of pollution control that is less effective than the best method. If it insists on the level of control appropriate to the best method, but chooses the poorer method, it can convert a social gain from control into a social loss. This possibility is illustrated in Figure 23.9.

If governments pursue their own objectives such as vote-

---

[2] 'Why worry?' you may ask. 'Isn't the small loss to each consumer a reasonable price to pay?' It may be in this one case. The problem, however, lies not in one such policy, but in the cumulative effects of many. If each of many special-interest groups secures a policy that costs each member of the public a small amount, the total bill over all such policies can be, and in many countries is, very large indeed.

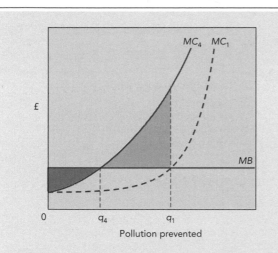

Figure 23.9 The effects of government failure

Choice of the wrong method of control will reduce the optimal amount of intervention and may convert the gains from intervention into losses. The MB and MC_1 curves are similar to those in Figure 23.8. Suppose the government specifies a method of pollution control that leads to the costs shown by MC_4 when costs shown by MC_1 could have been achieved by another method. The optimal level of prevention falls to q_4, with net benefits shown by the dark-shaded area. Government failure reduces the amount of prevention that is optimal.

The government will compound its failure if it insists on the level of prevention q_1 while requiring use of the inefficient method. The cost of every unit of pollution prevented beyond q_4 exceeds its benefits by the amount of the medium blue area. In the case shown, the result is worse than no intervention at all. (The medium blue area is larger than the dark blue area.) While the best possible government intervention would have produced a net gain, government failure in this case produces a net loss.

maximizing, they may sometimes fail to act in the public interest by design rather than by mistake. If government economists foresee that a politically popular policy will increase the degree of market failure in the long term, while seeming beneficial in the short term, the government may adopt the harmful policy, in spite of the unfavourable long-run consequences. The government could plead in such cases that it was only being democratic in following the public will. But if governments are to follow exactly where public opinion leads, they do not require experts who are able to foresee consequences that are not obvious to casual observers.

Government intervention today

Do governments intervene too little, or too much, in

response to market failure? This question reflects one aspect of the continuing debate over the role of government in the economy.

THE ROLE OF ANALYSIS

Economics can help to eliminate certain misconceptions that cloud and confuse the debate. We have earlier noted one such misconception: the optimal level of a negative externality, such as pollution, is not, as some urge, zero.

Another mistake is to equate market failure with the greed of profit-motivated corporations. Externalities do not require callous, thoughtless, or deliberately deceptive practices of private, profit-seeking firms; they occur whenever the signals to which rational decision-takers respond exclude significant benefits and costs. Local authorities and nationalized industries pollute just as much as privately owned industries when they neglect externalities in their operations, as they often do. More dramatically, pollution in the centrally controlled, former Soviet Union vastly exceeded the pollution in any industrialized Western market economy.

A third mistake is to think that the profits are related to externalities. Both a profitable industry (such as chemicals) and an unprofitable one (such as coal) are capable of spending too little on pollution control or on safety. They may also spend too much. The existence of profits provides no clue one way or the other.

THE ROLE OF IDEOLOGY

While positive analysis has a part to play, there are reasons why ideology plays a large role in evaluating government intervention. First, measuring the costs of government intervention is difficult, particularly with respect to indirect costs, because some of the trade-offs are inherently uncertain. How important and how unsafe is nuclear power? Does the ban on some pesticides cause so much malnutrition as to offset the gains in the ecology that it brings? What cannot be readily measured can be alleged to be extremely high (or low) by opponents (or supporters) of intervention.

Second, classifying the actual pattern of government intervention as successful or not is in part subjective. Has government safety regulation been (choose one) useful if imperfect, virtually ineffective, or positively adverse? All three views have been advocated.

Third, specifying what constitutes market failure is sometimes difficult. Does product differentiation represent market success (by giving consumers the variety they want) or failure (by foisting unwanted variations on them)?

In many of the advanced industrial countries in the mid-1980s, confidence in the existing mix of free-market and government regulation seems to be relatively low. No one believes that government intervention can, or should, be reduced to zero. But many governments seem to have become more cautious in evaluating the potential net gains from specific interventions and more willing to leave an increasing variety of decisions to be taken through the market mechanism.

Summary

1 Free markets can fail to achieve efficiency because of such influences as: monopoly power, a divergence of social from private costs caused by pollution, common property resources and congestion, the existence of public goods, the moral hazard and the adverse selection associated with insurance, and principal–agent problems.

2 Markets are sometimes also said to fail when they do not achieve other objectives held by members of the society, such as achieving a distribution of income regarded as equitable, protecting individuals from abuse by others (or sometimes by themselves), providing too few merit goods, and allowing transactions that violate those social obligations that transcend the market. Although no one would disagree that these reasons sometimes provide valid grounds for government intervention, they are a different kind of 'market failure' than inefficiencies, because they refer to failure to achieve results whose desirability depends on personal value judgements.

3 Governments may intervene in order to correct market failures using the tools of rules and regulations, nationalization of industry, expenditures, and taxes.

4 A rational assessment of government intervention requires an assessment of the costs as well as the potential benefits. Internal costs refer to the government's own costs of administering its policies. Direct external costs refer to the costs imposed on the non-government sector by these policies in such terms as extra production costs, costs of compliance, and losses in productivity. Indirect external costs refer to the efficiency losses that spread throughout the whole economy as a result of the alteration in price signals caused by government tax and expenditure policies.

5 As well as showing the potential for benefits to exceed costs in a world where the government functioned perfectly, it is necessary to consider the likely outcome in the imperfect world of reality. Government failure—not achieving some possible gains—can arise because of rigidities causing a lack of adequate response of rules and regulations to changing conditions, poorer foresight on the part of government regulators compared with private participants in the market, and government objectives—such as winning the next election—that conflict with such objectives as improving economic efficiency.

Topics for review

- Sources of market failure
- Public goods
- Externalities
- Common property resources
- Direct and indirect taxes
- Progressive, regressive, and proportional taxes
- The benefits and costs of government intervention
- Sources of government failure
- Public choice theory

≈ CHAPTER 24

Aims and objectives of government policy

GOVERNMENTS play a major role in all of the world's economies. Even in so-called free-market economies, the government's economic activities are widespread, and many individual markets are regulated and controlled. In the 1980s and 1990s, privatization and deregulation have been moving many countries, including Britain, towards a greater reliance on markets with a much reduced level of government presence in the economy. In this chapter, we study in detail the methods by which governments seek to achieve their three main goals of efficiency, equity, and growth.

Policy goals in outline

IN the previous chapter we saw that the various types of market failure provide a potential for useful government intervention into the workings of free markets. These market failures give rise to the two major goals of microeconomic policy, as traditionally seen by economists: *efficiency* and *equity*. In today's world, a third goal, *growth*, needs to be added to this list.

Efficiency   Recall from Chapters 16, 22, and 23 that efficiency is concerned with getting the most out of limited economic resources. When an economy is productively efficient, it is producing its current bundle of goods at the lowest possible resource cost. When an economy is allocatively efficient, the bundle of goods currently being produced is optimal. Achieving complete efficiency is an unattainable goal. Much government policy is devoted, however, towards increasing efficiency.

Equity   The second traditional goal of economic policy is equity. An equitable distribution of income is one that satisfies our ideas of justice or fairness. Notice that this is not necessarily an equal distribution. Many people feel that income differentials related to differentials in effort, or in contributions to output, are just. Others feel that justice calls for an equal distribution of income unrelated to people's work effort, and are willing to accept income differentials only where needed to avoid extreme inefficiencies.

Whatever their stand on the above issue, most people feel that social justice can be improved by making some alteration in the distribution of income that would result from the unhindered market. Thus, a major goal of government policy in all market economies is to influence the distribution of income.

Growth   A third major goal of policy is economic growth. In the recent past, growth has often been treated as a purely macroeconomic issue—the assumption being that growth depended mainly on such macroeconomic aggregates as total saving and total investment. In the last decade or two, under the influence of the so-called supply-side critics, economists have rediscovered the teaching of the classical economists:

As well as being related to such macro-magnitudes as total saving and total investment, growth is closely related to the micro-behaviour of the economy, to how well individual markets work, and to the extent to which government policy avoids distorting market signals.

Economics has traditionally recognized only two objectives of microeconomic policy: distribution and efficiency. Although governments have devoted much effort in the past two decades to examining the extent to which equity and efficiency policies may retard growth, we must still ask: is growth really a separate objective from distribution and efficiency? Is growth not just another dynamic aspect of efficiency so that the most efficient economies will be the fastest growing ones? The answer is that growth is best seen as a separate objective because it can conflict with the other two, forcing government policy-makers to make trade-offs between growth and distribution and static efficiency.

On the distribution side, it is clear that growth and equity may come into conflict. It is quite possible to argue, for example, as the famous American philosopher John Rawls has argued, that the only distribution of income that meets strict cannons of equity is absolute equality. Not everyone would agree, but for those who do there is a clear trade-off, since an equal distribution would leave no incentives for the entrepreneurial risk-taking associated with growth-creating innovations.

On the efficiency side, Joseph Schumpeter long ago pointed out that there is a potential conflict between the types of market structure that tend to encourage growth-creating innovation (particularly oligopoly) and the types of market structure that encourage static efficiency (price-taking with zero economic profits). The theory of biological evolution recognizes a trade-off between being highly adapted to the present environment and preserving enough variability to adjust quickly and flexibly to change. The best adjusted organisms may become too rigid to alter when circumstances require it and a less well adjusted organism may do better. Taking this lead, modern evolutionary theorists in economics, such as the American economists Nelson and Winter (whom we discussed in Chapter 17) and the Italian economist Giovanni Dosi, among many others, argue that there exists a trade-off between static efficiency, which maximizes real income at a moment in time, and costly, and often statically 'wasteful', experimentation, which is conducive to growth.

Given the possibility that there may be trade-offs between equity in distribution, efficiency in static resource allocation, and economic growth, it is simplest to see these as three separate policy objectives, each of which may respond differently to particular microeconomic policy measures.[1]

Two preliminaries Before proceeding, two preliminary points need mention. First, because most policies have more than one goal, the classification of policies according to goals cannot be exact. We deal as far as possible, however, with policies according to their major goal. Second, since the importance of microeconomic policy to growth has only recently been re-emphasized, few micro-policies have growth as their sole objective. Thus, growth effects are usually considered in the context of policies whose main objective is either efficiency or equity.

Efficiency

MANY government policies are designed to increase efficiency.

Improving knowledge and imposing standards

People cannot make maximizing decisions if they are poorly informed or deceived about the things they are buying or selling. Rules requiring that products and prices be described correctly are meant to improve the efficiency of choices by providing people with correct and relevant information.

In many cases where the consequences of errors are not dramatic, consumers can be left to discover, through trial and error, what is in their own best interests. In other cases, however, the results of error can be too drastic to allow consumers to learn from their own experiences which products are reliable and which unreliable. For example, botulism, caused by poorly preserved foods, can cause death. In such cases, the state intervenes to impose standards in consumers' own best interests.

Standards are also set in the workplace. The individualist might argue that firms should be left to set their own safety standards, in which case high-risk firms would have to pay wage premiums to induce workers to accept these risks voluntarily. Those who favour government regulation argue it on two grounds. First, firms are often better informed than workers on changing safety conditions in work, particularly in small factories. Government regulation compensates for the inefficiencies caused by this unequal access to information. Second, people who are desperate for work will take risks that are socially unacceptable, or that their own desperation causes them to assess imperfectly. In this case, the purpose of government intervention is either to impose social values not held by specific individuals or to act paternalistically in the belief that the state can assess the self-interests of the workers better than the workers themselves.

Provision of public goods

Because everyone can consume a public good once it is produced, private producers cannot usually market it. Lighthouses, weather notices broadcast to shipping, national defence, and a host of other similar public goods would not be provided in sufficient quantity, if at all, if the market were the sole determinant of production. Many economists have studied the problems raised by public goods, but the American Nobel Prize winner Paul Samuelson conducted probably the most path-breaking analysis in this area.

When should a public good be provided? To illustrate the

---

[1] Some call the conditions that promote growth the conditions for 'dynamic efficiency', which is acceptable as long as one accepts the possibility of a trade-off between static efficiency, which tends to maximize welfare at a moment in time, and dynamic efficiency, which tends to produce a relatively high rate of growth of welfare over time.

basic principle, consider a community composed of just two consumers. The government must decide whether or not to provide some public good which comes in a single indivisible unit; either it is produced, or it is not. Say that the first individual is prepared to pay £100 to have the use of the good, while the second individual is prepared to pay £75. On efficiency grounds, the good should be produced as long as its cost of production is no more than £175. Say it is £150. Producing the good provides services that the community values at £175 at an opportunity cost of only £150. There is a £25 gain on its production.

The optimal quantity of a public good   The above example reveals a key point about public goods.

If one person consumes a unit of an ordinary product, another person cannot also consume that unit. Thus, to satisfy all the demand at any given price, the *sum of all the quantities demanded* must be produced. With a public good, however, a given unit can be consumed by everyone. Thus, the demand for any unit of the good is represented by the sum of the prices that each individual consumer would be willing to pay for that unit. Therefore, the community's demand curve for a public good is the *vertical* sum of the demand curves of the individual consumers.

If the amount of a public good can be varied continuously, the optimal quantity to produce is that quantity for which the marginal cost of the last unit is just equal to the sum of the prices all consumers would be willing to pay for that unit.

This equilibrium, which is analysed in Figure 24.1, guarantees that the last unit of the public good costs as much to produce as the value that it gives to all its consumers.

Who pays?   One way to pay for a public good would be to charge each person the same fraction of the maximum amount he or she would be prepared to pay rather than go without the good, while fixing the fraction so as to cover the total costs of production. Consider, for example, a community of two persons, one of whom was prepared to pay £400 and the other £200 for some public good rather than go without. If the good costs £400 to produce, then each person might be charged two-thirds of his or her own maximum, making £267 for the first person and £133 for the second. Their payments would just cover total costs of production, leaving a consumers' surplus of £200.

The problem with any formula of this type lies in getting people to reveal what they would be willing to pay. Suppose, for example, that the government is considering building a public good to serve a community of 1,000 persons. It asks each of them how much he or she is prepared to pay. If I am one of those 1,000, it is in my interests to understate my true valuation, as long as everyone else does not do the same. Indeed, I might say I valued the good at zero, while others reported enough value to cover the costs. The public good would then be produced, and I would get the use of it for no payment at all.

This is the so-called **free rider problem**, the motivation of each person to understate the value of a public good to him- or herself in the hope that others will end up paying for it. The free rider problem makes it difficult to cover the costs of public goods by any formula based on people's individual valuations of that good. If enough people try to be free riders, the reported valuations will fall short of the cost. The public good then will not be built and everyone will be worse off than if they had told the truth and paid their share of the cost.

Two methods of overcoming the free rider problem are to cover the costs by either fees or taxes. Public parks, museums, and other public goods often have some or all of their costs covered by fees. This, however, leads to the prob-

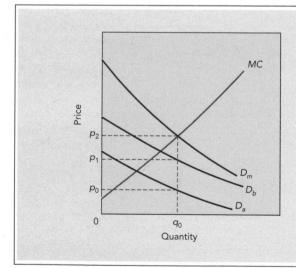

Figure 24.1   The optimal output of a public good

The society's demand curve for a public good is the vertical sum of the demand curves of all the individuals who consume that good. The demand curves D_a and D_b refer to two individual consumers of a public good. Their collective demand is shown by D_m, which is the vertical summation of D_a and D_b. For example, individual *a* would pay p_0 for quantity q_0, while individual *b* would pay p_1 for the same quantity. Together they are willing to pay the sum of p_0 and p_1, which is p_2.

The optimal quantity of the good to produce is q_0, where the marginal cost curve, *MC*, cuts the collective demand curve. At this point, the marginal cost of another unit is just equal to the sum of the values that each person places on that unit.

lem of *inefficient exclusion,* which means reducing social efficiency by excluding some people who value the good more than the cost of allowing them to consume it. The cost of allowing another person to consume an uncongested public good is zero. Charging a fee excludes all those who value their consumption at more than zero but less than the fee. This reduces total consumers' surplus below what it could be—and what it would be if no charge were levied for consuming the public good.

Because of the problem of free riders and inefficient exclusion, the cost of public goods is often met out of general taxation. The good is then provided free to all users, which achieves the efficient use of the good. Those who value a particular good higher than the average valuation gain more than those who value it below the average valuation. The hope is that, over a large number of public goods, these individual differences will cancel out. Everyone will then gain on balance as a result of the government's provision of public goods out of tax revenue.

Externalities: environmental regulation

Divergences between private and social costs and benefits are an important source of market failure. Firms that impose costs on society that they do not bear themselves will be motivated to produce too much. Firms that confer benefits on society for which they cannot receive payment will be motivated to produce too little.

Pollution is a negative externality. As a consequence of producing or consuming goods and services, 'bads' are produced as well. Steel plants produce heat and smoke in addition to steel. Farms produce chemical runoff as well as food. Households produce human waste and refuse as they consume goods and services. In all of these cases, the technology of production and consumption automatically generates pollution. Indeed, there are few human activities that do not have negative pollution externalities.

THE ECONOMIC RATIONALE FOR CONTROLLING POLLUTION

When firms use resources that they do not regard as scarce, they fail to consider the cost of those resources. This is a characteristic of most examples of pollution, including the case that is illustrated in Figure 24.2. When a paper mill produces pulp for the world's newspapers, more people are affected than its suppliers, employees, and customers. Its water-discharged effluent hurts the fishing boats that ply nearby waters, and its smog makes many resort areas less attractive, thereby reducing the tourist revenues that local motel operators and boat renters can expect. The profit-

maximizing firm neglects these external effects of its actions because its profits are not affected by them.

Allocative efficiency requires that the price (the value that consumers place on the marginal unit of output) be just equal to the marginal social cost (the value of resources that society gives up to produce the marginal unit of output). When there are harmful externalities, marginal social cost and *marginal private cost*, the cost borne by the producer, will diverge.

By producing where price equals marginal private cost, and thereby ignoring the externality, the firm is maximizing profits but producing too much output. The price that consumers pay just covers the marginal private cost but does not pay for the external damage. The *social benefit* of the last unit of output (the market price) is less than the social cost (marginal private cost plus the social cost

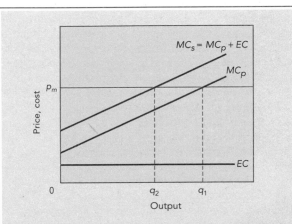

Figure 24.2 Pollution externalities

Internalizing an externality can correct market failure. The private marginal cost curve, MC_p, is the conventional marginal cost for a firm that is producing output in a competitive market. The external cost curve EC depicts marginal cost that the firm's production imposes on people other than its owners, employees, and customers. Because the firm is maximizing profits, it will ignore EC and produce output q_1, where the market price p_m equals private marginal cost. Adding EC and MC_p yields *social marginal cost*, MC_s. The socially optimal level of output is q_2, where price is equal to MC_s. Here the price is sufficient to pay for the private marginal cost of production, MC_p, and to compensate others for the external marginal cost imposed on them, EC.

Suppose that the firm is required to pay a tax of £EC per unit of output. Its MC_p curve will now become the MC_s curve. The externality will be *internalized,* and the profit-maximizing firm will be motivated to reduce its output to the socially optimal level, q_2. It does this because, with the tax added to its private marginal cost, q_2 is the profit-maximizing level of output.

imposed by the externality). Reducing output by one unit would reduce both social benefit and social cost, but would reduce social cost by more, because social cost is larger. Thus, reducing output by one unit would save economic resources and increase efficiency. The market fails to achieve efficiency because of the externality.

Making the firm bear the entire social cost of its production is called *internalizing* the externality. This will cause it to produce at a lower output. Indeed, at the optimal output, where the externality is completely internalized, consumer prices would just cover all of the marginal social cost of production—marginal private cost plus the externality. We would have the familiar condition for economic efficiency that marginal benefits to consumers are just equal to the marginal cost of producing these benefits. The difference here is that some of the marginal social cost takes the form of an externality.

Suppose that Warthog Industries PLC manufactures kitchen cabinets and that residue from painting the cabinets is washed into a stream that runs beside the plant. The stream is part of the municipal water supply, which is treated at a water purification plant before it is sent into people's homes. Suppose that each cabinet produced increases the cost of running the water treatment plant by £0.10. Then, in terms of the previous analysis, the external cost is £0.10 per unit, and *marginal social cost* will be exactly £0.10 above *marginal private cost*.

In practice, the external cost is often quite difficult to measure. This is especially so in the case of air pollution, where the damage is often spread over hundreds of thousands of square miles and can have real but small effects upon millions of people. Another difficulty arises because the cost that is imposed by pollution will generally depend on the mechanisms that are used to undo the damage that

it causes. Control mechanisms are themselves costly, and their costs also must be counted as part of the social cost of pollution. Nevertheless, the basic analysis of Figure 24.2 applies to these more difficult cases.

The socially optimal level of output is at the quantity where *all* marginal costs, private plus external, equal the marginal benefit to society.

Notice that the optimal level of output is not the level at which there is *no* pollution. Rather, it is the level at which the beneficiaries of pollution (the consumers and producers of Warthog Industries' kitchen cabinets, in our example) are just willing to pay the marginal social cost that is imposed by the pollution.

Unregulated markets tend to produce excessive amounts of environmental damage. Zero environmental damage, however, is neither technologically possible nor economically efficient.

POLLUTION CONTROL IN THEORY AND PRACTICE

The analyses of how much pollution to prohibit, and how much pollution to allow, are summarized in Figure 24.3, which depicts the benefits and costs of pollution control. It might be thought of as applying, for example, to water pollution in a specific watershed. It is drawn from the perspective of a public authority that has been charged with maximizing social welfare. The negatively sloped curve is the 'demand' for pollution to be abated (or prevented). The reason that we conduct the analysis in terms of pollution prevented is that pollution *abatement*, not pollution *cre-*

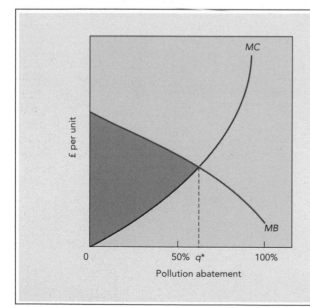

Figure 24.3 The optimal amount of pollution abatement

The optimal amount of pollution abatement occurs where the marginal cost of reducing pollution is just equal to the marginal benefits from doing so. *MB* represents the marginal benefit that is achieved by pollution prevention in some activity. *MC* represents the marginal cost of preventing pollution; it rises sharply as more and more pollution is eliminated. The optimal level of pollution control is q*, where *MB = MC*. *Notice that not all pollution is eliminated.* For all units up to q*, the marginal benefits derived from pollution abatement exceed the marginal costs. The total net benefit from the optimal amount of pollution abatement is given by the dark blue area—the sum of the difference between marginal benefit and marginal cost at each level of output. Any further reductions in pollution beyond q* would add more to costs than to benefits.

ation, is the service with positive economic value, and we are used to studying the supplies and demands for goods and services with positive values. If no pollution is abated, the watershed will be subject to the amount of pollution that would occur in an unregulated market. The greater the amount of pollution that is prevented, the smaller is the amount of pollution that remains.

The marginal cost of preventing pollution is often small at low levels of abatement but rises steeply after some point. (This is the shape shown in Figure 24.3.) There are two reasons for this shape. First is the familiar logic behind increasing marginal costs. For each firm that pollutes, there will be some anti-pollution measures that can be taken fairly easily, so the first portion of pollution reduction will be cheap relative to later portions. Second, pollution reduction of any degree is usually easier for some firms than for others. For example, new facilities usually run cleaner than old ones; reducing pollution from a factory that was designed in the era of environmental concern may be much easier than obtaining similar reductions from an older factory. After some point, however, the easy plants and the easy fixes are exhausted, and the marginal cost of reducing pollution further rises steeply.[2]

The marginal benefit of pollution reduction in Figure 24.3 is depicted as falling for much the same reason that the typical demand curve has a negative slope. Starting at any non-lethal level of pollution, people will derive some benefit from reducing the level of pollution, but the marginal benefit from a given amount of reduction will be lower, the lower is the existing level of pollution.

The optimal amount of pollution reduction occurs where the marginal benefit is equal to the marginal cost—where 'supply' and 'demand' in Figure 24.3 intersect. In trying to reach this optimum, the pollution control authority faces three serious problems.

First, although Figure 24.3 looks like a supply–demand diagram, we have already seen that the private sector will not by itself create a market in pollution control. Thus, the government must intervene in private-sector markets if the optimal level of control that is shown in Figure 24.3 is to be attained.

The second problem is that the optimal level of pollution abatement generally is not easily determined, because the marginal benefit and the marginal cost curves that are shown in Figure 24.3 are not usually observable. In practice, the government must estimate these curves. Accurate estimates are often difficult to obtain, especially when the technology of pollution control is changing rapidly and the health consequences of various pollutants (e.g., chemicals that are new to the market-place) are not known.

The third problem is that the available techniques for regulating pollution are themselves imperfect. Even when the optimal level of pollution control is known, there are both technical and legal impediments to achieving that level through regulation.

CONTROL THROUGH DIRECT REGULATION

Direct controls are the most common method of environmental regulations. Car emissions standards are direct controls that are familiar to most of us. Standards must be met by all new cars that are sold in the United Kingdom, and there are also standards that must be met by all cars over three years of age when they take their annual MOT test. They require that emissions of a number of noxious chemicals and other pollutants be less than certain specified amounts. The standards are the same no matter where the car is driven. The marginal benefit of reducing carbon monoxide emissions in rural Scotland, where there is relatively little air pollution, is certainly much less than the marginal benefit in London, where there is already a good deal of carbon monoxide in the air. Yet the standard is the same in both places.

Direct controls also often require that specific techniques be used in order to reduce pollution. Thus, coal-fired electricity generating plants are required to use devices called 'scrubbers' in order to reduce sulphur dioxide emissions, even in cases where other techniques could have achieved the same level of pollution abatement at lower cost.

Another form of direct control is the simple prohibition of certain polluting behaviours. Many cities and towns, for example, prohibit the private burning of leaves and other rubbish because of the air pollution problem that the burning would cause. The 1956 UK Clean Air Act obliged people to switch from coal to smokeless fuels. As a result of this Act, and some important changes in technology, smoke emissions in 1995 were less than one-quarter of their 1955 levels. Similarly, the government gradually reduced the amount of lead allowed in petrol and provided tax incentives for drivers to switch to unleaded petrol. Since the mid-1970s, petrol consumption has increased by about 50 per cent while lead emissions have fallen by about 75 per cent.

Problems with direct controls Direct controls are likely to be economically inefficient; more pollution can usually be abated by alternative methods at the same economic cost as that imposed by direct controls. Suppose that pollution of a given waterway is to be reduced by a certain amount. Regulators will typically apportion the required reduction among all of the polluters according to some roughly equitable criterion. The regulators might require that every polluter reduce its pollution by the same percentage; alternatively, every polluter might be required to install a certain type of control device or to ensure that each gallon of water that is dumped into the watershed meets certain quality criteria. Although any of these rules might seem rea-

---

[2] The World Bank has estimated that to bring about a 10 per cent reduction in CO_2 emissions below their 1988 levels would cost ECU 400 per tonne in Italy, ECU 200 per tonne in Denmark, and less than ECU 20 per tonne in the United Kingdom, France, or Germany!

sonable, unless the polluters face identical pollution abatement costs, each of them will be inefficient.

To illustrate the problem, consider two firms that face different costs of pollution abatement, as depicted in Figure 24.4. Suppose that firm A's marginal cost of pollution abatement is everywhere below firm B's. Such a circumstance is quite likely when one recalls that pollution comes from many different industries. It may be easy for one industry to cut back on the amount that it uses of some pollutant; in another industry the pollutant may be an integral part of the production process. The most efficient way to reduce pollution would be to have firm A cut back on its pollution until the marginal cost of further reductions is just equal to firm B's marginal cost of reducing its first (and cheapest to forgo) unit of pollution. Once their marginal costs of reducing pollution are equalized, *further* reductions in pollution will be efficient only if this equality is maintained.

To see this, suppose that the marginal costs of abatement are different for the two firms. By reallocating some pollution abatement from the high-marginal-cost firm to the low-marginal-cost firm, total pollution abatement could be kept constant while the real resources used to abate pollution would be reduced. Alternatively, one could hold the resource cost constant and increase the amount of abatement.

Direct pollution controls are usually inefficient in that they do not minimize the cost of any given amount of pollution abatement. This implies that they also do not abate the most pollution possible for any given cost.

Direct controls suffer from two other types of inefficiency. First, regulations tend to change only slowly: the regulators often will mandate today's best techniques tomorrow, even if something more effective has come along. Second, direct controls are expensive to monitor and to enforce.

None the less, direct controls are effective when it is important not to exceed certain dangerous thresholds. They are also useful in situations where production is undertaken by a very small number of publicly owned natural monopolies. In other cases, policies that structure economic incentives tend to be more effective than those that operate on the command principle.

CONTROL THROUGH EMISSIONS TAXES

The great English economist A. C. Pigou (1877–1959) did path-breaking work on externalities of all sorts, and was a pioneer in developing public policy tools for their control. His name is associated particularly with pollution taxes,

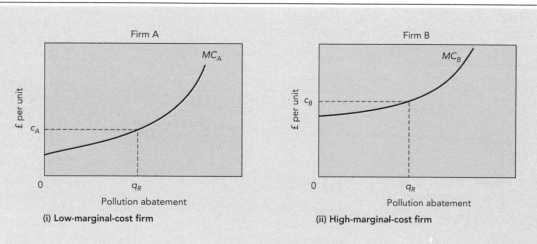

Figure 24.4 Potential inefficiency of direct pollution controls

Requiring equal amounts of pollution abatement from different polluters is likely to be inefficient.
Firm A is able to reduce its emissions according to the marginal cost curve MC_A. Firm B, which operates at the same scale but in a different kind of factory, has a higher marginal cost of abatement, MC_B. Suppose that a regulatory authority requires that the two firms reduce pollution by the same amount, q_R. Firm A will have a marginal cost of pollution abatement of c_A, whereas firm B's marginal cost will be c_B, which is larger than c_A.

To see that this outcome is inefficient, consider what happens if firm A increases its pollution abatement by one unit, while firm B is allowed to pollute one unit more. Total pollution remains the same, but total costs fall. Firm A incurs added costs of c_A, and firm B saves a greater amount, c_B. Because the total amount of pollution is unchanged, the total social cost of pollution and pollution abatement would fall.

which provide an alternative method to direct controls. The great advantage of such taxes is that they internalize the pollution externality, so that decentralized decisions can lead to efficient outcomes.

Again, suppose that firm A can reduce emissions cheaply, while it is more expensive for firm B to reduce emissions. If all firms are required to pay a tax of t on each unit of pollution, profit maximization will lead them to reduce emissions to the point where the marginal cost of further reduction is equal to t. This means that firm A will reduce emissions much more than firm B, and that in equilibrium both will have the same marginal cost of further abatement, which is required for efficiency. This is illustrated in Figure 24.5.

A second great advantage of using emissions taxes is that they do not require the regulators to specify anything about *how* polluters should abate pollution. Rather, polluters themselves can be left to find the most efficient abatement techniques. The profit motive will lead them to do so, because they will want to avoid paying the tax.

Emissions taxes can, in principle, perfectly internalize pollution externalities, so that profit-maximizing behaviour on the part of firms will lead them to produce the efficient amount of pollution abatement at minimum cost.

Emissions taxes in practice Emissions taxes can work only if it is possible to measure emissions accurately. For some types of pollution, this does not pose much of a problem, but for many other types of pollution, good measuring devices that can be installed at reasonable cost do not exist. Obviously, in these cases emissions taxes cannot work. One important example of such a case is automotive pollution. It would be very expensive to attach a reliable monitor to every car and lorry and then to assess taxes due based on readings from the monitor. In this case, as in many others, direct controls are the only feasible approach.

Another problem with emissions taxes involves setting the tax rate. Ideally, the regulatory agency would obtain an estimate of the marginal social damage caused per unit of each pollutant and set the tax equal to this amount. This would perfectly internalize the pollution externality. However, the information that is needed to determine the marginal social damage curves shown in Figures 24.2 and 24.3 is often difficult to obtain. If the regulatory agency sets the tax rate too high, too many resources will be devoted to pollution control. (The equilibrium will be beyond q^* in Figure 24.3.) If the tax is set too low, there will be too much pollution.

A potentially serious problem with emissions taxes is that information necessary to determine the optimal tax rate is often unavailable.

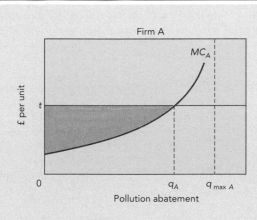
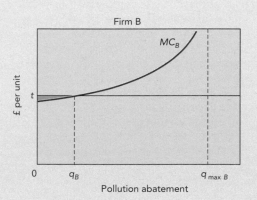

Figure 24.5 A tax on pollution

Taxes on pollution can lead to efficient pollution abatement. As in figure 24.4, firm A faces a lower marginal cost of pollution abatement than does firm B. Suppose that the regulatory authority imposes a tax of t per unit of pollution. Firm A will choose to reduce its pollution by q_A. Up to this point, the tax saved by reducing pollution exceeds the marginal cost of reducing pollution. If firm A chooses not to abate pollution at all, it would pay t times q_{max} in pollution taxes, where q_{max} is the firm's total pollution if it does nothing to prevent pollution. By reducing its pollution to $q_{max}-q_A$ (the same thing as abating pollution by q_A), firm A saves an amount that is given by the dark blue area in the panel on the left.

Firm B chooses to abate only a small amount of pollution, q_B. Any further abatement would require that the firm incur costs along MC_B, which would be greater than the benefits of taxes saved, t.

CONTROL THROUGH TRADABLE EMISSIONS PERMITS

One great advantage of direct controls is that the regulators can set the standards to limit the total quantity of pollution in a given geographic area. This can be done without knowing the details of either the marginal benefit or the marginal cost curves in Figure 24.3. The great advantage of emissions taxes is that they allow for decentralized decision-making, providing firms with an incentive to internalize the negative externality of pollution. *Tradable emissions permits* can combine both of these advantages, and thus they have the potential for being superior to either direct controls or emissions taxes.

In Figure 24.4, we noted that direct pollution controls would generally be inefficient because the marginal cost curves for pollution abatement would vary across firms. Tradable permits can solve this problem.

To use them, the regulator must redefine the problem from *how much pollution abatement to require* to *how much pollution to permit*. In Figure 24.4 the regulations required each firm to reduce its total pollution by Q_R. This is exactly the same as permitting the firms to pollute by their original amount of pollution minus Q_R. To pose the solution this way, the regulators issue to each firm a right to pollute by that amount. This has the same effect as ordering them to reduce pollution by Q_R.

Now, however, comes the new twist. A large efficiency gain can be achieved by making these rights to pollute *tradable*. This allows the firm with the low cost of pollution abatement to sell its right to pollute to the high-abatement-cost firm. Total pollution and total pollution abatement will be unchanged, but more abatement will be done by the firm with the low abatement cost (who sold its rights to pollute to the other firm), thus reducing the total cost of meeting the target for pollution reduction.

The firms will exchange rights to pollute, until their marginal abatement costs are equalized. At this point, there is no further gain from trading permits. Notice that the new equilibrium is identical to that depicted in Figure 24.5, with the equilibrium *price* of an emissions permit just equal to the emissions *tax* shown in that figure. However, with tradable permits, regulators do not need to calculate the optimal pollution tax. Given the permitted quantity of pollution, the market in permits will calculate the equivalent to the 'tax' through the voluntary trades of firms.

Tradable emissions permits can be used to achieve the same allocation of resources as would occur with emissions taxes, with much less information required of the regulatory authorities.

One problem with both pollution taxes and tradable permits is more political than economic, but it is certainly important in explaining why such policies are not used more often. Opponents of tradable permits often argue that by providing permits, rather than simply outlawing pollution above some amount, the government is condoning crimes against society. Direct controls, according to this argument, have much greater normative force, because they say that violating the standards is simply wrong. Emissions taxes and markets for pollution make violating the standards just one more element of cost for the firm to consider as it pursues its private goals.

Most economists find arguments of this kind unpersuasive. An absolute ban on pollution is impossible, and in choosing how much pollution to allow, society must trade pollution abatement against other valuable things. Economic analysis has a good deal to say about how a society might minimize the cost of *any* degree of pollution abatement, or maximize the amount of pollution abated for any given cost that the society is willing to bear.

Tradable emissions permits in practice   Tradable permits and emissions taxes pose formidable problems of implementation. Some of these involve technical difficulties in measuring pollution and in designing mechanisms to ensure that firms and individuals comply with regulations. Additionally, the potential efficiency gains arising from tradable permits cannot be realized if regulatory agencies are prone to change the rules under which trades may take place. This has been a problem in the past, but it is a problem that can be corrected.

Governmental creation of a 'market' in 'bads' may become one of the most promising strategies for efficiently overcoming the market failure that leads to environmental pollution.

Much environmental pollution is caused by the failure of markets to account for externalities. At the same time, market-like mechanisms can be effective in internalizing the externalities. Pollution is an example of a problem in which markets themselves can be used to correct market failure. Box 24.1 discusses some of the sources of opposition to using markets to address environmental issues.

CONCLUSION

The problem of externalities arises because of the absence of property rights. For example, the polluting firm uses the free air to dump its waste. If it owned the air, it would worry about the loss of the value of its property caused by the pollution. If those affected by the pollution owned the air, they would not allow it to be used unless they were paid sufficient compensation.

Many externalities arise from an absence of property rights. One way to internalize the externality is to create appropriate property rights.

BOX 24.1

Resistance to market-based environmental policies

Despite the many advantages that can be identified for market-based approaches to the environment, this approach often encounters resistance from firms, ordinary members of the public, and environmentalists. Why?

Producers

Opposition to market-based solutions sometimes comes from management. Some firms object to the costs they are asked to pay in terms of emissions taxes or the purchase prices of pollution rights. The introduction of market-based measures may, however, merely signal the end of a free ride that producers have been taking at society's expense. If the firms in an industry were bearing none of the cost of their pollution, almost any anti-pollution scheme will impose a burden on them—but only to the extent of forcing them to bear the costs of their own activities. The difference between the command solution and the market-based solution, however, is that the former will cost the industry, and hence the average firm in the industry, more than the market solution.

Market-based schemes do not ensure that *all* firms pay less than under a common scheme, only that the *average* firm does. When some firms pay more, they may oppose the measures out of self-interest or a feeling of injustice that they must pay more than some of their competitors. Of course, command solutions also have differential impacts on firms.

Finally, under market-based schemes, many firms feel a sense of unfairness because their competitors continue polluting while they must clean up. Their complaints ignore the fact that those who continue to pollute have paid for the right to do so, either by paying effluent taxes or by buying pollution rights, and that the complaining firm could do the same if it wished. (It does not do so because cleaning up is cheaper for it than paying to pollute, as the neighbours are doing.)

This points to a key issue in assessing market-based solutions: such solutions must not be judged in isolation. Given a government's decision to reduce pollution, the market solution must be compared with its alternatives.

The public

One source of public opposition is a moral reaction to giving anyone a right to pollute. Since it involves human survival, dealing in rights to pollute seems evil to many. This view makes difficult the rational evaluation of alternative plans for dealing with a serious social problem.

A further important source of opposition is found in the market-based solution's characteristic of allowing those who have the highest costs of cleaning up to go on polluting while those with the lowest costs do the cleaning up. Morality may dictate to many observers that the biggest polluters should do the cleaning up. Economists cannot show this reaction to be wrong; they can only point out the cost in terms of the higher prices, lower employment, unnecessary resource use, and less overall pollution abatement that follow from adopting such a position.

Environmentalists

Many, but of course not all, environmentalists are sceptical about the efficiency of markets. Some do not understand economists' reasoning as to why markets can be, and often are, efficient in their use of resources. Others understand the economists' case but reject it, although few complete the argument by trying to demonstrate that command-type allocation by government will be more effective.

Second, many environmentalists do not like the use of self-interest incentives to solve social issues. Economists who point to the voluminous evidence of the importance of self-interest incentives are often accused of ignoring higher motives such as social duty, self-sacrifice, and compassion. Although such motives are absent from the simple theories that try to explain the everyday behaviour of buyers and sellers (because it has not been found necessary to introduce such motives into these theories), economists since Adam Smith have been aware that these higher motives often do exert strong influences on human behaviour.

Such higher motives are very powerful at some times and in some situations, but they do not govern many people's behaviour in the course of day-to-day living. If we want to understand how people behave in the aftermath of a flood, or an earthquake, or a war, we need motives in addition to self-interest; if we want to understand how people behave day after day in their buying and selling, we need little other than a theory of the self-interested responses to market incentives. Since control of the environment requires influencing a mass of small, day-to-day decisions, as well as a few large ones, the appeal to self-interest is the only currently known way to induce the required behaviour through voluntary actions.

Another reason why many people reject market-based solutions is their belief that the market cannot be relied on to establish the right trade-off between present and future. As we saw in Chapter 19, many conservationists fear that relying on the free market to set production rates for resource products will cause resources to be exploited too quickly. They argue that government intervention is necessary to conserve the resource for the future. Although market failures in rates of extraction do occur, these failures can work towards extraction that is too slow as well as too fast. No one has succeeded in proving a general tendency for the market to extract resources too quickly. Further, the assumption that governments, dominated as they so often are by considerations of the next election, will none the less take a longer view than the market is by no means proven.

Finally, some people have a somewhat mystical view that resources are above mere monetary calculation and should thus be treated in special ways. The economist can point out that the use of the mystical view to justify departing from solutions based on calculations of market failures (which are measured in terms of failure to provide maximum economic value) ensures that measured material living standards will be lowered. If that is the understood and accepted price of regarding resources as mystical entities, then so be it!

Box 24.2 outlines some of the main policies that governments have used to give effect to desired environmental control.

Policy towards competition and monopoly

Most governments have policies concerning the behaviour of firms. These policies, which are designed to increase economic efficiency, usually have three main objectives, which we considered in Chapter 16: to prevent firms from colluding where competition is technically possible; to regulate the behaviour of natural monopolies; and to encourage activities that contribute to the long-run growth of the economy. Shifting views on how to achieve these objectives led, first, to the nationalization of many British industries in the middle of this century and heavy regulation of many that were left in private hands, and, second, to the privatization of many state-owned industries and the deregulation of many that were in private hands in the latter part of the century. We will say more about these policy shifts later in the chapter.

BOX 24.2

Policies for environmental regulation

Governments throughout the world are experimenting with many of the methods of environmental control discussed in the text. Here is a sampling of some of these policies.

Many current environmental policies use regulations. Standards are set for air or water quality, and the polluter is then left free to decide on how best to achieve these minimum standards. The regulator monitors the environment and takes action against any producers found to be violating the mandated standards.

In the United Kingdom, the Environmental Protection Act of 1989 laid down minimum standards for all emissions from thousands of chemical, waste incineration, and oil refining factories. Performance is monitored by HM Inspectorate of Pollution, the costs of which are paid for by the factory owners themselves. The Act also provides for public access to information on the pollution created by firms. The release of genetically engineered bacteria and viruses is also regulated. Stricter regulations have also been imposed on waste disposal operations and on most forms of straw and stubble burning, with local authorities required to keep public land clean. Litterers are subject to on-the-spot fines of up to £1,000.

Regulations have also played an important part in the 'Environmental Action Programmes' of the European Union. For example, specific standards have been set for minimum acceptable levels of water quality for drinking and for bathing. There is regular monitoring of bathing beaches.

Current governmental policy is to stabilize CO_2 emissions at their 1990 level by the year 2005. In practice, this will mean a reduction in CO_2 emissions in 2005 by between 20 and 50 per cent, compared with their estimated uncontrolled levels.

In the 1992 Copenhagen agreements nearly 100 countries agreed to phase out chlorofluorocarbons (CFCs) by the year 1996, four years earlier than had previously been agreed. The Copenhagen agreements also regulated other ozone-damaging substances, such as methyl bromide, used in preserving fruit and grain, the output of which is to be held at 1991 levels by the year 1995.

According to the 'polluter-pays' principle, adopted by the OECD in 1972, the polluter is to bear the cost of government-imposed measures designed to reduce pollution. This principle was to be adopted in all member-states so as to avoid the distortions in trade flows that could arise if countries tackled environmental problems in widely different ways with widely different effects on prices.

Under the United States Clean Air Act, utilities must cut emissions of sulphur dioxide from a national total of 19 million tonnes to 9 million tonnes by the year 2000. This is to be accomplished by issuing tradable permits to pollute to only that total amount. The Tennessee Valley Authority, for example, has agreed to buy allowances to emit 10,000 tonnes of sulphur dioxide from privately owned Wisconsin Power and Light. Similarly, Duquesne Light of Pittsburgh has bought allowances from the same Wisconsin company to emit between 15,000 and 25,000 tonnes of sulphur dioxide. This means that the target total amount of SO_2 will be eliminated, but Wisconsin Power and Light will do the job rather than the TVA and Duquesne Light.

In other cases, it is the sufferer who is paying. For example, Sweden assists Poland to reduce the acid rain that is damaging Swedish lakes and forests. Similarly, the Montreal Protocol includes provisions by which developing countries are to be compensated by richer countries for agreeing to limit their use of CFCs which damage the ozone layer.

Finally, consider the important resource of water. The UK strategy for water pricing gives water companies the freedom to pass on any extra costs of environmental improvements and ensures that those companies have an economic incentive to undertake such improvements. The policy violates the 'polluter-pays' principle by putting the costs on the consumer.

Non-market incentives are also widely applied to water. Under the UK Control of Pollution Act, a licence is required for the discharge of pollutants into rivers and coastal waters. These licences, called Discharge Consents, are issued by the National Rivers Authority. They specify the type and quantity of substances that may be discharged. However, in 1989 some 750 sewage works in England and Wales were found to be discharging more sewage than allowed in their Consents, proving that enforcement is critical if most schemes are to work.

Equity

GOVERNMENTS attempt to change the distribution of income in countless ways. Some attempts are general in their effects, but some arc quite specific and localized.

The functional distribution of income

Governments have many policies with respect to the functional distribution of income. In Britain, for example, personal income arising from labour services—which was called *earned income*—was until 1985 taxed at lower income tax rates than income arising from capital—which was called *unearned income*. This policy was designed to redistribute income among the owners of factors away from those who provided capital and in favour of those who provided labour. Also, by reducing the return on invested capital, it may have provided a disincentive to save and invest.

Governments also have policies affecting the distribution of income within the broad functional class of wage and salary income. Labour governments may try to redistribute income from professional–managerial and other middle-class groups to skilled and unskilled workers. Conservative governments may try to resist, or reverse, this redistribution.

Governments also change the distribution of income in favour of all sorts of relatively small special-interest groups. Special tax treatment, subsidies, legislation that restricts competition, and a host of other measures operate in many countries to turn the distribution of income in favour of various groups—small businessmen, farmers in general and poultry and milk producers in particular, households with large numbers of children, certain professional groups, some groups of skilled workers, and unmarried mothers are examples. The treatment afforded to many (but of course not all) of these special-interest groups is often hard to explain on grounds of efficiency or equity. Many such redistributive measures can, however, be explained by the theory of the vote-maximizing government. Such a government is tempted to adopt policies that greatly help each member of a small identifiable group, and slightly hurt each member of a large, diffuse, unorganized group. Those who are helped a lot will be grateful to the government, while those who are hurt just a little will be less likely to notice, and, hence, unlikely to blame the government for their losses.

The size distribution of income

In trying to alter the size distribution of income, the gov-ernment is concerned with large and small incomes, irrespective of the source of that income. Most governments seek to narrow the range of the size distribution, reducing the incomes of those at the upper end and raising the incomes of those at the lower end. In doing so, however, governments face a trade-off between equity and efficiency. Some jobs are more skilled, more difficult, more unpleasant, or more risky than others, and, unless the former are more highly paid than the latter, people will not be persuaded to do them. Even the former Communist governments of Eastern Europe had to allow major inequalities in the size distribution of income in order to provide the incentives needed to make the economic system function.

TAX POLICY

The first prong of any government's attempt to change the size distribution of income is its tax policy. A tax system that is progressive when viewed as a whole is helpful. Debate centres on the conflict between progressivity and adequate incentives.

EXPENDITURE POLICY

The second prong of redistributive policy is expenditure policy. The benefits received tend to vary with income. Many transfer payments benefit lower-income groups. Other expenditures, such as higher education, tend mainly to benefit middle-income groups.

The redistributive effects of expenditures depend on how the overall benefits are related to income. The redistributive effects of the overall tax system depend on how the balance between taxes paid and benefits received from expenditures varies with income. To take an extreme case, assume that government expenditure benefited people in proportion to the taxes they paid. The overall redistributive effect of the government's tax and expenditure system would then be zero: what it took away with one hand it would give back with the other. An effective redistribution scheme requires that the tax system be more progressive than the expenditure system. (A proportional tax system and a regressive expenditure system would do.)

Transfer payments help to fulfil this criterion, since many of them are welfare payments to various classes of needy such as the aged, the incapacitated, the unemployed, the unemployable, and the very young. Most of these expenditures are negatively related to incomes. For goods and services that are provided by the government at a subsidized, or zero, price, the case is not so clear. Education, for example, tends to be consumed more by higher- than by lower-income groups, since the higher a household's income, the more likely it is that its children will stay on beyond the minimum school-leaving age. This kind of relation, which exists for other products as well, means that much of the non-transfer part of the expenditure system is progressive, with benefits received tending to rise with income.

The distribution of wealth

It is sometimes argued that egalitarian economic policy should concern itself more with the distribution of *wealth* and less with that of *income* than it now does. Wealth confers economic power, and wealth is more unequally distributed than is income. Heavy estate duties in the United Kingdom, however, caused a gradual reduction in the inequality of wealth distribution earlier this century, although the trend has slowed, if not reversed, in the last decade or so.

There are two main ways in which the distribution of wealth can be made less unequal. The first is to levy taxes on wealth at the time that wealth is transferred from one owner to another, either by gifts during the lifetime of the owner or by bequest after death. In Britain, such transfers used to be subject to a capital transfer tax. The rate of tax was progressive and rose to 60 per cent on taxable transfers in excess of £2 million. Currently, however, gifts among individuals during their lifetime are potentially exempt of tax. They become taxable if made within seven years of the donor's death. Inheritance tax applies at the rate of 40 per cent on estates over £150,000 (in 1994).

The second method is an annual tax on the value of each person's wealth. A wealth tax of this sort has been considered in the past but it has not been actively debated since 1979.

Specific issues in distribution policy

In this section, we consider some specific issues that arise in attempts to narrow inequalities in the size distribution of income.

FREE GOODS AND SERVICES AS A REDISTRIBUTIVE DEVICE

Public goods must, by their very nature, be paid for out of general tax revenue. Many other goods and services that could be sold to cover costs are provided by the government at a subsidized price (zero in the limit). The shortfall between price and costs is then made up out of tax revenue. Such goods and services may be produced by a nationalized industry or by a private industry that receives a subsidy to cover the difference between its costs and the amount it

receives from selling its products below the free-market prices.

The grounds for adopting such policies are partly efficiency, partly equity, and possibly sometimes the mistaken belief that costs can be avoided. To the extent that the goal is to increase efficiency by encouraging the consumption of goods with positive externalities, there is no problem. The optimal policy is to provide a subsidy equal to the externality.

In what follows, we consider the provision of goods at a price below costs, which includes a price of zero in the extreme cases, as a device for redistributing income, and for avoiding costs.

The opportunity cost of 'free' goods   Voters sometimes opt to have the government subsidize a product, or even provide it free, because avoiding cost wherever possible seems a good idea. The opportunity cost of using resources to produce one product is the other products that could have been produced instead. The money measure of this cost is the market value of the resources being used. Whenever a product is provided 'free' by the government, the costs are met by taxes.[3] The taxpayers thus forgo what they would have consumed by spending their tax money, and the free product is consumed by its users instead. In so far as they are the same people, the consumers merely pay in a different form: taxes rather than purchase prices. In so far as they are different people, there is a transfer of income: from taxpayers to the consumers of the free product.

Providing a product free of charge does not remove the opportunity cost, it merely transfers it from consumers of the product to taxpayers.

The inefficiency of free goods   Consider a product that has neither positive nor negative externalities so that private and social costs and benefits coincide. If such a product is provided free and all demand is met, then people will go on consuming it until the last unit has a zero value to them. Thus, resources will have to be used up in producing units of the product which have zero value to each and every consumer. Since resources are scarce, they must be taken from the production of other goods that have positive values for all consumers (i.e. consumers would like to have more of them). Using scarce resources to produce products with low values, when the same resources could produce products with higher values, ensures that consumers will have a lower total value of consumption than they could have. If a price were charged for the product, its consumption would decline and resources would be freed to move to uses where their product would have higher values in the eyes of all consumers.

[3] This assumes that government expenditure is financed by taxes. We shall see in later chapters that there are other methods of finance. These do not, of course, avoid the cost; they merely shift it to yet other groups.

Providing a product free of charge, or at any price below marginal cost, is allocatively inefficient.

The magnitude of the resource waste depends on the elasticity of the demand curve for the subsidized product. With an inelastic demand curve, the policy induces only a small increase in output, so only a small amount of resources are inefficiently allocated. With an elastic demand, the quantity of misallocated resources is large.

The above discussion gives an intuitive statement of the argument for the inefficiency of a free-good policy. The formal case is given in Figure 24.6. It shows that:

Any given expenditure of state funds will increase people's satisfactions more if it is used to give them an income transfer than if it is used to subsidize the prices of some of the products that they consume.

The free-product policy has a second major shortcoming. Much of the money spent goes to subsidize the consumption of higher-income groups. Since there are few goods that are not bought by all income groups, the policy is much like shooting at a target with a shotgun—the bull's-eye will be hit, but so will everything else.

Transfer payments can be targeted at specific income groups; free goods cannot.

This lack of targeting makes the free-good policy an unnecessarily expensive way of helping low-income groups.

A third problem with free goods is that the government often does not provide sufficient quantity to meet the demand at zero price. Some alternative rationing scheme must therefore arise. Sometimes queues do the rationing. At other times suppliers' preferences do the job, as first dis-

cussed in Chapter 6. This happens, for example, when those considered most worthy by administrators or doctors are given expensive health care while others get cheaper alternatives.

The case for free goods   The case for providing some products, such as medical services and education, at a price below cost (zero in the limit) rests partly on a divergence between social and private costs that is an efficiency consideration, partly on compassion, and partly on more subtle welfare arguments which involve equity considerations.

To see what is involved, compare water with hospitals and schools. In some countries water is provided free, or at a flat rate that does not vary with consumption. Water has a highly elastic demand at low prices—even though its demand becomes highly inelastic as consumption falls towards the minimum needed to sustain life. Thus, a no-price policy causes significant amounts of the economy's scarce resources to be committed to producing units of water that have a very low value to consumers. There are no obvious positive or negative externalities from water and, since everyone consumes it, free water is an ineffective redistributive device. Here is a case where there is little rationale for the zero-price policy.

Now consider free hospital care and education. First, recall that the magnitude of the resource cost of a free-good policy depends on the elasticity of demand between the free-market price and the subsidized price (which in the limit will be zero). It is not clear, however, that many people waste free hospital care in the way they are observed to waste free water. Studies suggest low incidence of unnecessary hospitalization in a free-hospital system. In the case of education up to the statutory age, consumption is compulsory in any case.

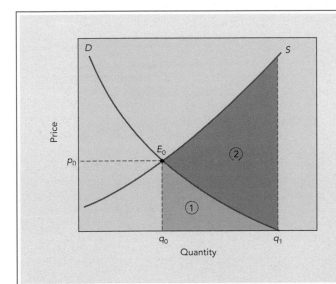

Figure 24.6 The case against free goods

It is allocatively inefficient to provide goods free. Competitive equilibrium is at E_0 with q_0 produced and sold at price p_0. If the government supplies the product free of charge, q_1 will be produced and consumed. The addition to consumers' surplus resulting from the extra consumption is equal to the medium blue area 1. But since every unit adds its marginal cost to the total costs of production, these costs rise by the sum of areas 1 and 2—the area under the supply curve which is the industry's marginal cost curve. By the definition of opportunity cost, these two areas give the values of other goods forgone when resources are drawn into the production of the subsidized good. Thus, the net loss of surplus to consumers is the dark blue area 2.

The steeper is the demand curve through E_0, the smaller will be the increase in quantity from q_0 to q_1 and hence the smaller will be the area of loss labelled 2.

Even if consumers do not waste free health care, there remains an allocation problem as long as (as is usually the case) the government is unwilling to supply all that is demanded at zero price. In Britain, the National Health Service has recently gone through a controversial introduction of an internal market mechanism. Patients get treatment free, but doctors have a notional budget and buy services from hospitals. Hospitals price operations, and these prices vary substantially over the country.

Second, in both educational and medical care, social and private costs and benefits are thought to diverge substantially: if I do not cure my infectious disease, the effects are not felt by me alone. If all children are better educated, not only do they and their parents gain, but everyone gains from the rise in output that results from an increase in their labour productivity. Thus, there are arguments for reducing the private costs of these services below the market rate by means of a subsidy.

Third, whereas it is not a great burden for a consumer to pay a commercial rate for all the water that is necessary for a moderately civilized life, charging a price that covers costs of production would deny medical and educational services to many who have either neglected to, or are unable to, obtain private insurance to cover the costs.

Finally, more subtle arguments concern social values. It has been argued that in richer societies decisions about basic medical care should be taken out of the economic arena. It is degrading for a person to have to balance medical care for a child against the other family needs. Therefore, it is argued, the inefficiency cost of providing basic medical care free is worth accepting in order to gain the creation of a society where choices about basic medical services are eliminated.

Notice the use of the word 'basic' in the previous paragraph. The above position is arguable if it is confined to basic services for all. Modern medical technology is so expensive that the state could not afford to make all conceivable services freely available to all. The more expensive services must be rationed. This can be done either by prices or by decisions about need taken by medical and hospital authorities.

MINIMUM WAGES AS A REDISTRIBUTIVE DEVICE

One other important market intervention designed to alter the size distribution of income is minimum wage laws, which were discussed on pp. 359–60 of Chapter 19. Minimum wages do not exist in Britain but they are an implicit part of the European Union's Social Chapter. A major reason for the UK government's opting out of that Chapter was to avoid having minimum wage laws in the United Kingdom.

For a large fraction of all employment covered by the law, the minimum wage is below the actual market wage. Where this is true, the wage is said to be 'not binding'. But some workers are in occupations where the free-market wage rate *is* below the legal minimum, and for them the minimum wage is said to be 'binding'.

The value of minimum wage laws is controversial. To the extent that they are effective, they raise the wages of employed workers. But, as our analysis in Chapter 6 predicted, an effective price floor may well lead to a market surplus—in this case, unemployment. Let us see to what extent this relationship applies to the minimum wage.

There are two main cases to consider. First, the minimum wage may be set in a market that is otherwise quite competitive, with many buyers and many sellers. Second, the wage may be set in a market where a few large employers buy from many unorganized sellers of labour services.

Effective minimum wages in a competitive market In Figure 19.6 on p. 358, we studied what happens when a union fixes a wage in an otherwise competitive market. The market outcome is unaffected by the identity of the organization fixing the wage—all that matters is that the wage is fixed. Thus, the results of the earlier analysis apply directly to the case of a government-imposed minimum wage law:

A minimum wage imposed on a competitive market will increase the wages of those employed, decrease employment, increase unemployment, and create incentives to evade the law by working for a rate that is below the legal minimum wage.

Effective minimum wages in a monopsonistic market In Figure 19.7 on p. 359, we studied what happens when a union fixes a wage in a market where monopsonistic employers were buying from unorganized labour. Since the source of the wage-fixing does not affect the outcome, the results of the earlier analysis apply to the minimum wage law introduced in this context:

A minimum wage imposed on a monopsonistic market can raise both wages and employment.

In this case the minimum wage can protect the unorganized worker against monopsony power in the same way that a union can. It is possible, however, that minimum wages will be set above the competitive level. If so, while wages of those employed will be raised, no prediction can be made as to whether employment will increase or decrease compared with the monopsony level. (It depends both on how high the wage is and on the shapes of the curves.)

Economic growth

OVER the long haul, economic growth is the most powerful determinant of living standards. Whatever the policies concerning efficiency and equity, people who live in economies with rapid rates of growth find their living standards rising on average faster than people who live in countries with low rates of growth. Over a decade or two, these growth-induced changes tend to swamp any changes due to altering the efficiency of resource allocation or redistributing the existing levels of income (see Table 33.1 on p. 633).

In the last half of this century, economists have viewed growth mainly as a macroeconomic phenomenon related to total savings and total investment. More recently, there has been a shift back to the perspective of earlier economists, who saw technological change as the engine of growth and individual entrepreneurs as the ones who introduced technological change by innovating. This is a microeconomic perspective, which is meant to add to, not replace, the macroeconomic stress on total savings and total investment. A sampling of the type of microeconomic policies that are debated in the growth context is given below. (We stress that this is only a brief sampling of a vast topic.)

Taxation policies for growth

Almost all taxes can affect growth by altering incentives either to save, to work, or to take risks.

Taxation of consumption or income Income taxes tax income when it is earned; spending taxes (such as the VAT) tax only that part of income that is spent on consumption.

Consider a woman in the 40 per cent marginal tax bracket who earns an extra £1,000 and pays £400 income tax. If she spends her after-tax income, she will be able to buy £600 worth of goods. If she saves the money, she will be able to buy a £600 bond. If the bond pays, say, a 4 per cent real return, she will earn £24 interest per year. But a 40 per cent tax must then be paid on the interest earnings, leaving only a £14.40 annual income. This is a 2.4 per cent after-tax return on the bond and a 1.44 per cent after-tax return on the original £1,000 income!

This 'double taxing' of saving is a disincentive to save. Economists who wish to encourage saving, which helps to finance growth-creating investment, argue for taxes on consumption, not on income, so that any income that is saved would be untaxed. Such a tax would be levied only when the interest earned on the savings was actually spent on consumption. In the 1980s the Conservative government took a major step in this direction by significantly reducing income tax rates and making up for the lost revenue by raising the VAT rate.

Avoid steeply progressive rates of tax Steeply progressive tax rates penalize people with fluctuating incomes, such as authors, self-employed builders, and small-scale innovators. Consider an innovator who tries something new each year and only covers costs on her first four attempts and then has a success that yields £250,000 in the fifth year. Her five-year income is the same as a salaried employee who earned £50,000 for each of these five years. Yet under a steeply progressive tax regime she will pay much more taxes than he will. This was a serious problem when the maximum rate of tax in the United Kingdom was 70 per cent. (Earlier still it had been over 90 per cent.) As we have already noted, in the 1980s the maximum rate was cut to 40 per cent, which greatly reduces the tax penalty paid by someone with a highly fluctuating income. But it is still there. In 1995, the lady innovator would have paid £96,295 in taxes, while over the same five-year period the salaried man would have paid £74,585 (assuming each had no dependants).

Here we see one of the many possible conflicts between growth and equity. One may favour progressive tax rates on grounds of equity but be persuaded to moderate the degree of progressivity in the interest of encouraging the risk-taking that is necessary for promoting growth.

Adjustment policies for growth

The innovations in products and production processes that underlie growth require continual changes and adaptations throughout the economy. If government policies discourage change, growth will be slowed. The realization that many policies designed to improve equity can discourage change has led to some reconsideration of policies intended to improve equity.

Labour market policies When people lose jobs because of economic change, the various measures that constitute the welfare safety net provide them with income support. Passive income support provides no incentive to change and sometimes can even discourages it.

An alternative is to make some or all of the support conditional on adjusting to change, for example by retraining or relocating. The government has, for example, funded Training and Enterprise Councils (TECs), through which all young people out of work and not in higher eduction are encouraged to undergo a period of training or work experience.

Support of firms and industries   Governments are always tempted to support declining industries. This reduces unemployment in the short run, but, if economic forces are leading to a continual decline, these policies are only costly ways of postponing the inevitable adjustments. Furthermore, the adjustment often comes suddenly, because the government support is withdrawn all at once when the growing cost of the support finally becomes unacceptable.

Industrial policies for growth[4]

Earlier we considered government policies towards industry that were directed primarily at efficiency. Other policies have long-term growth as their primary objective. Many of the disagreements over such policies depend on differing views on the micro-conditions needed to encourage growth-creating innovations. Some economists feel that maximizing the amount of competition at any point in time is the most important condition for growth. Others follow Schumpeter in holding that the existence of monopoly and oligopoly profits at any point in time is a powerful incentive to growth-creating innovations.

Patents   Some economists, who believe that competitive market structures best serve consumers by assuring them low prices, worry about a possible lack of incentives to innovate under competition. If an innovation can be easily copied, new firms may enter an industry so quickly that the innovating firm is not compensated for the costs and risks of innovation. The innovation is, in effect, a public good, and private firms are not motivated to produce it.

Patent laws are designed to provide the needed incentives. They create a temporary property right over the invention, extending the short-run period during which the invention's owner can earn profits as a reward for inventing. Once the patent expires, and sometimes even before other firms can copy the innovation. If there are no other barriers to entry, production will then expand until profits fall to normal.

Reduction of entry barriers   Those who accept Schumpeter's theory hold that anti-monopoly policy and public

utility regulations are unnecessary as policies to influence behaviour in the very long run. They worry that state intervention will inadvertently create entry barriers that will protect existing firms from the growth-creating process of creative destruction. They see government policies directed at minimizing entry barriers as the only ones that are needed.

Nationalization   Those who reject Schumpeter's theory often support anti-monopoly and public utility regulation policies. They feel that such policies are required to prevent monopolies from earning large profits at the expense of consumers.

Supporters of Schumpeter's theory argue that nationalization and public regulation will defeat their own purposes in the long term by inhibiting the process of creative destruction. A government monopoly provides the most enforceable entry barrier. It may inhibit the introduction of new products, and of new ways to produce old products, that would have occurred through new firms entering to attack the entrenched positions of existing firms. Supporters of this view point to the former Soviet Union's need to buy technology from Western countries, and argue that the rapid development of new products and processes in the oligopolistic and monopolistic industries operating in market-oriented economies gives some support to Schumpeter's view.

A short-term, long-term trade-off?   Economists who accept both the force of the argument that monopolistic firms can earn large exploitative profits in the short term *and* Schumpeter's argument about the very long run face a policy dilemma. In the short term, firms that gain monopoly power may earn very large profits at the expense of consumers. In the very long term, however, attempts to control these monopolies may inhibit the creative destruction that helps to raise living standards through productivity growth. For these economists,

The policy world is not a simple place, and policies that help to achieve desired goals over one time-span must be constantly scrutinized for undesired effects over other time-spans.

---

[4] Another growth-oriented objective of policy is so-called competitiveness. This issue is discussed in Chapter 33 on Economic Growth.

Conclusion: evaluating the role of government

ONE of the most difficult problems for the student of the economic system is to maintain perspective about the scope of government activity in the market economy. One pitfall is to become so impressed with the many ways in which government activity impinges on the individual that one fails to see that these only change market signals in a system that basically leaves individuals free to make their own decisions.

A different pitfall is to fail to see that most of the taxes paid by the private sector buy goods and services that add to the welfare of individuals or make transfers designed to alleviate many types of hardship.

A related pitfall is to believe that the government's alleged inability to improve efficiency implies an inability to improve equity. Throughout the world, governments are placing more reliance on markets in order to improve economic efficiency and prospects for growth. Accepting the market for efficiency reasons does not, however, require grinding the faces of the poor. A search for social justice through government interventions directed at equity is quite compatible—provided appropriate means are carefully chosen—with a search for efficiency through increased scope for market determination.

Yet another pitfall is failing to recognize that the public and private sectors both make claims on the resources of the economy. Government activities are not without opportunity costs, except in those rare circumstances in which they employ resources that have no alternative use.

Public policies in operation at any time are not the result of a single master plan that specifies precisely where and how the public sector shall seek to complement, or interfere with, the workings of the market mechanism. Rather, as individual problems arise, governments attempt to meet them by passing ameliorative legislation. These laws stay on the books, and some become obsolete and unenforceable. Since this is true of systems of law in general, it is easy to find outrageous examples of inconsistencies and absurdities in any system.

The amount and type of government interference that is desirable was one of the major political issues of the 1980s, and it is continuing in the 1990s. A free-market system is valued for its lack of coercion and its ability to allocate resources efficiently. But we need not be mesmerized by it; governments can intervene in pursuit of various social goals. When doing so, however, we need to recognize that some interventions have been both inefficient and ineffective.

Summary

1 The traditional goals of microeconomic policy of *efficiency* and *equity* are now augmented by *growth* as a result of the criticism of supply-side economists in the 1980s.

2 Efficiency-increasing policies include the provision of standards and knowledge, producing public goods, and dealing with externalities. The optimal quantity of a public good is provided when the marginal cost of production is equal to the sum of the prices that all its consumers would be willing to pay for the marginal unit produced. Externalities can be handled with rules and regulations, or by internalizing them through such measures as taxes and subsidies.

3 Most pollution problems can be analysed as negative externalities. Polluting firms and consumers going about their daily business do harm to the environment and fail to take account of the costs that they impose on others.

4 The economically efficient level of pollution in any activity is generally not zero; it is the level where the marginal cost of further pollution reduction is just equal to the marginal damage done by a unit of pollution. If producers or consumers face incentives that cause them to internalize fully the costs that pollution imposes, they will choose the economically efficient level of pollution.

5 Pollution can be regulated either directly or indirectly. Direct controls are used most often. Direct controls are often inefficient because they require that all polluters meet the same standard regardless of the benefits and costs of doing so. Indirect controls, such as taxes on emissions, are more efficient; ideally, they cause firms to internalize perfectly the pollution externality. Tradable emissions permits could have the same effect as taxes without requiring regulators to know as much about the technology of pollution abatement.

6 Governments use tax and expenditure policies in pursuit of equity objectives. All taxes have some disincentive effects, which must be balanced against their other benefits. Their incidence is often shifted from those who pay them, to a diffuse set of other persons that are often hard to identify. Free goods and services are often an unnecessarily costly redistributive device because their benefits

go to all consumers, rich and poor. They also lead to inefficiently large amounts of production and consumption. Nonetheless, the provision of free products can be justified on economic grounds whenever there are externalities, or where social values call for removing some basic choices from the economic arena in spite of the efficiency costs of doing so. Minimum wages can serve as a redistributive device, but they benefit some who stay on at the higher wage and harm those who lose jobs as a result.

7 Many macroeconomic policies have the potential to affect the country's overall rate of economic growth. Progrowth policies that are often advocated include taxing consumption rather than income, avoiding steeply progressive tax rates, encouraging the mobility of workers and firms, and encouraging firms to innovate.

8 Accepting that the private sector, working through the market economy, is a means to economic efficiency and economic growth does not require accepting the distribution of income that the market provides. Redistributive policies in pursuit of equity are quite compatible with privatization in pursuit of efficiency—and with regulation of natural monopolies and oligopolies whenever they arise out of private market forces.

Topics for review

- The goals of microeconomic policy
- Rules for providing and pricing public goods
- Costs and benefits of pollution abatement
- Emissions taxes
- Direct controls
- Efficient levels of pollution
- Tradable emissions permits
- The shifting and incidence of taxes
- Disincentive effects of taxes

PART SEVEN

International trade

✐ CHAPTER 25

The gains from trade

THE British buy Volkswagens, Germans take holidays in Italy, Italians buy spices from Tanzania, Africans import oil from Kuwait, Arabs buy Japanese cameras, and the Japanese depend heavily on American soybeans as a source of food. *International trade* refers to exchanges of goods and services that take place across international boundaries.

The founders of modern economics were concerned with foreign trade problems. The great eighteenth-century British philosopher and economist David Hume (1711–76), one of the first to work out the theory of the price system as a control mechanism, developed his concepts mainly in terms of prices in foreign trade. Adam Smith in his *Wealth of Nations* attacked government restriction of trade. David Ricardo (1772–1823) in 1817 developed the basic theory of the gains from trade that is studied in this chapter. The repeal of the Corn Laws—tariffs on the importation of grains into Great Britain—and

the transformation of that country during the nineteenth century from a country of high tariffs to one of complete free trade were to a significant extent the result of agitation by economists whose theories of the gains from trade led them to condemn all tariffs.

In this chapter, we enquire into the gains to living standards that result from trade. We find that the source of the gains from trade lies in differing cost conditions among geographical regions. World income is maximized when countries specialize in those products in which they have the lowest opportunity costs of production. These costs are determined partly by natural endowments, geographical and climatic conditions and partly by public policy. We then go on to discuss the terms on which trade takes place —which refers to the amount that must be exported to obtain a given amount of imports. Finally, we apply our demand and supply analysis to explain one country's exports and its imports.

Sources of the gains from trade

AN economy that engages in international trade is called an **open economy**. One that does not is called a **closed economy**. A situation in which a country does no foreign trade is called one of **autarky**. The advantages realized as a result of trade are called the **gains from trade**. The source of such gains is most easily visualized by considering the differences between a world with trade and a world without it. Although politicians often regard foreign trade differently from domestic trade, economists from Adam Smith on have argued that the causes and consequences of international trade are simply an extension of the principles governing domestic trade. What is the advantage of trade among individuals, among groups, among regions, or among countries?

Interpersonal, interregional, and international trade

Consider trade among individuals. Without trade, each person would have to be self-sufficient; each would have to produce all the food, clothing, shelter, medical services, entertainment, and luxuries that he or she consumed. A world of individual self-sufficiency would be a world with extremely low living standards.

Trade among individuals allows people to specialize in

those activities they can do well and to buy from others the goods and services they cannot easily produce. A good doctor who is a bad carpenter can provide medical services not only for his or her own family, but also for an excellent carpenter who lacks the training or the ability to practise medicine. Thus, trade and specialization are intimately connected. Without trade, everyone must be self-sufficient. With trade, everyone can specialize in what he or she does well and satisfy other needs by trading.

The same principles apply to regions. Without interregional trade, each region would be forced to be self-sufficient. With trade, each region can specialize in producing products for which it has some natural or acquired advantage. Plains regions can specialize in growing grain, mountain regions can specialize in mining and forest products, and regions with abundant power can specialize in manufacturing. Cool regions can produce wheat and other crops that thrive in temperate climates, and hot regions can grow such tropical crops as bananas, sugar, and coffee. The living standards of the inhabitants of all regions will be higher when each region specializes in products in which it has some natural or acquired advantage and obtains other products by trade than when all regions seek to be self-sufficient.

The same principle also applies to nations. Nations, like regions or persons, can gain from specialization. More of the goods in which production is specialized are produced than residents wish to consume, while less domestic production of other goods that residents desire is available.

International trade is necessary to achieve the gains that international specialization makes possible.

This discussion suggests one important possible gain from trade.

With trade, each individual, region, or nation is able to concentrate on producing those goods and services that it produces efficiently while trading to obtain goods and services that it does not produce efficiently.

Specialization and trade go hand in hand, because there is no motivation to achieve the gains from specialization without being able to trade the goods produced for goods desired. Economists use the term 'gains from trade' to embrace the results of both.

We shall examine two sources of the gains from trade. The first is differences among regions of the world in climate and resource endowment that lead to advantages in producing certain goods and disadvantages in producing others. These gains occur even though each country's costs of production are unchanged by the existence of trade. The second source is the reduction in each country's costs of production that results from the greater production that specialization brings.

The gains from specialization with given costs

In order to focus on differences in countries' conditions of production, suppose that there are no advantages arising from either economies of large-scale production or cost reductions that are the consequence of learning new skills. In these circumstances, what leads to gains from trade? To examine this question, we shall use an example involving only two countries and two products, but the general principles apply as well to the real-world case of many countries and many products.

A SPECIAL CASE: ABSOLUTE ADVANTAGE

The gains from trade are clear when there is a simple situation involving absolute advantage. **Absolute advantage** concerns the quantities of a single product that can be produced using the same quantity of resources in two different regions. One region is said to have an absolute advantage over another in the production of product *X* when an equal quantity of resources can produce more *X* in the first region than in the second.

Suppose region A has an absolute advantage over B in

one product, while region B has an absolute advantage over A in another. This is a case of *reciprocal absolute advantage*: each country has an absolute advantage in some product. In such a situation the total production of both regions can be increased (relative to a situation of self-sufficiency) if each specializes in the product in which it has the absolute advantage.

Table 25.1 provides a simple example, using hypothetical data for wheat and cloth production in the United States and the United Kingdom. In the example, total world production of both wheat and cloth increases when each country produces more of the good in which it has an absolute advantage. As a result, there is more wheat *and* more cloth for the same use of resources.

These gains from *specialization* make the gains from *trade* possible. The UK will now be producing more cloth and the US more wheat than when they were self-sufficient. Thus, the US will be producing more wheat and less cloth than US consumers wish to buy, and the UK will be producing more cloth and less wheat than UK consumers wish to buy. If consumers in both countries are to get cloth and

---

Table 25.1 Gains from specialization with absolute advantage

	Wheat (kg)	Cloth (metres)
(a) Amounts of wheat and cloth that can be produced with one unit of resources in the US and the UK		
US	10	6
UK	5	10
(b) Changes resulting from the transfer of one unit of US resources into wheat and one unit of UK resources into cloth		
US	+10	−6
UK	−5	+10
Total	+5	+4

When there is a reciprocal absolute advantage, specialization makes it possible to produce more of both products. Part *(a)* shows the production of wheat and cloth that can be achieved in each country by using one unit of resources. The US can produce 10 kg of wheat or 6 metres of cloth; the UK can produce 5 kg of wheat or 10 metres of cloth. The US has an absolute advantage in producing wheat, the UK in producing cloth. Part *(b)* shows the changes in production caused by moving one unit of resources out of cloth and into wheat production in the US and moving one unit of resources in the opposite direction in the UK. There is an increase in world production of 5 kg of wheat and 4 metres of cloth; worldwide, there are gains from specialization. In this example, the more resources that are transferred into wheat production in the US and cloth production in the UK, the larger the gains will be.

wheat in the desired proportions, the UK must export cloth to the US and import wheat from the US.

A FIRST GENERAL STATEMENT: COMPARATIVE ADVANTAGE

When each country has an absolute advantage over the other in a product, the gains from trade are obvious. But what if the US can produce both wheat and cloth more efficiently than the UK? In essence, this was David Ricardo's question, posed over 175 years ago. His answer underlies the theory of comparative advantage and is still accepted by economists as a valid statement of the potential gains from trade.

To start with, assume that US efficiency increases tenfold above the levels recorded in the previous example, so that a unit of US resources can produce either 100 kg of wheat or 60 metres of cloth. UK efficiency remains unchanged (see Table 25.2). It might appear that the US, which is now better at producing both wheat and cloth than is the UK, has nothing to gain by trading with such an inefficient foreign country. That it *does* have something to gain is shown in Table 25.2. Even though the US is 10 times as efficient as in the situation of Table 25.1, it is still possible to increase

---

Table 25.2 Gains from specialization with comparative advantage

	Wheat (kg)	Cloth (metres)
(a) Amounts of wheat and cloth that can be produced with one unit of resources in the US and the UK		
US	100	60
UK	5	10
(b) Changes resulting from the transfer of one-tenth of one unit of US resources into wheat and one unit of UK resources into cloth		
US	+10	–6
UK	–5	+10
Total	+5	+4

When there is comparative advantage, specialization makes it possible to produce more of both products. The productivity of UK resources is left unchanged from Table 25.1; that of US resources is increased tenfold. The UK no longer has an absolute advantage in producing either product. Total production of both products can none the less be increased by specialization. Moving 0.1 unit of US resources out of cloth and into wheat and moving 1 unit of resources in the opposite direction in the UK causes world production of wheat to rise by 5 kg and cloth by 4 metres. Reciprocal absolute advantage is not necessary for gains from trade.

---

world production of both wheat and cloth by having the US produce more wheat and less cloth, and the UK produce more cloth and less wheat.

What is the source of this gain? Although the US has an absolute advantage over the UK in the production of both wheat and cloth, the margin of advantage differs in the two products. The US can produce 20 times as much wheat as the UK by using the same quantity of resources, but only six times as much cloth. The US is said to have a **comparative advantage** in the production of wheat and a comparative disadvantage in the production of the cloth. (This statement implies another: the UK has a comparative disadvantage in the production of wheat, in which it is 20 times less efficient than the US, and a comparative advantage in the production of cloth, in which it is only six times less efficient.)

One of the theory's key propositions is:

The gains from specialization and trade depend on the pattern of comparative, not absolute, advantage.

A comparison of Tables 25.1 and 25.2 refutes the notion that the absolute *levels* of efficiency of two areas determine the gains from specialization. The key is that the margin of advantage that one area has over the other must differ between products. Total world production can then be increased if each area specializes in producing the product in which it has a comparative advantage.

Comparative advantage is necessary as well as sufficient for gains from trade. This is illustrated in Table 25.3, showing the US with an absolute advantage in both products and neither country with a comparative advantage over the other in the production of either product. The US is 10 times as efficient as the UK in the production of wheat and in the production of cloth. Now there is no way to increase the production of both wheat and cloth by reallocating resources within the US and within the UK. Part *(b)* of the table provides one example of a resource shift that illustrates this.

Absolute advantage without comparative advantage does not lead to gains from trade.

A SECOND GENERAL STATEMENT: OPPORTUNITY COSTS

Much of the previous argument has used the concept of a unit of resources. It assumes that units of resources can be equated across countries, so that statements such as 'The US can produce 10 times as much wheat with the same quantity of resources as the UK' are meaningful. Measurement of the real resource cost of producing products poses many difficulties. If, for example, the UK uses land, labour, and capital in proportions different from those used in the US, it may not be clear which country gets

Table 25.3 Absence of gains from specialization when there is no comparative advantage

	Wheat (kg)	Cloth (metres)
(a) Amounts of wheat and cloth that can be produced with one unit of resources in the US and the UK		
US	100	60
UK	10	6
(b) Changes resulting from the transfer of one unit of US resources into wheat and ten units of UK resources into cloth		
US	+100	−60
UK	−100	+60
Total	0	0

Where there is no comparative advantage, no reallocation of resources within each country can increase the production of both products. In this example, the US has the same absolute advantage over the UK in each product (tenfold). There is no comparative advantage, and world production cannot be increased by reallocating resources in both countries. Therefore, specialization does not increase total output.

Table 25.4 Opportunity cost of wheat and cloth in the US and the UK

	Wheat (kg)	Cloth (metres)
US	0.60 metre cloth	1.67 kg wheat
UK	2.00 metres cloth	0.50 kg wheat

Comparative advantages can be expressed in terms of opportunity costs that differ between countries. These opportunity costs can be obtained from Tables 25.1 or 25.2. The UK opportunity cost of 1 unit of wheat is obtained by dividing the cloth output of 1 unit of UK resources by the wheat output. The result shows that 2 metres of cloth must be sacrificed for every extra unit of wheat produced by transferring UK resources out of cloth production and into wheat. The other three cost figures are obtained in a similar manner.

Table 25.5 Gains from specialization with differing opportunity costs

	Changes resulting from each country's producing one more unit of a product in which it has the lower opportunity cost	
	Wheat (kg)	Cloth (metres)
US	+1.0	−0.6
UK	−0.5	+1.0
Total	+0.5	+0.4

Whenever opportunity costs differ between countries, specialization can increase the production of both products. These calculations show that there are gains from specialization given the opportunity costs of Table 25.4. To produce one more kilogram of wheat, the US must sacrifice 0.6 metre of cloth. To produce one more metre of cloth, the UK must sacrifice 0.5 kg of wheat. Making both changes raises world production of both wheat and cloth.

more output per unit of resource input. Fortunately, the proposition about the gains from trade can be restated without reference to so fuzzy a concept as units of resources.

To do this, go back to the examples of Tables 25.1 and 25.2. Calculate the *opportunity cost* of wheat and cloth in the two countries. When resources are assumed to be fully employed, the only way to produce more of one product is to reallocate resources and produce less of the other product. Table 25.1 shows that a unit of resources in the US can produce 10 kg of wheat *or* 6 metres of cloth. From this it follows that the opportunity cost of producing a unit of wheat is 0.60 unit of cloth, while the opportunity cost of producing a unit of cloth is 1.67 units of wheat. These data are summarized in Table 25.4. The table also shows that in the UK the opportunity cost of a unit of wheat is 2.0 units of cloth forgone, while the opportunity cost of a unit of cloth is 0.50 unit of wheat. Table 25.2 also gives rise to the opportunity costs in Table 25.4.

The sacrifice of cloth involved in producing wheat is much lower in the US than it is in the UK. World wheat production can be increased if the US rather than the UK produces it. Looking at cloth production, we can see that the loss of wheat involved in producing one unit of cloth is lower in the UK than in the US. The UK is the lower (opportunity) cost producer of cloth. World cloth produc-

tion can be increased if the UK rather than the US produces it. This situation is shown in Table 25.5.

The gains from trade arise from differing opportunity costs in the two countries.

Although Table 25.4 was calculated from Table 25.1 (or Table 25.2), we do not need to be able to compare real resource costs to calculate comparative advantages. The existence of a production-possibility boundary implies opportunity costs, and the existence of different opportunity costs implies comparative advantages and disadvantages.

The conclusions about the gains from trade arising from international differences in opportunity costs may be summarized.

1. Country A has a comparative advantage over country B in producing a product when the opportunity cost (in terms of some other product) of production in country A is lower. This implies, however, that it has a comparative disadvantage in the other product.

2. Opportunity costs depend on the relative costs of producing two products, not on absolute costs. (Notice that the examples in Tables 25.1 and 25.2 each give rise to the opportunity costs in Table 25.4.)

3. When opportunity costs are the same in all countries, there is no comparative advantage and there is no possibility of gains from specialization and trade. (You can illustrate this for yourself by calculating the opportunity costs implied by the data in Table 25.3.)

4. When opportunity costs differ in any two countries, and both countries are producing both products, it is always possible to increase production of both products by a suitable reallocation of resources within each country. (This proposition is illustrated in Table 25.5.)

Gains from specialization with variable costs

So far we have assumed that unit costs are the same whatever the scale of output, and we have seen that there are gains from specialization and trade as long as there are interregional differences in opportunity costs. If costs vary with the level of output, or as experience is acquired via specialization, *additional* sources of gain are possible.

SCALE AND IMPERFECT COMPETITION

Real production costs, measured in terms of resources used, generally fall as the scale of output increases. The larger the scale of operations, the more efficiently large-scale machinery can be used and the more a detailed division of tasks among workers is possible. Smaller countries such as Switzerland, Belgium, and Israel whose domestic markets are not large enough to exploit economies of scale would find it prohibitively expensive to become self-sufficient by producing a little bit of everything at very great cost.

Trade allows smaller countries to specialize and produce a few products at high enough levels of output to reap the available economies of scale.

Very large countries, such as the United States, have markets large enough to allow the production of most items at home at a scale of output great enough to obtain the available economies of scale. For them, the gains from trade arise mainly from specializing in products in which they have a comparative advantage. Yet even for such countries, a broadening of their markets permits achieving scale economies in subproduct lines, such as speciality steels or jeans.

One of the important lessons learned from patterns of world trade since the Second World War has concerned imperfect competition and product differentiation. Virtually all of today's manufactured consumers' goods are produced in a vast array of differentiated product lines. In some industries, many firms produce this array; in others, only a few firms produce the entire array. In either case, firms are not price-takers, and they do not exhaust all available economies of scale as a perfectly competitive firm must do (see Figure 12.11 on p. 230). This means that an increase in the size of the market, even in an economy as large as the United States, may allow the exploitation of some previously unexploited scale economies in individual product lines.

These possibilities were first dramatically illustrated when the European Common Market (now called the European Union, the EU) was set up in the late 1950s. Economists had expected that specialization would occur according to the classical theory of comparative advantage, with one country specializing in cars, another in refrigerators, another in fashion clothes, another in shoes, and so on. This is not the way it worked out. Instead, much of the vast growth of trade was in intra-industry trade. Today, one can buy French, English, Italian, and German fashion goods, cars, shoes, appliances, and a host of other goods in London, Paris, Bonn, and Rome. Ships loaded with Swedish furniture bound for London pass ships loaded with English furniture bound for Stockholm; and so on.

What free European trade did was to allow a proliferation of differentiated products, with different countries each specializing in different subproduct lines. Consumers have shown by their expenditures that they value this enormous increase in the range of choice among differentiated products. As Asian countries have expanded into European and American markets with textiles, cars, and electronic goods, European and American manufacturers have increasingly specialized their production and they now export textiles, cars, and electronic equipment to Japan even while importing similar but differentiated products from Japan.

LEARNING BY DOING

The discussion so far has assumed that costs vary only with the *level* of output. They may also vary with the accumulated experience in producing a good over time.

Early economists placed great importance on a factor that we now call learning by doing. They believed that, as countries gained experience in particular tasks, workers and managers would become more efficient in performing them. As people acquire expertise, costs tend to fall. There is substantial evidence that such learning by doing does occur.

The distinction between this phenomenon and the gains from economies of scale is illustrated in Figure 25.1. This is one more example of the difference between a movement along a curve and a shift of the curve.

Recognition of the opportunities for learning by doing leads to an important implication: policy-makers need not accept *current* comparative advantages as given. Through such means as education and tax incentives, they can seek to develop new comparative advantages.[1] Moreover, countries cannot complacently assume that their existing comparative advantages will persist. Misguided education policies, the wrong tax incentives, or policies that discourage risk-taking can lead to the rapid erosion of a country's comparative advantage in particular products. So, too, can developments in other countries.

Sources of comparative advantage

We have seen that comparative advantages are the source of the gains from trade. But why do comparative advantages exist? Why do different countries have different opportunity costs?

DIFFERENT FACTOR ENDOWMENTS

What has become the traditional answer to this question was provided early in this century by two great Swedish economists, Eli Heckscher (1879–1952) and Bertil Ohlin (1899–1979) and is now incorporated in the so-called Heckscher–Ohlin model. According to their theory, the international cost differences that lie behind comparative advantages arise because national factor endowments differ. To see how this works, consider an example.

[1] Of course, they can, foolishly, use such policies to develop industries in which they do not have, and will never achieve, comparative advantages.

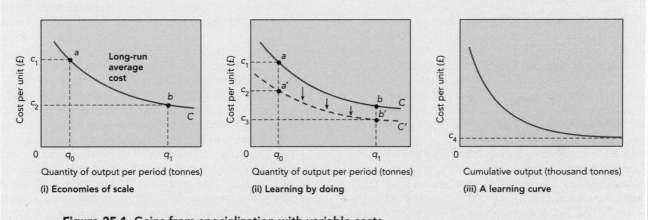

Figure 25.1 Gains from specialization with variable costs

Specialization may lead to gains from trade by permitting economies of larger-scale output, by leading to downward shifts of cost curves, or both. Consider a country that wishes to consume the quantity q_0. Suppose that it can produce that quantity at an average cost per unit of c_1. Suppose further that the country has a comparative advantage in producing this product and can export the quanity q_1–q_0 if it produces q_1. This may lead to cost savings in two ways. (i) The increased level of production of q_1 compared with q_0 permits it to *move along* its cost curve, C, from a to b, thus reducing costs per unit to c_2. This is an economy of scale. (ii) As workers and managements become more experienced, they may discover means of increasing productivity that lead to a downward shift of the cost curve from C to C'. This is learning by doing. The downward *shift*, shown by the arrows, lowers the cost of producing every unit of output. At output q_1 costs per unit fall to c_3. The movement from a to b' incorporates both economies of scale and learning by doing.

Part (iii) shows a learning curve, which is another way of showing the effects of learning by doing. This curve shows the relation between the costs of producing a given output per period and the total output over the whole time during which production has taken place. Growing experience with making the product causes costs to fall as more and more is produced. When all learning possibilities have been exploited, costs reach a minimum level, shown by c_4 in the figure.

A country that is well endowed with fertile land but has a small population will find that land is cheap while labour is expensive. It will, therefore, produce land-intensive agricultural goods cheaply, and labour-intensive goods, such as furniture, only at a high cost. The reverse will be true for a second country that is small in size but possesses abundant, and efficient, labour. As a result, the first country will have a comparative advantage in agricultural production, and the second in goods that use much labour and little land. Another country that is unusually well endowed with energy will have low energy prices. It will thus have a comparative advantage in such energy-intensive goods as chemicals and aluminium.

According to the Heckscher–Ohlin theory, countries have comparative advantages in the production of products that are intensive in the use of the factors of production with which they are abundantly endowed.

This is often called the *factor-endowment theory of comparative advantage.*

DIFFERENT 'CLIMATES'

Modern research suggests that this theory has considerable power to explain comparative advantages, but that it does not provide the whole explanation. One obvious additional influence comes from all those natural factors that can be called *climate* in the broadest sense. If you combine land, labour, and capital in the same way in Nicaragua and in Iceland, you will not get the same output of most agricultural goods. Sunshine, rainfall, and average temperature also matter. If you seek to work with wool, or cotton, in both dry and damp climates, you will get different results. (You can, of course, artificially create any climate you wish in a factory, but it costs money to create what is freely provided elsewhere.)

Climate, interpreted in the broadest sense, undoubtedly affects comparative advantage.

ACQUIRED ADVANTAGES

There is today a competing view. In extreme form, it says that comparative advantages are certainly there, but they are typically acquired, not nature-given—and they change. This view of comparative advantage is *dynamic* rather than static. New industries are seen to depend more on human capital than on fixed physical capital or natural resources. The skills of a computer designer, a videogame programmer, a sound mix technician, or a rock star are acquired by education and on-the-job training. Natural endowments of energy and raw materials cannot account for UK prominence in modern pop music and high-quality TV series, or for the leadership in computer technology of Silicon Valley in California. When countries such as the United Kingdom, and latterly the United States, find their former dominance (based on comparative advantage) declining in such smokestack industries as cars and steel, their firms need not sit idly by. Instead, they can begin to adapt by developing new areas of comparative advantage.

CONTRASTS

This modern view is in sharp contrast with the traditional assumption that cost structures are based largely on a country's natural endowments, which lead to a given pattern of international comparative advantage. The traditional view leads to the policy advice that a government interested in maximizing its citizens' material standard of living should encourage production to be specialized in those goods where it currently has a comparative advantage. When all countries follow this advice, the theory predicts that each will be specialized in a relatively narrow range of distinct products. The British will produce engineering products, Canadians will be producers of resource-based primary products, Americans will be farmers and factory workers, Central Americans will be banana growers, and so on.

There are surely elements of truth in both extreme views. It would be unwise to neglect resource endowments, climate, culture, social patterns, and institutional arrangements. But it would also be unwise to assume that all of these were innate and immutable.

To some extent, these views are reconciled by the theory of human capital discussed in Chapter 19. Comparative advantages that depend on human capital are consistent with traditional Heckscher–Ohlin theory. The difference is that this type of capital is acquired through conscious decisions relating to such matters as education and technical training.

The terms of trade

SO far, we have seen that world production can be increased when countries specialize in the production of the products in which they have a comparative advantage, and then trade with one another. We now ask: how will these gains from specialization and trade be shared among countries? The division of the gain depends on what is called the **terms of trade**, which relates to the quantity of imported goods that can be obtained per unit of goods exported. They are measured by the ratio of the price of exports to the price of imports.

A rise in the price of imported goods, with the price of exports unchanged, indicates a *fall in the terms of trade*; it will now take more exports to buy the same quantity of imports. Similarly, a rise in the price of exported goods, with the price of imports unchanged, indicates a *rise in terms of trade*; it will now take fewer exports to buy the same quantity of imports. Thus, the ratio of these prices measures the amount of imports that can be obtained per unit of goods exported.

In the example of Table 25.4, the UK domestic opportunity cost of 1 unit of wheat is 2 metres of cloth. If UK resources are transferred from cloth to wheat, 2 metres of cloth are given up for every kilogram of wheat gained. But, if the UK can obtain its wheat by trade on more favourable terms, there are gains in producing and exporting cloth to pay for wheat imports. Suppose, for example, that international prices are such that 1 kg of wheat exchanges for (i.e. is equal in value to) 1 metre of cloth. At those terms of trade, the UK can obtain 1 kg of wheat for every 1 metre of cloth exported. It gets more wheat per unit of cloth exported than it can obtain by moving resources out of cloth into wheat production at home. These terms of trade thus favour specializing in the production of cloth and trading it for wheat on international markets.

Similarly, in the example of Table 25.4, American consumers gain when they can obtain cloth abroad at any terms of trade more favourable than 1.67 units of wheat

sacrificed. If the terms of trade permit the exchange of 1 kg of wheat for 1 metre of cloth, the terms of trade favour the US obtaining its cloth by exporting wheat rather than producing it at home: a unit of cloth costs 1.67 units of wheat sacrificed when produced at home and only 1 unit of wheat when obtained through trade.

In this example, both the UK and the US gain from trade. Each can obtain units of the product in which it has a comparative disadvantage at a lower opportunity cost through international trade than through domestic production. The way in which the terms of trade affect the gains from trade is illustrated graphically in Box 25.1.

Because actual international trade involves many countries and many products, a country's terms of trade are computed as an index number:

$$\text{Terms of trade} = \frac{\text{index of export prices}}{\text{index of import prices}} \times 100.$$

A rise in the index is referred to as a *favourable* change in a country's terms of trade. A favourable change means that more can be imported per unit of goods exported than previously. For example, if the export price index rises from 100 to 120 while the import price index rises from 100 to 110, the terms-of-trade index rises from 100 to 109. At the new terms of trade, a unit of exports will buy 9 per cent more imports than at the old terms.

A decrease in the index of the terms of trade, called an *unfavourable* change, means that the country can import less in return for any given amount of exports or, equivalently, it must export more to pay for any given amount of imports. For example, the sharp rise in oil prices in the 1970s led to large unfavourable shifts in the terms of trade of oil-importing countries. When oil prices fell sharply in the mid-1980s, the terms of trade of oil-importing countries changed favourably. The converse was true for oil-exporting countries.

Trade in a small open economy

SO far, our discussion of the gains from trade has implicitly assumed that the two nations are about the same size. For many policy issues, however, we need a more realistic model.

The price-taking condition

Many countries, including the United Kingdom, are too small as actors on the international scene to influence the

BOX 25.1

The gains from trade illustrated graphically

International trade leads to an expansion of the set of goods that can be consumed in the economy in two ways: by allowing the bundle of goods consumed to differ from the bundle produced, and by permitting a profitable change in the pattern of production. Without international trade, the bundle of goods produced is the bundle consumed. With international trade, the consumption and production bundles can be altered independently to reflect the relative values placed on goods by international markets.

The graphical demonstration of the gains from trade proceeds in two stages.

Stage 1: Fixed production

In each part of the figure, the black curve is the economy's production possibility boundary. If there is no international trade, the economy must consume the same bundle of goods that it produces. Thus, the production possibility boundary is also the consumption possibility boundary. Suppose the economy produces, and consumes, at point a, with x_1 of good X and y_1 of good Y, as in part (i) of the figure.

Next, suppose that, with production point a, good Y can be exchanged for good X internationally. The consumption possibilities are now shown by the line tt drawn through point a. The slope of tt indicates the quantity of Y that exchanges for a unit of X on the international market.

Although production is fixed at a, consumption can now be anywhere on the line tt. For example, the consumption point could be at b. This could be achieved by exporting $y_1 - y_2$ units of Y and importing $x_2 - x_1$ units of X. Since point b (and all others

on line tt to the right of a) lies outside the production possibility boundary, there are potential gains from trade. Consumers are no longer limited by *their* country's production possibilities. Let us suppose they prefer point b to point a. They have achieved a gain from trade by being allowed to exchange some of their production of good Y for some quantity of good X and thus to consume more of good X than is produced at home.

Stage 2: Variable production

There is a further opportunity for the expansion of the country's consumption possibilities: with trade, the production bundle may be profitably altered in response to international prices. The country may produce the bundle of goods that is most valuable in world markets. That is represented by the bundle d in part (ii). The consumption possibility set is shifted to the line $t't'$ by changing production from a to d and thereby increasing the country's degree of specialization in good Y. For every point on the original consumption possibility set, tt, there are points on the new set, $t't'$, which allow more consumption of both goods; e.g. compare points b and f. Notice also that, except at the zero-trade point, d, the new consumption possibility set lies *everywhere above the production possibility curve*.

The benefits of moving from a no-trade position such as a to a trading position such as b or f are the *gains from trade* to the country. When the production of good Y is increased and the production of good X decreased, the country is able to move to a point such as f by producing more of good Y, in which the country has a comparative advantage, and trading the additional production for good X.

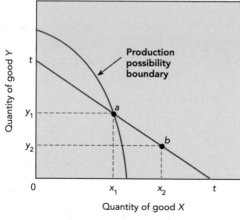

(i) Stage 1: fixed production

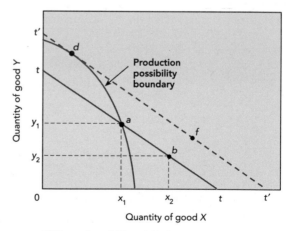

(ii) Stage 2: variable production

prices of most of the goods they import or export. The world prices of Swedish Volvos, Japanese tape-recorders, or IBM computers will be unaffected if consumers in the United Kingdom buy more or fewer of these products. Similarly, the prices of UK cars, aircraft, and engineering products are constrained by the existence of similar products produced elsewhere in the world. UK producers could not drive up the prices of these exports significantly by withholding some supplies from foreign markets. The United Kingdom thus comes close to being a price-taker in both its import and its export markets. UK goods and services are bought and sold under conditions that come closer to those of perfect competition than to those of monopoly.

These conditions, which face all small and most middle-sized economies in international markets, are formalized in the model of the **small open economy** (SOE). This is an economy that is a price-taker for both its imports and its exports. It must buy and sell at the world price, irrespective of the quantities involved.

Because a small open economy cannot, by its own actions, significantly influence the world price of traded products, it cannot influence its terms of trade.

Treating the United Kingdom as a SOE is a simplification. Manufactured goods are usually differentiated and sold under conditions of monopolistic competition or oligopoly. However, as a small actor on the world stage, and only one of many producers of differentiated products, the ability to alter prices and still maintain some sales is highly restricted by the existence of similar competing goods produced in other countries. Treating Britain as a SOE, therefore, comes closer to reality than treating it as a large trader

faced with negatively sloped demand curves for its exports and positively sloped supply curves for its imports.

Imports and exports in a small open economy

We can now use demand and supply analysis to show how the quantities of imports and exports are determined in a SOE. We first divide all goods into two types. **Tradables** are goods and services that enter into international trade. For a small economy, the prices of tradables are given since they are set on international markets. **Non-tradables** are goods and services that are produced and sold domestically but do not enter into international trade. Their prices are set on domestic markets by domestic supply and demand, and they are unaffected by market conditions for the same products in other countries.

Exports Figure 25.2 shows the domestic demand and supply curves for a typical product. For a small open economy, the world price is given and the country can buy or sell all that it wishes at that price. Notice that trade raises the price of the exported good above its autarky level. Notice also that the equilibrium is no longer where quantity demanded domestically equals domestic quantity supplied. Instead, the equilibrium price is the given world price, and the excess of domestic quantity supplied over domestic quantity demanded at that price is exported.

Imports Figure 25.3 gives the domestic demand and supply curves for a typical imported product. If imports are to occur, the world price must be below the autarky price.

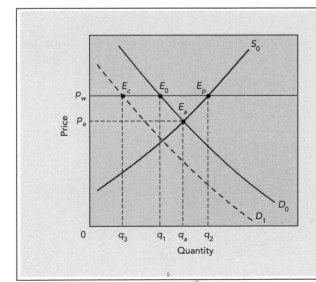

Figure 25.2 Exports in a small open economy

The exports of a SOE are the difference between the quantities supplied and demanded domestically at the world price. The curves D_0 and S_0 are the domestic demand and supply curves for a typical exported good. The autarky equilibrium is a E_a, where q_a is produced and consumed domestically at a price of p_a.

If trade can occur at the world price of p_w, consumption equilibrium will be at E_0, with q_1 consumed, while production equilibrium will be at E_p, with q_2 produced. The difference between domestic production and domestic consumption, q_2-q_1, is exported.

If domestic demand shifts to D_1, consumption equilibrium shifts to E_c, with q_3 consumed domestically. With unchanged domestic production, exports rise to q_2-q_3.

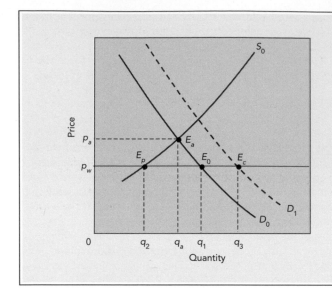

Figure 25.3 Imports in a small open economy

The imports of a SOE are the difference between the quantities demanded and supplied domestically at the world price. The curves D_0 and S_0 are the domestic demand and supply curves for a typical imported good. The autarky equilibrium is at E_a, where q_a is produced and consumed domestically at a price of p_a.

If trade can occur at a world price of p_w, consumption equilibrium will be at E_0, with q_1 consumed; while production equilibrium will be at E_p, with q_2 produced. The shortfall of domestic production below domestic consumption, $q_1–q_2$, is imported.

If domestic demand shifts to D_1, consumption equilibrium shifts to E_c, with q_3 consumed. With unchanged domestic production, imports rise to $q_3–q_2$.

Notice that trade lowers the price of the imported good below its autarky level. Notice also that the equilibrium is once again not where quantity demanded domestically equals quantity supplied domestically; price is given by the world price, and the excess of domestic quantity demanded over domestic quantity supplied at that price is met by imports.

For an open economy, equilibrium in particular markets is consistent with domestic demand for that product being different from domestic supply. If, at the world price, quantity demanded domestically exceeds quantity supplied domestically, the good will be imported; if quantity supplied domestically exceeds quantity demanded domestically, the good will be exported.

Effects of changes in domestic supply and demand   Suppose that domestic residents experience a change in tastes. At the given prices and values of the other variables that influence quantity demanded, they decide to consume less of their exported good and more of their imported good. This decision is shown in Figure 25.2, where the demand for the exported good shifts to the left, and in Figure 25.3, where the demand for imported goods shifts to the right. At the prevailing world prices, these shifts lead to an increase in the quantity of the good that is exported (Figure 25.2), and to an increase in the quantity of the good that is imported (Figure 25.3).

Since the economy we are studying is assumed to be small relative to the whole world, these demand shifts have no noticeable effects on world prices. The only results are changes in the *quantities* of imports and exports of that country. The assumption that world prices are constant means that, in effect, the country can buy, or sell, any quantities it wants in world markets.

The effects of a change in domestic supply can also be studied. For example, an increase in domestic wages would increase the home production cost of producing both the imported and the exported good. This would reduce the quantities that would be supplied domestically at each price; i.e. the domestic supply curves of both the import-competing and the exported good shift upwards. The reader can verify that *ceteris paribus* this would lead to an increase in the quantity of imports and a decrease in the quantity of exports. In Chapter 37 we shall see that these changes are not the end of the story. The rise in imports combined with a fall in exports would lead to exchange-rate adjustments that would restore the previous balance between imports and exports. In the meantime, we have reached a key result:

In a small open economy, other things being equal, shifts in domestic supply and demand lead to changes in quantities imported and exported rather than to changes in domestic prices.

We shall have occasion to use this model of the SOE many times throughout this book.

Summary

1 One country (or region or individual) has an absolute advantage over another country (or region or individual) in the production of a product when, with the same input of resources in each country, it can produce more of the product than can the other.

2 In a situation of reciprocal absolute advantage, total production of both products will be raised if each country specializes in the production of the product in which it has the absolute advantage. However, the gains from trade do not require absolute advantage on the part of each country, only comparative advantage.

3 Comparative advantage occurs whenever countries have different opportunity costs of producing particular goods. World production of all products can be increased if each country transfers resources into the production of the products in which it has a comparative advantage, which means those in which it has the lower opportunity cost.

4 The most important proposition in the theory of the gains from trade is that trade allows all countries to obtain the goods in which they do not have a comparative advantage at a lower opportunity cost than they would face if they were to produce all products for themselves; this allows all countries to have more of all products than they could have if they tried to be self-sufficient.

5 As well as gaining the advantages of specialization arising from comparative advantage, a nation that engages in trade and specialization may realize the benefits of economies of large-scale production and of learning by doing.

6 Classical theory regarded comparative advantage as being determined largely by natural resource endowments, and thus as difficult to change. Economists now believe that comparative advantage can be acquired and thus can be changed. A country may, in this view, influence its role in world production and trade. Successful intervention leads to a country acquiring a comparative advantage; unsuccessful intervention fails to develop such an advantage.

7 The terms of trade refer to the ratio of the prices of goods exported to those imported, which determines the quantity of imports that can be obtained per unit of exports. The terms of trade determine how the gains from trade are shared. A favourable change in the terms of trade—that is, a rise in export prices relative to import prices—means a country can acquire more imports per unit of exports.

8 A small open economy is a price-taker in markets for internationally traded goods and services. It will export goods for which its domestic supply exceeds its domestic demand at the world price and import goods for which domestic demand exceeds domestic supply at the world price.

Topics for review

- Interpersonal, interregional, and international specialization
- Absolute advantage and comparative advantage
- Gains from trade: specialization, scale economies, and learning by doing
- Opportunity cost and comparative advantage
- Dynamic comparative advantage
- Terms of trade
- Determination of imports and exports in a small open economy

∾ CHAPTER 26

The theory and practice of commercial policy

CONDUCTING business in a foreign country is always difficult. Differences in language, in local laws and customs, and in currency all complicate transactions. Our concern in this chapter is not, however, with these difficulties, but with the government's policy towards international trade, which is called its **commercial policy**.

In the past, economists spoke of 'trade policy', because tariffs and other measures imposed at a country's borders were the main impediments to international trade. Today, however, a much wider set of forces affects trade flows. Investment is often a complement rather than a substitute for trade, so domestic anti-monopoly policy and investment regulation can be an important impediment to trade. Environmental and labour standards affect international competitiveness, and countries often have trade policies that respond to such policies in other countries. In today's world of globalized competition and transnational corporations, almost any domestic policy can have an impact on foreign trade in goods and services.. This has given rise to what Canadian economist Sylvia Ostry has christened **systems frictions,** which means the international problems that arise when two or more countries' whole systems of what were formerly regarded as purely domestic policies

come into conflict with each other because of their actual or alleged impact on international trading and investment advantages and disadvantages. For these reasons, today's international policy analysts use the wider concepts of 'commercial policy' rather than the narrower one of 'trade policy'.

When we come to policies that may interfere with international trade through measures imposed at a country's borders such as tariffs and quotas, we can identify one important extreme case, which is called a policy of **free trade**, which means an absence of any form of government interference with the free flow of international trade. Any departure from free trade designed to give some protection to domestic industries from foreign competition is called **protectionism**.

In this chapter, we first reiterate the case for free trade and then go on to study various valid and invalid arguments that are commonly advanced for some degree of protectionism. After that, we study the many modern institutions designed to foster freer trade on either a global or a regional basis. We conclude by studying two such institutions, the North American Free Trade Agreement (NAFTA) and the European Union (EU).

The theory of commercial policy

TODAY, debates over commercial policy are as heated as they were 200 years ago when the theory of the gains from trade that we presented in Chapter 25 was still being worked out. Should a country permit the free flow of international trade, or should it seek to protect its local producers from foreign competition? Such protection may be achieved either by **tariffs**, which are taxes designed to raise the price of foreign goods, or by **non-tariff barriers**, which are devices other than tariffs that are designed to reduce the flow of imports; examples include quotas and customs procedures deliberately made more cumbersome than is necessary.

The case for free trade

The case for free trade is based on the analysis presented in Chapter 25. We saw there that, whenever opportunity costs differ among countries, specialization and trade will raise world living standards. Free trade allows all countries to specialize in producing products in which they have a comparative advantage.

Free trade allows the maximization of world production, thus making it possible for each consumer in the world to consume more goods than he or she could without free trade.

This does not necessarily mean that everyone *will* be better off with free trade than without it. Protectionism could allow some people to obtain a larger share of a smaller world output so that they would benefit even though the average person would lose. If we ask whether it is *possible* for free trade to improve everyone's living standards, the answer is 'yes'. But if we ask whether free trade does in fact *always* do so, the answer is 'not necessarily'.

There is abundant evidence that significant differences in opportunity costs exist and that large gains are realized from international trade because of these differences. What needs explanation is the fact that trade is not wholly free. Why do tariffs and non-tariff barriers to trade continue to exist two centuries after Adam Smith and David Ricardo stated the case for free trade? Is there a valid case for protectionism?

The case for protectionism

Two kinds of arguments for protection are commonly offered. The first concerns national objectives other than total income; the second concerns the desire to increase one country's national income, possibly at the expense of world national income.

OBJECTIVES OTHER THAN MAXIMIZING NATIONAL INCOME AS REASONS FOR PROTECTIONISM

It is possible to accept the proposition that national income is higher with free trade, and yet rationally to oppose free trade, because of a concern with policy objectives other than maximizing income.

Non-economic advantages of diversification Comparative advantage might dictate that a country should specialize in producing a narrow range of products. The government might decide, however, that there are distinct social advantages in encouraging a more diverse economy. Citizens would be given a wider range of occupations, and the social and psychological advantages of diversification would more than compensate for a reduction in living standards of, say, 5 per cent below what they could be with complete specialization of production according to comparative advantage.

Risks of specialization For a very small country such as Singapore, specializing in the production of only a few products—though dictated by comparative advantage—may involve risks that the country does not wish to take. One such risk is that technological advances may render its basic product obsolete. Everyone understands this risk, but there is debate about what governments can do about it. The pro-tariff argument is that the government can encourage a more diversified economy by protecting industries that otherwise could not compete. Opponents argue that governments, being naturally influenced by political motives, are, in the final analysis, poor judges of which industries can be protected in order to produce diversification at a reasonable cost.

National defence Another non-economic reason for protectionism concerns national defence. It used to be argued, for example, that the United Kingdom needed an experienced merchant navy in case of war, and that this industry should be fostered by protectionist policies even though it was less efficient than the foreign competition. The same argument is sometimes made for the aircraft industry.

Protection of specific groups Although free trade will maximize per capita GDP over the whole economy, some specific groups may have higher incomes under protection than under free trade. An obvious example is a firm or industry that is given monopoly power when tariffs are used to restrict foreign competition. If a small group of firms, and possibly their employees, find their incomes increased by, say, 25 per cent when they get tariff protection, they may not be concerned that everyone else's incomes fall by, say, 2 per cent. They get a much larger share of a slightly smaller total income and end up better off. If they gain from the tariff, they will lose from free trade.[1]

Tariffs tend to raise the relative income of a group of people who are in short supply domestically and to lower the relative income of a group of people who are in plentiful supply domestically. Free trade does the opposite.

In Chapter 21 we considered the consequences of opening trade in manufactures between the North and the South. When this happened, the South specialized in goods that needed mainly unskilled labour while the North specialized in goods that needed mainly skilled labour. As a result, wages in unskilled labour rose in the South and fell in the North. In the short term, unskilled workers in the North had gained by tariffs and lost by free trade. The reason was that unskilled workers were relatively scarce in the North but relatively plentiful in the world as a whole.

Conclusion Other things being equal, most people prefer more income to less. Economists cannot, however, say that it is irrational for a society to sacrifice some income in order to achieve other goals. Economists can, however, do three things when faced with such reasons for adopting protectionist measures. First, they can ask if the proposed measures really do achieve the ends suggested. Second, they can calculate the cost of the measures in terms of lowered living standards. Third, they can see if there are alternative means of achieving the stated goals at lower cost in terms of lost output.

MAXIMIZING NATIONAL INCOME AS A REASON FOR PROTECTIONISM

Next, we consider five important arguments for the use of tariffs when the objective is to make national income as large as possible.

---

[1] Models that show this possibility usually assume static technology and constant returns to scale. The presence of economies of scale, learning effects, and induced improvements in technology increases the total gain from free trade and makes it less likely that any large group will lose absolutely from that policy.

To alter the terms of trade   Trade restrictions can be used to turn the terms of trade in favour of countries that produce, and export, a large fraction of the world's supply of some product. They can also be used to turn the terms of trade in favour of countries that constitute a large fraction of the world demand for some product that they import.

When the OPEC countries restricted their output of oil in the 1970s, they were able to drive up the price of oil relative to the prices of other traded goods. This turned the terms of trade in their favour; for every barrel of oil exported, they were able to obtain a larger quantity of imports. When the output of oil grew greatly in the mid-1980s, the relative price of oil fell dramatically, and the terms of trade turned unfavourably for the oil-exploring companies. These are illustrations of how changes in the quantities of exports can affect the terms of trade.

Now consider a country that provides a large fraction of the total demand for some product that it imports. By restricting its demand for that product through tariffs, it can force the price of that product down. This turns the terms of trade in its favour because it can now get more units of imports per unit of exports.

Both of these techniques lower world output. They can, however, make it possible for a small group of countries to gain because they get a sufficiently larger share of the smaller world output. However, if foreign countries retaliate by raising their tariffs, the ensuing tariff war can easily leave every country with a lowered income.

To protect against 'unfair' actions by foreign firms and governments   Tariffs may be used to prevent foreign industries from gaining an advantage over domestic industries by use of predatory practices that will harm domestic industries and hence lower national income. Two common practices are subsidies paid by foreign governments to their exporters and price discrimination by foreign firms, which is called dumping when it is done across international borders. These practices are typically countered by levying tariffs called countervailing and anti-dumping duties. The circumstances under which dumping and foreign subsidization provide a valid argument for such tariffs are considered in detail later in this chapter.

To protect infant industries   The oldest valid argument for protectionism as a means of raising living standards concerns economies of scale. It is usually called the **infant industry argument**. If an industry has large economies of scale, costs will be high when the industry is small, but will fall as the industry grows. In such industries, the country first in the field has a tremendous advantage. A newly developing country may find that, in the early stages of development, its industries are unable to compete with established foreign rivals. A trade restriction may protect these industries from foreign competition while they grow up. When they are large enough, they will be able to produce as cheap-ly as foreign rivals and thus will be able to compete without protection.

To encourage learning by doing   Learning by doing, which we discussed in Chapter 25, suggests that the pattern of comparative advantage can be changed. If a country learns enough through producing products in which it currently is at a comparative *dis*advantage, it may gain in the long run by specializing in those products, and could develop a comparative advantage as the learning process lowers their costs.

Learning by doing is an example of what in Chapter 25 we called dynamic comparative advantages. The successes of such *newly industrializing countries* (the so-called NICs) as Brazil, Hong Kong, South Korea, Singapore, and Taiwan seemed to many observers to be based on acquired skills and government policies that create favourable business conditions. This gave rise to the theory that comparative advantages can change, and that they can be developed by suitable government policies.

Protecting a domestic industry from foreign competition may give its management time to learn to be efficient, and its labour force time to acquire the needed skills.

If this is so, it may pay in the very long run to protect the industry against foreign competition, while a dynamic comparative advantage is being developed.

Some countries have succeeded in developing strong comparative advantages in targeted industries, but others have failed. One reason such policies sometimes fail is that protecting local industries from foreign competition may make the industries unadaptive and complacent. Another reason is the difficulty of identifying the industries that will be able to succeed in the long run. All too often, the protected infant grows up to be a weakling requiring permanent tariff protection for its continued existence; or else the rate of learning is slower than for similar industries in countries that do not provide protection from the chill winds of international competition. In these instances, the anticipated comparative advantage never materializes.

To create or to exploit a strategic trade advantage   A major new argument for tariffs or other trade restrictions is to create a strategic advantage in producing or marketing some new product that is expected to generate pure profits. To the extent that all lines of production earn normal profits, there is no reason to produce goods other than ones for which a country has a comparative advantage. Some goods, however, are produced in industries containing a few large firms where large-scale economies provide a natural barrier to further entry. Firms in these industries can earn extra-high profits over long periods of time. Where such industries are already well established, there is little chance that a new firm will replace one of the existing giants.

The situation is, however, more fluid with new products. The first firm to develop and market a new product successfully may earn a substantial pure profit over all of its opportunity costs and become one of the few established firms in the industry. If protection of the domestic market can increase the chance that one of the protected domestic firms will become one of the established firms in the international market, the protection may pay off. This is the general idea behind the modern concept of strategic trade policy, and it is treated in more detail in the next section.

STRATEGIC TRADE POLICY AND COMPETITIVENESS AS REASONS FOR PROTECTIONISM

Implications of high development costs Many of today's high-tech industries have falling average total cost curves because of their large fixed costs of product development. For a new generation of civilian aircraft, silicon chips, computers, artificial-intelligence machines, and genetically engineered food products, a very high proportion of each producer's total costs go to product development. These are fixed costs of entering the market, and they must be incurred before a single unit of output can be sold.

In such industries, the actual costs of producing each unit of an already-developed product may be quite small. Even if average variable costs are constant, the large fixed development costs mean that the average total cost curve has a significant negative slope over a large range of output. It follows that the price at which a firm can expect to recover its total cost is negatively related to its expected volume of sales. The larger are the sales that it expects, the lower is the price that it can charge and still expect to recover its full costs.

In such industries, there may be room for only a few firms, and those firms may make large profits. A large number of firms, each of which has a relatively small output, could not recover their fixed costs. A small number of firms, each of which has a high output, can do so. Furthermore, it is possible for these firms to make large profits, whereas the entry of one more firm would cause everyone to suffer losses. In this case, the first firms that become established in the market will control it and will earn the profits.[2]

The production of full-sized commercial jet airplanes provides an example of an industry that possesses many of these characteristics. The development costs of a new generation of jet aircraft have risen with each new generation. If the aircraft manufacturers are to recover these costs, each of them must have large sales. Thus, the number of firms that the market can support has diminished steadily, until today there is room in the world aircraft industry for only two or three firms producing a full range of commercial jets.

Argument for subsidies The characteristics just listed are sometimes used to provide arguments for subsidizing the development of such industries. Suppose, for example, that there is room in the aircraft industry for only three major producers of the next round of passenger jets. If a government subsidizes a domestic firm, this firm may become one of the three that succeed. In this case, the profits that are subsequently earned may more than repay the cost of the subsidy. Furthermore, another country's firm, which was not subsidized, may have been just as good as the three that succeeded. Without the subsidy, however, this firm may lose out in the battle to establish itself as one of the three surviving firms in the market. Having lost this one battle, it loses its entire fight for existence. The firm, and the country's possibility of being represented in the industry, are gone for the foreseeable future.

This example is not unlike the story of the European Airbus. The European producers received many direct subsidies (and they charge that their main competitor, the Boeing 767, received many indirect ones). Whatever the merits of the argument, several things are clear: the civilian jet aircraft industry remains profitable; there is room for only two or three major producers; and one of these would not have been the European consortium if it had not been for substantial government assistance.

Argument for tariffs The argument for tariffs is that a protected domestic market greatly reduces the risks of product development and allows successful firms to achieve sufficient scale on the domestic market to be able to sell at competitive prices abroad. The classic example here is the victory in the 1970s of the Japanese semiconductor producers over their US rivals. From the beginning of the industry, US firms held a large competitive edge over all others. Then the Japanese decided to develop their industry. To do so, they shielded their domestic market from penetration by US firms. The Japanese, who at first were well behind the US firms, caught up, and were then able to penetrate the open US market. In the end, the Japanese succeeded with the next generation of silicon chips, and the once-dominant US industry suffered greatly. (This does not seem to have stopped the US firms from being successful in the round of competition over the next generation of chips in the 1990s.)

A combination of domestic subsidization and tariff pro-

---

[2] The reason for this is found in the indivisibility of product development costs. If, say, £500 million is required to develop a marketable product, a firm that spends only £300 million gets nothing. To see why this creates the potential for profits, assume that the market is large enough for the product to be sold at a price that would cover variable costs of production and also pay the opportunity costs of £1.25 billion worth of capital. Further, assume that the capital required for actual production is negligible. In this case two firms with a total of £1 billion of capital invested in development costs will enter the market and earn large profits. However, if a third firm entered, making the industry's total invested capital £1.5 billion, all three firms would incur losses.

tection allowed the Japanese semiconductor industry to score a major victory in terms of market share over their US competitors. The strategy, however, entailed large costs, both for product development and in aggressive, below-cost pricing policies. Currently, there is debate as to whether the long-run profits resulting from this policy were sufficient to cover all these costs.

Debate over strategic trade policy   Generalizing from this and similar cases, some economists advocate that their governments should adopt *strategic trade policies* more broadly than they now do. This means, for high-tech industries, government protection of the home market and government subsidization (either openly or by more subtle back-door methods) of the product development stage. These economists say that, if their country does not follow their advice, it will lose out in industry after industry to the more aggressive Japanese and North American competition—a competition that is adept at combining private innovative activity with government assistance.

Opponents argue that strategic trade policy is nothing more than a modern version of the age-old, and faulty, justifications for tariff protection.

Opponents argue that, once all countries try to be strategic, they will all waste vast sums trying to break into industries in which there is no room for most of them. Domestic consumers would benefit most, they say, if their governments were to let other countries engage in this game. Consumers could then buy the cheap, subsidized foreign products and export traditional, lower-tech products in return. The opponents of strategic trade policy also argue that democratic governments that enter the game of picking and backing winners are likely to make more bad choices than good ones. One bad choice, with *all* of its massive development costs written off, would require a great many good choices to be made, in order that sufficient profits would be made to allow taxpayers to break even overall.[3]

Advocates of strategic trade policy reply that a country cannot afford to stand by while others play the strategic game.

Advocates argue that there are key industries that have major 'spillovers' into the rest of the economy. If a country wants to have a high living standard, it must, they argue, compete with the best. If a country lets all of its key industries migrate to other countries, many of the others will follow. The country then risks being reduced to the status of a less developed nation.

Longer-run considerations   There are also some long-run political and economic arguments against the use of strategic trade policy that need to be considered. The rising world prosperity of the entire period following the Second World War has been built largely on a rising volume of relatively free international trade. There are real doubts that such prosperity could be maintained if the volume of trade were to shrink steadily because of growing trade barriers. Yet the pressure to use trade restrictions in troubled times is strong. If countries begin to raise barriers moderately when the initial economic costs are not large, the political forces involved are so strong that there is no telling where the process, once begun, will end.

In today's world, a country's products must stand up to international competition if they are to survive. Over time, this requires that they hold their own in competition for successful innovations. Over even so short a period as a decade, firms that do not develop new products (product innovation) and new production methods (process innovation) will fall seriously behind their competitors in many, possibly most, industries. Using case studies covering many countries, economists such as Michael Porter of Harvard University have shown that almost all firms that succeed in holding their own in competition based on innovation operate in highly competitive environments.[4]

Protection, by conferring a national monopoly, reduces the incentive for industries to fight to hold their own internationally. If any one country adopts high tariffs unilaterally, its domestic industries will become less competitive. Secure in its home market because of the tariff wall, the protected industries are likely to become less and less competitive in the international market.

As the gap between domestic and foreign industries widens, any tariff wall will provide less and less protection. Eventually, the domestic industries will succumb to the foreign competition.

Meanwhile, domestic living standards will fall relative to foreign ones, as an increasing productivity gap opens between domestic, tariff-protected industries and foreign, internationally oriented ones.

Although restrictive policies sometimes have been pursued following a rational assessment of the approximate cost, it is hard to avoid the conclusion that, more often than not, such policies are often pursued for political objectives, or on fallacious economic grounds, with little appreciation of the actual costs involved.

---

[3] Let each investment be £100 m and, when successful, return £125 m, for a 25 per cent return. Nine investments cost £900 m, and seven successes and two total losses yield £875 m. This is an overall loss of £25 m on a £900 m investment.

[4] Michael Porter, *The Competitive Advantage of Nations* (New York: Free Press, 1990). A 'highly competitive environment' refers to rivalrous behaviour among firms with significant market power, not to the existence of perfect competition.

The very high tariffs in the United States during the 1920s and 1930s are a conspicuous example. The current clamour for the European Union and the United States to do something about the competition from Japan, Korea, and other Pacific Rim countries may well be another.

Methods of protection

We have now studied some of the many reasons why governments may wish to provide some protection for some of their domestic industries. Our next task is to see how they do it. What are the tools that provide protection?

Two main types of protectionist policy are illustrated in Figure 26.1. Both cause the price of the imported good to rise and its quantity to fall. They differ, however, in how they achieve these results. The caption to the figure analyses these two types of policy.

POLICIES THAT DIRECTLY RAISE PRICES

The first type of protectionist policy directly raises the *price* of the imported product. A tariff, also often called an *import duty*, is the most common policy of this type. Other such policies include any rules or regulations that fulfil three conditions: they are costly to comply with; they do

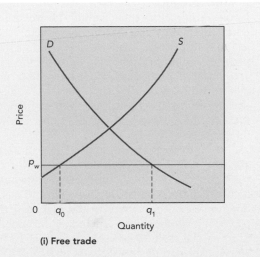
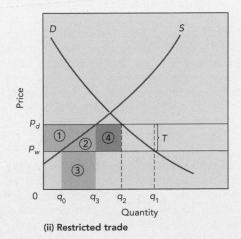

(i) Free trade

(ii) Restricted trade

Figure 26.1 Methods of protecting domestic producers

The same reduction in imports and increase in domestic production can be achieved by using either a tariff or a quantity restriction. In both parts of the figure, D and S are the domestic demand and supply curves, respectively, and p_w is the world price of some product that is both produced at home and imported.

Part (i) of the figure shows the situation under free trade. Domestic consumption is q_1, domestic production is q_0, and imports are q_0–q_1.

Part (ii) shows what happens when protectionist policies restrict imports to the amount q_3–q_2. When this is done by levying a tariff of T per unit, the price in the domestic market rises by the full amount of the tariff to p_d. Consumers reduce consumption from q_1 to q_2 and pay an extra amount, shown by the coloured areas 1, 2, and 4, for the q_2 that they now purchase. Domestic production rises from q_0 to q_3. Since domestic producers receive the domestic price, their receipts rise by the three medium blue areas, labelled 1, 2, and 3. Area 3 is revenue that was earned by foreign producers under free trade, while areas 1 and 2 are paid by domestic consumers because of the higher prices they now face. Foreign suppliers of the imported good continue to receive the world price, so the government receives as tariff revenue the extra amount paid by consumers for the q_3–q_2 units that are still imported (shown by the dark blue area, 4).

When the same result is accomplished by a quantity restriction, the government—through either a quota or a *voluntary export agreement (VER)*—reduces imports to q_3–q_2. This drives the domestic market price up to p_d and has the same effect on domestic producers and consumers as the tariff. Since the government has merely restricted the quantity of imports, both foreign and domestic suppliers get the higher price in the domestic market. Thus, foreign suppliers now receive the extra amount paid by domestic consumers (represented by the coloured area labelled 4) for the units that are still imported.

not apply to competing, domestically produced products; and they are more than is required to meet any purpose other than restricting trade.

As shown in part (ii) of Figure 26.1, tariffs affect both foreign and domestic producers, as well as domestic consumers. The initial effect is to raise the domestic price of the imported product above its world price by the amount of the tariff. Imports fall and, as a result, foreign producers sell less and so must transfer resources to other lines of production. The price received on domestically produced units rises, as does the quantity produced domestically. On both counts, domestic producers earn more. However, the cost of producing the extra output at home exceeds the price at which it could be purchased on the world market. Thus, the benefit to domestic producers comes at the expense of domestic consumers. Indeed, domestic consumers lose on two counts: first, they consume less of the product because its price rises; and second, they pay a higher price for the amount that they do consume. This extra spending ends up in two places: the extra that is paid on all units produced at home goes to domestic producers (partly in the resource costs of extra production and partly in profit), and the extra that is paid on units still imported goes to the government as tariff revenue.

POLICIES THAT DIRECTLY LOWER QUANTITIES

The second type of protectionist policy directly restricts the *quantity* of an imported product. A common example is the **import quota,** by which the importing country sets a maximum of the quantity of some product that may be imported each year. Increasingly popular, however, is the **voluntary export restriction (VER),** an agreement by an *exporting* country to limit the amount of a good that it sells to the importing country.

The European Union and the United States have used VERs extensively, and the European Union also makes frequent use of import quotas. Japan has been pressured into negotiating several VERs with the European Union and the United States in order to limit sales of some of the Japanese goods that have had the most success in international competition. For example, in 1983 the United States and Canada negotiated VERs whereby the Japanese government agreed to restrict total sales of Japanese cars to these two countries for three years. When the agreements ran out in 1986, the Japanese continued to restrain their car sales by unilateral voluntary action. VERs are further considered in Box 26.1.

Nominal and effective rates of tariff The rate of tariff charged on each product, called the **nominal rate of tariff,** does not necessarily show the degree of protection given to that product. Nominal rates frequently understate the degree of protection offered to domestic manufacturing industries, and a better measure is provided by what is called the **effective tariff rate.**

Nominal and effective rates of tariff differ whenever imported raw materials, or semi-finished goods, carry a lower rate of duty than do imports of the final manufactured goods that embody these intermediate products.

When the final good is made abroad, the duty for manufactured goods is applied to the entire price of that good, even though the price includes the values of the raw materials and semi-finished goods that it embodies. When the final good is produced domestically, the raw materials and semi-finished goods enter at the lower rate of tariff. For this reason, a tariff of, say, 10 per cent on the final good will protect a domestic producer that is much more than 10 per cent less efficient than its foreign competitor.

To illustrate this important point, consider an example. A wood product is manufactured in both Britain and Norway using Norwegian wood. The wood is assumed to enter Britain duty-free, but the manufactured good is subject to a 10 per cent tariff. Further, assume that when the product is manufactured in Norway the raw material accounts for half the cost of the final product and the other half is value added by the Norwegian manufacturer. Because of the 10 per cent tariff, a unit of output that costs £1 to produce in Norway will sell in the United Kingdom for £1.10.

Now consider the position of a UK manufacturer who is assumed to be less efficient than the Norwegian manufacturer. Let the UK firm's production costs be 20 per cent higher than those of the Norwegian firm. Thus, to produce one unit of output, the raw material costs the UK firm £0.50, but its other costs—including the opportunity costs of its capital—are £0.60 (i.e. 20 per cent higher than the Norwegian manufacturer's costs of £0.50). This gives the UK firm a final price of £1.10, which is just low enough to compete against the tariff-burdened Norwegian import.

In this example, a tariff of 10 per cent on the value of the final product is sufficient to protect a UK firm that is 20 per cent less efficient than its Norwegian competitor. To measure this effect, the effective rate of tariff expresses the tariff as a percentage of the *value added* by the exporting industry in question. Thus, the effective UK rate of tariff on the Norwegian manufacturing firm in the above example is 20 per cent, whereas the nominal tariff on manufactured goods is only 10 per cent.

TRADE REMEDY LAWS AND NON-TARIFF BARRIERS

As tariffs were lowered over the years since 1947, countries that wished to protect domestic industries began using, and abusing, a series of trade restrictions that came to be known as non-tariff barriers (NTBs). The original purpose of some of these was to remedy certain legitimate problems that arise in international trade. For this reason, they are often called *trade remedy laws*. All too often, however, they are

BOX 26.1

Import restrictions on Japanese cars: tariffs or quotas?

Voluntary export agreements (VERs) have been commonly used by the European Union and the United States to limit Japanese imports in key areas, such as cars and electronics, where the Japanese have a strong competitive advantage. The Japanese have agreed to such arrangements because, for any given volume of trade restrictions, VERs are far more profitable to the Japanese than most alternative arrangements. In 1994, they had agreed to restrict their exports to the United Kingdom to no more than 11 per cent of the UK market and had similar arrangements with other EU countries.

Those who believe in free trade criticize such arrangements, which certainly shield several European industries from intense Japanese competition and greatly raise the price of the affected products for European consumers and for producers who use any such goods as inputs.

The issue raised in this box concerns alternative methods of restricting trade in cars. Given that trade is to be restricted, what does economic theory predict to be the relative merits of VERs and tariffs? In both cases, imports are restricted, and the resulting scarcity supports a higher market price. With a tariff, the extra market value is appropriated by the government of the importing country—in this case the European Union. With a VER, the extra market value accrues to the goods' suppliers—in this case the Japanese car makers and their EU retailers.

Both cases are illustrated in the accompanying figure. We assume that the European market provides a small enough part of total Japanese car sales to leave the Japanese willing to supply all the cars that are demanded in the European Union at their fixed list price. This is the price p_0 in both parts of the figure. Given the European demand curve for Japanese cars, D, there are q_0 cars sold before restrictions are imposed.

In part (i) the EU places a tariff of T per unit on Japanese cars, raising their price in the EU to p_1 and lowering sales to q_1. Suppliers' revenue is shown by the medium blue area. Government tariff revenue is shown by the dark blue area.

In part (ii) a VER of q_1 is negotiated, making the supply curve

of Japanese cars vertical at q_1. The market-clearing price is p_1. The suppliers' revenue is the whole medium blue shaded area ($p_1 \times q_1$).

In both cases, the shortage of Japanese cars drives up their price, creating a substantial margin over costs. Under a tariff, the EU governments capture the margin; under a VER policy, however, the margin accrues to the Japanese manufacturers.

Although this is a simplified picture, it captures the essence of what actually happened. First, while sellers of EU cars were keeping prices as low as possible, and sometimes offering rebates on slow-selling models, Japanese cars were listed at healthy profit margins. Second, while it was always possible for the buyer of a EU car to negotiate a good discount off the list price, Japanese cars usually sold for their full list price. Third, because Japanese manufacturers were not allowed to supply all of the cars that they could sell in the EU, they had to choose which types of cars to supply. Not surprisingly, they tended to satisfy fully the demand for their more expensive cars, which have higher profit margins. This change in the 'product mix' of Japanese cars exported to the EU raised the average profit per car exported.

The VERs were thus costly to European consumers and profitable to Japanese car manufacturers. In North America, where the Japanese penetration of the local market was larger than in Europe and the VERs cut more deeply into Japanese sales, it was estimated that consumers paid about US$150,000 *per year* for each job that was saved in the US car industry, and that most of this went to Japanese producers! (This cost to consumers per job saved is typical of what is found in many industries where VERs or their equivalents have been used.) Of course, this amount is spread over many consumers, so each does not notice the amount of his or her contribution. None the less, $150,000 per year could do a lot of things, including fully retraining the workers and subsidizing their transfer to industries and areas where they could produce things that could be sold on free markets without government protection.

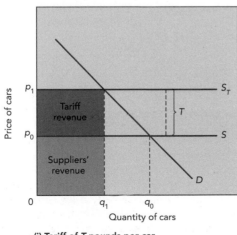

(i) Tariff of T pounds per car

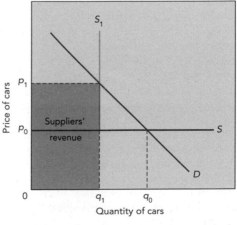

(ii) Quota of q₁ cars

misused to become potent methods of simple protectionism. When this happens they are called measures of *contingent protection*.

Escape clause   One procedure that can be used as a non-tariff barrier is the so-called escape clause action. A rapid surge of some imports may threaten the existence of domestic producers. These producers may then be given temporary relief to allow them time to adjust. This is done by raising tariff rates on the product in question above those set by international agreements. The trouble is that, once imposed, these 'temporary' measures are hard to eliminate.

Dumping   When a product is sold in a foreign country at a price that is lower than the price in the domestic market, it is called **dumping**. Dumping is a form of price discrimination studied in the theory of monopoly. Most governments have anti-dumping duties, which protect their own industries against unfair foreign pricing practices.

Dumping, if it lasts indefinitely, can be a gift to the receiving country. Its consumers get goods from abroad at less than their real cost. Dumping is more often a temporary measure, designed to get rid of unwanted surpluses, or a predatory attempt to drive competitors out of business. In either case, domestic producers complain about unfair foreign competition. In both cases, it is accepted international practice to levy anti-dumping duties on foreign imports. These duties are designed to eliminate the discriminatory elements in their prices.

Unfortunately, anti-dumping laws have been evolving over the last few decades in ways that allow anti-dumping duties to become barriers to trade and competition, rather than to provide redress for unfair trading practices. Two features of the anti-dumping system that is now in effect in many countries make it highly protectionist. First, *any* price discrimination is classified as dumping and therefore is subject to penalties. Thus, prices in the producer's domestic market become, in effect, minimum prices below which no sales can be made in foreign markets, whatever the circumstances in the domestic and foreign markets. Second, following a change in the US law in the early 1970s, many countries' laws now calculate the 'margin of dumping' as the difference between the price that is charged in that country's market and the foreign producers' 'full allocated cost' (average total cost). This means that, when there is global excess demand so that the profit-maximizing price for all producers is below average total cost (but above average variable cost), foreign producers can be convicted of dumping. This gives domestic producers enormous protection whenever the market price falls temporarily below average total cost.

Anti-dumping duties are very commonly used by many governments including the European Union, the United States, and Canada.

Countervailing duties   Countervailing duties, which are commonly used by the US government but much less so elsewhere, provide another case in which a trade relief measure can sometimes become a covert non-tariff barrier. The countervailing duty is designed to act not as a tariff barrier, but rather as a means of creating a 'level playing field' on which fair international competition can take place. Privately owned domestic firms rightly complain that they cannot compete against the seemingly bottomless purses of foreign governments. Subsidized foreign exports can be sold indefinitely at prices that would produce losses in the absence of the subsidy. The original object of countervailing duties was to counteract the effect on price of the presence of such foreign subsidies.

If a domestic firm suspects the existence of such a subsidy and registers a complaint, its government is required to make an investigation. For a countervailing duty to be levied, the investigation must find, first, that the foreign subsidy to the specific industry in question does exist and, second, that it is large enough to cause significant injury to competing domestic firms.

There is no doubt that countervailing duties sometimes have been used to remove the effects of 'unfair' competition that are caused by foreign subsidies. Many governments complain, however, that countervailing duties are often used as a thinly disguised barrier to trade. At the early stages of the development of countervailing duties, only subsidies whose prime effect was to distort trade were possible objects of countervailing duties. Even then, however, the existence of equivalent domestic subsidies was *not taken into account* when decisions were made to put countervailing duties on subsidized imports. Thus, the United States has some countervailing duties against foreign goods where the foreign subsidy is less than the US subsidy. This does not create a level playing field.

Over time, the type of subsidy that is subject to countervailing duties has evolved until almost any government programme that affects industry now risks becoming the object of countervailing duty. Because all governments, have many programmes that provide some direct or indirect assistance to industry, the potential for the use of countervailing duties as thinly disguised trade barriers is enormous.

Fallacious trade-policy arguments

We saw in Chapter 25 that there are gains from a high volume of international trade and specialization. We have also seen earlier in this chapter that there can be valid arguments for a moderate degree of protectionism. There are also many claims that do not advance the debate. Fallacious arguments are heard on both sides, and they colour much of the popular discussion. These arguments have been around for a long time, but their survival does not make them true. We will examine them now to see where their fallacies lie.

FALLACIOUS ARGUMENTS FOR FREE TRADE

Free trade always benefits all countries   This is not necessarily so. We saw above that a small group of countries may gain by restricting trade in order to get a sufficiently favourable shift in their terms of trade. Such countries would lose if they gave up these tariffs and adopted free trade unilaterally.

Infant industries never abandon their tariff protection   It is argued that granting protection to infant industries is a mistake because these industries seldom admit to growing up, and will cling to their protection even when fully grown. But infant-industry tariffs are a mistake *only* if these industries never grow up. In this case permanent tariff protection would be required to protect a weak industry never able to compete on an equal footing in the international market. But if the industries do grow up and achieve the expected scale economies, the real costs of production are reduced and resources are freed for other uses. Whether or not the tariff or other trade barriers remain, a cost saving has been effected by the scale economies.

FALLACIOUS ARGUMENTS FOR PROTECTIONISM

Prevent exploitation   According to the exploitation theory, trade can never be mutually advantageous; one trading partner *must* always reap a gain at the other's expense. Thus, the weaker trading partner must protect itself by restricting its trade with the stronger partner. By showing that both parties can gain from trade, the principle of comparative advantage refutes the exploitation doctrine of trade. When opportunity-cost ratios differ in two countries, specialization and the accompanying trade make it possible to produce more of all products. This makes it possible for both parties to consume more as a result of trade than they could get in its absence.

Keep the money at home   This argument says: if I buy a foreign good, I have the good and the foreigner has the money, whereas if I buy the same good locally, I have the good and our country has the money, too.

This argument is based on a misconception. It assumes that domestic money actually goes abroad physically when imports are purchased and that trade flows only in one direction. But when British importers purchase Japanese goods, they do not send sterling abroad. They (or their financial agents) buy Japanese yen and use them to pay the Japanese manufacturers. They purchase the yen on the foreign exchange market by giving up sterling to someone who wishes to use it for expenditure *in the United Kingdom.*

Even if the money did go abroad physically—that is, if a Japanese firm accepted a shipload of £5 notes—it would be because that firm (or someone to whom it could sell the notes) wanted them to spend in the only country where they are legal tender, i.e. the United Kingdom.

Sterling, or any other national currency, ultimately does no one any good except as purchasing power. It would be miraculous if UK money could be exported in return for real goods. After all, the Bank of England has the power to create as much new money as it wishes. It is only because UK money can buy UK products, and assets, that others want it.

Protect against low-wage foreign labour   Surely, this argument says, the products of low-wage countries will drive UK products from the market, and the high UK standard of living will be dragged down to that of its poorer trading partners. Arguments of this sort have swayed many voters through the years.

As a prelude to considering them, stop and think what the argument would imply if taken out of the international context and put into a local one, where the same principles govern the gains from trade. Is it really impossible for a rich person to gain from trading with a poor person? Would the local millionaire be better off if she did all her own typing, gardening, and cooking? No one believes that a rich person cannot gain from trading with those who are less rich.

Why then must a rich group of people lose from trading with a poor group? 'Well,' some may say, 'the poor group will price their goods too cheaply.' Does anyone believe that consumers lose from buying in discount houses or supermarkets just because the prices are lower there than at the old-fashioned corner shop? Consumers gain when they can buy the same goods at a lower price. If the Koreans pay low wages and sell their goods cheaply, *Korean* labour may suffer, but Britain will gain by obtaining imports at a low cost in terms of the goods that must be exported in return. The cheaper our imports are, the better off we are in terms of the goods and services available for domestic consumption.

Stated in more formal terms, the gains from trade depend on comparative, not absolute, advantages. World production is higher when any two areas, say Britain and Japan, specialize in the production of the goods for which they have a comparative advantage than when they both try to be self-sufficient.

Might it not be possible, however, that Japan will undersell Britain in all lines of production and thus appropriate all, or more than all, the gains for itself, leaving Britain no better off, or even worse off, than if it had no trade with Japan? The answer is no. The reason for this depends on the behaviour of exchange rates, which are discussed in Chapter 37. As we shall see in that chapter, equality of demand and supply in foreign exchange markets ensures that trade flows in both directions. In the meantime, the reason a country cannot import for long without exporting may be stated intuitively as follows.

Imports can be obtained only by spending the currency of the country that makes the imports. Claims to this currency can be obtained only by exporting goods and services, or by borrowing. Thus, lending and borrowing aside, imports must equal exports. All trade must be in two directions; we can buy only if we can also sell.

In the long run, trade cannot hurt a country by causing it to import without exporting.

Trade, then, always provides scope for international specialization, with each country producing and exporting those goods for which it has a comparative advantage and importing those goods for which it does not.

Exports raise living standards; imports lower them Exports create domestic income and employment; imports create income and employment for foreigners. Thus, other things being equal, exports tend to increase our total national income and imports to reduce it. Surely, then, it is desirable to encourage exports by subsidizing them and to discourage imports by taxing them.

This is an appealing argument, but it is incorrect. Exports raise national income by adding to the value of domestic output, but they do not add to the value of domestic consumption. In fact, exports are goods produced at home and consumed abroad, while imports are goods produced abroad and consumed at home. The standard of living in a country depends on the goods and services available for *consumption*, not on what is produced.

If exports were really good and imports really bad, then a fully employed economy that managed to increase exports without a corresponding increase in imports ought to be better off. Such a change, however, would result in a reduction in current standards of living, because, when more goods are sent abroad while no more are brought in from abroad, the total goods available for domestic consumption must fall.

The living standards of a country depend on the goods and services consumed in that country. The importance of exports is that they permit imports to be made. This two-way international exchange is valuable because more goods can be imported than could be obtained if the same goods were produced at home.

Create domestic jobs and reduce unemployment It is sometimes said that an economy with substantial unemployment, such as that of the United Kingdom in the 1930s and the 1980s, provides an exception to the case for freer trade. Suppose that tariffs or import quotas cut the imports of Japanese cars, Korean textiles, US computers, and Polish vodka. Surely, the argument maintains, this will create more employment in local industries producing similar products. The answer is that it will—initially. But the Japanese, Koreans, Americans, and Poles can buy from Britain only if they earn sterling by selling things to (or by borrowing sterling from) Britain.[5] The decline in their sales of cars, textiles, computers, and vodka will decrease their purchases of UK machinery, aircraft, insurance, and holidays in Britain. Jobs will be lost in UK export industries, and gained in those industries that formerly faced competition from imports. The likely long-term effect is that overall unemployment will not be reduced but merely redistributed among industries. In the process, living standards will be reduced because employment expands in inefficient import-competing industries and contracts in efficient exporting industries.

Industries and unions that compete with imports often favour protectionism, while those with large exports usually favour more trade. Protection is an ineffective means to reduce unemployment.

Commercial policy today

IN this second half of the chapter, we discuss commercial policy in the world today. We start with the many international agreements that govern current commercial policies and then look in a little more detail at the European Union.

Before 1947, any country was free to impose any tariffs on its imports. However, when one country increased its tariffs, the action often triggered retaliatory actions by its trading partners. The 1930s saw a high-water mark of world protectionism, as each country sought to raise its employment by raising its tariffs. The end result was lowered effi-

[5] They can also get sterling by selling to other countries and then using their currencies to buy sterling. But this only complicates the transaction; it does not change its fundamental nature. Other countries must have earned the sterling by selling goods to the UK (or borrowing from the UK).

ciency, less trade—but no increase in employment. Since that time, much effort has been devoted to reducing tariff barriers, on both a multilateral and a regional basis.

General Agreement on Tariffs and Trade (GATT)

One of the most notable achievements of the post-war era was the creation of the General Agreement on Tariffs and Trade (GATT). The principle of GATT is that each member-country agrees not to make unilateral tariff increases. This prevents the outbreak of tariff wars in which countries raise tariffs to protect particular domestic industries and to retaliate against other countries' tariff increases. Such wars usually harm all countries as mutually beneficial trade shrinks under the impact of escalating tariff barriers. The last such rounds of mutually destructive tariff wars occurred in the 1920s and 1930s. The GATT countries, which numbered 125 in 1994, also meet periodically to negotiate on matters affecting foreign trade and to agree on across-the-board tariff cuts.

The three most recently completed rounds of GATT agreements, the Kennedy round (completed 1967), the Tokyo round (completed 1979), and the Uruguay round (completed 1993), have each agreed to reduce world tariffs substantially, the first two by about one-third each, and the last by about 40 per cent.

The Uruguay round created a new body, the World Trade Organization (WTO), to replace GATT beginning in 1995. It also created a new legal structure for multilateral trading. Under this new structure, all members have equal mutual rights and obligations. Until the WTO was formed, developing countries who were in GATT enjoyed all the GATT rights but were exempt from most of its obligations to liberalize trade—obligations that applied only to the developed countries. Now, however, all such special treatments are to be phased out over seven years beginning in 1995. There is also a new dispute settlement mechanism with much more power to enforce rulings over non-tariff barriers than existed in the past.

There is to be a substantial reduction of tariffs—40 per cent across the board and more in some special cases. These are to be phased in between 1995 and 2000.

The Multifiber Agreement, which greatly restricts the ability of developing countries to export textiles in which they have a major comparative advantage, is to be phased out over 10 years. There are much stronger rules for trade in services, the protection of foreign investment, and intellectual property. The big failure was in not getting a major liberalization of trade in agricultural goods. The European Union resisted US pressure greatly to reduce its subsidization of agriculture production in, and exports from, its territory. These policies mainly hurt the developing countries,

many of whom have strong comparative advantages in agricultural goods but cannot compete against heavily subsidized exports from the European Union. The EU and a number of other countries that heavily protect their domestic agricultural sectors such as Canada finally agreed to a plan to end all import quotas which are needed to support policies that raise prices for domestic producers above the world price. These quotas are to be replaced with 'tariff equivalents'. These are tariffs that will restrict trade by the same amount as did the quotas. Often tariff equivalents had to be several hundred per cent to do the job done by quotas. The hope is that pressure will build up to reduce these very high tariffs over the next few decades.

All in all, however, the successful completion of the Uruguay round represents a major victory for the supporters of a strong, rules-based, multilateral trading system.

Types of regional agreement

Regional agreements seek to liberalize trade over a much smaller group of countries than the GATT membership. Three standard forms of regional trade-liberalizing agreements are free trade areas, customs unions, and common markets.

A **free-trade area (FTA)** is the least comprehensive of the three. It allows for tariff-free trade among the member-countries, but it leaves each member free to levy its own trade restrictions on imports from other countries. As a result, members must maintain customs points at their common borders to make sure that imports into the free-trade area do not all enter through the member that is levying the lowest tariff on each item. They must also agree on *rules of origin* to establish when a good is made in a member-country, and hence is able to pass duty-free across their borders, and when it is imported from outside the free-trade area, and hence is liable to pay duties when it crosses borders within the free-trade area.

A **customs union** is a free-trade area plus an agreement to establish common barriers to trade with the rest of the world. Because they have a common tariff against the outside world, the members need neither customs controls on goods moving among themselves nor rules of origin.

A **common market** is a customs union that also has free movement of labour and capital among its members.

TRADE CREATION AND TRADE DIVERSION

A major effect of regional trade liberalization is on resource reallocation. Economic theory divides these effects into two categories.

Trade creation occurs when producers in one member country find that they can export to another member-country as a result of the elimination of the tariffs. For example when the North American Free Trade Agreement

(NAFTA) comes into full force, some Mexican firms will find that they can undersell their US competitors in some lines of endeavour, while some US firms will find that they can undersell their Mexican competitors in others, now that tariffs are eliminated. As a result, specialization occurs and new international trade develops. This trade, which is based on (natural or acquired) comparative advantage, is illustrated in part (a) of Table 26.1.

Trade diversion occurs when exporters in one member-country replace foreign exporters as suppliers to another member-country. For example, US trade diversion occurs when Mexican firms find that they can undersell competitors from the rest of the world in the US market, not because they are the cheapest source of supply, but because their tariff-free prices are lower than the tariff-burdened prices of imports from other countries. This effect is a gain to Mexican firms but a cost to the United States—which now has to export more goods for any given amount of imports than before the trade diversion occurred. It is illustrated in part (b) of Table 26.1. Similarly, Mexican trade diversion occurs when US producers win out over competitors from the rest of the world in the Mexican market

because they are not subject to a tariff in that market while their non-member competitors are. This effect benefits US firms at the expense of Mexican consumers.

From the global perspective, trade diversion represents an inefficient use of resources.

From the narrower national point of view of Mexico and the United States, however, it brings some gain as well as some loss. In so far as there is a shared desire to increase domestic manufacturing production, trade diversion brings mutual benefit to both countries. It gives producers within the two countries an advantage over producers in the rest of the world, which has the effect of increasing the total amount of production and trade that occurs among the member-countries while reducing what comes in from third countries.

NAFTA and other free-trade areas

The first important free-trade area in the modern era was the European Free Trade Association (EFTA). It was formed in 1960 by a group of European countries that were unwilling to join the European Economic Community as the EU was then called because of its all-embracing character. Not wanting to be left out of the gains from trade, they formed an association whose sole purpose was tariff removal. First, they removed all tariffs on trade among themselves. Then each country signed a free-trade-area agreement with the EEC. This made the EEC–EFTA market the largest tariff-free market in the world (over 300 million people). Three of the EFTA countries were to enter the EU in 1995.

In 1985, the United States signed a limited free-trade agreement with Israel. In 1988, a sweeping agreement was signed between Canada and the United States, instituting free trade on all goods and most non-government services, and covering what is the world's largest flow of international trade between any two countries. In 1993, this agreement was extended into a North American Free Trade Agreement (NAFTA) by renegotiation of the Canada–US agreement to include Mexico. Provision is made within NAFTA for the accession of other countries with the hope that it may eventually evolve into a Western Hemisphere Free Trade Area (WHFTA) by taking in most, or even all, of the countries of Latin America and the Caribbean basin. Australia and New Zealand have also entered into an association that removes restrictions on trade in goods and services between their two countries. The countries of Latin America have been experimenting with free-trade areas for many decades. Most earlier attempts failed, but in the last few years more durable free-trade areas seem to have been formed. Whether these will remain stand-alone agreements or will evolve into a WHFTA remains to be seen.

Table 26.1 Trade creation and trade diversion

Producing country	US delivered price without tariffs	US delivered price with a 10% tariff
(a) Trade creation		
USA	$40.00	$40.00
Mexico	$37.00	$40.70
(b) Trade Diversion		
Taiwan	$20.00	$22.00
Mexico	$21.50	$23.65

Regional tariff reductions can cause trade creation and trade diversion. The table gives two cases. In the first case, a Mexican good, which could be sold for $37.00 in the United States, has its price increased to $40.70 by a 10 per cent US tariff. The US industry, which can sell the good for $40.00 with or without a tariff on imports, is protected against the more efficient Mexican producer. When the tariff is removed by NAFTA, the Mexican good wins the market by selling at $37.00. Trade is created between Mexico and the United States by eliminating the US inefficient production solely for a protected home market.

In the second case, Taiwan can undersell Mexico in the US market for another product when neither is subject to a tariff (first column) and when both are subject to a 10 per cent tariff (second column). But after NAFTA, the Mexican good is tariff-free and sells for $21.50 while the Taiwanese good, which is still subject to the tariff, continues to sell for $22.00. The Mexican good wins the market, and US trade is diverted from Taiwan to Mexico even though Taiwan is the lower cost supplier (ex tariff).

NAFTA OUTLINED

Since NAFTA builds on, and in many ways improves, the earlier Canada–US agreement, only NAFTA needs to be discussed. Because the agreement is for a free-trade area and not a customs union, each country retains its own external barriers to trade, and rules of origin are needed to determine when a good is made within the free-trade area and so is allowed to move freely among the members.

National treatment The fundamental principle that guides NAFTA is the principle of *national treatment.* This means that countries are free to establish any laws whatsoever, and that these can differ as much as desired among member countries, with the sole proviso that these laws must not discriminate on the basis of nationality. So the United States can have any tough environmental laws that it wishes, or standards for particular goods, but it must enforce these equally on Canadian and US-owned firms, and on both domestically produced and imported goods. The idea of national treatment is to allow a *maximum* of policy independence, while preventing national policies from being misused as concealed barriers to trade and investment.

This principle of maximizing policy independence subject to removing trade barriers is opposite to the European Union's philosophy, which seeks to harmonize as many policies as possible in order to create an embracing economic union.[6]

National treatment is, however, an important part of the European Union's financial integration (see below).

Other major provisions First, all tariffs on trade between the United States and Canada are to be eliminated by 1999. Canada–Mexico and Canada–US tariffs are to be phased out over a 15-year period starting in 1994. Also, a number of non-tariff barriers are eliminated or circumscribed.

Second, the Agreement guarantees national treatment to foreign investment once it enters a country, while permitting each country to screen a substantial amount of inbound foreign investment before it enters.

Third, all existing measures restricting trade and investment that are not explicitly removed are exempted so that only new restrictive measures are prohibited. This is probably the single most unfortunate aspect of NAFTA. Under it, a large rag-bag of restrictive measures is given indefinite life. A better alternative would have been to negotiate dates at which each would be eliminated. Even a 50-year extension would be preferable to an indefinite exemption.

Fourth, a few goods remain subject to serious non-tariff trade restrictions. The main examples are supply-managed agricultural products, beer, and textiles.

Fifth, trade in most non-governmental services is liberalized by giving service firms the *right of establishment* in all member-countries and the privilege of *national treatment.* There is also a limited opening of financial services to entry from firms based in other NAFTA countries.

Sixth, a significant amount, but by no means all, of government procurement is opened to cross-border bids.

Dispute settlement By far the biggest setback in the negotiations for the Canadians and Mexicans was the failure to get agreement on a common regime for countervailing and anti-dumping duties. In place of such a regime, a dispute settlement mechanism (DSM) was put in place. Under it, the domestic determinations that are required for the levying of anti-dumping and countervailing duties are subject to review by a panel of Canadians and Americans (and also Mexicans, once NAFTA comes into full force). This replaces appeal through the domestic courts. Panels are empowered to uphold the domestic determinations or to refer the decision back to the domestic authority—which in effect is a binding order for a new investigation. The referral can be repeated until the panel is satisfied that the domestic laws have been correctly and fairly applied.

This is pathbreaking:

For the first time in its history, the United States had agreed to submit the administration of its domestic laws to *binding* scrutiny of an international panel which would often contain a majority of foreigners.

Results By and large, both the Canada–US and the NAFTA agreements have worked as was expected, although it is still too early to determine their long-range effects. Business has clearly restructured in the direction of export orientation in all three countries. All three countries are importing more from, and exporting more to, each other.

It is hard to say how much trade diversion there will be. South East Asian exporters to the United States were clearly worried that Mexico would capture some of their markets by virtue of having the tariff-free access denied to their goods. Most estimates predict, however, that trade creation will dominate over trade diversion.

Foreign investment has increased, particularly in Canada and Mexico, although it will be years before the magnitude of the induced increase in foreign investment can be reasonably estimated.

Most difficulties are being felt in each country's import-competing industries, which is what theory predicts. An agreement such as NAFTA brings its advantages by encouraging a movement of resources out of protected but inefficient import-competing industries, which decline, and into efficient export industries, which expand because they have

---

[6] This principle was qualified to some extent by the negotiation, after the main treaty was signed, of a side agreement between the United States and Mexico establishing minimum standards of environmental protection in Mexico.

better access to the markets of other member-countries.

Finally, the dispute settlement mechanism has worked remarkably well. A large number of disputes have arisen and have been referred to panels. Panel members have reacted as professionals, not as nationals. Cases have been decided on merits, and there has been no serious allegation that issues were decided on national grounds.

Common markets: the European Union

By far the most successful common market, which is now referred to as a *single market*, is the European Union. Its origins go back to the period immediately following the Second World War in 1945. After the end of that war, there was a strong belief throughout Europe that the way to avoid future military conflict was to create a high level of economic integration between the existing nation-states. Later, the motivation switched to creating a powerful economic bloc which could be competitive with Japan and the United States.

In 1952, as a first step towards economic union, France, Belgium, West Germany, Italy, Luxembourg, and Holland formed the European Coal and Steel Community. This removed trade restrictions on coal, steel, and iron ore among these six countries. In 1957, the same six countries signed the Treaty of Rome. This created the European Economic Community (EEC), which later became the European Community (EC) and after 1993 the European Union (EU). In 1973 the United Kingdom, Denmark, and Ireland joined, and they were followed in 1981 by Greece and in 1986 by Spain and Portugal. Austria, Sweden, and Finland negotiated to enter in 1995.

In the first two decades of its existence, the main economic achievements of the EEC were the elimination of internal tariff barriers and the establishment of common external tariffs (in other words, the establishment of a customs union), and the establishment of the Common Agricultural Policy, which, for better or for worse, guarantees farm prices by means of intervention and an import levy (see Chapter 6). There were other significant EEC policies, such as regional aid and protection of competition, but they did not have great economic impacts early on.

By the mid-1980s, it was clear that the intended 'Common Market' had not been achieved. There remained many non-tariff barriers to trade and to the mobility of labour. These included quality standards, licensing requirements, and a lack of recognition of qualifications. In financial services, there were explicit exchange controls and other regulatory restrictions on cross-border trade. In response, a new push to turn the customs union into a genuine common market began in 1985.

THE SINGLE MARKET PROGRAMME

The *Single Market Act* was signed in 1986. Its intention was to remove all remaining barriers to the creation of a fully integrated single market by the end of 1992. The Single Market Act did not in itself create the single market. Rather, it was a statement (or treaty) of intent which instituted a simplified administrative procedure whereby most of the single market legislation needed only 'weighted majority' support, rather than unanimity. The single market itself was to be created by a large number of *Directives,* which are drafted by the European Commission (the EU civil service) and become Community law after they have been 'adopted' by the European Council (which is a committee of the heads of state of member-countries, or other ministers). They then have to be ratified in the law of each member-state. Once in force, they have precedence over the domestic laws of member-states if there is a conflict. There have been over 300 separate Directives adopted in the single market programme by 1994, and there are many more in the pipeline.

Eliminating non-tariff barriers has been approached on a product-by-product basis. Only in this way could minimum-quality standards be created which would permit cross-border trade without the threat of quality checks as a prerequisite to entry (a problem that plagues some branches of Canada–US trade). This has required a complicated set of negotiations on quality standards relating to everything from condoms to sausages and from toys to telecommunications. There is even a quality standard for the bacterial content of aqueous toys; these are transparent plastic souvenirs, containing, perhaps, a model of Big Ben or the Eiffel Tower, which, when shaken, create a snow scene.

All countries have such safety or quality standards for their products, and what has been happening is the harmonization of these standards, which is something that Canada and the United States have been trying to do since their Agreement was put in force in 1989. In Britain, however, this process has often been reported as an attempt by Brussels to dictate standards to Britain. Actually the Commission's job is only to draft the initial negotiating position; it is the Council of all ministers who must agree what the final standards should be.

The single market programme is an ongoing process, not a discrete jump. Some of the intended measures have been implemented, but many are still in the pipeline. The process will continue well into the twenty-first century.

Many important steps were achieved by the end of 1992, including the removal of some border checks. (At UK ports and airports, this means a blue channel through which EU citizens are permitted to carry as many goods as they like, if bought in other EU countries, so long as they are for personal use.) Although the single market movement has been genuinely trade-liberalizing, another view was often expressed: that the process was designed to build a wall of trade restrictions around the European Union, turning it into a 'Fortress Europe'. The forces that gave rise to this erroneous view are discussed in Box 26.2.

THE MAASTRICHT TREATY

Signed in 1992, the Maastricht treaty contained agreement for a common currency. Many people feel this is a key part of a common market, but others are concerned about passing monetary policy over to a single European central bank. (This is further discussed in Chapter 38.) The treaty also contained a Social Chapter, covering harmonization of policies with respect to labour markets and other social policies. The United Kingdom opted out of this Chapter because of concern over the government interference in the operation of its relatively free markets, particularly those for labour, that might result from the setting of Europe-wide social policy including a minimum wage for unskilled labour.

THE SINGLE MARKET IN FINANCIAL SERVICES

Perhaps the most significant achievements of the single market programme to date have been in the area of trade in financial services. Although the Treaty of Rome called for free movement of capital as well as goods, this was ignored until the mid-1980s. Most member-countries had exchange controls on capital movements until recently. These controls prohibited residents of each country from investing in any other country.

The Capital Liberalization Directive required all mem-

BOX 26.2

Fortress Europe?

The single market programme of the European Union was described in some quarters as an attempt to create a 'Fortress Europe', with free trade internally but greater barriers to trade with non-EU countries. Although the creation of new barriers for EU imports played no part in the design of the single market, three factors contributed to a false impression that they did.

1. The Common Agricultural Policy (CAP) does, indeed, involve major import restrictions which were defended by the EU trade negotiators in the Uruguay Round of the GATT. These GATT negotiations ran simultaneously with the implementation phase of the single market, and no doubt contributed to the European Union protectionist image. However, the CAP predates the single market initiative by over two decades and is separate from it. Furthermore some, very modest, phased reduction of agricultural protection within the EU was eventually agreed in the Uruguay Round. Although it did not do much to liberalize trade in agricultural goods, the single market programme introduced no new restrictions.

2. Although the 'Common Market' had already adopted a common set of external tariffs, many EU countries had other country-specific trade restrictions on imports from non-EU countries, such as quotas and voluntary export restraints (VERs). The plan to abolish internal customs checks within the European Union required that these restrictions should either be made common over the whole Union or be dropped. (It would be ineffective for, say, France to have a quota on Japanese car imports if these cars could enter France via Belgium without restriction.) These specific restrictions have been dealt with at the EU level on a case-by-case basis. In some cases all restrictions are being phased out, and in others a common EU external restriction replaces the existing country-by-country rules. Although some measures, such as those on imports of Japanese cars, remain quite restrictive, there was no general move to create new barriers to imports into the EU or to raise the average levels of those already in place.

3. An early draft of the Second Co-ordinating Banking Directive (which created the single 'driving licence' for EU banks) contained a clause, known as the 'reciprocity clause', which appeared to be designed to limit entry of foreign banks into the European Union after 1992. It would have implied, for example, that US banks would not have been allowed to establish branches in the European Union after 1992 unless the United States permitted EU banks to establish themselves in the United States and operate there as they could in the EU. This would have been impossible without a radical reform of US banking law. This proposal created the false impression that not just banks, but all foreign companies, would find it harder to establish themselves in the European Union after 1992.

Ironically, in the final analysis, this was not true even for banks. The final Directive which created the single banking market, had a reciprocity clause based upon national treatment, as discussed in the text. This means the foreign banks will be free to establish in the European Union so long as EU banks are not discriminated against in the respective foreign country. This means only that EU banks must be treated no worse than national banks in the country concerned. Even this reciprocity clause appeared in the banking Directive only because there was no global trade agreement covering services at the time. This is no longer true following the conclusion of the Uruguay Round. The GATT agreement has now adopted national treatment as its central principle governing trade in services.

If there is a Fortress Europe, it seems to have lowered rather than raised its drawbridge.

ber-states to abolish exchange controls by June 1990. Some member-states, such as Britain and Germany, had already abolished controls. France and Italy, which had not, were forced to do so by the directive. Spain, Portugal, Ireland, and Greece were given longer to comply. All except Greece fully abolished their controls by the end of 1992, and Greece abolished most of its controls by 1994.

Once exchange controls were abolished, it could be argued that nothing else had to be done to create a single market in financial services. Certainly, wholesale financial markets rapidly integrated with the global financial system, once they were free to do so. Indeed, this is one of the key elements of globalization that we discuss further in Box 35.3 on page 694.

However, agreement is still needed on how to facilitate greater cross-border competition in retail financial markets. Each country in isolation has already created a domestic regulatory regime designed, in part, to protect the consumer. How was the Community to encourage competition but maintain a sensible regime of consumer protection? (Financial services are particularly prone to fraud, because the profit margin for a crook is 100 per cent—even a used car salesman has to show you a car, but the seller of an investment product offers only future promises!)

The European Union adopted a pragmatic approach based upon assuming the competence of existing regulators. Firms in each sector were to be authorized as 'fit and proper' by their home-country regulator and they would then be presumed to be fit and proper to trade in any member-state. In effect, the home country gave a driving licence which then permitted an authorized company to 'drive' anywhere in the Community. This mutual recognition of regulators has been wrongly interpreted as permitting financial services firms to trade anywhere in the European Union on the basis of their home country's rules. A moment's thought will tell you why it has to be wrong. Imagine, for example, British drivers being permitted to drive on the left in France just because that is the law in Britain. It is just as disastrous to have banks in any one location trading under 12 different legal structures.

The single market in financial services is built on a dual set of principles: home-country authorization, and host-country conduct of business rules. This means that a firm can be authorized to trade throughout the Community by the home regulator, but the trade itself must obey the local laws in the country concerned.

Allowing home countries to regulate entry and host countries to regulate performance is a simple application of the principle of national treatment already discussed in the section on NAFTA.

The key directives creating the single market in banking were implemented at the end of 1992, but the completion of the single market in investment services (security trad-ing) and insurance (retail life and non-life) was not expected until after 1995 at the earliest.

The Cecchini (pronounced chuck-ee-knee) Report of 1989 estimated that the completion of the single market programme may increase the GDP of the European Union by up to 6 per cent. However, a well-known American economist, Richard Baldwin, has challenged that figure, suggesting that the gains could be at least twice as large (owing to economies of scale external to firms). And this is only the gain in one year. Similar gains will continue to flow in future years. Thus, while politically tortuous, the process of reducing trade barriers, even within groups of countries, is capable of creating considerable gains in economic efficiency.

The future of the multilateral trading system

At the end of the Second World War, the United States took the lead in forming GATT and in pressing for reductions in world tariffs through successive rounds of negotiations. Largely as a result of this US initiative, the world's tariff barriers have been greatly reduced, while the volume of world trade has risen steadily.

The next decade will be critical for the future of the multilateral trading system, which has served the world so well since the end of the Second World War. The dangers are, first, a growth of regional trading blocs that will trade more with their own member-countries and less with others, and second, the growth of state-managed trade.

The 1920s and 1930s provide a cautionary tale. Arguments for restricting trade always have a superficial appeal and sometimes have real short-term payoffs. In the long term, however, a major worldwide escalation of tariffs would lower efficiency and incomes and restrict trade worldwide, while doing nothing to raise employment. Both economic theory and the evidence of history support this proposition. Although most agree that pressure should be put on countries that restrict trade, the above analysis suggests that these pressures are best applied using the multilateral institution of GATT. Unilateral imposition of restrictions in response to the perceived restrictions in other countries can all too easily degenerate into a round of mutually escalating trade barriers.

It is notable that in the United States, one of the staunchest defenders of the free-market system, many voices are being raised to advocate moves that *reduce* the influence of market forces on international trade and increase the degree of government control over that trade. It is ironic to see enthusiasm for state-managed trade growing just as the former communist countries of Eastern Europe have at last agreed that free markets are better regulators of economic activity than is the government. The strength of the movement to manage trade will become clearer during the 1990s.

The European Union, although it has achieved something close to free trade within the union, has been equivocal on free trade with the rest of the world. Anti-dumping duties, voluntary export agreements, and other non-tariff barriers have been used with effect against successful importers—particularly the Japanese. Although these measures may bring short-term gains, both economic theory and historical experience suggest that they will bring losses in the long term. Protectionism reduces incomes because low-priced goods are excluded to the detriment of current consumers, particularly those with lower incomes. It also reduces employment because restrictions on imports are sooner or later balanced by restrictions on exports as other countries retaliate. It also inhibits the technological dynamism that is the source of long-term growth, by shielding domestic producers from the need that free international competition forces on them: to keep up with all foreign competitors.

Summary

1 The case for free trade is that world output of all products can be higher under free trade than when protectionism restricts regional specialization.

2 Protection can be urged as a means to ends other than maximizing world living standards. Examples of such ends are to produce a diversified economy, to reduce fluctuations in national income, to retain distinctive national traditions, and to improve national defence.

3 Protection also can be urged on the grounds that it may lead to higher living standards for the protectionist country than a policy of free trade would. Such a result might come about by using a monopoly position to influence the terms of trade, or by developing a dynamic comparative advantage by allowing inexperienced or uneconomically small industries to become efficient enough to compete with foreign industries.

4 A recent argument for protection is to operate a strategic trade policy whereby a country attracts firms in oligopolistic industries that, because of scale economies, can earn large profits even in equilibrium.

5 Domestic industries may be protected from foreign competition by tariffs and other policies, which affect the prices of imports, or by import quotas and voluntary export agreements, which affect the quantities of imports. Both sets of policies end up increasing prices in the domestic market and lowering the quantities of imports. Both harm domestic consumers and benefit domestic producers of the protected product. The major difference is that the extra money paid for imports goes to the domestic government under tariffs and to foreign producers under quantity restrictions.

6 As tariff barriers have been reduced over the years, they have been replaced in part by non-tariff barriers. Voluntary export agreements are straightforward restrictions on trade. Anti-dumping and countervailing duties can provide legitimate restraints on foreign unfair trading practices, but they can also be used as non-tariff barriers to trade.

7 Some fallacious free trade arguments are that, (a) because free trade maximizes world income, it will maximize the income of every individual country and (b) because infant industries seldom admit to growing up and thus try to retain their protection indefinitely, the whole country necessarily loses by protecting its infant industries.

8 Some fallacious protectionist arguments are that (a) mutually advantageous trade is impossible because one trader's gain must always be the other's loss; (b) buying abroad sends our money abroad, while buying at home keeps our money at home; (c) our high-paid workers must be protected against the competition from low-paid foreign workers; and (d) imports are to be discouraged because they lower national income and cause unemployment.

9 The General Agreement on Tariffs and Trade (GATT), whereby countries agree to reduce trade barriers through multilateral negotiations and not to raise them unilaterally, has greatly reduced world tariffs since its inception in 1947. It is being replaced in 1995 by the World Trade Organization.

10 Regional trade-liberalizing agreements such as free-trade areas and common markets bring efficiency gains through trade creation and efficiency losses through trade diversion.

11 The North American Free Trade Agreement (NAFTA) is the world's largest and most successful free-trade area, while the European Union is the world's largest and most successful common market (now called a single market).

Topics for review

- Free trade and protectionism
- Tariff and non-tariff barriers to trade
- Countervailing and anti-dumping duties
- General Agreement on Tariffs and Trade (GATT)
- World Trade Organization.
- Common markets, customs unions, and free-trade associations
- North American Free Trade Agreement (NAFTA)
- European Union (EU)

PART EIGHT

National income and output

❧ CHAPTER 27

An introduction to macroeconomics

INFLATION, unemployment, recession, competitiveness, and economic growth are everyday words. Governments worry about how to prevent recessions, reduce inflation, increase competitiveness, and stimulate growth. Adults of working age are anxious to avoid the unemployment that comes with recessions, and to obtain the rising incomes that usually accompany economic growth. Pensioners are keen to protect themselves against the hazards of inflation which can lower the value of their savings. Firms are concerned about how inflations, recessions, and foreign competition affect their profits and, perhaps, even their survival.

Each of these concerns plays a major role in macroeconomics. In this chapter we explain how macroeconomics differs in approach from the microeconomics of the first half of this book. We then introduce you to several of the topics that are of central concern in macroeconomics, such as the level and variability of national income and output, the level of unemployment, inflation and prices, interest rates, the exchange rate, and the balance of payments.

What is macroeconomics?

MACROECONOMICS is the study of how the economy behaves in broad outline without dwelling on much of its interesting, but sometimes confusing, detail. Macroeconomics is largely concerned with the behaviour of economic *aggregates*, such as total national product, total investment, and exports for the entire economy. It is also concerned with the average price of all goods and services, rather than with the prices of specific products. These aggregates result from activities in many different markets and from the behaviour of different groups such as consumers, governments, and firms. In contrast, *microeconomics* deals with the behaviour of individual markets, such as those for wheat, coal, or strawberries, and with the detailed behaviour of individual agents, such as firms and consumers.

In macroeconomics we add together the value of cornflakes, beer, coal, strawberries, haircuts, and restaurant meals along with the value of all other goods and services produced and study the movement of the aggregate *national product*. We also average the prices of all goods and services consumed and discuss the *general price level* for the entire economy—usually just called the price level. We know full well that an economy that produces much wheat and few cars differs from one that produces many cars but little wheat. We also know that an economy with cheap wheat and expensive cars differs from one with cheap cars and expensive wheat. Studying aggregates often means missing these important differences, but, in return for losing valuable detail, it allows us to view the big picture.

In macroeconomics, we look at the broad range of opportunities and difficulties facing the economy as a whole. When national product rises, the output of most products, and the incomes of most people, usually rise with it. When the price level rises, virtually everyone in the economy is forced to make adjustments, because of the lower value of money. When the unemployment rate rises, workers are put at an increased risk of losing their jobs and suffering losses in their incomes. These movements in economic aggregates are strongly associated with the economic well-being of most individuals: the health of the sectors in which they work and the prices of the goods that they purchase. These associations are why macroeconomic aggregates (particularly inflation, unemployment, and the balance of payments) are often in the news.

Why do we need macroeconomics?

WE need a separate subject called macroeconomics because there are forces that affect the economy as a whole which cannot be fully or simply understood by analysing individual markets and individual products. A problem that is affecting all firms or many workers in different industries may need to be tackled at the level of the whole economy. Certainly, if circumstances are common across many sectors of the economy, then analysis at the level of the whole economy may help us to understand what is happening. Let us look at some of the issues that are best thought about in a macroeconomic context.

Major macroeconomic issues

Business cycles   The economy tends to move in a series of ups and downs, called *business cycles*, rather than in a steady pattern. The 1930s saw the greatest worldwide economic depression in the twentieth century, with nearly one-fifth of the UK labour force unemployed for an extended period. In contrast, the 25 years following the Second World War was a period of sustained economic growth, with only minor interruptions caused by modest recessions. Then the business cycle returned in more serious form in the 1970s. The beginning and the end of that decade witnessed the two worst worldwide recessions since the 1930s. What fuelled the recovery of the mid-1980s? Why did another severe recession occur in 1990–3? Why was the recovery that started in 1993 so slow in developing momentum?

Overall living standards   As we saw in Chapter 1, both total and per capita output have risen for many decades in most industrial countries. These long-term trends have meant rising average living standards. Since the early 1970s, however, average living standards have grown much less rapidly than during the preceding decades of the twentieth century. Indeed, in the United States the *real wage*—the quantity of goods and services that can be purchased by the average hourly money wage—was lower in 1991 than it was in 1973. In the United Kingdom (see Figure 1.5), the real value of the average wage doubled in the 20 years between 1953 and 1973; it stagnated for a while in the 1970s but then grew rapidly again in the 1980s.

Although long-term growth gets less media attention than does the current inflation rate or unemployment rate, it is the predominant determinant of living standards and the material constraints facing a society from decade to decade and generation to generation. Among the most important issues in macroeconomics is how worldwide growth can be made to continue without the type of slowdown that happened in the 1970s or the serious recessions of the early 1980s and early 1990s.

Inflation and recession   The annual inflation rate in the United Kingdom was around 25 per cent in 1975. This was the highest level reached in peacetime for at least three centuries. The government of Mrs Thatcher was elected in 1979 on the promise of eliminating inflation from the British economy. Inflation did fall to below 5 per cent by 1984, but it rose again to around 10 per cent

before the end of the decade. By 1994, however, inflation had fallen to around 2 per cent, the lowest level since the early 1960s.

Accompanying these swings in inflation have been swings in economic activity. Generally, attempts by governments to control high inflation have helped to bring about recessions. However, the pattern of booms and recessions has been very similar across many different countries, so it cannot all be attributed to domestic government policy. Also, the relationship between inflation and recession seems to change over time. The 1980–1 recession was accompanied by inflation percentages in the mid-teens, while the 1990–3 recession was accompanied by only single-figure inflation. Will high inflation return? Or will the low inflation rates of the early 1990s persist into the twenty-first century?

Unemployment   A downturn in economic activity causes an increase in unemployment. Indeed, it was the high unemployment of the 1930s that led to the establishment of the subject now known as macroeconomics, and unemployment is still a central concern of economics. During the Great Depression of the 1930s, unemployment rose to nearly 20 per cent of the labour force. Although in the 1950s and 1960s it was consistently very low, in the 1980s and 1990s high unemployment has returned. Accordingly, the analysis of the causes of and potential cures for unemployment is very high on the agenda of macroeconomics today.

The solution for unemployment that economists came up with in the 1930s was for governments to increase their spending or reduce taxes. Why do governments seem reluctant to try such solutions today? What is the link between such fiscal stimuli and inflation? Why do some countries have much lower unemployment than others?

Government budget deficits   With the exception of two brief periods (1970 and 1988/9), the British government has had a *budget deficit* since the Second World War—it was spending more than it was raising in taxation. In the mid-1970s the budget deficit was at one time around 8 per cent of the gross domestic product (GDP), and in 1993/4 the budget was again in deficit by more than 7 per cent of GDP. These deficits had to be financed by government borrowing, which raised the national debt.

At one time, it was thought that budget deficits might be good for the economy because government spending creates jobs; but nowadays there is much concern about the potential burden of debt, the interest on which has to be paid by tax-payers and, therefore, keeps taxes high. This conflict over the role of the government budget is central to macroeconomics. Is it a good thing for governments to run budget deficits? Is the economy healthier if governments aim for a *balanced budget*? Can recessions be alleviated if governments deliberately run deficits?

Key macroeconomic phenomena

THE current macroeconomic state of the nation can be fairly fully described by the level and rate of growth of total and per capita output, the amount of employment, the unemployment rate, the inflation rate, the interest rate, the external value of the UK pound, and the balance of payments. We hear about each of these indicators on the daily news and read about them in newspapers; politicians give campaign speeches about them; economists theorize about them. In this chapter we discuss each of these variables, with an emphasis on why and how they affect our economic welfare. In Chapter 28 we expand the discussion to consider how the macroeconomic variables are measured. The remainder of this book is largely about the causes and consequences of changes in each of these variables.

Output and income

The most comprehensive measure of a nation's overall level of economic activity is the value of its total production of goods and services, called the *national product*. Since all the value that is produced must ultimately belong to someone in the form of a claim on that value, the national product is equal to the total income claims generated by the production of goods and services. Hence when we study national product, we are also studying *national income*. Figure 27.1 depicts national income and expenditure as a circular flow. It shows how national output also generates incomes—

wages, profits, and rents—so that the same activity that produces the output also produces incomes of equivalent value.

There are several related measures of a nation's total output and total income. Their various definitions, and the relationships among them, are discussed in detail in the next chapter. In this chapter we use the generic term *national income* to refer to both the value of total output and the value of the income claims generated by the production of that output.

AGGREGATING TOTAL OUTPUT

To measure total output, quantities of a variety of goods are *aggregated*. To construct such totals, we add up the *values* of the different products. We cannot add tons of steel to loaves of bread, but we can add the money value of steel production to the money value of bread production. Hence, by multiplying the physical output of a good by its price per unit and then summing this value for each good produced in a nation, we can calculate the quantity of total national output *measured in pounds sterling*.

REAL AND NOMINAL VALUES

The total that was just described gives the *money value* of national output, often called **nominal national income**. A change in this measure can be caused by a change in either

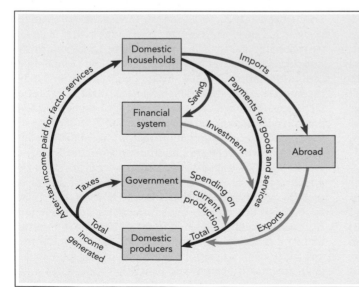

Figure 27.1 The circular flow of income and expenditure

The circular flow of income and expenditure implies that national income is equal to national product. If there were neither leakages (imports, saving, and taxes) nor injections (exports, investment, and government expenditure on goods and services), the flow would be a simple closed circuit, running from domestic households to domestic producers and back to households. Injections (shown in green) and leakages (also called withdrawals, and here shown in blue) complicate the picture but do not change the basic result: domestic production creates a claim on the value of that production; when all of the claims are added up, they must be equal to the value of all the production.

the physical quantities or the prices on which it is based. Economists wish to determine the extent to which any change is due to changes in quantities or to changes in prices. To do this, they distinguish between changes in **real national income**, which occurs only when the *quantities* of goods and services change, and changes in the *price level*. In order to measure real national income, economists must determine what would have happened to national income if prices had remained constant. To do this, they value all the quantities produced in each year at a constant set of prices that prevailed in some arbitrarily chosen *base year*. Thus, real national income measures the total value of all individual outputs, where each output is valued not at current prices, but at a set of base-year prices.

Nominal national income is often referred to as *money national income* or *national income at current prices*. Real national income is often called *national income at constant prices*. Denoted by the symbol Y, real national income tells us the value of current output measured at constant prices—the sum of the individual quantities each valued at prices that prevailed in the base year. Comparing real national incomes of different years provides a measure of the change in the quantity of output that has occurred during the intervening period, or of real economic growth.

Since its calculation holds prices constant, real national income changes only when quantities change.

Our interest is primarily in the *real* output of goods and services, so we shall use the terms 'national income' and 'national output' to refer to *real national income* and *real national output*, unless otherwise specified. (An example, illustrating the important distinction between real national income and money national income, is given in Box 28.3 on p. 541.)

POTENTIAL INCOME AND THE GDP GAP

Actual national income represents what the economy does, in fact, produce. An important related concept is **potential national income**, which measures what the economy could produce if all resources—land, labour, and productive capacity—were fully employed at their normal levels of utilization. This concept is usually referred to as 'potential income' but is sometimes called '*full-employment income*' (or '*high-employment income*').[1] We give it the symbol Y^* to distinguish it from actual national income, which is indicated by Y.

What is variously called the **output gap** or the **GDP gap** measures the difference between what would have been produced if potential, or full-employment, national income had been produced and what is actually produced, as measured by the current GDP. The gap is calculated by subtracting actual national income from potential national income ($Y^* - Y$).

When potential income exceeds actual income, the gap measures the market value of those goods and services that *could have been produced* if the economy's resources had been fully employed, but actually went unproduced. The goods and services that are not produced when the economy is operating below Y^* are permanently lost to the economy. Because these losses occur when employable resources are unused, they are often called the *deadweight loss* of unemployment. When the economy is operating below its potential level of output—that is, when Y is less than Y^*—the output gap is called a **recessionary gap**.

In booms, actual national income may exceed potential income, causing the output gap to become negative. Actual income can exceed potential income because potential income is defined for a *normal rate of utilization* of factors of production, and these normal rates can be exceeded temporarily. Labour may work longer hours than normal; factories may operate an extra shift or not close for routine repairs and maintenance. Although these expedients are only temporary, they are effective in the short term. When actual income exceeds potential income, there is generally upward pressure on prices. For this reason, when Y exceeds Y^* the output gap is called an **inflationary gap**.

Figure 27.2(i) shows potential income in the United Kingdom for the years 1970–93. The rising trend reflects the growth in productive capacity of the UK economy over this period. The figure also shows actual real national income, which has kept approximately in step with potential income. The distance between the two, which is the GDP gap, is plotted in Figure 27.2(ii). Fluctuations in economic activity are apparent from fluctuations in the size of the gap. The deadweight loss from unemployment over any time span is indicated by the overall amount of the gap over that time span. It is shown in part (ii) of Figure 27.2 by the shaded area between the curve and the zero line, which represents the level at which actual output equals potential output.

NATIONAL INCOME: THE HISTORICAL EXPERIENCE

One of the most commonly used measures of national income is called *gross domestic product*, or GDP. This can be measured in either real or nominal terms; we focus here on real GDP. The details of its calculation will be discussed in Chapter 28. *In this chapter we use the terms 'national income' and 'GDP' interchangeably to refer to the nation's total income and its total product.*

Part (i) of Figure 27.3 shows real GDP produced by the

---

[1] In everyday usage the words 'real' and 'actual' have similar meanings. In national income theory, however, their meanings are quite distinct. *Real* national income is distinguished from *nominal* national income, and *actual* national income is distinguished from *potential* national income. The latter both refer to real measures, so that the full descriptions are, in fact, 'actual real national income' and 'potential real national income'.

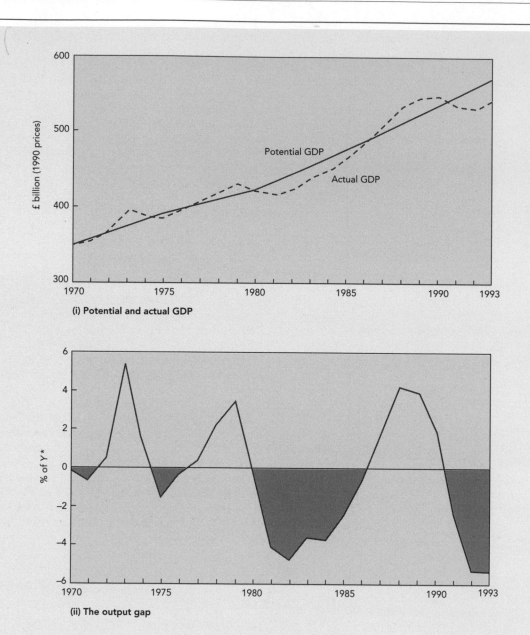

Figure 27.2 UK potential GDP and the output gap, 1970–1993

Potential and actual GDP have both displayed an upward trend in recent years but actual GDP fluctuates around its potential level.

(i) Growth in the economy has been such that both potential and actual GDP have increased by about 75 per cent since 1970. Both series are in real terms and are measured in 1990 pounds sterling. Measurement of potential GDP is controversial and there is no official UK series at present. These figures were calculated by the IMF.

(ii) The cycles in the economy are apparent from the behaviour of the output gap. Slumps in economic activity produce large recessionary gaps, and booms produce inflationary gaps. The zero line indicates where actual and potential GDP are the same. The shaded areas below the zero line indicate the deadweight loss that arises from unemployment during periods when there is a recessionary output gap. Notice the large recessionary gaps in the early 1980s and the early 1990s.

Source: International Monetary Fund.

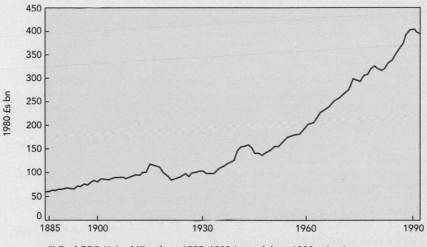

(i) Real GDP, United Kingdom, 1885–1993 (annual data, 1980 prices)

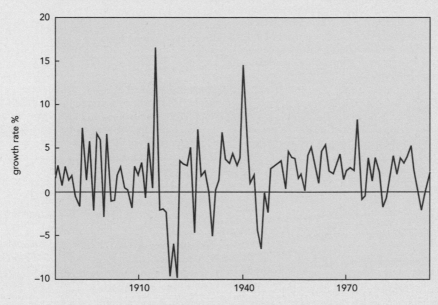

(ii) Annual growth rate of real GDP, United Kingdom, 1886–1993

Figure 27.3 UK real GDP and growth rate, 1885–1993

Real GDP, which measures the total production of goods and services for the whole economy over a year, has grown steadily over the last century.

(i) Long-term growth is reflected in the upward trend of real GDP. There were significant declines in real GDP after each of the world wars, there was a recession in the 1930s, and there were three noticeable recessions since 1970. Otherwise the trend dominates the cycle in the long term.

(ii) Real growth is measured by the annual rate of change of GDP. This has fluctuated sharply, but has generally been positive. The biggest swings in activity were the booms in output and subsequent slowdowns associated with the two world wars. However, the 1930s recession and the three recent recessions are clearly evident. Notice that the 1950s and 1960s were unusual in that, although there were cycles, annual GDP never fell.

Sources: 100 years of Economic Statistics, The Economist, 1989, and Economic Trends.

BOX 27.1

....

The terminology of business cycles

Trough

A trough is characterized by high unemployment and a level of demand that is low in relation to the economy's capacity to produce. There is thus a substantial amount of unused productive capacity. Business profits are low. For some individual companies they are negative. Confidence about economic prospects in the immediate future is lacking, and, as a result, many firms are unwilling to risk making new investments.

Recovery

The characteristics of a recovery, or expansion, are many—run-down equipment is replaced; employment, income, and consumer spending all begin to rise; and expectations become more favourable as a result of increases in production, sales, and profits. Investments that once seemed risky may be undertaken as the climate of business opinion starts to change from one of pessimism to one of optimism. As demand rises, production can be increased with relative ease merely by re-employing the existing unused capacity and unemployed labour.

Peak

A peak is the top of a cycle. At the peak, existing capacity is utilized to a high degree; labour shortages may develop, particu-larly in categories of key skills; and shortages of essential raw materials are likely. As shortages develop in more and more markets, a situation of general excess demand develops. Costs rise, but since prices rise also, business remains profitable.

Recession

A **recession**, or contraction, is a downturn in economic activity. Common usage defines a recession as a fall in the real GDP for two quarters in succession. Demand falls off, and, as a result, production and employment also fall. As employment falls, so do personal incomes. Profits drop, and some firms encounter financial difficulties. Investments that looked profitable with the expectation of continually rising demand now appear unprofit-able. It may not even be worth replacing capital goods as they wear out, because unused capacity is increasing steadily. In historical discussions, a recession that is deep and long-lasting is often called a **depression**.

Booms and slumps

Two nontechnical but descriptive terms are often used. The whole falling half of the cycle is often called a *slump*, and the whole rising half is often called a *boom*. These are useful terms to use when we do not wish to be more specific about the economy's position in the cycle.

UK economy since 1885; part (ii) shows its annual percentage change for the same period. The GDP series in part (i) shows two kinds of movement.

Long-term growth   The major movement in GDP is an upward trend that increased real output nearly sevenfold in just over a century from 1885 to 1993, and nearly three-fold since the Second World War. Because the trend has generally been upward in the modern era, it is referred to as *economic growth*.

The growth in real GDP is the source of the substantial increase in living standards that UK citizens have experienced throughout the post-war period.

Short-term fluctuations   A second feature of the real GDP series is the short-term fluctuations around the trend, often described as 'cyclical' fluctuations. Overall growth so dominates the real GDP series that the fluctuations are hardly visible in Figure 27.3(i). However, as can be seen in part (ii) of the figure, cyclical fluctuations in real GDP have been significant in the past.

The cyclical behaviour of real national income is shown by the annual fluctuations in the growth rate of real GDP.

The **business cycle** refers to these short-term fluctuations. It is the continual ebb and flow of business activity that occurs around the long-term trend after seasonal adjustments have been made.[2] When we study short-term fluctuations, it is convenient to regard potential income, Y^*, as constant. Since it changes very slowly, little harm is done by assuming it to be constant as long as our purpose is to study short-term fluctuations around Y^*.

Figure 27.4 shows stylized cycles that illustrate some useful terms. It is important to realize, however, that no two cycles are exactly the same. There are variations in duration and magnitude. Some expansions are long and drawn out, as was the one that began in 1981 and peaked in 1988;

---

[2] When economists wish to analyse monthly or quarterly data, they often make a *seasonal adjustment* to remove fluctuations that can be accounted for by the regular seasonal pattern evident in many economic series. For example, agricultural activity tends to be low in the winter months and high in the summer months, whereas sales of fuel oil tend to have the reverse seasonal pattern. Retail sales are highest in December.

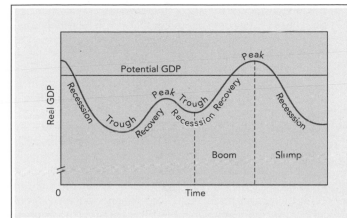

Figure 27.4 A stylized business cycle

Although the phases of business fluctuations are described by a series of commonly used terms, no two cycles are the same. Starting from a lower turning point, a cycle goes through a phase of recovery (or expansion), reaches an upper turning point, and then enters a period of recession. Cycles differ from one another in the severity of their troughs and peaks, and in the speed with which one phase follows another. Sometimes the entire rising half of the cycle is loosely referred to as a *boom* and the entire falling half is called a *slump*.

others come to an end after only a few years, as did the one that began in 1976. None the less, although they are neither smooth nor regular, fluctuations are systematic enough that it is useful to identify common factors in the four phases. Some of the most important of these are outlined in Box 27.1.

WHY NATIONAL INCOME MATTERS

National income is an important measure of economic performance in both the long run and the short run. Short-run movements in the business cycle receive the most attention in politics and in the press, but most economists agree that long-term growth, the rate of change of *potential income*, is in many ways the more important of the two.

Long-term growth In the long term, the course of real output is dominated by the growth in potential income while fluctuations around potential income are relatively unimportant. When studying long-term trends we cannot therefore regard Y^* as fixed.

The long-run trend in real national income per capita is the principal determinant of long-term improvements in a society's overall standard of living. When income per person grows, each generation can expect, on average, to be substantially better off than preceding ones. For example, if real income per capita grows at the relatively modest rate of 1.5 per cent per year, the average person's lifetime income expectancy will be *twice* that of his or her parents.

In the long run, national income can grow for two reasons. One is growth in the amount of output produced per hour of work. It is this growth—the *growth of labour productivity*—that has generally eliminated the low living standards that prevailed at the start of the Industrial Revolution in the mid eighteenth century. A second source of growth in income arises from *increases in the amount of labour supplied*. If the population grows (or the existing population works more hours), more output will be produced.

The difference between these two sources of growth is important. When productivity increases, more output is obtained for a given amount of effort. When the total amount of work increases, more output is obtained by using more resources; income rises, but the amount of income per person need not rise.

In the UK economy, almost all of the growth in income during the post-war period was due to increases in labour productivity. The size of the employed labour force was only 2.5 per cent higher in 1993 than in 1945, while real GDP had grown nearly three-fold. Corresponding to this growth in GDP, there was a greater than 2.5 fold increase in output per person for the UK economy over the same period. Particularly dramatic productivity growth was experienced in the manufacturing sector of the UK economy in the 1982–92 decade: in this period, output per worker rose 75 per cent.

This dramatic productivity growth in the UK economy is in marked contrast to what happened in some other industrial countries. Many had much better productivity growth than the United Kingdom in the 1950s and 1960s but experienced a slowdown in the 1970s and 1980s. Such contrasting international experience has raised a great deal of interest in the sources of growth, and this will be an important part of our discussions of macroeconomics.

Although economic growth makes people better off on average, it does not necessarily make every individual better off. Some people are harmed by the economic change that accompanies growth, although most people benefit.

It is also important to remember that national income is a far from perfect measure of economic well-being, in part because it fails to measure many things, such as leisure time, that matter to people. Chapter 28 contains a detailed discussion of how economists measure national income and an evaluation of the strengths and weaknesses of those measures.

Short-term fluctuations Recessions cause unemployment

and lost output. When actual income is below potential income, there is economic waste and human suffering as a result of a failure to use the economy's resources (including its human resources) at their normal intensity of use.

Booms, although associated with high employment and high output, can bring problems of their own. When actual national income exceeds potential income, strong inflationary pressure usually results, causing serious concern for any government that is committed to keeping the inflation rate low. Of course, inflation can be an even worse problem when governments are not committed to keeping it low.

Employment, unemployment, and the labour force

National income and employment (and, hence, unemployment) are closely related. If more is to be produced, either more workers must be used in production or existing workers must produce more. The first change means a rise in employment and actual national income; the second means a rise in labour productivity and in potential as well as actual income. In the short run, when the economy's potential income is fixed, the only way to produce more output is to employ more workers. Trend increases in productivity are a major source of economic growth, but their main effects are felt over longer periods of time.

The UK **labour force** is made up of the total number of adults (aged between 16 and retirement age and not in full-time education) who are either employed or unemployed. 'Employed' denotes the number of adult workers who hold jobs; 'unemployed' denotes the number of adult workers who are not employed but are actively seeking a job. The **unemployment rate**, usually represented by the symbol U, is unemployment expressed as a percentage of the labour force:

$$U = \frac{\text{Unemployed}}{\text{Labour force}} \times 100$$

The number of unemployed persons in the United Kingdom is calculated by the Department of Employment from the numbers of people claiming unemployment benefits. This number of estimated unemployed is then divided by the total number in the labour force (employed plus unemployed) to obtain the current unemployment rate, given as a percentage. Some problems connected with this measurement are discussed in Box 27.2. The official UK definition of unemployment has been changed frequently in the recent past, and the political motives for such changes have been a source of considerable controversy.

Consideration of employment and unemployment suggests another concept: that of *full employment*. One confusing thing about full employment is that it does *not* mean an absence of unemployment. This is why the concept is now often called *high employment* in North America, although

the long history of the use of the term 'full employment' in the United Kingdom guarantees that it will be widely used here for some time to come. We shall refer to the level of employment generated when GDP is at its potential level as **equilibrium employment**.

There are two main reasons why full employment is always accompanied by some unemployment. First, there is a constant turnover of individuals in given jobs and a constant change in job opportunities. New members enter the work-force; some people quit their jobs; others are made redundant. Although the number of vacant positions may equal the number of people looking for such positions, it takes time for these people to find jobs. So, at any point in time, there is unemployment due to the normal turnover of labour. Such unemployment is called **frictional unemployment**.

Second, because the economy is constantly changing and adapting, at any one time there will always be some mismatching between the characteristics of the labour force and the characteristics of the available jobs. This is a mismatching between the structure of the supplies of labour and the structure of the demands for labour. The mismatching may occur, for example, because labour does not have the skills demanded, or because workers are not in that part of the country where the demand is located. Unemployment that occurs because of a mismatching of the characteristics of the supply of labour and the demand for labour, even when the overall demand for labour is equal to the overall supply, is called **structural unemployment**. We will have more to say about these two types of unemployment in Chapter 41.

Full employment, or equilibrium employment, is said to occur when the only existing unemployment is frictional and structural. At less than full employment, other types of unemployment are present as well. One major reason for lapses from full employment lies with the business cycle. During recessions, unemployment rises above the minimum avoidable amount of frictional and structural unemployment. This excess amount is called **cyclical unemployment** (or, sometimes, *demand-deficient unemployment*).

The measured unemployment rate when the economy is at potential GDP is often called the **natural rate of unemployment** or the **NAIRU**.[3] Estimates of this rate are difficult to obtain and are often a source of disagreement among economists. Nevertheless, such estimates are a useful benchmark against which economists can gauge the current performance of the economy, as measured by the actual unemployment rate. Estimates indicate that the natural rate of unemployment rose from less than 2 per cent in the 1950s and early 1960s to around 5 or 6 per cent in the mid-

---

[3] *NAIRU* is an acronym for 'non-accelerating-inflation rate of unemployment'. The reasons for the use of this term will become clear in Chapter 40.

BOX 27.2

How accurate are the unemployment figures?

No measurement of unemployment is completely accurate. The unemployment figures that are calculated by the Department of Employment, however, have a number of shortcomings that reveal much about the concept of unemployment itself.

Measured unemployment may overstate or understate the number of people who would accept a job at the going wage rate if they were offered one. On the one hand, measured unemployment overstates true unemployment by including people who are voluntarily out of work. For example, unemployment benefit provides protection against genuine hardship, but it also induces some people to stay out of work and collect unemployment benefits for as long as the benefits last. Such people have, in fact, voluntarily withdrawn from the labour force, although, in order to remain eligible for unemployment payments, they must make a show of looking for a job by registering at the local job centre. Such people usually are included in the ranks of the unemployed because they are registered as claiming unemployment benefit and appear to be seeking work.

On the other hand, the measured figure understates unemployment by omitting some people who would accept a job if one were available but who are not currently claiming unemployment benefit. Someone, for example who lost his job last month and is actively looking for a new one, but has not bothered to register for unemployment benefit, would not be counted in the UK unemployment figures. Such people are, however, unemployed in the sense that they would willingly accept a job

if one were available. There is another category of people who are sometimes referred to as *discouraged workers*. These have voluntarily withdrawn from the labour market because they believe that they cannot find a job under current conditions. A good example would be someone who has effectively retired before the normal retirement age, who would be happy to work if a suitable opportunity arose, but who is not claiming unemployment benefit.

In addition, there are part-time unemployed people. Some people are working short hours because they want to. They are not unemployed. Others, however, are working six hours instead of eight hours per day because there is insufficient demand for the product that they help to make, then these workers are suffering 25 per cent unemployment even though none of them are reported as unemployed: 25 per cent of that group's potential labour resources are going unused. Part-time work is a major source of unemployment of labour resources that is not reflected in the official unemployment figures.

The official figures for unemployment are useful, particularly because they tell us the *direction* of changes in unemployment. It is unlikely, for example, that the figures will be rising when unemployment is really falling. For all of the reasons that we have just discussed, however, they can at times give under- or overestimates of the total number of persons who would be genuinely willing to work if they were offered a job at the going rate of pay.

1970s and to over 8 per cent in the late 1980s. (We shall discuss the reasons for these changes in Chapter 41.)

UNEMPLOYMENT: THE HISTORICAL EXPERIENCE

Figure 27.5(i) shows the trend in the employed labour force since 1900, and Figure 27.5(ii) shows unemployment since 1885. Employment rose particularly strongly during the two world wars. This largely reflected the greater participation of female workers. It is clear that the trend in employment growth is almost flat in the last two decades, despite considerable variation around the trend. This is in line with the slow growth of the overall UK population; there were about 50 million residents of the United Kingdom in 1945, and only about 57 million in 1993, a growth of 14 per cent.

Although the long-term growth trend dominates the employment figures, some unemployment is always present. Figure 27.5(ii) shows that the short-term fluctuations in the unemployment rate have been quite marked. The unemployment rate was as low as 0.3 per cent in 1943–4 and as high as 18 per cent in 1932; in the period following

the Second World War the unemployment rate fell as low as 1 per cent in 1955 and 1956 and remained in excess of 11.5 per cent during 1983–6.

The high unemployment rate of the Great Depression in the early 1930s tends to dwarf the fluctuations in unemployment that have occurred since then. None the less, the fluctuations in unemployment in recent decades have been neither minor nor unimportant. Although there has been an upward trend in unemployment since 1970, unemployment exhibits no upward or downward trend in the long term.

Unemployment can rise either because employment falls or because the size of the labour force increases. In recent decades the number of people entering the labour force has not greatly exceeded the number leaving it. The result has been that changes in employment and changes in unemployment have been very closely related. Rising employment is associated with falling unemployment.

WHY UNEMPLOYMENT MATTERS

The social and political significance of the unemployment

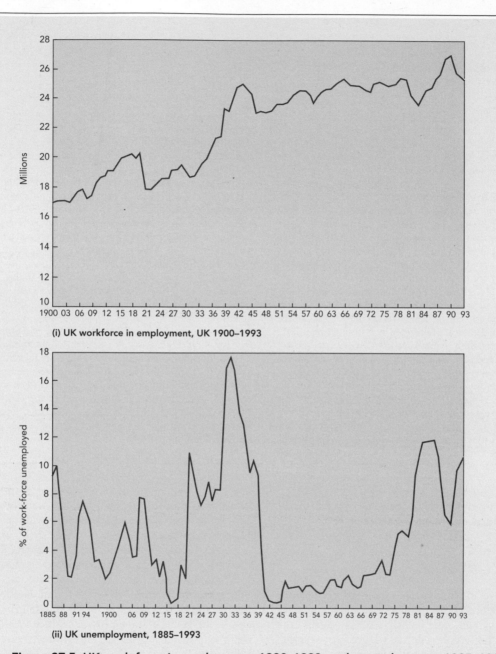

(i) UK workforce in employment, UK 1900–1993

(ii) UK unemployment, 1885–1993

Figure 27.5 UK work-force in employment, 1990–1993, and unemployment, 1885–1993

Employment grew up to 1945 but it has been flat in the post-war period. Unemployment was very high in the 1930s but was low for thirty years after the Second World War.

(i) The numbers in employment in 1993 were only a fraction higher than in 1945. A big increase in female participation rates has been offset by growing numbers of retired people and of unemployed. Overall, population growth has been very slow.

(ii) Unemployment varies cyclically with the level of economic activity though not in a uniform way. It fell to very low levels during the two world wars. After the First World War, it became very high and rose to even higher levels in the recession of the 1930s. However, after the Second World War it stayed very low throughout the 1950s and 1960s. In the 1980s it reached higher levels again.

Sources: 100 Years of Economic Statistics, The Economist, 1989, and Economic Trends.

INFLATION: THE HISTORICAL EXPERIENCE

Figure 27.6 shows the RPI and the inflation rate (measured by the annual rate of change in the RPI) from 1885 to 1993. What can we learn from this figure?

First, we learn that the price level is constantly changing. Second, we learn that in no year since the end of the Second World War in 1945 did the price level fall; in all years the inflation rate was positive. The average inflation rate between 1945 and 1993 was 6.4 per cent, and the lowest levels were achieved in 1959 and 1960 when inflation was 0.5 per cent. A falling price level was much more common before the Second World War. Prices fell in the early 1930s, and in 1922 they fell by over 20 per cent! The cumulative effect of this sequence of positive (though often small) price increases since 1945 is quite dramatic; in 1993 the price level was 20 times higher than it was in 1945. From 1980 to 1993 alone, prices more than doubled.

Third, we learn that, whereas the long-term increasing trend stands out when we look at the price level (especially the dramatic rise since 1970), the short-term fluctuations stand out when we look at the inflation rate. The sharp year-to-year swings in the inflation rate have sometimes been dramatic—especially the swing from positive to negative inflation that followed the end of the First World War. The increases in the inflation rate to double-digit levels in 1975 and again in 1979 were partly associated with major shocks to the world prices of oil and foodstuffs, and were experienced similarly in many other countries. The declines in inflation that followed were delayed responses to major recessions. (Note that, even when the inflation rate *falls*, as it did in 1982, for example, the price level continues to rise as long as inflation remains *positive*.) At the beginning of the 1990s the rate began to tumble, and by the end of 1994 it was around 2 per cent, a figure that had not been experienced since the early 1960s.

WHY INFLATION MATTERS

Money is the universal yardstick in our economy. We measure economic values in terms of money, and we use money to conduct our economic affairs. Things as diverse as wages, bank balances, the value of a house, and company accounts are all stated in terms of money. We value money, however, not for itself but for what we can purchase with it. The terms **purchasing power of money** and *real value of money* refer to the amount of goods and services that can be purchased with a given amount of money. A change in the price level affects us because it changes the real value of money.

The purchasing power of money is negatively related to the price level.

For example, if the price level doubles, a pound will buy only half as much, whereas if the price level halves, a pound will buy twice as much. Figure 27.6 shows that inflation has reduced the purchasing power of money over each of the last five decades.

If inflation reduces the real value of a given sum of money, it also reduces the real value of anything else whose price is *fixed* in money terms. Thus, the real value of a money wage, a savings account, or the balance that is owed on a mortgage or student loan is reduced by inflation.

A fully anticipated inflation It is possible to imagine an inflation that has no real effects of any kind. What is required for this to happen is, first, that everyone who is making any sort of financial arrangement knows what the inflation rate will be over the life of the arrangement and, second, that *all* financial obligations (including money itself) be stated in real terms. The real behaviour of the economy would then be exactly the same with, and without, the inflation.

Say, for example, that both sides of a wage contract agree that wages should rise annually by 3 per cent in real terms. If the inflation rate is expected to be zero, they would agree to a 3 per cent annual increase in money wages. If a 10 per cent inflation is expected, however, they would agree to a 13 per cent annual increase in money wages: 10 per cent would be needed to maintain the purchasing power of the money wages that would be paid, and 3 per cent would be needed to bring about the desired increase in purchasing power.[6]

Similarly, a loan contract would specify that the amount repaid on the loan be increased over the amount borrowed by the rate of inflation. Thus, if £100 is borrowed and the price level rises by 10 per cent, then £110 would have to be returned—plus any interest that might be paid on the loan. This would ensure that the real value of what is borrowed stays equal to the real value of what is returned.

Taxes would also have to be adjusted. For example, the personal allowance on income tax (the amount of income that each person can exempt from taxation) would have to be increased by 10 per cent to keep the real value of the exemption constant, given a 10 per cent inflation rate.

The result of all this would be a 10 per cent increase in everyone's money incomes and money assets, combined with a 10 per cent increase in all money prices and all money liabilities. Nothing real would have changed. People's higher money incomes would buy the same amount as before, and the real value of their assets and liabilities would be unchanged.

Once everything has adjusted, any one price level works as well as any other price level.

---

[6] This is only approximately correct, for reasons similar to those mentioned in fn. 5: the compounding of real and nominal increases is multiplicative rather than additive.

This is just what we should expect, since it would indeed be strange if altering the number of zeros that we use when stating monetary values could change anything real.[7]

A completely unanticipated inflation   At the opposite extreme from a fully anticipated inflation is a completely unanticipated inflation. No one sees it coming; no one is prepared to offset its consequences. The real value of all contracts that are specified in money terms will change unexpectedly. Who will gain and who will lose?

An unexpected inflation benefits anyone who has a debt (or future payment) fixed in money terms and harms anyone who is entitled to receive payment of a specific money sum.

For example, consider a wage contract that specifies a wage increase of 3 per cent on the assumption that the price level will remain constant. Both employers and employees expect that the purchasing power of wages paid will rise by 3 per cent as a result of the new contract. Now assume, however, that the price level unexpectedly rises by 10 per cent over the life of the wage contract. The 3 per cent increase in money wages now means a reduction in the purchasing power of wages of about 7 per cent. Employers selling goods whose prices rise at the average rate gain, because their wage payments represent a smaller part of the value of their output than they had expected. Workers lose, because their wages represent a smaller receipt of purchasing power than they had expected.

People who have borrowed money will pay back a smaller real amount than they borrowed. By the same token, people who have lent money will receive back a smaller real amount than they lent. Say, for example, that Jane lends Peter enough money to buy a medium-sized car, and the price level subsequently doubles. When Peter pays back the money that he borrowed, Jane finds herself with only half of the amount now required to buy the car.

Wage-earners and lenders will be able to adjust to the new price level when they make new contracts, but some people will be locked into their old money contracts for the rest of their lives. The extreme case is suffered by those who live on fixed money incomes. For example, some pension annuities pay a certain number of pounds per year for life. On retirement, this sum may look adequate, even generous. Twenty years later, however, inflation may have reduced its purchasing power to the poverty level. A person who retired on a fixed money income in 1973 would have found the purchasing power of that income reduced year by year, until in 1993 it would have been only 17 per cent of its original value. To understand the impact of this, imagine being told that, for every £1 that you now spend, only 17p can be spent 20 years from now. See Box 27.3 on p. 514 for a further discussion of this issue.

Intermediate cases   There are several reasons why virtually all real inflations fall somewhere between the two extremes (fully anticipated or complete surprise) that we have just discussed.

First, the inflation rate is usually variable and is seldom foreseen exactly, even though its general course may be anticipated. Thus, the actual rate will sometimes be higher than expected—to the benefit of those who have contracted to pay money. At other times, the inflation rate will be lower than expected—to the benefit of those who have contracted to receive money. Given the lack of certainty, different people will have different expectations.

Because it is hard to foresee accurately, inflation adds to the uncertainties of economic life. Highly variable inflation rates cause great uncertainty.

Second, even if the inflation rate is foreseen, all adjustments to it cannot occur at the same speed. As a result, inflation redistributes income, and it does so in a haphazard way. Those whose money incomes adjust more slowly than prices will lose; those whose money incomes keep ahead of the inflation will gain.

Third, even if the inflation rate is foreseen, the full set of institutions that would be needed for everyone to avoid its consequences does not exist. For example, some private pension plans are stated in money terms and others compensate for only up to 5 per cent inflation. Employees may have little choice but to take the plan that their employers make available to them. Thus, even when inflation is foreseen, some people will wind up living on fixed nominal incomes and thus will see their real incomes erode over time.

Fourth, much of the tax system is defined in nominal money terms, causing its effects to vary with the price level. For example, machinery and equipment owned by businesses wear out with use. The tax code in many countries, including the United Kingdom, allows for this by permitting firms to deduct *depreciation allowances* from their profits for tax purposes. The depreciation allowances are usually calculated as a certain fraction of the original purchase price of the machinery or equipment. If there has been a rapid inflation, the allowed depreciation may be much less than the real depreciation. This makes capital more expensive for firms and tends to reduce investment (and, as we shall see, economic growth).

Indexing   Some of the effects of inflation can be avoided by indexing. **Indexing** means linking the payments that are

---

[7] This is another way of stating the point that *only relative prices matter* for resource allocation. If all prices rise by 10 per cent, or by any other uniform percentage, relative prices are unchanged. The same relation holds in an open economy, where, in the face of an alteration in the domestic price level, the exchange rate changes to keep relative international prices and asset values unchanged.

made under the terms of a contract to changes in the price level. For example, a retirement pension might pay the beneficiary £10,000 per year starting in 1996, and it might specify that the amount paid will increase each year in proportion to the increase in the RPI. Thus, if the RPI turns out to rise by 10 per cent between 1996 and 1997, the pension that is payable in 1997 would rise by 10 per cent, to £11,000. If the RPI rose only 5 per cent, the pension would also rise by 5 per cent, to £10,500. In either case, indexing would hold the real purchasing power of the pension constant.

Indexing is potentially valuable as a defence against unforeseen changes in the price level, as a method of reducing uncertainty, and as a way of adapting institutions so that contracts can be made in real terms. In practice, however, indexing is used much less than it might be. Most of the tax code is not fully indexed, and the vast majority of contracts are written in nominal terms, putting them at risk for the consequences of unanticipated inflation. There are, however, some index-linked savings products available from the UK government (some via National Savings) which enable people to protect at least some of their savings against inflation. For example, in February 1994 you could buy on the London Stock Exchange (via a stockbroker or bank) any one of 13 different index-linked gilts. (UK government bonds are referred to as 'gilts' because they are very safe and are, therefore, gilt-edged.) These paid a guaranteed real interest rate of around 2.5 per cent and guaranteed to refund the original sum invested plus the percentage increase in the RPI between issue and redemption. (For example, suppose each bond (gilt) was issued for £100 in 1990 and redeemed in the year 2000. If the RPI rises by 150 per cent between 1990 and 2000, then the investor will receive £250 for each bond in the year 2000 (plus interest in the meantime).)

The interest rate

If a bank lends you money, it will usually ask you to agree to a schedule for repayment. Furthermore, it will charge you interest for the privilege of borrowing the money. If, for example, you are lent £1,000 today, repayable in one year's time, you may also be asked to pay £10 per month in interest. This makes £120 in interest over the year, which can be expressed (approximately) as an interest rate of 12 per cent per annum [(120/1,000) × 100 per cent].

The **interest rate** is the price that is paid to borrow money for a stated period of time and is expressed as a percentage amount per pound borrowed. For example, an interest rate of 12 per cent per year means that the borrower must pay 12p per year for every pound that is borrowed.

Just as there are many prices of goods, so there are many interest rates. The bank will lend money to an industrial customer at a lower rate than it will lend money to you—

there is a lower risk of its not being repaid. The rate charged on a loan that is not to be repaid for a long time will usually differ from the rate on a loan that is to be repaid quickly.

When economists speak of *the* interest rate, they mean a rate that is typical of all the various interest rates in the economy. Dealing with one interest rate suppresses much interesting detail. However, interest rates normally move together, so following the movement of one rate allows us to consider changes in the level of interest rates in general. The *base rate* of interest, the rate that banks use as a reference for all the rates they charge to different customers, may be thought of as *the* interest rate, since, when the base rate changes, most other rates change in the same direction. This is the rate that is quoted on the news when it changes as a result of a shift in government policy.

INTEREST RATES AND INFLATION

How does inflation affect the rate of interest? In order to begin developing an answer to this question, imagine that your friend lends you £100 and that the loan is repayable in one year. The amount that you pay her for making this loan, measured in money terms, is the **nominal interest rate**. If you pay her £108 in one year's time, £100 will be repayment of the amount of the loan (which is called the *principal*) and £8 will be payment of the interest. In this case, the nominal interest rate is 8 per cent ((8/100) × 100%).

How much purchasing power has your friend gained or lost by making this loan? As we have already noted in our discussion of the consequences of inflation, the answer will depend on what happens to the price level during the year. Intuitively, the more the price level rises, the worse your friend will do, and the better the transaction will be for you. This result occurs because, the more the price level rises, the less valuable are the pounds that you use to repay the loan. The **real rate of interest** measures the *real* return on a loan, in terms of purchasing power.

If the price level remains constant over the year, then the real rate of interest that your friend earns would also be 8 per cent, because she can buy 8 per cent more goods and services with the £108 that you repay her than with the £100 that she lent you. However, if the price level rises by 8 per cent, the real rate of interest would be zero, because the £108 that you repay her buys the same quantity of goods as the £100 that she originally gave up. If she is unlucky enough to lend money at 8 per cent in a year in which prices rise by 10 per cent, the real rate of interest that she earns is minus 2 per cent. The repayment of principal and nominal interest of 8 per cent will purchase 2 per cent *less*, in goods and services, than the amount originally lent.

If lenders and borrowers are concerned with real costs, measured in terms of purchasing power, the nominal rate of interest will be set at the real rate to which they agree as a return on their money *plus* an amount to cover any expected rate of inflation. Consider a one-year loan that is meant to earn a real return to the lender of 5 per cent. If the expected rate of inflation is zero, the nominal interest rate set for the loan will be 5 per cent; if a 10 per cent inflation is expected, the nominal interest rate will be 15 per cent.

To provide a given expected real rate of interest, the nominal interest rate must be set at the desired real rate of interest plus the expected annual rate of inflation.

The extra amount to cover the inflation is often called the *inflationary premium*. Thus, the nominal interest rate equals the real interest rate plus the inflationary premium.

Because they often overlook this point, many people are surprised at the high nominal rates of interest that exist during periods of rapid inflation. For example, when the nominal interest rates rose drastically in 1979, many commentators expressed shock at the 'unbearably' high rates. Most of them failed to notice that, with inflation running at about 18 per cent, an interest rate of 15 per cent represented a real rate of −3 per cent. Had the government given in to the pressure to hold interest rates to the more 'reasonable' level of 10 per cent, it would have been imposing an even larger *negative* real rate of interest of −8 per cent. With negative real interest rates, the purchasing power that lenders get back, including interest, is less than the purchasing power of the original amount that was lent.

The burden of borrowing depends upon the real, not the nominal, rate of interest.

For example, a nominal interest rate of 8 per cent, combined with a 2 per cent rate of inflation, is a much greater real burden on borrowers than a nominal rate of 16 per cent, combined with a 14 per cent rate of inflation. As discussed in more detail in Box 27.3, lenders often suffer from a similar confusion.

Figure 27.7 shows the nominal rate of interest paid on short-term government borrowing since 1900. Short-term interest rates were both high and volatile during the 1970s and 1980s. It also shows the real short-term interest rate, calculated as the three month rate on Treasury bills (short-term government borrowing) minus the inflation rate.[8]

WHY INTEREST RATES MATTER

As we shall see in Chapter 29, real interest rates help to

[8] Treasury bills are sold to the London money markets by the Bank of England acting as agent for the government. They normally have a life of three or six months. They are called 'bills' because they do not pay an explicit interest rate; rather, they are sold at a discount to their redemption value. For example, a bill that will be bought back for £100 in three months' time may be issued (sold) today for £98. The buyer gets a return on the bill because it appreciates in value over time. In this example, the rate of return would be 8.4 per cent per annum.

BOX 27.3

....

Does a fall in inflation hurt lenders?

In the early 1990s, the UK inflation rate fell to very low levels and nominal interest rates followed. Many retired persons complained that their incomes had fallen because their money, held in government bonds or bank and building society deposits, was producing a lower cash flow. Their mistake was in regarding the whole nominal interest as current income. By spending the inflationary premium, these pensioners were allowing the real purchasing power of their capital, and the real income it generates, to be reduced by the inflation rate. For example, a couple who spent the whole nominal interest earnings in the face of a 5 per cent inflation would find their real income halved in just over 14 years. To preserve the real value of capital and income, the inflationary premium needs to be saved and added to the sum lent out, thus keeping its real value constant.

To illustrate this, consider a retired couple who have £200,000 invested in government bonds that earn 10 per cent nominal interest in the face of a 5 per cent inflation. If they regard the entire £20,000 as income and spend it, the real purchasing power of this cash flow will fall by 5 per cent per year. At the end of 20 years, the prices of everything they buy will have risen by 2.65 times and they will be able to buy only about 38 per cent

([1/2.65] × 100) as much as 20 years before. Also, the real value of the £200,000 to be passed on to their heirs will be only 38 per cent of its original real value. This couple have consumed all of their income and much of their wealth.

A second couple who 'save' half of the interest earnings and spend the other half, will maintain real wealth and income over the 20 years. At the end of that period the nominal value of their wealth will be £530,000; nominal interest earnings will be £53,000 per year, which will have the same purchasing power as the original £20,000 (since £53,000/2.65 = £20,000).

The second couple have correctly regarded only the real return of £10,000 in the first year as income, and the other £10,000 as an inflationary premium to compensate for the loss of real value of capital. The first couple will have spent not only the real return, but also the inflationary premium. They will have suffered a slow reduction of real income and real wealth year by year.

Failure to understand these basic but subtle relations have led many a retired person down the path to poverty when inflation rates are even moderately high.

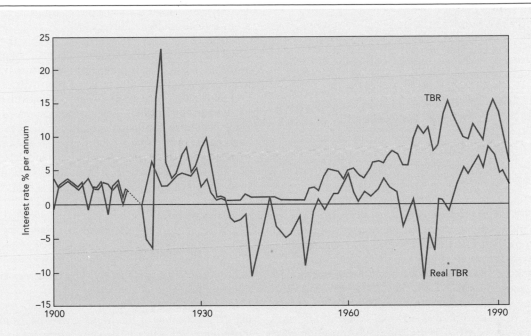

Figure 27.7 Real and nominal short-term interest rates, 1900–1993

The positive inflation of the post-war period means that nominal interest rates have generally exceeded real rates. However, real interest rates became very high, by historical standards, in the late 1980s. Real interest rates were at their highest level this century immediately after the First World War. This was because the inflation rate fell to –20 per cent, for a short while. Real interest rates were negative for much of the 1940s and 1950s, and then again in the mid-1970s.

The series used for nominal rates is the three-month Treasury bill rate (TBR). The real rate is calculated as the nominal rate minus the actual inflation rate. For some purposes in economic theory, the real rate of interest is defined as the nominal rate minus the *expected* rate of inflation. Data are not available for the period of the First World War.

Sources: 100 Years of Economic Statistics, The Economist, 1989, and Financial Statistics, CSO.

determine the amount of total investment expenditure. When real interest rates are high, it is costly to borrow, and there is less real investment than when interest rates are low. The greater is investment expenditure, the greater will be potential GDP in the future. Thus, real interest rates, through their effect on investment, affect long-term growth and *future* living standards.

Changes in investment can also cause swings in the business cycle. A slowdown in investment expenditure can trigger a slump; conversely, when investment increases sharply, GDP generally follows. Thus, via their effect on investment, real interest rates also affect unemployment and output in the short run. In addition, interest rates are an important determinant of the standard of living of many retired people who live on pensions or savings. For them, the higher are real interest rates, the higher will be the level of their real incomes.

Interest rates are also important for people who have

borrowed money, usually in the form of a mortgage, to buy a house or a flat. When interest rates are high mortgage repayments are also high, so people with such debts are worse off. In some countries fixed-interest-rate mortgages are common, so mortgage-holders are not affected by interest rate rises. In the United Kingdom, the vast majority of mortgages are *floating*-rate, so repayments tend to rise with the current level of market interest rates.

The international economy

The two important indicators of the UK position in the international economy are the *exchange rate*, which measures the international value of the pound, and the *balance of payments*, which records virtually all international economic transactions.

THE EXCHANGE RATE

If you are going on a holiday to Spain, you will need Spanish pesetas to pay for your purchases. Most banks, as well as any foreign exchange bureau, will make the necessary exchange of currencies for you. They will sell you pesetas in return for your pounds. If you get 200 pesetas for each pound that you give up, the two currencies are trading at a rate of £1 = Pta200 or, what is the same thing, Pta1 = £0.005.

The exchange rate refers to the price at which different currencies are traded for each other.

In particular, the **exchange rate** between the British pound and any foreign currency is the number of units of foreign currency that is needed to buy one pound. For example, on 31 December 1993 it took 1.48 US dollars, 2.57 German marks, or 8.74 French francs to buy one pound. The £/$ exchange rate was 1.48, the £/DM exchange rate was 2.57, and the £/Fr exchange rate was 8.74. Put the other way around, one US dollar was worth 0.68 pound, one Deutschmark was worth 0.39 pound, and one franc was worth 0.11 pound.

Actual exchange rates are prices for changing one currency into another, as above. However, when we talk about the value of a currency in general we talk about the **effective exchange rate**. This is an index of the value of one currency against a basket of all other major currencies. It is expressed relative to a value of 100 in some base year. The effective exchange rate for the pound is currently expressed relative to a base of 100 in 1985. Its value in mid-1993 was about 80.

Considerable confusion can arise in discussions of actual exchange rates, because the United Kingdom is the only major country that expresses its exchange rate as it does. The £/$ rate, for example, is in dollars per pound. In contrast, the Germans and the French (and most other countries, and economic theorists) express their rates as numbers of home currency units per dollar. Thus, the DM/$ exchange rate would be expressed as DM1.74 per dollar and the Fr/$ exchange rate as Fr5.9 per dollar. Hence in most countries a 'rise' in the exchange rate means a rise in the price of *foreign currency*, which is the same as a fall in the external value of the home currency; however, in the United Kingdom, a rise in the exchange rate means a rise in the external value of the home currency. In all cases, the term *appreciation* can be used to denote a rise in the external value of a currency (that is, the home currency is now

---

BOX 27.4

The exchange rate and cross rates

Although it is most common for exchange rates to be expressed against the US dollar, there is also a price (often implicit) at which any currency can be exchanged for any other. These other prices (sometimes referred to as *cross rates*) must all be consistent with one another; otherwise there arises an opportunity for currency traders to make money, through what is known as **arbitrage** (or triangular arbitrage).

The table sets out the exchange rates between the pound, dollar, Deutschmark, and franc on 31 December 1993. The first row has the exchange rates expressed as currency per pound, as discussed in the text. The numbers that appear in red in the second and third rows, however, are exchange rates which are implied by the numbers in the first row. For example, because there are $1.48 per £ and DM2.57 per £, there must be DM1.74 per $ (2.57/1.48 = 1.74). If the price of DM per $ were not 1.74 (while the other prices remained the same), then currency traders could make money by trading on this inconsistency. For example, suppose the DM/$ rate were DM2.00 per $. Let us start with $1,000. Buy Deutschmarks at DM2.00 per $. This gives DM2,000. Now buy pounds at DM2.57 per £. This gives £778.21 (2000/2.57). Now convert the pounds into dollars at $1.48 per £. This gives $1151.75. So we started with $1,000 and ended up with $1,151.75.

By doing this with larger sums we could get very rich very quickly. For this reason currency traders are always on the look-out for inconsistencies in cross rates, because when they find them they can make money—indeed, nowadays, they have their computers programmed to show up such trading opportunities. As a result, significant inconsistencies never arise, and even very small ones are eliminated quickly.

Note that the fact that all currency cross rates must be consistent does not mean that exchange rates cannot change; on the contrary, they are changing continuously while markets are open. What it does mean is that when the value of one currency falls—say the pound depreciates—then its value against the dollar will fall and the cross rates against all other currencies will depreciate as well.

	£	$	DM	Fr
£	1	1.48	2.57	8.74
$		1	1.74	5.91
DM			1	3.4
Fr				1

The first row expresses the exchange rate of the pound sterling against each of the other three currencies. It shows the number of units of foreign currency per pound. The red numbers are the cross rates between the other three currencies implied by the numbers in the first row. Thus, because there are $1.48 per £, and DM2.57 per £, there must be DM1.74 per $ (calculated as 2.57/1.48). A similar argument applies to the other cross rates.

worth more), while *depreciation* can be used to denote the reverse.

An appreciation in the exchange rate is the same thing as a rise in the external value of the domestic currency. A depreciation is the same thing as a fall in the external value of the domestic currency.

(The relationships between several currencies can be confusing; they are illustrated further in Box 27.4.)

The term **foreign exchange** refers to foreign currencies, or claims to foreign currencies, such as bank deposits, cheques, and securities, that are payable in foreign money. The **foreign exchange market** is the market where foreign currencies are traded—at prices expressed by the exchange rates.

The value of the UK pound can be looked at in two ways. The *internal value of the pound* refers to its power to purchase goods in UK domestic markets. We have already seen that the price level and the internal value of the pound are negatively related: the higher the price level, the lower the purchasing power of a pound. The *external value of the pound* refers to its power to purchase foreign currencies. This external value is expressed by the exchange rate, which, as you will recall, measures the foreign exchange cost of £1.

Figure 27.8 shows two indicators of the external value of the pound. The first is the US dollar price of £1 since 1900; the second is an index of the UK effective exchange rate, the cost of £1 in terms of a weighted basket of other currencies, from 1975 to mid-1994.

Up to 1976, the pound depreciated by both measures. However, from 1976 to 1981 the pound appreciated strongly. We will study the causes of exchange rate variations in Chapter 37. Whatever the cause, there is no doubt that this strong appreciation of sterling had a severe effect on the competitiveness of UK manufacturing and contributed to the early 1980 recession. The pound showed another period of strength against the US dollar in the period 1990–2, when the United Kingdom was a member of the EU Exchange Rate Mechanism (ERM). The pound fell sharply when the United Kingdom was forced to withdraw from the ERM in September 1992.

THE BALANCE OF PAYMENTS

In order to know what is happening to the course of international trade and international capital movements, governments keep an account of the transactions among countries. These accounts are called the **balance of payments accounts**. They record all international payments that are made for the buying and selling of both goods and services, as well as financial assets such as shares and bonds.

Figure 27.9 shows one part of the balance of payments that is most often the subject of controversy. This is the bal-ance of payments on the *traded goods and services*. It covers all trade in visible goods and in services. The balance is the difference between the value of UK exports and the value of UK imports. As can be seen from Figure 27.9, exports and imports both rose steadily in the 1970s and 1980s, but there was a large excess of imports over exports around 1990. Notice, however, that imports, exports, and the balance of trade are all reported in nominal rather than real terms. This means that, although the deficit during the Second World War was much bigger in real terms (and relative to real GDP) than the deficit in 1990, this is not apparent from part (ii) of the figure.

The **balance of trade** is a term used to refer specifically to the difference between visible exports and visible imports (sometimes referred to as 'merchandise trade'), while the **current account balance** includes the balance on visible trade, services, and flows of interest profits and dividends.[9] The size of balance of payments deficits is often a cause of political concern, although, as we shall discuss later, the balance of payments is much more of a problem for politicians under a fixed (or pegged) exchange rate regime than when the exchange rate is freely floating.

Cycles and trends

Why are the price level, national income, employment, and the value of the pound what they are today? What causes them to change? These are some of the questions that macroeconomics seeks to answer.

Before we begin to study these questions, it is useful to emphasize a distinction that has been made repeatedly in this chapter—the distinction between *cycles* and *trends*. Both are crucial to understanding the economy and evaluating its ability to provide goods, services, and opportunities.

Long-term trends The study of economic trends is the study of the economy over extended periods of time. Here we are concerned primarily with understanding the sources of long-term growth and the development of public policies that affect economic growth. Recent economic history has made the study of trends especially important. From the end of the Second World War until 1973, output per person employed in the United Kingdom grew at a rate of 2.3 per cent a year; since 1973 it has grown at a rate of 1.8 per cent a year. These differences matter: with productivity growing at 2.3 per cent a year, living standards double in 30 years; at an annual growth of 1.8 per cent a year, living standards double in about 40 years.

Notice, however, that the trend in productivity growth in the manufacturing sector of the UK economy has been in

---

[9] From here on, 'imports', 'exports', and the 'trade balance' will always refer to trade in goods *and services*.

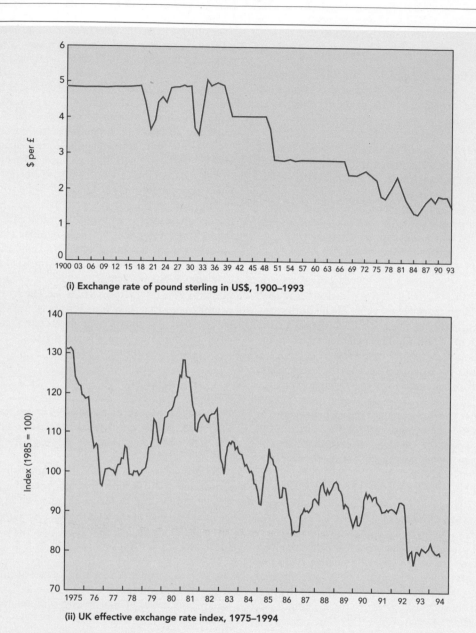

(i) Exchange rate of pound sterling in US$, 1900–1993

(ii) UK effective exchange rate index, 1975–1994

Figure 27.8 The UK exchange rate

The exchange rate is the value of one currency against another, or other currencies in general.
(i) In the early part of the century the exchange rate was nearly $5 per £1 sterling, but by 1994 it was only $1.5 per £1. After the Second World War it took $4.2 to buy £1. In 1949 the pound was devalued to $2.8, and in 1967 it was devalued again to $2.4. Otherwise, the £/$ exchange rate was constant during long periods of the so-called Bretton Woods system. Since 1972, sterling has floated against the US dollar. Note that there was not an effective market in foreign exchange during the two world wars, so the exchange rates during 1914–18 and 1939–45 are notional.
(ii) The effective exchange rate is an index of the value of the pound sterling against a weighted basket of other major currencies. The decline since 1981 reflects the fact that the pound has depreciated against the majority of other currencies. Between the end of 1992 and mid-1994, the pound maintained a very stable position against other currencies in general.

Sources: 100 Years of Economic Statistics, The Economist, 1989, and Datastream.

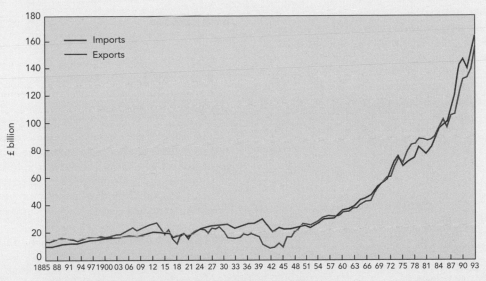

(i) UK exports and imports of goods and services, 1885–1993

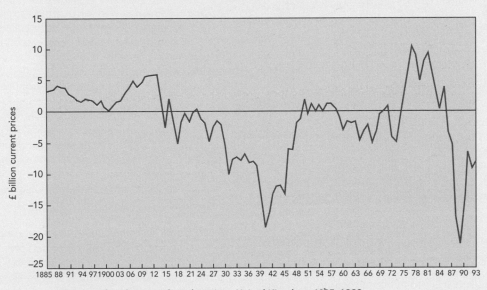

(ii) Balance of trade in goods and services, United Kingdom, 1885–1993

Figure 27.9 UK imports, exports, and the balance of trade, 1885–1993

The values of imports and exports tend to move together over time but thereare noticeable periods of deflict and surplus.

(i) The values of imports and exports more than doubled between 1980 and 1993. However, these figures are in nominal terms so they do not reflect changes in volume. Trade volumes have grown over time, but at nothing like the rate indicated here.

(ii) Substantial swings from surplus to deficit have occurred over the last century. In the early 1980s, the UK balance of trade was in substantial surplus. This was, in part, because of the emergence of Britain as an oil producer. In the late 1980s and early 1990s, however, there was a significant deficit. None the less, the 1990 deficit was only about 3.5 per cent of GDP, whereas the 1940–1 deficit was more than double GDP at the time.

Sources: 100 Years of Economic Statistics, The Economist, 1989, and Economic Trends.

marked contrast with the trend for the whole economy. From 1948 to 1980, productivity growth in manufacturing was 2.75 per cent per annum; from 1981 to 1993 this increased to 4.53 per cent per annum (though the numbers employed in manufacturing declined significantly, in line with many other countries). Hence we should be cautious about drawing too many conclusions without further detailed study. Clearly, however, the trend in productivity and the trend in potential GDP that is determined by productivity growth and population growth are the key objects of study for the long term.

In studying long-term trends, it is appropriate to ignore deviations from trend.

For trend analysis, this simplification does not cost us much, because over the long haul actual GDP moves quite closely with potential GDP. Moreover, over long time periods we are most interested in the evolution of the economy's *capacity* to produce (i.e. its potential output).

Short-term fluctuations   While trends greatly affect economic welfare over the long haul, at any given time what matters more is how the economy is doing relative to its *current* potential. To examine this, we study business cycles, i.e. shorter-term fluctuations away from trend growth. These fluctuations are important. When the economy is operating below its potential, unemployment is high, with its accompanying human suffering and economic waste; when the economy is operating above its potential, inflationary pressures are strong, with its accompanying economic distortions.

Changes in productivity and in the labour force dominate the long-term trends of output and employment, but productivity and the labour force generally change only slowly.

In studying short-term movements, it is appropriate to ignore long-term trends.

This is done with respect to national income by treating both the labour force and productivity as constant. Under these assumptions, a rise in output means a rise in employment and a fall in unemployment: output is positively associated with employment and negatively associated with unemployment. Taking productivity and the labour force as constant not only greatly simplifies our discussion but also reasonably approximates reality when we are dealing with the *short-term* behaviour of the economy.

Summary

1 Macroeconomics examines the behaviour of such broad aggregates and averages as the price level, national income, potential national income, the GDP gap, employment, and unemployment.

2 The value of the total production of goods and services in a nation is called national product. Since production of output generates income in the form of claims on that output, the total is also referred to as national income. One of the most commonly used measures of national income is gross domestic product (GDP).

3 Nominal national income evaluates output in current prices. Real national income evaluates output in base-period prices. Changes in real national income reflect changes in quantities of output produced.

4 Fluctuations of national income around its potential level are associated with the business cycle. Recoveries pass through peaks and become recessions, which in turn pass through troughs to become recoveries. Although these movements are systematic rather than random, they are by no means completely regular.

5 Potential real national income measures the capacity of the economy to produce goods and services when factors of production are employed at their normal intensity of use. The GDP gap is the difference between potential and actual real national income. A positive GDP gap is called a recessionary gap, while a negative GDP gap is called an inflationary gap.

6 The unemployment rate is the percentage of the labour force not employed but registered for unemployment benefit and actively searching for a job. The labour force and employment have both grown slowly for the past half century. The unemployment rate fluctuates considerably from year to year. Unemployment imposes serious costs on the economy in the form of economic waste and human suffering.

7 The price level is measured by a price index, which measures the cost of a set of goods in one year relative to their cost in an (arbitrary) base year.

8 The inflation rate measures the rate of change of the price level. Although it fluctuates considerably, the inflation rate has been positive in almost all years, which means that the price level has displayed a continual upward trend since 1939.

9 Other important macroeconomic variables include nominal and real interest rates; exchange rates, which refer to the cost of the pound in terms of foreign currency; and the balance of payments, which is a record of the aggregate of international transactions made by UK residents.

10 The dominant historical trends of the economy are growth of real output, and of the price level, over the long term. Output growth has never been entirely smooth. There have always been fluctuations in output, around the trend growth rate. The study of growth is simplified by ignoring these fluctuations and focusing on the broad trends. The study of the fluctuations is simplified by assuming that trends are zero so that all changes are fluctuations.

Topics for review

- National product and national income
- Real and nominal national income
- Potential and actual national income and the GDP gap
- Employment, unemployment, and labour force
- The price level and rate of inflation
- The effects of anticipated and unanticipated inflation
- The exchange rate
- Real and nominal interest rates
- The balance of payments
- The trade balance
- The current account balance

APPENDIX TO CHAPTER 27

....

How the RPI is constructed

TWO important questions must be answered when any price index is constructed. First, what group of prices should be used? This depends on the index. The retail price index (RPI), which is calculated by the Central Statistical Office (CSO), covers prices of commodities that are commonly bought by households. Changes in the RPI are meant to measure changes in the typical household's *cost of living*. (Other indexes, such as the wholesale price index or the producer price index, cover the prices of different groups of commodities. The implicit deflators of GNP and GDP cover all of the nation's output, not just consumer prices.)

Second, how should the movements in consumer prices be added up and summarized in one price index? If all prices change in the same proportion, this would not matter: a 10 per cent rise in every price would mean a 10 per cent rise in the average of all prices, no matter how the average was constructed. However, different prices usually change in different proportions. It then matters how much importance we give to each price change. Changes in the price of bread, for example, are much more important to the average consumer than changes in the price of caviar. In calculating a price index, each price is given a *weight* that reflects its importance.

Let us see how this is done for the RPI. Government statisticians periodically survey a representative group of households in what is called the Family Expenditure Survey. This shows how consumers spend their incomes. The average bundle of goods that is bought is determined, along with the proportion of expenditure that is devoted to each good. These proportions become the weights attached to the individual prices in calculating the RPI. As a result, the RPI weights rather heavily the prices of commodities on which consumers spend much of their income, and weights rather lightly the prices of commodities on which consumers spend only a little of their income. Table 27A.1 provides a simple example of how these weights are calculated.

Once the weights are chosen, the average price can be calculated for each period. This is done, as shown in Table 27A.2, by multiplying each price by its weight and summing the resulting figures. However, a single average price is not informative. Suppose, for example, you were told that the average price of all goods that were bought by consumers last year was £89.35. 'So what?' you might well ask, and the answer would be: 'So, not very much. By itself, this tells you nothing useful.' Now suppose you are told that this year's average price for the same set of consumers' purchases is £107.22. Now you know that, on average, prices paid by consumers have risen sharply over the year—in fact, the increase is 20 per cent.[1]

The average for each period is divided by the value of the average for the base period and multiplied by 100. The resulting series is called an index number series. By construction, the base-period value in this series equals 100; if prices in the next period average 20 per cent higher, the index number for that period will be 120. A simple example of how these calculations are carried out is given in Table 27A.2

[1] The change is £17.87, which is 20 per cent of the initial average price of £89.35.

Table 27A.1	Calculation of weights for a price index			
Commodity	Price (£)	Quantity	Expenditure (price × quantity) (£)	Proportional weight
A	5	60	300	0.50
B	1	200	200	0.33
C	4	25	100	0.17
Total			600	1.00

The weights are the proportions of total expenditure that are devoted to each commodity. This simple example lists the prices of three commodities and the quantities bought by a typical household. Multiplying price by quantity gives expenditure on each, and summing these gives the total expenditure on all commodities. Dividing expenditure on each good by total expenditure gives the proportion of total expenditure that is devoted to each commodity, as shown in the last column. These proportions become the weights for the price indexes that are calculated in Table 27A.2.

Table 27A.2   Calculation of a price index

Commodity	Weight	Price (£)			Price × weight (£)		
		1980	1985	1990	1980	1985	1990
A	0.50	5.00	6.00	14.00	2.50	3.00	7.00
B	0.33	1.00	1.50	2.00	0.33	0.495	0.66
C	0.17	4.00	8.00	9.00	0.68	1.36	1.53
Total	1.00				3.51	4.855	9.19

Index   1980 $\dfrac{3.51}{3.51} \times 100 = 100$

1985 $\dfrac{4.855}{3.51} \times 100 = 138.3$

1990 $\dfrac{9.19}{3.51} \times 100 = 261.8$

A price index expresses the weighted average of prices in the given year as a percentage of the weighted average of prices in the base year. The prices of the three commodities in each year are multiplied by the weights from Table 27A.1. Summing the weighted prices for each year gives the average price in that year. Dividing the average price in the given year by the average price in the base year and multiplying by 100 gives the price index for the given year. The index is, of course, 100 when the year is also taken as the given year, as is the case for 1980 in this example.

Price indexes are constructed by assigning weights to reflect the importance of the individual items being combined. The value is set equal to 100 in the base period.

Table 27A.2 shows the calculation of what is called a *fixed-weight index*. The weights are the proportion of income that is spent on the three goods in the base year. These weights are then applied to the prices in each subsequent year. The value of the index in each year measures exactly how much the base-year bundle of goods would cost at that year's prices.[2] Fixed-weight indexes are easy to interpret, but problems arise because consumption patterns change over the years; the fixed weights represent with decreasing accuracy the importance that consumers *currently* place on each of the commodities.

The RPI used to be calculated using fixed weights that were changed only every decade or so. Now they are revised annually. This avoids the problem of the fixed-weight index becoming steadily less representative of current expenditure patterns.

MEASURING THE RATE OF INFLATION

At the end of June 1994, the RPI was 144.7. (The average of the monthly values for 1987 = 100.) This means that at the end of June 1994 it cost just under 45 per cent more to buy a representative bundle of goods than it did in the base period, which in this case is taken as the average of prices prevailing in the year 1987. In other words, there was a 44.7 per cent *increase* in the price level over that period as measured by the RPI. The *percentage change* in the cost of purchasing the bundle of goods that is covered by any index is thus the level of the index minus 100.

The *inflation rate* between any two periods of time is measured by the percentage increase in the relevant price index from the first period to the second period. In the rare event of a drop in the price level, we speak of a *deflation*. When the amount of the rise in the price level is being measured from the base period, all that needs to be done is to substract the two indexes, as we have just done. When two other periods are being compared, we must be careful to express the change as a percentage of the index in the first period.

If we let P_1 indicate the value of the price index in the first period and P_2 its value in the second period, the inflation rate is merely the difference between the two, expressed as a percentage of the value of the index in the first period.

Inflation rate $= [(P_2 - P_1) \times 100]$.

(When P_1 is the base period, its value is 100, and the expression shown above reduces to $P_2 - 100$.) In other cases, the full calculation must be made. For example, the index went to 144.7 in June 1994 from 141.0 in June 1993, indicating a rate of inflation of 2.6 per cent over the year. The rise of 3.7

---

[2] To verify this, calculate the total expenditure required to buy 60 units of commodity A, 200 units of commodity B, and 25 units of commodity C in each of the three years for which price data are given in Table 27A.2. Divide the resulting amounts by £600, multiply by 100, and you will get exactly the index values shown in the table.

points in the index is a 2.6 per cent rise over its initial value of 141.0.

If the two values being compared are not a year apart, it is common to convert the result to an *annual rate*. For example, suppose the RPI is 135.2 in January 1998 and 135.6 in February 1998 (on a base of, say, 1993 = 100). This is an increase of 0.295 per cent over the month [(0.4/135.2) × 100]. It is also an *annual rate* of approximately 3.55 per cent (0.295 per cent × 12) over the year.[3] This means that, if the rate of increase that occurred between January and February 1998 did persist for a year, the price level would rise by approximately 3.55 per cent over the year.

[3] We say *approximately* because a 0.295 per cent rise each month that is *compounded* for 12 months will give rise to an increase over the year that is greater than 3.55 per cent. The appropriate procedure is to increase the index in January by 0.295 per cent 12 times (calculate $[(1.00295)^{12} - 1] \times 100$) rather than just to multiply it by 12. The two results are the difference between simple and compound interest rates.

☙ CHAPTER 28

Measuring macroeconomic variables

NATIONAL income and the national product are clearly concepts that matter. When they get bigger, the nation becomes better off, in some sense. Good times are associated with periods when national income and output are rising. Bad times are associated with periods when they are falling. Governments hope to have rising national income and output during their period in office so that they will be popular and be re-elected. Citizens want rising living standards and good employment prospects.

Macroeconomics has as its central goal the explanation of the determinants of national income and output. Indeed, from Chapter 29 onwards we spend a great deal of our time building up an analytical framework which helps us to understand the forces that influence national income and output. First, however, we have to understand what it is we are talking about. What exactly do we mean by national income and the national product? What do people mean when they refer to GDP, and how does it differ from GNP?

We start by discussing the measurement of national output, and find that, by summing the *value added* of each industry or sector, we arrive at a standard measure of national product. We then discuss how it is that we can arrive at the same measure of national product both from the expenditure side of the economy and from adding up factor incomes. An explicit result of this discussion is a demonstration of the equivalence of the concepts of national income and national product. Finally, we consider some limitations in the use of national income concepts as a measure of national well-being.

National output concepts

THE national output or the national product is related to the sum of all the outputs produced in the economy by individuals, firms, and governmental organizations. However, we cannot just add up all of the outputs of individual production units to arrive at the total national output.

Value added as output

The reason why getting a total for the nation's output is not quite so straightforward as it may seem at first sight is that one firm's output may be another firm's input. A maker of clothing buys cloth from a textile manufacturer and buttons, zips, thread, pins, hangers, etc., from a range of other producers. Most modern manufactured products have many ready-made inputs. A car or aircraft manufacturer, for example, will have hundreds of component suppliers.

Production occurs in stages. Some firms produce outputs that are used as inputs by other firms, and these other firms in turn produce outputs that are used as inputs by yet other firms.

If we merely added up the market values of all outputs of all firms, we would obtain a total that was greatly in excess of the value of the economy's actual output. The errors that would arise in estimating the nation's output by adding all sales of all firms is called **double counting**. 'Multiple counting' would be a better term, since, if we added up the values of all sales, the same output would be counted every time that it was sold from one firm to another.

The problem of double counting is solved by distinguishing between two types of output. **Intermediate goods and services** are outputs of some firms that are in turn inputs for other firms. **Final goods and services** are goods that are not, in the period of time under consideration, used as inputs by other firms. The term **final demand** refers to the purchase of final goods and services for consumption, for investment (including inventory accumulation), for use by governments, and for export. It does not include goods and services that are purchased by firms and used as inputs for producing other goods and services during the period under consideration.

If the sales of firms could be readily separated into sales for final use and sales for further processing by other firms, measuring total output would still be straightforward. It would equal the value of all *final goods and services* produced by firms, excluding all intermediate goods and services. However, when British Steel sells steel to the Ford Motor Company, it does not care, and usually does not know, whether the steel is for final use (say, construction of a new warehouse) or for use as an intermediate good in the production of cars. The problem of double counting must therefore be resolved in some other manner.

To avoid double counting, statisticians use the important concept of *value added*. Each firm's value added is the value of its output minus the value of the inputs that it purchases from other firms (which were in turn the outputs of those other firms). Thus, a steel mill's value added is the value of its output minus the value of the ore that it buys from the mining company, the value of the electricity and fuel oil that it uses, and the values of all other inputs that it buys from other firms. A bakery's value added is the value of the bread and cakes it produces minus the value of the flour and other inputs that it buys from other firms.

The total value of a firm's output is the gross value of its output. The firm's value added is the net value of its output. It is this latter figure that is the firm's contribution to the nation's total output. It is what its own efforts add to the value of what it takes in as inputs.

Value added measures each firm's own contribution to total output, i.e. the amount of market value that is produced by that firm. Its use avoids the statistical problem of double counting.

The concept of value added is further illustrated in Box 28.1. In this simple example, as in all more complex cases, the value of total output of final goods is obtained by summing all the individual values added.

The sum of all values added in an economy is a measure of the economy's total output. This measure of total output is called gross domestic product (GDP). It is a measure of all final output that is produced by all productive activity in the economy.

Table 28.1 gives the GDP by major industrial sectors for the UK economy in 1993.

Table 28.1 Gross domestic product for United Kingdom, 1993

Value added by sector	£ million	% of GDP
Agriculture, forestry, and fisheries	9,309	1.8
Mining, oil, and gas extraction	9,842	1.9
Manufacturing	114,698	22.3
Electricity, gas, and water supply	13,717	2.7
Construction	32,002	6.2
Wholesale and retail trade	72,549	14.1
Transport and communications	41,613	8.1
Finance and real estate	98,646	19.2
Public administration and defence	36,605	7.1
Education and health	52,509	10.2
Other services	32,892	6.4
Statistical discrepancy	359	
GDP at factor cost	514,741	100

The table shows value added by industrial sector in United Kingdom for 1993. The sector values added combine to make GDP at factor cost. As is explained later in the chapter, 'factor cost' means that it is the sum of factor incomes. The values added are calculated from the factor rewards attributable to each sector. Notice that manufacturing is the largest sector, but it produces only about 22 per cent of GDP. (*Note:* The original publications include a term, 'Adjustment for financial services'. This is deducted from total value added to avoid errors in the treatment of interest payments. Here we have deducted this term from the value added of the 'Finance and real estate' sector.)

Source: National Income Blue Book, 1994.

BOX 28.1

Value added through stages of production

Because the output of one firm often becomes the input of other firms, the total value of goods sold by all firms greatly exceeds the value of the output of final goods. This general principle is illustrated by a simple example in which firm R starts from scratch and produces goods (raw materials) valued at £100; the firm's value added is £100. Firm I purchases these raw materials valued at £100 and produces semi-manufactured goods which it sells for £130. Its value added is £30, because the value of the goods is increased by £30 as a result of the firm's activities. Firm F then purchases the semi-manufactured goods for £130 and works them into a finished state, selling them for £180. Firm F's value added is £50. The value of final goods, £180, is found either by taking the sales of firm F or by taking the sum of the values added by each firm. This value is less than the £410 that we obtain by adding up the market value of the commodities sold by each firm. The accompanying table summarizes this example.

Transactions between firms at three different stages of production

	Firm R	Firm I	Firm F		All firms
A: Purchases from other firms	£ 0	£100	£130		£230 = Total interfirm sales
B: Purchase of factors of production (wages, rent, interest, profits)	£100	£ 30	£ 50		£180 = Value added
Total A + B = value of product	£100	£130	£180	= Value of final goods and services	£410 = Total value of all sales

National-income accounting: gross domestic product

THE measures of national income and national product that are used in the United Kingdom derive from an accounting system called the National Income Accounts. The accounts, produced by the Central Statistical Office (CSO), provide a framework for studying national income. The National Income Accounts have a logical structure, based on the simple yet important idea that, whenever national product is produced, it generates an equivalent amount of national income.

Look again at Figure 27.1 (p. 504), which shows the circular flow of expenditure and income. The right half of the figure focuses on expenditure to purchase the nation's output in product markets, and the left half focuses on factor markets through which the receipts of producers are distributed to factors of production.

Corresponding to the two halves of the circular flow are two ways of measuring national income: by determining the value of what is produced, and by determining the value of the income claims generated by production. Both measures yield the same total, which is called **gross domestic product (GDP)**.[1] When it is calculated by adding up the total expenditure for each of the main components of final output, the result is called *GDP, expenditure-based*. When it is calculated by adding up all the incomes generated by the act of production, it is called *GDP, income-based*.

The conventions of double-entry bookkeeping require that all value produced must be accounted for by a claim that someone has to that value. For example, any expenditure you make must also be received by a supplier in exchange for the product bought. The value of what you spend is the expenditure; the value of the product sold to you is the output. Thus, the two values calculated on income and expenditure bases are identical conceptually and differ in practice only because of errors of measurement. Any discrepancy arising from such errors is then reconciled so that one common total is given as *the* measure of GDP. Both calculations are of interest, however, because each gives a different and useful breakdown. Also, having two independent ways of measuring the same quantity—in this case the sum of values added in the economy—provides a useful check on statistical procedures and on unavoidable errors in measurement.

GDP expenditure-based

GDP expenditure-based for a given year is calculated by adding up all the expenditures made to purchase the final output produced in that year. Total expenditure on final

output is the sum of four broad categories of expenditure: consumption, investment, government, and net exports. In the following chapters we will discuss in considerable detail the causes and consequences of movements in each of these four expenditure categories. In Chapter 29 we explain why these particular expenditure categories have received more attention in macroeconomics than have the net sector outputs listed in Table 28.1 and the income categories discussed below (Table 28.3). Here, we define these expenditure categories and explain how they are measured. Throughout, it is important to remember that they are exhaustive: they are defined in such a way that *all* expenditure on final output falls into one of the four categories.

CONSUMPTION EXPENDITURE

Consumption expenditure includes expenditure on all goods and services produced and sold to their final users during the year. It includes services, such as haircuts, medical care, and legal advice; nondurable goods, such as fresh meat, clothing, cut flowers, and fresh vegetables; and durable goods, such as cars, television sets, and microwave ovens. We denote actual, measured, consumption expenditure by the symbol C^a.

INVESTMENT EXPENDITURE

The next category of total expenditure is **investment expenditure,** which is defined as expenditure on the production of goods not for present consumption, but rather for their use in the future.[2] The goods that are created by this expenditure are called **investment (or capital) goods**. Investment expenditure can be divided into three categories: stockbuilding, fixed capital formation, and the construction of residential housing.

Stockbuilding   Almost all firms hold stocks of their inputs (raw materials) and their own outputs (finished products). These stocks are sometimes called *inventories*. Stocks of inputs and unfinished materials allow firms to maintain a steady stream of production in spite of short-term fluctuations in the deliveries of inputs bought from other firms. Stocks of outputs allow firms to meet orders in spite of temporary fluctuations in the rate of production or sales.

---

[1] Each of these totals must also equal the sum of value added in the economy, as discussed in the preceding section.
[2] In practice, there is no clear line between investment goods and consumption goods. Consumer durables such as cars and television sets produce consumption in the future as well as the present.

Modern 'just-in-time' methods of production pioneered by the Japanese aim to reduce stocks nearly to zero by delivering inputs just as they are needed. Most of the economy, however, does not achieve this level of efficiency and never will. Retailing, for example, would certainly not be improved if stores held no stocks.

An accumulation of stocks and unfinished goods in the production process counts as current investment because it represents goods produced (even if only half-finished) but not used for current consumption. A drawing down of stocks and work in progress, often called *destocking*, counts as a fall in investment because it represents a reduction in the stocks of finished goods (produced in the current period) that are available for future use. Stocks and work in progress are valued at what they will be worth on the market, rather than as what they have cost the firm so far. This is because the expenditure-based measure of national income includes the final value of these goods if they were sold, even though they have not yet been sold.

Fixed capital formation All production uses capital goods. These are manufactured aids to production, such as machines, computers, and factory buildings. The economy's total quantity of capital goods is called the **capital stock**. Creating new capital goods is an act of investment and is called *fixed investment*, or **fixed capital formation**. Much of the capital stock is in the form of equipment or buildings used by firms or government agencies in the production of goods and services. This would include not just factories and machines, but also hospitals, schools, and offices. Some capital stock is also owned by individuals; the most important example of this is housing.

Residential investment A house or a flat is a durable asset that yields its utility (provision of housing) over a long period of time. This meets the definition of investment that we gave earlier, so housing *construction* is counted as investment expenditure rather than as consumption expenditure. When a family purchases a house from another owner, the ownership of an already-produced asset is transferred, and that transaction is not a part of current national income. Housing construction is part of fixed capital formation in the UK definitions of national income.

Gross and net investment The total investment expenditure is called **gross investment** or **gross capital formation**. Gross investment is divided into two parts: replacement investment and net investment. **Replacement investment** is the amount of investment that just maintains the level of existing capital stock; in other words, it replaces the bits that have worn out. Replacement investment is classified as the **capital consumption allowance** or simply as **depreciation**. Gross investment minus replacement investment is **net investment**. Positive net investment *increases* the economy's total stock of capital, while replacement investment keeps the existing stock intact by replacing what has been used up.

All of gross investment is included in the calculation of national income. This is because all investment goods are part of the nation's total output, and their production creates income (and employment), whether the goods produced are a part of net investment or are merely replacement investment. Actual total investment expenditure is denoted by the symbol I^a.

GOVERNMENT EXPENDITURE ON GOODS AND SERVICES

When governments provide goods and services that households want, such as health care and street lighting, it is obvious that they are adding to the sum total of valuable output in the same way as do private firms that produce cars and video cassettes. With other government activities, the case may not seem so clear. Should expenditures by the government to negotiate over the political situation in Northern Ireland, or to pay a civil servant to help draft legislation, be regarded as contributions to national income? Some people believe that many (or even most) activities in Whitehall and in town halls are wasteful, if not downright harmful. Others believe that governments produce many of the important things of life, such as education, law and order, and pollution control.

National income statisticians do not speculate about which government expenditures are worth while. Instead, they include all government purchases of goods and services as part of national income. (Government expenditure on investment goods appears as public-sector capital formation, which is a part of total investment expenditure.) Just as the national product includes, without distinction, the outputs of both gin and Bibles, it also includes refuse collection and the upkeep of parks, along with the services of judges, members of Parliament, and even Inland Revenue inspectors. Actual government purchases of goods and services is denoted by the symbol G^a.

Government output typically is valued at cost rather than at market value. In most cases, there is really no choice. The output of public services is not (generally) sold in the market-place, so government output is not observed independently of the expenditures that produce it. What, for example, is the market value of the services of a court of law? No one knows. We do know, however, what it costs the government to provide these services, so we value them at their cost of production.

Although valuing at cost is the only possible way to measure many government activities, it does have one curious consequence. If, owing to an increase in productivity, one civil servant now does what two used to do, and the displaced worker shifts to the private sector, the government's measured contribution to national income will register a decline. On the other hand, if two workers now do what one worker used to do, the government's measured contribution will rise. Both changes could occur even though the services the government actually provides have not changed. This is an inevitable but curious consequence of measuring the value of the government's output by the cost of the factors, mainly labour, that are used to produce it—by inputs rather than by outputs.

It is important to recognize that only government expenditure on *currently produced goods and services* is included as part of GDP. A great deal of government expenditure is not a part of GDP. For example, when the Department of Health and Social Security (DHSS) makes a payment to an old-age pensioner, the government is not purchasing any currently produced goods or services from the retired. The payment itself adds neither to employment of factors nor to total output. The same is true of payments on account of unemployment benefit, welfare, student grants, and interest on the national debt (which transfers income from taxpayers to holders of government bonds). All such payments are examples of **transfer payments**, which are government expenditures that are not made in return for currently produced goods and services. They are not a part of expenditure on the nation's total output, and therefore are not included in GDP.[3]

Thus, when we refer to government expenditure as part of national income or use the symbol G^a, we include all government expenditure on currently produced goods and services, and we *exclude* all government transfer payments. (The term *total government spending* is often used to describe all government spending, including transfer payments.)

NET EXPORTS

The fourth category of aggregate expenditure, one that is very important to the UK economy, arises from foreign trade. How do imports and exports influence national income?

Imports   A country's GDP is the total value of final goods and services produced in that country. If you spend £12,000 on a car that was made in Germany, only a small part of that value will represent expenditure on UK production. Some of it represents payment for the services of the UK dealer and for transportation within this country; much of the rest is the output of German firms and expenditure on German products, though there may be component suppliers from several countries. If you take your next vacation in Italy, much of your expenditure will be on goods and services produced in Italy and, thus, will contribute to Italian GDP.

Similarly, when a UK firm makes an investment expenditure on a UK-produced machine tool that was made partly with imported materials, only part of the expenditure is on UK production; the rest is expenditure on the production by the countries that are supplying the materials. The same is true for government expenditure on such things as roads and dams; some of the expenditure is for imported materials, and only part of it is for domestically produced goods and services.

Consumption, investment, and government expenditure all have an import content. To arrive at total expenditure on UK output, we need to subtract from total UK residents' expenditure any expenditure on imports of goods and services, which is given the symbol IM^a.

Exports   If UK firms sell goods or services to German consumers, the goods and services are a part of German consumption expenditure but also constitute expenditure on UK output. Indeed, all goods and services that are produced in the United Kingdom and sold to foreigners must be counted as part of UK production and income; they are produced in the United Kingdom, and they create incomes for the UK residents who produce them. They are not purchased by UK residents, however, so they are not included as part of C^a, I^a, or G^a. Therefore, to arrive at the total value of expenditure on the domestic product, it is necessary to add in the value of UK exports. Actual exports of goods and services are denoted by the symbol X^a.

It is customary to group actual exports and actual imports together when calculating **net exports**. Net exports are defined as total exports of goods and services minus total imports of goods and services ($X^a - IM^a$), which will also be denoted NX^a. When the value of exports exceeds the value of imports, the net export term is positive; when, as in recent years, the value of imports exceeds the value of exports, the net export term becomes negative.

TOTAL EXPENDITURE

The expenditure-based measure of gross domestic product is the sum of the four expenditure categories that we have just discussed, or, in symbols:

$$GDP = C^a + I^a + G^a + (X^a - IM^a).$$

The actual expenditure components of GDP for the United Kingdom in 1993 are shown in Table 28.2.

GDP expenditure-based is the sum of consumption, investment, government, and net export expenditure on currently produced goods and services.

GDP income-based

The production of a nation's output generates income.

---

[3] Of course, the recipients of transfer payments spend their money on buying goods and services. Such spending then is measured as consumption expenditure, and thus as part of GDP, in the same way as any other consumption expenditure. We do not want to measure it twice, which is what we would be doing if we included both the government transfer and the spending by the recipient in GDP.

Table 28.2 Expenditure-based GDP and its components, 1993

Expenditure categories	£ million	% of GDP
1 Consumption	405,639	64.4
2 Government expenditure	138,224	21.9
3 Gross domestic fixed capital formation	94,715	
4 Increase in stocks and work in progress	– 197	
5 Gross investment (3) + (4)	94,518	15.0
6 Net exports	– 8,267	– 1.3
7 Statistical discrepancy	– 91	
GDP at market prices (Money GDP)	**630,023**	**100**
less taxes on expenditures	– 91,361	
plus subsidies	7,458	
GDP at factor cost	**546,120**	
GDP at market prices	£630,023	
Net property income from abroad	£3,062	
GNP at market prices	**£633,085**	

Expenditure-based GDP is made up of consumers' expenditure, government expenditure, investment, and net exports. Consumption is by far the largest expenditure category, equal to over 64 per cent of GDP; government accounted for just under 22 per cent and investment about 15 per cent. Whereas exports and imports are both quite large (each over 25 per cent of GDP), net exports are quite small; in 1993 they represented a mere (negative) 1.3 per cent of GDP. GDP at market prices is about 15 per cent more than GDP at factor cost. The difference is measured by net indirect taxes and represents the output of the economy that does not accrue to factors of production, but is transferred to other individuals. GNP at market prices is GDP at market prices plus net property income from abroad.

Source: CSO, National Income Blue Book 1994.

Labour must be employed, land must be rented, and capital must be used. The calculation of GDP from the income side involves adding up factor payments and other claims on the value of output until all of that value is accounted for. We have already noted that, because all value produced must be owned by someone, the value of production must equal the value of income claims generated by that production.

FACTOR PAYMENTS

National income accountants distinguish four main components of factor payments: income from employment, income from self-employment, rent, and profits.

Income from employment This consists of wages and salaries (which are usually just referred to as *wages*). It is the payment for the services of labour. Wages include take-home pay, taxes withheld, national insurance contributions, pension fund contributions, and any other fringe benefits. In other words, wages are measured gross. In total, wages represent that part of the value of production that is attributable to hired labour.[4]

Income from self-employment This category covers those people who are earning a living by selling their services or output but who are not employed by any one organization. It includes some consultants and those who work on short contracts but are not formally employees of an incorporated business. The income of the self-employed is little different in principle from employment income, though some of it could be thought of as profit rather than wages.

Rent Rent is the payment for the services of land and other factors that are rented. A major problem arises with housing. For the purposes of national income accounting, home owners are viewed as renting accommodation from themselves. The amount of rent in GDP thus includes payments for rented housing plus 'imputed rent' for the use of owner-occupied housing.

Profits Profits are net business incomes after payment has been made to hired labour and for material inputs. Some profits are paid out as **dividends** to owners of firms; the rest are retained for use by firms. The former are called *distributed profits*, and the latter are called *undistributed profits* or *retained earnings*. Both distributed and undistributed profits are included in the calculation of GDP.

Profits and rent together represent the payment for the use of the nation's capital (including land).

The various components of the income side of the GDP in the UK economy in 1993 are shown in Table 28.3. Note that one of the terms in the table is 'statistical discrepancy'. This is a small 'fudge factor' (which also appears with different value in Tables 28.1 and 28.2). It is there to make sure that the independent measures of income and product come to the same total. The statistical discrepancy is a clear indication that national income and product accounting is not error-free. It should also be noted that the term 'Stock appreciation' in Table 28.3 is not simply negative depreciation. Stock appreciation relates to valuation gains which firms receive when the goods they are holding go up in value. These capital gains add to profit but are not part of current output, so they are deducted from the sum of incomes when we measure GDP.

---

[4] The concepts of wages, rent, and profits that are used in macroeconomics do not correspond to the concepts with the same names that are used in microeconomics, but the details of the differences need not detain us.

GDP at factor cost The sum of the four components of factor incomes—wages, self-employment incomes, rent, and profits—is called **gross domestic product at factor cost**. It represents the share of total production that goes as income to the factors of production, labour, land, and capital. Notice that the measure of GDP arrived at in Table 28.3 is different from what we have labelled GDP (at market prices) in Table 28.2. This is because we have to take account of what is sometimes called the tax wedge.

NON-FACTOR PAYMENTS

Indirect taxes Taxes that are levied on transactions in goods and services are known as **indirect taxes**. They are contrasted with **direct taxes**, which are levied on a person's income or wealth independently of how such income is spent. When using incomes to calculate GDP, we distinguish between total income valued *at factor cost* and total income valued *at market prices*. The difference between the two is created by two intervening payments: indirect taxes and subsidies.

Suppose you spend £117.50 on a meal in a restaurant—hopefully for more than one person. Only £100 will be kept by the restaurant owner to cover costs of food, wages, etc.; the rest will go to the government in the form of value added tax, at the current rate of 17.5 per cent. (In earlier times, the tax might have been purchase tax, or what some countries today call sales tax.) A few goods, such as beer and cigarettes, have an additional tax on them known as excise duty. Clearly, whatever the indirect tax is called, its effect is to create a difference between what consumers actually spend and what is received by producers. The market price of a product is greater than the sum received by the factors of production (including in factor rewards all material and labour costs as well as profit).

Subsidies Some products have a government subsidy. The existence of a subsidy means that the market price may be less than the total rewards to factors. Conceptually, a subsidy is just a negative tax, though the way it is provided may make it hard to express as a tax rate. Suppose that a product costs £120 to make (including all input costs and profit) but sells in the shops for £100, with the other £20 being paid by the government: total factor rewards per unit exceed the market price.

Gross domestic product at market prices Adding indirect taxes to the four components of factor incomes (gross domestic product at factor cost) and subtracting subsidies gives the income-based measure of **gross domestic product at market prices**. Taxes and subsidies are sometimes combined into a single term, called *indirect taxes net of subsidies*.

Gross domestic product at market prices equals the sum of wages, income from self-employment, rent, profits, and indirect taxes net of subsidies.

Arriving at a measure of national output via the expenditure route leads naturally to the concept of GDP at market prices, since ultimate purchasers do pay out indirect taxes. Approaching the measure of GDP from the income or production side leads more naturally to GDP at factor cost, since this is what is received by factors of production. However, the former is the true measure of national output, since the latter excludes some output that is produced but that does accrue to factors. This difference is the indirect tax wedge, which is output taken by government and redistributed to individuals, but not on the basis of their factor inputs. For these reasons, GDP at market prices is the standard measure of the national product and national income. However, GDP at factor cost is a useful step on the road to measuring GDP at market prices from the data on factor rewards.

The difference between GDP at factor cost and GDP at market prices is illustrated in Table 28.2. It represents about 15 per cent of GDP (at factor cost). This is less than the VAT rate because not all goods—food, for example—are liable for VAT.

NET DOMESTIC PRODUCT

Depreciation The word 'gross' is in gross domestic product because no allowance has been made for depreciation. Depreciation, or capital consumption, is the value of capital that has been used up in the process of producing final output. It is part of gross profits, but, being that part needed to replace capital used up in the process of production, it is not part of *net* profits. Thus, depreciation is not income earned by any factor of production: instead it is value that must be reinvested just to maintain the existing stock of capital equipment. In the United Kingdom, factor incomes are normally reported before making allowance for depreciation.

Subtracting depreciation from gross domestic product gives **net domestic product**.

Net domestic product at factor cost, income-based, is the sum of the factor incomes that are generated in the process of producing final output *minus* depreciation.

Income produced and income received

GDP at market prices provides a measure of total output produced in the United Kingdom and of the total income generated as a result of that production. However, the total income received by UK residents differs from GDP, for two reasons. First, some domestic production creates factor earnings for non-residents who have previously invested in

Table 28.3   Components of GDP by income type, 1993

Income Type	£ million	% of GDP
Income from employment	352,896	64.6
Gross profits	81,048	14.8
Rent	52,872	9.7
Self employment	61,346	11.2
less stock appreciation	– 2,359	– 0.4
Statistical discrepancy	317	
GDP at factor cost	**546,120**	**100**

The income-based measure of GDP at factor cost is made up of income from employment, profits, rent, and income from self-employment (less stock appreciation). By far the largest income category is income from employment, which makes up nearly 65 per cent of GDP at factor cost. (Note that a figure of £3,942 million, which appears in the *Blue Book* as an imputed charge for consumption of non-trading capital, is included above under gross profits.)

Source: National Income Blue Book, 1994

the United Kingdom; on this account, income received by UK residents will be less than UK GDP. Second, many UK residents earn income on overseas investments; on this account, income received by UK residents will be greater than GDP.

While the GDP measures the output, and hence the income, that is *produced* in a country, the **gross national product, GNP**, measures the income that is *received* by a country. To convert GDP into GNP, it is necessary to add income received by domestic residents from assets owned abroad and to subtract income paid out to non-residents who own assets in the country. The difference between GDP and GNP is *net property income from abroad.*

Total output produced in the economy, measured by GDP, differs from total income received, measured by GNP, because of net property income from abroad.

Reconciling GDP with GNP   Table 28.2 shows the reconciliation of GDP with GNP. GNP is greater than GDP, but only by less than 0.5 per cent. This reflects slightly greater income from foreign assets held by UK residents than is being paid out to foreigners from their assets held in the United Kingdom. Clearly, GNP could be smaller than GDP if outward payments were greater than property income from abroad. Broadly speaking, countries that are net

debtors are likely to have a GNP lower than GDP, while countries that are net creditors are likely to have a GNP that exceeds GDP.

Figure 28.1 provides a visual representation of the information in Tables 28.1–28.3. It shows both the relations between GDP at (factor cost) and market prices, and the difference between GDP and GNP (at factor cost). Components of the three possible decompositions of GDP are also displayed.

Other income concepts

GDP and GNP (both at market prices) are the most commonly used concepts of national output and national income. Net domestic product is another not-uncommon measure. As we saw in building up the income approach, this is GDP minus the capital consumption allowance (depreciation). Net domestic product is thus a measure of the net output of the economy after deducting from gross output the amount needed to maintain intact the existing stock of capital. It is the maximum amount that could be consumed (out of domestic production) without running down the economy's capital stock. The term 'national income' used to have a very specific meaning in British national accounts: it was the net national product—GNP minus depreciation. However, this usage has gone out of fashion, and national income is now loosely used to refer to any of the standard national product measures. We also use 'national income' in this general sense. Once we move on to theory, it will be safe to assume that national income or national product are equivalent and refer to GDP at market prices unless told otherwise.

Personal income is income that is earned by or paid to individuals (the personal sector[5]) before allowing for personal income taxes on that income. Some personal income goes for taxes, some goes for savings, and the rest goes for consumption. **Personal disposable income** is the amount of current income that individuals have available for spending and saving; it is personal income minus personal income taxes and national insurance contributions.

Personal disposable income is GNP *minus* any part of it that is not actually paid to the personal sector (such as retained profits) minus personal income taxes plus transfer payments received by individuals.

[5] The UK personal sector actually contains some unincorporated businesses and non-profit organizations like charities. So in practice, it is not just the behaviour of private individuals that is being measured.

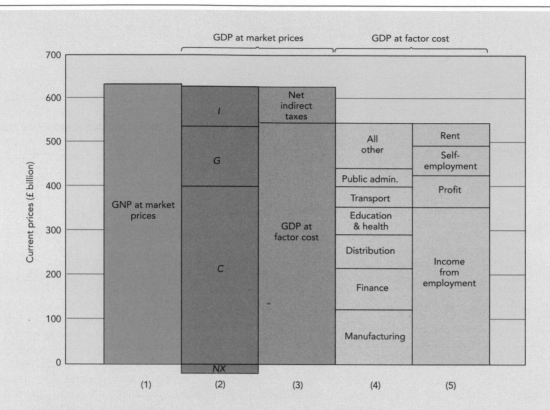

Figure 28.1 UK national income and output measures, 1993

Measurement of national income and output can be approached in three different ways, but they are all related. The figure shows the actual UK aggregates GNP at market prices, GDP at market prices, and GDP at factor cost for 1993. Column (1) is GNP at market prices. Columns (2) and (3) add up to GDP at market prices. Columns (4) and (5) add up to GDP at factor cost.

Column (1) (GNP) exceeds column (2) (GDP) by about 0.5 per cent. This difference is net property income from abroad. In 1993 this was positive but very small, so GNP and GDP were almost identical. Column (2) shows that GDP is made up of the expenditure components: consumption (*C*), investment (*I*), government spending (*G*), and net exports (*NX*). Notice that in 1993 net exports were negative, so *NX* has to be subtracted from the sum *C* + *I* + *G* to arrive at GDP. Column (3) shows that GDP at factor cost is equal to GDP at market prices minus net indirect taxes (indirect taxes less subsidies).

Column (4) shows that GDP at factor cost is made up of the sum of the values added of each of the production sectors of the economy; manufacturing, for example, produces nearly 22 per cent of GDP at factor cost. Column (5) shows that GDP at factor cost can also be broken down by income type. Income from employment amounts to about 65 per cent of this.

GDP at *market prices* is the 'true' measure of the output produced by the country as this is the value of goods available for consumption or investment. This exceeds GDP *at factor cost* because some of net output is redistributed by the government and does not accrue as a factor reward. Thus, GDP at factor cost is an underestimate of total current output, so long as net indirect taxes are positive.

Source: National Income Blue Book, 1994.

Interpreting national income measures

THE information provided by national income data is useful, but unless it is carefully interpreted it can be misleading. Furthermore, each of the specialized measures gives different information. Thus, each such measure may be the best statistic for studying a particular range of problems. Any statistical measure will be determined partly by some arbitrary decisions that might have been decided in another way. Some of these are discussed further in Box 28.2. The most important matters of interpretation will be dealt with now.

Real and nominal measures

In Chapter 27, we distinguished between real and nominal measures of national income and output. We learned that, when we add up money values of outputs, expenditures, or incomes, we end up with what are called *nominal values*. Suppose that we found that a measure of nominal GDP had risen by 70 per cent between 1980 and 1990. If we wanted to compare *real GDP* in 1990 with that in 1980, we would need to determine how much of that 70 per cent nominal

---

BOX 28.2

The significance of arbitrary decisions

National income accounting practices contain many arbitrary decisions. Goods that are finished and held in inventories are valued at market value, thereby anticipating their sale, even though the actual sales price may not be known. In the case of a Ford in a dealer's showroom, this practice may be justified, because the *value* of this car is perhaps virtually the same as that of an identical Ford that has just been sold to a customer. However, what is the correct market value of a half-finished house or an unfinished novel? Accountants arbitrarily treat goods in process at cost (rather than at market value) if the goods are being made by business firms. They ignore completely the value of the novel-in-progress. The arbitrary nature of these decisions is inevitable: Because people must arrive at some practical compromise between consistent definitions and measurable magnitudes, any decision will be somewhat arbitrary.

The definition of final goods provides further examples. Business investment expenditures are treated as final products, as are all government purchases. Intermediate goods purchased by businesses for further processing are not treated as final products. Thus, when a firm buys a machine or a lorry, the purchase is treated as a final good; when it buys a ton of steel, the steel is treated as a raw material that will be used as an input into the firm's production process. If the steel sits in inventory, however, it is regarded as a business investment and thus *is* a final good.

Such arbitrary decisions surely affect the size of measured GDP. Does it matter? The surprising answer is, for many purposes, no. In any case, it is wrong to believe that, just because a statistical measure falls short of perfection (as all statistical measures do), it is useless. Crude measures often give estimates to the right order of magnitude, and substantial improvements in sophistication may make only second-order improvements in these estimates.

In the third century BC, for example, the Alexandrian astronomer Eratosthenes measured the angle of the sun at Alexandria at the moment that it was directly overhead 500 miles south at Aswan, and he used this angle to calculate the circumference of the earth to within 15 per cent of the distance as measured today by the most advanced measuring devices. For the knowledge he wanted—the approximate size of the earth—his measurement was satisfactory, even though it would have been disastrously inadequate for launching a modern earth satellite.

Absolute figures mean something in general terms, although they cannot be taken seriously to the last pound. In 1993, UK GDP was measured as £630 billion. It is certain that the market value of all production in the United Kingdom in that year was neither £10 billion nor £10,000 billion, but it might well have been £600 billion or £650 billion had different measures been defined with different arbitrary decisions built in.

International and intertemporal comparisons, though tricky, may be meaningful if they are based on measures that contain roughly the same arbitrary decisions. Britain's per capita GDP is a little more than a third higher than the Spanish per capita GDP and about 20 per cent lower than the Japanese per capita GDP. Other measures might differ, but it is unlikely that any measure would reveal that the Spanish per capita GDP was higher than UK per capita GDP. UK output grew at about 2.2 per cent per year from 1983 to 1993; it is unlikely that another measure of output would have indicated a 6 per cent rate of increase. Japanese output grew at about 4 per cent per year over the same period. It is unlikely that another measure would change the conclusion that Japanese national output rose faster than UK national output during the decade in question.

increase was due to increases in prices and how much was due to increases in quantities produced. Although there are many possible ways of doing this, the basic principle is always the same. It is to compute the value of output, expenditure, and income in each period by using a common set of *base-period prices*. When this is done, we speak of real output, expenditure, or income as being measured in *constant pounds*, or, say, *1990 prices*.

GDP valued at current prices, i.e. money GDP, is a nominal measure. GDP valued at base-period prices is a real measure—in effect, an index number of the volume of national output and national income.

Any *change* in nominal GDP reflects the combined effects of changes in quantities and changes in prices. However, when real income is measured over different periods by using a common set of base-period prices, changes in real income reflect only changes in real output.

THE IMPLICIT DEFLATOR

If nominal and real GDP change by different amounts over some time period, this must be because prices have changed over that period. Comparing what has happened to nominal and real GDP over the same period implies the existence of a price index measuring the change in prices over that period. We say 'implies' because no price index was used in calculating real and nominal GDP. However, an index can be inferred by comparing these two values. Such an index is called an *implicit price index* or an *implicit deflator*. It is defined as follows:

$$\text{Implicit deflator} = \frac{\text{GDP at current prices}}{\text{GDP at base-period prices}} \times 100\%.$$

The implicit GDP deflator is the most comprehensive index of the price level, because it covers all the goods and services that are produced by the entire economy. Although some other indexes use fixed weights, implicit deflators are variable-weight indexes. They use the current year's 'bundle' of production to compare the current year's prices with those prevailing in the base period. Thus, the 1994 deflator uses 1994 output weights, and the 1995 deflator uses 1995 output weights. Box 28.3 illustrates the calculation of real and nominal national income and an implicit deflator for a simple hypothetical economy that produces only wheat and steel.

A change in any nominal measure of national income can be split into a change due to prices and a change due to quantities. For example, in 1993 UK nominal GDP ('money' GDP) was 5.4 per cent higher than in 1992. This increase was due to a 3.5 per cent increase in prices and a 1.9 per cent increase in real GDP. Table 28.4 gives nominal and real GDP and the implicit deflator for selected years since 1900.

Table 28.4   Nominal and real GDP at market prices, 1900–1993

Year	Money GDP (£ billion)	Real GDP (1990 prices)	Implicit GDP deflator (1990=100)
1900	1.9	109.5	1.7
1930	4.7	138.6	3.4
1950	13.1	200.4	6.5
1970	51.6	350.9	14.7
1980	231.2	426.8	54.2
1993	630.0	548.6	115.0

The data in the table are money GDP, real GDP, and the implicit GDP price deflator for selected years. The first column shows that money (nominal) GDP increased 330-fold between 1900 and 1993. However, the second column shows that there was only a five-fold increase in real GDP over the same period. The difference between the two is accounted for by the final column, which shows that the implicit price deflator for GDP rose 67-fold in this century. Since 1950, real GDP has increased 2.7-fold while the GDP price deflator has increased about 18-fold.

Sources: Economic Trends and *100 Years of Economic Statistics, The Economist,* 1989.

International comparisons of national income

One purpose to which national income measures are often put is for international comparisons of living standards or real income. It is natural to want to know if people are better-off in the United Kingdom or in, say, Germany. However, comparisons using measures such as GDP must be conducted with great care. We shall see below that there are many dimensions to living standards which are not measured by GDP or GNP. For some purposes, we may want to compare the absolute size of one economy relative to another, but normally we are interested in how well-off the average individual is in each country. For this purpose, we want to look at GDP per head or per capita (or perhaps at GNP per capita). To get this figure, we divide GDP by the total population of the country. This tells us the share of total national income that is available for the average citizen.

GDP in each country is measured in the local currency. So, to make comparisons, we have to convert different countries' nominal GDPs into the same currency. To do this, we have to use an exchange rate. This is problematic because exchange rates fluctuate, sometimes dramatically. In September 1992, for example, the exchange rate between US dollars and the UK pound moved from nearly $2 per pound to $1.5 per pound in a short time. Would we be happy to conclude that real UK incomes had fallen, relative

BOX 28.3

Calculation of nominal and real national income

To see what is involved in calculating nominal national income, real national income, and the implicit deflator, an example may be helpful. Consider a simple hypothetical economy that produces only two commodities, wheat and steel. Table (i) gives the basic data for output and prices in the economy for two years.

Table (i)   Data for a hypothetical economy

	Quantity produced		Prices	
	Wheat (bushels)	Steel (tons)	Wheat (£ per bu.)	Steel (£ per ton)
Year 1	100	20	10	50
Year 2	110	16	12	55

Table (ii) shows nominal national income, calculated by adding the money values of wheat output and of steel output for each year. In year 1 the value of both wheat and steel production was £1,000, so nominal income was £2,000. In year 2 wheat output rose, and steel output fell; the value of wheat output rose to £1,320, and that of steel fell to £880. Since the rise in value of wheat was greater than the fall in value of steel, nominal income rose by £200.

Table (ii)   Calculation of nominal national income

Year 1 (100 x 10) + (20 x 50) = £2,000
Year 2 (110 x 12) + (16 x 55) = £2,200

Table (iii) shows real national income, calculated by valuing output in each year by year 2 prices; that is, year 2 becomes the base year for weighting purposes. In year 2 wheat output rose, but steel output fell. Using year 2 prices, the value of the fall in steel output between years 1 and 2 exceeded the value of the rise in wheat output, and real national income fell.

Table (iii)   Calculation of real national income using year 2 prices

Year 1 (100 x 12) + (20 x 55) = £2,300
Year 2 (110 x 12) + (16 x 55) = £2,200

In Table (iv) the ratio of nominal to real national income is calculated for each year and multiplied by 100. This ratio implicitly measures the change in prices over the period in question and is called the *implicit deflator* or *implicit price index*. The implicit deflator shows that the price level increased by 15 per cent between year 1 and year 2.

Table (iv)   Calculation of implicit deflator

Year 1 (2,000/2,300) x 100 = 86.96
Year 2 (2,200/2,200) x 100 = 100.00

In Table (iv) we used year 2 as the base year for comparison purposes, but we could have used year 1. The implicit deflator would then have been 100 in year 1 and 115 in year 2, and the increase in price level would still have been 15 per cent. Or, the base year could be some earlier year. No matter what year is picked as the year in which the index had a value of 100, however, the change in the implicit deflator between year 1 and year 2 is 15 per cent.

to real US incomes, by 25 per cent? Even in normal conditions, it is not unusual for exchange rates to move by 10 per cent in a few days, but the move could easily be reversed a little later.

To solve the problem of making comparisons using unreliable or untypical exchange rates, economists make comparisons of national income using what they think are equilibrium exchange rates. These are estimated on the basis of what they think the exchange rate between two countries ought to be at a certain time if their economies had fully adjusted to their known economic environment. One approximation to the *equilibrium* exchange rates is the *purchasing power parity (PPP)* rate. This is the exchange rate that equates the prices of a representative bundle of goods in two countries. We shall discuss this concept more fully in Chapter 37.

Some comparisons of GDP per capita in 13 different countries (using PPP exchange rates) are given in Table 28.5. Figures are all expressed in US dollars. Several other indicators of material well-being are included in the table. Broadly speaking, they tell the same story as the GDP figures—the inhabitants of the richer countries can purchase more goods and services and tend to have a longer life expectancy. However, the rankings would be different for each possible indicator of well-being. The significance of this is that GDP per capita contains some useful information but there may be other important indicators which could tell a somewhat different story.

Table 28.5 International comparisons of living standards

	GDP per head (US$ 1991)	Real GDP growth: annual average (1983–92)	Telephones per 100 (1991)	Cars per 1,000 (1990)	Infant mortality per 1,000 live births (1991)	TVs per 1,000 (1991)	Life expectancy at birth (1991)	Doctors per 100,000 (1990)
USA	22,130	2.7	45	589	9	815	76	238
Germany	19,770	2.7	40	490	7	570	76	270
Japan	19,390	4.1	44	285	5	620	79	164
Canada	19,320	2.8	58	473	7	641	77	222
France	18,430	2.2	50	418	7	406	77	286
Australia	16,680	3.0	47	435	8	486	77	229
UK	16,340	2.2	44	403	7	435	75	164
Spain	12,670	3.2	32	308	8	396	77	357
Mexico	7,170	1.4	6	65	36	139	70	81
Russia	6,930	− 2.0	15	50	20	283	69	476
Brazil	5,240	1.9	6	104	58	213	66	93
China	1,680	9.4	1	2	38	31	69	99
India	1,150	5.2	1	2	90	32	60	41

The table shows eight different indicators of living standards for 13 countries. Most of the indicators tell the same story—wealthy countries have more goods and better life expectations. However, there are some interesting anomalies. Russia has more doctors per 100,000 people than any other country, yet life expectancy is the same as in China, which has only one-fifth as many doctors per person.

Source: The Economist, 25 December 1993.

What national income does not measure

National income measures the flow of economic activity in organized markets in a given year. But much economic activity takes place outside the markets that the national income accountants survey. Although these activities are not typically included in GDP or GNP, they nevertheless use real resources and satisfy real wants and needs.

Illegal activities GDP does not measure illegal activities, even though many of them are ordinary business activities that produce goods and services sold on the market and that generate factor incomes. Many forms of illegal gambling, prostitution, and drug trade come into this category. To gain an accurate measure of the *total* demand for factors of production in the economy, of *total* marketable output, or of total incomes generated, we should include these activities, whether or not we as individuals approve of them. The omission of illegal activities is no trivial matter: the drug trade alone is a multi-billion-pound business.[6]

Unreported activities A significant omission from measured GDP is the so-called 'underground' or 'black' economy. The transactions that occur in the underground economy are perfectly legal in themselves; the only illegality involved is that such transactions are not reported for tax purposes. One example of this is the carpenter who repairs a leak in your roof and takes payment in cash or in kind in order to avoid taxation. Because such transactions go unreported, they are omitted from GDP.

The growth of the underground economy is encouraged by the rising rates of taxation and is facilitated by the rising importance of services in the nation's total output. The higher the tax rates, the more there is to be gained by 'going underground'. It is also much easier for a self-employed carpenter or plumber to pass unnoticed by government authorities than it is for a manufacturing establishment.

Estimates of the scale of the underground economy show its importance growing in recent years. Estimates have put the UK underground economy at about 7 per cent of GDP. A recent Canadian study concluded that in 1992 15 per cent of Canadian GDP went unreported because it was produced in the underground economy. In other countries the figures are even higher. The Italian underground economy,

---

[6] Some illegal activities do get included in national income measures, although they are generally misclassified by industry. The income is included because people sometimes report their earnings from illicit activities as part of their earnings from legal activities. They do this to avoid the fate of Al Capone, a famous Chicago gangster in the 1920s and 1930s, who, having avoided conviction on many counts, was finally sent to prison for tax evasion.

BOX 28.4

....

GDP and economic growth

GDP is not a very good indicator of the long-term growth in welfare that accompanies long-term economic growth. The reason is that so many of the major benefits that growth provides are imperfectly measured, or not measured at all, by the GDP. This can be dramatically illustrated by looking at some of the most important changes that accompanied the first Industrial Revolution.

1. In early eighteenth century Europe, average life expectancy was around 30 years; in France, 1 in 5 children were dead by the end of the first year of life, and 50 per cent of registered children were dead by the age of 10! Life expectancy rose dramatically after the Industrial Revolution. In France today, infant mortality is only 7 per 1,000 live births and life expectancy at birth is 77 years.

2. Industrialization reduced famine and hunger. Not only did the average food intake rise, its year-to-year *variation* fell. It is of little consolation to a peasant that the average food consumption is above the subsistence level over the decades if fluctuations in harvests periodically drive it below the subsistence level, thus causing starvation.

3. The technological changes that accompanied the Industrial Revolution virtually eliminated many terrible diseases that had been common until that time, such as plague, tuberculosis, cholera, dysentery, smallpox, and leprosy.

4. The urbanization that accompanied industrialization increased literacy and other education, and broadened experience generally. In former times, poverty and a rural, peasant existence, with little or no communication between the village and the outside world, tended to encourage superstition, and restrict individual experience.

5. Privacy became possible when people moved from the one-room peasant dwelling, where the entire family lived, ate, and slept in one room, to multi-room urban dwellings.

6. The introduction of a market economy greatly increased the mobility of people among jobs. In the rural societies there are few options for employment, and customary behaviour—doing what one's parents did—dominated job selection.

7. The Industrial Revolution was based on mass production of goods sold mainly to low- and middle-income people. These changed the *quality* of consumption. For example, instead of wooden clogs, people adopted leather shoes; instead of rough, home-spun cloth, people had factory-made shirts and skirts; instead of mud floors and thatched roofs, people had wooden floors and slate roofs; instead of all living in one room, parents had a room separate from their children.

These things may seem trivial to us today, but they changed the way of life of ordinary people. Throughout the late eighteenth century and all of the nineteenth century, a succession of new products continued to alter the way ordinary people lived until, by the mid-twentieth century, the ordinary working person had a structurally different way of life from his or her counterpart in the mid-eighteenth century.

Statistics are the same whether a doubling of GDP takes the form of twice as much consumption of goods and services consumed before, or of new things that enhance the quality of life. The effect on living standards, however, is much greater when new commodities replace older ones rather than when more of the same ones become available.

Sources: J. Blum, *Our Forgotten Past: Seven Centuries of Life on the Land* (London: Thames & Hudson, 1982); F. Braudel, *Structures of Everyday Life, 15th–18th Century* (New York: Harper & Row, 1981); N. Rosenberg and L. E. Birdzell, Jr, *How The West Grew Rich* (New York: Basic Books, 1986).

---

for example, has been estimated at about 20 per cent of GDP; for Spain estimates are close to 25 per cent, and for Greece, 30 per cent!

Non-marketed activities If home owners hire a firm to do some landscaping, the value of the landscaping enters into GDP; if they do the landscaping themselves, the value of the landscaping is omitted from GDP. Other non-marketed activities include the services of those who do housework at home, any do-it-yourself activity, and voluntary work such as canvassing for a political party, helping to run a volunteer day-care centre, or coaching an amateur football team.

One important non-marketed activity is leisure itself. If a lawyer voluntarily chooses to work 2,200 hours a year instead of 2,400 hours, measured national income will fall by the lawyer's hourly wage rate times 200 hours. Yet the value to the lawyer of the 200 hours of new leisure, which is enjoyed outside of the market-place, must exceed the lost wages (because the leisure has been voluntarily chosen in preference to the extra work), so total economic welfare has risen rather than fallen. Until recently, one of the most important ways in which economic growth benefited people was by permitting increased amounts of time off work. Because the time off is not marketed, its value does not show up in measures of national income.

Economic bads When a coal-fired electricity generator sends sulphur dioxide into the atmosphere, leading to acid rain and environmental damage, the value of the electricity sold is included as part of GDP, but the value of the damage done by the acid rain is not deducted. Similarly, the petrol that we use in our cars is part of national income, but the damage done by burning that petrol is not deducted. To the extent that economic growth brings with it increases in pollution, congestion, and other disamenities of modern living, national income measures will overstate the value of the growth. They measure the increased economic output and income, but they fail to deduct the increased 'bads', or negative outputs, that generally accompany economic growth.

DO THE OMISSIONS MATTER?

GDP does a reasonable job of measuring the flow of goods and services through the market sector of the economy. Usually, an increase in GDP implies greater opportunities for employment for those households that sell their labour services in the market. Unless the importance of unmeasured economic activity changes rapidly, *changes* in GDP will do an excellent job of measuring *changes* in economic activity and economic opportunities. However, when the task at hand is measurement of the overall flow of goods and services available to satisfy people's wants, regardless of the source of the goods and services, then the omissions that we have discussed above become undesirable and potentially serious. Still, in the relatively short term, changes in GDP will usually be good measures of the direction, if not the exact magnitude, of changes in economic welfare.

The omissions cause serious problems when national income measures are used to compare living standards in structurally different economies, as was discussed above. Generally, the non-market sector of the economy is larger in rural than in urban settings and in less developed than in more developed economies. Be cautious, then, when interpreting data from a country with a very different climate and culture. When you hear that the per capita GDP of India is about US$1,150 per year, you should not imagine living in Manchester on that income. The average Indian is undoubtedly poorer than the average Briton, but perhaps not 14 times poorer, as the GDP figures suggest. The limitations of GDP are further considered in Box 28.4.

Is there a best measure of national income?

To ask which is *the* best income measure is like asking which is *the* best carpenter's tool. The answer depends on the job to be done. The decision concerning which measure to use will depend on the problem at hand, and solving some problems may require information provided by several different measures or information not provided by any conventional measures. If we wish to predict personal consumption behaviour, then personal disposable income may be the measure that we need to use. If we wish to account for changes in employment, then real GDP may be the measure that we want. For an overall measure of economic welfare, we may need to supplement or modify conventional measures of national income, none of which measures *the quality of life*.

Even if economists do develop new measures for some purposes, it is unlikely that GDP (and its relatives) will be discarded. Economists and policy-makers who are interested in changes in market activity and in employment opportunities for factors of production will continue to use GDP and other related measures because they are the ones that come closest to telling them what they need to know.

Summary

1 Each firm's contribution to total output is equal to its value added, which is the gross value of the firm's output minus the value of all intermediate goods and services—that is, the outputs of other firms—that it uses. Goods that count as part of the economy's output are called final goods; all others are called intermediate goods. The sum of all the value added produced in an economy is the economy's total output, which is called gross domestic product (GDP).

2 Gross domestic product (GDP) can be calculated in three different ways: (i) as the sum of all values added by all producers of both intermediate and final goods; (ii) as the expenditure needed to purchase all final goods and services produced during the period; and (iii) as the income claims generated by the total production of goods and services. By standard accounting conventions, these three aggregations define the same total.

3 From the expenditure side of the national accounts, $GDP = C^a + I^a + G^a + (X^a - IM^a)$. C^a comprises consumption expenditures of households. I^a is investment in fixed capital (including residential construction) and stock-building. Gross investment can be split into replacement investment (necessary to keep the stock of capital intact) and net investment (net additions to the stock of capital). G^a is government purchases of goods and services. $(X^a - IM^a)$ represents net exports, or exports minus imports; it will be negative if imports exceed exports.

4 GDP, income-based, adds up all factor rewards in production. Wages, income from self-employment, rent, and profits are the major categories. GDP at factor cost can be converted to GDP at market prices by adding indirect taxes net of subsidies. The deduction of depreciation, or capital consumption, converts gross domestic product into net domestic product (NDP).

5 UK GDP measures production that is located in the United Kingdom, and UK gross national product (GNP) measures income accruing to UK residents. The difference is due to net property income from overseas.

6 Real measures of national income are calculated to reflect changes in real quantities. Nominal measures of national income are calculated to reflect changes in both prices and quantities. Any change in nominal income can be split into a change in real income and a change due to prices. Appropriate comparisons of nominal and real measures yield implicit deflators.

7 Several related but different income measures are used in addition to GDP. Net domestic product measures total output after deducting the capital consumption allowance. Personal income is income received by individuals before personal taxes are deducted. Personal disposable income is the amount actually available for the personal sector to spend or to save—that is, income minus taxes.

8 GDP and related measures of national income must be interpreted with their limitations in mind. GDP excludes production resulting from activities that are illegal, that take place in the underground economy, or that do not pass through markets. Moreover, GDP does not measure everything that contributes to human welfare.

9 Notwithstanding its limitations, GDP remains a useful measure of the total economic activity that passes through the nation's markets and for explaining changes in the employment opportunities facing households that sell their labour services on the market.

Topics for review

- Value added
- GDP as the sum of all values added
- Intermediate and final goods
- Expenditure-based and income-based GDP
- GNP
- Personal disposable income
- Implicit deflator
- The significance of omissions from measured income

CHAPTER 29

Introduction to the theory of national income determination

WE now embark on the central task of macroeconomics: building a model of the economy as a whole. In Chapters 27 and 28, we encountered a number of important macroeconomic variables. We described how they are measured and how they have behaved in the past. We now turn to a more detailed study of what *causes* these variables to behave as they do, and how they are interrelated. In particular, we study the forces that determine national income (and hence employment and unemployment) and the price level.

It is important to realize that we are about to discuss *theory*. In this process, we will build up a conceptual model of the economy. The model will necessarily be simple. It needs to be simple so that we can understand how it works. In particular, we want to be able to answer questions like: what happens to national income when government spending is increased? or, under what conditions do we get inflation?

We shall proceed by starting from a very simple structure and then adding features to it as we go along. Some clearly stated assumptions will define our macroeconomic model. Some of these assumptions will be relaxed as we go along, others will remain throughout. The permanent or temporary nature of individual assumptions will be indicated as they are introduced.

Macroeconomics has been around, as a branch of economics, for over half a century. It has developed and changed a great deal in this time. It is going to take several chapters before we get close to understanding contemporary macroeconomics. Readers should be patient, therefore, and should not rush to draw policy conclusions too soon. By Chapter 39 we will have developed a powerful framework for analysis of current policy problems, but there are many small steps between here and there.

In this chapter we set out some of the conceptual foundations of macroeconomics. We then build the simplest possible model of national income determination, under some very special assumptions. Later chapters make our model increasingly realistic.

Key assumptions

IN the previous two chapters, we learned that national income and national output are the same thing. We also saw that we could arrive at a measure of GDP by three different routes. We could add up incomes of factors of production, we could add up the values added of each industrial sector, or we could add up total final expenditures. Now that we want to *explain* national income determination rather than just describing it, we have to decide which of these three classifications we are going to rely on to structure our theories. We shall learn very shortly that macroeconomics, as a subject, has developed by attempting to explain the major categories of final expenditure in the economy. We need to understand why this approach was adopted.

Suppose that we were to start our theory of national income by trying to explain the net output (value added) of each major industrial sector, such as manufacturing, agriculture, etc., as listed in Table 28.1. We could establish the capital stock and employment in each sector, and we could analyse demand forces for the output of each sector. In essence, we would be building a theory around demand and supply forces in each industry in the economy, and then we would add up the results to get total output.

One reason we do not do this in macroeconomics is that such an approach would not really be dealing with the aggregate economy at all. Models that explain output industry by industry do exist in economics, but they are microeconomic, and are not generally regarded as part of macroeconomics. Such models require so much detail that they make it difficult to handle many important issues that affect the whole economy simultaneously.

A second reason why we do not apply the tools of demand and supply on an industry-by-industry basis in macroeconomics is that the founders of macroeconomic theory thought that those tools were not appropriate for handling the important macro problems. In particular, macroeconomics as a subject was originally invented to explain why an economy might have unemployment and excess capacity for some time. In contrast, the microeconomic analysis of markets suggests that prices will move to clear markets. Macroeconomists also want to be able to study simultaneous (or near simultaneous) movements in output that are common to all sectors—the business cycle. An important question in macroeconomics is: what causes the business cycle, and can government policy stabilize it, that is, smooth out the cycles?

AGGREGATION ACROSS INDUSTRIES

In macroeconomics, we take the industrial structure of the

economy as fixed. When national output expands or contracts, all sectors expand and contract together. There is no consideration given to relative prices of different goods or services. In this respect, the economy is best thought of as being made up of many competitive firms, all producing the same type of product. These firms are all aggregated into a single productive sector. It is the behaviour of this single productive sector that will determine national output and national income.

In macroeconomics, we assume the existence of a single productive sector producing a homogeneous output.

This assumption will remain throughout our study of macroeconomics. We shall also analyse the behaviour of this single sector as if it were a manufacturing industry, though this is only a matter of convenience.

The fact that we assume a single production sector explains why we approach the determination of national income by focusing on expenditure categories: there are no subdivisions of output by type of product. However, an important implication for final expenditures is that, *in our model,* they are all spent on the same final good—the product of United Kingdom PLC. This means that, while different categories of expenditure may be differently motivated, they all have the same effect once implemented.

From time to time, we use concrete examples, such as: 'suppose the government increases spending on road building', or 'suppose firms decide to buy more machines (invest)'. The point to bear in mind is that all expenditures in the model have the same effect, once made, because they are all assumed in our model to be demands for the output of the single-product industrial sector. The only minor qualification to this general statement comes in Chapters 33 and 34 when we discuss growth. Here it is still true that the productive sector produces a single product. However, that product can be used in two ways. It can be consumed, and thereby used up, or it can be accumulated as increases in the capital stock. In effect, it is like seed corn, which can either be turned into bread and eaten, or be planted and turned into additional future output. For the rest of our discussion of macroeconomics, the capital stock is held constant, so all output is used up (consumed) in the current period—even that which is purchased through investment expenditure.[1]

The government sector Confusion can arise out of the assumption of a single sector when we come to discuss the role of government. In reality, part of government activity involves producing goods or services, such as health and education. However, in order to maintain the simplicity of the assumption that there is only one sector, in macroeconomics we ignore the fact that government is a producer and treat government as a purchaser of the output of the private industrial sector. In other words, we make no exceptions to our assumption about the homogeneity of productive activity so far as building a macro model is concerned. However, we do discuss what the government sector does in reality in Chapter 42.

Justification The extreme assumption that there is only one output is of course not meant as a description of reality. It is a theoretical abstraction meant to simplify our study without losing the essence of the problem in which we are interested. In this case, the one-product model captures the assumption that, for what we are interested in, the similarities between the effects of £1 spent in each sector of the real-world economy are more important than the differences. Note that it is only similarities with respect to the effects of expenditure that are in question. Causes of expenditure are not assumed to be the same. Indeed, much of our work is directed at developing consumption, investment, and net export functions that explain the *different* motives that determine the various expenditure flows.

Like all such simplifying assumptions, evaluation cannot be done by a priori reasoning. Only empirical observation can show whether a model based on the one-product assumption helps us to explain what we see in the real-world economy and to predict the consequences of various shocks that impinge on it. We will see throughout much of this book that often the answer is 'yes, it does'. In these cases, the similarities between the effects of the various expenditure flows will be more important than the differences.

In other cases, however, it is necessary to distinguish among some of the expenditure flows and to allow for different effects, say, on employment or on income. In such cases, the model needs to be extended to allow for these differences. We then speak of 'disaggregating' the flows to distinguish several sectors, in which, for example, capital–labour ratios may be different and some sectors may be operating at normal capacity while others have excess capacity. Macro models operate at various levels of disaggregation, running from two different sectors with different inputs and outputs to a hundred or more different sectors. As always, the test of each is pragmatic: does the cost of the added complexity pay off in terms of better understanding and predictions?

In this book, we stick with the theoretical model containing only one output. It is surprising how far that model

---

[1] It may seem strange to assume that investment expenditures are consumed. The justification is that investment in any one year is very small relative to the accumulated capital stock, and hence, for convenience, in the short run is presumed to leave the capital stock unchanged. In Chapter 33, we address capital accumulation explicitly. In practice, investment goods and consumer goods (and, indeed, the type of goods puchased by the government) are going to be different, but, since we do not have separate industries for each type of good in our model, they must all be treated as the same kind of output. Thus, *any* demand for final output is exactly the same as any other in terms of its repercussions on current national income.

can get us in understanding the real world. This is not because the real world has only one output, but because, in many circumstances, the differences between the effects of expenditure in each sector are unimportant relative to the similarities.

TIME SCALE

Macroeconomics has traditionally been concerned with the short-run behaviour of an economy, while growth theory has been concerned with long-run trends. In this book we discuss growth theory in the context of macroeconomics (Chapter 33), because it is clear that the trend is at least as important as the short-term fluctuations, even over relatively short time horizons. However, the point of this section is that the concepts of *short run* and *long run* have a different meaning in macroeconomics from the usage in microeconomics. Indeed, 'long run' itself will be used in two different senses, even within macroeconomics.

Short run   In microeconomics, 'short run' was used to analyse the behaviour of firms during the period in which their capital stock is taken as given and they can change only their variable inputs (labour and materials). In other words, the short run is a period during which the capital stock is fixed; none the less, firms are in equilibrium because they are producing their optimal output given their capital stock. In macroeconomics, the short run is a period during which the economy maintains a deviation of actual from potential output, or a GDP gap. It is associated with either the existence of excess capacity and unemployment, in the case of recession, or unsustainable output and inflation, in the case of a boom. In practice, the short run may be measured in terms of several years, so it is not necessarily short in the common-sense meaning of the term.

In its early days as a discipline, macroeconomics concentrated entirely on the short run, as we have just defined it. Recent developments, however, have restored a role for longer-run considerations.

Analysis of the short run in macroeconomics is concerned to explain why national output can deviate from its potential level. It is about the GDP gap and how to close it.

Long run   The long run is reached in macroeconomics when the economy returns to producing the level of potential (or full-employment) output. For analytical purposes (apart from in Chapters 33 and 34), we shall assume that the long-run level of output is constant and is associated with a fixed capital stock and a fixed level of technical knowledge. This contrasts markedly with the usage of 'long run' in microeconomics, where the term relates to a period long enough to permit the capital stock to vary. Thus, in macroeconomics there is really a 'long run' and a 'longer run', where the latter permits growth in productive capacity

and, therefore, growth in potential output. For the most part, we use the static concept of 'long run', unless we are explicitly discussing growth.

The long run in macroeconomics is the time period long enough for the economy to return to the level of potential GDP once it has been disturbed.

TEMPORARY ASSUMPTIONS

In order to get us started in building a theory of macroeconomics, we need to make a few additional assumptions, which will be relaxed in succeeding chapters.

The price level   At the outset, we shall assume that the price level, that is the money price of the output good produced by the economy, is fixed. All input prices are also fixed. Permitting the price level to vary simultaneously with output will be the main task addressed in Chapters 31 and 32. While the price level is held constant, all variables must necessarily be measured in real terms. But it is important to notice for the future that all expenditures (consumption, investment, government spending, and net exports) will continue to be defined in real terms, even when the price level is permitted to vary.

Excess capacity   Initially, we shall think of the economy as having excess capacity; it is not constrained from producing more output by shortage of capital stock or labour. In this context, the demand for output is the single determining factor. One reason we make this assumption is that this is the context in which macroeconomics as a subject got started. It was trying to explain how an economy could appear to get stuck (for some time at least) with high unemployment and excess capacity. When unemployment is approaching 20 per cent and GDP has fallen sharply, as in the early 1930s, this is a sensible assumption to make. It would not be regarded as a reasonable assumption when analysing an economy closer to potential output or full employment.

Another reason we start with the twin assumptions of a fixed price level and excess capacity is that it is a helpful simplification to begin in an environment where all changes in national income are changes in real national income. Explaining the division of increases in money GDP as between the price level and real GDP requires a more complicated model, which we come to in Chapter 31.

Closed economy   In this chapter alone, we shall ignore the fact that the output of our economy could be sold overseas and that domestic consumers could buy foreign produced goods. We assume an economy with no foreign trade, so domestic expenditure and domestic output are the same thing. This is not an assumption we shall need very long. It will be dropped in the next chapter.

No government A final simplifying assumption is that there is no government sector either demanding goods or raising money through taxes. (We have already made it clear that the government as a producer does not appear at any stage in our macro model, because, like everyone else, it is a purchaser of the single homogeneous product.) Again, we shall drop this assumption in the next chapter.

By now readers may be wondering what is left after we have assumed away so many potentially important things. It is worth summarizing all these assumptions. We have an economy with a single industrial sector, producing a homogeneous output, at a fixed price, in a closed economy, with no government. There is also excess capacity, so there are no resource constraints preventing the expansion of national output. What is left that we have not explicitly assumed away? The answer is: final demand, or expenditure

on the output of the economy. By explaining final expenditure, we are going to determine the national product and national income.

There is a very good reason for starting with an explanation of expenditure. This is that the original inventors of macroeconomics believed that the explanation of recessions was to be found in explaining *demand failure*, and even today we believe that sharp changes in aggregate demand can have major consequences for output and employment in the short run. Hence they focused explicitly on expenditure categories. The theory was not developed to explain these measures; rather, the way in which we measure these expenditure categories (see Table 28.2) was influenced by this theoretical reasoning.

Accordingly, we now turn to the task of explaining aggregate expenditure.

What determines aggregate expenditure?

BEFORE we can answer this question, we must deal with a few more important preliminaries.

SOME IMPORTANT PRELIMINARIES

From actual to desired expenditure In Chapter 28 we discussed how national income statisticians divide actual GDP, calculated from the expenditure side, into its components: consumption, investment, government, and net exports.

In this chapter and the next, we are concerned with a different concept. It is variously called *desired, planned*, or *intended* expenditure. Of course, all people would like to spend virtually unlimited amounts, if only they had the resources. Desired expenditure does not refer, however, to what people would like to do under imaginary circumstances; it refers to what people want to spend out of the resources that are at their command. The *actual* values of the various categories of expenditure are indicated by C^a, I^a, G^a, and $(X^a - IM^a)$. We use the same letters without the superscript *a* to indicate the *desired* expenditure in the same categories: C, I, G, and $(X - IM)$.

Everyone with income to spend makes expenditure decisions. Fortunately, it is unnecessary for our purposes to look at each of the millions of such individual decisions. Instead, it is sufficient to consider four main groups of deci-

sion-makers: individual consumers (or households), firms, governments, and foreign purchasers of domestic output. The actual purchases made by these four groups account for the four main categories of expenditure that we have studied in the previous chapter: consumption, investment, government, and net exports. Their desired expenditures, made up of desired consumption, desired investment, desired government purchases, and desired exports, account for total desired expenditure. (To allow for the fact that many of the commodities desired by each group will have an import content, we subtract expenditure on imports: see Chapter 28, p. 530.) The result is total desired expenditure on domestically produced goods and services, or **aggregate expenditure**, *AE*:

$$AE = C + I + G + (X - IM).$$

Desired expenditure need not equal actual expenditure, either in total or in any individual category. For example, firms may not plan to invest in the accumulation of stocks of finished goods this year but may do so unintentionally. If they produce goods to meet estimated sales but demand is unexpectedly low, the unsold goods that pile up on their shelves are undesired, and unintended, inventory accumulation. In this case, actual investment expenditure, I^a, will exceed desired investment expenditure, I.

National income accounts measure actual expenditure in each of the four categories: consumption, investment, government, and net exports. National income theory deals with desired expenditure in each of these four categories.

Recall, however, that these expenditure categories differ because different agents are doing the spending, and have different motivations for that spending. They are not different in the effects of their spending because they all generate spending on the final output of the single productive sector.

Autonomous and induced expenditure   In what follows, it will be useful to distinguish between *autonomous* and *induced* expenditure. Components of aggregate expenditure that do *not* depend on national income are called **autonomous expenditure,** or, sometimes, *exogenous* expenditure.[2] Autonomous expenditures can and do change, but such changes do not occur systematically in response to changes in national income. Components of aggregate expenditure that *do* change in response to changes in national income are called **induced expenditure,** or *endogenous* expenditure. As we will see, the induced response of aggregate expenditure to a change in national income plays a key role in the determination of equilibrium national income.

A simple model   To develop a theory of national income determination, we need to examine the determinants of each component of desired aggregate expenditure. In this chapter we focus on desired consumption and desired investment. Consumption is the largest single component of aggregate expenditure (about 65 per cent of UK GDP in 1993), and as we will see, it provides the single most important link between desired aggregate expenditure and national income. Investment is national income that is not used either for current consumption or by governments, and it is an important determinant of potential income in the future (though see footnote 1).

Desired consumption expenditure

We are now ready to study the determinants of desired expenditure flows. We start with consumption.

People can do one of two things with their disposable income: they can spend it on consumption, or they can save it. **Saving** is all disposable income that is not consumed.

By definition, there are only two possible uses of disposable income: consumption or saving. So when each individual decides how much to put to one use, he or she has automatically decided how much to put to the other use.

What determines the division between the amount that

people decide to spend on goods and services for consumption and the amount that they decide to save? The factors that influence this decision are summarized in the consumption function and the saving function.

THE CONSUMPTION FUNCTION

The **consumption function** relates the total desired consumption expenditure of the personal sector to the factors that determine it. It is, as we shall see, one of the central relationships in macroeconomics.

Although we are ultimately interested in the relationship between consumption and *national* income, the underlying behaviour of consumers depends on the income that they actually have to spend—their *disposable* income. Under the simplifying assumptions that we have made in this chapter, there are no taxes. All income that is generated is received by individuals.[3] Therefore, disposable income, which we denote by Y_d, is equal to national income, Y. (Later in our discussion, Y and Y_d will diverge, because taxes are a part of national income that is not at the disposal of individuals.)

CONSUMPTION AND DISPOSABLE INCOME

It should not surprise us to hear that a consumer's expenditure is related to the amount of income available. There is, however, more than one way in which this relationship could work. To see what is involved, consider two quite different types of individual.

The first behaves like the proverbial prodigal son. He spends everything he receives and puts nothing aside for a rainy day. When overtime results in a large pay cheque, he goes on a binge. When it is hard to find work during periods of slack demand, his pay cheque is small and his expenditures have to be cut correspondingly. This person's expenditure each week is thus directly linked to each week's take-home pay, that is, to his current disposable income.

The second individual is a prudent planner. She thinks about the future as much as the present, and makes plans that stretch over her lifetime. She puts money aside for retirement and for the occasional rainy day when disposable income may fall temporarily—she knows that she must expect some hard times as well as good times. She also knows that she will need to spend extra money while her children are being raised and educated and that her disposable income will probably be highest later in life when the children have left home and she has finally reached the peak of her career. This person may borrow to meet higher expenses earlier in life, paying back out of the higher income that she expects to attain later in life. A temporary, unexpected windfall of income may be saved. A temporary,

---

[2] 'Autonomous' means self-motivated, or independent. 'Exogenous' means determined outside the model.

[3] We are assuming here that all firms pass on all their profits to the persons who own them, so there is no retained profit.

unexpected shortfall may be cushioned by spending the savings that were put aside for just such a rainy day. In short, this person's current expenditure will be closely related to her expected average *lifetime income*. Fluctuations in her *current income* will have little effect on her current expenditure, unless such fluctuations also cause her to change her expectations of lifetime income, as would be the case, for example, if an unexpected promotion came along.

John Maynard Keynes (1883–1946), the famous English economist who developed the basic theory of macroeconomics—and, incidentally, gave his name to 'Keynesian economics'—peopled his theory with prodigal sons. For them, current consumption expenditure depended only on current income. To this day, a consumption function based on this assumption is called a *Keynesian consumption function*.

Later two US economists, Franco Modigliani and Milton Friedman, both of whom were subsequently awarded the Nobel Prize in economics, analysed the behaviour of prudent consumers. Their theories, which Modigliani called

the *life-cycle theory* and which Friedman called *the permanent income theory*, explain some observed consumer behaviour that cannot be explained by the Keynesian consumption function. (For more details, see the Appendix to this chapter.)

However, the differences between the theories of Friedman and Modigliani, on the one hand, and Keynes, on the other, are not as great as it might seem at first sight. To see why this is so, let us return to our two imaginary individuals and see why their actual behaviour may not be quite so divergent as we have described it.

Even the prodigal son may be able to do some smoothing of expenditure in the face of income fluctuations. Most people have some money in the bank and some ability to borrow, even if it is just from friends and relatives. As a result, not every income fluctuation will be matched by an equivalent expenditure fluctuation.

In contrast, although the prudent person wants to smooth her pattern of consumption completely, she may not have the borrowing capacity to do so. Her bank may not be willing to lend money for consumption when the

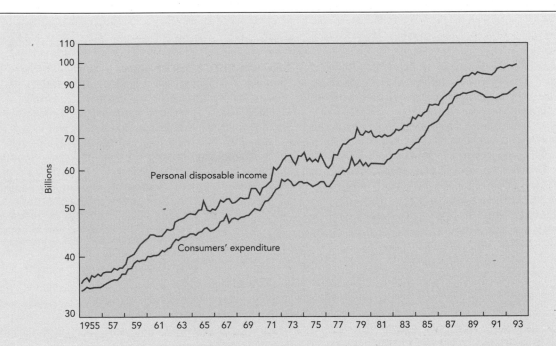

Figure 29.1 Consumers' expenditure and personal disposable income, United Kingdom, 1955–1993 (£ billion at constant prices, seasonally adjusted)

Consumer spending and income are closely related over time. The chart shows real consumption expenditure and real personal disposable income since 1955. Notice that the vertical axis has a log scale. This means that a constant growth rate appears as a straight line. The trend rate of growth of disposable income and consumption in real terms is between 2 and 2.5 per cent.

Source: Datastream.

Table 29.1 The calculation of average propensity to consume (APC) and marginal propensity to consume (MPC) (£ million)

(1) Disposable income (Y_d)	(2) Desired consumption (C)	(3) $APC = C/Y_d$	(4) Change in Y_d (ΔY_d)	(5) Change in C (ΔC)	(6) $MPC = \Delta C/\Delta Y_d$
0	100	—			
100	180	1.800	100	80	0.80
400	420	1.050	300	240	0.80
500	500	1.000	100	80	0.80
1,000	900	0.900	500	400	0.80
1,500	1,300	0.867	500	400	0.80
1,750	1,500	0.857	250	200	0.80
2,000	1,700	0.850	250	200	0.80
3,000	2,500	0.833	1,000	800	0.80

APC measures the proportion of disposable income that households desire to spend on consumption; *MPC* measures the proportion of any increment to disposable income that households desire to spend on consumption. The data are hypothetical. We call the level of income at which desired consumption equals disposable income the break-even level; in this example it is £500 million. *APC*, calculated in the third column, exceeds unity—that is, consumption exceeds income—below the break-even level; above the break-even level, *APC* is less than unity. It is negatively related to income at all levels of income. The last three columns are set between the lines of the first three columns to indicate that they refer to *changes* in the levels of income and consumption. *MPC*, calculated in the last column, is constant at 0.80 at all levels of Y_d. This indicates that, in this example, £0.80 of every additional £1.00 of disposable income is spent on consumption, and £0.20 is used to increase saving.

security consists of nothing more than the expectation that income will be much higher in later years. This may mean that, in practice, her consumption expenditure fluctuates more with her current income than she would wish.

This suggests that the consumption expenditure of both types of individual will fluctuate to some extent with their current disposable incomes and to some extent with their expectations of future disposable incomes. Moreover, in any economy there will be some people of both extremes—spendthrifts and planners—and aggregate consumption will be determined by a mix of the two types. As we develop our basic theory, we will often find it useful to make the simplifying assumption that consumption expenditure is determined primarily by current disposable income. That is, we will often use a Keynesian consumption function and then indicate how things change if we consider more sophisticated theories of consumer spending. Figure 29.1 shows UK personal disposable income and consumers' expenditure since 1955. It is clear that the two series are closely related.

The term *consumption function* describes the relationship between consumption and the variables that influence it; in the simplest theory, consumption is determined primarily by current disposable income.

When income is zero, a typical individual will still (via borrowing, or drawing down savings) consume some minimal amount.[4] This level of consumption expenditure is

autonomous because it persists even when there is no income. The higher a person's income, the more that person will want to consume. This part of consumption is *induced*; that is, it varies with disposable income and hence, in our simple model, with national income.

Consider the schedule relating disposable income to desired consumption expenditure for a hypothetical economy that appears in the first two columns of Table 29.1. In this example, autonomous consumption expenditure is fixed at £100 million throughout. Induced consumption is 80 per cent of disposable income, and so increases as income increases. In what follows we use this hypothetical example to illustrate the various properties of the consumption function.

Average and marginal propensities to consume   To discuss the consumption function concisely, economists use two technical expressions.

The **average propensity to consume** (*APC*) is total consumption expenditure divided by total disposable income: $APC = C/Y_d$. The third column of Table 29.1 shows the

[4] Many individuals have no income but continue to consume, for example such as dependent children or non-working spouses. In this case there is normally at least one earner in a household, and it is the household income that is relevant. The household would be the decision unit in that context. Such distinctions are important if we want to study the behaviour of individual spending units, but they are not critical in macroeconomics, which studies the aggregate behaviour of all consumers and relates their total spending to their total income.

APC calculated from the data in the table. Note that *APC* falls as disposable income rises.

The **marginal propensity to consume (*MPC*)** relates the *change* in consumption to the *change* in disposable income that brought it about. *MPC* is the change in disposable income divided into the resulting consumption change: $MPC = \Delta C/\Delta Y_d$ (where the Greek letter Δ, delta, means 'a change in'). The last column of Table 29.1 shows the *MPC* that corresponds to the data in the table. Note that, by construction, the *MPC* is constant.

The slope of the consumption function Part (i) of Figure 29.2 shows a graph of the consumption function, derived by plotting consumption against income using data from the first two columns of Table 29.1. The consumption function has a slope of $\Delta C/\Delta Y_d$, which is, by definition, the marginal propensity to consume. The positive slope of the consumption function shows that the *MPC* is positive; increases in income lead to increases in expenditure.

Using the concepts of the average and marginal propensities to consume, we can summarize the assumed properties of the short-term consumption function as follows:

1. There is a break-even level of income at which *APC* equals unity. Below this level, *APC* is greater than unity; above it, *APC* is less than unity. Below the break-even level consumption exceeds income, so consumers run down savings or borrow. Above the break-even level, income exceeds consumption, so there is positive saving.

2. *MPC* is greater than zero but less than unity for all levels of income. This means that, for each additional £1 of income, less than £1 is spent on consumption and the rest is saved. For a straight-line consumption function, the *MPC* is constant at all levels of income.

The 45° line Figure 29.2(i) contains a line that is constructed by connecting all points where desired consumption (measured on the vertical axis) equals disposable income (measured on the horizontal axis). Because both axes are given in the same units, this line has a positive slope of unity; that is, it forms an angle of 45° with the axes. The line is therefore called the **45° line.**

The 45° line makes a handy reference line. In part (i) of Figure 29.2 it helps to locate the break-even level of income at which consumption expenditure equals disposable income. The consumption function cuts the 45° line at the break-even level of income—in this instance (see Table 29.1) at £500 million. (The 45° line is steeper than the consumption function because the *MPC* is less than unity.)

THE SAVING FUNCTION

Individuals decide how much to consume and how much to save. As we have said, this is a single decision: how to divide disposable income between consumption and sav-

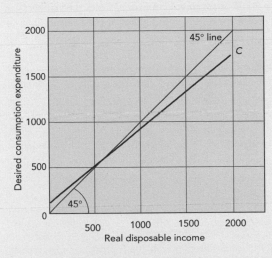

(i) Consumption function (£ million)

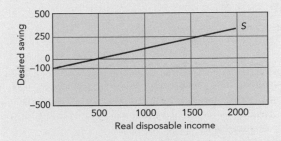

(ii) Saving function (£ million)

Figure 29.2 The consumption and saving functions

Both consumption and saving rise as disposable income rises. Line *C* in part (i) relates desired consumption expenditure to disposable income by using the hypothetical data from Table 29.1. Its slope, $\Delta C/\Delta Y_d$, is the marginal propensity to consume (*MPC*). The consumption line cuts the 45° line at the break-even level of disposable income, £500 million in this case. Note that the level of autonomous consumption is £100 million.

Saving is all disposable income that is not spent on consumption ($S = Y_d - C$). The relationship between desired saving and disposable income is derived in Table 29.2, and it is shown in part (ii) by line *S*. Its slope, $\Delta S/\Delta Y_d$, is the marginal propensity to save (*MPS*). The saving line cuts the horizontal axis at the break-even level of income. The vertical distance between *C* and the 45° line in part (i) is by definition the height of *S* in part (ii); that is, any given level of disposable income must be accounted for by the amount consumed plus the amount saved. Note that the level of autonomous saving is –£100 million. This means that at zero income consumers will draw down existing assets by £100 million a year.

Table 29.2   Consumption and saving schedules (£ million)

Disposable income	Desired consumption	Desired saving
0	100	– 100
100	180	– 80
400	420	– 20
500	500	0
1,000	900	+ 100
1,500	1,300	+ 200
1,750	1,500	+ 250
2,000	1,700	+ 300
3,000	2,500	+ 500
4,000	3,300	+ 700

Saving and consumption account for all household disposable income. The first two columns repeat the data from Table 29.1. The third column, desired saving, is disposable income minus desired consumption. Consumption and saving both increase steadily as disposable income rises. In this example, the break-even level of income is £500 million. At this level, all income is consumed.

ing. It follows that, once we know the dependence of consumption on disposable income, we also automatically know the dependence of saving on disposable income. (This is illustrated in Table 29.2.)

There are two saving concepts that are exactly parallel to the consumption concepts of *APC* and *MPC*. The **average propensity to save** (*APS*) is the proportion of disposable income that households want to save, derived by dividing total desired saving by total disposable income: $APS = S/Y_d$. The **marginal propensity to save** (*MPS*) relates the change in total desired saving to the *change* in disposable income that brought it about: $MPS = \Delta S/\Delta Y_d$.

There is a simple relationship between the saving and the consumption propensities. *APC* and *APS* must sum to unity, and so must *MPC* and *MPS*. Because income is either spent or saved, it follows that the fractions of incomes consumed and saved must account for all income (*APC* + *APS* = 1). It also follows that the fractions of any increment to income consumed and saved must account for all of that increment (*MPC* + *MPS* = 1). Calculations based on Table 29.2 will allow you to confirm these relationships in the case of the example given. *MPC* is 0.80 and *MPS* is 0.20 at all levels of income, while, for example, at an income of £2,000 million *APC* is 0.85 and *APS* is 0.15.

Figure 29.2(ii) shows the saving schedule given in Table 29.2. At the break-even level of income, where desired consumption equals disposable income, desired saving is zero. The slope of the saving line $\Delta S/\Delta Y_d$ is equal to the *MPS*.

WEALTH AND THE CONSUMPTION FUNCTION

The Keynesian consumption function that we have been analysing can easily be combined with the more recent 'permanent income' theories of consumption. According to the permanent income theories, households save in order to accumulate wealth that they can use during their retirement (or pass on to their heirs[5]). Suppose that there is an unexpected rise in wealth. This will mean that less of current disposable income needs to be saved for the future, and it will tend to cause a larger fraction of disposable income to be spent on consumption and a smaller fraction to be saved. Thus, the consumption function will be shifted upward and the saving function downward, as shown in Figure 29.3. A fall in wealth increases the incentive to save in order to restore wealth. This shifts the consumption function downward and the saving function upward.

Desired investment expenditure

Investment expenditure is the most volatile component of GDP, and changes in investment expenditure are strongly associated with economic fluctuations. For example, the Great Depression witnessed a major fall in investment: total investment fell by nearly a quarter between 1929 and 1932. A little less dramatically, at the trough of the recession of the early 1990s (in 1992), investment expenditure was 13 per cent less than the level two years earlier.

INVESTMENT AND THE REAL INTEREST RATE

Other things being equal, the higher is the real interest rate, the higher is the cost of borrowing money for investment purposes and the less is the amount of desired investment expenditure. This relationship is most easily understood if we disaggregate investment into its major parts: stock-building, business fixed capital formation, and residential house building.[6]

Stockbuilding   Changes in stocks of finished goods, work in progress, or raw materials represent only a small percentage of private investment in a typical year, but their average size is not an adequate measure of their impor-

---

[5] Empirical evidence suggests that there is a significant 'bequest motive' for saving. This means that individuals plan even further ahead than their own lifetime, because they want to leave money to their children.

[6] These represent different motives for investment, and, in practice, would create demand for different kinds of goods. However, recall that they will all end up creating demand for the output of the single production sector. Thus, the impact, in our model, of £1 worth of stockbuilding is the same as £1 worth of fixed capital formation and, indeed, of £1 worth of consumption. The reason we distinguish investment from consumption is that it is affected by different factors, the most important of which will be the interest rate.

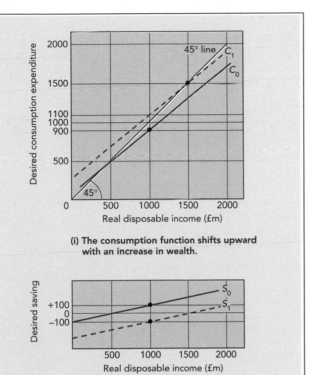

(i) The consumption function shifts upward with an increase in wealth.

(ii) The saving function shifts downward with an increase in wealth.

Figure 29.3 Wealth and the consumption function

Changes in wealth shift consumption as a function of disposable income. In part (i) line C_0 reproduces the consumption function from Figure 29.2(i). An increase in the level of wealth raises desired consumption at each level of disposable income, thus shifting the consumption line up to C_1. In the figure, the consumption function shifts up by £200, so with disposable income of £1000, for example, desired consumption rises from £900 to £1100. As a result of the rise in wealth, the break-even level of income rises to £1500.

The saving function in part (ii) shifts down by £200, from S_0 to S_1. Thus, for example, at a disposable income of £1000, saving *falls* from +£100 to −£100.

tance. They are one of the more volatile elements of total investment and therefore have a major influence on shifts in investment expenditure.

When a firm ties up funds by holding stocks, those same funds cannot be used elsewhere to earn income. As an alternative to investing in stock, the firm could lend the money out at the going rate of interest. Thus, the higher the real rate of interest (see p. 517), the higher will be the opportunity cost of holding stocks of a given size; the higher that opportunity cost, the smaller are the stocks that will be desired.

The higher the real rate of interest, the lower is the desired stock of goods and materials. Changes in the rate of interest cause temporary bouts of investment (or disinvestment) in stocks.

Residential housing construction Expenditure on new houses is also volatile. Between 1970 and 1993 it varied between 3.7 and 6.0 per cent of GDP in the United Kingdom and between 20 and 25 per cent of total investment. Because expenditure on housing construction is both large and variable, it exerts a major impact on the economy.

Most houses are purchased with money that is borrowed by means of mortgages. Interest on the borrowed money typically accounts for over one-half of the purchaser's annual mortgage payments; the remainder is repayment of the original loan, called the principal. Because interest payments are such a large part of mortgage payments, variations in interest rates exert a substantial effect on the demand for housing. During the mid-1980s interest rates fell sharply, and there was a boom in the demand for housing; that boom persisted until late 1988, when interest rates started to rise again. The housing market collapsed and house prices fell. The lower interest rates which arrived in 1992 and 1993 stopped the fall in house prices, but rates started to rise again in 1994, slowing any potential recovery.

Expenditure for residential construction tends to vary negatively with interest rates.

Business fixed capital formation Investment in fixed capital (factories, offices, and machines) by firms is the largest component of domestic investment. Over one-half of such investment is financed by firms' retained profits (profits that are *not* paid out to their shareholders). This means that current profits are an important determinant of investment.

The rate of interest is also a major determinant of investment. As became abundantly clear, both during the early 1980s and during 1989–92, high interest rates greatly reduce the volume of investment as more and more firms find that their expected profits from investment do not cover the interest on borrowed investment funds. Other firms which have cash on hand find that purchasing interest-earning assets provide a better return than investment in factories and machinery; for them, the increase in real interest rates means that the opportunity cost of investing in fixed capital has risen. Interest rates are determined in the monetary sector, so we do not incorporate interest rate effects until we have studied money in Chapter 36.

EXPECTATIONS AND BUSINESS CONFIDENCE

Investment takes time. When a firm invests, it increases its future capacity to produce output. If the new output can be sold profitably, the investment will prove to be a good one. If the new output does not generate profits, the investment will be a bad one. When the investment is undertaken, the firm does not know if it will turn out well or badly—it is betting on a favourable future that cannot be known with certainty.

When firms see good times ahead, they will want to invest so as to reap future profits. When they see bad times, they will not invest, because, given their expectations, there will be no payoff from doing so.

Business investment depends in part on firms' forecasts of the future state of the economy.

INVESTMENT AS AUTONOMOUS EXPENDITURE

We have seen that investment is influenced by many things. For the moment, we treat investment as autonomous, meaning only that it is uninfluenced by changes in national income. This allows us to study, first, how national income is determined when there is an unchanged amount of desired investment expenditure, and, second, how alterations in the amount of desired investment cause changes in equilibrium national income. (In later chapters, we will link changes in national income to changes in investment via induced changes in interest rates.)

The aggregate expenditure function

The aggregate expenditure function relates the level of desired real expenditure to the level of real income. Generally, total desired expenditure on the nation's output is the sum of desired consumption, investment, government, and net export expenditure. In the simplified economy of this chapter, aggregate expenditure is just equal to $C + I$:

$$AE = C + I.$$

Table 29.3 shows how the AE function can be calculated, given the consumption function of Tables 29.1 and 29.2 and a constant level of desired investment of £250 million. In this specific case, all of investment expenditure is autonomous, as is the £100 million of consumption that would be desired at zero national income (see Table 29.1). Total autonomous expenditure is thus £350 million, and induced expenditure is just equal to induced consumption, which is equal to 0.8Y. Thus, desired aggregate expenditure, whether thought of as $C + I$ or as autonomous plus induced expenditure, can be written as $AE = £350$ million $+ 0.8Y$. This aggregate expenditure function is illustrated in Figure 29.4.

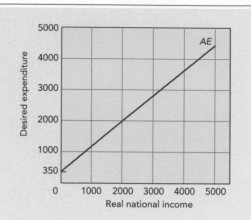

Figure 29.4 An aggregate expenditure function

The aggregate expenditure function relates total desired expenditure to national income. The *AE* curve in the figure plots the data from the first and the last columns of Table 29.3, which are repeated in Table 29.4. Its intercept (which in this case is £350) shows autonomous expenditure, which in this case is the sum of autonomous consumption of £100 and investment of £250. Its slope (which in this case is 0.8) shows the marginal propensity to spend.

The propensity to spend out of national income   The fraction of any increment to national income that will be spent on purchasing domestic output is called the economy's **marginal propensity to spend.** The marginal propensity to spend is measured by the change in aggregate expenditure divided by the change in income, or $\Delta AE/\Delta Y$, the slope of the aggregate expenditure function. In this book, we will denote the marginal propensity to spend by the symbol z, which will typically be a number greater than zero and less than one.

Similarly, the **marginal propensity not to spend** is the fraction of any increment to national income that does not add to desired aggregate expenditure. This is denoted $(1 - z)$; if z is the part of £1 of incremental income that is spent, $(1 - z)$ is the part that is not spent.[7]

In the example given in Table 29.3, z, the marginal propensity to spend, is 0.8. If national income increases by £1, 80p will go into increased spending; 20p (£1 times 0.2, the value of $(1 - z)$) will go into increased saving and will not be spent.

The marginal propensity to spend should not be confused with the marginal propensity to consume, which was

---

[7] More fully, these terms would be called the marginal propensity to spend *on national income* and the marginal propensity not to spend *on national income*. The marginal propensity not to spend $(1 - z)$ is often referred to as the *marginal propensity to withdraw*. Not spending part of income amounts to a *withdrawal* or a *leakage* from the circular flow of income, as is illustrated in Figure 27.1 on p. 504.

Table 29.3 The aggregate expenditure function in a closed economy with no government (£ million)

National income (Y)	Desired consumption expenditure (C = 100 + 0.8Y)	Desired investment expenditure (I = 250)	Desired aggregate expenditure (AE = C + I + G + (X – IM))
100	180	250	430
400	420	250	670
500	500	250	750
1,000	900	250	1,150
1,500	1,300	250	1,550
1,750	1,500	250	1,750
2,000	1,700	250	1,950
3,000	2,500	250	2,750
4,000	3,300	250	3,550

The aggregate expenditure function is the sum of desired consumption, investment, government, and net export expenditures. In this table, government and net exports are assumed to be zero, investment is assumed to be constant at £250 million, and desired consumption is based on the hypothetical data given in Table 29.2. The autonomous components of desired aggregate expenditure are desired investment and the constant term in desired consumption expenditure (£100 million). The induced component is the second term in desired consumption expenditure (0.8Y).

The marginal response of consumption to a change in national income is 0.8, the marginal propensity to consume. The marginal response of desired aggregate expenditure to a change in national income, $\Delta AE/\Delta Y$, is also 0.8, because all induced expenditure in the economy is consumption expenditure.

defined earlier in the chapter. The marginal propensity to spend is the amount of extra total expenditure induced when *national* income rises by £1, while the marginal propensity to consume is the amount of extra consumption expenditure induced when *personal disposable* income rises by £1. In the simple model of this chapter, the marginal propensity to spend is equal to the marginal propensity to consume, and the marginal propensity not to spend is equal to the marginal propensity to save. However, in later chapters, when we add government and the international sector, the marginal propensity to spend differs from the marginal propensity to consume. Both here and in later chapters, it is the more general measures of z and $(1 - z)$ that are important for determining equilibrium national income.

Equilibrium national income

WE are now ready to see what determines the *equilibrium* level of national income. Recall from Chapter 4 that equilibrium is a state of balance between opposing forces. When something is in equilibrium, there is no tendency for it to change; forces are acting on it, but they balance out, and the net result is *no change*. Any conditions that are required for something to be in equilibrium are called its *equilibrium conditions*.

Table 29.4 illustrates the determination of equilibrium national income for our simple hypothetical economy. Suppose that firms are producing a final output of £1,000 million, and thus national income is £1,000 million. According to the table, at this level of income aggregate desired expenditure is £1,150 million. If firms persist in producing a current output of only £1,000 million in the face of an aggregate desired expenditure of £1,150 million, one of two things must happen.[8]

One possibility is that consumers, firms, and governments will be unable to spend the extra £150 million that they would like to spend, so lines or waiting lists of unsatisfied customers will appear. These will send a signal to firms that they can increase their sales if they increase their production. When the firms increase production, national

---

[8] A third possibility—that prices could rise—is ruled out by assumption in this chapter.

Table 29.4 The determination of equilibrium national income (£ million)

National income (Y)	Desired aggregate expenditure (AE = C + I)	
100	430	
400	670	
500	750	Pressure on Y
1,000	1,150	to rise
1,500	1,550	↓
1,750	**1,750**	**Equilibrium Y**
2,000	1,950	↑
3,000	2,750	Pressure on Y
4,000	3,550	to fall

National income is in equilibrium where aggregate desired expenditure equals national income. The data are copied from Table 29.3. When national income is below its equilibrium level, aggregate desired expenditure exceeds the value of current output. This creates an incentive for firms to increase output and hence for national income to rise. When national income is above its equilibrium level, aggregate desired expenditure is less than the value of current output. This creates an incentive for firms to reduce output and hence for national income to fall. Only at the equilibrium level of national income is aggregate desired expenditure equal to the value of current output.

income rises. Of course, the individual firms are interested only in their own sales and profits, but their individual actions inevitably lead to an increase in GDP.

The second possibility is that all spenders will spend everything that they wanted to spend. Then, however, expenditure will exceed current output, which can happen only when some expenditure plans are fulfilled by purchasing stocks of goods that were produced in the past. In our example, the fulfilment of plans to purchase £1,150 million worth of commodities in the face of a current output of only £1,000 million will reduce stocks by £150 million. As long as stocks last, more goods can be sold than are currently being produced.[9]

Eventually, stocks will run out. But before this happens, firms will increase their output as they see their sales increase. Extra sales can then be made without a further depletion of inventories. Once again, the consequence of each individual firm's behaviour, in search of its own individual profits, is an increase in national income. Thus, the final response to an excess of aggregate desired expenditure over current output is a rise in national income.

At any level of national income at which aggregate desired expenditure exceeds total output, there will be pressure for national income to rise.

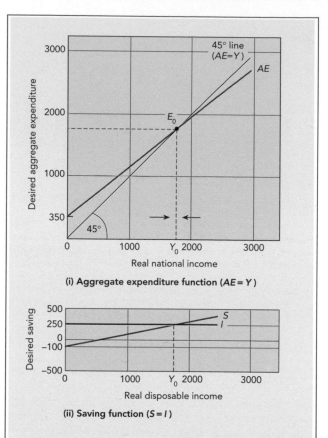

(i) Aggregate expenditure function (AE = Y)

(ii) Saving function (S = I)

Figure 29.5 Equilibrium national income

Equilibrium national income occurs at E_0, where the desired aggregate expenditure line intersects the 45°. If real national income is below Y_0, desired aggregate expenditure will exceed national income, and production will rise. This is shown in part (i) by the arrow to the left of Y_0. If national income is above Y_0, desired aggregate expenditure will be less than national income, and production will fall. This is shown by the arrow to the right of Y_0. Only when real national income is Y_0 will desired aggregate expenditure equal real national income.

When saving is the only withdrawal and investment is the only injection, the equilibrium Y_0 is also the level of national income at which saving equals investment, shown in part (ii). At levels of national income greater than Y_0 saving exceeds investment (withdrawals exceed injections), so aggregate spending is less than output and the economy contracts. At levels of national income below Y_0, investment exceeds saving (injections exceed withdrawals) so spending exceeds output and the level of national income increases. Parts (i) and (ii) are just two different ways of looking at the same phenomena.

[9] Notice that in this example actual national income is £1,000 million. Desired consumption is £900 million and desired investment is £250 million, but the reduction of inventories of £150 million is unplanned negative investment; thus, actual investment is only £100 million.

Box 29.1

A hydraulic analogue of national income determination

The key concept to understand in this chapter is how it is that national income achieves some static, or equilibrium, level (for given values of autonomous expenditures). This is one of the most important ideas in macroeconomics, because it explains how national income can be in equilibrium even when there is excess capacity in the economy.

Think of the economy as a water container, say a basin, which has inflows and outflows on a continuous basis—the tap is turned on and there is no plug in the plug hole. So the water is always changing, but there is some condition under which the water in the basin will stay at one level. This is when the volume of the inflow and the volume of the outflow are exactly equal.

Call the inflow 'investment', the outflow 'saving', and the level of water in the basin 'national income'. National income will stay at one level so long as the volume of investment just equals the volume of saving. If investment increases, the level of national income will rise until the increased water pressure is such that the volume of saving now equals the higher level of investment again. If investment falls, national income will fall until the lower pressure of water reduces saving to equal the new lower level of investment. (The same principle can be viewed in terms of the circular flow diagram, Figure 27.1, when there is no foreign trade and no government. Only when $I = S$ will the level of the circular flow be stable.)

What happens if the basin fills up to overflowing? That is the problem of capacity constraints and full employment which we discuss in later chapters. Hopefully, the basin will never run

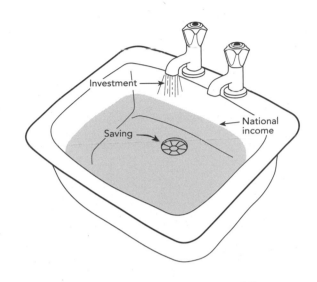

empty, because that means national income falls to zero—though the problem of the water getting undesirably low is exactly what macroeconomics was invented to avoid.

In later chapters, also, we shall see that investment is not the only inflow, or injection (government expenditure and exports will be added), and that saving is not the only leakage, or withdrawal (taxes and imports are also leakages).

Next, consider the £4,000 million level of national income in Table 29.4. At this level desired expenditure on domestically produced goods is only £3,550 million. If firms persist in producing £4,000 million worth of goods, £450 million worth must remain unsold. Therefore, stocks of unsold goods must rise. However, firms will not allow unsold goods to accumulate indefinitely; sooner or later they will reduce the level of output to the level of sales. When they do, national income will fall.

At any level of income for which aggregate desired expenditure is less than total output, there will be a pressure for national income to fall.

Finally, look at the national income level of £1,750 million in Table 29.4. At this level, and only at this level, aggregate desired expenditure is equal to national income. Purchasers can fulfil their spending plans without causing inventories to change. There is no incentive for firms to alter output. Because everyone wishes to purchase an amount equal to what is being produced, output and income will remain steady; they are in equilibrium.

The equilibrium level of national income occurs where aggregate desired expenditure equals total output.

This conclusion is quite general and does not depend on the numbers that are used in the specific example. Appendix B to Chapter 30 shows this by giving a more general derivation of equilibrium national income.

Figure 29.5 explains the determination of the equilibrium level of national income. In part (i) of that figure, the line labelled *AE* graphs the aggregate expenditure function given by the first and last columns of Table 29.3 and also shown in Table 29.4. The line labelled '45° line *(AE = Y)*' graphs the equilibrium condition that aggregate desired expenditure equals national income. Since in equilibrium the variables measured on the two axes must be equal, the line showing this equality is a 45° line. Anywhere along that line, the value of desired expenditure, which is measured on the vertical axis, is equal to the value of real national income, which is measured on the horizontal axis.[10]

Graphically, equilibrium occurs at the level of income at which the aggregate desired expenditure line intersects the 45° line. This is the level of income where desired expenditure is just equal to total national income and therefore is just sufficient to purchase total final output.

Exactly the same equilibrium is illustrated in part (ii), but in terms of the saving–investment balance. The line labelled S is equal to aggregate saving. In an economy without government and without international trade, i.e. the case we are studying here, aggregate saving is just equal to $Y - C$, the difference between national income and consumption. The line labelled I is investment, in this case assumed to be constant at all levels of income.

Notice that the vertical distance between S and I is just equal to the distance between the 45° line and AE. When desired investment exceeds desired saving, desired aggregate expenditure exceeds national income by the same amount. When desired investment is less than desired saving, desired aggregate expenditure is less than national income by the same amount. This is not a coincidence: they are showing the same feature in two different ways.

Now we have explained the determinants of the equilibrium level of national income at a *given price level*. A simple analogue, which will help you to understand why it is that equilibrium national income is associated with equality of desired investment and saving, is set out in Box 29.1. In the next section we shall study the forces that cause equilibrium income to change. We shall see that shifts in autonomous consumption and investment expenditure cause changes in national income.

Changes in national income

BECAUSE the AE function plays a central role in our explanation of the equilibrium value of national income, you should not be surprised to hear that shifts in the AE function play a central role in explaining why national income changes. (Remember that we continue to assume that the price level is constant.) To understand this influence, we must recall an important distinction first encountered in Chapter 4—the distinction between *shifts* in a curve and *movements along* a curve.

Suppose desired aggregate expenditure rises. This may be a response to a change in national income, or it may be the result of an increased desire to spend at each level of national income. A change in national income causes a *movement along* the aggregate expenditure function; an increased desire to spend at each level of national income causes a *shift in* the aggregate expenditure function. Figure 29.6 illustrates this important distinction.

SHIFTS IN THE AGGREGATE EXPENDITURE FUNCTION

For any specific aggregate expenditure function, there is a unique level of equilibrium national income. If the aggregate expenditure function shifts, the equilibrium will be disturbed and national income will change. Thus, if we wish to find the causes of changes in national income, we must understand the causes of shifts in the AE function.

The aggregate expenditure function shifts when one of its components shifts, that is, when there is a shift in the consumption function, in desired investment expenditure, in desired government expenditure on goods and services, or in desired net exports. In this chapter we consider only shifts in the consumption function and in desired investment expenditure. Both of these are changes in desired aggregate expenditure at every level of income.

Upward shifts   What will happen if households permanently increase their levels of consumption spending at each level of disposable income, or if, say, ICI invests in more fixed capital because of improved confidence about the future health of the economy? (Recall that an increase in any component of expenditure has the same effect, because it is an increase in demand for the output of the single production sector.) In considering these questions, remember that we are dealing with continuous flows mea-

---

[10] Because it turns up in many different guises, the 45° line can cause a bit of confusion until one gets used to it. The main thing about it is that it can be used whenever the variables plotted on the two axes are measured in the same units, such as pounds, and are plotted on the same scale. In that case, equal distances on the two axes measure the same amounts. One inch may, for example, correspond to £1,000 on each axis. In such circumstances, the 45° line joins all points where the values of the two variables are the same. In Figures 29.2 and 29.3, the 45° line shows all points where desired *consumption* expenditure in real terms equals real *disposable* income because these are the two variables that are plotted on the two axes. In Figure 29.4 and all those that follow it, the 45° line shows all points at which desired *total* expenditure in real terms equals real *national* income because those are the variables that are measured on the two axes of these figures.

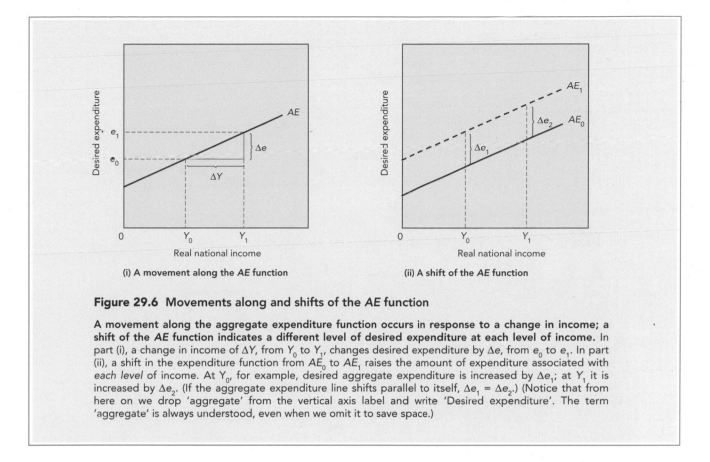

Figure 29.6 Movements along and shifts of the *AE* function

A movement along the aggregate expenditure function occurs in response to a change in income; a shift of the *AE* function indicates a different level of desired expenditure at each level of income. In part (i), a change in income of ΔY, from Y_0 to Y_1, changes desired expenditure by Δe, from e_0 to e_1. In part (ii), a shift in the expenditure function from AE_0 to AE_1 raises the amount of expenditure associated with *each level* of income. At Y_0, for example, desired aggregate expenditure is increased by Δe_1; at Y_1 it is increased by Δe_2. (If the aggregate expenditure line shifts parallel to itself, $\Delta e_1 = \Delta e_2$.) (Notice that from here on we drop 'aggregate' from the vertical axis label and write 'Desired expenditure'. The term 'aggregate' is always understood, even when we omit it to save space.)

sured as so much per period of time. An upward shift in any expenditure function means that the desired expenditure associated with each level of national income rises to and stays at a higher amount.

Because any such increase in desired expenditure shifts the entire aggregate expenditure function upward, the same analysis applies to each of the changes mentioned. Two types of shift in *AE* occur. First, if the same addition to expenditure occurs *at all levels* of income, the whole *AE* curve shifts parallel to itself, as shown in part (i) of Figure 29.7. Second, if there is a change in the propensity to spend out of national income, the *slope* of the *AE* curve changes, as shown in part (ii) of the figure. (Recall that the slope of the *AE* curve is *z*, the marginal propensity to spend.) A change such as the one illustrated in part (ii) would occur if consumers decided to spend more of every £1 of disposable income, that is, if the *MPC* rose.

Figure 29.7 shows that upward shifts in the aggregate expenditure function increase equilibrium national income. After the shift in the *AE* curve, income is no longer in equilibrium at its original level because at that level desired expenditure exceeds national income. Equilibrium national income now occurs at the higher level indicated by

the intersection of the new *AE* curve with the 45° line, along which aggregate expenditure equals real national income.

Downward shifts What happens to national income if there is a decrease in the amount of consumption or investment expenditure desired at each level of income? These changes shift the aggregate expenditure function downward. A constant reduction in desired expenditure *at all levels* of income shifts *AE* parallel to itself. A fall in the marginal propensity to spend out of national income reduces the *slope* of the *AE* function. When we use the saving–investment relation, we must note that a downward shift in the consumption function causes an upward shift in the saving function, reducing the equilibrium level of income, at which saving equals investment.

The results restated We have derived two important general propositions of the elementary theory of national income.

1. A rise in the amount of desired aggregate expenditure that is associated with each level of national income will increase equilibrium national income.

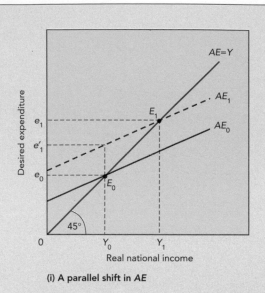
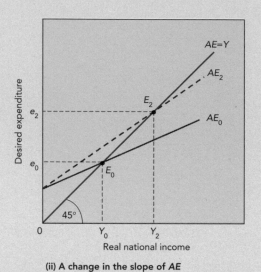

(i) A parallel shift in *AE*

(ii) A change in the slope of *AE*

Figure 29.7 Shifts in the *AE* curve

Upward shifts in the *AE* curve increase equilibrium income; downward shifts decrease equilibrium income. In parts (i) and (ii), the aggregate expenditure curve is initially AE_0 with national income Y_0. In part (i), a parallel upward *shift* in the *AE* curve from AE_0 to AE_1 means that desired expenditure has increased by the same amount at each level of national income. For example, at Y_0 desired expenditure rises from e_0 to e'_1 and therefore exceeds national income. Equilibrium is reached at E_1, where income is Y_1 and expenditure is e_1. *The increase in desired expenditure from e'_1 to e_1*, represented by a *movement along AE_1*, is an induced response to the increase in income from Y_0 to Y_1.
In part (ii), a non-parallel upward shift in the *AE* curve, say, from AE_0 to AE_2, means that the marginal propensity to spend at each level of national income has increased. This leads to an increase in equilibrium national income. Equilibrium is reached at E_2, where the new level of expenditure e_2 is equal to income Y_2. Again, the initial *shift* in the *AE* curve induces a *movement along* the new *AE* curve. Downward shifts in the *AE* curve, from AE_1 to AE_0 or from AE_2 to AE_0, lead to a fall in equilibrium income to Y_0.

2. A fall in the amount of desired aggregate expenditure that is associated with each level of national income will lower equilibrium national income.

THE MULTIPLIER

We have learned how to predict the direction of the changes in national income that occur in response to various shifts in the aggregate expenditure function. We would like also to predict the *magnitude* of these changes.

Economists need to know the *size* of the effects of changes in expenditures. During a recession, the government sometimes takes measures to stimulate the economy. If these measures have a larger effect than estimated, demand may rise too much and full employment may be reached with demand still rising. (We will see in Chapter 31 that this outcome will have an inflationary impact on the economy.) If the government greatly overestimates the effect of its mea-

sures, the recession will persist longer than is necessary. In this case, there is a danger that the policy will be discredited as ineffective, even though the correct diagnosis would be that too little of the right thing was done.

Definition   A measure of the magnitude of changes in income is provided by the *multiplier*. We have just seen that a shift in the aggregate expenditure curve will cause a change in equilibrium national income. Such a shift could be caused by a change in any autonomous component of aggregate expenditure, for example an increase or decrease in desired investment. An increase in desired aggregate expenditure increases equilibrium national income by a multiple of the initial increase in autonomous expenditure. The **multiplier** is the ratio of the change in income to the change in autonomous expenditure, that is, the change in national income *divided by* the change in autonomous expenditure that brought it about.

Why the multiplier is greater than unity   What will happen to national income if GEC spends £100 million per year on new factories? Initially the construction of the factory will create £100 million worth of annual new demand for the output of the production sector (recall that there is only one type of output), £100 million of new national income, and a corresponding amount of extra wages for workers and profits for firms (the income components of GDP). But this is not the end of the story. The increase in national income of £100 million will cause an increase in disposable income, which in turn will cause an induced rise in consumption expenditure.

Workers, who gain new income directly from the building of the factories, will spend some of it on consumer goods. (In reality, they would spend it on many different goods, such as beer and cinema visits. In the simplified world of our model, all spending is on the final output of the single industrial sector.) When output and employment expand to meet this demand, further new incomes will then be created for workers and firms. When they then spend these newly earned incomes, output and employment will rise still further. More income will be created, and more expenditure will be induced. Indeed, at this stage we might wonder whether the increases in income will ever come to an end. To deal with this concern, we need to consider the multiplier in somewhat more precise terms.

The simple multiplier defined   Consider an increase in autonomous expenditure of ΔA, which might be, say, £100 million per year. Remember that ΔA stands for *any* increase in autonomous expenditure; this could be an increase in investment or in the autonomous component of consumption. The new autonomous expenditure shifts the aggregate expenditure function upward by that amount. National income is no longer in equilibrium at its original level, because desired aggregate expenditure now exceeds income. Equilibrium is restored by a *movement along* the new *AE* curve.

The **simple multiplier** measures the change in equilibrium national income that occurs in response to a change in autonomous expenditure *at a constant price level*.[11] We refer to it as 'simple' because we have simplified the situation by assuming that the price level is fixed. Figure 29.8 illustrates the simple multiplier and makes clear that it is greater than unity. Box 29.2 provides a numerical example.

THE SIZE OF THE SIMPLE MULTIPLIER

The size of the simple multiplier depends on the slope of the *AE* function, that is, on the marginal propensity to spend, z. This is illustrated in Figure 29.9.

A high marginal propensity to spend means a steep *AE* curve (part (iii)). The expenditure induced by any initial increase in income is large, with the result that the final rise in income is correspondingly large. By contrast, a low mar-

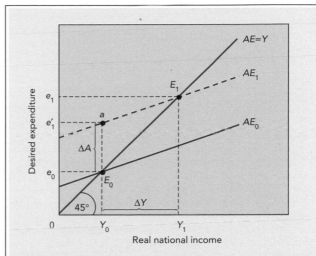

Figure 29.8 The simple multiplier

An increase in the autonomous component of desired aggregate expenditure increases equilibrium national income by a multiple of the initial increase. The initial equilibrium is at E_0, where AE_0 intersects the 45° line. At this point, desired expenditure, e_0, is equal to national income, Y_0. An increase is autonomous expenditure of ΔA then shifts the desired expenditure function upward to AE_1. If national income stays at Y_0, desired expenditure rises to e'_1. (The coordinates of point a are Y_0 and e'_1.) Because this level of desired expenditure is greater than national income, national income will rise.

Equilibrium occurs when income rises to Y_1. Here desired expenditure, e_1, equals income, Y_1. The extra expenditure of e_1 represents the induced increases in expenditure. It is the amount by which the final increase in income; ΔY, exceeds the initial increase in autonomous expenditure, ΔA. Because ΔY is greater than ΔA, the multiplier is greater than unity.

ginal propensity to spend means a relatively flat *AE* curve (part (ii)). The expenditure induced by the initial increase in income is small, and the final rise in income is not much larger than the initial rise in autonomous expenditure that brought it about.

The larger the marginal propensity to spend, the steeper is the aggregate expenditure function and the larger is the multiplier.

The precise value of the simple multiplier can be derived by using elementary algebra. (The derivation is given in

[11] It should be remembered also that we have assumed that there is excess capacity in the economy, so an increase in expenditure can lead to extra real activity. The situation is very different when we start out with resources already fully employed. We come to this situation in later chapters.

Box 29.2

The multiplier: a numerical example

Consider an economy that has a marginal propensity to spend out of national income of 0.80. Suppose that autonomous expenditure increases by £100 million per year because a large company spends an extra £100 million per year on new factories. National income initially rises by £100 million, but that is not the end of it. The factors of production involved in factory building that received the first £100 million spend £80 million. This second round of spending generates £80 million of new income. This new income, in turn, induces £64 million of third-round spending. And so it continues, with each successive round of new income generating 80 per cent as much in new expenditure. and each additional round of expenditure creating new income and yet another round of expenditure.

The table carries the process through 10 rounds. Students with sufficient patience (and no faith in mathematics) may compute as many rounds in the process as they wish; they will find that the sum of the rounds of expenditures approaches a limit of £500 million, which is five times the initial increase in expenditure.

Round of spending	Increase in expenditure (£m)	Cumulative total (£m)
Initial increase	100	100.0
2	80	180.0
3	64	244.0
4	51.2	295.2
5	41.0	336.2
6	32.8	369.0
7	26.2	395.2
8	21.0	416.2
9	16.8	432.8
10	13.4	446.2
11–20 combined	47.9	494.1
All others	5.8	500.0

The graph of the cumulative expenditure increases shows how quickly this limit is approached. The multiplier is thus 5, given that the marginal propensity to spend is 0.8. Had the marginal propensity to spend been lower, say, 0.667, the process would have been similar, but it would have approached a limit of three, instead of five, times the initial increase in expenditure. Notice that, since our model has only a single productive sector, it makes no difference what the initial spending goes on: that and all subsequent spending is on the output of this single industry. In reality, the impact of spending increases may vary slightly depending on the product first demanded.

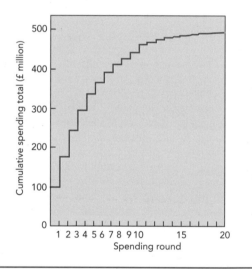

Box 29.3.) The result is that the simple multiplier, which we call K, is

$$K = \frac{\Delta Y}{\Delta A} = \frac{1}{1-z},$$

where z is the marginal propensity to spend out of national income. (Recall that z is the slope of the aggregate expenditure function.)

As we saw earlier, the term $(1-z)$ stands for the marginal propensity *not* to spend out of national income. For example, if £0.80 of every £1.00 of new national income is spent (z = 0.80), then £0.20 is the amount not spent. The value of the multiplier is then calculated as K = 1/(0.20) = 5.

The simple multiplier equals the reciprocal of the marginal propensity not to spend.

From this we see that, if $(1-z)$ is small (that is, if z is large), the multiplier will be large (because extra income induces much extra spending). What if $(1-z)$ is large? The largest possible value of $(1-z)$ is unity, which arises when z equals zero, indicating that none of any additional national income is spent. In this case the multiplier itself has a value of unity; the increase in equilibrium national income is confined to the initial increase in autonomous expenditure. There are no induced additional effects on spending, so national income increases only by the original increase in autonomous expenditure. The relation between $(1-z)$ and the size of the multiplier is illustrated in Figure 29.9.

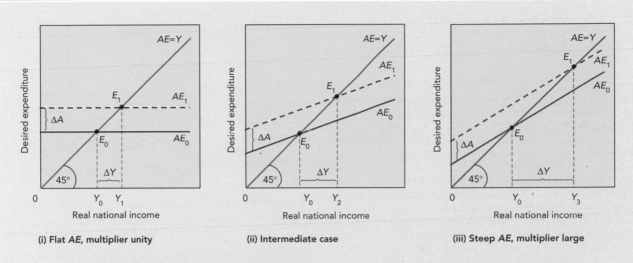

Figure 29.9 The size of the simple multiplier

The larger the marginal propensity to spend out of national income (z), the steeper is the AE curve and the larger is the multiplier. In each part of the figure, the initial aggregate expenditure function is AE_0, equilibrium is at E_0, with income Y_0. The AE curve then shifts upward to AE_1 as a result of an increase in autonomous expenditure of ΔA. ΔA is the same in each part. The new equilibrium is at E_1. In part (i), the AE function is horizontal, indicating a marginal propensity to spend of zero ($z = 0$). The change in income, ΔY, is only the increase in autonomous expenditure, because there is no induced expenditure by those who receive the initial increase in income. The simple multiplier is then unity, its minimum possible value.

In part (ii), the AE curve slopes upward but is still relatively flat (z is low). The increase in national income to Y_2 is only slightly greater than the increase in autonomous expenditure that brought it about.

In part (iii), the AE function is quite steep (z is high). Now the increase in income to Y_3 is much larger than the increase in autonomous expenditure that brought it about. The simple multiplier is quite large.

To estimate the size of the multiplier in an actual economy, we need to estimate the value of the marginal propensity not to spend out of national income in that economy, that is, $(1 - z)$. Evidence suggests that in the United Kingdom the value of the marginal propensity not to spend is much larger than 0.2. This is because there are other 'leakages' from the circular flow of income—income taxes and import expenditure (which will be added to our model in the next chapter). Allowing for these extra withdrawals leads to a realistic estimate of something around 0.65 for $(1 - z)$.[12] Thus, the simple multiplier for the United Kingdom is just over 1.4, rather than of the order of 5, as in the above example.

The simple multiplier is a useful starting point for understanding the effects of expenditure shifts on national income. However, as we shall see in subsequent chapters, many qualifications will arise, so the reader should not place too much policy significance on its value at this stage.

[12] This 0.65 is calculated using a marginal propensity to save of 0.2, a marginal propensity to import of 0.25, and an income tax rate of 0.25 (25p in the £). The formula is derived in Appendix B to Chapter 30.

Summary

1 Macroeconomics is concerned with the building of simple models of the economy as a whole which can explain the determination of real GDP and why actual GDP often deviates from its potential or long-term equilibrium level.

2 For simplicity, we aggregate all industrial sectors into one, so the economy produces only one type of output good. We approach the determination of national output (and income) through the major expenditure categories—consumption, investment, government spending, and net exports.

3 Desired aggregate expenditure includes desired consumption, desired investment, and desired government expenditure, plus desired net exports. It is the amount that economic agents want to spend on purchasing the

Box 29.3

The multiplier: an algebraic approach

Basic algebra is all that is needed to derive the exact expression for the multiplier. Readers who feel at home with algebra may want to follow this derivation. Others can skip it and rely on the graphical and numerical arguments that have been given in the text.

First, we derive the equation for the AE curve. Aggregate expenditure is divided into autonomous expenditure, A, and induced expenditure, N. In the simple model of this chapter, A is just equal to investment plus autonomous consumption. N is just equal to induced consumption.*

Thus, we can write

$$AE = N + A. \qquad \text{(i)}$$

Because N is expenditure on domestically produced output that varies with income, we can write

$$N = zY, \qquad \text{(ii)}$$

where z is the marginal propensity to spend out of national income. (z is a positive number between zero and unity. In the simple model of this chapter, with no government and no foreign sector, it is equal to the marginal propensity to consume.) Substituting equation (ii) into equation (i) yields the equation of the AE curve:

$$AE = zY + A. \qquad \text{(iii)}$$

Now we write the equation of the 45° line,

$$AE = Y, \qquad \text{(iv)}$$

which states the equilibrium condition that desired aggregate expenditure equals national income. Equations (iii) and (iv) are two equations with two unknowns, AE and Y. To solve them, we substitute equation (iii) in equation (iv) to obtain

$$Y = zY + A. \qquad \text{(v)}$$

Subtracting zY from both sides yields

$$Y - zY = A. \qquad \text{(vi)}$$

Factoring out Y yields

$$Y(1 - z) = A. \qquad \text{(vii)}$$

Dividing through by $1 - z$ yields

$$Y = \frac{A}{1 - z}. \qquad \text{(viii)}$$

This tells us the equilibrium value of Y in terms of autonomous expenditures A and the propensity not to spend out of national income $(1 - z)$. Now consider a £1 increase in A. The expression $Y = A/(1 - z)$ tells us that, if A changes by £1, the change in Y will be £$(1/(1 - z))$. Generally, for a change in autonomous spending of ΔA, the change in Y, which we call ΔY, will be

$$\Delta Y = \frac{\Delta A}{1 - z}. \qquad \text{(ix)}$$

Dividing through by ΔA gives the value of the multiplier, which we designate by K:

$$K = \frac{\Delta Y}{\Delta A} = \frac{1}{1 - z}. \qquad \text{(x)}$$

---

* When we add imports and government in the next chapter, N will include induced imports, and A will include government spending and exports. The derivation here is quite general, however. All that matters is that desired aggregate expenditure can be divided into one class of expenditure, N, that varies with income, and another class, A, that does not.

---

national product. In this chapter we consider only consumption and investment.

4 A change in disposable income leads to a change in consumption and saving. The responsiveness of these changes is measured by the marginal propensity to consume (MPC) and the marginal propensity to save (MPS), which are both positive and sum to one, indicating that all disposable income is either spent on consumption or saved.

5 A change in wealth tends to cause a change in the allocation of disposable income between consumption and saving. The change in consumption is positively related to the change in wealth, while the change in saving is negatively related to this change.

6 Investment depends, among other things, on real interest rates and business confidence. In our simple theory, investment is treated as autonomous.

7 In the simple theory of this chapter, investment expenditures and the constant term in the consumption function (that is, the level of consumption when income is zero, shown in Table 29.1) are both autonomous expenditures. The part of consumption that responds to income is called induced expenditure.

8 At the equilibrium level of national income, purchasers wish to buy an amount equal to what is being produced. At incomes above equilibrium, desired expenditure falls short of national income, and output will sooner or later be curtailed. At incomes below equilibrium, desired

expenditure exceeds national income, and output will sooner or later be increased.

7 In a closed economy with no government, desired saving equals desired investment at equilibrium national income.

8 Equilibrium national income is represented graphically by the point at which the aggregate expenditure curve cuts the 45° line, that is, where total desired expenditure equals total output. This is the same level of income at which the saving function cuts the investment function.

9 With a constant price level, equilibrium national income is increased by a rise in the desired consumption or investment expenditure that is associated with each level of the national income. Equilibrium national income is decreased by a fall in this desired expenditure.

10 The magnitude of the effect on national income of shifts in autonomous expenditure is given by the multiplier. It is defined as $K = \Delta Y/\Delta A$, where ΔA is the change in autonomous expenditure.

11 The simple multiplier is the multiplier when the price level is constant. It is equal to $1/(1 - z)$, where z is the marginal propensity to spend out of national income. Thus, the larger z is, the larger is the multiplier. It is a basic prediction of national income theory that the simple multiplier, relating £1 worth of spending on domestic output to the resulting increase in national income, is greater than unity.

Topics for review

- Aggregation across sectors
- Desired expenditure
- Consumption function
- Average and marginal propensities to consume and to save
- Aggregate expenditure function
- Marginal propensities to spend and not to spend
- Equilibrium national income at a given price level
- Saving–investment balance
- Shifts of, and movements along, expenditure curves
- The effect on national income of changes in desired expenditures
- The simple multiplier
- The size of the multiplier and slope of the AE curve

APPENDIX TO CHAPTER 29

The permanent income and life-cycle hypotheses of personal consumption

IN the Keynesian theory of the consumption function, current consumption expenditure is related to *current* income—either current disposable income or current national income. As we saw in this chapter, more recent theories relate consumption to some longer-term concept of income than income in the current period.

The two most influential theories of this type are the *permanent income theory (PIT)*, developed by Professor Milton Friedman, and the *life-cycle theory (LCT)*, developed by Professors Modigliani, Ando, and Brumberg. Although there are differences between these two theories, it is their similarities that are important. In particular, we note that, in both the PIT and the LCT, individual spending and saving behaviour tends to smooth the time pattern of consumption relative to that of disposable income. Later in this appendix we consider a potentially important difference between the two hypotheses.

In discussing this 'consumption-smoothing' issue, it is important to ask: What variables do these theories seek to explain? What assumptions do they make? What are the major implications of these assumptions?

VARIABLES

Three variables need to be considered: consumption, saving, and income. Keynesian-type theories seek to explain the amounts that people spend on purchasing goods and services for consumption. This concept is called *consumption expenditure*. Permanent income theories seek to explain the actual flows of consumption of the *services* that are provided by the commodities that consumers buy. This concept is called *actual consumption*.[1]

With services and nondurable goods, expenditure and actual consumption occur more or less at the same time, and the distinction between the two concepts is not important. Consumption of a haircut, for example, occurs at the time that it is purchased, and an orange or a packet of corn flakes is consumed very soon after it is purchased. Thus, if we knew when purchases of such goods and services were made (say, last year), we would also know last year's consumption of those goods and services.

This is not, however, the case with durable consumer goods. A car is purchased at one point in time, but it yields its services over a long period of time. The same is true of a personal computer, a watch, or a stereo system. For such products, if we know last year's purchases, we do not necessarily know last year's consumption of the services that the products yielded. Thus, one important characteristic of durable goods is that *expenditure* to purchase them is not necessarily synchronized with *consumption* of the stream of services that the goods provide. If in 1995 Ms Smith buys a car for £12,000, uses it for six years, and then discards it as worn out, her expenditure on cars is £12,000 in 1995 and zero for the next five years. Her consumption of the services of the car, however, is spread out at an average annual rate of £2,000 for six years. If everyone followed Ms Smith's example and bought a new car in 1995 and replaced it in 2001, the car industry would undergo wild booms in 1995 and 2001 with five intervening years of slump, even though the actual consumption of cars would be spread more or less evenly over time.

This example is extreme, but it illustrates the possibilities, where consumer durable goods are concerned, of quite different time-paths of *consumption expenditure*, which is the subject of Keynesian theories of consumption, and *actual consumption*, which is the subject of permanent income theory.

Now consider saving. The change in emphasis from consumption expenditure to actual consumption implies a change in the definition of saving. Saving is no longer income minus consumption expenditure: it is now income minus the *value* of actual consumption. When Ms Smith spent £12,000 on her car in 1995 but used only £2,000 worth of its services during that year, she was actually consuming £2,000 and saving £10,000. The purchase of a consumer-durable good is thus counted as saving in this theory, and only the value of its services actually consumed during the year in question is counted as consumption.

The third important variable is income. Instead of using *current* income, both PIT and LCT use a concept of *long-term* income. The precise definition varies, but basically it is related to the individual's expected income stream over a fairly long planning period. In the LCT it is the income that the individual expects to earn over his or her lifetime, called the *lifetime income*.

---

[1] Because Keynes's followers did not always distinguish carefully between the concepts of consumption expenditure and actual consumption, the word 'consumption' is often used in both contexts. We follow this practice, but where there is any possible ambiguity in the term we will refer to 'consumption expenditure' and 'actual consumption'.

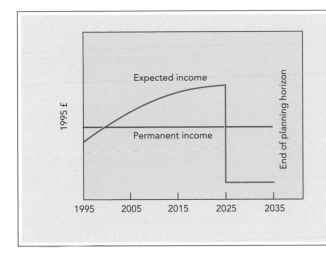

Figure 29A.1 Current income and permanent income

Expected current income may vary greatly over a lifetime, but expected permanent income is defined to be the constant annual equivalent. The graph shows a hypothetical expected income stream from work for a person whose planning horizon is 30 years from 1995. Current income rises to a peak and falls sharply on retirement. The corresponding permanent income is the amount that the person could consume at a steady rate over his or her lifetime, by borrowing early against future earnings (as do many newly married people), then repaying past debts, and finally saving for retirement when income is at its peak, without either incurring debt or accumulating new wealth to be passed on to future generations.

Every person is assumed to have a view of his or her lifetime income. This is not as unreasonable as it might seem. Students who are training to become doctors have a very different view of expected lifetime income from that of those who are training to become schoolteachers. And both of these expected income streams—for a doctor and for a schoolteacher—will be different from that expected by an assembly-line worker or a professional athlete. One possible lifetime income stream is shown in Figure 29A.1.

The individual's expected lifetime income is then converted into a single figure for annual **permanent income**. In the life-cycle theory, this permanent income is the maximum amount that the person could spend on consumption each year into the indefinite future without accumulating debts that are passed on to future generations. If people were to consume a constant amount that was equal to their permanent income each year, they would add to their debts or reduce their assets in years when current income was less than permanent income, and they would reduce their debt or increase their assets in years when their current income exceeded their permanent income. Over their lifetime, however, they would just break even, leaving neither accumulated assets nor debts to their heirs. If the interest rate were zero, permanent income would be just the sum of all expected incomes divided by the number of expected years of life. With a positive interest rate, permanent income will diverge from this amount because of the cost of borrowing and the extra income that can be earned by investing savings.

ASSUMPTION

The basic assumption of this type of theory, whether it is the PIT or LCT, is that the people's actual consumption is related to their permanent rather than to their current income; further, two individuals that have the same permanent income (and are similar in other relevant characteristics) will have similar consumption patterns, even though their current incomes may behave differently.

IMPLICATIONS

The major implication of these theories is that changes in a person's current income will affect his or her actual consumption only in so far as they affect his or her permanent income. Consider two income changes that could happen to a person with a permanent income of £30,000 per year and an expected lifetime of 30 or more years.

In the first case, suppose that the person receives an unexpected extra income of £2,000 *for this year only*. The increase in the person's permanent income is small. If the rate of interest were zero, the person in question could consume an extra £66.66 per year for the rest of his or her expected life span; with a positive rate of interest, the extra annual consumption would be more because money not spent this year could be invested and would earn interest. Still, the extra annual consumption enabled by the £2,000 would be very small relative to the current level of annual consumption.[2]

In the second case, suppose that the individual gets a totally unforeseen increase of £2,000 per year *for the rest of his or her life*. In this event, the person's permanent income has risen by £2,000 because the person actually can consume £2,000 more every year without accumulating new debts. Although in both cases current income rises by £2,000, the effect on permanent income is very different.

In the Keynesian consumption function, *consumption expenditure* is related to current income, and therefore the same change in this year's consumption expenditure is predicted for each of the cases just discussed. Permanent income theories relate *actual consumption* to permanent

---

[2] If the rate of interest were 7 per cent, the person could invest the £2,000, consume an extra £161 per year, and have nothing left at the end of 30 years.

income, and therefore predict different changes in actual consumption in each case; in the first case, there would be only a small increase in actual annual consumption; in the second case, there would be a large increase.

In the LCT and the PIT, any change in current income that is thought to be temporary will have only a small effect on permanent income and hence on actual consumption.

IMPLICATIONS FOR THE BEHAVIOUR OF THE ECONOMY

According to the permanent income and the life-cycle hypotheses, actual consumption is not affected much by temporary changes in income. Does this mean that aggregate expenditure, $C + I + G + (X – IM)$, is not affected much? Not necessarily. Consider what happens when people get a temporary increase in their incomes. If actual consumption is not greatly affected by this, then individuals must be saving most of this increase. However, from the point of view of these theories, people save when they buy a durable good just as much as when they buy a financial asset, such as a share or a bond. In both cases actual current consumption is not changed.

Thus, using a temporary increase in income either to increase savings or to buy a new car is consistent with both the PIT and the LCT, but it makes a great deal of difference to the short-run behaviour of the economy which one of these choices is made. If people increase their savings, aggregate expenditure on currently produced final goods will not rise when income rises temporarily; if they buy cars or any other durable consumer good, aggregate expenditure on currently produced final goods will rise when income rises temporarily. Thus, the PIT and the LCT leave unsettled the question that is critical in determining the size of the multiplier: what is the reaction of personal *expenditure* on currently produced goods and services, particularly durables, to short-term, temporary changes in income? Assume, for example, that a serious recessionary gap emerges and that the government attempts to stimulate a recovery by giving tax rebates and by cutting tax rates— both on an announced, temporary basis. This will raise current personal disposable incomes by the amount of the tax cuts, but it will raise their permanent incomes by only a small amount.

According to the PIT and the LCT, the flow of actual current consumption should not rise much. Yet it is quite consistent with the PIT and the LCT that people should spend their tax savings on durable consumer goods, the consumption of which can be spread over many years. In this case, even though actual consumption this year would not respond much to the tax cuts, expenditure would respond a great deal. Because current output and employment depend on expenditure rather than on actual consumption, the tax cut would be effective in stimulating the economy. However, it is also consistent with the LCT and the PIT that people spend only a small part of their tax savings on consumption goods and seek to invest the rest in bonds and other financial assets. In this case the tax cuts may have only a small stimulating effect on the economy.

It is important to note that the PIT and the LCT *do not predict unambiguously* that changes in taxes that are announced as only short-term measures will be ineffective in changing aggregate expenditure.

❧ CHAPTER 30

National income in an open economy with government

IN this chapter, we continue building a model of national income determination. So far, we have assumed a highly simplified environment. In building our model of Chapter 29, we maintained four simplifying, but temporary, assumptions: no government, no foreign trade, fixed price level, and excess capacity. The current chapter relaxes the first two of these. The following chapter relaxes the last two.

Our task in this chapter, then, is to add a government and a foreign sector to our simple model. Adding the government sector allows us to study *fiscal policy*, the ability of the government to use its taxing and spending powers to affect the level of national income. In an open economy, net foreign demand for domestic output is an important source of final expenditure, so it has to be included in any complete treatment of the expenditure components of national income. We proceed, first, to add the government. Then we add the foreign trade sector. Finally, we examine how these additions change both the structure of the model and its behaviour in response to changes in autonomous expenditures.

As we proceed, it is important to remember that the key elements of our theory of income determination are unchanged. The most important of these, which will remain true even after incorporating government and the foreign sector, are restated here.

1. Aggregate desired expenditure can be divided into autonomous expenditure and induced expenditure. Induced expenditure is expenditure that depends on the level of national income.
2. The equilibrium level of national income is the level at which the sum of autonomous-desired and induced-desired expenditure is equal to the level of national income. Graphically, this is where the aggregate expenditure line intersects the 45° line.
3. The simple multiplier measures the change in equilibrium national income that takes place in response to a unit change in autonomous domestic expenditure, with the price level held constant.

Recall that the expenditure-based measure of national income, or GDP, is made up of consumption, investment, government expenditure, and net exports. We have built a model of national income determination which includes consumption and investment. Now we are about to extend this model to include government spending and net exports.

Government spending and taxes

GOVERNMENT spending and taxing policies affect equilibrium national income in two important ways. First, government expenditure is part of autonomous expenditure. Second, in deriving disposable income, taxes must be subtracted from national income, and government transfer payments must be added. Because disposable income determines consumption expenditure, the relationship between desired consumption and national income becomes more complicated when a government is added. A government's plans for taxes and spending define its *fiscal policy*, which has important effects on the level of national income in both the short and the long run.

GOVERNMENT SPENDING

In Chapter 28 we distinguished between government *expenditure on goods and services* and government *transfer payments*. The distinction bears repeating here. Government expenditure on goods and services is part of GDP. When the government hires a civil servant, buys a paper clip, or purchases fuel for the navy, it is directly adding to the demands on the economy's current output of goods and services. Thus, desired government purchases, G, are part of aggregate expenditure. As explained in Chapter 29, in our model we treat government spending on goods and services as if it all went to buy output from a single industrial sector. This means that the effect of government spending on national income is exactly the same as the effect of any other component of autonomous expenditure.

The other part of government spending—transfer payments—also affects desired aggregate expenditure, but only indirectly. Consider, for example, state pensions, unemployment benefit, or student grants. These are payments (tranfers) made by government to individuals. The recipients may well then spend the money. However, that demand is recorded as personal consumption, so we don't want to count it twice, by recording it under G as well. We regard government transfer payments as affecting aggregate expenditure only through the effect that these payments have on *disposable* income. Transfer payments increase disposable income, and increases in disposable income, via the consumption function, increase desired consumption expenditure.

This distinction between transfers and government spending on goods and services is important when it comes to issues such as how much of national income is taken by government. Measuring the size of government to include transfers makes it look as though government's part in national output is much bigger than it really is. However, looking only at *G* makes the government's revenue needs look smaller than they are, since transfers must be financed by taxes or borrowing, just as expenditure on goods and services must be. We discuss the composition of government expenditure in more detail in Chapter 42.

TAX REVENUES

Tax revenues may be thought of as negative transfer payments in their effect on desired aggregate expenditure. Tax payments reduce disposable income relative to national income; transfers raise disposable income relative to national income. For the purpose of calculating the effect of government policy on desired consumption expenditure, it is the net effect of the two that matters.

We define **net taxes** to be total tax revenues received by the government minus total transfer payments made by the government, and we denote net taxes as *T*. (For convenience, when we use the term 'taxes' we will mean *net* taxes unless we explicitly state otherwise.) Since transfer payments are smaller than total taxes, net taxes are positive, and personal disposable income is less than national income. (It was 74 per cent of GDP at market prices in 1993.)

THE BUDGET BALANCE

The **budget balance** is the difference between total government revenue and total government expenditure; or, equivalently, it equals net taxes minus government spending, T – G. When revenues exceed expenditure, the government is running a **budget surplus**. When expenditure exceeds revenues, as it has for most of the post-war period (1988–9 and 1969–70 were the only exceptions), the government is running a **budget deficit**.[1] When the budget surplus (and deficit) is zero, the government has a **balanced budget**. When the budget is in deficit, the government is adding to the national debt since it must borrow to cover its deficit. When the budget is in surplus, the government is reducing the national debt since the surplus funds are used to pay off old debt.

The **Public Sector Borrowing Requirement (PSBR)** is

[1] When the government runs a budget deficit, it must borrow the excess of spending over revenues. It does this by *selling government bonds* (gilts). When the government runs a surplus, it uses the excess revenue to purchase outstanding government bonds. The stock of outstanding bonds is termed the *national* or *public debt*. (Public debt is the debt of the entire public sector, which includes local authorities and nationalized industries; national debt is the debt of the central government only.)

similar to the budget deficit but it differs from it by (minus) asset sales, and by borrowing by parts of the public sector other than central government. The budget deficit is the concept most relevant to macroeconomics because changes in the ownership of assets do not affect current GDP. Since the budget deficit is simply a negative budget surplus, we generally use 'budget surplus' to cover both cases, so bear in mind that the budget surplus can be negative.

TAX AND EXPENDITURE FUNCTIONS

We treat government expenditure as autonomous. The government is assumed to decide on how much it wishes to spend in real terms, and to hold to these plans whatever the

Table 30.1   The budget surplus function

National income (Y) (£m)	Government expenditure (G) (£m)	Net taxes (T = 0.1Y) (£m)	Government surplus (T – G) (£m)
500	170	50	– 120
1,000	170	100	– 70
1,750	170	175	5
2,000	170	200	30
3,000	170	300	130
4,000	170	400	230

The budget surplus is negative at low levels of national income and becomes positive at sufficiently high levels of national income. The table shows that the size of the budget surplus increases with national income, given constant expenditure and constant tax rates. For example, when national income rises by £1,000 million, the deficit falls or the surplus rises by £100 million in the example shown here.

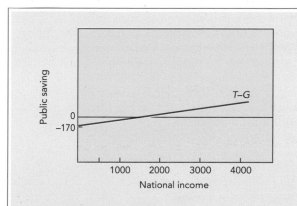

Figure 30.1   Budget surplus function

The budget surplus increases as national income increases. This figure plots the *T–G* column from Table 30.1. Notice that the slope of the surplus function is equal to the income tax rate of 0.1.

level of national income. We also treat *tax rates* as autonomous. The government sets its tax rates and does not vary them as national income varies. This, however, implies that *tax revenues* are induced, or endogenous. As national income rises, a tax system with given rates will yield more revenue. For example, when income rises, people will pay more income tax in total even though income tax *rates* are unchanged. For simplicity, in macroeconomic model-building we assume that the only tax is a tax on income, so there are no indirect taxes.

Table 30.1 and Figure 30.1 illustrate these assumptions with a specific example. They show the size of the government's surplus when its desired purchases (*G*) are constant at £170 million and its net tax revenues are equal to 10 per cent of national income. Notice that the government budget surplus (or public saving) increases with national income. This relationship occurs because net tax revenues rise with income but, by assumption, government expenditure does not. The slope of the budget surplus function is just equal to the income tax rate. The *position* of the function is determined by fiscal policy, as we discuss later in this chapter.[2]

The government budget surplus (public saving), for given tax rates, tends to increase as national income rises and to fall when national income falls.

Net exports

THE foreign trade sector of the UK economy is significant in relation to the size of GDP. Exports of goods and services in 1993 were just over 25 per cent of GDP at market prices. Although the total volume of trade is important for many purposes, such as determining the amount by which a country gains from trade, it is the balance between exports and imports (the current account balance) that is particularly important in national income determination. Data for the United Kingdom are shown in Figure 27.9 on p. 519.

THE NET EXPORT FUNCTION

In macroeconomics, we are interested in how the balance of trade responds to changes in national income, the price level, and the exchange rate. Our theory covers trade in goods *and services*. The effects on national income of selling a service to a foreigner are identical to those of selling a physical commodity. (Recall that we have only one type of product in our economy, and all expenditures are treated as demands for this product.)

Exports depend on spending decisions made by foreign consumers or firms that purchase UK goods and services. Typically, therefore, exports will not change as a result of changes in UK national income (or, at least, this is what we assume). They are autonomous, or exogenous, expenditures, from the point of view of UK national income.

Imports, however, depend on the spending decisions of domestic residents. Most categories of expenditure have an import content; British-made cars, for example, use large quantities of imported components and raw materials in their manufacture. Thus, imports rise when the other categories of expenditure rise. Because consumption rises with income, imports of foreign-produced consumer goods, and materials that go into the production of domestically produced consumer goods, also rise with income.

Desired net exports are negatively related to national income because of the positive relationship between desired imports and national income.

This negative relationship between net exports and national income is called the *net export function*. Data for a hypothetical economy with constant exports and with imports that are 25 per cent of national income are given in Table 30.2 and illustrated in Figure 30.2. In this example, exports form the autonomous component and imports form the induced component of the desired net export function. The formulation in the table implicitly assumes that all imports are for final consumption. Imports rise when income rises, but imports do not change when *other* categories of autonomous expenditure change, so there is no direct import content of *G*, *I*, and *X*. This simplification will prove useful in our development of the determination of equilibrium income and does not affect the essentials of the theory. The issue is further discussed in Appendix A.

SHIFTS IN THE NET EXPORT FUNCTION

We have seen that the net export function relates net

---

[2] The numerical example used here is designed only to illustrate the principles of income determination developed in this chapter. To avoid the appearance of direct applicability of overly simplified models, we have deliberately chosen not to use 'realistic' numbers. The example produces a GDP of £2,000 million, whereas UK money GDP in 1993 was a little over £600,000 million.

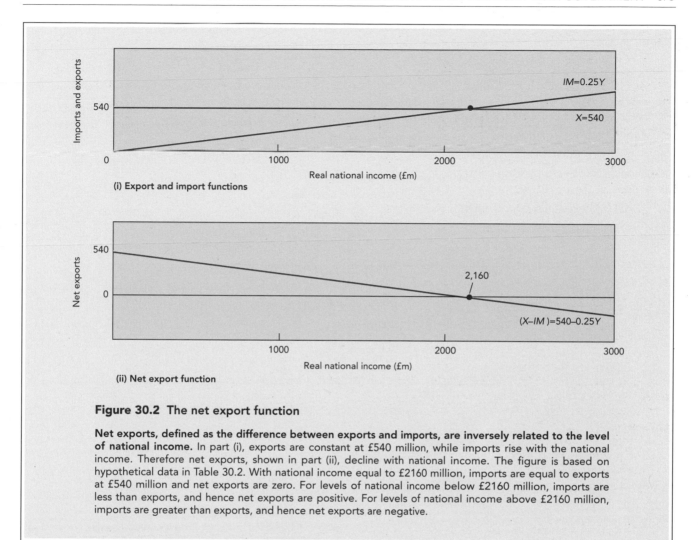

Figure 30.2 The net export function

Net exports, defined as the difference between exports and imports, are inversely related to the level of national income. In part (i), exports are constant at £540 million, while imports rise with the national income. Therefore net exports, shown in part (ii), decline with national income. The figure is based on hypothetical data in Table 30.2. With national income equal to £2160 million, imports are equal to exports at £540 million and net exports are zero. For levels of national income below £2160 million, imports are less than exports, and hence net exports are positive. For levels of national income above £2160 million, imports are greater than exports, and hence net exports are negative.

Table 30.2 The net export schedule

National income (Y) (£m)	Exports (X) (£m)	Imports (IM = 0.25Y) (£m)	Net exports (£m)
0	540	0	540
1,000	540	250	190
2,160	540	540	0
3,000	540	750	– 210
4,000	540	1,000	– 460
5,000	540	1,250	– 710

Net exports fall as national income rises. The data assume that exports are constant and that imports are 25 per cent of national income. In this case, net exports are positive at low levels of national income and negative at high levels of national income.

exports $(X - IM)$, which we also denote NX, to national income. It is drawn on the assumption that everything that affects net exports, except domestic national income, remains constant. The major factors that must be held constant are foreign national income, relative international price levels, and the exchange rate. A change in any of these factors will affect the amount of net exports that will occur at each level of national income and hence will shift the net export function.

Notice that anything that affects domestic exports will change the values in the 'Exports' column in Table 30.2 and so will shift the net export function parallel to itself, upward if exports increase and downward if exports decrease. Also notice that anything that affects the proportion of income that home consumers wish to spend on imports will change the values in the 'Imports' column in the table, and thus will change the slope of the net export function by making

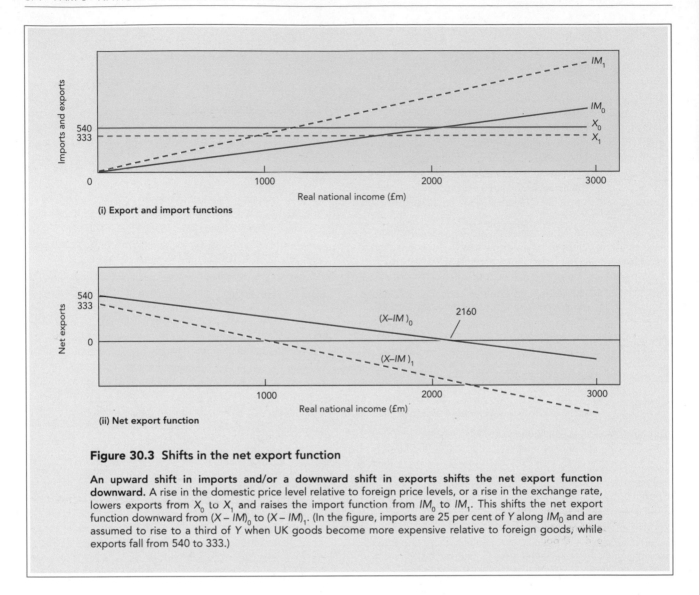

Figure 30.3 Shifts in the net export function

An upward shift in imports and/or a downward shift in exports shifts the net export function downward. A rise in the domestic price level relative to foreign price levels, or a rise in the exchange rate, lowers exports from X_0 to X_1 and raises the import function from IM_0 to IM_1. This shifts the net export function downward from $(X - IM)_0$ to $(X - IM)_1$. (In the figure, imports are 25 per cent of Y along IM_0 and are assumed to rise to a third of Y when UK goods become more expensive relative to foreign goods, while exports fall from 540 to 333.)

imports more or less responsive to changes in domestic income. What factors will cause such shifts?

Foreign income An increase in foreign income, other things being equal, will lead to an increase in the quantity of UK-produced goods demanded by foreign countries, that is to an increase in our exports. Because more exports will be sold whatever the level of UK national income, the increase is in the constant, X, of the net export function, causing NX to shift upward, parallel to its original position. A fall in foreign income leads to a parallel downward shift in the net export function.

Relative international prices Any change in the prices of home-produced goods relative to those of foreign goods

will cause both imports and exports to change. This will shift the net export function.

Consider first a rise in domestic prices relative to prices in foreign countries. On the one hand, foreigners now see UK goods as more expensive relative both to goods produced in their own country and to goods imported from other countries. As a result, UK exports will fall. On the other hand, we will see imports from foreign countries as cheaper relative to the prices of home-made goods. As a result, we will buy more foreign goods and imports will rise. Both of these shifts cause the net export function to shift downwards and change its slope, as shown in Figure 30.3.

Second, consider the opposite case of a fall in UK prices relative to prices of foreign-made goods. On the one hand, potential UK exports will now look cheaper in foreign markets relative both to their home-produced goods and to goods imported from third countries. As a result, UK exports rise. On the other hand, the same change in relative prices—British-made goods become cheaper relative to foreign-made goods—causes UK imports to fall. Thus, the net export function shifts upwards, in exactly the opposite way to the movement in Figure 30.3.

What kinds of things will cause relative international prices to change? Two important causes of changes in competitiveness, for a country as a whole, are international differences in inflation rates and changes in exchange rates.

Consider inflation rates first. Holding the sterling exchange rate constant, UK prices will rise relative to foreign prices if the UK inflation rate is higher than the inflation rates in other major trading countries. In contrast, UK prices will fall relative to foreign prices if the UK inflation rate is lower than the rates in other major trading countries.

Now consider exchange rates. Holding domestic and foreign price levels constant, a devaluation of sterling makes imports more expensive for domestic residents and our exports cheaper for foreigners. This is because we get less foreign currency for each pound sterling and foreigners get more pounds for each unit of their own currency. Both for-

eigners and domestic consumers will shift expenditure towards the home-produced goods, which have become cheaper relative to foreign goods. The net export function thus shifts upward.

An appreciation of sterling (holding price levels constant) has the opposite effect. It makes UK goods relatively expensive, thus shifting the net export function downward.[3]

The results of this important chain of reasoning are summarized as follows:

1. UK prices rise relative to foreign prices either if the UK inflation rate exceeds the rate in other major trading countries (with exchange rates fixed) or if the pound sterling appreciates (with price levels constant). This discourages exports and encourages imports, causing the net export function to shift downwards.

2. UK prices fall relative to foreign prices either if the UK inflation rate is less than the rates in competitor countries (with exchange rates fixed) or if the pound sterling depreciates (with price levels constant). This encourages exports and discourages imports, causing the net export function to shift upwards.

Equilibrium national income

WE are now ready to see how equilibrium national income is determined in our new model that includes a government and a foreign sector. As in Chapter 29, we can determine the equilibrium in two ways, which come to the same thing in the end: by relating income and expenditure, and by relating savings and investment.

The income–expenditure approach

In Chapter 29, we determined equilibrium national income by finding the level of national income where desired aggregate expenditure is equal to national income. The addition of government and the foreign sector changes the calculations that we must make but does not alter the basic principles that are involved. Our first step is to derive a new aggregate expenditure function that incorporates the effects of government and foreign trade.

RELATING DESIRED CONSUMPTION TO NATIONAL INCOME

Our theory of national income determination requires that

we relate each of the components of aggregate expenditure to national income. Personal income taxes cause personal disposable income to differ from national income (by the proportion of income taxation net of transfers). We shall simply assume that disposable income is always 90 per cent of national income.[4] Thus, whatever the relationship between C and Y_d, we can always substitute $0.9Y$ for Y_d. For example, if changes in consumption were always 80 per cent of changes in Y_d, changes in consumption would always be 72 per cent (80 per cent of 90 per cent) of changes in Y.

Table 30.3 illustrates how we can write desired consumption as a function of Y as well as of Y_d. We can then

[3] A depreciation of sterling that is exactly proportional to the excess of UK inflation over foreign inflation will leave the relative price of UK exports and imports unchanged. This would be referred to as a constant *real exchange rate*, or as preserving purchasing power parity (PPP). The real exchange rate is the relative price of home- and foreign-produced goods. It is also referred to as 'competitiveness' or the 'terms of trade'. A rise in the real exchange rate (fall in competitiveness) shifts the net export function down because it lowers exports and increases imports at each level of national income.

[4] In this case, T, desired net taxes, would be given by the function $T = 0.1Y$. Recall that, for simplicity, we ignore indirect taxes.

Table 30.3 Consumption as a function of disposable income and national income

National income (Y) (£m)	Disposable income ($Y_d = 0.9Y$) (£m)	Desired consumption ($C = 100 + 0.8Y_d$) (£m)
100	90	172
1,000	900	820
2,000	1,800	1,540
3,000	2,700	2,260
4,000	3,600	2,980

If desired consumption depends on disposable income, which in turn depends on national income, desired consumption can be written as a function of either income concept. The second column shows deductions of 10 per cent of any level of national income to arrive at disposable income. Deductions of 10 per cent of Y imply that the remaining 90 per cent of Y becomes disposable income. The third column shows consumption as £100 million plus 80 per cent of disposable income.

By relating the second and third columns, one sees consumption as a function of disposable income. By relating the first and third columns, one sees the derived relationship between consumption and national income. In this example, the change in consumption in response to a change in disposable income (i.e. the MPC) is 0.8, and the change in consumption in response to a change in national income is 0.72.

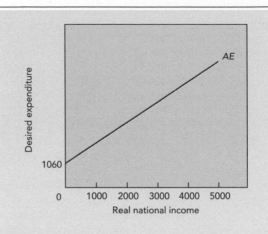

Figure 30.4 An aggregate expenditure curve

The aggregate expenditure curve relates total desired expenditure to national income. The AE curve in the figure plots the data from the first and last columns of Table 30.4. Its intercept shows £1,060 million of autonomous expenditure (£100 million autonomous consumption plus £250 million investment plus £170 million government, plus £540 million autonomous net exports). Its slope is the marginal propensity to spend (which, following the calculations in Table 30.4 is 0.47 in this case).

derive the marginal response of consumption to changes in Y by determining the proportion of any change in *national income* that goes to a change in desired consumption.

The marginal response of consumption to changes in national income ($\Delta C/\Delta Y$) is equal to the marginal propensity to consume out of disposable income ($\Delta C/\Delta Y_d$) multiplied by the fraction of national income that becomes personal disposable income ($\Delta Y_d/\Delta Y$).

We now have an equation that shows how desired consumption expenditure varies as national income varies, including the effects of taxes and transfer payments ($C = 100 + 0.72Y$; arrived at from $C = 100 + 0.8Y_d$ by substituting $0.9Y$ for Y_d). This is part of the aggregate expenditure function.

THE AGGREGATE EXPENDITURE FUNCTION

In order to determine equilibrium national income, we start by defining the aggregate expenditure function:

$$AE = C + I + G + NX.$$

Table 30.4 illustrates the calculation of the aggregate expenditure function. It shows a schedule of desired expenditure for each of the components of aggregate expenditure, and it shows total desired *aggregate* expenditure at each level of national income. Figure 30.4 shows this aggregate expenditure function, in graphical form.

THE MARGINAL PROPENSITY TO SPEND

The slope of the aggregate expenditure function is the *marginal propensity to spend* on national income (z). With the addition of taxes and net exports, however, the marginal propensity to spend is no longer equal to the marginal propensity to consume.

Suppose that the economy produces £1.00 of extra income and that the response to this is governed by the relationships in Tables 30.1 and 30.2, as summarized in Table 30.4. Since £0.10 is collected by the government as net taxes, £0.90 is converted into disposable income, and 80 per cent of this amount (£0.72) becomes consumption expenditure. However, import expenditure also rises by £0.25, so expenditure on domestic goods, that is aggregate expenditure, rises by only £0.47. Thus, z, the marginal propensity to spend out of national income, is 0.47. What is not spent on domestic output includes the £0.10 in taxes, the £0.18 of disposable income that is saved, and the £0.25

Table 30.4 The aggregate expenditure function

National income (Y)	Desired consumption expenditure ($C = 100 + 0.72Y$)	Desired investment expenditure ($I = 250$)	Desired government expenditure ($G = 170$)	Desired net export expenditure ($IM = 540 - 0.25Y$)	Desired aggregate expenditure ($AE = C + I + G + (X - IM)$)
(£m)	(£m)	(£m)	(£m)	(£m)	(£m)
0	100	250	170	540	1,060
100	172	250	170	515	1,107
500	460	250	170	315	1,195
1,000	820	250	170	290	1,530
2,000	1,540	250	170	40	**2,000**
3,000	2,260	250	170	– 210	2,470
4,000	2,980	250	170	– 460	2,940
5,000	3,700	250	170	– 710	3,410

The aggregate expenditure function is the sum of desired consumption, investment, government, and net export expenditures. The autonomous components of desired aggregate expenditure are desired investment, desired government spending, desired export expenditure, and the constant term in desired consumption (first row). These sum to £1,060 million in the above example. The induced components are the second term in desired consumption expenditure (0.72Y) and desired imports (0.25Y).

The marginal response of consumption to a change in national income is 0.72, calculated as the product of the marginal propensity to consume (0.8) times the fraction of national income that becomes disposable income (0.9). The marginal response of desired aggregate expenditure to a change in national income, $\Delta AE/\Delta Y$, is 0.47.

of import expenditure, for a total of £0.53. Hence, the marginal propensity not to spend, $1 - z$, is $1 - 0.47 = 0.53$.

DETERMINING EQUILIBRIUM NATIONAL INCOME

The logic of national income determination in our (now more complicated) hypothetical economy is exactly the same as in the closed economy without government, discussed in Chapter 29. We have added two new components of aggregate expenditure, G and $(X - IM)$. We have also made the calculation of desired consumption expenditure more complicated; taxes must be subtracted from national income in order to determine disposable income. However, *equilibrium national income is still the level of national income at which desired aggregate expenditure equals national income.*

The aggregate expenditure function can be used directly to determine equilibrium national income. In Table 30.4, the equilibrium is £2,000 million. When national income is equal to £2,000 million, it is also equal to desired aggregate expenditure.

Suppose that national income is less than its equilibrium amount. The forces leading back to equilibrium are exactly the same as those described on pp. 554–58 of Chapter 29. When domestic consumers, firms, foreign consumers, and governments try to spend at their desired amounts, they will try to purchase more goods and services than the eco-

nomy is currently producing. Thus, some of the desired expenditure must either be frustrated or take the form of purchases of inventories of goods that were produced in the past. As firms see that they are (or could be) selling more than they are producing, they will increase production, thereby increasing the level of national income.

The opposite sequence of events occurs when national income is greater than the level of aggregate expenditure desired at that income. Now the total of personal consumption, investment, government spending, and net foreign demand for the economy's output is less than the national product. Firms will notice that they are unable to sell all of their output. Their unsold stocks will be rising, and they will not let this happen indefinitely. They will seek to reduce the level of output until it equals the level of sales, and national income will fall.

Finally, when national income is equal to desired aggregate expenditure (£2,000 million in Table 30.4), there is no pressure for output to change. Consumption, investment, government spending, and net exports just add up to national product. Firms are producing exactly the quantity of goods and services that purchasers want to buy, given the level of income.

Equilibrium national income is determined where desired aggregate expenditure equals national income. In our extended model, aggregate expenditure includes consumption, investment, government spending, and net exports.

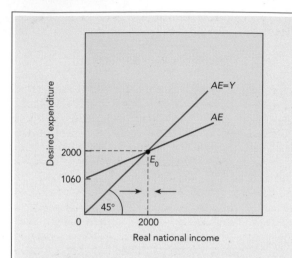

Figure 30.5 Equilibrium national income

Equilibrium national income occurs at E_0, where the desired aggregate expenditure line intersects the 45° line. Here the aggregate expenditure line is taken from Table 30.4; autonomous expenditure is £1,060, and the slope of AE is 0.47. If real national income is below £2,000, desired aggregate expenditure will exceed national income, and production will rise. This is shown by the arrow to the left of $Y = £2,000$. If national income is above £2,000, desired aggregate expenditure will be less than national income, and production will fall. This is shown by the arrow to the right of $Y = £2,000$. Only when real national income is £2,000 will desired aggregate expenditure equal real national income.

Graphical exposition   Figure 30.5 illustrates the determination of equilibrium and the behaviour of the economy when it is not in equilibrium. The line labelled AE is simply the aggregate expenditure function shown in Figure 30.4. The slope of AE is the marginal propensity to spend out of national income (0.47 in our example). Recall that AE plots the behaviour of desired purchases in the economy. It shows demand for the domestic product at each level of national income. (The AE curve is sometimes referred to as the 'aggregate demand curve' in this context. However, we reserve this term for another related concept in the next chapter, once we have permitted the price level to be variable.)

The line labelled $AE = Y$ (the 45° line) depicts the equilibrium condition that desired aggregate expenditure is equal to actual national income. Any point on this line *could* be an equilibrium, but only one is. Equilibrium occurs where behaviour (as depicted by the AE function) is consistent with equilibrium (as depicted by $AE = Y$). At the equilibrium level of income, desired expenditure is just equal to national income and is therefore just sufficient to purchase total national output.

The augmented saving–investment approach

An equivalent way of determining equilibrium national income is analogous to finding the point where desired saving equals desired investment. Finding the level of income where $S = I$ was appropriate in Chapter 29, where we were dealing with a closed economy with no government. Now we have to take account of the facts that there is government saving as well as private saving, and that net exports provide an injection of spending which plays a similar role to investment.

Additional injections and leakages   The reason why saving and investment had to be equal for national income to be in equilibrium is that this is the only point at which there is a balance of inflows and outflows (injections and leakages) in the circular flow of income. It may be helpful to review both the hydraulic analogue in Box 29.1, on p.557, and the circular flow of income, illustrated in Figure 27.1 on p. 500, at this stage. The principles involved are unchanged. Now, however, we have two additional sources of leakages and two additional sources of injections.

Saving was our only leakage of expenditure from the circular flow in Chapter 29. The marginal propensity to save told us how much was not spent out of each additional £1 of income received. Now we add personal income taxes. These are levied on individuals' gross incomes, and so they also represent a proportion of income earned that cannot be spent. The second additional leakage is imports. Imports are a leakage because they create demand for foreign output. This does not generate domestic income.

Investment was the only injection in our model in Chapter 29. In this chapter we have added government spending. This is received as income by the private sector and this extra income leads to further spending as before. Similarly, export demand comes from other countries, but it generates domestic incomes. Hence, export demand is our second new injection.

The condition for national income to be in equilibrium is now that the sum of desired injections must equal the sum of desired leakages (see Figure 27.1). We can write this condition as an equation, with the sum of all leakages (saving, S, plus taxes, T, plus imports, IM) equal to the sum of all injections (investment, I, plus government spending, G, plus exports, X):

$$S + T + IM = I + G + X.$$

An equilibrium condition for the determination of equilibrium national income equivalent to $AE = Y$ is that injections (investment plus government spending plus exports) must equal leakages (saving plus income taxes plus imports).

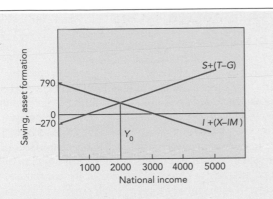

Figure 30.6 National saving and national asset formation

The economy is in equilibrium at Y_0, where desired national saving, $S+(T-G)$ equals desired national asset formation, $I+(X-IM)$. To the left of Y_0, desired national asset formation exceeds desired national saving. This implies that desired aggregate expenditure exceeds national income. Firms will respond to the imbalance by producing more, moving the economy toward equilibrium. To the right of Y_0, desired national asset formation is less than desired national saving, and aggregate expenditure is less than national income. Firms will cut back on output in order to avoid accumulating excess inventories, and the economy will move towards equilibrium.

Graphical exposition In order to illustrate the determination of national income via the equality of injections and leakages, it is convenient to rearrange the above equation slightly. The convenience is partly the creation of graphical simplicity, but also, there is an advantage in terms of economic intuition.

Subtracting G and IM from both sides of the above equation gives

$$S + (T - G) = I + (X - IM).$$

This is the same expression except that we have deducted G and IM from both sides. The brackets do not change the meaning of anything, but they do identify two terms we are already familiar with. $(T - G)$ is the government budget surplus. In this context it can be thought of as public-sector (government) saving. As S is private saving, $S + (T - G)$ is total domestic saving, or national saving. $(X - IM)$ is our old friend, net exports. When there is no net property income from abroad, that is when GNP and GDP are equal (as was approximately true in the United Kingdom in 1993), net exports equal the rate of accumulation of claims on foreigners. This is because, if we sell to foreigners more than we buy from them, we must acquire a financial claim against them. (This claim could be foreign money, but it could also be shares in foreign companies, foreign government bonds, etc.) Hence, net exports represent the net acquisition of foreign assets or overseas investment (but only in the special case where GNP = GDP). I is domestic investment, so $I + (X - IM)$ is domestic plus overseas investment, or national asset formation. Thus, the equation $S + (T - G) = I + (X - IM)$ can be interpreted as a generalization of the condition that saving equals investment, since it says that national saving equals national asset formation.

Figure 30.6 illustrates how national income is determined where the national saving and national asset formation schedules intersect. Notice that this is exactly the same level of national income at which $AE = Y$.

Changes in aggregate expenditure

CHANGES in any of the autonomous components of planned aggregate expenditure will cause changes in equilibrium national income. In Chapter 29 we investigated the consequences of shifts in the consumption function and in the investment function. Here we take a first look at fiscal policy—the effects of government spending and taxes. We also consider shifts in the net export function. First, we take account of the fact that the simple multiplier is reduced by the presence of taxes and the marginal propensity to import.

The simple multiplier revisited In Chapter 29 we saw that the *simple multiplier*, the amount by which equilibrium national income changes when autonomous expenditure changes by £1, was equal to $1/(1 - z)$. In the example considered throughout Chapter 29, z, the marginal propensity to spend, was equal to 0.8, and the multiplier was equal to 5, or $1/(0.2)$. In the example that we have developed in this chapter, with a marginal propensity to import of 0.25 and a marginal (net) income tax rate of 0.1, the marginal propensity to spend is 0.47 (Ten per cent of a £1 increase in

goes to taxes, leaving 90p of dispos-
marginal propensity to consume of
this, 25p is spent on imports, leaving a
spent on domestically produced con-
.) Thus, (1 − z) is (0.53), and the simple
(0.53) = 1.89.

Net exports and equilibrium national income

As with the other elements of desired aggregate expenditure, if the net export function shifts upward, equilibrium national income will rise; if the net export function shifts downward, equilibrium national income will fall.

Autonomous net exports Net exports have both an autonomous component and an induced component. Generally, exports themselves are autonomous with respect to domestic national income. Foreign demand for UK goods and services depends on foreign income, on foreign and UK prices, and on the exchange rate, but it does not depend on UK domestic income. Export demand could also change because of a change in tastes. Suppose that foreign consumers develop a taste for British-made goods (perhaps, in reality, Jaguars or Land Rovers, but in the model it is for the output of the single sector) and desire to purchase £500 million more per year of such goods than they had in the past. The net export function (and the aggregate expenditure function) will shift up by £500 million, and equilibrium national income will increase by £500 million times the multiplier.

Induced net exports The domestic demand for imports depends, in part, on domestic income. The greater is domestic income, the greater will be UK residents' demand for goods and services in general, including those produced abroad. Because imports are subtracted to obtain net exports (net exports equal $X − IM$), the greater is the marginal propensity to import, the lower will be the marginal propensity to spend on the domestic product, and the lower will be the multiplier, $1/(1 − z)$.

Fiscal policy

Fiscal policy involves the use of government spending and tax policies to influence total desired expenditure in order to influence the level of national income. In practical terms, this means trying to avoid unsustainable booms and recessions.

Since government expenditure increases aggregate desired expenditure and taxation decreases it, the *directions* of the required changes in spending and taxation are gen-

erally easy to determine once we know the direction of the desired change in national income. But the *timing, magnitude,* and *mixture* of the changes pose more difficult issues.

Any policy that attempts to stabilize national income at or near any desired level (usually potential national income) is called a **stabilization policy**. Here we deal only with the basic ideas of stabilization through fiscal policy. The main alternative to fiscal policy, monetary policy, will be discussed in Chapter 38, after we have added a monetary sector to our model of national income determination.

The basic idea of stabilization policy follows from what we have already learned. A reduction in tax rates or an increase in government expenditure shifts the *AE* curve upward, causing an increase in equilibrium national income. An increase in tax rates or a decrease in government expenditure shifts the *AE* curve downward, causing a decrease in equilibrium income.

If the government has some target level of GDP, it can use its taxation and expenditure as instruments to push the economy towards that target. First, suppose the economy is in a serious recession. The government would like to increase national income. The appropriate fiscal tools are to raise expenditure and/or to lower tax rates. Second, suppose the economy is 'overheated'. In the next two chapters, we will study what this means in detail. In the meantime, we observe that an 'overheated' economy has such a high level of national income that shortages are pushing up prices and causing inflation. Without worrying too much about the details, just assume that the current level of national income is higher than the target income that the government judges to be appropriate. What should the government do? The fiscal tools at its command are to lower government expenditure and to raise tax rates, both of which have a depressing effect on national income.

The proposition that governments can avoid recessions by deliberately stimulating aggregate demand created a major revolution in economic thought. This is still known as the Keynesian Revolution. We have already learned enough about macroeconomics to understand what this was all about. The idea was that an economy could reach an equilibrium level of national income that was well below the full-employment or potential level. The way out of this was for the government to use its fiscal policy to increase aggregate expenditure by increasing government spending or reducing taxes (or both).

The expenditure model of national income determination predicts that national income can get stuck at a level below its full potential. It also suggests how fiscal policy might be used to return the economy to its potential level of national income.

Now let us look in a little more detail at how this might work out. Bear in mind, however, that we are still dealing with a special case in which prices are fixed and there is excess capacity, so we are just looking at how our model, as developed so far, works, not at how the real world works.

CHANGES IN GOVERNMENT SPENDING

Suppose the government decides to increase its road building programme by £10 million a year.[5] Desired government spending (G) would rise by £10 million at every level of income, shifting AE upwards by the same amount. How much would equilibrium income change? This can be calculated, in our simple model, using the multiplier. Government purchases are part of autonomous expenditure, so a *change* in government purchases of ΔG will lead to a *change* in equilibrium national income of the multiplier times ΔG. In this example, equilibrium income would rise by £10 million times the simple multiplier, or £18.9 million. Figure 30.7 shows the effect on national income of an increase in government spending. It shows an upward parallel shift of the aggregate expenditure function, and a resulting increase in national income. The same analysis could be applied equally to an increase in any other autonomous expenditures, such as investment or exports.

Reducing government expenditure has the opposite effect of shifting the AE function downwards, parallel to itself, and reducing equilibrium national income. For example, if the government were to spend £2 million less on new roads, equilibrium national income would fall by £2 million times the simple multiplier, or £3.78 million.

A change in government spending, in this model, changes the equilibrium level of national income by the size of the spending change times the simple multiplier.

CHANGES IN TAX RATES

If tax rates change, the relationship between disposable income and national income changes. As a result, the relationship between desired consumption expenditure and national income also changes. For any given level of national income, there will be a different level of disposable income and thus a different level of consumption. Consequently, a change in tax rates will also cause a change in z, the marginal propensity to spend out of national income.

Consider a decrease in tax rates. If the government decreases its rate of income tax so that it collects 5p less out of every £1 of national income, then disposable income rises in relation to national income. Thus, consumption also rises at every level of national income. This results in a non-parallel upward shift of the AE curve, that is an increase in the slope of the curve, as shown in Figure 30.8. The result of this shift will be a rise in equilibrium national income.

A rise in taxes has the opposite effect. A rise in tax rates causes a decrease in disposable income, and hence in con-

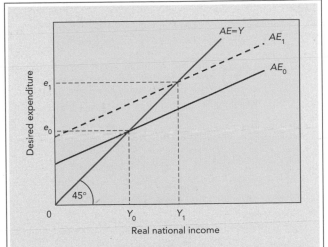

Figure 30.7 The effect of a change in government spending

A change in government spending changes national income by shifting the AE line parallel to its initial position. The figure shows the effect of an increase in government spending. The initial level of aggregate expenditure is AE_0 and the equilibrium level of national income is Y_0, with desired expenditures e_0. An increase in government spending shifts aggregate expenditure upwards to AE_1. As a result, national income rises to Y_1, at which level desired expenditures are e_1. The increase in national income from Y_0 to Y_1 is equal to the increase in government spending times the multiplier.

A reduction in government spending can be analysed in the same figure if we start with aggregate expenditure function AE_1 and national income Y_1. A reduction in government spending shifts the AE function downwards from AE_1 to AE_0 and, as a result, equilibrium national income falls from Y_1 to Y_0. The fall is equal to the change in government spending times the multiplier.

sumption expenditure, at each level of national income. This results in a non-parallel downward shift of the AE curve, and thus decreases the level of equilibrium national income.

Tax rates and the multiplier   We have seen that the *simple multiplier* is equal to the reciprocal of one minus the marginal propensity to spend. That is, the multiplier equals $1/(1 - z)$, where z is the marginal propensity to spend out of national income. The simple multiplier tells us how much equilibrium national income changes when autonomous expenditure changes by £1 and there is no change in prices.

---

[5] It does not matter what we assume the extra expenditure goes on. In our model it is always spent on the output of the single homogeneous industrial sector. Notice also that the value of the multiplier used in this section is hypothetical and based on the numerical example in Table 30.4.

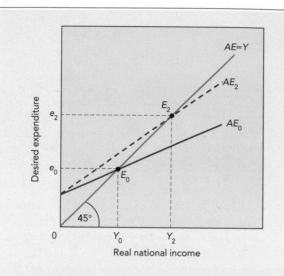

Figure 30.8 The effect of changing the tax rate

Changing the tax rate changes equilibrium income by changing the slope of the AE curve. A reduction in tax rates pivots the AE curve from AE_0 to AE_2. The new curve has a steeper slope, because the lower tax rate withdraws a smaller amount of national income from the desired consumption flow. Equilibrium income rises from Y_0 to Y_2, because at every level of national income desired consumption, and hence aggregate expenditure, is higher. If we take AE_2 and Y_2 to be the initial equilibrium, an increase in tax rates will reduce the slope of the AE curve, thereby reducing equilibrium income, as shown by AE_0 and Y_0.

When tax rates change, the multiplier also changes. Suppose that the *MPC* is 0.8 and the tax rate *falls* by 5p per pound of national income. This would increase the marginal propensity to spend by 4p per pound of national income. (Disposable income would rise by 5p per pound at each level of national income, and consumption would rise by the marginal propensity to consume, 0.8, times 5p, which is 4p.) The increase in the value of z, the marginal propensity to spend, would cause the multiplier to rise, making equilibrium income more responsive to changes in autonomous expenditure from any source. In our example, the multiplier has gone up from 1.89 to 1.96. ($(1 - z)$ has fallen from 0.53 to 0.51.)

The lower is the income tax rate, the larger is the simple multiplier.

National income may change as a result of a shift in any of the other exogenous components of expenditure—net exports, investment, or autonomous consumption. An increase in any of these would increase national income by the shift times the multiplier, as illustrated (for the case of a government spending increase) in Figure 30.7. An increase in any exogenous expenditure shifts the AE line vertically upwards by the amount of the expenditure increase. The new intersection with the 45° line determines the new level of national income, and its increase is measured relative to the original position on the horizontal axis. A reduction in any of these exogenous expenditures would shift the AE line downwards by the amount of the fall in spending.

Changes that would alter the slope of the AE line are a shift in the marginal propensity to consume, a shift in the rate of income tax, or a shift in the propensity to import. A fall in the marginal propensity to save (hence a rise in MPC, the marginal propensity to consume), a fall in the income tax rate, and a fall in the propensity to import all make the AE line steeper and increase the multiplier, as illustrated in Figure 30.8. A rise in any of these three has the opposite effect.

BALANCED BUDGET CHANGES

Another policy available to the government is to make a balanced-budget change by altering spending and taxes equally. Say the government increases tax rates enough to raise an extra £100 million that it then uses to purchase goods and services. Aggregate expenditure would remain unchanged if, and only if, the £100 million that the government takes from the private sector would otherwise have been spent by that sector. If so, the government's policy would reduce private expenditure by £100 million and raise its own spending by £100 million. Aggregate demand, and hence national income and employment, would remain unchanged.

But this is not the case in our model. When an extra £100 million in taxes is taken away from consumers, they reduce their spending on domestically produced goods by less than £100 million. If the marginal propensity to consume out of disposable income is, say, 0.75, consumption expenditure will fall by only £75 million. If the government spends the entire £100 million on domestically produced goods, aggregate expenditure will increase by £25 million. In this case, the balanced-budget increase in government expenditure has an expansionary effect, because it shifts the aggregate expenditure function upwards and thus increases national income.

A balanced-budget increase in government expenditure will have a mild expansionary effect on national income, and a balanced-budget decrease will have a mild contractionary effect.

The **balanced-budget multiplier** measures these effects. It is the change in income divided by the balanced-budget change in government expenditure that brought it about.

Thus, if the extra £100 million of expenditure (combined with the tax increases to finance it) causes national income to rise by £50 million, the balanced-budget multiplier is 0.5; if national income rises by £100 million, it is 1.0.

When government expenditure is increased with no corresponding increase in tax rates, we say it is deficit-financed. With a deficit-financed increase in government expenditure, there is no increase in tax rates, and hence no consequent decrease in consumption to offset the increase in government spending. With a balanced-budget increase in expenditure, however, the offsetting increase in tax rates and decrease in consumption does occur. Thus, the balanced-budget multiplier is much lower than the multiplier that relates the change in national income to a deficit-financed increase in government expenditure (with tax rates constant).

Lessons and limitations of the income–expenditure approach

In this and the preceding chapter, we have discussed the determination of the four categories of aggregate expenditure and seen how, simultaneously, they determine equilibrium national income. The basic approach, which is the same no matter how many categories are considered, was first presented in Chapter 29 and has been restated and extended in this chapter. Appendix B to this chapter provides an algebraic exposition of the model.

Any factor that shifts one or more of the components of desired aggregate expenditure will change equilibrium national income, *at a given price level.*

In the following chapters we augment the income–expenditure model by allowing the price level to change, in both the short run and the long run. When prices change, real income will change by amounts different from those predicted by the simple multiplier. We shall see that changes in desired aggregate expenditure generally change both prices *and* real national income. This is why the simple multiplier, derived under the assumption that prices do not change, is too simple.

However, there are three ways in which the simple income–aggregate expenditure model developed here remains useful, even when prices are incorporated. First, the simple multiplier will continue to be a valuable starting place in calculating actual changes in national income in response to changes in autonomous expenditure. Second, no matter what the price level, the components of aggregate expenditure add up to national income in equilibrium. Third, no matter what the price level, equilibrium requires that desired aggregate expenditure must equal national income in equilibrium, or, equivalently, that injections equal leakages.

Summary

1 Government spending is part of autonomous aggregate expenditure. Taxes minus transfer payments are called net taxes and affect aggregate expenditure indirectly. Taxes reduce disposable income, whereas transfers increase disposable income. Disposable income, in turn, determines desired consumption, according to the consumption function.

2 The budget balance is defined as government revenues minus government expenditures. When the result is positive, the budget is in surplus; when it is negative, the budget is in deficit.

3 When the budget is in surplus, there is positive public saving because the government is using less national product than the amount of income that it is withdrawing from the circular flow of income and product. When the government budget is in deficit, public saving is negative.

4 Since desired imports increase as national income increases, desired net exports decrease as national income increases, other things being equal. Hence, the net export function is negatively sloped.

5 National income is in equilibrium when desired aggregate expenditure, $C + I + G + (X - IM)$, equals national income.

6 The sum of investment and net exports is called national asset formation because investment is the increase in the domestic capital stock and net exports represent investment in foreign assets. At the equilibrium level of national income, desired national saving, $S + T - G$, is just equal to national asset formation, $I + X - IM$.

7 Equilibrium national income is negatively related to the amount of tax revenue that is associated with each level of national income. The size of the multiplier is negatively associated with the income tax rate.

8 Shifts in exogenous expenditures change national income by the value of the shift times the simple multiplier, so long as output is not limited by capacity constraints.

Topics for review

- Taxes and net taxes
- The budget balance
- Public saving
- The net export function
- The marginal propensity to spend
- National asset formation
- National saving
- Calculation of the simple multiplier
- Fiscal policy and equilibrium income

APPENDIX A TO CHAPTER 30

Import content of autonomous expenditure

TO simplify the treatment in the text, we assumed that all imports were embodied in consumption goods. Some of them may be final consumption goods, such as Japanese cars, and others may be foreign-made components of consumption goods assembled in the United Kingdom—such as printed circuits made in Singapore and incorporated into UK electrical goods. Formally, what we have assumed is that consumption is the only expenditure flow with any import content.

This simplifies the treatment by relating imports to national income but not to changes in autonomous expenditure. To understand the workings of the national income model, this is a useful simplification. In this appendix, we consider the effects of dropping this simplification. The appendix is mainly for those who may be worried by the assumption used in the text.

IMPORT CONTENT OF EXPENDITURE FLOWS

In practice, all categories of expenditure have an import content. Consider, first, an additional £100 million of domestic investment expenditure. When such expenditure goes to building factories, many of the materials used in the factory will be imported. Thus, the expenditure on domestically produced goods and services rises by less than £100 million, while new imports account for the rest. The same is true of all other categories of expenditure. If the government embarks on a new road-building programme, only part of the expenditure will be a net addition to the domestic circular flow, while the rest will leak out as expenditure on imports of many road-building materials. Even exports have a large import content. When UK firms sell an extra £100 million of new exports, this represents an injection of less than £100 million into the UK circular flow. The rest will be expenditure on imports of such things as components made in Taiwan and Indonesia that end up in the exported good.

Since we assumed in the text that only consumption expenditure had any import content, none of the categories of autonomous expenditure had any such content. The results derived in the text are exactly correct for this case. To apply it to the real world, we need to look in more detail at the import content of each expenditure flow.

AGGREGATE EXPENDITURE AND IMPORT CONTENT

The aggregate expenditure function is

$$Y = C + I + G + (X - IM).$$

We handle the import content of consumption by allowing both C and IM to depend on Y:

$$Y = cY + I + G + (X - mY).$$

Now we allow for the import content of autonomous expenditure by separating it out in each case:

$$Y = cY + (I - I_m) + (G - G_m) + [(X - X_m) - mY],$$

where I_m, G_m, and X_m are the import contents of investment expenditure, government expenditure, and exports.

There are two ways to handle the analysis from here on. First, we can deal with the terms in the parentheses, which means that each injection is defined as net of its import content. This was the approach taken by UK Nobel Laureate Professor James Meade, in his famous treatise on the balance of payments published in the 1950s. The main problem with this approach is that the magnitudes net of import content are not easy to relate to the published statistics. Also, it is not easy to use a model defined in these terms to deal with the effects of changes in autonomous expenditure on the trade balance.

Second, we can deal with gross spending in each category and gather up all the import-content terms into a single term for autonomous imports:

$$Y = cY + I + G + [X - (Z + mY)],$$

where Z is the autonomous component of imports, equal to $I_m + G_m + X_m$. The main problem with this approach is that, every time any element of autonomous expenditure changes, Z also changes by the import content of that autonomous expenditure.

In more advanced work, some decision must be made on how to handle the import contents of all expenditure flows when a model is constructed. In elementary treatments, it is simpler to avoid these complex problems of modelling by making the simplifying assumption used in the text that only consumption expenditure has an import content.

MULTIPLIERS OF LESS THAN UNITY

For most purposes of understanding the basic working of the model of the determination of national income, the above simplifying assumption is harmless. The one place in which it can be misleading, however, is in making us think that the multiplier is larger than it really is. Indeed, once an import content to autonomous expenditure flows is admitted, there is no need for the multiplier to exceed unity *where the change in injections is measured to include its import content.*

Consider, for example, a situation in which the government increases expenditure by £1 billion on projects that have an import content of 50 per cent. This means that the initial injection into the domestic circular flow is only £500

million—the rest goes to imports. If the multiplier is 1.8, the final change in national income will be £900 million, which is less than the original increase in government expenditure!

The above result does not contradict the theory. The theory refers to an injection into the *domestic circular flow*, which is clearly the *domestic content* of any increased expenditure. Once the import content is admitted, the theory predicts that the multiplier must exceed unity when applied to the domestic content of any injection of new expenditure, but not to the gross amount.

APPENDIX B TO CHAPTER 30

An algebraic exposition of the elementary income–expenditure model

We start with the definition of desired aggregate expenditure:

$$AE = C + I + G + (X - IM) \qquad (A1)$$

For each component of AE, we write down a behavioural function:

$$C = a + bY_d \text{ (consumption function)}, \qquad (A2)$$

where a is autonomous consumption spending and b is the marginal propensity to consume; then

$$I = I_0 \qquad (A3)$$

$$G = G_0 \qquad (A4)$$

$$X = X_0 \qquad (A5)$$

$$IM = mY \text{ (import function)} \qquad (A6)$$

where m is the marginal propensity to import. (Obviously, the 'behavioural' functions for investment, government spending, and exports are very simple: these are all assumed to be independent of the level of national income.)

Before deriving aggregate expenditure, we need to determine the relationship between national income (Y) and disposable income (Y_d), because it is Y_d that determines desired consumption expenditure. Y_d is defined as income after net tax collections, where net tax collections are total

tax collections minus government transfer payments. (Government transfers to households have exactly the same effect as tax reductions. They put money in the hands of the private sector without directly using goods and services.) In this chapter we examined a very simple linear income tax of the form $T = tY$. More generally, we might imagine autonomous net taxes T_0 and induced net taxes tY, so the tax function is given by

$$T = T_0 + tY. \qquad (A7)$$

Taxes must be subtracted from national income to obtain disposable income:

$$Y_d = Y - T_0 - tY = Y(1 - t) - T_0. \qquad (A8)$$

Substituting (A8) into the consumption function allows us to write consumption as a function of national income:

$$C = a - bT_0 + b(1 - t)Y. \qquad (A9)$$

Notice that autonomous consumption now has two parts, a and $-bT_0$, where the latter term is the effect of autonomous taxes on consumption.

Now we can add up all of the components of desired aggregate expenditure, substituting (A3), (A4), (A5), (A6), and (A9) into (A1):

$$AE = a - bT_0 + b(1 - t)Y + I_0 + G_0 + X_0 - mY. \quad (A10)$$

In equilibrium, aggregate expenditure must equal income, so, as an equilibrium condition,

$$AE = Y. \tag{A11}$$

Substitute (A11) into (A10):

$$Y = a - bT_0 + b(1 - t)Y + I_0 + G_0 + X_0 - mY. \tag{A12}$$

Group all the terms in Y on the right-hand side, and subtract them from both sides:

$$Y = Y[b(1 - t) - m] + a - bT_0 + I_0 + G_0 + X_0, \tag{A13}$$

$$Y - Y[b(1 - t) - m] = a - bT_0 + I_0 + G_0 + X_0. \tag{A14}$$

Notice that $[b(1 - t) - m]$ is exactly the marginal propensity to spend out of national income, defined earlier as z. When national income goes up by £1, only £$(1 - t)$ goes into disposable income, and only b of that gets spent on consumption. Additionally, m gets spent on imports, which are not expenditure on national income. Thus, $b(1 - t) - m$ gets spent on domestic output.

Substituting z for $b(1 - t) - m$ and solving (A14) for equilibrium Y yields

$$Y = \frac{a - bT_0 + I_0 + G_0 + X_0}{1 - z}. \tag{A15}$$

Notice that the numerator of (A15) is autonomous expenditure, A (see Box 29.3). Thus, (A15) can be rewritten as

$$Y = \frac{A}{1 - z}. \tag{A16}$$

Notice also that, if autonomous expenditure rises by some amount λA, Y will rise by $\lambda A/(1 - z)$. Thus, the simple multiplier is $1/(1 - z)$.

THE ALGEBRA ILLUSTRATED

The numerical example that was carried through Chapters 29 and 30 can be used to illustrate the preceding exposition. In that example, the behavioural equations are

$$C = 100 + 0.8Y_d \tag{A17}$$

$$I = 250 \tag{A18}$$

$$G = 170 \tag{A19}$$

$$X - IM = 540 - 0.25Y \tag{A20}$$

$$T = 0.1Y \tag{A21}$$

T_0 is 0, so, from (A8) disposable income is given by $Y(1 - t)$ $= 0.9Y$. Substituting this into (A17) yields

$$C = 100 + 0.72Y,$$

as in (A9).

Now, recalling that in equilibrium $AE = Y$, we add up all of the components of AE and set the sum equal to Y, as in (A12):

$$Y = 100 + 0.72Y + 250 + 170 + 540 - 0.25Y. \tag{A22}$$

Collecting terms yields

$$Y = 1,060 + 0.47Y. \tag{A23}$$

Subtracting $0.47Y$ from both sides gives

$$0.53Y = 1,060, \tag{A24}$$

and dividing through by 0.53, we have

$$Y = 1,060/0.53 = 2,000. \tag{A25}$$

This can also be derived by using (A16). Autonomous expenditure is 1,060, and z, the marginal propensity to spend out of national income, is 0.47. Hence $(1 - z)$ is 0.53. Thus, from (A16), equilibrium income is $1,060/(0.53) = 2,000$, which is exactly the equilibrium we obtained in Table 30.4.

❧ CHAPTER 31

National income and the price level in the short run

IN this chapter we abandon the assumption that the price level is constant. Virtually all expenditure shocks to the economy affect both national income *and* the price level; that is, they have both real and nominal effects, at least initially. To understand these effects, we need to develop some further tools, called the *aggregate demand curve* and *aggregate supply curve*.

In the process of making the price level endogenous, we are also going to need an explicit description of the supply side of our macroeconomic model. No longer will we maintain the assumption that national output is purely demand-determined. As a result, we shall be able to analyse more realistic situations where an economy operates close to potential output, or full employment.

We make the transition to a variable price level in two steps. First, we study the consequences for national income of *exogenous* changes in the price level—changes that happen for reasons that are not explained by our model of the economy. Then we use our model to explain endogenous movements in both national income *and* the price level.

Exogenous changes in the price level

WHAT happens to equilibrium national income when the price changes for some exogenous reason, such as a rise in the price of imported TV sets? To find out, we need to understand how the change affects desired aggregate expenditure.

Shifts in the *AE* curve

There is one key result that we need to establish. A rise in the price level *shifts* the aggregate expenditure curve downward, while a fall in the price level *shifts* it upward. In other words, the price level and desired aggregate expenditure are negatively related to each other. A major part of the explanation lies with how the change in the price level affects desired consumption expenditure and desired net exports.[1]

CHANGES IN CONSUMPTION

The link between a change in the price level and changes in desired consumption is provided by wealth. This link is in two parts.

The first part is provided by the effect of changes in the price level on the wealth of the private sector. Much of the private sector's total wealth is held in the form of assets with a fixed nominal money value. One obvious example is money itself—cash and bank deposits. Other examples include many kinds of financial instruments, such as Treasury Bills and company bonds. When a bill or a bond matures, the owner is repaid a stated sum of money. What that money can buy—its real value—depends on the price level. The higher the price level, the less the given sum of money can purchase. For this reason, a rise in the domestic price level lowers the real value of all assets that are denominated in money units.

How does this affect individuals? An individual who holds a bond has loaned money to the individual (or company) that issued it. When the real value of the asset falls, the individual who holds it has her wealth reduced. However, the individual that issued the bond has his real wealth increased. This is because the face value of the bond represents less purchasing power as a result of the rise in the price level. So the individual who has to repay the bond will part with less purchasing power to do so, and so has more wealth.

A change in the price level affects the wealth of holders of assets denominated in money terms in exactly the opposite way to how it affects the wealth of those who issued the asset.

Inside assets   An *inside asset* is one that is issued by someone (an individual or a firm) in the private sector and held by someone else in the private sector. It follows that, for inside assets, a rise in the price level lowers the real wealth of a bond-holder but raises the real wealth of the bond-issuer, who will have to part with less purchasing power when the bond is redeemed. With inside assets, therefore, the wealth changes are exactly offsetting: a rise in the price level lowers the real wealth of the person who owns any asset that is denominated in money, but it raises the real wealth of the person who must redeem the asset.

Outside assets   *Outside assets* are those held by someone in the domestic private sector but issued by some agent outside of that sector. In practice, this usually means the government or any foreign issuer. In this case, the only

---

[1] The effect on investment expenditure is also important, and it works in the same direction as the change in consumption and net exports. This is discussed in Chapter 36.

private-sector wealth-holders to experience wealth changes when the price level changes are the holders of the outside assets. There arc no offsetting private-sector wealth changes for the issuers of the assets, since they are not in the private sector. It follows that a change in the price level does cause a change in net private wealth held in outside assets denominated in nominal money units. A rise in the price level lowers the real wealth of holders of these assets.[2]

A change in the price level causes no net change in the wealth of the private sector with respect to inside assets, but it does cause a change with respect to outside assets, since the issuers are not in the private sector.

The second link in the chain running from changes in the price level to changes in desired consumption is provided by the relationship between wealth and consumption, which we stressed in Chapter 29 (see Figure 29.3 on p. 553). Whenever households suffer a decrease in their wealth, they increase their saving so as to restore their wealth to the level that they desire for such purposes as retirement. At any level of income, of course, an increase in desired saving implies a reduction in desired consumption. Conversely, whenever households get an increase in their wealth, they reduce their saving and consume more, causing an upward shift in the function that relates desired consumption expenditure and national income.

A rise in the domestic price level lowers the real value of total private-sector wealth by lowering the real value of outside assets denominated in money units; this leads to a fall in desired consumption, which, in turn, implies a downward shift in the aggregate expenditure curve. A fall in the domestic price level leads to a rise in wealth and desired consumption, and thus to an upward shift in the aggregate expenditure curve.

We have concentrated here on the direct effect of the change in wealth on desired consumption expenditure. There is also an indirect effect that operates through the interest rate. Although this effect is potentially very powerful, we cannot study it until we have studied the macroeconomic role of money and interest rates. Further discussion of this point must therefore be postponed until Chapter 36.[3]

CHANGES IN NET EXPORTS

When the domestic price level rises, domestically produced goods become more expensive relative to foreign goods. As we saw in Chapter 30, this change in relative prices causes UK consumers to reduce their purchases of domestically produced goods, which now have become relatively more expensive, and to increase their purchases of foreign goods, which now have become relatively less expensive. At the

same time, consumers in other countries reduce their purchases of the now relatively expensive UK goods. We saw in Chapter 30 that these changes can be summarized as a downward shift in the net export function.

A rise in the domestic price level shifts the net export function downward, which means a downward shift in the aggregate expenditure curve. A fall in the domestic price level shifts the net export function and the aggregate expenditure curves upward.

In simple language, if home-produced goods and services become more expensive, less of them will be bought, so total desired expenditure on UK output will fall; if home-produced goods and services become cheaper, more will be bought, and total desired expenditure on them will rise.[4]

Changes in equilibrium income

Because it causes downward shifts in both the net export function and the consumption function, a rise in the price level causes a downward shift in the aggregate desired expenditure curve, as shown in Figure 31.1. This figure also allows us to reconfirm what we already know from Chapter 30: when the *AE* curve shifts downward, the equilibrium level of real national income falls.

Because a rise in the domestic price level causes the aggregate expenditure curve to shift downward, it reduces equilibrium real national income—all other exogenous variables being held constant.

Now suppose that there is a fall in the UK price level. Because this is the opposite of the case that we have just studied, we can summarize the two key effects briefly. First, UK goods become relatively cheaper internationally, so net exports rise. Second, the purchasing power of some existing

[2] We are assuming that taxpayers do not include in their wealth calculations the real value of future tax liabilities. Taxpayers must pay taxes to service the national debt, and when a rise in the price level lowers its real value, it also lowers the real value of future tax liabilities by exactly the same amount. For the moment, we ignore this possible offsetting change, which we discuss in Chapter 42.

[3] Here is a brief summary of what is involved. When the price level rises, firms and households need to cover their increased money expenses between one payday and the next. This means that they need to hold more money on average. The increased demand for money bids up the price that must be paid to borrow money (the interest rate). Firms that borrow money to build factories and to purchase equipment, and households that borrow money to buy consumer goods and housing, respond to rising interest rates by choosing to spend less on a host of items such as capital goods, housing, cars, and many other durable goods. This means that there is a decrease in the aggregate demand for the nation's output.

[4] This assumes that the price elasticity of demand for traded goods exceeds unity. This standard assumption in the study of the balance of payments is discussed further in Chapter 37.

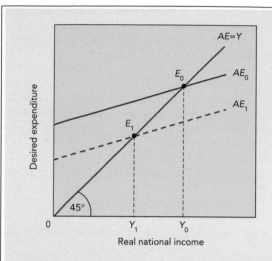

Figure 31.1 Aggregate expenditure and the price level

Changes in the price level cause the AE curve to shift and thus cause equilibrium national income to change. At the initial price level, the AE curve is given by the solid line AE_0, and hence equilibrium national income is Y_0. An increase in the price level reduces desired aggregate expenditure and thus causes the AE curve to shift downward to the dashed line, AE_1. As a result, equilibrium national income falls to Y_1. Starting with the dashed line, AE_1, a fall in the price level increases desired aggregate expenditure, shifting the AE curve up to AE_0 and raising equilibrium national income to Y_1.

assets that are denominated in money terms increases, so consumers spend more. The resulting increase in desired expenditure on domestic output causes the AE curve to shift upward and hence raises equilibrium real national income. This too is shown in Figure 31.1.

Because a fall in the domestic price level causes the aggregate expenditure curve to shift upward, it increases equilibrium real national income—all other exogenous variables being held constant.

The aggregate demand curve

We now know from the behaviour underlying the aggregate expenditure curve that the price level and real national income are negatively related to each other; that is, a change in the price level changes equilibrium national income in the opposite direction, holding all other exogenous variables (like government spending, tax rates, and investment) constant. This negative relationship can be shown in an important new concept, called the *aggregate demand curve*.

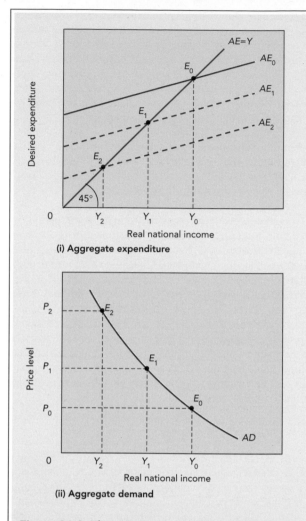

Figure 31.2 The AD curve and the AE curve

Equilibrium income is determined by the AE curve for each given price level; the level of income and its associated price level are then plotted to yield a point on the AD curve. When the price level is P_0, the AE curve is AE_0, and hence equilibrium national income is Y_0, as shown in part (i). (This reproduces the initial equilibrium from Figure 31.1.) Plotting Y_0 against P_0 yields the point E_0 on the AD curve in part (ii).

An increase in the price level to P_1 causes AE_0 in part (i) to shift downward to AE_1 and thus causes equilibrium national income to fall to Y_1. Plotting this new, lower level of national income, Y_1, against the higher price level, P_1, yields a second point, E_1, on the AD curve in part (ii). A further increase in the price level to P_2 causes the AE curve in part (i) to shift downward further, to AE_2, and thus causes equilibrium national income to fall further, to Y_2. Plotting Y_2 against P_2 yields a third point, E_2, on the AD curve in part (ii).

Thus, a change in the price level causes a shift in the AE curve in part (i) and a movement along the AD curve in part (ii).

Recall that the *AE* curve relates national income to desired expenditure for a given price level, plotting income on the horizontal axis. The **aggregate demand (*AD*) curve** relates equilibrium national income to the price level, again plotting income on the horizontal axis. Because the horizontal axes of both the *AE* and the *AD* curves measure *real* national income, the two curves can be placed one above the other so that the level of national income on each can be compared directly. This is shown in Figure 31.2.

Now let us see how the *AD* curve is derived. Given a value of the price level, equilibrium national income is determined in part (i) of Figure 31.2 at the point where the *AE* curve crosses the 45° line. In part (ii) of the figure, the combination of the equilibrium level of national income and the corresponding value of the price level is plotted, giving one point on the *AD* curve.

When the price level changes, the *AE* curve shifts, for the reasons just seen. The new position of the *AE* curve gives rise to a new equilibrium level of national income that is associated with the new price level. This determines a second point on the *AD* curve, as shown in Figure 31.2 (ii).

Any change in the price level leads to a new *AE* curve and hence to a new level of equilibrium income. Each combination of equilibrium income and its associated price level becomes a particular point on the *AD* curve.

Note that, because the *AD* curve relates equilibrium national income to the price level, changes in the price level that cause *shifts in* the *AE* curve cause *movements along* the *AD* curve. A movement along the *AD* curve thus traces out the response of equilibrium income to a change in the price level. Notice also that the only exogenous change we are permitting at present is a change in the price level. All other exogenous expenditures are, therefore, held constant along a given *AD* curve.

The aggregate demand curve shows for each price level the associated level of equilibrium national income for which aggregate desired expenditure equals total income.

THE SLOPE OF THE *AD* CURVE

Figure 31.2 shows that the *AD* curve is negatively sloped.

1. A rise in the price level causes the aggregate expenditure curve to shift downward and hence leads to a movement upward and to the left along the *AD* curve, reflecting a fall in the equilibrium level of national income.

2. A fall in the price level causes the aggregate expenditure curve to shift upward, and hence leads to a movement downward and to the right along the *AD* curve, reflecting a rise in the equilibrium level of national income.

BOX 31.1

The shape of the aggregate demand curve

In Chapter 4 we studied the demand curves for individual products. It is tempting to think that the properties of the aggregate demand curve arise from the same behaviour that gives rise to those individual demand curves. Unfortunately, life is not so simple. Let us see why we cannot take such an approach.

If we assume that we can obtain a negatively sloping aggregate demand curve in the same manner that we derived negatively sloping individual market demand curves, we would be committing the fallacy of composition. This is to assume that what is correct for the parts must be correct for the whole.

Consider a simple example of the fallacy. An art collector can go into the market and add to her private collection of nineteenth-century French paintings provided only that she has enough money. However, the fact that any one person can do this does not mean that everyone could do so simultaneously. The world's stock of nineteenth-century French paintings is fixed. It is not possible for *all* of us to do what any *one* of us with enough money can do.

How does the fallacy of composition relate to demand curves? An individual demand curve describes a situation in which the price of one commodity changes while the prices of all other commodities and consumers' money incomes are constant. Such an individual demand curve is negatively sloped, for two

reasons. First, as the price of the commodity rises, each consumer's given money income will buy a smaller *total* amount of goods, so a smaller quantity of each commodity will be bought, other things being equal. Second, as the price of the commodity rises, consumers buy less of it and more of the now relatively cheaper substitutes.

The first reason has no application to the aggregate demand curve, which relates the total demand for all output to the price level. All prices and total output are changing as we move along the *AD* curve. Because the value of output determines income, consumers' money incomes will also be changing along this curve.

The second reason does apply, but in a limited way, to the aggregate demand curve. A rise in the price level entails a rise in *all* domestic commodity prices. Thus, there is no incentive to substitute among domestic commodities whose prices do not change relative to each other. However, it does give rise, as we saw earlier in this chapter, to some substitution between domestic and foreign goods and services. Domestic goods and services rise in price relative to imported goods and services, and the switch in expenditure will lower desired aggregate expenditure on domestic output and hence will lower equilibrium national income.

In Chapter 4 we saw that demand curves for individual goods such as carrots and cars are negatively sloped. However, the reasons for the negative slope of the AD curve are different from the reasons for the negative slope of individual demand curves that are used in microeconomics; this important point is discussed further in Box 31.1.

POINTS OFF THE AD CURVE

The AD curve depicts combinations of national income and the price level that give equilibrium between aggregate desired expenditure and actual output in the sense that aggregate desired expenditure equals actual output. These points are said to be *consistent* with expenditure decisions.

The national income given by any point on the aggregate demand curve is such that, *if* that level of output is pro-duced, aggregate desired expenditure at the *given price level* will exactly equal the output.

Points to the left of the AD curve show combinations of national income and the price level that cause aggregate desired expenditure to exceed output. There is thus pressure for income to rise because firms could sell more than current output. Points to the right of the AD curve show combinations of national income and the price level for which aggregate desired expenditure is less than current income. There is thus pressure for income to fall because firms will not be able to sell all of their current output. These relationships are illustrated in Figure 31.3.

SHIFTS IN THE AD CURVE

Because the AD curve plots equilibrium national income as

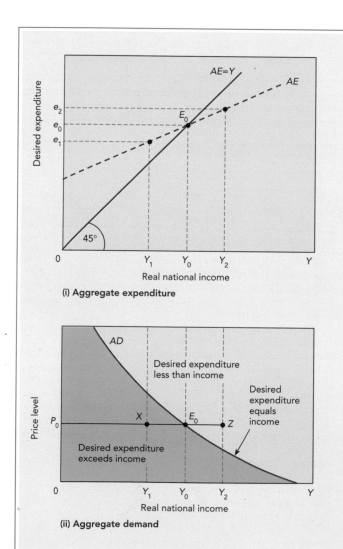

(i) Aggregate expenditure

(ii) Aggregate demand

Figure 31.3 The relationship between the AE and AD curves

The AD curve plots the price level against the level of national income consistent with expenditure decisions at that price level. With the price level P_0, equilibrium national income is Y_0, shown by the intersection of AE and the 45° line at E_0 in part (i) and by the point E_0 on the AD curve in part (ii).

With the price level constant at P_0, consider a level of national income of Y_1, which is less than Y_0. As can be seen in part (i), if national income were equal to Y_1, desired aggregate expenditure would be e_1, which is greater than Y_1. Hence Y_1 is not an equilibrium level of national income when the price level is P_0, and the combination (P_0, Y_1) is not a point on the AD curve in part (ii), as shown by point X. Now consider a level of national income of Y_2, which is greater than Y_0. As can be seen in part (i), if national income were equal to Y_2, desired aggregate expenditure would be e_2, which is less than Y_2. Hence Y_2 is not an equilibrium level of national income when the price level is P_0, and the combination (P_0, Y_2) is not a point on the AD curve in part (ii), as shown by point Z.

Repeating the same analysis for each given price level tells us that, for all points to the left of the AD curve (dark blue shaded area), income is tending to rise, because desired expenditure exceeds income, whereas, for all points to the right of the AD curve (light blue shaded area), income is tending to fall, because desired aggregate expenditure is less than income.

a function of the price level, anything that alters equilibrium national income *at a given price level* must shift the *AD* curve. In other words, any change in exogenous expenditures that we have been holding constant causes the *aggregate expenditure curve* to shift, and this will also cause the *AD* curve to shift. (Recall that a change in the price level causes *a movement along* the *AD* curve.) Such a shift is called an *aggregate demand shock*.

For example, a lowering of tax rates in the 1987 Budget led to an increase in the amount of UK consumption expenditure associated with each level of UK national income. This was an expansionary demand shock, which shifted the UK *AD* curve to the right. This stimulated a boom in the domestic economy. Domestic prices started to rise faster than those abroad. The extra domestic demand also spilled over into the balance of payments. Some of the increased domestic demand went into imports and the balance of payments went into deficit. In the context of our model, the net export function shifted downwards. The pick-up in domestic inflation later caused a reversal of the expansionary policy. Policy was aimed at shifting the *AD* curve down again. This was a major factor in the 1990–2 recession.

Using our new concepts, the conclusions on pp. 563–4 now can be restated as follows:

A rise in the amount of (autonomous) desired consumption, investment, government, or net export expenditure that is associated with each level of national income shifts the *AD* curve to the right. A fall in any of these expenditures shifts the *AD* curve to the left.

THE SIMPLE MULTIPLIER AND THE *AD* CURVE

We saw in Chapter 30 that the simple multiplier measures the magnitude of the *change* in equilibrium national income in response to a change in autonomous expenditure when the price level is constant. It follows that this multiplier gives the magnitude of the *horizontal* shift in the

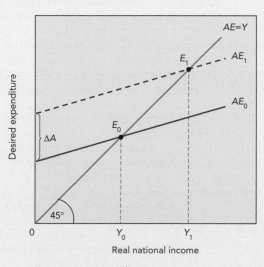

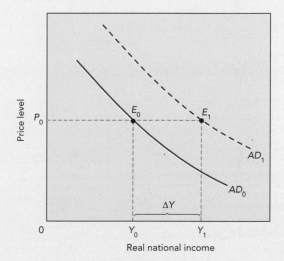

(i) Aggregate expenditure

(ii) Aggregate demand

Figure 31.4 The simple multiplier and shifts in the *AD* curve

A change in autonomous expenditure changes equilibrium national income for any given price level, and the simple multiplier measures the resulting horizontal shift in the aggregate demand curve. The original desired expenditure curve is AE_0 in part (i). Equilibrium is at E_0, with national income Y_0 at price level P_0. This yields point E_0 on the curve AD_0 in part (ii).

The *AE* curve in part (i) then shifts upward from AE_0 to AE_1, because of an increase in autonomous expenditure of ΔA. Equilibrium income now rises to Y_1, with the price level still constant at P_0. Thus, the *AD* curve in part (ii) shifts to the right to point E_1, indicating the higher equilibrium income Y_1, associated with the same price level P_0. The magnitude of the shift, ΔY, is given by the simple multiplier.

A fall in autonomous expenditure can be analysed by shifting the *AE* curve from AE_1 to AE_0, which shifts the *AD* curve from AD_1 to AD_0 at the price level of P_0. The equilibrium value of national income falls from Y_1 to Y_0.

AD curve in response to a change in autonomous expenditure. This is shown in Figure 31.4.

The simple multiplier measures the horizontal shift in the AD curve in response to a change in autonomous expenditure.

If the price level were to remain constant and firms were willing to supply everything that was demanded at that price level, the simple multiplier would still show the change in equilibrium income that would occur in response to a change in autonomous expenditure. However, it is worth bearing in mind at this stage that the size of the simple multiplier will be affected by feedback from the monetary sector. This will be explained in Chapter 36.

Equilibrium national income and the price level

S O far we have explained how the equilibrium level of national income is determined *when the price level is taken as given* and how that equilibrium changes as the price level is changed exogenously. We are now ready to take an important further step: adding an *explanation* for the behaviour of the price level. To do this, we need to take account of the supply decisions of firms.

The aggregate supply curve

Aggregate supply refers to the total output of goods and services that firms wish to produce, assuming that they can sell all that they wish to sell. Aggregate supply thus depends on the decisions of firms to use workers and all other inputs in order to produce goods and services to sell to consumers, governments, and other firms, as well as for export.

An *aggregate supply curve* relates aggregate supply to the price level. It is necessary to define two types of such curve. The **short-run aggregate supply (*SRAS*) curve** relates the price level to the quantity that firms would like to produce and to sell, on the assumption that the prices of all factors of production (inputs) remain constant. The *long-run aggregate supply (LRAS) curve*, which we will define more fully in the next chapter, relates the price level to desired sales after the economy has fully adjusted to that price level. For the remainder of this chapter, we confine our attention to the *SRAS* curve.

THE SLOPE OF THE SHORT-RUN AGGREGATE SUPPLY CURVE

To study the slope of the *SRAS* curve, we need to see how costs are related to output and then how prices and outputs are related.

Costs and output   Suppose that firms wish to increase their outputs above current levels. What will this do to their costs per unit of output—often called their **unit costs**? *The short-run aggregate supply curve is drawn on the assumption that the prices of all factors of production that firms use, such as labour, remain constant.* This does not, however, mean that unit costs will be constant. As output increases, less efficient standby machinery may have to be used, and less efficient workers may have to be hired, while existing workers may have to be paid overtime rates for additional work. For these and other similar reasons, unit costs will tend to rise as output rises, even when input prices are constant.[5]

Unit costs and output are positively related.

Prices and output   To consider the relationship between price and output, we need to consider firms that sell in two distinct types of market: those in which firms are price-takers, and those in which firms are price-setters. Some industries contain many individual firms. In these cases each one is too small to influence the market price, which is set by the overall forces of demand and supply; each firm must accept whatever price is set on the open market and adjust its output to that price. These firms are said to be *price-takers* and *quantity-adjusters*. When the market price changes, such firms will react by altering their production.

Because their unit costs rise with output, price-taking firms will produce more only if price rises and will produce less if price falls.

Many other industries, including most of those that produce manufactured products, contain a small enough number of firms that each can influence market prices. Most such firms sell products that differ from one another, although all are similar enough to be thought of as the

---

[5] Readers who have studied microeconomics will recognize the law of diminishing returns as one reason why costs rise in the short run as firms squeeze more output out of a fixed stock of capital equipment.

single commodity produced by one industry. For example, no two kinds of car are the same, but all cars are sufficiently alike that we have no trouble talking about the car industry and the commodity, cars. In such cases, each firm must quote a price at which it is prepared to sell each of its products; that is, the firm is a *price-setter*. If the demand for the output of price-setting firms increases sufficiently to take their outputs into the range in which their unit costs rise (e.g. because overtime is worked and standby equipment is brought into production), these firms will not increase their outputs unless they can pass at least some of these extra costs on through higher prices. When the demand falls, they will reduce output, and competition among them will tend to cause a reduction in prices whenever their unit costs fall.

Price-setting firms will increase their prices when they expand output into the range in which unit costs are rising.

This is the basic behaviour of firms in response to the changes in demand and prices when factor prices are constant, and it explains the slope of the *SRAS* curve, such as the one shown in Figure 31.5.

The actions of both price-taking and price-setting firms cause the price level and total output to be positively associated with each other; the graphical expression of this relationship is the positively sloped, short-run aggregate supply curve.

Real and nominal wages Another way of looking at why the *SRAS* curve is likely to be positively sloped is by focusing on the behaviour of real wages. Let us think in terms of the behaviour of firms that are price-takers, so that they are selling in competitive markets for their output. With given money prices of their inputs—we will concentrate on the labour input—and a given price at which they can sell their output, each firm will produce output at the level where its marginal cost equals its marginal revenue (and its average revenue, which is also equal to the market price of its output).

Now what happens if an increase in total demand for final output leads to a rise in the output price? Each firm will find that its marginal revenue curve (and average revenue) has shifted upwards. They will increase profits by expanding output up to the point where their new marginal revenue curve cuts their marginal cost curve. In the process, they will also increase employment. Thus, as the price level rises, output increases. This is the positively sloped *SRAS* curve.

Notice, however, what is happening to the real-wage rate. Money wages are fixed (by assumption) in money terms. As the price of final output goes up, workers will become worse off because their money wages will buy less goods. The *real wage* has fallen. This is why firms are happy

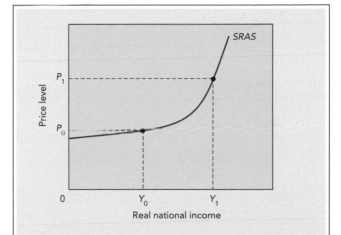

Figure 31.5 A short-run aggregate supply curve

The *SRAS* curve is positively sloped. The positive slope of the *SRAS* curve shows that, with the prices of labour and other inputs given, total desired output and the price level will be positively associated. Thus, a rise in the price level from P_0 to P_1 will be associated with a rise in the quantity of total output supplied, from Y_0 to Y_1.

Notice that the slope of the *SRAS* curve is fairly flat at low levels of income and very steep at higher levels. Box 31.3 provides a detailed explanation of this characteristic shape. Briefly, at low levels of income, where there is excess capacity in the economy, output can be increased with little change in cost. As the economy approaches potential income (somewhere between Y_0 and Y_1 in the figure), it becomes very difficult to increase real output in response to demand changes, and increased demand will mainly generate higher prices.

to hire more labour and expand output. The relative price of their inputs has fallen in comparison with the price of their output.

Of course, this will not be the end of the story. Workers will not accept a permanent fall in their real wage. Money wages will eventually start to rise and, as they do, the relative input and output prices faced by firms will tend to return to their initial level. So firms' output and employment will also return to their original level. But this is the long-run story, to which we return in Chapter 32.

As we move upwards along a given *SRAS* curve, the rise in the price level and output is associated with a fall in the real wage—that is, to a rise in the price of output relative to input prices.

SHIFTS IN THE *SRAS* CURVE

Shifts in the *SRAS* curve, which are shown in Figure 31.6, are called *aggregate supply shocks.* Two sources of aggregate

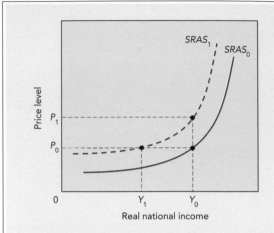

Figure 31.6 Shifts in the *SRAS* curve

A shift to the left of the *SRAS* curve reflects a decrease in supply; a shift to the right reflects an increase in supply. Starting from P_0, Y_0 on $SRAS_0$, suppose there is an increase in input prices. At price level P_0 only Y_1 would be produced. Alternatively, to get output Y_0 would require a rise to price level P_1. The new supply curve is $SRAS_1$, which may be viewed as being above and to the left of $SRAS_0$. An increase in supply, caused, say, by a decrease in input prices, would shift the *SRAS* curve downward and to the right, from $SRAS_1$ to $SRAS_0$.

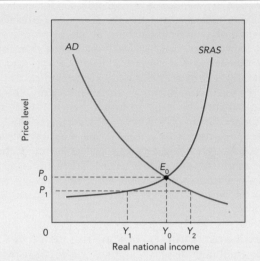

Figure 31.7 Macroeconomic equilibrium

Macroeconomic equilibrium occurs at the intersection of the *AD* and *SRAS* curves and determines the equilibrium values for national income and the price level. Given the *AD* and *SRAS* curves in the figure, macroeconomic equilibrium occurs at E_0, with national income equal to Y_0 and the price level equal to P_0. At P_0 the desired output of firms, as given by the *SRAS* curve, is equal to the level of national income that is consistent with expenditure decisions, as given by the *AD* curve.

If the price level were equal to P_1, less than P_0, the desired output of firms, given by the *SRAS* curve, would be Y_1. However, at P_1 the level of output that is consistent with expenditure decisions, given by the *AD* curve, would be Y_2, greater than Y_1. Hence, when the price level is P_1, or any other level less than P_0, the desired output of firms will be less than the level of national income that is consistent with expenditure decisions.

Similarly, for any price level above P_0, the desired output of firms, given by the *SRAS* curve, would exceed the level of output that is consistent with expenditure decisions, given by the *AD* curve.

The only price level where the supply decisions of firms are consistent with desired expenditure is a macroeconomic equilibrium. At P_0, firms wish to produce Y_0. When they do so, they generate a national income of Y_0; when income is Y_0, decision-makers wish to spend exactly Y_0, thus purchasing the nation's output. Hence all decisions are consistent with each other.

supply shocks are of particular importance: changes in the price of inputs, and increases in productivity.

Changes in input prices Factor prices are held constant along the *SRAS* curve, and when they change the curve shifts. If factor prices rise, firms will find the profitability of their current production reduced as their marginal and average cost curves shift upwards. For any given level of output to be produced, an increase in the price level will be required. If prices do not rise, firms will react by decreasing production. For the economy as a whole, this means that there will be less output at each price level than before the increase in factor prices. Thus, if factor prices rise, the *SRAS* curve shifts upward. (Notice that, when a positively sloped curve shifts upward, indicating that any given quantity is associated with a higher price level, it also shifts to the left, indicating that any given price level is associated with a lower quantity.)

Similarly, a fall in factor prices causes the *SRAS* curve to shift downward (and to the right). This increase in supply means that more will be produced and offered for sale at each price level.[6]

Increases in productivity If labour productivity rises, meaning that each worker can produce more, the unit costs of production will fall as long as wage rates do not rise suf-

ficiently to offset the productivity rise fully. Lower costs generally lead to lower prices. Competing firms cut prices

---

[6] Note that, for either the *AD* or the *SRAS* curve, a shift to the right means an increase, and a shift to the left means a decrease. Upward and downward shifts, however, have different meanings for the two curves. An upward shift of the *AD* curve reflects an increase in aggregate demand, but an upward shift in the *SRAS* curve reflects a decrease in aggregate supply.

in an attempt to raise their market shares, and the net result of such competition is that the fall in production costs is accompanied by a fall in prices.

Because the same output is sold at a lower price, this causes a downward shift in the SRAS curve. This shift is an increase in supply, as illustrated in Figure 31.6.

A rightward shift in the SRAS curve—brought about, for example, by an increase in productivity with no increase in factor prices—means that firms will be willing to produce more national income with no increase in the price level. This result has been the object of many government policies that seek to encourage increases in productivity.

A change in either factor prices or productivity will shift the SRAS curve, because any given output will be supplied at a different price level than previously. An increase in factor prices or a decrease in productivity shifts the SRAS curve to the left; an increase in productivity or a decrease in factor prices shifts it to the right.

Macroeconomic equilibrium

We have now reached our objective: we are ready to see how both real national income and the price level are simultaneously determined by the interaction of aggregate demand and aggregate supply.

The equilibrium values of national output and the price level occur at the intersection of the AD and SRAS curves, as shown by the pair Y_0 and P_0 that arise at point E_0 in Figure 31.7. We describe the combination of national income and price level that is on both the AD and the SRAS curves as a *macroeconomic equilibrium*, and its determination in Figure 31.7 should be studied carefully at this point.

To see why the pair of points, (Y_0, P_0), is the only macroeconomic equilibrium, first consider what Figure 31.7 shows would happen if the price level were below P_0. At this lower price level, the desired output of firms, as given by the SRAS

curve, is less than desired aggregate expenditure at that level of output. The excess desired aggregate expenditure will cause prices to be bid up, and national income will increase along the SRAS curve. Hence there can be no macroeconomic *equilibrium* when the price level is below P_0.

Similarly, Figure 31.7 shows that, when the price level is above P_0, the behaviour underlying the SRAS and AD curves is not consistent. In this case, producers will wish to supply more than the level of output that is demanded at that price level. If firms were to produce their desired levels of output, desired expenditure would not be large enough to purchase everything that would be produced.

Only at the combination of national income and price level given by the intersection of the SRAS and AD curves are spending (demand) behaviour and supply behaviour consistent.

When the price level is less than its equilibrium value, expenditure behaviour is consistent with a level of national income that is greater than the desired output of firms. When the price level is greater than its equilibrium value, expenditure behaviour is consistent with a level of national income that is less than the desired output of firms.

Macroeconomic equilibrium thus requires that two conditions be satisfied. The first is familiar to us because it comes from Chapters 29 and 30: at the prevailing price level, desired aggregate expenditure must be equal to national income, which means that households are just willing to buy all that is produced. The AD curve is constructed in such a way that this condition holds everywhere on it. The second requirement for equilibrium is introduced by consideration of aggregate supply: at the prevailing price level, firms must wish to produce the prevailing level of national income, no more and no less. This condition is fulfilled everywhere on the SRAS curve. Only where the two curves intersect, however, are both conditions fulfilled simultaneously.

Changes in national income and the price level

THE aggregate demand and aggregate supply curves now can be used to understand how various shocks to the economy change both national income and the price level.

A shift in the AD curve is called an **aggregate demand shock**. A *rightward* shift in the AD curve results from an *increase* in aggregate demand; it means that, at all price levels, expenditure decisions will now be consistent with a *higher* level of real national income. Similarly, a *leftward* shift in

the AD curve indicates a *decrease* in aggregate demand; it means that, at all price levels, expenditure decisions will now be consistent with a *lower* level of real national income.[7]

[7] The factors that could shift AD are the same as those that could shift AE (*apart from the price level*). An increase in autonomous consumption, an increase in government spending, an increase in investment, an increase in net exports, and a reduction in tax rates will all shift AD upwards to the right. The opposite shift in all of these will move AD downwards to the left.

Box 31.2

The Keynesian SRAS curve

Here we consider an extreme version of the *SRAS* curve, which is horizontal over some range of national income. It is called the Keynesian short-run aggregate supply curve, after John Maynard Keynes, who in his famous book *The General Theory of Employment, Interest, and Money* (1936) pioneered the study of the behaviour of economies under conditions of high unemployment.

The behaviour that gives rise to the Keynesian *SRAS* curve can be described as follows. When real national income is below potential national income, individual firms are operating at less than normal-capacity output, and they hold their prices constant at the level that would maximize profits if production were at normal capacity. They then respond to demand variations below that capacity by altering output. In other words, they will supply whatever they can sell at their existing prices as long as they are producing below their normal capacity. This means that the firms have horizontal supply curves and that their output is *demand-determined.**

Under these circumstances, the economy has a horizontal aggregate supply curve, indicating that any output up to potential output will be supplied at the going price level. The amount that is actually produced is then determined by the position of the aggregate demand curve, as shown in the figure. Thus, we say that real national income is demand-determined. If demand rises enough so that firms are trying to squeeze more than nor-

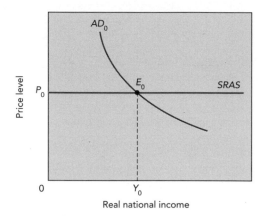

mal output out of their plants, their costs will rise, and so will their prices. Thus, the horizontal Keynesian *SRAS* curve applies, if at all, only to national incomes below potential income.

* The evidence is strong that many firms, particularly in the manufacturing sector, do behave like this in the short run. One possible explanation for this is that changing prices frequently is too costly, so firms set the best possible (profit-maximizing) prices when output is at normal capacity and then do not change prices in the face of short-term fluctuations in demand.

A shift in the *SRAS* curve is called an **aggregate supply shock**. A *rightward* shift in the *SRAS* curve results from an *increase* in aggregate supply: at any given price level, *more* real national income will be supplied. A *leftward* shift in the *SRAS* curve indicates a *decrease* in aggregate supply: at any given price level, *less* real national income will be supplied.[8]

What happens to real national income and to the price level when one of the aggregate curves shifts?

A shift in either the *AD* or the *SRAS* curve leads to changes in the equilibrium values of the price level and real national income.

Box 31.2 deals with the special case of a perfectly elastic *SRAS* curve. In that case, the aggregate supply curve determines the price level by itself, while the aggregate demand curve then determines real national income by itself. This is a special case which is unlikely to arise in practice, but it is the only case where the model of Chapter 30 (with fixed price level) would be adequate to determine real national income.

Aggregate demand shocks

Figure 31.8 shows the effects of an increase in aggregate demand. This increase could have occurred because of, say, increased investment or government spending; it means that more national output would be demanded at any given price level. For the moment we are not concerned with the source of the shock; we are interested in its implications for the price level and real national income. As is shown in the figure, following an increase in aggregate demand, both the price level and real national income rise.

Figure 31.8 also shows that both the price level and real national income fall as the result of a decrease in demand.

Aggregate demand shocks cause the price level and real

8 The distinction between movements along curves and shifts of curves, which we encountered in Chapter 4 and again in Chapter 29, is also relevant here. A *movement along* an aggregate demand curve indicates a change in the quantity demanded, whereas a *shift* in an aggregate demand curve indicates a change in demand. A similar distinction applies to the supply curve.

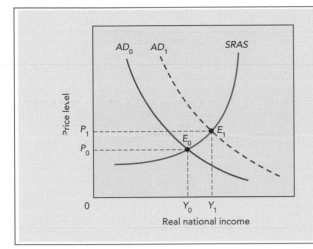

Figure 31.8 Aggregate demand shocks

Shifts in aggregate demand cause the price level and real national income to move in the same direction. An increase in aggregate demand shifts the AD curve to the right, say, from AD_0 to AD_1. Macroeconomic equilibrium moves from E_0 to E_1. The price level rises from P_0 to P_1 and real national income rises from Y_0 to Y_1, reflecting a movement along the $SRAS$ curve.

A decrease in aggregate demand shifts the AD curve to the left, say, from AD_1 to AD_0. Equilibrium moves from E_1 to E_0. Prices fall from P_1 to P_0, and real national income falls from Y_1 to Y_0, again reflecting a movement along the $SRAS$ curve.

national income to change in the same direction; both rise with an increase in aggregate demand, and both fall with a decrease in aggregate demand.

An aggregate demand shock means that there is a shift in the AD curve (for example, from AD_0 to AD_1 in Figure 31.8). Adjustment to the new equilibrium following an aggregate demand shock involves a movement along the $SRAS$ curve (for example, from point E_0 to point E_1).

THE MULTIPLIER WHEN THE PRICE LEVEL VARIES

We saw earlier in this chapter that the simple multiplier gives the extent of the horizontal shift in the AD curve in response to a change in autonomous expenditure. If the price level remains constant, and *if* firms are willing to supply all that is demanded at the existing price level (that is, if the aggregate supply curve is horizontal), then the simple multiplier gives the increase in equilibrium national income.

Now that we can use aggregate demand and aggregate supply curves, we can answer a more interesting question: what happens in the more usual case, in which the aggregate supply curve slopes upward? In this case, a rise in national income caused by an increase in aggregate demand will be associated with a rise in the price level. However, we have seen that a rise in the price level (by reducing net exports and lowering the real value of household wealth) shifts the AE curve downward, which lowers equilibrium national income, other things being equal. The outcome of these conflicting forces is easily seen using aggregate demand and aggregate supply curves.

Figure 31.8 shows that, when the $SRAS$ curve is positively sloped, the change in national income that has been caused by a change in autonomous expenditure is no longer equal to the size of the horizontal shift in the AD curve. A rightward shift of the AD curve causes the price level to rise, which in turn causes the rise in national income to be less than the horizontal shift of the AD curve. Part of the expansionary impact of an increase in demand is dissipated by a rise in the price level, and only part is transmitted to a rise in real output. Of course, there still is an increase in output, so a multiplier still may be calculated, but its value is not the same as that of the simple multiplier.

When the $SRAS$ curve is positively sloped, the multiplier is smaller than the simple multiplier.

Why is the multiplier smaller when the $SRAS$ curve is positively sloped? The answer lies in the behaviour that is summarized by the AE curve. To understand this, it is useful to think of the final change in national income as occurring in two stages, as shown in Figure 31.9.

First, with prices remaining constant, an increase in autonomous expenditure shifts the AE curve upward and therefore shifts the AD curve to the right. This is shown by a shift upward of the AE curve in part (i) of the figure and a shift to the right of the AD curve in part (ii). The horizontal shift in the AD curve is measured by the simple multiplier, but this cannot be the final equilibrium position because firms are unwilling to produce enough to satisfy the extra demand at the existing price level.

Second, we take account of the rise in the price level that occurs owing to the positive slope of the $SRAS$ curve. As we have seen, a rise in the price level, via its effect on net exports and on wealth, leads to a downward shift in the AE curve. This second shift of the AE curve partially counteracts the initial rise in national income and so reduces the size of the multiplier. The second stage shows up as a downward shift of the AE curve in part (i) of Figure 31.9 and a movement upward and to the left along the AD curve in part (ii).

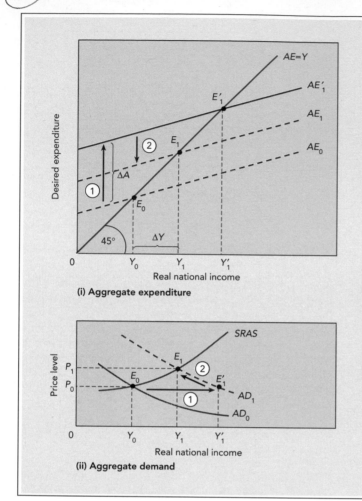

Figure 31.9 The *AE* curve and the multiplier when the price level varies

An increase in autonomous expenditure causes the *AE* curve to shift upward, but the rise in the price level causes it to shift part of the way down again. Hence the multiplier effect on income is smaller than when the price level is constant. Originally, equilibrium is at point E_0 in both part (i) and part (ii), with real national income at Y_0 and price level at P_0. Desired aggregate expenditure then shifts by ΔA to AE'_1, taking the aggregate demand curve to AD_1. These shifts are shown by arrow 1 in both parts. If the price level had remained constant at P_0, the new equilibrium would have been E'_1 and real income would have risen to Y'_1. The amount $Y_0Y'_1$ is the change called for by the simple multiplier.

Instead, however, the shift in the *AD* curve raises the price level to P_1, because the *SRAS* curve is positively sloped. The rise in the price level shifts the aggregate expenditure curve down to AE_1, as shown by arrow 2 in part (i). This is shown as a movement along the *AD* curve, as indicated by arrow 2 in part (ii). The new equilibrium is thus at E_1. The amount Y_0Y_1 is ΔY, the actual increase in real income, whereas the amount $Y_1Y'_1$ is the shortfall relative to the simple multiplier due to the rise in the price level.

The multiplier, adjusted for the effect of the price increase, is the ratio of $\Delta Y/\Delta A$ in part (i).

THE IMPORTANCE OF THE SHAPE OF THE *SRAS* CURVE

We now have seen that the shape of the *SRAS* curve has important implications for how the effects of an aggregate demand shock are divided between changes in real national output and changes in the price level. Figure 31.10 highlights this by considering *AD* shocks in the presence of an *SRAS* curve that exhibits three distinct ranges. Box 31.3 explores some possible reasons for such an increasing slope of the *SRAS* curve.

Over the *flat* range, from 0 to Y_0, any change in aggregate demand leads to no change in prices and, as seen earlier, to a response of output equal to that predicted by the simple multiplier.

Over the *intermediate* range, along which the *SRAS* curve is positively sloped, from Y_1 to Y_4, a shift in the *AD* curve gives rise to appreciable changes in both real income and the price level. As we saw earlier in this chapter, the change in the price level means that real income will change by less

in response to a change in autonomous expenditure than it would if the price level were constant.

Over the *steep* range, for output above Y_4, very little more can be produced, however large the demand is. This range deals with an economy near its capacity constraints. Any change in aggregate demand leads to a sharp change in the price level and to little change in real national income. The multiplier in this case is nearly zero.

How do we reconcile what we have just discovered with the analysis of Chapters 29 and 30, where shifts in *AE* *always* change national income? The answer is that each *AE* curve is drawn on the assumption that there is a constant price level and plenty of excess capacity. A rise in *AE* shifts the *AD* curve to the right. However, a steep *SRAS* curve means that the price level rises significantly (because there is little excess capacity), and this shifts the *AE* curve downward, offsetting some of its initial rise.

This interaction is seen most easily if we study the extreme case, shown in Figure 31.11, in which the *SRAS* curve is vertical. An increase in autonomous expenditure

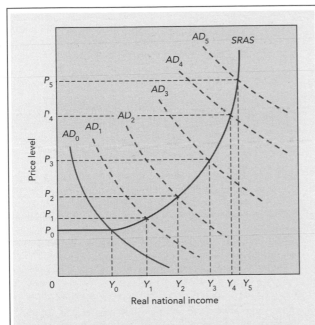

Figure 31.10 The effects of increases in aggregate demand

The effects of increases in aggregate demand are divided between increases in real income and increases in prices, depending on the shape of the *SRAS* curve. Because of the increasing slope of the *SRAS* curve, increases in aggregate demand up to AD_0 have virtually no impact on the price level. When aggregate demand increases from AD_0 to AD_1, there is a relatively small increase in the price level, from P_0 to P_1, and a relatively large increase in output, from Y_0 to Y_1. Successive further increases bring larger price increases and relatively smaller output increases. By the time aggregate demand is at AD_5, virtually all of the effect is on the price level.

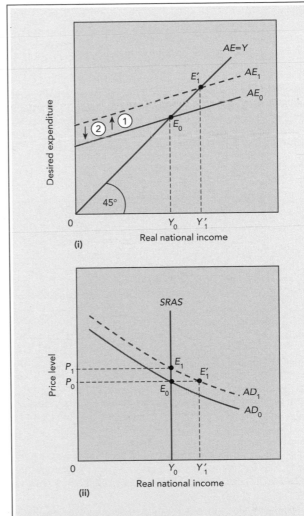

Figure 31.11 Demand shocks when the *SRAS* curve is vertical

If the *SRAS* curve were vertical, the effect of an increase in autonomous expenditure would be solely a rise in the price level. An increase in autonomous expenditure shifts the *AE* curve upward from AE_0 to AE_1, as shown by arrow 1 in part (i). Given the initial price level P_0, equilibrium would shift from E_0 to E'_1 and real national income would rise from Y_0 to Y'_1. (Primes are used on these variables because these results cannot persist; real national income cannot rise to Y'_1.) However, the price level does not remain constant. This is shown by the *SRAS* curve in part (ii). Instead, the price level rises to P_1. This causes the *AE* curve to shift back down all the way to AE_0, as shown by arrow 2 in part (i), and equilibrium income stays at Y_0. In part (ii) the new equilibrium is at E_1, with income at Y_0, which is associated with the new price level, P_1.

shifts the *AE* curve upward, thus raising the amount demanded. However, a vertical *SRAS* curve means that output cannot be expanded at all to satisfy the increased demand. Instead, the extra demand merely forces prices up, and as prices rise the *AE* curve shifts downward once again. The rise in prices continues until the *AE* curve is back to where it started. Thus, the rise in prices offsets the expansionary effect of the original shift and, as a result, leaves both real aggregate expenditure and equilibrium real income unchanged.

The discussion of Figures 31.10 and 31.11 illustrates a general proposition:

The effect of any given shift in aggregate demand will be divided between a change in real output and a change in the price level, depending on the conditions of aggregate

supply. The steeper is the *SRAS* curve, the greater is the price effect, and the smaller is the output effect.

Box 31.3

More on the shape of the SRAS curve

The *SRAS* curve relates the price level to the quantity of output that producers are willing to sell. Notice two things about the shape of the *SRAS* curve that is reproduced in Figure 31.5: it has a positive slope, and the slope increases as output rises.

Positive slope

The most obvious feature of the *SRAS* curve is its positive slope, indicating that a higher price level is associated with a higher volume of real output, other things being equal. Because the prices of all of the factors of production are being held constant along the *SRAS* curve, why is the curve not horizontal, indicating that firms would be willing to supply as much output as might be demanded with no increase in the price level?

The answer is that, even though *input prices* are constant, *unit costs of production* eventually rise as output increases. Thus, a higher price level for increasing output—rising short-run aggregate supply—is necessary to compensate firms for rising costs.

The preceding paragraph addresses the question: what has to happen to the price level if national output increases, with the price of factors of production remaining constant? Alternatively, one could ask: What will happen to firms' willingness to supply output if product prices rise with no increase in factor prices? Production becomes more profitable, and, since firms are interested in making profits, they will usually produce more.* Thus, when the price level of final output rises while factor prices are held constant, firms are motivated to increase their outputs. This is true for the individual firm and also for firms in the aggregate. This increase in the amount produced leads to an upward slope of the *SRAS* curve.

Thus, whether we look at how the price level will respond in the short run to increases in output or at how the level of output will respond to an increase in the price level with input prices being held constant, we find that the *SRAS* curve has a positive slope.

Increasing slope

A less obvious, but in many ways more important, property of a typical *SRAS* curve is that its slope *increases* as output rises. It is rather flat to the left of potential output and rather steep to the right. Why? Below potential output, firms typically have unused capacity—some plant and equipment are idle. When firms are faced with unused capacity, only a small increase in the price of their output may be needed to induce them to expand production—at least, up to normal capacity.

Once output is pushed far beyond normal capacity, however, unit costs tend to rise quite rapidly. Many higher-cost expedients may have to be adopted; standby capacity, overtime, and extra shifts may have to be used. Such expedients raise the cost of producing a unit of output. These higher-cost methods will not be used unless the selling price of the output has risen enough to cover them. The further output is expanded beyond normal capacity, the more rapidly unit costs rise and hence the larger is the rise in price that is needed to induce firms to increase output even further.

This increasing slope is sometimes called the *first important asymmetry* in the behaviour of aggregate supply. (The second, 'sticky wages', will be discussed in the next chapter.)

---

* Those who have already studied microeconomics can understand this in terms of perfectly competitive firms being faced with higher prices, and thus expanding output *along* their marginal cost curves until marginal cost is once again equal to price.

For reasons discussed in Boxes 31.2 and 31.3, many economists think that the *SRAS* curve is shaped like that in Figure 31.10, that is, relatively flat for low levels of income and becoming steeper as the level of national income increases (relative to potential national income). This shape of the *SRAS* curve implies that, at low levels of national income (well below potential), shifts in aggregate demand primarily affect output, and at high levels of national income (above potential) shifts in aggregate demand primarily affect prices.

Of course, as we have noted already, treating wages and other factor prices as constant is appropriate only when the time period under consideration is short. Hence the *SRAS* curve is used only to analyse short-run, or *impact*, effects. In the next chapter, we shall see what happens in the *long run* when factor prices respond to changes in national

income and the price level. First, however, our analysis of the short run needs to be finished off with a study of aggregate supply shocks.

Aggregate supply shocks

A decrease in aggregate supply is shown by a shift to the left in the *SRAS* curve and means that less national output will be supplied at any given price level. An increase in aggregate supply is shown by a shift to the right in the *SRAS* curve and means that more national output will be produced at any given price level.

Figure 31.12 illustrates the effects on the price level and real national income of aggregate supply shocks. As can be seen, following the decrease in aggregate supply, the price

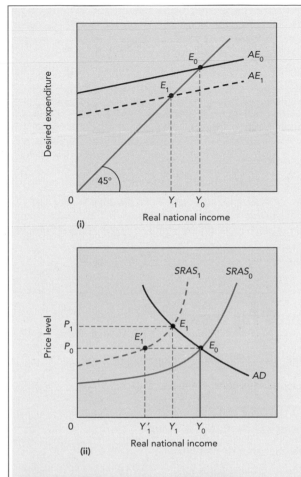

Figure 31.12 Aggregate supply shocks

Shifts in aggregate supply cause the price level and real national income to move in opposite directions. The original equilibrium is at E_0, with national income of Y_0 appearing in both parts of the figure. The price level is P_0 in part (ii), and at that price level the desired aggregate expenditure curve is AE_0 in part (i).

An aggregate supply shock now shifts the SRAS curve in part (ii) to $SRAS_1$. At the original price level of P_0, firms are now willing to supply only Y'_1. The fall in supply, with no corresponding fall in demand, causes a shortage that leads to a rise in the price level along $SRAS_1$. The new equilibrium is reached at E_1, where the AD curve intersects $SRAS_1$. At the new, and higher, equilibrium price level of P_1, the AE curve has fallen to AE_1, as shown in part (i), which is consistent with equilibrium national income of Y_1.

Figure 31.12 also shows that an increase in aggregate supply leads to an increase in real national income and a decrease in the price level.

Aggregate supply shocks cause the price level and real national income to change in opposite directions: with an increase in supply, the price level falls and income rises; with a decrease in supply, the price level rises and income falls.

An aggregate supply shock means that there is a shift in the SRAS curve (for example, from $SRAS_0$ to $SRAS_1$ in Figure 31.12). Adjustment to the new equilibrium following the shock involves a movement along the AD curve (for example, from E_0 to E_1 in the figure).

Oil prices have provided three major examples of aggregate supply shocks in recent decades. The economy is especially responsive to changes in the market for oil, because, in addition to being used to produce energy, oil is an input into plastics and many other materials that are widely used in the economy. Massive increases in oil prices during 1973–4 and 1979–80 caused leftward shifts in the SRAS curve.[9] National income fell while the price level rose, causing stagflation. In the mid-1980s oil prices fell substantially. This shifted the SRAS curve to the right, increasing national income and putting downward pressure on the price level. We can see now how a rightward shift in the SRAS curve, which is brought about by an increase in productivity or a fall in input prices, raises real national income and lowers the price level.

Summary

1 The AE curve shows desired aggregate expenditure for each level of income at a particular price level. Its intersection with the 45° line determines equilibrium national income for that price level, on the assumption that firms will produce everything that they can sell at the going price level. Equilibrium income then occurs where desired aggregate expenditure equals national income (output). A change in the price level is shown by a *shift* in the AE curve: upward when the price level falls, and downward when the price level rises. This leads to a new equilibrium level of national income.

level rises and real national income falls. This combination of events is called *stagflation*, a rather inelegant word that has been derived by combining *stagnation* (a term that is sometimes used to mean less than full employment) and *inflation.*

[9] In our model, with its single product assumption, we cannot show the positive effects on the supply of oil brought about by the higher price. Since Britain became a major oil producer in the 1970s, these effects were not unimportant. The net effect, however, on the economy as a whole, was still as discussed.

2 The *AD* curve plots the equilibrium level of national income that corresponds to each possible price level. A change in equilibrium national income following a change in the price level is shown by a *movement along the AD* curve.

3 A rise in the price level lowers exports and lowers consumers' spending (because it decreases consumers' wealth). Both of these changes lower equilibrium national income and cause the aggregate demand curve to have a negative slope.

4 The *AD* curve shifts when any element of autonomous expenditure changes, and the simple multiplier measures the magnitude of the shift. This multiplier also measures the size of the change in real equilibrium national income when the price level remains constant *and* firms produce everything that is demanded at that price level.

5 The short-run aggregate supply (*SRAS*) curve, drawn for given factor prices, is positively sloped because unit costs rise with increasing output and because rising product prices make it profitable to increase output. An increase in productivity or a decrease in factor prices shifts the curve to the right. A decrease in productivity or an increase in factor prices has the opposite effect.

6 Macroeconomic equilibrium refers to equilibrium values of national income and the price level, as determined by the intersection of the *AD* and *SRAS* curves. Shifts in the *AD* and *SRAS* curves, called aggregate demand shocks and aggregate supply shocks, change the equilibrium values of national income and the price level.

7 When the *SRAS* curve is positively sloped, an aggregate demand shock causes the price level and national income to move in the same direction. The division of the effects between a change in national income and a change in the price level depends on the shape of the *SRAS* curve. When the *SRAS* curve is flat, shifts in the *AD* curve primarily affect real national income. When the *SRAS* curve is steep, shifts in the *AD* curve primarily affect the price level.

8 An aggregate supply shock moves equilibrium national income along the *AD* curve, causing the price level and national income to move in opposite directions. A leftward shift in the *SRAS* curve causes stagflation—rising prices and falling national income. A rightward shift causes an increase in real national income and a fall in the price level. The division of the effects of a shift in *SRAS* between a change in national income and a change in the price level depends on the shape of the *AD* curve.

....

Topics for review

- Effects of a change in the price level
- Relationship between the *AE* and *AD* curves
- Negative slope of the *AD* curve
- Positive slope of the *SRAS* curve
- Macroeconomic equilibrium
- Aggregate demand shocks
- Effects of price level variation on the multiplier
- Aggregate supply shocks
- Stagflation

❧ CHAPTER 32

National income and the price level in the long run

EVERY employee knows that the best time to ask for a pay rise is during a boom, when the demand for labour is high. Workers also know that it is difficult to get significant wage increases during a recession, when high unemployment signals a low demand for labour. Every manager in industry knows that the cost of many materials tends to rise rapidly during business expansions, and to fall — often dramatically — during recessions. In short, factor prices change with economic conditions, and we need to allow for these effects.

It is necessary, therefore, to go beyond the assumption of fixed factor prices that we used to study the initial effects of aggregate demand and aggregate supply shocks in Chapter 31. To do this, we need to see what happens in a longer-term setting, when changes in national income *induce* changes in factor prices, especially wages. Once we have completed this task, we can use our model of the macro-economy to investigate the causes and consequences of business cycles and to continue our exploration of fiscal policy.

Induced changes in factor prices

WE begin by revising two key concepts that we first encountered in Chapter 27: potential income, and the output (or GDP) gap.

ANOTHER LOOK AT POTENTIAL INCOME AND THE GDP GAP

Recall that potential income is the total output that can be produced when all productive resources — labour and capital equipment in particular — are being used at their *normal rates of utilization*. When a nation's actual national income diverges from its potential income, the difference is called the GDP or output gap (see Figure 27.2 on p. 502).

Although growth in potential income has powerful effects from one decade to the next (see Chapter 33 for a discussion of the determinants of the growth of potential income), its change from one year to the next is small enough to be ignored when studying the year-to-year behaviour of national income and the price level. Therefore, in this discussion we will continue with the convention, first adopted in Chapter 27, of ignoring the small changes in potential income caused by year-to-year changes in productivity. This means that variations in the output gap are determined solely by variations in actual national income around a given potential national income.

Figure 32.1 shows actual national income being determined by the intersection of the *AD* and *SRAS* curves. Potential income is constant, and it is shown by identical vertical lines in the two parts of the figure. In part (i), the *AD* and *SRAS* curves intersect to produce an equilibrium national income that falls short of potential income. The result is called a *recessionary gap*, because recessions often begin when actual income falls below potential income. In part (ii), the *AD* and *SRAS* curves intersect to produce an equilibrium national income that exceeds potential

income, resulting in an *inflationary gap*. The way in which an inflationary output gap puts upward pressure on prices will become clear in the following discussion.

FACTOR PRICES AND THE OUTPUT GAP

The output gap provides a convenient measure of the pressure of demand on factor prices. When national income is high relative to potential income, demand for factors will also be high. When national income is low relative to potential income, demand for factors will be correspondingly low. This relationship is true of all factors. The discussion that follows is simplified, however, by focusing on one key factor—labour—and on its price—the wage rate.

When there is an inflationary gap, actual income exceeds potential income, and the demand for labour services will be relatively high. When there is a recessionary gap, actual income is below potential income and the demand for labour services will be relatively low.

Each of these situations has implications for wages. Before turning to a detailed analysis, we first consider a benchmark for the behaviour of wages. Earlier we referred to average costs per unit of output as *unit costs*; to focus on labour costs, we now use average wage costs per unit of output, which we refer to as *unit labour costs*.

Upward and downward wage pressures   In this section we consider the *upward* and *downward* pressures on wages that are associated with various output gaps. Inflationary gaps will exert upward pressure on wages, and recessionary gaps will exert downward pressure on wages. To what do the upward and downward pressures relate? One answer would

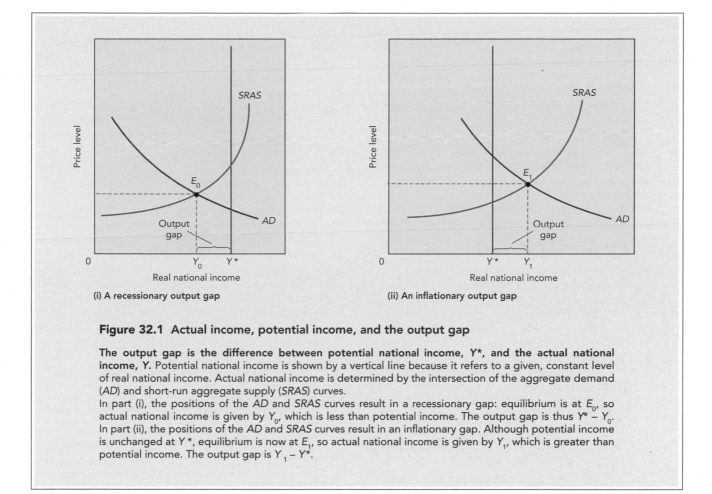

(i) A recessionary output gap

(ii) An inflationary output gap

Figure 32.1 Actual income, potential income, and the output gap

The output gap is the difference between potential national income, Y^*, and the actual national income, Y. Potential national income is shown by a vertical line because it refers to a given, constant level of real national income. Actual national income is determined by the intersection of the aggregate demand (AD) and short-run aggregate supply ($SRAS$) curves.

In part (i), the positions of the AD and $SRAS$ curves result in a recessionary gap: equilibrium is at E_0, so actual national income is given by Y_0, which is less than potential income. The output gap is thus $Y^* - Y_0$.

In part (ii), the positions of the AD and $SRAS$ curves result in an inflationary gap. Although potential income is unchanged at Y^*, equilibrium is now at E_1, so actual national income is given by Y_1, which is greater than potential income. The output gap is $Y_1 - Y^*$.

be that upward pressure means that wages would rise, and downward pressure means that wages would fall. However, most wage bargaining starts from the assumption that, other things being equal, workers will get the benefit of increases in their own productivity by receiving higher wages. Thus, when national income is at its potential level, so that there are neither upward nor downward pressures on wages caused by output gaps, wages will tend to be rising at the same rate as productivity is rising.[1] When wages and productivity change proportionately, *unit labour costs* remain unchanged. For example, if each worker produces 4 per cent more and earns 4 per cent more, unit labour costs will remain constant. This, then, is the benchmark:

When there is neither excess demand nor excess supply in the labour market, wages will tend to be rising at the same rate as labour productivity; as a result, unit labour costs will remain constant.

Note that, with unit labour costs remaining constant,

there is no pressure coming from the labour market for the $SRAS$ curve to shift and hence no pressure for the price level to rise or to fall.

In comparison with this benchmark, upward pressure on wages means that there is pressure for wages to rise faster than productivity is rising. Thus, unit labour costs will also be rising. For example, if money wages rise by 8 per cent while productivity rises by only 4 per cent, labour costs per unit of output will be rising by about 4 per cent. In this case, the $SRAS$ curve will be shifting to the left, reflecting upward pressure on wages coming from the labour market.

[1] Ongoing inflation would also influence the normal pattern of wage changes. Wage contracts often allow for changes in prices that are expected to occur during the life of the contract. (Of course, if wages merely rise to keep pace with product prices, there is no effect on unit labour costs; labour cost per £1 worth of output will be constant.) For now, we make the simplifying assumption that the price level is expected to be constant; hence changes in money wages also are expected to be changes in real wages. The distinction between changes in money wages and real wages, and the potentially important role played by expectations of price level changes, will be discussed later.

Downward pressure on wages means that there is pressure for wages to rise more slowly than productivity is rising. When this occurs, unit labour costs will be falling. For example, if productivity rises by 4 per cent while money wages rise by only 2 per cent, labour costs per unit of output will be falling by about 2 per cent. In this case, the *SRAS* curve will be shifting to the right, reflecting downward pressure on wages coming from the labour market.

Actual GDP exceeds potential GDP   Sometimes the *AD* and *SRAS* curves intersect where actual output exceeds potential, as illustrated in part (ii) of Figure 32.1. Firms are producing beyond their normal capacity output, so there is an unusually large demand for all factor inputs, including labour. Labour shortages will emerge in some industries and among many groups of workers, particularly skilled workers. Firms will try to bid workers away from other firms in order to maintain the high levels of output and sales made possible by the boom conditions.

As a result of these tight labour market conditions, workers will find that they have considerable bargaining power with their employers, and they will put upward pressure on wages relative to productivity. Firms, recognizing that demand for their goods is strong, will be anxious to maintain a high level of output. Thus, to prevent their workers from either striking or quitting and moving to other employers, firms will be willing to accede to some of these upward pressures.

The boom that is associated with an inflationary gap generates a set of conditions—high profits for firms and an unusually large demand for labour—that exerts upward pressure on wages.

Potential GDP exceeds actual GDP   Sometimes the *AD* and *SRAS* curves intersect where actual output is less than potential, as illustrated in part (i) of Figure 32.1. In this situation firms are producing below their normal capacity output, so there is an unusually low demand for all factor inputs, including labour. The general conditions in the market for labour will be the opposite of those that occur when actual output exceeds potential. There will be labour surpluses in some industries and among some groups of workers. Firms will have below-normal sales, and not only will resist upward pressures on wages, but also will tend to offer wage increases below productivity increases and may even seek reductions in money wages.

The slump that is associated with a recessionary gap generates a set of conditions — low profits for firms, an unusually low demand for labour, and a desire on the part of firms to resist wage demands and even to push for wage concessions — that exerts downward pressure on wages and unit labour costs.

Adjustment asymmetry   At this stage we encounter an important asymmetry in the economy's aggregate supply behaviour. Boom conditions, along with severe labour shortages, cause wages, unit labour costs, and the price level to rise rapidly. When there is a large excess demand for labour, wage (and price) increases often run well ahead of productivity increases. Money wages might be rising by 10 or 15 per cent, while productivity might be rising at only 2 or 3 per cent. Under such conditions, unit labour costs will be rising rapidly.

The experience of many developed economies suggests, however, that the downward pressures on wages during slumps often do not operate as quickly as do the upward pressures during booms. Even in quite severe recessions, when the price level is fairly stable, money wages may continue to rise, although their rate of increase tends to fall below that of productivity. For example, productivity might be rising at, say, 1.5 per cent per year while money wages are rising at 0.5 per cent. In this case, unit labour costs are falling, but only at about 1 per cent per year, so the rightward shift in the *SRAS* curve and the downward pressure on the price level are correspondingly slight. Money wages may actually fall, reducing unit wage costs even more, but the reduction in unit labour costs in times of the deepest recession has never been as fast as the increases that have occurred during several of the strongest booms.

Both upward and downward adjustments to unit labour costs do occur, but there are differences in the speed at which they typically operate. Excess demand can cause unit labour costs to rise very rapidly; excess supply often causes unit labour costs to fall only slowly.

In Chapters 40 and 41, we explore the consequences of this asymmetry for the relationship between unemployment (or the output gap) and inflation, which is one of the most important relationships in macroeconomics.[2]

Inflationary and recessionary gaps   By now it should be clear why the output gaps are named as they are. When actual national income exceeds potential national income, there will normally be rising unit costs, and the *SRAS* curve will be shifting upward. This, in turn, will push the price level up. Indeed, the most obvious event accompanying these conditions is likely to be a significant inflation. The larger is the excess of actual income over potential income, the greater will be the inflationary pressure. The term 'inflationary gap' emphasizes this salient feature, when actual output exceeds potential output.

When actual output is less than potential output, as we

---

[2] This is the second asymmetry in aggregate supply that we have encountered. The first refers to the variable slope of the *SRAS* curve, as discussed in Box 31.3.

have seen, there will be unemployment of labour and other productive resources. Unit labour costs will fall only slowly, leading to a slow downward shift in the *SRAS* curve. Hence the price level will be falling only slowly, so that *unemployment* will be the output gap's most obvious result. The term 'recessionary gap' emphasizes this salient feature that high rates of unemployment occur when actual output falls short of potential output.

The induced effects of output gaps on unit labour costs and the consequent shifts in the *SRAS* curve play an important role in our analysis of the long-run consequences of aggregate demand shocks, to which we now turn.

The long-run consequences of aggregate demand shocks

WE can now extend our study to cover the longer-run consequences of aggregate demand shocks, when incorporating changes in factor prices. We need to examine separately the effect of aggregate demand shocks on factor prices for expansionary and for contractionary shocks, since the behaviour of unit costs is not symmetrical for the two cases.

Expansionary shocks

Suppose that the economy starts with a stable price level at full employment, so actual income equals potential income, as shown by the initial equilibrium in part (i) of Figure 32.2.

Now suppose that this happy situation is disturbed by an increase in autonomous expenditure, perhaps caused by a sudden boom in investment spending. Figure 32.2(i) shows the effects of this aggregate demand shock in raising both the price level and national income. Now actual national income exceeds potential income, and there is an inflationary gap.

We have seen that an inflationary gap leads wages to rise faster than productivity, which causes unit costs to rise. The *SRAS* curve shifts to the left as firms seek to pass on their increases in input costs by increasing their output prices. For this reason, the initial increases in the price level and in real national income shown in part (i) of Figure 32.2 are *not* the final effects of the demand shock. As seen in part (ii) of the figure, the upward shift of the *SRAS* curve causes a further rise in the price level, but this time the price rise is associated with a fall in output.

The cost increases (and the consequent upward shifts of the *SRAS* curve) continue until the inflationary gap has been removed, that is until income returns to Y^*, its potential level. Only then is there no abnormal demand for labour, and only then do wages and unit costs, and hence the *SRAS* curve, stabilize.

This important expansionary demand-shock sequence can be summarized as follows:

1 Starting from full employment, a rise in aggregate demand raises the price level and raises income above its potential level as the economy expands along a given *SRAS* curve.

2. The expansion of income beyond its normal capacity level puts pressure on factor markets; factor prices begin to increase faster than productivity, shifting the *SRAS* curve upward, such that prices are higher at every level of output.

3. The shift of the *SRAS* curve causes national income to fall along the *AD* curve. This process continues *as long as* actual income exceeds potential income. Therefore, actual income eventually falls back to its potential level. The price level is now higher than it was after the initial impact of the increased aggregate demand, but inflation will have come to a halt.

The ability to wring more output and income from the economy than its underlying potential output (as in point 2) is only a short-term possibility. National income greater than Y^* sets into motion inflationary pressures that tend to push national income back to Y^*.

There is an adjustment mechanism that eventually eliminates any inflation caused by a one-time demand shock by returning output to its potential level and thus removing the inflationary gap.

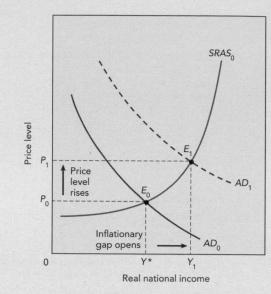
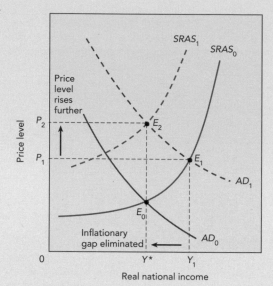
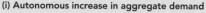

(i) Autonomous increase in aggregate demand

(ii) Induced shift in aggregate supply

Figure 32.2 Demand-shock inflation

A rightward shift of the *AD* curve first raises prices and output along the *SRAS* curve. It then induces a shift of the *SRAS* curve that further raises prices but lowers output along the *AD* curve. In part (i), the economy is in equilibrium at E_0, at its level of potential output $Y*$ and price level P_0. The *AD* curve then shifts to AD_1. This moves equilibrium to E_1, with income Y_1 and price level P_1, and opens up an inflationary gap of $Y*-Y_1$.

In part (ii), the inflationary gap results in an increase in wages and other input costs, shifting the *SRAS* curve leftward. As this happens, income falls and the price level rises along AD_1. Eventually, when the *SRAS* curve has shifted to $SRAS_1$, income is back to $Y*$ and the inflationary gap has been eliminated. However, the price level has risen to P_2.

Contractionary shocks

Let us return to that fortunate economy with full employment and stable prices. It appears again in part (i) of Figure 32.3, which is similar to part (i) of Figure 32.2. Now assume that there is a *decline* in aggregate demand, perhaps owing to a major reduction in investment expenditure, or to a fall in exports arising from a fall in income overseas.

The first effects of the decline are a fall in output and some downward adjustment of prices, as shown in part (i) of the figure. As output falls, unemployment rises. The difference between potential output and actual output is the recessionary gap that is shown in the figure.

Flexible wages   What would happen if severe unemployment caused wage rates to fall rapidly relative to productivity? For example, with productivity rising by 1 per cent per year, say that money wages fell by 4 per cent. Unit costs would then *fall* by 5 per cent. Falling wage rates would

lower unit costs, causing a rightward shift of the *SRAS* curve. As shown in part (ii) of Figure 32.3, the economy would move along its fixed *AD* curve, with falling prices and rising output, until full employment was restored at potential national income $Y*$. We conclude that, if wages were to fall rapidly whenever there was unemployment, the resulting fall in the *SRAS* curve would restore full employment.

Flexible wages that fell rapidly during periods of unemployment would provide an automatic adjustment mechanism that would push the economy back towards full employment whenever output fell below potential.

Box 32.1 takes up the interesting case of how the adjustment mechanism might work if the aggregate demand shock were anticipated in advance.

Sticky wages   Boom conditions, along with severe labour

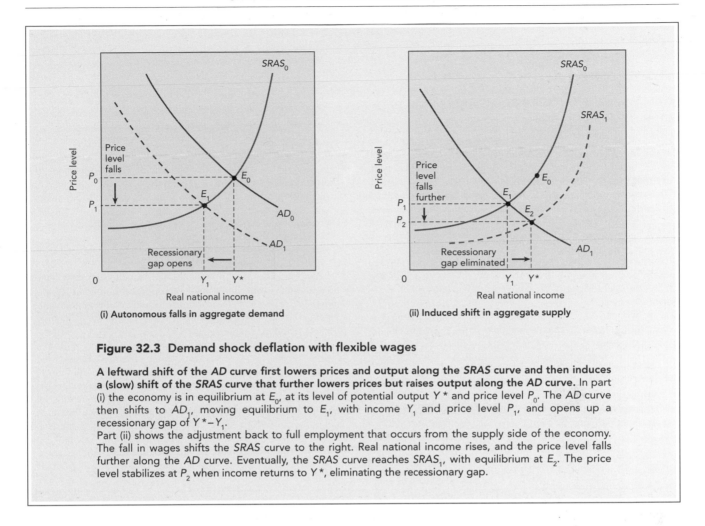

(i) Autonomous falls in aggregate demand

(ii) Induced shift in aggregate supply

Figure 32.3 Demand shock deflation with flexible wages

A leftward shift of the *AD* curve first lowers prices and output along the *SRAS* curve and then induces a (slow) shift of the *SRAS* curve that further lowers prices but raises output along the *AD* curve. In part (i) the economy is in equilibrium at E_0, at its level of potential output Y^* and price level P_0. The *AD* curve then shifts to AD_1, moving equilibrium to E_1, with income Y_1 and price level P_1, and opens up a recessionary gap of $Y^* - Y_1$.

Part (ii) shows the adjustment back to full employment that occurs from the supply side of the economy. The fall in wages shifts the *SRAS* curve to the right. Real national income rises, and the price level falls further along the *AD* curve. Eventually, the *SRAS* curve reaches $SRAS_1$, with equilibrium at E_2. The price level stabilizes at P_2 when income returns to Y^*, eliminating the recessionary gap.

shortages, do cause wages to rise rapidly, shifting the *SRAS* curve upward. However, as we noted earlier when we encountered the second asymmetry of aggregate supply behaviour, the experience of many economies suggests that wages typically do not fall rapidly in response to recessionary gaps and their accompanying unemployment. It is sometimes said that wages are 'sticky' in a downward direction. This does not mean that they never fall. In a recession, money wages often rise more slowly than productivity and some money wages even fall. But the gap between money wage changes and productivity changes is typically quite small during recessions. This means that unit labour costs will fall only slowly. This, in turn, means that the downward shifts in the *SRAS* curve occur slowly, and the adjustment mechanism that depends on these shifts will act sluggishly.

The weakness of the adjustment mechanism does not mean that slumps must always be prolonged. Rather, this weakness means that speedy recovery back to full employment must be generated mainly from the demand side. If the economy is to avoid a lengthy period of recession or stagnation, the force leading to recovery usually must be a rightward shift of the *AD* curve rather than a downward drift of the *SRAS* curve. The possibility that government *stabilization policy* might accomplish this is one of the more important and contentious issues in macroeconomics, one that we will return to often throughout the remainder of this book.

The *SRAS* curve shifts to the left fairly rapidly when national income exceeds Y^*, but it shifts to the right only slowly when national income is less than Y^*.

The asymmetry   This difference in speed of adjustment is a consequence of the important asymmetry in the behaviour of aggregate supply that was noted earlier in this chapter. This asymmetry helps to explain two key facts about our economy. First, unemployment can persist for quite long periods without causing decreases in unit costs and prices of sufficient magnitude to remove the unemployment.

BOX 32.1

....

Anticipated demand shocks

Suppose that the increase in aggregate demand that is illustrated in Figure 32.2 was widely anticipated well before it occurred. For example, an approaching election might have led to the wide-spread belief that the government would stimulate the economy in order to improve its electoral chances.

Further, suppose that most employers and employees believe that one of the effects of the demand stimulation will be infla-tion. Then workers might press for wage increases to prevent the purchasing power of their earnings from being eroded by the coming price increases. Firms might believe that the demand for their products was likely to rise, enabling them to raise their sell-ing prices; they might therefore be persuaded to grant wage increases now and pass these on to consumers in terms of higher prices.

A demand stimulus that was widely expected to occur and whose inflationary effects were widely understood could lead to upward pressure on wages, even without the opening of any inflationary gap.

If this were to occur, the leftward shift in the *SRAS* curve that is depicted in part (ii) of Figure 32.2 could occur quickly, per-haps accompanying, or even preceding, the rightward shift in the *AD* curve in part (i). Given *perfect* anticipation of the effects of the demand stimulus, and *full* adjustment to it in advance, the equilibrium would go straight from E_0 to E_2. The intermediate position, E_1, with its accompanying inflationary gap (with

national income in excess of potential income), would be com-pletely bypassed.

A similar story might be told for an anticipated fall in aggre-gate demand. The effects of an unanticipated fall are shown in the two parts of Figure 32.3. However, if the fall were widely anticipated and its effects were generally understood, firms might reduce their wage offers and workers might accept the decreases because they expect prices to fall as well. In this case, it is conceivable that the economy could bypass the recessionary stage and go straight to a lower price level at an unchanged level of real national income.

This possibility that anticipated demand shocks might have no real effects on real national income, and hence on unem-ployment, plays a key role in some important controversies con-cerning the effectiveness of government policies. We shall study these in detail in Chapters 41 and 43.

In the meantime, we may notice that, for the complete absence of real effects in the transitionary period, with the only change being in the price level, everyone must have full knowl-edge both of the exact amount of the stimulus that the govern-ment will induce and of the new equilibrium values of the relevant prices and wages. In other words, everyone knows what the new equilibrium will be and goes directly to it. Generally, people do not have such perfect knowledge and foresight, so there is some groping towards the equilibrium, and hence some real effects, until the final equilibrium set of wages and prices is reached.

Second, booms, along with labour shortages and produc-tion beyond normal capacity, do not persist for long peri-ods without causing increases in unit costs and the price level.

The long-run aggregate supply (*LRAS*) curve

The adjustment mechanism leads us to an important con-cept: the **long-run aggregate supply (*LRAS*) curve**. This curve relates the price level to real national income after wage rates and all other input costs have been fully adjust-ed to eliminate any unemployment or overall labour shortages.[3]

Shape of the LRAS curve   Once all the adjustments that are required have occurred, the economy will have eliminated any excess demand or excess supply of labour. In other words, full employment will prevail, and output will neces-

sarily be at its potential level, Y^*. It follows that the aggre-gate supply curve becomes a vertical line at Y^*, as shown in Figure 32.4. The *LRAS* curve is sometimes called the classi-cal aggregate supply curve because the classical economists were concerned mainly with the behaviour of the economy in long-run equilibrium.

Notice that the vertical *LRAS* curve does not represent the same thing as the vertical portion of the *SRAS* curve (see Figure 31.11). Over the vertical range of the *SRAS* curve, the economy is at its utmost limit of productive capacity, when no more can be squeezed out, as might occur in an all-out war effort. The vertical shape of the *LRAS* curve is due to the workings of an adjustment mechanism that brings the economy back to its potential output, even though output may differ from potential for considerable periods of time. It is called the long-run aggregate supply

---

[3] Notice that this use of the term 'long run' is different from its mean-ing in microeconomics, as we pointed out in Chapter 29. Note, however, the key similarity that in the long run more adjustment is completed than in the short run.

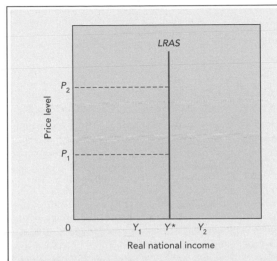

Figure 32.4 The long-run aggregate supply (*LRAS*) curve

The long-run aggregate supply curve is a vertical line drawn at the level of national income that is equal to potential income, *Y* *. It is a vertical line, because the total amount of goods that the economy produces when all factors are efficiently used at their normal rate of utilization does not vary with the price level. If the price level were to rise from P_1 to P_2 *and* wages and all other factor prices were to rise by the same proportion, the total desired output of firms would remain at *Y* *.

If income were Y_1, which is less than *Y* *, wages would be falling and the *SRAS* curve would be shifting rightward; hence the economy would not be on its *LRAS* curve. If income were Y_2, which is greater than *Y* *, wages would be rising and the *SRAS* curve would be shifting leftward; hence, again, the economy would not be on its *LRAS* curve.

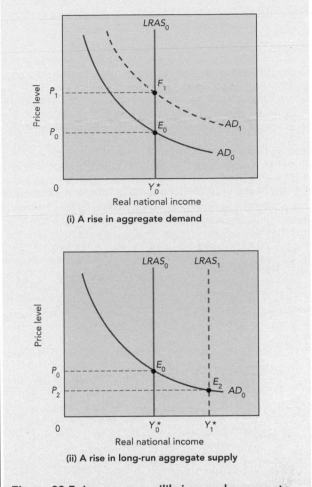

(i) A rise in aggregate demand

(ii) A rise in long-run aggregate supply

Figure 32.5 Long-run equilibrium and aggregate supply

When the *LRAS* curve is vertical, aggregate supply determines the long-run equilibrium value of national income at *Y**. Given *Y**, aggregate demand determines the long-run equilibrium value of the price level. In both parts of the figure, the initial long-run equilibrium is at E_0, so the price level is P_0 and national income is Y_0^*.

In part (i), a shift in the *AD* curve from AD_0 to AD_1, with the *LRAS* curve remaining unchanged, moves the long-run equilibrium from E_0 to E_1. This raises the price level from P_0 to P_1 but leaves national income unchanged at Y_0^* in the long run.

In part (ii), a shift in the *LRAS* curve from $LRAS_0$ to $LRAS_1$, with the aggregate demand curve remaining constant at AD_0, moves the long-run equilibrium from E_0 to E_2. This raises national income from Y_0^* to Y_1^* but lowers the price level from P_0 to P_2.

curve because it arises as a result of adjustments that take a significant amount of time.

Along the *LRAS* curve, all the prices of all outputs and all inputs have been fully adjusted to eliminate any excess demands or supplies. Proportionate changes in money wages and the price level (which, by definition, will leave real wages unaltered) will also leave equilibrium employment and total output unchanged. In the next section, we will ask what does change when we move from one point on the *LRAS* curve to another.

Long-run equilibrium

Figure 32.5 shows the equilibrium output and the price level as they are determined by the intersection of the *AD* curve and the vertical *LRAS* curve. Because the *LRAS* curve is vertical, shifts in aggregate demand change the price level

but not the level of equilibrium output, as shown in part (i). By contrast, a shift in aggregate supply changes both output and the price level, as shown in part (ii). For example, a rightward shift of the *LRAS* curve increases national income and leads to a fall in the price level.

With a vertical *LRAS* curve, in the long run total output is determined solely by conditions of supply, and the role of aggregate demand is simply to determine the price level.

What does change when the economy moves from one point on the *LRAS* curve, such as E_0 in part (i) of Figure 32.5, to another point, such as E_1? Although total output and total desired expenditure do not change, their *compositions* do change. The higher the price level, the lower is personal wealth (for a given nominal stock of assets), and hence the lower is consumption. (Recall from Chapter 29 that, the lower is wealth, the higher is saving and hence the lower is consumption.) Also, the higher the price level, the lower are exports and the higher are imports, and hence the lower are net exports.

Say the economy starts at a point on the *SRAS* curve and an increase in government expenditure then creates an inflationary gap. Money wages and the price level rise until the gap is removed. At the new long-run equilibrium, the higher level of government spending is exactly offset by lower consumption and net exports, leaving total output unchanged. A similar analysis holds for an increase in investment. In the new long-run equilibrium, the higher level of investment spending will be exactly offset by lower consumption spending and net exports.[4]

The vertical *LRAS* curve shows that, given full adjustment of input prices, potential income, Y^*, is compatible with any price level although its composition among consumption, investment, government, and net exports may be different at different price levels.

In Chapter 36 we will discover circumstances under which a rise in the price level has *no real effects*, so that, not only are total income and total expenditure the same at all points on the *LRAS* curve, but its composition among C, I, G and (X-IM) is also the same. We shall also learn, once we have added a monetary sector, that interest rate changes resulting from *AD* shocks have important effects on the composition of expenditure.

National income in the short and long run

WE have now identified two distinct equilibrium conditions for the economy:

1. In the short run, the economy is in equilibrium at the level of national income and the price level where the *SRAS* curve intersects the *AD* curve.

2. In the long run, the economy is in equilibrium at potential national income, the position of the vertical *LRAS* curve. The price level is that at which the *AD* curve intersects the *LRAS* curve.

When the economy is in long-run equilibrium, it is also in short-run equilibrium.

The *position* of the *LRAS* curve is at Y^*, which is determined by past economic growth. Deviations of actual income from potential income — output gaps — are generally associated with business cycles. Changes in total real output (and hence in employment, unemployment, and living standards) may take place as a result of either growth or the business cycle.

This discussion suggests a need to distinguish three ways in which GDP can be increased. These are illustrated in Figure 32.6.

Increases in aggregate demand   As shown in part (i) of Figure 32.6, an increase in aggregate demand will yield a one-time increase in real GDP. If that increase occurs when there is a recessionary gap, it will push GDP towards potential income and thus will short-circuit the working of the automatic adjustment mechanism, which eventually would have achieved the same outcome by depressing unit costs, as discussed earlier in this chapter.

If the demand shock pushes GDP beyond potential income, the rise in GDP above potential income will be only temporary; the inflationary gap will cause wages and other costs to rise, shifting the *SRAS* curve to the left. This will drive GDP back towards its potential level, so that the only lasting effect is on the price level. Box 32.2 gives a number of reasons why we might expect the effect of demand shocks on GDP to be cyclical, that is to cause GDP to move first one way, then the other.

Increases in aggregate supply   Increases in aggregate supply will also lead to an increase in GDP. Here it is useful to dis-

---

[4] Once we have studied the effect of interest rates on investment, in Chapter 36, we will see that an increase in government spending can also 'crowd out' investment via increases in interest rates.

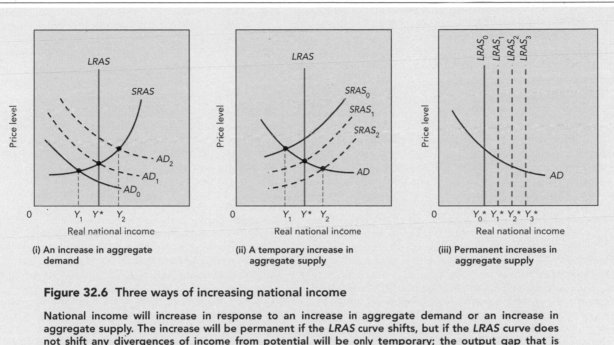

Figure 32.6 Three ways of increasing national income

National income will increase in response to an increase in aggregate demand or an increase in aggregate supply. The increase will be permanent if the *LRAS* curve shifts, but if the *LRAS* curve does not shift any divergences of income from potential will be only temporary; the output gap that is created will set in motion the wage adjustments that we studied earlier in this chapter. In part (i) of the figure the *AD* curve shifts to the right. If the initial level of income is Y_1, then the shift from AD_0 to AD_1 eliminates the recessionary gap and raises national income to Y^*. If the initial level of income is Y^*, then the shift from AD_1 to AD_2 raises national income to Y_2 and thereby opens up an inflationary gap. In part (ii) the *SRAS* curve shifts to the right. If the initial level of income is Y_1, then the shift from $SRAS_0$ to $SRAS_1$ eliminates the recessionary gap and raises national income to Y^*. If the initial level of income is Y^*, then the shift from $SRAS_1$ to $SRAS_2$ raises national income to Y_2 and thereby opens up an inflationary gap. In the cases shown in parts (i) and (ii), any increase in income beyond potential is temporary, since, in the absence of any additional shocks, the inflationary gap will cause wages and other factor prices to rise; this will cause the *SRAS* curve to shift upward and, hence, national income to converge to Y^*.

In part (iii) the *LRAS* curve shifts to the right, causing potential income to increase. Whether or not actual income increases immediately depends on what happens to the *AD* and *SRAS* curves. Since, in the absence of other shocks, actual income eventually converges to potential income, a rightward shift in the *LRAS* curve eventually leads to an increase in actual income. If the shift in the *LRAS* curve is recurring, then national income will grow continually.

tinguish between two possible kinds of increase that might occur: those that leave the *LRAS* curve unchanged, and those that shift it.

Part (ii) of Figure 32.6 shows the effects of a temporary increase in aggregate supply. This will shift the *SRAS* curve to the right but will have no effect on the *LRAS* curve and, therefore, none on potential income. The shock will thus cause GDP to rise relative to potential, but the increase will be eventually reversed.

Part (iii) of Figure 32.6 shows the effects of permanent increases in aggregate supply that shift the *LRAS* curve. A once-for-all increase arising from, say, a labour-market policy that reduces the level of structural unemployment will lead to a one-time increase in potential GDP. A recurring increase that is due, say, to population growth, capital accumulation, or ongoing improvements in productivity causes a continual rightward shift in the *LRAS* curve, giving rise to a continual increase in the level of potential GDP.

ECONOMIC GROWTH

A gradual but continual rise in potential GDP, or what we have called *economic growth*, is the main source of improvements in the standard of living over the long term.

Eliminating a severe recessionary gap could cause a once-for-all increase in national income of, say, 4 per cent, while eliminating structural unemployment will raise it by somewhat less. However, a growth rate of 3 per cent per year raises national income by 10 per cent in three years, *doubles* it in 24 years, and *quadruples* it in 48 years.

BOX 32.2

Demand shocks and business cycles

Aggregate demand shocks are a major source of fluctuations in GDP around Y^*. As we have seen, an expansionary demand shock, starting from a position of full employment, will lead to an increase in output, followed by a fall in output accompanied by an increase in prices as the adjustment mechanism restores the economy to equilibrium. Depending on the nature and magnitude of the shock, the adjustment will take many months, often stretching into one or two (or even more) years.

Suppose that the government increases spending on roads, or that economic growth in Germany leads to an increase in demand for UK exports. No matter what the source of growth in demand, the economy will not respond instantaneously. In many industries it takes weeks or months, or even longer, to bring new or mothballed capacity into production and to hire and train new workers. The multiplier process itself also takes time, as people and firms respond to the change in income that results from an initial increase in autonomous spending.

Because of these lags in the economy's response, changes in demand give rise to changes in output that are spread out over a substantial period of time. An increase in demand may lead to a gradual increase in output that builds up over several months. Then, as output does change, the adjustment mechanism comes into play. As an inflationary gap opens up, wages and costs start to rise, shifting the SRAS curve to the left.

Thus, a once-for-all positive demand shock gives rise to a *cyclical* output response, with GDP first rising because of the rightward shift in the AD curve, and then falling because of the upward shift in the SRAS curve. A negative demand shock is likely to play out even more slowly because of the asymmetry of response. Again, however, the behaviour of output will be cyclical: starting from potential output, GDP will fall over a period of time, because of a leftward shift in the AD curve, and then rise slowly as the adjustment mechanism shifts SRAS to the right.

Each major component of aggregate expenditure, consumption, investment, net exports, and government purchases is subject to continual random shifts, which are sometimes large enough to disturb the economy significantly. Adjustment lags convert such shifts into cyclical oscillations in national income.

In any given year, the position of the LRAS curve is at potential GDP, Y^*. The 'long run' to which the LRAS curve refers is thus one in which the resources available to the economy do not change, but in which all markets reach equilibrium. Economic growth moves the LRAS curve to the right, year by year. Here, there is no 'long run' in which everything settles down, because growth is a continuing process. Rather, the movement in LRAS is a continuing movement in Y^*.

Determinants of the long run shifts in potential national income, or economic growth, used to be regarded as beyond the scope of macroeconomics. However, it is such an important factor in determining living standards that we discuss it in more detail in the following chapter. Indeed, there is now a much stronger case for treating growth as an integral part of macroeconomics. This is that the forces of growth may be endogenous; that is, apparently short-term policies may have implications for long-term growth. No longer is it safe to assume that the determinants of growth are independent of the determinants of the short-term cycle (though we continue to assume so in this chapter).

CYCLICAL FLUCTUATIONS

Figure 32.6 allows us to distinguish the causes of trend growth in potential GDP, which is the gradual rightward shifting of the LRAS curve, from the causes of cyclical fluctuations, which are deviations from that trend.

Cyclical fluctuations in GDP are caused by shifts in the AD and SRAS curves that cause actual GDP to deviate temporarily from potential GDP.

These shifts, in turn, are caused by changes in a variety of factors, including interest rates, exchange rates, consumer and business confidence, and government policy. Although the resulting deviations of actual from potential GDP are described as 'temporary', recall from the discussion above that the automatic adjustment mechanism may work slowly enough that the deviations can persist for some time, perhaps several years.

Figure 32.7 shows three different output series. The three sectors shown are: manufacturing; construction; and food, drink, and tobacco. Each of these, as well as dozens of others that might be studied, tells us something about the general variability of the economy. Some move more than others, and no two move exactly together; yet all exhibit a cyclical pattern, and they tend to move approximately together. We will discuss such *business cycles* in more depth in Chapter 43. Economic growth is discussed in Chapter 33.

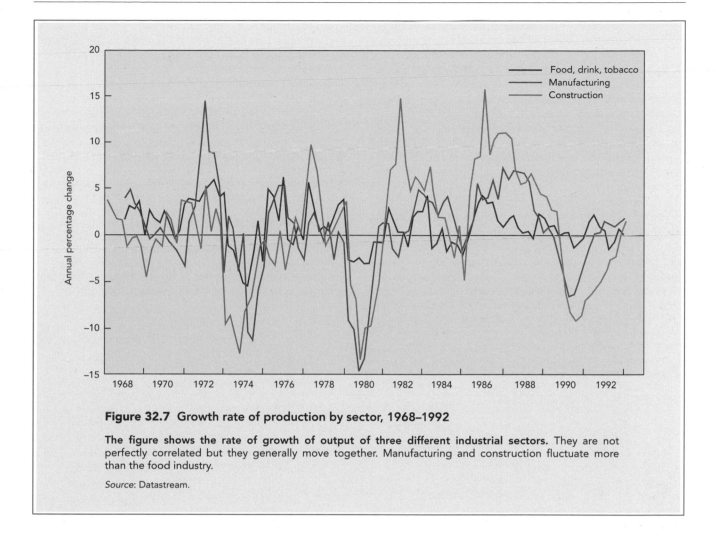

Figure 32.7 Growth rate of production by sector, 1968–1992

The figure shows the rate of growth of output of three different industrial sectors. They are not perfectly correlated but they generally move together. Manufacturing and construction fluctuate more than the food industry.

Source: Datastream.

Fiscal policy and the business cycle

MACROECONOMICS, as a formal discipline, was developed, not just to explain business cycles, but also to suggest policies that could be used to avoid the worst occurrences of recessions — where there is persistent high unemployment and excess capacity. Central to the so–called Keynesian Revolution in economic policy-making was the idea that government fiscal policy could be used in a countercyclical manner to stabilize the economy.

Accordingly, in the remainder of this chapter we discuss taxing and spending as tools of fiscal stabilization policy. In Chapter 38 we will return to the subject, because by then we shall also be able to discuss the role of monetary policy. We refer to deliberate changes in tax rates or government expenditure which are targeted on stabilizing the economy as *discretionary* fiscal policy.

Since government expenditure increases aggregate

demand and taxation decreases it, the *direction* of the required changes in spending and taxation is generally easy to determine once we know the direction of the desired change in national income. However, the *timing*, *magnitude*, and *mixture* of the changes pose more difficult issues.

There is no doubt that the government can exert a major influence on national income. Prime examples are the massive increases in military spending during major wars (see Figure 27.3). UK government expenditure during the Second World War rose from 13.4 per cent of GDP in 1938 to 49.2 per cent of GDP in 1944. At the same time, the unemployment rate fell from 9.2 to 0.3 per cent (see Figure 27.5). Economists agree that the increase in government spending helped to bring about the rise in GDP and the associated fall in unemployment. Similar experiences occurred during the rearmament of most European countries before, or just following, the outbreak of the Second World War in 1939 and in the United States during the Vietnam War in the late 1960s and early 1970s.

In the heyday of fiscal policy, from about 1945 to about 1970, many economists were convinced that the economy could be stabilized adequately just by varying the size of the government's taxes and expenditures. That day is past. Today most economists are aware of the many limitations of fiscal policy.

The basic theory of fiscal stabilization

A reduction in tax rates or an increase in government expenditure will shift the *AD* curve to the right, causing an increase in GDP. An increase in tax rates or a cut in government expenditure will shift the *AD* curve to the left, causing a decrease in GDP.

A more detailed look at how fiscal stabilization works will provide a useful review. It will also help to show some of the complications that arise in making fiscal policy.

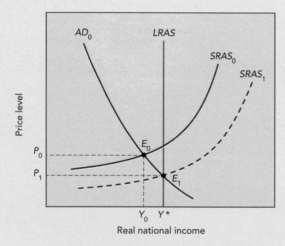

(i) A recessionary gap removed by a rightward shift in *SRAS*

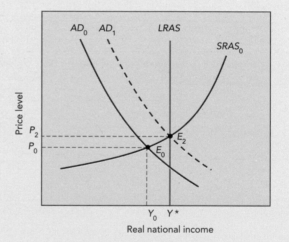

(ii) A recessionary gap removed by a rightward shift in *AD*

Figure 32.8 Removal of a recessionary gap

A recessionary gap may be removed by a (slow) rightward shift of the *SRAS* curve, a natural revival of private-sector demand, or a fiscal-policy-induced increase in aggregate demand. Initially, equilibrium is at E_0, with national income at Y_0 and the price level at P_0. The recessionary gap Y^*-Y_0.

As shown in part (i), the gap might be removed by a shift in the *SRAS* curve to $SRAS_1$. The increase in aggregate supply could occur as a result of reductions in wage rates and other input prices. The shift in the *SRAS* curve causes a movement down and to the right along AD_0. This movement establishes a new equilibrium at E_1, achieving potential income, Y^*, and lowering the price level to P_1.

As shown in part (ii), the gap might also be removed by a shift of the *AD* curve to AD_1. This increase in aggregate demand could occur either because of a natural revival of private-sector expenditure or because of a fiscal-policy-induced increase in expenditure. The shift in the *AD* curve causes a movement up and to the right along $SRAS_0$. This movement shifts the equilibrium to E_2, raising income to Y^* and the price level to P_2.

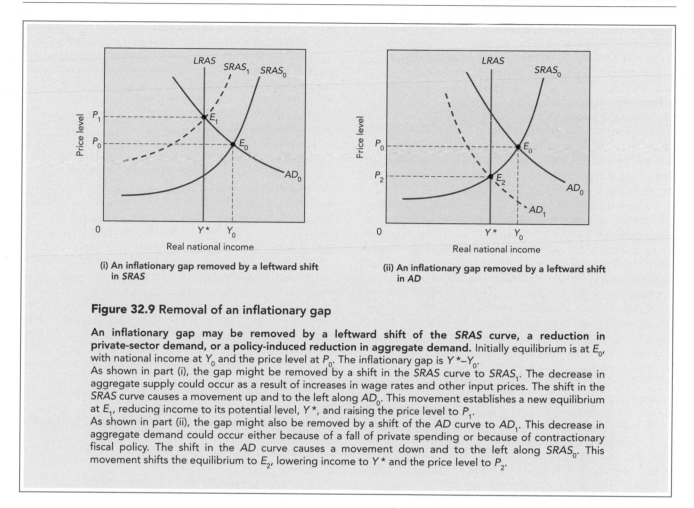

(i) An inflationary gap removed by a leftward shift in *SRAS*

(ii) An inflationary gap removed by a leftward shift in *AD*

Figure 32.9 Removal of an inflationary gap

An inflationary gap may be removed by a leftward shift of the *SRAS* curve, a reduction in private-sector demand, or a policy-induced reduction in aggregate demand. Initially equilibrium is at E_0, with national income at Y_0 and the price level at P_0. The inflationary gap is $Y^* - Y_0$.

As shown in part (i), the gap might be removed by a shift in the *SRAS* curve to $SRAS_1$. The decrease in aggregate supply could occur as a result of increases in wage rates and other input prices. The shift in the *SRAS* curve causes a movement up and to the left along AD_0. This movement establishes a new equilibrium at E_1, reducing income to its potential level, Y^*, and raising the price level to P_1.

As shown in part (ii), the gap might also be removed by a shift of the *AD* curve to AD_1. This decrease in aggregate demand could occur either because of a fall of private spending or because of contractionary fiscal policy. The shift in the *AD* curve causes a movement down and to the left along $SRAS_0$. This movement shifts the equilibrium to E_2, lowering income to Y^* and the price level to P_2.

A recessionary gap The removal of a recessionary gap is illustrated in Figure 32.8. There are two possible ways in which the gap may be removed.

First, the recessionary gap may eventually drive wages and other factor prices down by enough to shift the *SRAS* curve to the right and thereby reinstate high employment and potential income (at a lower price level). The evidence, however, is that this process takes a substantial period of time.

Second, the *AD* curve could shift to the right, restoring the economy to full employment and potential income (at a higher price level). The government can cause such a shift by using expansionary fiscal policy, lowering taxes or raising spending. The advantage of using fiscal policy is that it may substantially shorten what would otherwise be a long recession. One disadvantage is that the use of fiscal policy may stimulate the economy just before private-sector spending recovers on its own. As a result, the economy may overshoot its potential output, and an inflationary gap may open up. In this case, fiscal policy that is intended to promote economic stability can actually cause instability.

An inflationary gap Figure 32.9 shows the ways in which an inflationary gap can be removed.

First, wages and other factor prices may be pushed up by the excess demand. The *SRAS* curve will therefore shift to the left, eventually eliminating the gap, reducing income to its potential level, and raising the price level.

Second, the *AD* curve can shift to the left, restoring equilibrium GDP. The government, by raising taxes or cutting spending, can induce such a shift, reducing aggregate demand sufficiently to remove the inflationary gap. The advantage of this approach is that it avoids the inflationary increase in prices that accompanies the first method. One disadvantage is that, if private-sector expenditure falls owing to natural causes, national income may be pushed below potential, thus opening up a recessionary gap.

A key proposition This discussion suggests that, in circumstances in which the automatic adjustment mechanisms either fail to operate quickly enough or give rise to undesirable side effects such as rising prices, there is a potential stabilizing role for fiscal policy.

Government taxes and expenditure shift the *AD* curve and hence can be used to remove persistent GDP gaps.

THE PARADOX OF THRIFT

The theory of national income determination predicts that an increase in national saving will shift the *AD* curve to the left and hence *reduce* the equilibrium level of income in the short run. The contrary case, a general decrease in thrift and increase in expenditure, shifts the *AD* curve to the right and hence increases national income in the short run. This prediction is known as the *paradox of thrift*.[5]

The policy implication of this prediction is that substantial unemployment can be combated by encouraging governments, firms, and consumers to spend more, *not* to save more. In times of unemployment and depression, frugality will only make things worse. This prediction goes directly against the idea that we should tighten our belts when times are tough. The notion that it is not only possible but also acceptable to spend one's way out of a depression touches a sensitive point with people raised on the belief that success is based on hard work and frugality and not on prodigality; as a result, the idea often arouses great hostility.

The significance of the paradox of thrift for understanding the severity of the 1990–2 recession in the United Kingdom is discussed in Box 32.3.

Limitations   The paradox of thrift concentrates on shifts in aggregate demand that have been caused by changes in saving (and hence spending) behaviour. Hence it applies only in the short run, when the *AD* curve plays an important role in the determination of national income.

In the long run, when the economy is on its *LRAS* curve and hence aggregate demand is not important for the determination of real national income (see Figure 32.5), the paradox of thrift does not apply. The more people and governments save, the larger is the supply of funds available for investment.

The more people invest, the greater is the growth of potential income. Increased potential income causes the *LRAS* curve to shift to the right.

These longer-term effects were discussed briefly earlier in this chapter and are taken up in detail in Chapter 33 in the discussion of economic growth. Here, we concentrate on the short-run demand effects of saving and spending.

The paradox of thrift is based on the short-run effects of changes in saving and investment on aggregate demand.

AUTOMATIC STABILIZERS

The government budget surplus increases as national income increases because tax revenues rise, and some transfer payments, especially unemployment insurance, fall. Thus, net taxes move in the same direction as national income. (Unless there are changes in policy, government purchases are generally unaffected by cyclical movements in the economy.) With pro-cyclical net tax revenues, disposable income moves in the same direction as national income but does not move by as much. The government keeps a share of the increased national income when national income rises. When national income falls, the fall in net taxes makes disposable income fall by less.

In Chapter 30, for example, we assumed that the net income tax rate was 10 per cent of national income. This implies that a £1 rise in autonomous spending would increase disposable income by only 90p, dampening the multiplier effect of the initial increase. Generally, the wedge that income taxes place between national income and disposable income reduces the marginal propensity to spend out of national income, thereby reducing the size of the multiplier. The lower the multiplier, the less will equilibrium national income tend to change for a given change in autonomous expenditure. The effect is to stabilize the economy, reducing the fluctuations in national income that are caused by changes in autonomous expenditure. Because no policies need to be changed in order to achieve this result, the properties of the government budget that cause the multiplier to be reduced are called **automatic fiscal stabilizers**.

Even when the government does not undertake to stabilize the economy via discretionary fiscal policy, the fact that net tax revenues rise with national income means that there are fiscal effects that cause the budget to act as an *automatic stabilizer* for the economy.

Of course, it is possible that a government might try to tie its spending in each period to the tax revenues it raises. This would change the impact of fiscal policy in a major way. Thus, if a government follows a balanced-budget policy in every period, its fiscal policy becomes **pro-cyclical**. It will restrict its spending during a recession because its tax revenue is low, and it will increase its spending during a recovery when its tax revenue is rising. In other words, it moves with the economy, raising and lowering its spending in step with everyone else, exactly counter to the theory of fiscal stabilization that we just discussed. Some politicians have proposed to change the law so that governments must balance their budget in every year. However, those who understand macroeconomics rarely call for anything more restrictive than a policy whereby governments aim to balance their budget on average over the course of the business cycle. A budget that was balanced on average would still permit the automatic stabilizer that is built into fiscal policy to work.

---

[5] The prediction is not actually a paradox. Rather, it is a straightforward implication of the theory of income determination. The expectations that lead to the 'paradox' are based on the fallacy of composition: the belief that what is true for the parts is necessarily true for the whole.

BOX 32.3

The paradox of thrift in action

The contemporary relevance of the paradox of thrift is clearly illustrated by the behaviour of UK personal savings in the 1988 boom and the 1990–2 recession. The accompanying figure shows the personal saving ratio (personal savings as a percentage of personal disposable income) and unemployment (as a percentage of the work-force).

In the mid-1980s, the personal saving ratio fell to around 5 per cent from high of around 13 per cent in 1984. The fall in saving was associated with a consumer boom, a positive shift in *AD*, and an accompanying fall in unemployment. This boom peaked in 1988, which coincided with the trough in the saving ratio. A key element in the decline in the saving ratio was a sharp increase in personal borrowing — gross saving (acquisition of financial and real assets) did not fall at all. Rather, it was the increase in expenditures funded by borrowing that caused the overall saving ratio to fall. Borrowing was encouraged by low interest rates and rising house prices, so that people rushed to purchase dwellings before prices rose even further.

In 1988 the government raised interest rates and reduced the tax incentives on mortgages. The saving ratio recovered sharply. This represented a downward shift of *AD*. However, in the 1990 Budget the government (in the person of the then Chancellor, John Major) introduced further incentives for saving, in the form of Tax Exempt Special Savings Accounts (TESSAs). As a result of higher saving and lower spending, the economy slid into recession and unemployment rose sharply. A fall in house prices lowered personal wealth, and this lowered consumer spending still further.

This recession continued right through to the end of 1992. Other factors contributed to the severity of the 1990–2 recession, including low world demand and a high exchange rate. However, there is no doubt at all that swings in saving behaviour contributed importantly to a major boom and to the subsequent severe recession, exactly as predicted by the paradox of thrift.

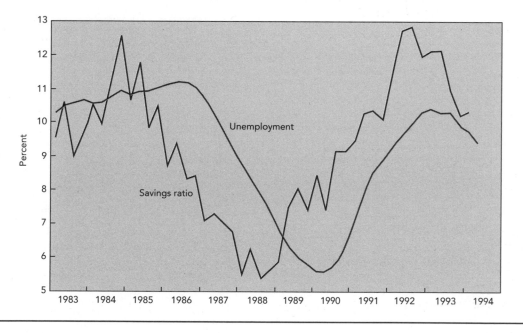

LIMITATIONS OF DISCRETIONARY FISCAL POLICY

According to the discussion of the previous few pages, returning the economy to high employment would simply be a matter of cutting taxes and raising government spending, in some combination. Why do many economists

believe that such policies would be 'as likely to harm as help'? Part of the answer is that the execution of discretionary fiscal policy is anything but simple.[6]

[6] Another part of the answer has to do with the long-term consequences of budget deficits. This subject is taken up in Chapter 42. Also, as we shall see in Chapter 39, international considerations may reduce (but not eliminate) fiscal policy's effectiveness as a stabilization tool.

Lags　To change fiscal policy, changes have to be made in taxes and government expenditure. The changes must be agreed upon by the Cabinet and passed by Parliament. Major changes are normally announced only once a year, in the November Budget Statement, although, 'mini-Budgets' are possible if crisis measures need to be taken at other times of year.

The political stakes in such changes are generally very large; taxes and spending are called 'bread and butter issues' precisely because they affect the economic well-being of almost everyone. Thus, even if economists agreed that the economy would be helped by, say, a tax cut, politicians may spend a good deal of time debating *whose* taxes should be cut and by *how much*. The delay between the initial recognition of a recession or inflation and the enactment of legislation to change fiscal policy is called a **decision lag**.

Once policy changes are agreed upon, there is still an **execution lag**, adding time between the enactment and the implementation of the change. Furthermore, once policies are in place, it will usually take still more time for their economic consequences to be felt. Because of these lags, it is quite possible that, by the time a given policy decision has any impact on the economy, circumstances will have changed in such a way that the policy is no longer appropriate. Figure 32.10 illustrates the problems that can arise in these circumstances.

To make matters even more frustrating, tax measures that are known to be temporary are generally less effective than measures that are expected to be permanent. If consumers know that a given tax cut will last for only a year, they may recognize that the effect on their long-run consumption possibilities is small and may adjust their short-run consumption relatively little. (See the Appendix to Chapter 29.)

The more closely household consumption expenditure is related to lifetime income rather than to current income, the smaller will be the effects on current consumption of tax changes that are known to be of short duration.

The role of discretionary fiscal policy　All of the above-mentioned difficulties suggest that attempts to use discretionary fiscal policy to fine-tune the economy are fraught with difficulties. **Fine-tuning** refers to the use of fiscal and monetary policy to offset virtually all fluctuations in private-sector spending and so hold national income at, or very near, its potential level at all times. However, neither economic nor political science has yet advanced far enough to allow policy-makers to undo the consequences of every aggregate demand shock. On the other hand, many economists would still argue that, when a recessionary gap is large enough and persists for long enough, gross-tuning may be appropriate. **Gross-tuning** refers to the occasional use of fiscal and monetary policy to remove large and persistent

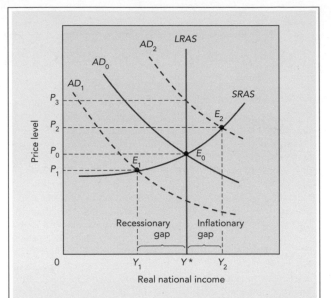

Figure 32.10　Effects of fiscal policies that are not reversed

Fiscal policies that are initially appropriate may become inappropriate when private expenditure shifts. The normal level of the aggregate demand function is assumed to be AD_0, leaving income normally at Y^* and the price level at P_0. Suppose a slump in private investment shifts aggregate demand to AD_1, lowering national income to Y_1 and causing a recessionary gap of Y^*-Y_1.

The government now introduces fiscal expansion to restore aggregate demand to AD_0 and national income to Y^*. Suppose that private investment then recovers, raising aggregate demand to AD_2. If fiscal policy can be quickly reversed, aggregate demand can be returned to AD_0 and income stabilized at Y^*. If the policy is not quickly reversed, equilibrium will be at E_2 and an inflationary gap Y^*-Y_2 will open up. This gap will cause wages to rise and thus will shift the *SRAS* curve leftward and eventually restore Y^* at price level P_3.

Now suppose that, starting from equilibrium E_0, a persistent investment boom takes AD_0 to AD_2. In order to stop the price level from rising in the face of the newly opened inflationary gap, the government introduces fiscal restraint, thereby shifting aggregate demand back to AD_0. Further assume, however, that the investment boom then comes to a halt, so that the aggregate demand curve shifts downward to AD_1. Unless the fiscal policy can be rapidly reversed, a recessionary gap will open up and equilibrium income will fall to Y_1.

GDP gaps. Advocates of gross-tuning hold that fiscal policy can and should be used to return the economy to full employment when a GDP is large and has persisted for a long time. Other economists believe that fiscal policy should not be used for economic stabilization under any circumstances. Rather, they would argue, tax and spending behaviour should be the outcome of public choices regarding the long-term size and financing of the public sector and should not be altered for short-term considerations. We return to these debates in Chapter 42.

Economic policy, economic stability, and economic growth

To get ahead of our story, the desirability of using fiscal policy to stabilize the economy depends a great deal on the speed with which the adjustment mechanism returns the economy to potential income. If the adjustment mechanism works quickly, there is no role for discretionary fiscal policy. If the adjustment mechanism works slowly, there may well be a role for policies that can be used to shift aggregate demand. Fiscal policy is one such policy. Monetary policy, which we take up in Part Nine, is another. Only when we have completed our study of the way in which money and monetary institutions fit into the overall macroeconomy can we fully outline the choices available to governments wishing to stabilize their economies.

Stabilization policy will generally have consequences for economic growth—for the movement of the *LRAS* curve over time. Given that an economy is at or near its potential GDP, then the more expansive is its fiscal policy, the lower will be national saving and national asset formation; thus, the lower will be economic growth. Of course, if the economy would otherwise stay in recession for a period of years, the gain in output in the short term could easily outweigh the longer-term consequences of a smaller stock of assets at full employment. (After all, and this was part of Keynes's message, the state of the world at full employment is not very interesting to members of a society who are a long way from it.)

Stability, growth, and the effect of economic policy on both are among the key subjects of this book. With the tools that we have developed thus far, we have been able to begin to see how they fit together. Once we add a better understanding of money and monetary policy, we will be able to complete the story of stabilization policy. However, before starting on monetary policy, we will look at the factors affecting the growth in potential income.

Summary

1 Potential income is treated as given and is represented by a vertical line at Y^*. The output gap is equal to the horizontal distance between Y^* and the actual level of income, as determined by the intersection of the *AD* and *SRAS* curves.

2 An inflationary gap means that Y is greater than Y^*, and hence demand in the labour market is relatively high. As a result, wages rise faster than productivity, causing unit costs to rise. The *SRAS* curve shifts leftward, and the price level rises.

3 A recessionary gap means that Y is less than Y^*, and hence demand in the labour market is relatively low. Although there is some resulting tendency for wages to fall relative to productivity, asymmetrical behaviour means that the strength of this force will be much weaker than that indicated in point 2 above. Unit costs will fall only slowly, so the output gap will persist for some time.

4 An expansionary demand shock creates the inflationary gap discussed in point 2. It causes wages to rise faster than productivity. Unit costs rise, shifting the *SRAS* curve to the left and resulting in a higher level of prices, with output eventually falling back to its potential level.

5 A contractionary demand shock works in the opposite direction by creating the recessionary gap discussed in point 3. Since factor prices tend to be sticky, the automatic adjustment process tends to be slow and a recessionary gap tends to persist for some time.

6 The long-run aggregate supply (*LRAS*) curve relates the price level and national income after all wages and other costs have been adjusted fully to long-run equilibrium. The *LRAS* curve is vertical at the level of potential income, Y^*.

7 Because the *LRAS* curve is vertical, output in the long run is determined by the position of the *LRAS* curve, and the only long-run role of the *AD* curve is to determine the price level. Economic growth determines the position of the *LRAS* curve.

8 GDP can increase (or decrease) for any of three reasons: a change in aggregate demand, a change in short-run aggregate supply, or a change in long-run aggregate supply which is called economic growth. The first two changes are typically associated with business cycles.

9 Demand shocks are an important source of business cycles. As the shock works its way through the economy and the adjustment mechanism comes into play, GDP will often exhibit a cyclical (up and down, or down and up) pattern.

10 In the long run, when the level of GDP is equal to Y^*, the higher is the level of national saving, the higher will be the level of national asset formation. Assets formed in the current period will yield increases in national income in the future.

11 In principle, fiscal policy can be used to stabilize the position of the *AD* curve at or near potential GDP. To remove a recessionary gap, governments can shift *AD* to the right by cutting taxes and increasing spending. To remove an inflationary gap, governments can pursue the opposite policies.

12 When the economy is in a recessionary gap, increases in desired savings on the part of firms, persons, and governments are likely to lead to further reductions in GDP, and may lead to reductions in actual saving. This phenomenon is often called 'the paradox of thrift'. In the long run, with the economy at Y^*, the paradox does not obtain, and increased thrift will lead to increased asset accumulation and economic growth.

13 Because government tax and transfer programmes tend to reduce the size of the multiplier, they act as automatic stabilizers. When national income changes, in either direction, disposable income changes by less because of taxes and transfers.

14 Discretionary fiscal policy is subject to decision lags and execution lags that limit its ability to take effect quickly. Some economists argue that these limitations are so severe that fiscal policy should never be used for stabilization because it will do more harm than good. Others argue that the automatic adjustment mechanism works so slowly that fiscal policy can play an important role in stabilizing the economy.

15 Fiscal policy has very different effects in the short and long run. The same fiscal policies (reduced taxes and increased spending) that stimulate the economy in the short run will, if pursued at full employment, reduce national saving, asset formation, and economic growth in the long run.

Topics for review

- The output gap and the labour market
- Inflationary gap
- Recessionary gap
- Asymmetry of wage adjustment
- Changes in aggregate demand and induced wage changes
- Wages, productivity, and unit costs
- Adjustment mechanism
- Long-run aggregate supply (*LRAS*) curve
- Economic stabilization
- Decision lags and execution lags
- Sources of long-run growth
- Automatic stabilizers

∾ CHAPTER 33

Economic growth

So far in this part we have taken the position of the *LRAS* curve as fixed while studying how actual income varied around potential income as a result of fluctuations in the *AD* and the *SRAS* curves. This is the theory of how income fluctuates in the short term around a given level of potential income. Now we complete our study of income changes by going one important step further: we consider long-term changes in potential national income, changes that typically shift the *LRAS* curve to the right, gradually but continually, over the years. This is the theory of *long-term* economic growth. The cumulative effects of these changes dominate the effects of fluctuations over any time span longer than a decade.

In this chapter, we first deal with the distinction between growth and other goals of economic policy. Then we discuss the costs and benefits of economic growth. This leads to a study of how the saving and investment flows that were dealt with in earlier chapters affect growth. After that, we outline some of the theories that economists have developed in an effort to understand the process of growth—first at a highly aggregated (or macro) level, then at a more disaggregated (or micro) level. Then we briefly consider the relation between a country's economic growth and its international competitiveness. We end with a brief discussion of possible limits to growth.

The nature of economic growth

ECONOMIC growth is the single most powerful engine for generating long-term increases in living standards. What happens to our material living standards over time depends primarily on the growth in national income (as measured, for example, by the GDP) in relation to the growth in population.

We saw in Chapter 1 that, throughout the first seven decades of the twentieth century, per capita GDP rose steadily while its distribution became somewhat less unequal. As a result, most citizens of most countries in the European Union became materially better off decade by decade, and children typically were substantially better off than their parents were at the same age. In the 1970s, however, the engine of growth faltered. Growth rates fell, and for various reasons the distribution of income stopped becoming less unequal. As a result, the real incomes of many European families remained relatively constant. Although we still live in one of the richest societies in all of human history, many have begun to speak of the end of the dream that each generation could expect to be much better off than its predecessors.

These changes in attitudes and perceptions brought about in the minds of ordinary, middle-class citizens by the mere slowdown of rapid growth shows how important a part that steady growth had played in people's minds and hearts over the decades of the nineteenth and twentieth centuries.

Shifts in aggregate demand and aggregate supply

In earlier chapters we outlined the effects of shifts in aggregate demand and aggregate supply. Economic growth concerns sustained shifts in aggregate supply; therefore, many of the points made in earlier chapters in the context of one-time shifts bear repeating in this new context.

Figure 33.1, which is similar to Figure 32.6 on p. 617, illustrates some important causes of rising national income.[1] If there is a recessionary gap, policies that increase aggregate demand will yield a once-for-all increase in national income. Once potential income is achieved, however, further increases in aggregate demand yield only transitory increases in real income but lasting increases in the price level.

Policies that reduce structural unemployment can also increase the employed labour force and thus can increase potential income.[2] The resulting increase in income might not be very large, but social benefits would result from the reduction in unemployment, especially in the long-term unemployment that occurs when people are trapped in declining areas, industries, or occupations. The increase, however, is once-for-all, as the total number of unemployed falls to a new, lower level. Similar results come from measures that increase economic efficiency. A once-for-all increase in potential output occurs as a given employed labour force works more efficiently.

Over the long run, the main cause of rising national income is *economic growth*—the increase in potential income arising from changes in factor supplies (labour and capital) and in the productivity of factors (output per unit of factor input). The removal of a serious recessionary gap or the elimination of all structural unemployment might

---

[1] The figures are not identical because they emphasize somewhat different points.

[2] See Chapter 27 p. 506 for a definition of structural unemployment.

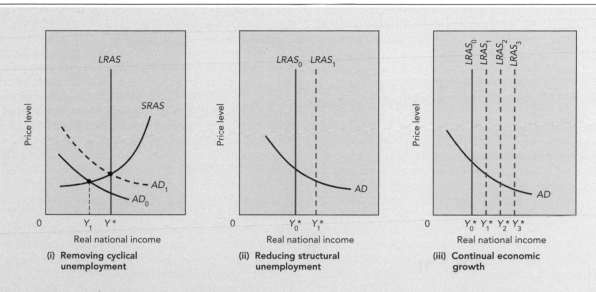

Figure 33.1 Ways of increasing national income

A once-for-all increase in national income can be obtained by raising aggregate demand to remove a recessionary gap or by shifting the *LRAS* curve, say, by cutting structural unemployment. Continual increases in national income are possible through continued economic growth, which shifts the *LRAS* curve. In part (i), with the aggregate demand curve at AD_0, there is a recessionary gap of $Y_1 Y^*$. An increase in aggregate demand from AD_0 to AD_1 achieves a once-for-all increase in national income from Y_1 to Y^*.

In part (ii) potential output rises from Y_0^* to Y_1^* owing to measures that reduce structural unemployment. The *LRAS* curve shifts from $LRAS_0$ to $LRAS_1$ because people who were formerly unemployed because of having the wrong skills or being in the wrong place are now better suited for employment.

In part (iii) increases in factor supplies and productivity lead to increases in potential income. This *continually* shifts the long-run aggregate supply curve outward. In successive periods it moves from $LRAS_0$ to $LRAS_3$, taking potential income from Y_0^* to Y_1^* to Y_2^*, and so on, as long as growth continues.

cause a once-for-all increase in national income by, at the very most, 5–10 per cent. However, a growth rate of 3 per cent per year raises potential income by 10 per cent in three years, *doubles* it in about 24 years, and quadruples it in 48 years. Even a 1 per cent growth rate doubles potential income over a normal lifetime of about 70 years.

Growth is a much more powerful method of raising living standards than is the removal of recessionary gaps, structural unemployment, or inefficiencies, *because growth can go on indefinitely.*

Table 33.1 illustrates the cumulative effect of what seem to be very small differences in growth rates. Notice that, if one country grows faster than another, the gap in their respective living standards will widen progressively. If, for example, countries A and B start from the same level of income, and if country A grows at 3 per cent per year while country B grows at 2 per cent per year, A's per capita

Table 33.1 The cumulative effect of growth

Year	Rate of growth per year				
	1%	2%	3%	5%	7%
0	100	100	100	100	100
10	110	122	135	165	201
30	135	182	246	448	817
50	165	272	448	1,218	3,312
70	201	406	817	3,312	13,429
100	272	739	2,009	14,841	109,660

Small differences in growth rates make enormous differences in levels of potential national income over a few decades. Let potential national income be 100 in year 0. At a rate of growth of 3 per cent per year, it will be 135 in 10 years, 448 after 50 years, and over 2,000 in 100 years. The compounding of sustained rates of growth is a powerful force!

income will be twice B's in 72 years. You may not think that it matters much whether the economy grows at 2 per cent or 3 per cent per year, but your children and grandchildren will!

Economic growth, efficiency, and redistribution

Observing that economic growth is the most important force for raising living standards over the long term in no way implies that policies designed to increase economic efficiency or redistribute income are unimportant.

Reducing inefficiency   If, at any moment in time, national income could be increased by removing certain inefficiencies, such gains would be valuable. After all, any increase in national income is welcome in a world where many wants go unsatisfied. Furthermore, inefficiencies may themselves serve to reduce the growth rate. For example, government supports for inefficient firms, which may be criticized on grounds of productive and allocative efficiency, may also lower growth rates by reducing the incentive to innovate.

Redistribution   Economic growth has made the poor vastly better off than they would have been if they had lived 100 years ago. Yet that is little consolation when they see that they cannot afford many things that are currently available to citizens with higher incomes. After all, people compare themselves with others in their own society, not with their counterparts at other times or in other places. Because many people care about *relative* differences among individuals, governments continue to have policies to redistribute income and to make such basic services as education and hospital care available to everyone, at least to some minimum acceptable degree.

Interrelations among the goals   Economists once assumed that the goals of redistributing income, increasing efficiency, and ensuring growth could be treated independently of each other. It is now understood, as we first observed in Chapter 24, that distribution, efficiency, and growth are interrelated. For example, policies that create extreme inefficiencies or a distribution of income unrelated to the market value of work can adversely affect the growth rate. It follows that policies designed to reduce inefficiencies or redistribute income need to be examined carefully for any effects that they may have on growth, while policies designed to affect growth need to be examined for their effects on economic efficiency and income distribution. A policy that reduces growth *may* be a bad bargain, even if it increases the immediate efficiency of the economy or creates a more equitable distribution of income.

Consider a hypothetical redistributive policy that raises the share of GDP going to poorer people by 5 per cent but lowers the rate of economic growth from 2 to 1 per cent. At the end of 10 years, those who gained from the policy would be no better off than if they had not received the redistribution of income while the growth rate had remained at 2 per cent. (And, of course, everyone who did not gain from the redistribution would be worse off from the outset.) After 20 years, those who had gained from the redistribution would have 5 per cent more of a national income that was 12 per cent smaller than it would have been if the growth rate had remained at 2 per cent.

Of course, not all redistribution policies have unfavourable effects on the growth rate. Some may have no effect, and others—by raising the health and educational standards of ordinary workers—may raise the growth rate.

Benefits and costs of growth

WE start by looking at the benefits of growth, and we then consider the costs. Boxes 33.1 and 33.2 outline some of the popular arguments on both sides of the growth debate. Although extreme in some cases, these are the sorts of arguments that are typically heard on both sides.

BENEFITS OF GROWTH

Growth and living standards   We have already observed that in the long term economic growth is the primary engine for raising general living standards. For those who share in it, growth is a powerful weapon against poverty. A family that is earning £25,000 today can expect an income of about £30,500 within 10 years (in constant pounds) if it shares in a 2 per cent growth rate, and £37,000 if that rate is 4 per cent.

The transformation of the lifestyle of ordinary workers in advanced industrial nations between 1870 and 1970 provides a notable example of the improvement in living standards that growth makes possible. Much of the concern today over economic problems facing UK families stems from the decline of growth that occurred in the 1970s, and in the recessions of the early 1980s and early 1990s. Partly because growth slowed in those periods and partly because the distribution of income has changed unfavourably for them, the real incomes of many working families have grown little over the last two decades.

Growth and income redistribution Not everyone benefits equally from growth. Many of the poorest are not even in the labour force and thus are unlikely to share in the higher wages that, along with profits, are the primary means by which the gains from growth are distributed. For this reason, even in a growing economy, redistribution policies will be needed if poverty is to be averted.

A rapid growth rate makes the alleviation of poverty easier politically. If existing income is to be redistributed, someone's standard of living will actually have to be lowered. However, when there is economic growth, and when the increment in income is redistributed (through government intervention), it is possible to reduce income inequalities without actually having to *lower* anyone's income. It is much easier for a rapidly growing economy to be generous towards its less fortunate citizens—or neighbours—than it is for a static economy.

Growth and lifestyle A family often finds that a big increase in its income can lead to a major change in the pattern of its consumption—that extra money buys important amenities of life. In the same way, members of society as a whole may change their consumption patterns as their average income rises. Not only do markets in a country that is growing rapidly make it profitable to produce more cars, but also the government is led to construct more highways and to provide more recreational areas for its newly affluent and mobile citizens. At yet a later stage, a concern about litter, pollution, and ugliness may become important, and their correction may then begin to account for a significant fraction of GDP. Such 'amenities' usually become matters of social concern only when growth has ensured the provision of the basic requirements for food, clothing, and housing of a substantial majority of the population.

COSTS OF GROWTH

Other things being equal, most people would probably regard a fast rate of growth as preferable to a slow one; but other things are seldom equal.

The opportunity cost of growth In a world of scarcity, almost nothing is free. Growth requires heavy investment of resources in capital goods, as well as in activities such as education. Often these investments yield no immediate

return in terms of goods and services for consumption; thus, they imply that sacrifices have been made by the current generation of consumers.

Growth, which promises more goods tomorrow, is achieved by consuming fewer goods today. For the economy as a whole, this sacrifice of current consumption is the primary cost of growth.

An example will suggest the magnitude of this cost. Suppose that a hypothetical economy has full employment and is experiencing growth at the rate of 2 per cent per year. Its citizens consume 85 per cent of the GDP and invest 15 per cent. They know that, if they immediately decrease their consumption to 77 per cent of GDP, they will produce more capital and thus will shift at once to a 3 per cent growth rate. The new rate can be maintained as long as they keep saving and investing 23 per cent of the national income. Should they do it?

Table 33.2 illustrates the choice in terms of time paths of consumption. Using the assumed figures, it takes 10 years for the actual amount of consumption to catch up to what

Table 33.2 The opportunity cost of growth

Year	(1) Level of consumption at 2% growth rate	(2) Level of consumption at 3% growth rate	(3) Cumulative gain (loss) in consumption
0	85.0	77.0	(8.0)
1	86.7	79.3	(15.4)
2	88.5	81.8	(22.1)
3	90.3	84.2	(28.2)
4	92.1	86.8	(33.5)
5	93.9	89.5	(37.9)
6	95.8	92.9	(40.8)
7	97.8	95.0	(43.6)
8	99.7	97.9	(45.4)
9	101.8	100.9	(46.3)
10	103.8	103.9	(46.2)
15	114.7	120.8	(28.6)
20	126.8	140.3	19.6
30	154.9	189.4	251.0
40	189.2	255.6	745.9

Transferring resources from consumption to investment goods lowers current income but raises future income. The example assumes that income in year zero is 100 and that consumption of 85 per cent of national income is possible with a 2 per cent growth rate. It is further assumed that, to achieve a 3 per cent growth rate, consumption must fall to 77 per cent of income. A shift from column (1) to column (2) decreases consumption for 10 years but increases it thereafter. The cumulative effect on consumption is shown in column (3); the gains eventually become very large.

BOX 33.1

An election manifesto for the Pro-Growth Party

Dear Voter:

You live in the world's first civilization that is devoted principally to satisfying *your* needs rather than those of a privileged minority. Past civilizations have always been based on leisure and high consumption for a tiny upper class, a reasonable living standard for a small middle class, and hard work with little more than subsistence consumption for the great mass of people.

The continuing Industrial Revolution is based on mass-produced goods for you, the ordinary citizen. You were born in a period of sustained economic growth that has dramatically raised consumption standards of ordinary citizens. Reflect on a few examples: travel, live and recorded music, art, good food, inexpensive books, universal literacy, and a genuine chance to be educated. Most important, there is leisure to provide time and energy to enjoy these and thousands of other products of the modern industrial economy.

Would any ordinary family seriously prefer to go back to the world of 150 or 500 years ago in its same relative social and economic position? Surely the answer is no. However, for those with incomes in the top 1 or 2 per cent of the income distribution, economic growth has destroyed much of their privileged consumption position. They must now vie with the masses when they visit the world's beauty spots, and be annoyed, while lounging on the terrace of a palatial mansion, by the sound of charter flights carrying ordinary people to inexpensive holidays in far places. Many of the rich complain bitterly about the loss of exclusive rights to luxury consumption, and it is not surprising that they find their intellectual apologists. Whether they know it or not, the anti-growth economists are not the social revolutionaries that they think they are. They say that growth has produced pollution and the wasteful consumption of all kinds of frivolous products that add nothing to human happiness. However, the democratic solution to pollution is not to go back to where so few people consumed luxuries that pollution was trivial, but rather to learn to control the pollution that mass consumption tends to create.

It is only through further growth that the average citizen can enjoy consumption standards (of travel, culture, medical and health care, etc.) now available only to people in the top 25 per cent of the income distribution—a group that includes the intellectuals who earn large royalties from the books that they write in which they denounce growth. If you think that extra income confers little real benefit, just ask those in the top 25 per cent to trade incomes with average citizens.

Ordinary citizens, do not be deceived by disguised élitist doctrines. Remember that the very rich and the élite have much to gain by stopping growth, and even more by rolling it back, but you have everything to gain by letting it go forward.

VOTE FOR GROWTH. VOTE FOR US.

---

it would have been had no reallocation been made. In the intervening 10 years, a good deal of consumption is lost, and the cumulative losses in consumption must be made up before society can really be said to have broken even. It takes an additional 9 years before total consumption over the whole period is as large is it would have been if the economy had remained on the 2 per cent path.[3]

Over a longer period, however, the payoff from the growth policy becomes enormous. Forty years on, the national income in the more rapidly growing economy is 35 per cent higher than in the slower growing economy. The total difference in consumption over those 40 years has become three times the annual amount of consumption in the faster-growing society at year 40.

Social and personal costs of growth   A growing economy is a changing economy. Innovation renders some machines obsolete and also leaves some people partly obsolete. No matter how well trained workers are at age 25, in another 25 years many will find that their skills are at least partly obsolete. A rapid growth rate requires rapid adjustments, which can cause much upset and misery to the people who are affected by it.

It is often argued that costs of this kind are a small price to pay for the great benefits that growth can bring. Even if this is true in the aggregate, these personal costs are very unevenly borne. Indeed, many of those for whom growth is most costly (in terms of lost jobs) share least in the fruits that growth brings.

---

[3] The time taken to break even is a function of the *difference* in growth rates, not their level. Thus, had 4 and 5 per cent or 5 and 6 per cent been used in the example, it still would have taken the same number of years. To see this quickly, recognize that we are interested in the ratio of two growth paths: $e^{r_1 t}/e^{r_2 t} = e^{(r_1 - r_2)t}$.

BOX 33.2

An election manifesto for the Anti-Growth Party

Dear Voter:

You live in a world that is being despoiled by a mindless search for ever-higher levels of material consumption at the cost of all other values. Once upon a time, men and women knew how to enjoy creative work and to derive satisfaction from simple activities. Today, the ordinary worker is a mindless cog in an assembly line that turns out more and more goods and services that the advertisers must work overtime to persuade the workers to consume.

Statisticians count the increasing flow of material output as a triumph of modern civilization. You arise from your electric-blanketed bed, clean your teeth with an electric toothbrush, and pop into your electric toaster a slice or two of bread baked from super-refined and chemically refortified flour; you climb into your car to sit in vast traffic jams on exhaust-polluted roads.

Television commercials tell you that by consuming more you are happier, but happiness lies not in increasing consumption, but in increasing the ratio of *satisfaction of wants* to *total wants*. Since, the more you consume, the more the advertisers persuade you that you *want* to consume, you are almost certainly less happy than the average citizen in a small town in 1950, whom we can visualize sitting on the front step, chatting with neighbours, and watching the local children skipping with pieces of old clothesline.

Today the landscape is dotted with endless factories that produce the plastic trivia of the modern industrial society. They drown you in a cloud of noise, air, and water pollution. The countryside is despoiled by open-cast mines, petroleum refineries, acid rain, and dangerous nuclear power stations, producing energy that is devoured insatiably by modern factories and motor vehicles. Worse, our precious heritage of natural resources is being rapidly depleted.

Now is the time to stop this madness. We must stabilize production, reduce pollution, conserve our natural resources, and seek justice through a more equitable distribution of existing total income.

A long time ago, Malthus taught us that, if we do not limit population voluntarily, nature will do it for us in a cruel and savage manner. Today the same is true of output: if we do not halt its growth voluntarily, the halt will be imposed upon us by a disastrous increase in pollution and a rapid exhaustion of natural resources.

Citizens, awake! Shake off the worship of growth, learn to enjoy the bounty that is yours already, and reject the endless, self-defeating search for increased happiness through ever-increasing consumption.

VOTE TO STOP GROWTH. VOTE FOR US.

Theories of economic growth

IN this section, we study some of the new theories that seek to explain economic growth. This is an exciting area. Ideas are changing rapidly as research of both a theoretical and an empirical nature expands our knowledge of the growth process. Our first step is to relate savings and investment, which we studied in detail in previous chapters, to the present subject of economic growth.

Saving, investment, and growth

Both saving and investment affect the level and rate of growth of real national income. To understand their influence, it is critical to distinguish between their short-run and long-run effects.

SHORT-RUN AND LONG-RUN EFFECTS OF INVESTMENT

The theory of national income determination that we studied in previous chapters is a short-run theory. It takes potential income as constant and concentrates on the effects of shifts in aggregate demand brought about by changes in various types of expenditure, including investment. These shifts cause actual national income to fluctuate around a given potential income. This short-term viewpoint is the focus of Figure 33.1(i).

In the long run, by adding to the nation's capital stock, investment raises potential income. This effect is shown by the continuing shift of the *LRAS* curve in Figure 33.1(iii).

The theory of economic growth is a long-run theory. It concentrates on the effects of investment in raising potential national income and ignores short-run fluctuations of actual national income around potential income.

The contrast between the short- and long-run aspects of investment is worth emphasizing. In the short run, any activity that puts income into people's hands will raise aggregate demand. Thus, the short-run effect on national income is the same whether a firm 'invests' in digging holes and refilling them or in building a new factory. The long-run growth of potential income, however, is affected only by the part of investment that adds to a nation's productive capacity—that is, by the factory, but not by the refilled hole.

Similar observations hold for public-sector expenditure, G. Any expenditure will add to aggregate demand and raise national income if there are unemployed resources, but only some expenditure increases potential income. Although public investment expenditure on such things as roads and health may increase potential national income, expenditure that shores up a declining industry in order to create employment may have an adverse effect on the growth of potential income. The latter expenditure may prevent the reallocation of resources in response to shifts both in the pattern of world demand and in the country's comparative advantage. Thus, in the long run, the country's capacity to produce commodities that are demanded on world markets may be diminished.

SHORT-RUN AND LONG-RUN EFFECTS OF SAVING

The short-run effect of an increase in saving is to reduce aggregate demand. If, for example, households or governments elect to save more, then they spend less. The resulting downward shift in the aggregate expenditure function lowers aggregate demand and thus lowers equilibrium national income.

In the longer term, however, higher national saving is necessary for higher investment. Firms usually reinvest their own savings, and the savings of households pass to firms, either directly through the purchase of stocks and bonds or indirectly through financial intermediaries. In the long run, the higher the level of national saving, the higher the level of investment; and, owing to the accumulation of more and better capital equipment, the higher the level of investment, the higher the level of real income. A high-saving economy accumulates assets faster, and thus grows faster, than does a low-saving economy.

In the long run, there is no paradox of thrift; societies with high rates of national saving have high investment rates and, other things being equal, high growth rates of real income.

Notice that the discussion refers to *national* saving: what the government saves or dissaves plus what the private sector saves. The amount of national saving available for private-sector investment is private-sector saving plus or minus the government's budget surplus or deficit: $S + (T - G)$, where, as we saw in Chapter 30, T is tax revenues net of transfer payments. This expression tells us that, if the government spends more than it raises in taxes, then it diminishes the pool of savings available for private investment. In contrast, if the government spends less than it raises in taxes, then it adds to the pool.[4]

DETERMINANTS OF GROWTH

Research suggests that four of the most important determinants of growth of total output are as follows:

1. *growth in the labour force,* such as occurs when the population grows or participation rates rise;[5]

2. *investment in human capital,* such as formal education and on-the-job experience;

3. *investment in physical capital,* such as factories, machines, transportation, and communications facilities;

4. *technological change,* brought about by innovation that introduces new products, new ways of producing existing products, and new forms of business organization.

One line of investigation studies how these four forces operate in what is called the **aggregate production function.** This is an expression for the relation between the total amounts of labour (L) and capital (K) employed and the nation's total output, its GDP:

$$GDP = f(L,K).$$

It is aggregate because it relates the economy's total output, its GDP, to the total amount of the two main factors that are used to produce that output.[6] (A micro-production function, such as is discussed in Chapters 10 and 11, relates the output of one firm or one industry to the factors of production employed by that firm or industry.) The function, indicated by the letter 'f', shows the relation between the inputs of L and K and the output of GDP. The production function tells us how much GDP will be produced for given amounts of labour and capital employed. For example, the function may tell us that, when 200 million units of labour

---

[4] It does this by paying off some of its debt and leaving these funds in the hands of private wealth-holders.

[5] Recall that the participation rate is the proportion of the total population that is in the labour force.

[6] Basic growth theory emphasizes the production of manufactured goods and services, where, in contrast to agriculture, land is rarely a limiting factor. All the relatively small amounts of land that are needed can be obtained, and hence nothing significant is lost by ignoring land in the analysis of an industrialized economy—although this could not be done for an agricultural economy.

and 300 million units of capital are used, the GDP will be 2,450 million.[7]

In growth theory, we ignore short-term fluctuations of income around its full-employment value. Thus, the GDP in the above production function can be interpreted as potential income.

We may now use this aggregate production function to discuss some theories of economic growth.

Neoclassical growth theory

One branch of neoclassical theory deals with growth when the stock of technological knowledge remains unchanged. There are no innovations—no new ways of making things, and no new products. As a result, the relation between inputs and output, as shown by the production function, does not change. The key aspects of what is called the neo-classical model are that the aggregate production function displays *decreasing returns* when either factor is increased on its own, and *constant returns* when both factors are increased together and in the same proportion.

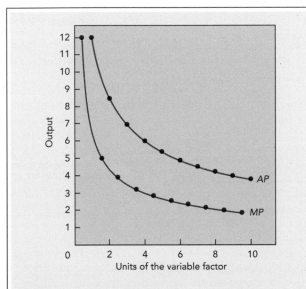

Figure 33.2 The average and marginal products of a variable factor

The average and marginal products of any variable factor decline as successive units of that factor are added to a fixed amount of another factor. This figure shows the marginal and average products of variable factor declining as more and more units of that factor are used. The marginal products are plotted between the units of the variable factor since they apply to a change from one amount to the next.

DECREASING RETURNS TO A SINGLE FACTOR

To start with, suppose that the population of the country grows while the stock of capital remains constant. More and more people go to work using the same fixed quantity of capital. The amount that each new unit of input adds to total output is called its *marginal product*. The operation of the famous **law of diminishing returns** tells us that the successive employment of equal additional amounts (or units) of labour will eventually add less to total output than the immediately previous unit of labour. In other words, sooner or later, each additional unit of labour will produce a diminishing marginal product. This famous relation is referred to as *diminishing returns to a single factor*. We first met it in Chapter 11, and it is illustrated in Figure 33.2.

The law of diminishing returns applies to any factor that is varied while the other factors are held constant. Thus, successive amounts of capital added to *a fixed supply of labour* will also eventually add less and less to GDP.

According to the law of diminishing returns, the increment to total production will eventually fall steadily whenever equal increases of a variable factor of production are combined with another factor of production whose quantity is fixed.[8]

CONSTANT RETURNS TO SCALE

The other main property of the neoclassical aggregate production function is **constant returns to scale**. This means that, if the amounts of both labour and capital are both changed in equal proportion, the total output will also change in that proportion. For example, 10 per cent increases in the amounts of both labour and capital used will lead to a 10 per cent increase in GDP.

SOURCES OF GROWTH IN THE NEOCLASSICAL MODEL

Now consider each of the sources of growth listed above. To begin with, we let each source operate with the others held constant.

Labour force growth In the long term, we can associate labour force growth with population growth (although in

---

[7] A simple example of a production function is $GDP = z(LK)^{1/2}$. This equation says that, to find the amount of GDP produced, multiply the amount of labour by the amount of capital, take the square root, and multiply the result by the constant, z. This production function has positive but diminishing returns to either factor. This can be shown using calculus by evaluating the first and second partial derivatives and showing the first derivatives to be positive and the second derivatives to be negative.

[8] In some production functions, marginal product may rise at first and begin to decline only after a certain critical amount of the variable factor is used. In the neoclassical, constant-returns production function, however, marginal product declines from the outset, as shown in Figure 33.2.

the short term, the labour force can grow if participation rates rise even though the population remains constant). As more labour is used, there will be more output and, consequently, a growth in total GDP. The law of diminishing returns tells us that, sooner or later, each further unit of labour to be employed will cause smaller and smaller additions to GDP. Eventually, not only will the marginal product of labour be falling, but the average product will fall as well. Beyond that point, although economic growth continues in the sense that total output is growing, living standards are falling in the sense that average GDP per head of population is falling. If we are interested in the growth in living standards, we are concerned with increasing GDP *per person*. Whenever diminishing average returns applies, increases in population on their own are accompanied by falling living standards.[9]

Human capital   Capital often means physical capital, i.e. the plants and equipment that embody current technological knowledge. But there is another kind of capital that is also of great importance to the growth process. This is *human* capital, i.e. the knowledge and skills embodied in people.

Human capital has several aspects. One involves improvements in the health and longevity of the population. Of course, these are desired as ends in themselves, but they also have consequences for both the size and the productivity of the labour force. There is no doubt that improvements in the health of workers have increased productivity per worker-hour by cutting down on illness, accidents, and absenteeism.

A second aspect of the quality of human capital concerns technical training—from learning to operate a machine to learning how to be a scientist. This training depends on the current state of knowledge, and advances in knowledge allow us not only to build more productive physical capital, but also to create more effective human capital. Training is clearly required if a person is to operate, repair, manage, or invent complex machines. More subtly, there may be general social advantages to an educated population. Productivity improves with literacy. The longer a person has been educated, the more adaptable, and thus the more productive in the long run, that person is in the face of new and changing challenges.

A third aspect of human capital is its contribution to growth and innovation. Not only can current human capital embody in people the best current technological knowledge, but, by training potential innovators, it leads to advances in our knowledge and hence contributes to growth.

Physical capital   Increases in the amount of physical capital on their own affect GDP in a manner similar to population growth alone. Eventually, each successive unit of physical capital will add less to total output than each previous unit of physical capital.

There is, however, a major contrast with the case of labour growth, because it is output per person that determines living standards, not output per unit of capital. Thus, as physical capital increases, living standards increase because output is rising while the population is constant. Indeed, per capita output can be increased by adding more physical capital as long as its marginal product exceeds zero. However, since the increases in output are subject to diminishing returns, successive additions to the economy's capital stock bring smaller and smaller increases in per capita output.

In the neoclassical model, the operation of diminishing returns means that physical capital accumulation on its own brings smaller and smaller increases in per capita GDP.

Balanced growth   Now consider what happens if labour and physical capital grow at the same rate. In this case, the neoclassical assumption of constant returns to scale means that GDP grows in proportion to the increases in inputs. As a result, per capita output (GDP/L) remains constant. Thus, growth in labour and capital leads to growth in total GDP but leaves per capita GDP unchanged.

This 'balanced growth path' is not, however, the kind of growth that concerns those interested in living standards. It is just more of the same: larger and larger economies, with more capital and more labour, doing exactly what the existing capital and the existing labour were already doing. There is nothing new.

Growth and living standards   In this constant-technology neoclassical model, the only way for growth to add to living standards is for the per capita (physical) capital stock to increase. The law of diminishing returns dictates, however, that the rise in living standards brought about by successive equal increases in capital will inexorably diminish. Raising living standards becomes more and more difficult as capital accumulation continues.

THE SOLOW RESIDUAL

In 1957 Robert Solow, who subsequently won the Nobel Prize in economics for his path-breaking work in growth and other fields of economics, decided to see what the data could tell him about the type of growth model we have just been discussing.

He took US data from 1909 to 1949, using measures of the total labour force, the total capital stock, and GDP, and

---

[9] In the neoclassical model, diminishing returns set in from the outset, so that there is no range over which population increases cause rising marginal or average product of labour. The issue of when diminishing returns set in need not concern us here, since all that matters for the text discussion is that increases in any one factor, other things held constant, must encounter diminishing returns sooner or later.

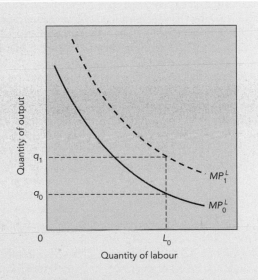 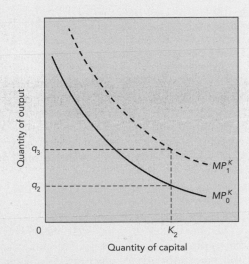

Figure 33.3 Shifts in the marginal products of labour and capital

Technological change shifts the marginal product curves such that each unit of the factor adds more to the total product than previously. The original marginal product curves are MP^L and MP^K. Technological change then alters the production function to allow any given amount of labour and capital to produce more. The marginal product of labour for a given amount of capital shifts to MP_0^L. The marginal product of each unit of labour therefore rises. For example, whereas the unit L_0 previously had a marginal product of q_0, its marginal product is now q_1. Similarly, the marginal product curve of capital for a given amount of labour shifts from MP_0^K to MP_1^K. Now each quantity of capital has a higher marginal product than it had previously. For example, the unit of K_2, which formerly had a marginal product of q_2, now has a marginal product of q_3.

applied it to the neoclassical production function given earlier in this section.[10] He made two important discoveries.

First, only about half of the growth in *total GDP* could be accounted for by growth in the inputs of labour and capital. Second, less than 20 per cent of the growth in *GDP per person employed* could be accounted for by the growth in the capital stock. The growth in GDP that could not be accounted for by increased use of capital and labour came to be called the *Solow residual*. It was assumed to be caused by technical change coming from innovation (although other influences on labour and capital not incorporated in Solow's measurements also turned out to have significant effects).

In the neoclassical model, technological change can be regarded as shifting the production function so that the same amount of labour and capital produces more GDP. This result is depicted in Figure 33.3 by rightward shifts in the *MP* curves of labour and capital: the same amount of input produces more output.[11]

MEASURED TECHNOLOGICAL CHANGE

New knowledge and inventions can contribute markedly to the growth of potential national income, even without cap-

ital accumulation. To illustrate this point, assume that the proportion of a society's resources that is devoted to the production of capital goods is just sufficient to replace capital as it wears out. Thus, if the old capital is merely replaced in the same form, the capital stock will be constant, and there will be no increase in the capacity to produce. However, if there is a growth in technology, so that as old equipment wears out it is replaced by different, more productive, equipment, national income will be growing.

Increases in productive capacity that are created by installing new and better capital goods are called **embodied technical change.** The historical importance of embodied technical change is clear: the assembly line and automation transformed most manufacturing industries, the airplane revolutionized transportation, and electronic devices now

---

[10] This was done by using standard statistical techniques to fit the production function to the data.

[11] In the neoclassical production function, which allows for growth, we have $GDP = z(L^\alpha K^{1-\alpha})$. The parameter z is a constant that relates given inputs of L and K to a specific GDP. Increases in factor productivity cause z to rise, so the given amounts of L and K are associated with higher GDP. Exogenous technical progress at a constant rate can be shown as $GDP_t = z^t(L_t^\alpha K_t^{1-\alpha})$, where z grows at a constant rate as time passes.

dominate the information technology industries. These innovations, plus lesser known but no less profound ones—for example, improvements in the strength of metals, the productivity of seeds, and the techniques for recovering basic raw materials from the ground—create new investment opportunities.

Less obvious but none the less important changes occur through **disembodied technical change**, that is, changes in the organization of production that are not embodied in particular capital goods. Examples are improved techniques of management, design, marketing, organization of business activity, and feedback from user experience to product improvement.

Most innovations involve both embodied and disembodied changes. They cause continual changes in the techniques of production and in the nature of what is produced. Looking back over the past century, firms produce very few products today in the same way that they did in the past, and much of what is produced and consumed is in the form of new or vastly improved products. Major innovations of the twentieth century include the development of such key products as the telephone, television, the mass-produced car, the airplane, plastics, coaxial cable, xerography, the electron microscope, the computer, the transistor, and the silicon chip. It is hard for us to imagine life without them.

The modern understanding that technological innovation is at the heart of the growth process has led to two important developments in many economists' views on growth. The first is that technological change is largely endogenous to the economic system. The second is that investment that increases the capital stock may encounter increasing rather than diminishing returns. These insights have led to new growth theories that go far beyond the neoclassical growth model.

TECHNOLOGICAL CHANGE IN THE MODEL

The neoclassical growth model can accommodate technological change along balanced growth paths if the changes are what is called *Harrod-neutral*. This means that the improvements increase the efficiency of labour, making labour grow at a constant exponential rate in efficiency units. This is called labour-augmenting technical change. The result is that there is no increase in output per efficiency unit of labour, but there is an increase in output per worker. The balanced growth path then has capital, efficiency of labour, and total and per capita output all growing at a constant rate.

Endogenous growth

In the neoclassical model, innovation shifts the production function but is itself unexplained. (It is assumed to be measured by the unexplained residual—the amount of income

growth that cannot be accounted for by anything else.) This view holds that technological change is *exogenous*. It has profound effects on economic variables, such as GDP, but it is not influenced by economic causes. It just happens.

Yet microeconomic research by many scholars over the last several decades has established that technological change *is* responsive to such economic 'signals' as prices and profits; in other words, it is *endogenous* to the economic system. Much of the earliest work on this issue was done in the United Kingdom by scholars associated with the Science Policy Research Unit (SPRU) at Sussex University. The most influential overall single study, however, was by the American professor, Nathan Rosenberg, whose pathbreaking book *Inside the Black Box* argued this case in great detail.[12]

Technological change stems from research and development (R&D) and from innovating activities that put the results of R&D into practice. These are costly and highly risky activities, undertaken largely by firms and usually in pursuit of profit. It is not surprising, therefore, that these activities respond to economic incentives. If the price of some particular input such as petroleum or skilled labour goes up, R&D and innovating activities will be directed to altering the production function to economize on these inputs.

This process does not involve a substitution of less expensive inputs for more expensive ones within the confines of known technologies; rather, it is the development of new technologies in response to changes in relative prices. Rosenberg shows, first, that R&D designed to apply known basic principles is responsive to economic signals, and, second, that *basic research* itself is responsive. One reason for the latter is that the basic research agenda is strongly influenced by practical issues of the day. For example, basic research in solid-state physics became popular, and was heavily funded, only after the development of the transistor.

There are many important implications of this new understanding that, to a great extent, growth is achieved through costly, risky, innovative activity which occurs to a significant extent in response to economic signals. We will now discuss some of these implications.

THE COMPLEXITY OF THE INNOVATION PROCESS

The pioneering theorist of innovation, Joseph Schumpeter, developed a model in which innovation flowed in one direction, starting from a pure discovery 'upstream', to more applied R&D, then to working machines, and finally to output 'downstream'.

[12] N. Rosenberg, *Inside the Black Box: Technology and Economics* (Cambridge University Press, 1982). See also the same author's *Exploring the black box: Technology, economics, and history* (Cambridge University Press, 1994).

In contrast, modern research shows that innovation involves a large amount of 'learning by doing' at all of its stages.[13] What is learned 'downstream' then modifies what must be done 'upstream'. The best innovation-managing systems encourage feedback from the more applied steps to the purer researchers and from users to designers.

This interaction is illustrated by the differences between the Japanese car manufacturers and their North American competitors in the handling of new models. North American design has traditionally been centralized: design production teams develop the overall design and then tell their production sections what to do, as well as asking for bids from parts manufacturers to produce according to specific blueprints. As a result, defects in the original design are often not discovered until production is under way, causing many costly delays and rejection of parts already supplied. Japanese firms, on the other hand, involve their design and production departments and their parts manufacturers in all stages of the design process. Parts manufacturers are not given specific blueprints for production but, rather, are given general specifications and asked to develop their own detailed designs. As they do so, they learn. They then feed information about the problems they are encountering back to the main designers while the general outlines are still being finalized. As a result, compared with North American car firms, the Japanese usually design a new product faster, at less cost, and with far fewer problems when production is finally put into place.[14]

THE LOCATION OF INNOVATION

Innovation typically takes place in different parts of the producer–user chain in different industries—as shown, for example, by the research of Eric von Hippel of the Massachusetts Institute of Technology (MIT) in his book *The Sources of Innovation*. Von Hippel describes how, while in some industries manufacturers make most of the product innovations, in other industries it is users that make most of them, and in yet others the innovating is done by those who supply components or materials to the manufacturer.

Unless these differences are appreciated, public policy designed to encourage innovation can go seriously astray. An example is provided by von Hippel in the following words:

Consider the current concern of US policymakers that the products of US semiconductor process equipment firms are falling behind the leading edge. The conventional assessment of this problem is that these firms should somehow be strengthened and helped to innovate so that US semiconductor equipment users (makers of semiconductors) will not also fall behind. But investigation shows that most process equipment innovations in this field are, in fact, developed by equipment *users*. Therefore, the causality is probably reversed: US equipment builders are falling

behind because the US user community they deal with is falling behind. If this is so, the policy prescription should change. Perhaps US equipment builders can best be helped by helping US equipment users to innovate at the leading edge once more.[15]

The message for economists and policy-makers is important: an understanding of the details of the innovating process in each industry is needed if successful innovation-encouraging policies are to be developed.

COSTLY DIFFUSION

The *diffusion* of technological knowledge from those who have it to those who want it is not costless (as it was assumed to be in Schumpeter's model). Firms need research capacity just to adopt the technologies developed by others. Some of the knowledge needed to use a new technology can be learned only through experience by plant managers, technicians, and operators. (Such knowledge is called *tacit knowledge*.) We often tend to think that, once a production process is developed, it can easily be copied by others. Indeed, some advanced economic theories use the hypothesis of replication, which holds that any known process can be replicated in any new location by using the same factor inputs and management as are used in the old location. In practice, however, the diffusion of new technological knowledge is not so simple.

For example, US economists Richard Nelson and Sidney Winter have argued that most industrial technologies require technology-specific organizational skills that can be 'embodied' neither in the machines themselves, nor in instruction books, nor in blueprints. Acquiring tacit knowledge requires a deliberate process of building up new skills, work practices, knowledge, and experience:

As an initial perspective on the problem, we would not recommend the [hypothesis of replication] ... but the following account from Polanyi: '... even in modern industries the indefinable knowledge is still an essential part of technology. I have myself watched in Hungary a new, imported machine for blowing electric lamp bulbs, the exact counterpart of which was operating successfully in Germany, failing for a whole year to produce a single flawless bulb[!]' ... [T]he creation of productive organizations is *not* a matter of implementing fully explicit blueprints by purchasing homogeneous inputs on anonymous markets, a firm that is already successful in a given activity is a particularly good

---

[13] This phenomenon, whereby costs per unit of output fall steadily over time as firms learn how to manage new technologies, is discussed in more detail in Chapter 24.

[14] A detailed account of this issue can be found in J. Womack, D. Jones, and D. Roos, *The Machine that Changed the World* (New York: Ransom Associates, 1990). North American firms have recently begun to adopt some of these Japanese practices.

[15] Eric von Hippel, *The Sources of Innovation* (New York: Oxford University Press, 1988), pp. 9–10.

candidate for being successful with new capacity of the same sort.[16]

The fact that diffusion is a costly, risky, and time-consuming business explains why new technologies take considerable time to diffuse, first through the economy of the originating country and then through the rest of the world. If diffusion were simple and virtually costless, the puzzle would be why technological knowledge, and best industrial practices, does not diffuse very quickly. As it is, decades can pass before a new technological process is diffused everywhere that it could be employed.

MARKET STRUCTURE AND INNOVATION

Because it is highly risky, innovation is encouraged by a strongly competitive environment and is discouraged by monopoly practices. Competition among three or four large firms often produces much innovation, but a single firm, especially if it serves a secure home market protected by trade barriers, seems much less inclined to innovate.[17]

Although the ideas of Joseph Schumpeter lie behind much of modern growth theory, this emphasis on competition seems on the surface to conflict with his ideas. The apparent conflict arises because the theories available to Schumpeter in his time offered only two market structures: perfect competition and monopoly. He chose monopoly as the structure more conducive to growth on the grounds that monopoly profits would provide the incentive to innovate, and innovation itself would provide the mechanism whereby new entrants could compete with established monopolies. (He called this latter process 'creative destruction'.) Modern economists, faced with a richer variety of theoretical market structures, find that competition among oligopolists is usually more conducive to growth-enhancing, technological change than is monopoly.

Government interventions that are designed to encourage innovation often allow the firms in an industry to work together as one. Unless great care is exercised, and unless sufficient foreign competition exists, the result may be a national monopoly that will discourage risk-taking rather than encourage it, as the policy intends.

The United Kingdom provides many examples of this mistaken view of policy. For example:

[UK policy in the 1960s] . . . operated under the faulty theory that encouraging British companies to merge would create world-class competitors. Consolidation of steel, automobiles, machine tools, and computers all led to notable failures. A program of research support for industry . . . proved disastrous. The British government tried to choose promising technologies and gave direct grants to firms to develop them. Most of the choices were failures. [In contrast] . . . unusually low levels of regulation in some service industries have avoided disadvantages faced by other nations and allowed innovation and change . . . in

auctioneering . . . trading and insurance. British firms in these industries have been among the most innovative in the world.[18]

SHOCKS AND INNOVATION

One interesting consequence of endogenous technical change is that shocks that would be unambiguously adverse to an economy operating with fixed technology can sometimes provide a spur to innovation that proves a blessing in disguise. A sharp rise in the price of one input can raise costs and lower the value of output per person for some time. But it may lead to a wave of innovations that reduce the need for this expensive input and, as a side-effect, greatly raise the productivity of labour.[19]

Sometimes individual firms will respond differently to the same economic signal. Those who respond by altering technology may do better than those who concentrate their efforts on substituting within the confines of known technology. For example, in *The Competitive Advantage of Nations*, Michael Porter tells of how US consumer electronics firms decided to move their operations abroad to avoid high, and rigid, labour costs. They continued to use their existing technology and went where labour costs were low enough to make that technology pay. Their Japanese competitors, however, stayed at home. They innovated away most of their labour costs—and then built factories in the United States to replace the factories of US firms that had gone abroad!

INNOVATION AS A COMPETITIVE STRATEGY

Managing innovation better than one's competitors is one of the most important objectives of any modern firm that wishes to survive. Firms often fail because they do not keep up with their competitors in the race to develop new and improved products and techniques of production and distribution.[20] Success in real-world competition often

[16] R. Nelson and S. Winter, *An Evolutionary Theory of Economic Change* (Cambridge, Mass.: Harvard University Press, 1982), p. 119.

[17] This is an important theme in much contemporary research, supported by evidence from such authors as Alfred D. Chandler, Jr (*Scale and Scope: The Dynamics of Industrial Capitalism*, Cambridge, Mass.: Harvard University Press, 1990), David Mowrey and Nathan Rosenberg (*Technology and the Pursuit of Economic Growth*, Cambridge University Press, 1989), and Michael Porter (*The Competitive Advantage of Nations*, New York: Free Press, 1990).

[18] Porter, *The Competitive Advantage of Nations*, p. 507.

[19] This is why in microeconomics we study three runs: the short run, the long run, and the very long run. Often, the very-long-run response to a change in relative prices is much more important than either the short-run response, limited by fixed capital, or the long-run response, limited by existing technology.

[20] The book *Made in America: Regaining the Competitive Edge*, by M. Dertouzous, R. Lester, and R. Solow (Cambridge, Mass.: MIT Press, 1989), gives a series of case studies illustrating why some US firms have lost out to the Japanese and why in other cases US firms have done better than their Japanese competitors.

depends more on success in managing innovation than on success in adopting the right pricing policies or in making the right capacity decisions from already-known technological possibilities.

Increasing returns theories

We saw earlier that neoclassical theories assume that investment is always subject to diminishing returns. New growth theories emphasize the possibility of *historical increasing returns to investment*: as investment in some new area, product, power source, or production technology proceeds through time, each new increment of investment is more productive than previous increments. A number of sources of increasing returns have been noted. These fall under the general categories of fixed costs and ideas.

FIXED COSTS

1. Investment in the early stages of development of a country or region may create new skills and attitudes in the work-force that are then available to all subsequent investors, whose costs are therefore lower than those encountered by the initial investors. In the language of Chapter 23, the early firms are conferring an externality on those who follow them.

2. Each new investor may find the environment more and more favourable to its investment because of the infrastructure that has been created by those who came before.

3. The first investment in a new product will encounter countless problems, both of production and of product acceptance among customers, that, once overcome, cause fewer problems to subsequent investors.

All of these cases, and many more that could be mentioned, are examples of a single phenomenon:

Many investments require fixed costs, the advantages of which are then available to subsequent investors; hence, the investment costs for 'followers' can be substantially less than the investment costs for 'pioneers'.[21]

More generally, many of the sources of increasing returns are variations on the following general theme: doing something really new is difficult, both technically and in terms of customer acceptance, whereas making further variations on an accepted and developed new idea becomes progressively easier.

We have already seen one reason for this rule: the costly knowledge developed by early pioneers often becomes available to followers at a much lower cost. A second reason concerns customers. When a new product is developed, customers will often resist adopting it, partly because they

may be conservative and partly because they know that new products often have teething troubles. Customers also need time to learn how best to use the new product—they need to do what is called 'learning by using'. The first firms in the field with a truly new idea, such as personal computers, usually meet strong customer resistance, but this resistance erodes over time.

Slow acceptance of new products by customers is not necessarily irrational. When a sophisticated new product comes on the market, no one is sure if it will be a success, and the first customers to buy it take the risk that the product may subsequently turn out to be a failure. They also incur the costs of learning how to use it effectively. Many potential users take the not-unreasonable attitude of letting others try a new product, following only after the product's success has been demonstrated. This makes the early stages of innovation especially costly and risky.

These points lead to the following overall result:

For many reasons, successive increments of investment associated with a new set of innovations often yield a range of increasing returns, as costs that are incurred in earlier investment expenditure provide publicly available knowledge and experience and as customer attitudes and abilities become more receptive to new products.

The implications of these ideas have been the subject of intense study ever since they were first embedded in modern growth models by Paul Romer of the University of California and Maurice Scott of Oxford University.[22] Probably the most important contrast between these new theories and the neoclassical theory concerns investment and income. In the neoclassical model, diminishing returns to capital implies a limit to the possible increase of per capita GDP. In the new models, investment alone can hold a constant population on a 'sustained growth path' in which per capita GDP increases without limit, provided that the investment embodies the results of continual advances in technological knowledge.

IDEAS

An even more fundamental change in the new theories is the shift from the economics of goods to the economics of ideas. The economics of ideas is profoundly different from the economics of physical goods, and the differences are only just beginning to be appreciated.

Physical goods, such as factories and machines, exist in one place at one time. The nature of this existence has two

---

[21] The general phenomenon discussed here has been the subject of intense study since the early 1970s.

[22] As with so many innovations, these new views have many historical antecedents, including a classic article in the 1960s by Nobel Prize winner Kenneth Arrow of Stanford University: 'The Economic Implications for Learning by Doing', *Review of Economic Studies*, 29 (1962).

consequences. First, when physical goods are used by someone, they cannot be used by someone else. Second, if a given labour force is provided with more and more physical objects to use in production, sooner or later diminishing returns will be encountered.

Ideas have different characteristics. First, once someone has an idea and develops it, it is available for use by everyone. Ideas can be used by one person without reducing their use by others. For example, if one firm is using a certain van, another firm cannot use that van at the same time; but one firm's use of a revolutionary design for a new suspension on a van or lorry does not prevent other firms from using that design as well. Ideas are not subject to the same use restrictions as goods.

Second, ideas are not necessarily subject to decreasing returns. As our knowledge increases, each increment of new knowledge does *not* inevitably add less to our productive ability than did each previous increment. A year spent improving the operation of semiconductors may be more productive than a year spent improving the operation of vacuum tubes (the technology used before semiconductors).

The evidence from modern research is that new technologies are usually absolutely factor-saving—in other words, they use less of all inputs per unit of output. Furthermore, there is no evidence that from decade to decade the factor saving associated with increments of new knowledge is diminishing.

Modern growth theories stress the importance of ideas in producing what can be called knowledge-driven growth. New knowledge provides the input that allows investment to produce increasing rather than diminishing returns. Since there are no practical boundaries to human knowledge, there need be no immediate boundaries to finding new ways to produce more output using less of all inputs.[23]

Classical and neoclassical growth theories gave economics the name 'dismal science' by emphasizing diminishing returns under conditions of given technology. The modern growth theories are more optimistic because they emphasize the unlimited potential of knowledge-driven technological change to economize on all resource inputs, and because they display increasing returns to investment with constant population.

In so far as these new ideas are true, however, they refer to long-term trends. The dynamics of market systems cause growth rates to vary from decade to decade for reasons that are not fully understood. Over the long haul, however, there seems no reason to believe that equal increments of human effort must inevitably be rewarded by ever-diminishing increments to material output.

Further causes of growth

So far, we have looked at increases in labour and capital and at innovation as causes of growth. Contemporary studies suggest that other causes of growth are also important. The effects of these other causes appear as shifts in the production function, so that any given number of hours of labour operating with a given amount of capital produce more and more output as time passes.

INSTITUTIONS

Almost all aspects of a country's institutions can foster or deter the efficient use of a society's natural and human resources. Social and religious habits, legal institutions, and traditional patterns of national and international trade are all important. So, too, is the political climate.

Historians of economic growth, such as Paul David and Nathan Rosenberg, attribute much of the growth of Western economies in the post-medieval world to the development of *new institutions*, such as the joint-stock company and limited liability. Many students of modern growth suggest that institutions are as important today as they were in the past. They suggest that the societies that are most successful in developing the new institutions that are needed in today's knowledge-intensive world of globalized competition will be those that are at the forefront of economic growth.

THE ROLE OF THE GOVERNMENT

Governments play an important role in the growth process.

First, the government needs to provide the framework for the market economy that is given by such things as well-defined property rights secure from arbitrary confiscation, security and enforcement of contracts, law and order, a sound money, and the basic rights of the individual to locate, sell, and invest where and how he or she decides.

Second, governments need to provide infrastructure. For example, transportation and communications networks are critical to growth in the modern globalized economy. Some of these facilities, such as roads, bridges, and harbours, are usually provided directly by governments; others, such as telecommunications, rail, and air services, can be provided by private firms, but government regulations and competition policy may be needed to prevent the emergence of growth-inhibiting monopolies in these areas.

Education and health (especially for the disadvantaged) are important forms of government expenditure. Creating the appropriate factors of production is critical to creating comparative advantages in products that can be exported. This requires general education, trade schools, and other appropriate institutions for formal education as well as policies to increase on-the-job training within firms.

Other possible government policies include favourable

---

[23] Possibly, at some distant date, we may know everything there is to know, but if that time ever comes, it is clearly going to be a long, long way in the future.

tax treatment of saving, investment and capital gains, R&D tax incentives and funding assistance, and policies to encourage some fraction of the large pools of financial capital held by pension funds and insurance companies to be used to finance innovation.

Finally, emphasis can be placed on poverty reduction for at least two reasons. First, poverty can exert powerful anti-growth effects. People living in poverty will not develop the skills to provide a productive labour force, and they may not even respond to incentives that are provided. Malnutrition in early childhood can affect a person's capacities for life. Second, although economic growth tends to reduce the incidence of poverty, it does not eliminate it.

Are there limits to growth?

MANY opponents of growth argue that sustained world growth is undesirable; some argue that it is impossible. A current slogan reads 'Economic growth a cancer on society'. Of course, all terrestrial things have an ultimate limit. Astronomers predict that the solar system itself will die when the sun burns out in another five billion or so years. To be of practical concern, a limit must be within our planning horizons.

RESOURCE EXHAUSTION

The years since the Second World War have seen a rapid acceleration in the consumption of the world's resources, particularly fossil fuels and basic minerals. World population has increased from under 2.5 billion to nearly 6 billion in that period; this increase alone has intensified the demand for the world's resources. Furthermore, the single fact of population growth greatly understates the pressure on resources. As economic development spreads to more and more countries, living standards are rising, in some cases at a rapid rate. As people attain higher incomes, they consume more resources. So not only are there more people in the world, but many of those people are consuming increasing quantities of resources.

The technology and resources available in the mid-1990s could not possibly support the world's population at a standard of living equal to that of the average European family; for example, to do so the annual consumption of oil would have to increase more than tenfold. It is evident that resources and our present capacity to cope with pollution and environmental degradation are insufficient to accomplish this rise in living standards with our present technology.

Most economists, however, agree that *absolute* limits to growth, based on the assumptions of constant technology and fixed resources, are not relevant. As modern growth theory stresses, technology changes continually, as do stocks of resources. For example, 40 years ago few would have thought that the world could produce enough food to feed its present population of nearly 6 billion people, let alone the 10 billion at which the population is projected to stabilize sometime in the mid-twenty-first century. Yet this task now seems feasible.

There will never be full protection from the vagaries of nature, nor from wilful or ignorant mismanagement. However, in the early 1990s, the developed world struggles not with a food shortage, but with a food glut. Farm support policies in the European Union have turned the countries of Europe into food exporters rather than food importers, as they had been in the past. These subsidies greatly hurt agricultural producers in countries that would export agricultural produce if free-market prices prevailed. A mere 3 per cent of European, US, and Canadian labour applied to limited farmland with modern technology is producing more food than the world markets can consume. The problem in the mid-1990s is how to reduce subsidized production, not how to produce more.

Although globally there is enough food for everyone, severe problems arise when primarily agricultural economies suffer drought and other natural disasters, or wars and other man-made disasters. The problem, then, is not to produce more food worldwide, but to be sure that it is available where it is needed.

It is possible that, 40 years from now, the global energy problem will be as much a thing of the past as the global food shortage problem is today. Technology could by then have produced a cheap, non-polluting energy source (possibly based on solar energy or nuclear fusion).

Furthermore, research into technological change shows that the typical innovation in production processes uses less of all inputs per unit of output. Thus, technological change is part of the *solution,* not part of the problem. The problem is too many people aspiring to levels of consumption that cannot be sustained *with existing technologies.*

The future is always uncertain, and it is instructive to recall

BOX 33.3

The Brundtland Commission and 'sustainable development'

In 1983 the United Nations created the World Commission on Environment and Development (called the Brundtland Commission after its chairman, Gro Harlem Brundtland) to examine global environmental and development problems and design solutions. In its 1987 report, *Our Common Future*, the Brundtland Commission outlined a broad agenda for integrating economic development and environmental policy. The Commission stressed the view that economic growth and environmental protection are interdependent: growth cannot long continue at the present rate of environmental degradation.

The report introduced the concept of *sustainable development*, defined as 'development that meets the needs of the present without compromising the ability of future generations to meet their own needs'.

The idea that economic growth is limited by 'nature' is not new. In the early 1970s, the Club of Rome focused on the limits to growth arising from the supply of natural resources: it extrapolated from the shortages in oil, caused by the formation of OPEC and the attendant price increases, that industrialized countries faced an imminent absolute limit to growth. This prediction was refuted by experience, as higher prices for fuel led to increases both in total supply and in the efficiency with which it has been used.

The bounds to growth envisioned by the Brundtland Commission are not absolute but rather are a function of the 'present state of technology' and the capacity of the 'biosphere to absorb the effects of human activity'. The environment imposes limits to the growth that can occur with any specific technology because it is the fundamental capital upon which economic development is based. As technology and economic organization improve, the stream of wealth that flows from this stock of 'environmental capital' can continue to increase. The concept of sustainable development stresses the role of the environment as capital that, if exhausted, cannot be replaced.

Regardless of whether an institution is a government agency, a small firm, or a transnational corporation, the Brundtland Commission's message applies: all institutions that affect the environmental base of the economy must respect the needs of future generations.

According to the Commission, governments need to expand their role in the collection and dissemination of information and, where possible, should produce an annual account of the nation's environment and resource base 'to complement the traditional annual fiscal budget and economic development plans'. The idea is that the environment is part of our capital, and when we degrade it, we reduce our ability to generate real income in the future, as occurs when a machine used for producing consumer goods depreciates.

Some of the Brundtland Commission's recommendations require increased government involvement in economies in order to produce and enforce environmental regulations. Although it recognizes the value of economic incentives in generating the cost reductions that flow from more efficient use of resources, the Commission also feels that there are limits to the ability of competitive industry to reduce waste voluntarily: 'Regulations imposing uniform performance standards are essential to ensure that industry makes the investments necessary to reduce pollution and waste and to enable them to compete on an even footing.'

In other cases, what is required is *less* government intervention, and the report calls on governments to examine whether existing policies and subsidies contribute to resource-efficient practices. For example, agricultural policies that protect farmers in the European Union and other industrialized countries are criticized for being 'studded with contradictions that encourage the degradation of the agricultural resource base and, in the long run, do more harm than good to the agricultural industry'. The solution lies in 'reducing incentives that force overproduction and noncompetitive production in the developed market economies and enhancing those that encourage food production in developing countries'.

Recommendations are made for reforming international organizations, in which an 'extensive institutional capacity exists that could be redirected towards sustainable development'. The efficacy of existing institutions is reduced by their 'fragmented' nature and a 'weakness of coordination'. Key to these reforms is the requirement that sustainable development be made central to the mandate of all international bodies such as UN agencies, the International Monetary Fund, and the World Bank.

Our Common Future is a hopeful document, but its hope is tempered with the realization that, unless major conservation initiatives are acted on quickly, the current serious rate of environmental degradation will soon start to harm the health and welfare of us all.

---

how many things that we accept as commonplace today would have seemed miraculous a mere 25 years ago.

Yet there is surely cause for concern. Although many barriers can be overcome by technological advances, such achievements are not instantaneous and are certainly not automatic. There is a critical problem of timing: how soon can we discover and put into practice the knowledge required to solve the problems that are made ever more imminent by the growth in the population, the affluence of the rich nations, and the aspirations of the billions who now live in poverty?

There is no guarantee that a whole generation will not be caught in transition between technologies, with enormous social and political consequences. One positive outgrowth of concern over environmental issues is the recent attention given to the concept of 'sustainable development', discussed further in Box 33.3.

RENEWABLE RESOURCES

One possible limitation to growth relates to renewable resources. The demands placed on them threaten to destroy their natural recuperative cycle. Throughout history, for example, fishermen were a small part of the predatory process. Now, the demands of nearly 6 billion people have made fish a scarce resource, threatening to destroy the fish-generating capacity of many oceans, as we saw in Box 23.1, p. 420.

POLLUTION

A further problem is how to cope with pollution. Air, water, and earth are polluted by a variety of natural activities, and through billions of years the environment has coped with these. The earth's natural processes had little trouble dealing with the pollution generated by its 1 billion inhabitants in 1800. But the nearly 6 billion people who now exist put demands on pollution abatement systems that threaten to become unsustainable. Smoke, sewage, chemical waste, hydrocarbon emissions, spent nuclear fuel, and a host of other pollutants threaten to overwhelm the earth's natural regenerative processes. Detailed analysis of how these problems may be dealt with was given in Chapters 23 and 24.

Conscious management of pollution and renewable resources was unnecessary when the world's population was 1 billion people, but such management has become a pressing matter of survival now that nearly 6 billion people are seeking to live in the same space and off the world's limited resources.

Conclusion

The world faces many problems. Starvation and poverty are the common lot of citizens in many countries and are not unknown in countries such as the United Kingdom and the United States, where average living standards are high. Growth has raised the average citizens of advanced countries from poverty to plenty in the course of two centuries—a short time in terms of human history. Further growth is needed if people in less developed countries are to escape material poverty, and further growth would help advanced countries to deal with many of their pressing economic problems.

Rising population and rising per capita consumption, however, put pressure on the world's natural ecosystems, especially through the many forms of pollution. Further growth must be sustainable growth, which in turn must be based on idea-driven technological change. Past experience suggests that new technologies will use less of all resources per unit of output. However, if they are to reduce dramatically the demands placed on the earth's ecosystems, price and policy incentives will be needed to direct technological change in more 'environmentally friendly' ways. Just as present technologies are much less polluting than the technologies of 100 years ago, the technologies of the twenty-first century must be made much less polluting than today's.

There is no guarantee that the world will solve the problems of sustainable growth, but there is nothing in modern growth theory and existing evidence to suggest that such an achievement is impossible.

Summary

1 Real national income can be increased on a once-for-all basis from the demand side by removing recessionary gaps and from the supply side by reducing structural impediments and economic inefficiencies. Sustained increases, however, are due mainly to economic growth, which continuously pushes the *LRAS* curve outward, thereby increasing potential income.

2 Investment has short-term effects on national income through aggregate demand and long-term effects through growth in potential national income. Saving reduces consumption and aggregate demand and therefore reduces national income in the short run, but in the long run saving finances the investment that leads to growth in potential income.

3 Growth is frequently measured by using rates of change of potential real national income per person or per hour of labour employed. The cumulative effects of even small differences in growth rates become large over periods of a decade or more.

4 The most important benefit of growth lies in its contribution to the long-run struggle to raise living standards and to escape poverty. Growth also facilitates the redistribution of income among people.

5 Growth, though often beneficial, is never costless. The opportunity cost of growth is the diversion of resources from current consumption to capital formation. For individuals who are left behind in a rapidly changing world, the costs are higher and more personal.

6   The aggregate neoclassical model displays diminishing returns when one factor is increased on its own and constant returns when all factors are increased together. In a balanced growth path, labour, capital, and national income all increase at a constant rate, leaving living standards unchanged.

7   When the neoclassical model was related to actual data, much of the observed growth in national income could not be explained by the growth in labour and capital. The unexplained growth, called the residual, was ascribed to technological change.

8   Modern growth theory treats technological change as an endogenous variable that responds to market signals. The diffusion of technology is also endogenous. It is costly and often proceeds at a relatively slow pace.

9   Some modern growth theories display increasing returns as investment increases on its own. This investment confers externalities such that successive increments of investment may add constant or even successively *increasing* amounts to total output.

10   Causes of growth, in addition to increases in the quantity of capital, labour, and technological change, are increases in the stock of human capital and changes in institutions.

11   The critical importance of increasing knowledge and new technology to the goal of sustaining growth is highlighted by the great drain on existing natural resources that has resulted from the explosive growth of population and output in recent decades. Without continuing technological change, the present needs and aspirations of the world's population cannot come anywhere close to being met.

12   Rising population and rising real incomes place pressure on resources. Although resources in general will not be exhausted, particular resources, such as petroleum, will be. Furthermore, resources that renewed themselves without help from humans when the world's population was 1 billion people can easily be exhausted unless they are consciously conserved now that the world's population exceeds 5 billion. This enormous increase in population has similar effects on pollution: the earth's environment could cope naturally with much of human pollution 200 years ago, but the present population is so large that pollution has outstripped nature's coping mechanisms.

Topics for review

- Short-run and long-run effects of investment and saving
- Cumulative nature of growth
- Benefits and costs of growth
- The neoclassical aggregate production function
- Balanced growth
- Endogenous technical change
- Increasing returns to investment
- Embodied and disembodied technical change
- The economics of goods and of ideas
- Resource depletion and pollution

∾ CHAPTER 34

Growth in developing countries

TRADITIONALLY in economics, the growth of high-income countries has been treated as a separate subject from the growth of lower-income countries (an inter-country distinction which is described in more detail below), and the latter subject is often not included in introductory courses. For this reason, this chapter has been made self-contained so that it can be skipped if desired.

We include this material at this point for two main reasons. First, the deeper understanding that economists are developing of the role that technological change plays in economic growth is blurring the traditional distinction between the forces that cause growth in high-income and in lower-income countries. Second, the growth successes of Japan earlier in this century and of several South-East Asian countries later in the century has blurred what earlier seemed to be a clear distinction between the high-income, largely industrialized, countries and all the rest. We now see what looks more like a continuous gradation from the very highest-income countries, which include the United States, most the countries of the European Union, and Japan at one end of the income scale, South Korea, Hong Kong, Singapore, Taiwan, some of the lower-income countries of the European Union (among others), and some of the higher-income countries of Latin America at the upper-middle end of the scale, countries such as Indonesia and Malaysia a little further back, followed by India and a rapidly growing China, with yet others, particularly many of the countries of sub-Saharan Africa, not only with very low incomes but also with static ones.

For these and other reasons, it no longer seems reasonable to assume that the forces that govern growth in rich countries are fundamentally different from the forces that govern growth in middle and lower-rank countries.

From the outset, development economics has had a micro component, concentrating on social and economic structures as influences on growth. Increasingly, while not forgetting the important macro influences of aggregate saving and investment, those economists who study technological change in high-income countries have come to place more emphasis on the microeconomic aspects of social and economic structure that encourage the innovation and diffusion of new technologies in the countries that they study. (See for example Box 34.1 on p. 662)

Probably the most important boundary that divides countries where different explanations of growth are required is between countries that have very low and static incomes, and all the rest. A country that has shown no significant economic growth for decades (or even for centuries) probably has economic and social structures, as well as fundamental direction to its economic policies, that are basically unfavourable to growth. If the people of that country wish to grow, they must contemplate fundamental structural changes, as well as major reversals in their economic policies. All the other countries, in which growth is occurring (although sometimes at a rate that is regarded as too low), face many common problems, whether they are low, middle, or high-income countries. The importance of individual forces may vary, but, overall, these countries face problems that have a significant degree of similarity. Of course, their underlying social and economic structures do affect their growth rates, but, since they are currently growing, they do not face the same urgent need to consider major alterations of their underlying structures as do the non-growing countries.

The uneven pattern of development

IN the civilized and comfortable urban life of today's developed countries, most people have lost sight of the fact that a short time ago—very short, in terms of the life span of the earth—people were nomadic food gatherers, existing as best they could from what nature threw their way. It has been only about 10,000 years since the Neolithic agricultural revolution, when people changed from food gatherers to food producers. Throughout most of subsequent human history, civilizations have been based on a comfortable life for a privileged minority and unremitting toil for the vast majority. It has been only within the last two centuries that ordinary people have become able to

expect leisure and high consumption standards—and then, only in the world's economically developed countries.

Close to 6 billion people are alive today, but the wealthy parts of the world—where people work no more than 40 or 50 hours per week, enjoy substantial leisure, and have a level of consumption at or near *half* that attained by the United States (the country with the highest per capita GDP)—contain no more than 20 per cent of the world's population. Many of the rest struggle for subsistence. Many exist on a level at or below that endured by peasants in ancient Egypt or Babylon.

The richest countries with the highest per capita incomes

are referred to by the United Nations as **developed countries**. These include the United States, Canada, most of the countries of Western Europe, South Africa, Australia, New Zealand, Japan, and a few others. The poorer countries are referred to by the UN as the **developing countries**[1] and include a diverse set of countries. Some, such as Vietnam, Argentina, and China, are growing very rapidly, while others, such as Ethiopia and Papua New Guinea, actually have negative growth rates of per capita real income. Between these two is another group of nations, variously called **newly industrialized economies (NIEs)** or newly industrialized countries (NICs); they include South Korea, Singapore, Taiwan, and Hong Kong. These countries have grown rapidly and typically have per capita incomes close to 50 per cent of those found in the developed nations. Several other countries in South East Asia are close behind the NICs, including Indonesia, Malaysia, and Thailand.

To see the problem of raising per capita incomes in one of the poorest countries as one of economic *development* is to recognize that the whole structure of its economy may need to be altered to create economic growth. This is a complex task; many countries remain undeveloped today in spite of decades of effort by their governments to get them on a path of sustained growth.

Data on per capita incomes throughout the world (converted to US dollars in Table 34.1) cannot be accurate down to the last $100.[2] Nevertheless, the data reflect enormous real differences in living standards that no statistical inaccuracies can hide. The *development gap*—the discrepancy between the standards of living in countries at either end of the distribution—is real and large.[3]

Figure 34.1 provides another way of looking at inequality. It shows the geographic distribution of per capita income. Modern political discussions of income distribution distinguish between richer and poorer nations as 'North' versus 'South'. The map reveals why.

The consequences of very low income levels can be severe. In a rich country such as the United Kingdom, variations in rainfall are reflected in farm output and farm income. In very poor countries, variations in rainfall are often reflected in the death rate. In these countries, many people live so close to a subsistence level that even slight fluctuations in the food supply can bring death by starva-

[1] The terminology of development is often confusing. 'Underdeveloped', 'less developed', and 'developing' do not mean the same thing in ordinary English, yet each has been used to describe the same phenomenon. For the most part, we shall use the term 'developing', which is the term currently used by the United Nations to describe the lower-income countries. Some of these countries are making progress in raising their living standards; that is, they are developing in the ordinary sense of that word. Others are not.

[2] There are many problems when we compare national incomes across countries. For example, home-grown food is vitally important to living standards in underdeveloped countries, but it is excluded, or at best imperfectly included, in the national income statistics of most countries. In Norway, significant amounts of GDP go to heating houses during cold winters. Such heating is not necessary in countries that have warm climates.

[3] You will find large discrepancies in international comparisons depending on the exchange rates that are used to convert GDPs valued in domestic currencies to a common currency unit. Use of rates based on the relative purchasing powers of national currencies (called purchasing power parity rates and described in Chapter 37) is more satisfactory, while use of current rates causes international standings to vary substantially from one year to the next.

Table 34.1 Income and population differences among groups of countries, 1992

Income groups by GNP per capita (US$)	(1) Number of countries	(2) GNP, (US$ million)	(3) Population (millions)	(4) GNP per capita (US$)	(5) World population (%)	(6) World GNP (%)
Low ($675 or less)	57	1,139,000	3,215	350	59.1	5.0
Lower–middle ($676–$2,695)	69	1,614,000	949	1,700	17.4	7.1
Upper–middle ($2,696–$8,355)	43	1,837,000	451	4,070	8.3	8.0
High ($8,356 or more)	38	18,297,000	828	22,100	15.2	79.9
World	207	22,887,000	5,443	4,200	100	100

The unequal distribution of world income is shown in columns (5) and (6). The poorest 60 per cent of the world's population earns only 5 per cent of world income; the richest 15 per cent earns 80 per cent of world income.

Source: World Bank Atlas 1994, World Bank, Washington, DC.

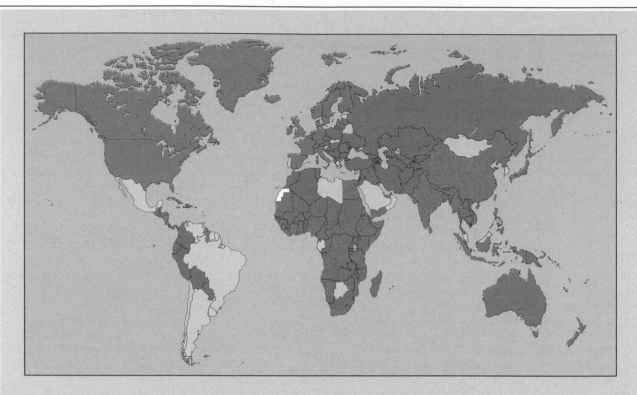

Figure 34.1 Countries of the world, classified by per capita GNP, 1992

There is a sharp geographical division between 'North' and 'South' in the level of income per capita. The nations of the world are classified here according to four levels of measured per capita GNP. The poorest group, shown in green, represents 59 per cent of the world's population. The lower-middle and upper-middle groups, shown in dark blue and light red, represent about 25 per cent of world population. The wealthiest group, shown in dark red, includes all of North America, Europe, Australasia, and Japan and represents only 15 per cent of the world's population. Areas in white indicate that no data are available. See Table 34.1 for more detail.

tion to large numbers. Other, less dramatic, characteristics of poverty include inadequate diet, poor health, short life expectancy, and illiteracy.

For these reasons, reformers in very low-income countries feel a sense of urgency not felt by their counterparts in higher-income countries. Yet, as Table 34.2 shows, some of the poorest countries in the world are among those with very low or negative growth rates of per capita GDP. As a result,

The development gap has been widening for the very poorest countries.

As we shall see, this is a problem of both output and population. It is also an international political problem. What are the causes of underdevelopment, and how may they be overcome?

Restraints on economic development

PER capita income grows when aggregate income grows faster than population. Many forces can impede such growth. Here we study a list of possible restraints that starts with natural resources and ends with international indebtedness. These can apply to countries at all income levels, but they tend to be most severe in the poorest countries.

INADEQUATE OR INEFFICIENTLY USED NATURAL RESOURCES

A country's supply of natural resources is important. A country with infertile land and inadequate supplies of natural resources will find growth in income more difficult to achieve than one that is richly endowed with such resources.

How these resources are managed also matters. When farmland is divided into many small parcels, it may be much more difficult to achieve the advantages of modern agriculture than when the land is available in huge tracts for large-scale farming. Fragmented land holdings may result from a dowry or inheritance system, or it may be politically imposed. One of the popular policies following the Mexican revolution early in the twentieth century was the redistribution of land from large landowners to ordinary peasants. Today, however, the fragmented land ownership prevents Mexican agriculture from producing many products at costs low enough to compete in international markets. The Mexican government now faces a difficult choice between allowing its popular land reforms to be reversed or continuing to protect a large agricultural sector whose inefficiency is increasing relative to competing suppliers.

Although abundant supplies of natural resources can assist growth, they are neither sufficient to ensure growth nor always necessary for it. Some countries with large supplies of natural resources have poor growth performances because the economic structure encourages waste; prime examples are the former Soviet Union, Argentina up until this decade, and Uganda. In contrast, other countries have enjoyed rapid rates of economic growth based on human capital and entrepreneurial ability in spite of a dearth of natural resources; prime examples are Switzerland in earlier centuries, Japan over the last 100 years, and Singapore, Hong Kong, and Taiwan in the last 40 years.

When one discusses inefficiency in resource use, it helps to distinguish between two kinds of economic inefficiency, which are studied in microeconomics. *Allocative inefficiency* occurs when factors of production are used to make an inefficient combination of goods. There is too much of some goods and too little of others. This means that the economy is at the 'wrong' point on its production possibility boundary. If resources are reallocated to produce less of some and more of other types of goods, some people can be made better off while no one will be made worse off.

Productive inefficiency occurs when factors of production are used in inefficient combinations. Given the prices of capital and labour, some production processes use too much capital relative to labour, while others use too little. This means that the economy is inside its production possibility boundary (as shown in Chapter 1). If factor combinations are altered, more of all goods can be produced.

Monopolistic market structures, as well as taxes, tariffs, and subsidies, are some important sources of the distortions that lead to both allocative and productive inefficiencies.

Another kind of inefficiency, called **X-inefficiency**, occurs either when firms do not seek to maximize their profits, or when owners of the factors of production do not seek to maximize their material welfare. X-inefficiency also puts the economy inside its production possibility boundary.

Professor Harvey Leibenstein of the University of California, the economist who developed the concept, has studied X-inefficiency in developing countries. He cites psychological evidence to show that non-maximizing behaviour is typical of situations in which the pressure that has been placed on decision-makers is either very low or very high. If the customary living standard can be obtained with little effort, according to this evidence, people are likely to follow customary behaviour and spend little time trying to make optimal decisions. When pressure builds up, so that making a reasonable income becomes more difficult, optimizing behaviour becomes more common. Under extreme pressure, however, such as very low living standards or a rapidly deteriorating environment, people become disoriented and once again do not adopt optimizing behaviour.

X-inefficiency may be typical of industries, and whole economies, where customary behaviour leads to acceptable living standards or where the challenges become overwhelming.[4]

---

[4] Although such behaviour is no doubt often found in some developing economies, it is also sometimes found in advanced countries. For example, studies of monopolies have often indicated a preference on the part of their managers and workers for the 'quiet life' rather than an active search for profit- and income-maximizing forms of behaviour.

INEFFICIENT AGRICULTURE

A developing country whose labour force is mainly devoted to agriculture has little choice but to accept this basic allocation of resources. It can build up its industrial sector, and if its efforts are successful the proportion of the population devoted to urban pursuits will rise. But the change will come slowly, leaving a large portion of the country's resources in rural pursuits for a long time to come.

It follows that policies to help the agricultural sector raise productivity are an important part of the development strategy in any agriculture-based, poor country. These can fill the dual purposes of raising the incomes of rural workers and reducing the cost of food for urban workers.

A developing country's government may choose to devote a major portion of its resources to stimulating agricultural production, for example by mechanizing farms, irrigating land, using new seeds and fertilizers, and promoting agricultural R&D. If successful, the country will stave off starvation for its current population, and it may even develop an excess over current needs and so have foodstuffs available for export. A food surplus can thereby earn foreign exchange to buy needed imports.

In the last two decades, India, Pakistan, Taiwan, and other Asian countries have achieved dramatic increases in food production by the application of new technology and the use of new seed in agricultural production. This has been labelled the *green revolution*.

The gains from this strategy, while large at first, are subject to diminishing returns. Further gains in agricultural production have an ever-higher opportunity cost, measured in terms of the resources needed to irrigate land and to mechanize production. Critics of reliance on agricultural output argue that newly developing economies must start at once to develop other bases for economic growth.

Many developing countries (as well as many developed ones) suffer from misguided government intervention in the agriculture sector. In India, for example, the government has encouraged crops such as oilseeds and sugar cane, in which India has a comparative disadvantage, and discouraged crops such as rice, wheat, and cotton, in which India has a strong comparative advantage. It has subsidized food prices, thus giving large benefits to the urban population. About 8 per cent of all Indian government spending is on subsidies that go to fertilizers, to farmers' debt payments, and to urban food consumption.

RAPID POPULATION GROWTH

Population growth is one of the central problems of economic development. For example, in the decade 1980–90, Ecuador, Ethiopia, and Papua New Guinea had growth rates of population of 2.7, 2.9, and 2.4 per cent per year alongside GDP growth rates of 2.2, 1.8, and 1.8 per cent, respectively. Hence they experienced *negative* rates of growth of GDP *per capita* (of − 0.5, − 1.1, and − 0.6 per cent per year). Many less developed countries have rates of population growth that are nearly as large as their rates of growth of GDP. As a result, their standards of living are barely higher than they were 100 years ago. They have made appreciable gains in aggregate income, but most of the gains have been literally eaten up by the increasing population. This is illustrated in Table 34.2.

The critical importance of population growth to living standards was perceived early in the nineteenth century by the Reverend Thomas Malthus. He asserted two relations concerning rates of increase. First, food production tends to increase in an arithmetic progression (e.g., 100, 103, 106, 109, 112, where the increments in this example are 3 units per period). Second, population tends to increase in a geometric progression (e.g., 100, 103, 106.09, 109.27, 112.55, where the increase in this example is 3 *per cent per period*).

Table 34.2   The relationship between the level and the rate of growth of per capita income, 1985–1992

Growth of GNP per capita, 1985–92 (%)	Number of countries	GNP, 1992 (US$ million)	Population, 1992 (millions)	GNP per capita, 1992 (US$)
Less than 0	51	1,108,000	661	1,630
0–0.9	24	1,681,000	262	6,420
1.0–1.9	26	8,083,000	875	9,240
2.0–2.9	18	5,287,000	386	13,700
3.0 or more	31	5,903,000	2,684	2,200
No data	57	852,000	576	1,480

The very poorest countries spend much of their increase in income on a rising population. Thus, their increase in income per capita is less than half that of the countries that are already richer. The gap in income between rich and many of the very poor countries is not closing. Notice that there are no consistent growth data for 57 of the poorest countries.

Source: World Bank Atlas 1994, World Bank, Washington, DC.

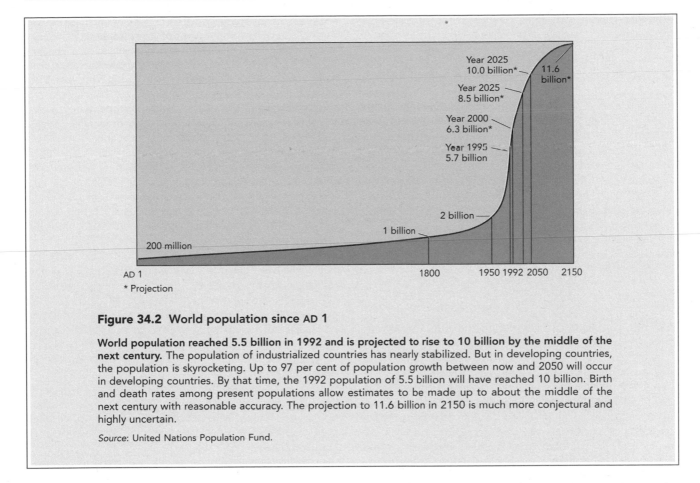

Figure 34.2 World population since AD 1

World population reached 5.5 billion in 1992 and is projected to rise to 10 billion by the middle of the next century. The population of industrialized countries has nearly stabilized. But in developing countries, the population is skyrocketing. Up to 97 per cent of population growth between now and 2050 will occur in developing countries. By that time, the 1992 population of 5.5 billion will have reached 10 billion. Birth and death rates among present populations allow estimates to be made up to about the middle of the next century with reasonable accuracy. The projection to 11.6 billion in 2150 is much more conjectural and highly uncertain.

Source: United Nations Population Fund.

As a result of these relationships, Malthus argued that population growth will always tend to outrun the growth in food supply. The difference in the above example may not seem like much after only 5 periods. But after 20 periods the arithmetic increase in food supply has increased it to 160 while the geometric increase in the population has increased it to 181.

Malthus's prediction gave economics the name of 'the dismal science'. In some poor areas of the world, the predictions seem all too accurate, even today. There, agricultural methods are fairly traditional, so that food production increases only slowly while population tends to increase at more rapid rates. The result is subsistence living, with population held in check by low life expectancies and periodic famines.

Fortunately, over most of the world Malthus's predictions have been proved false. Two reasons are paramount. First, Malthus underestimated the importance of technological change, which has increased productivity in agriculture at a *geometric* rate far higher than the rate at which the demand for food has been growing in most advanced countries. Second, he underestimated the extent of voluntary restrictions of population growth arising from the wide-spread use of birth control techniques. As a result, population has grown more slowly than has the production of food (and most other things) in developed countries. For them, living standards have been rising rather than falling.

For the more advanced industrialized countries, Malthusian pressures are not a problem today. However, for many poor countries, where people subsist on what they grow for themselves, the tendency for the growth in population to outstrip the growth in the food supply makes Malthusian pressures a current threat.

Figure 34.2 illustrates actual and projected world population. By now, the population problem is almost completely limited to the low-income countries. About 97 per cent of the expected growth in the world's population between now and 2050 will be in the developing countries of Africa, Asia, and Latin America.

INADEQUATE HUMAN RESOURCES

Numbers of people matter, and so does their training and experience. A well developed entrepreneurial class, motivated and trained to organize resources for efficient production, is often missing in poor countries. The cause may be that managerial positions are awarded on the basis of family status or political patronage (leading to X-inefficiency); it may be the presence of economic or cultural attitudes that do not favour acquisition of wealth by organizing productive activities; or it may simply be the absence of the quantity or quality of education or training that is required.

In today's world, much production is knowledge-intensive. This puts a premium on a well-educated work-force. The ability to read, do basic calculations, operate electronic equipment, and follow relatively complex instructions are important requirements for much modern labour. Failure to create such essential labour skills can be an important cause of lack of growth.

Poor health is another source of inadequate human resources. When the labour force is healthy, less time is lost and more effective effort is expended.

CULTURAL BARRIERS

Traditions and habitual ways of doing business vary among societies, and not all are equally conducive to high productivity. Often in developing countries, cultural forces are a source of X-inefficiency. Sometimes personal considerations of family, past favours, or traditional friendship or enmity are more important than market incentives in motivating behaviour. One may find a firm that is too small struggling to survive against a larger rival, and learn that the owner prefers to remain small because expansion would require use of nonfamily capital or leadership. To avoid paying too harsh a competitive price for built-in inefficiency, the firm's owners may then attempt to influence the government to prevent larger firms from being formed, or try to secure restrictions on the sale of output—and they may well succeed. Such behaviour will inhibit economic growth.

In a society in which people believe that it is more important who your father is than what you do, it may take a generation to persuade employers to change their attitudes, and another generation to persuade workers that times have changed. It is more difficult for the work-force to change its characteristics and to adapt to the requirements of growth, in a traditional society, in which children are expected to follow their parents' occupations, than in a society in which upward mobility is itself a goal. (These are aspects of the traditional economy that we first discussed in Chapter 1.)

Structuring incentives is a widely used form of policy action in market-oriented economies. However, if people habitually bribe the tax collector rather than pay taxes, they will not be likely to respond to policies that are supposed to work by raising or lowering taxes. All that will change is the size of the bribe.

Where social attitudes do not sanction the sacrifice of current living standards in order to generate a large volume of domestic saving, a government can impose compulsory saving. Such forced saving policies were one of the main aims of most of the development plans of communist governments, such as those of the former Soviet Union and China. The goal of such plans was to raise savings and thus lower current consumption below what it would be in a market economy. A less authoritarian method is to increase the national savings rate through fiscal and monetary policies. The object, however, is the same: to increase investment in order to increase growth, and thus to make future generations better off.

Unfortunately, even where the governments of developing countries have succeeded in raising their national savings rate, much of the savings were wasted in inefficient state-owned enterprises that could never become profitable. If the funds had been invested in the much needed infrastructure that only a government can create, then government intervention might have been effective in encouraging development.

There is lively debate about how much to make of differing cultural attitudes. Some analysts believe that traditional considerations dominate peasant societies to the exclusion of economic responses; others suggest that any resulting inefficiency may be relatively small. The fact that existing social, religious, or legal patterns may make growth more difficult does not in itself imply that such patterns are undesirable; instead, it suggests that the benefits of these patterns must be weighed against the costs, of which the limitation on growth is one. When people derive satisfaction from a religion whose beliefs inhibit growth, or when they value a society in which every household owns its own land and is more nearly self-sufficient than another society, they may be quite willing to pay a price in terms of growth opportunities forgone.

Many critics argue that development plans, particularly when imposed by economists from advanced countries, pay too little attention to local cultural and religious values. Even when they are successful as judged by rising GDP, it may be at too great a cost in terms of social upheaval for the current generation.

A country that wants development must accept some alteration in its traditional ways of doing things. However, a trade-off between speed of development and amount of social upheaval can be made. Critics argue that such a trade-off should be made by local governments and should not be imposed by outsiders who understand little of local customs and beliefs. An even more unfavourable possibility is that the social upheaval will occur without achieving even the expected benefits of a rising GDP. If the development policy does not take local values into account, the local population may not respond as predicted by Western economic theories. In this case, the results of the development effort may be disappointingly small.

INADEQUATE FINANCIAL INSTITUTIONS

The lack of an adequate, trustworthy, and trusted system of

financial institutions is often a restraint on development. Investment plays a key role in growth, and an important source of funds for investment is the savings of households and firms. When banks and other financial institutions do not function effectively, the link between private saving and investment may be broken, making it difficult to raise funds for investment.

Many people in poor countries do not trust banks—sometimes with good reason, but often without. Either they do not maintain deposits, or else they panic periodically, withdrawing their balances and seeking security for their money under mattresses, in gold, or in real estate. When banks cannot count on their deposits being left in the banking system, they cannot engage in the kind of long-term loans that are needed to finance investments. When this happens, savings do not become available for investment in productive capacity.

More importantly, a poorly functioning banking system, often one that is nationalized or dominated by a strong government-supported union, can seriously slow growth. India is still in this situation in 1995; although governments have introduced many market-oriented reforms over the last decade, they have so far been unwilling to take on the unions that dominate India's large, inefficient banking system.

INADEQUATE DOMESTIC SAVINGS

Although modern development strategies in many instances call for a large infusion of foreign capital imported by transnational corporations (TNCs), the rise of domestically owned firms, which will reap some of the externalities created by foreign technology, is one key to sustained development. And a supply of domestic savings is needed to finance the growth of domestic firms.

If more domestic capital is to be created by a country's own efforts, resources must be diverted from the production of goods for current consumption. This means a cut in present living standards. If living standards are already at or near subsistence level, such a diversion will be difficult. At best, it will be possible to reallocate only a small proportion of resources to the production of capital goods.

Such a situation is often described as the *vicious circle of poverty*: because a country has little capital per head, it is poor; because it is poor, it can devote few resources to creating new capital rather than to producing goods for consumption; because little new capital can be produced, capital per head remains low; and the country remains poor.

The vicious circle can be made to seem an absolute constraint on growth rates. Of course, it is not; if it were, we would all still be at the level of the early agricultural civilizations. The grain of truth in the vicious-circle argument is that some surplus must be available somewhere in the society to allow saving and investment. In a poor society

with an even distribution of income, in which nearly everyone is at the subsistence level, saving may be very difficult. But this is not the common experience. Usually, there is at least a small middle class that can save and invest if opportunities for the profitable use of funds arise. Also, in most poor societies today, the average household is above the physical subsistence level. Even the poorest households will find that they can sacrifice some present living standards for a future gain. For example, presented with a profitable opportunity, villagers in Ghana planted cocoa plants at the turn of the century, even though there was a seven-year growing period before any return could be expected.

An important consideration is that in less developed countries one resource that is often *not* scarce is labour. Profitable home or village investment that requires mainly labour inputs may be made with relatively little sacrifice in current living standards. Unfortunately, this kind of investment often does not appeal to local governments, which are too often mesmerized by large and symbolic investments, such as dams, nuclear power stations, and steel mills.

INADEQUATE INFRASTRUCTURE

Key services, such as transportation and a communications network, called **infrastructure**, are necessary to efficient commerce. Roads, bridges, railways, and harbours are needed to transport people, materials, and finished goods. Phone and postal services, a safe water supply, and sanitation are essential to economic development.

The absence, for whatever reason, of a dependable infrastructure can impose severe barriers to economic development.

Many governments feel that money spent on a new steel mill shows more impressive results than money spent on such infrastructure investments as automating the telephone system. Yet private, growth-creating, entrepreneurial activity will be discouraged more by the absence of good telephone communications than by the lack of domestically produced steel.

INTERNATIONAL DEBT

The 1970s and early 1980s witnessed an explosive growth in the external debt of many developing nations. Since the mid-1980s, most of these countries have experienced difficulties in making the payments required to service their debt. Debt rescheduling—putting off until tomorrow payments that cannot be made today—has been common, and many observers feel that major defaults are inevitable unless ways of forgiving the debt can be found.

The trend to increased debt started when OPEC quadrupled the world price of oil in 1973. Because many developing nations relied on imported oil, their balance of trade moved sharply into deficit. At the same time, the OPEC countries developed massive trade surpluses. Commercial banks helped to *recycle* the deposits of their OPEC customers into loans to the developing nations. These loans financed some necessary adjustments and some worthwhile new investment projects. However, a large part of the funds were used unwisely; wasteful government spending and lavish consumption splurges occurred in many of the borrowing countries.

A doubling of energy prices in 1979 led to a further increase in the debt of developing nations. The severe world recession that began in 1981 reduced demand for the exports of many of these countries. As a result, they were unable to achieve many benefits from the adjustments and investment expenditures that they had made. Furthermore, sharp increases in real interest rates led to increased debt service payments; as a result, many countries could not make their payments.

The lending banks had little choice but to reschedule the debt—essentially, lending the developing nations the money to make interest payments while adding to the principal of the existing loans. The International Monetary Fund played a central role in arranging these reschedulings, by making further loans and concessions conditional on appropriate policies of adjustment and restraint. These conditions were intended to limit wasteful government expenditure and consumption and thus to increase the likelihood that the loans eventually would be repaid. Critics of the IMF's role argued that much of the restraint resulted in reduced investment and, thus, that the IMF's conditions were counterproductive.

During the mid-1980s, the world economy recovered and interest rates fell. As a result, the LDCs' export earnings grew, their debt-service obligations stabilized, and the crisis subsided. The sharp *fall* in the price of oil, which started in late 1985, further eased the problems of the oil-importing nations, but it also created a new debt problem.

Throughout the period of rising energy prices in the 1970s, a number of *oil-exporting* developing nations—including Mexico, Venezuela, and Indonesia—saw in those high prices new opportunities for investment and growth. On the basis of their high oil revenues, their ability to borrow improved. Their external debt grew, and they were able to avoid many of the adjustments that the oil-importing developing nations had been forced to undertake. When oil prices fell, these oil exporters found themselves in very difficult positions. Today, although the debt is no longer rising, it remains an enormous burden on developing nations. Often the borrowed money has produced little or no benefit, going either to develop industries that did not turn out to be viable or to provide graft to the ruling classes. Today those who benefited little or not at all from the funds are saddled with the need to pay taxes to service the debt. This produces an enormous drag on further development.

Development policies[5]

THE past decade has seen a remarkable change in the views of appropriate policies for industrial development. The views that dominated development policies during the period from 1945 to the early 1980s have given way to a new set of views that reflect the experience of the earlier period.

The older view

The dominant views on appropriate development strategies from 1945 to the early 1980s were inward-looking and interventionist.

They were inward-looking in the sense that local industries were fostered primarily to replace imports. These local industries were usually protected with high tariffs (usually well into the three-digit range) and supported by large subsidies and favourable tax treatment. The exchange rate was almost always pegged, usually at an overvalued rate. As we shall see in Chapter 37, fixing the exchange rate above its free-market level raises the prices of exports and lowers the prices of imports, which leads to an excess demand for foreign exchange. The argument for keeping export prices high was that foreign demand for traditional exports was inelastic, so that (as we saw in Chapter 5) raising the prices of such exports would raise the amount received by their sellers. The excess demand for foreign exchange caused by the overvaluation of the currency led to a host of import restrictions and exchange controls, such as import licences and quotas issued by government officials.

Many governments were hostile to foreign investment and made it difficult for multinational firms to locate in their countries. For example, many had local ownership

[5] This section draws heavily from 'Globalization and Developing Countries', main Discussion Paper for the UN Symposium in The Hague, 30 March 1992, report by the Rapporteur.

rules, requiring that any foreign firm wanting to invest there must set up a subsidiary in which local residents would own at least half of the shares. Much new investment was undertaken by government-owned industries, while subsidization of privately owned, local industries was often heavy and indiscriminate. Industrial activity was often controlled, with a licence being required to set up a firm or to purchase supplies of scarce commodities. Much investment was financed by local savings, which were sometimes made voluntarily and sometimes enforced by the government. One way of doing the latter was for a state marketing board to be empowered to buy all the outputs of traditional export industries (such as cocoa in Ghana) at very low prices, sell them abroad at high prices, and use the profits so generated to finance government-owned industries.

This whole battery of measures is often referred to as being *inward looking* and based on *import substitution*. Strictly, 'import substitution' refers to the attempt to build local industries behind protectionist walls to replace imports. Often, however, the term is used to refer to the set of related measures just described.

These interventionist measures gave great power to government officials, and, not surprisingly, corruption was rife. Bribes were needed to obtain many things, including state subsidies, licences, and quotas. As a result, many resources were allocated to those who had the most political power and were willing to pay the highest bribes, rather than to those who could use the resources most efficiently.

Heavy subsidization of private firms and state investment in public firms required much money, and the tax structures of many poor countries could not provide sufficient funds. As a result, *inflationary finance* was often used.[6] Persistent inflation was a major problem in many of these countries. It was almost always in the two-digit range, and quite often soared to figures of several hundred per cent per year.

Most of the economies in which these policies were employed fell short of full central planning and full state ownership of resources. As a result, there was still some private initiative and some profit-seeking through normal market means. But the overall policy thrust was interventionist and inward-looking.

The rise of the new view

During the 1980s, four important events contributed to a reappraisal of this development model. First, developing countries that had followed these policies most faithfully had some of the poorest growth records. Second, the GDP growth rates of the more industrialized countries of Eastern Europe and the Soviet Union that had followed interventionist, non-market approaches to their own growth were visibly falling behind those of the market-based economies. Third, the countries of Taiwan, Singapore, South Korea,

and Hong Kong, which had departed from the accepted model by adopting more market-based policies, were prospering and growing rapidly. Fourth, the globalization of the world's economy led to an understanding that countries could no longer play a full part in world economic growth without a substantial presence of multinational corporations within their boundaries. Given the size of developing countries, this mainly meant the presence of foreign-owned multinationals. We discuss each of these four events in more detail in the next four sections.

THE EXPERIENCE OF THE DEVELOPING COUNTRIES

Highly interventionist economies fared poorly in the 1950s, 1960s, and 1970s. Economies as varied as Argentina, Myanmar, Tanzania, Ethiopia, and Ghana were all interventionist and all grew slowly, if at all. In Ethiopia, the emperor was overthrown, and the new government adopted rigid Soviet-style policies. Attempts to collectivize agriculture led, as they had fifty years earlier in the Soviet Union, to widespread famine. Some countries, such as Ghana and Nigeria, started from relatively strong economic positions when they first gained their independence, only to see their GDPs and living standards shrink. Other countries, such as India and Kenya, sought a middle way between capitalism and communism. They fared better than their more highly interventionist neighbours, but their development was still disappointingly slow.

THE EXPERIENCE OF THE COMMUNIST COUNTRIES

Underdevelopment is as old as civilization. Concern with it as a remediable condition, however, became a compelling policy issue only within the present century. One incentive behind this new attention to development was the apparent success of planned programmes of 'crash' development, of which the Soviet experience was the most remarkable, and the Chinese the most recent. Not surprisingly, therefore, the early successes of the growth policies of many communist countries provided role models for many of the early development policies of the poorer countries. Their governments sought to copy the planning techniques that appeared to underlie these earlier successes.

In recent decades, however, the more developed communist countries began to discover the limitations of their planning techniques. Highly planned government intervention seems most successful in providing infrastructure and developing basic industries, such as electric power and steel—where these are needed, and where the technology

---

[6] Under inflationary finance, the government sells newly created bonds to the central bank, which pays for them with newly created money. The large increase in money supply creates rapid inflation, as we shall see in Chapter 40.

can be copied from more market-oriented economies. It is now seen to be much less successful in providing the entrepreneurial activity, risk-taking, and adaptivity to change that are key ingredients to *sustained* economic growth and technological change.

The discrediting of the Soviet approach to development was given added emphasis when the countries of Eastern Europe and the former Soviet Union abandoned their system *en masse* and took the difficult path of rapidly introducing market economies. Although China, the last major holdout (apart from Cuba and North Korea), has been posting impressive growth figures, two very 'non-communist' reasons are important in explaining this performance. First, over 90 per cent of the population is engaged in basically free-market agriculture—because that sector has long been free of the central planning apparatus that so hampered agriculture in the former Soviet Union. Second, while the state-controlled industries suffer increasing inefficiencies and absorb ever-larger proportions of the state budget in subsidies, a major investment boom is going on in China's south-east coastal provinces. Here foreign investment, largely from Japan and the Asian NIEs, is introducing a rapidly growing, and highly efficient, industrialized market sector.[7]

THE EXPERIENCE OF THE NIEs

South Korea, Taiwan, Hong Kong, and Singapore are often called the Asian Tigers. All four have turned themselves from poor countries to relatively high-income, industrialized countries in the course of less than 40 years.

During the early stages of their development, their governments used import restrictions to build up local industries and to develop labour forces having the requisite skills and experiences. In the 1950s and early 1960s, however, each of the four abandoned many of the interventionist aspects of the older development model. They created market-oriented economies with less direct government intervention than other developing economies, who stuck with the accepted development model.

Korea and Singapore did not adopt a *laissez-faire* stance. Instead, both followed quite strong policies which targeted specific areas for development and encouraged those areas with various economic incentives. Hong Kong and Taiwan, in contrast, have had somewhat more *laissez-faire* attitudes towards the direction of industrial development.

After local industries had been established, all four of these countries adopted outward-looking, market-based, export-oriented policies. This tested the success of various policies to encourage specific industries by their ability to compete in the international market-place. With industries designed to serve a sheltered home market, it is all too easy to shelter inefficiency more or less indefinitely. With export-oriented policies *not based on subsidies,* the success of targeted firms and industries is tested in international

markets, and unprofitable firms fail.

Each country has experienced great successes and some failures of policy. Taiwan was typical in demonstrating the value of the new market-oriented approach when, in the period 1956–60, following the advice of the Western-trained Chinese economist S. C. Tsiang, they abandoned most of the apparatus of the older development model and moved to market-oriented policies. Before long their growth rate increased, and they started on a path that has taken them from a per capita GDP of about 10 per cent of that of the United States in 1955 to one of close to 50 per cent in the early 1990s. Today Taiwan has become a major foreign investor as its less skill-intensive industries migrate to mainland China and other locations in Southeast Asia. In Taiwan, wages are rising, making low-skill-intensive manufacturing uneconomic and pushing local industries to higher-value-added lines of production which can support higher wages and hence higher living standards for the workers.

Not far behind the NIEs is a second generation of Asian and Latin American countries which have also adopted more market-oriented policies and have seen substantial growth follow; Indonesia, Thailand, the Philippines, Mexico, Chile, and Argentina are examples. Even Vietnam and Laos are liberalizing their economies as communist governments come to accept that a market economy is a necessary condition for sustained economic growth.

GLOBALIZATION OF TRADE AND INVESTMENT BY TRANSNATIONALS

We discussed globalization briefly in Chapter 1; you may find it useful to reread the discussion on pp. 23–4 at this time.

At the heart of globalization lies the rapid reduction in transportation costs and the revolution in information technology that has characterized the last two decades. One consequence has been that the internal organization of firms, whether multinational or not, is changing to become less hierarchial and rigid, and more decentralized and fluid. Another consequence is that the strategies of transnational corporations (TNCs), which span national borders in their organizational structures, are driving globalization and much of economic development. Because most trade, and much investment, is undertaken by TNCs, no country can

---

[7] Karl Marx predicted that the state would wither away under communism, whereas it actually became ever more powerful. Ironically, communism may be withering away in China (rather than being swept away in one grand gesture, as it was in Eastern Europe). If the Communist government there continues to turn a blind eye to the growth of foreign investment and market-oriented production in its coastal regions, the government will soon be unable to eliminate this dynamic sector because it will be generating too large a proportion of China's GDP and employment. In contrast, the state-owned industries continue to languish, requiring ever larger subsidies merely to keep their inefficient operations in existence.

develop into an integrated part of the world economy without a substantial presence of TNCs within its borders. This is now recognized, and most aspiring developing countries generally put out a welcome mat for TNCs. A few countries, such as India, still put obstacles in the way of foreign investment; but even in these cases, the attitudes are softening so that foreign investment is increasingly tolerated, and even encouraged.

In industries that sell undifferentiated products such as steel and paper, and in industries with substantial scale economies such as aircraft, production tends to be concentrated in the home country while the output is exported. In contrast, foreign direct investment (FDI) tends to be high in industries selling differentiated products not subject to major scale economies, which includes many consumers goods. The FDI allows the local market to be served with suitable product variations and often creates multi-directional trade in different varieties of the same basic product, much of which is intrafirm trade.

TNCs increasingly operate in high-tech sectors, in complex manufacturing, and in services. TNCs that produce in these sectors tend to concentrate in countries where the productivity of capital is high, the business environment is favourable, and other investors are present. This FDI is often undertaken by domestic firms that have built up some advantage in the local market, such as patents and know-how, that gives them advantages when they move into foreign markets.

Although some countries, such as Japan and Taiwan, did industrialize without major infusions of FDI, they did so before the globalization of the world's economy. It is doubtful that many (or any) of today's poor countries could achieve sustained, rapid growth paths without a substantial amount of FDI brought in by foreign-owned transnationals. Without such FDI, both the transfer of technology and foreign networking would be difficult to achieve.

Developing countries have gradually come to accept the advantages in dropping their traditional hostility to foreign direct investment. First, the FDI often provides somewhat higher-paying jobs than might otherwise be available to local inhabitants. Second, it provides investment that does not have to be financed by local savings. Third, it links the local economy into the world economy in ways that would be hard to accomplish by new firms of a purely local origin. Fourth, it provides training in worker and management skills that come from working with large firms linked into the global market. Fifth, it can provide advanced technology that is not easily transferred outside of the firms that are already familiar with its use.

Today virtually all developing economies encourage foreign TNCs to locate within their borders. Where governments used to worry that their countries had too much FDI, they now worry that there may be too little.

Elements of the new view

As a result of the above experiences, a new consensus on development policy has emerged. The revised model calls for a more *outward-looking, international-trade-oriented, market-incentive-based, route to development*. It calls for accepting market prices as an instrument for the allocation of resources. This means abandoning both the heavy subsidization and the pervasive regulations that characterized the older approach.

One of the most important parts of this new consensus is an acceptance of the beneficial role played by competition (in its broadest sense) as a defender of the public interest and as a stimulus to growth-creating innovation. The other side of the coin is a recognition of the harmful role played by monopolies (in the broadest sense), whether of private firms, closed-shop union agreements, communications media, government institutions, or government-owned industries.

Another important part of the consensus is that it is more efficient to locate economic activities in the private rather than the public sector (unless there are compelling reasons for doing otherwise, as there may be with a range of 'social services' such as medical and hospital care). Some of the reasons that lie behind this presumption are: (1) the incentives for efficiency when managers are responsible to owners who are risking their own wealth; (2) the constraint provided by the need to be profitable, which acts as a rapid cutoff device when failure is evident; and (3) the corrective for inefficiency provided by the possibility of a hostile takeover.

Another part of the new consensus concerns those activities that are required of the government. Two basic classes of activity are important. First, the government needs to provide a framework for the market economy, which is given by such things as well defined property rights secure from arbitrary confiscation; security and enforcement of contracts; law and order; a sound money; ensuring the basic rights of the individual to locate, sell, and invest where, and how, he or she decides; and the provision of infrastructure.

Second, state activity is needed to resolve conflicts of interest, to handle market failures, and to redistribute income in line with currently accepted ideas of social justice. Redistributive policies cannot be judged in isolation (nor can growth policies). Instead, they must be constantly scrutinized for their impacts on growth, and, where these are significant, trade-offs need to be consciously made.

The new view has many aspects, and we can discuss only a few of the most important. The first concerns the changed attitude to foreign direct investment undertaken by TNCs. FDI is now understood to be capable of changing a country's comparative advantages and of improving its competitiveness in many ways.

THE IMPORTANCE OF FDI

FDI provides a major source of capital. This capital tends to be allocated to areas where experienced international operators feel that their chances of success are best. The capital brings with it up-to-date technology, which would be hard to develop domestically or even to transfer to home-owned firms. It would be difficult to generate this capital through domestic savings and, if it were so generated, it would be difficult to import the necessary technology from abroad. The modern growth research discussed in Chapter 33 has shown that the transfer of technology to firms with no previous experience of using it is a far more difficult, risky, and expensive task than was formerly thought. Also, when capital is obtained through loans or grants from foreign governments, there is a risk that its allocation will be in the hands of administrators inexperienced in commercial activities and motivated by political concerns.

Over a long period of time, FDI creates many externalities in the form of benefits available to the whole economy which the TNCs cannot appropriate as part of their own income.

These include transfers of general knowledge and of specific technologies in production and distribution, industrial upgrading, work experience on the part of the labour force, the introduction of modern management and accounting methods, the establishment of finance-related and trading networks, and the upgrading of telecommunications services. FDI in services affects the host country's absolute advantage and competitiveness by raising the productivity of capital and enabling host countries to attract new capital on favourable terms, and by creating services that can be used as strategic inputs in the traditional export sector to expand the volume of trade and to upgrade production through product and process innovation.

In today's world, the competitiveness of a country appears to be affected less and less by its relative factor endowments and the inherent abilities of its labour, and increasingly by the nature of its investment. It is difficult to compete in globalized trade without being a part of the vast, informal but powerful network of information and communications among TNCs.

By altering a country's comparative advantages and improving its competitiveness through technology transfer and the effects of myriad externalities, foreign as well as domestic investment can alter a country's volume and pattern of trade in many income-enhancing directions.

THE WASHINGTON CONSENSUS

What John Williamson of the Institute for International Economics in Washington, DC, has called the Washington Consensus describes the conditions that, according to the newer views, are necessary for a poorer country to get itself on a path of sustained development. These views are accepted by a number of international agencies, including the World Bank, the IMF, and several UN organizations. The main elements of this consensus are as follows.

1. Sound fiscal policies are required. Large budget deficits financed by bonds sold to the central bank can lead to rapid inflation and financial instability. For example, Brazil ended an excellent growth performance largely as a result of unsound macro policies.

2. The tax base should be broad, and marginal rates should be moderate.

3. Markets should be allowed to determine prices and the allocation of resources. Policies designed to affect resource allocation should work through price incentives rather than either the principles of a command economy (as described in Chapter 1) or price-distorting interventions. Exchange rates should be determined by market forces. Trade liberalization is desirable; in particular, import licensing, with its potential for corruption, should be avoided.

4. The desirability of free trade, however, is subject to the qualification of the infant industry justification discussed in Chapter 26. This allows targeted protection for specific industries and a moderate general tariff, say, 10–20 per cent, to provide a bias towards widening the industrial base of a less-developed country. Such protection should be for a specified period that is not easily extended.

5. In today's world, however, measures to insulate the home market by domestic protection should be held to the minimum possible consistent with developing strategic clusters of new industries. Industrial development should rely to an important extent on local firms and on attracting FDI and subjecting it to a minimum of local restrictions that discriminate between local and foreign firms. (Of course, restrictions will be required for such things as environmental policies, but these should apply to all firms, whether foreign-owned or locally owned.)

6. An export orientation provides a powerful impetus to the development of national capabilities (as long as exports do not rely on permanent subsidies). It provides competitive incentives for the building of skills and technologies geared to world markets; it permits the realization of scale economies; it furnishes the foreign exchange required for needed imports of capital; and it provides access to valuable information flows from buyers and competitors in advanced countries.

7. Education, health (especially for the disadvantaged), and infrastructure investment are desirable forms of public expenditure. Creating the appropriate factors of production is critical to creating comparative advantages in products that can be exported. This means general education,

trade schools, and other appropriate institutions for formal education as well as assistance to increase on-the-job training within firms. Because future demands are hard to predict and subject to rapid change, a balance must be struck between training for specific skills and training to develop generalized, and adaptive, abilities.

8. Finally, emphasis needs to be placed on the reduction of poverty, for at least two reasons. First, poverty can exert powerful anti-growth effects. People living in poverty will not develop the skills to provide an attractive labour force, and they may not even respond to incentives when these are provided; malnutrition in early childhood can affect a person's capacities for life. Second, although economic growth tends to reduce the incidence of poverty, it does not eliminate it. Commonly accepted views of equity call for some of the benefits of growth to be made available to those who do not gain from it through the normal operations of the market. Self-interest calls for avoiding growing inequality in the distribution of income as those who benefit from growth (including employed workers) enjoy rising incomes, while major groups are untouched by the growth process and suffer static or declining incomes.

Debate beyond the Washington Consensus

The basic Washington Consensus on outward-looking, market-oriented, fiscally sound economic policies provides what many people believe are necessary conditions for a country to achieve a sustained growth path in today's world—which in most cases will require that it is able to attract quite a large volume of FDI.

The policies suggested by the Washington Consensus relate primarily to the behaviour of governments themselves.

SUFFICIENT OR JUST NECESSARY?

There is substantial debate around one crucial issue: are the conditions of the Washington Consensus *sufficient* to encourage the kinds and volumes of both domestic and foreign investments needed to develop dynamic comparative advantages in higher-value-added industries, or are they merely necessary?

Some observers believe that they are sufficient. In their view, all a country needs to do is to meet these conditions; then domestic savings will finance domestic investments, FDI will flow in, and a sustained growth path will be established. Other economists worry that many countries may have only limited ability (1) to attract FDI, (2) to benefit from it, and (3) to create sufficient domestic investment, even after fulfilling the necessary conditions of the

Washington Consensus. The latter set of economists point to the experience of some African countries in which TNCs operated extractive industries, which despoiled the countryside and left little permanent benefit behind them; the corporations merely extracted the available resources and then left. Others point out that there is a major difference between pure extractive enterprises and manufacturing enterprises, the latter having more potential spillovers to the local economy than the former.

What does happen after the conditions of the consensus are fulfilled will depend partly on the existing endowments of the country in question. If large supplies of natural resources or cheap, reasonably well educated labour are available, fulfilling these conditions may be sufficient. Those who call for policies beyond those of the Washington Consensus argue that for some countries a past history of non-growth, plus the absence of externalities that go with a reasonably developed industrial sector, may call for the government to adopt a more active set of *integrated* trade, technology-transfer, and innovation policies. This set of policies would be aimed at encouraging the development of human and technological capabilities and building international competitiveness.

Policies that go beyond the Washington Consensus are directed at *the interactions between governments and the private sector*, particularly as represented by TNCs.

They relate, in British economist John Dunning's words, to the 'interface between the global strategies of TNCs designed to advance corporate profitability and growth, and the strategies of national governments intended to promote the economic and social welfare of their citizens'.

IMPLICATIONS OF MODERN GROWTH THEORY

What is at issue in the debate just described is related to the newer views on economic growth that were discussed in Chapter 33 and that are now gaining acceptance among many economists. The key new view is that *endogenous* technological innovation is the mainspring of economic growth. Things emphasized by economists for centuries, such as aggregate savings and investment, are still essential, but technological change is now seen to lie at the core of the growth process.

As we saw in Chapter 33, technological change is a costly process, one that is undertaken mainly by firms in pursuit of profit and that responds to economic incentives. Research and development are in their nature highly risky and highly uncertain activities. The technological path followed by firms and industries is evolutionary in the sense that it develops as experiments and errors are made.

For developing countries, one of the most important of the many new insights stemming from research into the growth process is that adopting someone else's technology

BOX 34.1

The importance of diffusion

In the past, one reason for making a clear distinction between the economics of developed and developing countries arose from the belief that advanced countries grew by innovating in new technologies, while poorer countries grew by copying technologies from the advanced countries—i.e. from the diffusion of technologies that had been fully developed in the advanced countries. If this were so, then the economics of growth in advanced countries would be the economics of innovation, while the economics of growth in poorer countries would be the economics of diffusion. This view was in line with early theories of technological change, which assumed that a new technology was invented and put in place in fully developed form by some innovator and that its use then diffused in more or less unchanged form to other firms, industries, and countries.

Modern research into invention, diffusion, and innovation has shown that this clear line does not exist in reality. A new technology almost always comes into existence in rudimentary form and operates at high cost. As the technology is used, it is developed continually, and its costs of operation fall while the quality of its performance and the range of its application rise.

For example, electronic computers were first developed for military applications during the early 1940s. By modern standards, these early computers were extremely limited in what they could do and were both slow and costly in doing it. When the first commercial applications were developed at the end of the Second World War, the world demand was thought to be for about 12 computers! The efficiency of computers was increased slowly over the decades, and it made a quantum leap when transistors were substituted for vacuum tubes as the switching device. At the same time, the costs were lowered and the range of applications was increased as computers became more varied and more flexible. These were not small improvements but orders-of-magnitude changes occurring every few years. Today, the product that was a technological curiosity 50 years ago is revolutionizing all of production, distribution, design, and just about every other economic activity.

A similar story can be told about the airplane. Its modern story began in 1903 with the first heavier-than-air flight (covering less than 100 yards). The airplane first became really suc-cessful commercially in 1936 with the introduction of the DC3. It improved through slow design changes and discontinuous innovations, such as the replacement of piston engines with jets, until by the 1970s it had become the dominant method of trans-porting people over long distances.

What is true of computers and aircraft is true of most major inventions. They typically begin in crude form with one or two applications; they then slowly diffuse through the economy; and as they diffuse, they are developed into more and more diverse, sophisticated, and efficient forms.

So the diffusion of technologies is not a flow that goes just from advanced to less advanced nations. Diffusion is a key part of technological change in advanced as well as developing nations and it follows similar patterns in each.

In any one high-income nation, most of the technological advances that come into use have been originally developed in other nations. Indeed, a small subset of the advanced nations do most of the development of fundamental new technologies which then diffuse to other high-income countries, being adapted and improved in the process.

It is true that a country just beginning to move from a subsis-tence to a market economy can grow quickly by adopting tech-noligies developed elsewhere (and adapting them to local conditions), but it is not true that the world's growth problems can be understood simply in terms of the conditions needed to invent technologies in rich countries and those needed to copy them in poor countries. Since many of the processes that govern the flow of technology and capital between rich and poor coun-tries also govern the flows among rich countries (and among sectors in each rich country), it is clear that many problems will be similar in the two groups of countries. Of course, institution-al arrangements will affect the diffusion and improvement of both major and minor innovations in developing countries. But they also do so in developed countries where forces such as com-petition policy, industrial concentration, national attitudes to risk-taking, support of R&D, and the organization of university research are thought to influence the development and diffusion of new technologies.

---

is not a simple, costless task. Substantial R&D capacity is needed to adapt other people's technology to one's own purposes, and to learn how to use it. For one reason, much of the knowledge required to use a technology is tacit; it can be obtained only from learning by doing and learning by using. This creates difficulties in imitating the knowledge, as well as uncertainty regarding which modifications will work in any new situation. This is true even when technol-ogy moves from one firm to another in the same industry and the same country. The problems are greater when tech-nology moves across industrial or national borders. The difficulties of adopting new technologies also become more difficult the more complex and information-intensive the technology becomes.

It follows that all knowledge is not freely tradable. Neither a firm nor a government can go out and buy it ready to use. Acquiring *working* technological knowledge requires both investment (sometimes in large, indivisible lumps) and the experience that allows workers and man-agement slowly to acquire the needed tacit knowledge.

Usable new knowledge comes to a less developed country through a slow, costly diffusion process.

The above discussion emphasizes the new understanding that diffusion is neither free, nor easy, nor instantaneous. Box 34.1 deals with another change in economists' understanding of diffusion: it is a key part of the growth process in all countries, whether they are developed or developing.

WHAT MAY BE NEEDED

The above view of technological change suggests to some economists a major reason why active government policies that go beyond the Washington Consensus may be needed. These would do more than just attract FDI and create favourable market conditions. It is argued that some countries have achieved this much but then got little technological spin-off from the TNCs to the local economy. When the TNCs subsequently moved away, little of lasting benefit was left behind. To avoid this result, the policies would be designed to encourage the diffusion of technological capacities into the local economy so that all parts of the economy could benefit and grow. For this, public assistance may well be necessary. This was provided in varying degrees by the governments of all four of the Asian Tigers.

Such policies work by developing the externalities that come from initial investment in the local economy, and that give benefits not captured by the firms that help to confer them. The policies also take account of the fact that technology is not bought in competitive markets and imported ready to go.

Experience suggests, however, that the appropriate set of policies is usually highly country-specific. What works well in one environment may fail in another. Many local details need to be assessed before appropriate policies can be designed for one country. These depend, among many other things, on location, size of economy, existing natural and human resources, infrastructure, social and cultural attitudes, and development stage.

Protection of the domestic market Such policies can work at the early stages by establishing a protected domestic market through tariffs and other import restrictions. Virtually every country that has moved to a sustained growth path in the past, including the United States, Canada, Japan, and all of the NIEs, has done so using import substitution in its early stages of industrialization. A protected home market provides a possible solution to the problem of coping with the enormous externalities involved in building up an infrastructure of physical and human capital as well as the required tacit knowledge and abilities. Even if not all the specific infants that are protected by the import substitution policy grow into self-sufficient adults, the externalities may still be created and become available for a second generation of more profitable firms.

Protection of the home market from international competition can, however, pose serious problems unless it is selective and temporary. Investment may occur mainly in areas where comparative advantage never develops. High costs of protected industries may create a lack of competitiveness of other domestic industries whose inputs are the outputs of the protected industries. Some potential comparative advantages may not be exploited because of the distorting effects of existing tariffs, and—as always—consumers bear much of the cost in terms of high prices of protected outputs.

Innovation policies Trade restrictions do not provide the only route to building an industrial and R&D capacity by encouraging technological diffusion and creating structural competitiveness. Other methods include the much-needed public investment in infrastructure and human capital and many other things, such as the provision of adequate financial schemes to favour investment in physical and intangible assets; procurement and tax incentives; provision of technical and marketing information; consulting services for assisting firms in industrial restructuring and in the adoption of new technologies and organizational techniques; support services in design, quality assurance, and standards; schemes for training and retraining personnel; and facilities for start-up companies.

Those who advocate such a policy package stress the importance of having the above incentives as a part of a more general innovation and competition policy in order to encourage technological transfer to the local economy. (Such transfers are riddled with market failures arising from their externalities.) Linkages among firms, and between firms and universities and research institutions, both within the country and with the rest of the world, are also important.

Policies that encourage the development of small and medium-sized enterprises are important to any development strategy. These tend to be locally owned and to be the vehicle by which know-how and best practices are transferred from TNCs to the local economy. They are also in the sector most vulnerable to excessive red tape, rules and regulations, profit taxes, and other interferences that raise the cost of doing business. This issue is discussed further in Box 34.2.

A cautionary note There is no doubt that the governments of many poor countries have been highly interventionist—and some still are. Thus, a good first strategy is often to diminish the government's place in the economy. There is no point adopting a new, relatively rational, technology-promotion strategy if existing government interventions are irrational and heavy. What is then needed is to clear away the unproductive interventions first. This does not demonstrate, however, that, if a government were starting from scratch, the best objective would be to minimize its place in the economy.

BOX 34.2

Rediscovering the middle of Africa

A recent article in *The Economist,* under the above box title, reports on a discussion paper called 'Africa's Entrepreneurs', written for the International Finance Corporation by Keith Marsden.

This article argues that many countries are learning that private-sector entrepreneurs are often a better engine of economic growth than is public-sector investment. These countries are also learning that it is important to reduce growth-inhibiting tax policies.

Development economists sometimes . . . complain about a 'missing middle': Africa, they say, has vast state companies and thousands of subsistence hustlers, but virtually nobody in between.

During the 1980s two-thirds of the countries south of the Sahara embarked on the market-freeing policies advocated by the IMF and the World Bank. They received more than US$1 billion a year in aid. Yet private capital has fled. After nearly a decade of reforming, some wonder if banks and businesses will ever return.

For the foreseeable future, few foreign companies are likely to invest in Africa to produce for the local market. It is simply too poor: the continent's combined GDP is a tenth of that of the seven countries of Eastern Europe.

Yet some countries have managed to attract investment aimed at export markets. Mauritania has drawn in so much that it no longer depends on huge injections of aid.

There are plenty of Africans running medium-sized firms. Botswana (population 1.1m) has 13 competing manufacturers of metal furniture; Tanzania has 5,000 registered road-transport companies.

These medium-sized African firms are efficient. A World Bank study in Kenya in 1986 found that private, Kenyan-owned enterprises earned an average return of 20%, compared with 18% for foreign private firms and 15% for public enterprises.

Entrepreneurs bring more expertise and motivation to such work than government consultants. Public funds, Mr Marsden suggests, are better spent on tax incentives that promote the private sector. In Botswana, for example, new investment projects attract tax relief and selective wage subsidies. This is probably the biggest reason why private employment has grown much faster there than in the highly taxed Ivory Coast.

Mr Marsden's main recommendation is for more lending to go to entrepreneurs rather than to governments. Many standard sorts of finance are denied to African businessmen: stock exchanges are scarce; banks lend according to a client's assets, rather than judging his business's potential. On top of all that, government borrowing often crowds out private requests— from institutions both domestic and foreign.

(*The Economist,* 8 December 1991)

Whatever methods are chosen, selective intervention is a delicate instrument, highly dangerous when used by inept hands; even when in practised hands, much damage can be done.

The intervention needs to be carefully tailored to get specific results and to reduce the opportunities for small groups to gain at the expense of others, and most assistance should, as a rule, be terminated after specified periods of time. It is also important to leave room for the market to generate, and support, unforeseen opportunities.

Box 34.3 provides a case study of South Korea's experience with some of the policies that go beyond the Washington Consensus.

Conclusion

According to the World Bank's *World Development Report* of 1991, about 1.1 billion residents of the developing countries were in poverty in the year 1985. In reviewing this report, *The Economist* argued: 'With luck and a lot of policy changes in rich and poor countries alike, that figure might be cut to about 800 million by the year 2000.'[8] That may not seem like a large change at first sight, but it is when put into the perspective of the rapidly growing world population; the 1.1 billion that the World Bank reckoned to be in poverty in 1985 made up about one-third of the developing countries' total population; the 800 million would be only 18 per cent of the estimated population of these same countries in the year 2000. The predicted change would substantially reduce the probability that a person born into the developing world in 2000 would be born into poverty and condemned to a life of acute deprivation.

According to *The Economist,* the World Bank's prescriptions fall into two categories:

Create new economic opportunities for the poor. Since the poor's main source of income is what they are paid for their labour, this means promoting labour-intensive economic growth.

Equip the poor to grasp these opportunities. This calls for adequate provision of basic social services such as primary education, health and family planning.

[8] All quotations from *The Economist* in this section are from 21 July 1991.

BOX 34.3

South Korea's development policy: a case study*

In the late 1950s South Korea seemed unable to generate adequate levels of exports and savings. Policy-makers solicited foreign aid and sought to manage the flow of imports. The currency was overvalued at a fixed rate on the foreign exchange market, tariff rates were high, and quantitative import restrictions abounded. These policies, which discouraged exports and encouraged import substitution, were close to the old model of appropriate development policy discussed in the text.

The economy was dominated by agriculture and mining, and the manufacturing sector supplied only simple consumer products. Exports amounted to about 3 per cent of GNP and consisted almost entirely of primary products and various minerals.

Then came policy reforms that stretched over several years, starting in 1960. These centred on fostering exports from both existing and new industries.

Today South Korea is dominated by its manufacturing sector. Major industries established since 1960 range from chemicals and electronics to cars and heavy electrical equipment. Exports exceed 40 per cent of GNP, with manufactured products constituting over 90 per cent of the total.

Existing industries

For well established industries, the reforms ensured that production for export would be no less profitable than production for the domestic market. This was accomplished by insulating export activity from the adverse consequences of policies motivated by domestic concerns.

Capital and intermediate inputs used in export production could be imported without tariffs and were not bound by the quotas that applied to imports for other purposes. Tradable inputs were exempt from indirect taxes. Exchange was managed at rates that were no longer overvalued.

The government enabled exporters to borrow working capital from state-owned banks in proportion to their export activity. Additional incentives were granted in the form of direct tax reductions, preferential interest rates, and privileged access to import licences. The export incentives were administered fairly uniformly across all industries. They were granted equally to 'indirect exports'—inputs produced and sold domestically for ultimate use in export production. (This policy was a major innovation rarely found in developing nations.)

The government also used publicly announced, quarterly export targets for individual commodities, markets, and firms. At a minimum, the targets have been useful in keeping the government well informed about export performance so that timely changes could be made in incentives.

These measures seem on balance to have been neutral among specific established export industries. They encouraged exports in general without the need for specific 'winners' having to be picked in advance. No doubt, however, the policies encouraged producers to move to the export sector from the competing import sector, where the distortional policies still applied.

New industries

The South Korean government has selectively intervened to promote targeted infant industries, typically by supporting the creation of large-scale establishments that were accorded temporary monopolies and received access to credit on preferential terms, as well as exemptions from most taxes (including tariffs).

Traditionally, it is protection of non-export sales that has been the dominant incentive to infant industries. Targeted industries have been protected by import controls, which have enabled them to practise discriminatory pricing. Export targeting requires that infant industries sell a swiftly growing proportion of their output at world prices, either as direct or indirect exports. This forces them to increase productivity rapidly.

The first producers of fertilizer, petrochemicals, and refined petroleum products in South Korea were public-owned enterprises. So was the first integrated steel mill, which is generally considered to be one of the most efficient mills in the world. New public enterprises have been expected to achieve international competitiveness quickly. They have been managed as autonomous profit-seeking entities and have contributed to government revenues.

The contribution of industrial policy

The South Korean experience shows that industrial policy can work. Selective intervention seems to have contributed to the nation's remarkable success by accelerating the rate of growth with little if any compensating loss in efficiency.

The enormous uncertainty involved in selecting infant industries for promotion was resolved by using information gained during the implementation of the industries to evaluate intentions, and by judging new industries on their ability to export (in a regime in which export promotion policies were neutral with respect to specific exports).

Viewing this apparently successful experience, an economist will naturally ask: what South Korean market failures has selective intervention successfully overcome?

Some economists argue that market imperfections associated with technological transfer are unimportant because less developed countries face an abundant supply of available technology. But (as we have seen in the text of Chapters 33 and 34) elements of technology are far from being perfectly tradable. Moreover, the tacitness of much technology creates problems in communication over long distances and across social boundaries, problems that can be overcome only at substantial cost:

BOX 34.3 *continued*

....

1. The tacitness of much knowledge makes some elements inherently non-tradable. Peculiarities in local resources, institutions, and local technological practices cannot be understood without being experienced.

2. Because of the imperfect tradability of technology, externalities related to technological development can be quite extensive. There are economies of scope in the application of many of the capabilities acquired in the course of industrialization.

3. An entrant's initial investment to master new technology may greatly reduce costs for subsequent entrants located nearby. The returns to particular technological efforts may be largely inappropriable because a significant share of them derives from the application of the newly acquired element in a cascade of subsequent technological changes.

In short, if used appropriately, selective intervention seems able to increase a country's ability to capture dynamic economies associated with the introduction and exploitation of modern technology.

Lessons

South Korea's industrial performance owes much to the gov-

ernment's reliance on free-market institutions to provide for flexibility in resource allocation. It has resulted in many highly profitable ventures that either were not foreseen or were not actively promoted by the government.

But South Korea's industrial performance also owes a great deal to the government's promotional policies towards exports and to its initiatives in targeting industries for development. Selective intervention has driven the fast-paced evolution of South Korea's industrial structure by fostering vertical integration at the national level and by promoting greater diversification of end-product mix.

The belief that selective intervention has outlived its usefulness has now led the South Korean government to alter its policies. Selective intervention has lost the support of the South Korean public, who prefer democratic government to economically enlightened dictatorship. The trend appears to be away from selective intervention, and it remains to be seen whether South Korea's economic performance will continue to be exceptional.

* This box is based on Larry E. Westphal, 'Industrial Policy in an Export-Propelled Economy: Lessons from South Korea's Experience', *Journal of Economic Perspectives*, Summer 1990.

The Bank also points out that one of the most damaging economic distortions in many developing countries is excessive taxation of farming. This hits the very part of the economy upon which most of the poor depend for their livelihood.

In sub-Saharan (i.e., black) Africa, 53 per cent of the population was above the poverty line while only 56 per cent of the current young attended primary school. This suggests that few of the poorer children were attending. Higher education is utilized almost exclusively by the middle- and upper-income groups. Commenting on these facts, *The Economist* argued:

It might, at first sight, seem crazy to argue that fees for education and hospital care are a good way to help the poor. In developing countries, however, they can indeed serve this purpose. If governments recovered the cost of higher education and hospital health-care from consumers, they would not be hurting the poor because they never set foot in universities and hospitals. The revenue could then be used for spending that really would help the poor—like better provision of cheap primary education and village health-posts. It used to be claimed that economic growth hurt the poor—a claim since disproved by the success of the Asian Tigers. Labour-intensive growth helps the poor, rest assured. However, governments do have a trade-off to wrestle with—not between overall growth and the well-being of the poor, but between the poor and the not-poor.

The World Bank's report and *The Economist*'s commentary suggest that a major reduction in poverty is possible worldwide. What is needed is the acceptance of the new consensus on the importance of market determination and of reducing state control and state ownership of business activity. This, plus a large dose of enlightened policies to bring education, health, and jobs to ordinary people and improved technology to the nations' firms, could pay enormous dividends in reducing poverty and suffering. The next decade will show how much of that hopeful potential will be realized.

....

Summary

1 About one-fourth of the world's population still exists at a level of bare subsistence, and nearly three-fourths are poor by US standards. Although some poorer societies have grown rapidly, the gap between the very richest and the very poorest remains large and is not decreasing.

2 Impediments to economic development include excessive population growth; resource limitations; inefficient use of resources, particularly those that are related to X-inefficiency; inadequate infrastructure; excessive govern-

ment intervention; and institutional and cultural patterns that make economic growth difficult.

3 The older model for development policies included (*a*) heavy tariff barriers and a hostility to foreign direct investment to protect the home market for local firms; (*b*) many government controls over, and subsidization of, local activities; and (*c*) exchange rates pegged at overly high values with imports regulated by licences.

4 During the 1980s, many governments became sceptical of this model after observing (*a*) the poor growth performances both of the planned economies and of those developing countries that adhered closely to this model; (*b*) the good performances of those who did not follow the model; and (*c*) the globalization of the world economy, which made transnational corporations and foreign direct investment increasingly important. Today, no developing country can play a part in the global trading system without some significant presence of TNCs within its borders.

5 The newer view holds that: (*a*) heavy indiscriminate protection of home markets should be avoided; (*b*) protection that does exist should be targeted to sectors that have a real chance of creating comparative advantage, and the protection should be for only a moderate period of time so that market tests of success and failure can be allowed to operate; (*c*) competition is an important spur to efficiency and innovation; (*d*) quantitative controls should be avoided and exchange rates set at a market-clearing value; and (*e*) production of most goods and services should be in the private sector, except where there are strong reasons for preferring the public sector, as might be the case in, say, medical and health services.

6 Part of this new view is given in the Washington Consensus, which calls for (*a*) sound fiscal and monetary policies; (*b*) broadly based taxes, levied at moderate rates; (*c*) market determination of prices and quantities; (*d*) discriminating use of infant industry protection for moderate time periods; (*e*) an acceptance of FDI and the presence of TNCs; (*f*) active government provision of education, health care, and infrastructure; and (*g*) anti-poverty programmes to help in human resource development and to aid those who are left behind by the growth process.

7 An active debate turns on whether the conditions of the Washington Consensus are sufficient, or just necessary, to establish a country on a sustained growth path. Those who regard it as sufficient feel that, once unleashed, natural market forces will create sustained growth.

8 Those who regard the conditions of the Washington Consensus as just necessary point to substantial externalities and pervasive market failures in the diffusion of technological knowledge from advanced to less advanced nations. They argue that foreign firms will not invest enough because they cannot capture in their profits many of the benefits they confer on the local economy (externalities) and that much of the technological know-how will not diffuse to local firms because such knowledge is not easy to transfer (market failure). These economists call for active government innovation policies to augment investment and to assist in the transfer of technological know-how and practice to the local economy.

Topics for review

- Barriers to development
- The vicious circle of poverty
- The NIEs
- TNCs and FDI
- The Washington Consensus
- Externalities and market failures in the diffusion of technology

PART NINE

Money, Banking, and Monetary Policy

❧ CHAPTER 35

The nature of money and monetary institutions

WHAT is the significance of money to the economy, and how did it come to play its present role? Many people believe that money is one of the more important things in life, and that there is never enough of it. Yet economists argue that increasing the world's money supply would not make the average person better off. Although money allows those who have it to buy someone else's output, the total amount of goods and services available for everyone to buy depends on the total output produced, not on the total amount of money that people possess. In the terminology of Chapter 32, an increase in the quantity of money will not increase the level of potential national income, Y^*.

In this chapter we do two important things. First, we discuss how money evolved and what role it plays in assisting economic activity. Secondly, we introduce some of the institutions that make up the monetary and financial sector of the economy. The most important of these sets of institutions for macroeconomics is the banking sector, because this has an important role in the determination of the money supply.

THE CLASSICAL VIEW

In the eighteenth century, economists articulated the independence of Y^* from monetary factors in terms of an economic theory that distinguished sharply between the 'real sector of economy' and the 'monetary sector'. This approach led to a view of the economy that is now referred to as the *classical dichotomy,* which meant that the real sector of the economy (the production and consumption of real goods and services) could be analysed separately from the monetary sector. In other words, economic forces originating in the monetary sector did not affect real activity.

According to these so-called classical economists, the allocation of resources, and hence the determination of real national income, is fully determined in the real sector. Further, they argued that it is *relative prices,* including the level of wages relative to the price of commodities, rather than money (nominal) prices, that matter for this process.

According to the classical economists, the allocation of resources, and the determination of real national income, depends only on relative prices.

These early economists argued that the price *level* is determined in the monetary sector of the economy. If the quantity of money were doubled, *other things being equal,* the prices of all commodities and money incomes would double. Relative prices would remain unchanged, and the real sector would be unaffected.

According to the classical economists, an increase in the money supply leads to a proportionate increase in all money prices, with no change in the allocation of resources or the level of real national income.

The doctrine that the quantity of money influences the level of money prices but has no effect on the real part of the economy is called the **neutrality of money**. Because early economists believed that the most important questions— How much does the economy produce? What share of it does each group in the society get?—were answered in the real sector, they spoke of money as a 'veil' behind which occurred the real events that affected material well-being. Of course, if the classical view were correct, we would not need to study monetary factors in trying to explain the determination of real national income.

THE MODERN VIEW

Most modern economists still accept the insights of the early economists that relative prices are a major determinant of the allocation of resources and that the quantity of money has a lot to do with determining the absolute level of prices. They accept the neutrality of money in long-run equilibrium when all the forces causing change have fully worked themselves out. However, they do not accept the neutrality of money when the economy is adjusting to the various forces that cause it to change, that is when the economy is not in a state of long-run equilibrium. Thus, they reject the classical dichotomy.

Money and the price level Modern economists stress that there is a strong link between money and the price level, especially over long periods of time, when the conditions of long-run equilibrium are apt to be most relevant. In Chapter 27 (see pages 509–513) we discussed the price level and inflation, and we presented some evidence from the United Kingdom's experience over the recent past. In the post-Second World War period, prices had a strong upward trend. Since 1970 alone, the price level has increased nearly sixfold in the United Kingdom.

Not all historical periods exhibit rising prices. Figure 35.1 records the course of an estimate of the price level in southern England over seven centuries. It shows that there was an overall inflationary trend, but that it was by no means evenly spread over the centuries. Prices fluctuated about a stable level between 1300 and 1500. There followed a period of rapid inflation, but prices were stabilized again from the late 1600s to the time of the Napoleonic wars, in the early 1800s. Prices actually fell for much of the nineteenth century, as they did again in the twentieth century, between the two world wars.

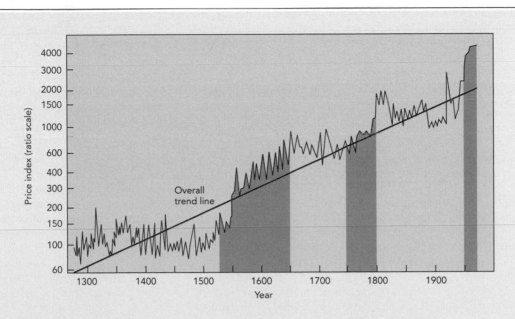

Figure 35.1 **A price index of consumables in southern England, 1275–1959**

Over the last seven centuries, long periods of stable prices have alternated with long periods of rising prices. This remarkable price series shows an index of the prices of food, clothing, and fuel in southern England from 1275 up to 1959. The trend line shows that the average change in prices over the whole period was 0.5 per cent per year. The shaded areas indicate periods of unreversed inflation. The series also shows that even the perspective of a century can be misleading, because long periods of stable or gently falling prices tended to alternate with long periods of rising prices.

Source: Lloyds Bank Review, no. 58 (October 1960).

The nature of money

WE have said, and we shall see why in detail in Chapter 36, that money affects the price level in the long run, and both the price level and the level of real income in the short run. But what exactly is money? There is probably more widespread misunderstanding of money and the monetary system than of any other aspect of the economy. In this section we describe the functions of money and briefly outline its history.

What is money?

In economics, **money** usually has been defined as any generally accepted medium of exchange. A **medium of exchange** is anything that will be widely accepted in a society in exchange for goods and services. Although being a medium of exchange is usually regarded as money's defining function, money can also serve other roles:

Money acts as a medium of exchange and can also serve as a store of value and a unit of account.

A medium of exchange If there were no money, goods would have to be exchanged by barter (one good being swapped directly for another). The major difficulty with barter is that each transaction requires a *double coincidence of wants;* anyone who specialized in producing one commodity would have to spend a great deal of time searching for satisfactory transactions. Thus, a thirsty economics lecturer would have to find a brewer who wanted to learn economics before he could swap a lesson in economics for a pint of bitter.

The use of money as a medium of exchange alleviates this problem. People can sell their output for money and subsequently use the money to buy what they wish from others. So a monetary economy involves exchanges of goods (and services) for money and of money for goods, but not (or not very often) of goods for goods.

The double coincidence of wants, which is required for barter, is unnecessary when a medium of exchange is used.

By facilitating transactions, money makes possible the benefits of specialization and the division of labour, which in turn contribute to the efficiency of the economic system. It is not without justification that money has been called one of the great inventions contributing to human freedom and well-being.

To serve as an efficient medium of exchange, money must have a number of characteristics. It must be readily acceptable and, therefore, of known value. It must have a high value relative to its weight (otherwise it would be a nuisance to carry around). It must be divisible, because money that comes only in large denominations is useless for transactions having only a small value. Finally, it must be difficult, if not impossible, to counterfeit.

A store of value Money is a convenient way to store purchasing power; goods may be sold today, and the money taken in exchange for them may be stored until it is needed. To be a satisfactory store of value, however, money must have a relatively stable value. A rise in the price level leads to a decrease in the purchasing power of money, because more money is required to buy a typical basket of goods. When the price level is stable, the purchasing power of a given sum of money is also stable; when the price level is highly variable, this is not so, and the usefulness of money as a store of value is undermined. Over the past three decades, inflation in the United Kingdom has been high enough and variable enough to diminish money's usefulness as a store of value.[1]

Although, in a non-inflationary environment, money can serve as a satisfactory store of accumulated purchasing power for a single individual, even in those circumstances it cannot do so for society as a whole. A single individual can accumulate money and, when the time comes to spend it, can command the current output of some other individual. However, if *all* individuals in a society were to save their money and then retire simultaneously to live on their savings, there would be no current production to purchase and consume. Society's ability to satisfy wants depends on goods and services being available; if some of this want-satisfying capacity is to be stored up for society as a whole, some goods that could be produced today must be saved

(in the form of real physical capital) for future periods. In other words, money may be accumulated as a savings, to help individuals buy future goods, but it is the future real capital stock and labour resources that will determine future real output. Money and real wealth should not be confused.

Money is a store of value for individuals but not for society as a whole.

A unit of account Money also may be used purely for accounting purposes, without having a physical existence of its own. For instance, a government store in a truly communist society might say that everyone had so many 'pounds' to spend or save each month. Goods could then be assigned prices and each consumer's purchases recorded, the consumer being allowed to buy until his or her allocated supply of pounds was exhausted. These pounds need have no existence other than as entries in the store's books, yet they would serve as a perfectly satisfactory unit of account.

Whether they could also serve as a medium of exchange between individuals depends on whether the store would agree to transfer credits from one customer to another at the customer's request. Banks will transfer pounds credited to current account deposits in this way, and so a bank deposit can serve as both a unit of account and a medium of exchange. Notice that the use of 'pounds' in this context suggests a further sense in which money is a unit of account. People think about values in terms of the monetary unit with which they are familiar.

A related function of money is that it can be used as a *standard of deferred payments*. Payments that are to be made in the future, on account of debts and so on, are reckoned in money. Money's ability to serve as a *unit of account over time* in this manner is much diminished by inflation.

Money is at the centre of the financial sector of an economy. Some other important financial concepts are discussed in Box 35.1.

The origins of money

The origins of money go far back in antiquity. Many primitive tribes seem to have made some use of it.

METALLIC MONEY

All sorts of commodities have been used as money at one time or another, but gold and silver proved to have great advantages. They were precious because their supplies were

---

[1] In 1994, £1 had about a sixth of the real purchasing power of £1 in 1970. This means that a bundle of specified goods that cost £1 in 1970 would have cost about £6 in 1994.

relatively limited, and they were in constant demand by the wealthy for ornament and decoration. Thus, these metals tended to have a high and stable price. Further, they were easily recognized, they were divisible into extremely small units, and they did not easily wear out.

Before the invention of coins, it was necessary to carry the metals in bulk. When a purchase was made, the requisite quantity of the metal was carefully weighed on a scale. The invention of coinage eliminated the need to weigh the metal at each transaction, but it created an important role for an authority, usually a monarch, who made the coins by mixing gold or silver with base metals to create convenient size and durability, and affixed his or her seal, guaranteeing the amount of precious metal that the coin contained.[2] This was clearly a great convenience, as long as traders knew that they could accept the coin at its 'face value'. The face value was nothing more than a statement that a certain weight of gold or silver was contained therein.

However, coins often could not be taken at their face value. A form of counterfeiting—clipping a thin slice off the edge of the coin and keeping the valuable metal—became common. This, of course, served to undermine the acceptability of coins—even if they were stamped. To get around this problem, the idea arose of minting the coins with a rough edge; the absence of the rough edge would immediately indicate that the coin had been clipped. This practice, called *milling,* survives on some coins (such as the current 5p, 10p, and £1 coins) as an interesting anachronism to remind us that there were days when the market value of the metal in the coin was equal to the face value of the coin.

Not to be outdone by the cunning of their subjects, some rulers were quick to seize the chance of getting something for nothing. The power to mint placed rulers in a position to work a *really profitable fraud.* They often used some suitable occasion—a marriage, an anniversary, an alliance—to remint the coinage. Subjects would be ordered to bring their coins into the mint to be melted down and coined afresh with a new stamp. Between the melting down and the recoining, however, the rulers had only to toss some further inexpensive base metal in with the molten gold. This *debasing* of the coinage allowed the ruler to earn a handsome profit by minting more new coins than the number of old ones collected, and putting the extras in the royal vault. To this day, the revenue generated from the power to create currency is know as *seigniorage.*[3]

The result of debasement was inflation. The subjects had the same number of coins as before, and hence could demand the same quantity of goods. When rulers paid their bills, however, the recipients of the extra coins could be expected to spend them. This caused a net increase in demand, which in turn bid up prices.

Debasing the coinage was a common cause of increases in prices.

It was the experience of such inflations that led early economists to stress the link between the quantity of money and the price level.

Gresham's law The early experience of currency debasement led to the observation known as **Gresham's law,** after Sir Thomas Gresham, an advisor to the Elizabethan court, who stated that 'bad money drives out good'.

When Queen Elizabeth I came to the throne of England in the middle of the sixteenth century, the coinage had been severely debased. Seeking to help trade, Elizabeth minted new coins that contained their full face value in gold. However, as fast as she fed these new coins into circulation, they disappeared. Why?

Suppose that you possessed one new and one old coin, each with the same face value, and had a bill to pay. What would you do? Clearly, you would use the debased coin to pay the bill and keep the undebased one. (You part with less gold that way.) Again suppose that you wanted to obtain a certain amount of gold bullion by melting down the gold coins (as was frequently done). Which coins would you use? Clearly, you would use new, undebased coins because you would part with less 'face value' that way. For these reasons, the debased coins would remain in circulation, and the undebased coins would disappear.

Gresham's insights have proven helpful in explaining the experience of a number of modern high-inflation economies. For example, in the 1970s, inflation in Chile raised the value of the metallic content in coins above their face value. Coins quickly disappeared from circulation as private citizens sold them to entrepreneurs who melted them down for their metal. Only paper currency remained in circulation and was used even for tiny transactions such as purchasing a box of matches. Gresham's law is one reason why modern coins, unlike their historical counterparts, are merely tokens that contain a metallic value that is only a minute fraction of their face value.

Gresham's law has had another modern interpretation, in regimes of pegged exchange rates, where the values of two currencies are pegged together artificially. If one currency is overvalued, and widely expected to have to be devalued, this causes people to spend it fast, while building up their holdings of the undervalued currency. The combination of hoarding one currency and running down balances of the other often brings about the devaluation that

---

[2] The earliest recorded coinage is attributed to the kings of Lydia in about the fourth century BC.

[3] Seigniorage was not normally revenue generated by debasement, but originally was an explicit duty, or tax, levied on the mint. In the modern context, the possibility of debasement does not enter, so the term applies to the revenue that accrues from the power to print bank notes (which have very low production costs relative to their face value) and from the fact that many central banks force banks to place non-interest-bearing deposits at the central bank (which finances the holding of interest-bearing securities). The term 'seigniorage' has also applied to a duty charged by a landlord on the output of mineral mines.

Box 35.1

Some financial terminology

In this and subsequent chapters, we shall encounter many different types of financial asset, or *security*. Securities are a liability to the issuer but an asset to the holder. All securities involve a written agreement, usually to repay a sum of money plus interest within a certain period of time. There are many varieties of such IOUs.

One important distinction is between equity and debt. *Equity* refers to assets such as ordinary shares that represent evidence of part ownership of a company, and hence are a claim on the earnings of that company. Equity is often called *real capital*, or just *capital*. Care must be taken to distinguish between 'real capital', used to refer to the physical machinery and buildings owned by a company, and its net worth, or the value of a claim on its future earnings.

Debt refers to the financial liabilities of a company other than to its owners. This may be loans due to a bank or traded securities such as bonds. A *bond* is a written promise to repay a certain sum of money (the principal) and at specific future time (typically, five to ten years at the time of issue), and to pay regular interest (the coupon) in the meantime. The repayment date is the *maturity date*, and the remaining life of a bond is its *term to maturity* or simply *term*. Some company bonds have attached to them an option to convert the debt into the equity of the company at a future date and a pre-specified price. Such bonds are known as *convertibles*, and the option to buy the company shares, when traded separately from the bond, is known as a *warrant*. A few government bonds, known as *perpetuities*, have no maturity date but continue to pay interest until the government chooses to buy them back, or *redeem* them. Debt represents a prior claim on a company's assets before the equity-holders can be paid.

A *bill* is a security with a short term (normally up to nine months), which is repaid in a lump sum but pays no interest during its life. A buyer of a bill is prepared to hold it only if it can be bought at a *discount*. This means that it is bought more cheaply than its redemption value. For example, a bill maturing in three months' time for £1,000 bought today for £980 would yield a return of 2 per cent over three months or about 8 per cent per annum. *Commercial bills*, or *bills of exchange* (sometimes also called trade bills), have been used for centuries to finance international trade. Suppose an exporter ships goods to Australia. The purchaser will pay for them when they arrive, but the exporter has to pay his work-force now. He could get a bank loan. Alternatively, he could draw up a bill which will be paid by the importer in, say, three months when the goods arrive. This bill can be sold, at a discount, in the money markets. Hence the exporter gets some money now. In effect, he has received a loan from the purchaser of the bill.

Merchant banks, or *acceptance houses*, used to specialize in guaranteeing, or accepting, commercial bills, earning a fee or a proportion of the discount for so doing. Bills guaranteed by top-quality merchant banks are known as *prime bank bills*. The government also issues bills, known as *Treasury bills*. However, these are not guaranteed by banks, as the government itself is regarded as the most creditworthy borrower. Short-term company IOUs which do pay interest are known as *commercial paper* (or sometimes as *notes*, especially Euro-notes). Similar securities issued by banks are known as *certificates of deposit* (CDs). These carry an interest rate, just like ordinary savings deposits, but the bank taking the deposit issues the depositor with a certificate stating that the deposit will be repaid at a specific future date. This CD is then resaleable in the money markets, so it gives the depositor greater liquidity (see below).

An important characteristic of financial assets is their *riskiness*, which refers to the possibility that the future payments will not be made in full. As typical investors are thought to be risk-averse, the riskier an asset is, the higher its expected yield will have to be to attract purchasers. The *liquidity* of an asset refers to the ease with which it can be converted into a ready means of payment. Money itself is perfectly liquid, but other assets vary in degree of liquidity. Assets whose market price can fluctuate over time are regarded as less liquid than those with a fixed money value because there will be times when it is hard to sell the asset without making a loss. In general, an asset that has a longer term to maturity will have greater potential fluctuations in its price than an asset with a short term. Hence, other things being equal, long-term assets are less liquid than short-term assets.

---

was feared—as, for example, when the pound sterling was forced to leave the European Exchange Rate Mechanism (ERM) in September 1992.

PAPER MONEY

The next important step in the history of money was the evolution of paper currency. One source was goldsmiths who required secure safes, and the public began to deposit their gold with such goldsmiths for safekeeping. Goldsmiths would give their depositors receipts promising to hand over the gold on demand. When any depositor wished to make a large purchase, she could go to her goldsmith, reclaim some of her gold, and hand it over to the seller of the goods. If the seller had no immediate need for the gold, he would carry it back to the goldsmith for safekeeping on his behalf.

If people knew the goldsmith to be reliable, there was no need to go through the cumbersome and risky business of physically transferring the gold. The buyer needed only to transfer the goldsmith's receipt to the seller, who would accept it as long as he was confident that the goldsmith would pay over the gold whenever it was needed. If the seller wished to buy a good from a third party, who also knew the goldsmith to be reliable, this transaction too could be effected by passing the goldsmith's receipt from the buyer to the seller. The deposit receipt was 'as good as gold'. The convenience of using pieces of paper instead of gold is obvious.

When it came into being in this way, paper money represented a promise to pay so much gold *on demand*. In this case, the promise was made first by goldsmiths and later by banks.[4] Such paper money, which became **bank notes,** was *backed* by precious metal and was *convertible on demand* into this metal.[5]

Fractionally backed paper money Early on, many goldsmiths and banks discovered that it was not necessary to keep a full ounce of gold in the vaults for every claim to an ounce circulating as paper money.

At any one time, some of the bank's customers would be withdrawing gold, others would be depositing it, and most would be trading in the bank's paper notes without indicating any need or desire to convert them into gold.

As a result, the bank was able to issue more money (initially notes, but later deposits) redeemable in gold than the amount of gold that it held in its vaults. This was good business, because the money could be invested profitably in interest-earning loans (often called *advances*) to individuals and firms. The demand for loans arose, as it does today, because some customers wanted credit to help them over hard times or to buy equipment for their businesses. To this day, banks have many more claims outstanding against them than they actually have in reserves available to pay those claims. We say that the currency issued in such a situation is *fractionally backed* by the reserves.

The major problem with a fractionally backed, convertible currency was maintaining its convertibility into the precious metal by which it was backed. The imprudent bank that issued too much paper money would find itself unable to redeem its currency in gold when the demand for gold was even slightly higher than usual. It would then have to suspend payments, and all holders of its notes would suddenly find that the notes were worthless. However, the prudent bank that kept a reasonable relationship between its note issue and its gold reserve would find that it could meet a normal range of demand for gold without any trouble.

If the public lost confidence and demanded redemption of its currency *en masse,* however, the banks would be unable to honour their pledges. The history of nineteenth- and early twentieth-century banking around the world is full of examples of banks that were ruined by 'panics', or sudden runs on their gold reserves. When this happened, the banks' depositors and the holders of their notes would find themselves with worthless pieces of paper.[6]

FIAT MONEY

As time went on, note issue by private banks became less common, and central banks took control of the currency. In time, *only* central banks were permitted to issue notes.[7] Originally, the central banks issued paper currency that was fully convertible into gold. In those days gold would be brought to the central bank, which would issue currency in the form of 'gold certificates' that asserted that the gold was available on demand. The gold supply thus set some upper limit on the amount of currency.

However, central banks, like private banks before them, could issue more currency than they had in gold because in normal times only a small fraction of the currency was presented for payment at any one time. Thus, even though the need to maintain convertibility under a gold standard put an upper limit on note issue, central banks had substantial discretionary control over the quantity of currency outstanding.

During the period between the two world wars, almost all of the countries of the world abandoned the gold standard; their currencies were thus no longer convertible into gold.[8] Money that is not convertible by law into anything valuable derives its value from its acceptability in exchange. **Fiat money** is widely acceptable because it is declared by government order, or *fiat,*[9] to be legal tender. **Legal tender** is anything that by law must be accepted when offered either for the purchase of goods or services or to discharge a debt.[10]

Today, almost all currency is fiat money.

---

[4] Banks grew out of at least two other trades in addition to that of the goldsmiths. There were scriveners, who had writing skills and sold their services managing other people's financial affairs; there were also merchant bankers, who started trading in commodities but ended up specialising in trade finance—Barings and Rothschilds started this way, and are still referred to as 'merchant banks' today.

[5] One of the earliest issuers of formal bank notes was the Riksbank of Sweden, established in 1668. Sweden's currency was based on copper rather than gold at the time. This bank is now the central bank of Sweden, though it acquired most of its central banking functions much later. It instituted the Nobel Prize for economics in 1968 to commemorate its tercentenary. It is thus 26 years older than the Bank of England, which was established in 1694. Other precursors to bank notes were letters of credit and bills of exchange, which were in use in European trade as early as the twelfth century

[6] In the early 1930s, about 10,000 banks, or a third of the total, went bust in the United States. The personal and corporate losses involved were a major contributor to the Great Depression.

[7] In England and Wales, no new banks have been permitted to issue notes since the 1844 Bank Charter Act, though in Scotland banks such as the Bank of Scotland, the Royal Bank of Scotland, and the Clydesdale Bank still issue the main notes in circulation. (Since 1845, however, the Scottish note issue has 100 per cent backing with Bank of England liabilities, and hence is fully under Bank of England direction.)

[8] The gold standard is discussed further in the Appendix to Chapter 37.

[9] Fiat means 'let there be' in Latin, and hence by 'decree'.

[10] Bank of England notes have been legal tender in England and Wales since 1833.

Bank of England notes still say on them 'I promise to pay the bearer on demand the sum of x pounds' and they are signed by the chief cashier, currently G. B. A. Kentfield. Until 1931 (apart from suspensions of convertibility for the Napoleonic (1797–1821) and First World Wars (1914–25), and temporary crises in the nineteenth century – 1847, 1857, and 1866), you could take these notes into the Bank of England and demand gold of equivalent value in return for your notes. Today, however, the promise is a quaint tradition rather than a real contract. The pound sterling, like all major currencies, is a fiat currency which is not backed by gold or any other commodity (though some people still argue for the return to a gold standard).

Fiat money is valuable because it is accepted (by convention and in law) in payment for the purchase of goods or services and for the discharge of debts.

Many people are disturbed to learn that present-day paper money is neither backed by nor convertible into anything more valuable—that it consists of nothing but pieces of paper whose value derives from common acceptance. Many people believe that their money should be more substantial than this. Yet money is, in fact, nothing more than pieces of paper.

If fiat money is acceptable, it is a medium of exchange. Further, if its purchasing power remains stable, it is a satisfactory store of value. And if both of these things are true, it will also serve as a satisfactory unit of account.

HOW DOES FIAT MONEY GET INTO THE ECONOMY?

When gold was the basis of money, it was not too difficult to imagine how more gold could get into circulation. It would either be produced from gold mines, converted from non-monetary uses (such as jewellery), or imported from other countries. However, it is not so obvious how fiat money gets into the economic system. In fact, it comes from the central bank—in the United Kingdom the Bank of England—but the central bank does not just drop it from the sky, or even just give it to the government to spend.

What the central bank has direct control over is referred to as *high-powered money, the cash base,* or *the monetary base.* (In the United Kingdom it is also defined as M0; see Box 38.1). This consists of currency (bank notes and coin) held by the public and the banks and of deposits held by the banks with the Bank of England. The monetary base is referred to as 'high-powered money' because it is the basis upon which a much bigger stock of monetary assets is built (including the biggest component of the money stock, bank deposits). High-powered money is an asset to anyone in the private sector who holds it, but to the central bank it is a liability.

The central bank gets high-powered money into the eco-

nomic system simply by buying securities (usually gilts or Treasury bills, but also private-sector securities). It pays for these purchases with newly issued high-powered money.

Hence, in creating new high-powered money, the central bank is expanding both sides of its own balance sheet. At the same time as it increases its liabilities, it purchases assets of equal value. There are two components of high-powered money: bankers' deposits with the central bank, and currency (notes and coin). Bankers deposits are the liability of the Banking Department of the Bank of England and currency is the liability of the Issue Department. The balance sheets of these two departments of the Bank of England are shown in Table 35.1.

It is simplest to think of the process of high-powered money creation in two steps. First, we shall discuss how the purchase of securities by the Bank of England (Banking Department) creates bankers' deposits. Then we shall see how currency gets into circulation.

Bankers' deposits   Consider a situation in which there are no net transactions going on between the Bank of England and the rest of the economy (either on the Bank's own behalf or on behalf of the government for which it is banker). The Bank now buys £1m worth of securities from the private sector. (It does not matter whether these securities are purchased from an individual person or, say, from a pension fund.) The seller receives a cheque for £1m from the Bank of England which is paid into the recipient's bank account at, say, Lloyds Bank. Lloyds' deposits rise by £1m but, at the same time, Lloyds receives an increase of £1m in its deposits at the Bank of England. This increase in its bankers' deposits at the Bank of England arises when Lloyds clears the cheque drawn on the Bank of England. (A cheque deposited in Lloyds drawn on the Midland Bank would simply transfer bankers' deposits from Midland to Lloyds, but a cheque drawn on the Bank of England creates new bankers' deposits at the Bank.)

This will not be the end of the story so far as Lloyds is concerned because it has now increased its reserves. We shall explain how the banking system can increase its deposits on the basis of larger reserves below. However, this is most of what we need to know about how the Bank of England expands the monetary base (high-powered money). Contraction of the monetary base simply reverses the process—the Bank sells securities. A member of the public then writes a cheque drawn on, say, Barclays Bank, payable to the Bank of England and Barclays transfers bankers' deposits to the Bank of an equivalent amount. The monetary base falls.

The only other serious complication arises from the role of the Bank of England as banker to the government. We assumed above that the Bank purchased a security from a member of the public. However, what would happen if the

Table 35.1 Bank of England Balance Sheet
(i) Balance Sheet of Bank of England Issue Dept., Oct 1994

Assets	(£m)	Liabilities	(£m)
Government securities	12,112	Notes in circulation	18,146
Other securities	6,038	Notes in Banking Dept.	4
Total assets	18,150	Total liabilities	18,150

(ii) Balance Sheet of Bank of England Banking Dept., Oct 1994

Assets	(£m)	Liabilities	(£m)
Government securities	1,255	Public deposits	1,042
Advances	4,055	Bankers' deposits	1,526
Premises	553	Reserves and other acs.	3,299
Notes and coin	4		
Total assets	5,867	Total liabilities	5,867

The Bank of England is divided into the Issue Department and the Banking Department. The table shows the balance sheets of these two departments at the end of October 1994. The only function of the Issue Department is to issue currency (bank notes and coins). It does this in exchange for purchases of securities, normally through a transaction with the Banking Department. The Banking Department acts as banker to the government and also holds deposits from the banks. In October 1994, the value of notes in circulation was £18,146 million.

Source: Financial Statistics, CSO.

Bank purchased a new security issued by the government? In this case, the government would acquire an increase in its deposits in the Banking Department of the Bank (which would acquire a matching security). As soon as the government writes a cheque (perhaps to pay civil service salaries) it transfers deposits to private individuals and banks acquire a corresponding increase in bankers' deposits at the Bank. Thus, when the central bank lends money to the government, by buying new government securities and creating new government deposits, it is increasing the monetary base. This is the nearest that governments can come to 'printing money' in the modern institutional environment. It is also known as *monetising the government debt*, a process often associated with inflation (See Chapters 40 and 42).

Currency   The above discussion explains how the Bank of England creates or destroys high-powered money. The composition of high-powered money, as between bankers' deposits and currency, is determined by the demand for currency on the part of the general public. If we choose to increase our currency holding, relative to bank deposits, we simply go to our bank and withdraw deposits in cash. The bank (if it did not have enough cash in its tills) would go to the Bank of England and withdraw some bankers' deposits in cash from the Banking Department. The Banking Department, in turn, would replenish its own stock of cash by selling securities to the Issue Department. Currency is

made available on demand to the economy in this way and is not restricted in supply by the Bank of England.

The stock of currency in circulation is determined entirely by the demands of the economy and is not set by any policy makers.

In the current UK financial system, the total stock of high-powered money is also demand determined. This is because the authorities choose to set short-term interest rates, and supply whatever high-powered money is demanded at those rates. The detailed discussion of the implementation of monetary policy is postponed until Chapter 38. However, for some illustrative purposes we shall assume that the Bank of England does set the value of the monetary base. This is a helpful simplification in the task of understanding the relationship between the monetary base (high-powered money) and the total money supply in a modern banking system.

Modern money

The creation of high-powered money is only part of the story of how the money supply is created, because most measures of the money supply include a wider range of assets than just the monetary base. In particular, money is usually defined to include bank deposits.

DEPOSIT MONEY

Today's bank customers frequently deposit coins and paper money with the banks for safekeeping, just as in former times they deposited gold. Such a deposit is recorded as a credit to the customer's account. A customer who wishes to pay a debt may come to the bank and claim the money in currency and then pay the money to other persons, who may themselves redeposit the money in a bank.

As with gold transfers, this is a tedious procedure. It is more convenient to have the bank transfer claims to money on deposit. As soon as cheques, which are written instructions to the bank to make a transfer, became widely accepted in payment for commodities and debts, bank deposits became a form of money called 'deposit money'. **Deposit money** is defined as money held by the public in the form of deposits in commercial banks that can be withdrawn on demand.[11] Cheques, unlike bank notes, do not circulate freely from hand to hand; thus, cheques themselves are not currency. However, a balance in a current account deposit *is* money; the cheque simply transfers that money from one person to another. Because cheques are easily drawn and deposited, and because they are relatively safe from theft, they have been widely used in the twentieth century. New technology has recently replaced many cheque transactions by computer transfer. Plastic cards, such as Visa, Mastercard, and Switch, enable holders of bank accounts to transfer money to another person's account in new ways.[12] The principle is the same, however: the balance in the bank account is the money that is to be transferred between customers, not the cheque or the plastic card.

When commercial banks lost the right to issue notes of their own, the form of bank money changed, but the substance did not. Today banks have money in their vaults (or on deposit with the central bank) just as they always did. Once it was gold; today it is the legal tender of the times—fiat money. It is true today, just as in the past, that most of the bank's customers are content to pay their bills by passing among themselves the bank's promises to pay money on demand. Only a small proportion of the transactions made by the bank's customers are made in cash.

Bank deposits are money. Today, just as in the past, banks can create money by issuing more promises to pay (deposits) than they have cash reserves available to pay out.

---

[11] For many years, government regulations created a sharp distinction among the various types of financial intermediaries by limiting the types of transaction each could engage in. The period from 1980 to the present has seen a sweeping deregulation of the financial system, so that many of these traditional distinctions no longer apply. Thus, when we speak of 'commercial banks', that term can be taken to extend to other financial intermediaries that create deposit money, notably building societies in the United Kingdom. (Other countries have different forms of savings banks, credit unions, or savings and loan associations (generally referred to as *thrifts*).)

[12] With credit cards such as Visa or Mastercard, if you buy, say, petrol today, the petrol company will receive a credit in its bank account after a few days and you will have to settle with the credit card company once a month. With so-called EFTPOS (electronic fund transfer at the point of sale) cards, however, like Switch, the funds are transferred directly from your account to the account of the petrol company very quickly. Planned innovations include 'smart' cards, which contain a silicon chip which carries with it all your account information and is updated every time you make a transaction. Thus, the technology of transactions is likely to keep advancing, though it does not fundamentally alter the nature of the bank account transfer which the technology facilitates.

Two models of banking

BANKS are firms that operate within a market-determined environment. We have already seen in the first half of this book that we need different models to understand how firms behave in different market environments—for example, monopolists behave differently from firms in perfectly competitive industries even though they are all profit-maximizers. So, also, is it useful to apply different models to explain different aspects of banks' behaviour. First, we shall explain a traditional analysis of banks which is useful for understanding the process of deposit creation on the basis of a given base of high-powered money (as, for example, in our goldsmith example above). However, this traditional model is insufficient for understanding other aspects of modern banking. Our second model is more suited to understanding both the forces of competition between banks themselves and the competition between banks and other channels of financial intermediation (such as securities markets). We shall also see (in Chapter 38) that our second model has important applications to the understanding of contemporary monetary policy in the United Kingdom.

Table 35.2 A new cash deposit

Liabilities	(£)	Assets	(£)
Deposit	100	Cash	100

A new cash deposit has 100 per cent backing. The balance sheet shows the changes in assets and liabilities resulting from a new cash deposit. Both cash assets and deposit liabilities rise by the same amount.

The ratios approach to the creation of deposit money

If you deposit cash with a bank, that deposit is an asset to you and a liability to the bank. The bank holds the cash as an asset, so its assets equal its liabilities. If it extends a loan to someone else on the basis of your cash, that will be an asset to the bank, but any deposit created will be a liability. (If a bank gives you a loan, it writes an extra balance into your account. This creates a deposit for you, but also it is a loan which you have to repay. So the process of overdraft or loan creation creates both deposits and loans simultaneously.) In general, banks' deposits are their liabilities, and whatever loans they make (or securities they purchase) constitute their assets. We will now see how banks can create deposits (and loans) that are some multiple of their cash reserves. Notice that 'cash' held by the banks can be currency or deposits at the central bank, but 'cash' for the public means currency.

Suppose that, in a system with many banks, each bank obtains new deposits in cash. Say, for example, that there are ten banks of equal size and that each receives a new deposit of £100 in cash. Each bank now has on its books the new entries shown in Table 35.2. The banks are on a fractional reserve system, and we assume for purposes of this illustration that they wish to hold 10 per cent reserves against all deposits. The new deposits put the banks into disequilibrium, since they each have 100 per cent reserves against these new deposits.

First, suppose that only one of the banks begins to expand deposits by making new loans (advances). When a bank makes a loan to a customer, it simply writes a larger balance into the customer's account, thereby increasing the size of its deposits. Now when cheques are written on these deposits, the majority will be deposited in other banks. Thus, of the amounts withdrawn the bank must expect much of its £100 in cash to drain away to other banks as soon as it creates new deposits for its own customers.

If, for example, one bank has only 10 per cent of the total deposits held by the community, then, on average, 90 per cent of any new deposits it creates will end up in other

Table 35.3 Restoration of a 10 per cent reserve ratio

Liabilities	(£)	Assets	(£)
Deposit	1,000	Cash	100
		Loans	900

With no cash drain, a new cash deposit will support a multiple expansion of deposit liabilities. The table shows the changes in assets and liabilities when all banks engage in deposit expansion after each has received a new cash deposit of £100. New assets are £900 and new deposits are £900. The accretion of £100 in cash now supports £1,000 in deposits, thus restoring the 10 per cent reserve ratio.

Table 35.4 Deposit expansion in expectation of a cash drain

Liabilities	(£)	Assets	(£)
Deposit	190	Cash	100
		Loans	90
	190		190

If all banks expand deposits in the expectation of a cash drain, they will end up with excess reserves. The table shows the position if all banks expand deposits on the basis of each receiving £100 in new cash deposits and in the expectation that 90 per cent of any new deposits will drain out of the bank in a cash flow. The banks obtain new assets of loans and bonds of £90 by creating new deposits of that amount. They expect £81 of these to be withdrawn in cash, leaving them with £19 to provide a 10 per cent reserve against £190 of deposits. Because there is no cash drain, they end up with cash reserves of close to 53 per cent.

banks. If other banks are not simultaneously creating new deposits, then this one bank will be severely restricted in its ability to expand deposits. The reason for the restriction is that the bank will suffer a major cash drain as cheques are written payable to individuals who deal with other banks.

One bank in a multi-bank system cannot produce a large multiple expansion of deposits based on an original accretion of cash, when other banks do not also expand their deposits.

Now assume, however, that *each* bank begins to expand its deposits based on its £100 of new reserves. On the one hand, since each bank does one-tenth of the total banking

Table 35.5   Deposit creation with a cash drain to the public

Liabilities	(£)	Assets	(£)
Deposit	500	Cash	50
		Loans	450
	500		500

A cash drain to the public greatly reduces the amount of new deposits that can be created on the basis of a given amount of cash. The table shows the balance sheet of the banking system on the assumption that there is £100 of cash in the system but the public desires cash holdings equal to 10 per cent of their bank deposits. The outcome which satisfies both banks' desired reserve ratio and the public's cash to deposit ratio is such that the banks hold £50 in reserves and issue £450 worth of loans. Total deposits are £500 and £50 is held in cash by the public. The total money stock is £550 (deposits plus cash held by the public). An example in which the banks' reserve ratio differs from the public's cash to deposit ratio is given in Table 35.6.

business, 90 per cent of the value of any newly created deposits will find its way into other banks as customers make payments by cheque to various members of the community. This represents a cash drain to these other banks. On the other hand, 10 per cent of the new deposits created by each *other* bank should find its way into this bank. Thus, if all banks receive new cash, and all start creating deposits simultaneously, no bank should suffer a significant cash drain to any other bank. All banks can go on expanding deposits without losing cash to each other; they need only worry about keeping enough cash to satisfy those depositors who occasionally require cash. Thus, the expansion can go on, with each bank watching its own ratio of cash reserves to deposits, expanding its deposits as long as the ratio exceeds 1 : 10 and ceasing to do so when it reaches that figure. Assuming no cash drain to the public, the process will not come to a halt until each bank has created £900 in additional deposits, so that, for each initial £100 cash deposit, there is now £1,000 in deposits backed by £100 in cash. Now *each* of the banks will have new entries in its books similar to those shown in Table 35.3.

It might help to think of this process as taking place in a series of hypothetical steps. In the first period, each bank gets £100 in new deposits and the books of each bank show new entries similar to those in Table 35.2. During the second period, each bank makes loans of £90, expecting that it will suffer a cash drain of £81 on account of these loans. Indeed, 90 per cent of the new deposits created by the loans made by bank A do find their way into other banks, but at the same time 10 per cent of the deposits created by each other bank find their way into bank A. Thus, there is no new movement of cash among banks. Instead of finding itself with its surplus cash drained away, each bank's books at the end of the day will contain the entries shown in Table 35.4.

Cash is now just over 50 per cent of deposits, instead of only 10 per cent as desired. Thus, each bank can continue to expand deposits in order to grant loans. As long as all banks do this simultaneously, no bank will suffer any significant cash drain to any other bank, and the process can continue until each bank has created £900 worth of new deposits and then finds itself in the position shown in Table 35.3.

A multibank system creates a multiple increase in deposit money when all banks with excess reserves expand their deposits in step with each other.

A COMPLICATION: CASH DRAIN TO THE PUBLIC

So far, we have ignored the fact that the public actually divides its money holdings in a fairly stable proportion between cash and deposits. This means that, when the banking system as a whole creates significant amounts of new deposit money, the system *will* suffer a cash drain as the public withdraws enough cash from the banks to maintain its desired ratio of cash to deposits.

An example   Assume that the public wishes to hold a proportion of cash equal to 10 per cent of the size of its bank deposits. This means that, for a given stock of cash in the system, the amount that will be held in bank reserves is reduced, so the maximum amount of deposit creation is also reduced. In this special case, in which banks have a reserve ratio of 10 per cent and the public hold cash to the value of 10 per cent of the size of their bank deposits, the outcome will be as in Table 35.5. Half of the cash in existence (assumed to be £100 in total) will be held in banks' reserves and the other half will be held by the public. On the basis of their £50 reserves, banks will extend £450 of loans, so total deposits will be £500. This is only half of the value of deposits which were created when the entire £100 of cash was held in bank reserves (as shown in Table 35.3).

A cash drain to the public reduces the expansion of deposit money that can be supported by the banking system.

The general case of deposit creation   The two ratios that we have discussed (the banks' reserve ratio and public's ratio of cash to deposits) can now be used to determine the total level of deposit creation in a formal way. Let R be the cash held in bank reserves, C be the cash held by the non-bank public, H (for high-powered money) be the total cash in the economy, and D be the size of bank deposits. Thus,

$$C + R = H. \tag{1}$$

This says that the total cash in the economy is held either by the banks or by the public.

Let the desired reserve ratio of banks be x. This allows us to write

$$R = xD. \qquad (2)$$

Finally, let the public hold a fraction, b, of its bank deposits in cash:

$$C = bD. \qquad (3)$$

Substituting the second and third equations into the first gives

$$bD + xD = H,$$

and solving for D yields:

$$D = H/(b + x). \qquad (4)$$

Equation (4) shows that if the public's desired cash ratio is zero, deposits rise by the reciprocal of the cash reserve ratio. (If the banks' reserve ratio were 0.1 (10 per cent), then deposits would be ten times the cash in the economy.) A positive b, however, means that the resulting cash drain lowers the increase in deposits since it raises the value of the denominator in (4).

The money multiplier   The total money supply, in an economy with a banking system is defined as $D+C$. (It does not include R, because the deposit that created the original bank reserves is already counted in with deposits D and should not be counted twice.) Hence the money supply M is

$$M = C + D. \qquad (5)$$

We can arrive at an expression that links M and H by substituting (2) into (5) for C and then (4) into (5) for D. This gives

$$M = \frac{b+1}{b+x} H. \qquad (6)$$

Expression (6) is known as the *money multiplier*, because it tells us how much bigger is the money supply than the cash base of the system. In the modern UK banking system, where reserve ratios and cash ratios are very small, the money multiplier could be of the order of 25 or greater.

The money multiplier should not be confused with the multiplier that links changes in exogenous spending with changes in national income. The same term is used for two different concepts.

The size of the money multiplier is greater, the smaller is the banks' desired reserve ratio x and the smaller is the public's desired cash ratio b.

A diagrammatic exposition of the above algebra is given in Figure 35.2. It shows that the two ratios, combined with a given cash base, can be used to determine the level of deposits that result and also the money supply. A numerical example of the same ideas is given in Table 35.6. We shall discuss this further in the context of monetary policy in Chapter 38.

A competitive banking system

The ratios approach to bank behaviour gives us important insights into how deposit money is created as some multiple of high-powered money, but it provides an inaccurate picture of how modern banks work. They do not just sit around waiting for cash deposits to be made and then, when a deposit is made, go out and lend some multiple of the deposit (though it is certainly true that their deposits are some multiple of their reserves). On the contrary, modern bankers usually start from the other end. They wait until they have found a profitable lending opportunity, and they then take steps to make sure that funds are available to make the loan. This they can do, either by offering higher interest on deposits, or by borrowing from the wholesale money markets (see below).

In the ratios world, banks passively receive deposits and then use these to make loans. In the modern world, however, banks are trading in highly competitive markets for both deposits and loans. In a competitive market, there will be a market-clearing interest rate for both deposit money and loans. Banks cannot expand their activity in either of these markets without taking into account the supply curve of deposits and the demand curve for loans which they face.

The market for bank loans is illustrated in Figure 35.3. This shows a positively sloped supply curve of loans and a negatively sloped demand curve for loans. The supply curve of loans is determined by two factors: the supply curve of deposits, and the *spread* (i.e. the difference between what the banks have to pay to borrow money and what they get by lending it, which has to cover staff costs, return on capital employed, and default risk). Remember that banks have to take in deposits in order to make loans. They borrow from one set of people or firms and lend to another.

The supply curve of deposits is positively sloped because, for given interest rates elsewhere in the economy, banks can attract more deposits by offering higher interest rates. (Not all deposits in banks pay interest, but the deposits that banks can increase by offering high interest rates—their marginal deposits—do.) The spread is assumed, for simplicity, to be of a constant absolute size, so that the supply curve of loans is drawn parallel to the supply curve of deposits, but above it by the constant size of the spread. This is a reasonable assumption to apply to the total market for loans; indeed, in reality, for each specific loan the per-

Table 35.6   High-powered money, deposits, and the money supply

Banks		Non-bank public		High-powered money ($H = C + R$)	Money supply ($M = C + D$)
Reserves (R) (1)	Deposits (D) (R x 20) (2)	Cash (C) (1,000 − R) (3)	Deposits (D) (C x 10) (4)	(5)	(6)
1,000	20,000	0	0	1,000	
900	18,000	100	1,000	1,000	
800	16,000	200	2,000	1,000	
700	14,000	300	3,000	1,000	
600	12,000	400	4,000	1,000	
500	10,000	500	5,000	1,000	
400	8,000	600	6,000	1,000	
333.3	**6,666.6**	**666.6**	**6,666.6**	**1,000**	**7,333.3**
300	6,000	700	7,000	1,000	
200	4,000	800	8,000	1,000	
100	2,000	900	9,000	1,000	
0	0	1,000	10,000	1,000	

For a given stock of high-powered money, the amount of bank deposits created will be the amount which is consistent with the banks' reserve ratio and the non-bank public's cash–deposit ratio. The table sets out a range of desired positions for banks and the non-bank public independently. Only one of these positions satisfies the desired positions for both the banks and the public, such that the deposits the banks wish to create are the same as the deposits the public wishes to hold.

The example assumes that high-powered money (the cash base or monetary base) is fixed at £1,000. This can be held in some proportion between the banks and public but it cannot be changed other than by the monetary authorities. Banks are assumed to have a reserve ratio of 5 per cent and the non-bank public is assumed to wish to hold cash at a level 10 per cent of their holding of bank deposits. Column (1) shows a range of possible levels of reserve holding for the banks, ranging from all of the £1,000 to none of it. Column (2) shows the level of deposits they would like to create (by making loans) in order to satisfy their desired reserve ratio, for each level of reserve holding in column (1). Column (3) shows the cash holding by the public that is implied for each level of banks' reserves in column (1), so it is equal to £1,000 minus the number in column (1). Column (4) shows the level of deposits that the public would like to hold given their cash holdings in column (3). Column (5) reminds us that the stock of high-powered money is fixed at £1,000 throughout. Column (6) show the value of the money supply for the unique position that satisfies the desires of both the banks and the public.

The actual outcome is the single position where the deposits that the banks wish to create are exactly equal to the deposits the public wish to hold. This is where the level of deposits is £6,666.6. At this point the banks hold £333.3 in reserves and the public hold £666.6 in cash. The money supply is £7,333.3 (deposits plus cash held by the public) and the money multiplier is 7.333 (M/H). We could also calculate this from equation (6) on p. 683: $(b + 1)/(b + x)$ is 1.1/.15 (where $b = 0.1$ and $x = 0.05$); this is 7.333.

centage spread will be inversely related to the size of the loan, other things being equal. In other words, the percentage spread on small loans is bigger than the percentage spread on large loans. Competition in banking drives the spread to the point where it is just enough to cover costs and return on capital, but does not involve any excess profit.

The demand curve for loans is negatively sloped because, as banks charge higher interest rates on loans, customers will opt to borrow less. At lower interest rates, customers will opt to borrow more. Equilibrium in the market for bank loans occurs where the demand and supply curves intersect. We will find this analysis of the market for bank loans very important below, when we discuss monetary

policy. The way in which the Bank of England seeks to control the UK money supply is via its ability to set interest rates. In effect, the Bank shifts the supply curve of deposits and this alters the interest rate in the loan market. By forcing up interest rates, the Bank lowers the demand for loans, and by lowering interest rates the Bank increases the demand for loans.

MONEY SUPPLY AND COMPETITIVE BANKING

The ratios approach to money supply creation and the competitive model of banking present two rather different ways of looking at the banking system, but they are compatible. Indeed, each helps us understand the other better,

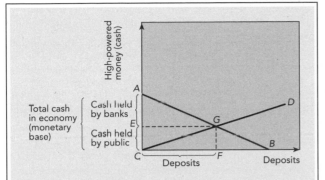

Figure 35.2 The ratios approach to the determination of the money supply

The money supply is determined by the stock of high-powered money (monetary base), the reserve ratio of the banks, and the cash–deposit ratio of the non-bank public. The diagram illustrates the size of deposit creation, given the banks' reserve ratio x (= AC/CB), the public's cash–deposit ratio b (= EC/CF), and the total cash in the economy AC. Deposits plus cash held by the public make up the total money supply. The total stock of high-powered money, or cash, in the economy has to be held by either the banks or the public. At point A, the public holds all the cash available so there are no bank deposits, and the total money supply is just AC which is all cash. At point C, the banks hold all the cash and on that reserve base they create deposits of CB. The line AB thus plots the level of deposit creation resulting from each level of cash reserves (where point A represents the point where banks have no cash or deposits and point C represents the point where all the cash in the economy is held in bank reserves and CB is the value of bank deposits created on that reserve base). The banks' reserve ratio AC/CB is thus equal to (minus) the slope of AB.

The line CD represents the cash–deposit ratio for the non-bank public. Its slope, measured by EC/CF, is equal to that cash–deposit ratio. For a given base of high-powered money (cash), deposit creation will be determined at the point where these two ratios are both satisfied. This will be where CD and AB intersect. So the actual outcome is at point G, where banks have AE cash in reserves and create CF of deposits. The public holds EC of cash and CF of deposits. The total money supply at G is given by CF plus EC.

Increases in the cash base in the economy shift AB upwards parallel to itself. A fall in banks' reserve ratios makes AB flatter with A fixed. Increasing the public's preference for cash over deposits makes CD steeper with C fixed. Notice that we use the terms 'cash', 'high-powered money', and 'monetary base' equivalently. In reality, cash for the public can be only currency (notes and coins), but for the banks it can be currency or deposits with the Bank of England.

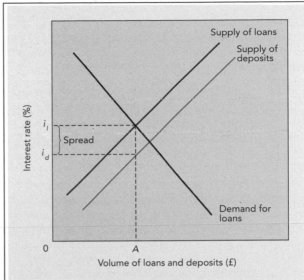

Figure 35.3 Competitive banking: supply and demand for loans

The volume of bank loans is determined by the intersection of the supply curve of loans and the demand curve for loans. The diagram shows the positively sloped supply curve of loans and the negatively sloped demand curve for loans. The supply curve of loans is determined by the supply curve of deposits and the spread, or the interest margin that banks require to cover costs and risk. For given interest rates elsewhere in the economy, the supply curve of deposits (which may not all be interest-bearing but are interest-bearing at the margin) is positively sloped because higher interest will attract more savings. The demand curve for loans is negatively sloped—high interest rates discourage borrowing and low rates encourage borrowing. Competition in banking drives the margin between deposit and loan rates to a level like i_l–i_d where the spread is just enough to allow banks to cover costs and make a normal return on capital. With the demand and supply curves shown there will be $0A$ deposits and loans, and depositors will receive an interest rate of i_d while borrowers pay the loan rate i_l.

and both are necessary for a complete understanding of modern monetary control techniques.

The ratios approach tells us that the total money supply is related to the stock of high-powered money, this relationship being determined by the reserve ratio of banks and the cash–deposit ratio of the public. For given reserve ratios, the total money supply would be determined if the authorities fixed the supply of high-powered money. However, in the United Kingdom the monetary authorities do not operate this way. Rather, they aim to control total deposits via the demand for bank loans. If they wish to lower deposits (and loans), they force up short-term interest rates, as shown in Figure 35.3. In other words, the authorities use the knowledge of the market demand curve for loans in order to influence the total stock of deposits and, therefore, also the money supply.

Having chosen what they think is the correct interest rate to generate the desired demand for loans, the UK monetary authorities supply whatever high-powered money is demanded at that going interest rate. So the authorities do not fix the supply of high-powered money; rather, this is demand-determined at the interest rate that policy-makers have set. The competitive model of banking helps us to see how this can be done by moving up or down the market demand curve for bank loans. We shall return to this issue in more detail below.

Before moving on, however, there are two other important insights provided by the competitive model of banking. First, in the absence of reserve requirements imposed on the banking system by the monetary authorities,[13] we can see that the reserve ratio that banks will choose will be the outcome of an internal optimization process. Banks will try to keep the level of reserves as low as possible, subject to the need to supply cash on demand when customers wish to withdraw deposits. This is because reserves earn no interest and banks would like to devote as much of their capital as possible to profitable uses. This means that, in the absence of high legal reserve requirements, banks' chosen reserve ratios tend to be very small, especially where they can access liquid funds very quickly by borrowing in the inter-bank market. The money multiplier has, as a result, got quite large (as discussed in Chapter 38).

Second, the competitive model helps us to understand that the banking system as a whole is in competition with other financial channels in the economy for the available amount of borrowing and lending (intermediation) business at any point in time. The real size of the banking sector, relative to other channels of finance (and, indeed, other industries), is determined by how efficient it is in supplying the intermediation services that the economy requires. Issues relating to the nominal size of bank deposits and the money supply should be kept separate from the question of the real relative size of the banking system.

Monetary institutions and markets

I N the following chapter we are concerned primarily with studying how monetary forces are involved with the macroeconomy, or, in other words, with how we can fit monetary factors into our discussion of national income determination. Before we proceed to this topic, however, it is useful to look more closely at some key monetary institutions, or sets of institutions. An understanding of institutions will help you to understand how policy decisions are actually put into practice.

Financial institutions

THE CENTRAL BANK

All major countries have a central bank. (The only exception is Hong Kong.) In the United Kingdom it is the Bank of England, in the United States it is the Federal Reserve System, in France the Banque de France, in Germany the Bundesbank. There are important differences in the way central banks operate from country to country, but they have one unique and common feature:

Central banks are the ultimate providers of high-powered money (cash) to the economy. As a result, they have the

job of controlling monetary conditions and are ultimately responsible for determining the value of a nation's currency, which is inversely related to the general price level.

The Bank of England was established in 1694 as a private joint-stock company. However, from the very beginning the Bank had a special relationship with the government. It was given a special charter in return for an agreement to lend money to the government. (The government had defaulted on its debt in 1672, so existing banks were reluctant to lend to it again.) The Bank of England was the only joint-stock bank, with limited liability for its shareholders—all other banks were permitted to have a maximum of just six partners, and these partners had unlimited liability. The Bank of England was also given a monopoly of government banking business. It, thus, became a very powerful bank in an environment where all other banks were necessarily small and under-capitalized. By 1826, when the restrictions on other banks began to be relaxed, the Bank of England was already evolving towards being the central bank in all but name. From that time on, the Bank increasingly focused on its role as banker to the government, and

---

[13] In the United Kingdom, reserves held with the Bank of England are currently required to be 0.40 per cent of deposits.

banker to the banks themselves, rather than seeking private-sector customers.

Two other important functions have also evolved from the special position the Bank has held. First, until 1931 (with two main breaks), the Bank of England operated under the gold standard (see pp. 738–9). This meant that its notes were convertible into gold at a fixed price. The Bank, therefore, had to maintain reserves of gold. These reserves were protected by excellent security (for many years there was an armed military guard), which led other bankers to deposit their gold with the bank as well. Hence the Bank held not only its own reserves, but also the reserves of the entire banking system. Gold, at the time, was also a major instrument for settling international debt. Hence this same gold reserve can be thought of, also, as the country's international reserve.

The Bank continued to hold gold reserves even after the gold standard was abandoned (and still does so today), but these ceased to be the domestic banking reserve: rather, they became part of international reserves. These international reserves (which today include foreign currency assets as well as gold) became the property of the UK Treasury when the Bank of England was nationalized in 1946. However, they are still operated by the Bank (in what is called the Exchange Equalization Account) on the Treasury's behalf. Thus, the Bank of England still has a role in foreign exchange markets, especially when the government is trying to influence foreign exchange rates (see Chapter 37).

The second important function of the Bank of England that derives from its specal position at the centre of the monetary system is as a *regulator* of the banking system. The Bank has for long had an informal role in monitoring and controlling the financial system, especially the City of London. Statutory responsibility for bank regulation was given to the Bank in the 1979 Banking Act, which resulted from the Secondary Banking Crisis of 1974, in which several fringe banks went bust.

Let us now summarize the main functions of the Bank of England:

The Bank of England has four main functions:

1 It is the ultimate supplier of cash to the monetary system, which it can literally print. As such, the Bank is sometimes referred to as 'Lender of Last Resort'. In this role, it implements monetary policy.

2 It is banker to the government and agent to the government for sales of government debt. It is also banker to the banks.

3 The foreign exchange reserve is operated by the Bank as agent for the Treasury.

4 The Bank of England is the regulator of all banks that trade under a UK banking licence. (Since 1 January 1993, EU banks may trade in other EU countries under a home-country banking licence.)

THE BANKING SYSTEM

The banking system is made up of *commercial banks* (or clearing banks[14]) and *investment banks* (or merchant banks). Commercial banks are primarily in the business of taking deposits and making loans. The commercial banking market in England and Wales is dominated by the big four High Street banks: NatWest, Barclays, Lloyds, and Midland. (In Scotland, the Bank of Scotland, the Royal Bank of Scotland, and Clydesdale are among the dominant group.) Investment banks specialize in raising capital for companies. They do some of this by making their own loans, but they also handle the issuance and trade in company debt (including equities). The long established investment banks in London, such as Barings and Rothschilds, have usually been called 'merchant banks' because they started as merchant banks and came to prominence through their expertise in trade finance.[15]

Until the 1980s, commercial banking was separated from many investment banking functions by traditional City conventions. However, the Big Bang reforms of 1986 allowed the major UK commercial banks to undertake investment banking operations. Thus, the functional distinction between UK commercial and investment banking no longer corresponds with discrete subsets of firms. In the United States, there has continued to be a legal separation of commercial and investment banking since the Glass–Steagall Act of 1933, although in practice this distinction has been fading and legal restrictions are currently being reformed.

Another useful distinction is between retail and wholesale banking. Retail banking is concerned with the deposit and loan business of personal or small business customers. In the personal market, the banks have considerable competition from *building societies*. Building societies are mutual organizations (which are owned by their members or customers) specializing traditionally in taking in savings deposits and offering loans (mortgages) for house purchase. The distinction between banks and building societies is shrinking slowly over time. In the 1980s banks started to compete with building societies for mortgage business, and the building societies, in turn, started to compete with banks by offering transactions services (chequebooks, cash cards, and credit cards) and loans unrelated to housing, as well as a range of other financial services. Indeed, the dividing line between banks and building societies became very confused in 1989, when the Abbey National Building Society converted into a bank. In 1994 Lloyds Bank launched a takeover of the Cheltenham and Gloucester Building Society, and in 1995 the Halifax and the Leeds building societies planned to merge and convert from mutual to PLC status (thereby becoming a bank).

[14] So called because they were members of London Clearing Banks Association.

[15] They are sometimes referred to as 'acceptance' houses because of their tradition of accepting or guaranteeing commercial bills.

BOX 35.2

The Eurodollar market

The Eurodollar market is a market in bank deposits and loans denominated in US dollars and located outside the United States. All the transactions handled in this market are of large denomination (wholesale), and they are made for specific periods of time, so deposits are not withdrawable on demand. Other currencies have become involved so the term 'Eurocurrency market' is also used, but the dollar is by far the dominant currency.

The main force driving the growth of the Eurodollar market was that it was dollar banking that avoided US Federal Reserve regulations. In the United States an interest rate ceiling on deposits (Regulation Q) was in force until 1981. There were also reserve requirements and deposit insurance subscriptions, which raised the margins (spreads) required on domestic as opposed to offshore business. Hence, Eurodollar deposits paid higher yields to savers, and Eurodollar loans were cheaper for borrowers, than their equivalent onshore products. A growing proportion of dollar banking business was thus attracted to the Eurodollar market and away from the banking system within the United States. A boost in turnover also came from the 1973 Oil Crisis; this gave oil producers substantial dollar balances which they wanted to lend, and other countries bigger payments deficits which they had to finance. The Euro-banking system took deposits from oil producers and made loans to oil importers. Much of the intermediation from one part of the world to another was channelled through the London interbank market.

Although it grew up to avoid US controls, the Eurodollar market also avoided UK banking controls in the 1960s and 1970s. For most of this time UK banks could not expand their sterling business because of official restrictions, but the dollar sector was uncontrolled (and was, therefore, effectively 'off-

shore'). This absence of control was one of the main reasons for the rapid growth of the Eurodollar market, especially in the two decades up to 1984. The importance of this activity for London can be seen in the chart from the fact that in 1984 dollar bank deposits in London were about four times the size of UK sterling bank liabilities. The relative importance of foreign currency banking (compared with domestic sterling banking) in London has since declined. The relative importance of domestic and foreign currency banking is illustrated in the chart.

The boom in Eurodollar banking ended in the 1980s, with the debt crisis that was triggered by Mexico defaulting on interest payments. Many banks (especially UK and US banks) had over-extended themselves in Eurodollar lending and had to write off substantial chunks of their assets. There were two important consequences of this crisis.

1. Many banks became very risky, and there was a serious possibility of major banks going bust. Risky borrowers have to pay a risk premium for borrowing in money and capital markets. As a result, banks became uncompetitive lenders, especially for large healthy corporations and for the governments of industrial countries. Accordingly, a process called *disintermediation* set in. This means that savers directed loans to ultimate borrowers through channels other than banks, notably securities markets. Creditworthy borrowers could borrow more cheaply by issuing their own debt than they could by borrowing from banks. For this reason, after 1982 the *Eurobond* market took over from the Eurocurrency market as the booming channel of finance. A Eurobond is a long-term debt instrument (normally dollar-denominated) issued by a company and launched outside that company's home capital markets. (Colourful terminology attaches to domestic bond issues in various currencies. Sterling

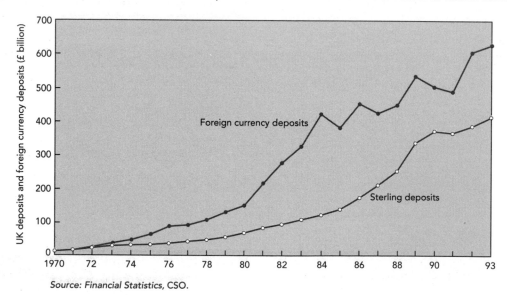

Source: Financial Statistics, CSO.

BOX 35.2 *continued*

issues are 'bulldogs', US dollars 'Yankees', Japanese yen 'samurai', Dutch guilder 'Rembrandts' etc.)

2. The world's bank regulators realized that they could no longer ignore the Eurodollar market, especially as what had happened there was threatening the survival of some of the world's major banks. The Basle Agreement of 1988 introduced a new regime of global bank regulation. Since its implementation, regulators have monitored their home-country banks on the basis of their global business, whereas before they had controlled only their domestic business. They also introduced a new set of minimum capital requirements which were to be standard for all major countries of the world.

In summary, the Eurodollar banking market was the product of a regulatory 'window' which arose in the transition from closed domestic financial systems to the global integrated financial system of today. The main regulatory loophole has now been closed. Banks face the same marginal capital requirements on offshore loans as on onshore ones. From now on, bankers will have to rediscover the skill of making good lending decisions rather than of outrunning the regulators.

Wholesale banking deals with large corporate customers, large governmental agencies, and other financial institutions. There are a substantial number (around 500) of foreign banks in London operating mainly in the wholesale market. Many were attracted to London by the growth of the Eurodollar market in the 1960s and 1970s (see Box 35.2) but most of these are now active in sterling as well as foreign currency money markets. Wholesale banking markets are highly competitive because there are a significant number of providers and it is an open international market.

The UK banking market has become increasingly competitive in recent years, because of competition between banks and building societies in the retail markets and competition from foreign banks in the wholesale markets.

THE DISCOUNT HOUSES

A feature of the UK monetary system which makes it different from most other countries is the role of a small set of financial institutions known as *discount houses*. There are around eight of these in London. They borrow money for very short periods (or 'at call', which means that it can be called back immediately) from banks, companies, and other financial institutions. The money they borrow is invested in the buying of commercial bills or Treasury bills. It is the fact that they buy and sell bills at a discount to their face value that earned them their label.

Discount houses would hardly rate a mention in an economics textbook were it not for the special role they play in the sterling money markets. In its operations in the sterling money markets, the Bank of England deals *only* with the discount houses. This dealing is often referred to as being through 'the discount window', but in fact, the representatives of the discount houses either meet Bank officials in an office or deal with them by telephone. The discount houses agree to take up any Treasury bills which the Bank wishes to sell (usually at a weekly tender). The Bank of England agrees to lend cash to the discount houses whenever they want it, but at an interest rate of the Bank's choosing. The

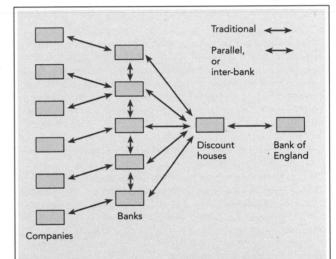

Figure 35.4 Traditional and parallel money markets

The traditional money market involves surplus funds flowing from banks (and companies) to the discount houses. The discount houses have access to borrowing (or rediscounting bills) from the Bank of England. In the parallel, or inter-bank, market, funds are channelled directly between the banks. Under present conventions, the banks are obliged to make some loans to discount houses.

Bank can always force the discount houses to borrow from it, by selling more bills than they would have chosen voluntarily to buy. (Recall that, by selling bills, the Bank is withdrawing high-powered money from the system.)

It is by forcing the discount houses to borrow (through the Bank's discount window) that the Bank of England sets interest rates in the sterling money markets. The interest rate set between the Bank of England and the discount houses is then transmitted very quickly to the rest of the monetary system, via the disount houses' dealing with the banks.

BOX 35.3

....

The globalization of financial markets

Technological innovations in communication and financial liberalization have led to a globalization of the financial service industry over the past two decades. Computers, satellite communication systems, reliable telephones with direct worldwide dialling, electronic mail, and fax machines—all coming into widespread use only within the past decade—have put people in instantaneous contact anywhere in the world.

As a result of these new technologies, borrowers and lenders can learn about market conditions and then move their funds instantly in search of the best loan rates. Large firms need transaction balances only while banks in their area are *open;* once banks close for the day in each area, the firms will not need these balances until the following day's reopening. Thus, the funds can be moved to another market, where they are used until *it* closes; they are then moved to yet another market. Funds are thus free to move from London to New York to Tokyo and back to London on a daily rotation. This is a degree of global sophistication that was inconceivable before the advent of the computer, when international communication was much slower and costlier than it now is. To facilitate the movement in and out of various national currencies, increasing amounts of bank deposits are denominated in foreign rather than domestic currencies.

One of the first developments in this movement towards globalization was the growth of the foreign currency markets in Europe in the 1960s. At first, the main currency involved was the US dollar, and so Eurodollar (see Box 35.2) markets were the first to develop. The progressive worldwide lifting of domestic interest-rate ceilings and other capital market restrictions that occurred in the 1980s led to a further globalization of financial markets. Particularly important was the abolition of exchange controls in country after country. The United Kingdom abolished its exchange controls in 1979, Japan did so in 1980; France and Italy in 1989, Spain in 1991, Portugal and Ireland in 1992, and Greece in 1994. Once such restrictions are abolished, the wholesale money markets integrate with the international money markets very quickly. This is because sophisticated borrowers and lenders dealing with large amounts of money have an incentive to shop around for the best terms.

The increasing sophistication of information transfer has also led to a breakdown of the high degree of specialization that had characterized financial markets in earlier decades. When information was difficult to obtain and analyse, an efficient division of labour called for a host of specialist institutions, each with expertise in a narrow range of transactions. As a result of the new developments in communication technology, economies of scale led to the integration of various financial operations within one firm. For example, in many countries banks have moved into the markets where securities are traded, while many security-trading firms have begun to offer a range of banking services. As the scale of such integrated firms increases, they find it easier to extend their operations geographically as well as functionally.

It has often been difficult for government regulations to keep up with these rapid changes. Governments that relaxed their regulations first in face of the evolving realities often allowed their financial institutions to gain important advantages in international competition. The UK government has been quick to react to these developments, and as a result London has retained its strong position in the international financial world. In contrast, the US government has been slow to adapt. For example, until 1994 it limited interstate banking, and it still keeps a separation of commercial and investment banking. As a result, the US banks have lost out to European and Japanese banks, although the 1994 abolition of interstate banking restrictions is likely to lead to a major merger movement in US banking and, thereby, to produce some of the worlds biggest banks.

The kinds of government intervention into domestic capital markets and government control over international capital flows that characterized the 1950s and 1960s is no longer possible. International markets are just too sophisticated. Globalization is here to stay, and, by removing domestic restrictions and exchange controls, governments in advanced countries are only bowing to the inevitable. However, globalization of regulation is now following market realities. The Basle Accord of 1988, for example, has introduced a new regime of global bank regulation.

Financial markets

The flows in the financial system are normally classified in broad categories depending upon the function they perform. Dividing lines are not precise, but the following terminology is commonly used.

MONEY MARKETS

The money markets are markets for short-term funds—typically, less than nine months and often just for a few

hours or overnight. These are important, because all companies and financial institutions find they have surplus funds on some days and deficits of cash flow on other days. The money markets enable surplus funds to be invested and to earn interest, while deficits can be funded easily (for a creditworthy borrower or 'good name').

The *traditional* money market is the one that links the banks via the discount house to the Bank of England (see Figure 35.4). The *parallel* money market is a market in short-term lending between the banks themselves, now more commonly called the inter-bank market. The latter is vastly more important in scale, but the existence of the former is essential for the transmission of interest rate signals from the Bank of England.

It is possible to imagine UK money markets operating without disount houses, but this would involve the Bank of England operating in the inter-bank market directly, probably by influencing the interest rates on overnight deposits. If the European Union ever adopts a single currency and the United Kingdom joins in, it is almost inevitable that discount houses will disappear, and the traditional London money market with them.

SECURITIES MARKETS

Securities markets differ from deposit and loan markets in that a tradable security or IOU changes hands. Securities that are issued for short periods (under nine months) are still classified as being part of the money market, because they are fulfilling the same need for short-term funding. Securities traded in money markets include commercial bills, Treasury bills, certificates of deposit (CDs), and commercial paper (CP). These are all just IOUs, but they vary in terms of risk and settlement terms.

We have mentioned corporate funding via bonds and equities earlier in this book (see Chapter 10). Here we do no more than point out that the equity and corporate bond markets are important sources of long-term finance for companies. London is one of the three main centres for trading corporate securities in what has now become an integrated global market (see Box 35.3). Markets for long-term finance are known collectively as *capital markets*.

One very important securities market is that in which the government does its long-term financing. In the financial year 1993/4 for example, the UK government had a Public Sector Borrowing Requirement (PSBR) of about £45 billion. This was funded largely by the sale of *gilt-edged securities*.[16] These are largely government bonds issued with fixed rates of interest which are redeemable in anything between 5 and 25 years. Other gilt-edged securities include the index-linked gilts, which pay a fixed real interest rate (that is, a specific rate on top of inflation) and are redeemed at a nominal value guaranteed in real terms.

The Bank of England acts as the agent for the government in conducting gilt sales, which it does via periodic public auctions. Occasionally, an issue of gilts will be held by the Bank of England and sold slowly to the market at the Bank's discretion. Such an issue is known as a 'tap' stock. The gilts market is different from the money market, in that it does not involve the discount market directly. However, the resulting payments from the private sector into the Bank of England do affect money flows into and out of the Bank of England

and hence determine whether the discount houses are going to have to go to the Bank to borrow. For this reason, what the Bank of England is doing via gilt sales cannot be entirely divorced from the ebb and flow of the money markets.

For example, suppose the Bank sold £100 million of gilts to the general public. The public would write cheques, which would be paid into the government's account at the Bank of England, and the commercial banks would lose the equivalent amount of deposits held at the Bank. They would then call back funds loaned to the discount market, and the discount houses would be forced to borrow from the Bank of England to make up this shortage.

In general, it is payments into or out of the government's account with the Bank of England, via debt sales, privatization issues, or tax payments, which create the need for active Bank of England participation in the money markets and create the opportunity for the Bank to set interest rates. If necessary, the Bank can create money shortages—and, therefore, a need for discount house borrowing—by appropriate sales of gilts.

THE FOREIGN EXCHANGE MARKET

Our discussion of financial markets would not be complete without mention of the foreign exchange markets. These are necessary because each nation-state has its own national currency. To trade with someone who lives in a different currency area from your own, you have to be able to change your local money (say, the pound sterling) into the money of the person whose goods you want to buy (say, the Deutschmark). The market in which currencies are exchanged for each other is the foreign exchange market.

London is the financial centre with the largest turnover of foreign exchange transactions. It trades not just the pound sterling against foreign currencies; the specific currency markets with the greatest volume of trade (for reasons we shall discuss in Chapter 37) are markets between the dollar and each of the other major currencies. We shall discuss exchange rates in more detail in Chapter 37. However, it is worth noting that trade in foreign exchange is one of the most important activities of the City of London. Its volume dwarfs many of the activities of the domestic financial sector.

The *daily* turnover in foreign exchange in London in 1994 averaged about $400 billion. This is not far short of the annual turnover of the UK equities market.

---

[16] So called because government debt is regarded as being very safe: the government always has the power to raise taxes to pay off its debts.

Summary

1 Money is a medium of exchange, a unit of account, and a store of value.

2 Money has evolved from being based primarily on a precious metal to being mainly in the form of bank deposits.

3 The existence of money frees the process of exchange from the constraint of the mutual coincidence of wants.

4 Banks create deposits to some multiple of their cash reserves.

5 In a competitive market, in which banks pay interest on deposits and loans, banks' behaviour is best understood in terms of demand and supply curves of deposits and loans. Banks must pay competitive interest rates to attract deposits, and they must charge competitive rates on their loans.

6 Central banks are the ultimate suppliers of cash to the monetary system and they have the power to set short-term interest rates in the money markets.

7 Money markets are the markets for short-term loans and deposits, whereas capital markets deal with the long-term funding needs of companies.

8 The gilt-edged market is the market for long-term government securities.

9 Discount houses have a special role in the sterling money markets because of their special access to the Bank of England.

10 The foreign exchange market enables one currency to be exchanged for another and hence permits international trade and investment flows in a world of many currencies.

Topics for review

- Functions of money

- Money multiplier

- Competitive banking systems

- The role of central banks

- Discount houses

- Money markets

- Securities markets

- Foreign exchange market

CHAPTER 36

The role of money in macroeconomics

I N this chapter we return to the theory of macroeconomics. In particular, we now focus on how monetary forces affect economic activity. We approach this issue via a number of steps. First, we discuss the factors that influence the demand and supply of money balances in the economy. Second, we ask how disequilibrium (excess demand or supply) in the monetary sector spills over into real activity. Having resolved that question, we are then able to accomplish the final task of integrating money and monetary policy into the aggregate demand and aggregate supply framework that we built up in Chapters 29–32. We start with some background material on financial assets and interest rates.

Financial assets

At any particular moment, people have a stock of wealth that they hold in many forms. Some of it may be money in the bank or building society; some may be cash in hand or under the mattress; some may be in shares; and some of it may be in property, such as a house.

To simplify our discussion, we will group wealth into just two categories, which we will call money and bonds. By 'money' we mean the assets that serve as a medium of exchange, that is, paper money, coins, and deposits on which cheques may be drawn.[1] By 'bonds' we mean all other forms of financial wealth; these include interest-earning financial assets *plus* claims on real capital.[2]

Money and bonds have different characteristics as assets. Bonds are risky because their price can rise or fall. The price of bonds is related to market interest rates, so our first task is to understand this relationship.

THE RATE OF INTEREST AND PRESENT VALUE

A bond is a financial asset that promises to make one or more interest payments and to repay a capital sum at a specified date in the future. The **present value** (PV) of a bond, or of any asset, refers to the value now of the future payment or payments to which the asset represents a claim. The concept of present value was first discussed in Chapter 20 on pp. 375–377.

Present value depends on the rate of interest, because when we calculate present value the interest rate is used to *discount* the future payments. This relationship between the rate of interest and present value can be seen by considering two extreme examples.

A single payment one year hence   We start with the simplest case. How much would someone be prepared to pay *now* to purchase a bond that will produce a single payment of £100 in one year's time?

Suppose that the interest rate is 5 per cent, which means that £1.00 invested today will be worth £1.05 in one year's

time. Now ask how much someone would have to lend in order to have £100 a year from now. If we use *PV* to stand for this unknown amount, we can write $PV(1.05)$ (which means *PV multiplied by* 1.05) = £100. Thus, $PV = £100/1.05$ = £95.24.[3] This tells us that the present value of £100 receivable in one year's time is £95.24; anyone who lends out £95.24 for one year at 5 per cent interest will get back the £95.24 plus £4.76 in interest, which sums to £100.

What if the interest rate had been 7 per cent? At that interest rate, the present value of the £100 receivable in one year's time would be £100/1.07 = £93.46, which is less than the present value when the interest rate was 5 per cent.

A perpetuity   Now consider another extreme case—a perpetuity that promises to pay £100 per year to its holder *for ever*. The *present value* of the perpetuity depends on how much £100 per year is worth, and this again depends on the rate of interest.

A bond that will produce a stream of income of £100 per year for ever is worth £1,000 at 10 per cent interest because £1,000 invested at 10 per cent per year will yield £100 interest per year for ever. However, the same bond is worth £2,000 when the interest rate is 5 per cent per year, because it takes £2,000 invested at 5 per cent per year to yield £100 interest per year. The lower the rate of interest obtainable on the market, the more valuable is a bond paying a fixed amount of interest.

Similar relations apply to bonds that are more complicated than single payments but are not perpetuities. Although in such cases the calculation of present value is more complicated, the same negative relationship holds between the interest rate and the present value.

The present value of any asset that yields a given stream of money over time is negatively related to the interest rate.

PRESENT VALUE AND MARKET PRICE

Present value is important because it establishes the market price for an asset.

The present value of an asset is the amount that someone would be willing to pay now to secure the right to the future stream of payments conferred by ownership of the asset.

---

[1] The precise definition of money is problematic and has changed frequently in the United Kingdom as a result of financial innovation. However, a further discussion of these problems will be found in Chapter 38.

[2] This simplification can take us quite a long way and is necessary in order to keep our model simple. However, for some problems it is better to treat debt and claims on capital as distinct assets, in which case at least three categories—money, debt (bonds), and equity (shares)—are used.

[3] Notice that in this type of formula the interest rate is expressed as a decimal fraction where, for example, 5 per cent is expressed as 0.05; so $(1 + i)$ equals 1.05.

To see this, return to our example of a bond that promises to pay £100 one year hence. When the interest rate is 5 per cent, the present value is £95.24. To see why this is the maximum that anyone would pay for this bond, suppose that some sellers offer to sell the bond at some other price, say, £98. If, instead of paying this amount for the bond, a potential buyer lends her £98 out at 5 per cent interest, she would have at the end of one year more than the £100 that the bond will produce: at 5 per cent interest, £98 yields £4.90 in interest, which when added to the principal makes £102.90. Clearly, no well-informed individual would pay £98—or by the same reasoning any sum in excess of £95.24—for the bond.

Now suppose that the bond is offered for sale at a price less than £95.24—say, £90. A potential buyer could borrow £90 to buy the bond and would pay £4.50 in interest on the loan. At the end of the year, the bond yields £100. When this is used to repay the £90 loan and the £4.50 in interest, £5.50 is left as profit. Clearly, it would be worth while for someone to buy the bond at £90 or, by the same argument, at *any* price less than £95.24.

This discussion should make clear that the present value of an asset determines its market price. If the market price of any asset is greater than the present value of the income stream that it produces, no one will want to buy it, and the market price will fall. If the market value is below its present value, there will be a rush to buy it, and the market price will rise. These facts lead to the following conclusion:

In a free market, the equilibrium price of any asset will be the present value of the income stream that it produces.

THE RATE OF INTEREST AND MARKET PRICE

The discussion above leads us to three important propositions. The first two stress the negative relationship between interest rates and asset prices:

1. If the rate of interest falls, the value of an asset producing a given income stream will rise.
2. A rise in the market price of an asset producing a given income stream is equivalent to a decrease in the rate of interest earned by the asset.

Thus, a promise to pay £100.00 one year from now is worth £92.59 when the interest rate is 8 per cent and only £89.29 when the interest rate is 12 per cent: £92.59 at 8 per cent interest (£92.59 × 1.08) and £89.29 at 12 per cent interest (£89.29 × 1.12) are both worth £100.00 in one year's time.

The third proposition focuses on the term to maturity of the bond:

3. The sooner is the maturity date of a bond, the less the bond's value will change with a change in the rate of interest.

To see this, consider an extreme case. The present value of a bond that is redeemable for £1,000 in one week's time will be very close to £1,000 no matter what the interest rate is. Thus, its value will not change much, even if the rate of interest leaps from 5 to 10 per cent during that week. Note that the interest-earning assets included in our definition of money are so short-term that their values remain unchanged when the interest rate changes.

As a second example, consider two bonds, one that promises to pay £100 next year and one that promises to pay £100 in ten years. A rise in the interest rate from 8 to 12 per cent will lower the value of £100 payable in one year's time by 3.6 per cent, but it will lower the value of £100 payable in ten years' time by 37.9 per cent.[4]

We now use what we have learned about the relationship between bond prices and interest rates to understand the factors affecting the choice between money and bonds.

The supply of money and the demand for money

The supply of money

The money supply is a *stock* (it is so many billions of pounds), not a *flow* of so many pounds per unit of time. In Chapter 35 we considered the factors that enable banks to create deposit money up to some multiple of the stock of high-powered money. We also saw that the stock of high-powered money could be directly controlled by the Bank of England. In Chapter 38 we shall discuss the realities of UK

monetary policy. Here, however, it is convenient to assume that the monetary authorities control the total money stock

---

[4] The example assumes annual compounding. The first case is calculated from the numbers of the previous example: (92.58 − 89.29)/92.58. The ten-year case uses the formula

$$\text{Present value} = \text{principal}/(1 + i)^n.$$

which gives £46.30 at 8 per cent and £28.75 at 12 per cent. The percentage fall in value is thus (46.30 − 28.75)/46.30 = 0.379, or 37.9 per cent.

directly, or, in other words, that the money stock is exogenously fixed by policy-makers. Our analysis therefore concentrates on the factors influencing money demand. It is important to notice that the money supply is a nominal variable, whereas the other variables in our macro model are measured in real terms.

The demand for money

The amount of wealth that everyone in the economy wishes to hold in the form of money balances is called the **demand for money**. Because people are choosing how to divide their given stock of wealth between money and bonds, it follows that, if we know the demand for money, we also know the demand for bonds. With a *given level of wealth*, a rise in the demand for money necessarily implies a fall in the demand for bonds; if people wish to hold £1 billion more of money, they must wish to hold £1 billion less of bonds. It also follows that, if households are in equilibrium with respect to their money holdings, they are in equilibrium with respect to their bond holdings.

When we say that on 31 December 1993 the quantity of money demanded was £550 billion, we mean that on that date the public wished to hold money balances that totalled £550 billion. But why do firms and individuals wish to hold money balances at all? There is a cost to holding any money balance. The money could have been used to purchase bonds, which earn higher interest than does money.[5] For the present, we assume no ongoing inflation, so there is no difference between real and nominal interest rates.

The opportunity cost of holding any money balance is the extra interest that could have been earned if the money had been used instead to purchase bonds.

Clearly, money will be held only when it provides services that are valued at least as highly as the opportunity cost of holding it. Three important services that are provided by money balances give rise to three different motives for holding money: the transactions, precautionary, and speculative motives. We examine each of these in detail.

THE TRANSACTIONS MOTIVE

Most transactions require money. Money passes from consumers to firms to pay for the goods and services produced by firms; money passes from firms to employees to pay for the factor services supplied by workers to firms. Money balances that are held to finance such flows are called **transactions balances**.

In an imaginary world in which the receipts and disbursements of consumers and firms were perfectly synchronized, it would be unnecessary to hold transactions balances. If, every time a consumer spent £10, she received

£10 as part payment of her wages, no transactions balances would be needed. In the real world, however, receipts and payments are not perfectly synchronized.

Consider the balances that are held because of wage payments. Suppose, for purposes of illustration, that firms pay wages every Friday and that employees spend all their wages on the purchase of goods and services, with the expenditure spread out evenly over the week. Thus, on Friday morning firms must hold balances equal to the weekly wage bill; on Friday afternoon the employees will hold these balances.

Over the week, workers' balances will be drawn down as a result of purchasing goods and services. Over the same period, the balances held by firms will build up as a result of selling goods and services until, on the following Friday morning, firms will again have amassed balances equal to the wage bill that must be met on that day.

The transactions motive arises because payments and receipts are not synchronized.

What determines the size of the transactions balances to be held? It is clear that in our example total transactions balances vary with the value of the wage bill. If the wage bill doubles for any reason, the transactions balances held by firms and households for this purpose will also double, on average. As it is with wages, so it is with all other transactions: the size of the balances held is positively related to the value of the transactions. It is the average value of money balances that people choose to hold over a particular period that is relevant for macroeconomics, but we need to know how money demand relates to national income rather than to total transactions. In fact, the value of all transactions exceeds the value of the economy's final output. When the miller buys wheat from the farmer and when the baker buys flour from the miller, both are transactions against which money balances must be held, although only the value added at each stage is part of national income.

Generally, there will be a stable, positive relationship between transactions and national income. A rise in national income also leads to a rise in the total value of all transactions and hence to an associated rise in the demand for transactions balances. This allows us to relate transactions balances to national income.

[5] As we mentioned in Chapter 35, many of the deposits that are included in money now yield interest. This complicates, but does not fundamentally alter, the analysis of the demand for money. In particular, it means that the opportunity cost of holding those interest-bearing components of money is not the *level* of interest rates paid on bonds, but the *difference* between that rate and the rate paid on money. Because the interest earned on deposits tends to fluctuate less than rates on marketable securities, the difference tends to move with the level of interest rates in the economy, rising when rates rise and falling when rates fall. For simplicity, we talk of the demand for money responding to the *level* of interest rates, but in reality it is the *difference* that is the opportunity cost of money. We shall deal with the problems created by the payment of interest on bank deposits more fully in Chapter 38.

The larger the value of national income, the larger is the value of transactions balances that will be held.

THE PRECAUTIONARY MOTIVE

Many expenditures arise unexpectedly, such as when your car breaks down, or when you have to make an unplanned journey to visit a sick relative. As a precaution against cash crises, when receipts are abnormally low or disbursements are abnormally high, firms and individuals carry money balances. **Precautionary balances** provide a cushion against uncertainty about the timing of cash flows. The larger such balances are, the greater is the protection against running out of money because of temporary fluctuations in cash flows.

The seriousness of the risk of a cash crisis depends on the penalties that are inflicted for being caught without sufficient money balances. A firm is unlikely to be pushed into insolvency, but it may incur considerable costs if it is forced to borrow money at high interest rates in order to meet a temporary cash crisis. Indeed, most firms have an overdraft facility with their bank precisely for this reason; it gives them the right to borrow money quickly when they are short of cash. (Of course, they still have to pay interest on what they borrow.)

The precautionary motive arises because households and firms are uncertain about the degree to which payments and receipts will be synchronized.

The protection provided by a given quantity of precautionary balances depends on the volume of payments and receipts. A £100 precautionary balance provides a large cushion for a person whose volume of payments per month is £800 and a small cushion for a firm whose monthly volume is £250,000. Fluctuations of the sort that create the need for precautionary balances tend to vary directly with the size of the firm's cash flow. In order to provide the same degree of protection as the value of transactions rises, more money is necessary.[6]

The precautionary motive, like the transactions motive, causes the demand for money to vary positively with the money value of national income.

For most purposes, the transactions and precautionary motives can be merged, as they both involve desired money holdings being positively related to income. Indeed, they both involve money being held in relation to planned or potential transactions.

THE SPECULATIVE MOTIVE

Money can be held for its characteristics as an asset. Firms and individuals may hold some money in order to provide a hedge against the uncertainty inherent in fluctuating prices of other financial assets. Money balances held for this purpose are called **speculative balances.** This motive was first analysed by Keynes, and the classic modern analysis was developed by Professor James Tobin, the 1981 Nobel Laureate in Economics.

Any holder of money balances forgoes the extra interest income that could be earned if bonds were held instead.[7] However, market interest rates fluctuate, and so do the market prices of existing bonds. (Their present values depend on the interest rate.) Because their prices fluctuate, bonds are a risky asset. Many individuals and firms do not like risk; they are said to be *risk-averse*.[8]

In choosing between holding money or holding bonds, wealth-holders must balance the extra interest income that they could earn by holding bonds against the risk that bonds carry. At one extreme, if individuals hold all their wealth in the form of bonds, they earn extra interest on their entire wealth, but they also expose their entire wealth to the risk of changes in the price of bonds. At the other extreme, if people hold all their wealth in the form of money, they earn less interest income, but they do not face the risk of unexpected changes in the price of bonds. Wealth-holders usually do not take either extreme position. They hold part of their wealth as money and part of it as bonds; that is, they *diversify* their holdings. The fact that some proportion of wealth is held in money and some in bonds suggests that, as wealth rises, so will desired money holding.

The speculative motive implies that the demand for money varies positively with wealth.

Although one individual's wealth may rise or fall rapidly, the total wealth of a society changes only slowly. For the analysis of short-term fluctuations in national income, the effects of changes in wealth are fairly small, and we shall ignore them for the present. Over the long term, however, variations in wealth can have a major effect on the demand for money.

Wealth that is held in cash or deposits earns less interest than could be earned by holding bonds; hence the reduction in risk involved in holding money carries an oppor-

---

[6] Institutional arrangements affect precautionary demands. In the past, for example, a traveller would have carried a substantial precautionary balance in cash, but today a credit card covers most unforeseen expenses that may arise during travelling.

[7] In Keynes's speculative motive, it is possible that money can be expected to have a higher return than bonds. This occurs if interest rates are low and *expected to rise*, so bond prices are expected to fall, creating a capital loss on bond holdings. In our analysis, which follows Tobin, interest rates are just as likely to rise or fall, irrespective of their current level. However, it is Keynes's analysis that gives rise to the term 'speculative', since it involves interest rate expectations.

[8] Recall that a person is risk-averse when he or she prefers a certain sum of money to an uncertain outcome for which the expected value is the same. See Chapter 9.

tunity cost in terms of forgone interest earnings. The speculative motive leads individuals and firms to add to their money holdings until the reduction in risk obtained by the last pound added is just balanced (in each wealth-holder's view) by the cost in terms of the interest forgone on that pound. A fall in the rate of return on bonds for the same level of risk will encourage people to hold more of their wealth as money and less in bonds. A rise in their rate of return for a given level of risk will cause people to hold more bonds and less money.

The speculative motive implies that the demand for money will be negatively related to the rate of interest.

The precautionary and transactions motives may also be negatively related to interest rates at the margin, because higher returns on bonds encourage people to economize on money-holding. However, in practice we observe only total money holdings, so we cannot distinguish the components held for different motives. Hence demand for money as a whole is likely to be positively related to national income and wealth, and negatively related to the interest rate.

REAL AND NOMINAL MONEY BALANCES

It is important to distinguish demand for real money balances from demand for nominal money. Real money demand is the number of units of purchasing power that the public wishes to hold in the form of money balances. For example, in an imaginary one-product (wheat) economy, this would be measured by the number of bushels of wheat that could be purchased with the money balances held. In a more complex economy, it could be measured in terms of the number of 'baskets of goods', represented by a price index such as the RPI, that could be purchased with the money balances held. When we speak of the demand for money in real terms, we speak of the amount demanded in constant pounds (that is, with a constant price level).

BOX 36.1

The quantity theory of money

The quantity theory of money can be set out in terms of four equations. Equation (i) states that the demand for money balances depends on the value of transactions as measured by nominal income, which is real income multiplied by the price level:

$$M^D = kPY. \qquad \text{(i)}$$

Equation (ii) states that the supply of money, M, is set by the central bank:

$$M^S = M. \qquad \text{(ii)}$$

Equation (iii) states the equilibrium condition that the demand for money must equal the supply:

$$M^D = M^S. \qquad \text{(iii)}$$

Substitution from (ii) and (iii) into Equation (i) yields:

$$M = kPY. \qquad \text{(iv)}$$

The original classical quantity theory assumes that k is a constant given by the transactions demand for money and that Y is constant because full employment is maintained. Thus, increases or decreases in the money supply lead to proportional increases or decreases in prices.

Often the quantity theory is presented by using the *equation of exchange*:

$$MV = PY. \qquad \text{(v)}$$

where V is the **velocity of circulation**, defined as national income divided by the quantity of money:

$$V = PY/M. \qquad \text{(vi)}$$

Velocity may be interpreted as showing the average amount of 'work' done by a unit of money. If annual national income is £400 billion and the stock of money is £100 billion, on average, each pound's worth of money is used four times to create the values added that compose the national income.

There is a simple relationship between k and V. One is the reciprocal of the other, as may be seen immediately by comparing (iv) and (vi). Thus, it makes no difference whether we choose to work with k or V. Further, if k is assumed to be constant, this implies that V also must be treated as being constant.

An example may help to illustrate the interpretation of each. Suppose the stock of money that people wish to hold equals one-fifth of the value of total transactions. Thus, k is 0.2 and V, the reciprocal of k, is 5. If the money supply is to be one-fifth of the value of annual transactions, each pound must be 'used' on average five times.

The modern version of the quantity theory does not assume that k and V are exogenously fixed. However, it does argue that they will not change in response to a change in the quantity of money.

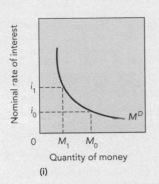
(i)

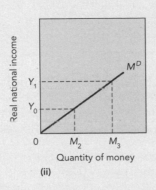
(ii)

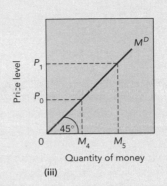
(iii)

Figure 36.1 The demand for money as a function of interest rates, income, and the price level

The quantity of money demanded varies negatively with the nominal rate of interest and positively with both real national income and the price level. In part (i) the demand for money is shown varying negatively with the interest rate along the money demand function. When the interest rate rises from i_0 to i_1, individuals and firms reduce the quantity of money demanded from M_0 to M_1.
In part (ii) the demand for money varies positively with national income. When national income rises from Y_0 to Y_1, individuals and firms increase the quantity of money demanded from M_2 to M_3.
In part (iii) the demand for money varies in proportion to the price level. When the price level doubles from P_0 to P_1, individuals and firms double the quantity of money demanded from M_4 to M_5.
In the text we refer to the M^D curve in (i) as the money demand function. It is drawn for given values of income, wealth, and the price level.

The real demand for money (or the demand for real money balances) is the nominal quantity demanded divided by the price level.

In the ten years from the end of 1983 to the end of 1993, the nominal quantity of money balances held in the United Kingdom roughly trebled, from just over £175 billion to £550 billion.[9] Over the same period, however, the price level, as measured by the RPI, rose by about 66 per cent. This tells us that the real quantity of money less than doubled, from £175 billion to about £332 billion, when measured in constant 1983 prices.

So far, we have held the price level constant, so we have been able to identify the determinants of the demand for real money balances as real national income, real wealth, and the interest rate. Now suppose that, with the interest rate, real wealth, and real national income being held constant, the *price level* doubles. Because the demand for real money balances will be unchanged, the demand for nominal balances must double: if the public previously demanded £300 billion in nominal money balances, it will now demand £600 billion. This keeps the real demand unchanged at £600/2 = £300 billion. The money balances of £600 billion at the new, higher price level represents exactly the same purchasing power as £300 billion at the old price level.

Other things being equal, the nominal demand for money balances varies in proportion to the price level; when the price level doubles, desired nominal money balances also double.

This is a central proposition of the quantity theory of money, which is discussed further in Box 36.1.

TOTAL DEMAND FOR MONEY

Figure 36.1 summarizes the influences of real national income, the nominal rate of interest, and the price level, the three variables that account for most of the short-term variations in the nominal quantity of money demanded. The function relating money demanded to the rate of interest is often called the **demand-for-money function**, even though the demand for nominal money depends also on income, wealth, and prices.

[9] This is the M4 definition of money, which is defined in Box 38.1 on p. 746.

Monetary forces and national income

WE are now in a position to examine the relationship between monetary forces, on the one hand, and the equilibrium values of national income and the price level, on the other. The first step in explaining this relationship is a new one: the link between monetary equilibrium and aggregate demand. The second is familiar from earlier chapters: the effects of shifts in aggregate demand on equilibrium values of national income and the price level.

Monetary equilibrium and aggregate demand

Monetary equilibrium occurs when the demand for money equals the supply of money. In Chapter 4 we saw that, in a competitive market for some commodity, such as carrots, the price will adjust so as to ensure equilibrium. The rate of interest does the same job with respect to money demand and money supply.

DETERMINATION OF THE INTEREST RATE

Figure 36.2 shows how the interest rate will change in order to equate the demand for money with its supply. When a few people find that they have less money than they wish to hold, they can sell some bonds and add the proceeds to their money holdings. This transaction simply redistributes given supplies of bonds and money among individuals; it does not change the total supply of either money or bonds.

Now suppose that all of the firms and households in the economy have excess demands for money balances. They all try to sell bonds to add to their money balances, but what one person can do, all cannot necessarily do. At any moment, the economy's total supply of money and bonds is fixed; there is just so much money and there are just so many bonds in existence. If everyone tries to sell bonds, there will be no one to buy them, and the price of bonds will fall.

We saw earlier in this chapter that a fall in the price of bonds means a rise in the rate of interest. As the interest rate rises, people will economize on money balances, because the opportunity cost of holding such balances is rising. This is what we saw in Figure 36.1(i), where the quantity of money demanded falls along the demand curve in response to a rise in the rate of interest. Eventually, the interest rate will rise enough that people will no longer be trying to add to their money balances by selling bonds. At that point there is no longer an excess supply of bonds, and the inter-est rate will stop rising. The demand for money again equals the supply.

Suppose now that all firms and households hold larger money balances than they would like. A single household or firm would purchase bonds with its excess balances, achieving monetary equilibrium by reducing its money holdings and increasing its bond holdings. However, just as in the previous example, what one individual can do, all cannot. At any moment, the total quantity of bonds is

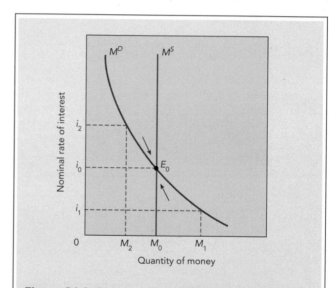

Figure 36.2 Determination of the interest rate

The interest rate rises when there is an excess demand for money and falls when there is an excess supply of money. The fixed quantity of money, M_0, is shown by the completely inelastic supply curve, M^S. The demand for money is M^D; its negative slope indicates that a fall in the rate of interest causes the quantity of money demanded to increase; it is drawn for given values of income, wealth, and the price level. Equilibrium is at E_0, with a rate of interest i_0. If the interest rate is i_1, there will be an excess demand for money of $M_0 M_1$. Bonds will be offered for sale in an attempt to increase money holdings. This will force the rate of interest up to i_0 (the price of bonds falls), at which point the quantity of money demanded is equal to the fixed available quantity, M_0. If the interest rate is i_2, there will be an excess supply of money $M_2 M_0$. Bonds will be demanded in return for excess money balances. This will force the rate of interest down to i_0 (the price of bonds rises), at which point the quantity of money demanded has risen to equal the fixed money supply, M_0.

fixed, so everyone cannot simultaneously add to personal bond-holdings. When all actors enter the bond market and try to purchase bonds with unwanted money balances, they bid up the price of existing bonds, and the interest rate will fall. Households and firms then become willing to hold larger quantities of money; that is, the quantity of money demanded increases along the money demand curve in response to a fall in the rate of interest. The rise in the price of bonds continues until firms and households stop trying to convert bonds into money. In other words, it continues until everyone is content to hold the existing supply of money and bonds.

Monetary equilibrium occurs when the rate of interest is such that the demand for money equals its supply, and hence the demand for bonds equals their supply.

The determination of the interest rate, depicted in Figure 36.2, is sometimes called the *liquidity preference theory* of interest and sometimes the *portfolio balance theory*.

As we shall see, a monetary disturbance—a change in either the demand for or supply of money—will lead to a change in the interest rate. However, as we saw in Chapter 31, desired aggregate expenditure is sensitive to changes in the interest rate. Here, then, is a link between monetary factors and real expenditure flows.

THE TRANSMISSION MECHANISM

The mechanism by which changes in the demand for and supply of money affect aggregate demand is called the **transmission mechanism.** The transmission mechanism operates in three stages: the first is the link between monetary equilibrium and the interest rate, the second is the link between the interest rate and investment expenditure, and the third is the link between investment expenditure and aggregate demand.

From monetary disturbances to changes in the interest rate
The interest rate will change if the equilibrium depicted in

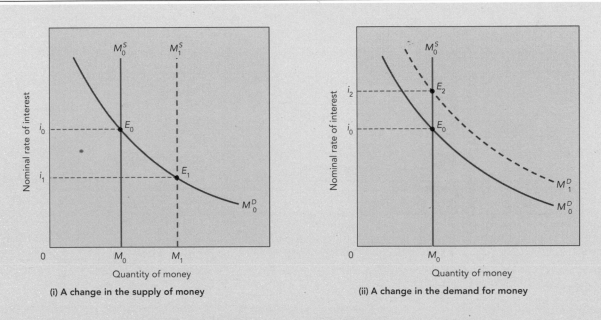

Figure 36.3 Monetary disturbances and interest rate changes

Shifts in the money supply or in the demand for money cause the equilibrium interest rate to change.
In both parts of the figure the money supply is shown by the vertical curve M_0^S and the demand for money is shown by the negatively sloped curve M_0^D. The initial equilibrium is at E_0, with corresponding interest rate i_0. In part (i) an increase in the money supply causes the money supply curve to shift to the right, from M_0^S to M_1^S. The new equilibrium is at E_1, where the interest rate is i_1, less than i_0. Starting at E_1, with M_1^S and i_1, it can be seen that a decrease in the money supply to M_0^S leads to an increase in the interest rate from i_1 to i_0. In part (ii) an increase in the demand for money causes the M^D curve to shift to the right from M_0^D to M_1^D. The new equilibrium occurs at E_2, and the new equilibrium interest rate is i_2, greater than i_0. Starting at E_2, we see that a decrease in the demand for money from M_1^D to M_0^D leads to a decrease in the interest rate from i_2 to i_0.

Figure 36.2 is disturbed by a change in either the supply of money or the demand for money. For example, as Figure 36.3(i) illustrates, an increase in the supply of money, with an unchanged money demand function, will give rise to an excess supply of money at the original interest rate. As we have seen, an excess supply of money will cause the interest rate to fall. Also, again as shown in Figure 36.3(i), a decrease in the supply of money will cause the interest rate to rise.

As we can see in Figure 36.3(ii), an increase in the demand for money, with an unchanged supply of money, will give rise to an excess demand for money at the original interest rate and will cause the interest rate to rise; also, a decrease in the demand for money will cause the interest rate to fall.

Monetary disturbances, which can arise from changes in either the demand for or the supply of money, cause changes in the interest rate.

From changes in the interest rate to shifts in aggregate expenditure The second link in the transmission mechanism relates interest rates to expenditure. We saw in Chapter 29 that investment, which includes expenditure on inventory accumulation, residential construction, and business fixed investment, responds to changes in the real rate of interest.

Other things being equal, a decrease in the real rate of interest makes borrowing cheaper and generates new investment expenditure.[10] This negative relationship between investment and the rate of interest is called the **investment demand function**, denoted I^D.

The first two links in the transmission mechanism are shown in Figure 36.4. We concentrate for the moment on changes in the money supply, although, as we have seen already, the process can also be set in motion by changes in the demand for money. In part (i), we see that a change in the money supply causes the rate of interest to change in the opposite direction. In part (ii), we see that a change in the interest rate causes the level of investment expenditure to change in the opposite direction.[11] Therefore, changes in the money supply cause investment expenditure to change in the same direction.

---

[10] In Chapter 29 we saw that purchases of durable consumer goods also respond to changes in the real interest rate. In this chapter we concentrate on investment expenditure, which may be taken to stand for *all* interest-sensitive expenditure, and we maintain our simplifying assumption that expected inflation is zero so that the real and nominal interest rates are equal.

[11] Recall that we have assumed that real and nominal interest rates are the same. Generally, as long as inflation expectations are constant, the change in the nominal interest rate determined in part (i) of Figure 36.4 is equal to the change in the real interest rate in part (ii).

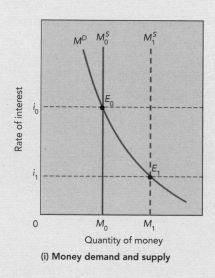

(i) **Money demand and supply**

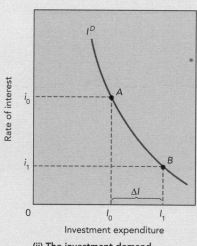

(ii) **The investment demand function**

Figure 36.4 The effects of changes in the money supply on investment expenditure

Increases in the money supply reduce the rate of interest and increase desired investment expenditure. Initial equilibrium is at E_0, with a quantity of money M_0 (shown by the inelastic money supply curve M_0^S), an interest rate of i_0, and an investment expenditure of I_0 (point A). The Bank of England then increases the money supply to M_1 (shown by the money supply curve M_1^S). This lowers the rate of interest to i_1 and increases investment expenditure by ΔI to I_1 (point B). A reduction in the money supply from M_1 to M_0 raises the interest rate from i_1 to i_0 and lowers investment expenditure by ΔI from I_1 to I_0.

An increase in the money supply leads to a fall in the interest rate and an increase in investment expenditure. A decrease in the money supply leads to a rise in the interest rate and a decrease in investment expenditure.

The change in investment expenditure shifts the aggregate expenditure curve, AE, as shown in Chapters 29 and 30.

From shifts in aggregate expenditure to shifts in aggregate demand   Now we are back on familiar ground. In Chapter 31 we saw that a shift in the aggregate expenditure curve leads to a shift in the AD curve; however, there the shifts in AE were caused by changes in exogenous expenditures. This is shown again in Figure 36.5.

A change in the money supply, by causing a change in desired investment expenditure (which earlier was assumed to be exogenous) and hence a shift in the AE curve, causes the AD curve to shift. An increase in the money supply causes an increase in investment expenditure and therefore an increase in aggregate demand. A decrease in the money supply causes a decrease in investment expenditure and therefore a decrease in aggregate demand. We had already established this link from AE to AD in Chapter 31. What is new here is the link from the money supply via interest rates to changes in investment, which in turn shift AE.

The transmission mechanism connects monetary forces and real expenditure flows. It works from a change in the demand for or the supply of money to a change in bond prices and interest rates, to changes in investment expenditure, and to a shift in the aggregate demand curve.

This is illustrated in Figure 36.6 for an expansionary monetary shock and a contractionary monetary shock. A preliminary discussion of how the openness of the economy affects the transmission mechanism is presented in Box 36.2. This discussion is extended in the following chapters.

An alternative derivation of the aggregate demand curve: *IS/LM*

We now set out a well-known derivation of aggregate demand. There are no new economic relationships or even different assumptions involved here, compared with our earlier discussions of aggregate demand. This particular diagrammatic exposition was devised by Nobel Laureate Sir John Hicks. It is so familiar to economists today that it is frequently quoted. Students who have followed the macroeconomics chapters this far already understand the economics behind the *IS/LM* model, but it is also helpful to

know what specific bit of analysis '*IS/LM*' refers to. The diagrammatic apparatus does, however, have one important payoff, in that it helps to make clear differences in the

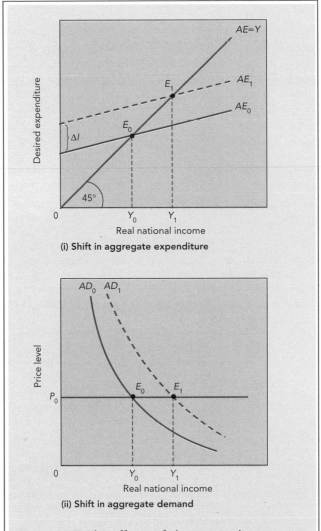

Figure 36.5 The effects of changes in the money supply on aggregate demand

Changes in the money supply cause shifts in the aggregate expenditure and aggregate demand functions. In Figure 35.4 an increase in the money supply increased desired investment expenditure by ΔI. Here, in part (i) the aggregate expenditure function shifts up by ΔI (which is the same as ΔI in Figure 35.4), from AE_0 to AE_1. At the fixed price level P_0, equilibrium income rises from Y_0 to Y_1, as shown by the horizontal shift in the aggregate demand curve from AD_0 to AD_1 in part (ii).
When the supply of money falls (from M_1^S to M_0^S in Figure 34.4), investment falls by ΔI, thereby shifting aggregate expenditure from AE_1 to AE_0. At the fixed price level P_0, this reduces equilibrium income from Y_1 to Y_0.

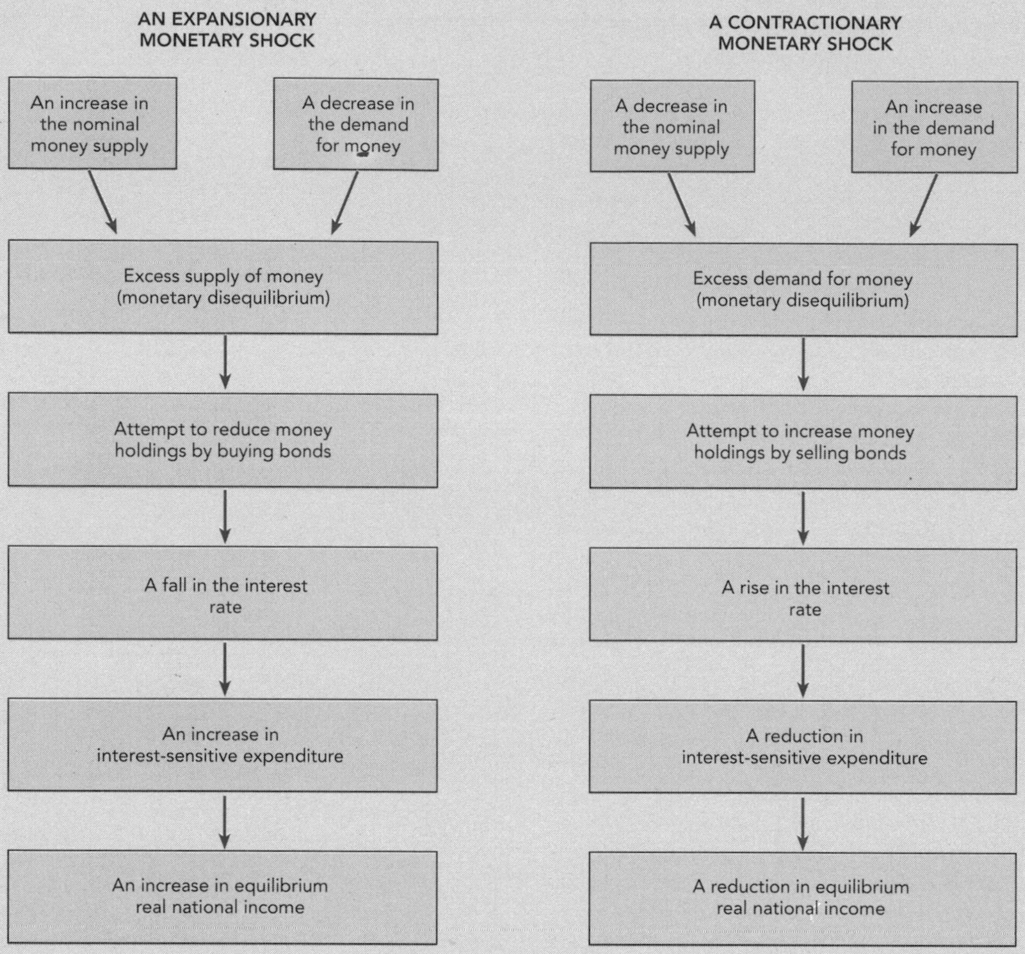

AN EXPANSIONARY MONETARY SHOCK

An increase in the nominal money supply	A decrease in the demand for money

Excess supply of money (monetary disequilibrium)

Attempt to reduce money holdings by buying bonds

A fall in the interest rate

An increase in interest-sensitive expenditure

An increase in equilibrium real national income

A CONTRACTIONARY MONETARY SHOCK

A decrease in the nominal money supply	An increase in the demand for money

Excess demand for money (monetary disequilibrium)

Attempt to increase money holdings by selling bonds

A rise in the interest rate

A reduction in interest-sensitive expenditure

A reduction in equilibrium real national income

Figure 36.6 The monetary transmission mechanism

The transmission mechanism causes monetary shocks to be translated into real expenditure effects. An expansionary shock arises from either an increase in the money supply or a decrease in the demand for money. Opposite changes cause contractionary shocks. The flow chart shows how the shock works through asset adjustments, to the interest rate, and to real expenditure flows.

transmission mechanism between monetary and fiscal policy. We shall use it in that context later in this chapter and again in Chapter 39 when comparing monetary and fiscal policy under different exchange rate regimes. It is also helpful to understanding some different approaches in macro-economics which are discussed in an appendix to this chapter.

For purposes of the present analysis, we assume that real wealth is constant and that there are no relative price changes between domestic and foreign goods—these were the factors that gave us a negatively sloped aggregate demand curve in Chapters 31 and 32. In our above discussion we have, in effect, demonstrated that interest rate linkages (our transmission mechanism of monetary policy) also imply a negatively sloped aggregate demand curve. What follows amounts to an explicit derivation of that negatively sloped *AD* curve.

THE *IS* CURVE

We saw above that investment expenditures were assumed to be related to the rate of interest. Figure 36.4(ii) plots the

Box 36.2

The transmission mechanism in an open economy

The text focuses on the interest rate as the channel through which the effects of monetary policy are transmitted to the economy. However, as we have observed in earlier chapters, the 'openness' of the economy to international trade and to capital flows means that two additional complications must be allowed for.* First, the effects of monetary contraction or expansion are weakened because UK interest rates are closely linked to interest rates in the rest of the world; this restricts the scope for domestic interest rates to change in response to monetary policy. (The strength of this restriction varies with the exchange rate regime—it is weakest under floating excxhange rates, stronger under pegged exchange rates, and would be overwhelming under a single EU currency.) Second, there is an added channel through which the effects of monetary policy are transmitted to real aggregate demand. This is through changes in the external value of the pound sterling on the foreign exchange market. (This effect applies almost exclusively to a floating exchange rate regime.)

The link between interest rates and the external value of the pound

If UK interest rates rise relative to those in other countries, the demand for sterling-denominated assets will also rise. UK residents will be less inclined to invest in assets of other countries, and foreign demand for high-yielding UK assets will increase. In order to invest in these assets, foreigners need to buy pounds, and their demand for these pounds on the foreign exchange rate will cause the pound to appreciate.

Low UK interest rates have the opposite effect. UK citizens will want to invest in foreign assets, and foreigners will be less anxious to invest in UK assets. Foreigners will demand fewer pounds, and people in the United Kingdom will be selling more pounds in order to obtain foreign currencies to invest in higher-yielding foreign assets. This will cause a depreciation of the pound on the foreign exchange market.

Other things being equal, the higher UK interest rates are, the higher will be the external value of the pound, and the lower UK interest rates are, the lower will be the external value of the pound.

The impact of changes in the money supply

Suppose that, in order to stimulate the economy, the Bank of England increases the money supply. The initial effects will be exactly the same as in the closed economy analysed in the text. Holders of money now find that they have excess money balances at the current levels of income, prices, and interest rates. Hence they increase their demand for bonds. This drives up the price of bonds and lowers the interest rate.

It is at this point that open-economy forces come into play. As UK interest rates fall, foreigners and UK citizens will start to sell UK assets in order to purchase foreign assets that now earn interest rates higher than those prevailing in the United Kingdom.

Because people are selling sterling assets, the fall in UK interest rates is mitigated. In this way, UK interest rates are constrained by those abroad; the availability of interest-earning assets in foreign currencies that investors think are substitutes for UK securities implies that UK interest rates do not move as much in response to changes in the money supply as they would in a closed economy.

People who have sold their sterling-denominated assets will now wish to sell pounds in order to buy foreign exchange which they will use to purchase foreign assets. This causes a depreciation of the pound on the foreign exchange market.**

An increase in the money supply will lead to a fall in domestic interest rates and a depreciation of sterling. A decrease in the money supply will have the opposite effects, resulting in an increase in interest rates and an appreciation of sterling.

The transmission mechanism

How are impacts on the interest rate and the external value of the pound transmitted into changes in the level of economic activity? The reduced response of interest rates to monetary policy implies less of an effect, for a given change in the money supply, on interest-sensitive expenditures. However, the induced changes in the value of the pound add a new channel by which monetary policy is transmitted to the economy, though clearly this applies only when the exchange rate is floating. A depreciation of the pound, other things being equal, makes UK-produced goods more competitive on world markets and thus increases exports and decreases imports.

Because an increase in the money supply leads to a depreciation of the pound sterling, it stimulates net exports and thereby raises aggregate demand. Similarly, a decrease in the money supply will lower aggregate demand because it leads to an appreciation of the pound and hence to a fall in net exports.

The operation of this channel of the transmission mechanism can be seen in terms of the definition of aggregate demand:

$$AD = C + I + G + (X - IM).$$

* These issues are discussed in more detail in Chapter 39.
** Equilibrium will occur when the pound has depreciated so much that people expect it to appreciate later (i.e., the exchange rate 'overshoots' its long-run value), and that expected appreciation compensates investors for the lower nominal interest rate on UK bonds. This theory is discussed in more detail in Chapter 37.

Box 36.2 *continued*

In a closed economy, monetary policy operates through changes in the interest rate influencing investment expenditure (I) as well as any interest-sensitive consumption expenditures (C); in the open economy that channel is weakened, but the effects on aggregate demand are reinforced through the effects of changes in the exchange rate on net exports ($X - IM$).

Although the channels are different, the ability of monetary policy to affect national income remains. In the rest of this chapter, we maintain the closed-economy emphasis for simplicity; we return to the open economy issues in Chapters 37 and 39.

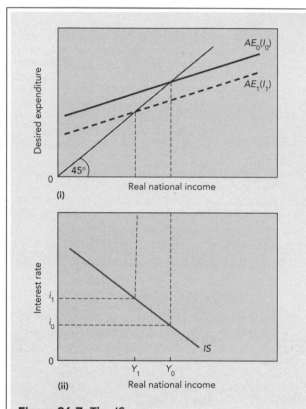

Figure 36.7 The *IS* curve

The *IS* curve shows the equilibrium level of national income associated with each given rate of interest. It shows combinations of the interest rate and income for which desired expenditure equals actual national income and output, and for which injections equal withdrawals. Part (i) shows a fall in AE resulting from a fall in investment from I_0 to I_1. This fall in I is caused by a rise in the interest rate from i_0 to i_1. The fall in investment produces a fall in the level of national income at which desired expenditure equals income from Y_0 to Y_1.

Part (ii) shows the resulting combinations of the interest rate and national income. For given values of exogenous expenditures, i_0 leads to a level of national income Y_0, and i_1 leads to level of national income Y_1. Choosing any other level of the interest rate and following through its effect on national income via investment produces all the other points on the *IS* curve.

negative relationship between interest rates and investment, called the investment demand function. We have also seen (in Figure 36.5) that an increase in investment shifts the *AE* curve upwards, and that this is associated with an increase in equilibrium national income.

The *IS* curve plots the relationship between the interest rate and the equilibrium level of national income, via the aggregate expenditure line *AE*. It tells us what the level of final expenditures, and therefore the equilibrium level of national income, will be for each rate of interest. The relationship is negative, because higher interest rates cause investment to fall, which shifts *AE* down and lowers equilibrium Y; and lower interest rates cause investment to rise, which shifts *AE* up and raises equilibrium Y. This relationship is plotted in Figure 36.7.

In a closed economy with no government, the *IS* curve would plot the combinations of the interest rate and national income for which saving and investment are equal, which is why it is called '*IS*'. However, in an open economy with a government, it plots the combinations of the interest rate and national income for which planned expenditure (*AE*) equals output, or for which injections equal withdrawals ($S + T + IM = I + G + X$).

The *IS* curve is the locus of interest rates and equilibrium levels of national income that are consistent with equilibrium between desired expenditures and output. It is drawn for given values of all other exogenous expenditures, such as G and X and for a given price level.

An increase in exogenous expenditures shifts the *IS* curve to the right (by the initial increase in expenditure times the multiplier), while a fall in exogenous expenditures shifts the *IS* curve to the left.

THE *LM* CURVE

Figure 36.2 illustrates equilibrium in the money market at the point where the money demand schedule M^D intersects the (policy-determined) money supply curve. The M^D curve plots the demand for money for given levels of income, the price level, and wealth. We continue to assume that wealth and the price level are constant, but what happens in that figure if income were to increase? The answer

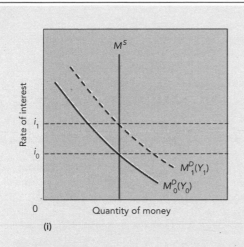
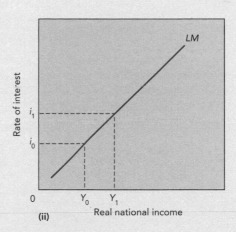

Figure 36.8 The *LM* curve

The *LM* curve shows the combinations of national income and the interest rate that are consistent with the equality of money demand and supply, for a given nominal money supply and given price level. Part (i) shows equilibrium in the money market with a fixed money supply and an M^D function that is negatively sloped. At an initial level of national income, Y_0, the demand for money is given by M_0^D and the equilibrium interest rate is i_0. At higher levels of national income the M^D curve shifts to the right. (Higher levels of national income cause a higher transactions demand for money.) When national income increases to Y_1, money demand shifts to M_1^D and the associated equilibrium interest rate rises to i_1.

In part (ii) the *LM* curve plots the equilibrium interest rate associated with each possible Y. This is a positively sloped curve. An increase in the nominal money supply shifts the *LM* curve parallel to the right and a decrease in the nominal money supply shifts the *LM* curve to the left.

is shown in Figure 36.8(i). As income increases, transactions and precautionary demand both increase, and so the M^D curve shifts to the right. At higher income levels, and with a given money supply, the equilibrium interest rate will rise. This is because, while the actual money supply is fixed, higher income has increased money demand. People will try to sell bonds (to get more money) until the price of bonds falls and interest rates, therefore, rise. The required rise in interest rates is the amount that is just sufficient to cause a fall in speculative demand that exactly offsets the rise in transactions demand.

The *LM* curve plots combinations of national income and the interest rate, for a given money supply and given price level, that are consistent with the equality of money demand and money supply.

The *LM* curve is plotted in Figure 36.8(ii). It shows a positive locus of combinations of national income and the interest rate consistent with money market equilibrium. An increase in the money supply shifts the *LM* curve to the right, while a decrease in the money supply shifts the *LM* curve to the left. To see this, shift the vertical money supply curve in part (i) of the figure. An increase in the money

supply produces a lower equilibrium interest rate for each level of Y (and therefore for each M^D curve), whereas a decrease in the money supply produces a higher equilibrium interest rate for each level of Y.

IS/LM AND AGGREGATE DEMAND

The *IS* and *LM* curves each tell part of the story of the determination of aggregate demand. The *IS* curve determines income for given interest rates, while the *LM* curve determines the interest rate for given levels of income. In effect, they are two simultaneous equations in income and the interest rate. One (*IS*) represents the set of equilibrium points for which desired expenditure equals national income; the other (*LM*) represents the set of equilibrium points for which money demand equals money supply. Equilibrium for the whole economy (but still excluding the supply side) must be on both the *IS* and *LM* curves. This will be where they intersect (see Figure 36.9).

In the past, the *IS/LM* model was widely used to analyse the effects of either changes in the money supply (shifts in *LM*) or changes in fiscal policy (shifts in *IS*) on national income. However, this framework has the limitation that it can be used (on its own) only for cases where either the

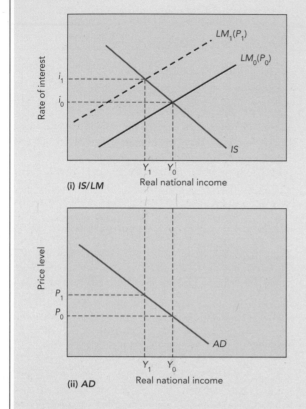

(i) IS/LM   Real national income

(ii) AD   Real national income

Figure 36.9 *IS–LM and aggregate demand*

The *AD* curve plots the *IS–LM* equilibrium level of national income for each given price level, holding all exogenous expenditures and the nominal money supply constant. Part (i) has the initial position as the intersection of LM_0 (which is drawn with price level P_0) with the *IS* curve. This gives the overall equilibrium levels of national income and the interest rate as Y_0 and i_0. At higher price levels the *LM* curve shifts to the left (because the real money supply falls). At price level P_1 the *LM* curve is given by LM_1, and this leads to equilibrium national income and the interest rate of Y_1 and i_1. Part (ii) plots out the resulting combinations of the price level and national income. This is the aggregate demand curve, *AD*. An increase in the money supply or exogenous expenditures will shift the *AD* curve to the right. A decrease in the money supply or of exogenous expenditures will shift the *AD* curve to the left.

To derive the *AD* curve, we take given *IS* and *LM* curves and ask the question: what happens to the level of national income (determined by their intersection) as the price level rises? The answer is that a higher price level shifts the *LM* curve to the left, and, for a given nominal money supply, and given all exogenous expenditures, leads to a lower level of national income. The reason why an increase in the price level shifts the *LM* curve to the left is that the fixed money supply is nominal but money is demanded in relation to its real purchasing power. This means that, as the price level rises, there will be an increase in the nominal quantity of money demanded to finance a given volume of real transactions. This would lead to an upward shift in the M^D curves in Figure 36.8(i) and so would lead to a higher equilibrium interest rate for each level of real national income. This shifts the *LM* curve (upwards) to the left. An alternative way of making the same point (that a higher price level shifts the *LM* curve leftwards) would be to draw Figure 36.8(i) with the *real* money stock on the horizontal axis. Then, an increase in the price level would simply reduce the *real* money supply and shift the M^S curve to the left. These two different ways of expressing the point are equivalent and lead to the same impact of price level changes on the *LM* curve. By taking different price levels, we plot out the aggregate demand curve. Notice that the *AD* curve is drawn for given levels of the money supply and exogenous expenditures, but *not* for given levels of endogenous variables, like the interest rate, consumption, investment, and income.

This derivation also helps us to understand the determinants of the slope of the *AD* curve. Since it is determined by the intersection of the *IS* and *LM* curves, it depends upon the slopes of both. These, in turn, depend on four factors: the interest and income elasticities of the demand for money, the interest elasticity of investment, and the size of the multiplier.

This reinforces our earlier argument, that the slope of the *AD* curve is not logically the same as any micro demand curve. The logic here is more tortuous—higher price level lowers real money supply; this raises interest rates; this lowers investment; and this lowers national income via the multiplier. In addition, there is the wealth effect and the effect of rising relative prices of domestic goods, which we studied in Chapter 31.

All that remains is to show that an increase in the money supply will shift the *AD* curve to the right (while a decrease in the money supply will shift the *AD* curve to the left). This can be done in Figure 36.9 simply by shifting the *LM* curve to the right for each price level. With a given *IS* curve, each higher money supply will be associated with a higher equilibrium level of national income. Therefore, a rightward shift of the *LM* curve leads to a rightward shift of the *AD* curve. Hence an exogenous increase in the nominal money supply shifts the *AD* curve to the right, and an exogenous decrease in the nominal money supply shifts the *AD* curve to the left.

price level is fixed and real income is variable, or where real income is fixed and the price level is variable. When output and prices are simultaneously variable, we need to move to the *AS/AD* framework to handle the analysis.

There is nothing wrong in the *IS/LM* model; it is just incomplete. Indeed, it can be used to derive the *AD* curve (thereby illustrating that the *IS/LM* model is consistent with our approach to *AD*). The *AD* curve implied by our *IS/LM* model is derived in Figure 36.9(ii).

Aggregate demand, the price level, and national income

WE have now completed a major task in macroeconomics, the addition of a monetary sector to our model of the macroeconomy. As a result, we are now able to analyse *monetary* influences on national income determination as well as all those other influences which we discussed in Chapters 29–32. However, by adding a monetary sector, we have also added to the economic linkages that affect the transmission of exogenous expenditure shocks (including fiscal policy). In particular, we have added a feedback mechanism involving interest rates. Accordingly, for the remainder of this chapter, we must first see how monetary shocks feed through the economy in the *AD/AS* framework, then re-examine how other shocks now influence national income in the presence of monetary feedbacks.

THE SLOPE OF THE *AD* CURVE REVISITED

Let us now review how the monetary transmission mechanism adds to the explanation (given in Chapter 31) of the negative slope of the *AD* curve, that is, we need to understand why equilibrium national income is negatively related to the price level (other things being held constant— including all exogenous expenditures and the money supply). In Chapter 31, when explaining the negative slope of the *AD* curve, we mentioned three reasons: the wealth effect, the substitution of domestic for foreign goods, and the effect operating through interest rates. Now that we have developed a theory of money and interest rates, we are able to understand in more detail the effect that works through the monetary sector. This effect is important because, empirically, the interest rate is a very important link between monetary factors and real expenditure flows.

The essential feature of this effect is that a rise in the price level raises the money value of transactions. This leads to an increased nominal demand for money, which brings the transmission mechanism into play. People try to sell bonds to add to their nominal money balances, but, collectively, all they succeed in doing is forcing up the interest rate. The rise in the interest rate reduces investment expenditure and so reduces equilibrium national income.

We now turn to an analysis of how the effects of monetary and expenditure shocks work their way through the economy. For simplicity, we consider the monetary shock to be a policy-induced change in the money supply. The expenditure shock is considered to be a fiscal policy change through a change in government spending.

THE EFFECT OF A MONEY SUPPLY CHANGE IN THE SHORT RUN

In order to consider the effects of a change in the money supply in our complete macroeconomic model, we need to put the *AD* curve together with the *AS* curve. To start with, we will consider the short-run *AS* curve as shown in Figure 36.10.

Let us take the case of an increase in the nominal money supply. This is represented by a rightward shift of the *LM* curve in part (i) and a rightward shift in the *AD* curve in part (ii). The economy moves to the intersection of the new *AD* curve with the *SRAS* curve. In the figure this looks very simple, but in reality there are several steps in the economic process that moves the economy between these two points:

1. The increase in the money supply means that people find that they have excess money balances, so they all attempt to shift from money into bonds. This is shown in Figure 36.10(i) by a rightward shift of the *LM* curve. This raises the price of bonds and lowers the rate of interest.

2. The lower interest rate causes an increase in investment which, via the multiplier effect, causes a further increase in desired expenditures (shown in Figure 36.10(i) as a movement along IS_0). This increase in desired expenditures is represented by the horizontal shift in *AD* in part (ii) of the figure. Notice that the size of the horizontal shift in *AD* is equal to the horizontal distance between the original intersection of LM_0 and IS_0 and the new intersection between LM_1 and IS_0.

3. Because desired expenditure exceeds actual output, there is an inflationary gap. The economy is trying to move to P_0Y_1 in part (ii). Excess demand for final output causes the price level to rise. In the short run, input prices (wages and raw materials) are fixed in nominal terms, so firms expand output.

4. The rise in the price level chokes off some of the increase in desired expenditure through the three effects that give a negative slope to *AD*: the decline in real wealth, the rise in the relative price of domestic goods, and the reduction in the real money supply. These effects shift both LM_1 and IS_0 leftwards slightly so that, after the rise in the price level from P_0 to P_1, the *IS* and *LM* curves intersect at point A (consistent with the level of income Y_2).

Steps 1 and 2 try to take the economy from *B* to *C* in Figure 36.10(ii). Steps 3 and 4 conceptually take the economy from *C* to *D*. The actual path may not go exactly from *B* to *C* to *D*, but neither will it necessarily go straight from *B* to *D*. The actual path followed depends upon the speeds of adjustment of all the bits of the process. Our analysis is powerful enough to tell us where we end up, but not to describe the precise path when the economy is out of equilibrium. The overall effect, however, has been an increase in output from Y_0 to Y_2 and a rise in prices from P_0 to P_1.

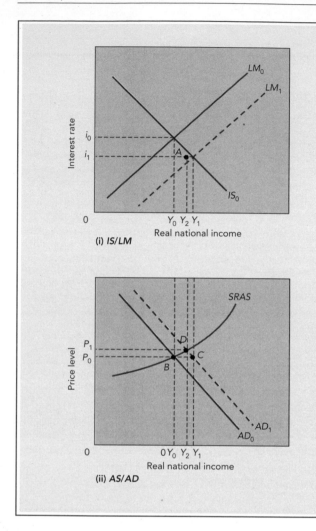

Figure 36.10 The short-run effects of an increase in the money supply

An increase in the money supply in the short run leads to an increase in real national income and the price level. The initial position is shown in part (i) as the intersection of IS_0 and LM_0, and in part (ii) as the intersection of AD_0 and the short-run aggregate supply curve $SRAS$, with associated national income and price level Y_0 and P_0. After an increase in the money supply, the LM curve shifts to LM_1 and the AD curve shifts to AD_1. Notice that horizontal shift in AD is equal to the distance Y_0Y_1, which is the horizontal between the original and the new intersections of IS and LM. The resulting increase in expenditures (resulting from lower interest rates and associated with higher investment) would, through the multiplier effect, tend to lead to national income of Y_1 indicated by point C. This would be the outcome only if the price level stayed constant and all the extra output demanded were forthcoming. However, excess demand for final output will lead to some increase in goods prices. As prices rise the real money supply falls, and there are also wealth effects and effects due to a rise in relative price of domestic goods. These shift the IS and LM curves back slightly to the left so that they intersect at a point like A. (The shifted curves are not shown as they are still very close to IS_0 and LM_1.) The combination of the stimulation to output caused by the initial expenditure increase and the negative feedback induced by a rising price level takes the economy from B to D, though the process can be analysed in two steps: B to C and C to D. So in the short run the economy moves to Y_2P_1. Clearly, the proportions in which national income and the price level rise are determined by the slope of $SRAS$. With a flat $SRAS$, most of the impact of an increase in AD falls on Y. With a steep $SRAS$, most of the impact falls on P.

Notice that whether this stimulus to aggregate demand affects mainly output or mainly prices depends entirely upon the slope of the short-run aggregate supply curve.

A fall in the money supply could be analysed in exactly the same way, except that we would have a leftward shift of the LM curve and a leftward shift of the AD curve rather than a rightward shift. In this case, we would get a rise in the interest rate leading to a fall in investment and a fall in desired expenditure. The fall in final demand would in turn lead to a fall in output and prices.

THE EFFECT OF A MONEY SUPPLY CHANGE IN THE LONG RUN

Steps 1–4 above are not the end of the story. If real national income at the initial point in Figure 36.10 was at its potential level, the short-run outcome at point D is at a point where current national income exceeds potential national income. This means that there is still an inflationary gap. What happens next is shown in Figure 36.11.

The adjustment that occurs in the long run involves a leftward shift in the aggregate supply curve. This is step 5:

5. While actual output is above potential output, there continues to be upward pressure on final goods prices. However, what shifts the $SRAS$ curve to the left is the upward adjustment of input prices, especially wages. In steps 3 and 4 above, workers suffer a fall in real wages, because the price of final goods has risen but money wages have been held constant. This is despite the fact that output has increased and firms' profits have risen. Wage rates will start to rise, both because demand for labour has temporarily risen and because employees (or their unions) will start to negotiate for a restoration of their real wage (or even for a real wage increase). Competitive firms will have to concede at least the restoration of real wages by granting money-wage increases. Accordingly, as the $SRAS$ curve shifts to the left, the price level rises further and real national income falls back to its potential level.

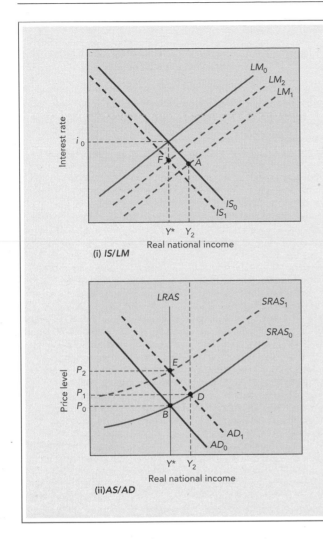

Figure 36.11 The effects of an increase in the money supply in the long run

Starting from full equilibrium, an increase in the money stock leads to no increase in national income in the long term but it does increase the price level. The initial increase in the money stock shifts the LM curve to the right, just as in Figure 36.10. Here we show LM_1, in part (i), as the LM curve after both the initial increase in the money stock and the resulting short-run increase in the price level from P_0 to P_1. (We neglect the possible shift in IS_0 that could also result from this initial rise in the price level.) The resulting rightward shift in the AD curve from AD_0 to AD_1 is shown in part (ii). The economy is initially in equilibrium at point B with price level P_0 and national income Y^*. The shift in AD moves the economy up the SRAS curve $SRAS_0$, so that in the short run the economy goes from point B to point D. However, the inflationary gap of Y^*Y_2 drives up wage rates, causing the SRAS curve to move up and to the left from $SRAS_0$ to $SRAS_1$. The price level rises to P_2, and this rise in the price level reduces the real money supply, so the LM curve shifts leftward in part (i). Wealth effects and the rising relative price of domestic goods also shift the IS curve leftward. If there were no wealth effects or relative price effects, then the IS and LM curves in part (i) would be back in their initial positions in full equilibrium, IS_0 and LM_0. The real money supply would have returned to its original level, and nothing else real (including the interest rate) would have changed. However, where these effects are present, the interest rate will go to a level like that at point F, which may be higher or lower than its initial position.

The process comes to a halt when national income has returned to its potential level, Y^*, with price level P_2. The economy, which started at point B in part (ii), ends up at point E via point D.

This latter adjustment does not all take place in the supply side of the economy. As the SRAS curve moves to the left, the economy is moving back up the AD curve. This movement involves a leftward shift of the IS curve owing to wealth effects, higher prices of domestic relative to foreign goods, and a rise in the interest rate, the latter having a further negative effect on investment. Indeed, it is possible that the long-run outcome will involve all real variables being restored to their original level and all nominal variables, including the price level, increasing in proportion to the initial increase in the money supply. We say 'possible' because this depends partly on the long-run wealth effect and on the effect of the higher price of domestic goods relative to foreign goods. As we shall see in later chapters, these two effects can be regarded as negligible in the long term, so the critical determinant of the outcome is what happens in the monetary sector. The general presumption, following from the quantity theory of money, is that, following a nominal increase in the money supply, the price

level will rise in the same proportion, so that the real money supply returns to its original level at LM_0. All nominal prices have accordingly risen, but all *relative* prices remain unchanged, so the real economy is returned exactly to its original point, with the IS curve at IS_0 and the economy at point E in Figure 36.11(ii).

This logic cannot be totally correct, since we have seen that, during the expansion that resulted from the nominal money supply increase, there was an increase in investment. This in turn will have led the capital stock to be greater than it was previously. This will have had some effect on potential income and output. Macroeconomics has traditionally neglected these effects. We have discussed them in Chapter 33. Also, note that we started with the economy in equilibrium at Y^*. If we had started with a recessionary gap, the increase in the money supply could have had the beneficial effect of returning the economy to Y^* more quickly than will occur eventually through downward pressure on prices and wages.

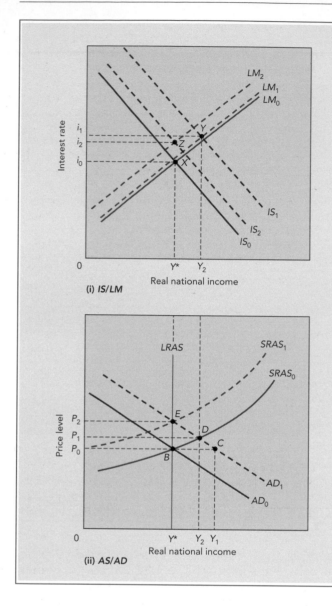

(i) IS/LM

(ii) AS/AD

Figure 36.12 The short-run and long-run effects of an expansionary fiscal policy

An expansionary fiscal policy, starting from equilibrium, has the same short- and long-run effects on national income and prices as an expansionary monetary policy, but it has different effects on the composition of expenditures. The economy starts in full equilibrium at point X in part (i) and point B in part (ii). An increase in government spending shifts the IS curve to the right in part (i) and the AD curve to the right in part (ii). The shift in AD with a given price level creates an inflationary gap, which means that the economy is trying to get to point C. However, this inflationary gap generates a short-term rise in the price level from P_0 to P_1. The new IS and LM curves, IS_1 and LM_1, are drawn to incorporate the effects of this initial rise in the price level. (Immediately after the rise in G but before the increase in P, the relevant IS curve would be to the right of IS_1 and the relevant LM curve would be LM_0.)

The result that the effect on the price level and output is the same as for monetary policy in both the short and the long run is illustrated in part (ii) by the path of the economy from point B to E (in the long run) via D (in the short run). However, what is different about the effects of fiscal policy can be seen in part (i). The increase in government expenditure increases the interest rate, initially from i_0 to i_1. This rise in the interest rate reduces investment, so government spending crowds out investment. Initially, the combination of national income and the interest rate moves from point X to point Y (as the price level rises from P_0 to P_1). In the long run, as the price level rises to P_2 and national income returns to Y^*, wealth effects and higher domestic prices shift the IS curve to IS_2 and the fall in the real money supply shifts the LM curve to LM_2. Thus, the long-run effect of a fiscal expansion is a permanently higher interest rate (like i_2 at point Z), which crowds out investment, and a higher price level, which could crowd out consumption (via wealth effects) and net exports (via a rise in domestic prices relative to foreign prices).

THE EFFECT OF A CHANGE IN FISCAL POLICY IN THE SHORT RUN

Let us now consider the effect of a fiscal policy expansion, which could come from an increase in government spending or a reduction in taxes. Just as with an increase in the money supply, an expansionary fiscal policy shifts the AD curve to the right, but via a rightward shift of IS rather than LM. As a result, the effect on output and prices will be the same as in Figure 36.10(ii). However, the steps, at least initially, are not quite the same, so it is helpful to go through them. We shall find in Chapter 39 that the impacts of monetary and fiscal policy can be quite different under different exchange rate regimes, but here we focus mainly on the internal adjustment mechanism. The impact of fiscal policy is shown in Figure 36.12.

Let us suppose that there has been an increase in government spending. What happens next?

1. The increase in G shifts the IS curve to the right by a horizontal distance equal to the increase in G times the multiplier. This is the multiplier that includes the effects of income taxes and import propensities (see p. 591). The AD curve shifts rightward by the horizontal distance between the original and new intersections of IS and LM.[12]

[12] Notice that the IS curve shifts initially by a horizontal distance equal to the simple multiplier, but the AD curve shifts by a smaller distance because it includes the negative feedback from higher interest rates. Thus, the multiplier becomes smaller once there is a monetary sector, even before we have added the aggregate supply curve (and price level effects).

2. The excess demand for final output in the economy (inflationary gap) causes the price level to rise and output to increase. This creates an excess demand for money, for two reasons. First, as prices rise, the real money supply falls with the nominal money supply held constant. Second, as output increases, the transactions demand for real money balances increases. This excess demand for money causes people to try to sell bonds, which lowers their price and raises interest rates, shown as a move from X to Y in Figure 36.12(i).

3. The higher interest rate lowers investment, which offsets some of the initial increase in aggregate demand. The rise in the price level also leads to wealth effects and relative price effects between domestic and foreign goods.

4. The economy in the short run moves to a point like D in Figure 36.12(ii). This is the same effect on national income and the price level as from a money supply increase, but important underlying differences are concealed. In particular, at point D, after a fiscal policy expansion the interest rate is higher and investment is lower than at B. With a monetary expansion the reverse is true—interest rates at D are lower and investment is higher than at B.

Thus, while fiscal and monetary policy expansions have the same analytical effect on the price level and real national income, they have very different effects on the composition of total expenditure. Part (i) of Figure 36.12 makes clear that a monetary policy expansion shifts the LM curve to the right, which lowers the equilibrium interest rate, while a fiscal expansion shifts the IS curve to the right, which raises the equilibrium interest rate. The remaining differences result from the fact that the former increases investment while the latter lowers it.

THE EFFECT OF A CHANGE IN FISCAL POLICY IN THE LONG RUN

The remaining adjustment from the short- to long-run case is the same for fiscal policy changes as for monetary policy, since it involves a leftward shift in the SRAS curve which results from increases in input prices, especially wages, as in step 5 above. There may be long-run implications of the fact that the government is now running a budget deficit when it was not before. Some of these issues are discussed in Chapter 42. However, there is more to be said about comparisons between the effects of monetary and fiscal policy in the context of Figures 36.11 and 36.12.

For the case of a monetary policy expansion, we argued that the economy will return to the same real equilibrium level with all real variables unchanged, subject to some minor qualifications. However, we cannot make the same claim for the outcome of a fiscal policy expansion. It is true, subject to the same qualifications as above, that real national income will return to its initial (potential) level.

However, our fiscal policy expansion involved a permanent increase in real government spending. If G has risen but Y is unchanged, some other component of final expenditure must have fallen. It is largely investment. Consumption could have fallen because higher prices reduce wealth, but wealth effects of modest price-level changes are unlikely to be large. Exports can have fallen only if there has been a permanent rise in the relative price of domestic goods, which is possible in the short run but unlikely in the long run, as the following chapter explains. So, in the long term, the most likely outcome is that the expansion of government spending replaces, or *crowds out*, investment expenditure via an increase in interest rates. In order to bring these higher interest rates about, the real money supply must be lower than in the initial position.

Thus, fiscal and monetary policies, while acting in similar ways via the shift in AD and having similar consequences for real national income and the price level, have quite different consequences for the composition of final expenditure. We shall learn in Chapter 39 that these effects are sensitive to the exchange rate regime and to the degree of capital mobility.

....

Summary

1 For simplicity, we divide all forms in which wealth is held into money, which is a medium of exchange, and bonds, which earn a higher interest return than money and can be turned into money by being sold at a price that is determined on the open market.

2 The price of existing bonds varies negatively with the rate of interest. A rise in the interest rate lowers the prices of all outstanding bonds. The longer its term to maturity, the greater will be the change in the price of a bond for a given change in the interest rate.

3 The value of money balances that the public wishes to hold is called the *demand for money*. It is a stock (not a flow), measured in the United Kingdom as so many billions of pounds.

4 Money balances are held, despite the opportunity cost of bond interest forgone, because of transactions, precautionary, and speculative motives. These have the effect of making the demand for money vary positively with real national income, the price level, and wealth, and negatively with the nominal rate of interest. The nominal demand for money varies proportionally with the price level.

5 When there is an excess demand for money balances, people try to sell bonds. This pushes the price of bonds down and the interest rate up. When there is an excess supply of money balances, people try to buy bonds. This pushes the price of bonds up and the rate of interest down. Monetary equilibrium is established when people are willing to hold the fixed stocks of money and bonds at the current rate of interest.

6 With given inflationary expectations, changes in the nominal interest rate translate into changes in the real interest rate. A change in the real interest rate causes desired investment to change along the investment demand function. This shifts the aggregate desired expenditure function and causes equilibrium national income to change. This means that the aggregate demand curve shifts.

7 Points 5 and 6 together describe the transmission mechanism that links money to national income. A decrease in the supply of money tends to reduce aggregate demand. An increase in the supply of money tends to increase aggregate demand.

8 The negatively sloped aggregate demand curve indicates that the higher the price level, the lower the equilibrium national income. The explanation lies in part with the effect of money on the adjustment mechanism: other things being equal, the higher the price level, the higher the demand for money and the rate of interest, the lower the level of investment and therefore the lower the aggregate expenditure function, and thus the lower the equilibrium income.

9 Combinations of the interest rate and equilibrium national income for which desired expenditure equals actual real national income can be represented by the *IS* curve, which is negatively sloped. Combinations of real national income and the equilibrium interest rate for which money demand equals money supply can be represented by the *LM* curve, which is positively sloped.

10 The *AD* curve can be derived from the *IS/LM* model, holding all exogenous expenditure and the nominal money supply constant. A rise in the price level lowers the real money supply, leading to higher interest rates and lower national income. A fall in the price level leads to an increase in the real money supply, which lowers interest rates and increases national income. Hence the *AD* curve is negatively sloped. This reinforces our earlier discussion of why *AD* has a negative slope.

11 Changes in the money supply affect national income via shifts in the *AD* curve; therefore, they have a positive relationship with national income in the short run but no effect on national income in the long run.

12 Fiscal policy has a similar effect to monetary policy so far as national income and the price level is concerned, but it has different effects on the composition of expenditure.

Topics for review

- Interest rates and bond prices

- Transactions, precautionary, and speculative motives for holding money

- Negative relationship between the demand for money M^D and the interest rate i

- Monetary equilibrium

- Transmission mechanism

- The investment demand function

- Money and the adjustment mechanism

- The *IS* and *LM* curves

- The slope of the *AD* curve

- The effects of monetary and fiscal policy in the short run and long run

APPENDIX TO CHAPTER 36

Schools of thought in macroeconomics

THE model we have built up since Chapter 29, and now extended to include a monetary sector, has been set out as if its relationships were generally accepted. In reality, there have been many fierce controversies about the appropriate model with which to describe the economy. This appendix outlines some of the disagreements between participants in macroeconomic debates. It is helpful to identify broad schools of thought within macroeconomics, even though no one may subscribe to these precise collections of views today.

Early Keynesians

Early, and more extreme, Keynesian models placed all their emphasis on explaining the expenditure categories ($C + I + G + NX$) and had no place for monetary influences. They used perfectly elastic (horizontal) LM and $SRAS$ curves. The perfectly elastic LM curve arose because the demand for money was assumed to be highly sensitive (in the limit, infinitely sensitive) to changes in the interest rate;[1] as a consequence, the expansionary effects of rightward shifts in the IS curve were not in the least crowded out through interest rate changes. The perfectly elastic $SRAS$ curve arose because wages and prices were assumed to be inflexible downward and the economy was at less than full employment; as a consequence, there was no crowding out of the effects of expenditure changes through changes in the price level.

This early Keynesian model has several characteristics, illustrated in Figure 36A.1. First, changes in aggregate desired expenditure caused large changes in income and employment, changes that were not damped by variations in either the interest rate or the price level. Second, changes in monetary aggregates did not affect income because the perfectly elastic LM curve was unaffected by changes in the quantity of money. (Recall that a change in the quantity of money shifts the LM curve to the left or to the right, which means that the perfectly elastic curve 'shifts into itself', and thus undergoes no visible change.) In an alternative version, investment was insensitive to the interest rate, so that, even if changes in the money supply did change the interest rate, they would not affect real expenditures. Third, there was no automatic adjustment mechanism to restore full employment, since the downward rigidity of wages and prices prevented the $SRAS$ curve from shifting downwards. In brief, both short- and long-run aggregate supply curves were

considered to be horizontal, and only changes in autonomous expenditures (not the money supply) would shift the aggregate demand curve.

The main policy implication of the early Keynesian model is that government fiscal policy is needed to restore full employment, whenever the economy shows signs of settling down into equilibrium with substantial unemployment.

Early monetarists

Early monetarists disputed these conclusions while accepting the underlying model. For example, when challenged to outline his model, Milton Friedman, the leader of the monetarist school, used an IS/LM model in which the LM curve was steep, rather than flat, and the $SRAS$ curve was flexible downwards, as well as upwards, because prices and wages were flexible downwards. The early versions of the extreme monetarist model, illustrated in Figure 36A.2, had a vertical LM curve because the demand for money depended only on income and not on the interest rate. The consequence of this was 100 per cent crowding out of any fiscal stimulus. Monetary policy, however, had powerful effects on the economy, because any shift in the LM curve had a large effect on the AD curve. The early monetarist model also had an easily shifted $SRAS$ curve because prices and wages were assumed to be quite flexible. This meant that any deviation from full employment would be corrected relatively quickly by adjustments in wages and prices that would shift the $SRAS$ curve back to intersect the AD curve at full employment.

Modern moderate monetarists and Keynesians

A great debate, accompanied by a vast amount of empirical work, raged between these two camps in the 1950s, 1960s,

---

[1] This horizontal LM curve was known as the *liquidity trap*, because when it occurred it meant that money and bonds were perfect substitutes, so an excess supply of money would not lead people to bid up the price of bonds and thereby lower the interest rate. Hence increases in the money supply would not be transmitted into increases in expenditure. This was expected to happen only in deep recessions when interest rates were very low—so low that it was not worth the effort to switch into bonds.

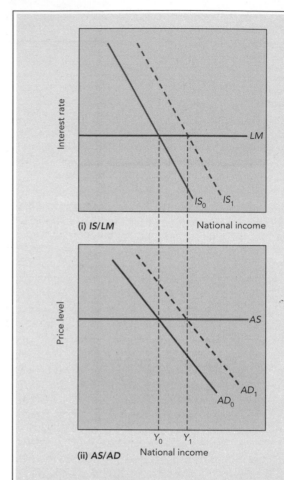

Figure 36A.1 The early or extreme Keynesian model

The early Keynesian model had a horizontal _LM_ curve and a horizontal aggregate supply curve. This meant that any shift in autonomous expenditures would have an effect on national income equal to the change in expenditure times the simple multiplier. This is illustrated in part (i) by a shift in the _IS_ curve from IS_0 to IS_1, which leads in part (ii) to a shift in the _AD_ curve of an equal amount from AD_0 to AD_1. National income increases from Y_0 to Y_1. Notice that early Keynesians did not use an _AD_ curve (they used _AE_ or _IS_), but according to their assumptions it would have been vertical, because they admitted no linkages from changes in the real money supply to interest rates, no relative price effects, and no wealth effects. _AD_ is drawn negatively sloped here, for familiarity; with a horizontal and fixed aggregate supply curve, it makes no difference.

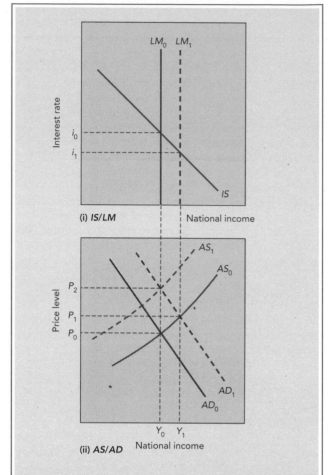

Figure 36A.2 The early monetarist model

The early monetarist model had a vertical _LM_ curve, which came from the assumption of a constant velocity of circulation. With a vertical _LM_ curve, shifts in the _IS_ curve (fiscal policy) would have no effect on _AD_, as they would be exactly crowded out by interest rate rises. An increase in the money supply would shift the _LM_ curve from LM_0 to LM_1, and the _AD_ curve from AD_0 to AD_1. National income would increase in the short run from Y_0 to Y_1, and the price level would increase from P_0 to P_1. However, inflationary pressure would eventually pass through into wages and the aggregate supply curve would shift from AS_0 to AS_1. The rise in the price level would return the _LM_ curve to LM_0. Thus, in the long run, prices would rise in proportion to the increase in the money stock, and all real variables would be left unchanged. The monetarist rule of thumb was that it took about one year for a change in the money supply to influence real output and a further year before it affected the price level.

and 1970s. One by one, as evidence accumulated, Keynesians and monetarists abandoned their extreme positions and moved towards a common ground, until finally little but rhetoric divided the two groups. This common ground is largely reflected in the model we have developed above, so we will not illustrate it again here.

Eventually, both sides had come to agree on a downward-sloping *IS* and an upward-sloping *LM* curve, which allowed the economy to respond to both monetary and real expenditure shocks. Keynesians agreed that there was some downward flexibility in wages and prices; they argued, however, that it acted too slowly to be an effective mechanism for restoring full employment quickly after a downward shift in aggregate desired expenditure. Monetarists agreed that wages and prices were sufficiently inflexible downwards to cause serious deviations from full employment when the economy was hit by either a monetary or an expenditure shock.

Early monetarists also argued against fine-tuning, saying that the lags in the economy's response to monetary shocks were long and variable, and that fine-tuning would be more likely to do harm than good. Keynesians came to accept this view but continued to hold that the system often settled into slumps that were prolonged enough for there to be plenty of time to diagnose the situation; corrective monetary and fiscal policies could then be applied at leisure, without having to worry about the pitfalls of fine-tuning against sharp, transitory fluctuations.

In 1980 the US Nobel Laureate James Tobin, one of the leaders of the moderate Keynesians, debated with the UK economist David Laidler, a moderate monetarist, in the pages of the *Economic Journal*. Neutral observers could find little real gulf between them. They disagreed, as one might expect, on matters of judgement about speeds of reactions and the precise slopes of some curves. They revealed, however, no discernible differences of underlying models or of fundamental assessment of what were the key relations that governed the economy's behaviour.

Indeed, the whole debate could have been regarded as a case study in positive economics. Although a great deal of heat had been generated over the decades, the end result was much light. Empirical evidence about such things as the income and interest elasticities of the demand for money, and wage and price flexibility, was amassed. The extreme positions of the two schools were moderated in the light of the accumulating evidence, until their differences were slight compared with their agreements.

Just as that apparently satisfactory situation was being reached, a new school became prominent. This was the *New Classical school*, whose intellectual leaders were the US economists Robert Lucas, Thomas Sargent, and Neil Wallace.

The New Classical school

Keynesians and monetarists had, all along, shared the presumption that macroeconomics was about explaining periods of *disequilibrium* (unemployment and excess capacity on the one hand, and inflationary gaps on the other). They certainly disagreed about adjustment speeds and appropriate policy responses, but they shared an assumption that recessions involved, at least temporary, market failure.

The New Classical school, in contrast, picked up the agenda of the *Austrian school*, which was to explain business cycles in an equilibrium model.[2] Thus, they assume that markets clear continuously, *as if* they were perfectly competitive. This makes full employment (no involuntary unemployment) the equilibrium position that would normally be achieved. The economy deviates from full employment either when mistakes are made or when rational agents (decision-takers are called 'agents') voluntarily decide to work less than the full-employment amount of work.

New Classical economics uses the theory of **rational expectations.** This assumes that agents form expectations based upon all available information about the future at the time they take decisions. So agents make only random errors in foreseeing the future course of market variables. Since markets always clear, and since agents do not make systematic errors, full-employment equilibrium is the normal state of the economy. Prices will always adjust to ensure that there are neither unsatisfied buyers nor unsatisfied sellers in any market, including the labour market. We will consider how this approach can be reconciled (if at all) with the observation of sustained periods of unemployment when we discuss business cycles in Chapter 43. An alternative 'equilibrium' approach to business cycles, known as 'real business cycles' , is also discussed in Chapter 43.

The critics of New Classical economics argue that markets do not always clear. They believe that, even when a shock is foreseen, so that no one misperceives what is happening, output will be affected because agents cannot anticipate all of the economy's reactions in advance. Agents cannot, therefore, establish the new equilibrium set of prices by anticipating what these will be. Instead, it is argued, agents' reactions have to be worked out slowly, and only as the price and quantity adjustments are observed to evolve over time.

Market-clearing There are many subtle differences between the different schools. The two most fundamental differences concern market-clearing and expectations formation. New Classical theorists assume that markets always clear; moderate monetarists assume that markets do not clear instantaneously, especially when downward adjustments are required. This sluggishness is sufficient to cause significant excess supplies to persist in goods and factor markets for some time. In the longer run, however, markets do tend to clear, and full-employment equilibrium is the point to which the economy gravitates.

[2] The Austrian school was founded by Carl Menger (1840–1921) and Eugen von Böhm-Bawerk (1851–1914). Its most influencial disciples were Ludwig von Mises (1881–1973), and Friedrich von Hayek (1899–1991). The UK economist Lionel (later Lord) Robbins (1898–1984) was also influenced by their ideas.

Moderate Keynesians agree with the moderate monetarists, but think that the adjustment takes a little longer than the monetarists think. As a result, they are inclined to give a place to demand management policies that will stabilize the economy against persistent recessionary and inflationary gaps—even if smaller, more transient, gaps must be accepted as unavoidable. Some extreme Keynesians believe that markets do not clear even in the long term and, thus, that government demand management must be used more or less continually to stabilize the economy at or near full employment. Modern, or New, Keynesians believe that unemployment (or a big chunk of it which cannot be removed by stimulating aggregate demand) is caused by rigidities in labour markets, and they seek solutions through structural reforms and supply-side intervention (in addition, perhaps, to aggregate demand policies). This contemporary 'Keynesian' approach is discussed in Chapter 41.

Expectations formation On expectations, the New Classical theorists believe in fully rational expectations, in which prediction errors are 'pure white noise'. Loosely, this means that systematic errors of prediction are not made. Since prices always clear all markets, and systematic mistakes are not made, deviations from full employment cannot be reduced by government intervention. Other economists believe that expectations are formed by some mixture of rational calculation, extrapolation from the past, and adaptive learning behaviour. Different economists vary on how they believe the typical mix combines the rational, the extrapolative, and the adaptive.[3] Those economists who believe that the economy is too complicated for contemporary economists to understand fully are inclined to believe that private decision-makers can make major, often systematic, mistakes. They ask: if economists disagree as much as they clearly do over how the economy behaves, how can private agents be expected to get this behaviour right on average?

It is important to be aware that the dividing lines in macroeconomic debates are perpetually shifting. Many modern Keynesians would not subscribe to many of the views we have attributed to the Keynesian school above. Indeed, much of the attention of what is now called New Keynesian economics is directed not at cyclical (demand-deficient) unemployment, but rather at what used to be called 'Classical' unemployment and is now referred to as 'equilibrium' unemployment. And the Keynesian policy solution for unemployment (fiscal stimulus) has shifted to supply-side measures (training, benefits structure, and wage bargaining institutions). These issues are examined in later chapters, but especially in Chapter 41.

---

[3] *Rational expectations* assumes that the expected value of a variable is equal to the mean of its statistical probability distribution, while the actual outcome will deviate from that expectation by a white-noise random error. *Extrapolative expectations* assumes that next period's expectation of the value of the variable will be equal to last period's value, or the extrapolation of some existing trend. *Adaptive expectations* assumes that agents adjust their expectations in proportion to the size and direction of the error in expectations (deviation between the expectation and the outturn) they made the last time.

∾ CHAPTER 37

The balance of payments and exchange rates

THIS chapter focuses on the linkages between the macroeconomy and the rest of the world. We have mentioned these linkages many times before, but here they become the main concern. There are financial (or monetary) linkages, through the international money and capital markets, and there are 'real' dimensions, through international trade and travel. The real and the monetary factors are not independent of each other. Real transactions cannot take place without money and finance, and are influenced by monetary forces; equally, money markets are influenced by the fundamentals of the real economy.

The discussion of these issues will bring together much material from earlier in this book: the theory of supply and demand (Chapter 4), the nature of money (Chapter 35), international trade (Chapter 25), and macroeconomics (Chapter 36). Indeed, we have had the exchange rate and the balance of payments (net exports of goods and services, *NX*) explicitly in our macroeconomic model since Chapter 30. Also we have seen in Box 36.2 that external linkages can have a critical effect on the transmission mechanism of macro policy. We now need to look at these issues in much greater detail, to prepare the ground for our policy discussions in the next two chapters.

In the first part of this chapter, we discuss the balance of payments. This is an important concept concerned with net transactions between one country and the rest of the world. We ask what the 'balance of payments' means, how it is measured, and whether it matters. In the second part we discuss the exchange rate—what role it plays in connecting the domestic economy with foreign economies, and what economic forces determine its value.

The balance of payments

THE balance of payments position of the UK economy has had a high profile in political arguments over economic policy throughout this century. We shall first explain how the balance of payments is recorded in the United Kingdom, and we shall then ask in what ways the balance of payments matters.

Balance of payments accounts

In order to know what is happening to the course of international trade, governments keep track of the transactions between countries. The record of such transactions is made in the *balance of payments accounts*. Each transaction, such as a shipment of exports or the arrival of imported goods, is classified according to the payments or receipts that would typically arise from it.

Transactions that lead to a receipt of payment from foreigners, such as a commodity export or a sale of an asset abroad, are recorded in the balance of payments accounts as a credit item with a positive sign. In terms of our later objective of analysing the market for foreign exchange, these transactions represent the supply of foreign exchange and the demand for sterling on the foreign exchange market, because foreigners have to buy our currency in order to pay us in sterling for the goods or assets they have bought. Transactions that lead to a payment to foreigners, such as a commodity import or the purchase of a foreign asset, are recorded as a debit item with a negative sign. These trans-

actions represent the demand for foreign exchange and the supply of sterling on the foreign exchange market, because we have to buy foreign currency with sterling in order to pay for our overseas purchases.

Balance of payments accounts are normally divided into two broad parts. One part deals with payments for goods and services, interest, and transfers. This is known as the **current account**. The other part records transactions in assets and is, accordingly, known as the **capital account**. A summary of the balance of payments accounts of the United Kingdom for 1993 is given in Table 37.1.

CURRENT ACCOUNT

The current account records transactions arising from trade in goods and services, from income accruing to capital owned by one country and invested in another, or from transfers by residents of one country to residents of another. The current account is divided into two main sections.

The first of these, variously called the **visible account**, the **trade account**, and the **merchandise account**, records payments and receipts arising from the import and export of tangible goods, such as computers, cars, wheat, and shoes. UK imports require payments to be made to foreign residents in foreign exchange, and hence are entered as debit items on the visible account. In 1993, UK residents spent just over £134 billion on buying goods imported from overseas. UK exports earn payments from foreign residents in foreign exchange (though the foreign exchange will be con-

Table 37.1   UK balance of payments, 1993 (£ million)

Visible trade balance	– 13,423
Exports	120,907
Imports	– 134,330
Invisibles balance	2,718
Services	5,145
Investment income	2,718
Transfers	– 5,110
Current account balance	– 10,670
Transactions in assets	– 162,768
Transactions in liabilities	171,668
Net transactions (capital flows)	8,900
Balancing item	1,770

The balance of payments accounts record transactions between the domestic economy and the rest of the world which cross the foreign exchanges. The trade balance is the difference in value between imports and exports. The current account includes also the balance of payments in invisibles. The capital account records net purchases and sales of assets and liabilities. If records were accurate, the current account balance and the capital account balance must be equal and of opposite sign. The balancing item is the measurement error in this set of accounts. Its presence is what makes the accounts balance in practice.

verted into sterling through the foreign exchange market), and hence are recorded as credit items. In 1993, UK exports amounted to about £121 billion. Exports represent goods leaving the country, but payment for those goods passes in the opposite direction. With imports, goods enter the country and payment has to be made to the foreign manufacturers. We can see that in 1993 there was a visible trade deficit of a little over £13 billion, which is the difference between the value of imports and exports.

The second part of Table 37.1, the **invisibles account**, records payments arising out of trade in services, payments for the use of capital, and transfers to persons. There are three components to invisibles: trade in such services as insurance, banking, shipping, and tourism; payments of interest, dividends, and profits that are made for capital used in one country but owned by residents of another country; and transfer payments, such as might arise when an Italian waiter in London sends money home to his mother in Turin, or when a UK pensioner receives her pension in the Costa del Sol.[1] The figures for invisibles in Table 37.1 are reported net. This means that, while for each category there are payments in both directions, it is only the balance that appears. So in 1993 the United Kingdom was a net recipient of payments for services (+£5.1 billion) and

investment incomes (+£2.7 billion), but made net transfers overseas (– £5.1 billion). Invisibles as a whole were in surplus to the value of £2.7 billion (calculated as £5.1 billion + £2.7 billion – £5.1 billion).

The UK trade account deficit in 1993, therefore, was £13.4 billion, while the invisibles surplus was £2.7 billion. The combination of this negative trade balance and positive invisibles balance gave an overall *current account balance* which was in deficit by nearly £10.7 billion.[2]

CAPITAL ACCOUNT

The other major component in the balance of payments is the **capital account**, which records transactions related to international movements of ownership of financial assets. It is important to notice right away that the capital account does not relate to imports and exports of physical capital: trade in such things as machine tools or construction equipment is part of the *visible trade account*. Rather, the capital account of the balance of payments relates only to cross-border movements in financial instruments, such as ownership of company shares, bank loans, or government securities.

UK purchases of foreign investments (which then become assets to the UK) are called a *capital outflow*. They use foreign exchange, in order to buy the foreign investment, and so they are entered as a debit (negative) item in the UK payments accounts.[3] Foreign investment in the United Kingdom (which, thereby, increases UK liabilities to foreigners) is called a *capital inflow*. It earns foreign exchange and so is entered as a credit (positive) item.

As shown in Table 37.1, in 1993 UK residents increased their investments abroad by nearly £163 billion, while foreigners increased their investments in the United Kingdom by over £171 billion. These may seem like very large amounts, and, indeed, they are. However, a high proportion of this activity is the international borrowing and lend-

[1] The symbols X and IM as used in this book refer to exports and imports of both tangible goods *and* services, but do not include payments of interest, dividends, and profits, or transfers.

[2] These were the first official full-year figures released for the United Kingdom for 1993. It is likely that there will be revisions to these figures in later official publications. In fact, later revisions are possible in all national income statistics. These revisions often have a significant effect on balance of payments figures. This is because the balance of payments records the difference between two large numbers. A small percentage revision on either side of the accounts can lead to a large percentage revision in the balance. For example, a 1 per cent rise in the value of exports would reduce the trade deficit by nearly 10 per cent.

[3] Capital outflows are sometimes also referred to as *capital exports*. It may seem odd that, whereas a merchandise export is a credit item on current account, a capital export is a debit item on capital account. To understand this terminology, consider the export of UK funds for investment in a German bond. The capital transaction involves the purchase, and hence the *import*, of a German bond, and this has the same effect on the balance of payments as the purchase, and hence the import, of a German good. Both items involve payments to foreigners, and both use foreign exchange. Both are thus debit items in UK balance of payments accounts.

ing of the financial institutions in the City of London, which is a major centre of international financial intermediation. The net capital inflow resulted in a surplus in the capital account of only about £9 billion. This means that there was a net increase in foreign liabilities of £9 billion.[4]

Short-term and long-term capital flows The capital account is often divided into two categories that distinguish between movements of short-term and long-term capital. Short-term capital is money that is held in the form of highly liquid assets, such as bank accounts and short-term Treasury bills. Long-term capital represents funds coming into the United Kingdom (a credit item) or leaving the United Kingdom (a debit item), to be invested in less liquid assets, such as long-term bonds, or in physical capital, such as a new car assembly plant.

Portfolio investment and direct investment The two major subdivisions of the long-term part of the capital accounts are direct investment and portfolio investment. **Direct investment** relates to changes in non-resident ownership of domestic firms and resident ownership of foreign firms. One form of direct investment, called greenfield investment, is the building of a factory in the United Kingdom by a foreign firm—for example, the Toyota car factory near Derby. Another form of direct investment, called brownfield investment, is a takeover, in which a controlling interest in a firm, previously controlled by residents, is acquired by foreigners—such as when BMW acquired a majority interest in the Rover Group from British Aerospace. **Portfolio investment,** on the other hand, is investment in bonds or a minority holding of shares that does not involve legal control. We have discussed the motives for foreign investment in Chapter 17 on page 315.

The meaning of payments balances and imbalances

We have seen that the payments accounts show the total of receipts of foreign exchange (credit items) and payments of foreign exchange (debit items) on account of each category of payment. It is also common to calculate the *balance* on separate items or groups of items. The concept of the balance of payments is used in a number of different ways, so we must approach this issue in a series of steps.

THE BALANCE OF PAYMENTS MUST BALANCE OVERALL

The notion that the balance of payments accounts must balance should present no great mystery. The accounts are constructed so that this has to be true. The idea behind this proposition is quite general. Take your own personal income and expenditure. Suppose you earn £100 by selling your services (labour) and you buy £90 worth of clothing. You have exports (of services/labour) worth £100, and imports (of clothing) worth £90. Your current account surplus is £10. However, that £10 surplus must be invested in holding a financial claim on someone else—if you hold cash, it is a claim on the Bank of England; if you deposit the money in a building society, it becomes a claim on the building society; and so on.

Whichever way you look at it, the £10 you have acquired is the acquisition of an asset. It represents a capital outflow from your personal economy which is the inevitable consequence of your current account surplus. So, you have a current account surplus of £10 and a capital account deficit (outflow) of £10. The only difference between your accounts and those for the economy as a whole is that with the latter, payments across the foreign exchange markets are involved. A country with a current account surplus in its balance of payments must, at the same time, have acquired net claims on foreigners to the same value.

The current and capital account balances are necessarily of equal and opposite size. When added together, they equal zero.

There is one important caveat to the above statement with regard to actual official accounts. This is that, while conceptually the current and capital account are defined to be equal and opposite, in practice, the national income statisticians are not able to keep accurate records of all transactions, and hence there are always errors in measurement. This means that a 'balancing item' is included in the balance of payments table. The balancing item stands for all unrecorded transactions and is defined to be equal to the difference between the measured current account and the measured capital account. So actually, it is the sum of the current account, the capital account, and the balancing item that is always zero by construction.

DOES THE BALANCE OF PAYMENTS MATTER?

The *balance of payments on current account* is the sum of the balances on the visible and invisible accounts. As a carryover from a long-discredited eighteenth-century economic doctrine called *mercantilism*, a credit balance on current account (where receipts exceed payments) is often called a **favourable balance,** and a debit balance (where payments exceed receipts) is often called an **unfavourable balance.** Mercantilists, both ancient and modern, hold that the gains from trade arise only from having a favourable balance of

---

[4] Note that this figure relates only to transactions in assets. It does not account for capital gains or losses resulting from valuation changes of existing asset holdings. Thus, the capital account balance is **not** a measure of the total change in indebtedness between the United Kingdom and the rest of the world.

BOX 37.1

The volume of trade, the balance of trade, and the new mercantilism

Media commentators, political figures, and much of the general public often judge the national balance of payments as they would the accounts of a single firm. Just as a firm is supposed to show a profit, the nation is supposed to secure a balance of payments surplus on current account, with the benefits derived from international trade measured by the size of that surplus.

This view is related to the exploitation doctrine of international trade: one country's surplus is another country's deficit. Thus, one country's gain, judged by its surplus, must be another country's loss, judged by its deficit.

People who hold such views today are echoing an ancient economic doctrine called *mercantilism*. The mercantilists were a group of economists who preceded Adam Smith. They judged the success of trade by the size of the trade balance. In many cases, this doctrine made sense in terms of their objective, which was to use international trade as a means of building up the political and military power of the state, rather than as a means of raising the living standards of its citizens. A balance of payments surplus allowed the nation (then and now) to acquire foreign exchange reserves. (In those days the reserves took the form of gold. Today they are a mixture of gold and claims on the currencies of other countries.) These reserves could then be used to pay armies, to purchase weapons from abroad, and generally to finance colonial expansions.

People who advocate this view in modern times are called *neo-mercantilists*. In so far as their object is to increase the military power of the state, they are choosing means that could achieve their ends. In so far as they are drawing an analogy between what is a sensible objective for a business, interested in its own material welfare, and what is a sensible objective for a society, interested in the material welfare of its citizens, their views are erroneous, because their analogy is false.

If the object of economic activity is to promote the welfare and living standards of ordinary citizens, rather than the power of governments, then the mercantilist focus on the balance of trade makes no sense. The law of comparative advantage shows that average living standards are maximized by having individuals, regions, and countries specialize in the things that they can produce comparatively best and then trading to obtain the things that they can produce comparatively worst. The more specialization there is, the more trade occurs.

On this view, the gains from trade are to be judged by the volume of trade. A situation in which there is a *large volume* of trade but in which each country has a *zero balance* of trade can thus be regarded as quite satisfactory. Furthermore, a change in commercial policy that results in a balanced increase in trade between two countries will bring gain, because it allows for specialization according to comparative advantage, even though it causes no change in either country's trade balance.

To the business interested in private profit, and to the government interested in the power of the state, it is the *balance* of trade that matters. To the person interested in the welfare of ordinary citizens, it is the *volume* of trade that matters.

---

trade. This misses the point of the doctrine of comparative advantage, which states that countries can gain from a *balanced increase* in trade because it allows each country to specialize according to its comparative advantage. The modern resurgence of mercantilism is discussed in Box 37.1.

It would be tempting to refer to a deficit on capital account as an unfavourable balance as well. However, by now it should be clear that this would be a nonsense, because a current account surplus is the same thing as a capital account deficit. Hence it is impossible for one to be 'good' and the other 'bad'. However, this discussion does have one important implication.

The terms balance of payments *deficit* and balance of payments *surplus* must refer to the balance on some part of the payments accounts. In the United Kingdom these terms almost always apply to the current account.

A current account deficit is just as likely to be the product of a healthy growing economy as it is of an unhealthy economy. Suppose, for example, that an economy has rapidly growing domestic industries which offer a high rate of return on domestic investment. Such an economy would be attracting investment from the rest of the world, and as a result it would have a capital account surplus (capital inflows) and a current account deficit. Far from being a sign of weakness, the current account deficit would indicate economic health. True, the economy is acquiring external debts; but if this debt is being used to finance rapid real growth, it can be repaid out of higher future output.[5]

In contrast, another economy may, indeed, have inefficient and unproductive domestic industry, and may be in a situation where domestic spending exceeds domestic output. (Recall from Chapter 30 that the current account balance is equal to the difference between total domestic expenditure and total domestic production.) Therefore, it will have a current account deficit and will be borrowing from abroad to finance the extra consumption.

---

[5] 'Debt' is used here in its general sense to refer to foreign liabilities rather than in the context of debt versus equity. These external debts could be in any specific form, including equity, bonds, or bank loans.

The existence of a current account balance of payments deficit tells only that an economy's total spending exceeds its total output and that it has a capital inflow. The existence of such a deficit is consistent both with healthy, growing economies and with unhealthy, inefficient economies.

Actual and desired transactions   The discussion in this section has focused on *actual* transactions as measured in the balance of payments accounts. It is the actual capital inflow that must equal the actual current account deficit. There is no reason at all, however, why *desired* (or planned) current account transactions should equal desired capital account transactions. In practice, it is movements in the exchange rate that play a key role in reconciling actual and desired transactions. We now turn to a discussion of the exchange rate and how it is determined.

The market for foreign exchange

THE foreign exchange markets are the markets in which one currency can be converted into another. We are used to thinking about markets in which goods are exchanged for money. In a foreign exchange market, it is one country's money that is exchanged for another country's money. As with all markets, the foreign exchange market can be analysed with the tools of demand and supply developed earlier in this book. Before proceeding with this exercise, it is helpful to remind ourselves why we need such markets.

Money is central to the efficient working of any modern economy that relies on specialization and exchange. Yet fiat money as we know it is a *national* matter, one that is closely controlled by national governments. Each nation-state has its own currency: if you live in Sweden, you earn kronor and spend kronor; if you run a business in Austria, you borrow schillings and meet your wage bill with schillings. The currency of a country is acceptable within the bounds of that country, but usually it will not be accepted by people and firms in another country. The Stockholm bus company will accept kronor for a fare, but not Austrian schillings; the Austrian worker will not take Swedish kronor for wages, but insists on being paid in schillings.

UK producers require payment in pounds sterling for their products. They need pounds to meet their wage bills, to pay for their raw materials, and to reinvest or distribute their profits. There is no problem when they sell to UK-based purchasers. However, if they sell their goods to, say, Indian importers, either the Indians must exchange their rupees to acquire pounds to pay for the goods, or the UK producers must accept rupees;[6] and they will accept rupees only if they know that they can exchange the rupees for pounds. The same holds true for producers in all countries; they must eventually receive payment in the currency of their own country.

Trade between nations typically requires the exchange of one nation's currency for that of another.

International payments involve the exchange of currencies between people who have one currency and require another. Suppose that a UK firm wishes to acquire ¥3 million for some purpose. (¥ is the currency symbol for the Japanese yen.) The firm can go to its bank and buy a cheque, or money order, that will be accepted in Japan as ¥3 million. How many *pounds* the firm must pay to purchase this check will depend on the value of the pound in terms of yen.

The exchange of one currency for another is a *foreign exchange transaction*. The term 'foreign exchange' refers to the actual foreign currency or various claims on it, such as bank deposits or promises to pay, that are traded for each other. The *exchange rate* is the value of the pound in terms of foreign currency; it is the amount of foreign currency that can be obtained with one unit of the domestic currency. For example, if one can obtain ¥150 for £1, the yen–pound exchange rate is 150.

A rise in the external value of the pound (that is, a rise in the exchange rate) results in an **appreciation** of the pound; for example, if one can now obtain ¥175 for £1, the pound has *appreciated*. A fall in the external value of the pound (that is, a fall in the exchange rate) is a **depreciation** of the pound; for example, if one can now obtain only ¥125 for £1, the pound has *depreciated*.[7]

---

[6] Some trade, especially in primary commodities such as wheat and oil, is conducted in US dollars, even when US residents are not involved. In this respect, the US dollar has a special role as an international medium of exchange or unit of account.

[7] When the external value of the currency changes as a result of explicit policy of the central bank, it is often said to have been *devalued* when it falls and *revalued* when it rises.

Because the exchange rate expresses the value of one currency in terms of another, when one currency appreciates, the other must depreciate.

The demand for and supply of pounds

The exchange rate is just a price, albeit a very important price, for the economy concerned. As with other prices, we shall approach the explanation of exchange rates from the perspective of demand and supply analysis. However, the exchange rate is potentially influenced by (and influences) all payments into and out of the national economy from abroad. Hence we need to be clear about what those payments are, before proceeding to discuss the determinants of the exchange rate.

For the sake of simplicity, we use an example involving trade between the United Kingdom and the United States and the determination of the exchange rate between their two currencies, the pound sterling[8] and the dollar. The two-country example simplifies things, but the principles apply to all foreign transactions. Thus, 'dollar' stands for foreign exchange in general, and the value of the pound in terms of dollars stands for the foreign exchange rate in general.

When £1 = $1.50, a US importer who offers to buy £1 million with dollars must be offering to sell $1.5 million. Similarly, a UK importer who offers to sell £1 million for dollars must be offering to buy $1.5 million.

Because one currency is traded for another in the foreign exchange market, it follows that a demand for foreign exchange implies a supply of pounds sterling, while a supply of foreign exchange implies a demand for pounds.

For this reason, a theory of the exchange rate between sterling and the dollar can deal either with the demand for and the supply of pounds or with the demand for and the supply of dollars: both need not be considered. We will concentrate on the demand, supply, and price of the pound (quoted in dollars).

We develop our example in terms of the demand-and-supply analysis first encountered in Chapter 4. To do so, we need only to recall that *in the market for foreign exchange*, transactions that generate a receipt of foreign exchange represent a demand for pounds, and transactions that require a payment of foreign exchange represent a supply of pounds. We focus on the demand and supply of pounds arising from both the current and capital accounts. Later we turn to the important role of official intervention by the Bank of England (acting as agent for the Treasury through the Exchange Equalization Account).

THE DEMAND FOR POUNDS

The demand for pounds arises from all international transactions that generate a receipt of foreign exchange.

UK exports One important source of demand for pounds in foreign exchange markets is foreigners who do not currently hold pounds but who wish to buy UK-made goods and services. A German importer of Scotch whisky is such a purchaser; an Austrian couple planning to take a holiday in Cornwall is another; the Chinese national airline seeking to buy Rolls Royce engines for its passenger aircraft is yet another. All are sources of demand for pounds, arising out of international trade. Each potential buyer wants to sell their own currency and buy pounds for the purpose of purchasing UK exports.

Capital inflows A second source of a demand for pounds comes from foreigners who wish to purchase UK assets. In order to buy UK assets, holders of foreign currencies must first buy pounds in foreign exchange markets.[9] These inflows may be of either long-term or short-term capital.

Reserve currency Governments often accumulate and hold foreign exchange reserves, just as individuals maintain savings accounts. The government of Nigeria, for example, may decide to increase its reserve holdings of sterling and reduce its reserve holdings of dollars; if it does so, it will be a demander of pounds (and a supplier of dollars) in foreign exchange markets. Sterling used to be a very important reserve currency, particularly for countries that were formerly British colonies. This role has been greatly reduced (relative to the US dollar), but it still creates a significant overseas demand for sterling. Currency reserves are almost always held in an interest-bearing asset, so it is the expected return on these assets that is likely to influence the choice, just as with private-sector capital flows.

THE TOTAL DEMAND FOR POUNDS

The demand for pounds by holders of foreign currencies is the sum of the demands for all of the purposes just discussed—for purchases of UK exports, for long- or short-term capital movements, or for adding to currency reserves.

Furthermore, because people, firms, and governments in all countries purchase goods from, and invest in, many other countries, the demand for any one currency will be the aggregate demand of individuals, firms, and governments in a number of different countries. Thus, the total demand for pounds, for example, may include Germans who are offering marks, Japanese who are offering yen,

---

[8] We use the words 'pounds', 'sterling', and 'pounds sterling' to refer to the UK currency. In the foreign exchange markets it is usually classified as GBP, while the dollar is USD. The foreign exchange market between the GBP and USD is referred to in the market as 'cable', because it grew to its present structure by use of one of the first transatlantic telephone cables.

[9] Capital inflows also arise when UK citizens sell foreign assets, because they enter the foreign exchange market and sell the foreign currency received for the assets and buy pounds.

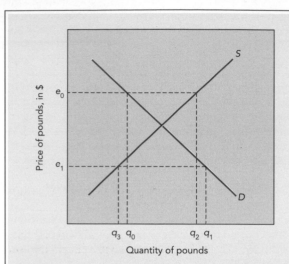

Figure 37.1 The market for foreign exchange

The demand for pounds is negatively sloped, and the supply of pounds is positively sloped, when drawn against the exchange rate, measured as the value of £1 in terms of foreign exchange. The demand for pounds in the market for foreign exchange is given by the negatively sloped line, D. It represents the sum of transactions giving rise to receipts of foreign exchange. When the exchange rate is e_0, the quantity of pounds demanded is q_0. A depreciation of the pound is indicated by a fall in the exchange rate to e_1; foreign demand for UK goods and assets rises, and hence the quantity of dollars demanded also rises, from q_0 to q_1. An appreciation has the opposite effect; a rise in the exchange rate from e_1 to e_0 causes the quantity of pounds demanded to fall from q_1 to q_0.

The supply of pounds in the market for foreign exchange is given by the positively sloped line, S. It represents the sum of transactions that require payments of foreign exchange. When the exchange rate is e_0, the quantity of pounds supplied is q_2. A depreciation of the pound causes the exchange rate to fall to e_1; UK demand for foreign goods and assets falls, and hence the quantity of pounds supplied to the foreign exchange market also falls, from q_2 to q_3. An appreciation has the opposite effect; a rise in the exchange rate from e_1 to e_0 causes the quantity of pounds supplied to rise from q_3 to q_2. (As discussed in footnote 10, we are assuming that the response of demand to the change in the exchange rate is *elastic*.)

Figure 37.1. This figure plots the value of the pound (measured in dollars) on the vertical axis and the quantity of pounds on the horizontal axis. Moving down the vertical scale, the pound is worth fewer dollars and hence is depreciating in the foreign exchange market. Moving up the scale, the pound is appreciating.

Why is the demand curve for pounds negatively sloped? Consider the demand for pounds that is derived from foreign purchases of UK exports. If the pound depreciates, the dollar price of UK exports will fall because holders of dollars require fewer of them to buy £1. US citizens will buy more of the cheaper UK goods and will require more pounds for this purpose. The quantity of pounds demanded will therefore rise. In the opposite case, when the pound appreciates, more dollars are required to buy £1, and so the price of UK exports rises in terms of dollars. US citizens will buy fewer UK goods and thus will demand fewer pounds.

Similar considerations affect other sources of demand for pounds. When the pound is cheaper, UK assets become attractive purchases, and the quantity purchased will rise. As it does, the quantity of pounds demanded to pay for the purchases will increase.

The demand curve for pounds in the foreign exchange market is negatively sloped when it is plotted against the dollar price of pounds.

THE SUPPLY OF POUNDS

The sources of supply of pounds in the foreign exchange market are merely the opposite side of the demand for dollars. (Recall that the *supply* of pounds by people who are seeking dollars is the same as the *demand* for dollars by holders of pounds.)

Who wants to sell pounds? UK residents seeking to purchase foreign goods and services or assets will be supplying pounds and purchasing foreign exchange for this purpose. In addition, holders of UK assets may decide to sell their UK holdings and shift them into foreign assets, and if they do they will sell pounds; that is, they will be supplying pounds to the foreign exchange market. Similarly, a country with some sterling reserves of foreign exchange may decide that the sterling assets offer a poor return and that it should sell pounds in order to buy another currency.

THE SHAPE OF THE SUPPLY CURVE OF POUNDS

When the pound depreciates, the sterling price of US exports to the United Kingdom rises. It takes more pounds to buy the same US goods, so UK residents will buy fewer of the now more expensive US goods. The amount of pounds being offered in exchange for dollars in order to pay for US exports to the UK (UK imports) will therefore fall.[10]

Greeks who are offering drachmas, and so on. For simplicity, however, we continue with our two-country example and use only the United Kingdom and the United States.

THE SHAPE OF THE DEMAND CURVE FOR POUNDS

The demand for pounds in terms of dollars is represented by a negatively sloped curve, such as the one shown in

---

[10] As long as the demand for imports is elastic (price elasticity greater than −1 (in absolute terms)), the fall in the volume of imports will swamp

In the opposite case, when the pound appreciates, US exports to the United Kingdom become cheaper, more are sold, and more pounds are spent on them. Thus, more pounds will be offered in exchange for dollars to obtain the foreign exchange needed to pay for the extra imports. The argument also applies to purchases and sales of assets.

The supply curve of pounds in the foreign exchange market is positively sloped when it is plotted against the dollar price of pounds.

This too is illustrated in Figure 37.1.

The determination of exchange rates

THE demand and supply curves in Figure 37.1 do not include official foreign exchange market intervention by the Bank of England, though they do include any transactions in sterling by foreign monetary authorities. In order to complete our analysis, we need to incorporate the role of domestic official intervention.[11] Three important cases need to be considered:

1. When there is no official intervention by the Bank of England, the exchange rate is determined by the equality between the supply and demand for pounds arising from the capital and current accounts. This is called a *flexible, or floating exchange rate*.

2. When official intervention is used to maintain the exchange rate at (or close to) a particular value, there is said to be a *fixed, or pegged, exchange rate*.

3. Between these two 'pure' systems are a variety of possible intermediate cases, including the *adjustable peg* and the *managed float*. In the adjustable peg system, governments set and attempt to maintain par values for their exchange rates, but they explicitly recognize that circumstances may arise in which they will change the par value. In a managed float, the central bank seeks to have some stabilizing influence on the exchange rate but does not try to fix it at some publicly announced par value. (Exchange rate regimes are discussed further in the appendix to this chapter.)

Flexible exchange rates

Consider an exchange rate that is set in a freely competitive market, with no intervention by the central bank. Like any competitive price, this rate fluctuates according to the conditions of demand and supply.

Suppose that the current price of pounds is so low (say, at e_1 in Figure 37.1) that the quantity of pounds demanded exceeds the quantity supplied. Pounds will be in scarce supply in the foreign exchange market; some people who require pounds to make payments to the United Kingdom will be unable to obtain them; and the price of pounds will be bid up. The value of the pound *vis-à-vis* the dollar will appreciate. As the price of sterling rises, the dollar price of UK exports to the United States rises and the quantity of pounds demanded to buy UK goods decreases. However, as the pound price of imports from the United States falls, a larger quantity will be purchased and the quantity of pounds supplied will rise. Thus, a rise in the price of the pound reduces the quantity demanded and increases the quantity supplied. Where the two curves intersect, quantity demanded equals quantity supplied, and the exchange rate is in equilibrium.

What happens when the price of pounds is above its equilibrium value? The quantity of pounds demanded will be less than the quantity supplied. With the pound in excess supply, some people who wish to convert pounds into dollars will be unable to do so.[12] The price of pounds will fall, fewer pounds will be supplied, more will be demanded, and an equilibrium will be re-established.

A foreign exchange market is like other competitive markets in that the forces of demand and supply lead to an equilibrium price in which quantity demanded equals quantity supplied.

---

the rise in price, and hence fewer pounds will be spent on imports. If the elasticity of demand for imports is less than − 1 (in absolute terms), the volume of imports will fall but the amount of domestic money spent on them will still rise. In what follows, we adopt the case of elastic demand, which is usual in this area. In a more general form, this is called the *Marshall–Lerner condition*, after two famous British economists who first studied the problem.

[11] Official intervention is included in the balance of payments accounts in Table 37.1 under 'Transactions in assets'. Official intervention used to be reported in the aggregate balance of payments figures under a separate category called 'Balance for official financing'. This practice is still followed in many other countries.

[12] Equivalently, we could say that there is an excess demand for foreign exchange.

In a floating exchange rate system, it is exchange rate adjustment that determines the actual current and capital account transactions, even though planned, or desired, trade and investment decisions may have been inconsistent. Suppose that, at the beginning of some period, importers and exporters had plans that would have created a current account deficit and domestic investors had plans to buy foreign securities (while foreigners had no such plans). The attempt to implement these plans would create a massive excess supply of sterling (demand for foreign exchange). This would force a sterling depreciation, which would continue until it moved far enough to force changes in plans. Indeed, it would depreciate just far enough so that any supply of sterling generated by a current account deficit was just balanced by a capital inflow (or any current account surplus was just balanced by a capital outflow).

Fixed exchange rates

When there is official intervention in the foreign exchange market to maintain a particular exchange rate, this stops some movement in the exchange rate that otherwise would have happened. In this way, it may prevent the exchange rate from adjusting sufficiently to guarantee that the current account balance and the (private-sector) capital account balance are equal and opposite. In this situation, any desired excess demand or supply of sterling by the private sector must be met by the Bank of England. In the process of intervention, the Bank will be building up or running down its foreign exchange reserves.

The official foreign exchange reserves are the stock of foreign-currency-denominated assets that the monetary authorities hold in order to be able to intervene in the foreign exchange markets.

When central banks peg their exchange rates, they do not do so at one specific rate, but, rather, within some range. In the post-war exchange regime that existed until 1972 (in the UK case) exchange rates were pegged within ± 1 per cent of a central (or 'par') rate. (± is the symbol meaning 'plus or minus'.) This is known as the Bretton Woods regime, after the town in the United States where the agreement was drawn up. In the European Exchange Rate Mechanism (ERM) of the 1980s and early 1990s, the range of permitted fluctuation was ± 2.25 per cent for some countries and ± 6 per cent for others (including the United Kingdom, from October 1990 to September 1992).

Let us consider a simplified analysis of how such pegged exchange rate regimes operate. Assume for simplicity that the Bank of England fixed the UK exchange rate between, say, $1.50 and $1.60. This case is illustrated in Figure 37.2. The Bank would then enter the market to prevent the rate from going outside this range. At the price of $1.50, the

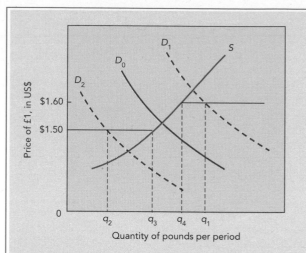

Figure 37.2 Managing fixed exchange rates

Under a fixed exchange rate regime, the central bank intervenes in the foreign exchange market to ensure that the exchange rate of the home currency stays within specified bands. The figures shows three possible outcomes when there is a given supply curve, and the bands within which the exchange rate is pegged are given by the range $1.50–$1.60. If the demand curve is given by D_0, the equilibrium exchange rate is within the bands so no intervention by the central bank is required. With demand curve D_1, the equilibrium exchange rate would be above $1.60. To stop the exchange rate rising above $1.60, the central bank has to sell $q_4 q_1$ pounds per period and buy dollars of equivalent value. (For every £100 it sells, it will acquire $160.) If the demand curve were D_2, the exchange rate would fall below $1.50 in a free market, so the central bank has to buy $q_2 q_3$ pounds per period with dollars. The dollars come out of official reserves. This is the case that causes most problems, because these reserve losses cannot be allowed to go on indefinitely. At some time reserves will run out. Here there has to be either a change of economic policy which shifts the D and S curves back to an intersection within the band, or a shift in the band (devaluation) such that it encompasses the current equilibrium price.

Bank offers to buy pounds (in exchange for dollars) in unlimited amounts. At the price $1.60, the Bank offers to sell pounds (in exchange for dollars) in unlimited amounts. When the bank buys foreign exchange (sells pounds) its exchange reserves rise, but when it sells foreign exchange (buys pounds) its foreign exchange reserves fall.

If, on average, the demand and supply curves intersect in the range $1.50–$1.60, then exchange reserves will be relatively stable. However, if demand for pounds intersected the supply curve below $1.50, the Bank would find itself losing reserves each period, and such a situation cannot be sustained indefinitely (because the Bank will run out of reserves). It must then either move the bands of fluctuation (devalue), or take action to shift the demand or supply curves. This could be done, for example, by trade restrictions, or by raising interest rates to attract short-term capital inflows.

In the remainder of this chapter, we focus on flexible exchange rates. However, before leaving fixed exchange rate regimes, it is worth noting that it is in a fixed exchange rate regime with an overvalued currency that balance of payments problems are directly felt by the monetary authorities. In this case, it is not necessarily a current account deficit that is the problem; rather, it is the overall excess supply of domestic currency (excess demand for foreign currency) in the foreign exchange market, which could arise from any of the components.

With fixed exchange rates and an overvalued currency, the monetary authorities will be suffering a loss of reserves. It is this that causes balance of payments crises for governments operating under fixed exchange rate regimes.

The problems associated with fixing the exchange rate provide a further example of the difficulties of price intervention listed in Chapter 6.

Changes in exchange rates

What causes exchange rates to move? The simplest answer to this question is: changes in demand or supply in the foreign exchange market. Anything that shifts the demand curve for pounds to the right or the supply curve for pounds to the left leads to an appreciation of the pound; anything that shifts the demand curve for pounds to the left or the supply curve for pounds to the right leads to a depreciation of the pound. This is nothing more than a restatement of the laws of supply and demand, applied now to the market for foreign currencies; it is illustrated in Figure 37.3.

What causes the shifts in demand and supply that lead to changes in exchange rates? There are many causes, some of which are transitory and some of which are persistent; we will discuss some of the most important ones.

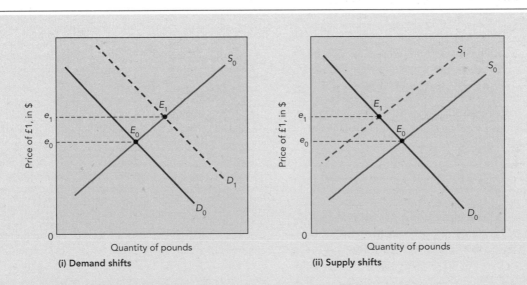

Figure 37.3 Changes in exchange rates

An increase in the demand for pounds or a decrease in the supply will cause the pound to appreciate; a decrease in the demand or an increase in supply will cause it to depreciate. The initial demand and supply curves, D_0 and S_0, are shown as solid lines. Equilibrium is at E_0 with an exchange rate of e_0. An increase in the demand for pounds, as shown by a rightward shift in the demand curve from D_0 to D_1 in part (i), or a decrease in the supply of pounds, as shown by a leftward shift in the supply curve from S_0 to S_1 in part (ii), will cause the pound to appreciate. In both parts the new equilibrium is at E_1, and the appreciation is shown by the rise in the exchange rate from e_0 to e_1.

A decrease in the demand for pounds, as shown by a leftward shift in the demand curve from D_1 to D_0 in part (i), or an increase in the supply of pounds, as shown by a rightward shift in the supply curve from S_1 to S_0 in part (ii), will cause the pound to depreciate. The equilibrium will shift from E_1 to E_0, and the depreciation is shown by the fall in the exchange rate from e_1 to e_0 in both parts.

A RISE IN THE DOMESTIC PRICE OF EXPORTS

Suppose that the sterling price of UK-produced telephone equipment rises. The effect on the demand for pounds depends on the price elasticity of foreign demand for the UK products.

If the demand is inelastic (say, because the United Kingdom is uniquely able to supply the product for which there are no close substitutes), then more will be spent; the demand for pounds to pay the bigger bill will shift the demand curve to the right, and the pound will appreciate. This is illustrated in Figure 37.3 (i).

If the demand is elastic, perhaps because other countries supply the same product to competitive world markets, the total amount spent will decrease and thus fewer pounds will be demanded; that is, the demand curve for pounds will shift to the left, and the pound will depreciate. This too is illustrated in Figure 37.3 (i), by a reverse of the previous shift.

A RISE IN THE FOREIGN PRICE OF IMPORTS

Suppose that the dollar price of US-produced videos increases sharply. Suppose also that UK consumers have an elastic demand for US videos because they can easily switch to UK substitutes. In this case they will spend fewer dollars for US videos than they did before. Hence they will supply fewer pounds to the foreign exchange market. The supply curve of pounds shifts to the left, and the pound will appreciate. If the demand for US videos were inelastic, spending on them would rise and the supply of pounds would shift to the right, leading to a depreciation of the pound. This is illustrated in Figure 37.3 (ii).

CHANGES IN PRICE LEVELS

Suppose that, instead of a change in the price of a specific exported product, there is a change in *all* prices because of inflation. What matters here is the change in the UK price level *relative to* the price levels of its trading partners. (Recall that, in our two-country example, the United States stands for the rest of the world.)

If UK inflation is higher than that in the United States, UK exports are becoming relatively expensive in US markets while imports from the United States are becoming relatively cheap in the United Kingdom. This will shift the demand curve for pounds to the left and the supply curve to the right. Each change causes the dollar price of pounds to fall, that is, causes the pound to depreciate.

If the price level of one country is rising relative to that of another country, the equilibrium value of its currency will be falling relative to that of the other country.

Indeed, the price level and the exchange rate are both mea-sures of a currency's value. The price level is the value of a currency measured against a typical basket of goods, while the exchange rate values a currency against other curren-cies.

CAPITAL MOVEMENTS

Major capital flows can exert a strong influence on exchange rates, especially as the size of capital flows (in the modern globalized financial system) can swamp trade pay-ments on any particular day. An increased desire by UK res-idents to invest in US assets will shift the supply curve for pounds to the right, and the pound will depreciate. This is illustrated in Figure 37.3 (ii).

A significant movement of investment funds has the effect of appreciating the currency of the capital-importing country and depreciating the currency of the capital-exporting country.

This statement is true for all capital movements—short-term and long-term. Because the motives that lead to large capital movements are likely to be different in the short and long terms, however, it is worth considering each separately.

Short-term capital movements   A major motive for short-term capital flows is a change in interest rates. International traders hold transactions balances just as domestic traders do. These balances are usually lent out on a short-term basis rather than being left in a non-interest-bearing deposit. Naturally, other things being equal, the holders of these balances will tend to lend them in those markets where interest rates are highest. Thus, if one major coun-try's short-term rate of interest rises above the rates in most other countries, there will tend to be an inflow of short-term capital into that country (or, at least, of deposits in major financial centres denominated in that country's cur-rency) in an effort to take advantage of the high rate, and this will tend to appreciate the currency. If these short-term interest rates should fall, there will most likely be a sudden shift away from that country as a location for short-term funds, and its currency will tend to depreciate.

A second motive for short-term capital movements is speculation about a country's exchange rate. If foreigners expect the pound to appreciate, they will rush to buy assets denominated in pounds; if they expect the pound to depre-ciate, they will be reluctant to buy or to hold UK financial assets.

Long-term capital movements   Long-term capital move-ments are largely influenced by long-term expectations about another country's profit opportunities and the long-run value of its currency. A US firm would be more willing to purchase a UK firm if it expected that the profits in pounds would buy more dollars in future years than the profits from investment in a US factory. This could happen if the UK business earned greater profits than the US alternative, with exchange rates remaining unchanged. It could also happen if the profits were the same but the US firm expected the pound to appreciate relative to the dollar.

STRUCTURAL CHANGES

An economy can undergo structural changes that alter the equilibrium exchange rate. 'Structural change' is an all-purpose term for a change in technology, the invention of new products, or anything else that affects the pattern of comparative advantage. For example, when a country's products do not improve in quality as rapidly as those of some other countries, that country's consumers' demand (at fixed prices) shifts slowly away from its own products and towards those of its foreign competitors. This causes a slow depreciation in the first country's currency, because the demand for its currency is shifting slowly leftward as illustrated in Figure 37.3 (i).

An important example of a structural change in recent UK history was the discovery of oil and gas in the North Sea. This reduced UK demand for imported oil, leading to a reduced supply of sterling in the foreign exchange market and an appreciation of sterling. (See discussion pertaining to Figure 37.4 below.)

The behaviour of exchange rates

The degree of exchange rate variability experienced since the early 1970s is generally thought to have exceeded that which can be explained by variations in the above determinants of exchange rates. (See Figure 27.8 on p. 518.)

Why have exchange rates been so volatile? This question remains at the centre of debate and controversy among researchers and policy commentators. In this section we provide only a cursory view of this and related questions about the behaviour of exchange rates.

First, we look at one measure of the value that the exchange rate would take on if it were subject to the influence of what might be called the underlying, or fundamental, market determinants. We can then compare this with the actual value of the exchange rate. Second, we provide one explanation for the divergence.

PURCHASING POWER PARITY

Purchasing power parity (PPP) theory holds that, over the long term, the average value of the exchange rate between two currencies depends on their relative purchasing power. The theory holds that a currency will tend to have the same purchasing power when it is spent in its home country as it would have if it were converted to foreign exchange and spent in the foreign country.

If, at existing values of relative price levels and the existing exchange rate, a currency has a higher purchasing power in its own country, it is said to be undervalued; there is then an incentive to sell foreign exchange and buy the domestic currency in order to take advantage of this higher purchasing power (that is, the fact that goods seem cheaper) in the domestic economy. This will put upward pressure on the domestic currency.

Similarly, if a currency has a lower purchasing power in its own country, it is said to be overvalued; there is then an incentive to sell the domestic currency and buy foreign exchange in order to take advantage of the higher purchasing power (cheaper goods) abroad. This will put downward pressure on the domestic currency.

The PPP exchange rate is determined by relative price levels in the two countries.

For example, assume that the UK price level rises by 20 per cent, while the US price level rises by only 5 per cent over the same period. The PPP value of the dollar then appreciates by approximately 15 per cent against sterling. This means that in the United States the prices of all goods (both US-produced and imported UK goods) will rise by 5 per cent, measured in dollars, while in the United Kingdom the prices of all goods (both UK-produced and imported US goods) will rise by 20 per cent, measured in pounds sterling.

The PPP exchange rate adjusts so that the relative price of the two nations' goods (measured in the same currency) is unchanged, because the change in the relative values of two currencies compensates exactly for differences in national inflation rates.

If the actual exchange rate changes along with the PPP rate, the competitive positions of producers in the two countries will be unchanged. Firms that are located in countries with high inflation rates will still be able to sell their outputs on international markets, because the exchange rate will adjust to offset the effect of the rising domestic prices. An exchange rate that adjusts in line with the PPP exchange rate is also referred to as a constant *real exchange rate*.[13] A simple model of the exchange rate implied by the quantity theory of money and PPP is set out in Box 37.2.

Figure 37.4 (i) shows an index of the UK real exchange rate for 1962–92. Figure 37.4 (ii) shows an alternative index

---

[13] The real exchange rate is the inverse of competitiveness. A country whose goods were becoming relatively cheap in world markets would be said to be improving its competitiveness but to be having a falling real exchange rate, and vice versa. The real exchange rate is not an actual price of currency: it is an index number of the relative prices of home and foreign goods.

BOX 37.2

Exchange rates and the quantity theory

A simple expression for the exchange rate can be derived from the quantity theory of money (as set out in Box 36.1) when there are two countries and an exchange rate that follows its PPP value.

Let the foreign country be denoted by an asterisk (*), so that it has an equation linking money, prices, income, and velocity:

$$M^*V^* = P^*Y^*. \qquad \text{(i)}$$

Using values for home money supply, prices, velocity, and income, we already had:

$$MV = PY. \qquad \text{(ii)}$$

All we need to add is the relationship implied by PPP. This is that prices will be the same in both economies when converted at the current exchange rate:

$$PE = P^*, \qquad \text{(iii)}$$

where P is the home country price level, P^* is the foreign country price level, and E is the exchange rate (number of units of foreign currency per pound sterling). Now all we do is rearrange (i) and (ii) as expressions for P and P^*, then substitute into (iii) and arrange as an expression for E. This gives†

$$E = \frac{M^*}{M} \cdot \frac{Y}{Y^*} \cdot \frac{V^*}{V} \qquad \text{(iv)}$$

This is an important equation which gives us some new insights into the exchange rate. The first term is the ratio of the home and foreign money supplies. E falls in proportion to the home money supply and rises in proportion to the foreign money supply. This means that, when the home money supply rises, the exchange rate depreciates in the same proportion. The logic of this has two steps. First, a rise in home money supply leads to a proportional increase in the home price level (for given levels of Y and V). Second, a rise in the home price level leads to a proportional depreciation of the home currency to preserve PPP.

The second term in (iv) has a very important implication. Domestic real national income is positively related to E. This means that, other things being equal, a rise in domestic national income leads to an appreciation of the home currency. The reason for this is that an increase in Y leads to an increased transactions demand for the home currency. As we have learned in this chapter, anything that increases demand for the home currency will tend to appreciate its exchange rate.

This simple model of exchange rates gives important insights, but it is only a beginning. Many more complicated factors affecting interest rates and expectations can easily be incorporated by a more detailed specification of the determinants of V. However, the main elements of (iv) are recognizable in many of the empirical exchange rate models of the last two decades.

† The steps are as follows:
1. $P^* = M^*V^*/Y^*$ and $P = MV/Y$.
2. Substituting into (iii), $E(MV/Y) = M^*V^*/Y^*$.
3. Rearranging gives (iv).

---

of the real exchange rate for the United Kingdom, the United States, and Germany for 1980–94. PPP requires that the real exchange rate should be constant in the long term. This is broadly true. Notice also, however, the large fluctuations around the PPP rate. The United Kingdom had a substantial rise in its real exchange rate in the late 1970s, associated with its emergence as an oil producer. This led to a sharp loss of competitiveness of the non-oil sectors of the economy (especially manufacturing) causing a sharp decline in UK manufacturing output which in turn contributed to the 1979–81 recession. The UK real exchange rate fell significantly between 1981 and 1986. The most dramatic swing in the 1980s, however, was in the US real exchange rate, which increased 50 per cent between 1980 and 1985, and then fell back to its 1980 level by 1987.

PPP governs exchange rate behaviour in the long term, but there often are significant deviations from PPP in the short to medium term.

Why have these wide fluctuations occurred? One of the most important reasons is associated with international differences in interest rates. Another, related reason—responses to new information—is discussed in Box 37.3.

EXCHANGE RATE OVERSHOOTING

Differences in interest rates between countries, arising from differences in monetary and fiscal policies, among other factors, can trigger large capital flows as investors seek to place their funds where returns are highest. These capital flows in turn will result in swings in the exchange rate between the two countries. Some economists argue that this is the fundamental reason for the wide fluctuations in exchange rates that have been observed.

To illustrate, suppose that an exogenous change in monetary policy causes UK interest rates to rise 4 percentage points above those in New York. The interest rate differential will lead to a capital inflow into the United Kingdom. UK and foreign investors alike will sell assets denominated

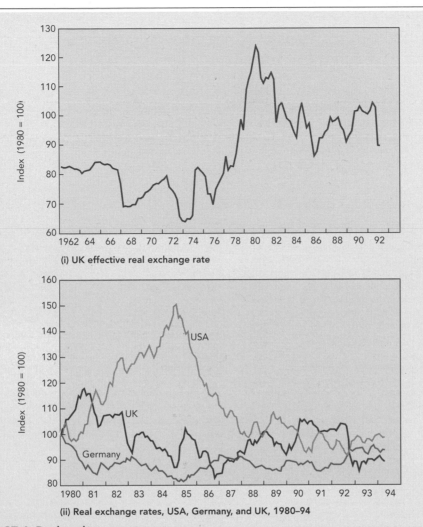

Figure 37.4 Real exchange rate

Deviations from PPP can be substantial in the short run, but over the long run exchange rates tend to converge to their PPP values. At the PPP exchange rate, the real exchange rate would be constant. Part (i) shows the UK real exchange rate from 1962 to 1992 (1980 = 100), calculated using value-added deflators (the price deflator for the GDP output measure of national income). It shows a substantial appreciation on the UK real exchange rate in the late 1970s, and a subsequent fall in the mid-1980s. This real exchange rate appreciation was a major cause of the collapse in manufacturing output in the 1979–81 recession.

Part (ii) shows real exchange rates for three countries (United States, Germany, and the United Kingdom) calculated by adjusting actual exchange rates by indexes of consumer prices, and set to a value of 100 in the first quarter of 1980.

The UK real exchange rate was already high (compared with the early 1970s) in 1980, as shown in part (i), but it continued to rise until early 1981. It then fell in stages. It rose again at the end of the 1980s but fell sharply after September 1992, when Britain left the ERM. The United States experienced a dramatic appreciation of its real exchange rate from 1980 to 1985, after which time it fell back; at the end of 1993, the US real exchange rate was roughly the same as in 1980. The real exchange rate of Germany fell in the early 1980s, but then cycled about a fairly constant level.

All of these figures are broadly consistent with the view that PPP holds in the long term. It is clear, however, that deviations from PPP can be sustained over lengthy periods—the US real exchange rate took nearly a decade to return to its long-run level. Also, the UK real exchange rate in the 1980s remained above that of the 1960s and early 1970s.

Source: Datastream

BOX 37.3

....

The organization of foreign exchange markets

Foreign exchange markets are rather different from markets in consumer goods. The vast bulk of trading takes place between professional foreign exchange dealers of banks. They do not meet the people they are trading with face to face. Rather, they do their transactions over the telephone, and the other party to the deal could be anywhere in the world. The structure of this market has two interesting implications.

Exchange rates respond to news

Deals done by the professional dealers are all on a large scale, typically involving sums no smaller than £1 million and often very much larger. Each dealer tends to specialize in deals between a small number of currencies, say, the pound and the Deutschmark. But the dealers in all currencies for each bank sit close together, in a dealing room, so that they can hear what is going on in other markets. When a big news event breaks, anywhere in the world, this will be shouted out to all dealers in the room simultaneously.

Each dealer is also faced with several TV screens and many buttons which will connect him or her very quickly by telephone to other dealers. Speed of transaction can be very important if you are dealing with large volumes of money in a market that is continuously changing the prices quoted. Latest price quotes from around the world appear on the screens. However, contracts are agreed over the telephone (and nowadays are recorded in case of disagreement) and the paperwork follows within two days.

As exchange rates are closely related to expectations and to interest rates, the foreign exchange dealers have to keep an eye on all major news events affecting the economic environment. Since all the players in the foreign exchange markets are professionals, they are all well informed, not just about what has happened but also about forecasts of what is likely to happen. Accordingly, the exchange rate, at any point in time, reflects not just history, but also current expectations of what is going to happen in future.

As soon as some future event comes to be expected, it will be reflected in the current exchange rate. Events expected to happen soon will usually be given more weight than distant events. The only component in today's news that will cause the exchange rate to change is what was *not* expected to happen. Economists attribute the unforecastable component of news to a random error. It is random in the sense that it has no detectable pattern to it and it is unrelated to the information available before it happened.

Some events are clearly unforecastable, like an earthquake in Japan or a head of state having a heart attack. Others are the pro-duction of economic statistics for which forecasts have generally been published. In the latter case, it is the deviation of announced figures from their forecast value which, if large, tend to move exchange rates.

Exchange rates are moved by news. Since news is random and unpredictable, exchange rates will tend to move in a random way.

Some people, observing the volatility of exchange rates, conclude that foreign exchange markets are inefficient. However, with well informed professional players, who have forward-looking expectations, new information is rapidly transmitted into prices. Volatility of exchange rates, therefore, reflects the volatility of relevant events around the world.

A medium of exchange in the foreign exchange markets

For the professional dealer, time is valuable. The quicker a particular transaction can be completed, the better. Banks typically sell foreign currency contracts to their customers, and then try to cover their own risk by buying the same currency from someone else. For obscure currencies, this may be difficult. So banks tend to make most deals (except deals in major currencies like the pound, yen, Deutschmark, and franc) in two steps, involving the US dollar. In this respect, the dollar is the medium of exchange of the foreign exchange markets. An example will help to clarify the point.

Suppose that NatWest has a customer who is exporting coffee from Brazil to Greece. The customer asks NatWest to provide a large volume of Brazilian cruzeiro in exchange for drachmas. NatWest accepts the drachmas, but then has to buy the cruzeiro from some other bank before it can deliver them to the customer. How does it do it? The problem is that there will be very few people in the market trying to make exactly the opposite deal. The bank could just wait for someone to turn up, but that is risky (especially if it has committed on a price to the customer). The NatWest dealer knows that there is an active market between the cruzeiro and the dollar, and also between the dollar and the drachma. So he does his deal in two steps: sell drachmas for dollars, and sells dollars for cruzeiro.

In the foreign exchange markets, there are not active cross-markets between all pairs of currencies, but this does not matter, because all currencies that have a market at all have one with the dollar. Hence, the dollar can be thought of as the medium of exchange of the.foreign exchange markets.

in US dollars and will buy UK assets that earn higher interest. These capital inflows will lead to an increased demand for pounds on the foreign exchange market as investors exchange dollars for pounds to buy UK assets. The increased demand will in turn lead to an appreciation of sterling.

A relative rise in domestic interest rates will cause a capital inflow and an appreciation of the home currency.

When will the process stop? It will stop only when expected return on UK and foreign assets are again roughly equalized; as long as the return on UK assets is above that on foreign assets, the capital inflows will continue, and the upward pressure on the pound will continue. The key is that the expected return includes not only the interest earnings, but also the expected gains or losses that might arise because of changes in the exchange rate during the period of the investment. A foreign investor holding a UK asset will receive pounds sterling when the asset is sold, and will at that time want to exchange pounds for foreign exchange. If the value of the pound has fallen, that will be a source of loss that has to be balanced against the interest income in assessing the net return on holding the asset.

Equilibrium occurs when the rise in value of the pound sterling in foreign exchange markets is large enough that investors will expect a future depreciation which just offsets the interest premium from investing funds in sterling-denominated assets.

Suppose investors believe that the PPP rate is £1 = US$1.50, but, as they rush to buy pounds to take advantage of higher UK interest rates, they drive the rate to, say, £1 = US$1.75. (Because £1 now buys more dollars, the pound has appreciated, and because it takes more dollars to buy £1, the dollar has depreciated.) They do not believe that this rate will be sustained and, instead, expect the pound to lose value in future periods. If foreign investors expect the pound to depreciate by 4 per cent per year, they will be indifferent between lending money in London and doing so in New York. The extra 4 per cent per year of interest that they earn in London is exactly offset by the 4 per cent that they expect to lose when they turn their money back into their own currency.

A policy that raises domestic interest rates above world levels will cause the external value of the domestic currency to appreciate enough to create an expected future depreciation that will be sufficient to offset the interest differential.

While interest differentials persist, the exchange rate must deviate from its equilibrium or PPP value; this is often referred to as exchange rate *overshooting*, because, at the time interest rates are raised, the exchange rate will jump beyond its long-run equilibrium level. This is illustrated in Figure 37.5.

The argument that a rise in domestic interest rates will cause an appreciation of the home currency requires an important proviso. The interest rate rise has to occur with all other factors—especially long-run inflation expecta-

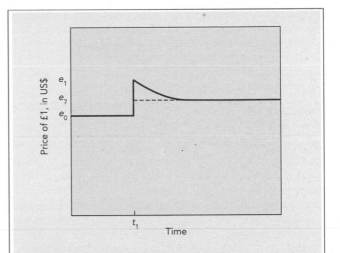

Figure 37.5 Exchange rate overshooting

The adjustment of exchange rates to policy changes often involves overshooting the long-run equilibrium. The figure illustrates how the exchange rate may move over time after the Bank of England tightens monetary policy by raising short-term interest rates. The tighter monetary policy will lower the domestic price level (relative to what it would otherwise have been) and will appreciate the nominal exchange rate, leaving the real exchange rate unchanged in the long run. However, higher interest rates will make the exchange rate jump (appreciate) to a point from which it will be expected to depreciate. The expected rate of depreciation will be just equal to the interest differential between home and foreign interest rates, assuming that domestic and foreign rates were equal to start with. The initial exchange rate is e_0. At time t_1, the Bank of England raises domestic interest rates and the exchange rate appreciates to e_1. Over time, it then depreciates back towards the new long-run equilibrium level of e_2. If the economy starts and finishes in full equilibrium, the appreciation from e_0 to e_2 will be proportional to the reduction in the price level caused by the tighter monetary policy and there will be no change in the real exchange rate. However, at e_1 there has been an appreciation of the real exchange rate, so the domestic economy has suffered a temporary loss in competitiveness.

tions—held constant. If, for example, it was a rise in expectations of future inflation that triggered off events, the story would be quite different. In this case, the interest rate rise would be responding to these expectations and to the consequent expectation of a long-run *depreciation* in the home currency. Now the change in the exchange rate would depend upon the size of the interest rate rise relative to the size of the expected long-run depreciation. In short, we need to be careful when applying economic analysis that works *holding other things constant* to a world where many things are changing simultaneously.

Implications of overshooting One policy implication of exchange rate theory is that a central bank that is seeking to use its monetary policy to attain its domestic policy targets may have to put up with large fluctuations in the exchange rate. Indeed, overshooting of the exchange rate in response to interest rate changes may be one of the most important elements of the monetary transmission mechanism.

In the case of a tightening of monetary policy which raises interest rates, the overshooting (appreciation) of the pound beyond its PPP rate would put export- and import-competing industries under temporary but severe pressure from foreign competition, because UK goods would become expensive relative to imported goods. The resulting fall in demand for UK goods would open up a recessionary gap, thus providing a further mechanism by which the restrictive monetary policy was transmitted to the rest of the economy. This is discussed further in Chapter 39.

The last two recessions in the United Kingdom both illustrate this mechanism at work. Both were associated with tight monetary policy and an overvalued exchange rate, although, as there were worldwide recessions at roughly the same time, domestic factors cannot be the whole story.

In the run-up to the 1979–81 recession, the pound had appreciated strongly. In 1979, interest rates were raised sharply and the pound appreciated further, as the Thatcher government implemented its commitment to control inflation by tight monetary policy. The high exchange rate meant that domestic producers became very uncompetitive, and so imports of cheaper foreign goods rose. Between late 1979 and early 1981, domestic manufacturing output fell by nearly 20 per cent and unemployment subsequently rose to over 3 million.

The high exchange rate cannot be blamed entirely on tight monetary policy alone, because this was also the time when the United Kingdom was emerging as an oil producer (and the price of oil had doubled in 1979). However, monetary policy (especially the sharp rise in interest rates in 1979) certainly contributed to the overshooting of sterling, and the extremely high exchange rate was undoubtedly a central element in the transmission mechanism between the monetary sector and the real economy.

The recession of 1991–3 was made worse by an attempt to maintain an overvalued exchange rate. From 1981 to 1988 the economy had seen a sustained recovery, but by 1988 inflationary pressures had built up. The government tightened monetary policy in the autumn of 1988 by raising interest rates. Higher interest rates created a higher foreign exchange value of the pound than would otherwise have happened. Then, in October 1990, the pound was pegged in the ERM. The onset of recession and fall of inflation, which was evident from 1991, would normally have permitted a reduction in interest rates (and a subsequent decline in the foreign exchange value of sterling), but ERM membership prevented this. This was because of the need to keep interest rates consistent with those of other ERM members, notably Germany. In September 1992 sterling was forced to leave the ERM by speculative pressure which caused reserve losses (as illustrated in Figure 37.2). This permitted a sharp fall in UK interest rates and was associated with a fall in the exchange rate. (Sterling fell from nearly $2.00 per pound in the summer of 1992 to around $1.50 after September, and stayed around that level for the next couple of years.) The fall in interest rates and in the exchange rate led fairly quickly to economic recovery by the spring of 1993.

A more detailed analysis of monetary policy follows in the next chapter. What we have learned in this chapter is that the exchange rate is an essential element of the transmission mechanism that turns monetary policy shocks into real shocks in an open economy under flexible exchange rates.

....

Summary

1 International trade normally requires the exchange of the currency of one country for that of another. The exchange rate between two currencies is the amount of one currency that must be paid in order to obtain one unit of another currency.

2 Actual transactions among the firms, consumers, and governments of various countries are recorded in the balance of payments accounts. In these accounts, any transaction that uses foreign exchange is recorded as a debit item, and any transaction that produces foreign exchange is recorded as a credit item. If all transactions are recorded, the sum of all credit items necessarily equals the sum of all debit items, because the foreign exchange that is bought must also have been sold.

3 Major categories in the balance of payments accounts are the trade account, the current account, and the capital account. When we talk about a balance of payments surplus or deficit, we are normally referring to the current account balance alone. A balance on the current account must be matched by a balance on capital account of equal magnitude but opposite sign.

4 There is nothing inherently good or bad about deficits or surpluses on the current account. Persistent deficits or surpluses involve a buildup or run-down of a country's net foreign assets.

5 The demand for pounds arises from UK exports of goods and services, long-term and short-term capital

flows into the United Kingdom, and the desire of foreign governments to use sterling assets as part of their reserves.

6 The supply of pounds to purchase foreign currencies arises from UK imports of goods and services, capital flows from the United Kingdom, and the desire of holders of sterling assets to decrease the size of their holdings.

7 The demand curve for pounds is negatively sloped and the supply curve of pounds is positively sloped when the quantities demanded and supplied are plotted against the price of pounds, measured in terms of a foreign currency.

8 When the central bank does not intervene in the foreign exchange market, there is a flexible exchange rate. Under fixed exchange rates, the central bank intervenes in the foreign exchange market to maintain the exchange rate within a specified range. To do this, the central bank must hold sufficient stocks of foreign exchange reserves.

9 Under a flexible, or floating, exchange rate, the exchange rate is market-determined by supply and demand for the currency.

10 Fluctuations in exchange rates can be understood as fluctuations around a trend value that is determined by the purchasing power parity (PPP) rate. The PPP rate adjusts in response to differences in national inflation rates. Deviations from the PPP rate are related, among other things, to international differences in interest rates.

11 Exchange rates tend to overshoot their long run equilibrium in response to shocks. A relaxation of monetary policy which lowers domestic interest rates will cause the exchange rate to depreciate. However, it will tend to depreciate to a point from which it can then appreciate at a rate sufficient to compensate for the interest rate fall. A rise in domestic interest rates will tend to make the exchange rate overshoot in the opposite direction (upwards).

Topics for review

- Balance of trade and balance of payments
- Current and capital account
- Mercantilist views on the balance of trade and volume of trade
- Foreign exchange and exchange rates
- Appreciation and depreciation
- Sources of the demand for and supply of foreign exchange
- Effects on exchange rates of capital flows, inflation, interest rates, and expectations about exchange rates
- Fixed and flexible exchange rates
- Adjustable pegs and managed floats
- Purchasing power parity
- Exchange rate overshooting

APPENDIX TO CHAPTER 37

The gold standard, Bretton Woods, and the ERM

TWO major international monetary regimes with fixed exchange rates occurred during the twentieth century. The gold standard, the origins of which are as old as currency itself, was dominant in the United Kingdom from about 1700 until 1931, though there were two significant breaks—for the Napoleonic Wars and the First World War. Other countries had currencies tied to gold for various periods. The United States, for example, was not on the gold standard from 1860 (the start of its Civil War) until 1873.[1] The period when the gold standard really was a global monetary system was, then, the four decades or so before the First World War.

The Bretton Woods system, which was the only global monetary system ever to be designed and established by conscious action, was born out of the Second World War and collapsed a little less than 30 years later. These histories are instructive, not least because many people continue to propose returning to one or the other of these systems.

The gold standard

The gold standard arose out of the general acceptance of gold as the commodity to be used as money. In most countries (at least for the period mentioned above) paper currency was freely convertible into gold at a fixed rate. In 1914 the US dollar was worth 0.053 standard ounce of gold, while the British pound sterling was worth 0.257 standard ounce of gold. This meant that the pound was worth 4.86 times as much as the dollar in terms of gold, thus making £1 worth US$4.86. (In practice, the exchange rate fluctuated within narrow limits set by the cost of shipping gold.) As long as all countries were on the gold standard, a person in one country could be sure of being able to make payments to a person in another.

The gold-flow, price-level mechanism

Under the gold standard, the balance of international payments was maintained by adjustments in price levels within individual countries. Consider a country that had a balance of payments deficit because the value of its imports (i.e. its purchases) from other countries exceeded the value of its exports (i.e. its sales) to other countries. The demand for foreign exchange would exceed the supply in this country's foreign exchange market. Some people who wished to

make foreign payments would need to convert their domestic currency into gold and ship the gold. Therefore, some people in a surplus country would receive gold in payment for exports. Thus, deficit countries would be losing gold, while surplus countries would be gaining it.

Under the gold standard, the whole money supply was linked to the supply of gold. The international movements of gold would therefore lead to a fall in the money supply in the deficit countries and a rise in the money supply in the surplus countries.

If full employment prevailed, changes in the domestic money supply would cause changes in domestic price levels. Deficit countries would thus have falling price levels, while surplus countries would have rising price levels. Indeed, it was the observation of links between gold inflows and price level rises that led to the formulation of the quantity theory of money. The exports of deficit countries would become relatively cheaper, while those of surplus countries would become relatively more expensive. The resulting changes in quantities bought and sold would move the balance of payments towards equilibrium. This mechanism was at one time known as the *price specie flow mechanism*, 'specie' being an old-fashioned word for a metal currency.

Actual experience of the gold standard

During the period before the First World War, the adjustment mechanism described above seemed to work well. Subsequent research has suggested, however, that the gold standard succeeded during that period mainly because it was not called on to do much work. No major trading country found itself with a serious and persistent balance of payments deficit, so no major country was called on to restore equilibrium through a large change in its domestic price level.

During the 1920s, the gold standard was called on to do a major job. It failed utterly, and it was abandoned. How did this happen? During the First World War most belligerent countries went off the gold standard. Most countries suffered major inflations, but the degree of inflation

---

[1] The US dollar was created by the Coinage Act of 1792, but it was defined in terms of both silver and gold. Because silver was undervalued and gold overvalued by the Act, silver coins circulated and gold was hoarded—Gresham's law in operation. Gold was restored to circulation by a revaluation in 1834. There were no national banknotes until after the Civil War—1865.

differed from country to country, which led to changes in the equilibrium (or purchasing power parity) exchange rates.

After the war, countries returned to the gold standard. Many returned to the pre-war rates. (The United Kingdom was taken back on to the gold standard in 1925 by the then Chancellor of the Exchequer, Winston Churchill. Keynes wrote a book called *The Economic Consequences of Mr Churchill*, in which he pointed out the deflationary consequences of this move.) This meant that some countries' goods were overpriced and other countries' goods were underpriced. Large deficits and surpluses in the balance of payments inevitably appeared, and the adjustment mechanism required that price levels should change in each of the countries in order to restore equilibrium. But exchange rates were not adjusted, and price levels changed very slowly. By the onset of the Great Depression in 1930, equilibrium price levels had not yet been attained. The financial chaos brought on by the Depression destroyed the existing international monetary system.

We may ask whether an altered gold standard, based on more realistic exchange rates, might not have succeeded. Some economists think that it would have; most others believe that the gold standard suffered from the key weakness that the price adjustment process worked too slowly and too imperfectly to cope with large and persistent disequilibrium.

Furthermore, gold as the basis for an international money supply suffered several disadvantages: a supply that could not be expanded as rapidly as increases in the volume of world trade required, an uneven distribution of existing and potential new gold supplies among the nations of the world, and a large and volatile speculative demand for gold during periods of crisis. These factors could cause disruptive variations in the supply of gold that was available for international monetary purposes.

The Bretton Woods system

The one lesson that everyone thought had been learned from the 1930s was that a system of either freely fluctuating exchange rates or fixed rates with easily accomplished devaluations was a sure route to disaster. In order to achieve a system of orderly exchange rates that would facilitate the free flow of trade following the Second World War, representatives of many major countries met at Bretton Woods, New Hampshire, in 1944.

The Bretton Woods system had three objectives: (1) to create a set of rules that would maintain fixed exchange rates in the face of short-term fluctuations; (2) to guarantee that changes in exchange rates would occur only in the face of 'fundamental' deficits or surpluses in the balance of payments; and (3) to ensure that, when such changes did occur, they would not spark a series of competitive devaluations.

The basic characteristic of the system was that US dollars, held by foreign monetary authorities, were made directly convertible into gold at a price fixed by the US government, while foreign governments fixed the prices at which their currencies were convertible into US dollars. It was this characteristic that made the system a **gold exchange standard**. Gold was the ultimate reserve, but other currencies were held as reserves, because, directly or indirectly, they could be exchanged for gold.

To maintain the convertibility of their currencies at fixed exchange rates, and to be able to support the exchange market, the monetary authorities had to have reserves of acceptable foreign exchange.[2] In the Bretton Woods system, the authorities held reserves of gold and claims on key currencies, mainly the US dollar and the UK pound sterling. When a country's currency was in excess supply, its authorities would sell dollars, pounds sterling, or gold; when a country's currency was in excess demand, its authorities would buy dollars or pounds sterling. If they then wished to increase their *gold* reserves, they would use the dollars to purchase gold from the Federal Reserve (the US central banking system established in 1913), thus depleting the US stock of gold.

The United States therefore needed to have enough gold to maintain fixed price convertibility of the dollar into gold, as demanded by foreign monetary authorities. Other countries needed to maintain convertibility (on either a restricted or an unrestricted basis) between their currency and the US dollar at a fixed exchange rate.

Problems of the adjustable peg system

Three key problems of the Bretton Woods system hampered its functioning and contributed to its eventual collapse.

Reserves to accommodate short-term fluctuations The Bretton Woods period witnessed a strong upward trend in the volume of overall international payments, and hence there was also a strong upward trend in the demand for foreign exchange reserves.

The ultimate reserve in the Bretton Woods system was gold, and this led to serious problems during the 1960s and early 1970s. The world's supply of monetary gold simply did not grow as fast as the volume of trade. The world's stock of monetary gold during the 1960s grew at less than 2 per cent per year while trade grew at nearly 10 per cent; gold, which had been 66 per cent of the total monetary reserves in 1959, was only 30 per cent by 1972. Over this period, reserve holdings of dollars and (to a lesser extent)

---

[2] The exchange rates were not quite fixed; they were permitted to vary by 1 per cent on either side of their par values. Later, the bands of permitted fluctuation were widened to 2.25 per cent on either side of their of par values.

pounds sterling rose sharply. At the same time, during this period the United States lost substantial gold reserves to other countries. By the late 1960s, the reduction in US reserves was sufficiently large to undermine confidence in the continued ability of the United States to maintain dollar convertibility.

Adjusting to long-term disequilibria   The second characteristic problem of a fixed-rate system is the adjustment to long-term disequilibria that develop because of secular shifts in the demand for and supply of foreign exchange.

These disequilibria developed slowly. At first they led to a series of speculative crises, as people expected a realignment of exchange rates to occur. Finally, they led to a series of realignments that started in 1967 (with the devaluation of sterling from $2.80 to $2.40). Each occurred amid quite spectacular flows of speculative funds that disrupted normal trade and payments flows.

Speculative crises   The adjustable peg system often leads to situations in which speculators are presented with one-way bets. In these disequilibrium situations, there is an increasing chance of an exchange rate adjustment in one direction, with little or no chance of a movement in the other direction. Speculators then have an opportunity to secure a large potential gain, with no corresponding potential for loss. Speculative crises, associated with the need to adjust to fundamental disequilibria, were the downfall of the system.

Collapse of the Bretton Woods system

Although the Bretton Woods system worked reasonably well (though with the help of capital controls) for nearly 20 years, the problems inherent in the adjustable peg system ultimately proved insurmountable. The system was beset by a series of crises of ever-increasing severity which reflected the system's underlying weaknesses.

The two key currencies in the system—the pound sterling and the dollar—each experienced speculative attacks that reflected a loss of confidence in the ability of the respective governments to maintain exchange rates at the stated par values. A devaluation of the pound in 1967 set off a series of other devaluations, and the subsequent period witnessed increasing flows of speculative funds out of dollars and into other currencies, including the German mark and the Japanese yen. In 1968 central banks stopped pegging the free-market price of gold, although the price for official settlements between central banks continued to be set at $35 an ounce. (The free-market price quickly soared above this level.) In August 1971 the United States suspended convertibility of the dollar in terms of gold, and this led quickly to a sharp devaluation of the dollar.

An agreement among the major trading nations was signed at the Smithsonian Institute in Washington, DC, in December 1971. The main element of the agreement was a 7.9 per cent devaluation of the dollar against their currencies. Following the Smithsonian agreement, the world was on a *de facto* **dollar standard**. Foreign monetary authorities held their reserves in the form of dollars and settled their international debts with dollars. However, the dollar was not convertible into gold.

The Smithsonian agreements did not lead to a new period of international financial stability. US inflation continued unchecked, and the deficit in the US balance of payments persisted. In January 1973 speculative movements of capital once again occurred, and in February 1973 the United States proposed a further 11 per cent devaluation of the dollar—to be accomplished by raising the official price of gold to $42.22 per ounce. Intense speculative activity followed the announcement.

Five member-countries of the European Community had decided to stabilize their currencies against each other in April 1972 (in narrower bands than was implied by their peg against the dollar), but in the spring of 1973 they decided to let them float together against the dollar. This joint float was called the Snake (originally it was the Snake in the Tunnel). Some other European countries soon joined the Snake, and other countries (notably, Italy, the United Kingdom, and Japan) announced their intention to allow their currencies to float in value.[3]

The Bretton Woods system effectively ended in the spring of 1973, though many of the institutions associated with it, such as the IMF, have survived. Since 1973, the dominant regime has been one of managed, or 'dirty', floating. This means that exchange rates are determined in the market but the authorities intervene from time to time to influence their course. Some groups of countries have set up specific arrangements to limit their mutual exchange rate fluctuations. One such arrangement is the European Exchange Rate Mechanism (ERM).

The European Exchange Rate Mechanism

The countries of the European Community (EC), now the European Union (EU), with varying degrees of commitment and varying degrees of success, have pursued a 'block' approach to fixed exchange rates over the past two decades, maintaining pegged exchange rates among themselves but

---

[3] In June 1972 the Bank of England had abandoned the *de facto* dollar standard with the announcement that it had 'temporarily' abandoned its commitment to support the pound sterling at a fixed par value against the US dollar. The events of 1973 led 'temporarily' to become 'indefinitely'. The United Kingdom had been a member of the Snake in the Tunnel when it began in April 1972, but left after about six weeks, following substantial losses in its reserves.

allowing their currencies to float as a block against other currencies such as the US dollar and the Japanese yen. In the early 1970s, the EC countries adopted the Snake, which worked well in 'normal' circumstances but was subject to speculative crises and increasingly frequent realignments of relative values of national currencies.

In the wake of these problems, there grew the perception of a need for a more formal arrangement with a stronger commitment to the agreed-upon parities. The Snake thus evolved, in 1979, into the European Exchange Rate Mechanism (ERM), which also spawned the European Currency Unit (ECU). The ECU was created as a weighted basket of existing national currencies. In principle, all countries were committed to intervention in order to maintain the parities against each other, but in practice, the German central bank, the Bundesbank, assumed a hegemonic role. The Bundesbank was a committed and proven 'inflation-fighter', and for a period of time the ERM functioned quite well, with other central banks apparently willing to take advantage of the Bundesbank's credibility. Indeed, in 1992 the Maastricht Treaty created considerable momentum towards creation of a currency union with a single European currency. (Whether or not the European Union will decide to proceed with this project will be determined by an EU intergovernmental conference to be convened in 1996.)

In September 1992, however, the momentum towards this goal suffered a sharp setback, with a speculative crisis that forced the pound and the lira out of the ERM. That crisis was led, at least in part, by the inconsistency of the monetary policies being pursued in the various countries with a commitment to fixed exchange rates. The United Kingdom, for example, faced a choice between raising interest rates to defend the pound or lowering them to stimulate the flagging economy. It tried the former, but in short order gave in to speculative pressures and adopted the latter. The crisis led to sharp changes in parities and interest rates. Many commentators felt that these events dealt a blow not only to the movement for the creation of a single European currency, but perhaps even to the survival of the ERM itself.

A further crisis developed in July 1993 as a result of a speculative attack on the French franc. It resulted in fluctuation bands being widened from 2.25 per cent for the core members (except for the guilder–DM rate, which continued within a 2.25 per cent band) to 15 per cent. Such margins are so wide that many think they are irrelevant. Because of the difficulties of pegging exchange rates between countries with different monetary policies, many people are urging the adoption of a single EU currency and (accordingly) a single monetary policy. The implications of such a move are discussed in Chapter 38.

❧ CHAPTER 38

Monetary policy

MONETARY policy seeks to influence economic activity using the tools available to the central bank: money supply, interest rates, and exchange rates. It is often contrasted with fiscal policy, which is associated with changes in government expenditure and taxation. However, both types of policy have their main impact through changes in aggregate demand. In this chapter we focus on the narrow question of what monetary policy is and how it works. In Chapter 36 we simply assumed that the monetary authorities fixed the money supply; now we look behind this convenient simplification. In the chapters that follow we return to the context of the macro model, in which monetary policy is only one of the potential policy instruments.

Money has special importance in a market economy. It is the commodity that provides the information about prices upon which much of the rest of the economy depends. When things go wrong with the monetary system—when there is inflation or a monetary collapse—the effect can be devastating to the real economy. Good monetary policy, therefore, is about providing an economy with a currency of stable value and avoiding disruption to the payments and banking system. Good monetary policy in itself cannot make an economy rich (only production of real goods and services can do that), but bad monetary policy does disrupt the real economy and, thereby, causes a loss of real output.

We start by noting how the nature of monetary policy changes significantly with the exchange rate regime. We then explain how monetary control is achieved at present and discuss how the authorities decide whether monetary policy should be tightened or loosened. Finally, we consider the pros and cons of the possible adoption of a single currency for the European Union.

The context of monetary policy

MONETARY policy choices are not independent of the institutional context. Particularly important, when it comes to determining such policy, is the exchange rate regime; the forces of competition and technical change in the financial system are also significant. Monetary policy has to change to suit the current environment in which it is operating.

The current regime of floating exchange rates is one of three major regimes that have operated during this century. Indeed, floating exchange rates have been the norm in the developed world, including the United Kingdom, only since the early 1970s. It is in this period that most controversy has surrounded monetary policy. Arguably, this is also the period in which monetary policy has been least successful—as UK prices have risen sixfold, and monetary policy has contributed to the three worst recessions since the Second World War. Let us see why monetary policy operates differently under other types of exchange rate regime.

THE GOLD STANDARD

In the world of the gold standard, the money supply in an economy is linked to the stock of gold. Banks issue notes that are convertible into gold (at a fixed price), and the total money supply is determined, as explained in Chapter 35, by the interaction of banks' reserve ratios and the public's choice of notes (or deposits) versus gold. The total stock of gold in the economy changes only as a result of net payments to foreigners (unless there are gold mines in the economy) via a balance of payments deficit or surplus.

There is no direct involvement of government in monetary policy under the gold standard. Preserving the convertibility of currency (notes and deposits) into gold is the job of all those banks that have issued notes. Monetary conditions are thus a combined product of the balance of payments and the working of the private banking system. Interest rates are determined by the supply of and demand for loans (including, in an open economy, demand and supply influences coming from overseas).

The Bank of England did have a special role in the English (and Welsh) monetary system under the gold standard. This was because of its dominant financial strength, which made it a place where other smaller banks chose to deposit their own gold reserves. Hence, the Bank of England could judge when there was a general run on gold reserves, and it had the financial power to raise interest rates in London so as to attract funds from abroad. Ultimately, however, the Bank's own ability to create money (its own notes and deposits) was limited by the fact that it had to maintain their convertibility into gold.

Under a gold standard regime, there is no need for government involvement in monetary policy. The money supply is determined by the interaction of international flows of gold and the domestic banking system. Interest rates are determined by market forces in the (international) markets for loans and deposits.

FIXED EXCHANGE RATES

Fixed exchange rates may appear to operate like the gold standard. Instead of fixing the value of domestic currency to gold, the value is fixed to some foreign currency. However, there is a major difference, and that is that under fixed exchange rate regimes (like the Bretton Woods system) the pegging of the domestic currency to foreign currency is a commitment of the domestic government. It is the government that has to hold reserves of foreign currency and intervene in foreign exchange markets (see Figure 37.2 on p. 728) to maintain a particular exchange rate.

Under the gold standard, the gold is held privately by individuals or in banks' reserves. This gold constitutes both the banking reserve (backing the note issue) and the international reserves (because it can be used to settle overseas debts). Under a pegged exchange rate (fiat money) system, however, the banking reserve contains central bank notes and deposits, but the international reserve consists of government-held balances of foreign currency (and foreign-currency-denominated assets). Hence, the move from a commodity currency system to the Bretton Woods regime necessarily involved the political authorities in key elements of monetary policy. In the UK context, foreign exchange reserves are held in the Exchange Equalization Account, which is owned by the Treasury but managed by the Bank of England as agent to the Treasury.

Fixed exchange rate regimes involve the use of government-owned foreign exchange reserves to buy and sell foreign exchange for domestic currency, in order to influence the exchange rate.

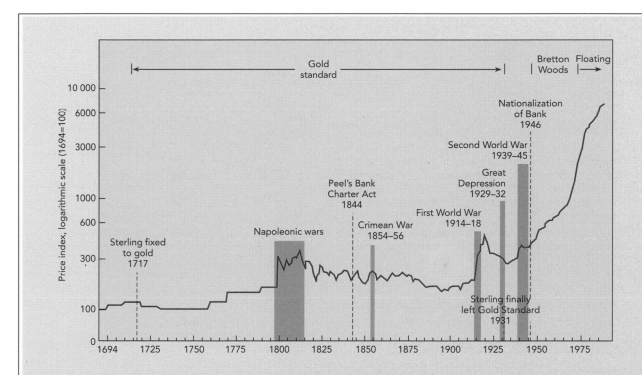

Figure 38.1 The RPI and monetary regimes over the last 300 years

The chart shows an index of retail prices since 1694. Data before 1800 are unreliable and are based substantially on food prices, although in 1700 two-thirds of household expenditure went on food, compared with less than a fifth today. It is noticeable that prices under the gold standard exhibited sharp rises only in times of war, when the link to gold was temporarily broken. Between 1694 and the end of the Second World War, prices had risen about threefold. Since then they have risen over twentyfold, with most of that rise coming in the floating exchange rate period. This illustrates the problem of controlling inflation when money is not guaranteed to be convertible into anything specific.

Source: Bank of England Quarterly Bulletin, May 1994.

An important implication of fixing the exchange value of the domestic currency to another currency is that it severely limits the independence of domestic monetary policy, especially if financial capital is internationally mobile. This is because tying two currencies together inevitably ties interest rates and inflation rates together to some extent. The fixed exchange rate case is not central to this chapter, since the current regime is one of floating exchange rates. However, it is important to understand that monetary policy is very different under such a regime. We discuss these differences more fully in Chapter 39.

FLOATING EXCHANGE RATES

Under floating exchange rates, the value of the domestic currency is not tied to the value of gold or to the value of foreign currency. Hence there is no external anchor for the value of domestic money, nor, therefore, for the domestic price level.

Under floating exchange rates, monetary policy is responsible for determining the value of domestic currency, in terms of both the domestic price level and the external exchange value.

A stable price level is the ultimate target of monetary policy. Neither the price level nor the exchange rate can be fixed directly by the monetary authorities under a floating regime. What can be fixed by the authorities is either the supply of high-powered money (currency plus bankers'

BOX 38.1

Definitions of UK monetary aggregates

The way in which 'money' is defined has changed a great deal over time and is likely to change again in future. In 1750, money would almost certainly have been defined as the stock of gold in circulation (specie). By 1850, it would probably have been defined as gold in the hands of the non-bank public plus bank notes in circulation. In 1950, the most likely definition would have been currency held by the public plus current account bank deposits. In 1995, money is usually defined to include currency held by the public plus all deposits (current and savings) in banks and building societies. By 2050, who knows?

There have been many changes in the definition of money even in the last few years. Many of these are the result of financial innovations of the 1980s. We cannot expect this to be the end of the story. Money measures such as M1 and £M3 (sterling M3), which were at the centre of monetary policy debates into the first half of the 1980s, have disappeared. These had to be dropped after 1989, when the Abbey National Building Society converted into a bank. Thereafter, any monetary aggregate that contained bank deposits but not building society deposits became distorted. M0 contains neither; M2 and M4 contain both.

The money measures current in 1994 were as follows:

- **M0** (the monetary base). This measure refers to all the currency in circulation outside the Bank of England plus bankers' deposits with the Bank of England.

- **M2.** This measure encompasses UK non-bank and non-building society holdings of notes and coins, plus sterling retail deposits with UK banks and building societies. ('Retail' effectively means 'held by individuals rather than companies'.) The definition of M2 was changed in 1992 to make it a subset of M4.

- **M4.** M4 is a measure of M2 plus all other private-sector sterling interest-bearing deposits at banks and building societies, plus sterling certificates of deposit (and other paper issued by banks and building societies of not more than five years' original maturity). (£M3 was effectively M4 minus building society deposits.)

The accompanying table presents data for these monetary aggregates for March 1994.

UK money supply, March 1994

	£ Million, not seasonally adjusted	
Notes and coin outside Bank of England	20,490	
Bankers' deposits at Bank of England	82	
M0	**20,572**	
Notes and coin with public (*part of* M0)		18,262
Non-interest-bearing bank deposits		35,146
Other retail bank deposits		149,319
Building society retail shares and deposits		198,758
M2		**401,485**
Wholesale bank deposits + CDs		137,397
Wholesale building society deposits + CDs		18,794
M4		**557,676**

Note: M0 is not a subset of M2 and M4 because it includes notes and coin held by banks, which are excluded from M2 and M4. If notes and coin held by banks were included in the latter, there would be double counting, because notes and coins held by banks are assets, and the deposits (liabilities) that are counterparts to those assets are included in M2 and M4 already.

Source: Financial Statistics.

reserves at the central bank) or the interest rate at which the money markets can borrow from the central bank. The comparatively poor record of the UK monetary authorities at controlling the price level under floating exchange rates is shown in Figure 38.1.

The monetary authorities also have to bear in mind that their actions, in trying to maintain the long-run value of the currency, also have an impact on the cycles about the trend in potential GDP. The importance of the inflation target relative to cyclical concerns has been a source of controversy since the advent of floating exchange rates in 1972.

Monetary policy has been an important object of controversy since the early 1970s, precisely because it is only under a floating exchange rate regime that the domestic monetary authorities have complete discretion over what monetary policy should be. Under fixed exchange rates and the gold standard, the convertibility constraint severely restricts the authorities' actions.

It is easy to state the goals of monetary policy—a stable valued currency and minimal monetary shocks to the real economy. However, it is far from simple to decide how these goals should be achieved in practice. The remainder of this chapter deals with these problems of implementation.

Before proceeding to the next section, readers will find it useful to revise our earlier discussion of models of the banking firm and the structure of the money markets in Chapter 35 on pp. 680–91. This is also a good time to become familiar with the definitions of various monetary aggregates used in the United Kingdom which are summarized in Box 38.1; some knowledge of these is essential for what follows.

Techniques of monetary control

FOR much of the post-war period, monetary control was achieved by direct controls, in the form of both specific limits on bank lending, and exchange controls (which segmented the domestic monetary system from the rest of the world). Temporary abandonment of controls on bank lending in 1971 (in the reforms known as Competition and Credit Control) led to a surge in monetary growth and rapid inflation (see Figure 38.2). Quantitative limits, known as the Corset, were re-imposed in 1973 in slightly different form, but all attempts at direct controls were finally abandoned in 1980.[1] Since then, the UK monetary authorities have attempted to achieve monetary control by influencing short-term interest rates. We shall consider this policy shortly. However, before doing so it is necessary to review the traditional textbook explanation of how the money supply is controlled.

Money supply and the money multiplier

In Chapter 35 (p. 684) we derived a relationship known as the money multiplier. This was expressed as

$$M = \frac{(b+1)}{(b+x)} H,$$

where M is the money stock, H is the monetary base (alternatively referred to as the cash base, or high-powered money), b is the proportion of cash relative to bank deposits chosen by the public, and x is the banks' reserve ratio. This expression is known as the money multiplier because the term $(b + 1)/(b + x)$ must be greater than one, as long as x is less than one. For example, if both b and x were 0.1 (a 10 per cent ratio), then the value of the money multiplier would be just over 5. This says that the total money supply will be about five times the value of the monetary base, H.

If the money multiplier could be relied upon to be stable, the monetary authorities could control the money supply by influencing H, the stock of high-powered money in the system. (Recall that H, or equivalently the official aggregate M0, is currency held by the banks or the public, plus banks' deposits with the Bank of England.) The way they would do this is through *open-market operations*.

Open-market operations By means of open-market operations, the Bank of England buys or sells securities (government bonds (gilts), Treasury bills, or commercial bills) with

---

[1] The Corset put a limit on the rate of growth of banks' interest-bearing liabilities. In effect, this put a limit on the rate of growth of their lending because it stopped them expanding their interest-bearing borrowings. Exchange controls were abolished in October 1979 because of the excessive appreciation of sterling in foreign exchange markets, and the abolition of the Corset soon followed. Once exchange controls had been abolished, banks were free to do whatever business they liked offshore, so quantitative ceilings on domestic business became ineffective.

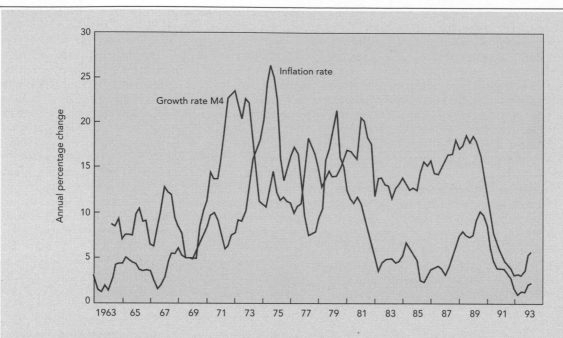

Figure 38.2 The growth rate of broad money (M4) and inflation 1963–1993

The chart shows the rate of growth of M4 and the rate of growth of the RPI since the early 1960s. The surge in monetary growth after the Competition and Credit Control reforms is clearly evident. The growth rate of £M3 was somewhat higher than that of M4 at this time (not shown), but the general pattern was very similar for the two aggregates. Also clear from the chart is that the rapid growth in M4 in the early 1980s coincided with a period of sharply falling inflation. Indeed, the rate of growth of M4 substantially exceeded the inflation rate throughout the 1980s. Inflation did pick up towards the end of the decade, but the data suggest that the relationship between M4 and inflation was a very imprecise one.

Source: Datastream.

the specific intention of altering the stock of high-powered money held by the private sector.

Suppose, for example, that the authorities wanted to reduce the money supply. They would sell securities in the London market. These could be bought either by private citizens or by banks. The payment for the securities would involve a transfer from the clearing banks' deposits with the Bank of England to the government's account. This thereby lowers H, through its effect of lowering banks' deposits with the Bank of England . To maintain their reserve ratios, banks would then have to reduce their loans, perhaps by calling in overdrafts which are recallable on demand, and the money supply would fall.

In the case of an expansion of the money supply, the Bank of England would buy securities from the London money markets, thereby increasing the reserves of the banking system. Banks would then find they have excess reserves and would accordingly attempt to increase their loans.

Other techniques   A similar goal of controlling the money supply could be achieved by changing the required reserve ratio of the banks. For example, increasing the required reserve ratio would reduce the size of the money multiplier, and thus would reduce M for any given H.

Exactly the same effect can be achieved by calling on the banks to make *special deposits* with the Bank of England. Special deposits are deposits made by banks at the Bank of England which may not be counted as part of their reserve assets. This has exactly the same effect as calling for a higher reserve ratio. Calls for special deposits or increases in required reserve ratios have not been used in the United Kingdom for many years.

Monetary base control   The method of controlling the money supply via controlling the quantity of high-powered money is known as *monetary base control*. There was a debate in the United Kingdom in the early 1980s about whether monetary policy should be implemented by this means, but monetary base control was rejected in favour of the policy of influencing interest rates.

There are three reasons why monetary base control was rejected. The first is that it would have destroyed the traditional relationship between the Bank of England and the discount market. The Bank of England has always stood ready to provide cash to the discount market (in exchange for bills), but at a price. If the Bank were to close this discount window, it would, in effect, lose its traditional finger on the pulse of the London money markets. It would also mean that short-term interest rates would be determined solely by market forces. This could make short-term interest rates more volatile. (The Bank of England has had a traditional role of maintaining orderly financial markets. Base control might conflict with this.)

The second reason why base control was rejected is that the Bank of England believes it can achieve the same goals by setting interest rates as by setting the monetary base. The authorities can set either a quantity or a price, but not both. Whether setting the interest rate or the monetary base are equivalent is discussed further below.

A final reason why monetary base control has become impractical is because the money multiplier has become a very large and unpredictable number. If we take M4 as the standard measure of broad money and M0 as the measure of the monetary base (see Box 38.1), in 1968 M4 was about six times the size of M0. This means that the money multiplier was 6. In 1994, however, M4 was over 26 times the size of M0 (and M2 was about 20 times the size of M0). The money multiplier had grown to over 26. There is no reason to believe that this number has an upper bound—or, indeed, any stable value to which it must return. Indeed, we saw in Chapter 35 that competitive forces in a modern banking system (in the absence of legal reserve requirements) lead to banks choosing very small reserve ratios. The cash–deposit ratio of the public is also falling as the payment technology changes. Hence, trying to control M4 by limiting M0 is about as practicable as trying to control the flow of water in the Thames by means of a tap near Oxford! We shall, however, return to the point that M0 might be an interesting indicator of monetary conditions. This is, however, different from the argument that it should be controlled in order to control the broader money supply.

The traditional approach to monetary control, via operating on the monetary base, is an approach that has been rejected by the UK monetary authorities.

Monetary control via banks' assets

The strategy adopted by the UK monetary authorities for monetary control since 1980 (apart from the brief excursion into the ERM between October 1990 and September 1992) has been, and continues to be, based upon controlling, but only indirectly, the assets of the banking system. The main liabilities of banks are their deposits, and the main assets are their loans. Since balance sheets must balance, assets and liabilities must always be equal. Hence it is a matter of practical convenience which side of the balance sheet is controlled. Measures of the money supply contain as their major components bank deposits (liabilities). However, these deposits will have their counterparts in banks' assets.

The assets of the banking sector can be conveniently divided into two parts: loans to the public sector and loans to the private sector.[2]

Public-sector loans Bank lending to the public sector is controlled by a two-pronged policy. The first prong involves using fiscal policy to keep the government borrowing under control. The amount that the public sector has to borrow each year is known as the *public sector borrowing requirement* (PSBR),[3] and the plan introduced at the beginning of the 1980s gradually to eliminate the PSBR over time was known as the *medium-term financial strategy* (MTFS). This would have removed the need for government borrowing in general, and hence any need for government borrowing from the banking system.

The second prong of the policy to control bank lending to the public sector is a suitable policy of gilt sales. By funding the PSBR through sales of long-term government securities, the authorities can raise loans for the government which will not lead to increases in the money supply. Gilts sold to the non-bank private sector achieve the goal of raising loans for the government independently of the banking system.

One form of funding the government deficit which directly increases the supply of high-powered money occurs when the Bank of England itself buys newly issued government securities, say Treasury bills. In exchange for the bills, the government receives a credit in its account at the Bank of England which it then transfers to the private sector by writing cheques, perhaps to pay wages. The citizens receiving these cheques pay them into their banks and, when the cheques clear, the banks receive an increase in deposits at the Bank of England, which is an increase in

---

[2] Strictly speaking we must include also loans to the overseas sector, but the method of control here is little different from that applied to private-sector loans, so we leave out unnecessary complications.

[3] The PSBR is equal to the government budget deficit (which we have discussed in the context of our macroeconomic models), minus public-sector asset sales. The budget deficit is the difference between current government receipts and expenditures, and excludes capital transactions. Thus, the PSBR was reduced by privatization proceeds, while the budget deficit would have been unaffected. The original MTFS did succeed in eliminating the PSBR by 1988/9, but it had soared again by 1993/4. A new strategy for eliminating the PSBR was put in place in 1992/3 but it is no longer referred to as the MTFS.

BOX 38.2

....

The yield curve

The monetary authorities can fix short-term interest rates, but they cannot fix the yield on long-term securities. As a result, the relationship between long-term interest rates and short-term interest rates can vary considerably over time.

The two figures illustrate what is known as the yield curve at different points in time. Both show yields on government securities on two different days. Figure (i) shows the ends of months August and November 1989. Figure (ii) shows dates at the ends of December 1993 and March 1994. The range of maturities shown is from two years to over 20 years.

In late 1989 the yield curve was downward-sloping; this means that yields on government securities with a long time to maturity were lower than those with a shorter life. In early 1994, the reverse was true.

What accounts for the difference between these two periods is that in 1989 short-term interest rates were abnormally high, but were expected to fall. In 1994 they were abnormally low, but were expected to rise. The important economic lesson from this is that the monetary authorities can set the level of short-term interest rates, but long-term rates are set by market forces. The principle factors that are believed to influence long-term rates are inflation expectations and the expected future course of short-term interest rates.

Long-term rates are important in the investment decisions of large firms that can borrow by issuing bonds. But short-term rates are more important for persons (especially via the mortgage rate) and small companies dependent upon bank finance.

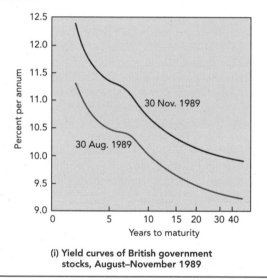

(i) Yield curves of British government
stocks, August–November 1989

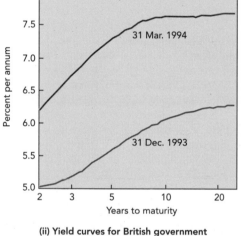

(ii) Yield curves for British government
stocks, December 1993–March 1994

their reserves. This process is known as *monetizing the government debt*. It is the nearest that governments, in the UK institutional context, can come to 'printing money' to pay their debts. Fortunately, it does not happen on any significant scale in the United Kingdom, though there are many examples in other countries where it has happened. (See Box 40.1 on p.792, which gives an example of the hyperinflation that can result in extreme cases.)

Private-sector lending   The control of lending to the private sector is achieved by means of interest rates. The Bank of England determines the interest rate at which it will buy (rediscount) bills offered to it by the discount houses (see Chapter 35, pp. 689). This sets the approximate level of interest rates in the short-term money markets. (It is 'approximate' because there will be minor variations about

the general level for different sectors of the market.) The level of interest rates at which banks can borrow and lend in the wholesale money markets determines the deposit and loan rates they set for all their customers. Most retail and small business customers pay loan rates that are linked to the banks' *base rate*. The base rate is the rate that banks publish which provides a reference rate for most of their retail and small business loans. It is held constant, sometimes for long periods, and changes only when the general level of market rates shifts significantly.[4] (Money market

---

[4] It is precisely because base rates are moved only occasionally and in discrete jumps that they achieve media attention. A rise in base rates is taken as a sign that the Bank of England has made it clear, through the money markets, that it wants short-term interest rates to rise. Similarly, a fall in base rates is taken as a signal that the monetary authorities want rates to fall.

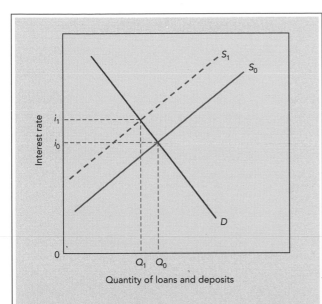

Figure 38.3 Use of interest rates to control banks' assets

By changing interest rates, the Bank of England can influence the demand for loans and, therefore, also the money supply. The figure shows the demand curve and supply curve for loans. The initial equilibrium is at i_0Q_0, where the supply curve S_0 intersects with the demand curve D_0. By forcing up the interest rate in the money markets, the Bank of England effectively shifts the supply curve of loans leftward to S_1. The quantity of loans demanded falls from Q_0 to Q_1 and there is a corresponding fall in bank deposits and the money stock.

rates, in contrast, move continuously while the market is open, but usually only by small amounts.) A high-quality customer may borrow at base rate plus 2 per cent, whereas a more risky loan may be made at base rate plus 4 per cent.

In effect, by forcing short-term money market rates up or down, the Bank of England is moving the interest rates charged (and offered) by banks to all their customers. If the Bank of England wishes to tighten monetary policy, it will force up short-term interest rates. Banks will accordingly raise their base rates. This will raise the cost of borrowing from banks, which will, in turn, reduce the demand for loans (other things being equal). This will be contractionary on economic activity through the transmission mechanism outlined in Chapter 36. A contraction of loans will also have a counterpart in a contraction (or slowdown in the rate of growth) of deposits and, therefore, also of the money supply.

Changing short-term interest rates does not necessarily alter long-term rates. To find out what happens to them, we need to consider the *yield curve*. This is discussed in Box 38.2.

This mechanism by which the Bank of England uses

interest rates to control bank lending is illustrated in Figure 38.3. The figure (which is similar to Figure 35.3) shows the demand curve for the total stock of outstanding loans and the supply curve of loans. Recall that all loans have their counterpart on the liability side of banks' balance sheets, so the total stock of loans (assets) will be equal to the total stock of deposits (liabilities). The banks face a given demand curve for loans which is partly determined by the private-sector investment demand (see Chapter 36). Bank of England policy on interest rates shifts the supply curve of deposits and, therefore, also the supply curve of loans—by influencing the interest rate at which banks can borrow in the money markets. (Deposit rates in general will rise as banks compete with each other for deposits.) No profitable bank will lend at interest rates less than it pays to borrow.

A tightening of monetary policy shifts the supply curve of loans to the left, thereby raising loan rates and reducing the quantity of loans demanded. A relaxation of monetary policy shifts the supply curve of loans to the right, lowering loan rates and increasing the quantity of loans demanded. A reduction in the stock of outstanding loans also implies a reduction of deposits and, therefore, of the money supply. An increase in the stock of loans implies an increase in deposits and in the money supply.

A completely analogous analysis could be conducted in the context of Figure 36.2. This latter way of looking at the problem is more common in macroeconomics because it relates explicitly to money demand and supply. By setting a higher interest rate, the monetary authorities reduce the quantity of money demanded. They then have to let the money supply adjust so that it intersects money demand at the required interest rate. In practice, this means that the Bank of England has to provide whatever level of high-powered money is demanded at the level of the interest rate chosen.

Whichever way we choose to look at it, the monetary authorities can undoubtedly influence economic activity by their control of interest rates. Forcing interest rates up is contractionary—it shifts the aggregate demand curve down, through both the investment and exchange rate effects. The reverse is true when the authorities lower interest rates—aggregate demand shifts up.

Monetary control is achieved in the United Kingdom by the ability of the Bank of England to determine the level of short-term interest rates in the money markets. Monetary tightening involves forcing interest rates up. Relaxation of monetary policy is associated with bringing interest rates down. The monetary base is demand-determined; it is not fixed exogenously by the monetary authorities.

THE INTEREST RATE AND AGGREGATE DEMAND

In Chapter 36, we talked about monetary policy involving

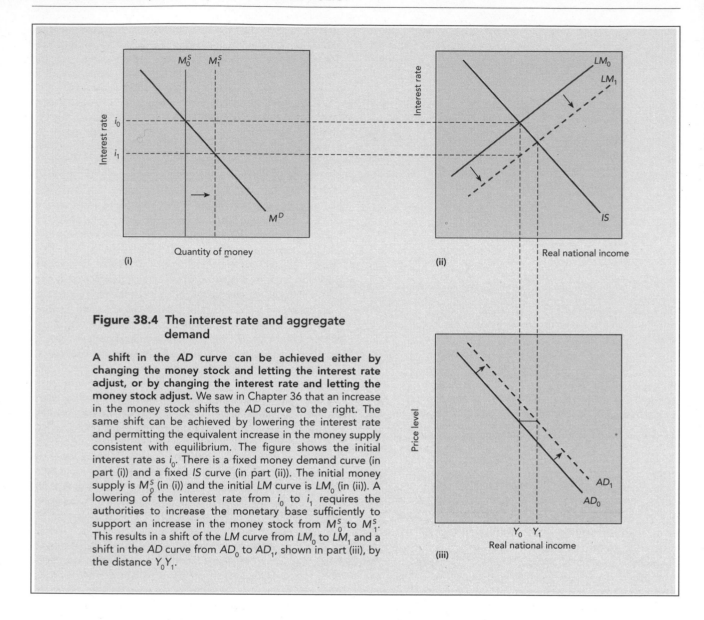

Figure 38.4 The interest rate and aggregate demand

A shift in the *AD* curve can be achieved either by changing the money stock and letting the interest rate adjust, or by changing the interest rate and letting the money stock adjust. We saw in Chapter 36 that an increase in the money stock shifts the *AD* curve to the right. The same shift can be achieved by lowering the interest rate and permitting the equivalent increase in the money supply consistent with equilibrium. The figure shows the initial interest rate as i_0. There is a fixed money demand curve (in part (i)) and a fixed *IS* curve (in part (ii)). The initial money supply is M_0^S (in (i)) and the initial *LM* curve is LM_0 (in (ii)). A lowering of the interest rate from i_0 to i_1 requires the authorities to increase the monetary base sufficiently to support an increase in the money stock from M_0^S to M_1^S. This results in a shift of the *LM* curve from LM_0 to LM_1 and a shift in the *AD* curve from AD_0 to AD_1, shown in part (iii), by the distance Y_0Y_1.

changes in the money supply, but we have now discovered that the UK authorities do not actually control the money stock, or even the monetary base (high-powered money). Rather, they set short-term interest rates. We have already seen that, for a given money demand curve, setting the interest rate and fixing the money stock are equivalent. What we now wish to establish is that these policies can have the same effect on the aggregate demand curve, so that we can talk about expanding the money supply and lowering interest rates as equivalent policies.

It is important to be clear from the start that this equivalence is true only when the money demand curve is fixed and known with certainty *and* when all exogenous expenditures are held constant (the *IS* curve is fixed). Later in this chapter we shall discover that setting the interest rate and fixing the money stock are not equivalent when *either* money demand is volatile *or* the exogenous expenditures shift about.

The equivalence of interest-rate changes and money supply changes on *AD* is shown in Figure 38.4. Part (ii) of the figure shows the *IS* and *LM* curves and part (iii) the associated *AD* curve—drawn for a given nominal money stock and given exogenous expenditures. An increase in the money stock, illustrated in part (i), shifts the *LM* curve to the right, and shifts the *AD* curve to the right by the same horizontal distance as between the old and new intersection of *IS* and *LM*. At the same time, the equilibrium interest rate has fallen.

If instead we start with the authorities lowering the market interest rate, what happens? At the lower interest rate there will be an increased quantity of money demanded (because the opportunity cost of holding money has fallen), and so the authorities will have to permit an expansion of the money supply to that which is demanded at the new lower interest rate.[5] The outcome is exactly the same as above, in that the *LM* curve shifts by an identical amount in both cases, as does *AD*. Hence, in this case at least, they are equivalent policies.

For a given money demand function and given exogenous expenditures, the policies of setting interest rates or fixing the money stock are equivalent.

Targets and indicators

THE monetary authorities have the power to tighten and loosen monetary policy. The next question we have to address is: how should the authorities decide at any particular time whether it is appropriate to tighten or loosen monetary policy?

It is helpful to distinguish between the *instruments* and ultimate *goals* of monetary policy, and between intermediate *targets* and useful *indicators*. The instruments of policy are what the authorities actually can change or control exactly, such as the interest rate at which the Bank of England lends to the discount market. The goals of policy are what they really *want to* control or influence, such as the rate of inflation or the level of real economic activity. Intermediate targets are economic variables that policy-makers attempt to control, even though these variables do not matter in themselves, because they believe that controlling the intermediate target will help them to achieve the ultimate goals. Targeting the money supply in order to control inflation is an example. Useful indicators are economic variables that are not targeted but are none the less monitored for the information they contain about the state of the economy.

There is little disagreement that the ultimate goal of monetary policy is to achieve a low inflation rate. Inflation itself can be the sole target of monetary policy, but it cannot be the sole indicator, because inflation takes time to build up, so by the time inflation becomes a problem, monetary policy has already failed. It is a lagging indicator. What intermediate targets or indicators of monetary policy should be used to signal the need for a change in policy stance early enough that inflation never arises?

Monetary targets

One school of economists regards control of the money stock as a necessary and sufficient condition for controlling inflation. These economists, known as *monetarists*, are united in their belief in the significance of changes in the money supply as the cause of inflation.

The policy recommendation of the monetarists is that policy-makers should aim to achieve a stable rate of growth of the money supply in order to control inflation.[6] In effect, there should be an intermediate target, which is the rate of growth of money. Let us briefly review the reasoning behind the original monetarist position.

Monetarists take it as well established that 'inflation is always and everywhere a monetary phenomenon', in the words of leading monetarist, Milton Friedman. At one level, it is hard to argue with this, because inflation is, by definition, a fall in the value of money. Indeed, no one doubts that money and the price level are intimately related. The issue is: can changes in one be regulated in order to stabilize the other? Monetarists have no doubt that the answer is: yes.

Monetarists also maintain that monetary 'shocks', that is rapid monetary expansions and contractions, are a major cause of cycles in the economy. However, active counter-cyclical monetary policy (or fine-tuning) is not recommended. This is because the effects of monetary policy are felt by the real economy 'with long and variable lags'. Hence attempts to use active discretionary monetary policy to stabilize the cycle are likely to make things worse. For example, if we were currently experiencing a recession, a relaxation of monetary policy today will have its main impact in about two years' time. By this time the economy may already have recovered, so the monetary policy relaxation would then be adding fuel to the fire.

---

[5] In the UK institutional context, the Bank of England will have to supply the extra high-powered money required to sustain higher total deposits and loans demanded at the lower interest rate. The latter increases arise both because people choose to hold more money (deposits) relative to bonds and because there is an increased demand for loans at lower interest rates, so banks can expand both sides of their balance sheets.

[6] The term 'Monetarism' was coined by a leading monetarist, the late Karl Brunner (1916–89) in an article published in the Federal Reserve Bank of St Louis *Review* in 1968.

Thus, monetarists opt for policy *rules* as opposed to the policy-makers' *discretion*. The policy rule they recommend is to set a stable growth rate for the money supply.

For monetarists, the goals of controlling inflation and of minimizing monetary shocks to the economy are both achieved by setting and sticking to a target rate of growth of the money supply.

A critical assumption that lies behind the monetarist approach is that there is a stable money demand function. If this were the case, it would be possible to predict accurately the long-term inflation consequences of money supply increases. There was some empirical support for this proposition up to the late 1970s, but the events of the 1980s undermined the credibility of this entire rule-based approach to monetary policy.

MONETARY TARGETING IN PRACTICE

Official targeting of monetary aggregates was introduced in the United Kingdom in 1976, by the Labour Chancellor of the Exchequer Denis Healey. This followed the fairly persuasive evidence that the high inflation of 1974–5 was the result (in large part) of the rapid monetary growth of 1971–3. Indeed, this episode gave support to the monetarist rule of thumb that rapid monetary growth affects output after about a year and prices after about two years (with

Table 38.1 Monetary targets under the MTFS (%)

Target year	Year of announcement								Actual %	
	1979	1980	1981	1982	1983	1984	1985	1986		
£M3										
1979/80	7–11								16.2	
1980/81		7–11							18.4	
1981/82		6–10	6–10						12.8	
1982/83		5–9	5–9	8–12					11.1	
1983/84		4–8	4–8	7–11	7–11				9.5	
1984/85				6–10	6–10	6–10			11.9	
1985/86					5–9	5–9	5–9		16.3	
1986/87						4–8	4–8	11–15	18.7	
1987/88						3–7	3–7			
1988/89						2–6	2–6			
									M1	*PSL2*
M1 & PSL2										
1982/83				8–12					12.3	11.5
1983/84				7–11	7–11				14	12.4
1984/85				6–10	6–10					
1985/86				5–9						

Target year	Year of announcement							Actual %
	1984	1985	1986	1987	1988	1989	1990	
MO								
1984/85	4–8							5.4
1985/86	3–7	3–7						4.1
1986/87	2–6	2–6	2–6					3.5
1987/88	1–5	1–5	2–6	2–6				6.4
1988/89	0–4	0–4	1–5	1–5	1–5			6.8
1989/90			1–5	1–5	1–5	1–5		5.0
1990/91					0–4	0–4	1–5	3.2
1991/92					0–4	0–4	0–4	1.2
1992/93						–1–3	0–4	5.1
1993/94							–1–3	6.8

There have been a variety of aggregates targeted since the late 1970s, and with varying success. The first aggregate to be targeted was £M3. However, targets for this aggregate were consistently exceeded in the early 1980s. Targets for £M3 were abandoned in 1985/6. Targeting of M1 and PSL2 survived an even shorter period. Post-1992 policy involves reference ranges for MO and M4 (latter not shown) but not formal targets for these aggregates. Inflation is the ultimate target, and there are no official intermediate targets.

Source: David Heathfield, 'Monetary Policy, 1947–91', *Economic Review* (April 1992), and *Financial Statistics*.

output then falling back). Figures 36.10 and 36.11 on pp. 710 and 711 illustrate this process in the *AD/AS* framework.

The targeted monetary aggregate was the then standard broad money measure, £M3. The same aggregate was targeted by the Conservative government of Margaret Thatcher from 1979 onwards. Ironically, the Thatcher government was labelled 'monetarist' even though it did little more than carry forward the monetary targets of the previous Labour government.[7] Indeed, before too long this government abandoned monetary targets.

Table 38.1 shows the target ranges that were in place for £M3 in the 1980s. Looking down the columns, we can see that the intention was always to reduce the rate of growth of £M3 gradually over time. In 1980, for example, the announced target ranges for £M3 growth for future years were: 1980/81, 7–11 per cent; 1981/2, 6–10 per cent; 1982/3, 5–9 per cent; 1983/4, 4–8 per cent. These targets were rarely achieved, as the figures for actual £M3 growth, in the last column of Table 38.1, indicate.

One reason for failure to stay within the target ranges for monetary growth was the abolition of the Corset in June 1980. This permitted banks to compete more aggressively for deposits and resulted in the growth rate of £M3 rising to over 18 per cent in 1980/81, at a time when the target range was 6–10 per cent. However, at this time the economy was in recession and unemployment was rising rapidly. This rapid growth of broad money did not lead to an upturn in inflation.

This episode did much to destroy the credibility of monetary targets in the United Kingdom. However, the problems for monetary targeting did not end there.

Financial innovation   The new regime of the 1980s generated a new regulatory and competitive environment for the UK financial system. Many other changes followed as competitive forces and further regulatory changes encouraged innovation in financial products and services. Particularly relevant to monetary policy was the growing competition between banks and building societies. Building society deposits were increasingly held as transactions balances, and banks found themselves having to pay increased interest rates on both current and savings accounts.

Two things followed from this. First, as the characteristics of bank deposits changed, so the demand for £M3 shifted. As higher interest rates were paid on deposits, more deposits were held for savings purposes rather than for transactions. This meant that people held more money for any given level of income, so the velocity of circulation of money fell. Second, as building society deposits became very close substitutes for bank deposits, it became increasingly hard to justify targeting a monetary aggregate which included bank but not building society deposits.

Policy-makers paid less and less attention to the £M3 target as time went by. At first, it was supplemented by other targeted aggregates, M1 and PSL2 (later to be renamed M5,

which itself was dropped in 1991, to be replaced by 'liquid assets outside M4'). From 1984, growth ranges for M0 were announced. These have been continued to date, but, as we have seen, M0 is small relative to broad money and it is unlikely ever to become the single intermediate target, or even the sole indicator of monetary conditions. The official view is that M0 is a useful leading indicator of retail sales (because the supply of cash is demand-determined and people draw cash only shortly before going out to spend), but cannot be the sole guide of monetary policy.

It is true, however, that M0 has a closer correlation with the UK price level than any of the other previously targeted aggregates. This relationship is shown in Figure 38.5. This does not imply that prices are caused by M0; since M0 is demand-determined, the reverse is likely to be true. Neither does it imply that controlling the supply of M0 would control inflation—rather it could encourage growth in close substitutes.

In 1986 formal targeting was officially abandoned, though in reality it had been abandoned much earlier. The financial innovations of the 1980s made the application of monetary targeting virtually impossible. This was because there appeared to be no plausible monetary aggregate with a stable underlying demand function. Such was the disenchantment with £M3 that the Bank of England even stopped reporting it after 1989 (along with several other standard measures, including M1).[8] The two main money measures are now M0 and M4, though, as Box 38.1 shows, M2 also exists in current official definitions.

Monetary targeting was abandoned in 1986, in the United Kingdom, because of the perceived instability of the money demand function. Financial innovation did much to contribute to these problems.

Exchange rate targets   After the abandonment of monetary targeting in 1986, there was a period in which the authorities attempted to substitute an exchange rate target. In 1987–8, Conservative Chancellor Nigel Lawson followed an unstated (but later admitted) policy of maintaining the value of the pound sterling close to DM3. A more formal attempt to peg the pound to the Deutschmark was tried from October 1990 to September 1992, when the pound

---

[7] The monetarist label stuck to the Thatcher government more because of its anti-inflation rhetoric, and also, perhaps, because of its *fiscal* policy. Sir Geoffrey Howe raised taxes in 1981, at a time when the economy was in the depths of the worst recession (up to that time) since the Second World War, in order to satisfy the perceived needs of the MTFS. A total of 364 economists signed a letter to *The Times* condemning the policy, but the economy grew strongly for the rest of the decade! This is not to say that the policy was, therefore, correct—merely that what policy makers do may not always be so important.

[8] This was made inevitable by the conversion of the Abbey National Building Society into a bank. Bank deposits were in M1 and £M3 but building society deposits were not, so the conversion created an arbitrary jump in both M1 and £M3 which had no economic significance.

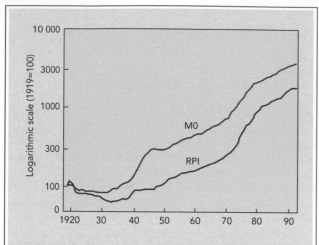

Figure 38.5 M0 and the RPI, 1920–1994

M0 and the price level are closely correlated. The chart shows an index of the log of the RPI and the monetary base (M0) since 1920. M0 exhibited a surge relative to the RPI in the early years after the Second World War, and the RPI grew faster than M0 in the mid-1970s. Otherwise their trends are nearly parallel. With a vertical scale in natural logarithms, parallel lines indicate identical rates of growth.

Source: Bank of England Quarterly Bulletin, May 1994.

became a member of the Exchange Rate Mechanism of the European Monetary System.

Both these episodes were attempts to find a guiding principle for monetary policy to fill the vacuum left by the failure of monetary targeting. Since the United Kingdom has left the ERM, the problem of providing appropriate indicators of monetary policy stance remains.

INTEREST RATE VERSUS MONEY STOCK CONTROL

We now return to an analysis of the differences between setting the interest rate and fixing the money supply. In our earlier example, these were equivalent because, under the assumed conditions, a specific money stock generated a unique interest rate and vice versa. We have now discovered, however, that part of the problem for monetary policy in the United Kingdom in the 1980s and 1990s has been instability of money demand. In such circumstances, the tools we have developed generate a powerful conclusion. This is that, even with an unstable money demand function, setting the interest rate also fixes the AD curve in one position, whereas fixing the money supply transmits disturbances in money demand on to aggregate demand.

This proposition is demonstrated in Figure 38.6. Start in part (i), which shows money demand and money supply.

The problem is caused by the fact that the money demand curve is not fixed in one place but is fluctuating (in an unpredictable way) between M_0^D and M_1^D. We want to compare the outcome of the policy alternatives of fixing the money supply and fixing the interest rate.

With a fixed money supply (at the level M_0^S) the equilibrium interest rate will fluctuate between i_0 and i_1, and as a result the LM curve will oscillate between LM_0 and LM_1. This is the same thing as AD moving about between AD_0 and AD_1. Such fluctuations in AD would induce volatility in national income in the range Y_0 to Y_1. In other words, the instability in money demand is transmitted into instability in national income—a clearly undesirable effect.

In contrast, if the interest rate is pegged, the money stock fluctuates endogenously, exactly to match the fluctuations in money demand. The LM curve remains at its initial position, as does AD, and so there is no effect on national income. In other words, fixing the interest rate cuts off the transmission of disturbances to the real economy that originate in unstable money demand.

If money demand is unstable, fixing the interest rate insulates the real economy from the effects of these disturbances, while fixing the money stock does not.

This result provides a powerful case for a policy of interest rate pegging in a period such as the 1980s in the United Kingdom, when there was possible instability in money demand. However, this does not mean that it must always be the best policy. Indeed, it is easy to show that, if the instability lies in the IS curve (as a result of either instability in exogenous expenditures or instability in one of the expenditure functions), rather than in money demand, fixing the money supply will be preferred to fixing the interest rate, for reasons of stability.

Figure 38.7 demonstrates this point in the IS/LM framework. Fixing the money supply (with a stable money demand curve) is equivalent to fixing the LM curve. With a given LM curve and fluctuating IS curve, aggregate demand will fluctuate between Y_2 and Y_1. (This is the range of horizontal shifts in AD, not shown.) However, the policy of pegging the interest rate would involve shifts in the LM curve. (To stop the interest rate changing, money supply has to change.) This would result in aggregate demand fluctuating between Y_3 and Y_4. Hence under this scenario national income would be more unstable under the fixed interest case than with a fixed money supply.

The intuition of this result is as follows. Instability of expenditures causes instability in national income through the multiplier. With a fixed money supply, interest rates rise when expenditure is abnormally high. This creates a decrease in investment, which reduces the expansionary effect of the initial high expenditures. This is what engineers call negative feedback. The rise in interest rates reduces the tendency to expand. Similarly, when expendi-

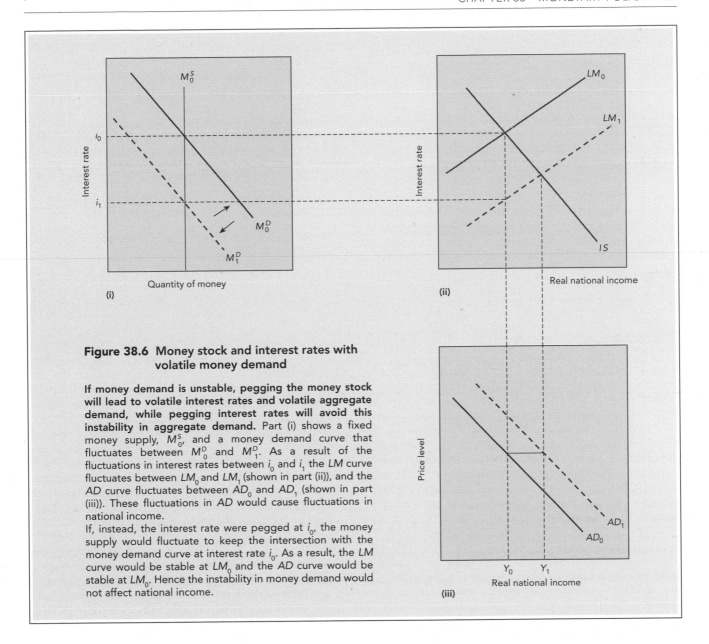

Figure 38.6 Money stock and interest rates with volatile money demand

If money demand is unstable, pegging the money stock will lead to volatile interest rates and volatile aggregate demand, while pegging interest rates will avoid this instability in aggregate demand. Part (i) shows a fixed money supply, M_0^S, and a money demand curve that fluctuates between M_0^D and M_1^D. As a result of the fluctuations in interest rates between i_0 and i_1 the LM curve fluctuates between LM_0 and LM_1 (shown in part (ii)), and the AD curve fluctuates between AD_0 and AD_1 (shown in part (iii)). These fluctuations in AD would cause fluctuations in national income.

If, instead, the interest rate were pegged at i_0, the money supply would fluctuate to keep the intersection with the money demand curve at interest rate i_0. As a result, the LM curve would be stable at LM_0 and the AD curve would be stable at LM_0. Hence the instability in money demand would not affect national income.

tures fall, interest rates fall and thereby increase investment, which offsets the original fall in spending.

Fixing the interest rate cuts out this stabilizing effect of the monetary sector. When expenditures rise (at a fixed interest rate), the money supply rises (to satisfy the higher transactions demand for money at a constant rate of interest) and so there is no negative feedback.

Fixing the interest rate is the best policy for stabilizing national income when money demand is unstable, but fixing the money supply is preferable if instability originates in real expenditures.

The analysis we have just been through tells us something about how monetary policy should be conducted in the face of some instability that will be self-reversing, so that shifts in underlying functions are only temporary. From time to time, the authorities need to react to shifts in fundamentals which are sustained. This brings us back to the problem of reacting quickly enough, so that inflation or recession does not take hold in the economy in a significant way. This is the unsolved problem. What we can say is that its solution requires reliable indicators, which would warn at an early stage of impending inflation or recession.

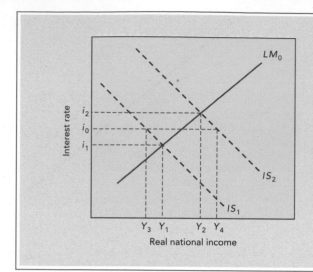

Figure 38.7 Money stock versus interest rate control with a volatile *IS* curve

If it is the *IS* curve that exhibits instability, pegging the money stock will lead to smaller fluctuations in *AD* than will pegging the interest rate. This figure shows only the *IS* and *LM* curves. It is assumed that the *IS* curve is fluctuating between *IS₁* and *IS₂*. If the money stock is fixed so that the *LM* curve is given by *LM₀*, then the *AD* curve will fluctuate by the horizontal distance $Y_1 Y_2$. However, if the interest rate is pegged at i_0, the *LM* curve will fluctuate to maintain the stable interest rate at each level of *IS*. This means that the *AD* curve will fluctuate by the distance $Y_3 Y_4$. So if the *IS* curve is unstable, fluctuations in national income will be lower under a policy of pegging the money supply than under a policy of pegging interest rates.

Monetary indicators

Since leaving the ERM, the UK government has adopted a judgemental approach to monetary policy. It eschews explicit targets for either monetary aggregates or the exchange rate, but it does state 'monitoring ranges' of the only two official traditional monetary aggregates published, M0 and M4. However, it also states explicitly that a wide range of other economic indicators will be monitored as well. We shall return to the problems of judgemental methods below. However, there are some new features of the post-1992 monetary regime which are worthy of comment.

THE MONETARY SERVICES INDEX

The reason we expect money to be a key indicator of inflation is that it plays a special role in transactions, and we expect people to wish to hold a stable proportion of their income in real money balances. Part of the explanation of shifts in money demand (which discredited monetary targeting) lies in the financial innovations which led to interest being paid on most deposits. Interest on bank deposits encouraged people to hold money for savings purposes, in addition to their normal transactions balances. Some economists argued that, if we could find a measure of the transactions component of the money stock, the rate of growth of transactions-related (as opposed to savings-related) money might provide a superior monetary indicator of future inflation.

One available index of the transactions services of money is known as the Divisia index, after the French mathematician François Divisia (1889–1964), who invented the index in the 1930s. The application of the Divisia index to

monetary economics was first proposed by a US economist working at the Federal Reserve Board in the late 1970s, William Barnett.

The idea behind the Divisia index is that potential components of the money stock should be weighted according to the extent to which they deliver transactions services as opposed to pure asset services (in the form of interest yield). Traditional monetary aggregates give a weight of one to all included components and a weight of zero to all excluded components. In contrast, Divisia index numbers weight a component according to the difference between its interest yield and the yield on a safe benchmark asset. Thus, currency and non-interest-bearing deposits have a weight of one in the Divisia index, whereas high-interest savings deposits would have a weight closer to zero—because they bear close to market interest rates.

In this way, the Divisia index attempts to measure the transactions services of money and gives greater weight to those components that are clearly held for transactions purposes. The Bank of England has accepted the principle behind the Divisia index and has calculated such a series back to 1977. It is updated every quarter in the Bank of England *Quarterly Bulletin*. However, it is too early to say whether the availability of this new indicator (and others that may be invented) will improve monetary policy in the future.

Figure 38.8 shows the growth rate of M4 and the growth rate of the Divisia index of money (both lagged 8 quarters) alongside the inflation rate. Rapid M4 growth between 1980 and 1982, at a time of falling inflation, did much to discredit M4 as a monetary indicator. Divisia money, which was falling over this period, did a better job of leading inflation, but only relatively so. The collapse of the growth rate of Divisia money after 1988 predated the collapse of M4 by

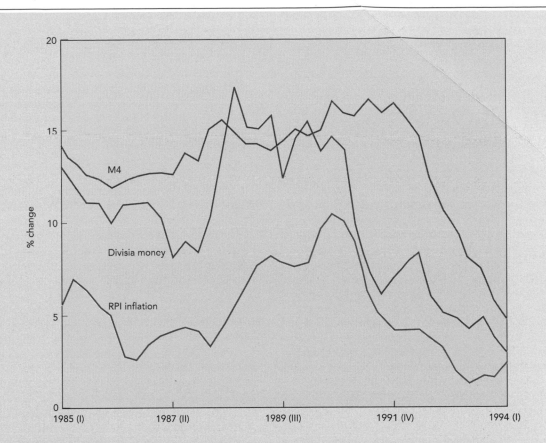

Figure 38.8 The growth of M4, Divisia money, and the level of inflation, 1985–1994

The growth rate of the Divisia index of money proved to be a good indicator of impending inflation in the late 1980s, but M4 did not. The chart shows growth rates of Divisia money and M4 lagged by eight quarters, and contemporaneous inflation as measured by the RPI. Money growth rates are shifted back in time because rapid money growth is traditionally expected to cause inflation with about a two-year lag. The chart shows that Divisia money growth does have a noticeable relationship with inflation (when shifted back two years). M4, however, shows no obvious leading indicator properties. Of course, the evidence from one specific episode should not be given too much weight. A different monetary indicator may be best correlated with inflation in the next cycle.

several quarters, and may therefore have been a better leading indicator of the 1991–3 recession and subsequent fall in inflation. Such conclusions remain speculative and require a great deal more research before firm policy conclusions can be drawn.

Monetary policy may be improved in future by the production of index numbers of the transactions services of money. But, to date, the value of such indicators remains to be proven.

The economic theory behind the need for a Divisia-style index is, perhaps, more important than the index itself.

What happened in the 1980s was a regime change which brought about changes in economic behaviour. These changes were susceptible to economic analysis. For example, taking off quantitative restrictions on banks' liabilities was always likely to lead to greater competition in deposit and loan markets—indeed, greater competition was intended. However, changes in the nature of financial institutions' products alter the links between the monetary system and the real economy. In the face of such changes, any attempt to run monetary policy on the basis of rigid rules inherited from historical relationships which worked in the old regime is not very sensible.

This does not imply that sensible policy analysis is

impossible; it merely says that attempting to guide policy by rigid rules is misguided.[9] At the very least, the rules must adapt to the innovations in behaviour.

MONETARY POLICY IN THE 1990s

Monetary policy in the United Kingdom in the late 1980s and early 1990s was partly responsible for an exaggerated consumer boom, followed by a pick-up of inflation. The attempts to control inflation then led to a long and deep recession.

The anatomy of this latest boom–bust cycle goes back to the failures of monetary policy in 1987–8. The authorities for too long disregarded the warning signs of a buildup in inflation, which included not only rapid monetary growth but also booming share and property prices and booming consumer spending. Interest rates were permitted to fall too far for too long—this error was later admitted by the Governor of the Bank of England in his famous Durham speech. Inflation rose from under 5 per cent in the mid-1980s to around 10 per cent by the end of the decade.

Monetary policy was tightened severely from the autumn of 1988, when interest rates were forced up from 9 to (eventually) 15 per cent. The speculative boom in the property market was burst very quickly by this policy reversal, but, as predicted by the old monetarist rule of thumb, output in general did not turn down until 1990. Monetary tightening was sustained after October 1990 when the United Kingdom joined the ERM. This involved tying sterling to the Deutschmark at a time when German interest rates were high because of the costs of reunification of East and West Germany. As a result of this policy, the UK monetary stance stayed tight for longer than was necessary on domestic grounds. Only after withdrawal from the ERM in September 1992 were UK interest rates permitted to fall sharply. Recovery in output followed from around the second quarter of 1993.

Policy-makers are, of course, determined not to make the same mistakes again. However, where judgement is involved, it would be foolish to assume that future policy-makers will be any wiser than their predecessors. The central problem remains that simple policy rules cannot be trusted in a changing world, while the policy-maker who looks at 'a wide range of indicators' can prevaricate until the case for action is overwhelming. By then, it may be too late to avoid destabilizing policy actions.

In policy-making, there are both *decision lags* and *execution lags*. Decision lags arise because most economic data take time to be collected and processed. Even when the data come in, it takes time to analyse them, and different series may be telling conflicting stories. Policy-makers are usually cautious and will change policy only after many figures point to the same conclusion. Execution lags, on the other hand, arise because policy changes take time to impact on economic behaviour. Suppose, for example, that the

authorities were to raise interest rates today. It would be many months before some mortgage holders had to pay increased monthly payments, and perhaps months after that before they adjusted their other spending patterns to accommodate the new increased cash drain.

This long execution lag of monetary policy makes monetary fine-tuning difficult and possibly destabilizing. This is because the impact of the policy is felt much later than the time the policy decision is made, and circumstances may have changed in the meantime.

Monetary policy is capable of exerting expansionary and contractionary forces on the economy, but it operates with a time lag that is long and unpredictably variable.

The existence of long and variable lags in monetary policy was used by monetarists as the basis of their argument for monetary rules. However, we have also discovered that reliable rules are hard to find.

An independent central bank?   One proposal to improve monetary policy is to give greater independence to the Bank of England. Throughout the post-war period, the Chancellor of the Exchequer has been responsible to Parliament for the conduct of monetary policy. The Bank of England has an advisory role in policy formation, as well as responsibility for implementation.

The problem, it is alleged, is that making elected politicians responsible for monetary policy creates the temptation to take a short-term view. Politicians are worried, it is alleged, by the next election, so they are more likely to encourage a pre-election boom, even though the longer-term consequences may be higher inflation. An independent central bank would, it is argued, be able to take monetary policy decisions with the long-term inflation goal in mind, and would, therefore, deliver a better long-term inflation performance.

There is some, though not overwhelming, evidence to support the proposition that independent central banks control inflation better. Examples supporting the case for central bank independence include Germany and Switzerland, where independent central banks have delivered lower-than-average inflation rates in the floating exchange rate era. New Zealand also has had low inflation since its central bank was given some degree of independence in the early 1990s.

Some steps have been taken in the United Kingdom to give the Bank of England a more independent voice on monetary policy. In 1993, the Bank started to produce a

---

[9] The point we are making here is essentially the same as the point made by Robert Lucas which is known as the Lucas critique. Basing policy on empirical regularities which were true only in a previous regime is likely to create mistakes. After the move to floating exchange rates, for example, in the early 1970s, many policy mistakes were made, such as failure to anticipate rapid inflation.

quarterly 'Inflation Report'. This is intended to represent the Bank's independent view of the prospects for inflation. Greater transparency has also been introduced into the process of monetary policy formation. Chancellor of the Exchequer Kenneth Clark, in the spring of 1994, started to publish the minutes of the Treasury's monetary policy committee (with a few weeks' lag). This may seem like a trivial policy move, but it does have the implication that it will place disagreements between the Bank of England and the Treasury in the public domain. In future, it will at least be possible to say whether bad monetary policy was the fault of elected politicians, or whether it was due to bad economic advice from officials, including the Governor of the Bank of England.

By the next century, it is possible that the United Kingdom will cease to be a separate currency area. At the time of writing this does not seem likely, at least not by the year 2000. However, it is certain that the issue will be debated extensively in the years to come. For this reason, it is necessary to have some understanding of the economic issues raised by the possible adoption of a single currency.

The costs and benefits of a single currency for the European Union

THERE are two major aspects to the single currency question. First, what are the main differences between the current monetary system, where each EU member-state has its own currency and exchange rate, and an alternative monetary system, in which the European Union has one currency? The second issue is: if we agree that we want to go from the current multi-currency system to a single currency, how should we get there? What is the transition process?

Before discussing these two big issues, it is helpful to dismiss one misconception about the single currency. This is the belief that we would lose our banknotes with the Queen's head on them and, instead, have to have ECU notes, the same as everybody else in the European Union. To see that this is not so, look at the case of Scotland. Scotland has had full currency harmonization with England since 1845, yet Scottish bank notes are issued by private banks such as the Bank of Scotland, the Royal Bank of Scotland, and the Clydesdale Bank, just as they were before the Scottish and English currency systems were unified. Indeed, Scotland continues to have a £1 note, whereas the smallest note in England is £5.

What matters, in this example, is that both sets of notes are convertible (in a bank) at no cost to the public. Remarkably, Scottish notes are rarely seen in the south of England, though they are more common in those northern towns where Scots can go on a day trip.

The EU single currency proposal is compatible with the continuation of distinctive banknotes in member-states. What matters is that those notes be convertible into each other at a known price, at no cost to the public.

BENEFITS AND COSTS

In this section we avoid problems of transition and ask: what would be the main differences before and after a single currency had been adopted?

The main benefit of a single currency is the reduction in transactions costs for intra-EU trade and travel, and the enhanced efficiency of the price mechanism that results from prices across the European Union being readily comparable. Some people have argued that current transactions costs are quite small (especially on wholesale trade) so the savings here would not be big. However, the correct calculation is not just the saving on transactions costs of existing trade patterns: rather, you have to include the potential gains from the reorganization of industry and commerce that would follow from the elimination of both exchange rate costs and exchange rate uncertainty. Of course, the EU currency would still be floating against other world currencies, so there would still be external currency risk.

The main cost of moving to a single currency is the loss of the possibility for an independent monetary policy. After the adoption of a single currency, monetary policy will have to be determined by a European central bank, so UK interest rates will have to be those that are suitable on average across Europe.[10] If the UK economy were in recession while the rest of the EU member-states were not, there would be no possibility of lowering UK interest rates or even of devaluing the UK currency, in order to stimulate the economy. Of course, this is already the position faced by a region within an existing currency area, say, Yorkshire. Regional imbalance must accordingly be tackled by fiscal policy, or not at all (that is, left to market forces). However,

---

[10] There could also be problems for the role of the City of London as a financial centre if the EU central bank operated mainly in another financial centre. Certainly there would be institutional changes, as the discount market would be unlikely to survive. However, the City could also lose out if other EU countries go for a single currency while the United Kingdom stays out of the system; this would encourage the development of other financial centres which could possibly take business from London.

some fear that the whole of the United Kingdom might become a depressed region and monetary policy would not be available to correct the imbalance, while other tools may be inadequate for the task.

For those who do not believe in using monetary policy as an active countercyclical stabilization tool, the loss of monetary independence should not matter too much, so long as the EU central bank delivers low inflation. However, for those who believe in active management of domestic aggregate demand in order to maintain GDP close to its potential level, the loss of an independent monetary policy would be important.

Ironically, in the United Kingdom the politicians seem to have taken inconsistent positions. The right wing of the Conservative Party (who believe in using monetary policy to achieve low inflation and are opposed to fine-tuning) are strongly opposed to the single currency, whereas left-of-centre Tories, the Liberal Democrats, and the right wing of the Labour Party (all of whom generally support active countercyclical monetary policy) are more sympathetic to the idea of a single currency.[11]

THE TRANSITION TO A SINGLE CURRENCY

Even if it were agreed to introduce a single currency at some future date, there is still a problem of how to go from here to there. The agreed EU policy, as set out in the Maastricht Treaty of 1992 and outlined in the Delors Report of 1989, is to insist upon a process of gradual convergence. The single currency is (supposedly) to be introduced by 1999 (1997 at the earliest), with a final decision coming by the end of 1996. In order to qualify for membership of the new currency area, member-states are supposed to meet all of the following 'convergence criteria':

1. They must have been members of the ERM with narrow bands for at least two years before the adoption of the single currency.

2. They must have long-term interest rates not more than 1.5 per cent above the average of the three lowest.

3. They must have inflation rates not more than 2 per cent above the average of the three lowest.

4. The government budgets deficit must be no more than 3 per cent of GDP.

5. Total public debt must not exceed 60 per cent of GDP.

The idea behind these criteria is that countries must have achieved a high degree of monetary policy convergence, and a controlled fiscal position (small deficit and low debt), in the context of a pegged exchange rate regime before qualifying for the currency union. None of the member-states satisfied all of these criteria in 1993/4, and some with high public debt levels, like Italy and Belgium, will be unlikely ever to meet them. As a result, the criteria may be relaxed as the reality of a single currency comes closer.

Alternatively, the currency area may initially be formed by a subset of EU countries, or it may be accomplished over a longer time scale.

The problems with the strategy of slow convergence are twofold. First, there are always shocks to the real economy which blow convergence off course; so convergence can never be guaranteed to arrive within a given time-scale. Second, the transition regime is harder to maintain than either floating exchange rates or the single currency. This is because the narrow ERM requires central banks to intervene in foreign exchange markets to maintain exchange rates within prescribed bands. When the markets take a different view from the authorities, as in September 1992, the markets often win. Once the single currency is in place, there are no exchange rates to speculate against. Hence neither a floating regime nor the single currency require active price fixing. Hence the two extreme regimes cannot be destroyed by speculators once in force.

It can be seen that the transition problems are considerable, especially if transition proceeds along the lines set out in the Maastricht Treaty. There is no point in speculating on alternative routes since the whole operation may not take place at all. Indeed, the problems of transition may themselves be prohibitive.

All of this discussion of the single currency for the EU is highly speculative. What we can say is that, if it ever happens, and if the United Kingdom becomes a member of the system, it will shift monetary policy responsibility away from the UK authorities to the European central bank. It will also change the financial environment in ways that are currently hard to predict. Only when and if the institutional structure gets established will we be able to analyse its effects in detail. The debate in the next few years is going to be more about the principle; the detail will come later, if at all.

....

Summary

1 The nature of monetary policy is critically affected by the exchange rate regime. Under a gold standard regime, there is no need for government involvement. Convertibility of notes into gold is achieved by private banks.

[11] Some aspects of this curious state of affairs must remain a mystery, but part of the explanation undoubtedly lies in politics rather than economics. The 'free markets' ideology of the Tory right finds conflict with the more corporatist and interventionist ideology of many other EU countries. Hence any encroachment by 'Brussels Bureaucrats' is to be opposed. There is also the belief that those controlling our affairs should be accountable to the UK Parliament, which would not be the case with an EU central bank, though it would be accountable to both the Commission (and perhaps the Council) and the European Parliament.

2 Fixed exchange rate regimes, with fiat money, require governments to intervene in foreign exchange markets. They run down reserves and buy domestic money when the home currency is under selling pressure, and they build up reserves by selling domestic currency and buying foreign currency when the home currency is in excess demand.

3 Under floating exchange rate regimes, the constraints requiring that either domestic notes are convertible into gold, or that domestic currency is convertible into foreign currency at a fixed price, disappear.

4 Until 1980, with a break in 1971–3, the UK authorities had direct quantitative controls on parts of bank balance sheets. Only since 1980 have they had to achieve monetary control purely by means of market intervention.

5 The UK authorities instituted a method of monetary control in the 1980s which neither attempted to control the monetary base, nor attempted to control banks' reserves. The central plank of the control strategy was to control private-sector bank lending by means of short-term interest rates.

6 Monetary targets were used for a while, but they were abandoned because of doubts about the stability of demand functions for the various monetary aggregates.

7 Fixing the money stock and fixing the interest rate are equivalent, for a given money demand function and given *IS* curve.

8 In the face of an unstable money demand function, fixing the interest rate stabilizes aggregate demand, but fixing the money stock does not. However, instability in the *IS* curve will lead to less instability of national income with a given money stock than with a given interest rate.

9 If the European Union moves towards a single currency, monetary policy for the whole of the Union will be set by the new European central bank.

10 A single currency for the European Union reduces transactions costs and increases the transparency of the price mechanism. The main cost is that it removes the possibility of using monetary policy (interest rates or devaluation) in a member-state to control or stimulate demand.

Topics for review

- Monetary policy and the exchange rate regime
- Monetary base control
- Open-market operations
- Asset-based controls
- Policy goals and intermediate targets
- Monetary indicators
- Monetary services index (Divisia)
- Independent central bank
- Single EU currency

CHAPTER 39

Macroeconomic policy in an open economy

THE economies of all modern advanced industrial nations (and many developing nations) are open to large volumes of foreign trade and capital movements. In this chapter we study the complications that this openness creates for fiscal and monetary policies.

In Chapter 36, we expanded our model of the economy to incorporate monetary forces in the determination of aggregate demand. In that analysis, we did make some allowances for openness, as net exports were a component of aggregate demand, and Box 36.2 discussed the topic of financial openness. In this chapter, we incorporate financial capital flows explicitly into our model and then go on to reconsider the impact of monetary and fiscal policies, under the alternative regimes of fixed and floating exchange rates.

Before proceeding, you should revise the last section of Chapter 36 on pp. 709–13, in which we set out the steps in the chain of causation, from policy changes to national income, in the short run and the long run. In that chapter, we neglected the role of external influences, such as capital flows and the exchange rate, in the adjustment process. Now they must be incorporated in order to complete our formal development of the model of the macroeconomy.

Why does openness matter?

THERE are three reasons why we have to take a much closer look at the interactions between our macro model and the rest of the world. First, while we have always had net exports in our model, we have not paid attention to the possible implication of trade imbalances. Second, we have mentioned several times in earlier chapters the fact that financial markets have become more integrated around the world. We refer to this as *globalization*. Yet in our discussions of money demand and supply, our analysis focuses exclusively on domestic monetary conditions. In reality, the high international mobility of financial capital implies that money markets in one country are not independent of world financial markets. Third, in Chapters 37 and 38, we learned that the exchange rate regime matters for the conduct of monetary policy. We shall see that it also affects fiscal policy.

Let us expand a little on each of these three factors before we proceed to an explicit analysis of the macro model in which capital flows are included, and explicit attention is paid to the trade balance.

NET EXPORTS

Our macro model, from Chapter 30 onwards, included net exports, *NX*. The first thing we learned about the *NX* function was that it is negatively sloped. This means that net exports fall as national income rises—because induced imports rise while autonomous exports are constant.

We also discovered that the net export function will shift if there is an exogenous (autonomous) change in export demand and if there is a change in domestic prices relative to foreign prices (caused either by an exchange rate change with given price levels, or a price level change with given exchange rates). An autonomous rise in exports increases net exports (shifts the *NX* function upwards for each level of national income—see Figures 30.2 and 30.3 on pages 573–4). A rise in domestic relative prices reduces net exports (shifts the *NX* function down and changes its slope).

When we studied how fiscal and monetary policy can be used to alter national income (see pp. 709–13), we ignored any repercussions that might be induced by changes in the balance of trade. We can no longer do so. We now repeat the analysis of monetary and fiscal policies, taking explicit account of the forces that are put in play by the deterioration of the trade balance (a falling surplus or a rising deficit) as national income rises.

The nature of these effects, however, is influenced by the degree of mobility of financial capital and by the exchange rate regime. We shall focus on the case of highly mobile financial capital, because this conforms most closely to the modern world. The analysis of Chapter 36 would be adequate, however, for a world of flexible exchange rates and *immobile* capital. Under such a regime (which might apply to a country that maintained restrictions on capital flows such as those abolished in the United Kingdom in 1979), the exchange rate would move to maintain equality of imports and exports, so net exports (and capital flows) could be ignored for analytical purposes.

MOBILE CAPITAL

Recall that, when we talk about capital flows in the context of the balance of payments, we are not talking about imports and exports of capital goods, such as machine tools and heavy equipment; rather, we are talking about international flows of borrowing and lending, or trade in assets and liabilities, such as share and bond sales or lending by banks in one country to customers in another.

Capital flows matter for two reasons. First, as we saw in Chapter 36, net capital flows must equal (with opposite sign) net exports. This relationship is true by definition so it must always hold. It is important to realize, however, that the economic causation between net exports and capital flows is not unidirectional. Changes affecting capital flows will have implications for net exports (possibly via exchange rate changes), just as shifts affecting net exports will have implications for the capital account. We will be more specific about these linkages below.

The second reason capital flows matter for the macro model is that they influence the domestic interest rate. If domestic residents are free to borrow and lend internationally, and foreign residents are free to borrow and lend in this country, they will borrow where the interest rate is lowest and lend where it is highest. Mobile capital tends to drive the domestic interest rate towards the level of interest rates in world markets. In effect, the domestic economy is a price-taker in world financial markets. The price involved here is the interest rate on loans and deposits.

We shall examine how this works in detail below. The key point to notice now is that, in an open economy with mobile financial capital, we cannot analyse the determination of the domestic interest rate using domestic demand and supply factors alone. (The globalization of financial markets was discussed earlier in Box 35.3.) Changes in the

---

BOX 39.1

Historical approaches to open-economy adjustment

Balance of payments adjustment in our full model can work in many different ways. Several of these were identified by economists in the past, in a piecemeal way, and were given different labels. In this box we explain some of these earlier approaches.

The classical price–specie flow mechanism

This approach, associated especially with David Hume (1711–76), applied to the world of the gold standard. Current account balance of payments surpluses led to gold inflows which caused domestic prices to rise. The rise in domestic prices made domestic goods relatively expensive compared with foreign goods, so imports rose and exports fell. By this means, a balance of payments surplus would be eliminated.

The monetary approach to the balance of payments

The central proposition of this approach is that excess demand or supply of money is important in explaining official reserve changes, under fixed exchange rates, and exchange rate changes, under floating. Professor Harry Johnson (1923–77) popularized this modern interpretation of the classical approach in the 1970s. He reinterpreted the links between the money supply and the balance of payments to fit with modern monetary institutions. The result, that increases in the money supply lead to proportional currency depreciation and price-level increases, is consistent with the monetary approach. However, one important insight of the monetary approach was that an economy that is growing faster than the rest of the world, but is subject to restricted domestic money creation, could have a sustained current account surplus under fixed exchange rates, or a continuing appreciation under floating exchange rates.

The absorption approach

Invented by S. S. Alexander at the IMF in the early 1950s, this approach emphasized that, for a devaluation to improve the current account of the balance of payments, it must reduce domestic expenditure relative to domestic output (or be accompanied by other policies that did so). This view is based upon the fact that net exports are identical to the difference between domestic expenditure and domestic output (GDP). So, for net exports to become positive, total expenditure must be reduced below GDP.

The elasticities approach

This was associated with Alfred Marshall (1842–1924), Abba Lerner (1903–82), and Joan Robinson (1903–83). It approached balance of payments adjustment from the perspective of changes in the relative prices of imports and exports. The famous *Marshall–Lerner condition* for a devaluation to improve the trade balance is that the sum of the elasticities of demand for imports and exports must be less than −1. It means that the quantities must have adjusted more than in proportion to the change in relative prices. We have assumed, through most of our analysis, that the Marshall–Lerner condition holds, so a rise in the relative price of domestic goods shifts the net export function downwards; that is, a rise in the relative price of domestic goods lowers the volume of net exports.

The Keynesian approach

This is the name attached to a focus on balance of payments based upon the net export function that we have in our model. For given autonomous exports and a given import propensity, it focuses on the change in net exports induced by changes in national income.

domestic interest rate brought about by domestic shocks or policy changes will generate reactions through capital flows and net exports, which will inevitably complicate the picture.

THE EXCHANGE RATE REGIME

The exchange rate regime matters because it determines which variables are free to adjust. Clearly, under fixed exchange rates, the exchange rate is not free to adjust. But fixing the exchange rate ties down other variables as well. Fixed exchange rates tie together the value of domestic and foreign money. This means that the domestic price level cannot deviate from the foreign price level in the long run.

Fixed exchange rates, with mobile capital, also mean that domestic and foreign interest rates are tied together because there is no exchange rate uncertainty. In such circumstances, the domestic monetary authorities have no discretion in the setting of the domestic money supply or domestic interest rates. The money supply is endogenously determined by demand, at whatever interest rate is dictated by world money markets. This explains why monetary policy was less important than fiscal policy under the Bretton Woods fixed exchange rate regime of the 1950s and 1960s (though capital controls gave some degree of monetary independence). It also explains why the UK authorities had

no discretion to lower interest rates (as would have been dictated by internal considerations alone) during October 1990–September 1992, when the United Kingdom was a member of the ERM.

In general, the monetary authorities can fix any one (and only one) of the interest rate, the exchange rate, and the money supply; but, once they choose one of these, the other two become endogenous. Fixing the exchange rate is one possible monetary policy, but, having done this, the authorities cannot also control either the interest rate or the money supply.

Under floating exchange rates, much of the adjustment to shocks comes through exchange rate changes and the resulting effect on the relative price of domestic and foreign goods (and assets). In contrast, under fixed exchange rates, much more of the adjustment to shocks is worked out via aggregate demand, money stock, and output changes at given relative prices. These differences will become clearer as we work through specific examples below. Some of the key steps in the history of the evolution of the analysis of open-economy adjustment are discussed in Box 39.1.

We now turn to a discussion of how the macro model is modified by the inclusion of capital flows, and how the presence of capital flows alters the impact of monetary and fiscal policies.

Macro policy in a world with perfect capital mobility

A S we have seen, capital flows in the balance of payments accounts include net cross-border sales of a wide variety of domestic and foreign assets—shares, Treasury bills, bonds, etc. To keep things as simple as possible, we assume that there are just two types of asset: domestic bonds and foreign bonds. Domestic bonds are denominated in pounds sterling and foreign bonds are denominated in US dollars. (Which foreign currency we select is not critical, so long as it represents the rest of the world.)

Capital flows into the home economy when asset holders switch from foreign bonds to domestic bonds. Capital flows out of the home economy when asset holders switch from domestic bonds to foreign bonds. The process of switching involves sales of one currency for the other, so it creates a demand or supply of foreign exchange in the foreign exchange market.

An important assumption we make throughout is that net exports and the current account of the balance of payments are identical. In effect, this means that we are ignoring net property income from abroad. This would be a

reasonable assumption for the United Kingdom in 1993, for, as Table 28.2 on p. 531 shows, net property income from abroad was less than 0.5 per cent of GDP in that year. Even if this item were not so small, it could be ignored for analytical purposes, because it does not vary much in response to short-run changes in exchange rates or national income.

We now wish to incorporate capital flows into the macro model.

THE MACRO MODEL WITH CAPITAL FLOWS

Two relationships must be kept in mind when incorporating capital flows into our model. The first is that net capital flows must be of equal size and opposite sign to the current account balance of payments surplus. This means that, if there were capital inflows, there must be a current account deficit of equal size.

The second relationship that we need to bear in mind is the foreign demand for domestic bonds. This will depend

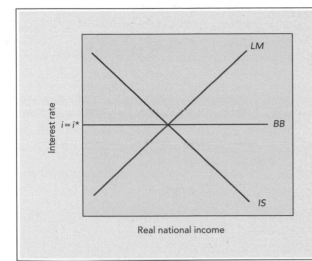

Figure 39.1 The macroeconomic implications of perfect capital mobility

With perfect capital mobility, the domestic interest rate must be equal to the foreign interest rate in equilibrium. The *BB* line shows the combinations of interest rates and national income for which a current surplus (deficit) equals the associated capital outflow (inflow). The *BB* line is drawn horizontally at the point where the domestic interest rate is equal to the foreign rate i^*. The shape of *BB* means that any size of current account deficit can be financed by borrowing at the going interest rate on world capital markets. For a given net export function, the current account balance deteriorates as national income increases. Actual capital flows in any period will always be equal and opposite to the current account balance.

upon the differential in interest rates between domestic and foreign bonds. We need to make some assumption about how sensitive demand for domestic bonds will be to this interest differential. The analysis of Chapter 36 implicitly assumed immobile capital (and flexible exchange rates), so that there would be no switching between domestic and foreign bonds at any feasible interest rate.

Now we make the other extreme assumption, which is that foreign demand for domestic bonds is perfectly elastic with respect to the interest differential. In effect, we are assuming that domestic and foreign bonds are perfect substitutes.[1] This is only one of several possible assumptions, but it is close to the realities of the modern world of globalized finance and highly mobile international capital. Hence it is a reasonable simplifying assumption to make in the UK context, though it will be inappropriate for economies that still have official exchange controls affecting capital flows.

Perfect substitutability between domestic bonds and foreign bonds is called *perfect capital mobility*. Its implications are illustrated in Figure 39.1, which shows the familiar *IS/LM* diagram, with the addition of a horizontal line labelled *BB*. Points on the *BB* line represent combinations of the interest rate and national income for which there is an equality between the current account balance of payment and capital flows. It joins short-run balance of payments equilibrium points. Its horizontal shape reflects our present assumption that the domestic interest rate must equal the foreign interest rate i^*.[2] This is because, if they were not equal, there would be an enormous excess supply or demand for domestic bonds. If the return on domestic bonds were slightly higher than on foreign bonds, there would be immediate huge demand for them; this would drive up the price of domestic bonds and drive down their yield. Similarly, if domestic bonds had a yield below foreign bonds, holders would sell them to buy foreign bonds; this would drive their price down and their yield up. The com-

mon sense of this is that any two commodities that are perfect substitutes must have a common price (because they are, in effect, one commodity).

It is important to notice that the *BB* curve does not represent points for which the current account balance is zero. Indeed, for a given net export function, the current account balance deteriorates as we move to the right (national income increases). If this involves a deficit, however, this can be financed by borrowing from abroad at the going world rate of interest. Thus, any point on *BB* for which there is a current account imbalance will also be associated with an equal and opposite capital account imbalance. The horizontal shape of *BB* reflects the perfectly elastic supply curve of capital, as discussed above.

How can we be sure that the *BB* line cuts the *IS* and *LM* curves at their intersection? The answer is that initially it may not do so, but, if it does not, there will be adjustments of exchange rates and/or real money supply; these will shift either the *IS* or the *LM* curve (or both) until all three have a common intersection. We will shortly be discussing cases where policy changes create such non-intersections, and we will then see in detail how such adjustment works. The process is not independent of the exchange rate regime.

The assumption that domestic and foreign interest rates are equal requires further comment. Recall that domestic and foreign bonds are denominated in different currencies.

[1] Since corporate bonds vary in riskiness, at best there will be perfect substitutability only between the bonds issued by governments of major industrial countries, as these are virtually riskless.

[2] Because the domestic economies of most countries, including the United Kingdom, are each a small part of the world economy, each country is a price-taker in world financial markets; i.e. the foreign interest rate is exogenous to the domestic economy. If capital flows were imperfect, the *BB* line would be positively sloped. This is because net exports decrease as national income increases, and the higher capital flows required to finance an increasing current account deficit could be attracted only at *increasing* interest rates.

When exchange rates are fixed (and expected to remain fixed), this causes no complications. The comparative yield will be given by the interest differential, and perfect capital mobility does indeed require exact equality of domestic and foreign interest rates at all times.

However, under floating exchange rates, where exchange rates are expected to change, the position is more complicated. Here there can be a differential in nominal interest rates which will be equal to the expected rate of change of the exchange rate. This effect is associated with exchange rate overshooting, and was discussed in Chapter 37 and illustrated in Figure 37.5 on p.735. Suppose, for example, that holders of bonds expect sterling to depreciate against the US dollar by 5 per cent over the next year. If the yield on US bonds is 10 per cent per year, they will need a yield of about 15 per cent on sterling bonds to compensate for the expected currency depreciation. In this case, the expected returns would be equal, but the nominal interest rates would not.[3]

This means that, when we discuss floating exchange rates, points on the horizontal *BB* line represent the full equilibrium, when there are no further expectations of exchange rate changes, but we can deviate from it during the adjustment process. With fixed exchange rates, on the other hand, we must be on it all the time.

Perfect capital mobility means that, with fixed exchange rates, the domestic interest rate must always equal the foreign interest rate. With floating exchange rates, any interest differential must equal the expected exchange rate change. This will be zero in full static equilibrium.

The explicit addition of capital flows to our model introduces a new adjustment mechanism which reconciles differences in the desired trade surplus and desired net capital flows via either official reserve changes (under fixed exchange rates) or exchange rate changes (under floating rates). This we shall explain in the context of specific examples.

Policy changes with fixed exchange rates

Now we can trace through the effects of monetary and fiscal policy changes in a model that allows for perfect capital mobility. Of particular interest will be the changes in predictions that follow from the addition of capital flows to the model.

To make it easier to understand how the adjustment mechanism works with capital flows included, initially we consider the effects of policy changes starting from a position of full equilibrium, where $Y = Y^*$. This, of course, is somewhat artificial, since policy changes would normally

be made to correct a disequilibrium. The difficulty that would arise if we started from disequilibrium is that there can be many different reasons for disequilibrium, and the effect of policy changes may depend upon what has caused the deviation of Y from Y^*. However, there should be no surprise, when we start at Y^*, to find that eventually we return to Y^*. What matters is to understand how the adjustment mechanism works when perfect capital mobility is assumed. We shall discuss how the result might change if we start with disequilibrium later. We start with a fixed exchange rate regime.

MONETARY POLICY

Starting with an economy in full equilibrium, we assume that the monetary authorities increase the money stock (or, equivalently, reduce interest rates). The analysis, which is shown in Figure 39.2, is simple under a fixed exchange rate regime.

The policy change shifts the *LM* curve to the right. However, we do not bother to translate this shift into an aggregate demand shift, because it will be reversed immediately. As soon as domestic interest rates dip slightly below world rates, there will be a massive sale of domestic bonds. This will create an excess supply of sterling in the foreign exchange market (because holders are selling sterling bonds and converting the proceeds into dollars to buy dollar bonds), and the authorities will have to buy sterling (and sell reserves) in order to stop the exchange rate from falling.

As they buy back sterling, the domestic money supply is reduced and the *LM* curve shifts back to its initial position. The conclusion is that, with perfect capital mobility and fixed exchange rates, the monetary authorities have control over neither domestic interest rates nor the stock of money. If they do not provide the money stock that is demanded at the ruling world interest rate, they are swamped with massive inflows or outflows of financial capital (bond sales or purchases).

Capital flows do not change the ultimate outcome of an increase in the money supply under fixed exchange rates, but they do speed up the adjustment process—so much so that the policy will have been reversed long before it is able to stimulate national income. Indeed, perfect capital mobility will force the reversal of the money supply increase within hours (at most), while, without capital flows, the reversal can take months or even years. Thus, perfect capital mobility means that it is impossible to use monetary policy to influence real economic activity under fixed exchange rates. With no (or severely restricted) capi-

---

[3] The exact expression that must hold for expected yields on the two different currency-denominated bonds to be equal is: $(1 + i) = (1 + i^*)$ (e_t/e_{t+1}), where i is the yield on UK bonds (expressed as a decimal, so 10 per cent is 0.1), i^* is the yield on foreign bonds, e_t is the exchange rate (\$ per £) at the beginning of the holding period, and e_{t+1} is the exchange rate expected to hold at the end of the holding period.

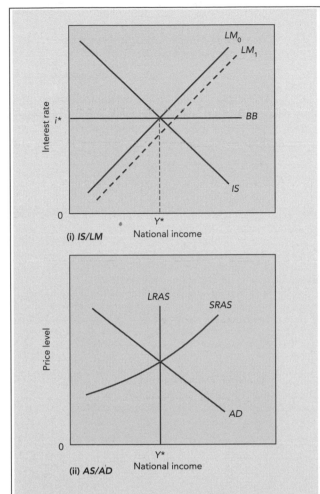

(i) IS/LM

(ii) AS/AD

Figure 39.2 Monetary policy with fixed exchange rates and perfect capital mobility

Monetary policy is powerless to influence economic activity under fixed exchange rates and perfect capital mobility. An increase in the money supply shifts the *LM* curve to the right from LM_0 to LM_1. However, the smallest fall in domestic interest rates causes a massive desired capital outflow. This puts downward pressure on the exchange rate. The monetary authorities are forced to buy sterling immediately, in order to stop the exchange rate falling, and the *LM* curve shifts back to its original position, LM_0. Thus, monetary policy, under fixed exchange rates and perfect capital mobility, is powerless to achieve any influence over the real economy, even in the very short run.

tal flows, limited temporary monetary policy influences may be achieved.[4]

Monetary policy under fixed exchange rates and perfect capital mobility cannot exert any independent influence over real economic activity.

FISCAL POLICY

The analysis of what happens when fiscal policy changes is much more complicated than in the case of a monetary policy change. It is also very different from events in the absence of capital flows. The course of events is set out in Figure 39.3.

Again, we start with the economy in full equilibrium. The assumed fiscal policy change is an increase in government spending. The initial effect of this increase is to shift the *IS* curve to the right. With a given nominal money stock (given *LM* curve), this will put upward pressure on domestic interest rates. However, even the smallest rise in domestic interest rates generates a capital inflow (foreign demand for domestic bonds) and creates excess demand for sterling in the foreign exchange markets. To stop the exchange rate rising, the monetary authorities have to sell sterling and buy foreign currency. These sales of sterling increase the supply of high-powered money and shift the *LM* curve to the right.

Thus, the initial rightward shift of the *IS* curve has been reinforced by a rightward shift of the *LM* curve. The *AD* curve would have shifted right as a result of each of these shifts. The combined effect is shown in part (ii) of the figure. This is a bigger shift of *AD* than would have resulted from a shift in the *IS* curve alone. Indeed, the size of the horizontal shift of *AD* is equal to the full value of the simple (open-economy) multiplier, because there is no negative feedback from the monetary sector. This comes about because interest rates cannot rise, so the authorities have to increase the money supply to avoid an interest rate rise (or an exchange rate appreciation).

Of course, this is not the end of the story. The increase in aggregate demand has created an inflationary gap, as is indicated by the fact that the new aggregate demand curve intersects the initial short-run aggregate supply curve at a level of national income well above its potential level. This causes a short-term boom in the economy, and real national income rises temporarily above its potential level.

The inflationary gap, once created, puts upward pressure on the domestic price level. Initially this is felt only in output prices. The increase in output prices, combined with the increase in real national income, creates a trade deficit. The trade deficit increases because (induced) imports increase with income. The price level rise reinforces this increase because (with a fixed exchange rate and given for-

---

[4] In the absence of capital flows, all the adjustment has to take place through the current account of the balance of payments. The increase in the money supply leads, via excess money balances, to lower interest rates. The lower interest rates lead to higher investment, and the resulting increase in national income leads to greater imports. The increase in imports generates an excess supply of domestic currency (excess demand for foreign currency) in the foreign exchange market, so the authorities have to buy sterling with dollars to stop the exchange rate falling. This purchase of sterling reduces the stock of high powered money, and so reverses the initial increase in the money supply.

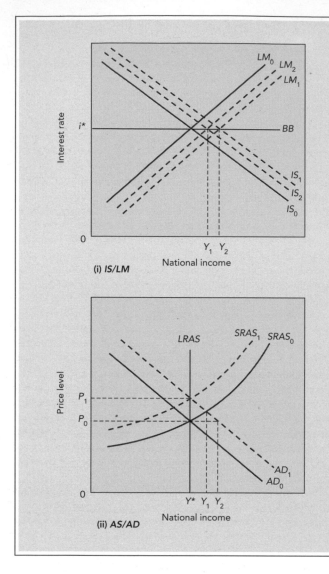

Figure 39.3 Fiscal policy with fixed exchange rates and perfect capital mobility

Starting from full equilibrium, an increase in government spending under fixed exchange rates and perfect capital mobility creates a significant stimulus to real activity in the short run, but in the long run it leads to a higher price level and a balance of payments deficit. The increase in government spending shifts the IS curve from IS_0 to IS_1 in part (i). With a given money supply, this puts upward pressure on domestic interest rates. The slightest rise in domestic interest rates causes a massive capital inflow, which puts upward pressure on the exchange rate. To stop the exchange rate rising, the monetary authorities sell sterling in the foreign exchange market. This increases the money supply, and shifts the LM curve to the right, from LM_0 to LM_1. The combined effect of the IS and LM curves shifting is that AD shifts right, from AD_0 to AD_1, as shown in part (ii). There is no negative feedback from the monetary sector, because interest rates cannot rise.

The increase in aggregate demand causes national income to increase from Y^* to Y_1 in the short run, and there is a small initial increase in the price level. (This price level rise shifts the IS and LM curves slightly leftward to IS_2 and LM_2 so that they intersect at Y_1 rather than Y_2.) Net exports become negative. (There is a current account balance of payments deficit because national income has increased and the domestic price level has risen relative to the foreign price level.) In the long run, inflationary pressure causes the price level to rise to P_1 as the $SRAS$ curve shifts up to $SRAS_1$ and national income returns to Y^*. However, the sustained rise in the price level (for given foreign prices) causes a permanent trade deficit, which is equal to the budget deficit. At price level P_1 the real money supply has fallen, so the LM curve shifts back to LM_0. The higher price of domestic goods causes net exports to shift downwards, so IS also shifts back to its original position, IS_0.

eign prices) domestic goods become more expensive relative to foreign goods, so there is a change in import propensity and a shift in export demand. Indeed, it is this price level rise that moves the economy back up the AD curve and reduces the impact on national income, compared with the full impact of the simple multiplier (as measured by the horizontal shift in AD).

In the longer term, inflationary forces pass through to input prices, and the short-run aggregate supply curve shifts up to the left. This raises the price level further, as the economy moves back up the AD curve and national income returns to its potential level. The higher price level reduces the real money supply, and so the LM curve shifts back leftwards to its initial position. It also further increases the trade deficit, and this downward shift in net exports also shifts the IS curve back leftwards to its original position.

Thus, instead of crowding out investment (as happened in Chapter 36 in the absence of capital flows), the increase in government spending has led to a trade deficit of equal value. (Real national income returns to its original level but real national expenditure has risen by the amount of extra government spending. The excess of national expenditure over national output is equal to the trade deficit.)

An increase in government spending (starting at full equilibrium), with fixed exchange rates and perfect capital mobility, creates a short-run economic boom, but the long-run effect is an increase in the domestic price level and a trade deficit.

This trade deficit will be equal to the government budget deficit if the initial position was one of budget balance and trade balance. Notice, also, that the mechanism that brought about the trade deficit was a rise in domestic prices (relative to foreign prices). This is equivalent to a rise in the real exchange rate, even though the nominal exchange rate is fixed. However, in this case there has been no crowding out of investment because fiscal policy is powerless to influence interest rates. In effect, domestic investment can be financed at the going world interest rate. The trade deficit is matched by a capital inflow (foreign purchases of domestic bonds) of equal size.

This is the end of the story in our model, but it cannot be the end of the story in reality. We have an equilibrium in which there is a current account deficit on the balance of payments and, therefore, continuing capital inflows. The domestic economy is borrowing from the rest of the world to finance the excess of spending over output.

If this borrowing finances current consumption (government consumption, in this case), the wealth of the economy will be falling (relative to the initial trend position), and this cannot go on for ever. At some point the wealth effects will lead to either a shift in domestic expenditures (downward) or a reversal of government policy. (The government cannot build up infinite debt, and any financing problems may cause reserve losses.) The modelling of such wealth effects is beyond the scope of this book. Readers should merely note that some further adjustment must happen.

However, if the borrowing finances real investment (or if an equivalent amount of real investment takes place anyway), the story could be quite different. If the return on real investment were greater than the interest rate on foreign borrowing, this economy would be increasing its wealth over time. So long as investment returns continued to exceed interest costs, this position could be sustained and potential income would be growing over time, as discussed in Chapter 33. Therefore, one cannot assume that a current account balance of payments deficit is always undesirable. This reinforces the point first stated in Chapter 37.

Policy changes with floating exchange rates

We now turn to the analysis of policy changes under a regime of floating exchange rates. This is the current regime in the United Kingdom, so this analysis is the one that is appropriate for analysing the effects of macroeconomic policy in the UK economy today. It represents the culmination of all our efforts to build a macroeconomic model.

MONETARY POLICY

Again, we start with an increase in the money supply (or, equivalently, a reduction in the interest rate) initiated by the domestic monetary authorities from a position of full equilibrium, as illustrated in Figure 39.4. This shifts the LM curve downward to the right.

The fall in domestic interest rates, with perfect capital mobility, would normally cause a massive capital outflow. However, since the exchange rate is floating, the emergence of an excess supply of sterling causes an immediate drop in the exchange rate. It drops to the point where it is expected to appreciate at a rate sufficient to compensate for the lower domestic interest rate; in other words, it overshoots its long-run equilibrium in a downward direction. We discussed this notion of overshooting in Chapter 37, pp. 732–36.

The fall in the nominal exchange rate also represents a fall in the real exchange rate, because the domestic price level does not change quickly, while the exchange rate has fallen instantaneously. So the relative price of domestic goods has fallen. This leads to an upward shift in the net export function, which causes a shift of the IS curve to the right. The combined effect of the rightward shifts of the LM and IS curves causes a rightward shift in the AD curve.

The increase in aggregate demand takes national income beyond its potential level and creates an inflationary gap. In the short run, the economy experiences a boom in output and a small increase in the domestic price level. This increase in prices reduces the real money supply slightly and also offsets a little the upward shift in net exports; so both IS and LM curves shift back a fraction relative to their new positions. However, the full adjustment takes place in the longer term, when inflationary pressure works through into input costs and the short run aggregate supply curve shifts upwards.

As the price level rises to its long-run equilibrium, the real money supply returns to its original level, so the LM curve shifts back to its initial position, reversing the initial interest rate fall. Also, the real exchange rate returns to its initial position (the price level rises in proportion to the long-run currency depreciation), so net exports shift back to where they started. Notice, however, that during the adjustment period the current account has been in surplus because of the lower real exchange rate (and, therefore, there have been capital outflows), and so there has been an accumulation of net foreign assets (a rundown of foreign liabilities). This accumulation reflects the fact that national expenditure has been less than national output during the adjustment process (i.e., there has been a trade surplus). The current account is back in balance at the long-run equilibrium.

An expansionary monetary policy (increased money supply or lower interest rate) under floating exchange rates with perfect capital mobility causes a boom in real economic activity in the short run, but the long-run effect is a higher price level and a depreciation of the nominal

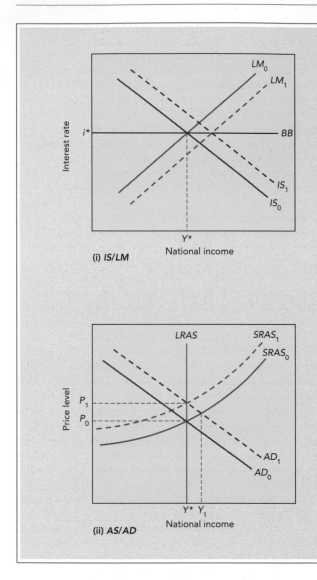

Figure 39.4 Monetary policy with floating exchange rates and perfect capital mobility

Starting at full equilibrium, an increase in the money supply causes an output boom in the short run, but in the long run causes only higher prices and currency depreciation. An increase in the money supply puts downward pressure on domestic interest rates, by shifting the LM curve to the right. Any fall in the domestic interest rate causes the exchange rate to depreciate to a point from which it is expected to appreciate at an annual rate equal to the annual interest differential. To be expected to appreciate, the exchange rate must fall beyond its new long-run equilibrium level (given the increased money stock). This involves overshooting, and a fall in the real exchange rate. This fall in the real exchange rate shifts the net export function upwards, so, as part (i) shows, there is a shift in the IS curve from IS_0 to IS_1 accompanying the initial shift in the LM curve, from LM_0 to LM_1. The combined effect of these two shifts on aggregate demand is shown in part (ii) as the shift from AD_0 to AD_1.

The increase in aggregate demand creates an inflationary gap. National income increases from Y^* to Y_1 in the short run, and the price level starts to rise to the level indicated by the intersection of AD_1 and $SRAS_0$. Eventually, inflationary pressure works through to input prices and the short-run aggregate supply curve shifts upwards to $SRAS_1$. The price level rises to P_1 and national income falls back to Y^*. The LM curve shifts back to LM_0 as the rise in price level reduces the real money supply. The IS curve shifts back to IS_0 as higher domestic prices (and the expected appreciation of the exchange rate) raise the relative price of domestic goods and the net export function shifts downwards. The long-run outcome is an increase in prices (and a depreciation of the home currency) in proportion to the initial increase in the money supply; but in the short run the economy has had a stimulus to real activity.

exchange rate, with no permanent gain in real output and an unchanged real exchange rate.

Although we assume, in the context of our model, that national income returns to its potential level, in practice, there may be some long-run real effects (even in the case that starts and finishes at Y^*). These arise from the fact that there is a change in national wealth. This change has two components. First, during the period when domestic interest rates were lower, there would have been a temporary increase in investment. Second, we have already noted the increase in net foreign assets arising from the cumulative trade surplus. These effects are ignored in our model, but in reality they may be significant.

Notice, also, the change in the monetary adjustment mechanism when there is perfect capital mobility (in con-

trast to the case discussed in Chapter 36). In the absence of capital flows, the monetary expansion creates a desired current account deficit (because it increases national income), whereas in the presence of capital flows it creates an exchange rate depreciation, which results in an *actual* current account surplus and a capital outflow. In the long run, the outcome is the same (a higher price level and proportional depreciation of the currency with the same real national income), but external payments adjustment during the transition to full equilibrium is quite different.

FISCAL POLICY

The case of a fiscal policy expansion under floating exchange rates with perfect capital mobility is illustrated in

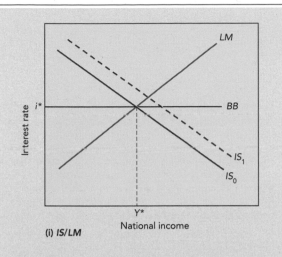

(i) IS/LM

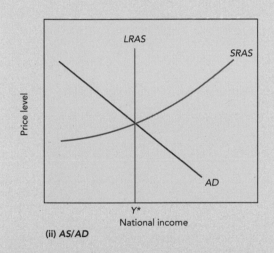

(ii) AS/AD

Figure 39.5 Fiscal policy with floating exchange rates and perfect capital mobility

Starting at full equilibrium, a fiscal expansion leads to a currency appreciation which crowds out an equivalent volume of net exports, causing a current account deficit but little or no stimulus to national income. The initial increase in government spending shifts the IS curve to the right from IS_0 to IS_1. But the resulting appreciation of the exchange rate (real and nominal) shifts the net export function downwards, which shifts the IS curve back to the left. The short-run effect of these countervailing forces is ambiguous, but we show it as if the net effect on aggregate demand is neutral. The only long-run effect is that the increase in government spending causes a trade deficit which is brought about by the sustained increase in the real exchange rate. The trade deficit is equal to the budget deficit. Thus, fiscal policy has little impact on domestic real activity under floating exchange rates and perfect capital mobility, at least when we start in full equilibrium.

Figure 39.5. Again, we take as our policy change an increase in government spending at full equilibrium.

The increase in government spending shifts the IS curve to the right. With a given money supply (fixed LM curve), this puts upward pressure on domestic interest rates. Any rise in domestic interest rates creates massive desired capital inflows (foreign demand for domestic bonds) and, thereby, puts upward pressure on the exchange rate. The exchange rate immediately appreciates (overshoots upwards) to a point from which it can be expected to depreciate at a rate equal to the interest differential.

The exchange rate appreciation, for a given initial price level, also appreciates the real exchange rate, which means that domestic goods become more expensive than foreign goods. This rise in the relative price of domestic goods shifts the net export function downwards, and therefore also shifts the IS curve back towards its original position. In other words, it causes a current account balance of payments deficit, which is matched by net capital inflows.

There is ambiguity about the precise course of aggregate demand in the short run. The increase in government spending shifts AD to the right, but the downward shift in net exports shifts it back to the left. Depending on the extent of upward exchange rate overshooting and on the adjustment speed of net exports, it is possible that AD will move slightly to the right, but it is also possible that it will move slightly to the left. On balance, the likely outcome is that it will remain roughly at its initial position, though it may, first, move right in the short run as government expenditure increases, and then, later, return to its initial position as net exports fall. The factors affecting the adjustment of net exports to an exchange rate change are discussed in Box 39.2. In any event, the effect on real national income, even in the short run, may well be negligible.

The long-run outcome is that there is a trade deficit that matches the government budget deficit. There is also a permanent increase in the real exchange rate, brought about by a sustained appreciation of the nominal exchange rate (though less than the appreciation achieved during the overshooting phase).

The difference between short-run adjustment to a fiscal policy expansion (under floating exchange rates) with perfect capital mobility as opposed to no capital flows is significant. With no capital flows, the increase in G creates an inflationary gap and a currency *depreciation*, the domestic price level rises, and interest rates rise (thereby crowding out investment). With capital flows, the same increase in the relative price of domestic output is brought about by exchange rate *appreciation*, but there is no interest rate rise (except the short-run rise during the exchange rate overshooting) and no sustained crowding out of investment. There is, however, a trade deficit which matches the budget deficit.

Again, this cannot be the end of the story, because there is ongoing borrowing by the government and increasing

---

BOX 39.2

....

The J-curve

In this chapter we consider what happens when there is a change in monetary or fiscal policy under fixed or floating exchange rates. We do not ask what happens under a fixed exchange rate regime if there is a discrete devaluation. In such a devaluation, there is a sudden fall in the exchange rate at which the currency is pegged.

The purpose of such devaluations is usually to improve the current account of the balance of payments (trade balance) and, thereby, reduce outflows of official international reserves. However, the effect on the current account is often not immediately positive. A common pattern is for the current account first to deteriorate further, but later to improve. This pattern is known as the J-curve because of the J-like curve the current account traces over time. The figure plots the path of the current account over time, starting in deficit. A devaluation at time t_0 initially makes the deficit worse but eventually it leads to a surplus after a lag of perhaps two years.

The reason for the initial deterioration in the current account is that volumes of imports and exports take time to adjust to the new relative prices. Devaluation makes domestic goods cheaper than foreign goods and if volumes did not change at all, the domestic currency value of exports would stay the same but the domestic currency value of imports would rise (because their price has gone up in domestic-currency terms).

It is only when the volumes of imports and exports adjust more than in proportion to the change in relative goods prices that the current account of the balance of payments improves.

After the 1967 devaluation of sterling, it took between eighteen months and two years for the current account to move into surplus.

The J-curve is applicable to a world of floating exchange rates after there has been a sudden sustained exchange rate change. It helps us to understand that it takes many months, if not years, for the trade account fully to adjust to such exchange rate changes. When exchange rates change in small steps, the economic adjustments are still there, but they are harder to detect.

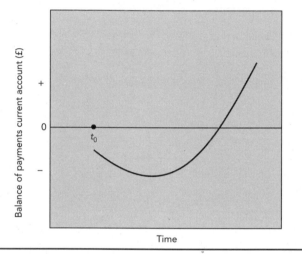

---

indebtedness to foreigners. Thus, similar wealth effects arise, as we discussed in the context of fiscal policy under fixed exchange rates (and perfect capital mobility). The big difference, however, is that under floating exchange rates a fiscal expansion creates a minimal stimulus to real national income, whereas under fixed rates a fiscal expansion leads to a short-run boom.

An expansionary fiscal policy, under floating exchange rates and with perfect capital mobility, has little impact on real national income in the short run; rather, it causes an exchange rate appreciation and a trade deficit. In the long run, there is a permanent appreciation of the real exchange rate, and the government budget deficit is equal to the trade deficit.

Let us now summarize what we have learned about the adjustment to monetary and fiscal policy changes in the presence of perfect capital mobility, assuming that we start in full equilibrium. We will then see whether starting in disequilibrium makes any difference.

1. *Under fixed exchange rates,* monetary policy is powerless to influence real economic activity. The money supply is demand-determined and the authorities have no discretion over interest rates. A fiscal policy expansion under fixed exchange rates causes a short-run boom in real activity, but this leads to inflation; the long-run effect is a permanent rise in the domestic price level (and the real exchange rate), a budget deficit, and a trade deficit (financed by capital inflows).

2. *Under floating exchange rates,* an expansionary monetary policy creates an inflationary boom in real activity in the short run; in the long run, the price level rises in proportion to the money stock increase, and the nominal exchange rate depreciates in the same proportion. A fiscal policy expansion under floating exchange rates creates little or no increase in real national income, even in the short run; in the long run, there is a sustained real and nominal exchange rate appreciation, and the government budget deficit is matched by a trade deficit (financed by capital inflows).

Policy changes to correct disequilibrium

We now need to check if our conclusions are specific to the case in which the economy is initially in equilibrium. In reality, policy-makers will want to use monetary and fiscal policies as tools for returning the economy to equilibrium, not for moving it away. There are many possible examples, but we can get a feel for the significance of the equilibrium assumption by studying a few illustrative cases in depth. We shall look closely only at flexible exchange rates, as that is the current UK situation, and we shall consider only the response to a negative aggregate demand shock. However, the fixed-exchange-rate case is easy to summarize, and we shall now do that before proceeding.

Let us suppose that the economy is in a situation where Y is less than Y^*, and that this has come about because of an autonomous fall in domestic investment. Under a fixed exchange rate regime with perfect capital mobility, monetary policy can do nothing to change this situation. The monetary authorities cannot lower interest rates (because of the horizontal BB curve), nor can they increase the money supply. Hence the conclusion about the impotence of monetary policy under fixed exchange rates is robust, even when we start in disequilibrium.

Fiscal policy can, however, have a beneficial effect. The fall in investment will have shifted the IS and AD curves to the left. An increase in government spending can shift these two curves back to their initial position without any of the longer-term harmful effects that arise when G is increased at full equilibrium. (There is no real exchange rate appreciation or crowding out of the balance of payments, though there is a budget deficit.) Certainly, government spending has replaced investment expenditure in equilibrium GDP, but this is not crowding out since the causation is reversed—G is filling the gap left by an autonomous fall in I. (Crowding out involves higher G causing lower I through higher interest rates.)

Of course, if the initial negative demand shock had been an exogenous fall in export demand, rather than an autonomous fall in investment, the increase in G (and the budget deficit) would be matched by a current account balance of payments deficit in equilibrium. But, again, this could not be called crowding out, because of the reversed causality. Also, whether the increase in G really improves the outcome will depend on it being timed correctly. This point also arises under a floating exchange rate, so let us now look more closely at policy responses to a negative demand shock under floating exchange rates.

MONETARY POLICY

Let us suppose, again, that a negative demand shock results from an autonomous fall in investment with a given initial money stock. The situation created by this investment fall is illustrated in Figure 39.6. The fall in investment shifts the IS curve to the left. This is associated with a shift to the left of the AD curve. The leftward shift of AD leads to a small fall in the price level, given an upward-sloping $SRAS$ curve, so the LM curve shifts slightly to the right (assuming that the monetary authorities hold the nominal money stock constant) as the real money stock has risen. Hence the effect of the fall in investment is to lower national income from Y^* to Y_1 in the figure.[5]

If, with the economy at Y_1, the monetary authorities do nothing (that is, keep the nominal money stock fixed), an automatic adjustment process will start to work. Because the domestic interest rate has fallen, desired capital outflows will cause the exchange rate to depreciate (to the point where it is expected to appreciate at just the right rate to compensate for the lower domestic interest rate). The currency depreciation, combined with the lower price level, means that domestic goods have fallen in price relative to foreign goods. (There has been a real exchange rate depreciation.) This causes an upward shift in the net export function and an associated current account balance of payments surplus (combined with capital outflows).

The upward shift in the net export function shifts the IS curve back to the right, and this could be sufficient to return the economy to equilibrium at Y^*. However, it is possible that the initial recessionary gap may also cause the $SRAS$ curve to shift to the right, via a reduction in money wage rates. Both of these responses, however, take some time, so the monetary authorities could, in principle, speed up the return to Y^* by increasing the nominal money supply, which would shift the LM curve to the right.

The advisability of such a monetary response depends upon the authorities being able to achieve their effects quickly. (Recall from Chapter 38 that many economists believe that monetary policy works with long and variable lags.) If the effects of this monetary stimulus are not felt until the economy has already returned to a national income level close to potential, then, rather than help end the recession, they could cause the economy to overshoot into an inflationary boom. In any event, the monetary stimulus would have to be reversed at some stage if inflation is to be avoided in the longer term.

Thus, monetary policy can be used in the short term to offset the recessionary effects of a negative demand shock, but whether this can be done with enough accuracy to improve on the automatic adjustment mechanisms is controversial.

---

[5] The initial fall in national income would be much greater if the monetary authorities were pegging the interest rate rather than the nominal money stock. In that case, national income would initially fall to Y_2 in the figure. The authorities would have to abandon this pegged interest rate policy in order to use monetary policy to stimulate the economy, so we revert to the assumption of an initially fixed nominal money supply.

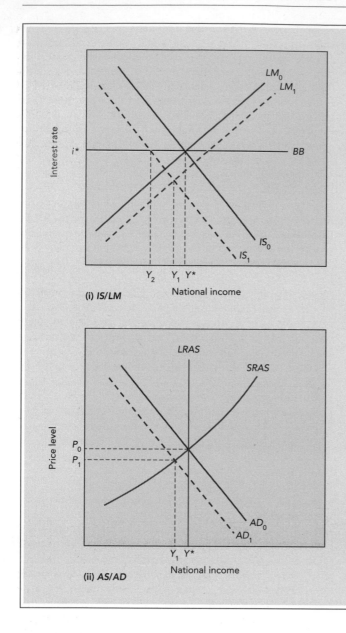

(i) IS/LM

(ii) AS/AD

Figure 39.6 Macro policies to correct a disequilibrium

Monetary and fiscal policy can help the economy recover from a negative demand shock, so long as they are appropriately timed. The negative demand shock is assumed to be an autonomous fall in investment. The economy is initially in full equilibrium at Y^*. The fall in investment shifts the IS curve from IS_0 to IS_1 in part (i), and it shifts the AD curve from AD_0 to AD_1 in part (ii). The resulting fall in the price level from P_0 to P_1 increases the real money supply (assuming that the authorities are fixing the nominal money stock), which shifts the LM curve to LM_1. (There is also a small upward shift in the net export function which shifts the IS curve back up slightly; this is not shown.) The economy thus goes to national income level Y_1, where there is a recessionary gap.

In the absence of policy changes, there are two forces that will eventually bring national income back to Y^*. First, the fall in the domestic interest rate below i^* will cause a currency depreciation (both real and nominal). This will shift the next export function upwards and so will shift the IS and AD curves back to the right. Second, the recessionary gap will cause a fall in money wages which will shift the SRAS curve to the right.

If correctly timed, monetary policy can speed up this adjustment process by lowering domestic interest rates further and causing a larger currency depreciation in the short term, although the policy will later have to be reversed if inflation is to be avoided. Fiscal policy can cut out the automatic adjustment. An increase in government spending shifts the IS and AD curves back to their original position, though there is a budget deficit (and lower investment) at Y^*, compared with the initial position. There is also a smaller trade surplus than would have occurred without the fiscal intervention.

Monetary policy exerts leverage via the exchange rate overshooting mechanism, but timing this correctly is difficult.

FISCAL POLICY

Now let us consider the possibilities of a fiscal reaction to the same negative demand shock that is illustrated in Figure 39.6. As a result of the fall in investment, national income has fallen from Y^* to Y_1 (assuming that the authorities are fixing the nominal money stock, rather than pegging interest rates).

An increase in government spending (of the appropriate magnitude) would shift the IS and AD curves back to their initial positions and, thereby, restore national income to Y^*. If this could be timed exactly to coincide with the fall in investment, there would be no fall in interest rates and no exchange rate depreciation, and so there would be no shift in the net export function. The only change at full equilibrium would be lower investment and a budget deficit (assuming that the budget was in balance before the increase in government spending).[6]

---

[6] If the negative demand shock had been caused by an exogenous fall in net exports, rather than investment, the net effect would be a sustained budget deficit and a balance of payments deficit in full equilibrium.

However, as with monetary policy, there is the problem of getting the timing right. If the increase in government expenditure takes effect after the automatic adjustment process does its job, then the increased spending could create an inflationary gap (as happens when G is increased with the economy starting at Y^* as above).

There is, however, an important difference between fiscal and monetary stabilization in response to this same negative demand shock. Monetary stabilization policy speeds up the automatic response mechanism by lowering the interest rate and exchange rate further than they would otherwise go (with a fixed money stock). If monetary policy is timed accurately, the long-run outcome is the same as if automatic stabilizing forces did the work. Monetary policy just helps to get the economy to full equilibrium more quickly.

By contrast, (accurate) fiscal policy cuts out the automatic adjustment mechanism and leads to a different composition of final demand in equilibrium. In general, the increased budget deficit will crowd out an equivalent volume of net exports *relative to what would have happened if the automatic adjustment had been left alone*. This is because the fiscal stimulus stops the exchange rate fall (nominal and real) which would otherwise have shifted the net export function upwards.

In the case of an initial fall in investment, the automatic adjustment mechanism would have created a current account balance of payments surplus at full equilibrium. A fiscal stimulus replaces this with a budget deficit (and a current account balance at full equilibrium). Of course, if the initial negative demand shock had been caused by a fall in export demand (a downward shift of the net export function), the automatic adjustment mechanism would have restored current account balance at full equilibrium, but an offsetting fiscal stimulus would mean that there was both a current account deficit and a budget deficit at full employment.

In short, starting the economy at less than potential national income and flexible exchange rates makes it possible that both monetary and fiscal policy could be used to speed up the adjustment of national income back to its potential level.

However, whether actual fiscal and monetary policies improve on the automatic adjustment mechanism in practice depends crucially on timing. If the impact of policy is felt too late, it will push the recovery of national income beyond potential national income and into an inflationary boom, even though it was conceived as a response to an earlier recessionary gap.

Some implications

READERS will probably have found the material in this chapter hard going, on first reading. However, the effort is worth while because we have now reached a very advanced level of understanding of a coherent model of the macroeconomy and how it works under a variety of circumstances. In the following chapters we shall be discussing a number of important policy issues. Before doing so it is worth drawing together some of the implications of what we have already learned.

The transmission of monetary policy

When we first introduced a monetary sector into our macro model in Chapter 36, we discussed the way in which changes in monetary policy are transmitted to the real economy via changes in domestic interest rates.

The *transmission mechanism* was set out as follows: starting from full equilibrium, an increase in the money supply creates an excess demand for bonds, which raises the price of bonds and lowers the interest rate. The lower interest rate increases investment, which, via the multiplier, increases desired aggregate expenditure. This increase in desired aggregate expenditure is moderated by negative feedback from the monetary sector (as interest rates adjust back upwards, but not by the full extent of their initial fall), but translates into an increase in aggregate demand. The increase in aggregate demand then leads to an increase in national income and a rise in the price level. As the price level rises further, in response to inflationary pressure, the real money stock falls and national income returns to its potential level at a higher price level.

We have now learnt that the transmission of monetary policy cannot work like this in most forms of open economy. With fixed exchange rates, monetary policy is powerless to influence the real economy, because excess supply of the home currency in the foreign exchange market will rapidly force a policy reversal. This happens especially quickly in the modern world of highly mobile financial capital.

Box 39.3

International policy co-ordination?

The analyses of macroeconomic policy in this chapter have taken place in the context of a single economy. However, openness to foreign trade and the globalization of financial markets have meant that all major countries in the world have been influenced at least as much by global economic forces as by local conditions. No country has been able to insulate itself from the effects of a worldwide recession, of which there have been three since 1970 (1974–5, 1980–2, and 1990–2).

The correlation between GDP growth rates in the United Kingdom, Germany, and the United States is shown in the chart. The UK and US cycles have been very closely related over the last quarter-century. The German economy managed to delay its recession at the end of the 1980s, relative to most other countries. This was partly the result of the massive fiscal expansion associated with the reunification of East and West Germany.

Open economies are ultimately constrained by world aggregate demand, and appear unable significantly to offset swings in world demand by local monetary or fiscal policy changes. No one country acting alone (except, perhaps, the United States, or the EU countries acting together) can influence world aggregate demand substantially. So the only possibility of stabilizing world aggregate demand is for countries to co-ordinate their macroeconomic policies.

Ronald McKinnon of Stanford University has suggested that the United States, Germany, and Japan should aim to stabilize their joint aggregate money supply, thereby stabilizing the major component of the world money supply.

In the 1980s, policy co-ordination was a topic that the Group of Seven (G7) major countries took seriously. In 1985, there was a bout of co-ordinated intervention in foreign exchange markets, following the Plaza Agreement, to stop the foreign exchange value of the US dollar rising. In 1987 there was a further bout of co-ordinated intervention, following the Louvre Accord, to stop the dollar falling.

Much theoretical work studied the benefits of policy co-ordination. There were also many simulation exercises performed by linking forecasting models of all the major countries. The balance of the academic argument supported the proposition that co-ordinated policies *could* work to improve the stability of the world economy.

However, the realities of the politics of policy formation create formidable obstacles to further action. There are already decision lags and implementation lags in the policy formation process in each country. These would be magnified if policy were to be determined at the supra-national level. Realistically, explicit co-ordination of macroeconomic policies is not going to happen in the foreseeable future. This may mean that the global business cycle is a phenomenon countries will have to continue to live with.

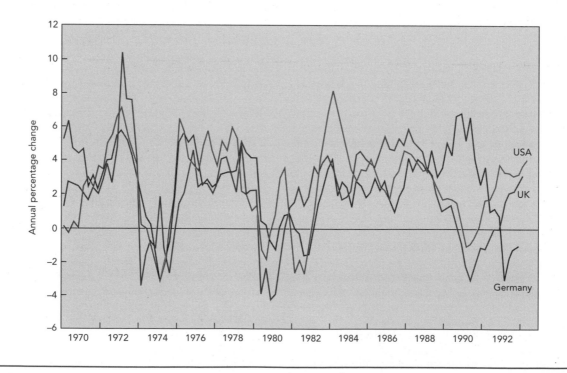

Under floating exchange rates with perfect capital mobility, monetary policy is able to stimulate real activity in the short run. It does so partly because a monetary policy expansion depreciates the real exchange rate, which thus stimulates net exports. Deliberate use of monetary policy can be helpful in speeding the adjustment to a negative demand shock. In our model, nominal interest rates fall temporarily and this stimulates investment. However, in the real world this fall in nominal interest rates will not necessarily be matched by a fall in expected real interest rates (because inflation will be expected to rise, especially if we start close to potential income), and so the effect in investment in practice may be small. Hence it is probable that the principal link in the transmission mechanism from the monetary sector to real activity in an open economy, with floating exchange rates, is through the exchange rate to net exports.

The efficacy of fiscal policy

We have found that fiscal policy is a very powerful tool for stimulating real activity in the short run, in an economy with fixed exchange rates and mobile international capital. In that case, the monetary authorities are forced (by capital inflows) to reinforce the fiscal expansion with an increase in the money supply.

Under floating exchange rates, with mobile capital starting in full equilibrium, however, the expansionary fiscal policy creates a currency appreciation, which neutralizes the stimulation to real activity. With floating rates, but limited capital mobility, an expansionary fiscal policy may have a short-run stimulating effect; but this is not the world in which we currently live.

The long-run effect of a fiscal expansion, with no capital flows, is to crowd out investment. But, with mobile capital, a fiscal expansion crowds out net exports via an appreciation of the real exchange rate.

There is a potential role for fiscal policy in offsetting the negative demand shocks that cause recessionary gaps. In such cases, at best, fiscal adjustment would replace the automatic adjustment mechanism of the economy and would lead to a deterioration of the budget balance in equilibrium. However, there may be situations in which this is preferable to waiting for recovery.

In general, the role of fiscal policy in influencing macroeconomic activity is much more limited in a world of floating exchange rates and mobile international capital than it would be under a fixed exchange rate regime, or in the world of restricted capital flows.

Global transmission of cycles

Small countries may be price-takers in globalized financial markets, so that they have only limited free ence domestic nominal interest rates, and e dom to influence domestic real interest rates. not mean that the *world* interest rates will not n it means that interest rates around the world w end to move up and down together as the demand and supply of credit moves up and down at the world level.

At the world level, interest rate movements will be transmitted to real activity through our original transmission mechanism. Correlation of interest rate movements around the world also causes correlation of the cyclical movements in real activity. See the chart in Box 39.3, which shows the growth rates of GDP for the United States, Germany, and the United Kingdom. Hence we should not be surprised to find that cycles about the trend of potential income in most of the industrial countries of the world follow a very similar pattern. This suggests that a stabilization of cycles cannot be achieved at the level of individual countries, but rather must be tackled, if at all, by co-ordinated stabilization policy among groups of countries or at the world level.

This argument should not be taken to mean that domestic macro policies do not matter; rather, the point is that they are not the only things that matter. External influences are much more important today than they were, say, in the 1950s. But there are, certainly, many things that domestic policy-makers can do that affect the performance of their home economy for better or worse. Despite the clear existence of a global business cycle, there have been widely differing experiences, with regard to inflation and unemployment, among economies more or less equally exposed to external forces. It is to the causes and cures of inflation and unemployment that we now turn.

Summary

1 Openness of the economy matters because the trade balance and capital flows influence real activity, international financial markets influence domestic money markets, and the exchange rate regime partly determines which variables are free to move.

2 Perfect capital mobility can be represented by a horizontal *BB* line in the *IS/LM* diagram.

3 Starting from any position, an expansionary monetary policy under fixed exchange rates and perfect capital mobility is rapidly reversed through losses of foreign exchange reserves. It has no real impact.

4 Starting from equilibrium national income, an increase in government spending, under fixed exchange rates and perfect capital mobility, creates an inflationary gap and a significant stimulus to real national income in the short run. In the long run, there is a rise in the relative price of domestic goods (through a higher domestic price level), a budget deficit, and a trade deficit.

5 Starting from equilibrium, a monetary policy expansion, under floating exchange rates and perfect capital mobility, creates a currency depreciation and an inflationary gap (associated with an increase in real national income above its potential level). In the long run, the price level rises in proportion to the money supply increase and the exchange rate depreciates in the same proportion.

6 Starting from equilibrium, an increase in government spending, with floating exchange rates and perfect capital mobility, creates little or no stimulus to real national income. However, it does lead to a currency appreciation and a trade deficit. The budget deficit and the trade deficit are of equal size.

7 Starting with a recessionary gap, both monetary and fiscal polices may speed up the return to potential national income if they are timed correctly. Fiscal policy can be used to increase final demand while monetary policy can lower interest rates and/or the exchange rate.

Topics for review

- Monetary policy
- Fiscal policy
- Fixed exchange rates
- Floating exchange rates
- Capital mobility
- Overshooting
- Crowding out

❧ PART TEN

Macroeconomic issues

CHAPTER 40

Inflation

INFLATION, unemployment, and growth are the big macroeconomic issues of our time. We have already discussed growth. In this chapter we focus on inflation, while the following chapter concentrates on unemployment. But it is important to know right away that the two issues are closely related, at least in the short run. Attempts to reduce unemployment have often been accompanied by a rise in inflation, and attempts to reduce inflation have usually led to increased unemployment. Macroeconomic policy, in effect, is an attempt to walk a tightrope with inflation on one side and unemployment on the other.

Inflation is bad (especially when unexpected) because it distorts the working of the price system, creates arbitrary redistribution from debtors to creditors, creates incentives for speculative as opposed to productive investment activity, and is usually costly to eliminate. Unemployment is bad because it disrupts lives and is associated with an irrecoverable loss of real output.

The recent history of inflation and unemployment in the United Kingdom is set out in Figure 40.1. In the 1950s and 1960s, inflation and unemployment were both low.

Inflation averaged about 3.5 per cent and unemployment was always below 750,000, averaging about 1.5 per cent of the work-force. However, this picture changed dramatically in the 1970s. Inflation rose to over 25 per cent in 1975 (the highest peace-time inflation rate in the United Kingdom for at least 300 years) and unemployment fluctuated about a rising trend, reaching 1.5 million in 1977, and over 3 million by 1983. Inflation fell to under 5 per cent by the mid-1980s, but it rose again to around 10 per cent as a result of the late-1980s boom. This boom also brought unemployment down to around 1.5 million. However, it rose again to around 3 million in the recession of the early 1990s; at the same time, inflation fell to around 2 per cent. The negative relationship between inflation and unemployment, at least since the end of the 1970s, is evident from the figure.

In this chapter we shall first use the macroeconomic model we have built up to investigate how inflation can arise. We shall then set out a theoretical framework for analysing the trade-off between inflation and unemployment. Finally, we shall discuss the implications of our analysis for counterinflationary policy-making.

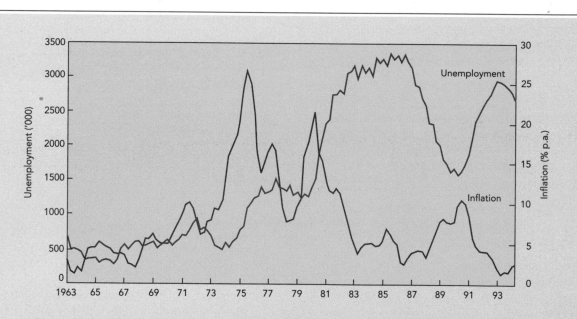

Figure 40.1 Inflation and unemployment in the United Kingdom, 1963–1993

Inflation and unemployment are negatively related, but not perfectly so. Unemployment and inflation were both very low in the 1960s, though inflation started to rise after the 1967 devaluation of sterling. Three major bursts of inflation are shown; 1972–5, 1979–81, and 1988–90. Unemployment trebled in the 1974–6 recession, from 500 000 to 1.5 million, and it doubled again as a result of the 1980–1 recession, from 1.5 million to over 3 million. By 1994, inflation was down to around 2 per cent, but unemployment was still a major problem.

Sources: Datastream and CSO, *Economic Trends*.

Inflation in the macro model

I T is important to distinguish between the forces that cause a once-for-all increase in the price level, and the forces that can cause a continuing (or sustained) increase. However, we refer to any increase in the price level as an inflation and distinguish between inflations of various durations.

Any event that tends to drive the price level upwards is called an **inflationary shock**. To examine these, we begin with an economy in long-run macroeconomic equilibrium. The price level is stable, and national income is at its potential level. It is an economy operating under a flexible exchange rate regime.[1] We then study the economy as it is buffeted by different types of inflationary shock.

Supply shocks

Suppose there is a negative shock to short-run aggregate supply; that is, the *SRAS* curve shifts up and to the left. This might be caused, for example, by a rise in the costs of imported raw materials, or by a rise in domestic wage costs per unit of output. The price level rises and output falls. The rise in the price level shows up as a temporary burst of inflation. What happens next depends, first, on whether the shock to the *SRAS* curve is an isolated event or one of a series of recurring shocks, and, second, on how the central bank reacts. If it responds by increasing the money supply, we say that the supply shock has been *accommodated*. If it holds the money supply constant, the shock is not accommodated.

ISOLATED SUPPLY SHOCKS

Suppose that the leftward shift in the *SRAS* curve is an isolated event. It might, for example, be caused by a once-for-all increase in the cost of imported raw materials.

No monetary accommodation The leftward shift in the *SRAS* curve causes the price level to rise and pushes income below its full-employment level, opening up a recessionary gap. Market pressures tend to cause wages and other factor costs to fall relative to productivity. When this happens, the *SRAS* curve shifts downward, causing a return of income to full employment, and a fall in the price level. The period of inflation accompanying the original supply shock is followed by a period of deflation, which continues until long-run equilibrium is re-established. This sequence is illustrated in Figure 40.2. Since money wages tend to react only sluggishly to excess supply in the labour market, unit costs of production fall only slowly, so the recovery to full employment may take a long time.

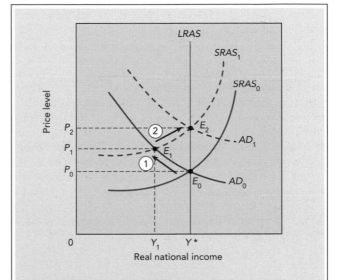

Figure 40.2 A single supply shock

The final effect of a single supply shock depends on whether or not it is accommodated by monetary expansion. A supply shock causes the *SRAS* curve to shift leftward from $SRAS_0$ to $SRAS_1$, as shown by arrow 1. Short-run equilibrium is established at E_1. If there is no monetary accommodation, the unemployment would exert a downward pressure on wage costs, causing the *SRAS* curve to shift slowly back to the right to $SRAS_0$. Prices would fall, and ouput would rise, until the original equilibrium was restored at E_0. If there is monetary accommodation, the *AD* curve shifts from AD_0 to AD_1, as shown by arrow 2. This re-establishes full-employment equilibrium at E_2, but with a higher price level, P_2.

Monetary accommodation Now suppose that the central bank reacts by increasing the money supply. This shifts the *AD* curve to the right, causing both the price level and output to rise. (Part of this adjustment may come from a currency depreciation, causing an upward shift of the net export function.) When the recessionary gap is eliminated, the price level, rather than falling back to its original value, will have risen further. These effects are also shown in Figure 40.2.

The monetary authorities might decide to accommodate

---

[1] For most purposes, the analysis followed here is consistent with the existence of perfect capital mobility. The interest rate can deviate from the world interest rate, but such deviations will be associated with exchange rate overshooting. The monetary authorities are assumed to fix the domestic money supply rather than the domestic interest rate.

the supply shock because relying on cost deflation to restore full employment forces the economy to suffer an extended slump.

Monetary accommodation can return the economy to full employment relatively quickly, but at the cost of a once-for-all increase in the price level.

REPEATED SUPPLY SHOCKS

As an example of a repeated supply shock, assume that powerful unions are able to raise money wages faster than productivity is increasing, even in the face of a significant excess supply of labour. Firms then pass these higher wages on in the form of higher prices. This type of supply shock causes what is called a **wage-cost push inflation**—an increase in the price level due to increases in money wages that are not associated with an excess demand for labour.

No monetary accommodation   Suppose the central bank does not accommodate these supply shocks. The initial effect of the leftward shift in the SRAS curve is to open up a recessionary gap, as shown in Figure 40.2. If unions continue to negotiate increases in wages, subjecting the economy to further supply shocks, prices continue to rise while output and employment continue to fall. Eventually, the trade-off between higher wages and unemployment will become obvious to everyone. Long before everyone is unemployed, unions will cease forcing up wages in order to maintain jobs for those who are still employed.

Once the wage-cost push ceases, there are two possibilities. First, the unions may succeed in holding on to their high real wages, but not push for further increases of money wages in excess of productivity increases. The economy will then come to rest with a stable price level and a large recessionary gap. Second, the persistent unemployment may eventually erode the power of the unions, so that real wages and hence unit costs begin to fall, because money wages rise more slowly than productivity is rising. In this case, the supply shock is reversed, and the SRAS curve will shift downward until full employment is eventually restored.

Non-accommodated wage-cost push tends to be self-limiting because the rising unemployment that it causes tends to restrain further wage increases.

Monetary accommodation   Now suppose that the central bank accommodates the shock with an increase in the money supply, thus shifting the AD curve to the right, as shown in Figure 40.3. In the new full-employment equilibrium, where national income is at its potential level, both money wages and prices have risen. The rise in wages has been offset by a rise in prices. Workers are no better off than they were originally, although those who remained in jobs were temporarily better off in the transition period when wages had risen (taking equilibrium to E_1 in Figure 40.2) but before the price level had risen enough to restore full employment (taking equilibrium to E_2).

The stage is now set for the unions to try again. If they succeed in negotiating further increases in money wages, they hit the economy with another supply shock. If the central bank again accommodates the shock, full employment is maintained, but at the cost of a further round of inflation. If this process goes on repeatedly, it can give rise to a continual wage-cost push inflation as shown in Figure 40.3. The wage-cost push tends to cause a stagflation, with rising prices and falling output. Monetary accommodation tends to reinforce the rise in prices and to offset the fall in output. It will also be associated with repeated currency depreciation.

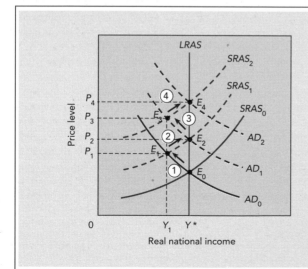

Figure 40.3   Monetary accommodation of a repeated supply shock

Monetary accommodation of a repeated supply shock causes a continuous inflation in the absence of excess demand. The initial equilibrium is at E_0. A supply shock then takes equilibrium to E_1, just as in Figure 40.2. This is the stagflation phase of rising prices and falling output; it is indicated by arrow 1. If the central bank then accommodates the supply shock by increasing the money supply, the AD curve shifts to AD_1, taking equilibrium to E_2. This is the expansionary phase of rising prices and rising output (arrow 2). A second supply shock takes equilibrium to E_3 (arrow 3), and a second round of monetary accommodation takes it to E_4 (arrow 4). As long as the supply shocks and the monetary accommodation continue, the inflation continues.

There are two requirements for continuing wage-cost push inflation. First, powerful groups, such as industrial unions or government employees, must press for, and employers must grant, increases in money wages in excess of productivity growth, even in the absence of excess demand for labour and goods. Second, the central bank must accommodate the resulting inflation by increasing the money supply, in order to prevent the rising unemployment that would otherwise occur. The process set up by this sequence of wage-cost push and monetary accommodation is often called a *wage–price spiral*.

Is monetary accommodation desirable? Once started, a wage–price spiral can be halted only if the central bank stops accommodating the supply shocks that are causing the inflation. The longer it waits to do so, the more entrenched will become the expectations of continuing inflation. These entrenched expectations may cause wages to continue to rise after accommodation has ceased. Because employers expect prices to rise, they go on granting wage increases. If expectations are firmly enough entrenched, the wage push can continue for quite some time, in spite of the downward pressure caused by the rising unemployment associated with the growing recessionary gap.

Because of this possibility, some economists argue that the process should not be allowed to begin. One way to ensure this is to refuse to accommodate any supply shock whatsoever.[2]

Some people fear that accommodating any supply shocks risks setting off a wage–price spiral. Others are willing to risk accommodating isolated shocks, in order to avoid the recessions that otherwise accompany them.

This may not seem like a big issue in the 1990s, but it certainly was important in the 1970s, and may recur in the future. Notice also that wage shocks are not the only type of possible supply shock. The energy price rises of 1973 and 1979 (oil shocks) were very important, and their effects can be analysed just as above. Equally, a price rise in any imported materials would have a similar effect. Exchange rate depreciations contribute to input price shocks because the price of imported materials rises; but exchange rate changes have demand dimensions as well (as they shift the net export function), and they are exogenous only in a fixed exchange rate regime.

Demand shocks

Now suppose that an initial equilibrium is disturbed by a rightward shift in the aggregate demand curve, a shift that could have been caused by either an increase in some category of autonomous expenditure or an increase in the money supply. This causes the price level and output to rise. If the central bank reacts to an increase in autonomous expenditure by increasing the money supply, it is said to be validating the shock. (Notice that this terminology distinguishes between the central bank's response to a supply shock, which is described as *accommodating* the shock, and its response to a demand shock, which is described as *validating* the shock.)

No monetary validation This is the standard case of a once-for-all increase in aggregate demand, such as shown in Figure 36.12 on page 712. Because the initial *AD* shock takes output above the full-employment level, an inflationary gap opens up. The pressure of excess demand soon causes wages to rise faster than productivity, shifting the *SRAS* curve upwards. As long as the central bank holds the money supply constant, the rise in the price level moves the economy upwards along its fixed *AD* curve. The rise in the price level thus eventually eliminates the inflationary gap. In this case, the initial period of inflation is followed by further inflation which continues until the new long-run equilibrium is reached. Full-employment national income and a stable price level are then restored.

The monetary adjustment mechanism We have just described a process whereby demand inflation is halted because the *SRAS* curve shifted upwards along a fixed, negatively sloped *AD* curve, removing the inflationary gap. This is an important process. It is one whose operation is often misunderstood, and therefore it is worth going through again.

The basis of the proposition that the rise in the price level removes the inflationary gap is the negative slope of the *AD* curve. This, we saw in Chapter 36, is due to the monetary transmission mechanism, which links the real and the monetary parts of the economy. Let us recall how it works. (We concentrate here on the adjustment process, which is internal to the economy, and neglect the complications of exchange rate adjustment and capital flows discussed in Chapter 39. The analysis here applies easily to cases with floating exchange rates where the shock is monetary in origin.)

As the price level rises, more money is needed for transactions and precautionary purposes. (Real money supply falls.) The attempt to obtain money balances by selling bonds bids up the interest rate. This reduces interest-sensitive expenditures, and so reduces equilibrium national income. The process continues until national income is restored to its potential level, which means that the inflationary gap is removed.

The monetary sector is important in this process. The rise in the price level creates an increased demand for

---

[2] One of the main arguments in favour of a fixed exchange rate is that it gives a strong signal in advance that the monetary authorities *cannot* accommodate any domestic inflation shocks.

money. If this demand is not satisfied by the creation of new money, the shortage of money will eventually end the inflation. What happens is that the rise in the price level pushes up the interest rate and crowds out enough expenditure (especially investment and net exports) to remove the excess demand.

This mechanism is sometimes called the *monetary adjustment mechanism*. It is really just an aspect of the monetary transmission mechanism. But since this aspect is so important, there is no harm in giving it a name of its own as long as it is not thought to be some new force, different from the transmission mechanism.

A sufficiently large rise in the price level will eliminate any inflationary gap, provided the nominal money supply remains constant.

Monetary validation   Next, suppose that, once the initial demand shock has created an inflationary gap, the central bank frustrates the monetary adjustment mechanism by increasing the nominal money supply when output starts to fall. This is the case illustrated in Figure 40.4. Two forces are now brought into play. Spurred by the inflationary gap, the wage increases cause the SRAS curve to shift to the left. Fuelled by the expansionary monetary policy, the AD curve shifts to the right. As a result of both of these shifts, the price level rises, but if the shift in the AD curve offsets the shift in the SRAS curve, the inflationary gap does not diminish. The validation of an isolated demand shock thus creates a series of repeated demand shocks that permit the inflation to continue.

Validation of a demand shock turns what would have been a transitory inflation into a sustained inflation fuelled by monetary expansion.

We can now see two reasons why a rise in the price level may not remove an inflationary gap. First, the central bank may choose, as a matter of policy, to validate the inflation by increasing the nominal money supply at the same rate as prices are rising, thus holding the real money supply constant. Second, the central bank might have insufficient control over the money supply. If the money supply expands endogenously to meet any demand for it (perhaps, because the central bank is pegging interest rates and does not pick up the warnings of impending inflation), there is no monetary adjustment mechanism to eliminate the inflationary gap. As the price level rises, the nominal money supply rises sufficiently to keep the real money supply constant, and the inflationary gap is not reduced.

Although there is controversy over how much control the central bank can have over the money supply, few economists doubt that a determined enough anti-inflationary policy can stop the nominal money supply from expanding as fast as prices are rising. Most central banks have done so

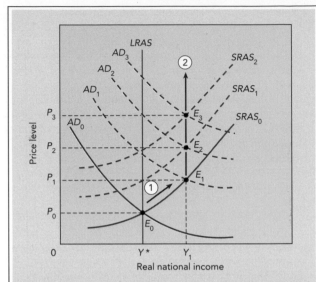

Figure 40.4 A validated demand-shock inflation

Monetary validation will cause the AD curve to shift, offsetting the leftward shift in the SRAS curve, and maintaining an inflationary gap in spite of the ever-rising price level. An initial demand shock shifts equilibrium from E_0 to E_1 (along the path indicated by arrow 1), taking income to Y_1 and the price level to P_1. The resulting inflationary gap then causes the SRAS curve to shift to the left. This time, however, the money supply is increased, shifting the AD curve to the right. By the time the aggregate supply curve has reached $SRAS_1$, the aggregate demand curve has reached AD_2, taking equilibrium to E_2. Income remains constant at Y_1, while the price level rises to P_2.

The persistent inflationary gap continues to push the SRAS curve to the left, while the continued monetary validation continues to push the AD curve to the right. By the time the aggregate supply reaches $SRAS_2$, the aggregate demand has reached AD_3. The price level has risen still further to P_3, but, because of the frustration of the monetary adjustment mechanism, the inflationary gap remains unchanged at $Y_1–Y^*$. As long as this monetary validation continues, the economy moves along the vertical path of arrow 2.

at one time or another over the past few decades, thereby ending an inflation in their own country.[3] Thus, in the world in which we live, inflations cannot go on indefinitely unless they are validated by policy decisions taken by the central bank.

Figure 40.5 summarizes all the cases of supply and demand shock with or without accommodation or validation.

[3] The UK authorities tightened monetary policy sharply in late 1988, as a result of the surge in inflation shown in Figure 40.1. This brought inflation down from around 10 per cent to about 2 per cent. But it took time—it was 1993 before the resulting recession began to end.

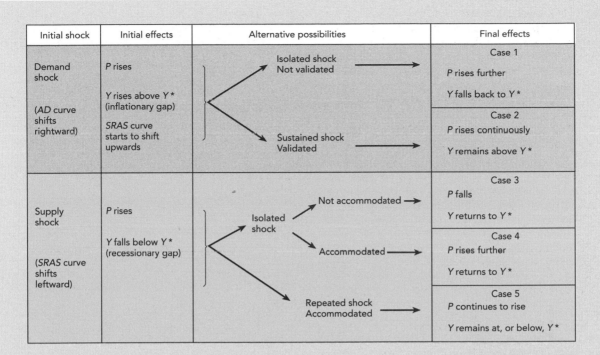

Figure 40.5   The effects of inflationary shocks

Demand and supply shocks have different final effects, depending on whether or not they are isolated or sustained and are validated or accommodated. This figure summarizes the analysis of each of the five cases given in the text. It should be referred to after reading the text discussion of each of the cases. All comparisons assume that national income starts at its potential level and that initially the price level is stable.

The initial effects of a demand shock are to raise national income and the price level. If the shock is isolated, the price level continues to rise until national income falls back to its potential level (case 1). If the shock is sustained and validated (validation turns an isolated shock into a sustained shock), the price level continues to rise while national income stays above its potential level (case 2).

The initial effects of a supply shock are to raise the price level but to reduce national income. Once the shock is over, national income will return to its potential level, with a lowered price level, if there is no accommodation (case 3), and with a higher price level if there is accommodation (case 4). If the shock is sustained and accommodated, the price level can continue to rise, with or without a persistent recessionary gap (case 5).

INFLATION AS A MONETARY PHENOMENON

Economists have debated the extent to which inflation is a monetary phenomenon. Does it have purely monetary causes—increases in the supply of money? Does it have purely monetary consequences—only the price level is affected? One slogan stating an extreme position on this issue was made popular by the US economist Milton Friedman: 'Inflation is *everywhere* and *always* a monetary phenomenon.' This could be a mere tautology, since inflation is by definition a fall in the purchasing power of money. However, avoiding semantics, let us summarize what we have already learned about the *causes* of inflation.

1. Many forces can cause the price level to rise. On the demand side, anything that shifts the *AD* curve to the right will have this result—*ceteris paribus*, increases in desired expenditure on exports, government, investment and consumption, as well as increases in the money supply or decreases in money demand. On the supply side, anything that increases unit costs of production will shift the *SRAS* curve to the left and cause the price level to rise.

2. Such inflations can continue for some time without any increases in the money supply.

BOX 40.1

Hyperinflation

Monetary validation of ongoing inflation sometimes gets out of hand. In extreme cases it leads to hyperinflation, in which inflation is so rapid that money ceases to be useful as a medium of exchange and a store of value. Inflation rates of 50, 100, and even 200 per cent or more per year have occurred year after year in some countries, and have proven to be manageable as people adjust their contracts in real terms. Although there are strains and side-effects, the evidence shows such situations to be possible without causing money to become useless.

Does this mean that there is no reason to fear that rapid inflation will turn into a hyperinflation that will destroy the value of money completely? The historical record is not entirely reassuring. There have been a number of cases in which prices began to rise at an ever-accelerating rate until a nation's money ceased to be a satisfactory store of value, even for the short period between receipt and expenditure, and hence ceased also to be useful as a medium of exchange.

The index of wholesale prices in Germany during and after the First World War is given in the table. The index shows that a product purchased with one 100-mark note in July 1923 would have required *10 million* 100-mark notes for its purchase only four months later! Although Germany had experienced substantial inflation during the war, averaging more than 30 per cent per year, the immediate post-war years of 1920 and 1921 gave no sign of an explosive inflation; indeed, during 1920 price stability was experienced. In 1922 and 1923, however, the price level exploded. On 15 November 1923, the mark was officially repudiated, its value wholly destroyed. How could this happen?

When an inflation becomes so rapid that people lose confidence in the purchasing power of their currency, they rush to spend it. People who have goods become increasingly reluctant to accept the rapidly depreciating money in exchange. The rush to spend money accelerates the increase in prices until people finally become unwilling to accept money on any terms. What was once money ceases to be money.

The price system can then be restored only by repudiation of the old monetary unit and its replacement by a new unit. This destroys the value of monetary savings and of all contracts specified in terms of the old monetary unit.

There are about a dozen documented hyperinflations in world history, among them the collapse of the continental† during the American War of Independence; the rouble during the Russian Revolution; the drachma during and after the German occupation of Greece in the Second World War; the pengo in Hungary during 1945–6; and the Chinese national currency during 1946–8. Every one of these hyperinflations was accompanied by great increases in the money supply; new money was printed to give governments the purchasing power that they could not or would not obtain by taxation. Further, every one occurred in the midst of a major political upheaval in which grave doubts existed about the stability and the future of the government itself.

Date	German wholesale price index (1913=1)
January 1913	1
January 1920	13
January 1921	14
January 1922	37
July 1922	101
January 1923	2,785
July 1923	74,800
August 1923	944,000
September 1923	23,900,000
October 1923	7,096,000,000
November 1923*	750,000,000,000

* The mark was repudiated on 15 November 1923 in a currency reform.

Is hyperinflation likely in the absence of civil war, revolution, or collapse of the government? Most economists think not. Further, it is clear that high inflation rates over a period of time do not mean the inevitable or even likely onset of hyperinflation.

However, do not assume that hyperinflation is a curiosity only to be found in the history books. The following is an extract from a newspaper report on events in Serbia in 1993 and 1994:

Worried that Serbian cities might starve during the winter, the government announced [in July 1993] that it would buy a million tons of the wheat harvest from private farmers at guaranteed prices. . . . The entire country, now highly attuned to living with an unstable currency, realised what this would mean. The government could only pay by printing a lot more money, which the peasants would switch into marks the moment they were paid. It would, in short, kill the currency.

Sure enough, three times during July, the dinar/mark exchange rate lurched downwards. Then it spun out of control.

The exponential growth of inflation during these months still astonishes even the Yugoslav economists who had seen it coming. Between July and the end of the year it went from 500 per cent to 2,000 per cent a month, to 20,000 per cent, then 500,000 per cent and onwards. By January, prices were rising faster than 100 per cent an hour.

At the final assessment before the recovery plan was put into effect on January 24th [1994], the monthly inflation rate had reached a mind-blowing 302 million per cent. Compare that with the inflation rate in Germany, which at its height in 1923 reached only 332 per cent per month, while inflation in Latin American countries during the 1980s never went beyond 300 per cent per year.

Independent on Sunday, 9 October 1994, p. 9.

† This is the name given to the notes issued by the American Continental Congress at that time.

3. The rise in prices must eventually come to a halt, unless monetary expansion occurs.

Points 1 and 2 indicate that a *temporary* burst of inflation may or may not be a monetary phenomenon; it need not have monetary causes, and it need not be accompanied by monetary expansion. Point 3 implies that a *sustained* inflation must be a monetary phenomenon; if a rise in prices is to continue, it must be accompanied by continuing increases in the money supply (or decreases in money demand). This is true regardless of the cause that set the rise in prices in motion. What happens when monetary validation gets out of hand is discussed in Box 40.1.

Now let us summarize what we have learned about the *consequences* of an inflation, assuming that the economy begins from a situation of full employment and a stable price level.

1. In the short run, a demand-shock inflation tends to be accompanied by an increase in national income.
2. In the short run, a supply-shock inflation tends to be accompanied by a decrease in national income.
3. When all adjustments have been fully made (so that the relevant supply-side curve is the *LRAS* curve), shifts in either the *AD* or *SRAS* curves leave national income unchanged and affect only the price level.

Points 1 and 2 are saying that inflation is not, in the short run, a purely monetary phenomenon; it has real consequences for output and employment. Point 3 states that, from the point of view of long-run equilibrium, inflation is a purely monetary phenomenon.

We have now established three important conclusions.

1. Without monetary accommodation, supply shocks cause temporary bursts of inflation accompanied by recessionary gaps. The gaps are removed if, and when, unit costs of production fall, restoring equilibrium at potential income and at the initial price level.
2. Without monetary validation, demand shocks cause temporary bursts of inflation accompanied by inflationary gaps. The gaps are removed as wages rise, returning income to its potential level, but at a higher price level.
3. With an appropriate response from the central bank, an inflation initiated by either supply or demand shocks can continue indefinitely; an ever-increasing money supply is necessary for an ever-continuing inflation.

The Phillips curve, or how fast does the *SRAS* curve shift?

UP to now, it has been enough to say that an inflationary gap implies excess demand for labour, low unemployment, pressure on wages to rise faster than productivity, and, hence, an upward-shifting *SRAS* curve. But now we need to look in more detail at the influence of wages on inflation. To do this, we make use of a famous relation called the Phillips curve, which we first present in its original form and then transform into a form more applicable to the *AD–AS* model. Since the original curve uses *unemployment* rather than *national income* as its indicator of excess demand in labour markets, we must first show the relation between the two.

The NAIRU We saw in Chapter 27 that, when current national income is at its potential level, unemployment is not zero, even though we refer to this situation as 'full employment'. Instead, there may be a substantial amount of frictional unemployment, caused by the movement of people among jobs, and structural unemployment, caused by a mismatch between the characteristics of the demand for labour and the characteristics of its supply. The amount of frictional and structural unemployment that exists when national income is at its potential level is called the **NAIRU** or the **natural rate of unemployment** (U^*).[4] We use the term NAIRU rather than natural rate because the latter term may create the erroneous impression that nothing can be done to reduce unemployment below a rate that is 'natural'.

It follows from the definition of the NAIRU that, when national income exceeds potential income ($Y > Y^*$), unemployment will be less than the NAIRU ($U < U^*$). When national income is less than potential income ($Y < Y^*$), unemployment will exceed the NAIRU ($U > U^*$).

[4] 'NAIRU' is an acronym for *non-accelerating-inflation rate of unemployment*. The reason for this name will become apparent later in the chapter. We talk about the natural rate of unemployment and the NAIRU as if they were the same concept. For most purposes they are. However, some economists would reserve the former term for equilibrium in a *perfectly competitive* economy, whereas the NAIRU can also apply under imperfect competition. On this interpretation, the natural rate is a special case of the NAIRU.

We can now use the NAIRU terminology to restate our earlier assumptions about the pressure that is put on wage rates, and through them on the *SRAS* curve, by inflationary and recessionary gaps.

When the unemployment rate is below the NAIRU, demand forces put pressure on wages to rise faster than productivity. When the unemployment rate is above the NAIRU, demand forces put pressure on wages to rise more slowly than productivity, or even to fall. When unemployment is at the NAIRU, demand forces exert neither upward nor downward pressure on wages relative to productivity.

The theory of the Phillips curve

In the 1950s, the late Professor A. W. Phillips (1914–75) was doing research on stabilization policy at the London School of Economics. He was interested in the question of the speed with which input prices responded to excess demand and excess supply. To study this question, he looked at the rate of change of money-wage rates in the United Kingdom over a period of 100 years. By relating these wage changes to the level of unemployment, he discovered a remarkable relationship which came to be known as the Phillips curve. This was an empirical relationship which later theoretical work tried to explain. We shall incorporate the key elements of Phillips curve theory into the context of our macro model.

The **Phillips curve** relates the percentage rate of change of money-wage rates (measured at an annual rate) to the level of unemployment (measured as the percentage of the labour force unemployed). Unemployment is plotted on the horizontal axis, and wage changes on the vertical axis. Thus, any point on the curve relates a particular level of unemployment to a particular rate of increase of money wages.

So far in this book we have dealt with the levels of variables. The Phillips curve relates the amount of unemployment to the *rate of change* of money wages. Letting ΔW stand for the change in money-wage rates from one year to the next, and W for the level of wage rates in the first year, the equation of the Phillips curve is:

$$(\Delta W/W)100 = f(U), \qquad (1)$$

where 'f' stands for a functional relation. Hereafter we denote $(\Delta W/W)100$ by the symbol $\dot{W}$, which is a commonly used symbol for the percentage rate of change of a variable.

A numerical example of a Phillips curve is shown in Figure 40.6. The numbers on the figure are hypothetical. The original curve became negative at high rates of unem-

ployment. We shall see that, appropriately interpreted, the Phillips curve can handle all of the causes of inflation. For the moment, we shall concentrate on the influence of demand forces.

THE SHAPE OF THE PHILLIPS CURVE

A negative slope Note first that the Phillips curve has a negative slope, showing that, the lower is the level of unemployment, the higher is the rate of change of money wages. This should not surprise us. Low rates of unemployment are associated with boom conditions, when excess demand for labour will be causing money wages to rise rapidly. High rates of unemployment, on the other hand, are associated with slump conditions, when the slack demand for labour will lead to low increases in money wages, or possibly even to decreases.

A flattening slope Moving along the Phillips curve from left to right, the curve gets flatter. This shape is another way of showing the asymmetry of aggregate supply, namely that input prices change more rapidly upwards than downwards. Let us recall why.

First, assume that a growing boom is increasing the excess demand for labour. As the boom develops, the unemployment rate will decrease towards, but will never reach, zero. (There will always be *some* frictional and structural unemployment.) At the same time, the growing excess demand for labour will be bidding up wage rates more and more rapidly. This behaviour causes the Phillips curve to get very steep and to lie far above the horizontal axis at its left-hand end. The further the curve is above the axis, the faster wages are rising.

The steepness of the curve in the range of low unemployment shows that wage inflation is very responsive to changes in unemployment in that range.

Second, consider a growing recession that raises unemployment. This recession restrains wage increases. As a result, the Phillips curve comes closer and closer to the horizontal axis, indicating less and less upward pressure on wages the higher the level of unemployment. If the curve fell below the axis, then money wages would actually be falling over some range of high unemployment. We do not show this case in the figure but instead assume that, as unemployment gets very high, the rate of increase in money wages approaches zero but never becomes negative.

The flatness of the Phillips curve in the range of high unemployment shows that the rate of wage inflation is relatively unresponsive to changes in unemployment over that range.

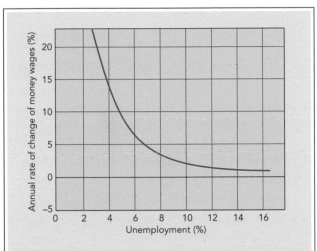

Figure 40.6 A Phillips curve

The Phillips curve relates the level of unemployment to the rate of change of money wage rates. The figure shows a numerical example of a Phillips curve. According to the example, an increase in unemployment by four percentage points, from 8 to 12 per cent, will lower wage inflation from 3 to 2 per cent, while a reduction in unemployment by four percentage points, from 8 to 4 per cent, will raise wage inflation from 3 to 14 per cent.

The Phillips curve and the *SRAS* curve

To see what is happening to unit costs of production, we need to relate the increase in wage rates to the increase in labour productivity. For simplicity in the rest of the discussion, we will assume that labour is the only variable factor used by firms. This allows us to associate the labour costs of each unit of output with total variable costs per unit of output. (We could equally well have assumed that all input prices change at the same rate as does the price of labour.)

What happens to unit costs of production now depends only on the *differences* between what labour costs the firm and what labour produces for the firm. To illustrate what is involved, we repeat in part (i) of Figure 40.7 the Phillips curve from Figure 40.6. We then add to it a horizontal line labelled g, for growth in output per unit of labour input, which shows the rate at which labour productivity is growing year by year. In the hypothetical example of the figure, we have assumed that productivity is rising at 3 per cent per year. The intersection of the Phillips curve and the productivity line at the point x now divides the graph into an inflationary and a deflationary range described in the numbered points below. Given the assumptions about wage behaviour made earlier, point x must occur at the NAIRU (labelled U^*)—which corresponds to a level of output equal to potential national income, Y^*.

1. At unemployment rates less than at the intersection point, wages are rising faster than productivity and, thus, unit costs of production (input costs per unit of output) are rising. If unit costs are rising, the *SRAS* curve must be shifting upwards.

2. At unemployment rates greater than at the intersection point, money-wage rates are rising more slowly than productivity is rising. Thus, unit costs are *falling*. If unit costs are falling, the *SRAS* curve must be shifting downwards.

Notice that, although we have drawn the Phillips curve to show complete downward inflexibility of money wages, this does not imply complete downward inflexibility of *unit costs*. As long as money wages rise less than productivity rises, unit costs of production will be falling, and the *SRAS* curve will be shifting downwards. Complete downward inflexibility of unit costs—and thus the total absence of the equilibrating mechanism that comes from downward shifts in the *SRAS* curve—requires more than the downward inflexibility of money wages: it requires that money wages never rise by *less than* the increase in productivity.

We shall now derive from the Phillips curve a new curve that expresses the verbal argument just given.

Part (ii) of Figure 40.7 shows a new curve, which relates the rate of unemployment to the change in unit costs, rather than to the change in money-wage rates. The new curve still measures unemployment on the horizontal axis, but now it measures the rate of increase in unit costs on the horizontal axis. Since this is merely the rate of increase in money-wage rates *minus* the rate of increase of productivity, the new diagram is the same as part (i) of the figure, except that the origin on the vertical axis has been shifted by the rate of productivity growth.

The new curve tells us the rate at which unit costs of production are changing—and thus the rate at which the *SRAS* curve is shifting upwards or downwards—at each level of unemployment.

So far, we have followed Phillips in plotting unemployment on the horizontal axis. The *SRAS* curve, however, plots national income on its horizontal axis. To get a curve that relates the change in unit costs of production to the level of national income, we recall that unemployment is negatively related to the level of national income. As national income rises, unemployment tends to fall.

To make the relation precise, we assume that the labour force remains constant. Now any short-run increase in national income, which means that more labour is employed, must mean that less labour is *un*employed. In this case, any *increase* in national income must mean a *decrease* in unemployment.

We can now transform the curve in part (ii) of Figure 40.7, which plots changes in unit costs of production against the *unemployment rate*, into a new relation, shown in part (iii) of the figure. This curve shows the same rate of

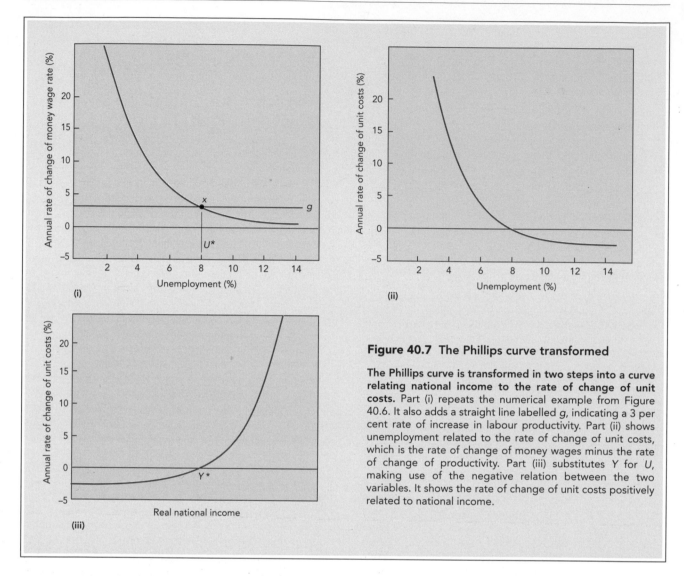

Figure 40.7 The Phillips curve transformed

The Phillips curve is transformed in two steps into a curve relating national income to the rate of change of unit costs. Part (i) repeats the numerical example from Figure 40.6. It also adds a straight line labelled *g*, indicating a 3 per cent rate of increase in labour productivity. Part (ii) shows unemployment related to the rate of change of unit costs, which is the rate of change of money wages minus the rate of change of productivity. Part (iii) substitutes *Y* for *U*, making use of the negative relation between the two variables. It shows the rate of change of unit costs positively related to national income.

change in unit costs of production, but plots it against the level of national income. Since national income and unemployment vary negatively with each other, the curve in part (iii) of the figure has the opposite slope to the curve in part (ii) of the same figure.[5] We call this new curve the *transformed Phillips curve*. (Notice that, to emphasize that we are dealing with rates of change, we place a dot over the variable to indicate its annual percentage rate of change—in this case the symbol is *ċ*.)

SHIFTS IN THE *SRAS* CURVE EXPLAINED

Figure 40.8 (i) shows the familiar aggregate demand/aggregate supply diagram. Part (ii) shows the transformed Phillips curve (*PC*), relating the rate of change of unit costs to national income. Both parts have national income on their horizontal axes, and by lining these up we can com-

pare one with the other. The *AD* and *SRAS* curves in part (i) determine the short-run levels of prices and national income. Given the national income so determined, the transformed Phillips curve tells us the rate at which the *SRAS* curve is shifting. Since from now on we will always be working with this transformed curve, we will just call it a Phillips curve.

The long-run equilibrium of the economy is at potential income. All that the curve in part (ii) tells us is how fast the *SRAS* curve in part (i) is shifting, moving the economy towards its long-run equilibrium. The steepness of the

---

[5] We have started with the relation $\Delta W/W = f(U)$, which is the original Phillips curve. We then subtracted productivity growth, *g*, to get a unit-cost-increase curve: $\Delta c/c = f(U) - g$. Then we substituted a relation between unemployment and national income, $U = u(Y)$, to get a curve relating the rate of increase in unit costs to the level of unemployment: $\Delta c/c = f(u(Y))$.

curve for Y greater than Y^* (i.e. above equilibrium) shows the rapid adjustment towards equilibrium after a single expansionary shock. The flatness of the curve below equilibrium shows the slowness of adjustment towards equilibrium after a single contractionary shock.

The nonlinearity of the transformed Phillips curve expresses the asymmetry of aggregate supply: that costs, and hence prices, rise rapidly in the face of an inflationary gap, but fall only slowly in the face of a recessionary gap.

THE MICRO UNDERPINNINGS OF THE ASYMMETRY

The micro behaviour that lies behind the flat part of the Phillips curve to the left of Y^* is explained in two parts. The first concerns the theory of short-run oligopoly pricing described in Chapter 14—firms absorb cyclical demand fluctuations by varying their outputs rather than their prices. The second concerns the theory that money wage rates do not fall rapidly in the face of an excess supply of labour, although they can rise rapidly in the face of excess demand for labour. This issue of wage inflexibility is central to the modern new Keynesian attempts to understand labour markets, and will be discussed in Chapter 41.

The overall microeconomics of wage behaviour is thought to be as follows. When demand falls, firms reduce their outputs and their demands for labour, holding their mark-ups approximately constant. The unemployment does not force money wage rates down significantly, so firms' unit costs, and hence their prices, fall no faster than productivity is rising. There will also be some downward pressure on money wages (particularly in non-unionized markets) and on prices in more competitive markets, and the result will be a slow downward drift of the price level. When demand rises above potential income, firms try to expand output by hiring more labour, and the labour shortages that develop cause wages to rise. As costs rise, firms pass these on in higher prices. This is a *continuing process*, which goes on as long as excess demand holds income above its full-employment level.

Expectational forces

We must now consider influences on costs and prices other than demand. A second force that can influence wage costs is *expectations*. Suppose, for example, that both employers and employees expect a 4 per cent inflation next year. Unions will start negotiations from a base of a 4 per cent increase in money wages, which would hold their real wages constant. Firms also may be inclined to begin bargaining by conceding at least a 4 per cent increase in money wages, since they expect that the prices at which they sell their products will rise by 4 per cent. *Starting from that base,*

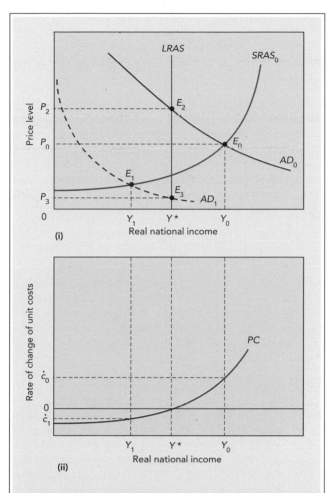

Figure 40.8 The Phillips curve and the AS–AD relation

The transformed Phillips curve shows the speed with which the SRAS curve is shifting upwards. When the curves are AD_0 and $SRAS_0$ in part (i), they intersect at E_0 to produce equilibrium national income of Y_0. Part (ii) shows that when income is Y_0, unit costs, and hence the rate of increase in the SRAS curve, is $\dot{c}_0$ per cent per year. Thus, equilibrium national income is moving rapidly towards Y^* as the point of macroeconomic equilibrium moves up the fixed AD curve towards the long-run equilibrium at E_2. When the curves are AD_1 and $SRAS_0$ in part (i), equilibrium is at E_1, with income Y_1. Part (ii) shows that when income is Y_1, unit costs, and hence the SRAS curve, will be shifting downwards at the rate of $\dot{c}_1$ per cent per year. Thus, equilibrium national income is moving slowly along AD_1 towards a long-run equilibrium at E_3. Each long-run equilibrium has the same level of national income, but a different price level.

unions will attempt to obtain some desired increase in their real wages. At this point, such factors as profits, productivity, and bargaining power become important.

The general expectation of an x per cent inflation creates pressures for wages to rise by x per cent more than productivity, and hence for the *SRAS* curve to shift upwards by x per cent.

The key point is that the *SRAS* curve can be shifting upwards even if there is no inflationary gap. As long as people *expect* prices to rise, their behaviour will push money wages and unit costs up. This brings about the rise in prices that was expected. This is another example of the phenomenon of self-realizing expectations—if everyone thinks that event x is going to occur, their actions in anticipation of x may make x occur.

EXPECTATIONS FORMATION

We have already discussed expectations in Chapter 37, in the context of exchange rate determination. Expectations are also important in investment behaviour, since firms invest in the expectation of increasing future profits. Here we consider the importance of expectations in the context of the Phillips Curve.

Backward-looking theories   Keynesian theories of expectations assume that expectations are slow to change. The theory of **extrapolative expectations** says that expectations depend on extrapolations of past behaviour and respond only slowly to what is currently happening to costs. In one simple form of the theory, the expected future inflation rate is merely a moving average of past actual rates. The rationale is that, unless a deviation from past trends persists, firms and workers will dismiss the deviation as transitory. They do not let it influence their wage- and price-setting behaviour.

The theory of **adaptive expectations** states that the expectation of future inflation rates adjusts to the error in predicting the current rate. Thus, if you thought the current rate was going to be 6 per cent and it turned out to be 10 per cent, you might revise your estimate of the next period's inflation rate upwards by, say, half of your error, making the new expectation 8 per cent.

These two theories make expectations about future inflation depend on past actual rates. In an obvious sense, such expectations are backward-looking, since the expectation can be calculated using data on what has happened already.

Forward-looking theories   **Rational expectations** are forward-looking. The rational expectations hypothesis assumes that people do not continue to make persistent, systematic errors in forming their expectations. Thus, if the economic system about which they are forming expectations remains stable, their expectations will be correct *on average*. Any individual's expectations at any time about

next year's price level can thus be thought of as the actual price level that will occur next year, plus a random error term which has a mean of zero.

Rational expectations have the effect of speeding up the adjustment of expectations. Instead of being based on past inflation rates, expected inflation is based on an informed forecast of the outcome of existing (and expected) policies.

Backward-looking expectations are overly naïve. People do look ahead to the future and assess future possibilities rather than just blindly reacting to what has gone before. Yet the assumption of unbiased forward-looking expectations requires that workers and firms have a degree of understanding of inflation forecasting that few economists would claim to have. It is possible that, in reality, wage-setting is a mixture of rational, forward-looking behaviour and expectations based on the experience of the recent past. Depending on the circumstances, expectations will sometimes tend to rely more on past experience, and at other times to rely more on present events whose effects are expected to influence the future.

Of course, people will not make the error of consistently underpredicting (or overpredicting) the inflation rate for decades, but it can happen for several years, whenever people do not fully understand the causes of current inflation. Every past period of inflation has led to intense debate among economists about its causes, cures, and probable future course. If professionals are uncertain, it would be surprising if wage- and price-setters got these matters right on average. None the less, economists can use assumptions such as rational expectations in their models and then test the predictions to see if they are consistent with the data.

Random shocks

Wage changes are also affected by forces other than excess demand and expectations of inflation. These forces can be positive, pushing wages higher than they otherwise would go, or negative, pushing wages lower than they otherwise would go. One such shock occurs when an exceptionally strong union, or an exceptionally weak management, comes to the bargaining table and produces a wage increase that is a percentage point or two higher than would have occurred under more typical bargaining conditions.

One simple theory assumes that there are many sources of shock, and that they are independent of one another. This means that, overall, they exert a random influence on wages—sometimes speeding wage changes up a bit, sometimes slowing them down a bit, but having a net effect that more or less cancels out when taken over several years. Over the long term, they may be regarded as random events and are referred to as *random shocks*.

Random shocks may have a large positive or negative

effect in any one year. Over the period of a sustained infla-tion, however, positive shocks in some years will tend to be offset by negative shocks in other years so that, overall, they contribute little to the long-term trend of the price level.

The overall effect on wages

The overall change in wage costs is a result of the three basic forces just studied. We may express this as follows:

$$\begin{array}{c}\text{Percentage}\\\text{increase}\\\text{in unit}\\\text{wage costs}\end{array} = \begin{array}{c}\text{demand}\\\text{effect}\end{array} + \begin{array}{c}\text{expectational}\\\text{effect}\end{array} + \begin{array}{c}\text{shock}\\\text{effect}\end{array} . \quad (2)$$

The expectations-augmented Phillips curve

We can now add the forces of expectations and random shocks to the Phillips curve determining the behaviour of unit labour costs. The Phillips curve in Figure 40.7 shows the effects only of demand pressures. It will predict actual inflation only if the expected inflation rate is zero and there are no random shocks.

The relation shown in (2) above defines a whole set of Phillips curves. Each curve is drawn for zero shocks and a given expected rate of inflation, which enters as an additive constant. At Y^* there are no demand pressures on wages, so the height of the Phillips curve above the axis at that point is determined by the expected rate of inflation. The whole Phillips curve then shows how much the rate of change of unit costs varies from the expected inflation rate as a result of excess demand or excess supply in the labour market. Any particular Phillips curve drawn for a given expected rate of inflation is called a **short-run Phillips curve** (*SRPC*) or an **expectations-augmented Phillips curve**.

Figure 40.9 gives an example of one short-run curve, and uses it to illustrate the relations shown in equation (2). It shows unit costs rising as a result of increases in wage costs brought about by demand pressures (shown by the Phillips curve), expectations of inflation (which determine the

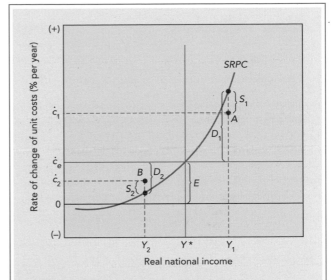

Figure 40.9 The components of cost inflation illustrated

The rate of cost inflation can be separated into three components: expectational inflation, demand inflation, and shock inflation. The Phillips curve is drawn for a given expected rate of inflation and hence is labelled a short-run Phillips curve. The given expected inflation rate, $\dot{c}_e$, is shown by the height of the horizontal solid blue line. Point A indicates a national income of Y_1 combined with a rate of cost inflation of $\dot{c}_1$. This rate is composed of a rate to match expected inflation, shown by the brace E; a positive demand component, shown by the brace D_1 (determined by the shape of $SRPC$); and a negative shock component, shown by the brace S_1. Point B indicates a national income of Y_2 combined with a rate of cost inflation of $\dot{c}_2$. This rate is composed of: a rate to match expected inflation, once again shown by the brace E; the demand component, shown by the brace D_2, which is now negative (since income Y_2 is less than Y^*); and a positive shock component, shown by the brace S_2.

height of the Phillips curve above the axis at Y^*), and ran-dom shocks (which are shown as deviations from the Phillips curve).

Rising inflation

NOW consider attempts to sustain a steady inflation. Assume that the economy starts out in macro equilibrium at potential income and steady prices, as shown in Figure 40.10. The government then increases its expenditure. This shifts the *AD* curve to the right, raising national income above its potential level, so that unemployment falls below the NAIRU. Inflation then sets in at a rate determined by the Phillips curve, and by validating that inflation low unemployment and high output can be achieved.

If that were the end of the story, the outcome might seem like a reasonable bargain. At the cost of some inflation, extra output and extra employment have been obtained. Indeed, this is what many governments thought they could do in the 1960s. Governments that wanted lower unemployment could have it, but at the cost of higher inflation.

We now know, however, that there is more to the story. Whatever theory of the formation of inflationary expectations we adopt, any persistent inflation will come to be expected sooner or later. The expected inflation rate will then rise, and the *SRPC* will shift upward. If the same level of national income is to be maintained, the central bank will have to raise its rate of monetary expansion to prevent the more rapid inflation rate from shifting the *AD* curve to the left (by lowering the real money supply).

This is not all. Ignoring random inflation shocks, we know that the actual inflation rate is the sum of the expect-

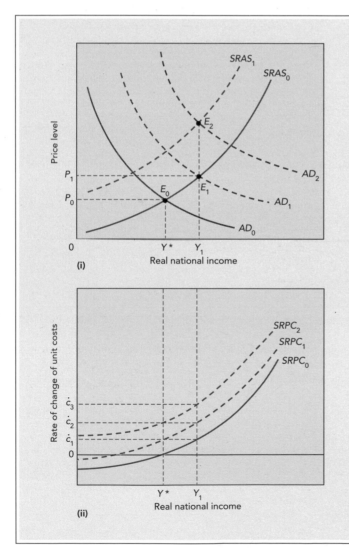

Figure 40.10 Rising inflation

The attempt to hold national income above its potential level and unemployment below the NAIRU will lead to an ever-rising inflation. Macroeconomic equilibrium is originally at E_0 with income Y^* and a stable price level of P_0. The government then adopts measures to shift the *AD* curve to AD_1, taking national income to Y_1 and the price level to P_1. Now, however, units costs begin to rise at a rate of $\dot{c}_1$. This shifts the *SRAS* curve to the left and, to offset its effects, the government validates the inflation with monetary expansion. As long as the Phillips curve in part (ii) stays constant, inflation proceeds at a constant rate. When the curves in part (i) have reached, say, $SRAS_1$ and AD_2, people come to expect the inflation to continue at the rate $\dot{c}_1$. The short-run Phillips curve now shifts upwards to $SRPC_1$, which passes through the point $(Y^*,\dot{c}_1)$. With income at Y_1, the inflation rate now rises to $\dot{c}_2$. The *SRAS* curve now shifts upwards more rapidly and, to maintain income at Y_1, the rate of monetary validation must be increased to allow the *AD* curve to shift more rapidly. (Further shifts in *SRAS* and *AD* are not shown in the figure.)

Sooner or later, the inflation rate of $\dot{c}_2$ comes to be expected and the Phillips curve shifts to $SRPC_2$, which passes through the point $(Y^*,\dot{c}_2)$. The inflation rate now rises to $\dot{c}_3$, and the rate of monetary expansion must be further increased to hold income at Y_1.

ed rate and the demand component. We also know that, when national income is above Y^*, the demand component is positive. It follows that, whenever actual income exceeds potential income, actual inflation must exceed expected inflation. It also follows that the expected rate will itself continue to rise as it adjusts towards the actual rate. This means that the short-run Phillips curve will continue to shift upward.

Upward shifts of the Phillips curve mean that any given level of national income is associated with higher and higher rates of inflation. To maintain that national income level, the central bank must then engage in a faster and faster rate of monetary expansion.

This gives us what is called the *accelerationist* hypothesis, because when inflation rises the price level accelerates:

If the central bank validates any rate of inflation that results when national income is held above its potential level, then the inflation rate itself will rise continuously; and the rate of monetary expansion required to frustrate the monetary adjustment mechanism will also rise continuously.

The long-run Phillips curve

Is there any level of income in this model that is compatible with a constant rate of inflation? The answer is yes: potential income. When income is at Y^*, the demand component of inflation is zero, as shown in Figure 40.8. This means that actual inflation equals expected inflation. There are no surprises. No one's plans are upset, so no one has any incentive to alter plans as a result of what actually happens to inflation.

Provided the inflation rate is fully validated, any rate of inflation can persist indefinitely as long as income is held at its potential level.[6]

We now define the **long-run Phillips curve** (*LRPC*) as the relation between *national income and stable rates of inflation* that neither accelerate nor decelerate. This occurs when the expected and actual inflation rates are equal. On the theory just described, the long-run Phillips curve is vertical, because only at Y^* can the expected and actual rates of inflation be equal. The long-run Phillips curve is shown in Figure 40.11.

Maintaining a point on the *LRPC* leads to steady inflation at the expected rate. This is illustrated in Figure 40.12, which shows a positive expected inflation rate being fully accommodated by the central bank's monetary expansion. Because national income is at its potential level, there is no demand effect on inflation. Thus, the actual and the expected inflation rates are equal. As a result, the situation is sustainable (as long as the central bank continues to accommodate the inflation). The *SRAS* curve shifts upwards at a constant rate while the short-run Phillips curve stays stable. Since everyone's expectations are being fulfilled, there is no reason for anyone to change their behaviour.

The long-run Phillips curve is vertical at Y^*; only Y^* is compatible with a stable rate of inflation; and any stable rate is, if fully accommodated, compatible with Y^*.

---

[6] We now see why the level of unemployment associated with potential income is called the *non-accelerating-inflation rate of unemployment* (NAIRU). At any lower level of unemployment, income exceeds potential income and the inflation rate will tend to rise. At any higher level of unemployment, income is below potential income and inflation will tend to fall. (Money-wage increases are lower than the rate of productivity growth.)

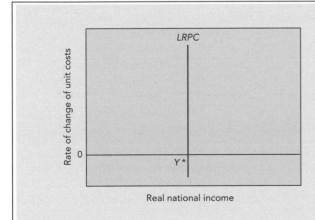

Figure 40.11 The vertical long-run Phillips curve

When actual inflation equals expected inflation, there is no trade-off between inflation and unemployment. In long-term equilibrium, the actual rate of inflation must remain equal to the expected rate (otherwise expectations would be revised). This can occur only at potential income Y^*, that is, along the *LRPC*. At Y^* there is no demand pressure on the price level; hence the only influence on actual inflation is expected inflation. Any stable rate of inflation (provided it is accommodated by the appropriate rate of monetary expansion) is compatible with Y^* and its associated NAIRU.

Breaking an entrenched inflation

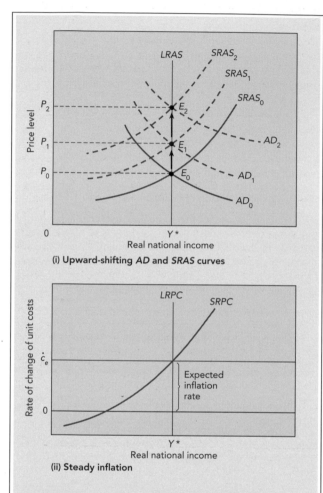

Figure 40.12   Monetary accommodation and steady inflation

Positive expected inflation means that unit costs will be rising even when income is only at its potential level; monetary accommodation can then keep national income constant and sustain the inflation rate. The expected inflation rate is shown in part (ii) by $\dot{c}_e$, which determines the height of the short-run Phillips curve above the axis at Y^*. This translates into an $SRAS$ curve that is shifting upward at a constant rate from $SRAS_0$ to $SRAS_1$ to $SRAS_2$ in part (i). Monetary accommodation means that the AD curve in (i) also shifts upward, from AD_0 to AD_1 to AD_2. As drawn, the monetary accommodation just keeps national income constant at Y^* so inflation persists at the expected rate $\dot{c}_e$. The inflation of unit costs in part (ii) is reflected in a constant rate of price increase, with the price level going from P_0 to P_1 to P_2 in part (i). Since the economy is on its $LRPC$, expected inflation is constant and the $SRPC$ is stable.

WHEN an inflation has been going on for a long time, can it be reduced without inflicting major hardships in terms of unemployment and lost output?

This question caused great concern in the early 1980s, when the UK government set out to lower inflation rates which were then in the high teens. The problem recurred towards the end of the 1980s, when the inflation rate approached 10 per cent. The issue was then, and may be again in the future, how to reduce inflation when people have adapted their behaviour to the belief that the rate will continue.

Our analysis begins with a situation of a continuing, fully validated inflation, with actual national income above its potential level. The inflation has been going on for some time, and people expect it to continue. These firmly held expectations of a continuation of the current inflation rate are what leads to the concept of an *entrenched inflation*. What is entrenched is the expectation of further inflation.

Now suppose that the central bank decides to reduce the inflation rate by reducing its rate of monetary validation. The events that follow such a decision fall into three phases.

Phase 1: Removing the inflationary gap   The first phase of the anti-inflationary policy, illustrated in Figure 40.13, consists of slowing the rate of monetary expansion below the current rate of inflation. This slows the rate at which the aggregate demand curve is shifting upward, and begins to eliminate the inflationary gap. To illustrate what happens, in the figure we take an extreme case where the rate of monetary expansion is cut to zero, so that the upward shift in the AD curve is halted suddenly.

Under the combined influence of an inflationary gap and expectations of continued inflation, wages will continue to rise and the $SRAS$ curve thus will continue to shift upwards. Income returns to Y^* as the inflationary gap is removed. If the only influence on wage costs were current demand, that would be the end of the story. At Y^* there is no inflationary gap and hence no upward demand pressure on wages relative to productivity. Wage costs would stop rising, the $SRAS$ curve would be stabilized, and the economy would remain at full employment with a stable price level.

Phase 2: Stagflation   Governments around the world have many times wished that things were really that simple. However, instead of settling into full employment and stable prices, economies tend to overshoot and develop a recessionary gap. The reason for this overshooting, as we have already seen, is that wages depend not only on current excess demand, but also on inflationary expectations. Once inflationary expectations have been established, it is not

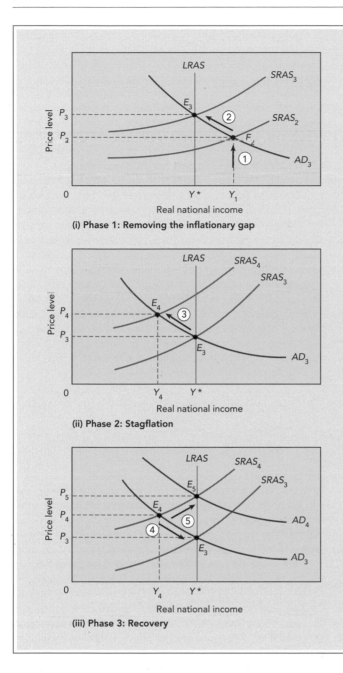

(i) Phase 1: Removing the inflationary gap

(ii) Phase 2: Stagflation

(iii) Phase 3: Recovery

Figure 40.13 Eliminating an entrenched inflation

When monetary restraint is used to stop an entrenched inflation, a period of stagflation will usually be suffered. A fully validated inflation of the type shown in Figure 40.4 is taking the economy along the path shown by arrow 1 here. When the curves reach $SRAS_2$ and AD_3, the central bank stops expanding the money supply, thus stabilizing aggregate demand at AD_3.

(i) Phase 1: Wages continue to rise faster than productivity, taking the $SRAS$ curve leftward. The economy moves along arrow 2, with income falling and the price level rising. When aggregate supply reaches $SRAS_3$, the inflationary gap has been removed, national income is Y^*, and price level is P_3.

(ii) Phase 2: Expectations of inflation cause wages to continue to rise faster than productivity. Unit costs continue to rise, leading to stagflation, with a growing recessionary gap and continuing inflation. The economy moves along the path shown by arrow 3. The driving force is the $SRAS$ curve, which continues to shift because of inflationary expectations. The recessionary gap grows as income falls. The inflation continues, but at a diminishing rate. If wages stop rising faster than productivity when national income has reached Y_4 and the price level P_4, the stagflation phase is over, with equilibrium at E_4.

(iii) Phase 3: After expectations are revised, recovery takes income to Y^* and the price level is stabilized. There are two possible scenarios for recovery. In the first, the recessionary gap causes wage costs to fall (slowly), taking the $SRAS$ curve back to $SRAS_3$ (slowly) as shown by arrow 4. The economy retraces the path originally followed in part (ii) back to E_3. In the second scenario, the central bank increases the money supply sufficiently to shift the AD curve to AD_4. The economy then moves along the path shown by arrow 5. This restores potential income at the cost of a further temporary inflation that takes the price level to P_5. Full employment and a stable price level are now achieved at equilibrium E_5.

always easy to get people to revise them downward, even in the face of changed monetary policies. Thus, the $SRAS$ curve continues to shift to the left, causing the price level to rise and income to fall further.

Expectations may cause an inflation to persist after its original causes have been removed. What was initially a demand inflation, resulting from an inflationary gap, becomes a purely expectational inflation, fuelled by the expectation that it will continue.

We have now entered phase 2, shown in part (ii) of Figure 40.13. Even though the inflationary gap has been eliminated, the expectation of further inflation leads to further wage increases. This shifts the $SRAS$ curve to the left. The price level continues to rise in spite of a growing recessionary gap. This is the stagflationary phase.

The growing recessionary gap has two effects. First, there is rising unemployment. Thus, the demand influence on wages becomes negative. Second, as the recession deepens, people revise their expectations of inflation downward.

When they have no further expectations of inflation, there are no further increases in wage costs and the *SRAS* curve stops shifting upwards. The stagflationary phase is over. The inflation has come to a halt, but a large recessionary gap now exists.

Keynesian and monetarist economists have often differed strongly on what they expect in a typical phase 2 period. Keynesians tend to be pessimistic and to expect a severe slump. Monetarists tend to be optimistic and to expect a relatively mild recession.

The main reason for these differences lies in a disagreement over what determines the expected inflation rate. Keynesians tend to believe that people adjust their expected inflation rates quite slowly, even in the face of substantial recessionary gaps. They believe, therefore, that phase 2 tends to be quite long. Monetarists are more likely to believe that downward adjustments in the expected rate can occur quite rapidly, and hence that phase 2 can often be quite short.

Phase 3: Recovery   The final phase is the return to full employment. When the economy comes to rest at the end of the stagflationary phase, the situation is exactly the same as when the economy is hit by an isolated supply shock (see Figure 40.2). The move back to full employment can be accomplished in one of two ways. Either the recessionary gap can be relied on to reduce wage costs, thus shifting the *SRAS* curve to the right to eliminate the effects of the overshooting caused by inflationary expectations; or the money supply can be increased sufficiently to shift the *AD* curve to a level consistent with full employment. These two possibilities are illustrated in part (iii) of Figure 40.13.

Those economists who worry about waiting for wages and prices to fall fear that the process will take a very long time. Those who worry about a temporary burst of monetary expansion fear that expectations of inflation may be rekindled when the central bank increases the money supply. If inflationary expectations are revived, the central bank will then have an unenviable choice. Either it must let another severe recession develop to break these new inflationary expectations, or it must validate the inflation in order to reduce unemployment. In the latter case, it is back where it started with a validated inflation on its hands.

Three UK inflation cycles

THE UK economy has been through three major boom–bust cycles since 1970. These can be seen very clearly by reference to the inflation rate, as shown in Figure 40.1 on page 786. Each of these cycles was different, though they shared the following characteristics: output boom, followed by falling unemployment, followed by rising prices (inflation), followed by falling output, followed by rising unemployment.

THE BARBER BOOM, 1971–7

In the late 1960s, the UK economy was tightly constrained by aggregate demand controls designed to correct a balance of payments deficit. There was a devaluation of sterling in 1967 which was accompanied by a tight fiscal policy designed to reduce domestic absorption. (See Box 39.1 for a discussion of absorption.) The policy was successful in that by 1970 there was a balance of payments surplus and a government budget surplus. However, unemployment hit a post-war high in 1971.

In August 1971, President Richard Nixon floated the dollar temporarily. The UK government took this as a signal that the constraint of fixed exchange rates had gone. Ministers believed that they could now stimulate real economic growth by boosting aggregate demand, without having to worry about the balance of payments (and reserve losses). What they were yet to learn was the inflationary consequences of boosting aggregate demand under floating exchange rates.

Monetary policy was relaxed in September 1971, when controls on bank lending were removed. Fiscal policy was relaxed in the Budget of March 1972 by the Chancellor of the Exchequer, Anthony (later Lord) Barber. This domestic monetary and fiscal stimulation came on top of a boom in the world economy, caused in part by US expenditure on the war in Vietnam. The combination of these influences amounted to a very significant positive demand shock. A short, but very sharp, boom in output opened up an inflationary gap which was followed by a rapid rise in inflation.

The turning point in the output boom was triggered by a major negative supply shock—the quadrupling of oil prices in late 1973. This further boosted inflation, while knocking output back. Policy was reversed in late 1973, with quantitative controls being re-imposed on the banking system; this ended monetary validation. Unemployment rose from about 500,000 at the end of 1973 to around 1.5 million in 1977.

The inflation in retail prices had been preceded by a boom in house prices and commercial properties. This boom also burst at the end of 1973, and there were collapses of both property development companies and the financial institutions that had lent to them (secondary banks).

SECOND OIL SHOCK, 1977–83

The Labour government maintained tight monetary and fiscal policies from 1975 until 1978. There was a modest recovery of output in 1978 and 1979, but this was largely through the internal dynamics of the private sector rather than through any strong boost to aggregate demand coming from monetary or fiscal policies. Monetary policy was relaxed somewhat in 1978, but not dramatically so.

Inflation picked up sharply, from around 7 per cent at the end of 1978 to around 20 per cent by late 1980. However, there was only a modest growth of output (for a cycle peak) in 1979 and unemployment fell only marginally. This was not, therefore, a simple demand-induced cycle such as the previous (and subsequent) one. Indeed, the elements of this cycle are hard to disentangle and are still subject to controversy.

The two significant boosts to inflation in 1979/80 were both negative supply shocks. The first was a catch-up in money wages for many groups that had their pay held back (by official wage controls) in earlier years and were now looking for compensation for accumulated cuts in real wages. The second was a further doubling of the price of oil.

The effect of the second oil price shock was complicated in the United Kingdom by the fact that Britain itself had become a significant producer of oil by this time. This makes it impossible to analyse all the effects in a single-sector model, because the impact on the oil sector was very different from that on the rest of the economy. Indeed, the presence of oil led to a very strong appreciation of the UK real exchange rate (see Figure 37.4 on page 733), which, if anything, ameliorated the inflation but made a major contribution to the subsequent recession.

The onset of recession was triggered by the combination of the oil price rise and a sharp tightening of UK monetary policy in late 1979, combined with the real exchange rate appreciation. The energy price shock, of course, affected the economy worldwide, so world recession followed in 1981/2. (The UK economy was ahead of the rest of the world, however, in that UK output stopped falling in early 1981 whereas other major countries experienced their worst slowdown in 1982.) This recession was heavily concentrated on the manufacturing sector in the United Kingdom. Manufacturing output fell by nearly 20 per cent between late 1979 and the first quarter of 1981, owing to the severe loss of competitiveness that domestic manufacturers suffered as a result of real exchange rate appreciation.

What is still controversial is the extent to which the real exchange rate appreciation was caused by North Sea Oil as opposed to the monetary policies of the government of Mrs Thatcher (elected in 1979). Suffice it to note that this real exchange rate appreciation started in 1976, and the Labour

Chancellor, Dennis Healey, gave up trying to stop the appreciation of sterling in 1978. Notice also, however, that the emergence of an oil sector involves a structural change in the supply side of the economy, rather than a simple supply shock to a single homogeneous sector of the form we have discussed above.

THE LAWSON BOOM, 1983–93

In the first half of the 1980s the economy recovered slowly from the recession, partly through the natural recovery processes (discussed in Chapter 39, where it was called the automatic adjustment mechanism), and partly through the positive supply shock of falling oil prices. However, it started with a recessionary gap. Financial liberalization, combined with a relaxation of monetary policy, gave a clear boost to aggregate demand in the mid-1980s, but the GDP gap was so great to begin with that it took a long time for the inflationary consequences to come through. In other words, the demand stimulus initially served to close a recessionary gap, but later created an inflationary gap. The early warning sign was a speculative boom in asset prices—house prices, commercial property prices, and share prices. This was rather similar to the pattern in 1971–3, but more prolonged.

Output growth was positive from 1983 until 1988, but by 1988 the level of national income was clearly above potential as inflation started to climb (see Figure 27.2 on page 502). Another indicator of the scale of the expansion in activity is that unemployment fell sharply, from well over 3 million in 1986 to just over 1.5 million in 1990.

The inflationary gap was made larger by a further relaxation of monetary policy in the early months of 1988 and tax-cutting budgets in 1987 and 1988. In other words, a positive demand shock was added to an existing inflationary gap. On top of this, the UK internal cycle was reinforced by the fact that the world economy was also booming in the last few years of the 1980s. This was probably because the second oil shock had made the 1982 world recession a general event. By the mid-1980s, most economies were recovering together.

The bursting of the boom was initiated in late 1988 by a sharp tightening of UK monetary policy. Interest rates stayed high until 1992. This tightening was reinforced by the UK entry into the ERM in October 1990, which resulted in the UK real exchange rate being held up (by linking to the Deutschmark) and interest rates staying higher longer than internal considerations might have required.[7] The

[7] In the 1988–90 period, interest rates were deliberately forced up by the UK authorities. As explained in Chapter 39, with perfect capital flows, the main transmission mechanism is through currency appreciation (overshooting) shifting the net export function downwards, thereby introducing a negative demand shock. Once in the ERM, the UK authorities were subject to the fixed exchange rate regime constraints that they could not lower interest rates, even though the recessionary gap that emerged would have justified such interest rate reductions by about 1991.

result was a long recession, with unemployment rising to around 3 million by 1993.

The positive outcome of this recession was that inflation fell to under 2 per cent. The authorities were confident that they had learned from the three previous inflationary booms, and that they could keep inflation low in future. The remaining challenge was how to get unemployment down while preserving low inflation. It is to this issue that we now turn.

Summary

1 A shift in the *SRAS* curve is called a supply shock, while a shift in the *AD* curve is called a demand shock.

2 A single leftward shift in the *SRAS* curve causes a rise in the price level and a fall in national income. Full employment can be restored either by a fall in unit wage costs, which shifts the *SRAS* curve to the right, or by a monetary expansion, which shifts the *AD* curve to the right.

3 Repeated supply shocks in terms of leftward shifts of the *SRAS* curve carry their own restraining force in terms of ever-rising unemployment if they are not accommodated by monetary expansion. If accommodated, they can give rise to a sustained supply-side inflation.

4 An isolated expansionary demand leads to a temporary rise in income and a rise in the price level. If it is not validated, income will fall while the price level rises when national income returns to its potential level.

5 Sustained demand shocks that are validated by monetary expansion lead to sustained inflation with income remaining above potential.

6 The original Phillips curve relates wage inflation to the level of unemployment; suitably transformed, it relates unit-cost inflation to national income. It thus determines the rate at which the *SRAS* curve is shifting.

7 Unit-cost inflation depends on the state of demand—being positive when $Y > Y^*$ and negative when $Y < Y^*$—and on expectations of inflation and random shocks. The expectations-augmented Phillips curve relates national income to unit-cost inflation and is displaced from the zero-demand-inflation point at $Y = Y^*$ by the amount of expectational inflation.

8 When $Y > Y^*$, actual inflation must exceed expected inflation. If expected inflation adjusts towards actual inflation, then the expectations-augmented Phillips curve must be shifting upwards. Hence if national income is held above potential by a constant amount, inflation must be rising.

9 A sustained inflation at a constant rate is possible only when $Y = Y^*$ and the monetary authorities accommodate the inflation. Expected inflation is then equal to actual inflation.

10 The economy reacts to break a sustained inflation in three phases. First, the rate of monetary accommodation is slowed until the inflationary gap is removed. Second, expectations of continued inflation cause the *SRAS* curve to continue shifting upwards, causing a stagflation, with income falling below Y^* while prices continue to rise. Third, when expectations are fully adjusted, prices stop rising and full employment is restored, either by a single *AD* shock, or by a downward drift of unit costs causing a rightward shift in *SRAS*.

Topics for review

· Causes and consequences of demand and supply shocks

· Once-for-all and sustained inflations

· The NAIRU

· The original, the transformed, and the expectations-augmented Phillips curves

· Starting and stopping sustained inflations

· Stagflation

◆ CHAPTER 41

Employment and unemployment

Unemployment is probably the most widely feared phenomenon of our times. It touches all parts of society. There are 35 million people unemployed in OECD countries (about 8.5 per cent of the labour force). Perhaps another 15 million have either given up looking for work or unwillingly accepted a part-time job. As many as a third of young workers in some OECD countries have no job.

Economic growth will play a part in reducing unemployment. But beyond the cyclical component of unemployment is a structural element that persists even into recovery. This is harder to reduce and is even more troubling.

Structural unemployment grows from the gap between the pressure on the economies to adapt to change and their ability to do so. Adaptation is fundamental to progress in a world of new technologies, globalisation and intense national and international competition.[1]

THE Keynesian revolution was about the use of counter-cyclical aggregate demand policies to cure unemployment. The simple message that unemployment can be cured by stimulating demand is no longer accepted in its original form. Most unemployment policies did not distinguish between cyclical unemployment and equilibrium unemployment (frictional plus structural). Early Keynesian macroeconomics focused mainly on cyclical (demand-deficient) unemployment. We now know that unemployment would still be high (by historical standards) if the economy were at its potential income level and the level of unemployment were at the non-accelerating-inflation rate of unemployment (NAIRU), discussed in Chapter 40. Hence we need explanations both of deviations from the NAIRU and of changes in the NAIRU itself.

In this chapter we first set out some of the stylized facts relating to unemployment. Then we study cyclical unemployment. Finally, we consider the NAIRU in much more detail, asking such questions as: Why does the NAIRU change? Can government policy do anything to reduce the NAIRU?

Employment and unemployment characteristics

IN Figure 40.1, on p. 786, it looks as though there is a rising trend in UK unemployment in successive cycles. However, a longer perspective (as shown in Figure 27.5 on p. 508) suggests that there is no long-term upward trend. Rather, there is a high degree of persistence. (Once high it stays high; once low it stays low.) In the inter-war period unemployment was consistently high, but in the 1950s and 1960s it was consistently low. In the 1980s it has been high, but not as high as in the 1930s.

Unemployment varies much more *between* business cycles than *within* business cycles. Compare, for example, the 1920s and 1930s, when unemployment cycled about a high average level, with the 1950s, when it cycled about a low level. Also, compare the low average unemployment levels of the 1960s and early 1970s with the high levels of the 1980s. This evidence suggests there are long-term changes in social institutions affecting employment and unemployment, and, perhaps, that big shocks to the economic system (a major war being the obvious example) have long-lasting effects.

Total employment in the United Kingdom has been remarkably stable in the post-war period (also shown in Figure 27.5). The numbers in employment in 1993 were about the same as in 1966. However, this figure disguises big shifts between sectors (a decline in manufacturing employment and a rise in services), changes in the composition of the labour force, and some cyclical variation. Figure 41.1 shows the changing proportions of males and females in employment. Increased female participation rates have been offset by declining male employment, and by higher proportions of retired and unemployed workers (population growth was positive but small), although 45 per cent of female employment is part-time as opposed to just over 6 per cent for males.

International comparisons

As the *OECD Jobs Study*, quoted above, makes clear, unemployment is not a problem unique to the United Kingdom; indeed, UK experience is no worse than some (but not all) other European countries. Hence international comparisons are instructive.

There is a dramatic contrast over the last three decades

---

[1] *The OECD Jobs Study: Facts, Analysis and Strategies*, OECD, Paris, 1994. OECD member-countries are: Australia, Austria, Belgium, Canada, Denmark, France, Finland, Germany, Greece, Iceland, Ireland, Italy, Japan, Luxembourg, Mexico, the Netherlands, New Zealand, Norway, Portugal, Spain, Sweden, Switzerland, Turkey, the United Kingdom, and the United States.

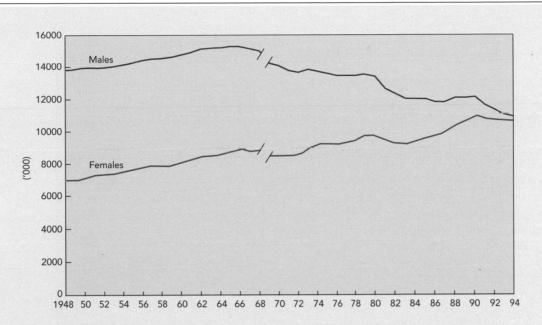

Figure 41.1 Numbers of males and females in employment, in the United Kingdom, 1948–1994

Female employment has cycled around a rising trend, while male employment peaked in the mid-1960s and has cycled about a declining trend since. In the mid-1960s about 15 million males were in employment, but by 1994 the figure was just over 10 million. By contrast, the number of females in employment has risen since 1948 from about 7 million to just over 10 million, though this includes part-time employment. The self-employed are excluded. Data are for June of each year, though the 1994 figure is for March. Also note that there is a break in the data series between 1968 and 1969.

Sources: Monthly Digest of Statistics, CSO, and *British Labour Statistics: Historical Abstract,* Department of Employment/HMSO, 1971.

between employment growth in North America (United States and Canada) and Oceania (Australia and New Zealand) and employment growth in Europe. Total employment grew by only 10 per cent in EU countries between 1960 and 1994, whereas in North America total employment grew by over 80 per cent in the same period. This is shown in Figure 41.2.

In part, this reflects slow population growth in Europe, compared with high levels of immigration into North America. In addition, however, in the latter part of the period there have been declines in the real wages of low-paid workers in Canada, the United States, and Australia, whereas in Europe real wages of the low paid have increased significantly, as shown in Figure 41.3.

Unemployment varies between countries, even within the European Union (in 1993, for example, unemployment was 2.6 per cent in Luxembourg and 22.4 per cent in Spain), and it is dangerous to make comparisons when countries may be at different stages of the business cycle.

However, there is one broad generalization which will be helpful in our attempt to understand the causes of equilibrium unemployment.

Unemployment is the result of the balance of two continuous flows: the inflow of potential workers into unemployment (leaving employment but seeking work, or joining the labour force but not finding employment) and the outflow of workers from unemployment (finding jobs, or withdrawing from the labour force).

In EU countries, the flow into unemployment is quite small and does not change much over time. However, the outflow is also small, so a very high proportion of workers who are unemployed have been unemployed for a long time. For example, in Belgium, Ireland, and Italy, around 60 per cent of the unemployed (in 1992) had been unemployed for more than 12 months; the figures for Germany, France, and the United Kingdom were all around 35 per cent. This contrasts with Canada and the United States, where long-term unemployment was only just over 10 per

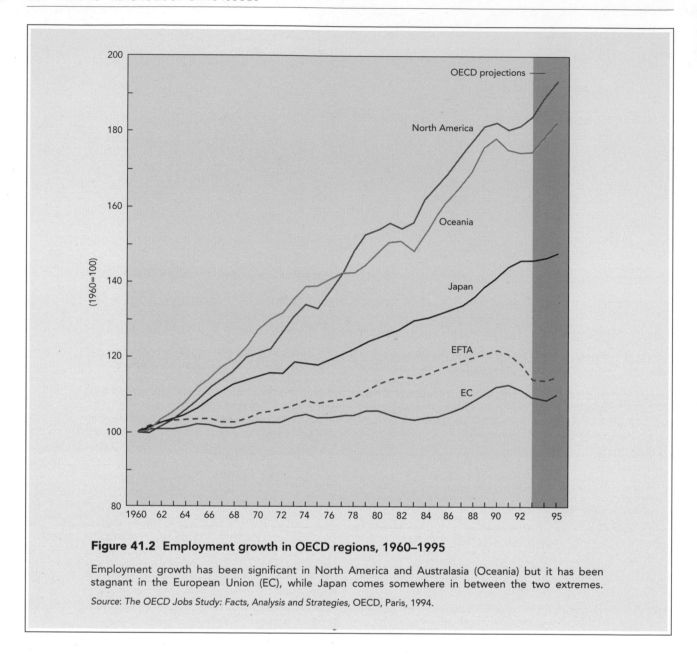

Figure 41.2 Employment growth in OECD regions, 1960–1995

Employment growth has been significant in North America and Australasia (Oceania) but it has been stagnant in the European Union (EC), while Japan comes somewhere in between the two extremes.

Source: The OECD Jobs Study: Facts, Analysis and Strategies, OECD, Paris, 1994.

cent. In the United States, in particular, flows into unemployment are high, but flows out are just as high so the level of long-term unemployment is low.

This may give an important clue as to the causes of the higher persistence of unemployment in the European Union. Skills and human capital deteriorate during periods out of employment, so the long-term unemployed are perceived (rightly or wrongly) as being less employable than those who have recently been in work.

A common pattern across countries is that unemployment is highest among the low-skilled. Low-skilled workers are four or five times more likely to be unemployed than

skilled or professional workers. About 75 per cent of unemployed men are manual workers. This suggests that it is the unemployment of manual workers that should be the main focus of study.

Older workers are less likely to be unemployed than young workers. Youth unemployment is universally higher than adult unemployment—extreme cases include Spain, with 43 per cent youth unemployment, and Italy, with 30 per cent; the UK figure was 17 per cent in 1992.

In most EU countries, female unemployment is greater than male unemployment. The United Kingdom is the exception, with 7.5 per cent female unemployment com-

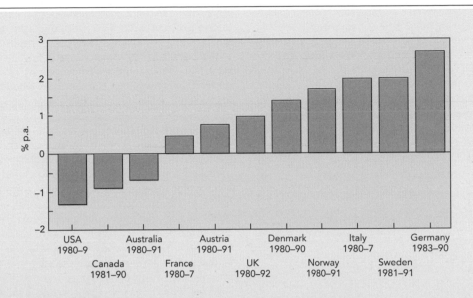

Figure 41.3 Growth in real wages of low-paid workers in the 1980s

Real wages of low-paid workers fell in the United States, Canada, and Australia but they rose in most European countries. These figures, combined with those from Figure 41.1, suggest an inverse relationship between real wage growth and job creation. This does not mean that jobs can be created only if real wages fall. What it does suggest is a greater responsiveness of real wages to excess labour supply (unemployment) in some countries compared with others. Canada, the United States, and Australia have experienced significant population growth in the last thirty years, whereas EU countries have not.

Source: The OECD Jobs Study: Facts, Analysis and Strategies, OECD, Paris, 1994.

pared with around 12.3 per cent for males (although a high proportion of female employment is part-time[2]).

Another universal feature of unemployment is that movement into the ranks of the unemployed is predominantly the result of redundancy rather than voluntary job-leaving. This may seem obvious, but it is important from an economic theory perspective because the New Classical school has attempted to explain unemployment as a voluntary choice made by workers. There is certainly some element of choice involved in deciding when to accept a job offer rather than remain unemployed, but this is very different from having chosen to be unemployed in the first place. Hence, most economists believe that the majority of those who are recorded as unemployed are involuntarily unemployed *in the sense that they would accept an offer of work in jobs for which they are trained, at the going wage rate, if such an offer were made.*

Consequences of unemployment

Involuntary unemployment is a social 'bad' just as much as output is a social 'good'. The harm caused by such involuntary unemployment is measured in terms of the output lost to the whole economy and the harm done to the individuals who are affected.

Lost output Every involuntarily unemployed person is someone willing and able to work but unable to find a job. The unemployed are valuable resources whose potential output is wasted. The material counterpart of unemployment is the recessionary gap—potential GDP that is not produced. The cumulative loss of UK output in the three years 1991–3 alone was £70 billion[3] (at 1990 prices); this is about £1,200 for every member of the population, or about £2,700 for each member of the labour force. In a world of scarcity with many unsatisfied wants, this loss is serious. It represents goods and services that could have been produced but are gone for ever.

---

[2] Of the females in part-time jobs in the spring of 1993, 80 per cent did not want full-time employment, 10 per cent could not find a full-time job, and most of the rest were studying part-time. Among the much smaller group of males in part-time jobs, 30 per cent would have preferred a full-time job (*source: Social Trends*, CSO, 1994, Table 4.13).

[3] This figure is calculated using the IMF estimates of actual and potential GDP shown in Figure 27.2 on p. 502. The loss is just the sum of the gaps between actual and potential output in each of these three years.

Personal costs   A social welfare system, designed to alleviate the short-term economic consequences of unemployment, has been extended in the post-war period. Being unemployed in the United Kingdom, even for some substantial period of time, is no longer quite the life-threatening disaster that it once was. But the longer-term effects of high unemployment rates for the disillusioned, who have given up trying to make it within the system and who contribute to social unrest, should be a matter of serious concern to the haves as well as the have-nots. As UK economists Richard Layard, Stephen Nickell, and Richard Jackman put it,

Unemployment matters. It generally reduces output and aggregate income. It increases inequality, since the unemployed lose more than the employed. It erodes human capital. And, finally, it involves psychic costs. People need to be needed. Though unemployment increases leisure, the value of this is largely offset by the pain of rejection.[4]

Kinds of unemployment

For purposes of study, the unemployed can be classified in various ways. They can be grouped by personal characteristics, such as age, sex, degree of skill or education, or ethnic group. They can also be classified by geographical location, by occupation, by the duration of unemployment, or by the reasons for their unemployment.

In the rest of this chapter we are concerned with explanations of unemployment. Although it is not always possible to say why a particular person does not have a job, it is usu-ally possible to test hypotheses about the causes of aggregate unemployment differences, both over time for one country, and between countries at the same point in time.

In Chapter 27 (see Box 27.2 on p. 507), we noted that the recorded figures for unemployment may significantly understate or overstate the numbers who are actually willing to work at the existing set of wage rates. We noted that overstatement arises because the measured figure for unemployment includes people who are not interested in work but who say they are in order to collect unemployment benefits. We also noted that understatement arises because people who would like to work but have ceased to believe that suitable jobs are available voluntarily withdraw from the labour force. Although these people may not be measured in the unemployment figures (which include only those people actively looking for work and registering for benefits), they are unemployed in the sense that they would accept a job if one were available at the going wage rate. People in this category are referred to as **discouraged workers**. They have voluntarily withdrawn from the labour force, not because they do not want to work, but because they believe that they cannot find a job given current labour market conditions.

In Chapter 27 we also distinguished three types of unemployment: cyclical, frictional, and structural. Both frictional and structural unemployment exist even when national income is at its potential level, and hence when there is neither a recessionary nor an inflationary gap. Together, these two types of unemployment make up the NAIRU, and can, therefore, be called *equilibrium unemployment*. We study first cyclical unemployment and then equilibrium unemployment.

Cyclical unemployment

THE term *cyclical unemployment* (or demand-deficient unemployment) refers to unemployment that occurs whenever total demand is insufficient to purchase all of the economy's potential output, causing a recessionary gap in which actual output is less than potential output. Cyclical unemployment can be measured as the number of persons currently employed minus the number of persons who would be employed at potential income. When cyclical unemployment is zero, all existing unemployment is either structural or frictional, and the rate of unemployment is the NAIRU. Notice that cyclical unemployment can be less than zero, because national income can be above potential national income, at least temporarily.

Macroeconomic theory has traditionally sought to explain only cyclical unemployment.

Equilibrium unemployment was once presumed to be outside the scope of macroeconomics. However, we shall see below that it is unwise to try to make a simple dichotomy between cyclical unemployment, which has macro causes, and equilibrium unemployment, which has micro

---

[4] Richard Layard, Stephen Nickell, and Richard Jackman, *The Unemployment Crisis*, Oxford University Press, 1994. This is a readable summary and update of their more technical study, *Unemployment: Macroeconomic Performance and the Labour Market*, Oxford University Press, 1991.

causes. There are both micro and macro factors contributing to both cyclical unemployment and equilibrium unemployment. (The microeconomics of labour markets was discussed in Chapter 19.) Indeed, we shall find that a strong case can be made for the view that high cyclical unemployment (in some contexts) raises the level of equilibrium unemployment for some time. Hence, we must caution against the presumption that cyclical unemployment and equilibrium unemployment have different causes, or, indeed, that they are unrelated.

None the less, it is convenient for most purposes to think of cyclical unemployment as that which results from deviations of national income from its potential level, and hence is linked to the theory of national income that we have developed above.

However, fluctuations in national income are not sufficient to guarantee fluctuations in involuntary unemployment. We need something else. Suppose, for example, that aggregate demand is fluctuating, causing national income to fluctuate around its potential level. This fluctuation will cause the demand for labour to fluctuate as well, rising in booms and falling in slumps. If the labour market had fully flexible wage rates, then wages would fluctuate to keep quantity demanded equal to quantity supplied. We would observe cyclical fluctuations in employment (and, therefore, also voluntary unemployment) and in the wage rate, but no changes in involuntary unemployment. Employment and wages would vary pro-cyclically (i.e. rising in booms and falling in slumps), but there would be no significant amounts of involuntary unemployment. Such behaviour is shown for a typical labour market in Figure 41.4.

The hypothetical situation we have just described is not what we actually observe. Instead, we see cyclical fluctuations not only in employment, but also in involuntary unemployment. Furthermore, the changes in wage rates that do occur are insufficient to equate demand and supply, as is shown in Figure 41.5. Unemployment exceeds the NAIRU in slumps and is below it in booms. Although wages do tend to vary over the cycle (pro-cyclically), the fluctuations are not sufficient to remove all cyclical variations in unemployment. Why is this so?

Two types of explanation have been advanced over the years. The line that we consider first is associated with the

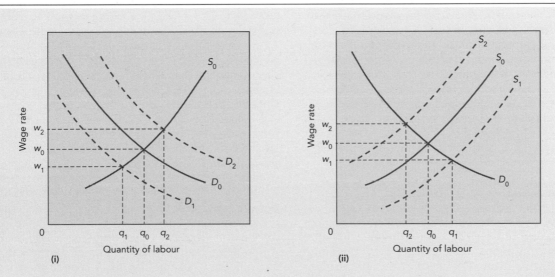

Figure 41.4 Employment and wages in a single competitive labour market

In a perfectly competitive labour market, wages and employment fluctuate in the same direction when demand fluctuates and in opposite directions when supply fluctuates; in both cases, there is no involuntary unemployment. The figure shows a single perfectly competitive market for one type of labour. In part (i), the demand curves D_1, D_2, and D_0 are the demands for this market when there is a slump, a boom, and when aggregate income is at its potential level. As demand rises from D_1 to D_0 to D_2, wages rise from w_1 to w_0 to w_2, and employment rises from q_1 to q_0 to q_2. At no time, however, is there any involuntary unemployment.

In part (ii), the supply of labour fluctuates from S_1 to S_0 to S_2, and wages fluctuate from w_1 to w_0 to w_2. In this case, wages fall when employment rises and vice versa, but again there is no involuntary unemployment.

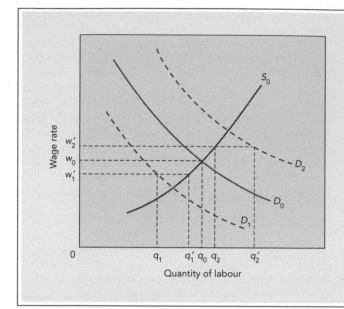

Figure 41.5 Unemployment in a single labour market with sticky wages

When the wage rate does not change enough to equate quantity demanded and quantity supplied at all times, there will be unemployment in slumps and labour shortages in booms in each individual labour market. When demand is at its normal level, D_0, the market is cleared with wage rate w_0, employment is q_0, and there is no unemployment. In a recession, demand falls to D_1, but the wage falls only to w_1'. As a result, q_1 labour is demanded, but q_1' is supplied. Employment is determined by the quantity demanded at q_1; the remainder of the supply for which there is no demand, q_1q_1', is unemployed. In a boom, demand rises to D_2, but the wage rate rises only to w_2'. As a result, the quantity demanded is q_2', whereas only q_2 is supplied. Employment rises to q_2, i.e. the amount supplied; the rest of the demand cannot be satisfied, making an excess demand for labour of q_2q_2'.

New Classical school. The explanation assumes that labour markets are always in equilibrium in the sense that quantity demanded is continually equated with quantity supplied. While the New Classical approach is hard to accept as a description of the causes of unemployment, for reasons already mentioned (like the assumption of no involuntary lay-offs), the methods adopted set down a challenge which was picked up under the umbrella of what we call the *New Keynesian agenda*. Also, in the tradition of positive economics, it is worth noting that the predictions of New Classical models and New Keynesian models, while based on very different assumptions, are difficult to distinguish empirically.

The New Classical approach

The New Classical approach tries to explain unemployment in a context in which agents continuously optimize and markets continuously clear; hence there can be no involuntary unemployment. Notice the contrast with traditional Keynesian (and early monetarist) macroeconomics, which assumed that unemployment was a sign of market failure, associated with non-market-clearing prices and/or wages, and that a high proportion (usually all) of unemployment was involuntary.

One New Classical explanation of cyclical fluctuations in employment assumes that they are caused by fluctuations in the willingness of people to supply their labour, as shown in part (ii) of Figure 41.4. If the supply curve of labour fluctuates cyclically, this will lead to cyclical variations in employment. This explanation of cyclical behaviour in the labour market has two problems. First, the wage will tend to rise in slumps and fall in booms, which is not what we

observe. Second, there will still be no systematic cyclical *involuntary unemployment*, since labour markets always clear, leaving everyone who wishes to work actually working. Supply-induced fluctuations in employment form part of the basis of what is called real business cycle theory, which will be discussed in Chapter 43. However, the real supply shocks that trigger 'real' business cycles cause changes in the NAIRU, so at best, this explains variations in equilibrium but not cyclical unemployment.[5]

A second line of explanation lies in errors on the part of workers and employers in predicting the course of the price level over the business cycle. To understand the argument, start by assuming that each of the economy's markets is in equilibrium, that there is full employment, that prices are stable, and that the actual and the expected rates of inflation are zero. Now suppose that the government increases the money supply (unexpectedly, so that inflation expectations are unaffected) by 5 per cent. People find themselves with unwanted money balances, which they seek to spend. For simplicity, assume that the increased money supply leads to an increase in desired expenditure on *all* commodities. The demand for each commodity shifts to the right, and all prices, being competitively determined, rise. Individual decision-makers see their selling prices go up and mistakenly interpret the increase as a rise in their own relative price.[6] This is because they expect the overall infla-

[5] The distinction here is semantic if the NAIRU is cyclical. We do not pursue the argument further because, although supply shocks are undoubtedly important, the assumption of continuous market-clearing seems unnecessarily restrictive and implausible.

[6] The critical relative price for firms' output decisions is the output price relative to input prices. For firms to increase output, they have to think that their marginal revenue curve has shifted upwards while their marginal cost curve is unchanged (or shifted less).

tion rate to be zero. Firms will produce more, and workers will work more, because both groups think they are getting an increased *relative* price for what they sell. Thus, total output and employment rise.

When both groups eventually realize that their own relative prices are in fact unchanged, output and employment fall back to their initial levels. The extra output and employment occur only while people are being fooled. When they realize that *all* prices have risen by 5 per cent, they revert to their initial behaviour. The only difference is that now the price level has risen by 5 per cent, leaving relative prices unchanged.

A similar argument shows that an unanticipated decrease in the money supply would cause output to fall below its full-employment level.

All New Classical explanations assume that labour markets clear, and then look for reasons why employment fluctuates. They all imply, therefore, that people who are not working have voluntarily withdrawn from the labour market, i.e. that there is no involuntary unemployment.

The New Keynesian agenda

Many economists find New Classical explanations implausible. They believe that people correctly read market signals but react in ways that do not cause markets to be in equilibrium at all times. These economists believe that many who are recorded as unemployed are involuntarily unemployed, as described above.

However, the New Classical approach has attractions. It assumes rational agents who are always optimizing. In other words, it has rigorous micro-foundations which are attractive to economists trained to analyse the utility-maximizing behaviour of agents interacting in clearing markets. Economists so trained are uncomfortable with the early Keynesian assumptions of arbitrary price and wage stickiness (in the face of sustained excess supply) and markets that do not clear. Those who are unhappy to assume no involuntary unemployment therefore seek to explain why there could be a labour market *equilibrium* in which there is an excess supply of labour at the going wage. We refer to this as the New Keynesian 'agenda' rather than 'theory', because there are many different theories encompassed by it and it is ongoing.[7]

Most attempts to explain involuntary unemployment examine the forces that determine wage-setting and hiring decisions in realistic labour market institutions. They look for reasons (consistent with optimizing behaviour by participants) why wages do not respond quickly to shifts in supply and demand in the labour market. So, quantity supplied and quantity demanded may *not* be equated for extended periods of time. Labour markets will then display unemployment during recessions and excess demand dur-

ing booms. This is shown for one typical labour market in Figure 41.5.

These theories start with the everyday observation that wage rates do not change every time demand or supply shifts. When unemployed workers are looking for jobs, they do not knock on employers' doors and offer to work at lower wages than are being paid to current workers. Instead, they answer job advertisements and hope to get the jobs offered, but often are disappointed. Similarly, employers, seeing an excess of applicants for the few jobs that are available, do not go to their current workers and reduce their wages until there is no one who is looking for a job.[8]

In discussing New Keynesian approaches, it is helpful to divide them into two groups. The first seeks to explain nominal wage and price rigidities that slow the adjustment towards full equilibrium. The second focuses on real wage rigidities which are not eliminated over time, but continue in full equilibrium. We shall associate the former approaches with long-term relationships, and menu costs; the latter we shall discuss in the context of efficiency wages and union bargaining models.

LONG-TERM RELATIONSHIPS

One set of theories explains the familiar observation that money wages do not adjust to clear labour markets as resulting from the advantages to both workers and employers of relatively long-term, stable employment relationships. Workers want job security in the face of fluctuating demand; employers want workers who understand the firm's organization, production, and marketing plans. Under these circumstances, both parties care about things in addition to the wage rate, and wages become somewhat less sensitive to fluctuations in current economic conditions. Wages are, in effect, regular payments to workers over an extended employment relationship, rather than a device for fine-tuning the current supplies and demands for labour. Given this situation, the tendency is for employers to 'smooth out' the income of employees by paying a steady money wage and letting profits and employment fluctuate to absorb the effects of temporary increases and decreases in demand for the firm's product.

A number of labour-market institutions work to achieve these results. Employment contracts provide for a schedule of money wages over a period of several years. Fringe benefits, such as membership of the company pension scheme, a

---

[7] Many economists working in this area might not accept the label 'Keynesian'. Indeed, some of the new approaches explain why real wages may be held 'too high' to generate employment for all those seeking work at the going wage. This used to be called 'Classical' unemployment. 'Keynesian' used to be reserved for demand-deficient unemployment. Thus, much of the new work makes these old taxonomies irrelevant.

[8] This observation concerns cyclical variations in the demand for labour. It does not conflict with the different observation that, when firms get into long-term competitive trouble, workers sometimes renegotiate contracts and agree to wage cuts in order to save the firm, and their jobs.

company car, and perhaps private health insurance, tend to bind workers to their employers. A worker's pay tends to rise with years of service. Such features help to bind the employee to the company, whereas redundancy pay, related to years of service, tends to bind the employer to the long-term worker, who would cost the firm more to dismiss.

These practices tend to encourage long-term employment, despite the known fact that the output attributable to workers rises rapidly as they gain experience, reaches a peak, and then falls off as their age advances. Under gradually rising wages, experienced workers tend to get less than the value of their marginal product when they are young and more than the value of their marginal product as they near retirement. But over the long haul they are paid, on average, the value of their marginal product, just as microeconomic theory predicts.

In labour markets characterized by long-term relationships, the wage rate does not fluctuate to clear the market. Wages are written over what has been called the long-term 'economic climate' rather than the short-term 'economic weather'. Some conclude that optimizing firms in such an environment will adjust employment rather than wages during the cycle. However, it is not clear why employees would prefer to be laid off rather than accept a lower wage. So it is still not clear why sticky wages are optimal for both workers and firms.

MENU COSTS AND WAGE CONTRACTS

A typical large manufacturing firm sells differentiated products numbered in the thousands and employs hundreds of different types of labour. Changing prices and wages in response to every minor fluctuation in demand is a costly and time-consuming activity. Firms find it optimal to keep their price lists (*menus*) constant for significant periods of time. Since all manufacturing firms are operating in imperfectly competitive markets, they have some discretion over price. Hence it may be optimal for firms to respond to small changes in demand by holding prices constant and responding with changes in output and employment. If many firms are behaving this way, output and employment will respond to changes in aggregate demand.

The UK evidence is consistent with the existence of sluggish price adjustment by manufacturers.[9] This, of course, is where Keynesian economics came in. However, the New Keynesian literature, rather than assuming price stickiness to be arbitrary, attempts to model it as an optimal response to adjustment costs and adverse customer reactions.

Money wages tend to be inflexible in the short term because wage rates are generally set on an annual basis. In some other countries they are set for longer periods—three years is not uncommon with union contracts in North America. Inflexibility of wages, particularly in the face of negative supply shocks, such as the oil price shocks of 1973 and 1979, will lead to increases in unemployment.

We now turn to a discussion of the New Keynesian approaches that focus on real rigidities in labour markets.

EFFICIENCY WAGES

The idea of the *efficiency wage* forms the core of a strand of thinking about why it may be optimal for firms to set wages permanently above the level that would clear the labour market. Efficiency wage theory applies to hiring, to productivity on the job, and to worker turnover.

Workers are not homogeneous. There are good workers and bad workers, but there is *asymmetrical information*: firms do not know the characteristics of a specific worker until after they have sunk costs into hiring and training her. Good workers know who they are and are likely to have a higher reservation wage (the wage at which they are prepared to work) than bad workers. By lowering the wage they offer, firms will significantly lower the average ability of the workers who apply to them for jobs, and so they could find that paying lower wages makes them worse off. This is known as *adverse selection*. It is a concept we have already met in the context of insurance (see p. 168), but it is also an essential feature of labour markets.

In labour markets with informational asymmetries, where unobserved characteristics of workers are correlated with the reservation wage, it may not be optimal for firms to pay the market-clearing wage.

Once in employment, workers are likely to give greater effort if they feel they are being well rewarded and the costs of losing their job are high. If wages are so low that workers are just indifferent between staying and losing their jobs, they are likely to please themselves how hard they work and they will not be afraid of getting the sack. Employers have a problem of monitoring and enforcing efficient work practices—this is another case of the principal–agent problem discussed on p. 318. Paying a high wage reduces the problem, both because workers will expect to be much worse off if they lose their current job, and because there will be a queue of good-quality workers prepared to work for the higher wage. The high wage improves efficiency—hence the term *efficiency wages*.

Another way in which higher wages may improve productivity is through the direct effects on worker nutrition and general health. By improving the physical well-being of the worker, the marginal productivity of workers may be increased. This is a very important effect in developing countries, but it may also apply in some sectors of developed economies.[10] However, an effect that clearly does

[9] See Simon Price, 'Costs, Prices, and Profitability in UK Manufacturing', *Applied Economics* (23), 1991, pp. 839–49.

[10] Important work on this topic was done by Christopher Bliss and Nicholas Stern. However, the major recent contribution is by Partha Dasgupta, *An Inquiry into Well-Being and Destitution*, Oxford University Press, 1993.

apply in developed countries is that workers who are paid well above their best alternative wage have an incentive to invest in self-education and skill acquisition in order to secure their continued employment prospects.

Finally, firms for which high quit rates are costly will be reluctant to lower the wages of existing workers, even in the face of an excess supply of labour. It is possible for firms to pay lower wages to new workers, but tiered wage structures, in which several people doing the same job get different rates of pay, often cause morale problems. This does not say that experienced workers cannot be paid more; rather, it says that firms cannot respond to job queues by offering new workers a lower lifetime earnings profile than that enjoyed by existing workers.

Efficiency wage theory says that firms may find it advantageous to pay high enough wages so that working is a clearly superior alternative to being laid off. This will improve the quality of workers' output without firms having to spend heavily to monitor workers' performance.

Efficiency wage theory helps us to understand a lot more about labour markets. It also explains why firms may wish to pay wages above market-clearing levels. This helps to explain why involuntary unemployment can persist in equilibrium, that is when national income is at its potential level.

UNION BARGAINING

The final theoretical approach to be considered under the New Keynesian agenda assumes that those already in employment ('insiders') have more say in wage bargaining than those out of work ('outsiders'). Typically, those in employment are represented by a union which negotiates the wage rate with firms. The union will generally represent the interests of its members, the bulk of whom will be in employment. It will not necessarily reflect the interests of those excluded from employment.

It is easy to see that insiders will wish to bid up wages even though to do so will harm the employment prospects of outsiders. Hence, this framework can generate an outcome to the bargaining process between firms and unions at which the wage is set higher than the market-clearing level, just as with the efficiency wage.

Again, these models help explain the existence of involuntary unemployment even when national income is at its potential level. However, they do add one important new

insight into the causes of international differences in unemployment.

In some countries unions bargain at the level of the firm; in others they bargain at the level of the whole industry or the whole economy. Where bargaining is decentralized, the union can push for higher wages for the insiders without worrying about effects on the rest of the economy or on outsiders. However, where bargaining is centralized, the effects on the rest of the economy tend to get internalized into the bargaining process, because union negotiators are bargaining on behalf of all workers (and potential workers), rather than just those in one firm.

The conclusion is that decentralized bargaining with strong unions will lead to higher than market-clearing wages, and the outsiders will be excluded from jobs, whereas centralized bargaining will produce an outcome closer to the market-clearing outcome (because outsider concerns are voiced), so unemployment will be low.

The third alternative to centralized and decentralized union bargaining is no union bargaining at all (i.e. low unionization or weak unions). This too will produce an outcome close to the free market (in the absence of efficiency wage considerations). This analysis may explain why unemployment is relatively high in EU countries (strong unions but decentralized bargaining) and lower in Scandinavia (strong unions and centralized bargaining) and the United States (weak unions).

The basic message of New Keynesian theories of unemployment is that labour markets cannot be relied on to eliminate involuntary unemployment by equating current demand for labour with current supply.

However, it is not yet clear that these approaches provide the basis of an understanding of the causes of cyclical unemployment, which amounts to a lot more than the traditional assumption of nominal price and (especially) wage stickiness in the face of fluctuations in aggregate demand and supply. Nor do these approaches offer a new justification for the traditional Keynesian remedy for unemployment, namely expansionary fiscal policy. This is not to say that the efforts have been a failure. On the contrary, they have generated a vast increase in the level of understanding of labour markets. This understanding has already shifted the main focus of attention away from cyclical unemployment and towards the determinants of equilibrium unemployment. Here there are many solutions on offer, but they are very different from the traditional Keynesian ones.

Equilibrium unemployment: the NAIRU

WE now turn to a consideration of equilibrium unemployment, or the NAIRU, which, as we have seen, is composed of frictional and structural unemployment.

FRICTIONAL UNEMPLOYMENT

As we saw in Chapter 27, *frictional unemployment* results from the normal turnover of labour. An important source of frictional unemployment is young people who enter the labour force and look for jobs. Another source is people who are in the process of changing their jobs and are caught between one job and the next. Some may quit because they are dissatisfied with the type of work or their working conditions; others may be sacked. Whatever the reason, they must search for new jobs, which takes time. People who are unemployed while searching for jobs are said to be frictionally unemployed or, alternatively, in *search unemployment.*

The normal turnover of labour would cause some frictional unemployment to persist, even if the economy were at potential income and the structure of jobs in terms of skills, industries, occupations, and location were unchanging.

STRUCTURAL UNEMPLOYMENT

Structural adjustments can cause unemployment. When the pattern of demand for goods changes, the pattern of the demand for labour changes. Until labour adjusts fully, *structural unemployment* develops. Such unemployment may be defined as unemployment caused by a mismatch between the structure of the labour force—in terms of skills, occupations, industries, or geographical locations—and the structure of the demand for labour.

ENDOGENOUS CHANGE

Changes that accompany economic growth shift the structure of the demand for labour. One of the more dramatic recent structural changes in the economy has been in the organization of the firm. Manufacturing firms used to be organized much like an army, with a pyramid command structure. Most key strategic decisions were made near the top, with lesser ones concerning implementation made at lower levels. This structure required an array of middle-level managers who passed information upward to the top level and downward to the production level and who made various secondary decisions themselves. Recent changes pioneered among Japanese firms have led to a much looser organization with much more local autonomy among the subsections of the firm. As a result, large numbers of middle managers have been made redundant. They find themselves on the labour market at middle age and with many of their skills rendered obsolete.

Another key structural change in the United Kingdom (and many other economies) has been the decline in employment in manufacturing. Employment in this sector has been declining since the late 1950s, but the real exchange rate appreciation of the late 1970s and early 1980s (partly associated with another structural change, the emergence of North Sea oil production—see Figure 37.4 on p. 733), accelerated this adjustment. Many factories closed in the early 1980s, or were replaced by capital-intensive rather than labour-intensive plant.

Increases in international competition can have effects similar to those of economic growth and change. As the geographical distribution of world production changes, so does the composition of production and of labour demand in any one country. Labour adapts to such shifts by changing jobs, skills, and locations, but until the transition is complete, structural unemployment exists.

Structural unemployment will increase if there is either an increase in the speed at which the structure of the demand for labour is changing or a decrease in the speed at which labour is adapting to these changes.

POLICY INFLUENCES

Government policies can influence the speed with which labour markets adapt to change. Some countries have adopted policies that discourage movement among regions, industries, and occupations. These policies tend to raise structural unemployment, though state subsidies may disguise it for a while. The EU Common Agricultural Policy (CAP), for example, is intended (partly) to resist the decline of incomes and employment in agriculture, even though employment in agriculture has been declining in Europe since the late eighteenth century. Other countries, such as Sweden, have done the reverse and have encouraged workers to adapt to change. Partly for this reason, Sweden's unemployment rates were well below the European and North American norms during the 1980s.

Policies that discourage firms from replacing labour with machines may protect employment over the short term. However, if such policies lead to the decline of an industry because it cannot compete effectively with innovative foreign competitors, serious structural unemployment can result in the long run. Box 41.1 gives a further view on this issue.

BOX 41.1

*Industrial change: an economist's cautionary tale**

The audience hushed as the members of the government's investigating commission filed into the room. The chief forecasting wizard (behind his back, some called him the economic soothsayer) began his report: 'I have identified beyond reasonable doubt the underlying trends now operating,' he declared to the expectant audience. 'The nation's leading industry, industry X, is in a state of decline. From its current position of employing close to 50 percent of our work force, it will, within the duration of one lifetime, employ only 3 percent.'

'Over 40 percent of the nation's jobs destroyed within one lifetime!' proclaimed the newspaper headlines.

'Where can new jobs possibly come from at so rapid a pace?' asked a union leader.

'The government must protect industry X; we just cannot let all these jobs go down the tubes,' argued an employer.

'Perhaps we should identify and promote new "sunrise industries",' said a senior bureaucrat. Indeed, it had been widely believed that a new high-tech product, product Z, would become the wave of a future new transportation revolution. A call went out for subsidies and tax breaks to back its development.

'Is there any hope that the private sector might provide the new jobs?' someone asked.

'Possibly,' said a junior economist, more out of desperation than hope, 'the new product Y that is being produced by a few people in backyard sheds might grow to be a significant employer.'

He was immediately pounced on by a pride of self-proclaimed realistic thinkers. 'Product Y! It's noisy, it's smelly, and it's a plaything for the rich. Surely *it* will never provide significant employment.'

All of the economic facts in the above tale are true; only the government commission and the policy initiatives are fictitious.

The country was the United States. The time was 1900. Industry X, the employer of close to 50 percent of the work force, was agriculture. Product Z, the sunrise industry, was the large, powered, lighter-than-air craft known as the zeppelin. Product Y, the scorned plaything of the rich, was the motor car.

The decline of some traditional industries is always a cause for concern. Some of them are suffering a temporary decline, and some are declining permanently. In either event, the hardships on those losing their jobs are severe. The tale just told has a serious message. Here are a few of the lessons that can be gained from comparing the economy in 1900 and in 1995.

First, the economy is constantly changing. Indeed, the motto of any market economy could be that 'nothing is permanent'. New products appear continually; others disappear. At the early stage of a new product, total demand is low, costs of production are high, and many small firms are each trying to get ahead of their competitors by finding the twist that appeals to consumers or finding the technique that slashes costs. Sometimes new products never get beyond that phase; they prove to be passing fads. Others, however, do become items of mass consumption.

Successful firms in growing industries buy up, merge with, or otherwise eliminate their less successful rivals. Simultaneously,

their costs fall, owing to scale economies. Competition drives prices down along with costs. Eventually, at the mature stage, a few giant firms often control the industry. They become large, conspicuous, and important parts of the nation's economy. Sooner or later, new products arise to erode the position of the established giants. Demand falls off, and unemployment occurs as the few firms run into financial difficulties.

A large, sick, declining industry may appear to many as a national failure and a disgrace. At any moment, however, firms can be found in all phases—from small firms in new industries to giant firms in declining industries. Large, declining industries are as much a natural part of a healthy, changing economy as large, stable industries and small, growing ones.

Second, the policy of shoring up the declining industries of the 1990s could be just as destructive of our living standards as the policy of protecting the agricultural sector from decline in 1900 would have been. (Policies that ease the human cost of the adjustment are not, however, in this category.)

Third, to tell where the new employment will come from requires the kind of crystal ball that our young economist would have needed in 1900 to stick by his wild guess of identifying the new plaything of the rich as the massive motor car industry 30 years later. Economists are continually being asked: 'Where will the new employment come from?' The answer 'we don't know' is *wrongly* taken to mean 'it won't come.' In the past, the new jobs have come, and we see no new, identifiable forces that would prevent their coming in the future. For example, in the course of the current recovery, many people gaining employment are starting in *new* jobs—jobs with firms and in locations that did not exist or would not have been predicted even 5 years ago. Who in the 1960s could have predicted that anyone would currently be employed in any of: the off-shore oil industry, the PC (software or hardware) industry, the mobile phone industry or satellite television?

Fourth, picking winners and backing them with government policy is a likely way to waste public funds and inhibit the development of the real winners. People risking their own money and diversifying risks over many ventures are probably a better route to employment creation than governments that risk taxpayers' money, mesmerized by fads and fashion. This is not to say that government participation in industry is always wrong—Singapore and South Korea, for example [see Chapter 34] show that government involvement with industry can be beneficial.

Fifth, the industrial policy that is needed is one that encourages private initiatives and risk-taking. Small businesses are often, if not always, the route to the creation of new employment. Risk-taking and the growth of small firms should not be discouraged by such things as complicated regulatory rules and tax laws.

The general point is not that *laissez-faire* is always the best policy. It is merely that attempting to protect employment by slowing down economic change will often have the opposite effect, in the long term, to that intended.

* Copyright 1984 by R. G. Lipsey and D. D. Purvis. Reprinted and adapted by permission of the *Financial Post*.

Minimum wage laws can cause structural unemployment by pricing low-skilled labour out of the market. As explained in Chapter 19, minimum wage laws have two effects when they are imposed on competitive markets: (1) they reduce employment of the unskilled, and (2) they raise the wages of the unskilled who retain their jobs.

Why does the NAIRU change?

We have noted that structural unemployment can increase because the pace of change accelerates or the pace of adjustment to change slows down. An increase in the rate of growth, for example, usually speeds up the rate at which the structure of the demand for labour is changing. The adaptation of labour to the changing structure of demand may be slowed by such diverse factors as a decline in educational achievement, and regulations that make it harder for workers in a given occupation to take new jobs in other areas or occupations. Any of these changes will cause the NAIRU to rise. Changes in the opposite direction will cause the NAIRU to fall.

DEMOGRAPHIC CHANGES

Because people usually try several jobs before settling into one for a longer period of time, young or inexperienced workers have higher unemployment rates than experienced workers. The proportion of inexperienced workers in the labour force rose significantly as the post-war baby boom generation entered the labour force in the late 1960s and 1970s, along with an unprecedented number of women who elected to work outside the home. In the 1980s youth unemployment became an even bigger problem, because school-leavers found it hard to get a foothold on the career ladder when unemployment was rising and even experienced workers were being paid off.

Even if youth unemployment should fall in future, many observers worry about the long-term consequences for some individuals. Learning through on-the-job experience is a critical part of developing marketable labour skills, and those who suffered prolonged unemployment during their teens and twenties have been denied that experience early in their working careers. These workers may have little option later in life but to take temporary jobs at low pay and with little future job security, or drop out of the labour force entirely.

The significant increase in female participation rates, and the related increase in the number of households with more than one income-earner, has also affected the NAIRU. When both husband and wife work, it is possible for one to support both while the other looks for 'a really good job', rather than accepting the first job offer that comes along, or spends time in retraining. This can increase recorded unemployment while not inflicting excessive hardship on those involved.

HYSTERESIS

Recent models of unemployment show that the size of the NAIRU can be influenced by the *size* of the actual current rate of unemployment. Such models get their name from the Greek word **hysteresis**, meaning 'coming late'.[11] In economics it means that the current equilibrium is not independent of what has gone before—it is path-dependent. This means that the NAIRU will be higher after periods of high unemployment than after periods of low unemployment. If this is correct, we have to distinguish between the short-run NAIRU and the long-run NAIRU. The latter is the true long-run equilibrium towards which the short-run NAIRU will adjust slowly over time.

One mechanism that can lead to hysteresis in labour markets has already been noted. It arises from the importance of experience and on-the-job training. Suppose, for example, that a period of recession causes a significant group of new entrants to the labour force to have unusual difficulty in obtaining their first jobs. As a result, the unlucky group will be slow to acquire the important skills that workers generally learn in their first jobs. When demand increases again, this group of workers will be at a disadvantage relative to workers with normal histories of job experience, and the unlucky group may have unemployment rates that will be higher than average. Thus, the NAIRU will be higher than it would have been had there been no recession.

Another force that can cause such effects is insider–outsider segregation in a heavily unionized labour force, discussed above. In times of high unemployment, people who are currently employed (insiders) may use their bargaining power to ensure that their own status is maintained and prevent new entrants to the labour force (outsiders) from competing effectively. In an insider–outsider model of this type, a period of prolonged high unemployment—whatever its initial cause—will tend to become 'locked in'. If outsiders are denied access to the labour market, their unemployment will fail to exert downward pressure on wages, and the NAIRU will tend to rise.

Hysteresis is part of the explanation of the high levels of persistence of unemployment in many EU countries, including the United Kingdom.

INCREASING STRUCTURAL CHANGE

The amount of industrial restructuring, both locally and internationally, increased in the 1980s and appears to be carrying on through the 1990s. In part, this is the result of the increasing integration of the UK economy with the European Union and the rest of the world, and the globalization of world markets. Most observers feel that this inte-

---

[11] It was first used in electronics to relate to effects coming after their causes, i.e. lagged effects.

gration has been beneficial overall. One less fortunate consequence, however, is that labour markets are increasingly affected by changes in demand and supply conditions anywhere in the world.

The following numerous structural changes have created a continuing need for rapid adjustments:

- the collapse of communism and the conversion of the countries of Eastern Europe to market economies;
- increases in the supply of agricultural products owing to the green revolution in less-developed countries and heavy agricultural subsidization in the European Union;
- enormous OPEC-induced increases in the price of oil in the 1970s and early 1980s, followed by almost equally precipitous declines in the mid-1980s that carried through into the 1990s;
- the emergence of several Asian countries as industrial economies of which China will, in the long run, be the most important;
- the communications revolution, leading to the decentralization of industry, with components produced in various countries and assembled in others;
- robotization, which increased industrial productivity and reduced the demand for assembly-line workers;
- the growth of knowledge-intensive industries, which require highly educated and geographically mobile workforces;
- the globalization of competition, with fewer and fewer domestic markets that are sheltered by artificial barriers;
- changes in the organization of firms;
- the privatization of large sections of formerly state-owned industries;
- the decline of employment in manufacturing;
- the enormous growth in service employment.

Although evidence is difficult to obtain, some observers argue that the increasing pace and the changing nature of technological change since the mid-1970s has contributed to an increase in the level of structural unemployment.

Mismatch Structural change that creates unemployed workers with the wrong characteristics (skills, experience, location) for the available jobs is known as *mismatch*. As we saw above, the biggest mismatch is likely to be that modern industry requires skilled and flexible workers while the majority of the unemployed are unskilled. Intuitively this makes sense—a metal worker made redundant in Sheffield in 1980 is unlikely to have found work (quickly) as an advertising executive, even if vacancies existed.

Researchers studying UK unemployment have found mismatch to be important in increasing the NAIRU, but mismatch does not appear to have increased markedly since the early 1970s.[12] Thus, it explains the rise in the NAIRU between the 1960s and 1970s but not subsequent rises. It could be that mismatch has been important but that it is not amenable to accurate measurement.

UNEMPLOYMENT BENEFITS

Workers who lose their jobs receive unemployment benefit. The size of the benefits paid, relative to pay levels in work, is known as the **replacement ratio**. A high replacement ratio raises the NAIRU. It affects the willingness of the unemployed to accept job offers and it affects the intensity with which they search for work.

Changes in the replacement ratio do have significant statistical effects in increasing the NAIRU, but Layard, Nickell, and Jackman[13] find that it explains only 0.8 percentage point of the 6.2 percentage point rise in equilibrium unemployment between the 1960s and 1980s.

However, differences in benefit systems between countries do seem to play a very important role in explaining international differences in unemployment. It is not just the replacement ratio faced by a newly unemployed worker that matters; also important is the duration for which that benefit is provided (if it is for a short period the worker has an incentive to find work very quickly) and the degree to which the benefit is conditional on job-seeking activity. Countries with only temporary benefits and both incentives and assistance with finding work tend to have lower equilibrium unemployment rates.

OTHER EFFECTS

Two other factors are often reported to have at least a temporary effect on the NAIRU. The first is the *tax wedge*. This is the difference between what an employer has to pay to hire a worker and what the worker receives in take-home pay. Increasing the tax wedge for a given quantity of labour demanded reduces take-home pay. This is likely to increase wage bargaining pressure, resulting from workers' reluctance to accept lower real wages. In effect, this shifts up the short-run Phillips curve, thereby worsening the inflation–unemployment trade-off in the short run. However, this has no long-run effect on the NAIRU, as the tax wedge cannot keep increasing.

The second effect is associated with terms-of-trade loss, or real exchange rate depreciation. This is argued to have a similar effect; because it raises import prices, it also reduces real wages. Real wage resistance shifts the short-run Phillips curve upwards and we get the same result as in the previous paragraph, but it will not change the equilibrium level of unemployment.

Explaining unemployment

By combining the analysis of demand and supply shocks

[12] The econometric evidence on factors affecting the UK NAIRU has been surveyed by Roy Cromb, 'A Survey of Recent Econometric Work on the NAIRU', *Journal of Economic Studies*, 20 (1993), pp. 27–51.

[13] Layard *et al.*, op. cit. fn. 4.

and the Phillips curve of Chapter 40 with what we have learned about labour markets above, we can now produce an explanation for the unemployment experience which we summarized at the beginning of this chapter. This explanation is broadly that set out by Layard, Nickell, and Jackman.[14]

Supply shocks Most countries were subjected to two major supply shocks, associated with the oil price rises of 1973 and 1979. Countries with more centralized wage bargaining suffered less unemployment than others, because wage negotiators were more prepared to accept cuts in real wages. The shock was complicated in the United Kingdom by structural adjustment resulting from the emergence of an oil-producing sector. The pace of technological and organizational change has speeded up and affected unemployment most in those countries with inflexible labour market institutions and regulations.

Demand shocks Governments reacted to high inflation in the 1970s with tight monetary and fiscal policies. Slow downward adjustment of inflation expectations, combined with negative demand shocks, created recessionary gaps and rising unemployment. (The adjustment to negative demand shocks was discussed in Chapter 39, and the adjustment to positive demand and supply shocks was analysed in Chapter 40.) The short-run impact of these demand shocks on unemployment was less, the more flexible were wage contracts. (The contribution of policy-makers to exaggerating the UK business cycle was outlined in the last section of Chapter 40.)

Persistence Unemployment became persistent in those countries with open-ended unemployment benefits and, once in place, was sustained by hysteresis effects. Countries that did least to get the long-term unemployed back to work suffered most in terms of rising equilibrium unemployment rates.

Reducing unemployment

OTHER things being equal, all governments would like to reduce unemployment. The questions are: 'Can it be done?' and 'If so, at what cost?' Some commonly aired 'solutions' which will almost certainly not help are discussed in Box 41.2.

In this section, we review the policies that governments could introduce to help the unemployment problem. The simple (if flippant) solution, in view of what we have learnt about persistence, is: don't start from here!

DEMAND MANAGEMENT

The traditional macroeconomic solution to unemployment is a policy-induced stimulus to aggregate demand. We now know that this will cure the problem, if at all, only if the NAIRU is low so that the unemployment is recent, or cyclical. This suggests that the authorities should act quickly to accommodate the effects of a negative shock to aggregate supply.

An increase in aggregate demand (with national income close to its potential level) intended to reduce equilibrium unemployment, however, would rapidly lead to a rise in inflation. By definition, inflation will start to accelerate once unemployment falls below the NAIRU.

This means that the most that demand management can do about equilibrium unemployment is to try to make sure that it does not rise as a result of major deflations.

Unfortunately, it was attempts to eliminate inflation rapidly by restrictive aggregate demand policies that contributed to high unemployment in the first place.

Once inflation is low and the unemployment level is close to the NAIRU, aggregate demand policy should be neutral; that is, it should aim to maintain national income at its potential level.

REDUCING PERSISTENCE

The reduction of persistence and hysteresis effects is a major challenge. It probably requires both a reform of the benefits system and active policies to ensure that those in danger of long-term unemployment get work experience and training.

The feature of the benefits system that seems to be most harmful (in the sense of creating long-term unemployment) is an indefinite period of benefit. This reduces the incentive of the recently unemployed to seek work urgently. Some commentators advocate compulsory public-sector work for the unemployed after some period of time; others advocate state subsidies towards private-sector employment as a way of getting people back into the labour market. The general point, however, is that, whatever the

[14] Layard *et al.*, op. cit. fn. 4, p. 816.

BOX 41.2

False trails: what won't cure unemployment

The existence of high unemployment prompts many well-meaning but ill considered suggestions for solving the problem. The most common error made when thinking about unemployment is to assume that there is a fixed number of jobs available to be shared out. This leads to proposals for compulsory job sharing and enforced early retirement to divide existing jobs among available workers, proposals to halt new technology 'destroying' jobs, and protectionism to stop 'our jobs' being taken by low-wage foreigners.

The following arguments against these false presumptions are all drawn from the 1994 *OECD Jobs Study*, referred to earlier in this chapter.

Job sharing

Enforced job sharing and involuntary early retirement reduce potential national income because they prevent those who are willing and able to work productively from doing so. It makes the individuals so restricted worse off and it makes society as a whole worse off. Indeed, it is a form of forced unemployment.

As the *OECD Jobs Study* puts it (p. 27):

Legislated, across-the-board, work-sharing addresses the unemployment problem not by increasing the number of jobs through more economic activity, but through rationing gainful work. Enforced work-sharing has never succeeded in cutting unemployment significantly, not least because of workers' resistance to reduced income.

This is not to say that flexible working practices, which *enable* part-time working for those who would otherwise be unable to work, are a bad thing; on the contrary, the key is that each individual should be able to maximize his or her productive activity in the manner most suited to his or her needs and commitments. Anything that limits the opportunities to work is harmful.

Technology

In 1811 Nottinghamshire frameworkers (led by the, probably mythical, Ned Ludd) smashed new machinery. This was because they thought that the new technology of the industrial revolution was doing them out of a livelihood. Before that time real wages were constant, possibly for centuries. Since that time real wages have multiplied at least tenfold even for manual workers, and job opportunities have multiplied in incalculable ways.

To quote the OECD study again (p. 29):

history has shown that when technological progress accelerates, so do growth, living standards and employment. Technological progress would lead to high unemployment only in a world of saturated wants or perpetual restriction of demand, conditions that have not occurred in the past, and seem unlikely in the foreseeable future. Furthermore, worries about a new era of 'jobless growth' appear unfounded: the current upswing in the United States and a number of other countries has brought job growth in its train, and broadly in line with past relationships between growth and employment.

Protectionism

It is an erroneous but widely held view in Europe that competition from low-wage countries, especially in Asia, is responsible for much of the current unemployment. This is an argument that the OECD economists are able to dismiss (p. 28):

The weight of low-wage countries' exports in the overall expenditure of OECD countries on goods and services is only about 1.5 per cent. The number of markets which they contest is greater, and their effect on the intensity of competition is increasing. But the judgement on present evidence is that the overall impact both of imports from these countries and their contestation of OECD markets is too small to account for a significant part of either current unemployment or falling relative wages of the low-skilled. On the other hand, these countries represent a large and growing potential market for OECD exports of goods and services, and hence represent an important source of current and future growth and employment.

On the case for using protectionism to 'keep jobs at home', the OECD has no doubts (p. 29):

Protectionism reduces overall economic welfare; increases costs to consumers, often hurting most those with lowest incomes; penalises successful enterprise; harms exports; encourages tariff factories; harms developing countries' trade; and increases the pressures for international migration. It encourages domestic monopolies, while cutting the economy from mainstream developments in the world outside. Producers, dependent on protection for their survival, ultimately become prepared to spend large sums to preserve its continuance. Lobbying, and even bribery and corruption, become more widespread.

---

policies are, they have to be targeted on the unemployed directly, rather than in the form of general reflation.

Another aspect of persistence is mismatch. Policies to reduce this must involve making it easier for workers to change occupations by assistance for retraining and relocation. It could be argued that it is the responsibility of individuals or firms to finance retraining. However, individuals may be financially constrained, and firms may feel that it is not worth training a worker who may go elsewhere. The state funds education for the young, so there is no reason, in principle, why those needing retraining should be treated differently.

LABOUR MARKET REFORM

A third class of policies that may help to reduce unemployment involves labour market reforms, especially the structure of wage bargaining. We have seen that insiders may hold wage rates high, to the detriment of outsiders. We have also seen that centralized wage bargaining may generate lower unemployment than decentralized bargaining. However, union structures have evolved over decades, and it is no easy matter in a free society to scrap the lot and start again.

Conclusion

Unemployment is a major problem of our time. We have been able to understand, with a combination of the tools provided by the macro model and our new understanding of labour markets, how unemployment came about and why it is characterized by persistence. We have also learned why the traditional macroeconomic approach to reducing unemployment is no longer adequate.

The bad news is that reducing equilibrium unemployment is likely to take many years. The good news is that persistence does not mean permanence. Normal economic change and new economic policies can make progress against persistence which need not be accepted as inevitable.

Summary

1 Employment has grown little in Europe in the last three decades and unemployment has appeared to have an upward trend. However, unemployment is untrended in the long run.

2 It is useful to distinguish among several kinds of unemployment: (a) cyclical unemployment, which is caused by too low a level of aggregate demand; (b) frictional unemployment, which is caused by the length of time it takes to find a first job and to move from job to job as a result of normal labour turnover; and (c) structural unemployment, which is caused by the need to reallocate resources among occupations, regions, and industries as the structure of demands and supplies change. Together, frictional unemployment and structural unemployment make up equilibrium unemployment, the NAIRU, which is then expressed as a percentage of the total labour force.

3 New Classical theories look to explanations that allow the labour market to be cleared continuously. Such theories can explain cyclical variations in employment but do not explain involuntary unemployment, that is the unemployment of workers who would like to work at the going wage rates but for whom jobs are not available.

4 Recent New Keynesian theories have focused on the long-term nature of employer–worker relationships and on the possibility that it is efficient for employers to pay wages that are above the level that would clear the labour market.

5 The NAIRU will always be positive because it takes time for labour to move between jobs both in normal turnover and in response to changes in the structure of the demand for labour. Government policies can also influence the NAIRU.

6 Unemployment insurance helps to alleviate the human suffering that is associated with inevitable unemployment, but it also increases unemployment by encouraging persistence in unemployment.

7 Cyclical unemployment can be reduced by aggregate demand policies. Equilibrium unemployment can be reduced by lowering benefits (level and duration), imposing active manpower policies, and reforming wage bargaining institutions. However, in a growing, changing economy, populated by people who wish to change jobs for many reasons, it is neither possible nor desirable to reduce unemployment to zero. Most important is the avoidance of the buildup of long-term unemployment.

Topics for review

- Cyclical unemployment
- Frictional unemployment
- Structural unemployment
- Efficiency wages
- Hysteresis
- Persistence
- Determinants of the size of the NAIRU
- Policies to reduce unemployment

❧ CHAPTER 42

The government budget

IN early Keynesian macroeconomics, concerned as it was with curing recessions, it seemed like a good thing for the government to create a budget deficit (through an increase in government spending or a reduction in tax rates), because it provided an injection of net spending into the economy, which through the multiplier would lead to an increase in national income. Such a shift in fiscal policy might help to close a recessionary gap, but, if started when the economy was at potential national income, it would, of course, create an inflationary gap. When a monetary sector was added to the simple Keynesian income–expenditure model, it was seen that a budget deficit could crowd out private investment expenditure, and, by lowering private investment, could lower long-term growth. In Chapter 39, we saw that a budget deficit in an open economy with perfect capital mobility (starting in full equilibrium) would not stimulate national income at all, but rather would crowd out net exports, leading to an increase in foreign debt. Thus, the attitude to budget deficits has swung more towards the view that they are harmful, except in the relatively rare situation of prolonged major recessionary gaps.

Many major countries, notably Italy, Canada, and (to a lesser extent) the United States, have had substantial and sustained budget deficits in recent years and this has led to big buildups of public debt. Economists have worried about the long-term implications of this debt buildup. In the European Union, the 1992 Maastricht Treaty called for countries to have deficits of less than 3 per cent of GDP and public debt of less than 60 per cent of GDP by the end of the 1990s, in preparation for the possible adoption of a single EU currency. The single currency may never happen, but pressures to get (and keep) the public finances in 'balance' certainly will.[1]

The UK budget position in the recent past has not been problematic, by international standards. However, the deficit was over £40 billion in 1993/4, or about 7 per cent of GDP, and the United Kingdom is not immune from taxpayer (and voter) pressure to keep tax rates low and the budget under control.

This chapter studies the government budget and debt. First, we take a closer look at government spending and taxes. Then we look at the budget deficit and the resulting stock of debt. We ask: do debt and deficits matter? We then review, briefly, some arguments relating to the appropriate size of the public sector in a modern economy, and conclude by outlining some problems that will have to be faced in future relating to the demands likely to be put on the public purse.

The UK budget and the national debt

IN this section we look at some of the facts about the level and composition of government expenditure in the United Kingdom and the European Union. We look also at the main sources of tax revenue and the evolution of the budget deficit. Finally, we examine the national debt over the last century.

GOVERNMENT EXPENDITURE

In building our macroeconomic model, we included government expenditure, G. Recall that this is government current expenditure on goods and services. Total government spending, however, includes also government capital formation and transfers (including debt interest). Implicitly, we have included government investment in I, along with private investment; but transfers are not modelled explicitly, because they turn up in personal disposable income. (They were deducted from gross taxes to get net taxes.)

However, total government spending is the figure that has ultimately to be financed through taxation, so it is an important number as far as the government finances and taxpayers are concerned. The history of government spending as a proportion of GDP over the last century is shown in Figure 42.1. The figure shows both total government spending and spending on goods and services (the G of our theory).

Several features of this chart are worthy of comment. First, however, it should be noted that total government spending could, in principle, exceed 100 per cent of GDP and so it does not represent the share of the national 'cake' taken by the government.[2]

Not surprisingly, government expenditure rose sharply during the two world wars. It is also noticeable that spending settled at a new higher level after each of the wars. This has been referred to as the **displacement effect**.[3] The logic

---

[1] What 'balance' means in this context will be discussed below.

[2] Transfers are resources taken from the private sector and given back to the private sector. Government consumption, G, plus its investment is the part of national income not available for private use.

[3] The term was coined by UK economists Alan Peacock and Jack Wiseman in *The Growth of Public Expenditure in the United Kingdom* (Princeton University Press, 1961).

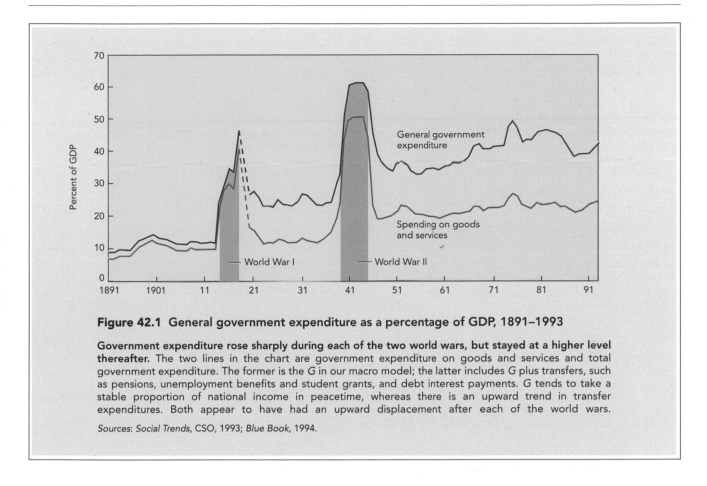

Figure 42.1 General government expenditure as a percentage of GDP, 1891–1993

Government expenditure rose sharply during each of the two world wars, but stayed at a higher level thereafter. The two lines in the chart are government expenditure on goods and services and total government expenditure. The former is the G in our macro model; the latter includes G plus transfers, such as pensions, unemployment benefits and student grants, and debt interest payments. G tends to take a stable proportion of national income in peacetime, whereas there is an upward trend in transfer expenditures. Both appear to have had an upward displacement after each of the world wars.

Sources: Social Trends, CSO, 1993; Blue Book, 1994.

of this is that government increased its participation in the economy during each war, but did not unwind it fully afterwards. Spending on goods and services stays broadly constant, as a proportion of GDP, in peacetime, though there was a rise between the early 1960s and mid-1970s. Since then G has stayed at just over 20 per cent of GDP, rising slightly as GDP falls in recessions, and falling as GDP rises in booms.

Total government spending, however, has been on a rising trend in the post-war period because of rising social security expenditure. Transfer payments are more cyclical than G, because of the inclusion of unemployment benefits; hence the fall in transfers in the late 1980s, and the subsequent rise in 1992 and 1993. A major reason for the upward trend in transfers, in addition to the high unemployment of the 1980s and early 1990s, is the growing proportion of pensioners in the population.

The composition of UK government spending by function is given in Table 42.1. It can be seen that social security payments have risen to about a third of total government spending. This massive component of the budget amounted to over £70 billion in 1993, or nearly £3,000 for every member of the work-force, and it considerably exceeded the

total expenditure on the National Health Service and education combined. The other component of expenditure to take a rising proportion of spending is health.

The composition of expenditures in the EU budget is shown in Table 42.2. This shows the cost of agricultural intervention polices at the EU level. Support for agriculture and fisheries takes around 60 per cent of total EU expenditure. The next largest category is regional policy with under 14 per cent, and then social policy with just over 8 per cent. Notice, however, that the EU budget is only about one-fifth the size of the UK government budget.

TAXATION

Government spending has to be financed. Tax revenue is not equal to government spending in every (or even most) year, but over the long run it has the same trend as total government spending. The contribution of different kinds of taxation to total tax revenue in 1993 is shown in Figure 42.2. Taxes on expenditure (mainly VAT and excise duties) are the largest single category, but if national insurance contributions (which are levied on income) were added to taxes on income the latter would be the largest category.

Table 42.1   UK general government expenditure by function, 1981–1992 (%)

	1981	1986	1991	1992
Defence[a]	10.8	11.8	9.2	9.7
Public order and safety	3.7	4.2	5.6	5.5
Education	12.2	11.9	12.9	12.7
Health	11.4	11.8	13.7	13.8
Social security	26.6	30.8	32.3	33.1
Housing and community amenities	6.1	5.0	4.0	4.3
Recreational and cultural affairs	1.4	1.5	1.7	1.6
Fuel and energy	0.3	–0.7	–1.5	–0.6
Agriculture, forestry, and fishing	1.4	1.3	1.2	1.1
Mining, mineral resources, manufacturing, and construction	3.0	1.2	0.7	0.5
Transport and communication	3.6	2.3	3.0	2.5
General public services	3.9	3.9	4.9	4.8
Other economic affairs and services	2.5	2.5	2.0	2.0
Other expenditure	13.1	12.7	9.4	9.1
Total expenditure (£ billion) (= 100%)	111.7	162.3	228.3	254.1

[a] Includes contributions by other countries towards the United Kingdom's cost of the Gulf conflict—£2.1 billion in 1991.

The proportions of total government spending going to health and social security have risen, while the proportion spent on defence and housing has fallen. The table shows the breakdown of general government expenditure by subsector. Health and education are the two largest components of government spending on goods and services. But, out of general government total spending, health and education combined are dwarfed by social security payments. Notice that the figures in columns are percentages, but the number at the foot of each column is the money value of the total. The money value of social security spending in, say, 1981 can be calculated as 26.6 per cent of £117.1 billion, which is £31.15 billion.

Source: Social Trends, CSO, 1994.

Table 42.2   European Community (now European Union) expenditure by sector, 1981–1993 (%)

	1981	1986	1991	1992
Agriculture and fisheries	65.5	66.0	61.6	58.8
Regional policy	13.6	7.1	11.8	13.6
Social policy	3.5	7.0	7.5	8.3
Co-operation with developing countries	4.2	3.0	4.1	4.6
Research, energy, industry, and transport	1.8	2.2	3.2	3.4
Administration	5.3	4.4	5.0	5.2
Other	6.2	10.2	4.0	1.8
Total expenditure (£ billion) (= 100%)	9.8	23.2	37.6	49.4

By far the largest category of EU expenditure is on the Common Agricultural Policy (CAP). Expenditure on agriculture and fisheries accounts for nearly 60 per cent of the EU budget. Regional policy is next largest, with under 14 per cent of total spending. Notice, however, that the EU budget is only about one-fifth the size of the UK government budget, though it is spread around (currently) 12 countries. This indicates that EU federal governmental activity is still small compared to the governmental activity of member states.

Source: Social Trends, CSO, 1994.

Taxes on income consist of about 75 per cent personal income tax and 20 per cent corporation tax; the rest is made up of capital gains tax and inheritance tax.

THE BUDGET DEFICIT

Before considering the budget deficit, we need to clarify what we mean by 'government'. There are three broad concepts of the government in the United Kingdom. The government sector that we have been referring to so far is sometimes called the 'general government' sector, to dis-tinguish it from 'central government'. The difference is that central government excludes local authorities. A third category, which is even broader than general government, is the 'public sector'. This includes central government, local authorities, and publicly owned institutions and industries. Central government is by far the largest component of these other two sectors, but it is important to avoid confusing them.

In macroeconomic theory, 'government' always corresponds to general government, but UK policy discussions of the budget deficit usually relate to the deficit of the public sector. This makes some sense from a financial markets perspective, since the public-sector deficit influences how much the government will want to borrow. However, even here confusion arises because there is a difference between the commonly quoted Public Sector Borrowing Requirement (PSBR) and the public-sector financial deficit. The latter is the difference between public-sector current expenditures and receipts, whereas the PSBR may be reduced (relative to the public-sector deficit) by asset sales such as privatizations.

The public-sector financial surplus as a proportion of GDP, since 1963, is shown in Figure 42.3. A surplus is a positive number, while a deficit is negative. For most of the period there has been a deficit, but there were two short periods of surplus: 1969/70 and 1988/9. In general, for given tax and benefit rates, the deficit will increase in a recession and fall in a boom. This is because tax revenue

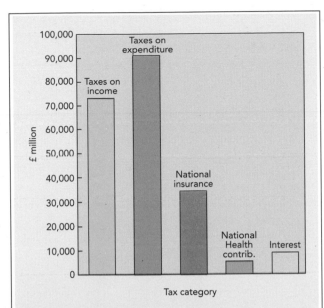

Figure 42.2 Sources of government revenue, United Kingdom 1993

The main categories of taxation are taxes on income, taxes on expenditure, and national insurance contributions. The figure shows the amounts of money raised by these different forms of taxation. Taxes on income come largely from personal income taxes, but also include corporation tax and capital gains tax. Taxes on expenditure are dominated by VAT, but also include excise duties on drink and tobacco, and import duties. National insurance contributions are really another tax on income but they have an upper limit so they are not paid at the margin on high incomes.

Source: Economic Trends, CSO.

automatically rises (for given tax rates) as national income rises and social security expenditure falls as unemployment falls; hence the deficits during the 1974–5 and 1990–3 recessions and the surplus at the time of the 1988 boom.

GOVERNMENT DEBT

Deficits have to be financed by borrowing, and borrowing creates debt, so the outstanding stock of debt is the result of accumulations arising from past deficits. A similar confusion arises in the definition of debt as it did for the deficit. There are two commonly used classifications for government debt: the **national debt** is the debt of the central government, while the **public-sector debt** is the debt of the entire public sector. Confusion arises because it sounds as if the national debt is the debt of the whole country, rather than just of the central government. The national debt is

smaller than the public-sector debt (though not substantially so).

Figure 42.4 shows the national debt as a percentage of GDP since 1885. We use the national debt rather than the public-sector debt, because historical data are more readily available, and the long-term trends in the two would be almost identical. Clearly, the dominant events this century were the increases in debt associated with the two world wars. Notice, however, that debt grew higher after the First World War, whereas it was reduced back to its pre-1914 level in the thirty years after the Second World War. The difference between these two episodes is due to the fact that in the inter-war period the price level fell, so that the real value of the nominal debt rose. After the Second World War the price level rose, not rapidly (until the mid-1970s) but consistently, so that debt fell as a percentage of nominal national income, even though the government was usually running a deficit and, therefore, increasing its nominal debt.

The real revenue stream accruing to the government from inflation eroding the real value of its debt is known as the **inflation tax**. It improves the financial position of the government just as if it had raised real tax revenue at constant prices. The inflation tax revenue is paid by holders of government debt, who see the real value of their savings fall. In recent years, the government has issued some of its debt with a rate of return and capital value guaranteed in real terms (index-linked gilts), but these were not available to investors who helped finance the Second World War.

Governments worry about debt because it can get out of control so that they end up having to set high tax rates just to pay the interest on the debt. It is for this reason also that they worry about sustained deficits; for, with a constant price level, deficits increase the level of debt.

The UK fiscal position was not especially worrying in this regard in 1994, notwithstanding the 1993/4 deficit of around 7 per cent of GDP. This is because the UK national debt is low by international standards, at less than 40 per cent of GDP. Countries with more serious problems include Italy and Belgium, which have public debts in excess of 100 per cent of GDP. However, UK deficits on the 1993/4 scale sustained for five years (at zero inflation and slow real GDP growth) could double the debt–GDP ratio.

Evaluating the deficit

To judge the importance of the deficit, economists look at the different forces that influence it. This allows them to define several different deficits whose separate behaviours shed light on the deficit as a whole.

The most serious problem in judging either the long-run importance of the deficit or how well it is doing its job as a short-term built-in stabilizer arises from the fact that the deficit is determined partly exogenously, by the govern-

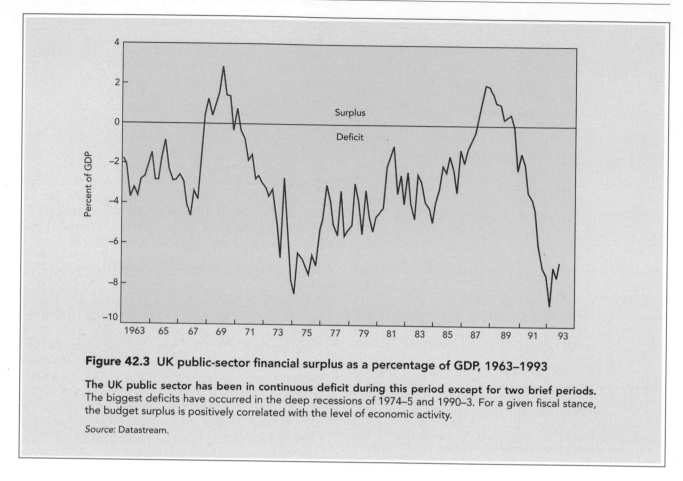

Figure 42.3 UK public-sector financial surplus as a percentage of GDP, 1963–1993

The UK public sector has been in continuous deficit during this period except for two brief periods.
The biggest deficits have occurred in the deep recessions of 1974–5 and 1990–3. For a given fiscal stance,
the budget surplus is positively correlated with the level of economic activity.

Source: Datastream.

ment's fiscal policy, and partly endogenously, by the state of the economy. Let us see why this is so. We now return to thinking of the government budget balance as it is defined in our macro model, i.e. as the difference between government spending on goods and services and taxes *net of transfers.*

Government tax revenues, as we have just seen, are related to the performance of the economy. For a given tax rate, tax revenues will rise when national income rises and fall when national income falls. Because government expenditure on goods and services is relatively insensitive to the level of national income, the budget surplus will rise (the budget deficit will fall) as national income rises. This relationship is given by the *budget surplus function*. This function is illustrated in Figure 42.5 by the curves labelled $B = T - G$, where B stands for budget surplus.

With a given spending and taxing policy, as national income changes, the budget surplus changes in the same direction.

When the government makes its plans for spending and taxing, it determines the position of the budget surplus

function. The higher the net tax rate, the higher and steeper will be the curve in Figure 42.5. (Recall that the net tax rate includes taxes net of transfer payments; typically, tax revenues rise *and* transfer payments fall as income rises.) The lower the level of planned government spending, the higher will be the budget surplus function. The higher is the budget surplus function, the higher will be the surplus (the lower the deficit) *at any given level of national income.*

Fiscal policy determines the *position* of the budget surplus (or deficit) function.

The actual budget surplus (or deficit)   Tax rates were not cut in the early 1990s, yet the budget balance went from a small surplus in 1989 to a massive deficit in 1993. This happened almost entirely because the economy went into a deep recession. Thus, while there was no shift in the budget surplus function, the economy moved to the left along the existing curve. The outcome was an increase in the deficit. Part (i) of Figure 42.5 illustrates how, with a given budget surplus function, a fall in national income will raise the budget deficit or lower the surplus, while a rise in national income will lower the deficit or raise the surplus.

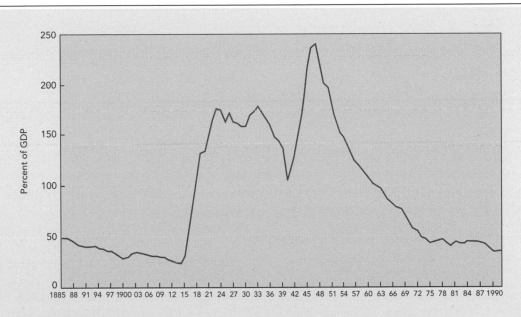

Figure 42.4 The ratio of national debt to GDP, United Kingdom, 1885–1992

The national debt rose dramatically as a result of the two world wars, but by the 1980s it was down to pre-1914 levels in relation to GDP. However, in the inter-war period the debt–GDP ratio stayed high because the price level fell. After the Second World War the debt–GDP ratio fell consistently because of steady inflation. As a result, even though there were consistent deficits (apart from a brief period at the end of the 1980s), the debt ratio stayed down around pre-1914 levels.

Sources: B. R. Mitchell, *British Historical Statistics*, Cambridge University Press, 1988; Datastream.

The actual level of the budget surplus (or deficit) depends on both fiscal policy, which determines the location of the budget surplus function, and the level of national income, which determines a specific point on the budget surplus function.

The cyclically adjusted surplus (or deficit) Because it depends in part on the level of national income, the actual budget deficit is a poor measure either of the effect of fiscal policy on the economy or of the long-term deficit problem. For example, if national income fell by enough, the budget deficit could increase at the same time that fiscal policy became more restrictive. In order to measure the fiscal stance independently of the level of national income, it is necessary to develop a measure of the budget balance that is also independent of the level of national income.

Economists have developed the concept of the **cyclically adjusted surplus** (CAS) and **cyclically adjusted deficit** (CAD). These are also known as the *structural surplus* (or *deficit*), defined as the budget surplus (or deficit) that would obtain if the economy were operating at potential national income.[4]

Fixing the level of income at which the surplus is measured removes the changes in the actual deficit that are caused by changes in income. The structural surplus measures the position of the budget surplus function, which is determined solely by fiscal policy.

Parts (ii) and (iii) of Figure 42.5 illustrate how the CAD can be used to judge the stance of fiscal policy. The higher is the structural deficit, the higher is the government's net contribution to aggregate expenditure at that level of income.

Some economists have also proposed calculating an inflation adjustment as well as a cyclical adjustment to the government budget. The logic of an *inflation-adjusted surplus* is that it incorporates the impact of the inflation tax. Therefore, it shows the change in the real financial balance of the government, rather than its nominal value. It is the real financial balance that is appropriate for macro theory.

---

[4] The concept used to be called the *full-employment surplus* or *deficit*. The change from 'full-employment' to 'cyclically adjusted' came during the 1970s, when the amount of unemployment associated with potential income rose so much that referring to it as 'full-employment' became embarrassing.

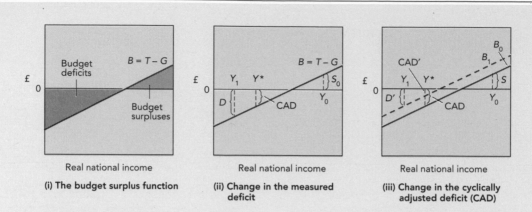

Figure 42.5 The budget surplus (deficit) function

The budget surplus can change either because of a change in fiscal policy or because of a change in national income. Parts (i) and (ii) illustrate the same budget surplus function, showing that the budget surplus increases (budget deficit falls) as national income rises.

Part (ii) defines the cyclically adjusted surplus (or deficit) (CAS or CAD) as the budget balance that obtains at potential national income, Y^*. In the example, the CAD is a deficit. At a sufficiently high income Y_0, the actual budget would be in surplus by an amount S_0. At incomes lower than Y^*, such as Y_1, the actual budget would be in deficit by D, more than the amount of the CAD. Throughout the curve in part (ii), fiscal policy is unchanged. The deficit and surplus change only because national income changes. Part (iii) shows how the actual deficit (or surplus) might move in a different direction from the CAD or CAS. Suppose the economy starts at Y_0, with fiscal policy given by B_0. If fiscal policy is made more restrictive, through some combination of higher taxes and lower government spending, the budget balance will now behave according to B_1. At the same time, if income should fall to Y_1, the budget surplus of S will turn into a deficit of D'. By looking at the actual budget balance, one would see the budget move from surplus to deficit, suggesting, incorrectly, that the fiscal policy had become more stimulative of the economy. Focusing on the CAD, however, the level of budget balance at Y^*, makes it clear that B_1 is more restrictive than B_0—that CAD' is smaller than CAD at Y^* (and at every level of income) with the fiscal policy given by B_1.

Why worry about deficits?

So much for the size of deficits and their appropriate measurement. The next question is: should we worry about them?

Postponed tax liability

Suppose that the government decides to make £1 billion of additional expenditure. It can raise tax rates until its revenues rise by £1 billion, and the matter ends there. Or it can borrow £1 billion by selling £1 billion worth of gilts. As long as that debt exists, the interest on it is the cost of postponing the payment of £1 billion. At an interest rate of 6 per cent, this would be £60 million per annum. When the debt is redeemed, £1 billion of current tax revenue is used at that time to pay for the original expenditure (assuming that the debt is not rolled over by further borrowing). As Professor Milton Friedman once put it, 'There is no such thing as a free lunch.' Government expenditure must be paid for: either it is paid for by current tax payments, or the liability is passed on to the future. The current cost of passing the tax liability on is the current interest bill that must be paid on the debt incurred to finance the expenditure.

Debt is a postponed tax liability, and the interest paid on that debt is the cost of postponing the liability.

Ricardian neutrality

Some economists have argued that, *for a given level of real government spending,* the size of the deficit has no important effects on the economy. This idea is known as the **Ricardian neutrality proposition**, or **Ricardian equivalence.**[5] Its main modern advocate is Harvard economist Robert Barro.

Suppose that the government has plans for real expenditure that involve an increase in spending next year. The issue is: does it make any difference to the real impact of this expenditure increase if it is financed by borrowing rather than increasing next year's taxes? For most macroeconomists the answer is that, at least in the short run, the expenditure increase financed by borrowing will increase aggregate demand more than the increase financed by taxes. (The effect of an expenditure increase financed by taxes is not zero because of the balanced budget multiplier, discussed in Chapter 30.)

For the Ricardian, these two alternatives have an identical impact on private-sector behaviour. The reason is that the present value of the taxes to be paid is the same either way. Citizens either have to pay taxes next year equal to the expenditure increase, or they have to pay taxes plus interest at some future date. Discounting (through net present value calculations) the future tax liability back to the same point in time (using the same interest rate as the rate on government debt) produces the same result. So the present value of citizens' future tax liabilities is the same either way. Hence their behaviour should be the same: they should adjust their consumption behaviour *as if* their personal disposable incomes had fallen by the present value of the extra taxes; that is to say, they should save enough today to pay their taxes in future.

Notice that this theory does *not* say that different paths of real government spending, however financed, will *not* have different real effects. It merely says that, for given government expenditure plans, the way in which those plans are financed in a perfect capital market make no difference to their real effects.

Ricardian equivalence has been mistakenly interpreted as saying that whatever the government does with its budget makes no difference. This is a mistaken interpretation. Even the correct interpretation could be wrong if capital markets were imperfect, individuals were myopic (i.e. discounted the future at a rate higher than the market interest rate), or behaved as if they had finite horizons (so that they did not care about the debts of future generations). However, the approach does alert us to one important possibility. This is that it is the *level* of government activity in an economy that matters most for its impact on the private sector, rather than the way in which that activity is financed. We shall return to this issue below.[6]

A less formal, and somewhat different, argument — that the national debt is of no concern to the nation as a whole

since it is something that we as citizens owe to ourselves—is discussed in Box 42.1.

Effects of deficits

For most economists, the relevant question is not whether deficits have effects, but the form and magnitude of those effects.

One way in which deficits influence the economy is through their short-run stabilizing or destabilizing effects.

This stabilization role was emphasized in Chapter 32. Figure 42.5 shows the complications that arise when the current deficit is used to judge the stance of fiscal policy for stabilization purposes. However, the effect of deficits in the macro model arises through its effect on current spending decisions. What we have learned in this chapter is that, whether or not the financing implications are neutral as the Ricardians think, the cumulative effects of a deficit via a buildup of debt do have to be taken seriously.

A second way in which deficits can influence the economy is through their potential to affect income and welfare adversely in the long run.

We have already seen in Chapter 39 that a budget deficit (in full equilibrium) will crowd out investment in the absence of capital flows (or with imperfect capital flows) by forcing up interest rates, and that it will crowd out net exports, in the presence of capital mobility, by causing a real exchange rate appreciation. Hence we must recall that the impact of a deficit on the macro model is not independent of the external regime within which it is operating.

WILL A DEFICIT CAUSE INFLATION?

Neither economic theory nor the available evidence suggests that deficits by themselves are sufficient to cause inflation. The worry that persistent deficits may cause inflation arises out of the fear that a persistent deficit will eventually cause the Bank of England to increase the money supply, which, as we saw in Chapter 40, is a necessary condition for a sustained inflation.

---

[5] The originator of the idea was the English economist David Ricardo (1772–1823). His main work was *Principles of Political Economy and Taxation* (1817). He also put forward the idea that 'comparative costs' determined the pattern of international trade. He was a Member of Parliament from 1819 to 1823, in which capacity he contributed to the campaign for free trade.

[6] When increased current taxes pay for the increase in government spending G, personal disposable income Y_d is reduced. When debt sales are used to finance the increase in G, personal wealth W is reduced by the discounted present value of future taxes. Since W appears in a fully specified consumption function, both of these changes reduce consumption expenditure.

BOX 42.1

....

Does the national debt matter? The owe-it-to-ourselves view

A few economists have argued that, since the national debt simply involves a debt of some UK citizens payable to other UK citizens, it imposes no net burden on the country. Of course, these economists recognize that the debt is a burden to taxpayers in general, who ultimately must provide the funds for the government to make interest payments on the debt. But, the 'owe-it-to-ourselves' argument holds, that burden is exactly offset by the interest payments that are made to Britons who own government bonds.

The owe-it-to-ourselves view thus argues that the major effect of the national debt is that interest payments on it merely redistribute income from the general taxpayer towards bond-holders. Since government bonds are widely held, being a major component of most public and private pension funds, the argument holds that even this redistribution of income is not a serious matter.

This contention raises several issues.

Crowding out

First, suppose that the basic facts alleged in the owe-it-to-ourselves view are true—that is, that virtually all UK government debt is in fact held by Britons. Even in this case, it does not follow that there is no net burden to the UK economy arising from the government debt.

Economic theory and evidence suggest that government bonds are held instead of claims on income streams produced by real capital. That is, if the debt did not exist, people would still wish to hold assets to provide income in the future; in the absence of government debt, they would invest in corporations engaged in producing goods and services. Thus, the bonds, which on balance contribute nothing to the economy but merely redistribute income from one group to another, crowd out investment in real capital, which would have created wealth and income for UK citizens.

Furthermore, taxes must be levied to pay the interest on the national debt. High tax rates can become counterproductive in driving people and capital either abroad or into the underground economy. This can have serious effects on the economy.

Finally, if the debt gets so large that lenders fear the tax base cannot support it, they will demand large risk premia, which will put further pressure on the tax system and could, as it has with some other governments, lead to a fiscal crisis where further money cannot be borrowed at an acceptable interest rate.

International capital mobility

The basic contention that the debt is merely owed to ourselves is not completely true. Though most UK government securities

(gilts) are held by UK citizens, they are also sold on international markets, and a rising proportion is held by foreigners. Accordingly, the interest payments on some of these securities, which must be financed by UK taxpayers, accrue to overseas residents.

The fact that some UK government debt is held abroad is enough to upset the owe-it-to-ourselves view. But the situation is even more complicated—and more damaging to this view.

Suppose that a UK company wishes to float a new debt issue in order to finance a new factory. Although it might normally expect to sell a large fraction of the new bonds on the London market, the volume of the UK government's gilt sales to finance its budget deficit may force the company to sell much of its debt abroad. Given the total amount of debt issued by the UK government, there may not be enough UK savings to finance the borrowing requirements of both the government and the private sector. It is thus inevitable that many new issues of shares and bonds are sold to foreigners.

Again, there will be a burden to the national debt not in the form of a reduced capital stock in the United Kingdom, but in the form of reduced income and wealth for UK residents. Foreign nationals will now own claims to the income from the new UK investment projects, and some of the income from these projects will accrue to those foreign nationals.

In this case, the burden to the national debt arises *indirectly* because of the need that it creates for UK firms to finance their investment by selling bonds and equities abroad. Once this indirect effect is recognized, simply looking at the share of foreign ownership of the national debt does not give a good indication of how much is owed to ourselves and how much is actually owed to foreign nationals.

What limits the acceptable size of the deficit?

If the owe-it-to-ourselves view were correct, there should be no limit to an acceptable level of government debt. Surely the politicians would like that, as it would allow them to avoid many of the difficult decisions involved in restraining expenditure and raising taxes. However, since the debt represents postponed tax liabilities, a debt that grows faster than GDP will eventually exceed the capacity of taxpayers to finance the growing interest bill which is the current cost of postponing these liabilities. When this happens, a crisis will suddenly stop further borrowing. Drastic spending cuts and tax increases will have to be imposed rapidly. Such a crisis hit New Zealand, which tumbled from boasting the world's third highest living standard to the twenty-third highest in the course of a very few years, and in the process was forced to reduce drastically its whole income support system.

To date, however, this has not been a problem, as the deficit has been financed by government borrowing in pri-

vate-sector capital markets. Only if it were financed by selling government securities to the Bank would the growth rate in the money supply be increased. (When this happens, the Bank *creates* the money to finance the deficit by giving the government new deposits in return for its new securities.) If this increase in the money supply is too rapid, then—as we saw in Chapter 40—it will cause inflation.

WILL THE NATIONAL DEBT HARM FUTURE GENERATIONS?

In a closed economy, or in an open economy with limited capital flows, public debt crowds out private debt. This will harm long-term growth if the borrowed resources are spent on consumption or if they are invested less productively in the public sector than they would have been in the private sector. Many economists think that public-sector resource use is normally less efficient than that in the private sector, and it is partly this presumption that has driven the recent wave of privatizations.

In an open economy, under flexible exchange rates with mobile capital, deficits increase borrowing from abroad. Payments of interest and dividends on liabilities owed abroad will lower GNP (defined in Chapter 28) in relation to GDP (i.e. net property income from abroad is negative), since some of the income generated in the home economy will accrue to foreign residents in the form of interest payments. These payments will lower GNP relative to what it would have been without the deficits, unless, of course, the deficit was due to public investment which had a higher rate of return than the interest on the debt.

Borrowing from abroad entails a transfer of purchasing power to domestic residents when the borrowing occurs, and a transfer back to foreign residents when interest payments and repayments of principal occur.

Future generations have either to repay the debt or continue to pay interest on it. Thus, they are either paying the tax bill for things their parents and grandparents received from the government, or they are paying the interest cost of postponing the bill to a yet later date. If their parents and grandparents saved to offset the deficit (as in Ricardian equivalence), later generations might inherit the wealth to offset their extra tax burden. Equivalently, if the government invested the resources in projects that had a rate of return at least as high as the interest rate on their debt, then national income would grow at sufficient rate to meet the future tax burden without difficulty. In cases where government investment is paid for out of current taxation (is not debt-financed), current taxpayers could be paying for capital formation which will benefit their children and grandchildren.

Proposals to control the deficit

As we have seen, government deficits (under standard non-Ricardian theory) contribute to aggregate demand and hence can play a useful role in damping cyclical fluctuations in the economy. As we have seen also, government deficits at potential national income either crowd out domestic investment or increase foreign borrowing, and thereby lead to a reduction in future living standards of the average UK resident (subject to the proviso above).

This conflict, between the short-term stabilization role of deficits and the long-term adverse effects, has been a subject of constant debate among economists and others who are concerned with government policy. Views range from those who dismiss the long-run costs of deficits to those who believe that deficits should never be used for short-term stabilization. We now look at some of the specific proposals that have been put forward. Some of the possibilities are illustrated in Figure 42.6.

AN ANNUALLY BALANCED BUDGET

Much of the rhetoric of fiscal restraint urges governments to balance the budget. In some countries there have been calls for constitutional changes requiring that the budget always be balanced. The discussion earlier in this chapter suggests that an annually balanced budget would be extremely difficult, perhaps impossible, to achieve. With fixed tax rates, tax revenues fluctuate as national income fluctuates. Much government expenditure is fixed by past commitments, and most of the rest is hard to change quickly.

Yet suppose an annually balanced budget, or something approaching it, were feasible. What would its effects be? Would it be desirable?

A government sector whose expenditures on goods and services are not very sensitive to the cyclical variations in national income acts as a built-in stabilizer for the economy, because tax revenue increases as national income increases (see Chapter 32). To insist that annual government expenditure be tied to annual tax receipts would be to abandon the present built-in stability provided by the government. Government expenditure would then become a major *destabilizing* force. Tax revenues necessarily rise in booms and fall in slumps. An annually balanced budget would force government expenditure to do the same. Changes in national income would then cause induced changes not only in household consumption expenditure, but also in government expenditure. This would greatly increase the economy's marginal propensity to spend and hence would increase the value of the multiplier. In the terminology of Chapter 32, this would serve as a *built-in destabilizer*!

An annually balanced budget would accentuate the swings in national income that accompany changes in such autonomous expenditure flows as investment and exports.

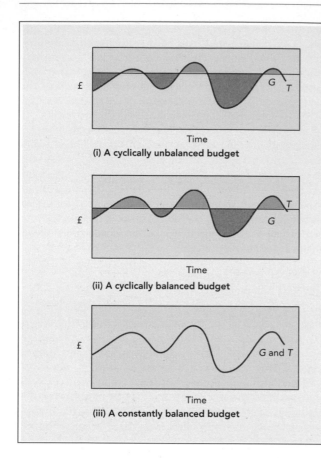

Figure 42.6 Balanced and unbalanced budgets

An annually (constantly) balanced budget is a destabilizer; a cyclically balanced budget is a stabilizer. The flow of tax receipts, T, is shown varying over the business cycle; in parts (i) and (ii) government expenditure, G, is shown at a constant rate.

In part (i) deficits (red areas) are common and surpluses (blue areas) are rare, because the average level of expenditure exceeds the average level of taxes. Such a policy will tend to stabilize the economy against cyclical fluctuations, but there is likely to be debt accumulation.

In part (ii) government expenditure has been reduced until it is approximately equal to the average level of tax receipts. The budget is now balanced cyclically. The policy still tends to stabilize the economy against cyclical fluctuations because of deficits in slumps and surpluses in booms. However, the average fiscal stance is neither strongly expansionary nor strongly contractionary.

In part (iii) a balanced budget has been imposed. Deficits have been prevented, but government expenditure now varies over the business cycle, which tends to destabilize the economy by accentuating the cyclical swings in aggregate expenditure.

A CYCLICALLY BALANCED BUDGET

An alternative policy—one that would prevent continual deficits (and could also inhibit the growth in the size of the government sector)—would be to balance the budget over the business cycle. This would be more feasible than an annually balanced budget, and it would not make government expenditure a destabilizing force.

Although more attractive in principle than the annually balanced budget, a cyclically balanced budget would present problems of its own. One government might well spend in excess of its revenue in one year and then lose power, leaving the next government to have to spend less than current revenue in following years. Could such an obligation to balance over a period of several years be made binding? It could be made a legal requirement through an Act of Parliament, but future Parliaments would be able to change the rules.[7]

Perhaps even more of a problem is that there is always room for some disagreement about the current state of the business cycle. A requirement to balance the budget over the business cycle can only be implemented on the basis of some forecast of future economic conditions. Forecasting of the level of economic activity is an imperfect science, to say the least, and there will be genuine disagreement among economists about what stage of the business cycle the economy is in and where the economy is headed. Compounding the difficulty that arises from such uncertainty is the fact that politicians will have a stake in the economic forecast. Those who favour increased government spending will tend to argue that *this* year is an unusually bad one and that the deficits of this year can be made up by the surpluses in (better) years to come. On the other side, some will always tend to find *this* year to be unusually good —a time to run surpluses against the hard times to follow.

Although a budget balanced over the course of the business cycle is in principle an acceptable way of reconciling short-term stabilization and long-term concerns with national saving, it may not be possible in practice to define the business cycle well enough to make the proposal operational.

Allowing for growth   A further problem is that the goal of budget *balance*, whether applied annually or over the cycle,

[7] The United States for many years has had a law limiting the size of the government debt, but it has never had much effect. Every time the national debt approaches the 'debt ceiling', fixed in some prior year, Congress raises the ceiling and the President signs the new ceiling into law.

BOX 42.2

Debt, deficits, and sustainability

One way of checking whether concern about persistent government budget deficits is justified is to ask whether the current fiscal plan is *sustainable*. A sustainable fiscal plan is one that will not lead to unlimited growth in the debt–GDP ratio.

An unsustainable fiscal plan leads to debt and interest payments which are an ever increasing fraction of GDP. If the present fiscal plan is unsustainable, the government will eventually have to introduce some fiscal correction; otherwise, its deficit will eventually absorb all of the tax revenue in interest payments on the debt.

To examine this issue more fully, we need to introduce a fundamental equation that describes the evolution of the debt–GDP ratio over time. To do this, we let B stand for the size of the government debt, Y stand for national income as measured by GDP, and b for the ratio of the two; that is, $b = B/Y$, the debt–GDP ratio. Next let b' stand for the change in the debt–GDP ratio over time. A positive value for b' means that the ratio is increasing, and a negative value for b' means that the ratio is decreasing. b' can be expressed as the sum of the two terms in the following equation:

$$b' = (g - t) + (i - n)b.$$

The first term on the right-hand side is called the *primary deficit*, and it shows the difference between government expenditure and tax revenue, each as a fraction of GDP. The second term is the debt–GDP ratio b multiplied by the difference between the interest rate i and the rate of growth of GDP, n.

To see the role of these two terms, we consider each in isolation. First, suppose that the primary deficit is zero ($g = t$). The equation shows that in this case the change in the debt–GDP ratio is equal to the term $(i - n)b$. This tells us that there are two competing pressures on b'. Interest payments (ib) have to be financed by issuing new debt, so there is upward pressure of this amount on b. This tends to make b' positive. However, since we are concerned with the ratio of debt to GDP, growth in GDP serves to reduce the ratio. The term $(-nb)$ puts downward pressure on the ratio and hence tends to make b' negative. Thus, whether the ratio rises or falls depends on whether the interest rate i is greater than or less than the growth rate n.

Now suppose that the interest rate i is just equal to the growth rate n. This makes the second term in the equation zero, so the change in the ratio is equal to $g - t$. This means that the primary deficit will cause the debt–GDP ratio to rise over time. A primary surplus means that the debt–GDP ratio will fall over time.

We can now examine the conditions that must be met if the 'deficit' is to be sustainable. There are two cases, depending on the relation between the interest rate i and the growth rate n.

First, consider the case where the interest rate i is less than the growth rate n. In this case, even if there is a primary deficit ($g > t$) that makes b' positive, the ratio will eventually turn down. Initially, the primary deficit will cause the debt–GDP ratio to grow. However, this growth in b increases the weight given to the second term in the equation, which is negative. As this second term grows in absolute size, the rate at which the debt grows, given by b', falls. Eventually, b' will reach zero, and hence the ratio b will be constant.

Second, consider the case where the interest rate i is greater than the growth rate n. In this case, the second term in the equation is positive. For b' to be zero now requires a primary surplus, so that a negative value of $g - t$ offsets the positive value of $(i - n)b$.

A further difficulty arises in this second case because it involves an inherent instability. Any increase in b—say, arising from a temporary primary budget deficit—will tend to make b' positive and thus cause further increases in b. This is because the initial rise in b increases the weight given to the second term in the equation (where the interest payment effect ib outweighs the growth effect nb). In order to limit this self-reinforcing and potentially explosive effect, the government would have to undertake discretionary fiscal actions to create a primary surplus, so that the negative effects of the first term again offset the positive effects of the second term.

Since interest rates normally exceed the rate of growth of GDP, this sounds very pessimistic for the possibilities of sustainable budget deficits. However, a glance back at Figure 42.4 should serve to remind us that this analysis applies to real (inflation-adjusted) deficits rather than to nominal deficits. Equivalently, the interest rate in question should be seen as the real interest rate, not the nominal rate. It is much more common for the real rate to be less than the rate of growth than for the nominal rate, though real rates have been high in the 1990s in comparison with, say, the 1970s.

is, in fact, stricter than is required to avoid a rising debt–GDP ratio. Growth in GDP (due either to growth in real output or to inflation) means that some growth in the debt, and hence a (small) deficit, is consistent with a stable debt–GDP ratio.

For economists who think of a stable debt–GDP ratio as the appropriate indicator of fiscal prudence, *budget bal-*

ance means a deficit such that the debt grows at the same rate as nominal GDP.

The need for fiscal prudence is accepted by virtually everyone. How to evaluate it and enforce it, however, is still subject to controversy. Indeed, there is serious doubt that the idea of a balanced budget over any time period is operational. Many economists believe that a superior alternative to insisting on a precise balance is to pay attention to the balance without making a fetish of never adding to the national debt.

Some further aspects of the concern about growth in the debt–GDP ratio are discussed in Box 42.2.

THE POLITICAL ECONOMY OF THE DEBT

Almost all economists accept that, if the debt got so large that it could not be serviced without either putting a crushing burden on taxpayers or forcing the government to create new money to service it, there would be serious problems. This is not a current problem in the United Kingdom, but it could be in the future, and it is in some other countries. Others think that the overriding principle is that the debt should be allowed to vary according to the needs of stabilization policy.

An alternative view is what has come to be called *fiscal conservatism*. The main premiss of fiscal conservatives is that governments are not passive agents that do what is necessary to create full employment and maximize social welfare: rather, they are composed of individuals—elected officials, legislators, and civil servants—who, like everyone else, seek mainly to maximize their own well-being. Their welfare is best served by a big role for government and by a satisfied electorate. Thus, they tend to favour spending and

to resist tax increases. This creates a persistent tendency towards deficits which is quite independent of any consideration of a sound fiscal policy. It is the fiscal conservatives who are most in favour of legal restrictions on the budget deficit.

The debate reflects deeply held views about the role of government, the nature and motivation of public officials, and the desirability of stabilization. Keynesians are more likely to emphasize the potential benefits from active fiscal policy and to regard substantial government intervention as essential to an effective and humane society. Fiscal conservatives are likely to see public intervention, however well motivated, as probably inept and ultimately destabilizing.

The deficits of the past decade in many countries have also received so much public attention that the majority of both Keynesians and fiscal conservatives consistently argue that deficits must be controlled. In spite of the fact that deficit reduction is politically uncontroversial in principle, it has proved very difficult to effect in practice. This is not entirely surprising. As we have seen, most of the harm that will arise from deficits will appear only over the very long term, in the form of reduced living standards in the future. To do something about deficits, politicians must raise taxes and cut spending today, imposing real costs on today's voters, when the uncertain benefits of those actions will be reaped only in the relatively distant future.

How big should government be?

MOST of this chapter has been about the financing of government activity, with concerns about debt and deficits. However, behind all this lies a deeper issue, which is: what should be the *level* of government activity? Many of the issues involved in answering this question take us beyond the bounds of macroeconomic policy. But it is important to remember that there are good reasons why some activity has evolved within the government sector.

In macroeconomics, we treat G as if it were purchases by the government of the output of the domestic industrial sector, which then disappears into a black hole. In reality, government expenditure is on the production of goods and services that are usually freely provided to the public, such as health and education (see Table 42.1 on p. 828).

In the private sector, if consumers want to consume more of a product, they express their desires through the market and producers respond by supplying more output. In the non-market public sector, however, that mechanism is not (usually) available. The level of provision of these ser-

vices is decided through the political process rather than through the market. This means that it is quite possible that the politically determined supply will be either too little or too much, compared with some notional economic optimum.

PUBLIC GOODS

In Chapter 23 (see p. 420), we discovered that there are some goods, known as public goods, which cannot be provided by the normal market mechanism. This is because they are jointly consumed, so that, once provided, everybody gets the benefit whether they like it or not. More importantly, since you benefit whether you pay or not, there is an incentive not to pay. If payment is linked to benefit, there is an incentive to lie about how much you benefit. This is known as the *free-rider problem*.

All this means that pure public goods such as defence systems and law and order will usually have to be provided through the political process rather than the market, and to be paid for out of taxation.

More controversial is the extent to which goods such as health services and education, which are not pure public goods, should be provided free by the state, or through the market. With health and education, it is normally argued that there are external benefits (social benefits) as well as private benefits to be had from a suitable level of provision, which justify state involvement. There may also be a case for public provision of health and education on grounds of equity. Both justifications can be debated, but the important point here is that the state has taken these on board (in the United Kingdom and many other countries), and the problem is to decide on the right rate of growth of the provision of these services.

It could be that people would choose a higher national expenditure on these services than that generated through the political process if there were some other channel for expressing their preferences.

WAGNER'S LAW

What seems to happen in most industrial countries, as Figure 42.1 indicates, is that in peace-time governments plan the growth of their expenditures on goods and services so that they maintain a roughly constant share of national income.[8]

This proportionality between state activity and national income was observed over a century ago by the German economist Adolf Wagner (1835–1917), and hence it is known in some quarters as **Wagner's law**. Wagner has mistakenly been interpreted as having said that state activity would grow for ever as a proportion of national activity—his proposition is sometimes referred to as the *law of increasing state activity*. Clearly, this cannot be possible, as the proportion is bounded from above. However, what Wagner actually said was that after growth in the proportion of state activity during the development phase of an economy, there would be a maximum proportion of state activity in the national economy that would not permanently be exceeded:

There is thus a proportion between public expenditure and national income which may not be permanently overstepped. This only confirms the rule that there must be some sort of balance in the individual's outlays for the satisfaction of his various needs. For in the last resort, the state's fiscal requirements covered by taxation figure as expenditures in the household budget of the private citizen.[9]

Clearly, one of the main constraints on the ability of governments to increase the level of their services is the acceptable level of taxation needed to finance those services. The irony is that citizens of a growing economy may rationally choose to spend a growing proportion of their income on health care and education, if the appropriate choice mechanisms were available, but the political process may not be able to deliver such an outcome.

REDISTRIBUTION

The above discussion applied strictly to government provision of goods and services. Table 42.1 showed us that an expanding proportion of total government spending is devoted to social security. Some of this rise in social security expenditure is the result of the high unemployment of the 1980s and early 1990s. However, even if equilibrium unemployment were to return to the levels of the 1960s, there is still a major problem, which will get worse over the next twenty or thirty years.

The problem is the growing proportion of retired people in the population. This is not generally bad news; it means that most of us have greater life expectancy. It is only a problem for state finances, because more and more people will become dependent on state pensions and will live longer to draw them. (Elderly people also place greater demands on the health service.) This is a big problem in the United Kingdom, but it is much worse in some other European countries, notably France, where a bigger proportion of pension liabilities are unfunded state obligations, which will have to be met by future taxpayers.[10] In the United Kingdom, many people have been encouraged by tax incentives to pay into a company pension scheme or a personal pension plan. This reduces the problem somewhat, but it is still the case that future taxpayers will have to make much greater tax contributions just to support future pensioners, unless the real value of the state pension is steadily reduced.

Transfers do not take net resources out of the private sector, other than the resources required to effect them (they

[8] This has been labelled the *permanent income* approach to government consumption, because real government consumption growth is planned on the basis of the trend growth in real national income. This means that G rises as a proportion of Y when Y is below trend and falls as proportion when Y is above trend. See J. E. Alt and K. A. Chrystal, *Political Economics*, University of California Press and Wheatsheaf, Brighton, 1983.

[9] *Finanzwissenschaft*, 1883; translated and reprinted as 'Three Extracts on Public Finance' in *Classics on the Theory of Public Finance*, edited by R. A. Musgrave and A. T. Peacock, Macmillan, London, 1962.

[10] People who pay into a company pension scheme or a personal pension plan are building up a stock of investments (a fund) which will be used, once they retire, to pay out a pension until they (and their spouses) die. This fund is usually managed by an insurance company or fund manager, which invests the accumulated moneys in company shares and government bonds. The state pension, in contrast, is not paid out of any accumulated fund. Rather, it is part of general government expenditure and is paid out of current taxation (or borrowing, if there is a deficit). Hence, it is *unfunded*, and claims to future pensions are a liability for future taxpayers. In 1993, pension funds in the United Kingdom and the United States had assets equivalent to about 60 per cent of GDP. In Germany the figure was only 6 per cent, and in France, only 2 per cent.

are taken and then returned), but they do have to be financed by taxes. Therefore, they do affect how much governments will willingly spend on goods and services, as high taxes are unpopular. The prospects are for continued pressure on the state purse well beyond the recovery phase of the current business cycle.

In short, government activity in the provision of services and redistribution is an important part of a modern economy. The level of this activity is the outcome of a political process that attempts to balance the needs for adequate social provision with the financing made available through the politically acceptable level of taxation. We have seen that the level of provision of state services tends to rise during the early development phase of an economy. The economics of development in general was discussed in Chapter 34. In the following chapter, we return to the issue of cycles in the economy.

Summary

1 The recent record of persistent, large government budget deficits in many countries has generated heated debate over the policy options. The deficit position in the United Kingdom has not been bad by international standards, though the 1993/4 deficit reached the unsustainable level of 7 per cent of GDP.

2 Deficits influence the economy through their short-run stabilizing or destabilizing role and through their potential to affect income and welfare adversely in the long run. The latter effects arise from the buildup of the debt–GDP ratio.

3 The UK debt–GDP ratio fell to pre-1914 levels in the post-war period, largely as a result of inflation. Persistent real deficits are a cause for concern for several reasons, including inflation (if financed through money creation), the crowding out of investment and net exports, and the reduction of national income in the long run.

4 An annually balanced budget would be unfeasible; even if it were possible, it would destabilize the economy. A cyclically balanced budget would act as a stabilizer and would also curb the growth of the government sector.

5 In a growing economy, the concept of budget balance allows for a small but positive deficit such that the stock of debt grows at the same rate as nominal GDP.

6 Keynesians tend to take a relatively sanguine view of the effect of active fiscal policy on the national debt. As long as the national debt does not grow rapidly as a proportion of national income, they view its short-term fluctuations as a stabilizing device and its long-term upward trend as a reasonable price to pay for economic stability.

7 Fiscal conservatives mistrust government and view insistence on a balanced budget as the only effective means of curtailing reckless government spending which wastes scarce resources and feeds the fires of inflation.

8 Governments are providers of important services to the economy, and it could be optimal for these services to grow as a proportion of national income. However, government services tend to be planned as a stable proportion of GDP.

9 All developed countries face growing long-term problems with social security provisions, because of the growing proportion of retired people in the population. This is most problematic where the population is heavily dependent on unfunded state pensions. Here, future taxpayers will have to foot the bill.

Topics for review

- Short-run and long-run effects of deficits
- The relationship between deficits and the national debt
- Debt interest payments
- Debt–GDP ratio
- The inflation tax
- Cyclically balanced budget
- Keynesian and fiscal conservative views of debt
- Wagner's law

❧ CHAPTER 43

Business cycles

BUSINESS cycles have been observed for almost as long as recorded history. The Old Testament, for example, talks about a pattern in which seven good years are followed by seven lean years. In more recent times, the cyclical nature of economic activity has been equally apparent, and scholars have long tried to establish regularities in the data.

Some have tried to make a case for the existence of a *long-wave* cycle, with a duration of about fifty years from peak to trough. These long waves are usually labelled *Kondratief cycles*, after the Russian economist N.D.Kondratief (1892–1931). However, when we refer to the business cycle today, we are talking about the shorter-term cycles in GDP, which usually have something in the range of five to ten years from peak to peak; recent cyclical peaks in the United Kingdom came in 1973, 1979, and 1988.

The macro model we have built up in previous chapters was a static model. In that model, a one-off shock leads to a period of adjustment, with the economy eventually settling back to the potential level of national income. The shock has, in effect, produced one phase in a cycle. Keynesian economists adopted the static analysis because they argued that the economy could come to rest with excess capacity and unemployment. It is possible, however, to approach output and employment variations with the apparatus of dynamic models, which can generate cycles as ongoing phenomena. In such models, a single shock may generate cycles for some time, or cycles may be an intrinsic characteristic of the models even without external shocks.

In this chapter, we first look at some of the empirical regularities in business cycles. Then we review some of the economic analysis underlying many explanations of business cycles. Finally, we outline the approaches of four different schools of thought in economics, and discuss the possibility that electoral considerations may contribute to policy cycles. The distinguishing characteristics of these different schools were first discussed in the Appendix to Chapter 36.

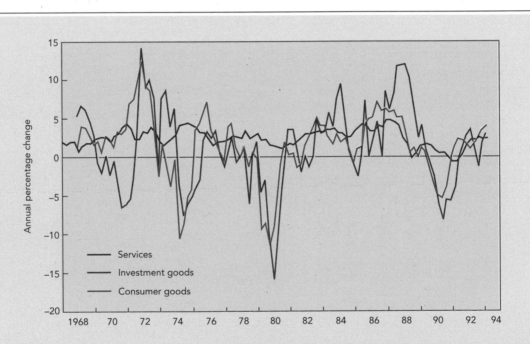

Figure 43.1 Growth rate of output of capital goods, consumer goods, and services, United Kingdom, 1968–1994

Output in most sectors moves together over the business cycle, but the investment goods sector tends to show greater swings than final goods sectors. The figure shows growth rates of output for the capital (investment) goods, consumer goods, and services sectors, measured as the percentage change in the output index over the same quarter a year earlier. The consumer goods sector tends to lead the investment goods sector out of recession.

Source: Datastream.

Characteristics of business cycles

NO two business cycles are quite the same, but there is a surprising number of similarities in most recent cycles. Some of the terminology of business cycles was set out in Figure 27.4 on page 505.

COMMON PATTERNS

One of the reasons why business cycles are important for society as a whole is that almost all sectors of the economy are affected by them. Most sectors (or industries) tend to have an increase in output during a boom and a fall in output during a recession. Figure 32.7 on p. 619 showed the strong correlation in output growth of three specific industries. Figure 43.1 also shows the growth rates of output of three industrial sectors, but this time the sectors have been selected to give us more information about the cyclical pattern in different types of industry.

The three sectors shown are those producing investment goods (capital), consumer goods, and services. It is obvious that the fluctuations in the growth rate of the services sector are minor in comparison with both investment and consumer goods. Also, the growth rate of investment goods generally fluctuates more than the growth rate of consumer goods. As we shall see shortly, this contrast would be even greater if we were to exclude durable goods from the consumer sector. The reasons for this greater volatility of investment goods industries will be discussed below (in the context of what is known as the *accelerator*).

Another pattern worthy of notice is the tendency for consumer goods output to lead investment goods output in the cycle. This is especially obvious in recoveries, where the pick-up in output of consumer goods typically precedes that of investment goods by at least one quarter. The reason is that producers of consumer goods are more likely to

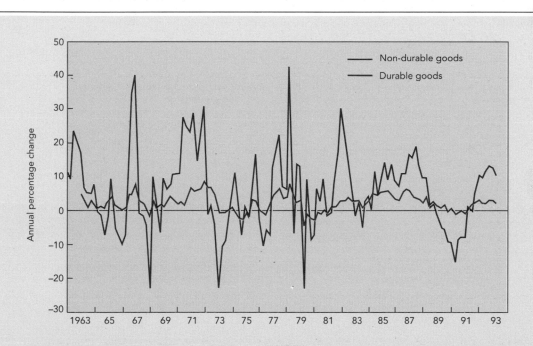

Figure 43.2 Growth rate of real consumers' expenditure on durable and non-durable goods, United Kingdom, 1963–1993

Expenditure on consumer durables shows much greater variability than expenditure on non-durables. This is because durable goods are lumpy and their purchase can be postponed when the economic environment is depressed or uncertain. Even in hard times, people continue to eat and consume basic services. When times improve, expenditure on basics does not rise dramatically, but demand for 'big ticket' items shows a sharp pick-up.

Source: Datastream.

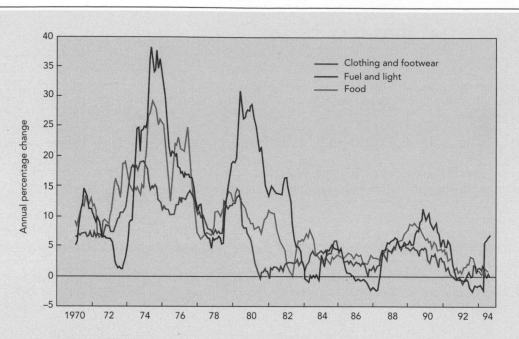

Figure 43.3 Changes in UK prices of food, clothing and footwear, and fuel and light, 1970–1994

Prices in many sectors tend to move together, pro-cyclically, but with a lag of about a year behind output. The dominant feature in the figure is the sharp rise in energy prices in 1973–4 and 1979–80. However, there was already an inflationary cycle under way in both periods even before the energy price rises. The resulting supply shocks helped create a downturn in activity, but there would have been a cyclical downturn at some stage anyway. A more normal, demand-led, cycle is the one in the late 1980s. The pick-up of energy prices in 1994 was due to the introduction of VAT on heating oil and power supplies.

Source: Datastream.

increase their capacity (or even replace old machines) once they have seen an upturn in final demand. This desired increase in capacity is what translates into a demand for investment goods, with a lag—it is a *derived* demand.

We have already hinted at an important difference between consumers' expenditure on durables and on nondurables. This is clearly evident from Figure 43.2, which shows growth rates (in real terms) of these two components of final demand. Durable goods expenditure is highly volatile relative to nondurable goods expenditure. The reason for this is that purchases of durable goods (e.g. cars, TVs, and stereo equipment) can be postponed when times are hard, although when times are good a high proportion of extra spending will go on these luxury items. Necessities such as food and shelter, however, will be purchased come what may. Thus, industrial sectors producing consumer durables will generally see much greater fluctuations in demand across the business cycle than sectors providing nondurable consumption goods.

Just as output moves together in many sectors, so do the prices of a wide variety of goods and services, though prices tend to lag behind output by about a year. Figure 43.3 shows the percentage changes in the prices of food, clothing and footwear, and fuel and light. These are positively correlated, though far from perfectly. Rises tend to come at the tail end of a boom and falls tend to follow recessions. Notice, however, the rapid increases in fuel prices (in 1973–4 and 1979) that followed the two oil price shocks. These are often thought of as exogenous (since the price of oil was set by the OPEC cartel). Both of these oil price increases came when the world economy (and the UK economy) were already experiencing inflationary booms. Hence it is likely that energy prices would have risen to some extent in a free market, although not as much. A more typical pattern may be that shown in the business cycle from the mid-1980s onward; in this later period, price changes for different sectors are clearly pro-cyclical, rising as a result of a boom and falling after a recession.

A final common pattern in business cycles is that profits tend to be highly variable and pro-cyclical. This is illustrat-

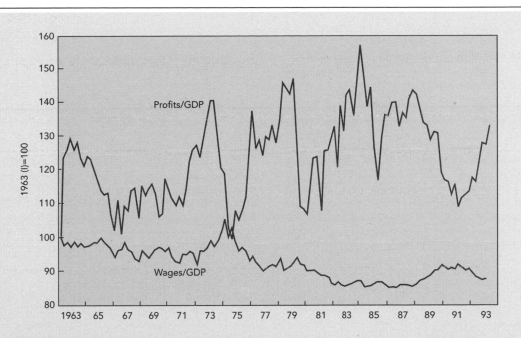

Figure 43.4 Indexes of wages and profits as a proportion of GDP, United Kingdom, 1963–1993

Profits (as a share of GDP) are strongly pro-cyclical and highly variable, while wages (as a share of national income) are mildly counter-cyclical but stable. The ratios of profits (of industrial and commercial companies) to GDP and wages and salaries (of the whole economy) to GDP are both expressed as index numbers with the respective values set equal to 100 in the first quarter of 1963. Thus, the chart shows volatility relative to the base period for each of these two variables. The figure cannot be used to make comparisons of the absolute changes in wages and profits, as wages are a much larger proportion of GDP (over 50 per cent) than are profits (about 10 per cent). The measure of profit used here is not that used in national income accounts; even if it were, wages and profits would not add up to GDP, not least because GDP at market prices, rather than factor cost, is used.

Source: Datastream.

ed in Figure 43.4, which shows the ratio of profits (of industrial and commercial companies) to GDP and the ratio of wages and salaries (for the whole economy) to GDP, both expressed as an index number (with 1963 (I) = 100). Profits fall in recessions (such as 1974–5, 1980–1, and 1990–2) and rise in booms. In contrast, the share of wages in GDP is mildly counter-cyclical, rising in recessions and falling in booms. This is despite the fact that *wage rates* (both nominal and real) are generally pro-cyclical. The reasons for this are linked to the existence of sticky wages, which was discussed in Chapter 41.

Notice that Figure 43.4 compares profits and wages (as a proportion of GDP) relative to a base period but *not rela-tive to each other* in absolute size. Wages and salaries comprise about 50 per cent of GDP, while profits (of industrial and commercial companies) account for only about 10 per cent. This is why a large percentage change in the share of profits is matched by only a small percentage change in the share of wages.

Box 43.1 addresses a further empirical issue relating to the UK business cycle. This is the question of why business cycles since the 1970s have displayed much greater amplitude than those of the 1950s and 1960s.

We now turn to some theoretical explanations of business cycles.

BOX 43.1

Why did the business cycle return?

In the 1950s and 1960s, it was widely believed that the business cycle had been abolished. Many economists thought that the newly invented tools of macroeconomic stabilization policy meant that recessions could be avoided. Indeed, the 1950s and 1960s were a period of relative stability. Unemployment and inflation were both low, and, although there were cycles in activity (see the chart, which shows the growth rate of UK GDP annually from 1948 to 1993), these cycles did not involve any major fall in output, but only variations in positive growth rates.

In contrast, since the early 1970s there have been three recessions during which output fell (1974–5, 1980–1, and 1991–2). We have already seen, in Chapter 41, the impact of these recent recessions on unemployment.

What is the reason for this change in experience since the early 1970s? Is it the abandonment of Keynesian counter-cyclical stabilization policy by governments and the accompanying abandonment of the commitment to 'full employment'? Or is it some other change in the environment?

We cannot give definitive answers to these questions, but we can dismiss the simple argument that stabilization policy worked in the 1950s and 1960s and was responsible for the relative stability of that period.

From the Second World War until 1972, the United Kingdom operated under a fixed exchange rate regime. This meant that there was virtually no discretion in the operation of monetary policy (though exchange controls gave limited monetary independence), and that fiscal policy was heavily constrained by recurrent balance of payments crises (reserve losses). These occurred whenever there was a tendency for domestic demand to expand too fast (relative to domestic output). Certainly, there were 'stop–go' cycles in fiscal policy stance, but the evidence supports the view that fiscal policy, on balance, was *destabilizing* in the 1950s and 1960s. (See e.g. the study by J. C. R. Dow for the National Institute.*)

This is important, because it suggests that the stability of the 1950s and 1960s was not the result of active stabilization policies at all, but rather, was due to the absence of major exogenous shocks. The world economy was growing in a stable fashion, with low inflation; there were no major demand or supply shocks coming from the international economy; neither were there any real exchange rate shocks (until the 1967 devaluation) coming from swings in the nominal exchange rate.

The first major demand shock came in the late 1960s and early 1970s, and resulted from US expenditure on the war in Vietnam. This created inflationary gaps in many countries simultaneously in the early 1970s. On top of this, in the United Kingdom, was added the positive demand shock resulting from the expansionary monetary and fiscal policies associated with the Barber boom (see pp. 804–05). The first oil shock compounded the subsequent recession, which would have occurred anyway once validation of the ongoing inflation ceased.

The recession of 1980–1 was also affected by exogenous energy shocks, combined with an internal (and worldwide) cycle and compounded by mistimed policy interventions. In contrast, the most recent cycle, leading to the 1990–2 recession, was not affected significantly by energy shocks, but it was made worse by the UK government's aggregate demand policies. These permitted an increase in aggregate demand in 1987–8, when there was already an inflationary gap, and reduced aggregate demand in 1990–2, when the economy was already in recession.

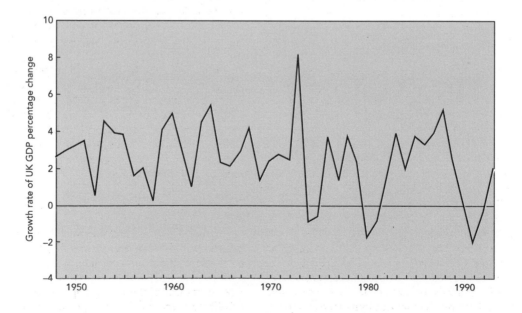

BOX 43.1 *(continued)*

Thus, it is reasonable to conclude that a contribution to the greater amplitude of business cycles since 1970 has come from the demand and supply shocks that have affected the world economy, especially the two energy price shocks. However, there is undoubtedly a contribution from inappropriate domestic aggregate demand policies. These have certainly not been what any Keynesian would have recommended, but neither have they been monetarist. Monetarists recommend stable monetary growth across the cycle (and generally support cyclically balanced budgets); Keynesians recommend counter-cyclical fiscal and (perhaps) monetary policy. No school of thought, so far as we are aware, recommends pro-cyclical aggregate demand policies (as were clearly in evidence during the Barber and Lawson booms).

Could it be that governments always get it wrong? The differ-ence between the 1950s and 1960s and the floating exchange rate era could be that in the earlier period governments just had less room for discretionary policy (because of the fixed exchange rate and the balance of payments constraint). Under floating rates, they were free to make much bigger mistakes.

The optimistic outcome is that policy-makers will learn from past mistakes, and, at least, will not add fuel to the inflationary fire next time around. So, in the absence of major external shocks, the next cycle may be less severe than the last. Realistically, however, the business cycle is back, and the 1950s and 1960s were just an abnormal conjunction of circumstances which is unlikely to be repeated.

* J. C. R. Dow, *The Management of the British Economy, 1945-1960*, Cambridge, 1964.

Theories of the cycle

THERE are two components to any theory of cycles. The first is a pattern of shocks or disturbances which hits the economy from outside. The second is a model of the dynamic behaviour of the endogenous variables (national income, consumption, investment, etc.) that generate cycles over time. Let us look at each of these components in turn.

SYSTEMATIC OR RANDOM SHOCKS

One way in which cycles could be generated is if there were cycles in the exogenous shocks hitting the economy. Before the industrial revolution, where agriculture was the main activity, cycles could have been caused by weather patterns, over-planting followed by under-planting ('hog-cycles'), or perhaps even incidences of crop disease. In industrial economies, cycles could result from patterns of innovation (product cycles) or waves of productivity improvements. There are certainly, also, cycles in demand for exports of open economies resulting from cycles in the rest of the world. (The correlation of cycles in different countries is shown in Box 39.3 on p. 780.)

For a small open economy such as the United Kingdom, there are undoubtedly systematic movements in exogenous variables, notably world demand. None the less, most effort in the economic analysis of cycles has been directed towards how cycles can result from random external shocks (or discrete changes in exogenous variables) which then trigger some cyclical internal adjustment mechanism.

Most theories of this type rely on lags. Many empirical macro models that are designed to fit the data have quite long lags in their behavioural relations. For example, if a fall in the rate of interest makes a new investment programme profitable, it may take six months to plan it, three months to let contracts, six more months before spending builds up to its top rate, and another two years to complete the project.

A pioneering study by two US economists, Irma and M. A. Adelman, established that, if occasional random shifts in exogenous expenditures disturb a system of expenditure-determining equations, all of which contain long lags, a cycle is generated. Here the disturbing influences are random or erratic, but the consequences are a cyclical path for the major endogenous macro variables such as national income and unemployment.

Each of the major components of aggregate expenditure has sometimes undergone shifts large enough to disturb the economic system significantly. The long lags in expenditure functions can then convert these shifts into cyclical oscillations in national income.

A recent line of theorizing has developed what are called equilibrium theories of the business cycle. (Some of these fall into the New Classical camp, but others are now in a group known as the *real business cycle* school; both are discussed below.) These rely on microeconomic models of markets which are always in equilibrium—a micro underpinning of cycle theory that has yet to gain general acceptance. None the less, they rely on the basic process used in the Keynesian empirical models where random shocks have systematic effects resulting from long lags that spread these effects out over time.

An even more recent line of research models the dynamic behaviour of the economy in complex nonlinear systems of equations. These systems are known as *chaotic* (as they are related to a branch of mathematics known as *chaos theory*). What is interesting about them is that they can generate ongoing cycles without a need for external shocks of any kind. This line of inquiry is highly technical and is in its infancy. We shall not discuss it further.

CYCLICAL ADJUSTMENT MECHANISMS

There may be many ways of formulating a dynamic model of the economy so that it generates cycles. Here we outline one simple mechanism which can generate cycles in response to discrete changes in exogenous variables. It is called the multiplier-accelerator mechanism. No one believes any longer that it provides *the* explanation of cycles; many economists still accept, however, that it captures one major element of cyclical fluctuations. To understand it, we need to return to a discussion of the causes of variations in investment.

The accelerator theory of investment   In our macroeconomic model above, we have investment changing in response to changes in interest rates. The **accelerator theory of investment** relies on another determinant of investment which can be formalized only in a dynamic model. This theory relates investment to national income. The possibility of systematic fluctuations arises because the *level* of investment is related to *changes* in national income.

The demand for machinery and factories is obviously derived from the demand for the goods that the capital equipment is designed to produce. If there is a demand that is expected to persist, and that cannot be met by increasing production with existing industrial capacity, then new plant and equipment will be needed.

Investment expenditure occurs while the new capital equipment is being built and installed. If the desired stock of capital goods increases, there will be an investment boom while the new capital is being produced. But if nothing else changes, and even though business conditions continue to look rosy enough to justify the increased stock of capital, investment in new plant and equipment will cease once the larger capital stock is achieved.

This makes investment depend on changes in sales, and hence on changes in national income, as illustrated in Table

43.1. The more formal derivation of the theory is outlined below.

Let there be a simple relationship between the GDP and the amount of capital needed to produce it:

$$K = \alpha Y \qquad (1)$$

where K is the required capital stock. The coefficient α (the Greek letter alpha) is the capital–output ratio; $\alpha = K/Y$ and is also called the accelerator coefficient. Taking changes in (1), and noticing that investment is, by definition, the change in the capital stock, yields

$$I = \Delta K = \alpha \Delta Y. \qquad (2)$$

This says that investment is some constant times the change in national income. This is called the 'simple', or sometimes the 'naïve', accelerator. Figure 43.5 illustrates what happens to investment under the accelerator theory when national income rises from one constant level to another.

Table 43.1   An illustration of the accelerator theory of investment

(1) Year	(2) Annual sales	(3) Change in sales	(4) Required stock of capital[a]	(5) Net investment increase in required capital stock
1	£10	£0	£50	£0
2	10	0	50	0
3	11	1	55	5
4	13	2	65	10
5	16	3	80	15
6	19	3	95	15
7	22	3	110	15
8	24	2	120	10
9	25	1	125	5
10	25	0	125	0

[a]Assuming a capital–output ratio of 5:1.

With a fixed capital–output ratio, net investment occurs only when it is necessary to increase the stock of capital in order to change output. Assume that it takes £5 of capital to produce £1 of output per year. In years 1 and 2 there is no need for investment. In year 3 a rise in sales of £1 requires investment of £5 to provide the needed capital stock. In year 4 a further rise of £2 in sales requires an additional investment of £10 to provide the needed capital stock. As columns (3) and (5) show, the amount of net investment is proportional to the *change* in sales. When the increase in sales tapers off in years 7–9, investment declines. When sales no longer increase in year 10, net investment falls to zero because the capital stock of year 9 is adequate to provide output for year 10's sales.

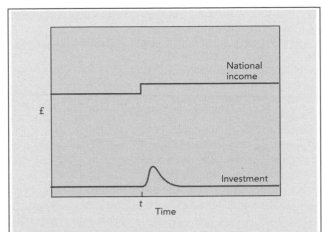

Figure 43.5 The accelerator and investment

When there is a change in the level of final output, there is a much bigger percentage change in the rate of investment. The figure illustrates the path over time of national income and investment. We assume that national income is constant but that at time *t* it jumps to a new higher level, and then continues at this level. Replacement investment carries on at some constant level while national income is constant, but the increase in national income requires a higher capital stock. This in turn requires a burst of *new investment*. Once this burst of new investment is over (shown as being spread out over time), the level of new investment returns to zero, so total investment is only at the level required for replacements. Hence, at the time that income rose, a small percentage increase in national income induced a large percentage increase in investment. However, even though national income (hypothetically) stays at its new higher level, investment subsequently falls. In a full dynamic model, this fall in investment would induce a fall in national income, causing the downturn in the cycle, as described in the text.

The main insight that the accelerator theory provides is its emphasis on the role of net investment as a *disequilibrium* phenomenon—something that occurs when the stock of capital goods differs from what firms and households would like it to be. Thus the accelerator its particular importance in connection with *fluctuations* in national income. As we shall see, it can itself contribute to those fluctuations.

Taken literally, the simple accelerator posits a mechanical and rigid response of investment to changes in sales (and thus, aggregatively, to changes in national income). It does this by assuming a proportional relationship between changes in income and changes in the desired capital stock, and by assuming a fixed capital–output ratio. Each assumption is to some degree questionable.

The accelerator does not by itself give anything like a complete explanation of variations in investment in capital goods, and it should not be surprising that a simple accel-

erator theory provides a relatively poor overall explanation of changes in investment. Yet accelerator-like influences do exist, and they play a role in the cyclical variability of investment. Figure 43.1 above shows the relative volatility of output of investment goods that is predicted by the accelerator relationship. (The reasons for this excess volatility are explained in Figure 42.5.) Modern investment theories often include a flexible version of the accelerator, in which the coefficient α is a function of other variables such as interest rates.

Multiplier–accelerator interaction   The theory linking systematic fluctuations in national income to systematic fluctuations in investment expenditure unites the accelerator theory just discussed with the version of the Keynesian multiplier theory that sees the multiplier as a process working over time as successive rounds of induced expenditure build up in response to some initiating shock (see Box 29.2 on p. 562).

This **multiplier-accelerator theory** of the cycle is divided into three steps. First, a theory of cumulative upswings and downswings explains why, once started, movements tend to carry on in the same direction. Second, a theory of floors and ceilings explains why upward and downward movements are eventually brought to a halt. And third, a theory of instability explains how, once a process of upward or downward movement is brought to a halt, it tends to reverse itself.

Why does a period of expansion or contraction, once begun, tend to develop its own momentum? First, the multiplier process tends to cause cumulative movements. As soon as a revival begins, some unemployed people find work again. These people, with their newly acquired income, can afford to make much-needed consumption expenditures. This new demand causes an increase in production and creates new jobs for others. As incomes rise, demand rises; as demand rises, incomes rise. Just the reverse happens in a downswing. Unemployment in one sector causes a fall in demand for the products of other sectors, which leads to a further fall in employment and a further fall in demand.

A second major factor is the accelerator theory. New investment is needed to expand existing productive capacity and to introduce new methods of production. When consumer demand is low and there is excess capacity, investment is likely to fall to a very low level; once income starts to rise and entrepreneurs come to expect further rises, investment expenditure may rise very rapidly. Furthermore, when full employment of existing capacity is reached, new investment becomes one of the few ways available for firms to increase their output.

A third major explanation for cumulative movements is expectations. All production plans take time to fulfil. Current decisions to produce consumer goods and investment goods are very strongly influenced by business expectations. Such expectations can sometimes be volatile, and sometimes self-fulfilling. If enough people think, for example, that bond prices are going to rise, they will all buy bonds in anticipation of the price rise, and these purchases will themselves cause prices to rise. If, on the other hand, enough people think that bond prices are going to fall, they will sell quickly at what they regard as a high price, and thereby actually cause prices to fall. This is the phenomenon of *self-realizing expectations*. It applies to many parts of the economy. If enough managers think the future looks rosy and begin to invest in increasing capacity, this will create new employment and income in the capital-goods industries, and the resulting increase in demand will help to create the rosy conditions whose vision started the whole process. One cannot lay down simple rules about so complicated a psychological phenomenon as the formation of expectations, but there is a bandwagon effect. Once things begin to improve, people expect further improvements, and their actions, based on this expectation, help to cause further improvements. On the other hand, once things begin to worsen, people often expect further worsening, and then their actions, based on this expectation, help to make things worse.

The multiplier-accelerator process, combined with changes in expectations that cause expenditure functions to shift, can explain the cumulative tendencies of recessions and recoveries.

The next question that arises is: why do these upward and downward processes ever come to an end?

A very rapid expansion can continue for some time, but it cannot go on for ever because eventually the economy will run into bottlenecks (or ceilings) in terms of some resources. This will happen when firms cannot take on more workers without paying much higher wages to attract them from other firms. Inflation will pick up, and either the government will put interest rates up or firms will cut

investment in anticipation of a downturn. This expectation itself becomes self-fulfilling.

A rapid contraction, too, is eventually brought to an end. Firms can postpone investment and run down stocks, and consumers can put off buying new clothes and new cars, but eventually confidence returns and a small upturn in spending leads to the start of an upswing of the cycle, through the interaction of the multiplier and accelerator together.

Indeed, the accelerator can explain reversals of direction of expansions and contractions. We have seen that the accelerator causes the desired level of *new* (not replacement) investment to depend upon the rate of change of income. If income is rising at a constant rate, then investment will be at a constant *level*; if there is a slackening in the speed at which income is rising, the level of investment will decline. This means that a *levelling off* in income at the top of a cycle may lead to a *decline* in the level of investment. The decline in investment at the upper turning-point will cause a decline in the level of income. This will be intensified through the multiplier process.

The accelerator thus provides one theory of the upper turning-point, or cyclical peak.

What about the possible stabilization of income at a floor? Investment theory predicts that, sooner or later, an upturn will begin. If nothing else causes an expansion of business activity, eventually there will be a revival of replacement investment. As existing capital wears out, the capital stock will fall to the level required to produce current output. At this stage new machines will eventually have to be bought to replace those that are wearing out. The rise in the level of activity in the capital-goods industries will then cause, by way of the multiplier, a further rise in income. The economy will have turned the corner. An expansion, once started, may trigger the sort of cumulative upward movement already discussed.

Cyclical controversies

MANY of the different schools of thought in economics have had their own approach to explaining business cycles; indeed, attempts to document and explain the cycle in economic activity predate modern macroeconomics. We concentrate here on the views of the major macro schools of thought, first outlined in the Appendix to Chapter 36.

THE MONETARIST APPROACH

Monetarists believe that the economy is inherently stable, because private-sector expenditure functions are relatively stable and price adjustment will bring the economy back to potential output. In addition, they believe that shifts in the aggregate demand curve are due mainly to policy-induced changes in the money supply.[1]

The view that business cycles have mainly monetary causes originally relied partly on the evidence advanced by Milton Friedman and Anna Schwartz in their classic study, *A Monetary History of the United States, 1867–1960*. They purported to have established a strong correlation between changes in the money supply and changes in economic activity. Major recessions have been associated with absolute declines in the money supply and minor recessions with the slowing of the rate of increase in the money supply below its long-term trend.

More recent work has shown that the Friedman–Schwartz relations are not as close, even in the United States, as these authors tried to show. Attempts to establish a similar close relation for the United Kingdom have not been successful. None the less, there is a broad association —even if a loose one—between changes in the money supply and changes in money national income. When, for example, the latter rises rapidly during an inflation, the former rises as well.

The rough correlation between changes in the money supply and changes in the level of economic activity is accepted by many economists. But there is controversy over how this correlation is to be interpreted. Do changes in money supply cause changes in the level of aggregate demand and hence of business activity, or vice versa?

Friedman and Schwartz maintained that changes in the money supply cause changes in business activity. They argued, for example, that the severity of the Great Depression was due to a major contraction in the money supply, which shifted the aggregate demand curve far to the left.

According to monetarists, fluctuations in the money supply cause fluctuations in national income.

This leads the monetarists to advocate a policy of stabilizing the growth of the money supply. In their view, this would avoid policy-induced instability of the aggregate demand curve.

THE KEYNESIAN APPROACH

The traditional Keynesian explanation of cyclical fluctuations in the economy has two parts. First, it emphasizes variations in investment as a cause of business cycles and stresses the non-monetary causes of such variations, such as expectations or, as Keynes put it, 'animal spirits'.[2]

Keynesians reject what they regard as the extreme monetarist view that only money matters in explaining cyclical fluctuations. Many Keynesians believe that both monetary and non-monetary forces are important in explaining cycles. Although they accept serious monetary mismanagement as one potential source of economic fluctuations,

they do not believe that it is the only, or even the major, source of such fluctuations. Thus, they deny the monetary interpretation of business cycle history given by Friedman and Schwartz. They believe that most fluctuations in the aggregate demand curve are due to variations in the desire to spend on the part of the private sector and are not induced by government policy.

Keynesians also believe that the economy lacks strong natural corrective mechanisms that will always force it easily and quickly back to full employment. They believe that, while the price level rises fairly quickly to eliminate *inflationary* gaps, prices and wages fall only slowly in response to recessionary gaps. As a result, Keynesians believe that recessionary gaps can sometimes persist for long periods of time unless they are eliminated by an active stabilization policy.

The second part of the Keynesian view on cyclical fluctuations concerns the alleged correlation between changes in the money supply and changes in the level of economic activity. In so far as this correlation exists, the Keynesian explanation reverses the causality suggested by the monetarists. Keynesians argue that changes in the level of economic activity often cause changes in the money supply.

Certainly, Keynesians are on strong ground when there is a fixed exchange rate regime, because, as we saw in Chapter 39, the money stock is endogenously determined by demand under this regime. However, it is also true under floating exchange rates where monetary authorities operate monetary policy by pegging short-term interest rates, as in the United Kingdom. For a given interest rate, changes in national income will cause changes in the money stock rather than vice versa.

According to Keynesians, fluctuations in national income are often caused by fluctuations in autonomous expenditures. Further, they believe that fluctuations in national income usually cause fluctuations in the money supply.

Nevertheless, most Keynesians also agree that deliberate changes in monetary policy can cause national income to change. However, notice that the monetarist approach makes the monetary authorities the main cause of cycles—

---

[1] The view that fluctuations often have monetary causes is not new. The English economist R. G. Hawtrey (1879–1971), the Austrian Nobel Laureate F. A. von Hayek, (1899–1991), and the Swedish economist Knut Wicksell (1851–1926) were prominent among those who have given monetary factors an important role in explaining the turning points in cycles and/or the tendency for expansions and contractions, once begun, to become cumulative and self-reinforcing. Modern monetarists carry on this tradition.

[2] Like the monetarists, the Keynesians are modern advocates of views that have a long history. The great Austrian (and later American) economist Joseph Schumpeter (1883–1950) stressed such explanations early in the present century. Knut Wicksell and the German Arthur Spiethoff (1873–1957) both stressed this aspect of economic fluctuations before the emergence of the Keynesian school of thought.

hence the recommendation that they should be constrained to follow a rigid policy rule. For many Keynesians, it is fluctuations in private-sector investment behaviour (and, perhaps, exports) that matter, and the authorities are the 'good guys' who can offset this privately generated instability. It is for this reason that Keynesians are often interventionist and monetarists are usually non-interventionist.

A shift of emphasis within the Keynesian school has come out of the New Keynesian research agenda, discussed in Chapter 41. Early Keynesians focused mainly on the use of aggregate demand (especially fiscal) policies to stabilize the cycle; New Keynesians hope to see national income kept close to its potential level by whatever means possible, but place more stress on supply-side (labour market) policies to eliminate persistent (equilibrium) unemployment than did their Keynesian predecessors.

THE NEW CLASSICAL APPROACH

The New Classical approach to explaining business cycles has something in common with the monetarists, in that the shock that sets off the cycle is a change in the money supply. However, what happens next in the New Classical story is quite different from traditional (monetarist or Keynesian) business cycle theory, because the New Classical school wanted a model in which markets were always in equilibrium. An alternative approach to modelling business cycles in 'equilibrium' models, which does not rely on monetary shocks, is discussed below.

The Lucas aggregate supply function The key element in the New Classical approach is a particular specification of the aggregate supply function, which was formulated by US economist Robert Lucas.

In Chapter 31, where we first set out the *SRAS* curve, we assumed that in the short run output prices are variable (they can respond to changes in demand in the current period) while input prices (we shall concentrate here on wages) are fixed. In the long run, if output prices rise, wages get negotiated upwards to catch up with prices. This is what makes the *LRAS* curve vertical.

In the Lucas approach, wages are not just given on the basis of last period's equilibrium; rather, they are set at the beginning of the current period at the market-clearing level for *given expectations of what output prices in the current period will be.* In other words, they are set on the basis of forward-looking expectations of what the market outcome will be.

This may seem like a harmless modification of our original assumption, but it turns out to have fundamental implications. Figure 43.6 illustrates the implications for aggregate supply behaviour. The key point is that any shift in aggregate demand that is expected at the time wages are set, such as an announced (or anticipated) increase in the

money supply, will lead to the *SRAS* curve shifting up immediately. The economy will, therefore, experience an immediate increase in the price level and no increase in national income. Only an *unexpected* increase in *AD* will lead to an increase in national income in the short run. Lucas assumed that this shock to *AD* would be an unexpected increase in the money supply.

In the New Classical approach, cycles in real economic activity are triggered only by unexpected increases in the money supply.

We have already noted above that the New Classical economists assume that expectations are formed rationally. This means that the expectational errors that trigger cycles cannot be systematic. (If they were systematic, agents could learn from the pattern of mistakes and improve their forecasts.) It would be tempting to conclude from this that deviations from potential output must, therefore, be random—which is clearly contradicted by evidence. However, to avoid this erroneous implication, Lucas added a lagged adjustment process to his model. This meant that, once shocked, it behaved like any of the other cycle models described above. Hence, it is difficult to distinguish this approach from others on the basis of observations of real-world cycles.

Policy invariance A perhaps surprising implication of the New Classical approach is that changes in monetary or fiscal policy, which may be intended to influence economic activity by shifting the *AD* curve, will have real effects only if they are unexpected. For example, a stimulus to demand involving an announced increase in the money supply will create expectations of rising prices. These expectations will influence wage-setting, so the *SRAS* curve will shift up immediately and prices will rise straight away with no temporary increase in output. This outcome is illustrated in Figure 43.6 by the fact that an anticipated money supply increase shifts *AD* to the right and *SRAS* to the left, the net effect being that the economy moves straight up the *LRAS* curve, the price level rising but real national income remaining unchanged.

According to the New Classical approach, only unanticipated policy changes lead to changes in real national income. Systematic policy changes will be predictable and will have no real effects.

Most economists do not accept the proposition that only unexpected policy changes will have real effects. One reason is that there is so much inertia in price- and wage-setting behaviour that very few contracts can be renegotiated as soon as a policy change is announced. Hence the policy-makers certainly have some leverage over real activity, even when they are making policy changes that are predictable.

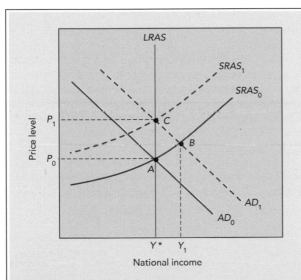

Figure 43.6 The Lucas aggregate supply curve

In the new classical approach, a given *SRAS* curve applies only to unexpected shifts in *AD*. Suppose there is a shift in aggregate demand from AD_0 to AD_1. If the shift in aggregate demand is unexpected, the economy will move from the initial position at point *A* to point *B*, at the intersection of $SRAS_0$ and AD_1. This is the normal short-run outcome in the model we developed in earlier chapters. However, if the shift in *AD* is expected, agents will negotiate higher wages immediately on the basis of this expectation, and the *SRAS* curve will shift up to $SRAS_1$. The price level will go straight from P_0 to P_1, and the economy will move from *A* to *C*, with no increase in national income. Policy ineffectiveness follows from the same analysis. Any predictable change in monetary or fiscal policy, causing a change in aggregate demand, such as the shift in *AD* from AD_0 to AD_1, will lead to an immediate rise in prices from P_0 to P_1, and will have no effect on real national income. (The economy goes direct from *A* to *C*.) An unexpected policy change of the same magnitude, however, would take the economy from point *A* to point *B* in the short run, and to *C* only in the long run.

A second reason is that the massive complexity of the economy makes it impossible for individual agents to know how some shock will affect their prices and quantities over any specified period of time. Leaving aside most of the complexities, let us just concentrate on the direct effects of an increase in the money supply. Say that the monetary authorities implement a 20 per cent increase in the stock of high-powered money. Will the money multiplier turn out to be 5 or 25 this time? If I anticipate the change by altering my prices and/or quantities tomorrow, will others wait, or will they too act tomorrow? If they do act, will they expect the same money multiplier as I do? Given the variety of contracts in the economy, what will be the time sequence of

all other reactions? The idea of everyone knowing the exact nature of some policy disturbance and solving the equations of the economy to determine the exact outcome of their acting to anticipate these seems far-fetched to many. After all, the great virtue of the price system is that it co-ordinates activity without the need for some far-seeing body of central planners to solve for equilibrium and set all prices and quantities.

However, the New Classical presumption that private agents have expectations of what policy-makers are going to do, and that this influences private behaviour, is important. Without assuming omniscience, just reasonable approximate expectations, private anticipation of government action can affect the outcome of policies. This realization has had a fundamental impact on macroeconomic policy analysis. In both Keynesian and monetarist models, the government was exogenous to the model. However, in the New Classical framework, the government and the private sector interact by trying to guess what the other is going to do. The conduct of policy becomes more like a 'game', where strategy and perception of the other players matters.

This change in perception of policy as interactive rather than exogenous has two important implications.

Policy credibility　If private agents are watching the government and trying to form expectations of its future behaviour, not only does it matter what the government does, but it also matters what agents think it will do in future. This means that a government needs more than just the correct current policies. It also needs to establish **credibility** that it will follow the correct policies in future.

Suppose, for example, that a government enters office with a commitment to control inflation. It introduces tight monetary and fiscal policies, which in due course succeed in bringing down inflation. Now, however, there is an election approaching, and the government would like to increase real national income to improve its chances of re-election. It may be tempted to break its original commitment to anti-inflationary policies.[3] However, private agents know that this incentive exists, so it matters to the outcome whether the private agents anticipate the government breaking its word or not. In other words, the government's credibility actually affects private behaviour. Of course, once the government has broken its commitments, it will be very hard for it to establish credibility again—at least, without a change in personnel.

The Lucas critique　The assumption that private agents are forming expectations of government behaviour has important implications for how economic models can be used to predict the effects of changes in policy.

[3] The fact that it may now be rational for the government to renege on its commitments was labelled *time inconsistency* by F. Kydland and E. Prescott.

A great deal of effort over the last thirty years has gone into building empirical econometric macroeconomic models of the economy for forecasting purposes (such as the National Institute model and the Treasury model). Lucas pointed out that such models contain estimates of key behavioural parameters that were estimated from past data. These data were collected under particular policy regimes.

Any attempt to use such a model to predict the consequences of significant policy changes may be erroneous. This is because the behaviour of private agents may change when the behaviour of policy-makers changes, as they are interdependent in some areas.

An example might be the Phillips curve. In the 1950s and 1960s, the government could make inflation/unemployment policy choices assuming the existence of a single stable (short- and long-run) Phillips curve. This seemed to be stable over decades of historical data. However, the periods for which it was stable were periods of a fixed exchange rate regime (the gold standard and the Bretton Woods regime), during which inflation was low and stable. Once the authorities abandoned fixed exchange rates (in 1972) and tried to boost activity at a high level of employment, the short-run Phillips curve shifted upwards (because people came to expect higher inflation) and an unpredicted serious inflation resulted.

Another example might be the failure of the government to understand (and the forecasters to forecast) the buildup of inflationary pressures in the economy in the late 1980s, following the financial innovations of the mid-1980s.

The Lucas critique suggests that there will be shifts in many private-sector behaviour functions when there are significant changes in the policy regime. Hence the effects of such regime changes will be impossible to forecast accurately using conventional models.

The New Classical approach to business cycles clearly supports a non-interventionist approach to macroeconomic policy. Governments can initiate shocks, but systematic attempts to stabilize cycles will be frustrated by their very predictability.

REAL BUSINESS CYCLES

Another group has taken up the task of explaining business cycles in the context of equilibrium models of the economy. According to Professor Alan Stockman of the University of Rochester, 'The purpose of real business cycle (RBC) theory is to explain aggregate fluctuations in business cycles without reference to monetary policy.'[4]

Real business cycle research has evolved from the New Classical attempt to explain cyclical fluctuations in the context of models in which equilibrium prevails at all times. In this sense, the models can be seen as an extension of the New Classical approach. The researchers' desire to model

equilibrium outcomes because they believe that the channels through which monetary policy affects real outcomes in the traditional macro model are not clearly understood. The focus on *real* disturbances also reflects their attempt to build a more convincing supply side to macro models.

The view of the business cycle found in RBC models is that fluctuations in national income are caused by fluctuations in the vertical *LRAS* curve. In contrast, the traditional theory of fluctuations is based on fluctuations in the *AD* curve.

The explanation of cyclical fluctuations that arises in RBC models is based on the role of supply (productivity) shocks originating from sources such as oil price changes, technical progress, and changes in tastes.

In this view, output is always equal to potential national income, but it is potential national income itself that fluctuates.

Key propositions and criticisms   The RBC approach is controversial. The major claims in favour of it include the following:

1. It has been able to mimic the recent behaviour of the US economy quite well statistically, while disavowing any role for aggregate demand fluctuations in the business cycle.

2. It suggests that an integrated approach to understanding cycles and growth may be appropriate, since both reflect forces that affect the *LRAS* curve. The distinction it makes is some shocks are temporary (and thus have cyclical effects) and some are permanent (and therefore affect the economy's growth).

3. It provides valuable insights into how shocks, regardless of their origin, spread over time to the different sectors of the economy. By abstracting from monetary issues, it is possible to address more details concerning technology and household choice, involving intertemporal trade-offs between consumption, labour supply, and leisure.

4. It has focused on integrating the explanation of a number of facts that other approaches have ignored, such as seasonal and cyclical fluctuations, consumption varying less than output over the business cycle, and pro-cyclical movements of hours worked and of average labour productivity.

Critics of the approach focus on some implausible results, express concern about its assumed underlying behaviour, and argue that the phenomena mentioned in point 4 have

[4] Alan C. Stockman, 'Real Business Cycle Theory: A Guide, an Evaluation, and New Directions', *Federal Reserve Bank of Cleveland Monthly Review* (1988), pp. 24–47.

already been given satisfactory explanations. More importantly, they are sceptical about a model in which monetary issues are completely ignored. For example, they point out that RBC models are unable to provide insights into the correlation between money and output that is at the heart of the traditional macro model. Furthermore, RBC models are unable to provide insights into empirical regularities involving nominal variables, such as prices that apparently vary less than quantities and nominal prices that vary pro-cyclically. On top of this, as we saw in Chapter 41, any model of the cycle that *assumes* the absence of involuntary unemployment, even in deep recessions, is unlikely to achieve widespread acceptance, although some RBC models have recently incorporated some Keynesian features, such as sticky prices, in some sectors.

Policy implications Because the approach gives no role to aggregate demand in influencing business cycles, it provides no role for stabilization operating through monetary and fiscal policies. Indeed, the models used by this school to date predict that the use of such demand management policies can be harmful.[5]

The basis for this prediction is the proposition in RBC models that cycles represent *efficient* responses to the shocks that are hitting the economy. Policy-makers may mistakenly interpret cyclical fluctuations as deviations from full-employment equilibrium that are caused by fluctuations in aggregate demand. The policy-makers may try to stabilize output and thereby distort the maximizing decisions made by households and firms. In turn, this distortion will cause the responses to the real shocks (as opposed to nominal, monetary shocks) to be inefficient.

Although only a minority of economists espouse these models as complete or even reasonable descriptions of the business cycle, and thus only a minority take seriously the strict implications for policy, many accept the view that real disturbances can play an important role in business cycles. It is, of course, highly controversial to argue that, whatever the cycles in the economy, they are an optimal response to shocks, upon which no policy actions can improve. Indeed, if this were the case, macroeconomics as a subject has no purpose, invented, as it was, to help policy-makers cure recessions and alleviate unemployment; and Europe's 30 million unemployed have been voluntarily idle, either because they have preferred leisure to work at correctly perceived real wage rates, or, in contradiction of rational expectations, they have been systematically underpredicting the real wage rate for many years in succession.

THE POLITICAL BUSINESS CYCLE

As early as 1944, the Polish-born Keynesian economist Michael Kalecki (1899–1970) warned that, once governments had learned to manipulate the economy, they might engineer an election-geared business cycle. In pre-election periods they would raise spending and cut taxes. The resulting expansionary demand shock would create high employment and good business conditions, which would gain voters' support for the government. But the resulting inflationary gap would lead to a rising price level. So, after the election was won, the government would depress demand to remove the inflationary gap, also providing some slack for expansion before the next election.

This theory invokes the image of a vote-maximizing government, manipulating employment and national income solely for electoral purposes. Few people believe that governments deliberately do this all the time, but the temptation to do it some of the time, particularly before close elections, may prove irresistible. In the UK electoral system, where the length of parliaments is flexible, it is also natural for the government to seek a general election at a time favourable to itself, within the maximum five-year horizon.

A naïve political business cycle, in which private agents never learn to anticipate that politicians are going to boost the economy before a general election, is impossible to justify in a world of rational expectations, or almost any theory of expectations in which agents learn. This is because there is no reason for voters to be fooled, certainly not repeatedly. Just as they form inflation expectations in relation to their wage-setting behaviour (in the expectations augmented Phillips curve; see Chapter 40), so they can use those same expectations to inform their voting behaviour, and to punish a government that deliberately creates an inflationary gap, even though the full effects of the inflation may be to come. Credibility now matters, and probably always did.

However, a political cycle can follow from electoral considerations, even where expectations are rational, so long as the rival political parties have different policy agendas. The approach of an election, combined with a changing probability that a different party will come to power, influences expectations of what future policy will be and, thereby, changes behaviour even before the election has happened. This *partisanship* approach does not predict a simple pattern of pre-election boom and post-election slump (which is not supported by evidence anyway[6]). Rather, it merely

[5] In reality, it is more of an assumption than a prediction because it is implicit in the assumption of continuous market-clearing. This makes whatever happens to the economy, in response to real shocks, an optimal (equilibrium) adjustment, with which policy changes can only interfere. This is not a result of analysis of actual policy, but it is a result of the assumption of equilibrium.

[6] There have been eight general elections in the United Kingdom since 1960. (The two in 1974 are counted as one.) Three took place in relative boom conditions, but in two of these (1964 and 1979) the incumbent government was defeated. This leaves 1987 as the only clear case of a pre-election boom that was followed just over a year later by severe policy-tightening. In 1983 and 1992, the government was returned to power despite recessions and high unemployment. In 1970 and 1974 (Feb.), governments called elections in recessions (1970 was the tail end of a recession, 1974 was during the onset of recession) and lost. In 1966 there was a relative slowdown and a balance of payments crisis, but the incumbent government won.

says that expectations of electoral outcomes matter and that they may cause shocks to the system at almost any time, via changes in the expectations of firms and consumers relating to the future.

STOP–GO

A policy-induced cycle may occur even in the absence of electoral considerations and partisan differences. Government and private agents need only be rather short-sighted. In this theory, when there is a recession and relatively stable prices, the public and the government identify unemployment as the Number One economic problem. The government then engineers an expansionary demand shock. This, plus such natural cumulative forces as the multiplier and the accelerator, expands the economy and cures unemployment. But, as national income rises above its potential level, the price level begins to rise. At this point the unemployment problem is declared cured. Now inflation is seen as the nation's Number One economic problem and a contractionary policy shock is engineered. The natural cumulative forces again take over, reducing income to a recessionary level. The inflation subsides but unemployment rises, setting the stage once again for an expansionary shock to cure the unemployment problem.

Many economists have criticized government policy in the past for causing fluctuations by shortsightedly pursuing first expansion to cure unemployment (or achieve real growth), and then contraction to cure inflation. This phenomenon has occurred often enough in the United Kingdom for it to be termed the **stop–go policy**, or more simply just *stop–go*.

We have cast the stop–go cycle in its modern form of alternating concern over inflation and unemployment.[7] Historically, when the United Kingdom operated under a fixed exchange rate, the two competing policy goals were the balance of payments and full employment. The balance of payments could always be improved by depressing national income and so reducing imports, which are positively related to income; but this would raise unemployment. The conflict encouraged policy swings, whereby income was depressed to remove a balance of payments deficit, and then expanded to remove the heavy unemployment.

SUPPLY SHOCKS

Monetarist, Keynesian, and New Classical approaches to the business cycle all assume that cycles are triggered by demand shocks—changes in the money supply, changes in autonomous investment, and money surprises. Only the real business cycle school, of the approaches we have dis-

cussed, emphasizes shocks coming from the supply side of the economy. Clearly, however, any shock that disturbs the equilibrium of the economy can generate a cyclical response so long as there is some lagged adjustment process within the economy.

The idea that supply shocks can cause cycles in real activity has a long pedigree in economics. In the nineteenth century, for example, serious credence was given to the theory that 'sun spots' triggered business cycles on earth. The logic of this was that changes in the intensity of the sun's rays, associated with the observation of spots on the sun, affected the quality of the harvest on earth. Variations in harvest would provide a shock to the real incomes of farmers, and variations in food prices would affect real wages in other sectors. Such shocks could take several seasons to work through the system.

Notice also, as is clear from part (ii) of Figure 27.3, on p. 503, that the two most extreme cycles in economic activity in this century were associated with the First and Second World Wars. The impact of a war on the economy is complex, but it has both demand- and supply-shock elements. There were also lesser shocks to the world economy caused by the Korean War in the early 1950s and the Vietnam War in the late 1960s and early 1970s.

In the recent past, the most important supply shocks have been changes in energy prices associated with the 1973 and 1979 OPEC oil price rises. (Fuel price changes are shown in Figure 43.3.) The fact that all major countries were affected by these energy price shocks simultaneously did much to ensure that the 1974–5 and 1980–2 recessions were worldwide phenomena which could not be explained by domestic demand shocks alone. The economic cycle in Germany (and perhaps in much of Europe) has also been affected by the fall of the Berlin wall in 1989 and the massive costs of reconstruction that followed. (This is both a demand and a supply shock.)

Most economists now agree that supply shocks and demand shocks can both be important, that most of the factors we have discussed can contribute to cycles, but that no two economic cycles are ever quite the same. This means that explanations based upon a single key causal factor will never be adequate for every case. The long-term trend in real GDP is upwards, but, despite over half a century of macroeconomic analysis of stabilization policy, cycles about the trend appear to be endemic. In principle, policy-makers have the tools to reduce fluctuations in the economy, but in practice they frequently make things worse.

---

[7] It might be argued that unemployment was abandoned as a target by the 1980s Conservative government. However, the 1985–8 boom (the Lawson boom), fuelled by tax cuts and rapid money supply increases, followed by a sharp raising of interest rates and tax increases, is the most dramatic go–stop cycle of all.

Summary

1 Output in different sectors tends to move together over the business cycle.

2 Output of investment goods tends to fluctuate more than that of consumer goods and services. Demand for durable goods fluctuates more than for nondurables.

3 Prices tend to move pro-cyclically but with a lag of about a year behind output movements.

4 Profits are strongly pro-cyclical, but the share of wages in national income is mildly counter-cyclical.

5 Cycles in the economy may result from random exogenous shocks or from discrete changes in exogenous variables combined with the dynamic interaction of the multiplier and the accelerator (or many other possible lagged adjustment mechanisms).

6 Monetarists think that the dominant cause of business cycles is changes in the money supply. Many Keynesians think that it is swings in autonomous expenditures (investment and exports).

7 The New Classical school emphasizes that only unexpected shifts in aggregate demand will have real effects. Real business cycle theorists assume that supply-side shocks trigger the cycle in a market-clearing model.

8 Systematic aggregate demand policies cannot affect national income in the New Classical model.

9 Policy credibility is important once it is perceived that private agents' behaviour is influenced by their expectations of the government's future policy actions.

10 Both demand and supply shocks can trigger cycles, but no two cycles are ever exactly the same.

Topics for review

- Cyclical behaviour of sectors
- Durable and nondurable expenditures
- The share of profits and wages in GDP
- The accelerator
- Multiplier–accelerator interaction
- Lucas aggregate supply curve
- Money surprises
- Policy invariance
- Credibility
- The political business cycle
- Stop–go

❧ CHAPTER 44

Macroeconomics in retrospect and prospect

MACROECONOMICS in its modern form has been around for about sixty years. In that time, it has developed enormously in apparent sophistication. Early models could be written down in a handful of equations, while modern forecasting models often have hundreds of equations. (Some might argue that the greater complexity has not greatly increased our understanding of the economy.)

We believe that the study of macroeconomics has increased our understanding of aggregate economic phenomena considerably, and that this level of understanding is continuing to improve as rapidly today as it ever has. Many of the valid insights generated by the study of macroeconomics are simple, apply at the aggregate level, and can be explained either in words or in simple two-dimensional diagrams.

Attempts to make advances in understanding the macro-economy by a reductionist strategy,[1] especially where this requires all agents to be continually optimizing (such as in New Classical and real business cycle models) in equilibrium market structures, may be intellectually attractive, but ultimately may not prove fruitful. All sciences are about looking for simple patterns, not about trying to build up a model so complex that it cannot easily be understood.

Science makes progress by debate, by argument and counter-argument, so the observation that economists disagree does not suggest that economics is a worthless subject. Rather, it indicates that it is a healthy and rapidly moving discipline. Ultimately theories have to be tested against the data.

In this chapter, we review some of the broad issues that have been, or still are, the focus of debate. First, we approach macro debates from the policy perspective: can policy-makers improve things by active intervention? We then review key aspects of macro models, and how they have evolved over time. Finally, we remind ourselves that positive economics is about adapting theory in the light of evidence.

Interventionists versus non-interventionists

ONE simple way of classifying approaches to macroeconomics is between those who believe that active government policy interventions can improve economic outcomes and those who believe that they cannot. It is common to categorize Keynesians as interventionists, and monetarists (plus New Classicists and real business cycle theorists) as non-interventionists. This may be broadly correct, but not always so. Some modern Keynesians, for example, may be quite happy to focus monetary policy on the control of the inflation rate, and not to attempt to use it to fine-tune economic activity in the short run.

THE NON-INTERVENTIONIST VIEW

Non-interventionists believe that the free-market economy performs quite well on its own. Although shocks do hit the system, they lead rather quickly, and often painlessly, to the adjustments dictated by the market system. For example, relative prices in booming sectors rise, drawing in resources from declining sectors or regions. As a result, resources (and particularly labour) usually remain fully employed, so there is no need for full-employment policies. Indeed, according to some (extreme) views, all unemployment is voluntary.

Non-interventionists hold that macroeconomic performance will be most satisfactory if it is determined solely by the workings of the free market.

Some would concede that involuntary unemployment does exist, but none the less would maintain that the market system works well enough to preclude any constructive role for policy. In addition, many non-interventionists believe that policy instruments are so crude that their use is often counterproductive. A policy's effects may be so uncertain, with regard to both strength and timing, that often it may impair rather than improve the economy's performance.

In a modern economy some government presence is inevitable. Thus, a stance of no intervention is impossible; rather, what is advocated by non-interventionists is minimal direct intervention in the market system, except where the intervention increases the flexibility of the market economy by removing institutional rigidities. (Examples might include Mrs Thatcher's trade union reforms, and the privatization of nationalized industries both of which reduce previous interventionist policies.) The government is, however, responsible for providing a *stable environment* in which the private sector can function.

---

[1] Reductionism means explaining aggregate behaviour by explaining the behaviour of sub-components of the aggregate. This means seeking 'micro-foundations' for all aggregate behaviour. Even in science this is not always successful. No amount of study of individual oxygen and hydrogen atoms would help us predict how they would behave when combined into water molecules. Some stable relationships in the aggregate may have no correspondence in the individual behaviour of components. These issues are controversial. The point is just that we do not necessarily have to seek regularities in economic behaviour by continual disaggregation.

A key component of the non-interventionist view is that macroeconomic policy cannot affect the level of potential national income. This view is based on the belief that, at any point in time, the economy has a unique equilibrium level of national income and employment which cannot be altered by policy.

It is sometimes thought that uniqueness of full-employment equilibrium is the same thing as a vertical *LRAS* curve. This is incorrect, because the argument for the perfectly inelastic *LRAS* curve (see Chapter 32) does not require a unique equilibrium. Instead, it is based solely on the absence of money illusion. To see this, assume that there is an equilibrium level of national income consistent with some equilibrium in each of the economy's markets. If we now add a zero to all prices, nothing real changes and the same real equilibrium will be consistent with the new price level. This argument shows that any single equilibrium income that exists is consistent with any price level—provided only that there is no money illusion. In other words, any given equilibrium real national income is associated with a vertical *LRAS* curve, showing that income level to be independent of the price level. This does not, however, prove uniqueness, because the argument applies to *any* equilibrium income, no matter how many equilibria there may be.

Non-interventionists argue that potential income is unaffected by the cyclical behaviour of the economy. Thus, there is no need to worry about what happens to potential national income and equilibrium employment when the economy is left to follow whatever cyclical path is produced by private-sector market forces. The economy will always return to the same equilibrium (path). Government policy can thus be left to concentrate on controlling inflation and providing a stable climate in which private firms can flourish.

THE INTERVENTIONIST VIEW

Interventionists believe that the functioning of the free-market economy is often far from satisfactory. Sometimes markets show weak self-regulatory forces and the economy settles into prolonged periods of high unemployment. At other times markets tend to 'overcorrect', causing the economy to lurch between the extremes of large recessionary and large inflationary gaps. However:

Interventionists hold that, although interventionist policies are imperfect, they are good enough to improve the functioning of the economy.

The interventionist view starts by criticizing the assumption that the economy's macroeconomic equilibrium is unique. No one has yet proved that there is a unique equilibrium in a model that captures the mixture of perfectly competitive, oligopolistic, and monopolistic markets that characterizes real modern economies. Without such a proof, there is no theoretical prediction of uniqueness of

macroeconomic equilibrium for modern industrial economies. Indeed, the microeconomic evidence on endogenous technological change, reviewed in Chapter 33, suggests the absence of uniqueness. If the shocks that hit an economy influence the amount and direction of its firms' research and development, identical economies hit by different shocks, *which are then removed,* will not return to identical starting-points.[2]

A further part of the interventionist critique is based on the development of theories that cast doubt on the uniqueness assumption as it applies to labour markets. These theories have arisen partly out of attempts to explain the prolonged recessions that beset most of the EU countries during the early 1980s and early 1990s.

One class of such theories is based on the idea of hysteresis (discussed in Chapter 41), which describes situations in which the equilibrium state of a system depends on the path by which that equilibrium is approached. In such cases, the equilibrium is said to be *path-dependent*. Of course, it cannot then be unique.

One way in which an equilibrium can be path-dependent is via capital. To see what is involved, let the economy start from a position of macroeconomic equilibrium and then consider two cases. In case 1 there is a short recession, followed by a return to potential national income and full employment. In case 2 there is a prolonged recession, lasting most of a decade, followed by a return to potential national income and full employment.

Consider, first, the effect on physical capital. During the short recession, physical capital and labour will both be unemployed. When the recovery quickly follows, the unemployed capital and labour will be put back to work and the new full-employment equilibrium will be the same as the original one. In the long recession, however, physical capital may not be replaced as it wears out, since demand may be too low to employ all of the existing capital. When the economy eventually recovers, the remaining capital stock will become fully employed, while there will still be substantial unemployed labour. Thus, potential national income will be met at a lower level of employment than after the short recession because the capital stock will be smaller as a result of the longer period of the recession. (This argument assumes a fixed capital–labour ratio embodied in existing capital.)

Similar results can occur with human capital. A short recession will have little effect on human capital. A prolonged recession, however, will cause many young people

---

[2] New theories of endogenous economic growth are behind the so-called 'new economics' which has been influential in forming a new policy strategy for the UK Labour Party, announced in September 1994. This involves government encouragement for training and infrastructure investment, among other things. The key idea of the endogenous growth literature is that there are externalities to capital formation. Thus, government investment can increase the productivity of private capital, and faster growth today creates faster growth tomorrow (because tomorrow's capital will be working with more capital around it).

entering the labour force for the first time to remain for years without a job, thus losing the opportunities for on-the-job training that goes with early job experience. When the recovery comes, they will have become different people, with different attitudes and less human capital, than if they had worked during their early formative years. Those who did have jobs during the recession may have been less inclined to invest in further human capital because the prospects of moving to a better job were bleak. Since capital is productive, less human capital implies less output from any given amount of employment. When recovery finally comes, full-employment national income will thus be lower than it would have been if the recession had been short-lived. Furthermore, those who have lost out on the chance of developing human capital may remain in the ranks of the unemployed or semi-employed for a much longer period—even for the rest of their lives.

To see the other side of this coin, consider a period of boom characterized by an inflationary gap, with national income *above* potential and employment *above* full employment. (Recall that 'full employment' refers to the level of employment that exists when national income is at its potential level.) The boom may lead people to acquire more human capital than they would do under full employment. When normal conditions return, potential income may be higher, because more human capital means more output from a given amount of employment. Furthermore, the equilibrium employment may be higher, because a better trained work-force has a higher marginal productivity, which generates higher demand for labour at any given real wage.

These possibilities provide reasons for the interventionist position that the government should use stabilization policies to prevent prolonged periods of slump and, perhaps, should provide retraining and/or work experience for those who would otherwise stay unemployed for long periods. They also provide reasons for believing that occasional recessionary gaps, with their accompanying unemployment, are more serious than occasional inflationary gaps, with their mild inflations and high employment.

Another source of non-uniqueness of macroeconomic equilibrium arises from possible union behaviour. Suppose unions understand the conflict between higher wages and higher employment that follows from a negatively sloped demand curve for labour. Suppose, however, that they care only about their members. A short recession leads to lay-offs, but those without jobs stay in the union and are re-employed when the recovery occurs. Now let there be a prolonged recession. Once again employment falls, but this time the unemployed drift out of the union. The union, which cares only about its current members, will then wish to protect the existing level of wages. The unemployed will have no say in the matter because they are not union members. Having got to a period of low employment, the economy will tend to stay there because the union is protecting the interests of those currently employed, who have no desire to cut wages to increase the employment of non-members. Insider–outsider models of labour markets give one possible explanation of why wages do not adjust to clear labour markets: they are the outcome of negotiation between employers and insiders only.

This provides a possible rationale for altering institutions to give more representation in wage bargaining to the unemployed. But, in the absence of such a major reform, it also provides a rationale for government intervention to prevent the emergence of prolonged periods of unemployment—periods that prevent the unemployed from having a say in making the trade-off between higher employment and higher wages.

The assumption of the uniqueness of macroeconomic equilibrium at any point of time is just that—an assumption, which does not follow from any general equilibrium theory describing the economy as we know it, and which is contradicted by the evidence in favour of hysteresis and endogenous growth.

The role of policy

The non-interventionist and interventionist diagnoses of the economy's ills lead, not surprisingly, to very different prescriptions about the appropriate role of economic policy.

NON-INTERVENTIONIST PRESCRIPTIONS

It is not necessary to distinguish non-interventionist policies with respect to full employment and stable prices. This is because non-interventionists believe that both goals will be achieved by the same basic policy: provision of a stable environment in which the free-market system can operate.

Providing a stable environment   Creating a stable environment by inactivity, as the non-interventionists advocate, may be easier said than done. We shall focus on the prescriptions for establishing stable fiscal and monetary policies.

One major problem to keep in mind is that macro-variables are interrelated. The stability of one may imply the instability of another. In such cases, a choice must be made. How much instability of one aggregate can we tolerate to secure stability in another, related, aggregate?

Assume, for example, that the government decides to adopt the goal of stability in the budget balance as part of the stable environment. This 'stability' requires great *instability* in tax and expenditure policy. Tax revenues depend on the interaction between tax rates and the level of national income. With given tax rates, tax revenues change with the ebb and flow of the cycle. A stable budget balance would require that the government raise tax rates and cut expenditure in slumps, and lower tax rates and raise expenditure in booms.

Not only does this squander the budget's potential to act as a stabilizer, but great instability of the fiscal environment is caused by continual changes in tax rates and expenditure levels. A stable fiscal environment requires substantial stability in government expenditure and tax rates. Stability is needed so that the private sector can plan for the future within a climate of known patterns of tax liabilities and government demand.

Any target budget balance must be some average over a period long enough to cover a typical cycle. Stability from year to year should be found in tax rates and expenditure programmes, not in the size of the budget balance.

This in turn requires that the government budget vary cyclically, showing its largest deficits in slumps and its largest surpluses in booms.

Advocates of a stable monetary environment are actually advocating stable inflation. Whether or not a *zero* rate is feasible is still debatable. The monetary policy urged by non-interventionists in the 1970s and 1980s was to set a target rate of increase in the money supply and hold it. To establish such a target, the central bank needs to estimate the rate at which the demand for money would be growing if actual income equalled potential income and the price level were stable. As a first approximation, this can be taken to be the rate at which potential income itself is growing. This then becomes the target rate of growth of the money supply. The key proposition is that the money supply should be changing gradually along a stable path that is independent of short-term variations in the demand for money caused by cyclical changes in national income.

Would a monetary growth rule really provide monetary stability? The answer is, not necessarily.

Assuring a stable rate of monetary growth does not assure a stable monetary environment. Monetary shortages and surpluses depend on the relation between the supply of and the demand for money.

The rule for monetary growth looks after supply, but what about demand? Problems arise when the demand for money shifts. For example, the payment of interest on current accounts increased the demand for these accounts. In this event, if the Bank of England had adhered to a rigid rule for monetary growth, there would have been an excess demand for money and interest rates would have risen. In this way, contractionary pressures can be put on the economy.

Should the Bank commit itself to a specific percentage growth rule, or should it merely work towards unannounced and possibly variable targets? The announced rule makes it easier to evaluate how well the Bank is doing its job. It also helps to prevent the Bank from succumbing to the temptation to fine-tune the economy.

One disadvantage of the announced rule, however, is that it sets up possible speculative behaviour. If, for example, when monthly money supply figures are announced there is too much money, speculators know that the Bank will sell more bonds to reduce the surplus. This will depress the price of bonds. Speculators are thus induced to sell bonds, hoping to rebuy them at bargain prices once the Bank acts.

Stable pre-announced monetary targets can introduce instability into interest-rate behaviour.

A second disadvantage of such a rule is that the Bank, in order to preserve its credibility, may fail to take discretionary action that would otherwise be appropriate. For example, after an entrenched inflation is broken, the economy may come to rest with substantial unemployment and a stable price level. There is then a case for a once-for-all discretionary expansion in the money supply to get the economy back to potential national income. The fixed money growth rule precludes this, condemning the economy to a prolonged slump.

Despite these problems, many non-interventionists believe that a money growth rule is superior to any known alternative. Some would agree that, in principle, the central bank could improve the economy's performance by occasional bouts of discretionary monetary policy to offset such things as major shifts in the demand for money. But they also believe that, once given such discretion, the central bank would abuse it in an attempt to fine-tune the economy. The resulting instability would, they believe, be much more than any instability resulting from the application of a rigid money growth rule in an environment subject to some change.

The difficulties of monetary growth targeting in the United Kingdom in the face of financial innovation, which shifted the money demand function (discussed in Chapter 38), led an allegedly monetarist government to abandon fixed rules for monetary growth. The non-interventionist position has accordingly shifted to support the cause of central bank independence, and to impose on the central bank the single target of price stability. The reason for central bank independence is to remove the central bank from short-term political pressures, with the intention of removing any incentive to generate short-term booms (especially in the run-up to an election). Again, however, it is an act of faith that, if it could be achieved, price stability would aid the stability of real economic activity better than a policy that preserved discretion for countercyclical policy changes.

An alternative strategy for monetary policy is to return to a fixed exchange rate regime (or even to a commodity standard, such as the gold standard). At one time, this might have been regarded as the non-interventionist strategy, since it removes all possibility of countercyclical discretionary monetary policy. This was the policy that was in place during the stable years in the 1950s and 1960s. However, in the Thatcher era, fixed exchange rates were regarded as highly interventionist. The put-down for such a strategy was: 'You can't buck the market.' Certainly, there can be no guarantee that a fixed exchange rate regime will deliver more stability of the real economy than would a floating regime, as the UK experience with the ERM has emphasized. Equally, the gold standard delivered long-term price stability, but it was unable to deliver stability during the turbulent period of the 1920s.

A single EU currency, if ever implemented, would remove monetary policy entirely from the discretion of both UK politicians and the Bank of England. Ironically, it is the non-interventionists (monetarists and right-wing Conservatives) who are most strongly opposed to this, and the interventionists (left-wing Conservatives, the Labour Party, and the Liberal Democrats) who are most in favour. The economics of the issue suggests that the interventionists should be most troubled by a single currency, as it removes the possibility of using monetary policy for countercyclical purposes at the level of the UK economy. Of course, which route delivers the more stable economic environment is highly controversial.

Long-term growth Non-interventionists want to let growth take care of itself. They argue that governments cannot improve the workings of free markets and that their interventions can interfere with market efficiency. Thus, they push for reducing the current level of government intervention as the best pro-growth policy. Indeed, they argue for as little government involvement in industry as possible, and for privatization wherever the market can possibly deliver a good or service.

INTERVENTIONIST PRESCRIPTIONS

Interventionists call for different policies for the three policy goals of high employment, price stability, and growth. As we consider their prescriptions, we give their reasons for rejecting the non-interventionist case.

High employment There are two levels of interventionist policies relating to employment. The traditional Keynesian line calls for discretionary fiscal and monetary policies (aggregate demand policies) to offset significant inflationary and recessionary gaps, that is, to return national income to its potential level and to return unemployment to the NAIRU. Some of the major problems associated with effective discretionary stabilization policy have been discussed in earlier chapters.

The newer line of argument relates to 'supply-side' interventions, designed to lower the NAIRU (equilibrium unemployment) and to raise the trend growth rate of potential national income. These policies include such measures as changing the structure of wage bargaining institutions, altering the benefits system, and introducing active labour market policies to improve job skills and training.

A stable price level Some interventionists, particularly a group called *post-Keynesians*, believe that it may be impossible to achieve full employment and stable prices simultaneously. This is because they accept a wage-cost push theory of inflation (discussed in Chapter 40), even though wage push can cause sustained inflation only if accommodated by the monetary authorities.

Some post-Keynesians have called for **incomes policies** to restrain the wage-cost push and so make full employment compatible with stable prices. Some still believe that such policies should become permanent features of the economic landscape.

Wage–price controls might work as temporary measures to break inflationary inertia, but as permanent features they would introduce inefficiencies and rigidities.

More permanent incomes policies might be of the type commonly used in past decades but now out of favour, i.e. a *social contract*. This entails annual consultations between labour, management, and the government to agree on target wage changes. These are calculated to be non-inflationary, given the government's projections for the future and its planned economic policies.

Some interventionists argue that high employment should be the dominant objective, and that this should not be compromised even if it does lead to somewhat higher inflation. The problem with this line of reasoning was set out in Chapters 40 and 41. Unemployment can certainly be reduced below the NAIRU in the short term, but keeping it there will lead not to stable, but to ever rising (and eventually hyper-), inflation. We also know that, once high inflation has set in, only unemployment above the NAIRU can bring it down, and this is often a long, slow, and costly process. In short, the interventionists are on shaky ground if they try to argue for employment targets that ignore the inflationary conequences. As has been said, 'There is no such thing as a free lunch'!

Growth Traditional policies to increase growth rates seek to alter the general economic climate in a way favourable to growth. They typically include subsidization or favourable tax treatment for research and development, for purchase of plant and equipment, and for other profit-earning activities. Measures to lower interest rates temporarily or permanently are urged by some as favourable to investment and growth.

Further policies concern the diffusion of new technologies. Earlier economic models assumed that, once an innovation was made, it was freely available to everyone. More recent research shows that the diffusion of technological knowledge is a slow and costly business. One reason is that the cost of learning what is currently available is high, particularly for small firms. Another reason is that innovations made by other firms often require further R&D to adapt them to similar but not identical uses. OECD governments have been devoting much attention in recent years to policies to aid and speed up the process of diffusion of the constantly changing best-practice technologies among the firms in their own economies.

Some also support more specific intervention, usually in the form of what is called *picking and backing winners* in one way or another. Advocates of this view want governments to pick the industries, usually new ones, that have potential for future success and then to back them with subsidies, government contracts, research funds, and all of the other encouragements at the government's command.

Opponents argue that picking winners requires foresight, and that there is no reason to expect the government to have better foresight than private investors. Indeed, since political considerations inevitably get in the way, the government may be less successful than the market in picking winners. If so, channelling funds through the government rather than through the private sector may hurt rather than help growth.

The modern case for active intervention to boost growth is based upon the economic analysis of endogenous growth and of hysteresis. Endogenous growth theory suggests that appropriate investments by the public sector may boost productivity of capital in the private sector. Hysteresis applied to labour markets shows that the NAIRU would be lower (over the medium term, but not in the very long run) if unemployment were never allowed to rise in the first place. Related arguments suggest that the NAIRU can be lowered, once it is high, by policies directed at boosting the job skills of the long-term unemployed, through periods of work experience and retraining.

Non-interventionists might concede the theoretical possibility of such beneficial interventions but be sceptical that any real government could make such intervention work in a reasonable time period, at least without causing other problems, such as higher taxes, inflation, or large budget deficits. The intention to improve growth is not new, but in the past, long-term intentions have been buried by financial crises or other short-term problems.

The evolution of macroeconomics

MACROECONOMIC theory has changed over time, and the consensus view of the best current theory tends also to influence the tenor of policy recommendations made by economists. Clashes between interventionists and non-interventionists predate modern economics by hundreds of years,[3] even though we relate these arguments to the more recent debate between monetarists and Keynesians. In recent times, changes in the 'standard' macroeconomic model have swung the balance of the argument first to the Keynesians (interventionists), then to the monetarists (non-interventionists), and most recently to the New Keynesians (interventionists). In this section, we highlight some of these key steps in the evolution of the theory.

THE CONCEPT OF EQUILIBRIUM

In our macro model since Chapter 32 we have assumed a single, completely inelastic, long-run aggregate supply (*LRAS*) curve. This curve defines a single level of national income towards which the economy gravitates in the long run. The associated level of unemployment is called the non-accelerating-inflation rate of unemployment (NAIRU), or the natural rate of unemployment. Equilibrium unemployment is frictional plus structural unemployment in a growing, changing economy.

The view that the economy has a unique macroeconomic equilibrium was generally accepted in the 1970s. As we have seen, however, the idea has come under serious criticism from recent developments in New Keynesian economics.

To understand the modern debate, we need to review how the concept of macroeconomic equilibrium has

[3] In the early nineteenth century, the two schools were the bullionists and anti-bullionists. The former were forebears of monetarists, in that they wanted paper currency issue tied to gold (a monetary rule). Later in the nineteenth century the bullionists turned into the currency school. Their opponents, the banking school, were Keynesian, in the sense that they wanted the money supply to expand in line with the needs of real economic activity.

evolved since the beginning of Keynesian economics. The evolution had been towards allowing less and less scope for interventionist policies; however, recent developments have started to shift the balance back towards focused interventions.

Dominated by the experience of the Great Depression of the 1930s, macroeconomic theory started off assuming excess supply, so that demand deficiency was the problem and increasing aggregate demand was the solution. It then moved to an assumption of market-clearing (either always or eventually), so that policies could do little more than speed up adjustments.[4] Finally, the agenda has shifted towards 'supply-side' interventions which can change the nature of the real equilibrium, possibly for the better.

Phase 1: The diagonal cross   The earliest Keynesian models were of the type set out in Chapters 29 and 30. Equilibrium national income occurred where the aggregate desired expenditure curve (*AE*) cut the 45° line. This equilibrium income would be equal to potential income (originally called 'full-employment income') only by accident. Whenever it was less than potential income, there was a place for expansionary fiscal policy, designed to make the two coincide.

Phase 2: The simple Phillips curve   In the 1960s, the Phillips curve was added to the Keynesian model. As long as wage costs were flexible upwards and downwards, the long-run equilibrium level of national income was now uniquely determined at the non-inflationary level of unemployment and national income. This is where the Phillips curve cuts the productivity growth line or, what is the same thing, where the unit-cost inflation curve cuts the zero axis (see pp. 795–97).

In this model, however, the government could permanently achieve an inflationary level of national income as long as it was willing to validate the inflation with the necessary monetary expansion. In other words, the appropriate interventionist policy would allow the government to achieve any desired point on the Phillips curve. To do this, fiscal policy would be used to shift the *AD* curve so that it intersected the *SRAS* curve at the desired level of real income. Monetary policy would then be used to prevent the resulting inflation from shifting the *LM* curve to the left. This is done by increasing the nominal money supply at the same rate as the price level is rising, thus holding the real money supply constant. In effect, as the *SRAS* curve shifts leftwards, the *AD* curve would be shifted rightward to preserve the inflationary gap.

Phase 3: The expectations-augmented Phillips curve   The accelerationist hypothesis removed the above-mentioned possibility by adding the expected inflation rate to the simple Phillips curve. If the government tried to hold the economy at any point on the expectations-augmented Phillips curve associated with some positive rate of inflation, the Phillips curve would begin to shift upwards. This is because the expected rate of inflation would be continually rising to catch up with the actual rate. Maintaining the target level of income and employment would thus require accepting an ever-increasing rate of inflation. Since, sooner or later, such a policy would have to be abandoned, a return of the economy to the unique NAIRU, and to the associated potential level of national income, was the only viable objective for aggregate demand policy. Thus, interventionist policy could not affect the level of income and employment at which the economy settled. All it could do, at best, was to speed up the adjustment back towards equilibrium, when exogenous shocks and cyclical forces caused national income to deviate from potential income and unemployment to deviate from the NAIRU. Interventionists called for such a stabilization policy; non-interventionists rejected it because they felt it was likely to be perverse in its effects and because the economy's natural adjustment forces were thought to be strong enough.

Phase 4: Hysteresis   Recent advances in the understanding of labour markets suggest that the equilibrium levels of unemployment (the NAIRU) and of national income are path-dependent. After periods when high unemployment has been allowed to build up, the NAIRU will be higher than it was previously, and, accordingly, the potential level of national income will be lower than it otherwise might have been. This means that reducing the amplitude of the cycle could raise the level of potential output and lower the NAIRU (compared with a counterfactual case, where significant recessions are permitted).

This analysis concludes that successful stabilization policy would be beneficial in raising the sustainable potential level of national income. Of course, it does nothing to say how stabilization policy can be better conducted to achieve those goals. But it is still more favourable to the principle of active intervention than a theory stating that the equilibrium is unaffected by the size and duration of disequilibrium.

Phase 5: Integration of trend and cycle   A possible further extension of phase 4 arises out of the endogenous growth literature. The analysis of hysteresis suggests that active stabilization policy can generate a once-for-all parallel upward shift in the time trend in (the log of) potential output. The theory of endogenous growth poses the possibility that specific interventions can raise the trend growth rate of national income, that is, raise the slope of the time trend of (the log of) potential national income.

To date, macroeconomics has concentrated on cycles about the trend in national income, and has assumed that

---

[4] Actually this was more like a reversion to classical economics, but it took a long time for counter-arguments to emerge.

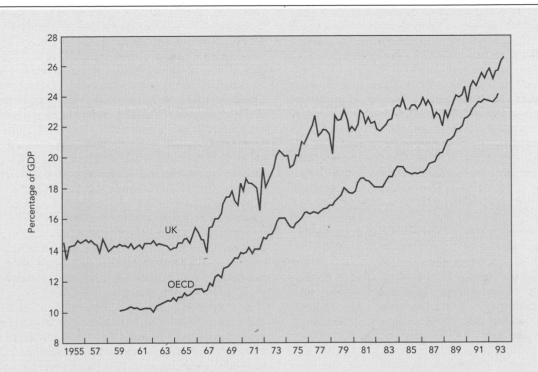

Figure 44.1 Openness of economies

The importance of trade in most developed economies has increased significantly since the late 1950s.
The chart shows exports as a percentage of GDP for the United Kingdom (1955–93) and for OECD countries as a whole (1960–93). UK exports have risen from about 14 per cent of GDP in the late 1950s to about 27 per cent in 1993. For OECD countries as a whole, the percentage has risen from about 10 per cent in 1960 to around 24 per cent today.
Data are the ratios (×100) of the (constant-price) volume measures of GDP and exports, seasonally adjusted. Note that using the values of exports and GDP at current prices would produce a much more volatile series, as exchange rate swings create considerable volatility in export values.

Source: Datastream.

the determinants of the trend itself are beyond the bounds of the subject. We have recognized the potential for ending this dichotomy by bringing the study of economic growth into the core of macroeconomics (see Chapter 33).

The full integration of theories of the trend and of the cycle still has a long way to go. None the less, we can recognize this as a distinct possibility over the next few years. If the endeavour is successful, economic growth will become truly endogenous to macroeconomics. Indeed, the real business cycle school is already building models that explain both trend and cycle.

OPENNESS

Another important respect in which the perception of the suitable setup of the macro model has changed over time

is with regard to linkages with the rest of the world. Substantial changes have been necessary because the world itself has changed substantially.

When Keynesian macro models were being developed in the 1950s, international trade was much less than it is today and was affected by direct controls (even for the major industrial countries, with the exception of the United States). Financial capital flows were almost universally even more severely restricted by exchange controls, so for a while most economies had a reasonable degree of monetary independence, even though the Bretton Woods system (which lasted from the Second World War until 1973) was a regime of almost universal fixed exchange rates. Currencies were tied to the US dollar, and US inflation was low.

In this environment, a fixed-price closed-economy model may capture many of the key elements of what is happening. Imports and exports were there in most models from early on, but in the world of the 1950s the level of trade was low relative to domestic activity. Figure 44.1 shows the ratio of exports to GDP for the United Kingdom and for OECD countries as a whole.

Things started to change in the 1960s, as trade in goods and services was liberalized and world trade grew rapidly relative to aggregate GDP. Figure 44.1 shows the percentage of exports in UK GDP rising from about 14 per cent in the late 1950s to about 27 per cent today. The comparable rise for OECD countries as a whole is from about 10 per cent to about 25 per cent. International linkages became more important. For a while in the post-war literature these linkages were modelled entirely through net exports (and components of trade), but in the early 1970s the role of financial flows (and asset stocks) was emphasized by the monetary approach to the balance of payments (see Box 39.1).

After 1973, an important task was to incorporate the external adjustment mechanisms associated with floating exchange rates into the macro model. This, combined with rational expectations, produced the overshooting theories which we first met in Chapter 37 and integrated into our macro model in Chapter 39. Floating also permitted some countries (e.g. the United Kingdom) to get into trouble with high inflation, so monetary policy became important and fixed-price models would no longer do.

Another step on the long road towards increasing openness came with the widespread abolition of exchange controls. This happened at different times in different countries (United Kingdom 1979, Japan 1980, France 1989, Spain 1991, Portugal 1992, Ireland 1992), but the overall effect was to increase the level of financial integration around the world.[5] We have referred to this as the process of globalization.

The impact of globalization on the macro model is akin to the assumption of perfect capital mobility which we discussed in Chapter 39. In effect, each country becomes a price-taker in world financial markets, because it is a small player in a big market. As we saw, the assumption of perfect capital mobility changes our perception of the transmission mechanism resulting from policy changes and the effect of those changes when the system returns to equilibrium. It also affects perceptions of the power of policy in individual countries when open economies are so affected by world market conditions. It should come as no surprise that many countries have experienced very similar cycles over the last two decades and that their domestic policy-makers did not seem able to do much about it (see Box 39.3).

It may be that domestic monetary and fiscal policy-makers are just not powerful enough to offset, with the tools available, the cycles in demand and real interest rates transmitted through trade and financial flows. Whether successful stabilization policy can be co-ordinated at the supranational level is doubtful, but this may be the only solution if future global business cycles are to be limited.

The progress of economics

IT is difficult to predict major shifts in the approach that is to be used by any science. Such major shifts in the way of looking at things are often called paradigm shifts.

Whatever its current paradigm, useful economics must be related in some clear way to what we see in the real world. Applying the scientific method is not, however, a simple matter in economics. We lack laboratory conditions. We cannot get the holders of opposing views to agree on critical tests and then repeat them over and over until everyone must agree on the results. The call for economics to try to be a science is a plea for economists to try to relate their theories to observations. If we hold that the truth of economic theories is totally independent of successful empirical applications, it is difficult to see how economics can claim to be in any way useful in interpreting the world around us.

In economics, general acceptance that theories should be tested by confronting their predictions with the available evidence is only half a century or so old. At many points, we have raised the question of how various parts of macroeconomic theory could be tested; we have also discussed some of the tests that have been conducted and some of the resulting changes in the theory. However, not everyone agrees on what methodology should apply to accepting or rejecting theories.

There is no doubt that, since economics first began, some progress, albeit irregular and halting, has been made in

---

[5] It should be emphasized that the trend towards greater openness that we have described applies only to the period since the Second World War. Much of what happened did little more than restore the degree of openness experienced before the First World War in many countries.

relating theory to evidence. This progress has been reflected in the superior ability of governments to achieve their policy objectives. The unsuccessful efforts of successive UK governments to deal with the economic catastrophe that overwhelmed the country after the return to the gold standard in the 1920s, and even more so during the Great Depression of the 1930s, constitute a record of measures adopted in all sincerity which in most cases actually served to make things worse. Across the Atlantic, President Roosevelt's attempts to reduce US unemployment in the same decade were greatly hampered by the failure of most economists to realize the critical importance of budget deficits in increasing aggregate demand and hence national income.

The debate between monetarists and Keynesians is another illustration of the value of the rule of evidence. Monetarists have several times had to revise their positions in the face of evidence. For example, they no longer hold that the demand for money is completely interest-inelastic, or that fiscal policy cannot affect aggregate expenditure. The anti-inflation experiments of the early 1980s and early 1990s have been closely watched and heavily documented. Already we have hard evidence on several issues on which economists could only conjecture ten to fifteen years ago. Those monetarists, Keynesians (and New Keynesians), New Classicists, and real business cycle theorists who are emotionally fully committed to their present views will never abandon their basic positions; however, those who have open minds, by testing their specific positions, really will learn about the economy.

In the mid-1970s, the new disease of stagflation burst on the world's economies. The coexistence of falling output and accelerating inflation seemed utterly paradoxical to observers familiar with the concept of a stable Phillips curve, along which inflation increased on cyclical upswings and decreased on cyclical downswings. Many observers spoke of the end of conventional economics, and the need to develop entirely new models for understanding the economy's radically new behaviour.

Such was the pace of theoretical and empirical research, however, that within a very few years the phenomenon of stagflation was explained by, and incorporated into, conventional macro models. Today, a satisfactory explanation of what seemed so paradoxical to observers in the 1970s has found its way into standard first-year university textbooks —as readers of this book well know.

The process of understanding, and explaining, stagflation greatly enriched economists' knowledge in a number of ways. First, economists are now much more aware of the importance of supply-side phenomena, compared with earlier days when most attention was focused on the demand side of macro models. Second, they are more aware of the influence of sectoral price shocks. In the 1970s, Milton Friedman, along with many other monetarists, argued that the oil price shock would not be inflationary because other prices would fall so as to hold the general price level constant. This proved to be completely wrong. It is now clear that, in the face of equal amounts of excess supply and excess demand, prices do not fall as fast as they rise, so that a major sectoral price shock raises the whole price level. Thus, it shifts the *SRAS* curve upwards, giving the economy a contractionary supply-side shock. Third, economists are more aware of the dangers of treating supply-side, stagflationary shocks as if they were demand-side shocks. The US government made this mistake in 1974–5 and exacerbated an already severe contractionary, supply-side shock by imposing restrictive demand measures.

A further challenge was posed by the persistence of high unemployment in many European countries in the 1980s, which continued even during an inflationary boom. This experience differed from stagflation in that output was growing fast but unemployment refused to fall to anything like 1960s levels. New theories of hysteresis helped economists to understand this phenomenon, and new policy measures emerged from the analysis. By questioning the uniqueness of equilibrium, New Keynesian economics made macroeconomics interesting again. It also offered the hope that policy measures could actually improve long-run outcomes.

It is in such important policy areas as the curing of major recessions and the handling of major inflations that the general thrust of our theories is tested, even if all their specific predictions are not. In some general sense, then, economic theories have always been subjected to empirical tests. When they were wildly at variance with the facts, the ensuing disaster could not but be noticed, and the theories were discarded or amended in the light of what was learned.

What we do not know covers vast areas, which should give all economists a sense of humility. But those who believe that we know nothing need only involve themselves in a policy-making situation with non-economists to lose some of their feelings of inferiority. First, we really do know many things about the behaviour of the economy that help us to evaluate policy choices. Second, many non-economists do not understand how price systems work, and thus fail to understand how decentralized decision-taking can be both co-ordinated and relatively efficient. This leads them to misinterpret much of the economic behaviour that they observe, and to advocate policies that would work only if the price system did not. Third, economists have a method of looking at problems that is potentially enlightening to almost any problem, whether or not it is conventionally described as economic.

The advance of economics in this century partly reflects a change in economists' attitudes towards empirical observation. Today, we are much less likely to dismiss theories just because we do not like them and to refuse to abandon theories just because we do like them. We are more likely to try to base our theories as much as possible on empirical observation, and to accept empirical relevance as the ultimate arbiter of the value of those theories. As human beings, we suffer much anguish at the upsetting of a pet theory; as scientists, we should try to train ourselves to take pleasure in it because of the new knowledge we gain thereby. It has been said that one of the great tragedies of science is the continual slaying of beautiful theories by ugly facts. As economists, we are all too often swayed by aesthetic considerations. In the past, we have too often clung to our theories because they were beautiful or because we liked their political implications; as scientists, we must always remember that, when theory and fact come into serious conflict, it is theory, not fact, that will eventually give way.

Summary

1 Approaches to macroeconomics can be classified according to whether they are interventionist or non-interventionist.

2 Keynesians and New Keynesians are interventionist, while monetarists, New Classicists, and real business cycle theorists are non-interventionist.

3 Non-interventionists generally assume that policy cannot affect the level of potential national income.

4 Interventionists believe that there are real output gains available from active policy in both the short run and the long run.

5 Theories of hysteresis and endogenous growth create a theoretical possibility that policy interventions can improve both equilibrium national income and/or its growth rate. However, this does not guarantee that actual policies will have the intended effects.

6 It is not always clear what non-intervention means or what the non-interventionist policy should be. Not intervening with respect to one variable may create instability of another.

7 Interventionists generally give high employment and output a higher priority than low inflation.

8 The concept of equilibrium in macroeconomics has changed several times as the subject has evolved.

9 The changing environment has meant that macro models have had to evolve to accommodate openness to trade and the globalization of finance.

10 Theories have to evolve in the light of evidence generated by data from the real world.

Topics for review

- Interventionists
- Non-interventionists
- Equilibrium concepts
- Uniqueness
- Hysteresis
- Endogenous growth
- Trend and cycle
- Theories and evidence

Glossary

absolute advantage The advantage that one region is said to have over another in the production of some commodity when an equal quantity of resources can produce more of that commodity in the first region than in the second.

absolute price The price of a good or a service expressed in monetary units; also called a *money price*

absorption approach Analysis of the balance of payments based upon comparing domestic expenditure with domestic output.

accelerator theory of investment The theory that the level of investment depends on the rate of change of national income.

acceptance houses Financial institutions in London which accept, or guarantee, *bills of exchange* by stamping their own name on the back of the bill. Now more commonly called *merchant banks*.

accommodation Said to occur when the monetary authorities increase the money supply in response to a negative *aggregate supply shock*. It has the effect of offsetting the downward impact of the shock on real national income at the cost of a permanently higher price level.

actual consumption The consumption of the flow of services that are provided by the commodities that households buy.

actual expenditure See *realized expenditure*.

AD curve See *aggregate demand curve*.

ad valorem tariff A tariff levied as a percentage of the price of the product.

ad valorem tax A tax levied as a percentage of the value of some transaction.

adaptive expectations The expectation of a future variable, formed on the basis of an adjustment which is some proportion of the error in expectations made last period. The error is the difference between what was expected last period and what actually happened.

adjustable peg system A system with these two characteristics: (i) the exchange rate is pegged at a publicly announced par value; (ii) the exchange rate is adjusted from time to time in the face of fundamental disequilibria.

administered price A price that is set by the decisions of individual firms rather than by impersonal market forces.

advances Bank loans.

adverse selection The tendency for people most at risk to insure, while people least at risk do not, so that the insurers get an unrepresentative sample of clients within any one fee category.

agents Decision-makers, including consumers, workers, firms and government bodies.

aggregate demand (AD) The total desired purchases of all the nation's buyers of final output.

aggregate demand curve A curve that plots all combinations of the price level and national income that yield equilibrium in the goods and the asset markets — i.e. that yield *IS–LM* equilibrium.

aggregate demand shock A shift in the *aggregate demand curve* resulting from an autonomous change in exogenous expenditures or the money supply (or equivalently, a policy-induced change in interest rates).

aggregate desired expenditure (AE) The total amount of purchases of currently produced goods and services that all spending units in the economy wish to make.

aggregate production function The technical relationship which expresses the maximum national output that can be produced with each possible combination of capital, labour and other resource inputs. See also *production function*.

aggregate supply (AS) The total desired output of all the nation's producers.

aggregate supply curve A curve relating the economy's total desired output, Y, to the price level, P.

aggregate supply shock A shift in the *aggregate supply curve* resulting from an exogenous change in input prices or from technical change (exogenous or endogenous). Most common example is the oil price shocks of the 1970s.

allocative efficiency The situation occurring when resources cannot be reallocated to produce a different bundle of goods which will then allow someone to be made better off while no one is made worse off.

appreciation When a change in the free-market exchange rate raises the value of one currency.

arbitrage Trading activity based upon buying where a product is cheap and selling where it has a higher price (from the French word 'arbitrer': to referee or arbitrate). Arbitrage activity helps to bring prices closer in different segments of the market. The term 'arbitrageurs' (often shortened to arbs) has been erroneously applied in the United States to traders who attempted to profit from inside information or to *speculate*.

arc elasticity A measure of the average responsiveness of quantity to price over an interval of the demand curve. For analytical purposes it is usually defined by the formula

$$\eta = \frac{\Delta q/q}{\Delta p/p} \,.$$

An alternative formula often used where computations are involved is

$$\eta = \frac{(q_2 - q_1)/(q_2 + q_1)}{(p_2 - p_1)/(p_2 + p_1)} \,,$$

where p_1 and q_1 are the original price and quantity and p_2 and q_2 are the new price and quantity. With negatively sloped demand curves, elasticity is a negative number. The above expressions are therefore sometimes multiplied by -1 to make measured elasticity positive. See also *point elasticity*.

asset disequilibrium See *portfolio disequilibrium*.

asset equilibrium See *portfolio equilibrium*.

asymmetric information A situation in which some economic agents have more information than others. The two most common examples in economics are: (i) in labour markets, where workers have less (or different) information about output markets than do firms (employers), and (ii) in the theory of the firm, where there is a separation of ownership (shareholders) from control (managers). In the latter case see also *principal–agent problem*.

Austrian school of economics A group of economists, originally led by Menger and Bohm-Bawerk in Vienna, which tried (but failed) to build a theory of the business cycle on the basis of microeconomic (market-clearing) principles.

autarky Situation existing when a country does no foreign trade.

automatic fiscal stabilizers Stablizers that arise because the value of some tax revenues and benefits changes with the level of economic activity. For example, income tax revenue rises as personal incomes rise, corporation tax revenue increases with company profits, and unemployment benefit falls as employment increases.

autonomous variable See *exogenous variable.*

average fixed cost (AFC) Total fixed costs divided by the number of units produced.

average product (AP) Total output divided by the number of units of the variable factor used in its production.

average propensity to consume (APC) Total consumption expenditure divided by total income, *C/Y.*

average propensity to import Total imports divided by total income, *IM/Y.*

average propensity to save (APS) Total saving divided by total income, *S/Y.*

average propensity to tax The total tax revenue divided by total national income, *T/Y.*

average revenue (AR) The total revenue divided by the number of units sold.

average total cost (ATC) The total cost of producing any given output divided by the number of units produced, i.e. the cost per unit.

average variable cost (AVC) Total variable cost divided by the number of units produced; also called *unit cost.*

balanced budget A situation in which current revenue is exactly equal to current expenditure.

balanced-budget multiplier Measures the change in income divided by the balanced-budget change in government expenditure that brought it about.

balance of payments accounts A summary record of a country's transactions that involve payment or receipts of foreign exchange.

balance of trade The difference between imports and exports.

bank notes Paper currency originally issued as a receipt for deposits of gold or silver. Later created by banks on a fractional reserve basis. Now almost universally issued by *central banks.*

barriers to entry Anything that prevents new firms from entering an industry that is earning profits.

barter The trading of goods directly for other goods.

base period See *base year.*

base rate The interest rate quoted by UK banks as the reference rate for much of their loan business. For example, a company may be given a loan at 'base plus 2%'. Base rate changes periodically when the monetary authorities signal that they wish money market rates in general to change. The equivalent term used by US banks is *prime rate.*

base year A year, or other point in time, chosen for comparison purposes in order to express or compute index numbers. Also called *base period.*

Basle Agreement An agreement reached in 1988 between the bank regulators of all the major countries. It established that banks would be monitored by their home bank regulator on the basis of their worldwide activities. It also introduced a minimum risk–asset ratio of 8 per cent. This means that banks have to hold £8 of capital for each £100 of private-sector loans.

BB line The locus of levels of the interest rate and real national income for which the desired current account balance of payment surplus (deficit) just equals the desired capital account deficit (surplus).

bill A tradable security, usually with an initial maturity of up to six months, which pays no explicit interest and so trades at a discount to its maturity value. See also *Treasury bills* and *bills of exchange.*

bills of exchange Written orders to pay a sum of money to another party at a future date, usually in exchange for the delivery of goods. Widely used in the finance of international trade because they enable exporters to receive finance (minus a discount) as soon as the goods are shipped while the importer does not pay until the goods have been received. Also known as commercial bills and trade bills. Bills of exchange that have been *accepted*, or guaranteed, by a good name in the City of London become *prime bank bills* and are eligible to be rediscounted via the discount market at the Bank of England.

black market A market in which goods are sold illegally at prices that violate the legal restrictions on prices.

bond In economic theory, any evidence of a debt carrying a legal obligation to pay interest and repay the principal at some stated future time.

boom Periods of high output and high employment.

break-even price The price at which a firm is just able to cover all of its costs, including the opportunity cost of capital.

Bretton Woods system The fixed exchange rate regime introduced after the Second World War. It broke down in the early 1970s when several major countries floated their exchange rates. (For the United Kingdom this happened in June 1972.) So called because it was the outcome of an agreement reached in July 1944 in a town called Bretton Woods, in the US state of New Hampshire.

broad money A money stock measure which includes interest-bearing savings deposits as well as current account deposits and cash. The standard measure of broad money today is M4. In the 1970s it would have been M3.

budget deficit The shortfall of current revenue below current expenditure, usually with reference to the government.

budget deficit function Function relating the government budget deficit, or the PSBR, to national income.

budget line Shows all those combinations of commodities that are just obtainable, given the household's income and the prices of commodities.

budget surplus The excess of current revenue over current expenditure, usually with reference to the government.

building societies Financial institutions which take savings deposits and make loans (mortgages) for house purchase. The recent trend has been for them to diversify and become more like banks. Originally they were clubs which would disband once all members had a house. Modern societies are 'permanent'. They are the British equivalent of US saving and loan institutions, also referred to as thrifts.

built-in stabilizer Anything that reduces the economy's cyclical fluctuations and that is activated without a conscious government decision. See also *automatic fiscal stabilizers*.

bundle Any collection. Specifically, in consumption theory, any collection of goods represented by a point on an indifference curve or a budget line is a 'bundle of goods'. Also called a *combination*.

business cycles Fluctuations in the general level of activity in an economy which affect many sectors at roughly the same time, though not necessarily to the same extent. In recent times, the period from the peak of one cycle to the peak of the next has varied in the range of five to ten years. Used to be known as trade cycles.

buyout When a group of investors buys up a controlling interest in a firm.

capacity The output that corresponds to the minimum short-run average total cost.

capital account Record of international transactions related to movement of long- and short-run capital.

capital consumption allowance An estimate of the amount by which the capital stock is depleted through its contribution to current production. Also called *depreciation*.

capital deepening Increasing the ratio of capital to labour.

capital goods All those man-made aids to further production, such as tools, machinery and factories, which are used up in the process of making other goods and services rather than being consumed for their own sake.

capital inflow Arises when overseas residents buy assets in the domestic economy or domestic residents sell claims on foreign assets.

capital–labour ratio The ratio of the amount of capital to the amount of labour used to produce any given output.

capital markets Bond and equity markets in which companies and governments sell securities to finance their long-term needs.

capital outflow Arises when overseas residents sell assets in the domestic economy or domestic residents buy foreign assets.

capital–output ratio The number of units of capital required to produce each unit of output. Most commonly appears in macroeconomics in the *accelerator theory of investment*.

capital stock The total quantity of capital.

capital widening Increasing the quantity of capital without changing the proportions in which the factors are used.

cartel A group of firms that agree to act as if they were a single seller.

cash base See *high-powered money*.

central authorities See *government*.

central bank A bank that acts as banker to the commercial banking system and often to the government as well. In the modern world, usually a government-owned and -operated institution that controls the banking system and is the sole money-issuing authority.

centrally planned economy See *command economy*.

certificate of deposit (CD) A tradable IOU (debt instrument) issued by a bank in exchange for a deposit of money, repayable with interest at a specific date.

ceteris paribus Other things being equal, as when all but one independent variables are held constant so as to study the influence of the remaining independent variable on the dependent variables.

change in demand A *shift* in the whole demand curve, that is, a change in the amount that will be bought at *each* price.

change in the quantity demanded An increase or decrease in the specific quantity bought at a specified price, represented by a movement along a demand curve; sometimes called an *extension* (increase) or a *contraction* (decrease) in demand.

chaos theory Branch of mathematics in which nonlinear equation systems can generate data series which have no pattern detectable by traditional methods.

circular flow of income The flow of expenditures on output and factor services passing between domestic (as opposed to foreign) firms and domestic households.

classical dichotomy Concept in classical economics that monetary forces could influence the general price level but had no effect on real activity. Related to the concept of *neutrality of money*.

classical economics Usually refers to the body of thought on economics which had built up in the hundred years or so before the 1930s; often associated (probably incorrectly) with the notion that government policy cannot influence the level of economic activity. Contrasted with *Keynesian economics*, which attempted to break down the *classical dichotomy*.

clearing banks The UK name for *commercial banks* that were members of the London Clearing Banks Association, which organized the clearing of cheques for member banks.

clearing house A place where interbank debts are settled.

closed economy An economy that does not engage in international trade (autarky).

closed shop Firm in which only union members can be employed. Closed shops may be either 'pre-entry', where the worker must be a member of the union before being employed, or 'post-entry', where the worker must join the union on becoming employed.

collective consumption goods See *public goods.*

combination See *bundle.*

command economy An economy in which the decisions of the central authorities (as distinct from households and firms) exert the major influence over the allocation of resources and the distribution of income.

commercial banks Banks that take deposits from the general public and make loans. In the United States, commercial banking has been legally separated from *investment banking*, but in many other countries banks have both commercial and investment banking operations in the same entity, sometimes referred to as universal banking.

commercial bills See *bills of exchange.*

commercial paper Short-term interest-bearing debt instruments issued by companies.

commercial policy The government's policy towards international trade, investment, and related matters.

commodities In the world of commerce, a term that usually refers to basic goods, such as wheat and iron ore, which are produced by the primary sector of the economy. Sometimes also used by economists to refer to all goods and services. See also *products.*

common market An agreement among a group of countries to have free trade among themselves, a common set of barriers to trade with other countries, and free movement of labour and capital among themselves.

common property resource A resource that is owned by no one and may be used by anyone.

comparative advantage The ability of one nation (or region or individual) to produce a commodity at a lesser opportunity cost in terms of other products forgone than another nation.

comparative statics Short for *comparative-static equilibrium analysis*; studying the effect of some change by comparing the positions of static equilibrium before and after the change is introduced.

competition policy Policies designed to prohibit the acquisition and exercise of monopoly power by business firms. Also called *anti-monopoly policy.*

competitive devaluations When several countries devalue their currencies in an attempt to gain a competitive advantage over one another.

complements Two goods for which the quantity demanded of one is negatively related to the price of the other.

concentration ratio The fraction of total market sales (or some other measure of market occupancy) controlled by a specific member of the industry's largest firms, four-firm and eight-firm concentration ratios being most frequently used.

conglomerate merger When firms selling quite unrelated products merge; also called *lateral merger.*

constant returns Situation existing when a firm's output increases exactly as fast as its inputs increase.

consumer Anyone who consumes goods or services to satisfy his or her wants.

consumers' surplus The difference between the total value consumers place on all units consumed of a commodity and the payment they must make to purchase that amount of the commodity.

consumption The act of using goods and services to satisfy wants.

consumption expenditure The amount that individuals spend on purchasing goods and services for consumption.

consumption function The relationship between personal planned consumption expenditure and all of the forces that determine it.

contestable market A market is perfectly contestable if there are no sunk costs of entry or exit, so that potential entry may hold profits of existing firms to low levels — zero in the case of perfect contestability.

convertibles Usually refers to *bonds* that carry an option to convert the debt into the issuing company's *equity* at a specified price and within a specific period of time. The option to buy equity, if stripped from the bond and traded separately, is referred to as a *warrant*.

co-operative solution A situation in which existing firms co-operate to maximize their joint profits.

cost minimization An implication of profit maximization that the firm will choose the method that produces specific output at the lowest attainable cost.

creative destruction Schumpeter's theory that high profits and wages, earned by monopolistic or oligopolistic firms and unions, are the spur for others to invent cheaper or better substitute products and techniques that allow their suppliers to gain some of these profits.

credibility The extent to which actors in the private sector of the economy believe that the government will carry out the policy it promises in the future. It is important in policy analysis in macro models which assume *rational expectations*, since expectations of future policy action influence current behaviour.

cross-elasticity of demand The responsiveness of demand for one commodity to changes in the price of another commodity, defined as the percentage change in quantity demanded of one commodity divided by the percentage change in price of another commodity.

crowding-out effect The lowering of interest-sensitive expenditure because a rise in national income causes a rise in the interest rate. It explains the difference between the values of the interest-constant and the interest-sensitive multipliers.

current account Account recording all international transactions related to goods and services.

customs union A group of countries who agree to have free trade among themselves and a common set of barriers against imports from the rest of the world.

cyclical fluctuations Periodic (auto-correlated) oscillations of any economic time-series around its trend.

cyclical unemployment See *demand-deficient unemployment*.

cyclically adjusted deficit (CAD) An estimate of expenditures minus revenues, not as they actually are, but as they would be if potential national income had been achieved (i.e. if there were neither an inflationary nor a recessionary gap). Also called *full-employment deficit* and *high-employment deficit*.

cyclically balanced budget Budget that is balanced over the period of one cycle.

debt instruments Any written documents that record the terms of a debt, often providing legal proof of the conditions under which the principal and interest will be repaid.

decision lag The time it takes to assess a situation and decide what corrective action should be taken.

decreasing returns A situation in which output increases less than proportionately to inputs as the scale of production increases.

deficit The shortfall of current revenue below current expenditure.

deflation A decrease in the general price level.

degree of risk A measurement of the amount of risk associated with some action such as lending money or innovating. When the nature of the risk is known, the degree can be measured by the variance of the probability distribution describing the possible outcomes.

demand The entire relationship between the quantity of a commodity that buyers wish to purchase per period of time and the price of that commodity, other things being equal.

demand curve A graphical relation showing the quantity of some commodity that households would like to buy at each possible price.

demand-deficient unemployment Unemployment that occurs because aggregate desired expenditure is insufficient to purchase all of the output of a fully employed labour force. Also called *cyclical unemployment*.

demand deposit See *sight deposit.*

demand for money The amount of wealth everyone in the economy wishes to hold in the form of money balances.

demand function A functional relation between quantity demanded and all of the variables that influence it.

demand management Policies that seek to shift the aggregate demand curve by shifting either the *IS* curve (fiscal policy) or the *LM* curve (monetary policy).

demand schedule A numerical tabulation showing the quantities that are demanded at selected prices.

deposit accounts See *time deposits.*

deposit money Bank deposits on which cheques can be drawn.

depreciated Reduced value of a currency, resulting from a change in the free-market exchange rate.

depreciation (1) The loss in value of an asset over a period of time due to physical wear and tear and obsolescence. (2) A fall in the free-market value of domestic currency in terms of foreign currencies. See also *capital consumption allowance.*

depression A prolonged period of very low economic activity with very high unemployment and high excess capacity.

derived demand The demand for a factor of production that results from the demand for the products it is used to make.

desired expenditure See *planned expenditure.*

developed countries Usually refers to the rich industrial countries of North America, Western Europe, Japan and Australasia.

developing countries See *less developed countries.*

differentiated product A product that is produced in several varieties, or brands, all of which are sufficiently similar to distinguish them, as a group, from other products (e.g. cars).

diminishing marginal rate of substitution The hypothesis that the less of one commodity that is presently being consumed by a household, the less willing will the household be to give up a unit of that commodity to obtain an additional unit of a second commodity; its geometrical expression is the decreasing absolute slope of an indifference curve as one moves along it to the right.

direct investment See *foreign direct investment.*

direct taxes Taxes levied on persons that can vary with the status of the taxpayer.

dirty float See *managed float.*

discount houses Specialized financial institutions, which borrow money at call (i.e. repayable on demand), or at very short notice, from banks and other lending institutions. They use this money to purchase short-dated financial assets such as Treasury bills and bills of exchange.

discount market The sector of the London *money markets* in which the *discount houses* are active.

discount rate The difference between the current price of a bill and its maturity value expressed as an annualized interest rate.

discouraged worker Someone of working age who has withdrawn permanently from the labour force because of the poor prospects of employment.

discretion Policy made by judgmental methods rather than following rigid rules. Used especially in the context of the old debate between *monetarists* and *Keynesians* in which monetarists called for a monetary growth rule and Keynesians recommended policy discretion.

diseconomies of scale See *decreasing returns to scale*.

disembodied technical change Technical change that is the result of changes in the organization of production that are not embodied in specific capital goods, e.g. improved management techniques.

disequilibrium A state of imbalance between opposing forces so that there is a tendency to change.

disintermediation Process in which financial flows from savers to borrowers shift from passing through financial intermediaries (like banks and building societies) and instead are channelled through securities markets.

displacement effect Refers to the observed tendency of government expenditure to rise during war-time and to stay at a higher than pre-war level even after hostilities have long ceased.

disposable income The after-tax income that households have at their disposal to spend or to save.

distribution of income The division of national income among various groups. See also *size* and *functional distribution of income*.

dividends Profits that are paid out to shareholders.

Divisia index Invented by French mathematician François Divisia, its modern application is an index of the money supply which gives variable weights to included assets, depending upon the interest rate paid on each asset. Traditional monetary aggregates attach a weight of unity to all included assets and zero to all excluded assets. The index may help to identify the transactions services of money as opposed to the savings services.

division of labour The breaking up of a production process into a series of repetitive tasks, each done by a different worker.

double counting In national income accounting, adding up the total outputs of all the sectors in the economy so that the value of intermediate goods is counted in the sector that produces them *and* every time they are purchased as an input by another sector.

dumping When a commodity is sold in a foreign country at prices below its domestic sale price for reasons not related to costs.

duopoly An industry containing exactly two firms.

dynamic differentials See *disequilibrium differentials*.

economic growth The positive trend in the nation's total output over the long term.

economic models A term used in several related ways: sometimes as a synonym for theory, sometimes for a specific quantification of a general theory, sometimes for the application of a general theory to a specific context, and sometimes for an illustrative abstraction designed to illustrate some point but not meant as a full theory on its own.

economic profits or losses The difference between the revenues received from the sale of output and the opportunity cost of the inputs used to make the output. Negative economic profits are economic losses. Also called *pure profits* or *pure losses*, or simple *profits* or *losses*.

economic rent An excess that a factor is paid above what is needed to keep it in its present use.

economies of scale See *increasing returns.*

economies of scope Economies achieved by a firm that is large enough to engage efficiently in multi-product production and associated large-scale distribution, advertising, and purchasing.

economy Any specified collection of interrelated marketed and non-marketed productive activities.

ECU The European Currency Unit. Invented in 1979 with the establishment of the *EMS*, it is valued as a weighted basket of *EMS* member-currencies.

effective exchange rate An index number of the value of a country's currency relative to a weighted basket of other currencies. Whereas an *exchange rate* measures the rate of exchange of a currency for one other currency, changes in the effective exchange rate indicate movements in a single currency's value against other currencies in general.

effective tariff rate The tax charged on any imported commodity expressed as a percentage of the value added by the exporting industry.

efficiency wage A wage rate above the market-clearing level which enables employers to attract and keep the best workers as well as providing employees with an incentive to perform (i.e. not get sacked). It helps to explain why wage rates do not adjust to clear labour markets.

elastic Describes the situation where the percentage change in quantity is greater than the percentage change in price (elasticity greater than one).

elasticities approach Analysis of the balance of payments based upon the *price elasticities of demand* for imports and exports.

elasticity of demand See *price elasticity of demand.*

elasticity of supply See *price elasticity of supply.*

embodied technical change A technical change that is the result of changes in the form of particular capital goods.

employed Status of those persons working for others and paid a wage or a salary.

EMS The European Monetary System, established in 1979 to limit the fluctuations between member-countries' exchange rates.

endogenous variable A variable that is explained within a theory; also called an *induced variable.*

entrepreneur One who innovates, i.e. one who takes risks by introducing both new products and new ways of making old products.

entry barrier Any natural barrier to the entry of new firms into an industry, such as a large minimum efficient scale for firms, or any firm-created barrier, such as a patent.

envelope Any curve that encloses, by being tangent to, a series of other curves. In particular, the *envelope cost curve* is the *LRAC* curve, which encloses the *SRAC* curves by being tangent to each without cutting any of them.

equation of exchange $MV = PT$, where M is the money stock, V is the velocity of circulation, P is the average price of transactions, and T is the number of transactions. As usually defined, it is an identity which says that the value of money spent is equal to the value of goods and services sold. However, with additional assumptions it provides a basis for the *quantity theory of money.*

equilibrium A state of balance between opposing forces so that there is no tendency to change.

equilibrium differentials Differentials in the prices of factors that persist in equilibrium without generating forces to eliminate them.

equilibrium employment (unemployment) The level of employment (unemployment) achieved when national income is at its potential level. Traditionally referred to as full employment, equilibrium unemployment (*frictional* plus *structural*) is made up of total unemployment minus *cyclical unemployment*.

equilibrium price The price at which quantity demanded equals quantity supplied.

equilibrium quantity The amount that is bought and sold at the equilibrium price.

equities Certificates indicating part ownership of a joint stock company.

ERM The Exchange Rate Mechanism of the *EMS*.

EU The European Union, formerly known as the European Community (EC).

eurobonds Typically, dollar-denominated bonds issued outside the United States; in general, any bonds issued in the international capital markets outside the country whose currency is involved. Very important financial instruments in *globalized* financial markets.

eurodollar market A market in wholesale bank deposits and loans which grew rapidly in the 1960s and 1970s. The bulk of the business was denominated in dollars and it was done outside the control of US banking regulations.

ex ante **expenditure** See *planned expenditure*.

ex post **expenditure** See *realized expenditure*.

excess capacity theorem Theorem stating that each firm in a monopolistically competitive industry is producing its output at an average cost that is higher than it could achieve by producing its capacity output.

excess demand The amount by which quantity demanded exceeds quantity supplied at some price; negative excess supply.

excess supply The amount by which quantity supplied exceeds quantity demanded at some price; negative excess demand.

exchange rate The rate at which two national currencies exchange for each other. Often expressed as the amount of domestic currency needed to buy one unit of foreign currency.

execution lag The time it takes to initiate corrective policies and for their full influence to be felt.

exhaustive expenditures Government purchases of currently produced goods and services; also called *government direct expenditures*.

exogenous variable A variable that influences other variables within a theory but is itself determined by factors outside the theory; also called an autonomous variable.

expectations-augmented Phillips curve See *short-run Phillips curve*.

expected value The most likely outcome if a procedure is repeated over and over again; the mean of the probability distribution expressing the possible outcomes.

expenditure See *planned expenditure*.

explicit collusion When firms explicitly agree to co-operate rather than compete. See also *tacit collusion*.

external balance When the value of the balance of payments is equal to some target level.

external economies Economies of scale that arise from sources outside of the firm.

externalities Costs of a transaction that are incurred by members of the society, or benefits that are received by them, but not considered by the parties to the transaction.

extrapolative expectations Expectation formation based upon the assumption that a past trend will continue into the future. The simplest form of extrapolation would be to assume that next period's value of a variable is expected to be the same as this period's.

factor markets Markets where factor services are bought and sold.

factor services The services of factors of production.

factors of production Resources used to produce goods and services; frequently divided into the basic categories of land, labour, and capital. Sometimes entrepreneurship is distinguished as a fourth factor; sometimes it is included in the category of labour.

fiat money Inconvertible paper money that is issued by government order (or fiat).

final products The outputs of the economy after eliminating all double counting.

financial capital The funds used to finance a firm, including both equity capital and debt (also called *money capital*).

financial innovation Occurs when new products are introduced in the financial system, or when existing suppliers behave in new ways. Changes are often a complex interaction of (i) regulatory changes, (ii) changing technology, and (iii) competitive pressures.

financial intermediaries Financial institutions that stand between those who deposit money and those who borrow it.

fine-tuning The attempt to maintain national income at, or near, its full-employment level by means of frequent changes in fiscal and/or monetary policy.

firm The unit that employs factors of production to produce commodities that it sells to other firms, to households, or to the government.

fiscal policy Attempts to influence the aggregate demand curve by altering government expenditures and/or government revenues, thus shifting the *IS* curve.

fixed capital formation See *fixed investment*.

fixed cost A cost that does not change with output. Also called *overhead cost*, *unavoidable cost*.

fixed exchange rate Exchange rate that is held within a narrow band around some pre-announced par value by intervention of the country's central bank in the foreign exchange market.

fixed factors Inputs whose amount available in the short run is fixed.

fixed investment Investment in plant and equipment.

floating exchange rate Exchange rate that is left free to be determined on the foreign exchange market by the forces of demand and supply.

floating interest rate One that moves continuously in line with current market conditions.

floating rate note (FRN) A bond on which the interest rate changes periodically in line with market interest rates. On a normal, or 'straight', bond the coupon interest rate is fixed for the full maturity of the bond.

foreign direct investment (FDI) Non-resident investment in the form of a takeover or capital investment in a domestic branch, plant, or subsidiary corporation in which the investor has voting control. See also *portfolio investment*.

foreign exchange Foreign currencies and claims to them in such forms as bank deposits, cheques and promissory notes payable in the currency.

foreign exchange market The market where foreign exchange is traded — at a price that is expressed by the exchange rate.

free-market economy An economy in which the decisions of individuals and firms (as distinct from the central authorities) exert the major influence over the allocation of resources.

free rider problem The problem that arises because people have a self-interest in not revealing the strength of their own preferences for a public good in the hope that others will pay for it.

free trade An absence of any form of government interference with the free flow of international trade.

free-trade area An agreement among two or more countries to abolish tariffs on all, or most, of the trade among themselves, while each remains free to set its own tariffs against other countries.

frictional unemployment Unemployment that is associated with the normal turnover of labour.

full-capacity output The highest output at which minimum costs can be obtained.

full-cost pricing Refers to the situation where, instead of equating marginal revenue with marginal cost, firms set prices equal to average cost at normal-capacity output, plus a conventional mark-up.

full-employment output See *potential output*.

function Loosely, an expression of a relationship between two or more variables. Precisely, Y is a function of the variables $X_1, \ldots, X_n$ if, for every set of values of the variables $X_1, \ldots, X_n$, there is associated a unique value of the variable Y.

functional distribution of income The distribution of income among major factors of production.

gains from trade Advantages realized as a result of specialization made possible by trade.

GDP See *gross domestic product*.

GDP gap See *output gap*.

general price level The average level of the prices of all goods and services produced in the economy; usually just called the *price level*.

Giffen good A good with a positively sloped demand curve.

gilt-edged securities UK government bonds; so called because they are considered to carry lower risk than private-sector debt.

given period Any particular period that is being compared with a base period.

globalization The process by which most economies around the world have become more interdependent. The term is applied especially to the increased integration of financial markets that has occurred over the last three decades as a result of reducing regulatory barriers to international financial flows.

GNP See *gross national product*.

GNP gap See *output gap*.

gold exchange standard A monetary system in which US currency was directly convertible into gold, and other countries' currencies were indirectly convertible into the gold-backed US dollar at a fixed rate.

gold standard Currency standard whereby a country's money is convertible into gold.

Goodhart's law The view that many statistical relations (particularly those established by monetarists) cannot be used for policy purposes because they do not depend on causal relations and are, therefore, unstable.

goods Tangible production, such as cars or shoes.

goods markets Markets where goods and services are bought and sold.

government In economics, all public agencies, government bodies and other organizations belonging to, or owing their existence to, the government; sometimes (more accurately) called the *central authorities*.

government direct expenditures See *exhaustive expenditures*.

government failure Where the government achieves less than the benefits it could achieve through perfectly efficient action.

Gresham's law Bad money (i.e. money whose intrinsic value is less than its face value) drives good money (i.e. money whose intrinsic value exceeds its face value) out of circulation.

gross domestic product (GDP) The value of total output actually produced in the whole economy over some period, usually a year (although quarterly data are also available).

gross investment The total value of all investment goods produced in the economy during a stated period of time.

gross national product (GNP) Income earned by UK residents in return for contributions to current production, whether production is located at home or abroad. Equal to GDP plus net property income from abroad.

gross return on capital The market value of output minus all non-capital costs, divided into depreciation, pure return, risk premium, and pure profit.

gross tuning Use of monetary and fiscal policy to attempt to correct only large deviations from potential national income. It is contrasted with *fine tuning*, which aims to adjust aggregate demand frequently in order to keep national income close to its potential level at all times.

high-employment deficit An estimate of expenditures minus tax revenues, not as they actually are, but as they would be if potential national income had been achieved (i.e. if there were neither an inflationary nor a recessionary gap). Also called *full-employment* or *cyclically adjusted deficit*.

high-employment national income (output) See *potential national income*.

high-powered money The monetary magnitude that is under the direct control of the central bank. It is composed of cash in the hands of the public, bank reserves of currency, and clearing balances held by the commercial banks with the Bank of England.

hog cycles A term used to characterize cycles of over- and under-production because of time lags in the production process. For example, high prices for pork today lead many farmers to start breeding pigs; when the pigs mature there will be an increased supply of pork which will drive down its price; so fewer farmers will breed pigs and the price will later rise again, starting the cycle over again.

homogeneous product A product is homogeneous when, in the eyes of purchasers, every unit is identical to every other unit.

horizontal merger Union or merger of firms at the same stage of production.

household All the people who live under one roof and who take, or are subject to others taking for them, joint financial decisions.

human capital The capitalized value of productive investments in persons. Usually refers to value derived from expenditures on education, training, and health improvements.

hyperinflation Episodes of very rapid inflation.

hysteresis The lagging of effects behind their causes. In economics, the term has come to relate to persistence or irreversibility of effects. An example is the difficulty of returning the long-term unemployed to work because their skills have deteriorated. It also implies path dependency, which means that the ultimate equilibrium is not independent of how the economy gets there (i.e. it is not unique).

identification problem The problem of how to estimate both demand and supply curves from observed market data on prices and quantities actually traded.

immobile capital Applies to financial capital which is not free to move from one country to another, usually because of government regulations.

import quota A maximum amount of some product that may be imported each year.

import substitutions A policy of producing goods domestically that were previously imported.

imputed costs The costs of using factors of production already owned by the firm, measured by the earnings they could have received in their best alternative employment.

incidence In tax theory, where the burden of a tax finally falls.

income-consumption line On an indifference-curve diagram, a line showing how consumption bundles change as income changes, with prices held constant.

income effect The effect on quantity demanded of a change in real income, relative prices held constant.

income-elastic Describes the situation where the percentage change in quantity demanded exceeds the percentage change in income.

income elasticity of demand The responsiveness of quantity demanded to a change in income.

income-inelastic Describes the situation where the percentage change in quantity demanded is smaller than the percentage change in income.

incomes policies A wide range of policies running from the government's setting of voluntary guidelines for wage and price increases, through consultation on wage and price norms between unions, management, and government, to compulsory controls on wages, prices, and profits.

increasing returns A situation in which output increases more than in proportion to inputs as the scale of a firm's production increases. A firm in this situation, with fixed factor prices, is a decreasing-cost firm.

incremental ratio When Y is a function of X, the incremental ratio is the change in Y divided by the change in X that brought it about, $\Delta Y/\Delta X$. The limit of this ratio as ΔX approaches zero is the derivative of Y with respect to X, dY/dX.

index of retail prices See *retail price index*.

indexation When a contract, for wages, pensions or repayment of debt, is specified in real terms. Any specified money payment would be increased to compensate for actual inflation. More generally, the term applies to any contingent contract tied to an index number.

indicators Variables that policy-makers monitor for the information they yield about the state of the economy.

indifference curve A curve showing all combinations of commodities that yield equal satisfaction to the household.

indifference map A set of indifference curves.

indirect tax A tax levied on a thing, and paid by an individual by virtue of his or her association with that thing.

individualism The belief that individuals are the best judges of their own interests.

induced Anything that is determined from within a theory; the opposite of autonomous or exogenous, also called *endogenous*.

induced expenditure Any expenditure flow that is related to national income (or to any other variable explained by the theory).

induced variable See *endogenous variable*.

industrial unions All workers in a given industry belonging to a single union, whatever their trade.

industry A group of firms that sell a well-defined product or closely related set of products.

inelastic Describes the situation where the percentage change in quantity is less than the percentage change in price (elasticity is less than one).

infant industry argument The argument that new domestic industries with potential economies of scale need to be protected from competition from established low-cost foreign producers so that they can grow large enough to achieve costs as low as those of foreign producers.

inferior good A commodity with a negative income elasticity; its demand diminishes when income increases.

inflation An increase in the general price level.

inflation-adjusted budget surplus (deficit) The *budget surplus (deficit)* when the *inflation tax* is incorporated.

inflation tax The implicit revenue to the government which accrues from the fall in real value of its outstanding debt resulting from inflation.

inflationary gap A negative output gap, i.e. actual national income exceeds potential national income.

inflationary shock Any autonomous shift in aggregate demand or aggregate supply which causes the price level to rise.

infrastructure The basic facilities (especially transportation and communications systems) on which the commerce of a community depends.

injection Income received, either by domestic firms or domestic households, that does not arise from the spending of the other group.

inputs The materials and factor services used in the process of production.

inside assets Assets that are the liability of other agents in the same sector or economy so that they net out for the sector or economy as a whole.

insider–outsider models Any analysis of labour markets which gives more influence over market outcomes to those in employment (usually via trade union representation) than to the unemployed.

instruments The variables that policy-makers can control directly. (In econometrics, instruments are proxy variables used in regression equations because of their desirable statistical properties — usually independence from the equation error.)

interest The amount paid each year on a loan, usually expressed as a percentage (e.g. 5 per cent) or as a ratio (e.g. 0.05) of the principal of the loan.

intermediate products All goods and services used as inputs into a further stage of production.

internal balance When real national income is at its target level.

internal economies Economies of scale that arise from sources within the firm.

internalizing an externality Doing something that makes an externality enter into the firm's own calculations of its private costs and benefits.

invention The discovery of something new, such as a new production technique or a new product.

inventories See *stocks*.

investment The act of producing goods that are not for immediate consumption.

investment banks US term for banks that specialize in corporate finance, especially trading and underwriting securities. UK terminology for the same type of institution is *merchant bank*.

investment demand function A negative relationship between the quantity of investment per period and the interest rate, holding other things constant. It used to be more commonly called the *marginal efficiency of investment*.

investment expenditure Expenditure on capital goods.

investment goods Goods produced not for present consumption, i.e. capital goods, inventories, and residential housing.

invisibles Services, i.e. those things that we cannot see, such as insurance and freight haulage and tourist expenditures.

involuntary unemployment Unemployment that occurs when a person is willing to accept a job at the going wage rate, but cannot find such a job.

IS curve The locus of combinations of the interest rate and the level of real national income for which desired aggregate expenditure equals actual national income. So called because, in a closed economy with no government, it also reflects the combinations of the interest rate and national income for which investment equals saving, $I = S$. In general, it reflects points for which injections equal withdrawals.

IS/LM model A diagrammatic representation of a model of aggregate demand determination based upon the locus of equilibrium points in the aggregate expenditure sector (IS) and the monetary sector (LM). It is incomplete as a model of national income determination because it does not include an aggregate supply curve.

iso-cost line A line showing all combinations of inputs that have the same total cost to the firm.

isoquant A curve showing all technologically efficient factor combinations for producing a specified output.

isoquant map A series of isoquants from the same production function, each isoquant relating to a specific level of output.

J-curve Pattern usually followed by the *balance of trade* after a devaluation of the domestic currency. Initially the trade balance deteriorates, and then, after a lag, it improves.

joint stock company A firm regarded in law as having an identity of its own. Its owners are not personally responsible for anything that is done in the name of the firm; called a *corporation* in North America.

Keynesian economics Economic theories based on *AE*, *IS*, *LM*, *AD*, and *AS* curves and assuming enough short-run price inflexibility that *AD* and *AS* shocks cause substantial deviations of real national income from its potential level.

Keynesian revolution Adoption of the idea that government could use monetary and fiscal policy to control aggregate demand and thereby influence the level of national income. For a while it was believed that Keynesian economics had found ways in which policy-makers could smooth business cycles and eliminate unemployment.

Kondratief cycles Long cycles in economic activity of around fifty years' duration. Sometimes referred to as long waves.

labour All productive human resources, mental and physical, both inherited and acquired.

labour force See *working population.*

labour force participation rate The percentage of the population of working age that is actually in the labour force (i.e., either working or seeking work).

labour productivity Total output divided by the labour used in producing it, i.e. output per unit of labour.

Laffer curve A curve relating total tax revenue to the tax rate.

land Those free gifts of nature, such as land, forests, minerals, etc., sometimes called natural resources.

lateral merger See *horizontal merger.*

law of diminishing returns Law stating that, if increasing quantities of a variable factor are applied to a given quantity of a fixed factor, the marginal product, and the average product, of the variable factor will eventually decrease.

leakages See *withdrawals.*

legal tender Currency that is recognized in law as the acceptable medium for payment of debts. Bank of England notes became legal tender in England and Wales in 1833.

less developed countries (LDCs) The lower-income countries of the world, most of which are in Asia, Africa and South and Central America. Also called *underdeveloped countries* and *developing countries.*

leveraged buyout (LBO) A buyout of a firm largely financed by borrowed money.

life-cycle theory A theory that relates the household's actual consumption to its expected lifetime income.

limited partnership A form of business organization in which the firm has two classes of owners: general partners, who take part in managing the firm and who are personally liable for all of the firm's actions and debts, and limited partners, who take no part in the management of the firm and who risk only the money that they have invested.

liquidity The ease with which an asset can be converted into money. Sometimes refers to money itself — *liquidity preference* used to be widely used in economics as an expression meaning *demand for money.*

liquidity preference The demand to hold wealth as money rather than as interest-earning assets. Also called the *demand for money.*

LM curve The locus of combinations of the interest rate and real national income for which money demand equals money supply. So called because it represents the points where *liquidity preference* equals the *money supply.*

logarithmic scale A scale in which equal proportional changes are shown as equal distances (for example, 1 inch may always represent doubling of a variable, whether from 3 to 6 or 50 to 100). Also called *log scale, ratio scale.*

long run A period of time in which all inputs may be varied, but the basic technology of production is unchanged.

long-run aggregate supply curve (LRAS) A curve that relates the price level to equilibrium real national income, after all input costs, including wage rates, have been fully adjusted to eliminate any excess demand or supply.

long-run average cost curve (LRAC) Curve showing the least-cost method of producing each level of output when all inputs can be varied. Also called long-run average total cost curve.

long-run industry supply curve (LRS) Curve showing the relation between equilibrium price and the output that all the firms in the industry will be willing to supply after all the desired entry or exit has occurred.

long-run Phillips curve (LRPC) The relation between national income and stable rates of inflation that neither accelerate nor decelerate.

long wave See *Kondratief cycles.*

Lorenz curve A graph showing the extent of departure from equality of income distribution.

Lucas aggregate supply curve An aggregate supply curve which is positively sloped for unexpected increases in the price level but vertical for anticipated increases in the price level. Also known as the *'surprise' aggregate supply curve.*

Lucas critique The proposition that forecasts and simulations using empirical macro models will be inaccurate when used to predict the effects of changes in policy. This is because the behaviour of agents will be different under different policy regimes.

M0 Currency held by the non-bank public plus bankers' deposits with the central bank. Also known as the monetary base, the cash base or *high-powered money.*

M1 A measure of the money stock which includes currency plus current account bank deposits. This measure is no longer reported by the Bank of England.

M2 Currency held by the public plus retail current and savings accounts in banks and building societies.

M3 Measure of *broad money* no longer used by UK authorities. It was equal to M1 plus all savings deposits in banks.

M4 Currency in circulation plus all deposits in banks and building societies.

macroeconomic policy Any measure directed at influencing such macroeconomic variables as the overall levels of employment, unemployment, national income and the price level.

macroeconomics The study of the determination of economic aggregates and averages, such as total output, total employment, the general price level, and the rate of economic growth.

managed float Intervention in the foreign exchange market by a country's central bank in pursuit of an unofficial exchange rate target, but not to maintain a publicly announced par value. Also called a *dirty float*.

marginal cost (MC) The increase in total cost resulting from raising the rate of production by one unit.

marginal cost pricing Method of pricing where price is set equal to marginal cost.

marginal efficiency of capital The rate at which the value of the stream of output of a marginal unit of capital must be discounted to make it equal to £1.

marginal efficiency of capital schedule A schedule that relates the marginal efficiency of each additional £1's worth of capital to the size of the capital stock.

marginal efficiency of investment The relation between desired investment and the rate of interest, assuming all other things are equal.

marginal physical product (MPP) See *marginal product*.

marginal product (MP) The change in total product resulting from using one more (or less) unit of the variable factor. Also called *marginal physical product*. Mathematically, the partial derivative of total product with respect to the variable factor.

marginal propensity not to spend The proportion of each additional £1 of income that is not passed on in spending, and instead leaks out of (i.e. is withdrawn from) the circular flow of income. Also called the *marginal propensity to withdraw* and the *marginal propensity to leak*.

marginal propensity to consume (MPC) The proportion of each new increment of income that is spent on consumption, $\Delta C/\Delta Y$.

marginal propensity to import The proportion of any new increment of income that is spent on imports, $\Delta M/\Delta Y$.

marginal propensity to leak See *marginal propensity not to spend*.

marginal propensity to save (MPS) The proportion of any new increment of income that is saved, $\Delta S/\Delta Y$.

marginal propensity to spend The ratio of any increment of induced expenditure to the increment in income that brought it about.

marginal propensity to tax The proportion of an increment in income that is taxed away by the government, $\Delta T/\Delta Y$.

marginal propensity to withdraw See *marginal propensity not to spend*.

marginal rate of substitution (MRS) The rate at which one factor is substituted for another with output held constant; graphically, the slope of the isoquant.

marginal rate of transformation The slope of the production possibility curve, indicating the rate of substitution of one good for another.

marginal revenue The change in total revenue resulting from a unit change in the sales per period of time. Mathematically, the derivative of total revenue with respect to quantity sold.

marginal revenue product The addition to a firm's revenue resulting from the sale of the output produced by an additional unit of the variable factor.

marginal utility The change in satisfaction resulting from consuming one unit ʼ ʼor one unit less of a commodity.

market An area over which buyers and sellers negotiate the exchange of commodity.

market economy A society in which people specialize in productive ac

most of their material wants through exchanges voluntarily agreed upon by the contracting parties.

market failure Any market performance that is judged to be less good than the best possible performance.

market for corporate control An interpretation of conglomerate mergers, leveraged buyouts, and hostile takeovers as mechanisms that place the firm in the hands of those who are able to generate the greatest value of output.

market rate of interest The actual rate of interest that rules in the market.

market sector That portion of an economy in which producers must cover their costs by selling their output to consumers.

market structure The characteristics of a market that influence the behaviour and performance of firms that sell in the market. The four main market structures are perfect competition, monopolistic competition, oligopoly, and monopoly.

Marshall–Lerner condition Condition specifying that, for the balance of payments to improve as a result of a devaluation of the home currency, the sum of the elasticities of demand for imports and exports must exceed unity in absolute size.

maturity The length of time until the *redemption date* of a security such as a *bond*.

medium of exchange A commodity or token which is widely accepted in payment for goods and services.

medium term financial strategy (MTFS) The combined monetary and fiscal policy goals introduced by the Conservative government of Mrs Thatcher after 1979, with the aim of bringing down inflation and eliminating the budget deficit.

menu costs Costs associated with changing prices, such as the costs of reprinting catalogues or menus. These costs make it rational for producers to keep output prices fixed until input prices have changed significantly, or to respond only periodically.

mercantilism The doctrine that the gains from trade are a function of the balance of trade, in contrast with the classical theory, in which the gains from trade are a function of the volume of trade.

merchandise trade Trade in physical products.

merchant banks British name for *investment banks*. Usage arose because the banks involved started out as traders in commodities and then moved over to specialize in trade finance. Modern merchant banks are involved in a wide range of securities trading and corporate finance.

merger When two or more formerly independent firms unite. See *horizontal, vertical* and *conglomerate mergers*.

merit goods Goods, of which the government decides that more should be produced than people would choose to consume left to themselves.

microeconomics The study of the allocation of resources and the distribution of income as they are affected by the working of the price system and by the policies of the central authorities.

minimum efficient scale (MES) The smallest level of output at which long-run average cost is at a minimum; the smallest output required to achieve the economies of scale in production and/or distribution.

mismatch See *structural unemployment*.

mixed economy An economy in which some decisions about the allocation of resources are made by firms and households and some by the central authorities.

mobile capital Financial capital which is free to move to the market where expected returns are highest.

monetarism The doctrine that monetary magnitudes exert powerful influences in the economy, and that control of these magnitudes is a potent means of affecting the economy's macroeconomic behaviour.

monetary approach to the balance of payments Analysis linking the excess demand for money to the international payments balance or exchange rate change.

monetary base control Policy of controlling the money stock by means of fixing the stock of *high-powered money*; also known as the monetary base. Not used in the United Kingdom as a method of implementing monetary policy.

monetary equilibrium A situation in which there is no excess demand for or supply of money.

monetary policy Policy traditionally seen as working through the *LM* curve, shifting aggregate demand by altering the supplies of monetary aggregates, and regulating the terms and availability of credit.

monetary transmission mechanism The mechanism that turns a monetary shock into a real expenditure shock and thus links the monetary and the real side of the economy.

money Any generally accepted medium of exchange, i.e. anything that will be accepted in exchange for goods and services.

money demand function The function that determines the demand to hold money balances.

money income A household's income as measured in terms of some monetary unit.

money markets The markets in which banks, companies and the public sector finance or invest their short-term financial surpluses and deficits. It is contrasted with capital markets (bonds and equities), in which long-term financing is achieved.

money multiplier The ratio of the money stock to the monetary base (high-powered money).

money national product See *nominal national product.*

money price See *absolute price.*

money rate of interest The rate of interest as measured in monetary units.

money stock See *supply of money.*

money substitutes Things that serve as temporary media of exchange but are not stores of value, e.g. credit cards.

money supply See *supply of money.*

monopolist A single seller in any market.

monopolistic competition A market structure in which there are many sellers and freedom of entry but in which each firm sells a product somewhat differentiated from the others, giving it some control over its price.

monopoly A market structure that exists when an industry is in the hands of a single producer.

monopsonist A single purchaser in any market.

moral hazard Hazard that arises from people taking actions that increase social costs because they are insured against private loss.

most favoured nation An agreement between two countries according to which each will give the other's goods treatment that is at least as favourable as the most favourable treatment given to any other country's goods (where 'more favourable' means lower tariffs).

multinational enterprises (MNEs) See *transnational corporations.*

multiplier The ratio of the change in national income to the change in autonomous expenditure that brought it about.

multiplier accelerator theory The theory that business cycles are caused by the interaction of the multiplier and the accelerator.

NAIRU The amount of unemployment (all of it *frictional* and *structural*) that exists when national income is at its potential level and which, if maintained, will result in a stable rate of inflation.

Nash equilibrium In the case of firms, an equilibrium that results when each firm in an industry is currently doing the best that it can, given the current behaviour of the other firms in the industry.

national debt The debt of the central government.

national income In general, the value of the nation's total output, and the value of the income generated by the production of that output.

national product A generic term for the nation's total output which might be measured more specifically by *GNP* or *GDP*.

natural monopoly An industry whose market demand is sufficient to allow only one firm to produce at its minimum efficient scale.

natural rate of unemployment The level of unemployment in a competitive economy which corresponds to potential national income, and is associated with stable inflation. For most purposes it is equivalent to the *NAIRU*, but the latter applies to imperfectly competitive economies as well.

natural scale A scale in which equal absolute amounts are represented by equal distances.

near money Anything that fulfils the store-of-value function, and is readily convertible into a medium of exchange, but is *not* itself a medium of exchange.

negatively related Refers to the relationship where an increase in one variable is associated with a decrease in the other.

net domestic product *Gross domestic product* minus an allowance for *depreciation* (or *capital consumption*).

net exports Total exports minus total imports $(X - M)$.

net investment Gross investment minus replacement investment, which is new capital that represent net additions to the capital stock.

net taxes Total tax receipts net of *transfer payments*.

neutrality of money Hypothesis that the level of real national income is independent of the level of the money stock.

New Classical theory A theory that assumes that the economy behaves as if it were perfectly competitive with all markets always clearing; where deviations from full employment can occur only if people make mistakes and, given rational expectations, these mistakes will not be systematic.

New Keynesian economics Recent research agenda which has focused on explaining why prices do not adjust to clear markets, especially the labour market. It differs from the traditional Keynesian approach in its concern for *equilibrium unemployment* as well as *cyclical unemployment*.

newly industrialized countries (NICs) Formerly underdeveloped countries that have become major industrial exporters in recent times. Sometimes called newly industrialized economies (NIEs).

nominal interest rate Actual interest rate in money terms. It is contrasted with the *real interest rate*, which is the nominal interest rate minus the inflation rate (or expected inflation rate).

nominal money supply The money supply measured in monetary units.

nominal national product Total output valued at current prices.

nominal rate of tariff The tax charged on any imported commodity, expressed as a percentage of the price of the commodity.

non-cooperative equilibrium An equilibrium reached when firms calculate their own best policy without considering competitors' reactions.

non-market sector That portion of an economy in which producers must cover their costs from some source other than sales revenue.

non-renewable or exhaustible resources Any productive resource that is available as a fixed stock that cannot be replaced once it is used, such as petroleum.

non-strategic Behaviour which does not take account of the reactions of others, as when a firm acts in *perfect* or *monopolistic competition*.

non-tariff barriers Devices other than tariffs that are designed to reduce the flow of imports.

non-tradables Goods and services that are produced and sold domestically but do not enter into international trade.

normal capacity output The level of output that the firm expects to maintain on average.

normal good A commodity whose demand increases when income increases.

normative Statements concerning what ought to be; they depend on our *value judgements*.

NX Symbol used in the macroeconomics sections of this book for net exports, which is exports minus imports.

OECD Organization for Economic Co-operation and Development. A Paris-based economics research institute and policy forum supported by the major industrial countries. For a list of members see fn. 1 on p. 812.

official financing Refers to items that represent international transactions involving the central bank of the country whose balance of payments is being recorded.

oligopoly An industry that contains only a few firms.

open economy An economy that engages in international trade.

open-market operations Sales or purchases of securities by the central bank aimed at influencing monetary conditions.

open shop A place of employment in which a union represents its members but does not have bargaining jurisdiction for all workers in the shop, and where membership of the union is not a condition of getting or keeping a job.

opportunity cost The cost of using resources for a certain purpose, measured by the benefit given up by not using them in their best alternative use.

output gap The difference between actual output and potential output ($Y^* - Y$); positive output gaps are called *recessionary gaps*; negative output gaps are called *inflationary gaps*.

outputs The goods and services that result from the process of production.

outside assets Assets held by a sector or economy which are the liabilities of agents in another sector or economy.

overshooting Occurs when the impact effect of a shock takes a variable beyond its ultimate equilibrium level. Most widely applied to the exchange rate. A characteristic of a wide class of exchange rate models under rational expectations is that when monetary policy is, say, tightened the exchange rate initially appreciates to a point from which it will depreciate towards its long-run equilibrium level.

parallel money market In the traditional London money market, banks lent short-term surpluses to the *discount houses*. The parallel money market arose when banks started to trade directly with each other. It is more widely known today as the inter-bank market.

Pareto efficiency See *Pareto optimality*.

Pareto optimality A situation in which it is impossible, by reallocating production or consumption activities, to make at least one person better off without making anyone worse off. Also called *Pareto efficiency*.

partisanship Influences on economic policy (or expected economic policy) coming from the differences in priority and constituency of political parties. It is an important component in some modern theories of the *political business cycle.*

partnership An enterprise with two or more joint owners, each of whom is personally responsible for all of the partnership's debts.

paternalism The belief that the individual is not the best judge of his or her own self-interest; someone else knows better.

path dependence Non-uniqueness of equilibrium resulting from the possibility that what happens in one period affects the stock of physical and human capital for a long time subsequently. Sometimes referred to as *hysteresis.*

per capita economic growth The growth of per capita national income (national income divided by the population).

per-unit tax See *specific tax.*

perfect capital mobility Arises when there are no artificial barriers to the movement of financial capital and investors regard domestic and foreign securities (riskless) as perfect substitutes.

perfect competition A market structure in which all firms in an industry are price-takers and in which there is freedom of entry into, and exit from, the industry.

permanent income The maximum amount that a person can consume per year into the indefinite future without reducing his or her wealth.

permanent income theory A theory that relates actual consumption to permanent income.

perpetuity A bond that pays a fixed sum of money each year for ever and has no redemption date; sometimes called a consol.

personal disposable income (PDI) The gross income of the personal sector less all direct taxes and national insurance contributions.

Phillips curve Relates the percentage rate of change of money wages (measured at an annual rate) to the level of unemployment (measured as the percentage of the labour force unemployed).

planned expenditure What people intend to spend.

point elasticity Uses the derivative at a point on the demand curve $(\mathrm{d}q/\mathrm{d}p)/(p/q)$. (See also *arc elasticity.*)

policy invariance A proposition associated with the *New Classical School,* which states that systematic changes in monetary and fiscal policy cannot affect real national income. It implies that only unexpected changes in aggregate demand policy affect real national income. The conditions required for this to be true are not generally thought likely to hold.

political business cycles Cycles in the economy resulting from the political goals of incumbent (or potentially incumbent) politicians. The simplest form of this is the deliberate pre-election boom, though modern theories are more subtle.

poll tax A tax which takes the same lump sum from everyone.

portfolio balance See *portfolio equilibrium.*

portfolio disequilibrium Situation existing when wealth-holders have too much of some assets and too few of others in the current portfolios.

portfolio equilibrium Situation existing when wealth-holders have the desired proportion of assets in their current portfolios; also called *portfolio balance.*

portfolio investment Investment in bonds and other debt instruments that do not imply ownership, or in minority holdings of shares that do not establish legal control.

positive Refers to statements concerning what is, was or will be; they assert alleged facts about the universe in which we live.

positively related Refers to the relationship where an increase in one variable is associated with an increase in the other.

potential output (national income), Y^* The level of output at which there is a balance between inflationary and deflationary forces. It is also the level of output at which there is no *cyclical unemployment* (the economy is at the *NAIRU*) and the existing capital stock is being run at its normal rate of utilization.

precautionary balances The amount of money people wish to hold because of uncertainty about the exact timing of receipts and payments.

present value The value now of a sum to be received in the future. Also called *discounted present value*.

price-consumption line A line on an indifference curve diagram showing how consumption changes as the price of one commodity changes, *ceteris paribus*.

price controls Anything that influences prices by laws, rather than market forces.

price discrimination Situation arising when firms sell different units of their output at different prices for reasons not associated with differences in costs.

price elasticity of demand The percentage change in quantity demanded divided by the percentage change in price that brought it about; often called *elasticity of demand*.

price elasticity of supply The percentage change in quantity supplied divided by the percentage change in price that brought it about; often called *elasticity of supply*.

price index A statistical measure of the average percentage change in some group of prices over some base period.

price level See *general price level*.

price-makers Firms that administer their prices. See *administered price*.

price-specie-flow mechanism The automatic balance of payments adjustment mechanism under the *gold standard*. A balance of payments surplus leads to an inflow of gold which raises the domestic money supply, and this, in turn, raises domestic prices. Domestic residents accordingly switch to purchases of foreign goods, and the balance of payments surplus disappears (or turns into a deficit).

price system An economic system in which prices play a key role in determining the allocation of resources and the distribution of the national product.

price-taker A firm that can alter its rate of production and sales within any feasible range without having any effect on the price of the product it sells.

prime bank bills A *bill of exchange* which has been accepted (guaranteed) by a *merchant bank* which has a 'good name'. Such bills are eligible for being rediscounted with the Bank of England, via the *discount market*.

prime rate US terminology for *base rate*.

principal The amount of a loan, or the individual (or firm) who takes ownership of a transaction.

principal–agent problem The problem of resource allocation that arises because contracts that will induce agents to act in their principals' best interests are generally impossible to write or too costly to monitor.

principle of substitution The idea that methods of production will change if relative prices of inputs change, with relatively more of the cheaper input and relatively less of the more expensive input being used.

private cost The value of the best alternative use of the resources used in production as valued by the *producer*.

private sector That portion of an economy in which the organizations that produce goods and services are owned and operated by private units such as households and firms.

pro-cyclical Positively correlated with the *business cycle*.

producer Any unit that makes goods or services.

producers' surplus Total revenue minus total variable cost; the market value that the firm creates by producing goods, net of the value of the resources currently used to create these goods.

production The act of making goods and services.

production function A functional relation showing the maximum output that can be produced by each and every combination of inputs.

production possibility boundary A curve that shows the alternative combinations of commodities that can just be attained if all available productive resources are used; it is the boundary between attainable and unattainable output combinations.

productive efficiency Production of any output at the lowest attainable cost for that level of output.

productivity Output per unit of input employed.

products A general term referring to all goods and services. Sometimes also referred to as *commodities*.

profit (1) In ordinary usage, the difference between the value of outputs and the value of inputs. (2) In microeconomics, the difference between revenues received from the sale of goods and the value of inputs, which includes the opportunity cost of capital: also called *pure profits* or *economic profits*. (3) In macroeconomics, excluding interest on borrowed capital but not the return on owner's capital.

profit-maximizing output The level of output that maximizes a firm's profits. Sometimes also called the *optimal output*.

progressive tax A tax that takes a larger percentage of people's income the larger is their income.

progressivity The general term for the relation between income and the percentage of income paid in taxes.

proportional tax A tax that takes the same percentage of people's income whatever the level of their income.

protectionism Any departure from free trade designed to give some protection to domestic industries from foreign competition.

proxy An order from a stockholder that passes the right to vote to a nominee, usually an existing member of the board of a firm.

PSBR See *public sector borrowing requirement*.

public corporation A body set up to run a nationalized industry. It is owned by the state but is usually under the direction of a more or less independent, state-appointed board.

public goods Goods and services which, once produced, can be consumed by everyone in the society; also called *collective consumption goods*.

public sector That portion of an economy in which production is owned and operated by the government or by bodies created by it, such as nationalized industries.

public sector borrowing requirement (PSBR) The combined excess of expenditure over revenue of the central government, the local authorities, and public corporations, minus asset sales.

public-sector debt The outstanding debt of central government, local authorities, and public corporations.

purchasing power of money The amount of goods and services that can be purchased with a given amount of money.

purchasing power parity (PPP) exchange rate The exchange rate between two currencies that equates their purchasing powers and hence adjusts for relative inflation rates.

purchasing power parity theory The theory that the equilibrium exchange rate between two national currencies will be the one that equates their purchasing powers.

pure profit Any excess of a firm's revenue over all opportunity costs including those of capital; also called *economic profit*.

pure rate of interest See *pure return on capital.*

pure return on capital The amount that capital can earn in a riskless investment; also called the *pure rate of interest.*

quantity actually bought and sold The amount of a commodity that consumer and firms actually succeed in purchasing and selling.

quantity actually purchased See *quantity actually bought and sold.*

quantity demanded The amount of a commodity that households wish to purchase in some time-period.

quantity supplied The amount of a commodity that firms offer for sale in some time-period.

quantity theory of money Theory predicting that the price level and the quantity of money vary in exact proportion to each other — i.e. changing M by X% changes P by X%.

quasi-rent Factor payments which are economic rent in the short run and transfer earnings in the long run.

ratio scale See *logarithmic scale.*

rational expectations The theory that people understand how the economy works and learn quickly from their mistakes, so that, while random errors may be made, systematic and persistent errors are not made.

reaction curve Curve showing one firm's profit-maximizing output for each given quantity sold by its competitor.

real business cycles An approach to the explanation of business cycles which uses dynamic equilibrium market-clearing models and relies upon productivity shocks as a trigger. In such models, all cycles are an optimal response to the real shock and there are no deviations from potential output: rather, it is the full equilibrium that fluctuates over time.

real capital Physical assets that constitute factories, machinery, and stocks of material and finished goods; also called *physical capital.*

real exchange rate An index of the relative prices of domestic and foreign goods.

real income The purchasing power of money income.

real money supply The money supply measured in purchasing-power units.

real national product Total output valued at base-year prices.

real product wage The proportion of the sale value of each unit that is accounted for by labour costs (including the pre-tax nominal wage rate, benefits, and the firm's national insurance contributions).

real rate of interest The money rate of interest minus the inflation rate, which expresses the real return on a loan.

real wage The money wage deflated by a price index to measure the wage's purchasing power.

realized expenditure What people actually succeed in spending.

reallocation of resources Some change in the uses to which the economy's resources are put.

recession A sustained drop in the level of economic activity.

recessionary gap A positive output gap, when actual national income falls short of potential national income.

redemption date The time at which the principal of a loan is to be repaid.

regressive tax A tax which takes a smaller percentage of people's incomes the larger their income is.

relative price Any price expressed as a ratio of another price.

renewable resources Productive resources that can be replaced as they are used up, as with physical capital; distinguished from non-renewable resources, which are available in a fixed stock that can be depleted but not replaced.

replacement investment Investment which replaces capital as it wears out. It is equal to *depreciation*, or *capital consumption*, but does not increase the capital stock.

replacement ratio Benefits received by those out of work as a proportion of the wage of those in employment.

resource allocation The allocation of the economy's scarce resources among alternative uses.

retail price index (RPI) An index of the general price level based upon the consumption pattern of typical consumers.

Ricardian equivalence (neutrality proposition) Proposition stating that, for a given path of real government spending, it makes no difference to private expenditures whether this spending is financed by taxes or borrowing (future taxes), since the present value of the tax liability is the same either way.

risk-averse Desirous of avoiding risks, persons will only play games that are sufficiently biased in their favour to overcome their aversion to risk; they will be unwilling to play mathematically fair games, let alone games that are biased against them.

risk-loving Describes people who are willing to play some games that are biased against them, the extent of the love of risk being measured by the degree of bias that they are willing to accept.

risk-neutral Indifferent about playing a mathematically fair game. Risk-neutral persons will willingly play a game that is biased in their favour, but will not play one that is biased against them.

risk premium The return on capital necessary to compensate owners of capital for the risk of loss of their capital.

rules Policy-making based upon a rigid formula.

satisficing Refers to firms that strive to achieve certain targets for their profits, but, having achieved them, will not strive to improve their profit position further.

saving Income received by households that they do not pass back to firms through consumption expenditure.

seigniorage The revenue that accrues to the issuer of money.

self-employed Those people who work for themselves.

sellers' preferences Allocation of commodity in excess demand by the decisions of sellers.

services Intangible production such as haircuts and medical services.

shares See *equities*.

shifting The passing of tax incidence from the person who initially pays it to someone else.

short-run The period of time over which the inputs of some factors cannot be varied.

short-run aggregate supply (SRAS) curve The total amount that will be produced and offered for sale at each price level on the assumption that all input prices are fixed.

short-run equilibrium Generally, equilibrium subject to fixed factors or other things that cannot change over the time-period being considered.

short-run Phillips curve Any particular Phillips curve drawn for a given expected rate of inflation.

short-run supply curve A curve showing the relation of quantity supplied to price when one or more factor is fixed; under perfect competition it is the horizontal sum of marginal cost curves (above the level of average variable costs) of all firms in an industry.

shut-down price The price that is equal to a firm's average variable costs, below which it will produce no output.

sight deposit A deposit that can be transferred to others by means of a cheque and can be converted into cash on demand. Also called *demand deposit*.

simple multiplier Usually applies to the value of the *multiplier* in the aggregate expenditure system before any account is taken of the feedback from the monetary sector and from aggregate supply.

single proprietorship An enterprise with one owner who is personally responsible for everything that is done. More commonly called a *sole trader*.

size distribution of income A classification of income according to the amount of income received by each individual irrespective of the sources of that income.

slump A period of low output and low employment.

small open economy (SOE) An economy that is a price-taker for both its imports and its exports. It must buy and sell at the world price, irrespective of the quantities that it buys and sells.

social cost The value of the best alternative use of resources that are available to the whole society.

sole trader A non-incorporated business operated by a single owner. Modern UK terminology for a *single proprietorship*.

special drawing rights (SDRs) Financial liabilities of the IMF held in a special fund generated by contributions of member-countries. Members can use SDRs to maintain supplies of convertible currencies when these are needed to support foreign exchanges.

specialization of labour An organization of production in which individual workers specialize in the production of particular goods or services (and satisfy their wants by trading) rather than producing everything they consume (and satisfying their wants by being self-sufficient).

specific tariffs Tariffs that are so much on each unit of the imported product, independent of its price.

specific tax A tax expressed as so much per unit, independent of its price; also called a *per-unit tax*.

speculation Taking a financial position that will yield profits if prices move in a particular direction in future, but will yield losses if they move the other way.

speculative motive The motive that leads agents to hold money in reaction to the risks inherent in a fluctuating price of bonds. More generally, it refers to the asset motive, as opposed to the transactions motive, for holding money.

SRAS curve See *short-run aggregate supply curve*.

stabilization policy The attempt to reduce fluctuation in national income, employment, and the price level by stabilizing national income at its full-employment level, if possible.

stagflation The simultaneous occurrence of a recession (with its accompanying high unemployment) and inflation.

stock See *equities*.

stock variable A variable that does not have a time dimension. It is contrasted with a flow variable.

stockbuilding The process of building *stocks*.

stocks Accumulation of inputs and outputs held by firms to facilitate a smooth flow of production in spite of variations in delivery of inputs and sales of outputs. Sometimes called *inventories*.

stop–go policy Fluctuations caused by shortsightedly pursuing expansion to cure unemployment, then contraction to cure inflation.

strategic Behaviour which takes into account the reactions of others to one's own actions, as when the firm makes decisions in oligopolistic situations.

structural unemployment Unemployment that exists because of a mismatching between the characteristics of the unemployed and the characteristics of the available jobs in terms of region, occupation, or industry.

substitutes Two goods are substitutes if the quantity demanded of one is positively related to the price of the other.

substitution effect The change in quantity demanded of a good resulting from a change in the commodity's relative price, eliminating the effect of the price change on real income.

supply The whole relation between the quantity supplied of some commodity and its own price.

supply curve The graphical representation of the relation between the quantity of some commodity that producers wish to make and sell per period of time and the price of that commodity, *ceteris paribus.*

supply function A functional relation between the quantity supplied and all the variables that influence it.

supply of effort The total number of hours people in the labour force are willing to work; also called *supply of labour.*

supply of labour See *supply of effort.*

supply of money The total amount of money available in the entire economy; also called the *money supply* or the *money stock.*

supply schedule A numerical tabulation showing the quantity supplied at a number of alternative prices.

supply-side policies Policies that seek to shift either the short-run or the long-run aggregate supply curve.

supply shocks A shift in any aggregate supply curve caused by an exogenous change in input prices or technology.

surprise aggregate supply curve See *Lucas aggregate supply curve.*

takeover When one firm buys another firm.

targets The variables in the economy which the policy-makers wish to influence. Typical policy targets might be inflation, unemployment and real growth.

tariffs Taxes designed to raise the price of imported goods.

tax wedge The difference between what employers pay out for each employee and the amount of that money that ends up in the employees' pockets.

tender offer An offer to buy directly, for a limited period of time, some or all of the outstanding common stock of a corporation from its shareholders at a specified price per share, in an attempt to gain control of the corporation. Also called *takeover bid.*

term The amount of time between a bond's issue date and its redemption date.

terms of trade The ratio of the average price of a country's exports to the average price of its imports.

theory of games The theory that studies rational decision-making in situations in which one must anticipate the reactions of one's competitors to the moves one makes.

theory of income determination The theory explains the size of, and changes in, national income.

third-party effects See *externalities.*

time deposits An interest-earning bank deposit, legally subject to notice before withdrawal (the notice requirement is not normally enforced) and, until recently, not transferable by cheque.

time inconsistency Problem that arises in rational expectation models when policy-makers have an incentive to abandon their commitments at a later time. The existence of this incentive is generally understood by private-sector agents and it may influence their current behaviour.

total cost (TC) The total of all costs of producing a firm's output, usually divided into fixed and variable costs.

total final expenditure The total expenditure required to purchase all the goods and services that are produced domestically, when these are valued at market prices.

total fixed costs The total of a firm's costs that do not vary in the short run.

total product (TP) Total amount produced by a firm during some time period.

total revenue (TR) The total amount of money that the firm receives from the sale of its output.

total utility The total satisfaction derived from consuming some amount of a commodity.

total variable costs The total of those of the firm's costs that do vary in the short run.

tradables Goods and services that enter into international trade.

trade bills See *bills of exchange.*

trade creation Trade between the members of a customs union or free trade area where previously protected industries served their own home markets.

trade cycles See *business cycles.*

trade diversion The diversion of the source of a member-country's imports from outside sources to other union members as a result of the preferential removal of tariffs consequent on the formation of a customs union or a free trade area.

trade or craft union An organization of workers with a common set of skills, no matter where, or for whom, they work.

trade-weighted exchange rate The average of the exchange rates between a particular country's currency and those of each of its major trading partners, with each rate being weighted by the amount of trade with the country in question.

transactions demand for money The amount of money that people wish to hold in order to finance their transactions.

transfer earnings The amount that a factor must earn in its present use to prevent it from moving (i.e. transferring) to another use.

transfer payments Payments not made in return for any contribution to current output, such as unemployment benefits.

transmission mechanism See *monetary transmission mechanism.*

transnational corporations (TNCs) Firms that have operations in more than one country. Also called *multinational enterprises (MNEs).*

Treasury bill A promise to repay a stated amount at some specified date between 90 days and 1 year from the date of issue, issued by the Treasury at a discount to redemption value.

underdeveloped countries See *less developed countries.*

unemployment The percentage of the workforce out of work but seeking employment. In UK statistics, must also be registered and claiming benefit.

unit cost See *average variable cost.*

unity elasticity An elasticity with a numerical measure of one, indicating that the percentage change in quantity is equal to the percentage change in price (so that total expenditure remains constant).

utility The satisfaction that a household receives from consumption.

utils An imaginary measure of utility used in the exposition of marginal utility theory which assumes that utility is cardinally measurable.

validation Term used when the authorities sustain an ongoing inflation by increasing the money supply.

value added The value of a firm's output *minus* the value of the inputs that it purchases from other firms.

value of money See *purchasing power of money.*

variable Any well-defined item, such as the price of a commodity or its quantity, that can take on various specific values.

variable cost A cost that varies directly with changes in output. Also called *direct cost, avoidable cost.*

variable factors Inputs whose amount can be varied in the short run.

velocity of circulation The number of times an average unit of money is used in transactions within a specific period. Defined as the ratio of nominal national income to the money stock.

vertical merger Union or merger of firms at different stages of production.

very long run A period of time over which the technological possibilities open to a firm are subject to change.

vicious circle of poverty Describes the situation existing when a country has little capital per head, so is poor; because it is poor, it can devote few resources to creating new capital rather than to producing goods for consumption; because little new capital can be produced, capital per head remains low, and the country remains poor.

visibles Goods, i.e. things such as cars, pulpwood, aluminium, coffee and iron ore, that we can see when they cross international borders.

visible trade Trade in physical products. Same as *merchandise trade.*

voluntary export restriction (VER) Restriction whereby an exporting country agrees to limit the amount it sells to a second country.

voluntary unemployment Unemployment that occurs when there is a job available, but the unemployed person is not willing to accept it at the existing wage rate.

wage-cost-push inflation An increase in the price level due to increases in money wages that are not associated with excess demand for labour.

wage-price spiral The process set up by a sequence of wage-cost pushes that shifts the *SRAS* curve to the left and monetary accommodation that shifts the *AD* curve to the right.

Wagner's law Generally stated as saying that government activity will be an ever increasing proportion of the national product. However, the actual prediction was of a growing proportion of state activity during the development phase and a constant proportion for a mature economy.

warrant The option component of a convertible bond. When separated from the bond, it is a call option on a company's equity.

withdrawals Income received by either firms or households that is not passed on to the other group by buying goods or services from it. Also called *leakages.*

working population The total of the employed, the self-employed, and the unemployed, i.e. those who have a job plus those who are looking for work.

X-inefficiency Failure to use resources efficiently within the firm so that firms are producing above their relevant cost curves and the economy is inside its production possibility boundary.

yield curve A graph plotting the yield on securities against the term to maturity.

Index

*Head words in blue refer to subjects which are defined in the Glossary. Page numbers of subjects covered in boxes are shown in **bold** type; page numbers in italic type are to references in the appendices.*

Index compiled by Margaret Cronan